Dreamweaver® 4 Bible

Joseph W. Lowery

Hungry Minds™

Hungry Minds, Inc.

New York, NY ✦ Cleveland, OH ✦ Indianapolis, IN

Dreamweaver® 4 Bible

Published by
Hungry Minds, Inc.
909 Third Avenue
New York, NY 10022
www.hungryminds.com

Library of Congress Control Number: 2001089091

ISBN: 0-7645-3569-2

Printed in the United States of America

10 9 8 7 6 5 4 3 2

1B/RY/QU/QR/IN

Distributed in the United States by Hungry Minds, Inc.

Distributed by CDG Books Canada Inc. for Canada; by Transworld Publishers Limited in the United Kingdom; by IDG Norge Books for Norway; by IDG Sweden Books for Sweden; by IDG Books Australia Publishing Corporation Pty. Ltd. for Australia and New Zealand; by TransQuest Publishers Pte Ltd. for Singapore, Malaysia, Thailand, Indonesia, and Hong Kong; by Gotop Information Inc. for Taiwan; by ICG Muse, Inc. for Japan; by Intersoft for South Africa; by Eyrolles for France; by International Thomson Publishing for Germany, Austria, and Switzerland; by Distribuidora Cuspide for Argentina; by LR International for Brazil; by Galileo Libros for Chile; by Ediciones ZETA S.C.R. Ltda. for Peru; by WS Computer Publishing Corporation, Inc., for the Philippines; by Contemporanea de Ediciones for Venezuela; by Express Computer Distributors for the Caribbean and West Indies; by Micronesia Media Distributor, Inc. for Micronesia; by Chips Computadoras S.A. de C.V. for Mexico; by Editorial Norma de Panama S.A. for Panama; by American Bookshops for Finland.

For general information on Hungry Minds' products and services please contact our Customer Care department within the U.S. at 800-762-2974, outside the U.S. at 317-572-3993 or fax 317-572-4002.

For sales inquiries and reseller information, including discounts, premium and bulk quantity sales, and foreign-language translations, please contact our Customer Care department at 800-434-3422, fax 317-572-4002 or write to Hungry Minds, Inc., Attn: Customer Care Department, 10475 Crosspoint Boulevard, Indianapolis, IN 46256.

For information on licensing foreign or domestic rights, please contact our Sub-Rights Customer Care department at 212-884-5000.

For information on using Hungry Minds' products and services in the classroom or for ordering examination copies, please contact our Educational Sales department at 800-434-2086 or fax 317-572-4005.

For press review copies, author interviews, or other publicity information, please contact our Public Relations department at 650-653-7000 or fax 650-653-7500.

For authorization to photocopy items for corporate, personal, or educational use, please contact Copyright Clearance Center, 222 Rosewood Drive, Danvers, MA 01923, or fax 978-750-4470.

 is a trademark of Hungry Minds, Inc.

Dreamweaver® 4
Bible

About the Author

Joseph W. Lowery has been writing about computers and new technology since 1981. He is the author of the previous editions of *Dreamweaver Bible* and *Fireworks Bible* as well as *Buying Online For Dummies* (all from Hungry Minds, formerly IDG Books Worldwide). He recently co-wrote a book on Flash with designer Hillman Curtis and has also written books on HTML and using the Internet for business. Joseph is currently Webmaster for a variety of sites and is also a Web design trainer and consultant. Joseph and his wife, dancer/choreographer Debra Wanner, have a daughter, Margot.

Credits

Acquisitions Editor
Michael Roney

Project Editor
Julie M. Smith

Technical Editor
Derren Whiteman

Copy Editors
Kelly Campbell Hogue
Nancy Rapoport
Roxane Marini

Project Coordinator
Dale White

Quality Control Technicians
Laura Albert
John Bitter
Valery Bourke
David Faust
Angel Perez
Nancy Price
Linda Quigley
Marianne Santy

Graphics and Production Specialists
Sean Decker
Stephanie Jumper
Kristin Pickett
Kendra Span
Brian Torwelle
Erin Zeltner

Senior Permissions Editor
Carmen Krikorian

Media Development Manager
Laura Carpenter

Media Development Supervisor
Rich Graves

Media Development Specialist
Megan Decraene

Media Development Coordinator
Marisa Pearman

Proofreading and Indexing
York Production Services, Inc.

Foreword

We live in a time of great change, and I feel privileged to have the opportunity to affect the expression of a new medium, the Internet. Everything about the Web is evolving quickly — the design, the tools, and even the medium itself. Dreamweaver is an evolutionary product for Macromedia as well as a revolutionary one. Not only is Dreamweaver the state-of-the-art Web authoring tool used by more professionals than any other, it has also evolved into an application platform central to Macromedia's ever-expanding Internet vision.

I think one of the reasons Dreamweaver was so successful from the beginning is that it grew out of a community. Before Dreamweaver, there was a growing community of professional Web developers that no one was listening to. Developers cried, "Leave my code alone!" but all of the available visual editors altered their code. Developers pleaded, "Help me create tables," but no integrated tool could help. Developers demanded, "I need cutting-edge features," only to get the previous year's fading standards.

Macromedia decided to listen. The Dreamweaver project relied on an advisory board of designers and developers to identify the most desirable features. The development effort, however, was far more than a committee voting on a wish list. An entire culture was evolving, and the Dreamweaver team came out of that culture and remains a part of it still. Throughout the year we listen to our customers — both current and potential — to gather their reactions to the present release as well as to better understand their requirements for the future.

One of the key underpinnings of Dreamweaver is its extensibility layer. By constantly expanding the core customizability of Dreamweaver, we enable our customers to streamline their workflow. We think it's better that the product adapt to the way you work rather than that you have to adapt to the product. The community of extension builders has taken Dreamweaver to unforeseen heights in creating a new set of power tools for its use. In fact, Macromedia itself has taken advantage of Dreamweaver's extensibility to craft a new product, Dreamweaver UltraDev.

What's in the future for Dreamweaver? Macromedia is committed to making tools for every aspect of what we call the Web Content Life Cycle. The most effective Web sites are continually developing and changing in response to their visitors' needs and reactions. We see Dreamweaver as a core element in Macromedia's mission to empower developers and their companies to create entertaining, educational, and effective Web content — and to successfully use that content to communicate and refine their message.

One person whose message needs no refining is Joseph Lowery. From the beginings of Dreamweaver, Joe has provided the Dreamweaver community with remarkable works of clarity and substance. *Dreamweaver® 4 Bible* is the definitive resource for the Web authoring professional, not only because it covers the product in exhaustive detail but also because the book provides a much-needed context for understanding new technologies. We're glad that Joe has shared his talents and energies with Macromedia and the Dreamweaver community, and we look forward to growing together.

Kevin Lynch
President Products and Office of the President, Macromedia

Preface

Web designers are relentless explorers in the ever-expanding frontier that is the World Wide Web. Boundary-pushing is not only the norm, it's practically a job requirement — which is one of the reasons Dreamweaver is the leading Web design program today. Dreamweaver provides the tools you need to build any type of Web site you can imagine. Imagination, however, is not enough. A cutting-edge site requires cutting-edge resources — and that's the reason *Dreamweaver 4 Bible* was written.

Among other accolades, Macromedia's Dreamweaver has one of the most appropriate product names in recent memory. Web page design is a blend of art and craft; whether you're a deadline-driven professional or a vision-filled amateur, Dreamweaver is the perfect tool for many Web designers. Dreamweaver is not only the first Web authoring tool to bring the ease of visual editing to an HTML code–oriented world, it also brings a point-and-click interface to complex JavaScript coding.

To use this book, you need only two items: the Dreamweaver software and a desire to make cutting-edge Web pages. (Actually, you don't even need Dreamweaver to begin; the CD-ROM that accompanies this book contains a fully functional trial version.) From quick design prototyping to ongoing Web site management, Dreamweaver automates and simplifies much of a Webmaster's workload. Unfortunately, even Dynamic HTML, which Dreamweaver handles elegantly, cannot accomplish all the tasks of a modern Web page. As a result, this book contains step-by-step instructions on how to handle every Web design task — through Dreamweaver's visual interface or its integrated HTML code editors.

Underneath its simple, intuitive interface, Dreamweaver is a complex program that makes high-end Web concepts (Dynamic HTML, Cascading Style Sheets, and JavaScript behaviors) accessible for the first time. *Dreamweaver 4 Bible* is designed to help you master every nuance of the program. Are you creating a straightforward layout with the visual editor? Do you need to extend Dreamweaver's capabilities by building your own custom objects? With Dreamweaver and this book, you can weave your dreams into reality for the entire world to experience.

What's New in Dreamweaver 4

Since its inception, Dreamweaver has strived to serve two masters: professional Web developers, savvy in technique and used to hand-coding, and beginning designers looking to overcome their lack of HTML and JavaScript expertise.

Dreamweaver 4 attempts to continue the balancing act of satisfying the two different markets—and, in large part, succeeds. Innovations in Dreamweaver 4 can be categorized into three areas: team development, code enhancements, and layout tools.

In a major coup for enterprise Web developers, Dreamweaver 4 supports two source control systems: Visual SourceSafe and WebDAV. Connecting to a Visual SourceSafe server is well integrated into Dreamweaver; simply define the VSS server as your remote site and add the necessary connection information. WebDAV, although perhaps less well known than VSS, offers an equally powerful and more available content management solution. More important, Macromedia has developed the source control solution as a system architecture enabling other third-party content management or version control developers to use Dreamweaver as their front end. You'll find complete coverage of Visual SourceSafe and WebDAV integration—as well as the other team-oriented features—in Chapter 35, new to this edition.

Advanced coders tied to their simple text editor will be mightily tempted by Dreamweaver 4's new code editor. Rewritten from the ground up, the editor now features auto-indenting, punctuation balancing, and live syntax coloring for HTML as well as for JavaScript. Accessing the editor is also easier than ever as Dreamweaver adds two new modes to the current Design view. Now you can see both the code and the layout simultaneously in one window via the Split view or just the code in the Code view. All modes are immediately accessible—along with numerous key options—through the new Toolbar. You'll discover how to make the most of the new coding tools in Chapter 8.

Dreamweaver has always made it easy for designers new to the Web to build nice-looking, interactive Web pages without having to know HTML or JavaScript. The new version expands on that theme with two developments: Layout mode and Flash objects. Layout mode allows designers to draw tables and cells directly on the screen for positioning content. Once drawn, cells can be modified by dragging borders or moving the entire cell; nested tables may also be included. Chapter 13 explains how it all comes together.

Just as Dreamweaver behaviors may add JavaScript interactivity to a page without the developer's knowing JavaScript, the new Flash objects offer the potential for including highly attractive navigation elements without your having to master a vector-based animation program. Two different types of Flash objects are available: Flash buttons and Flash text. A Flash button is actually a Macromedia Generator template with full animation and sound capabilities. Because it's a template, the layout artist may customize it with text and a link. Dreamweaver ships with numerous examples, but anyone with Flash 5 can create his or her own template. Flash text, on the other hand, does not handle any animation other than a simple color rollover. However, it provides an effective way to include a heading or other page element in a specific font—a far better solution, with more market penetration, than materializing from Dynamic HTML. Both types of Flash objects are detailed in Chapter 23.

Dreamweaver appeals to both the expert and the novice Web designer. Although the program is extraordinarily powerful, it's also fairly intuitive. Nonetheless, designers new to the Web often find the entire process overwhelming and under-standably so. To give folks a bird's-eye view of the overall use of Dreamweaver in Web site design and production, this edition includes a Quick Start in Chapter 2. In this chapter, you'll see how one designer — yours truly — works with Dreamweaver in every aspect of building Web pages and constructing a site. Special emphasis is given to Dreamweaver 4's new Layout view feature.

Who Should Read This Book?

Dreamweaver attracts a wide range of Web developers. Because it's the first Web authoring tool that doesn't rewrite original code, veteran designers are drawn to using Dreamweaver as their first visual editor. Because it also automates compli-cated effects, beginning Web designers are interested in Dreamweaver's power and performance. *Dreamweaver 4 Bible* addresses the full spectrum of Web profession-als, providing basic information on HTML if you're just starting as well as advanced tips and tricks for seasoned pros. Moreover, this book is a complete reference for everyone working with Dreamweaver on a daily basis.

What Hardware and Software Do You Need?

Dreamweaver 4 Bible includes coverage of Dreamweaver 4. If you don't own a copy of the program, you can use the trial version on this book's CD-ROM. Written to be platform-independent, this book covers both Macintosh and Windows versions of Dreamweaver 4.

Macintosh

Macromedia recommends the following minimum requirements for running Dreamweaver on a Macintosh:

- ✦ Power Macintosh PowerPC (G3 or higher recommended)
- ✦ MacOS 8.6 or 9.*x*
- ✦ 32MB of available RAM
- ✦ 135MB of available disk space
- ✦ Color monitor capable of 800 × 600 resolution
- ✦ CD-ROM drive

Windows

Macromedia recommends the following minimum requirements for running Dreamweaver on a Windows system:

✦ Intel Pentium processor, 166MHz or equivalent (Pentium II or higher recommended)

✦ Windows 9*x*/ME, NT 4.0 (with Service Pack 3), or Windows 2000

✦ 32MB of available RAM

✦ 110MB of available disk space

✦ 256-color monitor capable of 800 × 600 resolution

✦ CD-ROM drive

Note   These are the minimum requirements. As with all graphics-based design tools, more capability is definitely better for using Dreamweaver, especially in terms of memory and processor speed.

How This Book Is Organized

Dreamweaver 4 Bible can take you from raw beginner to full-fledged professional if read cover to cover. However, you're more likely to read each section as needed, taking the necessary information and coming back later. To facilitate this approach, *Dreamweaver 4 Bible* is divided into eight major task-oriented parts. Once you're familiar with Dreamweaver, feel free to skip around the book, using it as a reference guide as you build up your own knowledge base.

The early chapters present the basics, and all chapters contain clearly written steps for the tasks you need to perform. In later chapters, you encounter sections labeled "Dreamweaver Techniques." Dreamweaver Techniques are step-by-step instructions for accomplishing specific Web designer tasks — for example, building an image map that uses rollovers, or eliminating underlines from hyperlinks through Cascading Style Sheets. Naturally, you can also use the Dreamweaver Techniques as stepping stones for your own explorations into Web page creation.

If you're running Dreamweaver while reading this book, don't forget to use the CD-ROM. An integral element of the book, the accompanying CD-ROM offers a vast number of additional Dreamweaver behaviors, objects, commands, browser profiles, and other extensions in addition to relevant code from the book.

Part I: Getting Started with Dreamweaver

Part I begins with an overview of Dreamweaver's philosophy and design. To get the most out of the program, you need to understand the key advantages it offers over other authoring tools and the deficiencies in them that Dreamweaver addresses. Part I takes you all the way to setting up your first site. In Chapter 2, you'll get an overview of the Web development process as a quick start to Dreamweaver.

The other opening chapters give you a full reference to the Dreamweaver interface and all of its customizable features. You also learn how you can access Dreamweaver's full-bodied online Help and find additional resources on the Web. Chapter 6 takes you from the consideration of various Web site design models to publishing your finished site on the Internet while Chapter 7 shows you how to make the most of Dreamweaver's FTP Site window.

Part II: Using Basic HTML in Dreamweaver

Although Dreamweaver is partly a visual design tool, its roots derive from the language of the Web: HTML. Part II gives you a solid foundation in the basics of HTML, even if you've never seen code. Chapter 8 covers HTML theory, describing how a Web page is constructed and alerting you to some potential pitfalls to look out for.

The three fundamentals of Web pages are text, images, and links. You explore how to incorporate these elements to their fullest extent in Chapters 9, 10, and 11, respectively. Chapter 12 examines another fundamental HTML option: lists. You study the list in all of its forms: numbered lists, bulleted lists, definition lists, nested lists, and more.

Part III: Incorporating Advanced HTML

Part III begins to investigate some of the more advanced structural elements of HTML as implemented in Dreamweaver. Chapter 13 examines the various uses of tables — from a clear presentation of data to organizing entire Web pages. Here you learn how to use Dreamweaver 4's greatly enhanced visual table editing capabilities to resize and reshape your HTML tables quickly.

Chapter 14 is devoted to image maps and shows how to use Dreamweaver's built-in Image Map tools to create client-side image maps. The chapter also explains how you can build server-side image maps and demonstrates a revised technique for creating image map rollovers. Forms are the focus of Chapter 15, where you find all you need to know about gathering information from your Web page visitors. Chapter 16 investigates the somewhat complex world of frames — and shows how Dreamweaver has greatly simplified the task of building and managing these multifile creations, particularly with the new Frame objects. You also learn how to handle more advanced design tasks such as updating multiple frames with just one click.

Part IV: Extending HTML Through Dreamweaver

HTML is a language with extensive capabilities for expanding its own power. Part IV begins with Chapter 17, which introduces you to the world of CGI programs, external plug-ins, Java applets, ActiveX controls, and scripting with JavaScript and VBScript. You also find techniques for ensuring a secure middle ground of cross-browser compatibility in the ongoing browser wars.

With its own set of objects and behaviors, Dreamweaver complements HTML's extensibility. Chapter 18 shows you how you can use the built-in objects to accomplish most of your Web page–layout chores quickly and efficiently—and when you're ready for increased automation, the chapter explains how to build your own custom objects. Chapter 19 offers an in-depth look at the capabilities of Dreamweaver behaviors. Each standard behavior is covered in detail with step-by-step instructions. If you're JavaScript-savvy, Chapter 20 gives you the material you need to construct your own behaviors and reduce your day-to-day workload. Finally, Chapter 21 explores the brave new world of Dreamweaver extensibility, with complete coverage of using and building commands as well as custom tags, translators, floaters, and C-level Extensions.

Part V: Adding Multimedia Elements

In recent years, the Web has moved from a relatively static display of text and simple images to a full-blown multimedia circus with streaming video, background music, and interactive animations. Part V contains the power tools for incorporating various media files into your Web site.

Graphics remain the key medium on the Web today, and Macromedia's Fireworks is a top-notch graphics generator. Chapter 22 delves into methods for incorporating Fireworks graphics—with all the requisite rollover and other code intact. Special focus is given to the Dreamweaver-to-Fireworks communication link and how your Web production efforts can benefit from it.

In addition to Dreamweaver, Macromedia is perhaps best known for one other contribution to Web multimedia: Flash. Chapter 23 explores the possibilities offered by incorporating Flash and Shockwave movies into Dreamweaver-designed Web pages and includes everything you need to know about configuring MIME types. You also find step-by-step instructions for building Shockwave inline controls and playing Shockwave movies in frame-based Web pages, as well as how to add Flash buttons, Flash text, and Generator objects

Chapter 24 covers digital video in its many forms: downloadable AVI files, streaming RealVideo displays, and panoramic QuickTime movies. Chapter 25 focuses on digital audio, with coverage of standard WAV and MIDI sound files as well as the newer streaming audio formats, like MP3. A special section covers the exciting possibilities offered by Beatnik and the Rich Music Format, with full coverage of the Beatnik ActionSet.

Part VI: Working with Dynamic HTML and Dreamweaver

Dynamic HTML brought a new world of promises to Web designers — promises that went largely unfulfilled until Dreamweaver was released. Part VI of *Dreamweaver 4 Bible* examines this brave new world of pixel-perfect positioning, layers that fly in and then disappear as if by magic, and Web sites that can change their look and feel at the click of a mouse.

Chapter 26 provides an overview of Dynamic HTML and explores the different implementations by the major browsers — with new information on how to embed cross-platform, cross-browser fonts in your Web pages. Chapter 27 takes a detailed look at the elegance of Cascading Style Sheets and offers techniques for accomplishing the most frequently requested tasks, such as creating an external style sheet. Many of the advantages of Dynamic HTML come from the use of layers, which enable absolute positioning of page elements, visibility control, and a sense of depth. You discover how to handle all these layer capabilities and more in Chapter 28. Chapter 29 focuses on timelines, which have the potential to take your Web page into the fourth dimension. The chapter concludes with a blow-by-blow description of how to create a multiscreen slide show, complete with layers that fly in and out on command.

Part VII: Creating Next-Generation Code with Dreamweaver

The Web is one fast-moving train, and if you're not running when you try to board, you're going to get left behind. Keeping up with the latest technological developments is essential for working Web designers. Sooner or later, your clients are going to demand the cutting edge, and Part VII is here to help you create the sharpest sites online.

I can't think of any new technology on the Web that has so quickly gained the widespread acceptance that XML has. In a nutshell, XML (short for Extensible Markup Language) enables you to create your own custom tags that make the most sense for your business or profession. Although XML doesn't enjoy full browser support as of this writing, it's only a matter of time — and little time at that. Chapter 30 shows you how to apply this fast-approaching technology of tomorrow in Dreamweaver today.

The Web has become one vast information junkie: the more data you put online now, the more information will be required tomorrow. Part of this tremendous growth is due to the explosion of electronic commerce (e-commerce) — the Internet is almost at the point where if you can buy it, you can buy it online. To manage this overwhelming flood of info, Web designers are turning to database-driven pages and sites. Dreamweaver 4 now offers numerous connectivity and e-commerce solutions, surveyed in Chapter 31, to help Web designers create such active content.

Part VIII: Enhancing Web Site Management and Workflow in Dreamweaver

Although Web page design gets all the glory, Web site management pays the bills. In Part VIII, you see how Dreamweaver makes this essential part of any Webmaster's day easier to handle. Chapter 32 starts off the section with a look at the use of Dreamweaver Templates and how they can speed up production while ensuring a unified look and feel across your Web site. Chapter 33 covers the Library, which can significantly reduce any Webmaster's workload by providing reusable — and updateable — page elements. Finally, Chapter 34 describes Dreamweaver's built-in tools for maintaining cross- and backward-browser compatibility. A Dreamweaver Technique demonstrates a browser-checking Web page that automatically directs users to appropriate links.

Until now, individual Web developers have been stymied when attempting to integrate Dreamweaver into a team development environment. File locking was all too easily subverted, allowing revisions to be inadvertently overwritten, site reports were limited in scope and output only to HTML, and, worst of all, version control was nonexistent. Dreamweaver 4 addresses all of these concerns while laying a foundation for future connectivity. In Chapter 35, you'll see how you can tie Dreamweaver into an existing Visual SourceSafe or WebDAV version control system. Other new features covered include custom file view columns and enhanced Design Notes accessibility.

Appendixes

Appendix A describes the contents of the CD-ROM that accompanies this book. Throughout this book, whenever you encounter a reference to files or programs on the CD-ROM, please check Appendix A for more information.

Dreamweaver comes with a fully functional internal HTML editor, and the full version of the program is bundled with two industrial-strength external HTML editors: BBEdit for the Macintosh and HomeSite for Windows. Although both editors offer extensive online help, an abbreviated user's manual for both programs appears in Appendixes B and C. Each appendix also has detailed information on integrating the external editors with Dreamweaver.

One special area of the Web — online learning — has experienced so much explosive growth that it has been granted its own special extension of Dreamweaver: CourseBuilder for Dreamweaver. Appendix D dives into this unique application and provides an overview of its most vital features.

Conventions Used in This Book

I use the following conventions throughout this book.

Windows and Macintosh conventions

Because *Dreamweaver 4 Bible* is a cross-platform book, it gives instructions for both Windows and Macintosh users when keystrokes for a particular task differ. Throughout this book, the Windows keystrokes are given first; the Macintosh are given second in parentheses, as follows:

To undo an action, press Ctrl+Z (Command+Z).

The first action instructs Windows users to press the Ctrl and Z keys in combination, and the second action (in parentheses) instructs Macintosh users to press the Command and Z keys together.

Key combinations

When you are instructed to press two or more keys simultaneously, each key in the combination is separated by a plus sign. For example:

Ctrl+Alt+T (Command+Option+T)

The preceding tells you to press the three listed keys for your system at the same time. You can also hold down one or more keys and then press the final key. Release all the keys at the same time.

Mouse instructions

When instructed to *click* an item, move the mouse pointer to the specified item and click the mouse button once. Windows users use the left mouse button unless otherwise instructed. *Double-click* means clicking the mouse button twice in rapid succession.

When instructed to select an item, you may click it once as previously described. If you are selecting text or multiple objects, click the mouse button once, press Shift, and then move the mouse to a new location and click again. The color of the selected item or items inverts to indicate the selection. To clear the selection, click once anywhere on the Web page.

Menu commands

When instructed to select a command from a menu, you see the menu and the command separated by an arrow symbol. For example, when instructed to execute the Open command from the File menu, you see the notation File ⇨ Open. Some menus use submenus, in which case you see an arrow for each submenu, as follows: Insert ⇨ Form Object ⇨ Text Field.

Typographical conventions

I use *italic* type for new terms and for emphasis, and **boldface** type for text that you need to type directly from the computer keyboard.

Code

A special typeface indicates HTML or other code, as demonstrated in the following example:

```
<html>
<head>
<title>Untitled Document</title>
</head>
<body bgcolor="#FFFFFF">
</body>
</html>
```

This code font is also used within paragraphs to designate HTML tags, attributes, and values such as `<body>`, `bgcolor`, and `#FFFFFF`. All HTML tags are presented in lowercase, as written by Dreamweaver, although browsers are not generally case-sensitive in terms of HTML.

The ¬ character at the end of a code line means you should type the next line of code before pressing the Enter (Return) key.

Navigating Through This Book

Various signposts and icons are located throughout *Dreamweaver 4 Bible* for your assistance. Each chapter begins with an overview of its information and ends with a quick summary.

Icons appear in the text to indicate important or especially helpful items. Here's a list of the icons and their functions:

Tips provide you with extra knowledge that separates the novice from the pro.

Notes provide additional or critical information and technical data on the current topic.

 Sections marked with a New Feature icon detail an innovation introduced in Dreamweaver 4.

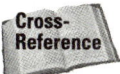 Cross-Reference icons indicate places where you can find more information on a particular topic.

 The Caution icon is your warning of a potential problem or pitfall.

 The On the CD-ROM icon indicates that the accompanying CD-ROM contains a related file in the given folder. See Appendix A for more information about where to locate specific items.

Further Information

You can find more help for specific problems and questions by investigating several Web sites. Macromedia's own Dreamweaver Web site is the best place to start:

    www.dreamweaver.com

I heartily recommend that you visit and participate in the official Dreamweaver newsgroup:

    news://forums.macromedia.com/macromedia.dreamweaver

You're also invited to visit my Web site for book updates and new developments:

    www.idest.com/dreamweaver

You can also e-mail me:

    jlowery@idest.com

I can't promise instantaneous turnaround, but I answer all my mail to the best of my abilities.

Acknowledgments

Whoever said "writing is a lonely business" never wrote a computer book. Sometimes I feel like the point man of a large swing band filled with seasoned pros. All the folks in this group can both play their parts exceedingly well, supporting the main theme, and are ready to solo at the drop of a hat. And now it's time to introduce, and applaud, the band.

If this book feels richer, more dense in detail (not to mention a pound or two heavier) than the previous edition, a great deal of the credit goes to my technical editor, Derren Whiteman. Derren has been absolutely top notch in providing insightful background comments, on-the-money tips, and real-world work experience. It also doesn't hurt that Derren is, as my Grandma used to say, persnickety about the details.

You can always identify people who have only read about the Internet when they despair about how the Internet increases our isolation. Baloney. I've got more colleagues and friends around the world now than I ever did. The Dreamweaver community has been especially gracious and giving of their time and expertise to further the goals of this book. I'd like to express my gratitude to the growing pool of developers who have taken their valuable time to create Dreamweaver extensions and offer them freely to the public. While the group has literally become too numerous to mention, I would like to highlight a few luminaries: Andrew Wooldridge, Massimo Foti, Jaro von Flocken, Brendan Dawes, Taylor, and Al Sparber. I'm particularly grateful because all of these authors (and many others) have kindly permitted their work to be included on this book's CD-ROM. I now owe a good 40 percent of the user base a drink.

Macromedia has been wonderfully supportive of my efforts to bring out the most detailed *Bible* possible. I can only imagine the collective groan that goes up when yet another e-mailed question from me — with a deadline, no less — arrives. Warm thanks and heartfelt appreciation to Dave George, Sho Kuwamoto, Hava Edelstein, Heidi Bauer, Darrick Brown, and all the other Dreamweaver engineers and techs who opened up their brains for me to pick. A special "Gawd, what would I have done without you?" award goes to Lori Hylan for help above and beyond the call of duty. I'd also like to single out the Dreamweaver Technical Support staff, whose answers to users' queries have been tremendous sources of information. And who's that in the back of the room? Macromedia management — in the form of David Mendels, Beth Davis, Eric Ott, Matt Brown, and others — has opened many, many doors to me and should stand up and take a bow. And finally, I and the rest of the

Dreamweaver community are beholden to Kevin Lynch and Paul Madar for their vision and hard work in bringing this dream home.

To me, there's no higher compliment than to be told that I know my business. Well, the folks I work with at Hungry Minds (known as IDG Books Worldwide when I started this effort) sure know their business: acquisitions editor Mike Roney; project editor Julie Smith; copy editors Kelly Campbell Hogue, Nancy Rapoport, and Roxane Marini; and all the additional support staff. And to someone whose business is to know my business, a double thank you with a cherry on top for my agent, Laura Belt of Adler & Robin Books.

One last note of appreciation—for all the people who took a chance with some of their hard-earned money and bought the previous editions of this book. That small sound you hear in the background is me applauding you as thanks for your support. I hope my efforts continue to be worthy.

Contents at a Glance

Contents

· ·

Part II: Using Basic HTML in Dreamweaver   225

Chapter 8: Understanding How HTML Works 227

Chapter 9: Adding Text to Your Web Page 259

Part III: Incorporating Advanced HTML   385

Chapter 13: Setting Up Tables 387

Chapter 14: Making Client-Side Image Maps 431

Chapter 15: Interactive Forms 449

Part IV: Extending HTML Through Dreamweaver   501

Part VI: Working with Dynamic HTML and Dreamweaver — 825

Part VIII: Enhancing Web Site Management and Workflow in Dreamweaver · 967

Getting Started with Dreamweaver

What Is Dreamweaver?

Dreamweaver, by Macromedia, is a professional Web site development program. Among its many distinctions, Dreamweaver was the first Web development program to take advantage of the capabilities of the latest generation of browsers, making it easy for developers to use advanced features such as Cascading Style Sheets and Dynamic HTML.

Dreamweaver is truly a tool designed by Web developers for Web developers. Designed from the ground up to work the way professional Web designers do, Dreamweaver speeds site construction and streamlines site maintenance. Throughout this chapter, you can see the philosophical underpinnings of the program and get a better sense of how Dreamweaver blends traditional HTML with cutting-edge techniques. You also learn some of the advanced features that Dreamweaver offers to help you manage a Web site.

The Real World of Dreamweaver

Dreamweaver is a program very much rooted in the real world. For example, Dreamweaver recognizes the problem of incompatible browser commands and addresses by producing cross-browser compatible code. Dreamweaver even includes browser-specific HTML validation so you can see how your existing or new code works in a particular browser.

Dreamweaver 4 extends the real-world concept to the workplace. Features such as the Assets panel streamline the production and maintenance process on large Web sites. Dreamweaver's advanced Layout view makes it possible to quickly structure whole pages during the design stage, while keeping your pages backwardly browser-compatible when published. Dreamweaver's commands capability enables Web designers to automate their most difficult Web creations.

Integrated visual and text editors

In the early days of the World Wide Web, most developers "hand-coded" their Web pages using simple text editors such as Notepad and SimpleText. The second generation of Web authoring tools brought visual design or WYSIWYG ("what you see is what you get") editors to market. What these products furnished in ease of layout, they lacked in completeness of code. Professional Web developers found they still needed to hand-code their Web pages, even with the most sophisticated WYSIWYG editor.

Dreamweaver acknowledges this reality and has integrated a superb visual editor — rewritten from the ground up for version 4 — with its browser-like document view. You can work graphically in Design view or programatically in Code view. You even have the option of a split-screen view, which shows the Design and Code views simultaneously. Figure 1-1 shows Dreamweaver's visual editor and code editor working together. Any change made in the Design view is reflected in the Code view and vice versa. If you'd prefer to work with a code editor you're more familiar with, Dreamweaver enables you to work with any text editor. Moreover, the program includes two of the best: a full-version of HomeSite for Microsoft Windows developers and a trial version of BBEdit for Macintosh developers. Dreamweaver enables a natural, dynamic flow between the visual and code editors.

Figure 1-1: Dreamweaver enables you to work with a visual WYSIWYG editor and a code editor simultaneously.

Dreamweaver further tightens the integration between the visual design and the underlying code with the Quick Tag Editor. Web designers frequently need to adjust the HTML code minutely — changing an attribute here or adding a single tag there. The Quick Tag Editor, which appears as a small pop-up window in the Design view, makes these code tweaks quick and easy.

Roundtrip HTML

Most Web authoring programs modify any code that passes through their system — inserting returns, removing indents, adding `<meta>` tags, uppercasing commands, and so forth. Dreamweaver's programmers understand and respect that Web developers all have their own particular coding styles. An underlying concept, Roundtrip HTML, ensures that you can move back and forth between the visual editor and any HTML text editor without your code being rewritten.

Web site maintenance tools

Dreamweaver's creators also understand that creating a site is only a part of the Webmaster's job. Maintaining the Web site can be an ongoing, time-consuming chore. Dreamweaver simplifies the job with a group of site management tools, including a library of repeating elements and a file-locking capability for easy team updates.

In Dreamweaver, Web site maintenance is easier than ever — and very visual. Take note of the Site Map feature that enables you to view your Web site structure at a glance and to access any file for modification. Links are updated automatically, or are under user control, if a file moves from one directory to another. And, you can not only access a library of repeating elements to be inserted in the page, but also define templates to control the entire look and feel of a Web site — and modify a single template to update all the pages sitewide.

Team-oriented site building

Until now, individual Web developers have been stymied when attempting to integrate Dreamweaver into a team development environment. File locking was all too easily subverted, enabling revisions to be inadvertently overwritten, site reports were limited in scope and only output to HTML, and, most notable of all, version control was nonexistent. Dreamweaver 4 addresses all of these concerns while laying a foundation for future connectivity.

In a major coup for enterprise Web developers, Dreamweaver 4 supports two source control systems: Visual SourceSafe (VSS) and WebDAV. Connecting to a Visual SourceSafe server is well integrated into Dreamweaver; simply define the VSS server as your remote site and add the necessary connection information. WebDAV, although perhaps less well known than VSS, offers an equally powerful and more available content-management solution. More importantly, Macromedia has developed the source-control solution as a system architecture enabling other third-party content management or version control developers to use Dreamweaver as their front end.

Extensible architecture also underlies Dreamweaver's new site reporting facility. Dreamweaver ships with the ability to generate reports on usability issues such as missing Alt text or documents without an HTML title, or workflow concerns, such as showing who has what files checked out. However, users can also develop custom reports on a project-by-project basis.

The Dreamweaver Interface

When creating a Web page, Webmasters do two things over and over: They insert an element—whether text, image, or layer—and then they modify it. Dreamweaver excels at such Web page creation. The Dreamweaver workspace combines a series of windows, panels, and inspectors to make the process as fluid as possible, thereby speeding up the Webmaster's work.

Easy text entry

Although much of the World Wide Web's glitz comes from multimedia elements such as images and sound, Web pages are primarily a text-based medium. Dreamweaver recognizes this and makes the text cursor the default tool. To add text, just click in Dreamweaver's main workspace—the Document window—and start typing. As shown in Figure 1-2, the Text Property Inspector enables you to change characteristics of the text, such as the size, font, position, or color.

One-stop object modification

You can select Web page elements other than text from the Objects panel. Adding a picture to a Web page is as easy as clicking the Insert Image button from the Objects panel. Dreamweaver asks you to select the file for the image, and your image appears in your current cursor position. Once your graphic is onscreen, selecting it brings up the appropriate Property Inspector to enable you to make modifications. The same technique holds true for any other inserted element— from horizontal rules to Shockwave movies.

Access and manage resources

One standout addition to Dreamweaver's interface is the new Assets panel, shown in Figure 1-3. The Assets panel gathers all the various elements used in an individual site: images, background and text colors, external URLs, included scripts, Flash movies, Shockwave content, and QuickTime media, as well as Dreamweaver templates and library items. Sizeable thumbnails of graphics and media are displayed in the preview pane of the Assets panel—you can even play Flash, Shockwave, and QuickTime elements in preview before dragging them onto the page. Moreover, often-used resources can be listed in a Favorites category, distinguishing them from the rest of the assets found in the sight.

Figure 1-2: Use the Text Property Inspector to change the format of the selected text.

Figure 1-3: Preview a Flash movie with the Assets panel before placing it on the Dreamweaver page.

Complete custom environment

Dreamweaver enables you to customize your workspace to suit you best. A handy Launcher opens and closes various windows, panels, and inspectors, all of which are movable. Just drag them wherever you want them onscreen. Want to see your page by itself? You can hide all windows at the touch of a function button; press it again, and your controls are revealed.

Dreamweaver's customization capabilities extend even further. If you find that you are inserting something over and over, such as a QuickTime video or .wav sound file, you can add that element to your Objects panel. Dreamweaver even enables you to add a specific element — a Home button, for example — to the Objects panel. In fact, you can add entire categories of objects if you like. Moreover, Dreamweaver 4 exposes the entire menu structure for customization — you can not only change keyboard shortcuts, but also add custom menus.

Cross-Reference   For more information on customizing your Objects panel, see Chapter 18. Information about changing the menu system is found in Chapter 21.

Managing keyboard shortcuts

Keyboard shortcuts are great in theory: just press an easy-to-remember key combination to activate your favorite feature. The problem is that, in reality, there are too many essential features, too few single-purpose keys on the keyboard and, most importantly, too few brain cells to retain all the widely varied keyboard combinations from all the programs the working designer must master.

New Feature   Macromedia has moved to ease keyboard shortcut overload across their entire product line, and Dreamweaver's no exception. Dreamweaver now offers a Keyboard Shortcut Editor that enables you to both standardize and customize the key combinations used in the program. Choose from a Macromedia standard set — common to Dreamweaver, UltraDev, Fireworks, and Flash — or use a set taken from a previous version of Dreamweaver. You can even select a set from an entirely different program such as HomeSite or BBEdit. Best of all, any keyboard shortcut can be personalized to represent a combination that's easy for you to remember.

Simple selection process

As with most modern layout programs, in order to modify anything in Dreamweaver, you must select it first. The usual process for this is to click an object to highlight it or to click and drag over a block of text to select it. Dreamweaver adds another option for this process with the Tag Selector feature. Click anywhere on a Web page under construction and then look at Dreamweaver's status bar. The applicable HTML tags appear on the left side of the status bar.

In the example shown in Figure 1-4, the Tag Selector shows

```
<body> <table> <tr> <td> <div> <p>
```

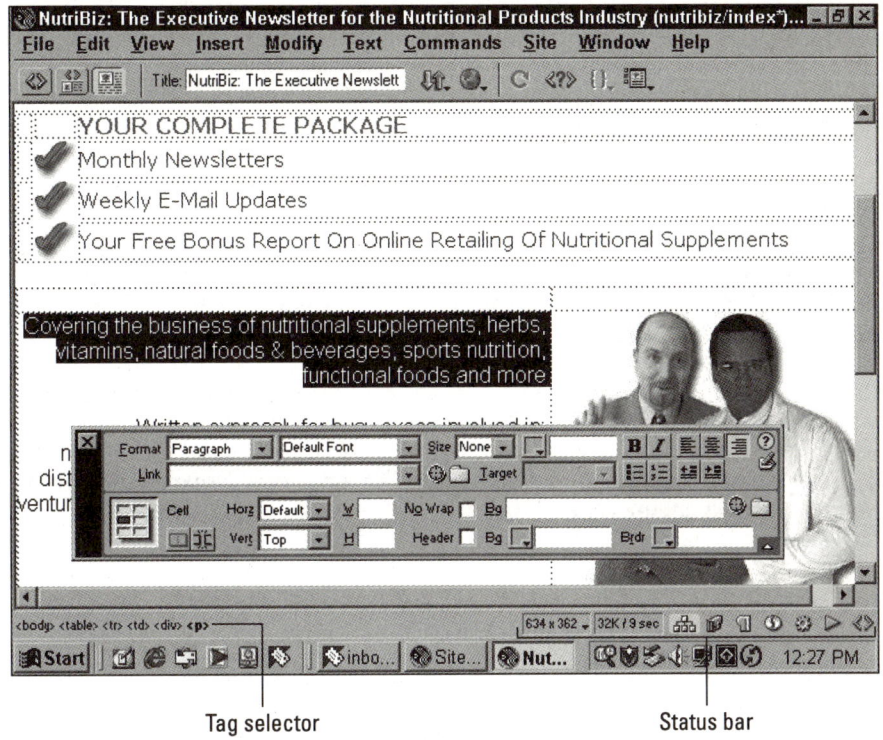

Figure 1-4: Choosing the <p> tag in Dreamweaver's Tag Selector is a quick and easy way to highlight the current paragraph on your Web page.

Click one of these tags, and the corresponding elements are selected on your page, ready for modification. The Tag Selector is a terrific time-saver; throughout this book, I point out how you can use it under various circumstances.

Enhanced layout options

Dreamweaver works much more like a desktop publishing program than do many other visual HTML editors. Today's browser capabilities permit images and text to be placed in specific locations on the Web page—a concept known as *absolute positioning*. To enable you to take full advantage of this power, Dreamweaver includes both rulers and grids. You can specify the type of measurement to be used (inches, pixels, or centimeters), as well as the spacing and appearance of the grid lines. You can even have objects snap to the grid for easy alignment.

New Feature Dreamweaver has always made it easy for designers new to the Web to build nice-looking interactive Web pages without having to know HTML. Dreamweaver 4 expands on that theme with Layout view. Layout view enables designers to draw tables and cells directly on the screen for positioning content. Once drawn, cells can be modified by dragging borders or moving the entire cell. Nested tables may also be included.

Cross-Reference To find out more about absolute positioning, see Chapter 28; you can learn more about Layout view in Chapter 13.

Active content preview

In order for a browser to display anything beyond standard format graphics, a plug-in is generally required. Plug-ins extend the capability of most browsers to show animations, play music, or even explore 3D worlds. Dreamweaver is one of the first Web authoring tools to enable you to design your Web page with an active plug-in playing the extended file; with all other systems, you have to preview your page in a browser to see the active content.

The active content feature in Dreamweaver enables the playback of plug-ins such as Macromedia Flash, Shockwave, and others. However, this feature extends far beyond that. Many Web pages are coded with server-side includes, which traditionally required the page to be viewed through a Web server. Dreamweaver translates much of the server-side information so that the entire page — server-side includes and all — can be viewed in its entirety at design time.

Extended Find and Replace

The Web is a fluid medium. Pages are constantly in flux, and because changes are relatively easy to effect, corrections and additions are the norm. Quite often a Web designer needs to update or alter an existing page — or series of pages. Dreamweaver's enhanced Find and Replace feature is a real power tool when it comes to making modifications.

Find and Replace works in the Document window, whether in Design View or Code View, as well as in the Code Inspector to alter code and regular content. Moreover, changes are applicable to the current page, the working site, selected Web pages, or an entire folder of pages, regardless of the number. Complex Find and Replace queries can be stored and retrieved later to further automate your work.

Up-to-Date HTML Standards

Most Web pages are created in HyperText Markup Language (HTML). This programming language — really a series of tags that modify a text file — is standardized by an organization known as the World Wide Web Consortium, or W3C (www.w3.org). Each new release of HTML incorporates an enhanced set of commands and features. The current version, HTML 4, is recognized by the majority of browsers in use today. Dreamweaver writes clear, easy-to-follow, real-world browser-compatible HTML 4 code whenever you insert or modify an element in the visual editor.

Straightforward text and graphics support

Text is a basic building block of any Web page, and Dreamweaver makes formatting your text a snap. Once you've inserted your text, either by typing it directly or pasting it from another program, you can change its appearance. You can use the generic HTML formats, such as the H1 through H6 headings and their relative sizes, or you can use font families and exact point sizes.

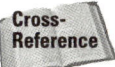

Chapter 9 shows you how to work with text in Dreamweaver.

Additional text support in Dreamweaver enables you to add both numbered and bulleted lists to your Web page. The Text Property Inspector gives you buttons for both kinds of lists as well as easy alignment control. Some elements, including lists, offer extended options. In Dreamweaver, clicking the Property Inspector's Expander arrow opens a section from which you can access additional controls.

Graphics are handled in much the same easy-to-use manner. Select the image or its placeholder to enable the Image Property Inspector. From there, you can modify any available attributes, including the image's source, its width or height, and its alignment on the page. Need to touch up your image? Send it to your favorite graphics program with just a click of the Edit button.

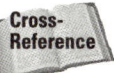

You learn all about adding and modifying Dreamweaver images in Chapter 10.

Enhanced table capabilities

Other features — standard, yet more advanced — are similarly straightforward in Dreamweaver. Tables are a key component in today's Web pages, and Dreamweaver gives you full control over all their functionality. Dreamweaver changes the work of resizing the column or row of a table, previously a tedious hand-coding task, into an easy click-and-drag motion. Likewise, you can delete all the width and height values from a table with the click of a button. Figure 1-5 shows the Table Property Inspector, which centralizes many of these options in Dreamweaver.

Tables are flexible in Dreamweaver. Font changes can be applied to any number of selected cells, rows, or columns. Standard commands enable you to automatically format or sort a table as well.

Easy form entry

Forms, the basic vehicle for Web page data exchange, are just as easy to implement as tables in Dreamweaver. Switch to the Forms category of the Objects panel and insert any of the available elements: text boxes, radio buttons, checkboxes, and even pop-up menus or scrolling lists. With the Validate Form behavior, you can easily specify any field as a required field and even check to ensure that the requested type of information has been entered.

Figure 1-5: The Table Property Inspector is just one of Dreamweaver's paths to a full range of control over the appearance of your table.

Click-and-drag frame setup

Frames, which enable separate Web pages to be viewed on a single screen, are often considered one of the most difficult HTML techniques to master. Dreamweaver employs a click-and-drag method for establishing your frame outlines. After you've set up your frame structure, open the Frames panel (see Figure 1-6) to select any frame and modify it with the Property Inspector. Dreamweaver writes the necessary code for linking all the HTML files in a frameset, no matter how many Web pages are used. Dreamweaver keeps frame creation simple with the Frames category of the Objects panel.

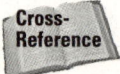

Cross-Reference   For more information on creating frame-based Web pages, see Chapter 16.

Multimedia enhancements

Dreamweaver enables you to drop in any number of multimedia extensions, plug-ins, applets, or controls. Just click the appropriate button on the Objects panel and modify with the Property Inspector. Two multimedia elements, Shockwave movies and Flash files — both from Macromedia — warrant special consideration in Macromedia's Dreamweaver. When you insert either of these objects,

Dreamweaver automatically includes the necessary HTML code to ensure the widest browser acceptance, and you can edit all the respective properties.

Macromedia has formed partnerships with numerous cutting-edge multimedia companies such as RealNetworks, IBM, and Beatnik. Dreamweaver fully supports the fruits of those partnerships: custom objects that enable complex images, audio, and presentations to be easily inserted and displayed in Web pages.

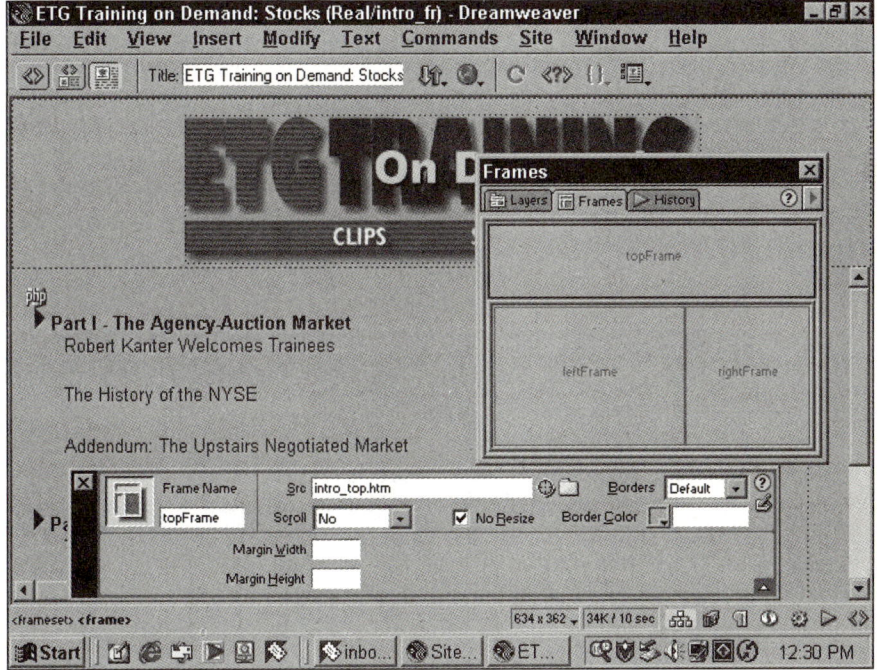

Figure 1-6: In Dreamweaver you use the Frames panel to choose which frame you want to modify through the Property Inspector.

Next-Generation Features

Dreamweaver was among the first Web authoring tools to work with the capabilities brought in by the 4.0 generation of browsers. Both Netscape Communicator 4+ and Microsoft Internet Explorer 4+ include variations of Dynamic HTML (DHTML). Moreover, both of these browsers adhere to the Cascading Style Sheet (CSS) standards to some degree, with support for absolute and relative positioning. Dreamweaver gives Web developers an interface that takes these advanced possibilities and makes them realities.

3D layers

One particular Dynamic HTML feature enables Dreamweaver to be called "the first 3D Web authoring tool." Until Dynamic HTML, Web pages existed on a two-dimensional plane — images and text could only be placed side by side. Dreamweaver supports control of Dynamic HTML layers, meaning that objects can be placed in front of or behind other objects. Layers can contain text, graphics, links, controls — you can even nest one layer inside another.

You create a layer in Dreamweaver by clicking the Draw Layer button on the Objects panel. Once created, layers can be positioned anywhere on the page by clicking and dragging the selection handle. As with other Dreamweaver objects, you can modify a layer through the Property Inspector.

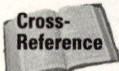 Detailed information on using Dynamic HTML in Dreamweaver starts in Chapter 26.

Animated objects

Objects in layers can be positioned anywhere on the Web page under construction, and they can also be moved when the page is viewed. Dreamweaver takes this capability and adds its Timelines panel, becoming a 4D Web authoring tool! The Timelines panel, shown in Figure 1-7, is designed along the lines of Macromedia's world-class multimedia creation program, Director. With timelines, you can control a layer's position, size, 3D placement, and even visibility on a frame-by-frame basis. With Dreamweaver, you no longer have to plot a layer's path on a timeline — now you can just draw it using the Record Path of Layer feature.

Dynamic style updates

Dreamweaver completely supports the Cascading Style Sheet (CSS) specification agreed upon by the World Wide Web Consortium. CSS gives Web designers more flexible control over almost every element on their Web pages. Dreamweaver applies CSS capabilities as if they were styles in a word processor. For example, you can make all the <h1> tags blue, italic, and in small caps. If your site's color scheme changes, you can make all the <h1> tags red — and you can do this throughout your Web site with one command. Dreamweaver gives you style control over type, background, blocks, boxes, borders, lists, and positioning.

Dreamweaver enables you to change styles online as well as offline. By linking a CSS change to a user-driven event such as moving the mouse, text can be highlighted or de-emphasized, screen areas can light up, and figures can even be animated. And it can all be done without repeated trips to the server or huge file downloads.

 Details on using Cascading Style Sheets begin in Chapter 27.

Figure 1-7: Use the Timelines panel to animate objects in layers using Dreamweaver's advanced Dynamic HTML features.

JavaScript behaviors

Through the development of JavaScript behaviors, Dreamweaver combines the power of JavaScript with the ease of a drag-and-drop interface. A behavior is defined as a combination of an event and an action — whenever your Web page user does something and then something else happens, that's a behavior. What makes behaviors extremely useful is that they require no programming whatsoever.

Behaviors are JavaScript-based, and this is significant because JavaScript is supported to varying degrees by existing browsers. Dreamweaver has simplified the task of identifying which JavaScript command works with a particular browser. You simply select the Web page element that you want to use to control the action, and open the Behaviors panel from the Launcher. As shown in Figure 1-8, Dreamweaver enables you to pick a JavaScript command that works with all browsers, a subset of browsers, or one browser in particular. Next, you choose from a full list of available actions, such as go to a URL, play a sound, pop up a message, or start an animation. You can assign multiple actions and even determine when they occur.

Cross-Reference   For complete details on working with JavaScript behaviors, see Chapter 19.

Figure 1-8: Dreamweaver offers only the JavaScript commands that work with the browser you specify.

Flash and Fireworks integration

Dreamweaver 4 has upped the ante for integration with Macromedia's graphics engine, Fireworks. Now, images derived from Fireworks are identified as such, both in the Property Inspector and in the Assets panel. Graphics may be optimized to alter the file size, cropping, transparency, or many other aspects right from within Fireworks. If more extensive modification is required, selecting the Edit button sends the graphic back to Fireworks. More impressively, sliced images — maintained as a borderless table in HTML — may be edited in their entirety. Fireworks even respects HTML alterations to a degree, such as changes to URLs or converting an image slice to a text block. This degree of integration lends an amazing fluidity to the workflow.

New Feature

Just as Dreamweaver behaviors may add JavaScript interactivity to a page without the developer knowing JavaScript, the new Flash objects offer the potential for including highly attractive navigation elements without mastering that vector-based animation program. Two different types of Flash objects are available: Flash buttons and Flash text. A Flash button (see Figure 1-9) is actually a Macromedia Generator template with full animation and sound capabilities. Because it's a template, the layout artist may customize it with text and a link. Dreamweaver ships with numerous examples, but anyone with Flash 5 can create their own template.

Figure 1-9: Flash buttons make it easy to add animated, sound-capable navigation elements to any page.

Flash text, on the other hand, does not handle any animation other than a simple color rollover. However, it is an effective way to include a heading or other page element in a specific font—a far better solution, with more market penetration, than materializing from Dynamic HTML. Moreover, Flash text weighs far less than an equivalent GIF image.

Roundtrip XML

A new type of markup language has excited a wide cross section of Web designers, intranet developers, and corporate users. XML, which stands for Extensible Markup Language, has piqued the interest of many because of its underlying customizable nature. With XML, tags are created to describe the use of the information, rather than its appearance.

Dreamweaver is capable of exporting and importing XML tags, no matter what the tag definition. As XML grows in popularity, Dreamweaver is ready to handle the work.

Cross-Reference To learn more about XML and its use in Dreamweaver, see Chapter 30.

Program Extensibility

One of Dreamweaver's primary strengths is its extensibility. Virtually no two Web sites are alike, either in their design or execution. With such a tremendous variety of end results, the more flexible a Web authoring tool, the more useful it is to a wider group of designers. When it was introduced, Dreamweaver broke new ground with objects and behaviors that were easily customizable. Now, Dreamweaver lengthens its lead with custom floaters, commands, translators, and Property Inspectors. The basic underpinnings of Dreamweaver can even be extended with the C-Level Extensibility options.

Objects and behaviors

In Dreamweaver parlance, an *object* is a bit of HTML code that represents a specific image or HTML tag such as a `<table>` or a `<form>`. Dreamweaver's objects are completely open to user customization, or even out-and-out creation. If you'd rather import structured data into a table without a border instead of with the standard 1 pixel border, you can easily make that modification to the Insert Tabular Data object file — right from within Dreamweaver — and every subsequent table is inserted as you'd prefer.

Objects are a terrific time-saving device, essentially enabling you to drop in significant blocks of HTML code at the click of a mouse. Likewise, Dreamweaver behaviors enable even the most novice Web designer to insert complex JavaScript functions designed to propel the pages to the cutting edge. Dreamweaver ships with a full array of standard behaviors — but that's only the tip of the behavior iceberg. Because behaviors, too, are customizable and can be built by anyone with a working knowledge of JavaScript, many Dreamweaver designers have created custom behaviors and made them publicly available.

On the CD-ROM   You can find a large assortment of custom objects, behaviors, and commands on the CD-ROM that accompanies this book.

Commands and floating panels

Objects and behaviors are great ways to help build the final result of a Web page, but what about automating the work of producing that page? Dreamweaver employs commands to modify the existing page and streamline production. A great example is the Sort Table command, standard with Dreamweaver. If you've ever had to sort a large table by hand — meticulously moving data, one row at a time — you can appreciate the power of commands the first time you alphabetize or otherwise re-sort a table using this option.

Commands hold a great promise—they are, in effect, more powerful than either objects or behaviors combined. In fact, some of the more complex objects, such as the Rollover Image object, are actually commands. Commands can also extract information sitewide and offer a powerful programmable language within Dreamweaver.

Creating a Dreamweaver command is now easier than ever, thanks to the History panel. Aside from displaying every action you undertake as you build your Web page, the History panel enables you to select any number of those actions and save them as a command. Your new command is instantly available to be called from the menu whenever you need it.

After only a few moments with Dreamweaver, you become accustomed to its use of floating panels. In Dreamweaver 4, custom floating panels can be created. These custom panels can show existing resources or provide a whole new interface for modifying an HTML element.

Custom tags, translators, and Property Inspectors

In Dreamweaver, almost every part of the user interface can be customized—including the tags themselves. Once you've developed your custom third-party tags, you can display and modify their current properties with a custom Property Inspector. Moreover, if your custom tags include content not typically shown in Dreamweaver's Document window, a custom translator can be built, enabling the content to be displayed.

Programs such as Dreamweaver are generally built in the programming language called C or C++, which must be compiled before it is used. Generally, the basic functions of a C program are frozen solid; there's no way you can extend them. This is not the case with Dreamweaver, however. Dreamweaver offers a C-Level Extensibility that permits programmers to create libraries to install new functionality into the program. Translators, for example, generally rely on new C libraries to enable content to be displayed in Dreamweaver that could not be shown otherwise. Companies can use the C-Level Extensibility feature to integrate Dreamweaver into their existing workflow and maximize productivity.

Automation Enhancements

Web site design is the dream job; Web site production is the reality. Once a design has been finalized, its execution can become repetitive and burdensome. Dreamweaver offers a number of ways to automate the production work, keeping the look of the Web pages constant with the minimum work required.

Applying HTML Styles

Designers in every field depend on the consistency and flexibility of styles. Until recently, the only styles available to Web designers came through a Cascading Style Sheet (CSS). While CSS is, for many, an ideal solution, numerous clients are hesitant to authorize its use, for fear of alienating users with older browsers that don't support CSS. The Dreamweaver engineers have come up with a solution that maintains backward-compatibility while simplifying text formatting: HTML Styles.

The HTML Styles panel enables you to define, manage, and apply any combination of text formatting. You can apply your new style to either a selection or an entire paragraph — styles can be defined either to add formatting to the existing tags or to replace them. While redefining an existing HTML Style does not cause text to update, HTML Styles are sitewide and can be used to enforce a consistent look and feel without CSS limitations.

Importing office documents

Much of the Web's content originates from other sources — in-house documents produced by a word processor or spreadsheet program. Dreamweaver bridges the gap between the offline and online world with two useful import features: Import Word HTML and Import Tabular Data.

Microsoft Word, perhaps the premier word processor, is great at creating and storing word processing documents but not so accomplished at outputting standard HTML. An HTML file derived from Word is, to put it mildly, bloated with extraneous and repetitive code. Dreamweaver's Import Word HTML feature strips out the unnecessary code and even permits you to format the code like your other Dreamweaver files. The Import Word HTML command offers a wide range of options for cleaning up the code.

Of course, not all Web content derives from word processing documents — databases and spreadsheets are the other two legs of the modern office software triangle. Dreamweaver includes the capability to incorporate data from any source that can export structured text files through the Import Tabular Data command. Just save your spreadsheet or database as a comma, tab, or otherwise delimited file and bring it directly into Dreamweaver in the table style of your choice.

Reference panel

Even the most advanced coder needs to refer to a reference when including seldom-used HTML tags or arcane JavaScript functions. Dreamweaver now includes a built-in reference with HTML, JavaScript, and Cascading Style Sheet details. Taken from O'Reilly's *Dynamic HTML, The Definitive Reference* by Danny Goodman, Dreamweaver's guide is context-sensitive; highlight a tag or function in Code view and hit Shift+F1 to get a breakdown on syntax and browser compatibility.

History panel

The repetitiveness of building a Web site is often a matter of repeating the same series of commands over and over again. You might, for example, need to add a vertical margin of 10 pixels and a horizontal margin of 5 around most, but not all, of the images on a page. Rather than selecting each image and then entering these values time and again in the Property Inspector, you can now enter the values once and then save that action as a command.

The feature that brings this degree of automation to Dreamweaver is found in the History panel. The History panel shows each step taken by a designer as the page is developed. Although this visual display is great for complex, multilevel undos, the capability to save any number of your steps as an instantly available command is truly time-saving.

Site Management Tools

Long after your killer Web site is launched, you'll find yourself continually updating and revising it. For this reason, site management tools are as important as site creation tools to a Web authoring program. Dreamweaver delivers on both counts.

Object libraries

In addition to site management functions that have become traditional, such as FTP publishing, Dreamweaver adds a whole new class of functionality called *libraries*. One of the truisms of Web page development is that if you repeat an element across your site, you're sure to have to change it — on every page. Dreamweaver libraries eliminate that drudgery. You can define almost anything as a Library element: a paragraph of text, an image, a link, a table, a form, a Java applet, an ActiveX control, and so on. Just choose the item and open the Library panel (see Figure 1-10). Once you've created the Library entry, you can reuse it throughout your Web site. Each Web site can have its own library, and you can copy entries from one library to another.

Being able to include "boilerplate" Web elements is one issue, being able to update them across the site simultaneously is quite another! You can easily change a Library entry through the Library panel. Once the change is complete, Dreamweaver detects the modification and asks if you want to update your site. Imagine updating copyright information across a 400+ page Web site in the wink of an eye, and you start to understand the power of Dreamweaver libraries.

Cross-Reference To find out more about making site-wide changes with Library items, see Chapter 33.

Figure 1-10: Use Dreamweaver's Library feature to simplify the task of updating elements repeated across many Web pages.

Templates

The more your Web site grows, the more you'll find yourself using the same basic format for different pages. Dreamweaver enables the use of Web page templates to standardize the look and feel of a Web site and to cut down on the repetitive work of creating new pages. A Dreamweaver template can hold the basic structure for the page — an image embedded in the background, a navigation bar along the left side, or a set-width table in the center for holding the main text, for example — with as many elements predefined as possible.

But Dreamweaver templates are far more than just molds for creating pages. Basically, templates work with a series of locked and editable regions. To update an entire site based on a template, all you have to do is alter one or more of the template's locked regions. Naturally, Dreamweaver enables you to save any template that you create in the same folder, so that your own templates, too, are accessible through the File ➪ New from Template command. (You can find more about using and creating templates in Chapter 32.)

Browser targeting

Browser targeting is another site management innovation from Dreamweaver. One of the major steps in any site development project is to test the Web pages in various browsers to look for inconsistencies and invalid code. Dreamweaver's Browser Targeting function enables you to check your HTML against any existing browser's profile. Dreamweaver includes predefined profiles for several browsers, and you can create a profile for any browser you'd like to check.

 Cross-Reference To learn how you can set up your own profile for Browser targeting, see Chapter 34.

You can also preview your Web page in any number of browsers. Dreamweaver enables you to specify primary and secondary browsers that can display your page at the press of a function key. You can install up to 18 other browsers for previewing your Web page. The entire list of browsers is available through the Preview in Browser command under the File menu.

Converting Web pages

Although Web site designers may have access to the latest HTML tools and browsers, much of the public uses older, more limited versions of browsers. Dreamweaver gives you the power to build Web pages with the high-end capabilities of fourth-generation browsers — and then convert those pages so that older browsers can also read what you've created. Moreover, you can take previously designed Web pages that use tables and "upgrade" them to take advantage of the latest HTML features with the Tables to Layers command. Dreamweaver goes a long way toward helping you bridge the gap between browser versions.

Verifying links

Web sites are ever-evolving entities. Maintaining valid connections and links amid all that diversity is a constant challenge. Dreamweaver includes a built-in link checker so you can verify the links on a page, in a directory, or across your entire site. The Link Checker quickly shows you which files have broken links, which files have links to external sites, and which files may have been "orphaned" (so that no other file connects with them).

FTP publishing

The final step in Web page creation is publishing your page on the Internet. As any Webmaster knows, this final step is one that happens over and over again as the site is continually updated and maintained. Dreamweaver includes an FTP (File Transfer Protocol) publisher that simplifies the work of posting your site. More importantly, Dreamweaver enables you to synchronize your local and remote sites with one command.

You can work with sites originating from a local folder, such as one on your own hard drive. Or, in a collaborative team environment, you can work with sites being developed on a remote server. Dreamweaver enables you to set up an unlimited number of sites to include the source and destination directories, FTP user names and passwords, and more.

The Dreamweaver Site window, shown in Figure 1-11, is a visual interface in which you can click and drag files or select a number of files and transfer them with the Get and Put buttons. You can even set the preferences so the system automatically disconnects after remaining idle for a user-definable period of time.

Figure 1-11: The FTP Site window enables you to publish your Web site directly from within Dreamweaver.

Site Map

Web sites can quickly outgrow the stage in which the designer can keep all the linked pages in mind. Dreamweaver includes a visual aid in the Web site management toolbox: the Site Map. With the Site Map, the Web designer can see how the entire Web site is structured. However, you can use the Site Map to do far more than just visualize the Web.

The Site Map, shown in Figure 1-12, can be used to establish the structure of the Web site in addition to viewing it. New pages can be created, and links can be added, modified, or deleted. In fact, the Site Map is so powerful, it becomes a site manager as well.

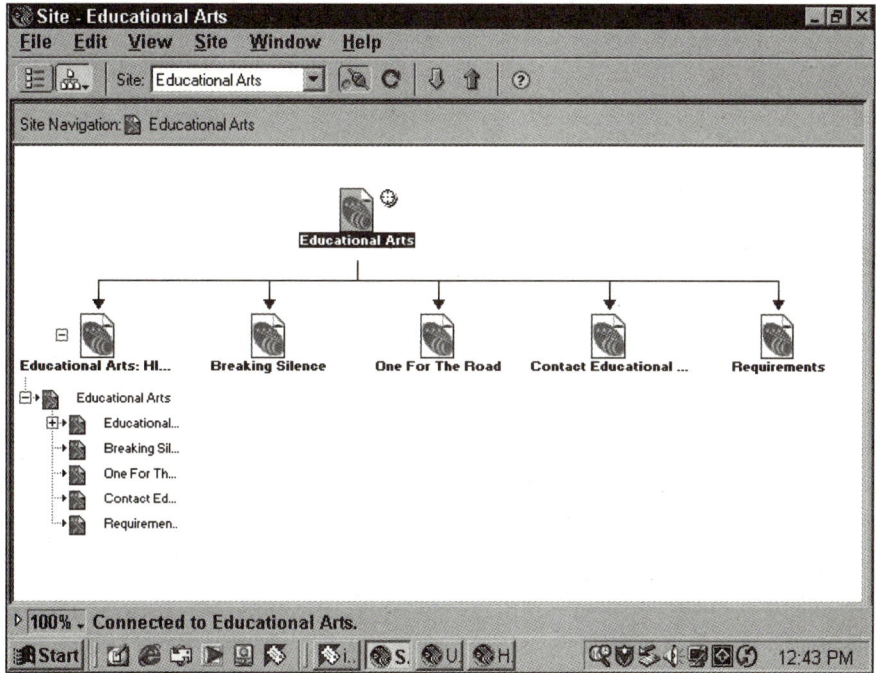

Figure 1-12: Use the Site Map to get an overall picture of your site — and then add new pages or links, right on the map.

File check in/check out

On larger Web projects, more than one person is usually responsible for creation and daily upkeep of the site. An editor may need to include the latest company press release, or a graphic artist may have to upload a photo of the newest product — all on the same page. To avoid conflicts with overlapping updates, Dreamweaver has devised a system under which Web pages can be marked as "checked out" and locked to prevent any other corrections until the file is once again "checked in."

Dreamweaver places a green checkmark over a file's icon in the Site Files window when it has been checked out by you, and a red mark if it has been checked out by another member of your team. And, so you won't have to guess who that team member is, Dreamweaver displays the name of the person next to the filename. You can also keep track of who last checked out a particular Web page (or image) — Dreamweaver keeps an ongoing log listing the file, person, and date and time of the check out.

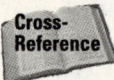

Cross-Reference   You can learn all about Dreamweaver's Web publishing capabilities in Chapter 7.

Summary

Building a Web site is half craft and half art, and Dreamweaver is the perfect tool for blending these often dueling disciplines. Dreamweaver's visual editor enables quick and artful page creation, and at the same time, its integrated text editors offer the detail-oriented focus required by programmers. Dreamweaver's key features include the following:

✦ Dreamweaver works the way professional Web developers do, with integrated visual and text editors. Dreamweaver won't convert your HTML code when it's used with preexisting Web pages.

✦ Dreamweaver supports HTML standard commands with easy entry and editing of text, graphics, tables, and multimedia elements.

✦ Dreamweaver makes cutting-edge features, such as Dynamic HTML and Cascading Style Sheets, easy to use.

✦ Dreamweaver offers you a variety of reusable JavaScript behaviors, object libraries, commands, and templates to streamline your Web page creation.

✦ Dreamweaver's wide range of site management tools include FTP publishing with a file-locking capability that encourages team creation and maintenance, as well as a built-in Link Checker and visual Site Map.

In the next chapter, you hit the ground running with a quick-start guide to Dreamweaver.

✦   ✦   ✦

QuickStart for Beginners

Designing a Web site is a big job, and Dreamweaver is a big program; both can be overwhelming when you first approach them. If you're new to Web design in general or to Dreamweaver in particular, the best way to learn about either of them is to build several sample sites. I've found that working on a project helps most people absorb all the little nuances of a program needed to be productive.

This chapter presents an overview of how I use Dreamweaver to begin building a Web site. A hallmark of any world-class software program such as Dreamweaver, is its capability to be used in many ways by many different people. Don't get the idea that what follows is the only way to construct a site; it is, however, the basic methodology that I've used successfully over the years.

If you are totally new to Web-site creation or to Dreamweaver, I recommend reading through the chapter in one sitting. Doing so will give you an overview of both the process and the program. Throughout this chapter, you can find many cross-references to other sections of the book where step-by-step instructions are detailed. As you begin to build your sites, use this chapter as a jumping-off place to delve deeper into each topic.

Setting up a Site

The first phase of designing a Web site involves pure input. You need to gather as much information from your client as possible. Some of this information relates to the overall message of the Web site along with its purpose, intended audience, and goals. Other elements, such as logos, textual content, and prior marketing materials are more tangible. I've found it best to get up front as much information — in both categories — as possible.

Tip

Whenever possible, get your data in digital format; the images ideally should be in a format that your graphics program can read and the content should be in a standard word processing file. Your workflow will be greatly enhanced if you don't have to spend time recreating logos or keying in faxed text.

As you are sketching out design ideas for the look of the site (on paper and in your head), you can begin to set up the structure of the site on your computer. Dreamweaver uses a folder on your hard drive as the local site root; when the site goes live on the Internet, the local site is mirrored on the Web server, also known as the *remote site*. So the very first physical step is to create a folder with the site or client name. All you need is a single folder to define a site in Dreamweaver and to begin building your Web site. Here's one way to start:

1. Using the system file manager, create a folder on your local hard drive and give it a unique name, reflective of the client or site.

2. In Dreamweaver, open the Site window, as shown in Figure 2-1, by choosing the Show Site button from the Launcher. Alternatively, you could select Window ➪ Site Files or use the keyboard shortcut F8.

Figure 2-1: Use Dreamweaver's Site window to lay out the structure of your Web site.

3. From the site list, choose Define Sites. The Define Sites dialog box opens, displaying a list of your currently available sites, if any.

4. Select the New button to set the parameters of your new site.

5. In the Site Definition dialog box, enter the name of the new site, its local root folder, its HTTP address, and the name of the home page.

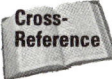 **Cross-Reference**   A detailed breakdown of the process of defining a site can be found in Chapter 6.

After the site is initially defined, you have a folder and a single file set up as the home page, as shown in the Site Map view displayed in Figure 2-2. Dreamweaver's Site Map is not just a useful tool for maintaining a Web site; it is also useful when developing the site structure. I recommend that you use it to develop the entire structure of your Web site before you begin adding content.

Figure 2-2: The Web site is defined and the home page is created.

Using the techniques outlined in Chapter 6, you can then create new blank files, already linked to your home page. These new pages act as placeholders for content to come. They also help to ease the building of the site by providing existing pages to link to and to preview the navigation of your site. To function properly, many of Dreamweaver's commands depend on a file being saved. So, by prebuilding your site pages, you avoid unnecessary delays and warning dialog boxes. By the time you're finished, your Web site is beginning to take form, as shown in Figure 2-3.

Figure 2-3: Dreamweaver's Site window is a valuable Web-site prototyping tool.

Note   While it's not necessary to create all the pages a site might use, I find it helpful to make the primary ones linked to the home page. Then, when I work on each section, such as Products, I use the Site window to create the pages in that division.

Creating Your Home Page Layout

With the site's structure beginning to emerge, it's time to turn your attention to the page that most visitors' first see at the Web site: the home page. Although any page can act as a doorway to your site, the home page is by far the most commonly used entrance. I like to start my design on the home page for another reason also—I frequently reuse core elements from the home page, such as the logo and navigation system, throughout the site. By setting these designs early—and getting approval for them—I can save myself a fair amount of work down the road while maintaining a consistent look-and-feel to the site.

Starting with the \<head\>

One of the most important sections of a Web page is also one of those most frequently—and wrongly—ignored: the \<head\> section. Under normal circumstances, the \<head\> area (as opposed to the \<body\>) is not seen, but its effect is enormous. The \<head\> section contains vital information about the page and the site itself, including the page's title, its description, and the keywords used to describe the page for search engines. Much of this information is contained in a page's `<meta>` tags. I like to add this information at the beginning of my Web site development, partly to get the chore out of the way, but primarily so that I don't forget to do it! Dreamweaver offers an easy way to input `<head>` information:

1. Change the Title field in the Toolbar from Unnamed Document to whatever you'd like to appear in the browser title bar. Remember that a page's title is a primary criterion that search engines use to rank a site.

2. Choose View ➪ Head Content from the main menu or choose Head Content under the View Options button on the Toolbar. The `<head>` section appears at the top of the Document window as shown in Figure 2-4.

Figure 2-4: The `<head>` area holds important information for search engines.

3. From the Head category of the Objects panel insert both a Keywords and a Description object, and fill them out appropriately. I prefer that my clients supply both the keywords and the description whenever possible. They know their business best and how best to market it.

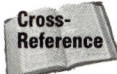

Cross-Reference For a detailed description of the `<head>` section and its various tags, turn to Chapter 8.

4. Close the Head Content view by deselecting that option under the View Options button of the Toolbar.

Specifying page colors

After the first *Dreamweaver Bible* was published, I received an irate e-mail from a beginning Web designer who was infuriated by one of Macromedia's practices. By default, Dreamweaver pages all specify a white background color — and nothing else. The gentleman who was complaining set his browser colors to have a black background with white lettering — an austere look, but it was his preference. Whenever he previewed default Dreamweaver pages with his browser, his text seemed to disappear. His text was still there, of course, but because it was white text on a white background, it was invisible. The moral of this story is to always specify your background, text, and link colors if you want your Web pages to maintain your designed look.

After entering the `<head>` content, I next define the page's colors and margins through Dreamweaver's Page Properties dialog box, shown in Figure 2-5. Choose Modify ➪ Page Properties to set these parameters. This is also the location for setting up a background image, if you're using one. I often alter these settings several times in the home page design stage as I try out different looks, so I've memorized the keyboard shortcut Ctrl+J (Command+J).

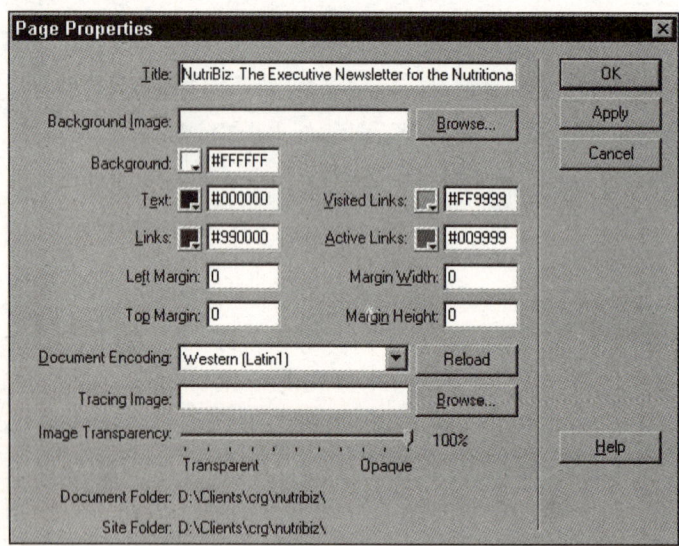

Figure 2-5: Be sure to set your page colors through the Page Properties dialog box.

Tip   Not sure about your color combinations? Dreamweaver has a useful command, Set Color Scheme, which contains background, text, and link color selections that are designed to work together.

Initial graphic layout

Like many small-shop Web designers, I create the majority of the graphics to use on my pages myself, and the Dreamweaver/Fireworks Studio has been a major boon to my productivity. Typically, I create or modify the logo for the home page in Fireworks while Dreamweaver is open, for instant placement and integration. Although the use of layers is always a possibility for placement, I prefer to lay out my pages with tables for most situations. Many designers new to the Web — especially those from a print background — prefer the exact positioning of layers and can use Dreamweaver's excellent layers-to-tables conversion features. The approach that is used is up to you, but remember that many clients still balk at using layers for fear of excluding visitors with older browsers.

Dreamweaver 4 includes a new feature that makes composing the basic layout of a page very straightforward: the Layout View. Here's how a typical home page is developed using this new tool:

1. Start by creating a logo for the Web in your favorite graphics editor. Remember that Web graphics are of a particular format, usually GIF or JPEG with a screen resolution of 72 dpi. Although most Web page visitors' monitors display thousands of colors, it's still good practice to use Web-safe colors wherever possible.

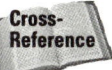 You can find an explanation of Web graphic formats and Web-safe colors in Chapter 10.

2. In Dreamweaver, choose the Layout View from the bottom of the Objects panel. With Layout View enabled, both the Draw Layout Cell and Draw Layout Table tools, also on the Objects panel, become available.

3. Select Draw Layout Cell and drag out the initial cell for holding the logo. Dreamweaver automatically creates a layout table — a borderless table that is the full width of your window — around the layout cell.

4. Press the Ctrl (Command) key to continue drawing out other layout cells for your navigational elements and any other upfront information such as company name.

   Although your layout is likely to be different from mine, in the example shown in Figure 2-6, I start with a two-row by two-column configuration and modify it as needed.

 Tables are an important layout tool for Web designers. Chapter 13 shows you how to create and modify tables in Dreamweaver.

Figure 2-6: Placing the logo in a table to begin laying out the page.

5. Place your logo in the layout cell by choosing Insert Image from the Objects panel or dragging the graphic into place from the Assets panel.

6. Add background color to the table or rows, if desired, by picking a color from the Property Inspector.

   Using a table's background color features is a good, no overhead way to add color to your page. Dreamweaver enables me to sample colors directly from the logo to begin to tie the page together graphically.

7. If desired, adjust the positioning of the logo by using the Align option on the Property Inspector.

I continue to add and modify elements to the logo area until I'm satisfied. In the case of the example site, I added right-justified contact information on one side of the table and then added navigation elements below the logo, as shown in Figure 2-7. I used a contrasting background color for the second smaller row to set off the navigation bar. Initially, the navigation bar is just text and not graphics; this enables me to prototype the page quickly, and I can always replace the text with images at a later date. Cascading Style Sheets or Dreamweaver 's HTML Styles control the look of the text.

Figure 2-7: All the graphic elements are now in place in the logo area.

Note

One advantage of using tables instead of layers is that tables can adjust in width more consistently across browsers than layers can. Dreamweaver's layout tables are set to 100 percent width. If I use the Page Properties dialog to change the margins to zero, I can be sure the background color will stretch across the page, regardless of the user's browser window size.

Including Client Text

Now that your home page is beginning to attract some eyeballs with its graphic look, it is time to throw in some content to get the message across. Text from a client comes in many forms: from the headings and paragraphs of a marketing brochure to bulleted copy points written especially for the Web, and everything in between. Your job as a Web designer is to make it all flow together in a logical, attractive, understandable fashion.

Many print designers coming to the Internet are appalled at the lack of typographic control on the Web. Particular fonts are, for the most part, suggested rather than specified, with alternatives always available. Sizes are often relative and line spacing — outside of Cascading Style Sheets — is nonexistent. A typical first response is to render blocks of text into graphics to achieve exactly the look desired. In a word, don't. Graphics, unlike text, aren't searchable, and displaying text as graphics defeats much of the purpose of the Web. Moreover, large blocks of graphics can take a long time to download. It's far better to learn the ins and outs of HTML text and take advantage of its universality. Besides, Cascading Style Sheets are increasingly a real option and give the Web designer almost as much control as the print designer.

To facilitate including client-generated text in my Web page designs, I often work with my word processing program and Dreamweaver open simultaneously. This arrangement enables me to quickly cut and paste text from one to the other.

Note   If you have a great deal of already-formatted client text to include on your page —and a copy of Microsoft Word — take advantage of Dreamweaver's new Import Word HTML feature. When you run the command, Dreamweaver brings the Word-generated HTML document into a new page, and you can copy the needed sections (or all of it, if you like) and paste them directly into the home page. Dreamweaver preserves all the coding during the copy-and-paste operation.

I generally adopt a top-down approach when inserting text: I place the headings followed by the body copy. Then I can try different heading sizes, independently of the main paragraphs.

Tip   If you're copying multiple paragraphs from your word processing document, make sure that your paragraphs are separated by two returns. When pasted into Dreamweaver, the paragraph breaks will be preserved. If you just have a single return between paragraphs, Dreamweaver converts the paragraphs to line breaks.

Although it depends on the design, I rarely let the text flow all the way across the page. If my page margins are set at zero—which they often are for the graphics I use—the text then bumps right up against the edge of the browser windows. I frequently use two techniques in combination. First, I place the text in a table that is set at 95 percent width or less and that is centered on the page. This assures me that some "air" or gutter-space is on either side of my text, no matter how the browser window is sized. I'm also fond of the <blockquote> tag, which indents text by a browser-defined amount. You can access the <blockquote> tag by selecting your text and choosing the Indent button on the Property Inspector. The text blocks on the example page shown in Figure 2-8 use both techniques.

I feel that it's important to style your text in some fashion to maintain the desired look. Unless you specify the font, size, and color, you're at the mercy of your visitors' browser preferences — which can totally wreck your layout. You have two methods for defining text formatting: standard HTML tags and Cascading Style Sheets (CSS). Whenever possible, I use CSS because of its greater degree of control and flexibility. With CSS, if a client doesn't like the color of body text I've chosen or its size, I can modify it sitewide with one alteration. HTML tags, on the other hand, offer backward compatibility with 3.0 browsers. However, for most clients, the relatively small percentage of visitors still using the earlier browser versions is a fair trade-off for the power of CSS.

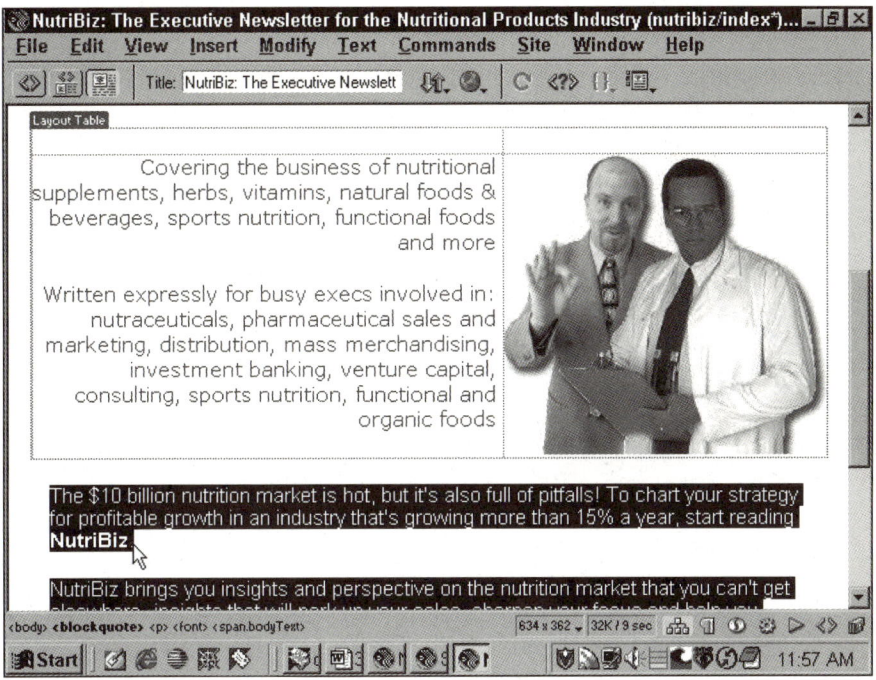

Figure 2-8: The text in the top paragraph (next to the image) is set within a centered table, whereas the text below is indented with the `<blockquote>` tag.

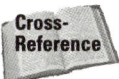
Cross-Reference To get the full scope of what CSS can do for you and your Web sites, see Chapter 27.

Activating the Page

Study after study has proven that an engaged viewer remembers your message better than a passive viewer. One method of grabbing people's attention is to activate your Web page in some fashion, so that some element of the page reacts to the visitor's mouse movements. This reaction could be anything from a simple rollover to the complete rewriting of a frame. Activating a page typically requires a combination of HTML and JavaScript, frequently beyond the programming skill level — or interest — of the Web designer. Luckily, Dreamweaver makes such effects possible through behaviors.

After I have the basic layout of a page done, I go back and activate the page in a fitting manner. As with any effect, too many behaviors can be more distracting than attractive; it's best to use them only when called for. At the very least, I typically use some form of rollover for the navigation bar; this is especially feasible now with Dreamweaver's tighter integration with Fireworks. But even without Fireworks, Dreamweaver enables you to construct a complete multistate navigation bar, or you can just use the Swap Image behavior to create your own.

Here's one method of activating your page:

1. In Fireworks, or another graphics program, create a series of rollover buttons with one image for each state.

   You need at least two states (Up and Over) and as many as four (Up, Over, Down, and Over While Down).

2. In Dreamweaver, remove the temporary text links for the navigation bar.

3. If you've created your rollover buttons in Fireworks, you can just choose Insert Fireworks HTML from the Objects panel.

   Dreamweaver inserts a table of sliced images, such as those in Figure 2-9, complete with all the necessary code.

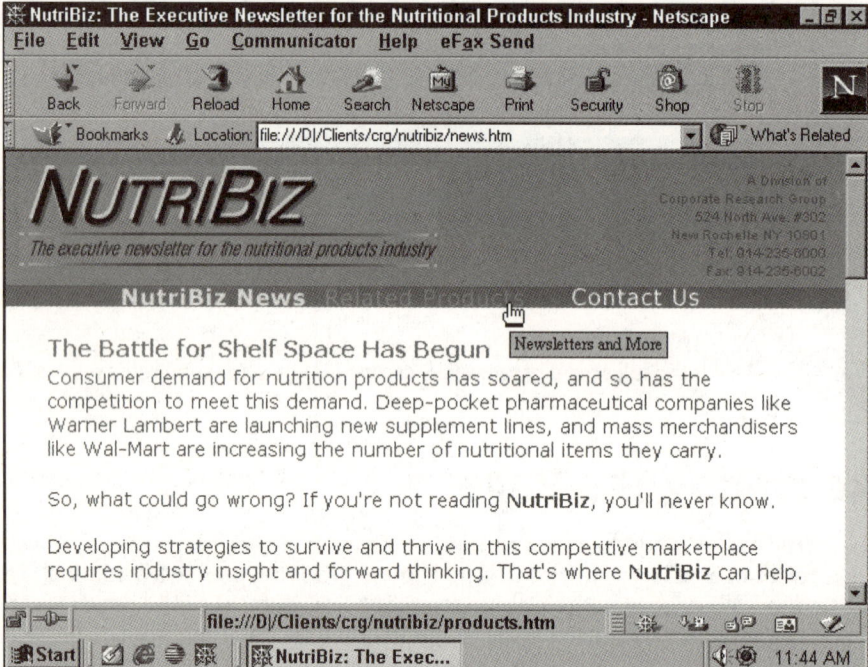

Figure 2-9: These rollover buttons were imported directly from Fireworks-generated HTML.

4. If you're working with separate images for the various rollover states, either use the Swap Image behavior or insert a Navigation Bar object. Either method enables you to select the separate images for your rollover states.

Cross-Reference   All of Dreamweaver's standard behaviors are covered in Chapter 19; information on the Navigation Bar object can be found in Chapter 10.

If I'm using tables for my layouts, I tend to nest the table containing the Navigation Bar inside the cell of another table. This technique gives me a fluid design that resizes and realigns well to match the user's browser window. For instance, in the NutriBiz example site, I merged all the columns in the row beneath the logo and then centered the table containing the navigation buttons.

New Feature Another alternative, sure to give your page some pizzazz, are the new Flash Button objects. A *Flash Button* is a predesigned graphic template with animation and possibly sound that uses your specified text. Flash Buttons are great for quickly turning out a professional quality navigation system. Because the are actually Flash animations, they depend on the user having the Flash Player plugin installed — which, as of this writing, is the case in over 92 percent of the systems running.

After I've completed the initial elements of my page, I take advantage of one of Dreamweaver's key features: Library items. By turning my Navigation Bar into a Library item, I can easily reuse it on the same page (as I do in the example page at the bottom), and on every other page of the site. Not only does this keep consistent elements on every page — an important consideration for design — but if I ever need to update the navigation system by changing a link or adding more buttons, I can do it in one step. Moreover, Dreamweaver's Library items, if activated with behaviors, retain all the necessary code.

Cross-Reference Library items are extremely useful for cutting your production time. Learn more about them in Chapter 33.

Previewing and Posting the Page

No matter how beautiful or spectacular your home page design, it's not a Web page until it's viewed through a Web browser and posted on the Web. Now, "the Web" could just as easily be a company intranet or the Internet. But chances are that if the page is intended to be viewed by numerous people, it will be seen under a number of different circumstances. Different operating systems, browsers, screen sizes, and resolutions are just some of the variables you have to take as a given — which is why previewing and testing your Web page is vitally important.

Here are a few pointers for initially testing your pages in development:

✦ At the very least, you should look at your Web page through versions of both major browsers. Dreamweaver enables you to specify up to 13 browsers with its Preview in Browser feature; I currently have 5 available on my system.

✦ During the initial building phase, my routine is to preview my page with both my primary browser (as of this writing, Netscape 4.7) and secondary browser (Internet Explorer 5.5) whenever I add a major component to the page.

✦ I make it a point to resize the page several times to see how my layout is affected by different screen sizes. If the client has specified maximum browser compatibility as a site requirement, I also look at the page under various screen resolutions.

✦ When a page is largely completed, I run Dreamweaver's Check Target Browsers command to make sure I'm not committing some grievous error. If incompatibilities do appear — as they do especially when checking the earliest browsers as shown in Figure 2-10 — I have to decide whether to keep the offending tag or risk the page being visited by users with those browsers.

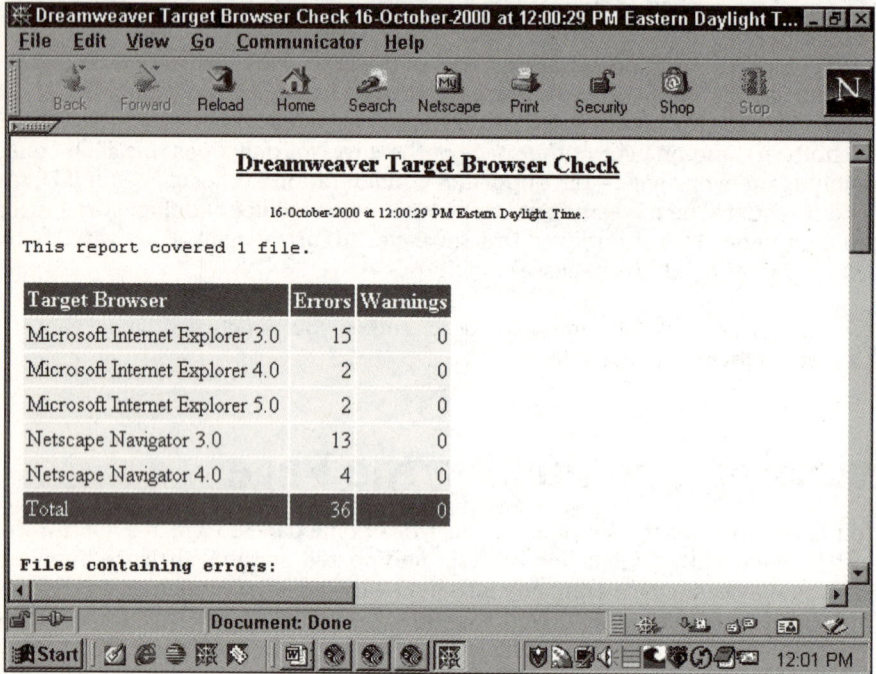

Figure 2-10: Errors from the Check Target Browser command are not uncommon when checking early browser versions.

I also make it a habit to routinely check the Download Stats found in Dreamweaver's status bar. The Download Stats show the "weight" of a page — its file size and the download time at a set speed. By default, the speed is set for a 28.8 Kbps modem, but you can alter that in the Status Bar category of Preferences. Remember that the Download Stats include all the dependent files (images and other media) as well as the size of the page itself.

To be sure that all my ducks are in a row and that all my links are valid, I run Dreamweaver's Check Links Sitewide command. Not only does this give me a report of broken links, but it also displays orphaned files and offers a list of external links that I can verify from its report.

My final testing phase is always conducted online. Here's a procedure that you can use for uploading your site and testing it:

1. Choose Window ⇨ Site Files to open the Site window. By this time you've already established a domain with an Internet host and edited your site definition to include the necessary FTP information.

2. Select the Connect button on the Site window. Dreamweaver logs in to the remote system and displays the remote files in the category opposite the local files.

3. Select the HTML files for the completed Web pages.

4. Choose the Put button.

5. By default, Dreamweaver asks if you'd like to include the dependent files; click Yes.

   Dreamweaver begins to transfer the HTML files and all the dependent files. All necessary subfolders (images, media) are created to replicate the local site structure on the remote site.

Note If the Include Dependent Files dialog box does not appear, then open Preferences and, on the Site FTP category, select the Dependent Files: Prompt on Put/Check In option.

6. After the file transfer is complete, open a browser and connect to the URL for the site.

7. Navigate to every page and try all links and user actions, including rollovers. Note any "files not found" or other errors.

8. If errors occurred, return to Dreamweaver and verify the links for the problem files.

9. If necessary, repair the links and re-upload the HTML file. In most cases, you will not need to resend the dependent files.

10. Repeat Steps 6 through 9 with all available browsers and systems.

Tip If the site is publicly viewable on the Internet, be sure to view the pages through an America Online (AOL) browser. Although AOL uses an Internet Explorer-derived browser, it also compresses graphics with its own algorithm and tends to open with smaller-than-normal windows. If you find problems, consult AOL's Webmaster Site at http://webmaster.info.aol.com.

Summary

When people ask me what I like about designing Web sites, I tell them that it appeals to me because it engages both my left and right brain. Web site design is, at turns, both creative and pragmatic, and Dreamweaver balances that equation with grace. Although everyone works differently, these are some of the points I try to keep in mind as I'm working:

✦ The more time spent in planning, the less time spent in revision. Get as much information as possible from the client before you begin designing.

✦ Use Dreamweaver's Site Map to prototype the site; the existing structure saves time as you begin to fill in the content.

✦ Work from the home page out. The home page is primarily used to succinctly express the client's message, and it often sets the tone for the entire site.

✦ Include some interactivity in your Web page. A static page may be beautiful to behold, but an active page enables the visitor to interact and leaves a more lasting impression.

✦ Preview your pages early and often during the development phase. It's far better to discover an incompatibility with the page half done than when you're demoing for the client.

In the next chapter, you get an in-depth tour of all of Dreamweaver's features.

✦   ✦   ✦

Touring Dreamweaver

CHAPTER

Dreamweaver's user interface is clean, efficient, and powerful. By offering streamlined tools and controls, Dreamweaver helps you focus on the most important area of the screen: your Web page design. This chapter provides a detailed overview of the Dreamweaver workspace so you know where all the tools are when you need to use them.

Many other Web authoring programs surround your page-in-progress with numerous menu strips, icons, and other interface paraphernalia. Dreamweaver takes a more streamlined approach, however, which enables you to keep the focus on your workspace as your page develops. Dockable panels further reduce onscreen clutter; in Dreamweaver, every panel is dockable, including the Code Inspector.

Viewing the Document Window

Dreamweaver's primary workspace is the Document window. When you first start Dreamweaver, you see what is essentially an empty canvas, as shown in Figure 3-1. This is where you create your Web pages by typing in headlines and paragraphs, inserting images and links, and creating tables, forms, and other HTML elements.

The Web design process consists of creating your page in Dreamweaver and then previewing the results in one or more browsers. As your Web page begins to take shape, Dreamweaver shows you a close representation of how the page looks when viewed through a browser such as Netscape Communicator or Internet Explorer. You can do this as often as you like — Dreamweaver displays the page in your favorite browser with the press of a button. You can even view active elements, such as QuickTime movies or Shockwave and Flash files, in your Web page as you're building it.

Menus   Document window   Objects palette

Tag selector   Window size   Launcher

Download indicator

Figure 3-1: Dreamweaver's opening window is designed to maximize your workspace with a minimum of distracting tools and windows.

Dreamweaver surrounds your "empty canvas" with the tools you need to create your Web masterpiece. We start our tour with the first of these: the status bar.

Working with the Status Bar

The status bar is found at the bottom of the Document window. Embedded here are four important tools: the Tag Selector, the Window Size pop-up menu, the Download Indicator, and the Launcher. Beyond displaying useful information such as which windows are open, these status bar tools are extremely helpful and provide the Web designer with several timesaving utilities.

Tip If you don't see the status bar at the bottom of your screen, check the View menu. Make sure there's a checkmark next to the status bar item; if not, select it with your mouse to enable it.

Tag Selector

The Tag Selector is an excellent example of Dreamweaver's elegant design approach. On the left side of the status bar, you see a listing of the current HTML tags. When you first open a blank page in Dreamweaver, you see only the <body> tag. If you type a line of text and then press Enter (Return), the paragraph tag <p> appears. Your cursor's position in the document determines which tags are displayed in the Tag Selector. The Tag Selector constantly keeps track of where you are in the HTML document by displaying the tags surrounding your current cursor position. This becomes especially important when you are building complex Web pages that use such features as nested tables.

As its name implies, the Tag Selector does more than just indicate a position in a document. Using the Tag Selector, you can quickly choose any of the elements surrounding your current cursor. Once an element is selected, you can quickly modify or delete it. If you have the Property Inspector (described later in this chapter) onscreen, choosing a different code from the Tag Selector makes the corresponding options available in the Property Inspector.

Tip If you want to quickly clear most of your HTML page, choose the <body> tag and press Delete. All graphics, text, and other elements you have inserted through the Document window are erased. Left intact is any HTML code in the <head> section, including your title, <meta> tags, and any preliminary JavaScript. The <body> tag is also left intact.

In a more complex Web page section such as the one shown in Figure 3-2, the Tag Selector shows a wider variety of HTML tags. As you move your pointer over individual codes in the Tag Selector, they are highlighted; click one, and the code becomes bold. Tags are displayed from left to right in the Tag Selector, starting on the far left with the most inclusive (in this case the <body> tag) and proceeding to the narrowest selection (here, the italic <i> tag) on the far right.

As a Web page developer, you're constantly selecting elements in order to modify them. Rather than relying on the click-and-drag method to highlight an area — which often grabs unwanted sections of your code, such as <font> tags — use the Tag Selector to unerringly pick just the code you want. Dreamweaver's Tag Selector is a subtle but extremely useful tool that can speed up your work significantly.

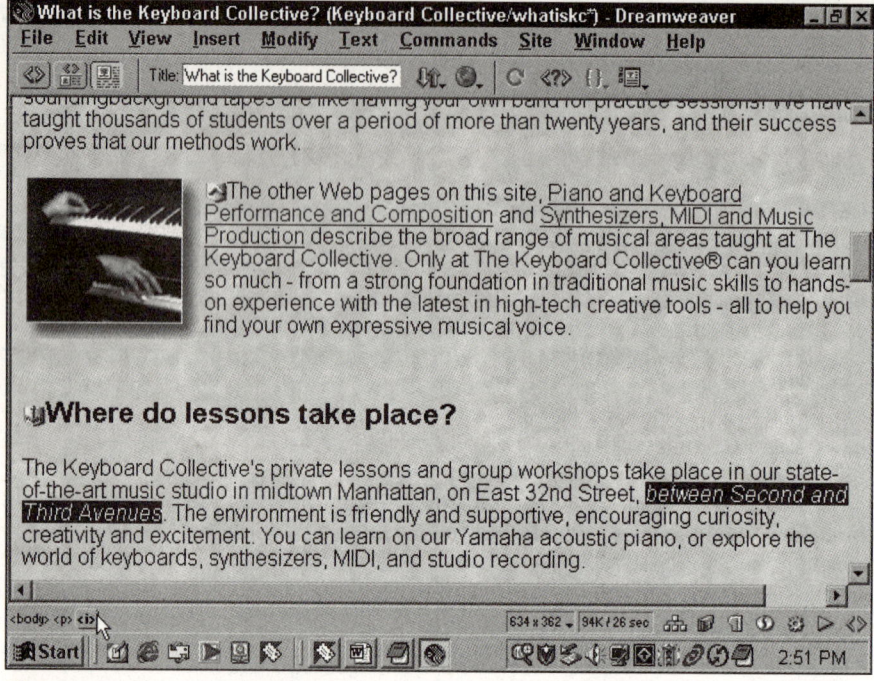

Figure 3-2: The Tag Selector enables you to highlight just the code you want. Here, selecting the ⟨i⟩ tag chooses only the italicized portion of the text.

Window Size pop-up menu

The universality of the Internet enables virtually any type of computer system from anywhere in the world to access publicly available Web pages. Although this accessibility is a boon to global communication, it forces Web designers to be aware of how their creations look under various circumstances—especially different screen sizes.

The Window Size pop-up menu gives designers a sense of how their pages look on different monitors. Located just right of center on the status bar, the Window Size pop-up menu indicates the screen size of the current Document window, in pixels, in *width×height* format. If you resize your Document window, the Window Size indicator updates instantly. This indicator gives you an immediate check on the dimensions of the current page.

But the Window Size pop-up menu goes beyond just telling you the size of your screen—it also enables you to quickly view your page through a wide variety of monitor sizes. Naturally, your monitor must be capable of displaying the larger screen dimensions before they can be selected. To select a different screen size, follow these steps:

1. Click once on the expander arrow to the right of the displayed dimensions.

   A menu listing the standard sizes, shown in Figure 3-3, pops up.

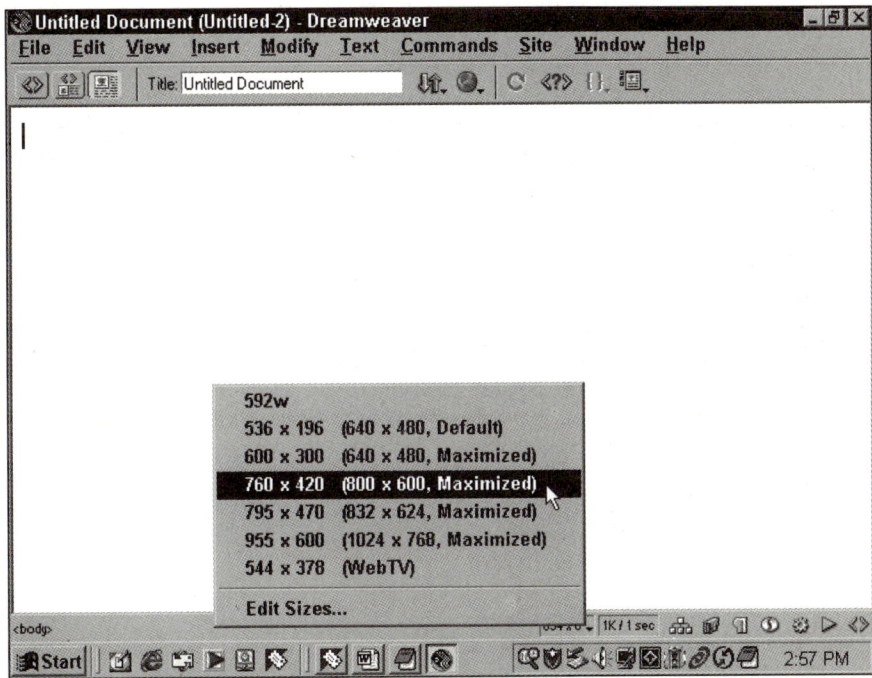

Figure 3-3: You can change your current screen size to any of seven standard sizes — or add your own custom sizes — with the Window Size pop-up menu.

2. Holding down the mouse button, move your mouse over a desired screen size.

3. To select a size, release the mouse button.

The standard sizes, and the machines most commonly using them, are as follows:

✦ 592w

✦ 536×196 (640×480, Default)

✦ 600×300 (640×480, Maximized)

✦ 760×420 (800×600, Maximized)

✦ 795×470 (832×624, Maximized)

✦ 955×600 (1024×768, Maximized)

✦ 544×378 (WebTV)

The first option, 592w, is the only option that does not change the height as well as the width. Instead, this choice uses the current window height and just alters the width.

Tip You can set up your own custom screen settings by choosing Edit Sizes from the Window Size pop-up menu. This option opens the Status Bar category of the Preferences dialog box. How you modify the pop-up list is described in Chapter 4.

The dimensions offered by the Window Size pop-up menu describe the entire editable area of a page. The Document window has been carefully designed to match specifications set by the primary browsers. Both the left and right margins are the same width as both the Netscape and Microsoft browsers, and the status bar matches the height of the browser's bottom row as well. The height of any given browser environment depends on which toolbars are being used; however, Dreamweaver's menu strip is the same height as the browsers' menu strips.

Tip If you want to compensate for the other browser user interface elements, such as the toolbar and the Address bar (collectively called "chrome"), you can increase the height of your Document window by approximately 72 pixels. Combined, Navigator's toolbar (44 pixels high) and Address bar (24 pixels) at 68 pixels are slightly narrower than Internet Explorer's total chrome. Microsoft includes an additional bottom separator that adds 6 pixels to its other elements (toolbar, 42 pixels; and Address bar, 24) for a total of 72 pixels. Of course, with so many browser variables, the best design course is to leave some flexibility in your design.

Download Indicator

So you've built your Web masterpiece, and you've just finished uploading the HTML, along with the 23 JPEGs, eight audio files, and three Flash movies that make up the page. You open the page over the Net and — surprise! — it takes five minutes to download. Okay, this example is a tad extreme, but every Web developer knows that opening a page from your hard drive and opening a page over the Internet are two vastly different experiences. Dreamweaver has taken the guesswork out of loading a page from the Web by providing the Download Indicator.

The Download Indicator is located to the right of the Window Size pop-up menu on the status bar. As illustrated in Figure 3-4, Dreamweaver gives you two values, separated by a slash character:

✦ The cumulative size of the page, including all the associated graphics, plug-ins, and multimedia files, measured in kilobytes (K).

✦ The time it takes to download at a particular modem connection speed, measured in seconds (sec).

Tip   You can check the download size of any individual graphic by selecting it and looking at the Property Inspector—you can find the file size in kilobytes next to the thumbnail image on the left.

Figure 3-4: Take notice of the Download Indicator whenever you lay out a page with extensive graphics or other large multimedia files.

The Download Indicator is a handy real-world check. As you build your Web pages, it's a good practice to keep an eye on your file's download size—both in kilobytes and seconds. As a Web designer, you ultimately have to decide what your audience will deem is worth the wait and what will have them reaching for that Stop button. For example, the graphic shown in Figure 3-4 is attractive, but at 35K it's on the borderline of an acceptable size. Either the graphic should probably be reduced in size or the number of colors lessened to lower the overall "weight" of the page.

Cross-Reference   Not everybody has the same modem connection. If you are working with an intranet or on a broadband site, you can set your connection speed far higher. Likewise, if your site gets a lot of traffic, you can lower the connection speed. You change the anticipated download speed through Dreamweaver's Preferences dialog box, as explained in Chapter 4.

Launcher

On the far right of the status bar, you find the Launcher — or, rather, one of the Launchers. In addition to the one on the status bar (known as the Mini-Launcher), Dreamweaver offers an independent, draggable panel with larger, named buttons that is also known as the Launcher. Both Launchers open and close the same windows by default: Site, Assets, HTML Styles, CSS Styles, Behavior, History, and Code Inspector. A key feature of the Launcher is that it's completely customizable.

As with the Tag Selector, each one of the buttons in the Mini-Launcher lights up when the pointer passes over it and stays lit when selected. You can also use the Launcher to close the windows it has opened — just click the highlighted button. Dreamweaver enables you to keep open any or all of the different windows at the same time.

Clicking a Launcher or Mini-Launcher button when a window is already open has one of two effects. If the window for the button is on top, the window closes. If the window is hidden behind another floating window, the window corresponding to the button is brought forward.

Tip   If you don't want the Mini-Launcher to appear in the status bar, you can turn it off. Choose Edit ➪ Preferences and then select the Status Bar category. Click Show Launcher in Status Bar to remove its checkmark and then click OK. Naturally, you can turn the Launcher back on by rechecking its box.

The features of the various windows controlled through the Mini-Launcher are discussed in the section "Using the Launcher," later in this chapter.

Accessing the Toolbar

Regardless of the job — whether it's hanging a picture or fixing a faucet — work goes faster when your tools are at your fingertips. The same principle holds true for Web site building: the easier it is to accomplish the most often required tasks, the more productive you'll be as a Web designer. Dreamweaver puts a number of the repetitive tasks, such as previewing your page in a browser, just a function key away. However, there are far more necessary operations than there are function keys. In an effort to put needed functionality right up front, Dreamweaver incorporates the toolbar.

New Feature   The toolbar appears across the top of the Document window, whether in Design or Code view. On the toolbar you'll find some of the most frequently used commands that affect the entire document. The toolbar itself is toggled by choosing View ➪ Toolbar or by choosing Ctrl+Shift+T (Command+Shift+T). One of the best features of the toolbar is its quick and easy access to changing your Web page's title, as shown in Figure 3-5.

Figure 3-5: The toolbar offers easy access to an important element of a Web page, the title.

The first set of buttons is dedicated to the various views: Code, Code and Design, and Design view. These buttons are mutually exclusive as only one view can be shown at a time. Next to the view buttons is a text field for displaying and altering the title of your document. Dreamweaver, by default, titles every new page "Untitled Document." Not only is it considered bad form to keep this default title, search engines rely on a relevant title to properly index a site. To change a page title, enter the new text in the Title field and press Enter (Return) to confirm your modification.

Managing Files

The File Management button, next to the Title field, contains Web publishing–related commands. While maintaining a Web site, you'll often be required to make small alterations such as changing a bit of text or rescaling an image. I prefer to post these changes as quickly as possible to get the work off my virtual desk. The Get and Put options, along with Check In and Check Out, found on the toolbar under File Management, greatly simplify the process and speed my work. Under the File Management button you'll find:

✦ **Turn off Read Only:** Unlocks the current file for editing.

✦ **Get:** Transfers the remote file to a local site.

✦ **Check Out:** Marks the file as checked out and gets the remote file.

✦ **Put:** Transfers the local file to the remote site.

✦ **Check In:** Marks the file as checked in and puts the file to the remote site.

✦ **Undo Check Out:** Replaces the local version of the page with the remote version effectively undoing any changes made on the local file.

✦ **Design Notes:** Opens the Design Notes dialog box for the current page.

✦ **Locate in Site:** Selects the current page in the file listings of the Site window.

Previewing and debugging your file

Although Dreamweaver gives you a good representation of what your page will look like when rendered in a browser, it's not perfect. There are so many variations among the different browser programs—not to mentions versions—that you absolutely must test your page throughout the development process. Dreamweaver gives you the tools for both previewing your page and debugging it, should JavaScript errors appear—and you can access those tools right from the toolbar.

Selecting the Preview/Debug in Browser button on the toolbar presents a dynamic list of available browsers. All of the browsers entered in Preferences appear first, with the primary and secondary browsers leading the list. After the preview commands, Dreamweaver displays Debug options for all the supported browsers installed on the local system.

 Note   Dreamweaver can preview in any browser you assign—however, the debugger only works with specific browsers.

The final entry under the toolbar's Preview/Debug in Browser button is Edit Browser List. When invoked, this command opens the Preview in Browser category of Preferences to enable you to add, remove, or otherwise manage the browsers on your system in relation to Dreamweaver.

Easy Refresh and Reference

The next two options on the toolbar are the Refresh and the Reference buttons. Use the Refresh button when you've altered code directly in the Code view to apply those changes in the Design view; this option is especially useful when the split-screen Code and Design view is in operation. The Reference button, as you might expect, opens the Reference panel. If a tag, attribute, JavaScript object, or CSS style rule is selected, choosing the Reference button causes the Reference panel to open to the pertinent entry.

Straight-away Code Navigation

Dreamweaver's code editor offers a number of key features for programming and debugging Web pages with increasingly complex JavaScript routines. Several of these features are grouped under the Code Navigation button found on the toolbar. One such feature is the ability to set *breakpoints*. Breakpoints are markers that temporarily halt the execution of the code when running the JavaScript Debugger. Once the program execution is stopped, the current values of variables and other information can be retrieved.

While you can set breakpoints directly in the JavaScript Debugger, you can also set them in Dreamweaver's Code view. Position the cursor where you'd like the program to stop during debugging and choose Set Breakpoint from the Code Navigation button. After the first breakpoint is set, two additional commands are dynamically added: Remove Breakpoint and Remove All Breakpoints. Remove Breakpoint is only active when placed on the code line where a breakpoint was previously applied.

The remainder of the menu items under the Code Navigation button display JavaScript functions in the current page. Selecting any of these functions positions the cursor directly on that piece of code in the Code view. This capability makes it easy to quickly move from function to function; it also tells you at a glance which functions are included in a page.

View Options

View Options is a welcome but somewhat schizophrenic button found all the way to the right on the toolbar. The options that it makes available depend on the view mode currently employed. If, for example, you're in Design view and choose View Options, you're given the option to hide the various visual aids, such as table or frame borders, individually or all at once. If, on the other hand, you're in Code view, the View Options button toggles code-oriented functions, such as Word Wrap and Line Numbers. Best of all, if you're in the split-screen Code and Design view, you get both sets of view options!

The view options, all of which act as toggles, under Design view are:

- ✦ Hide All Visual Aids
- ✦ Visual Aids ⇨ Table Borders, Layer Borders, Frame Borders, Image Maps, and Invisible Elements
- ✦ Head Content
- ✦ Rulers
- ✦ Grid
- ✦ Tracing Image
- ✦ Design View on Top

When in Code view, the view options are:

- ✦ Word Wrap
- ✦ Line Numbers
- ✦ Highlight Invalid HTML
- ✦ Syntax Coloring
- ✦ Auto Indent

Selecting Items from the Objects Panel

The Objects panel holds the items most often used—the primary colors, as it were—when designing Web pages. Everything from images to ActiveX plug-ins to HTML comments can be selected from the Objects panel. Moreover, the Objects panel is completely customizable—you can add your own favorite items and even set up how the Objects panel is organized.

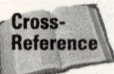

Cross-Reference   To see how you can build your own Dreamweaver objects and modify the Objects panel, turn to Chapter 18.

The Objects panel is divided into seven separate categories of objects: Characters, Common, Forms, Frames, Head, Invisibles, and Special. The initial view is of the Common category. To switch from one category to another, select the small expander arrow at the top of the Objects panel (see Figure 3-6) and then choose an option from the resulting pop-up menu. Each category is described in detail in the following sections.

Drag bar   Close button

Objects   Available panels

Figure 3-6: The Objects panel acts as a toolbox for holding your most commonly used Web page elements.

The Objects panel has taken on a new role in Dreamweaver 4. In addition to providing access to the most commonly used elements, the Objects panel also contains the mechanism for switching between Standard view and Layout view. Layout view, itself new in Dreamweaver 4, allows Web designers to quickly structure their page by drawing special tables and cells to hold content. Once the Layout view is selected, two additional tools become available, Draw Layout Cell and Draw Layout Table. Two standard objects (Insert Table and Draw Layer) are not accessible in Layout view. To find out more about how to use Layout view, see Chapter 13.

If the Objects panel is not available when you first start Dreamweaver, you can enable it by choosing Window ➪ Objects or the keyboard shortcut, Ctrl+F2 (Command+F2). Likewise, choosing Window ➪ Objects (or the shortcut) again deselects it and closes the Objects panel. You can also remove the Objects panel from your screen by clicking its Close button.

Mac users have the added advantage of being able to windowshade the Objects panel by selecting the Collapse button.

To reposition the Objects panel — or any of the Dreamweaver windows or floating toolbars — just place your cursor over the drag bar at the top of the window and drag it to a new location. The Objects panel can be placed anywhere on the screen, not just inside the Document window. Some Web designers like to size their Document window to a standard width that renders well across a variety of platforms and resolutions, and then place the Objects panel outside of that window so they have a clear canvas with which to work.

You can reshape the Objects panel by positioning your pointer over the panel's border so that a double-headed arrow appears. Click and drag the rectangle into a new size or shape, and the icons within the Objects panel rearrange themselves to fit. If your resized Objects panel is too small to contain all the objects, a small scroll arrow is displayed. Select the arrow, and the Objects panel scrolls to show additional objects; at the same time, another arrow appears at the opposite side of the window to indicate more hidden objects. Mac users can only resize the Objects panel by dragging the lower-right corner.

Common objects

The most often-used HTML elements, aside from text, are accessible through the Common Objects category of the Objects panel. Table 3-1 explains what each of the Common Objects icons represents.

Note   In Dreamweaver 4, the number of objects has increased to the point where, to show them all, the standard Objects panel is widened to two columns. The following tables describe the icons in a left-to-right, top-to-bottom order.

		Table 3-1 **Common Objects Category**	
Icon	*Name*	*Description*	*Detailed Information*
	Insert Image	Use for including any graphic (including animated GIFs) at the cursor position	See Chapter 10
	Insert Rollover Image	Inserts an image that changes into another image when the user's mouse moves over it	See the section "Inserting Rollover Images" in Chapter 10
	Insert Table	Opens a dialog box for creating a table at the cursor position	See Chapter 13
	Insert Tabular Data	Imports delimited data exported from a spreadsheet or database program	See the section "Importing Tabular Data" in Chapter 13
	Draw Layer	Enables you to drag out a layer of specific size and shape at a specific location	See Chapter 28
	Insert Navigation Bar	Inserts a series of images with links used as buttons for navigation	See Chapter 10
	Insert Horizontal Rule	Draws a line across the page at the cursor position	See the section "Dividing the Web Page with Horizontal Rules" in Chapter 10
	Insert E-mail Link	Inserts a text link that opens an e-mail form when selected	See the section "Adding an E-mail Link" in Chapter 11
	Insert Date	Inserts the current date in a user-selected format	See the section "Incorporating Dates" in Chapter 9
	Insert Server-Side Include	Opens the dialog box for inserting a server-side include	See the section "Applying Server-Side Includes" in Chapter 33

Icon	Name	Description	Detailed Information
🌀	Insert Fireworks HTML	Inserts images and code generated by Fireworks	See Chapter 22
🌸	Insert Flash	Use to include a Flash movie	See Chapter 23
🖼	Insert Flash Button	Creates a Flash button based on a template	See the section "Creating Flash Buttons and Crafting Templates" in Chapter 23
🅰	Insert Flash Text	Makes a Flash headline or other text	See the section "Working with Flash Text" in Chapter 23
ⅢⅢ	Insert Shockwave	Use to include a Shockwave movie	See Chapter 23
⚙	Insert Generator	Inserts a Generator template file with optional parameters	See the section "Adding Generator Templates" in Chapter 23

All of the common objects except for Insert Horizontal Rule and Draw Layer open a dialog box that enables you to browse for a file or specify parameters.

Tip   If you'd prefer to enter all your information, including the necessary filenames, through the Property Inspector, you can turn off the automatic appearance of the file requester when you insert any object through the Objects panel or the menus. Choose Edit ➪ Preferences and, from the General Category, select Show Dialog When Inserting Objects to uncheck it.

Character objects

Certain special characters — such as © (the copyright symbol) — are represented in HTML by codes called *character entities*. In code, a character entity is either a name (such as © for the copyright symbol) or number (©). Each character entity has its own unique code.

Dreamweaver eases the entry of these complex, hard-to-remember codes with the Characters category. Nine of the most commonly used characters are included as separate objects and a tenth object opens a dialog box with 99 special characters to choose from. Table 3-2 details the new Characters category objects. The Characters category also contains objects for inserting a line break and a non-breaking space.

Table 3-2
Characters Category

Icon	Name	Description	Detailed Information
	Insert Line Break	Puts in a ` ` tag that causes the line to wrap at the cursor position	See the section "Working with Paragraphs" in Chapter 9
	Insert Non-Breaking Space	Inserts a hard space in the current cursor position	See the section "Inserting Symbols and Special Characters" in Chapter 8
	Insert Copyright	Inserts the code for the copyright symbol	See the section "Inserting Symbols and Special Characters" in Chapter 8
	Insert Registered Trademark	Inserts the code for the registered trademark symbol	See "Inserting Symbols and Special Characters" in Chapter 8
	Insert Trademark	Inserts the code for the trademark symbol	See "Inserting Symbols and Special Characters" in Chapter 8
	Insert Pound	Inserts the code for the pound currency symbol	See "Inserting Symbols and Special Characters" in Chapter 8
	Insert Yen	Inserts the code for the yen currency symbol	See "Inserting Symbols and Special Characters" in Chapter 8
	Insert Euro	Inserts the code for the Euro currency symbol	See "Inserting Symbols and Special Characters" in Chapter 8
	Insert Left Quote	Inserts the code for the opening curly quote symbol	See "Inserting Symbols and Special Characters" in Chapter 8
	Insert Right Quote	Inserts the code for the closing curly quote symbol	See "Inserting Symbols and Special Characters" in Chapter 8
	Insert Em Dash	Inserts the code for the em dash symbol	See "Inserting Symbols and Special Characters" in Chapter 8
	Insert Other Character	Opens the dialog box for inserting special characters	See "Inserting Symbols and Special Characters" in Chapter 8

Form objects

The form is the primary method for implementing HTML interactivity. The Forms category of the Objects panel gives you nine basic building blocks for creating your Web-based form. Table 3-3 describes each of the elements found in the Forms category.

Table 3-3
Forms Category

Icon	Name	Description	Detailed Information
	Insert Form	Creates the overall HTML form structure at the cursor position	See Chapter 15
	Insert Text Field	Places a text box or a text area at the cursor position	See the section "Using Text Boxes" in Chapter 15
	Insert Button	Inserts a Submit, Reset, or user-definable button at the cursor position	See the section "Activating Your Form with Buttons" in Chapter 15
	Insert Check Box	Inserts a checkbox for selecting any number of options at the cursor position	See the section "Providing Checkboxes and Radio Buttons" in Chapter 15
	Insert Radio Button	Inserts a radio button for making a single selection from a set of options at the cursor position	See the section "Providing Checkboxes and Radio Buttons" in Chapter 15
	Insert List/Menu	Enables either a drop-down menu or a scrolling list at the cursor position	See the section "Creating Form Lists and Menus" in Chapter 15
	Insert File Field	Inserts a text box and Browse button for selecting a file to submit	See the section "Using the Hidden Field and the File Field" in Chapter 15
	Insert Image Field	Includes an image that can be used as a button	See the section "Activating Your Form with Buttons" in Chapter 15
	Insert Hidden Field	Inserts an invisible field used for passing variables to a CGI or JavaScript program	See the section "Using the Hidden Field and the File Field" in Chapter 15
	Insert Jump Menu	Opens a dialog box for building a pop-up menu that activates a link	See the section "Navigating with a Jump Menu" in Chapter 15

As demonstrated in Figure 3-7, you can use a table inside a form to get objects to line up properly. All forms return user input via a CGI or JavaScript program. See Chapter 15 for more detailed information.

Form outline   Forms panel

Figure 3-7: Dreamweaver puts a distinctive dashed line around any form if you have View Visual Aids ⇨ Invisible Elements checked.

Frame objects

In HTML terms, a *frame* is a collection of separate pages arranged on a single screen. Frames are contained within framesets, which until Dreamweaver could be created only by dragging frame borders into position or selecting a menu option. Because it involves multiple pages, creating a frameset often proved difficult for the novice designer.

The process for making standard framesets is greatly simplified when using the Frames category objects. Eight of the most commonly used designs are now immediately available. Select any frame object, and that frameset is made, incorporating the existing page.

The blue symbol in the frame object icons indicates which frame on the current page is placed when the frameset is created. For example, if you create a single page with the text "Table of Contents" and then choose the Insert Top Frame object, "Table of Contents" is moved below the newly inserted top frame. All of the Frames category objects are explained in Table 3-4.

	Table 3-4 **Frames Category**		
Icon	**Name**	**Description**	**Detailed Information**
	Insert Left Frame	Inserts a blank frame to the left of the current page	See Chapter 16
	Insert Right Frame	Inserts a blank frame to the right of the current page	See Chapter 16
	Insert Top Frame	Inserts a blank frame above the current page	See Chapter 16
	Insert Bottom Frame	Inserts a blank frame below the current page	See Chapter 16
	Insert Left, Top-Left Corner, and Top Frames	Makes a frameset with four frames where the current page is in the lower right	See Chapter 16
	Insert Left and Nested Top Frames	Makes a frameset where the top spans the lower two frames	See Chapter 16
	Insert Top and Nested Left Frames	Makes a frameset where the left spans the two rightmost frames	See Chapter 16
	Split Frame Center	Creates a frameset with four equal frames	See Chapter 16

Head objects

General document information — such as the title and any descriptive keywords about the page — is written into the `<head>` section of an HTML document. The objects of the Head category enable Web designers to drop in these snippets of code in a handy object format. These objects insert `<meta>` tags with keywords for search engines, specify refresh times, and do many more tasks that impact a Web site's overall performance.

While Dreamweaver enables you to see the `<head>` objects onscreen via the View ⇨ Head Content menu option, you don't have to have the `<head>` window open to drop in the objects. Simply click any of the six objects detailed in Table 3-5, and a dialog box opens, prompting you for the needed information.

<table>
<tr><td colspan="4" align="center">Table 3-5
Head Objects Category</td></tr>
<tr><td>*Icon*</td><td>*Name*</td><td>*Description*</td><td>*Detailed Information*</td></tr>
<tr><td></td><td>Insert Meta</td><td>Includes document information usable by servers and browsers</td><td>See the section "Understanding <meta> and other <head> tags" in Chapter 8</td></tr>
<tr><td></td><td>Insert Keywords</td><td>Inserts keywords used by search engines to catalog the Web page</td><td>See the section "Understanding <meta> and other <head> tags" in Chapter 8</td></tr>
<tr><td></td><td>Insert Description</td><td>Provides a description of the current page</td><td>See the section "Understanding <meta> and other <head> tags" in Chapter 8</td></tr>
<tr><td></td><td>Insert Refresh</td><td>Sets a tag to refresh the current page or redirect the browser to another URL</td><td>See the section "Refreshing the page and redirecting users" in Chapter 8</td></tr>
<tr><td></td><td>Insert Base</td><td>Specifies the base address of the current document</td><td>See the section "Understanding <meta> and other <head> tags" in Chapter 8</td></tr>
<tr><td></td><td>Insert Link</td><td>Declares a relationship between the current document and another object or file</td><td>See the section "Linking to other files" in Chapter 8</td></tr>
</table>

Invisible objects

As any experienced Web designer knows, what you see onscreen is, increasingly, a small part of the code necessary for the page's generation. Often you need to include an element that Dreamweaver categorizes as an Invisible. The Invisibles category of the Objects panel gives you quick access to the most commonly inserted behind-the-scenes tags, as described in Table 3-6.

<table>
<tr><td colspan="4" align="center">Table 3-6
Invisible Objects</td></tr>
<tr><td>*Icon*</td><td>*Name*</td><td>*Description*</td><td>*Detailed Information*</td></tr>
<tr><td></td><td>Insert Named Anchor</td><td>Puts a hyperlink at a particular place on a Web page</td><td>See the section "Navigating with Anchors" in Chapter 11</td></tr>
</table>

Icon	Name	Description	Detailed Information
	Insert Script	Inserts JavaScript or VBScript either directly or from a file	See the section "Adding JavaScript and VBScript" in Chapter 17
	Insert Comment	Places HTML comment tags inside your script; these comments are ignored by the browser	See the section "Commenting Your Code" in Chapter 9

Tip   Invisible elements can be turned on or off through the Preferences dialog box. Choose Edit ⇨ Preferences and then select the Invisible Elements category. A list of 11 options (including the objects listed in the Invisibles category except for Insert Non-breaking Space) is displayed. To turn off an option, click once to remove the checkmark from the option's checkbox. For a complete description of all the Invisible elements and other preferences, see Chapter 4.

Special objects

As noted throughout this book, part of the power of HTML is its ability to go beyond its native capabilities by including special objects. Dreamweaver facilitates the inclusion of these external elements — Java applets, plug-ins, and ActiveX controls — through the objects found in the Special category of the Objects panel. Each of these objects inserts a placeholder on the page to assist with layout; files requiring plug-ins can be played within Dreamweaver while applets and ActiveX controls must be viewed in the browser. Table 3-7 details the three Special objects.

Table 3-7 Special Objects Category			
Icon	**Name**	**Description**	**Detailed Information**
	Insert Applet	Includes a Java applet at the cursor position	See the section "Adding Java Applets" in Chapter 17
	Insert Plug-in	Use for including a file that requires a plug-in	See the section "Incorporating Plug-ins" in Chapter 17
	Insert ActiveX	Puts a placeholder for an ActiveX control at the cursor position, using the `<object>` tag	See the section "Working with ActiveX Components" in Chapter 17

Getting the Most out of the Property Inspector

Dreamweaver's Property Inspector is your primary tool for specifying an object's particulars. What exactly those particulars are — in HTML these are known as *attributes* — depends on the object itself. The contents of the Property Inspector change depending on which object is selected. For example, click anywhere on a blank Web page, and the Property Inspector shows text attributes for format, font name and size, and so on. If you click an image, the Property Inspector displays a small thumbnail of the picture, and the image's attributes for height and width, image source, link, and alternative text. Figure 3-8 shows a Property Inspector for a line of text with an attached hyperlink.

Figure 3-8: The Property Inspector takes many forms, depending on which HTML element you select.

Manipulating the Property Inspector

The Property Inspector is enabled by choosing Window ➪ Properties or selecting the keyboard shortcut, Ctrl+F3 (Command+F3). As with the Objects panel, the Property Inspector can be closed by selecting the Close button, unchecking Window ➪ Properties, or choosing the keyboard shortcut again. On the Mac, you can also windowshade the Property Inspector so that only the title bar is left showing by clicking the Collapse button on its window.

You can reposition the Property Inspector in one of two ways. You can click and drag the title bar of the window and move it to a new location, or — unlike the Objects panel — you can click and drag any open gray area in the inspector itself. This is handy for quickly moving the inspector aside, out of your way. However, it only works for Windows.

The Property Inspector initially displays the most typical attributes for a given element. To see additional properties, click the expander arrow in the lower-right corner of the Property Inspector. Virtually all the inserted objects have additional parameters that can be modified. Unless you're tight on screen real estate, it's a good idea to keep the Property Inspector expanded so you can see all your options.

Tip   In addition to using the expander arrow, you can reveal (or hide) the expanded attributes by double-clicking any open gray area of the Property Inspector.

Property Inspector elements

Many of the attributes in the Property Inspector are text boxes; just click in any one and enter the desired value. If a value already appears in the text box, whether number or name, double-click it (or click and drag over it) to highlight the information and then enter your new data — the old value is immediately replaced. You can see the effect your modification has had by pressing the Tab key to move to the next attribute or by clicking outside of the Property Inspector.

Dreamweaver enables you to make small additions to the code without opening up the Code Inspector through the Quick Tag Editor. Located on the right of the Property Inspector just below the Help button, the Quick Tag Editor pops open a small window to display the code for the currently selected tag. You can swiftly change attributes or add special parameters not found in the Property Inspector. The Quick Tag Editor is covered in depth in Chapter 8.

The Property Inspector also uses scrolling list boxes for several attributes that provide a limited number of responses for you to choose. To open the drop-down list of available options, click the arrow button to the right of the list box. Then choose an option by highlighting it.

Tip   Some options on the Property Inspector are a combination drop-down list and text box — you can select from available options or type in your own values. For example, when text is selected, the font name, size, and color options are all combination list/text boxes.

If you see a Folder icon next to a text box (see the Folder icon in the inspector, shown in Figure 3-8), you have the option of browsing for a filename on your local or networked drive, or manually inputting a name. Clicking the folder opens a standard Open File dialog box (called Select File in Dreamweaver); after you've chosen your file and clicked Open, Dreamweaver inputs the name and any necessary path information in the correct attribute.

Dreamweaver enables you to quickly select an onscreen file in either a Document window or a Site window as a link, with its Point to File icon, found next to the Folder icon. Just click and drag the Point to File icon until it touches the file (or the filename from the Site window) you want to reference. The path is automatically written into the Link text box.

Cross-Reference   Dreamweaver can handle all forms of absolute and relative addressing. For more information on specifying HTML pages, be sure to read Chapter 6.

Certain objects such as text, layers, and tables enable you to specify a color attribute. The Property Inspector alerts you to these options with a small color swatch next to the text box. You can type in a color's name (such as "blue") or its six-figure hexadecimal value ("#3366FF") or select the color swatch. Choosing the color swatch displays a color picker, shown in Figure 3-9, with the 212 colors common to both the Netscape and Microsoft browsers — the so-called browser-safe colors. (Some of the 212 Web-safe colors are duplicated to create a more user-friendly interface.) You can go outside of this range by clicking the small painter's palette in the lower-right corner of the color picker. This opens a full-range Color dialog box in which you can choose a color visually or enter its red, green, and blue values or its hue, saturation, and luminance values.

Eyedropper tool

Figure 3-9: Dreamweaver's color picker enables you to choose from a wide selection of colors, right from the palette or right off the desktop, with the Eyedropper tool.

The color picker in Dreamweaver is very flexible. Not only can you choose from a series of color swatches, but you can also select any color onscreen with Dreamweaver's Eyedropper tool. The Eyedropper button has two modes: By default, the Eyedropper snaps the selected color to its nearest Web-safe neighbor; if you deselect Snap to Web Safe from the color picker's context menu, colors are sampled exactly. If you'd like to access the system color picker, the color wheel button opens it up for you. There's also a Default Color tool, which deletes any color choice previously inserted. Finally, you can use the color picker's context menu to change the swatch set shown. By default, the Color Cubes view is shown, but you may also see the swatches in a Continuous Tone configuration as well as restricted to Windows OS, Macintosh OS, or Grayscale colors. While these options may not be used frequently by the Web designer, Macromedia standardized the color picker across its product line to make it easier to switch between applications.

One final aspect of the Property Inspector is worth noting: The circled question mark in the upper-right corner of the Property Inspector is the Help button. Selecting this button invokes online help and displays specific information about the particular Property Inspector you're using. The Help button is also available throughout all of the panels opened by the Launcher, as described in the next section.

Using the Launcher

Dreamweaver's third main control panel, along with the Objects panel and the Property Inspector, is called the Launcher, shown in Figure 3-10.

Close button

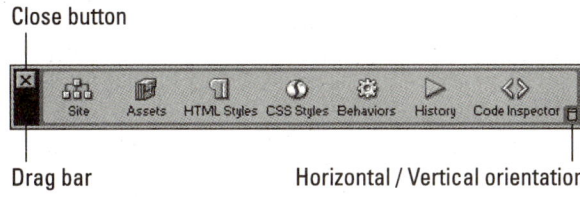

Drag bar   Horizontal / Vertical orientation

Figure 3-10: The Launcher gives you access to seven different Dreamweaver functions, and up to thirteen if you customize it.

The Launcher opens and closes seven default windows, each of which handles a different aspect of the program:

✦ The Site window handles all elements of publishing to the Web, as well as basic file maintenance such as moving and deleting folders.

✦ The Assets panel puts the resources — images, colors, links, Flash movies, Shockwave movies, QuickTime and MPEG movies, scripts, templates, and Library items — of a site right up front, where they can be dragged and dropped with ease right onto the page.

✦ The HTML Styles panel applies standard HTML formatting to text and paragraph selections.

✦ The CSS Styles panel coordinates the Cascading Style Sheet modifications on each Web page and, if used in conjunction with an external style sheet, throughout your entire Web site.

✦ The Behaviors panel assigns one or more JavaScript actions to a JavaScript event selected from a browser-targeted list.

✦ The History panel shows a list of the user actions that can be replayed, undone, or saved as a command.

✦ The Code Inspector is one view of Dreamweaver's internal code editor, which appears in a separate floating window.

Similar to the other control panels, the Launcher can be started by choosing Window ➪ Launcher, and closed by either selecting the Close button or choosing Window ➪ Launcher again. A standard title bar is available on the Launcher for dragging the panel into a new position. The Launcher also includes a small button in the lower-right corner (refer to Figure 3-10) that serves to change the panel's orientation from a horizontal shape to a vertical one, and vice versa.

The free-floating Launcher panel functions identically to the status bar Launcher. Each one of the Launcher buttons is highlighted when the pointer passes over it, and remains highlighted when chosen. As noted, the Launcher can be used to close the windows or bring them to the front as well as open them — just click the highlighted button. Any or all of the windows can be "launched" simultaneously.

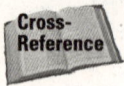 **Cross-Reference**   Both the floating Launcher and status bar Launcher are customizable. You can display the icon for any or all of the 13 standard panels. See the section "Panels Preferences" in Chapter 4.

Site window

The Site window is your gateway to the Web. Through it, you can transfer files from the development folder on your local drive to your online Web server. Any member of your development team can check out a file to work on with no fear that another member is making changes at the same time. The team leader can even check Dreamweaver's log to see who is working on what.

Web sites can become quite complex very quickly, and it's often difficult to remember how pages are linked together. Dreamweaver offers a visual representation of your Web site through its Site Map window. The Site Map window not only enables you to quickly review the structure of a site, you can also use it to add, move, or modify links. You can learn all the details about the Site Map feature in Chapter 7.

Open the Site window by choosing the Site button, on either the Launcher panel or the status bar Launcher, by selecting Window ⇨ Site Files or by pressing F8. As you can see in Figure 3-11, the Site window is two-paned: Local files are shown on the right side, and remote files are displayed on the left. The headings across the top of each pane and the panes themselves can be resized. Position your pointer over a border until a double-headed arrow appears and then click and drag the border to a new position.

 Tip   The files of both local and remote folders can be sorted by name, file size, file type, date modified, or checkout status — all the options corresponding to the headings across each pane. For example, to display your files in A-to-Z alphabetical order, click the Name button once. To show them in descending (Z-to-A) order, click the Name button again. If you're constantly updating your site, it's good practice to have your folders sorted in descending date order so that your most recently modified files appear at the top of each pane.

Site Map button   Remote panel   Local panel

Figure 3-11: Dreamweaver's Site window handles the Webmaster's site management chores.

The major operations performed in the Site window include the following:

Site Window Function	Site Window Action
Connecting to the site	When your site is properly configured, the Connect button automatically calls your remote site and uses whatever login and password are necessary to get you online. After the connection is confirmed, the button changes into a Disconnect button.
Transferring files	To move files between your local drive and the remote server, use the Get and Put buttons. The Get button copies whatever files are highlighted in the Remote pane to the local folder, and the Put button copies files highlighted in the Local pane to the remote directory. To stop a transfer, select the Stop Current Task button — the stop sign in the lower-right corner of the window.

Continued

Site Window Function	Site Window Action
Locking files	When a team of Web designers is working on a site, you have to be able to prevent two people from working on the same file simultaneously. The Checked In/Checked Out indicator not only shows that a file is in use, but who has the file.
Site Map representation	As a site grows in complexity, it is often helpful to get an overview of a site's structure and its links. The Site Map feature gives a visual representation of the complete site and can be chosen by selecting the Site Map button.

Cross-Reference   Maintaining a Web site is a major portion of a Webmaster's responsibility. To learn more about Dreamweaver's site management features, see Part VIII.

Assets panel

For most Web pages, an HTML file is just one of the elements necessary for the page's rendering in a browser. In addition to the code, the typical page may require GIFs, JPEGs, Flash movies and other multimedia, external CSS files and added JavaScript files to be complete. Dreamweaver now includes a center for all the resources included in a site: the Assets panel, shown in Figure 3-12.

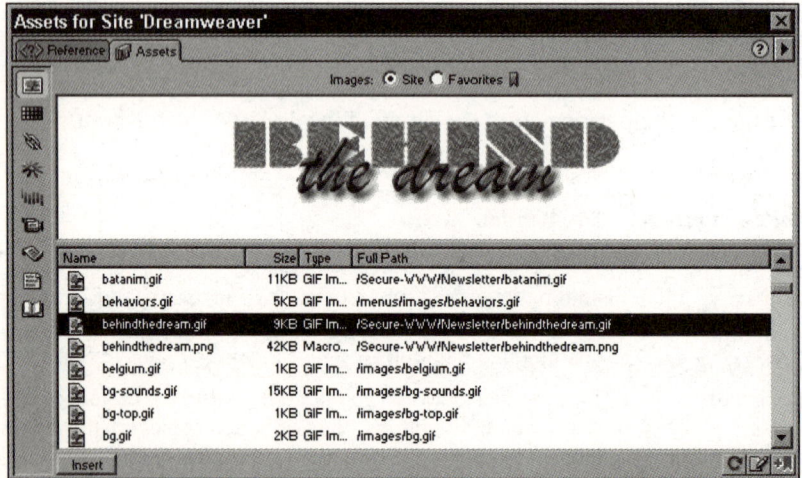

Figure 3-12: The Assets panel tracks almost all the components used within any given site.

New Feature The Assets panel not only catalogs all the current elements within a site, it makes them extremely easy to include. To add a previously used company logo to a page, just drag it from the Assets panel onto the page. A copy of the image is placed on the page while the logo remains available for further use in the Assets panel. There are nine categories of assets, each represented by an icon on the side of the panel: images, colors, URLs, Flash movies, Shockwave movies, multimedia movies, scripts, templates, and Library items. Each category of the Assets panel accepts a particular file type; Table 3-8 details what you'll find in each category.

Table 3-8
Assets Panel Categories

Category	Types of Elements Cataloged
Images	Standard Web images: GIF, JPEG, and PNG formats
Colors	Colors applied to backgrounds, text, links (including `alink` and `vlink` attributes) in HTML or CSS styles
URLs	Absolute links using any of these protocols: HTTP:, HTTPS:, FTP:, JavaScript:, gopher:, mailto:, or file:
Flash	Flash player movies (.swf)
Shockwave	All Shockwave movie formats
Movies	MPEG or QuickTime
Scripts	External JavaScript and VBScript files included using the `scr` attribute of the `<script>` tag
Templates	Pages saved as a template in Dreamweaver (.dwt files)
Library	Dreamweaver Library items (.lbi files)

There are several ways to display the Assets panel. Select the Show Assets button from the Launcher or choose Window ⇨ Assets. You can also use the keyboard shortcut, F11. Once opened, you'll see that the Assets panel is divided into two areas, a preview and a listing. Images and multimedia are shown as a proportionate thumbnail; Flash, Shockwave, and Movie category previews can be played by selecting the Play button that appears in the preview area when a file is selected.

Dreamweaver keeps track of the assets in a site through the use of the site cache, which is enabled when the site is defined. When you open a page in a site and display the Assets panel, the site cache is read and all the available resources are listed. When you add an asset, such as an image or new background color, it appears in the Assets panel automatically the next time a page from the site is opened. You can hasten the process and manually refresh the site cache by selecting the Refresh Site List button on the bottom of the Assets panel. The same procedure holds true for assets removed from your pages.

Tip
If, after selecting Refresh Site List, you still don't see your asset, Ctrl+click (Command+click) Refresh Site List. This action rebuilds the site cache from the ground up so it may take a moment or two, but it ensures that all of your assets are categorized.

Site assets

There are two ways to use an asset on a page, both very straightforward:

✦ Drag the preview of the asset from the Assets panel and drop it in the desired place on the page. You can also drag-and-drop the listing of the asset.

✦ Position the cursor where you'd like the asset to appear, choose the listing from the Assets panel, and then select the Insert or Apply button.

The assets from the media categories — Images, Flash, Shockwave, and Movies — insert the proper code as well as references to specific media files. Colors are applied to selected text via a `<font>` tag; if you drop a color from the Assets panel where no text is selected, the next text you type at that location will take on the specified color. URL assets are similar: Drop a URL asset on selected text to add that link while inserting a URL asset on a cursor position inserts the link using the URL as the text. For example, if you were to drag the URL asset mailto:jlowery@ idest.com on the page, the following code would be inserted:

```
<a href="mailto:jlowery@idest.com">mailto:jlowery@idest.com</a>
```

Dragging either a script or Library asset onto the page inserts the necessary code at the selected position. However, inserting a template from the Assets panel applies that template to the current page.

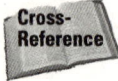

Cross-Reference
When a template is applied to a page, all the elements on that page must be placed into an editable region of the template or discarded. For more details on working with templates, see Chapter 32.

If you'd like to alter an asset before placing on the page, you can choose to edit any item in all of the categories except for Colors and URLs. Select the Edit button on the Assets panel to invoke the editor, as selected for that file type in Preferences, for the selected asset. After making your modifications and saving the file in the editor, the change is reflected in the Assets panel.

Caution
When editing graphic assets for which Fireworks 4 is the chosen editor, you won't see the Launch and Edit interface as you do when selecting the Edit Image in Fireworks 4 command or choosing the Edit button from the Property Inspector. In Fireworks, choose File ➪ Export to update changed GIFs, JPEGs, and exported PNGs; and File ➪ Save to modify Fireworks source PNGs. You'll have to navigate to the proper file location during export or save to store the image in the same place.

Often designers reuse elements from one site in another. The Assets panel allows you to easily copy any selected asset from one site to any other defined site. To copy an asset from one site to another, follow these steps:

1. Select the desired asset(s) in the Assets panel.

   Ctrl+click (Command+click) additional assets to extend your selection.

2. From the context menu, choose Copy to Site ➪ Sitename, where Sitename designates the site you want to copy the asset to.

   Dreamweaver informs you that the asset has been placed in the Favorites category of the Assets panel.

3. To view your moved asset, choose Site ➪ Open Site to switch to the other site and then select Favorites from the Assets panel.

When Dreamweaver copies an asset from one site to another, it moves it to the same relative location. For example, if I were to copy a file with the relative address of /images/logos/mainLogo.gif to another site, Dreamweaver would put the file in the same folders, creating any that did not already exist.

Tip If you have documents open from a number of defined sites, the Assets panel switches to show the assets in the site that the document is from.

To make it easier to find a particular asset, you can sort your entries by any of the headings found in the listings area of the Assets panel. To find all your GIF images, for example, select the Type heading. Select the heading once to sort the files in an ascending order (A–Z) and again to sort in a descending order (Z–A).

Note Unfortunately, the Assets panel is one aspect of Dreamweaver that is not customizable. You can't alter the existing categories to accept additional file types or add new categories.

Favorite Assets view

The Assets panel categories are available in both Site and Favorites views, as controlled by the radio buttons on top of the panel. When the Site view is selected, all the resources within the defined site are visible; on even medium-sized sites, the number of assets can be substantial. To make it easy to locate often-used assets, Dreamweaver provides a Favorites view, which contains only selected assets. Select either the Site or Favorites views at the top of the Assets panel to switch between these two options. To create a Favorite asset, select the asset (or assets) in the Site view and choose the Add to Favorites button found on the bottom of the Assets panel. To delete the entry in the Favorites view, select it and choose Remove From Favorites.

The Favorites view has a number of special properties. First, you can label any asset with an alias or, as it's called in Dreamweaver, a *Nickname*. Giving an asset a Nickname, such as Main Logo, makes retrieval very easy and does not rename the original file. To give a Favorite asset a Nickname, slowly click the filename of the asset twice — do not double-click. The original filename will be highlighted and available for you to enter a new name, as shown in Figure 3-13.

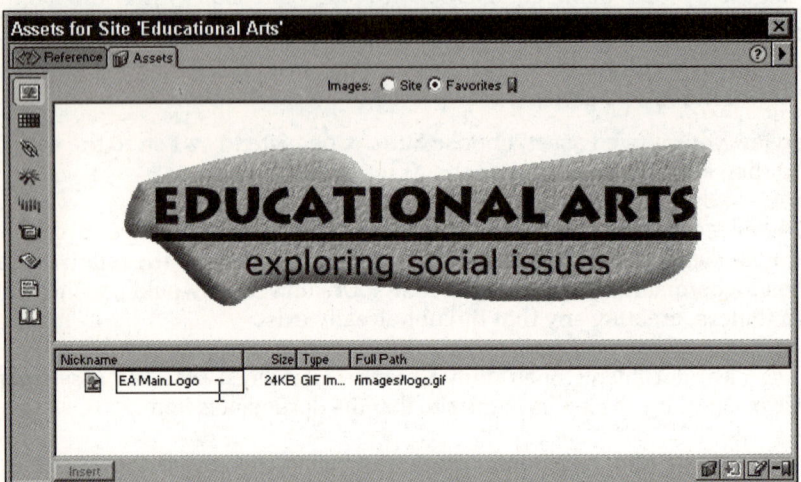

Figure 3-13: In a site with many assets, use the Favorites view to isolate the most frequently used ones; you can give any Favorite asset a Nickname to make it more identifiable.

The Favorites view of the Assets panel gives you another organizational tool with the capability to group assets. In the standard Site view of the Assets panel, all assets are listed equally, one after another. In the Favorites view, you can create a folder by selecting the New Favorites Folder button and then drag any assets into it. Favorites folders can be created in any asset category.

Finally, the Favorites view may be used to create new assets, not just list existing ones. In the Favorites view of the Assets panel, you can create a new:

✦ **Color:** In the Color category, choose the New Color button and select one from the standard color picker.

✦ **URL:** In the URLs category, select the New URL button and enter the desired link and Nickname.

Tip　You can use the New URL option to store relative links in the Assets panel; generally only absolute URLs are treated as assets.

✦ **Template:** In the Templates category, select the New Template button. This creates a blank template; you'll need to choose the Edit button to add content and mark editable regions for the template to be useful.

✦ **Library:** In the Library category, select the New Library Item button; again this creates a blank Library item, which will have to be edited to be made useful. You can also drag any selection from the current document into the Library category of the Assets panel to create a new Library item.

HTML Styles panel

Although Cascading Style Sheets are powerful, they have two major drawbacks: They're not compatible with 3.0 browsers, and they're difficult to master. To offset these disadvantages — and still make it easy to apply formatting to text and paragraphs — Dreamweaver offers HTML styles.

The HTML Styles panel lists all available styles and is used primarily to apply and remove formatting. Two basic types of HTML styles exist: paragraph and selection. A paragraph style is denoted by the ¶ symbol, while styles, which only affect a selection, are marked with an underlined, lowercase *a*, as shown in Figure 3-14. Styles with a plus sign (+) next to them add their formatting to the existing tags; those styles without the plus sign replace the original formatting.

Defined HTML styles

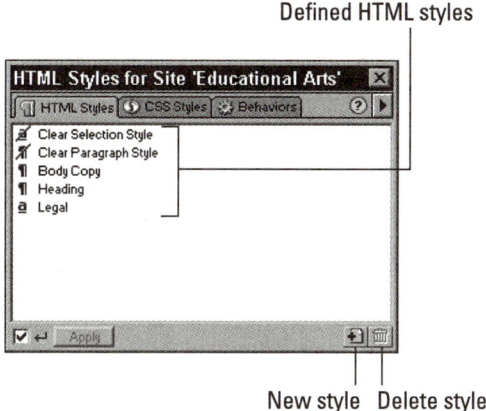

New style Delete style

Figure 3-14: The HTML Styles panel offers an easy way to apply consistent formatting to any text selection or paragraph.

Features of the HTML Styles panel are listed in the following table:

HTML Styles *Panel Function*	*Document Window Action*
Defining styles	New styles can be defined through the Define HTML Style dialog box, which is opened when the New Style button is selected.
Applying styles	All available styles are listed in the panel and applied by selecting one, if the Apply option is enabled. If the Apply option is not selected, you'll have to choose the style and then click the Apply button.
Removing styles	Existing HTML text formatting, whether applied through the HTML Styles panel or another means, can be removed by choosing either Clear Selection Style or Clear Paragraph Style.
Editing styles	Double-clicking an existing HTML style reopens the Define HTML Style dialog box. Styles that are already applied are not affected by any changes.

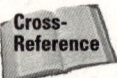

Cross-Reference   HTML styles are explained fully in the section "Using HTML Styles" in Chapter 9.

CSS Styles panel

Through the CSS Styles panel, Dreamweaver makes creating and applying Cascading Style Sheets easy. Style sheets give the Web designer a terrific degree of control over the appearance of text and other elements, throughout the creation stage and when the Web site is live. Styles can be used in conjunction with a single Web page or an entire site.

The CSS Styles panel, shown in Figure 3-15, is accessed by clicking the Show CSS Styles button from either the Launcher panel or the status bar Launcher. You can also open the CSS Styles panel by choosing Window ⇨ Styles or by pressing Shift+F11. You can drag or resize the CSS Styles panel with the mouse.

The CSS Styles panel has the following three key uses:

CSS Styles *Panel Function*	*Document Window Action*
Defining styles	Through the Style Sheet button on the CSS Styles panel, you can create, modify, and remove CSS formats. CSSs either redefine existing HTML tags or create new user-defined classes.
Applying styles	Once your CSS styles are defined, you can easily apply them to any selected text throughout your Web page. Just click the desired style in the CSS Styles panel, if you have the Apply option selected; otherwise, you'll have to also click the Apply button.
Viewing styled tags	It can be difficult to tell which style has already been applied to which tag. With the CSS Styles panel, pick any text or item on the screen, and the applied style (if any) is highlighted.

Defined CSS Styles

Apply Style

Attach Style Sheet

New Style

Edit Style Sheet

Delete Style

Figure 3-15: The CSS Styles panel displays custom styles and gives you access to Dreamweaver's point-and-click CSS editing capabilities.

For more detailed information on how to use the CSS Styles panel, see Chapter 27.

Behaviors panel

The Behaviors panel enables nonprogrammers to build cutting-edge Web pages through prebuilt JavaScript actions. Briefly, behaviors are composed of two parts: an action and an event that triggers the action. Dreamweaver includes 25 standard behaviors, and because behaviors can be custom-built, hundreds more are available on the Web — and, of course, on the CD-ROM that accompanies this book. Macromedia also maintains the Dreamweaver Exchange, which is instantly accessible through the Get More Behaviors menu item.

The Behaviors panel is browser-savvy and won't allow you to assign a JavaScript event that only works on 4.0 browsers when you need 3.0 compatibility. With the Behaviors panel, not only can you link several actions to a single event, but you can also specify the order of the actions.

Use the Show Behaviors button on either Launcher (panel or status bar) to open the Behaviors panel. You can also press Shift+F3 or choose Window ➪ Behaviors. Like the other windows, you can resize or reposition the Behaviors panel with the mouse using the click-and-drag technique. As shown in Figure 3-16, the Behaviors panel displays the events in the left column and the actions in the right column.

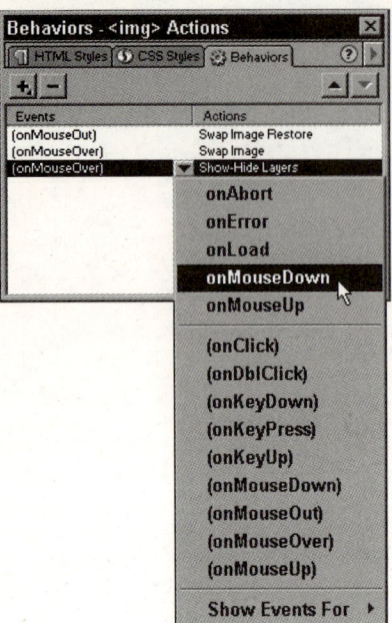

Figure 3-16: Linking an action to an event creates a JavaScript behavior in the Behaviors panel.

Use the Behaviors panel to perform the functions outlined in the following table:

Behaviors Panel Function	Document Window Action
Specifying a browser	The various browsers and browser versions understand specific JavaScript commands. You can target individual browsers by manufacturer or version number, or a combination of the two, by using the Browser pop-up menu.
Picking an action	Behaviors are linked to specific HTML tags; not all HTML tags have behaviors associated with them. Selecting the Behavior pop-up menu (by clicking the + button) displays a list of available actions. Remove an action by highlighting it and clicking the – (minus) button.
Changing an event	The events listed under the Events pop-up menu (the arrow button in between the action and the event) are determined by what's selected in the Browser pop-up menu.
Order the actions	Because you can assign more than one action to an event, Dreamweaver enables you to rearrange the order of the actions. Use the up/down-arrow keys to rearrange the order of your action list for each event.

Behaviors are user-definable. In Chapter 19, you learn how to create your own actions.

On the CD-ROM Be sure to check out the Behaviors section of the CD-ROM that accompanies this book to add to your list of Dreamweaver action capabilities.

History panel

Web design is largely a process of experimentation and repetition. You try one approach, and if you're not satisfied, you undo what you've done and try something else. Then, when you find something you like, you do it over and over. In the earliest versions of Dreamweaver, this process was performed rather blindly, if at all: You had little idea of what steps you were undoing, and automation was not an option.

The History panel tracks every action taken by the user — from deleting text to inserting and resizing a layer. A slider, shown in Figure 3-17, points to the last action performed. Dragging the slider up undoes each step in turn; dragging the slider back down redoes the steps. Selected steps can be quickly repeated in the same document by selecting the Replay button. You can save any selection of steps as a Command for application at any other time, in any other document.

Steps

Replay button   Copy steps

Save As command

Figure 3-17: Undo or redo any series of actions by moving the slider in the History panel.

The primary functions of the History panel are covered in the following table:

History Panel Function	Document Window Action
Undo actions	Reverses each action the slider passes over as it is dragged up the History panel.
Redo actions	Reapplies each action the slider passes over as it is dragged down the History panel.
Replay selected steps	Choosing the Replay button repeats selected steps, in sequence.
Save As selected steps as a command	Stores the selected actions under a user-selected name, which is dynamically added to the Command menu.

Code Inspector

The last default window controlled by the Launcher is the Code Inspector (shown in Figure 3-18) — the internal editor designed to complement Dreamweaver's visual layout facility. Although you can opt to use an external editor such as the bundled BBEdit or HomeSite for extensive coding, the Code Inspector is great for making spot edits or quickly checking your code. The tight integration between Dreamweaver's text and visual editors enables simultaneous input and instant updating. The Code Inspector opens in a separate window, unlike the Code or Code and Design view in which code appears in the Document window. Which one you use is a matter of personal preference.

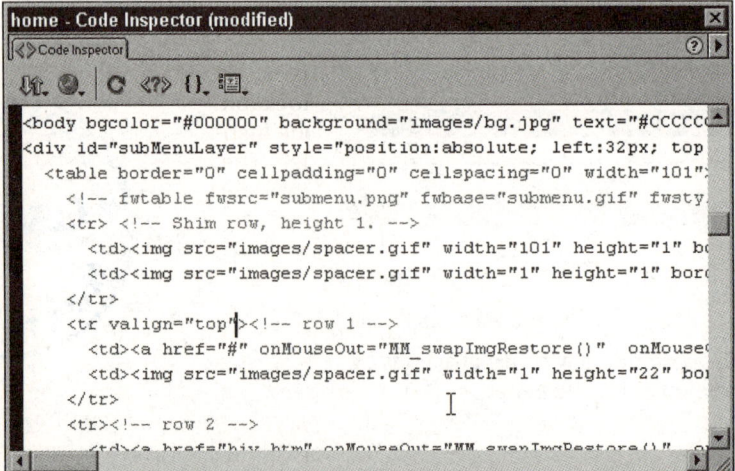

Figure 3-18: The Code Inspector gives you instant access for tweaking your code — or adding entirely new elements by hand.

Tip You can see the tight integration between the visual editor and the Code Inspector when you have both windows open and you select an object in the Document window. The corresponding code is instantly displayed in the Code Inspector. This feature is useful for quickly finding a specific HTML element for alteration.

Clicking the Code Inspector button on either Launcher opens and closes the Code Inspector, as does choosing Window ⇨ Code Inspector or pressing F10. Once the Code Inspector is open, changes made in the Document window are incorporated in real time. However, in order to properly check the code, any changes made in the Code Inspector are not updated in the Document window until the Document window is activated. You can alternate between the two windows by pressing Ctrl+Tab (Option+Tab).

By design, the Code Inspector's layout is simple, to give maximum emphasis to your code. A toolbar along the top of the window replicates the functions found in the Document window's toolbar: File Management, Preview/Debug in Browser, Refresh, Reference, Code Navigation, and View Options.

Tip You might notice that the code in the Code Inspector is colored. The color coding (no pun intended) is set by the HTML Colors category of the Preferences dialog box — you can even modify the background color of the Inspector.

Customizing Your Workspace with Dockable Panels

Dreamweaver is known for its powerful set of tools: Objects, Behaviors, Layers, Timelines, and so much more. To be truly useful, each tool needs its own panel; but the more tools you use, the more cluttered your workspace can become.

To reduce the amount of screen real estate taken up by the individual windows, but still keep their power, Dreamweaver incorporates dockable panels. All of Dreamweaver's 13 floating panels (including the Code Inspector) can be grouped into a single window — or several windows, if you like. The dockable panel system is completely customizable to give you optimum control over your workflow.

Whenever one panel is docked with another, each becomes accessible by clicking the representative tab. Selecting the tab moves the panel's display to the front of the other docked panels. Grouping panels together is very straightforward. Simply drag one panel by its tab on top of another panel. When you see a border appear inside the stationary panel, release your mouse button. A new tab is created to the right of the existing tab, or tabs. To remove a panel from a docked group, click the tab and drag the panel clear of the others. When you release the mouse button, the panel returns to being an independent floating panel but retains the size and shape of the group it was previously docked with.

Note A couple of restrictions apply when docking panels. First, while you can't dock the Objects panel on another panel, you can combine any other panel in the Objects panel's window. Second, neither the Property Inspector nor the Launcher can be docked.

Dreamweaver displays a symbol for the panel and its name on each tab. When too many panels are combined to fit within the docking window, Dreamweaver shows just the symbols to make room for more tabs. If you add an additional panel to a docking window that is too small, Dreamweaver automatically expands the docking window.

Tip As noted earlier, when you remove a panel from a docked group, the panel retains the size and shape of the group it was docked with. To resize any panel, click and drag its borders. On the Mac, you only resize from the bottom-right corner of a window by dragging the resize handle.

Accessing the Menus

Like many programs, Dreamweaver's menus duplicate most of the features accessible through panels. Certain features, however, are available only through the menus or through a corresponding keyboard shortcut. This section offers a reference guide to the menus when you need a particular feature or command. (Note to Windows users: The menus referred to here are those for the Document window and not the Site window; those menu options particular to the Site window are covered in Chapter 7.)

Tip Almost every element placed in the Document window has a contextual menu associated with it. To access a contextual menu, right-click (Control+click) any area or object. The contextual menus change according to which object or area is selected. Using the contextual menus can enhance your productivity tremendously.

The File menu

The File menu contains commands for file handling and overall site management. Table 3-9 describes the commands and their keyboard shortcuts.

Table 3-9			
File Menu Commands			
Command	*Description*	*Windows*	*Macintosh*
New	Adds a new Document window	Ctrl+N	Command+N
New from Template	Creates a document based on an existing template	N/A	N/A

Command	Description	Windows	Macintosh
Open	Displays the Open dialog box for opening an existing file	Ctrl+O	Command+O
Open in Frame	Opens an existing file in the selected frame	Ctrl+Shift+O	Command+Shift+O
Close	Closes the current window	Ctrl+W or Ctrl+F4	Command+W
Save	Saves the current document, or displays the Save As dialog box for an unnamed document	Ctrl+S	Command+S
Save As	Displays the Save As dialog box before saving the document	Ctrl+Shift+S	Command+Shift+S
Save As Template	Stores the current document as a template in the Templates folder of the current site	N/A	N/A
Save Frameset	Saves a file describing the current frameset, or displays the Save As dialog box for an unnamed document	N/A	N/A
Save Frameset As	Displays the Save As Frameset before saving the current frameset	N/A	N/A
Save All Frames	Saves all documents in a frameset	N/A	N/A
Revert	Loads the previously saved version of the current page	N/A	N/A
Import ➪ Import XML into Template	Creates a new document by inserting an XML file into the current template	N/A	N/A
Import ➪ Import Word HTML	Opens an HTML file saved in Microsoft Word, and optionally, cleans up the code	N/A	N/A
Import ➪ Import Tabular Data	Inserts a table derived from a file with delimited data	N/A	N/A
Export ➪ Editable Regions as XML	Saves the current template's editable regions as an XML file	N/A	N/A
Export ➪ CSS Styles	Creates an external style sheet based on CSS styles in the current document	N/A	N/A

Continued

Table 3-9 *(continued)*

Command	Description	Windows	Macintosh
Export ⇨ Table	Saves data in the current table as a delimited text file	N/A	N/A
Convert ⇨ 3.0 Browser Compatible	Creates a new Web page, converting all layers to tables	N/A	N/A
Preview in Browser ⇨ Your Browser List	Displays a list of browsers established in Preferences; choose one to preview the current page using that browser	F12 (Primary) Shift+F12 (Secondary)	F12 (Primary) Shift+F12 (Secondary)
Preview in Browser ⇨ Edit Browser List	Displays the Preview in Browser category of Preferences, where the user can add, edit, or delete additional preview browsers	N/A	N/A
Debug in Browser ⇨ Your Browser List	Displays a list of browsers established in Preferences; choose one to debug the current page using JavaScript debugger with that browser	Alt_F12 (Primary) Ctrl+Alt+F12 (Secondary)	Option+F12 (Primary) Command+ Option+F12 (Secondary)
Debug in Browser ⇨ Edit Browser List	Displays the Preview in Browser category of Preferences, where the user can add, edit, or delete additional preview browsers	N/A	N/A
Check Links	Verifies hypertext links for the current document	Shift+F8	Shift+F8
Check Target Browsers	Displays the Check Target Browsers dialog box, where the user can validate the current file against installed browser profiles	N/A	N/A
Design Notes	Displays the Design Notes dialog box for the current document	N/A	N/A
Your Last Opened Files	Displays the last four opened files; select any name to reopen the file	N/A	N/A
Exit (Quit)	Closes all open files and quits	Ctrl+Q or Alt+F4	Command+Q

The Edit menu

The Edit menu gives you the commands necessary to quickly modify your page — or recover from a devastating accident. Many of the commands (Cut, Copy, and Paste) are standard in other programs; others, such as Paste As Text, are unique to Dreamweaver. Table 3-10 lists all of the features found under the Edit menu.

	Table 3-10		
	Edit Menu Commands		
Command	*Description*	*Windows*	*Macintosh*
Undo	Reverses the last action; the number of times you can Undo is determined by a Preferences setting	Ctrl+Z	Command+Z
Redo/Repeat	Repeats the last action	Ctrl+Y	Command+Y
Cut	Places a copy of the current selection on the clipboard, and removes the selection from the current document	Ctrl+X	Command+X
Copy	Places a copy of the current selection on the clipboard, and leaves the selection in the current document.	Ctrl+C	Command+C
Paste	Copies the clipboard to the current cursor position	Ctrl+V	Command+V
Clear	Removes the current selection from the document	Delete or Backspace	Delete
Copy HTML	Copies the current selection onto the clipboard with the HTML codes	Ctrl+Shift+C	Command+ Shift+C
Paste HTML	Pastes the current selection from the clipboard as HTML	Ctrl+Shift+V	Command+ Shift+V
Select All	Highlights all the elements in the current document or frame	Ctrl+A	Command+A
Select Parent Tag	Chooses the tag surrounding the current selection	Ctrl+Shift+<	Command+ Shift+<
Select Child	Chooses the first tag contained within the current selection	Ctrl+Shift+>	Command+ Shift+>
Find and Replace	Displays the Find and Replace dialog box for modifying the current document	Ctrl+F	Command+F
Find Next (Find Again)	Repeats the previous Find operation	F3	Command+G

Continued

Table 3-10 *(continued)*

Command	Description	Windows	Macintosh
Indent Code	Indents selected code (Code view only)	Ctrl+]	Command+]
Outdent Code	Removes indentations for selected code (Code view only)	Ctrl+[	Command+[
Balance Braces	Selects code within the nearest surrounding parentheses or braces (Code view only)	Ctrl+'	Command+'
Set/Remove Breakpoint	Toggles the insertion and removal of a marker that stops the execution of the JavaScript code (Code view only)	Ctrl+Alt+B	Command+Option+B
Remove All Breakpoints	Eliminates all breakpoints previously set in the code (Code view only)	N/A	N/A
Edit with External Editor (Menu entry specifies external editor when defined)	Opens the External HTML Editor as defined in Preferences ➪ External Editors	Ctrl+E	Command+E
Preferences	Displays the Preferences dialog box	Ctrl+U	Command+U
Keyboard Shortcuts	Opens the Keyboard Shortcuts dialog box to allow customization of the keyboard shortcuts	N/A	N/A

The View menu

As you build your Web pages, you'll find that it's helpful to be able to turn certain features on and off. The View menu centralizes all these commands and switches between the Design and Code views. One of the handiest commands hides all the Visual Aids with a keyboard shortcut, Ctrl+Shift+I (Command+Shift+I). Table 3-11 describes each command under the View menu.

Table 3-11
View Menu Commands

Command	Description	Windows	Macintosh
Code	Displays the code of the current page	N/A	N/A
Design	Displays the browser view of the current page	N/A	N/A

Command	Description	Windows	Macintosh
Code and Design	Splits the view, showing Code and Design views simultaneously; also known as Split view	N/A	N/A
Switch Views	Activates the alternate view in Split view	Ctrl+Tab	Option+Tab
Refresh Design View	Applies changes made in Code view to the Design view	F5	F5
Design View on Top	When selected, shows the Design view above the Code view	N/A	N/A
Head Content	Displays symbols for elements inserted in the `<head>` section of the current document	Ctrl+Shift+W	Command+ Shift+W
Table View ⇨ Standard View	Displays the Standard view in the Document window	Ctrl+Shift+F6	Command+ Shift+F6
Table View ⇨ Layout View	Engages Layout view for creating layout cells and tables	Ctrl+F6	Ctrl+F6
Table View ⇨ Show Layout Table Tabs	Shows outlines and tabs marking layout cells and tables	N/A	N/A
Visual Aids ⇨ Hide All	Toggles all the visual aids on or off	Ctrl+Shift+I	Command+ Shift+I
Visual Aids ⇨ Layer Borders	Toggles the border outlining an unselected layer	N/A	N/A
Visual Aids ⇨ Table Borders	Toggles the border outlining an unselected table	N/A	N/A
Visual Aids ⇨ Frame Borders	Toggles borders in a frameset	N/A	N/A
Visual Aids ⇨ Image Maps	Displays/hides the overlays for defined image maps	N/A	N/A
Visual Aids ⇨ Invisible Elements	Controls whether the symbols for certain HTML tags are shown	N/A	N/A
Code View Options ⇨ Word Wrap	Toggles word wrapping at the window's edge	N/A	N/A
Code View Options ⇨ Line Numbers	Displays a number for every line of code	N/A	N/A
Code View Options ⇨ Highlight Invalid HTML	Shows a yellow highlight for incorrect HTML	N/A	N/A

Continued

Table 3-11 *(continued)*

Command	Description	Windows	Macintosh
Code View Options ⇨ Syntax Coloring	Toggles code coloring according to function	N/A	N/A
Code View Options ⇨ Auto Indent	Forces the line after a return to indent to the position of the current line	N/A	N/A
Rulers ⇨ Show	Displays the horizontal and vertical rulers	Ctrl+Alt+R	Command+ Option+R
Rulers ⇨ Reset Origin	Resets the rulers' 0,0 coordinates to the upper-left corner of the window	N/A	N/A
Rulers ⇨ Pixels/ Inches/Centimeters	Sets the rulers to a selected measurement system	N/A	N/A
Grid ⇨ Show	Displays a background grid using the current settings	Ctrl+Alt+G	Command+ Option+G
Grid ⇨ Snap To	Forces inserted objects to align with the nearest snap setting	Ctrl+Alt+ Shift+G	Command+ Option+ Shift+G
Grid ⇨ Edit Grid	Displays the Grid Settings dialog box	N/A	N/A
Tracing Image ⇨ Show	Displays the image chosen as the Tracing Image according to the Page Properties settings	N/A	N/A
Tracing Image ⇨ Align with Selection	Aligns the top-left corner of the Tracing Image with the top-left corner of the selected object	N/A	N/A
Tracing Image ⇨ Adjust Position	Enables the Tracing Image to be moved using the cursor keys or numerically	N/A	N/A
Tracing Image ⇨ Reset Position	Resets the position of the Tracing Image to the upper-left corner of the document	N/A	N/A
Tracing Image ⇨ Load	Displays the Open File dialog box for inserting the tracing	N/A	N/A
Plug-ins ⇨ Play	Plays the selected plug-in	Ctrl+Alt+P	Command+ Option+P
Plug-ins ⇨ Stop	Stops the selected plug-in from playing	Ctrl+Alt+X	Command+ Option+X
Plug-ins ⇨ Play All	Plays all plug-ins on the current page.	Ctrl+Alt+ Shift+P	Command+ Option+ Shift+P

Command	Description	Windows	Macintosh
Plug-ins ⇨ Stop All	Stops all plug-ins on the current page from playing	Ctrl+Alt+ Shift+X	Command+ Option+Shift+X
Hide Panels	Closes all open panels	F4	F4
Toolbar	Enables the toolbar to be shown	Ctrl+Shift+T	Command+Shift+T

The Insert menu

The Insert menu contains the same items available through the Objects panel. In fact, if you add additional objects (as discussed in Chapter 18), you can see your objects listed on the Insert menu the next time you start Dreamweaver. All objects are inserted at the current cursor position.

Table 3-12 lists the items available to be inserted in the standard Dreamweaver.

Table 3-12 Insert Menu Commands			
Command	**Description**	**Windows**	**Macintosh**
Image	Opens the Insert Image dialog box that enables you to input or browse for a graphics file	Ctrl+Alt+I	Command+ Option+I
Interactive Images ⇨ Rollover Image	Opens the Rollover dialog box for inserting a Rollover button	N/A	N/A
Interactive Images ⇨ Navigation Bar	Opens the Navigation Bar dialog box for creating a series of Rollover buttons with links	N/A	N/A
Interactive Images ⇨ Flash Button	Inserts an animated button based on a Flash template	N/A	N/A
Interactive Images ⇨ Flash Text	Includes a Flash object for displaying text	N/A	N/A
Interactive Images ⇨ Fireworks HTML	Imports HTML and JavaScript generated by Fireworks	N/A	N/A
Media ⇨ Flash	Opens the Insert Flash Movie dialog box so you can either type in or browse for a movie file	Ctrl+Alt+F	Command+ Option+F

Continued

Table 3-12 *(continued)*

Command	*Description*	*Windows*	*Macintosh*
Media ⇨ Shockwave	Opens the Insert Shockwave dialog box for you to input or browse for a Director file	Ctrl+Alt+D	Command+ Option+D
Media ⇨ Generator	Opens the Insert Generator dialog box to include a Generator template	N/A	N/A
Media ⇨ Applet	Opens the Insert Applet dialog box that permits you to input or browse for a Java class source	N/A	N/A
Media ⇨ Plug-in	Opens the Insert Plug-in dialog box so you can either input or browse for a plug-in.	N/A	N/A
Media ⇨ ActiveX	Inserts an ActiveX placeholder	N/A	N/A
Table	Opens the Insert Table dialog box for establishing a table layout	Ctrl+Alt+T	Command+ Option+T
Layer	Inserts a layer of a preset size	N/A	N/A
Frames ⇨ Left/Right/ Top/Bottom/Left and Top/Left Top/Top Left/Split	Inserts the selected frameset	N/A	N/A
Form	Creates the form structure on your Web page	N/A	N/A
Form Object ⇨ Text Field/Button/Check Box/Radio Button/ List/Menu/File Field/ Image Field/Hidden Field	Inserts the selected form object at the current cursor position	N/A	N/A
Form Object ⇨ Jump Menu	Opens the Jump Menu dialog box for creating a list box with links	N/A	N/A
Server-Side Include	Opens the dialog box for inserting a server-side include	N/A	N/A
E-mail Link	Opens the Insert E-mail Link dialog box to create a mailto: link	N/A	N/A
Date	Opens the Insert Date dialog box for entering the current date	N/A	N/A
Tabular Data	Inserts a table derived from a file with delimited data	N/A	N/A

Command	Description	Windows	Macintosh
Horizontal Rule	Inserts a horizontal line the width of the current window	N/A	N/A
Invisible Tags ⇨ Named Anchor	Displays the Insert Named Anchor dialog box	Ctrl+Alt+A	Command+ Option+A
Invisible Tags ⇨ Script	Displays the Insert Script dialog box	N/A	N/A
Invisible Tags ⇨ Comment	Displays the Insert Comment dialog box	N/A	N/A
Head Tags ⇨ Meta/ Keywords/Description/ Refresh/Base/Link	Displays the appropriate dialog box for inserting the selected HTML tag in the `<head>` section	N/A	N/A
Special Characters ⇨ Line Break	Inserts a line break ` ` tag	Shift+Enter	Shift+Return
Special Characters ⇨ Non-breaking Space	Inserts a hard space	Ctrl+Shift+ spacebar	Command+ Shift+spacebar (or Option+ spacebar)
Special Characters ⇨ Copyright/Registered/ Trademark/Pound/ Yen/Euro/Em-Dash/ Left Quote/ Right Quote	Inserts the HTML code for the selected character entity	N/A	N/A
Special Characters ⇨ Other	Opens the Insert Other Character dialog box to choose a special character	N/A	N/A
Get More Objects	Connects to the Dreamweaver Online Resource Center	N/A	N/A

The Modify menu

Inserting objects is less than half the battle of creating a Web page. Most Web designers spend most of their time adjusting, experimenting with, and tweaking the various elements. The Modify menu lists all the commands for altering existing selections. Table 3-13 lists all the Modify options.

Table 3-13
Modify Menu Commands

Command	Description	Windows	Macintosh
Page Properties	Opens the Page Properties dialog box	Ctrl+J	Command+J
Selection Properties	Displays and hides the Property Inspector	Ctrl+Shift+J	Command+Shift+J
Quick Tag Editor	Displays the Quick Tag Editor for the current selection; repeating the keyboard shortcut toggles between the three Quick Tag Editor modes	Ctrl+T	Command+T
Make Link	Presents the Select HTML File dialog box for picking a linking file	Ctrl+L	Command+L
Remove Link	Deletes the current link	Ctrl+Shift+L	Command+Shift+L
Open Linked Page	Opens the linked page in Dreamweaver	N/A	N/A
Link Target ⇨ Default/ _blank/_parent/ _self/_top	Selects the target for the current link	N/A	N/A
Link Target ⇨ Set	Enables you to name a target for the link	N/A	N/A
Table ⇨ Select Table	Highlights the entire table surrounding the current cursor position	Ctrl+A	Command+A
Table ⇨ Merge Cells	Merges selected cells using spans	Ctrl+Alt+M	Command+Option+M
Table ⇨ Split Cell	Splits cells into rows or columns	Ctrl+Alt+S	Command+Option+S
Table ⇨ Insert Row	Adds a new row above the current row	Ctrl+M	Command+M
Table ⇨ Insert Column	Adds a new column before the current column	Ctrl+Shift+A	Command+Shift+A
Table ⇨ Insert Rows or Columns	Opens the Insert Rows/Columns dialog box that enables multiple rows or columns to be inserted relative to the cursor position	N/A	N/A
Table ⇨ Delete Row	Removes the current row	Ctrl+Shift+M	Command+Shift+M
Table ⇨ Delete Column	Removes the current column	Ctrl+Shift +– (minus sign)	Command+Shift+– (minus sign)

Command	Description	Windows	Macintosh
Table ⇨ Increase Row Span/Decrease Row Span	Increases or decreases by one row the span of the current cell	N/A	N/A
Table ⇨ Increase Column Span/ Decrease Column Span	Increases or decreases the column span of the current cell by one column	Ctrl+Shift+] (Increase Column Span) Command+ Shift+] (Increase Column Span)	Ctrl+Shift+[(Decrease Column Span)\ Command+ Shift+[(Decrease Column Span)
Table ⇨ Clear Cell Heights	Removes specified row height values for the entire selected table	N/A	N/A
Table ⇨ Clear Cell Widths	Removes specified column width values for the entire selected table	N/A	N/A
Table ⇨ Convert Widths to Pixels	Changes column widths from percents to pixels for the entire selected table	N/A	N/A
Table ⇨ Convert Widths to Percent	Changes column widths from pixels to percents for the entire selected table	N/A	N/A
Frameset ⇨ Edit No Frames Content not support frames	Opens a new window for content to be seen by browsers that do	N/A	N/A
Frameset ⇨ Split Frame Left/Split Frame Right/Split Frame Up/Split Frame Down	Moves the current frame in the specified direction, and adds a new frame opposite	N/A	N/A
Navigation Bar	Opens the Navigation Bar dialog box for editing the selected Navigation Bar	N/A	N/A
Arrange ⇨ Bring to Front	Places selected layers or hotspots in front of all other layers or hotspots	N/A	N/A
Arrange ⇨ Send to Back	Places selected layers or hotspots behind all other layers or hotspots	N/A	N/A
Arrange ⇨ Prevent Layer Overlaps	Stops newly created layers from overlapping	N/A	N/A
Align ⇨ Left	Aligns grouped layers or hotspots on the left edge	Ctrl+Shift+1	Command+ Shift+1

Continued

Table 3-13 *(continued)*

Command	*Description*	*Windows*	*Macintosh*
Align ⇨ Right	Aligns grouped layers or hotspots on the right edge	Ctrl+Shift+3	Command+ Shift+3
Align ⇨ Top	Aligns grouped layers or hotspots on the top edge	Ctrl+Shift+4	Command+ Shift+4
Align ⇨ Bottom	Aligns grouped layers or hotspots on the bottom edge	Ctrl+Shift+6	Command+ Shift+6
Align ⇨ Make Same Width	Changes the width of grouped layers or hotspots to that of the last selected layer	Ctrl+Shift+7	Command+ Shift+7
Align ⇨ Make Same Height	Changes the height of grouped layers or hotspots to that of the last selected layer.	Ctrl+Shift+9	Command+ Shift+9
Convert ⇨ Tables to Layers	Places all content on the page in layers	N/A	N/A
Convert ⇨ Layers to Tables	Places all content in layers in tables	N/A	N/A
Library ⇨ Add Object to Library	Opens the Library category, and adds the selected object	Ctrl+Shift+B	Command+ Shift+B
Library ⇨ Update Current Page/Update Pages	Replaces any modified Library items in the current page or current site	N/A	N/A
Templates ⇨ Apply Template to Page	Enables the selection of a template to be overlaid on the current page	N/A	N/A
Templates ⇨ Detach from Template	Breaks the link between the template and the current page	N/A	N/A
Templates ⇨ Open Attached Template	Opens the current template for editing	N/A	N/A
Templates ⇨ Update Current Page	Automatically updates the page with template changes	N/A	N/A
Templates ⇨ Update Pages	Enables the updating of an entire site or of all pages using a particular template	N/A	N/A
Templates ⇨ New Editable Region	Inserts the placeholder for a new editable region	Ctrl+Alt+V	Command+ Option+V

Command	Description	Windows	Macintosh
Templates ⇨ Remove Editable Region	Converts the selected region from editable to locked	N/A	N/A
Templates ⇨ No Editable Regions	Displayed in menu until editable regions are created and is then replaced by editable region names	N/A	N/A
Timeline ⇨ Add Object to Timeline	Opens the Timelines panel, and inserts the current image or layer	Ctrl+Alt+ Shift+T	Command+ Option+Shift+T
Timeline ⇨ Add Behavior to Timeline	Opens the Timeiines panel, and inserts an onFrame event using the current frame	N/A	N/A
Timeline ⇨ Record Path of Layer	Plots the path of a dragged layer onto a timeline	N/A	N/A
Timeline ⇨ Add Keyframe	Inserts a keyframe at the current Playback Head position	F6	F6
Timeline ⇨ Remove Keyframe	Deletes the currently selected keyframe	Shift+F6	Shift+F6
Timeline ⇨ Change Object	Applies a timeline path to another object	N/A	N/A
Timeline ⇨ Remove Object/Remove Behavior	Deletes the currently selected object or behavior	N/A	N/A
Timeline ⇨ Add Frame/ Remove Frame	Inserts or deletes a frame at the current Playback Head position	N/A	N/A
Timeline ⇨ Add Timeline/Remove Timeline/Rename Timeline	Inserts an additional timeline, deletes the current timeline, or renames the current timeline	N/A	N/A
Translate ⇨ Date	Updates the date and time code inserted by the Date object	N/A	N/A

The Text menu

The Internet was initially an all-text medium, and despite all the multimedia development, the World Wide Web hasn't traveled far from these beginnings. The Text menu, as described in Table 3-14, covers overall formatting as well as text-oriented functions such as spell-checking.

Table 3-14
Text Menu Commands

Command	Description	Windows	Macintosh
Indent	Marks the selected text or the current paragraph with the `<blockquote>` tag to indent it	Ctrl+Alt+]	Command+ Option+]
Outdent	Removes a `<dir>` or `<blockquote>` surrounding the selected text or current indented paragraph	Ctrl+Alt+[	Command+ Option+[
Paragraph Format ⇨ None	Removes all HTML formatting tags surrounding the current selection	Ctrl+0 (zero)	Command+0 (zero)
Paragraph Format ⇨ Paragraph	Converts the selected text to paragraph format	Ctrl+Shift+P	Command+ Shift+P
Paragraph Format ⇨ Heading 1–6	Changes the selected text to the specified heading format	Ctrl+1–6	Command+ 1–6
Paragraph Format ⇨ Preformatted Text	Formats the selected text with a monospaced font	N/A	N/A
Align ⇨ Left	Aligns the selected text to the left of the page, table, or layer	Ctrl+Alt+ Shift+L	Command+ Option+ Shift+L
Align ⇨ Center	Aligns the selected text to the center of the current page, table, or layer	Ctrl+Alt+ Shift+C	Command+ Option+ Shift+C
Align ⇨ Right	Aligns the selected text to the right of the page, table, or layer	Ctrl+Alt+ Shift+R	Command+ Option+ Shift+R
List ⇨ None	Changes a list item into a paragraph	N/A	N/A
List ⇨ Unordered List	Makes the selected text into a bulleted list	N/A	N/A
List ⇨ Ordered List	Makes the selected text into a numbered list	N/A	N/A
List ⇨ Definition List	Converts the selected text into alternating definition terms and items	N/A	N/A
List ⇨ Properties	Opens the List Properties dialog box	N/A	N/A
Font ⇨ Default	Changes the current selection to the default font	N/A	N/A
Font ⇨ Your Font List	Displays fonts in your current font list	N/A	N/A

Command	Description	Windows	Macintosh
Font ⇨ Edit Font List	Opens the Font List dialog box for adding or deleting fonts from the current list	N/A	N/A
Style ⇨ Bold	Makes the selected text bold	Ctrl+B	Command+B
Style ⇨ Italic	Makes the selected text italic	Ctrl+I	Command+I
Style ⇨ Underline	Underlines the selected text	N/A	N/A
Style ⇨ Strikethrough	Surrounds the selected text with the `<s>...</s>` tags for text with a line through it	N/A	N/A
Style ⇨ Teletype	Surrounds the selected text with the `<tt>...</tt>` tags for a monospaced font	N/A	N/A
Style ⇨ Emphasis	Surrounds the selected text | with the `<emp>...</emp>` tags for slightly emphasized, usually italic, text	N/A	N/A
Style ⇨ Strong	Surrounds the selected text with the `<strong>...</strong>` tags for more emphasized, usually bold, text	N/A	N/A
Style ⇨ Code	Surrounds the selected text with HTML code for depicting programming code	N/A	N/A
Style ⇨ Variable	Surrounds the selected text with HTML code for depicting a variable in programming, typically in italic	N/A	N/A
Style ⇨ Sample/Keyboard	Surrounds the selected text with HTML code for depicting monospaced fonts	N/A	N/A
Style ⇨ Citation	Surrounds the selected text with HTML code for depicting cited text, usually in italic	N/A	N/A
Style ⇨ Definition	Surrounds the selected text with HTML code for depicting a definition, usually in italic	N/A	N/A
HTML Styles ⇨ Clear Selection Style	Removes text formatting tags around the current selection	N/A	N/A
HTML Styles ⇨ Clear Paragraph Style	Removes text formatting tags for the paragraph containing the current selection	N/A	N/A

Continued

Table 3-14 *(continued)*

Command	Description	Windows	Macintosh
HTML Styles ➪ New Style	Displays the HTML Styles dialog box to create a new text style	N/A	N/A
CSS Styles ➪ None/ Your Style List	Applies a user-defined style to selected text. The None option removes previously applied styles	N/A	N/A
CSS Styles ➪ New Style	Displays the New Style dialog box for creating a new CSS style	N/A	N/A
CSS Styles ➪ Edit Style Sheet	Opens the Edit Style Sheet dialog box for adding, deleting, or modifying custom styles	Ctrl+Shift +E	Command+ Shift+E
CSS Styles ➪ Attach Style Sheet	Displays the Select File dialog box and links the selected CSS file to the current document	N/A	N/A
CSS Styles ➪ Export CSS Styles	Copies in-document defined CSS styles to an external style sheet	N/A	N/A
Size ➪ Default ➪ 1–7	Converts the selected text to the chosen font size	N/A	N/A
Size Change ➪ +1 through +7	Increases the size of the selected text relative to the defined basefont size (default is 3)	N/A	N/A
Size Change ➪ +1 through +4 / −1 through −3	Changes the size of the selected text relative to the defined basefont size (default is 3)	N/A	N/A
Color	Opens the operating system's Color dialog box to alter the color of selected or following text	N/A	N/A
Check Spelling	Opens the Spell Check dialog box	Shift+F7	Shift+F7

The Commands menu

Commands are user-definable code capable of affecting almost any tag, attribute, or item on the current page—or even the current site. Commands increase your productivity by automating many of the mundane, repetitive tasks in Web page creation.

Dreamweaver comes with several handy commands, but they are truly just the tip of the iceberg. Commands are written in a combination of HTML and JavaScript and can be created and modified by any capable JavaScript programmer.

Table 3-15 describes the standard Dreamweaver commands.

Table 3-15
Commands Menu

Command	Description	Windows	Macintosh
Start/Stop Recording	Begins remembering the sequence of user commands; toggles with Stop Recording	Ctrl+Shift +X	Command+ Shift+X
Play Recorded Command	Executes the last recorded command	Ctrl+P	Command+P
Edit Command List	Opens the Edit Command List dialog box for arranging and deleting custom items from the Commands menu.	N/A	N/A
Get More Commands	Connects to the Dreamweaver Online Resource Center	N/A	N/A
Manage Extensions	Opens the Extension Manager for installing and removing extensions	N/A	N/A
Apply Source Formatting	Structures the current page according to the Source Format Profile	N/A	N/A
Clean Up HTML	Processes the current page according to various options to remove extraneous HTML	N/A	N/A
Clean Up Word HTML	Processes the current page according to various options to remove extraneous HTML inserted by Microsoft Word	N/A	N/A
Add/Remove Netscape Resize Fix	Inserts or deletes code to compensate for the bug affecting layers in Netscape 4+ browsers	N/A	N/A
Optimize Image in Fireworks	Displays the Optimize Image dialog box for processing images. Requires Fireworks 4	N/A	N/A
Create Web Photo Album	Uses Fireworks to make a thumbnail catalog of a folder of images. Requires Fireworks 4	N/A	N/A
Set Color Scheme	Selects a color scheme for the current page, affecting background color, text color, and the link colors	N/A	N/A
Format Table	Enables a predesigned format to be set on the current table	N/A	N/A

Continued

Table 3-15 *(continued)*			
Command	**Description**	**Windows**	**Macintosh**
Sort Table	Sorts the current table alphabetically or numerically	N/A	N/A
Your Commands	Automatically lists new commands added to the Commands folder	N/A	N/A

You can find a number of new commands on the CD-ROM that accompanies this book. Chapter 21 gives you information on how to build your own commands.

The Site menu

Web designers spend a good portion of their day directly interacting with a Web server: putting up new files, getting old ones, and generally maintaining the site. To ease the workflow, Dreamweaver includes the most commonly used commands in the Document window menu as well as the Site window menu.

The Site menus are very different on the Windows and Macintosh platforms. Because of these differences, the commands are listed in two different tables. All the commands found in the Windows Site menu are described in Table 3-16.

Table 3-16 Site Menu Commands (Windows)		
Command	**Description**	**Windows**
Sites Files	Displays the Site window	F8
Site Map	Displays the current site map	Alt+F8
New Site	Presents the Site Definition dialog box for creating a new site	N/A
Open Site ➪ Your Site List	Displays a user-definable list of sites; when one is selected, the Site window opens pointing to the selected site	N/A
Define Sites	Displays the Site Information dialog box for setting up a new site, or for modifying or deleting an existing site	N/A

Command	Description	Windows
Get	Transfers the selected files from the remote site to the local folder	Ctrl+Shift+D
Check Out	Marks selected files on the remote site as checked out	Ctrl+Alt+Shift+D
Put	Transfers the selected files from the local folder to the remote site	Ctrl+Shift+U
Check In	Marks selected files as checked in	Ctrl+Alt+Shift+U
Undo Check Out	Removes the Check Out designation on selected files	N/A
Reports	Opens the Reports dialog box for running the currently available interactive reports	N/A
Check Links Sitewide ⇨ Selected	Verifies hypertext links for the current or selected documents	Ctrl+F8
Locate in Local Site	Selects the current document in the Site Files list Local pane	N/A
Locate in Remote Site	Selects the current document in the Site Files list Remote pane	N/A

The Macintosh Site menu is set up somewhat differently from the Windows version, although the functionality is the same. Table 3-17 details the Site menu for Macintosh systems.

Table 3-17 Site Menu Commands (Macintosh)		
Command	**Description**	**Macintosh**
New Site	Presents the Site Definition dialog box for creating a new site	N/A
Open Site ⇨ Your Site List	Displays a user-definable list of sites; when one is selected, the Site Window opens pointing to the selected site	N/A
Define Sites	Displays the Site Information dialog box for setting up a new site, or for modifying or deleting an existing site	N/A

Continued

Table 3-17 *(continued)*

Command	Description	Macintosh
Connect	Connects to the current site online	N/A
Refresh	Refreshes the selected pane in the Site window	F5
Site Files View ➪ New File	Creates a new HTML file in the current site	Command+Shift+N
Site Files View ➪ New Folder	Creates a new folder in the current site	Command+Shift+Option+N
Site Files View ➪ Refresh Local	Rereads and displays the current local folder	Shift+F5
Site Files View ➪ Refresh Remote	Rereads and displays the current remote folder	Option+F5
Site Files View ➪ Select Checked Out Files	Highlights files that have been Checked Out	N/A
Site Files View ➪ Select Newer Local	Highlights files that have been modified locally but not transferred to the remote site	N/A
Site Files View ➪ Select Newer Remote	Highlights files that have been modified remotely but not transferred to the local site	N/A
Site Files View ➪ File View Columns	Opens Preferences to the File View Columns category	N/A
Site Map View ➪ View as Root	Makes the selected file the starting point for the map	Command+Shift+R
Site Map View ➪ Link to New File	Creates a new file and adds a link to the selected page	Command+Shift+N
Site Map View ➪ Link to Existing File	Adds a text link to an existing file to the selected page	Command+Shift+K
Site Map View ➪ Change Link	Selects a new page to use as a link instead of the selected file and updates the link	Command+L
Site Map View ➪ Remove Link	Deletes the selected link	Command+Shift+L
Site Map View ➪ Show/Hide Link	Marks a file and all its dependent files as hidden or displayable	Command+Shift+Y

Command	Description	Macintosh
Site Map View ⇨ Open Source of Link	Opens the HTML file containing the selected link in Dreamweaver	N/A
Site Map View ⇨ New Home Page	Makes the selected file the starting point for the Site Map	N/A
Site Map View ⇨ Set as Home Page	Presents a Select File dialog box to choose a file that becomes the new starting point for the Site Map	N/A
Site Map View ⇨ Save Site Map ⇨ Save Site Map as PICT | JPEG	Stores the current site map as a graphic file in the chosen format	N/A
Site Map View ⇨ Show Files Marked as Hidden	Displays all hidden files with the filename in italics	N/A
Site Map View ⇨ Show Dependent Files	Shows all the graphic and other additional files associated with the HTML pages	N/A
Site Map View ⇨ Show Page Titles	Displays icons identified by page titles instead of by filenames	Command+Shift+T
Site Map View ⇨ Layout	Opens the Layout dialog box that determines the structure of the Site Map	N/A
Site Map View ⇨ Refresh Local	Redraws the Site Map	Shift+F5
Get	Transfers the selected files from the remote site to the local folder	Command+Shift+D
Check Out	Marks selected files on the remote site as checked out	Command+Option+Shift+D
Put	Transfers the selected files from the local folder to the remote site	Command+Shift+U
Check In	Marks selected files as checked in	Command+Option+Shift+U
Undo Check Out	Removes the Check Out designation on selected files	N/A
Open	Loads a selected file into Dreamweaver	Command+Option+Shift+O
Rename	Renames the selected file	N/A
Unlock	Makes selected read-only files accessible	N/A
Locate in Local Site	Selects the current document in the Site Files list Local pane	N/A

Continued

Table 3-17 *(continued)*

Command	Description	Macintosh
Locate in Remote Site	Selects the current document in the Site Files list Remote pane	N/A
Reports	Opens the Reports dialog box for running the currently available interactive reports	N/A
Check Links Sitewide	Verifies hypertext links for the current or selected documents	Command+F8
Change Link Sitewide	Opens a dialog box to specify a link to change	N/A
Synchronize	Transfers files between the local and remote sites so that the latest version of all selected files are on both sites	N/A
Recreate Site Cache	Rebuilds the Site Cache to enable quicker updates	N/A
FTP Log	Opens the FTP Log window	N/A
Tool Tips	Enables long filenames or page titles to be displayed when passed over by the pointer	N/A

The Window menu

The Window menu manages both program and user-opened windows. Through this menu, described in Table 3-18, you can open, close, arrange, bring to the front, or hide all of the additional Dreamweaver screens.

Table 3-18
Window Menu Commands

Command	Description	Windows	Macintosh
Objects	Opens the Objects panel	Ctrl+F2	Command+F2
Properties	Shows the Property Inspector for the currently selected item	Ctrl+F3	Command+F3
Launcher	Opens the Launcher panel	N/A	N/A
Sites Files	Displays the Site window	F8	F8
Site Map	Displays the current site map	Alt+F8	Alt+F8

Command	Description	Windows	Macintosh
Assets	Shows the various resources for the current site	F11	F11
Behaviors	Shows the Behaviors panel	Shift+F3	Shift+F3
Code Inspector	Displays the Code Inspector	F10	F10
CSS Styles	Opens the CSS Styles panel	Shift+F11	Shift+F11
Frames	Opens the Frames panel	Shift+F2	Shift+F2
History	Displays the History panel	Shift+F10	Shift+F10
HTML Styles	Opens the HTML Styles panel	Ctrl+F11	Command+F11
Layers	Opens the Layers panel	F2	F2
Library	Opens the Assets panel with the Library category selected	N/A	N/A
Reference	Displays the Reference panel	Ctrl+Shift +F1	Command+ Shift+F1
Templates	Opens the Assets panel with the Templates category selected	N/A	N/A
Timelines	Shows the Timelines panel	Shift+F9	Shift+F9
Arrange Panels	Moves all open panels to their preset positions	N/A	N/A
Show/Hide Panels	Displays/hides all open panels	F4	F4
Minimize All (Windows only)	Reduces all open windows to their smallest size	Shift+F4	N/A
Restore All (Windows only)	Expands all windows to their previous size	Alt+Shift+F4	N/A
Your Open Windows	Displays a list of the currently open document windows	N/A	N/A

Tip All the commands for Dreamweaver's various panels and inspectors are toggles. Select a command once to open the window; select again to close it.

The Help menu

The final menu, the Help menu, offers access to Dreamweaver's excellent online help, as well as special examples and lessons. Table 3-19 explains each of these useful options.

Table 3-19
Help Menu Commands

Command	Description	Windows	Macintosh
Welcome	Opens the Welcome screen	N/A	N/A
Using Dreamweaver	Opens the Dreamweaver online help system in your primary browser	F1	F1
Reference	Opens the Reference panel to the selected code, if any	Shift+F1	Shift+F1
What's New	Displays the What's New section of the Welcome screen	N/A	N/A
Guided Tour	Displays the Guided Tour section of the Welcome screen	N/A	N/A
Lessons	Displays the available Lessons	N/A	N/A
Dreamweaver Exchange	Connects to the Dreamweaver Online Resource Center	N/A	N/A
Manage Extensions	Opens the Extensions Manager	N/A	N/A
Dreamweaver Support Center	Connects to Macromedia's Dreamweaver Support Center	N/A	N/A
Macromedia Online Forums	Connects to Macromedia's Online Forums page	N/A	N/A
Extending Dreamweaver	Opens the Extending Dreamweaver online documentation in your primary browser	N/A	N/A
Creating and Submitting Extensions	Opens the help pages for using the Extension Manager to package extensions	N/A	N/A
Register Dreamweaver	Goes online to register your copy of Dreamweaver	N/A	N/A
About Dreamweaver	Displays the opening splash screen with credits and registration and version information	N/A	N/A

Summary

In this chapter, you've observed Dreamweaver's power and had a look at its well-designed layout. From the Objects panel to the various tools controlled through the Launcher, Dreamweaver offers you an elegant, flexible workspace for creating next-generation Web sites. This chapter covered the following important points:

✦ The Document window is your main canvas for visually designing your Dreamweaver Web pages. This workspace includes simple, powerful tools such as the Tag Selector and the status bar Launcher.

✦ The Objects panel is Dreamweaver's toolbox. Completely customizable, the Objects panel holds the elements you need most often, in seven initial categories: Characters, Common, Forms, Frames, Head, Invisibles, and Special. The Objects panel also switches between Standard view and Layout view.

✦ Dreamweaver's mechanism for assigning details and attributes to an HTML object is the Property Inspector. The Property Inspector is context-sensitive, and its options vary according to the object selected.

✦ The Launcher is the control center for Dreamweaver's specialized functions: the Site window, the Assets panel, the HTML Styles panel, the CSS Styles panel, the Behaviors panel, the History panel, and the Code Inspector. You have two Launchers to choose from: one free-floating panel and the one accessible through the status bar.

✦ Dreamweaver 4 introduces two new panels: the Assets and Reference panels.

✦ Dreamweaver's full-featured menus offer complete file manipulation, a wide range of insertable objects, the tools to modify them, and extensive online — and on-the-Web — help. Many menu items can be invoked through keyboard shortcuts.

In the next chapter, you learn how to customize Dreamweaver to work the way you work by establishing your own preferences for the program and its interface.

✦　　✦　　✦

Setting Your Preferences

Everyone works differently. Whether you need to conform to a corporate style sheet handed down from the powers that be or you think "it just looks better that way," Dreamweaver offers you the flexibility to shape your Web page tools and your code output. This chapter describes the options available in Dreamweaver's Preferences and then details how you can tell Dreamweaver to format your source code your way.

Customizing Your Environment

The vast majority of Dreamweaver's settings are controlled through the Preferences dialog box. You can open Preferences by choosing Edit ⇨ Preferences or by using the keyboard shortcut Ctrl+U (Command+U). Within Preferences, you find 16 different categories listed on the left side of the screen. As you switch from one category to another by selecting its name from this Category list, the options available for that category appear in the main area of the dialog box. Although this chapter covers all the options available in each category, the categories are grouped by function, rather than examined in the same order as they appear in the Category list.

Most changes to Preferences take effect immediately after you close the window by clicking OK or the Close button. The following two preferences only are not updated instantly:

✦ The Show Only Site Window on Startup option goes into effect on the next running of Dreamweaver.

✦ If you elect to modify the Source Format, as described in the section "Understanding the Source Format," later in this chapter, you should complete this modification outside of Dreamweaver (in a text editor), save your work, and then start the program.

General Preferences

Dreamweaver's General Preferences, as shown in Figure 4-1, cover program appearance, user operation, and fundamental file settings. The appearance of the program's interface may seem to be a trivial matter, but Dreamweaver is a program for designers — to whom appearance is extremely important. These user-operation options are based purely on how you, the user, work best.

Figure 4-1: Dreamweaver's General Preferences enable you to change your program's appearance and certain overall operations.

File options

The first area of the General category, File Options, determines how you work with HTML and other files.

Tip   In choosing all the preferences, including the General ones, you can work in two ways. If you are a seasoned Web designer, you probably want Dreamweaver to work with your established manner to minimize your learning curve. If you're just starting out as a Web page creator, work with the default options for a while and then go back to try other options. You'll want to know right away the styles that work for you.

Show Only Site Window on Startup

Some Web designers prefer to use the Site window as their "base of operations," rather than the Document window. For them, it's easier to construct and maintain their Web pages from the sitewide perspective offered through the Site window. Dreamweaver offers you the option to begin a Web authoring session with the Site window only.

Selecting the Show Only Site Window on Startup option displays the Site window the next time you open Dreamweaver. The Site window is shown in the configuration used the last time you opened it — with or without the Site Map enabled and with the various columns positioned in the same manner. To bring up the Document window, choose File ➪ New Window from the Site window menu.

Open Files in New Window (Windows only)

Select the Open Files in New Window option when you need to have several Web pages open simultaneously. Alternatively, if you want to free up some of your system resources (such as memory) and you need only one Dreamweaver window, you can deselect this option.

Note If this option is not selected and changes are made to the current file, Dreamweaver asks if you'd like to save the current page when you attempt to load a new file.

Warn when Opening Read-Only Files

Read-only files are locked to prevent accidental overwriting. As an option, Dreamweaver warns you when such a file is opened. The warning is actually more than an alert, however. Dreamweaver provides an option on the warning dialog box to make the file writable. Alternatively, you can just view the file.

Although Dreamweaver enables you to edit the file either way, if the document is still read-only when you save your changes, the Save As dialog box appears, prompting you to store the file under a new name.

Add Extension when Saving

HTML files originally were identified — cleverly enough — by their .html filename extension. When Microsoft jumped on the Internet bandwagon, it reduced the extension to three letters, .htm, to fit its pre-Windows 95 format. But now many different Web file formats and extensions have exploded onto the Internet — .asp, .shtml, .stm, and .phtml, to name just a few. In early versions of Dreamweaver (prior to 2), the .htm extension was not only the default, but a difficult one to change at best. Today, Dreamweaver includes the capability to save your files using any filename extension you specify.

The Add Extension when Saving option is straightforward. Just enter the extension of your choosing in the text box and make sure the option is selected. For example, if you are building nothing but Active Server Pages for a particular Web site, you would change the Add Extension when Saving text box to .asp and select OK in the Preferences dialog box. Now, to save a file, you have to enter only the initial part of the filename, and the appropriate extension is automatically appended.

Update Links when Moving Files

As your site grows in complexity, you'll find that keeping track of the various links is an increasingly difficult task. Dreamweaver has several enhanced features to help you manage links, and the Update Links when Moving Files option is one of them. Dreamweaver can check each link on a page when a file is moved — whether it is the Web page you're working on or one of the support files, such as an image, that goes on the page. The Update Links when Moving Files option determines how Dreamweaver reacts when it notes an altered link.

By default, the Update Links when Moving Files option is set to Prompt, which causes Dreamweaver to alert you to any link changes and requires you to "OK" the code alterations by selecting the Update button. To leave the files as they are, you choose the Don't Update button. You can elect to have Dreamweaver automatically keep your pages up to date by selecting the Always option from the Update Links when Moving Files drop-down list. Finally, you can select the Never option, and Dreamweaver ignores the link changes necessary when you move, rename, or delete a file.

As a general rule, I keep my Update Links when Moving Files option set to Always. It is a very rare circumstance when I intentionally want to maintain a bad link on my Web page. Likewise, I recommend using the Never option with extreme caution.

Editing options

The second main section of the General Preferences screen consists of numerous checkbox options you can turn on or off. Overall, these options fall into the user-interaction category or "What's good for you?" Take the Show Dialog when Inserting Objects option, for example. Some Web creators prefer to enter all their attributes at one time through the Property Inspector and would rather not have the dialog boxes appear for every inserted object. Others want to get their file sources in immediately and modify the rest later. Your selection depends on how you want to work.

The following sections describe the listed options.

Show Dialog when Inserting Objects

By default, almost all the objects that Dreamweaver inserts — via either the Objects panel or the Insert menu — open an initial dialog box to gather needed information. In most cases, the dialog box enables you to input a URL or browse for a source file. Turning off the Show Dialog option causes Dreamweaver to insert a default-sized object, or a placeholder, for the object. You must then enter all attributes through the Property Inspector.

Faster Table Editing (Deferred Update)

When you enter text into a table, the current column width automatically expands while the other columns shrink correspondingly. If you're working with large tables, this updating process can slow your editing. Dreamweaver gives you the choice between faster input or instantaneous feedback.

When the Faster Table Editing preference is turned on, Dreamweaver updates the entire table only when you click outside the table, or if you press Ctrl+spacebar (Command+spacebar). If you prefer to see the table form as you type, turn this option off.

Tip

Two other ways to update tables: Select any tag in the Tag Selector (a useful approach when working with a very large table), or resize the Document window.

Rename Form Items when Pasting

Designing forms can be highly repetitive—and somewhat tedious—work. Moreover, if you do not name each form element uniquely, your efforts will be for thwarted; most form actions require each field to be individually identified. The Rename Form Items when Pasting option is intended to eliminate some of the tedium as well as some of the risks from form design.

New Feature

When the Rename Form Items when Pasting option is selected, as it is by default, any copied form element, such as a text field or checkbox, is automatically renamed, each time it is pasted. This facility allows you to copy a single checkbox once and paste it as many times as necessary. Each time the checkbox is pasted, an incrementing number is added. For example, if I copy a checkbox named `beersCB`, the first checkbox I pasted is named `beersCB2` and the next, `beersCB3`, and so on. If this option were disabled, each checkbox would be named `beersCB`, causing problems during processing.

Enable Double-Byte Inline Input

Some computer representations of languages, primarily Asian languages, require more raw descriptive power than others. The ideogram for "snow," for example, is far more complex than a four-letter word. These languages need twice the number of bytes per character and are known as *double-byte languages*. In versions of Dreamweaver before 2, all double-byte characters had to go through a separate text input window instead of directly into the Document window.

Dreamweaver now simplifies the page creation process for double-byte languages with the Enable Double-Byte Inline Input option. Once selected, this option enables double-byte characters to be entered directly into the Document window. To use the old method of inserting such characters, deselect this option.

Maximum Number of History Steps

Before Dreamweaver 3, the number of undo steps was limited by a system's memory—but there was no visual indication of what those steps were. The History panel now shows exactly what actions have been taken. A limit exists, however, to the number of steps that can be tracked. By default, the limit is set to 50.

Although 50 history steps are more than enough for most systems, you can alter this number by changing the Maximum Number of History Steps value. When the maximum number of history steps is exceeded, the oldest actions are wiped from memory and unrecoverable. The history steps are not discarded when a file is saved, unlike the previous undo steps.

Objects panel

Learning a new software program can be tough—simply memorizing which icon means what can increase your learning curve. With Dreamweaver, you don't have to try to remember all of the Object symbols right off the bat. If you like, you can opt to have the name of an Object next to its icon—or even just the name itself. You make this choice in the Objects panel option.

By default, the Objects panel is composed only of icons. When you pass your mouse over each one, a ToolTip appears that names the object. However, if you don't want to hunt for your object, you can select Icons and Text (or Text Only) from the Objects panel option. Whichever option you select, when you exit from Preferences, the Objects panel changes size and shape to accommodate the new format, as shown in Figure 4-2.

Figure 4-2: The Objects panel can display each object's name along with its icon.

Spelling Dictionary

The Spelling Dictionary option enables you to select a spell-checking dictionary from any one of those installed. In addition to the standard English-language version, which has three options—English (US), English (UK-ise), and English (UK-ize)—additional versions of dictionaries exist online. As of this writing, dictionaries in the following languages are also available: German, Spanish, Swedish, French, Italian, Brazilian-Portuguese, and Catalan. You can download these dictionaries from Macromedia's Dreamweaver Object Exchange at `www.macromedia.com/support/dreamweaver/dictionary.html`. Once downloaded, save the .dat file in the Configuration\Dictionaries folder and restart Dreamweaver.

To select a different dictionary for spell-checking, select the Spelling Dictionary option button and choose an item from the drop-down list. Dreamweaver also maintains a Personal dictionary (although it's not visible on the list) to include those words you wish Dreamweaver to learn during the spell-checking process.

Preferences for invisible elements

By their nature, all HTML markup tags remain unseen to one degree or another when presented for viewing through the browser. You may want to see certain elements while designing a page, however. For example, adjusting line spacing is a common task, and turning on the visibility of the line break tag <BR> can help you understand the layout.

Dreamweaver enables you to control the visibility of 11 different codes — or rather their symbols, as shown in Figure 4-3. When, for example, a named anchor is inserted, Dreamweaver shows you a small gold shield with an anchor emblem. Not only does this shield indicate the anchor's position, but you can also manipulate the code with cut-and-paste or drag-and-drop techniques. Moreover, double-clicking a symbol opens the pertinent Property Inspector and enables quick changes to the tag's attributes.

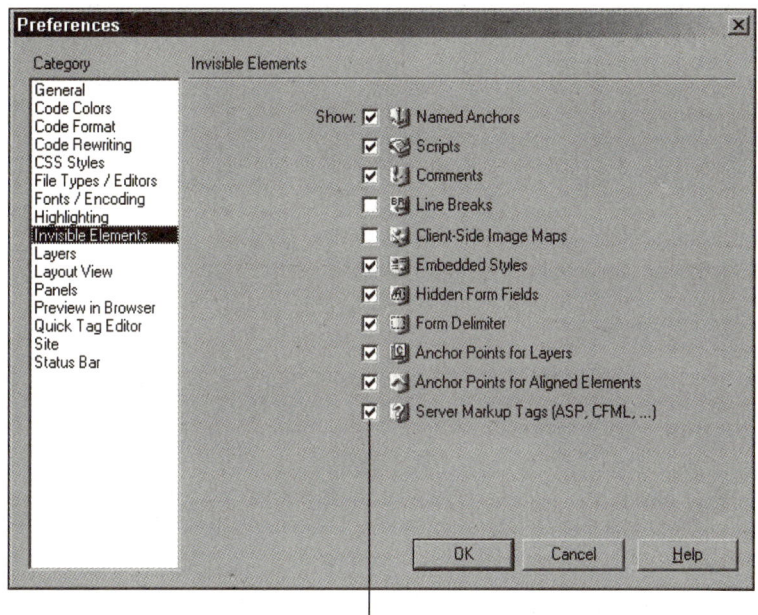

Server Markup tags

Figure 4-3: You can show or hide any or all of the 11 invisible elements listed in the Preferences dialog box.

Tip You can temporarily hide all invisible elements by deselecting View ➪ Visual Aids ➪ Invisible Elements.

The 11 items controlled through the Invisible Elements category are as follows:

✦ Named anchors

✦ Scripts

✦ Comments

✦ Line Breaks

✦ Client-Side Image Maps

✦ Embedded Styles

✦ Hidden Form Fields

✦ Form Delimiter

✦ Anchor Points for Layers

✦ Anchor Points for Aligned Elements

✦ Server markup tags (ASP, CFML, . . .)

Most of the Invisible Elements options display or hide small symbols in Dreamweaver's visual Document window. Several options, however, show an outline or another type of highlight. Turning off Form Delimiter, for example, removes the dashed line that surrounds a form in the Document window.

Tip You may have noticed that the Cold Fusion tags and Active Server Page tags are combined into one symbol, Server markup tags. Dreamweaver's capability to handle dynamic pages generated by databases makes these invisible elements essential.

Panels preferences

Although the various panels and inspectors are convenient, sometimes you just want a clear view of your document. The Panels category of Preferences enables you to choose which of Dreamweaver's accessory screens stay on top of the Document window. As shown in Figure 4-4, you can adjust 14 different elements. By default, they are all set to float above the Document window. The last option, All Other Panels, is used to control the behavior of any custom panels you might end up using.

Tip You can use the Show/Hide Panel key to bring back any screen element that has gone behind the Document window. Just press F4 twice.

All Other Floaters

Add   Up

Delete   Down

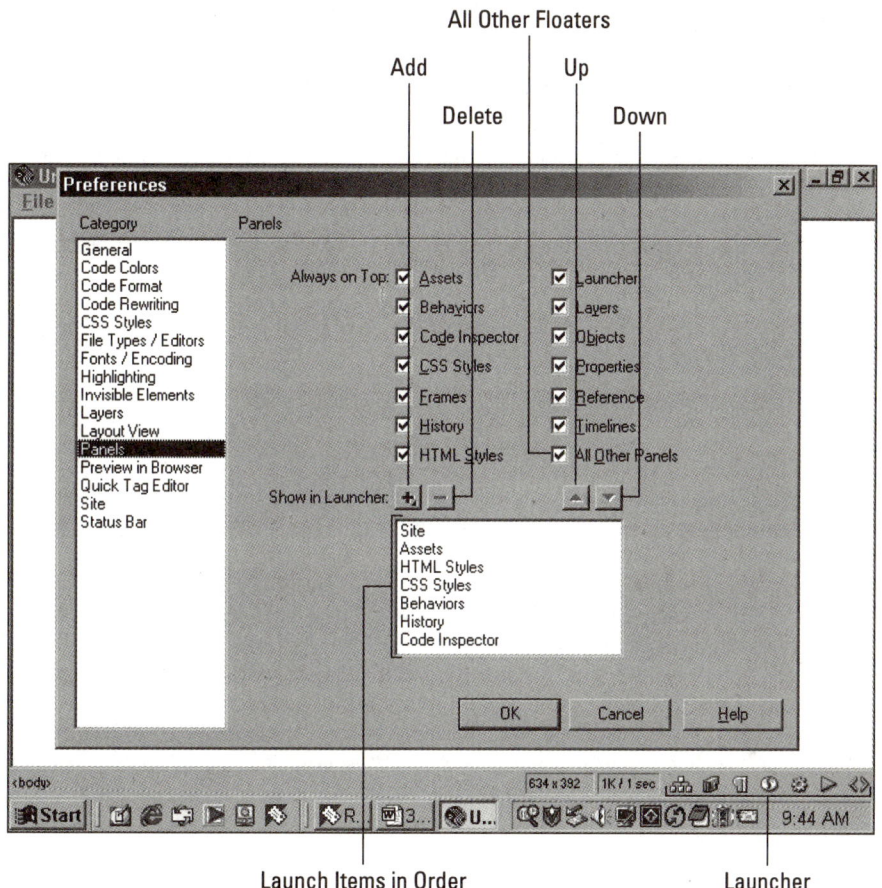

Launch Items in Order   Launcher

Figure 4-4: If you deselect any of the floating panels, they move behind the Document window.

If you prefer to use the Code Inspector rather than the Code view, you might consider taking it off the "always on top" list. Then, after you've made your HTML code edits, click in the Document window. This sequence updates the visual document, incorporating any changes, and simultaneously pushes the Code Inspector behind the Document window. You can switch between the two views of your Web page by using the Ctrl+Tab (Option+Tab) key combination.

The Launcher (both the floating panel and the status bar versions) displays a series of icons for quickly opening and closing various Dreamweaver panels. The Launcher is completely customizable — you can add or remove icons for any of the available panels. Moreover, the order of their appearance is up to you as well.

To add a new icon to the Launcher, follow these steps:

1. Click the Add (+) button and choose an available floating panel from the drop-down list.

   The chosen panel is added to the end of the list, and the icon appears on the right of the Launcher.

2. You can reposition the icon by using the up and down arrows with the panel's name selected.

To remove an icon from the Launcher, select the panel in the list and choose the Delete (-) button.

Highlighting preferences

Dreamweaver is extremely extensible—custom functions are better handled, server-side markup is more acceptable, and more third-party tags are supported. Many of these features depend on "hidden" capabilities that are not noticeable in the final HTML page, but the Web designer must take them into account. Dreamweaver uses user-selectable highlighting to mark areas on a Web page under construction.

The Highlighting category of the Preferences dialog box, shown in Figure 4-5, enables you to choose the highlight color for four different types of extended objects: Editable and Locked Regions, both used in templates; Library Items; and Third-Party Tags. In each case, to choose a highlight color, select the color swatch to open Dreamweaver's color picker. Then use the Eyedropper to pick a color from the Web-safe palette or from your desktop. After you've chosen an appropriate color, make sure to select the related Show checkbox so that the highlighting is displayed.

Note   You'll only notice the Locked Region highlight in Templates if you open the Code view; the Display view only highlights Editable Regions.

Quick Tag Editor preferences

The Quick Tag Editor is designed to bridge the gap between the visual layout and the underlying code. With the Quick Tag Editor, you can quickly edit a tag or wrap the selection in a whole new tag, without opening the Code Inspector. The Quick Tag Editor pops open a small draggable window when invoked, and its preferences, shown in Figure 4-6, control the appearance and behavior of that window.

The Quick Tag Editor has three modes: Edit Tag, Insert HTML, and Wrap Tag. The first option, Apply Changes Immediately While Editing, affects only the Edit Tag mode. When this option is disabled, the Enter (Return) key must be pressed to confirm the edits. In the other two modes, you always must confirm your additions with the Enter (Return) key.

Figure 4-5: Use the Highlighting preferences to control how template regions, library items, and third-party tags appear in the Document window.

The second option, Enable Tag Hint Dropdown, works in all three modes. A short time after the Quick Tag Editor is invoked, a list of possible tags appears. To reduce your typing, when the first letter of the tag is typed, the list scrolls to the tags starting with that letter. For example, if you want to wrap a `<blockquote>` tag around a paragraph, typing a *b* brings the list to the `<b>` (bold) tag; type the next letter, *l*, and the list scrolls to `<blockquote>`—at this point, all you have to do is press Enter (Return) to confirm your choice. The Tag Hint list does not appear at all if Enable Tag Hint Dropdown is unchecked. You can also control the speed at which the Tag Hint list appears by moving the Delay slider; the range is from .5 seconds to 5 seconds.

Tip   If you like using the Tag Hint list, set the Delay slider to .5 second; with that setting, the list pops up almost immediately and speeds your work.

Status bar preferences

The status bar is a handy collection of four different tool sets: the Tag Selector, the Window Size pop-up menu, the Connection Speed Indicator, and the Mini-Launcher. The Status Bar category of the Preferences dialog box, shown in Figure 4-7, controls options for all of these tools except the Tag Selector.

Control the speed of Tag Hints

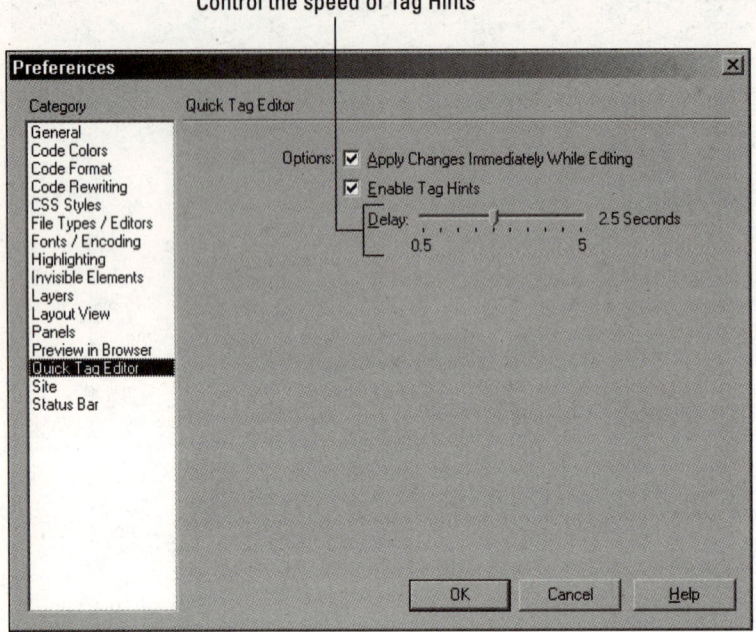

Figure 4-6: Adjust the Quick Tag Editor preferences to suit the way you like to add code to a page.

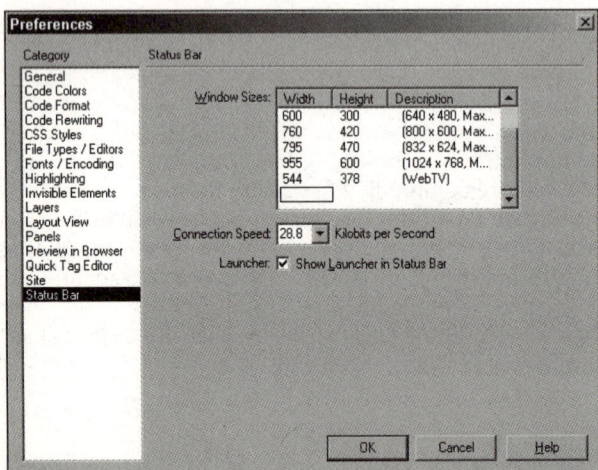

Figure 4-7: Use the Status Bar category to evaluate your real-world download times.

Window Sizes

The Window Sizes list at the top of the Status Bar category shows the current options for the Window Sizes pop-up menu. This list is completely user editable and enables you to add new window sizes, modify existing dimensions, add descriptions, or delete little-used measurements.

As discussed in Chapter 3, the Window Sizes pop-up is a feature in Dreamweaver that enables you to instantly change your screen size so that you may view and build your page under different monitor conditions. To change any of the current dimensions, simply click the measurement you wish to alter and enter a new value. You can also change any description of the existing widths and heights by clicking in the Description column and entering your text. While you can enter as much text as you like, it's not practical to enter more than about 15 to 20 characters.

To enter a new set of dimensions in the Window Sizes list box, follow these steps:

1. From the Status Bar category of the Preferences dialog box, locate the last entry in the current list.

   If the last entry is not immediately available, use the vertical scroll bar to move to the end.

2. Click once in the Width column on the line below the last entry.

3. Enter the desired width of the new window size in pixels.

4. Press Tab to move to the Height column.

5. Enter the desired height for the new window size. Press Tab again.

6. Optionally, you can enter short descriptive text in the Description column. Press Tab when you're finished.

7. To continue adding new sizes, repeat Steps 2 through 6. Click OK when you finish.

Caution   You don't have to enter the word *pixels* or the abbreviation *px* after your values in the Width and Height columns of the Window Sizes list box, but you can. If you enter any dimensions under 20, Dreamweaver converts the measurement to its smallest possible window size, 20 pixels.

Connection Speed

Dreamweaver understands that not all access speeds are created equal, so the Connection Speed option enables you to check the download time for your page (or the individual images) at a variety of rates. The Connection Speed setting evaluates the download statistics in the status bar. You can choose from seven preset connection speeds, all in kilobits per second: 14.4, 28.8, 33.6, 56, 64, 128, and 1,500. The lower speeds (14.4 through 33.6) represent older dial-up modem connection rates — if you are building a page for the mass market, you should consider selecting one of these slower rates. Although 56K modems are widespread on the market today, the true 56K connection is a rare occurrence. Use the 128 setting if your audience connects through an ISDN line. If everyone views your page through a direct LAN connection, change the connection speed to 1,500.

You are not limited to these preset settings. You can type any desired speed directly into the Connection Speed text box. You could, for example, specify a connection speed more often experienced in the real world, such as 23.3. If you find yourself designing for an audience using DSL or cable modems, you could change the Connection Speed to 150 or higher.

Show Launcher in Status Bar

The default setting enables the status bar Launcher. When this option is disabled, you always have to access the Launcher by choosing Window ⇨ Launcher from the menus.

File Types/Editors preferences

Refinement is often the name of the game in Web design, and giving you quick access to your favorite modification tools — whether you're modifying code, graphics, or other media — is one of Dreamweaver's key features. The File Types / Editors category, shown in Figure 4-8, is where you specify the program you want Dreamweaver to call for any file type you define.

Open in Code View

It's no longer just an HTML world — many other code types may be found on a Web designer's palette. Dreamweaver's internal code is full-featured enough to handle a wide variety of code and, with the Open in Code View option, you can determine which types you'd like it to handle. By default, JavaScript (.js), text (.txt) and Active Server Application (.asa) files are automatically opened in Code view. Dreamweaver attempts to open any other selected file type in the Design view.

If you find yourself hand-editing other file types, such as XML files, you can add their extension to the Open in Code View field. Separate extensions with a space and ensure that you begin each one with a period.

Note   Although Macintosh systems do not require extensions, you still use them in the Open in Code View feature.

External Code Editor preferences

Dreamweaver recognizes the importance of your choice of a text editor. Although Dreamweaver ships with two extremely robust code editors — as well as its excellent built-in code editor — you can opt to use any other program. To select your editor, enter the path in the External Code Editor text box or select the Browse button to choose the appropriate executable file.

Add   Add

Delete   Delete

File Types by Extension   Editors   Make Primary

Figure 4-8: Assign your favorite HTML, graphics editors, and more through the newly extended File Types / Editors category of the Preferences dialog box.

The two included editors, BBEdit for Macintosh and HomeSite for Windows, are integrated with Dreamweaver to varying degrees. Both of the editors can be called from within Dreamweaver, and both have "Dreamweaver" buttons for returning to the main program — switching between the editor and Dreamweaver automatically updates the page. Like Dreamweaver's internal HTML editor, BBEdit highlights the corresponding code to a selection made in Dreamweaver; this property does not, however, extend to HomeSite.

You specify and control your external editor selection with the following options.

Enable BBEdit Integration (Macintosh only)

Dreamweaver for Macintosh ships with this option activated. If you prefer to use another editor or an older version of BBEdit that lacks the integration capabilities, deselect this option.

Reload Modified Files

The drop-down list for this setting offers three options for working with an external editor:

✦ **Prompt:** Detects when files are updated by another program and enables you to decide whether to update them within Dreamweaver.

✦ **Always:** Updates the file in Dreamweaver automatically when the file is changed in an outside program.

✦ **Never:** Assumes that you want to make all updates from within Dreamweaver yourself.

Personally, I prefer to have Dreamweaver always update my files. I find it saves a couple of mouse clicks — not to mention time.

Save on Launch

Any external HTML editor — even the integrated HomeSite or BBEdit — opens and reads a previously saved file. Therefore, if you make any changes in Dreamweaver's visual editor and switch to your editor without saving, the editor shows only the most recently saved version. To control this function, you have the following three options:

✦ **Prompt:** Determines that unsaved changes have been made and asks you to save the file. If you do not, the external editor reverts to the last saved version.

✦ **Always:** Saves the file automatically before opening it in the external editor.

✦ **Never:** Disregards any changes made after the last save, and the external editor opens the previously saved file.

Here again, as with Reload Modified Files, I prefer to always save my files when switching back and forth. Keep in mind, however, that saving a file clears Dreamweaver's undo memory and the changes cannot be undone.

Tip   If you try to open a file that has never been saved in an external editor, Dreamweaver prompts you to save it regardless of your preference settings. If you opt not to save the file, the external editor is not opened because it has no saved file to display.

File Types Editor preferences

Dreamweaver has the capability to call an editor for any specified type of file at the touch of a button. For example, when you import a graphic, you often need to modify its color, size, shape, transparency, or another feature to make it work correctly on the Web page. Rather than force you to start your graphics program independently, load the image, make the changes, and resave the image, Dreamweaver enables you to send any selected image directly to your editor. After you've made your modifications and saved the file, the altered image appears automatically in Dreamweaver.

The capability to associate different file types with external editors applies to more than just images in Dreamweaver. You can link one or more editors to any type of media — images, audio, video, even specific kinds of code. The defined external editor is invoked when the file is double-clicked in the Site window. Because the editors are assigned according to file extension as opposed to media type, one editor could be assigned to GIF files and another to JPEGs. The selection is completely customizable.

Note If you have the same file type defined to Open in Code View and set up in the editor list, the file defaults to opening in Code view.

When a file is double-clicked in the Site window, that file type's primary editor runs. Dreamweaver offers the capability to define multiple editors for any file extension. You might, for instance, prefer to open certain JPEGs in Fireworks and others in Photoshop. To choose an alternative editor, right-click (Control+click) the filename in the Site window and select the desired program from the Open With menu option. The Open With option also enables you to browse for a program.

To assign an editor to an existing file type, follow these steps:

1. Select the file type from the Extensions list.

2. Click the Add (+) button above the Editors list.

   The Add External Editor dialog box opens.

3. Locate the application file of the editor and click Open when you're ready.

   You can also select a shortcut or alias to the application.

4. If you want to select the editor as the primary editor, click Make Primary while the editor is highlighted.

To add a new file type, click the Add button above the Extensions list and enter the file extension — including the period — in the field displayed at the bottom of the list. For multiple file extensions, separate each extension with a space, such as this:

```
.doc .dot .rtf
```

Tip Looking for a good almost-all-purpose editor? The QuickTime Pro Player makes a great addition to Dreamweaver as the editor for AIFF, AU, WAV, MP3, AVI, MOV, and animated GIF files and others. The Pro Player is wonderful for quick edits and optimization especially with sound files. It's available from the Apple Web site (www.apple.com/quicktime) for both platforms for around $30.

Finally, to remove an editor or a file extension, select it and click the Delete (-) button above the corresponding list. Note that removing a file extension also removes the associated editor.

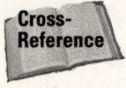

Cross-Reference Be sure that your graphics program is adept at handling the three graphic formats used on the Web: GIFs, JPEGs, and PNG images. Macromedia makes Fireworks, a graphics editor designed for the Web that integrates nicely with Dreamweaver. In fact, it integrates so nicely, this book includes an entire chapter on it, Chapter 22.

Adjusting Advanced Features

Evolution of the Web and its language, HTML, never ends. New features emerge often from leading browser developers. A competing developer can introduce a similar feature that works in a slightly different way. The HTML standards organization — the World Wide Web Consortium, also known as the W3C — can then endorse one approach or introduce an entirely new method of reaching a similar goal. Eventually, one method usually wins the approval of the marketplace and becomes the accepted coding technique.

To permit the widest range of features, Dreamweaver enables you to designate how your code is written to accommodate the latest Web features: layers and style sheets. The default preferences for these elements offer the highest degree of cross-browser and backward compatibility. If your Web pages are intended for a more specific audience, such as a Netscape-only intranet, Dreamweaver enables you to take advantage of a more specific feature set. Furthermore, Dreamweaver also gives you control over its new Layout view, enabling you to set global options as well as some site-by-site.

Layout View preferences

In Layout view — new in Dreamweaver 4 — a column in a table may be set to automatically match the size of the browser window; if the window is resized, the column is stretched or shrunk accordingly. To maintain the structure of such tables and other complex layout devices, professional designers often include an added row on the top or bottom of the table. This additional row is sized to be one pixel high with the same number of cells as the table itself. Within each cell (except for the resizeable cell) is a transparent GIF image, sized to match the cell's dimensions. This image is sometimes called a *spacer*. One of the major functions of the Layout View category of Preferences is to manage these spacers.

Dreamweaver automatically includes spacers if a column is set to Autostretch and the Autoinsert Spacers When Making Autostretch Tables is selected, as it is by default (see Figure 4-9). If you decide not to include spacers, select Never. Which should you choose? I find that spacers definitely help and, unless you have a compelling reason not to use them — such as a corporate edict — I'd advise you to go with the default option. Because a spacer is an actual graphic image, albeit a small one, you must include such a file in every site. Dreamweaver will create one for you if you like or you can select an existing one. The option for creating or locating a spacer is offered when an autostretch table is designated. However, if you'd prefer not to worry about spacers each time you create an autostretch table, you can pre-select an existing image to use through the Layout View category of Preferences. This option is set on a sitewide basis.

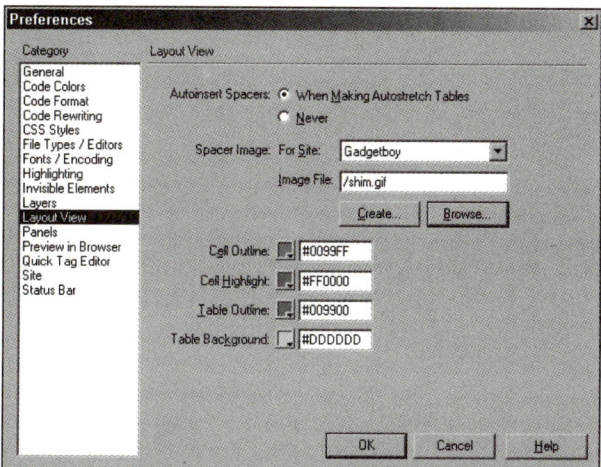

Figure 4-9: Spacer images are used to maintain a table's complex layout; you can set which spacer is used on a site-by-site basis through the Layout View category of Preferences.

To set a spacer image for a site, follow these steps:

1. In the Layout View category of Preferences, choose the site to be affected from the Spacer Image For Site drop-down list.

2. If you do not have a transparent, single pixel GIF image available, select Create.

   Dreamweaver opens the Save Spacer Image File As dialog box.

3. Select a location within your site to store the spacer file.

   If you like, you can also rename the file from spacer.gif to something else.

4. If a graphic on your site is using a transparent, single pixel GIF image, select Browse to locate the graphic.

The remaining options found under the Layout View category are concerned with the various colors used as follows:

✦ **Cell Outline** is the color of the layout cell when it is selected; the default is dark blue.

✦ **Cell Highlight** is the color used to designate an unselected layout cell when the designer's mouse rolls over it, red by default.

✦ **Table Outline** is the color of the outline surrounding the entire table; the outline is initially set to dark green.

✦ **Table Background** is the color of the layout table where no layout cell has been drawn; a light gray is the default background.

Should your site design make any of the colors unusable — if, for example, your page background was the same light gray as the default table background — you can alter the colors by selecting the color swatch and choosing a new color from the standard color picker.

Layers preferences

Aside from helping you control the underlying coding method for producing layers, Dreamweaver enables you to define the default layer. This capability is especially useful during a major production effort in which the Web development team must produce hundreds of layers spread over a Web site. Being able to specify in advance the initial size, color, background, and visibility saves numerous steps — each of which would have to be repeated for every layer. Figure 4-10 shows the layout of the Layers category of the Preferences dialog box.

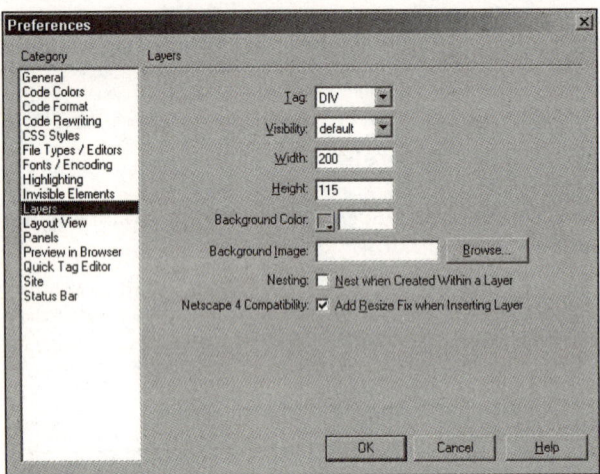

Figure 4-10: In the Layers category, you can predetermine the structure of the default Dreamweaver layer.

The controls accessible through the Layers category include the following:

Tag

Select the arrow button to see the tags for the four HTML code methods for implementing layers: `<div>`, `<span>`, `<layer>`, and `<ilayer>`. The first two, `<div>` and `<span>`, were developed by the W3C as part of their Cascading Style Sheets recommendation and are supported by version 4.0 (and above) of both Netscape and Internet Explorer. Netscape developed the latter two HTML commands, `<layer>` and `<ilayer>`; currently only Netscape 4.x supports these tags.

Dreamweaver uses the ⟨div⟩ tag for its default. Supported by both major 4.0 and above browsers, the ⟨div⟩ element offers the widest cross-browser compatibility. You should use only one of the other Tag options if you are building a Web site intended for a specific browser.

To learn more about the uses of the various positioning tags, see Chapter 28.

Visibility

Layers can be either visible or hidden when the Web page is first loaded. A layer created using the default visibility option is always displayed initially; however, no specific information is written into the code. Selecting Visible forces Dreamweaver to include a visibility:visible line in your layer code. Likewise, if you select Hidden from the Visibility options, the layer is initially hidden.

Use the Inherit option when creating nested layers. Creating one layer inside another makes the outer layer the parent, and the inner layer the child. If the parent layer is visible and the child layer is set to visibility:inherit, then the child is also visible. This option makes it possible to affect the visibility of many layers with one command—hide the parent layer, and all the inheriting child layers disappear as well.

Width and Height

When you choose Draw Layer from the Objects panel, you drag out the size and shape of your layer. Choosing Insert ⇨ Layer puts a layer of a default size and shape at your current cursor position. The Width and Height options enable you to set these defaults. Select the text boxes and type your new values. Dreamweaver's default is a layer 200 pixels wide by 115 pixels high.

Background Color

Layers can have their own background color independent of the Web page's overall background color (which is set as a ⟨body⟩ attribute). You can define the default background color of any inserted layer through either the Insert menu or the Objects panel. For this preference setting, type a color, either by its standard name or as a hexadecimal triplet, directly into the text box. You can also click the color swatch to display the Dreamweaver browser-safe color picker.

Note that while you can specify a different background color for the layer, you can't alter the layer's default text and link colors (except on a layer-by-layer basis) as you can with a page. If your page and layer background colors are highly contrasting, be sure your text and links are readable in both environments. A similar caveat applies to the use of a layer's background image, as explained in the next section.

Background Image

Just as you can pick a specific background color for layers, you can select a different background image for layers. You can type a file source directly into the

Background Image text box or select your file from a dialog box by choosing the Browse button. The layer's background image supersedes the layer background color, just as it does with the HTML page. Also, just as the page's background image tiles to fill the page, so does the layer's background image.

Nesting

The two best options about layers seem to be directly opposed: overlapping and nesting layers. You can design layers to appear one on top of another, and you can code layers so that they are within one another. Both techniques are valuable options, and Dreamweaver enables you to decide which one should be the over-riding method.

If you are working primarily with nested layers and plan on using the inheritance facility, check the Nest when Created Within a Layer option. If your design entails a number of overlapping but independent layers, make sure this option is turned off. Regardless of your preference, you can reverse it on an individual basis by pressing the Ctrl (Command) key when drawing out your layers.

Netscape 4.x Compatibility

Netscape 4.x has a particularly annoying problem displaying Web pages with layers. When the user resizes the browser, all of the CSS positioning information is lost — in other words, all your layers lose their exact positioning and typically align them-selves on the left. The only fix is to force Netscape to reload the page after the browser has been resized.

When the Netscape 4 Compatibility option is enabled, Dreamweaver automatically includes a small JavaScript routine to handle the resizing problem. The code is inserted in the `<head>` section of the page when the first layer is added to the page. If additional layers are added, Dreamweaver is smart enough to realize that the workaround code has already been included and does not add more unnecessary code.

Many Web designers run into this problem as they begin to explore the possibilities of Dynamic HTML. Although the problem has been fixed with the release of Netscape 6, I highly recommend that you enable this option to offset any problems with the large number of Netscape 4.x browsers still in use.

CSS Styles preferences

The CSS Styles category (see Figure 4-11) is entirely devoted to how your code is written. As specified by the W3C, Cascading Style Sheets (CSS) declarations — the specifications of a style — can be written in several ways. One method displays a series of items, separated by semicolons:

```
H1 { font-family: helvetica; font-size: 12pt; line-height: 14pt; ¬
font-weight: bold;}
```

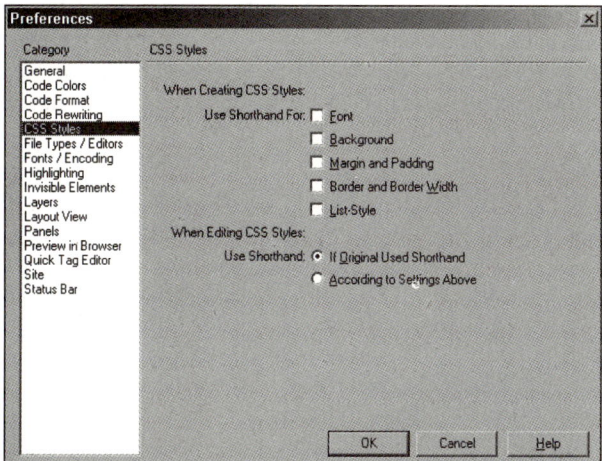

Figure 4-11: The CSS Styles category enables you to code the style sheet sections of your Web pages in a graphics designer–friendly manner.

Certain properties (such as font) have their own grouping shorthand, developed to be more readable to designers coming from a traditional print background. A second, "shorthand" method of rendering the preceding declaration follows:

```
H1 { font: helvetica 12pt/14pt bold }
```

With the CSS Styles category, you can enable the shorthand method for any or all of the five different properties that permit it. Select any of the checkboxes under Use Shorthand For to have Dreamweaver write your style code in this fashion.

The second option in the CSS Styles category determines how Dreamweaver edits styles in previously coded pages. If you want to retain the format of the original page, click Use Shorthand If Original Used Shorthand. If you want Dreamweaver to write new code in the manner that you specify, select Use Shorthand According to Settings Above.

Caution Although the leading varieties of the 4.0 and above browsers can read the style's shorthand with no difficulty, Internet Explorer 3.0 does not have this capability. IE3 is the only other mainstream browser that can claim support for Cascading Style Sheets, but it doesn't understand the shorthand form. If you want to maintain browser backward-compatibility, don't enable any of the shorthand options.

Making Online Connections

Dreamweaver's visual layout editor offers an approximation of your Web page's appearance in the real world of browsers — offline or online. After you've created the initial draft of your Web page, you should preview it through one or more browsers. And when your project nears completion, you should transfer the files to a server for online, real-time viewing and further testing through a File Transfer Protocol program (FTP). Dreamweaver gives you control over all these stages of Web page development, through the Site and Preview in Browser categories.

Site preferences

As your Web site takes shape, you'll spend more time with the Site window portion of Dreamweaver. The Site category, shown in Figure 4-12, enables you to customize the look and feel of your site, as well as enter essential connection information.

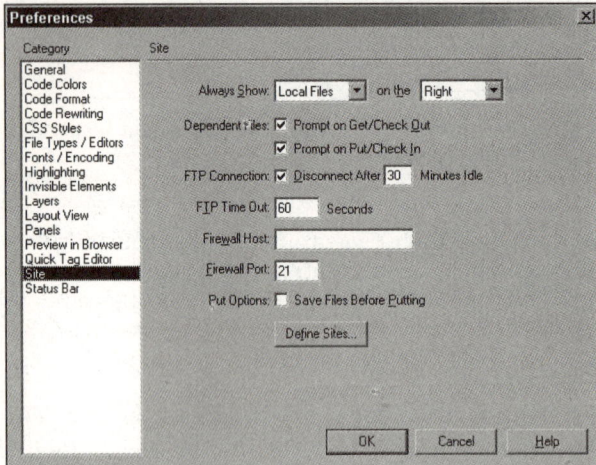

Figure 4-12: Options for Dreamweaver's Site window are handled through the Site category.

The available Site preferences are described in the following sections.

Always Show Local/Remote Files on the Right/Left

The Site window is divided into two panes: one showing local files and one showing remote files on the server. By default, Dreamweaver puts the Local pane on the right and the Remote pane on the left. However, Dreamweaver enables you to customize that option. Like many designers, I'm used to using other FTP programs in which the Remote files are on the right and the Local files on the left; Dreamweaver enables me to work the way I'm used to working.

To switch the layout of your Site window, select the file location you want to change to (Local Files or Remote Files) from the Always Show drop-down list or select the pane you want to change to (Right or Left) from the "on the" drop-down list. Be careful not to switch both options, or you end up where you started!

Dependent files

Web pages are seldom just single HTML files. Any graphic — whether it's in the background, part of your main logo, or used on a navigational button — is uploaded as a separate file. The same is true for any additional multimedia add-ons such as audio or video files. If you've enabled File Check In/Check Out when defining your site, Dreamweaver can also track these so-called dependent files.

Enabling the Prompt checkboxes causes Dreamweaver to ask you if you'd like to move the dependent files when you transfer an HTML file. You can opt to show the dialog box for Get/Check Out, Put/Check In, or both.

Tip You're not stuck with your Dependent Files choice. If you turn off the Dependent Files prompt, you can make it appear by pressing the Alt (Option) key while clicking the Get or Put button.

FTP Connection: Disconnect After __ Minutes Idle

You can easily forget you're online when you are busy modifying a page. You can set Dreamweaver to automatically disconnect you from an FTP site after a specified interval. The default is 30 minutes; if you want to set a different interval, you can select the FTP Connection value in the Disconnect After text box. Dreamweaver then asks if you want to continue to wait or to disconnect when the time limit is reached, but you can maintain your FTP connection regardless by deselecting this option.

FTP Time Out

Client-server communication is prone to glitches. Rather than hanging up your machine while trying to reach a server that is down or slow, Dreamweaver alerts you to an apparent problem after a set period. You can determine the number of seconds you want Dreamweaver to wait by altering the FTP Time Out value. The default is 60 seconds.

Firewall information

Dreamweaver enables users to access remote FTP servers outside their network firewall. A firewall is a security component that protects the internal network from unauthorized outsiders, while enabling Internet access. To enable firewall access, enter the Firewall Host and External Port numbers in the appropriate text boxes; if you do not know these values, contact your network administrator.

Caution If you're having trouble transferring files through the firewall via FTP, make sure the Use Firewall (in Preferences) option is enabled in the Site Definition dialog box. You can find the option in the Remote Info category.

Put options

Certain site operations, such as putting a file on the remote site, are now available in the Document window. It's not uncommon to make an edit to your page and then quickly choose the Site ⇨ Put command — without saving the file first. In this situation, Dreamweaver prompts you with a dialog box to save your changes. However, you can avoid the dialog box and automatically save the file by choosing the Save Files Before Putting option.

Preview in Browser preferences

Browser testing is an essential stage of Web page development. Previewing your Web page within the environment of a particular browser gives you a more exact representation of how it looks when viewed online. Because each browser renders the HTML slightly differently, you should preview your work in several browsers. Dreamweaver enables you to select both a primary and secondary browser, which can both be called by pressing a function key. You can name up to 18 additional browsers through the Preview in Browser category shown in Figure 4-13. This list of preferences is also called when you choose File ⇨ Preview in Browser ⇨ Edit Browser List.

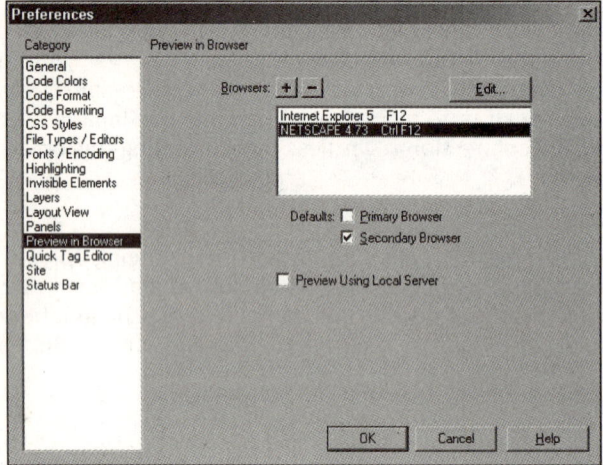

Figure 4-13: The Preview in Browser category lists browsers currently available for preview and enables you modify the list.

If you are developing on Windows, your Web page is using site root relative paths for links, and you have a local server setup, enable the Preview Using Local Server option. This capability ensures that your previews link correctly. The other method to preview sites using site root relative paths places the files on a remote server.

To add a browser to your preview list, follow these steps:

1. Choose Edit ⇨ Preferences or press the keyboard shortcut: Ctrl+U (Command+U).

2. Select the Preview in Browser category.

3. Select the Add (+) button.

4. Enter the path to the browser file in the Path text box or click the Browse button to pick the file from the Select Browser dialog box.

5. After you have selected your browser application, Dreamweaver fills in the Name field. You can alter this name if you wish.

6. If you want to designate this browser as your Primary or Secondary browser, select one of those checkboxes in the Defaults section.

7. Click OK when you have finished.

8. You can continue to add browsers (up to a total of 20) by following Steps 3 through 7. Click OK when you have finished.

Once you've added a browser to your list, you can modify your selection by following these steps:

1. Open the Preview in Browser category and highlight the browser you want to alter.

2. Select the Edit button to get the Edit Browser dialog box.

3. After you've made your modifications, click OK to close the dialog box.

Tip   You can quickly make a browser your Primary or Secondary previewing choice without going through the Edit screen. From the Preview in Browser category, select the desired browser and check either Primary Browser or Secondary Browser. Note that if you already have a primary or secondary browser defined, this action overrides your previous choice.

You can also easily remove a browser from your preview list:

1. Open the Preview in Browser category and choose the browser you want to delete from the list.

2. Select the Remove (–) button and click OK.

Customizing Your Code

For all its multimedia flash and visual interactivity, the Web is based on code. The more you code, the more particular about your code you are likely to become. Achieving a consistent look and feel to your code enhances its readability and, thus, your productivity. In Dreamweaver, you can even design the HTML code that underlies a Web page's structure.

Every time you open a new document, the default Web page already has several key elements in place, such as the language the page is to be rendered in. Dreamweaver also enables you to customize your work environment by selecting default fonts and even the colors of your HTML code.

Fonts/Encoding preferences

In the Fonts / Encoding category, shown in Figure 4-14, you can control the basic language of the fonts as seen by a user's browser and the fonts that you see when programming. The Default Encoding section enables you to choose Western-style fonts for Web pages to be rendered in English, one of the Asian languages — Japanese, Traditional Chinese, Simplified Chinese, or Korean — or another language, such as Cyrillic, Greek, or Icelandic Mac.

Dreamweaver 4 has extended the number of encoding options to 10, as well as adding a generic Other category. Many of the encodings have platform-specific configurations, such as Icelandic Mac. Be sure to examine all the choices before you make a selection.

Figure 4-14: Use the Fonts / Encoding category to set both the font encoding for each Web page and the fonts you use when programming.

In the bottom portion of the Fonts / Encoding category, you can alter the default font and size for three different fonts:

✦ **Proportional Font:** This font option sets the default font used in Dreamweaver's Document window to depict paragraphs, headings, and lists.

✦ **Fixed Font:** In a fixed font, every character is allocated the same width. Dreamweaver uses your chosen fixed font to depict preformatted styled text.

✦ **Code Inspector:** The Code Inspector font is used by Dreamweaver's built-in text editor. You should probably use a monospaced font such as Courier or Monaco. A monospaced font makes it easy to count characters, which is often necessary when debugging your code.

Select any one of the three font options by clicking the list and highlighting your choice of font. Change the font size by selecting the value in the Size text box or by typing in a new number.

Caution Don't be misled into thinking that by changing your Proportional Font preference to Arial or another font, all your Web pages are automatically viewed in that typeface. Changing these font preferences affects only the default fonts that you see when developing the Web page; the default font that the user sees is controlled by the user's browser. To ensure that a different font is used, you have to specify it for any selected text through the Text Property Inspector or by choosing Text ➪ Font ➪ Edit Font List from the menus.

Code Rewriting preferences

The exception to Dreamweaver's policy of not altering imported code occurs when HTML or other code is incorrectly structured. Dreamweaver automatically fixes tags that are nested in the wrong order or have additional, unnecessary closing tags — unless you tell Dreamweaver otherwise by setting up the Code Rewriting preferences accordingly (see Figure 4-15).

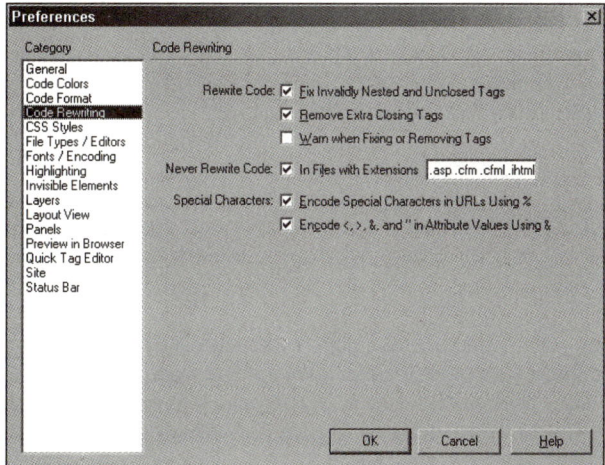

Figure 4-15: The Code Rewriting category can be used to protect nonstandard HTML from being automatically changed by Dreamweaver.

Dreamweaver accommodates many different types of markup languages, not just HTML, through the Never Rewrite Code in Files with Extensions option. Moreover, you can prevent Dreamweaver from encoding special characters, such as spaces, tildes, and ampersands, in URLs or attribute values.

Following are descriptions of the particular controls of the Code Rewriting preferences.

Fix Invalidly Nested and Unclosed Tags

When enabled, this option repairs incorrectly placed tags. For example, if a file contained the following line:

```
<h3><b>Welcome to the Monkey House!</h3></b>
```

Dreamweaver rewrites it as follows:

```
<h3><b>Welcome to the Monkey House!</b></h3>
```

Open that same file while the Fix option is turned off, and Dreamweaver highlights the misplaced code in the Document window. Double-clicking the code brings up a window with a brief explanation.

Caution   If a browser encounters nonstandard HTML, the code is probably ignored. Dreamweaver does not follow this protocol, however. Unless Dreamweaver is familiar with the type of code you are using, your code could be altered when the page is opened. If you are using specially formatted database tags or other non-standard HTML programming, be sure to open a test page first.

Remove Extra Closing Tags

When you're editing your code by hand, it's fairly easy to miss a closing tag. Dreamweaver cleans up such code if you enable the Remove Extra Closing Tags option. You may, for example, have the following line in a previously edited file:

```
<p>And now back to our show...</p></i>
```

Notice that the closing italic tag, </i>, has no matching opening partner. If you open this file in Dreamweaver with the Remove option enabled, Dreamweaver plucks out the offending </i>.

Tip   In some circumstances, you want to make sure your pages remain as originally formatted. If you edit pages in Dreamweaver that are preprocessed by a server unknown to Dreamweaver prior to the display of the pages, make sure to disable both the Fix Invalidly Nested and Unclosed Tags option where possible and the Remove Extra Closing Tags option.

Warn When Fixing or Removing Tags

If you're editing a lot of Web pages created on another system, you should enable the Warn when Fixing or Removing Tags option. If this setting is turned on, Dreamweaver displays a list of changes that have been made to your code in the HTML Corrections dialog box. As you can see from Figure 4-16, the changes can be quite extensive when Dreamweaver opens what it regards as a poorly formatted page.

Figure 4-16: Dreamweaver can automatically catch and repair certain HTML errors. You can set Dreamweaver to send a report to the screen in the HTML Corrections dialog box.

Caution Remember that once you've enabled these Rewrite Code options, the fixes occur automatically. If this sequence happens to you by mistake, immediately close the file (without saving it!), disable the Code Rewriting preference options, and reopen the document.

Never Rewrite Code preferences

Many of the database connectivity programs, such as Cold Fusion or Lasso, use proprietary tags embedded in a regular Web page to communicate with their servers. Dreamweaver enables you to explicitly protect file types, identified with a particular file extension.

To enter a new file type in the Never Rewrite Code options, select the In Files with Extensions field. Enter the file extension of the file type, including the period, in the end of the list. Be sure to separate your extensions from the others in the list with a space on either side.

Special Character preferences

In addition to the rewriting of proprietary tags, many middleware vendors faced another problem when trying to integrate with Dreamweaver. By default, earlier versions of Dreamweaver encoded all URLs so that they could be understood by Unix servers. The encoding converted all special characters to their decimal equivalents, preceded by a percent sign. Spaces became %20, tildes (~) became %7E, and ampersands were converted to &. Although this is valid for Unix servers, and helps to make the Dreamweaver code more universal, it can cause problems for many other types of application servers.

Dreamweaver gives you the option to disable the URL encoding, if necessary. Moreover, Dreamweaver also enables you to turn off encoding that is applied to special characters in the attributes of tags. This latter issue can be particularly vexing because, while you can rewrite the attributes in the Code Inspector, if you select the element in the Document window with the Property Inspector open, the attributes are encoded. You can prevent this from happening with the selection of a single checkbox.

In general, however, it's best to leave both of the Special Characters encoding options enabled unless you find your third-party tags being rewritten destructively.

Code Colors preferences

HTML code is a combination of the tags that structure the language and the text that provides the content. A Web page designer often has difficulty distinguishing swiftly between the two — and finding the right code to modify. Dreamweaver enables you to set color preferences for the code as it appears in the Code view or Code Inspector. You can not only alter colors for the background, default tags, and text and general comments, but also specify certain tags to get certain colors.

To modify any of the basic elements (Background, Text, Comments, or Tag Default) or any of the Script colors (Reserved Keywords, Other Keywords, or Strings), select the color swatch next to the corresponding name, as illustrated in Figure 4-17. Select a color from any of the 216 displayed in the color picker or choose the small palette icon to select from the full range of colors available to your system. You can also use the Eyedropper tool to pick a color from the Document window.

To select a different color for a specific tag, first select the tag from the Tag Specific list box. Then choose either the Default option (which assigns the same color as specified for the Tag Default) or a custom color by clicking the color swatch and choosing the color. If you want to set all of the code and text enclosed by the selected tag to the same color, choose the Apply Color to Tag Contents option.

Code Format preferences

Dreamweaver includes two other tools for customizing your HTML. The first is an easy-to-use, point-and-click preferences category called Code Format. The second is a text file called the Source Format (SourceFormat.txt), which must be modified by hand and controls the output of every HTML tag. You can modify your HTML using either or both techniques. All of the options controlled by the Code Format category are written out to the text file.

Figure 4-17: Use the Code Colors category to custom color–code the HTML Inspector.

Most of your HTML code parameters can be controlled through the Code Format category. The only reason to alter the SourceFormat.txt text file by hand is if you want to control the appearance of your HTML code at the tag level.

In the Code Format category, you can decide whether to use indentations — if so, whether to use spaces or tabs and how many of each — or to turn off indents for major elements such as tables and frames. You can also globally control the case of your HTML tags and their attributes. As you can see in Figure 4-18, the Code Format category is full featured.

To examine the available options in the Code Format category, let's separate them into four areas: indent control, line control, case control, and centering.

Indent control

Indenting your code generally makes it more readable. Dreamweaver defaults to indenting most HTML tags with two spaces, giving extra indentation grouping to tables and frames. All these parameters can be altered through the Code Format category of the Preferences dialog box.

Figure 4-18: The Code Format category enables you to shape your HTML to your own specifications.

The first indent option enables indenting, and you can switch from spaces to tabs. To permit indenting, make sure a checkmark is displayed in the Indent checkbox. Of the 52 separate HTML tags Dreamweaver identifies in its Source Format, 29 tags are designed to be indented. If you prefer your code to be displayed flush left, turn off the Indent option altogether.

To use tabs instead of the default spaces, click the Use arrow button and select tabs from the drop-down list. If you anticipate transferring your code to a word processing program for formatting and printing, you should use tabs; otherwise, stay with the default spaces.

Dreamweaver formats both tables and frames as special indentation groups. Within each of these structural elements, the related tags are indented (or nested) more than the initial two spaces. As you can see in Listing 4-1, each table row (`<tr>`) is indented within the table tag, and the table data tags (`<td>`) are nested within the table row.

Listing 4-1: **An Indented Code Sample**

```
<table border="1" width="75%">
 <tr>
 <td>Row 1, Column 1</td>
 <td>Row 1, Column 2</td>
 <td>Row 1, Column 3</td>
 </tr>
 <tr>
 <td>Row 2, Column 1</td>
```

```
<td>Row 2, Column 2 </td>
<td>Row 2, Column 3</td>
</tr>
</table>
```

If you want to disable the special indentation grouping for tables, deselect Table Rows and Columns in the Code Format category. Turn off frame indenting by unchecking Frames and Framesets (this option is selected by default).

The other two items in the indent control section of Code Format preferences are Indent Size and Tab Size. Change the value in Indent Size to establish the size of indents using spaces. To alter the size of tab indents, change the Tab Size value.

Line control

The browser is responsible for ultimately formatting an HTML page for viewing. This formatting includes wrapping text according to each user's screen size and the placement of the paragraph tags (`<p>...</p>`). Therefore, you control how your code wraps in your HTML editor. You can turn off the automatic wrapping feature or set it for a particular column through the line control options of the Code Format category.

To turn off the automatic word-wrapping capability, deselect AutomaticWrapping. When you are trying to debug your code and looking for specific line numbers and character positions, enable this option. You can also set the specific column for the word wrap to take effect. Be sure AutomaticWrapping is enabled and then type your new value in the After Column text box.

Tip   If you're using the Code view or Inspector, selecting the Word Wrap option overrides the Automatic Wrapping setting in Code Format.

The Line Breaks setting determines which line break character is appended to each line of the page. Each of the major operating systems employs a different ending character: Macintosh uses a carriage return (CR), Unix uses a line feed (LF), and Windows uses both (CR LF). If you know the operating system for your remote server, choosing the corresponding line break character helps the file to appear correctly when viewed online. Click the arrow button next to Line Breaks and select your system.

Caution   The operating system for your local development machine may be different from the operating system of your remote server. If so, using the Line Breaks option may cause your HTML to appear incorrectly when viewed through a simple text editor (such as Notepad or vi). The Dreamweaver Code Inspector, however, does render the code correctly.

Case control

Whether an HTML tag or attribute is in uppercase or lowercase doesn't matter to most browsers — the command is rendered regardless of case. Case is only a personal preference among Web designers. That said, some Webmasters consider case a serious preference and insist on their codes being all uppercase, all lowercase, or a combination of uppercase and lowercase. Dreamweaver gives you control over the tags and attributes it creates, including control over case conversion for files that Dreamweaver imports.

The Dreamweaver default for both tags and attributes is lowercase. Click the arrow button next to Case for Tags and/or Case for Attributes to alter the selection. After you have selected OK from the Code Format category, Dreamweaver changes all the tags in any currently open file. Choose File ⇨ Save to write the changes to disk.

Tip   Lowercase tags and attributes are also less fattening, according to the W3C. Files with lowercase tag names and attributes compress better and thus transmit faster.

You can also use Dreamweaver to standardize the letter case in tags of previously saved files. To alter imported files, select the Override Case Of Tags and/or the Override Case Of Attributes options. When enabled, these options enforce your choices made in the Case for Tags and Case for Attributes option boxes in any file Dreamweaver loads. Again, be sure to save your file to keep the changes.

Centering

When an object — whether it's an image or text — is centered on a page, HTML tags are placed around the object (or objects) to indicate the alignment. Since the release of HTML 3.2, the `<center>` tag has been deprecated by the W3C in favor of using a `<div>` tag with an align="center" attribute. By default, Dreamweaver uses the officially preferred method of `<div align="center">`.

Many Web designers are partial to the older `<center>` tag and prefer to use it to align their objects. Dreamweaver offers a choice with the Centering option in the Code Format category. To use the newer method, select the Use DIV Tag option (the default). To switch to the older `<center>` method, select the Use CENTER Tag option. Although use of `<center>` has been officially discouraged, it is so widespread that all browsers continue to support it.

Understanding the Source Format

As noted earlier, Dreamweaver pulls its code configuration guidelines from a text file named SourceFormat.txt. When Dreamweaver is installed, this file is put in the Dreamweaver\Configuration folder. When you make a modification to the Code Format category, the initial profile is renamed as SourceFormat.backup and then Dreamweaver writes a new SourceFormat.txt.

Tip You can restore the default Source Profile settings at any time. When Dreamweaver is closed, delete SourceFormat.txt and then make a copy of the SourceFormat.original file. Finally, rename the copy as SourceFormat.txt.

Dreamweaver uses a specialized Code Format to create a SourceFormat.txt that can be viewed and edited in any text editor. Three main sections exist, each denoted with a `<?keyword>` format: `<?options>`, `<?elements>`, and `<?attributes>`. Prior to each section, Dreamweaver uses the HTML comment tags to describe them. The file closes with the `<?end>` keyword.

The Source Format (see Listing 4-2) starts with two HTML comments. The first describes the overall document (`Dreamweaver source formatting profile`), followed by the Options section.

Listing 4-2

```
<!-- Dreamweaver source formatting profile -->

<!-- options

    INDENTION      : indention options
        ENABLE       - allows indention
        INDENT       - columns per indention
        TABS         - columns per tab character
        USE          - TABS or SPACES for indention
        ACTIVE       - active indention groups (IGROUP)

    LINES          : end-of-line options
        AUTOWRAP     - enable automatic line wrapping
        BREAK        - CRLF, CR, LF
        COLUMN       - auto wrap lines after column

    OMIT           : element omission options
        OPTIONS      - options

    ELEMENT        : element options
        CASE         - "UPPER" or "lower" case
        ALWAYS       - always use preferred element case
(instead of original case)

    ATTRIBUTE      : attribute options
        CASE         - "UPPER" or "lower" case
        ALWAYS       - always use preferred attribute case
(instead of original case)

-->
<?options>
<indention enable indent="2" tabs="4" use="spaces"
active="1,2">
```

Continued

Listing 4-2 *(continued)*

```
<lines autowrap column="76" break="CRLF">
<omit options="0">
<element case="lower">
<attribute case="lower">
<colors text="0x00000000" tag="0x00000000"
unknowntag="0x00000000" comment="0x00000000"
invalid="0x00000000" object="0x00000000">
<directives break="1,0,0,1">
<directives delimiter="%3C%25=" break="0,0,0,0"> <!-- no line
breaks surrounding a "<%=" script block -->

<!-- element information
    line breaks                  : BREAK  = "before, inside start,
inside end, after"
    indent contents              : INDENT
    indent group                 : IGROUP = "indention group
number" (1 through 8)
    specific name case           : NAMECASE = "CustomName"
    prevent formatting           : NOFORMAT
-->
<?elements>
<address break="1,0,0,1">
<applet break="0,1,1,0" indent>
<area break="1,0,0,1">
<base break="1,0,0,1">
<blockquote break="1,0,0,1" indent>
<body break="1,1,1,1">
<br break="0,0,0,1">
<caption break="1,0,0,1">
<center break="1,1,1,1" indent>
<cfabort break="1,0,0,1">
<cfapplet break="1,0,0,1">
<cfapplication break="1,0,0,1">
<cfassociate break="1,0,0,1">
<cfauthenticate break="1,0,0,1">
<cfbreak break="1,0,0,1">
<cfcache break="1,0,0,1">
<cfcatch break="1,1,1,1" indent>
<cfcase break="1,1,1,1">
<cfcol break="1,0,0,1">
<cfcollection break="1,0,0,1">
<cfcontent break="1,0,0,1">
<cfcookie break="1,0,0,1">
<cfdefaultcase break="1,1,1,1">
<cfdirectory break="1,0,0,1">
<cferror break="1,0,0,1">
<cfexit break="1,0,0,1">
<cffile break="1,0,0,1">
<cfform break="1,1,1,1" indent>
<cfftp break="1,0,0,1">
```

```
<cfgrid break="1,1,1,1" indent>
<cfgridcolumn break="1,0,0,1">
<cfgridrow break="1,0,0,1">
<cfgridupdate break="1,0,0,1">
<cfheader break="1,0,0,1">
<cfhtmlhead break="1,0,0,1">
<cfhttp break="1,1,1,1" indent>
<cfhttpparam break="1,0,0,1">
<cfif break="1,1,1,1">
<cfelse break="1,0,0,1">
<cfelseif break="1,1,1,1">
<cfinclude break="1,0,0,1">
<cfindex break="1,0,0,1">
<cfinput break="1,0,0,1">
<cfinsert break="1,0,0,1">
<cfldap break="1,0,0,1">
<cflocation break="1,0,0,1">
<cflock break="1,1,1,1" indent>
<cfloop break="1,1,1,1" indent>
<cfmail break="1,1,1,1" indent>
<cfmodule break="1,0,0,1">
<cfobject break="1,0,0,1">
<cfoutput indent>
<cfparam break="1,0,0,1">
<cfpop break="1,0,0,1">
<cfprocparam break="1,0,0,1">
<cfprocresult break="1,0,0,1">
<cfquery break="1,1,1,1">
<cfregistry break="1,0,0,1">
<cfreport break="1,1,1,1" indent>
<cfscript break="1,1,1,1">
<cfschedule break="1,0,0,1">
<cfsearch break="1,0,0,1">
<cfselect break="1,1,1,1" indent>
<cfset break="1,0,0,1">
<cfsetting break="1,0,0,1">
<cfslider break="1,0,0,1">
<cfstoredproc break="1,1,1,1" indent>
<cfswitch break="1,1,1,1" indent>
<cftable break="1,1,1,1" indent>
<cfthrow break="1,0,0,1">
<cftextinput break="1,0,0,1">
<cftransaction break="1,1,1,1" indent>
<cftree break="1,1,1,1" indent>
<cftreeitem break="1,0,0,1">
<cftry break="1,1,1,1" indent>
<cfupdate break="1,0,0,1">
<dd break="1,0,0,1" indent>
<dir break="1,0,0,1" indent>
<div break="1,0,0,1" indent>
<dl break="1,0,0,1" indent>
<dt break="1,0,0,1" indent>
```

Continued

Listing 4-2 *(continued)*

```
<embed break="0,1,1,0" indent>
<form break="1,1,1,1" indent>
<frame break="1,0,0,1">
<frameset break="1,0,0,1" indent igroup="2">
<h1 break="1,0,0,1" indent>
<h2 break="1,0,0,1" indent>
<h3 break="1,0,0,1" indent>
<h4 break="1,0,0,1" indent>
<h5 break="1,0,0,1" indent>
<h6 break="1,0,0,1" indent>
<head break="1,1,1,1">
<hr break="1,0,0,1">
<html break="1,1,1,1">
<ilayer break="1,0,0,1">
<input break="1,0,0,1">
<isindex break="1,0,0,1">
<layer break="1,0,0,1">
<li break="1,0,0,1" indent>
<link break="1,0,0,1">
<map break="1,0,0,1" indent>
<menu break="1,0,0,1" indent>
<meta break="1,0,0,1">
<object break="0,1,1,0" indent>
<ol break="1,1,1,1" indent>
<option break="1,0,0,1">
<p break="1,0,0,1" indent>
<param break="1,0,0,1">
<pre break="1,0,0,1" noformat>
<script break="1,0,0,1" noformat>
<select break="1,1,1,1" indent>
<mm:treecontrol break="1,1,1,1" indent>
<server break="1,0,0,1" noformat>
<style break="1,0,0,1" noformat>
<table break="1,1,1,1" indent igroup="1">
<td break="1,0,0,1" indent igroup="1">
<textarea break="1,0,0,1" noformat>
<th break="1,0,0,1" indent igroup="1">
<title break="1,0,0,1">
<tr break="1,0,0,1" indent igroup="1">
<ul break="1,1,1,1" indent>
<jsp:getProperty break="1,0,0,1" namecase="jsp:getProperty">
<jsp:setProperty break="1,0,0,1" namecase="jsp:setProperty">
<jsp:useBean break="1,0,0,1" namecase="jsp:useBean">
<jsp:forward break="1,0,0,1">
<jsp:include break="1,0,0,1">
<jsp:plugin break="1,1,1,1">
<jsp:params break="1,1,1,1" indent>
<jsp:param break="1,0,0,1">
<jsp:fallback break="1,0,0,1">
```

```
<!-- attribute information
     specific name case         : NAMECASE = "CustomName"
     values follow attr case    : SAMECASE
-->
<?attributes>
<onAbort namecase="onAbort">
<onBlur namecase="onBlur">
<onChange namecase="onChange">
<onClick namecase="onClick">
<onDragDrop namecase="onDragDrop">
<onError namecase="onError">
<onFocus namecase="onFocus">
<onKeyDown namecase="onKeyDown">
<onKeyPress namecase="onKeyPress">
<onKeyUp namecase="onKeyUp">
<onLoad namecase="onLoad">
<onMouseDown namecase="onMouseDown">
<onMouseMove namecase="onMouseMove">
<onMouseOut namecase="onMouseOut">
<onMouseOver namecase="onMouseOver">
<onMouseUp namecase="onMouseUp">
<onMove namecase="onMove">
<onReset namecase="onReset">
<onResize namecase="onResize">
<onSelect namecase="onSelect">
<onSubmit namecase="onSubmit">
<onUnload namecase="onUnload">
<onDblClick namecase="onDblClick">
<onAfterUpdate namecase="onAfterUpdate">
<onBeforeUpdate namecase="onBeforeUpdate">
<onHelp namecase="onHelp">
<onReadyStateChange namecase="onReadyStateChange">
<onScroll namecase="onScroll">
<onRowEnter namecase="onRowEnter">
<onRowExit namecase="onRowExit">
<align samecase>
<checked samecase>
<codetype samecase>
<compact samecase>
<ismap samecase>
<frame samecase>
<method samecase>
<multiple samecase>
<noresize samecase>
<noshade samecase>
<nowrap samecase>
<selected samecase>
<shape samecase>
<type samecase>
<valign samecase>
<visibility samecase>
<?end>
```

Options

The Options section parallels the options set in the Code Format category. Either you can use Dreamweaver's point-and-click interface by choosing Edit ⇨ Preferences and then selecting the Code Format category, or you can edit the `<?options>` section of the SourceFormat.txt file. In the Options description, five parameters are outlined: indention, lines, omit, element, and attribute.

The indention item denotes the indent options:

```
ENABLE - allows indention
INDENT - columns per indention
TABS - columns per tab character
USE - TABS or SPACES for indention
ACTIVE - active indention groups (IGROUP)
```

The final indention option, ACTIVE, relates to the special grouping function that Dreamweaver calls IGROUPS. By default, Dreamweaver assigns `IGROUP #1` to Table Rows and Columns and `IGROUP #2` to Frames and Framesets.

The line options are detailed as follows:

```
AUTOWRAP - enable automatic line wrapping
BREAK - CRLF, CR, LF
COLUMN - auto wrap lines after column
```

As mentioned earlier, the BREAK options are used to insert the type of line break character recognized by your Web server's operating system. Use CRLF for Windows, CR for Macintosh, and LF for Unix.

The next Options section, `OMIT`, is reserved by Dreamweaver for further expansion and is not currently used.

The Element and Attribute sections control the case of HTML elements (or tags) and attributes:

```
CASE - "UPPER" or "lower" case
ALWAYS - always use preferred element case (instead of original
case)
```

If the `ALWAYS` keyword is used, Dreamweaver alters the case of tags and/or attributes when you import a previously saved file.

The following section of the Source Format that starts with `<?options>` contains the actual options read by Dreamweaver at startup. This listing shows the default options from the default SourceFormat.txt file for Dreamweaver 4:

```
<?options>
<indention enable indent="2" tabs="8" use="spaces"
active="1,2">
<lines autowrap column="76">
```

```
<omit options="0">
<element case="lower">
<attribute case="lower">
```

Elements

The Element information in the next section of the Source Format describes the syntax and options for individually controlling each HTML tag.

```
line breaks : BREAK = "before, inside start, inside end, after"
indent contents : INDENT
indent group : IGROUP = "indention group number" (1 through 8)
specific name case : NAMECASE = "CustomName"
prevent formatting : NOFORMAT
```

break

The syntax for break refers to the number of line breaks surrounding the opening and closing HTML tags. For example, the default syntax for the <h1> tag follows:

```
<h1 break="1,0,0,1" indent>
```

The preceding produces code that looks like the following:

```
<h1>Welcome!</h1>
```

If you want to display the opening and closing tags on their own lines, you could change the break value as follows:

```
<h1 break="1,1,1,1" indent>
```

The preceding gives you the following result:

```
<h1>
 Welcome!
</h1>
```

Use zero in the "before" and "after" positions when you want a tag to appear in line with the other code, as in this map tag:

```
<map break="0,1,1,0" indent>
```

The Elements list only contains tags that have opening and closing elements, which are also known as *container tags*. Any single-element tags, such as the image tag, <img>, are presented in line with other elements.

Note　　For all of the Source Format's comprehensiveness, one type of tag is unavailable: comment tags. While you can't adjust their spacing, you can alter the color of comments through Preferences, in the Code Colors category.

You're not restricted to using 1 and 0 values for break. If you want to isolate a tag so that it really stands out, use 2 in the "before" and "after" positions. For example:

```
<p break="2,1,1,2" indent>
```

The preceding produces completely separated paragraphs such as the following:

```
<p>
Synapse Advertising is your first choice for the best in
subliminal advertising.
</p>

<p>
Call Synapse when you want your clients to come a-knockin' at
your door -- ¬
and have no idea why!
</p>
```

indent

The indent keyword ensures that the text contained between the opening and closing tags wraps to the same text column as the tag, rather than appearing flush left. The difference is apparent when you compare almost any text format tag, from paragraph <p>, to any heading <h1> through <h6> tag, to the preformatted tag <pre>.

```
<p>Four score and seven years ago our fathers brought forth ¬
on this continent, a new nation, conceived in liberty, and ¬
dedicated to the proposition that all men are created ¬
equal.</p>

<pre>The above speech was offered by President Abraham Lincoln
and is known as ¬
the Gettysburg Address. Now recognized by many as the leading
speech of the ¬
Lincoln presidency, the Gettysburg Address was initially
received to mixed ¬
reviews...</pre>
```

igroup

The igroup keyword is used only when applied to special indentation groups such as tables and frames. For example, all the elements contained in a table have igroup="1" as part of their source profile, as shown in the following:

```
<table break="1,1,1,1" indent igroup="1">
<td break="1,0,0,1" indent igroup="1">
<th break="1,0,0,1" indent igroup="1">
<tr break="1,0,0,1" indent igroup="1">
```

The igroup attribute in the indention option activates the indentation set for all the tags in that group. For example, if the `indention` option read as follows:

```
<indention enable indent="2" tabs="8" use="spaces" active="2">
```

then indenting would be turned off for igroup number 1, tables.

The active igroup causes each element to use the indentation level of the outermost group member as its left margin — and indent from there. Thus, with the indented `<table>...</table>` pair as the outer igroup member, the `<tr>...</tr>` pair is indented two more spaces and the `<td>...</td>` pair is indented another two spaces, so it looks like the following:

```
<table border="2" width="50%">
 <tr>
 <td>Symbol</td>
 <td>Element</td>
 </tr>
 <tr>
 <td>H</td>
 <td>Hydrogen</td>
 </tr>
</table>
```

You can currently define up to six igroups, in addition to the preset tables and frames.

namecase

You can override the general case conventions for any element with the namecase keyword. If you want to use a title case or mixed case for certain tags, you define them in the following way:

```
<applet break="0,1,1,0" indent namecase="Applet">
<blockquote break="1,0,0,1" indent namecase="BlockQuote">
```

You may also use the namecase keyword when defining a custom tag for use in conjunction with a new object. Let's say you've created a series of objects for use with ColdFusion and you want them to stand out in the code. To accentuate your new tag pair, `<cfif>...</cfif>`, you could add the following line to your Source Format:

```
<cfif break="1,1,1,1" indent namecase="CFIf">
```

This line ensures that a ColdFusion "if" tag is always inserted in the specified mixed case.

Note   In addition to a large number of ColdFusion tags included in the Source Format file, Dreamweaver also supports eight different JavaServer Page tags. You'll find these listed at the end of the `<?elements>` section with the `jsp:` prefix.

noformat

As the name implies, the noformat keyword presents the tag-surrounded text without any additional formatting. This keyword is primarily used when the tag is used to reproduce verbatim information, such as when using the preformatted tag `<pre>`. The noformat keyword is also used when the element requires attributes and values in a specific format, such as with `<style>` or `<script>`.

Attributes

The Attributes section has only two options: namecase, which works as previously described in the "Elements" section, and samecase. The namecase option is used to maintain a consistent mixed case approach to JavaScript events, such as `onKeyDown`. The samecase option ensures that an attribute and its value use the same case as its tag. If the `<input>` tag is uppercase, then the named attribute and the value are uppercase.

Caution   Never use the samecase option with any attribute that requires a case-sensitive value. The most common instance of this situation is an attribute such as src that takes a filename as its value — which, in most cases, is case-sensitive.

Case is generally determined for all attributes by the following line found in the Objects section:

```
<attribute case="lower">
```

As with elements, you can alter the case of attributes individually by specifying them in this section. For example, if you always want the source attribute of the image tag to be uppercase, you can include the following line in the Attributes section:

```
<src namecase="SRC">
```

The preceding produces code such as the following:

```
<img SRC="logo.gif>
```

This capability is handy when you are scanning your code and quickly want to find all the source files.

Modifying the Source Format

Because you have to restart Dreamweaver in order for any Source Format modifications to take effect, it's best to edit the file with Dreamweaver closed. You can use any editor capable of saving an ASCII or regular text file. If you want to preserve the previous profile, you can use the Save As feature of your editor to save the file under a different name, such as SourceFormat.backup, prior to making any changes. Then, after you complete your alterations, use Save As again and name it SourceFormat.txt.

Make your changes only to those sections marked with the `<?keyword>`, such as `<?options>` or `<?elements>`. Remember that Dreamweaver is not case-sensitive when it comes to changing commands — other than with the namecase keyword — so you can write lines such as the following:

```
<element case="LOWER">
```

In the preceding example, all your tags are still created, as specified, in lowercase.

Dreamweaver is fairly protective of its Source Format. If you accidentally misspell a keyword (for example, "ident" instead of "indent"), Dreamweaver ignores and then deletes the misspelled keyword. Likewise, misplaced keywords — for instance, using the enable keyword when defining an element instead of an option — are removed from the file when Dreamweaver loads.

One of the Dreamweaver commands enables you to apply the Source Format to an existing page — typically one created outside of Dreamweaver. To use this capability, you first make changes to the Source Format and save it. Then restart Dreamweaver and open the page you want to affect. Finally, choose Commands ⇨ Apply Source Formatting. Whatever modifications you made to the Source Format are written to the existing code.

The Source Format is an HTML tinker's paradise. You can shape your code as precisely as necessary, and Dreamweaver outputs it for you. Feel free to experiment and try different code arrangements. Just be sure to have a copy of the original Source Format available as a reference.

Summary

Creating Web pages, like any design job, is easier when the tools fit your hands. Through the Preferences and the Source Format, you can make Dreamweaver work the way you work. The following highlights the basic areas for personalization:

✦ Dreamweaver enables you to customize your Web page design and HTML coding environment through a series of easy-to-use, point-and-click categories.

✦ You can decide how best to use cutting-edge features, such as layers and style sheets, depending on the degree of cross-browser and backward compatibility you need.

✦ Dreamweaver gives you plenty of elbow room for previewing and testing by providing for 20 selections on your browser list.

✦ The Source Format can be modified. You can make alterations, from across-the-board case changes to tag-by-tag presentation, to define the way Dreamweaver writes your HTML code.

In the next chapter, you learn how to get online and offline help from Dreamweaver.

✦   ✦   ✦

Using the Help System

Dreamweaver includes a multifaceted Help system that you can rely on in any number of situations:

+ To provide quick context-sensitive answers to questions about how to use specific Dreamweaver features

+ To learn the program using step-by-step instructions presented in a tutorial format

+ To explain various concepts and capabilities through the hyperlinked Help pages and their embedded Show Me movies

+ To detail the syntax for specific HTML, JavaScript and Cascading Style Sheet code

+ To seek specific programming assistance from the peer-to-peer network of the online newsgroups or the Dreamweaver technical support team at Macromedia

Whether you're a novice Web designer or a Dreamweaver master upgrading to the latest version, you'll need the Help system at some point. In this chapter, we'll cover the Help pages, included tutorials and lessons, Dreamweaver 4's new Reference feature, and the online help options.

Navigating the Help Screen

To assist your understanding of Dreamweaver — in both the short term and the long term — Macromedia includes a full electronic manual with the program._To access this searchable guide, choose Help ⇨ Using Dreamweaver or press the keyboard shortcut F1 to open the Dreamweaver HTML Help pages.

If you have defined a primary browser in Dreamweaver through the Preferences, or with File ⇨ Preview in Browser ⇨ Edit Browser List, that browser opens and the Help pages are loaded. Otherwise, Dreamweaver uses your system's default browser to display the Help pages.

The Dreamweaver Help pages are presented within an HTML frameset as shown in Figure 5-1. The frame on the far left changes according to the current mode (Contents, Index, or Search). The main portion of the frame is reserved for showing the Help pages themselves. Along the top and bottom of each page is a set of navigation arrows for moving from topic to topic within a section.

Figure 5-1: The Dreamweaver Help pages comprise a hyperlinked manual that is displayed in your primary or default browser.

Note   Dreamweaver includes a whole other level of online help documentation for the advanced user: Extending Dreamweaver. The Extending Dreamweaver Help pages are the online edition of a second manual that comes with Dreamweaver, and they explain how to customize various aspects of the program. The Extending Dreamweaver Help pages are available from the Help menu or by choosing the Extending Dreamweaver option from the standard Help pages themselves.

Browsing the Help contents

To get the most benefit from the Help pages, maximize your browser window. You can alternate between the Contents and Index by selecting one or the other control button. When you choose Contents, the frame on the left side provides a list of main Dreamweaver subjects and a handy scroll bar for moving through the list.

Selecting any main topic — displayed in bold — in the Help Contents reveals another list of subtopics. You can collapse the main topic by selecting it again or by choosing another main topic. Note that you must click a subtopic to load the information into the main viewing frame. If there is too much information to be displayed on a single screen, another scroll bar appears on the far-right side of the frame. To see the additional text, you can drag the scroll bar or select the frame and use your PgUp and PgDn keys.

Dreamweaver takes advantage of your browser's HTML capabilities, and many Help pages contain hyperlinks to other Help screens. If you follow a hyperlink to a new section from the main screen, the Contents updates to reflect your new position.

Using the navigational controls

As you browse through the Help pages, you find you can use your browser's Back and Forward buttons to revisit pages you have already viewed. You can also use the Help pages' own navigational system to move back and forth from topic to topic.

The Next and Previous arrows, shown in Figure 5-2, are tied to the Help pages' content structure and only display current subtopics within each major subject. As you would expect, selecting the Next arrow displays the next topic or subtopic, and Previous arrow displays the prior ones.

If you reach the last subtopic and attempt to use the Next arrow, you get a JavaScript alert saying you are at the end of the section. A similar event occurs when you are looking at the first subtopic and try to view the Previous one. To go to another major subject, you have to select it from the Contents listing and then select one of the subtopics.

Using the Help index

Selecting the Index control button switches to an alphabetical listing of topics covered in the Dreamweaver Help pages. To find the subject you need, select the first letter of the topic you're seeking from the A-B-C . . . letters shown in Figure 5-3; each letter is actually a link that loads the relevant section of the index when selected. For example, if I were looking for information on activating a timeline in Dreamweaver, I would select T. Once the specific letter's index has loaded, scroll down the list by dragging the scroll bar at the near right.

Figure 5-2: Move from topic to topic with the Next and Previous arrows.

Tip   If you'd like to see the entire index, choose the A–Z option. You can also click any-where in the index frame and use your system's PgUp and PgDn keys or wheel-mouse to navigate through the index.

When you find your subject, select it from the list. The corresponding Help page appears in the main frame. Note that when an index listing is divided into a topic and related subtopics, you must choose one of the subtopics to get the related Help page. In this case, the topics themselves are not linked to any specific Help page.

Note   The A–Z index is quite extensive and can take several moments to completely load. Be sure to wait until the browser indicates that the frame is completely loaded before scrolling all the way down.

Searching the Help files

Dreamweaver has included a search function with the Help pages. As designed by Macromedia, the search engine is actually a Java applet that runs within your browser displaying the Help pages. One major advantage to this approach is that it enables you to keep the search window available as you look for the material you need.

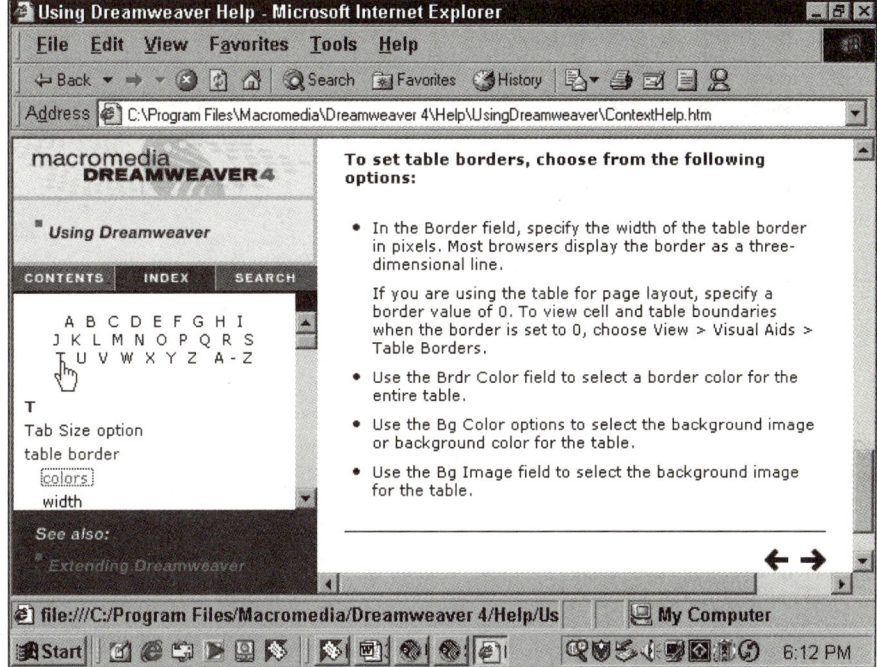

Figure 5-3: Quickly navigate to any index item by choosing its first letter from the A-B-C . . . links visible in Index mode.

To search the Help pages for a particular topic, follow these steps:

1. Select the Search button found at the top of the leftmost frame.

2. In the Search window (see Figure 5-4), enter keywords in the upper text box.

- To search for a phrase, enter the words as you would normally, for example, "shockwave" (without the quotes).

- To search for several related keywords that do not have to appear next to each other, enter the words with a plus sign between them, like this: template + behavior

- By default the search is not case-sensitive. To turn on this feature, select the Case sensitive checkbox.

3. After you've entered your search criteria, select the List Topics button.

As each page is searched, pages matching your search criteria are displayed in the results window.

Figure 5-4: Quickly find the topics you're looking for with the Help pages search engine.

4. To see an individual page, double-click its title in the results window. You can also select the title of the page and click the Display button.

The page linked to the title is displayed in the main frame of the Help pages.

5. Repeat Steps 2 through 4 to continue searching.

6. Click the Cancel button to close the Search window.

To return to either the Contents or the Index listing, select the Contents or Index command buttons, respectively.

Stepping Through the Tutorial

The Dreamweaver Help pages include a step-by-step tutorial that demonstrates how to use the latest Dynamic HTML features to create a Web page. To access the tutorial, choose Help ⇨ Tutorial or, from the Help pages, select the Dreamweaver Tutorial topic.

The Dreamweaver 4 Tutorial takes the form of a complete sample Web site for a fictitious travel company, Compass. In the process of building its Web pages, you get to try your hand at defining a local site, designing a page in Layout view, editing existing pages, working with templates, using the Assets panel, attaching behaviors, and even adding in Flash objects.

To see the sample Web site, in your browser, choose File ⇨ Open and locate the Dreamweaver 4\Tutorial\Compass_Site folder. Then select the CompassHome.html file to open it. The example home page, shown in Figure 5-5, should be previewed in a 4.0 or above browser to understand how the various pages link together.

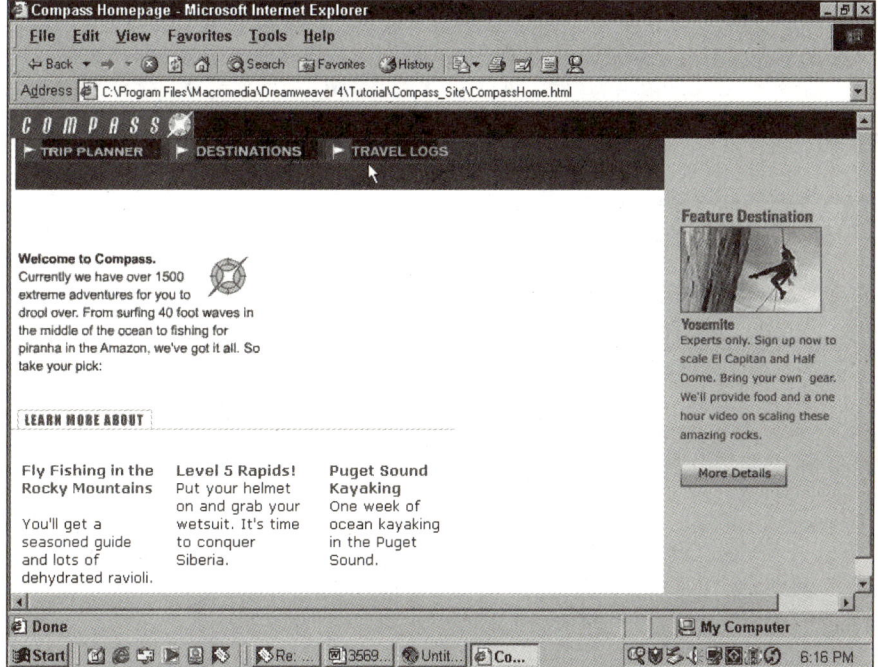

Figure 5-5: Dreamweaver includes a tutorial that demonstrates how to use the program to build an advanced Web page, step by step.

Note   The tutorial folder holds both completed and semicompleted pages. The completed pages are included to give you an idea of how the site should ultimately look. The semicompleted files enable you to work on specific techniques during the tutorial without having to build every page from the ground up each time. For easy identification, the filenames for the pages-in-progress begin with the prefix "DW4," for example, DW4_Destinations.html.

Getting the Guided Tour

Building a Web site is a big job and Dreamweaver is a big program with a large number of features. One of the most common issues faced by newcomers to the field — and the program — is not knowing where to start. To help novices scale the initial learning curve, Dreamweaver offers a series of features that introduce Web building in general and Dreamweaver in particular.

New Feature

When you run Dreamweaver for the first time, a floating Welcome panel appears displaying four topics (see Figure 5-6): What's New, Guided Tours, Tutorial, and Lessons. The Tutorial link opens the Help Pages section in your default browser but the other three subjects display material in a different Welcome panel. With a combination of text, images, and Flash movies, key concepts and new features are introduced. The Welcome panel appears automatically the first time you run Dreamweaver; however you can view the material at any time by choosing Help ⇨ Welcome.

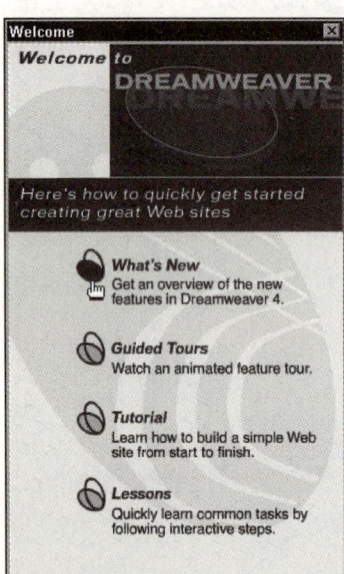

Figure 5-6: Get up-to-speed quickly by exploring Dreamweaver's Welcome panel.

Each of the descriptions shown in the Welcome panel takes a similar approach. Follow these steps to explore a Welcome panel topic:

1. If the Welcome panel is not displayed, choose Help ⇨ Welcome to open it.

Caution

The Welcome panel is actually a series of Flash movies, so you'll need the Flash Player installed before accessing this feature.

2. Select the primary topic you're interested in:

- **What's New** examines the new features in Dreamweaver 4.

- **Guided Tours** offers an overview of the Web-building process in Dreamweaver.

- **Lessons** describes techniques for accomplishing specific goals in Dreamweaver.

    Subtopics for each category are displayed next for both Guided Tours and Lessons.

3. Unless you've selected What's New, choose the subtopic you'd like to see.

    Each screen of information includes some text along with an image, a movie camera icon, or an image symbol.

4. To view an embedded Flash movie click the movie camera symbol.

 Tip
Be sure the sound is turned up on your system when running the movies. All the movies punctuate their actions with sound.

5. To see an image, select the image symbol.

    Some images display helpful screens of information when you move your mouse over them. Along the bottom of the panel, you'll notice that navigational aids have appeared: (from left to right) Home, Rewind, Previous and Next.

6. When you're finished viewing one page, select the Next button.

7. You can review prior screens by selecting the Previous button.

8. To view the topic from the start, select the Rewind button.

9. If you'd like to look at more topics in the current category, select the Home button.

10. To see topics in another category, first select the Home button and then choose the Back button on the lower-left of the Welcome panel.

The lessons found in the Welcome panel — which can be directly accessed by choosing Help ⇨ Lessons — includes a couple of additional features, shown in Figure 5-7, not found in the Guided Tours. First, you'll see a step-by-step list of the process covered (for example, Creating an image map) at the start of each lesson. Not only does this give you an overview of the procedure, but the steps themselves are clickable so that you can go directly to the information you need. Within the lessons, a special steps navigation button appears, which, when selected, displays a navigable list of all the steps in that lesson. Select any step to display that screen of information.

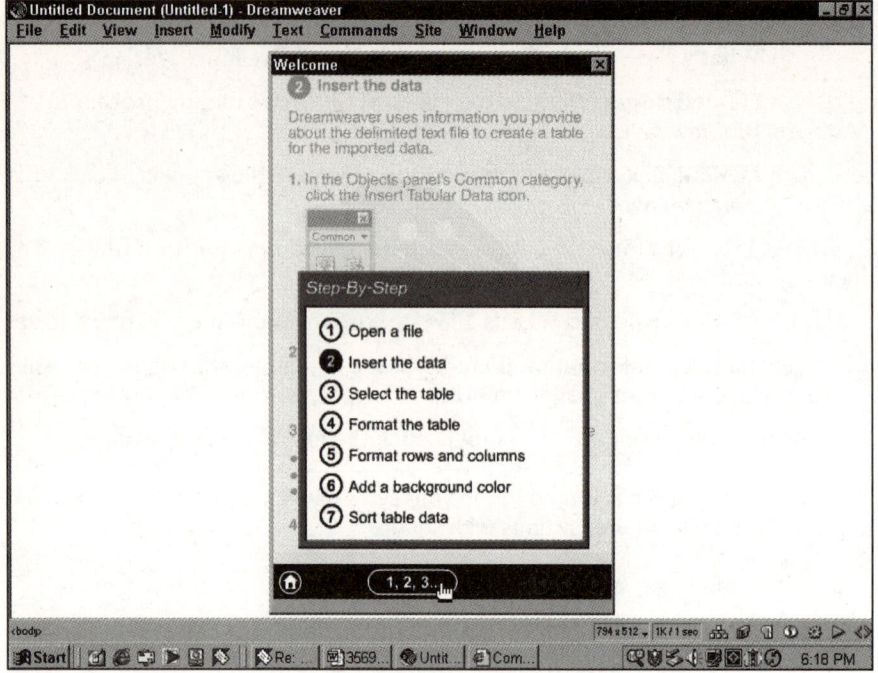

Figure 5-7: Dreamweaver lessons offer step-by-step navigation.

Lessons also offer a tool for trying out the described techniques right away. Dreamweaver comes with a practice page ready for you to work with. On the first page of each lesson, select the Open Practice Page button to load a predesigned HTML page into Dreamweaver. All of the steps in the lesson refer to the practice page and it's a great tool for quickly mastering the concepts described.

Tip   Be sure to use File ⇨ Save As to store your practice page under another name rather than Save so you can revisit the unchanged example page if necessary.

Using the Reference Panel

Pop quiz: What value of a form tag's `enctype` attribute should you use if the user is submitting a file? Is it:

A. application/x-www-form-urlencoded

B. multipart/form-data

C. multipart/data-form

Chances are, unless you've recently had to include such a form in a Web page, you'd have to pull down that well-worn HTML reference book you keep handy and look up the answer to be sure. All code for the Web — including HTML, JavaScript, and Cascading Style Sheets (CSS) — must be precisely written or it will, at best, be ignored; at worst, an error will be generated whenever the user views the page. Even the savviest of Web designers can't remember the syntax of every tag, attribute, and value in HTML or every function in JavaScript or every style rule in CSS. A good reference is a necessity in Web design. (By the way, the answer to the pop quiz is B.)

New Feature

Macromedia has lightened the load on your bookshelf considerably with the addition of the Reference panel in Dreamweaver 4, as shown in Figure 5-8. With the Reference panel, you can quickly look up any HTML tag and its attributes as well as JavaScript objects and CSS style rules. The Reference panel uses content from Danny Goodman's *Dynamic HTML: The Definitive Reference*, published by O'Reilly & Associates, a superb guide to Web technology. Not only does the Reference panel offer the proper syntax for any code in question, it also displays the level of browser support. Moreover, you don't have to dig through the tag lists to find the info you need — just highlight the tag or object in question and press the keyboard shortcut, Shift+F1.

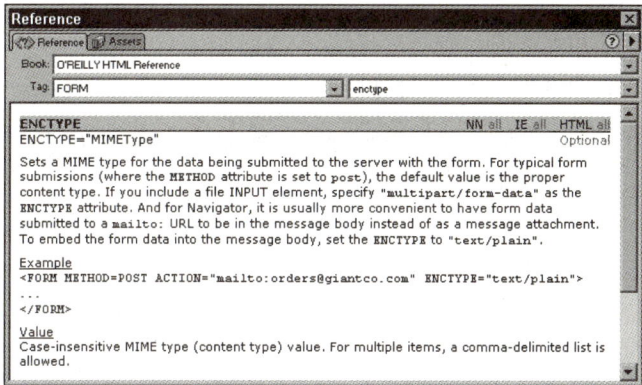

Figure 5-8: To quickly look up a tag, select it in the Tag selector or in Code view and then choose Shift+F1 to open the Reference panel.

There are four different ways to open the Reference panel:

✦ Choose Window ⇨ Reference

✦ Select the Reference button on the toolbar.

✦ Use the Shift+F1 keyboard shortcut.

✦ Use the Ctrl+Shift+F1 (Command+Shift+F1) keyboard shortcut.

What's the difference between the two shortcuts? Shift+F1 is used for context-sensitive help; select any tag (or just place your cursor within text enclosed by the tag) and then choose Shift+F1 to display the entry for the selected tag in the Reference panel. The other shortcut, Ctrl+Shift+F1 (Command+Shift+F1), is not context-sensitive, but rather toggles the Reference panel open and closed — and opens the panel to the last entry viewed.

Tip　To find reference details for the attributes of an HTML tag, a JavaScript object or a CSS style rule included on a Web page, open the Code view and select the code in question prior to choosing Shift+F1 or selecting the Reference button from the toolbar.

To look for information on code not included in the page, follow these steps:

1. Display the Reference panel by choosing Window ➪ Reference or using the keyboard shortcut Ctrl+Shift+F1 (Command+Shift+F1).

2. Select the required guide from the Book drop-down list. The standard options are:

   • O'Reilly CSS Reference

   • O'Reilly HTML Reference

   • O'Reilly JavaScript Reference

3. Choose the primary topic from the Style/Tag/Object drop-down list. The list heading changes depending which Book is selected.

Tip　Windows users can move quickly to a topic by selecting the drop-down list and then pressing the key for the first letter of the term being sought. Then they can use the down arrow to move through items that start with that letter. For example, if you were looking for information on the JavaScript regular expressions object, you could press "r" and then the down arrow to reach RegExp.

4. If desired, you can select a secondary topic from the second drop-down list for HTML and JavaScript elements.

   If you've chosen an HTML tag, the secondary list displays all the available attributes for that tag. If you've chosen a JavaScript object, the secondary list shows the available properties for that object.

The information shown depends, naturally, on the book, topic, and subtopic chosen. At the top of each entry, you'll find the name of the subject and details on how it relates to browsers and standards:

   ✦ The CSS reference shows whether the style is supported in Netscape Navigator (NN) or Internet Explorer (IE). You'll also see which level of the Cascading Style Sheet specification (CSS 1 or CSS 2) the style is derived from and whether it is inherited or not.

✦ The HTML reference tells you which version of Netscape Navigator or Internet Explorer supports the selected tag. The HTML version in which the tag was introduced and information about whether an end tag is required is also displayed.

Note The book on which the Reference panel is based was published in 1998 and only covers 4.0 browsers and below.

✦ The JavaScript reference details which version of the two main browsers as well as which version of the Document Object Model (DOM) or ECMA (the standard on which JavaScript is based) introduced the selected object.

The Reference panel's context menu allows you to switch between three different font sizes: small, medium, and large. This capability is especially useful when working at resolutions higher than 800×600. You'll also find an option to connect directly to O'Reilly Books Online.

Getting Help Online

Without a doubt, one of the factors that has helped the Web to grow so rapidly is the fact that it is largely self-documenting. Want to learn more about developing Web pages? Find out on the Web! The same holds true for Dreamweaver. An extensive array of information about Dreamweaver is available online — and more is added every day.

Macromedia has done — and continues to do — an excellent job of supporting Dreamweaver on the Web. To that end, Macromedia has developed and continues to sponsor two Web sites: the Dreamweaver Support Center and the Dynamic HTML Zone. The Dreamweaver Support Center is part of the general Macromedia site and focuses exclusively on providing support for Dreamweaver. Let's take a look at this one first.

Note As with many popular Web sites, the Macromedia sites are constantly in a state of revision. The following information was current when written, but some of the content or structure may have changed by the time you read it. If all else fails, you should always be able to find assistance by starting at `www.macromedia.com` and looking for the Dreamweaver support area.

Dreamweaver Support Center

Macromedia's primary help center on the Web for Dreamweaver is a terrific resource. Visit the Dreamweaver Support Center at `www.macromedia.com/support/dreamweaver/` to find the latest technical data, free downloads, and peer-to-peer connections — and it's all specific to Dreamweaver, naturally. One of the most impressive aspects of the site is its multilevel approach; there's material here for everyone, from rank beginner to the savviest code jockey.

When you visit the Dreamweaver Support Center, you find various areas of help as well as a search facility. Macromedia generally updates the site, shown in Figure 5-9, on a monthly or better basis. It's definitely worth bookmarking in your browser and visiting often.

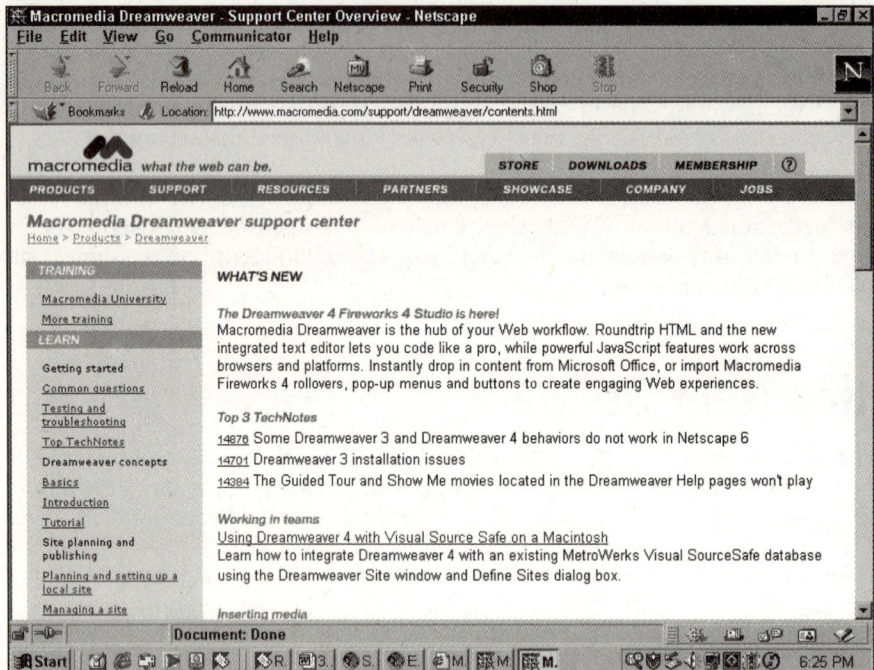

Figure 5-9: The Dreamweaver Support Center Web site is a central resource for gathering the newest information and software related to Dreamweaver.

Dynamic HTML Zone

The Dynamic HTML Zone, at www.dhtmlzone.com, is another extremely valuable online resource center. This site is also hosted by Macromedia, but here the focus is less on Dreamweaver than on implementing Dynamic HTML features in your Web pages. The Dynamic HTML Zone, shown in Figure 5-10, is a great jumping-off place for learning about DHTML through a variety of methods. The following is just some of what you can find at "the DZone."

Articles

The Dynamic HTML Zone contains a collection of some of the finest technical papers about creating DHTML pages on the Web. Both browser-specific and cross-browser features are explained by experts in the field. Sample articles include "Creating Multimedia with Dynamic HTML: An Overview," "Cross-Browser Dynamic HTML," and "Techniques for Building Backward Compatible DHTML."

Figure 5-10: Visit the Dynamic HTML Zone for the latest information on building your Web pages with cutting-edge DHTML capabilities.

Tutorials

Learning from tutorials can be dry and tedious — but not at the DZone! Visit SuperFly Fashions and learn helpful general techniques, such as working with CSS layers and initializations. You also find more advanced methods, such as pull-down menus and scrolling text. The tutorials come with an overview as well as a line-by-line analysis of the JavaScript subroutines and other needed HTML code.

Resources

The Resources area is a collection of links to articles, reference guides, demos, various tutorials, and browser data — all related to DHTML. Pulling equally from the Microsoft and Netscape camps, as well as independent organizations such as C|Net and the W3C, these links are a great jumping-off place for all things DHTML.

Spotlight

Want to see what else is being accomplished with Dynamic HTML? Check out the Spotlight area. In addition to the site that's currently "in the spotlight," this page maintains an archive of past sites so honored.

Shockwave in DHTML

Combining the interactivity of Shockwave with the flexibility of Dynamic HTML is an exciting concept, and this area of the DZone gives you all the tools you need to make this marriage happen. You can find both technical white papers and full-featured demos to learn from.

Summary

Dreamweaver is a full-featured program incorporating many new technologies. This chapter describes the substantial alternatives available to you for shortening your learning curve. Key methods include the following:

✦ The expansive electronic manual, Dreamweaver Help pages, which explains how to accomplish specific Web page building tasks through hyperlinked text and embedded multimedia.

✦ Built-in tutorials for learning how to get started with Dreamweaver, by making a Web page with some of the latest effects.

✦ Lessons showing how to use the most popular HTML features as created in Dreamweaver.

✦ The Reference panel offers detailed descriptions of HTML, JavaScript, and CSS syntax.

✦ A wealth of information, online. Constantly updated, always available, Dreamweaver's online resources are a tremendous benefit to any Web designer or developer, no matter what your level of skills.

In the next chapter, you see how to set up your first Dreamweaver site, step by step.

✦   ✦   ✦

Setting Up Your First Site

In This Chapter

Web site design and structure

Making a local site

Generating and saving pages

Previewing your Web site

Publishing online

✦ ✦ ✦ ✦

Web sites — especially those integrating Web applications — are far more than collections of HTML documents. Every image — from the smallest navigational button to the largest image map — is a separate file that must be uploaded with your HTML page. And if you use any additional elements, such as an included script, background sound, digital video, or Java applet, their files must be transferred as well. To preview the Web site locally and view it properly on the Internet, you have to organize your material in a specific manner.

In Dreamweaver, the process of creating a site also involves developing Web applications in a particular server model. Dreamweaver is unique in its ability to author sites for a variety of application servers. While it is feasible to mix pages developed for different server models, it's not really practical. Dreamweaver enables you to select one server model for each site.

Each time you begin developing a new site, you must define several initial parameters, including the chosen server model, as described in this chapter. These steps lay the groundwork for Dreamweaver to properly link your local development site with your remote online site as well as linking properly to your data sources. For those who are just starting to create Web sites, this chapter begins with a brief discussion of approaches to online design. The remainder of the chapter is devoted to the mechanics of setting up your site and basic file manipulation.

Planning Your Site

Planning in Web design, just as in any other design process, is essential. Not only will careful planning cut your development time considerably, but it also makes it far easier to achieve a uniform look and feel for your Web site — and thus make it friendlier and easier to use. This first section briefly covers some of the basics of Web site design: what to focus on, what options to consider, and what pitfalls to avoid. If you are an established Web site developer who has covered this ground before, feel free to skip this section.

Primary considerations

Even before you choose from various models to design your site, you'll need to address the all-important issues of message, audience, and budget.

What do you want to say?

If I had to pick one overriding concern for Web site design, it would be to answer the following question: "What are you trying to say?" The clearer your idea of your message, the more focused your Web site will be. To this end, I find it useful to try to state the purpose of a Web site in one sentence. "I want to create the coolest Web site on the planet" doesn't count. Although it could be regarded as a goal, it's so open-ended that it's almost no concept at all.

Here are some examples of clearly stated Web site concepts:

✦ "To provide the best small-business resource center focused on Microsoft's Office software."

✦ "To chronicle the world's first voyage around the world by hot air balloon."

✦ "To advertise music lessons offered by a collective of keyboard teachers in New York City."

Who is your audience?

Right behind a site's concept — some would say neck-and-neck with it — is the site's audience. Who are you trying to reach? Quite often a site's style is heavily influenced by a clear vision of the site's intended audience. Take, for example, Macromedia's Dynamic HTML Zone (www.dhtmlzone.com). This is an excellent example of a site that is perfectly pitched toward its target; in this case, the intended audience is composed of professional developers and designers. Hence, you'll find the site snazzy but informative and filled with exciting examples of cutting-edge programming techniques.

In contrast, a site that is devoted to mass-market e-commerce must work with a very different group in mind: shoppers. Everyone at one time or another falls into this category, so we're really talking about a state of mind, rather than a profession. Many shopping sites use a very straightforward page design — one that is easily maneuverable and comforting in its repetition, and one that enables visitors to quickly find what they are looking for and, with as few impediments as possible, buy it.

What are your resources?

Unfortunately, Web sites aren't created in a vacuum. Virtually all development work happens under real-world constraints of some kind. A professional Web designer is accustomed to working within a budget. In fact, the term *budget* can apply to several concepts.

First, you have a monetary budget — how much is the client willing to spend? This translates into a combination of development time (for designers and programmers), materials (custom graphics, stock photos, and the like), and ongoing maintenance. You can build a large site with many pages that pulls dynamically from an internal database and requires very little hands-on upkeep. Or you can construct a small, graphics-intensive site that must be updated by hand weekly. Yet it's entirely possible that both sites will end up costing the same.

Second, budget also applies to the amount of time you can afford to spend on any given project. The professional Web designer is quick to realize that time is an essential commodity. The resources needed when undertaking a showcase for yourself with no deadline are very different from contracting on June 30th for a job that must be ready to launch on July 4th.

The third real-world budgetary item to consider is bandwidth. The Web, with faster modems and an improved infrastructure, is slowly shedding its image as the "World Wide Wait." That means today's Webmaster must keep a steady eye on a page's weight — how long it takes to download under typical modem rates. Of course, you can always decide to include that animated video masterpiece that takes 33 minutes to download on a 28.8 modem — you just can't expect anyone to wait to see it.

In conclusion, when you are trying to define your Web page, filter it through these three ideas: message, audience, and the various faces of the budget. The time spent visualizing your Web page in these terms will be time decidedly well spent.

Design options

Many Web professionals borrow a technique used extensively in developing other mass-marketing forms: *storyboarding*. Storyboarding for the Web entails first diagramming the various pages in your site — much like the more traditional storyboarding in videos or filmmaking — and then detailing connections for the separate pages to form the overall site. How you connect the disparate pages determines how your visitors will navigate the completed Web site.

There are several basic navigational models; the modern Web designer should be familiar with them all because each one serves a different purpose and they can be mixed and matched as needed.

The linear approach

Prior to the World Wide Web, most media formats were linear — that is, one image or page followed another in an unalterable sequence. In contrast, the Web and its interactive personality enable the user to jump from topic to topic. Nevertheless, you can still use a linear approach to a Web site and have one page appear after another, like a multimedia book.

The linear navigational model, shown in Figure 6-1, works well for computer-based training applications and other expository scenarios in which you want to tightly control the viewer's experience. Some Web designers use a linear-style entrance or exit from their main site, connected to a multilevel navigational model. One advantage that Dynamic HTML brings is that you can achieve the effects of moving through several pages in a single page through layering.

Figure 6-1: The linear navigational model takes the visitor through a series of Web pages.

Keep in mind that Web search engines can index the content of every page of your site separately. Each page of your site — not just your home page — then becomes a potential independent entrance point. So be sure to include, on every page, navigation buttons back to your home page, especially if you use a linear navigational model.

The hierarchical model

Hierarchical navigational models emerge from top-down designs. These start with one key concept that becomes your home page. From the home page, users branch off to several main pages; if needed, these main pages can, in turn, branch off into many separate pages. Everything flows from the home page; it's very much like a company's organization chart, with the CEO on top followed by the various company divisions.

The hierarchical Web site, shown in Figure 6-2, is best known for maintaining a visitor's sense of place in the site. Some Web designers even depict the treelike structure as a navigation device and include each branch traveled as a link. This enables visitors to quickly retrace their steps, branch by branch, to investigate different routes.

The spoke-and-hub model

Given the Web's flexible hyperlink structure, the spoke-and-hub navigational model works extremely well. The hub is, naturally, the site's home page. The spokes projecting out from the center connect to all the major pages in the site. This layout permits fairly immediate access to any key page in just two jumps — one jump always leading back to the hub/home page and one jump leading off to a new direction. Figure 6-3 shows a typical spoke-and-hub structure for a Web site.

Figure 6-2: A hierarchical Web layout enables the main topics to branch into their own subtopics.

The main drawback to the spoke-and-hub structure is the constant return to the home page. Many Web designers get around this limitation by making the first jump off the hub into a Web page using frames, in which the navigation bars are always available. This design also enables visitors using nonframes-capable browsers to take a different path.

The full Web design

The approach that seems the least structured for a Web site — fullWeb — takes the most advantage of the Web's hyperlink capabilities. This design enables virtually every page to connect to every other page. The full Web design, shown in Figure 6-4, works well for sites that are explorations of a particular topic because the approach encourages visitors to experience the site according to their own needs, not based on the notions of any single designer. The danger in using full Web for your site design is that the visitor can literally get lost. As an escape hatch, many Web designers include a link to a clickable site map, especially for large-scale sites of this design.

Figure 6-3: This storyboard diagram for a zoo's Web site shows how a spoke-and-hub model might work.

Defining a Site

Now that you've decided on a design and mapped your site, you're ready to set it up in Dreamweaver. When you define a site, you are telling Dreamweaver where to store your Web pages locally, where to transfer them to remotely, as well as the style of code in which to write them. Defining a site is an essential first step.

The Site Definitions dialog box is comprised of five categories of information. Only the first two—Local Info and Remote Info—are essential for site definition and are detailed in the remainder of this section.

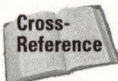

Cross-Reference   The other categories in the Site Definition dialog box (File View Columns, Site Map Layout, and Design Notes) are helpful for working in a team environment and working visually with Dreamweaver's Site Map. You can find more information on these features in Chapter 7.

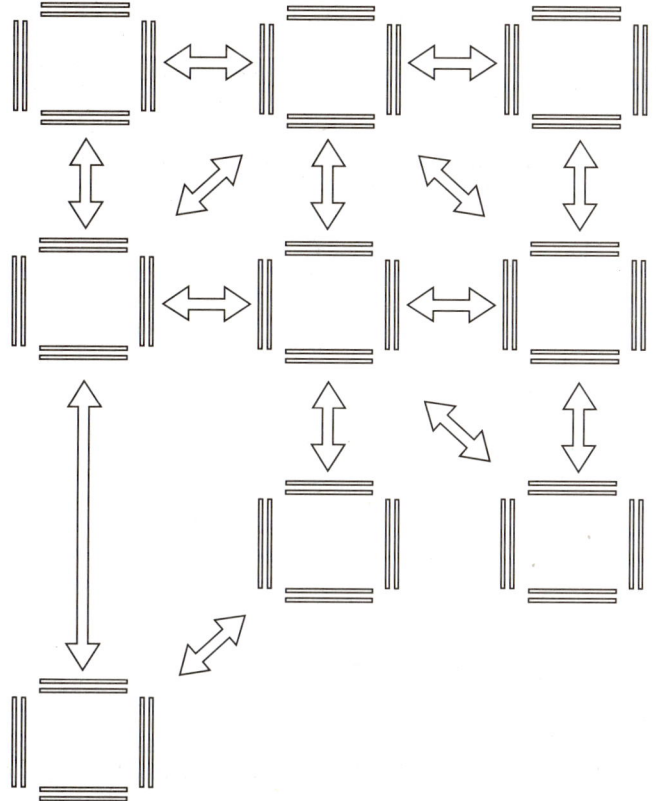

Figure 6-4: In a full Web design, each page can have multiple links to other pages.

There are three main steps to defining a site in Dreamweaver:

1. Locate the folder to be used for the local, development site.
2. Enter the remote site information.
3. Specify the application server model to be used for the site.

Establishing local connections

Once your site is on your Web server and fully operational, the site consists of many files — plain HTML, graphics and other media files — that make up the individual Web pages. All of these associated files are kept on the server in one folder, which may use one or more subfolders. This main folder is called the *remote site root*. In order for Dreamweaver to properly display your linked pages and embedded images — just as they are displayed online — the program creates a mirror of your remote site on your local development system. This primary mirror folder on your system is known as the *local site root*.

It's necessary for you to establish the local site root at the beginning of a project. This ensures that Dreamweaver duplicates the complete structure of the Web development site when it comes time to publish your pages to the Web. One of Dreamweaver's key site-management features enables you to select just the HTML pages for publication; Dreamweaver then automatically transfers all the associated files, creating any needed folders in the process. The mirror images of your local and remote site roots are critical to Dreamweaver's ability to expedite your workload in this way.

Tip

If you do decide to transfer an existing Web site to a new Dreamweaver local site root, run Dreamweaver's Link Checker after you've consolidated all your files. Choose File ➪ Check Links or press the keyboard shortcut, Shift+F8. The Link Checker tells you of broken links and orphan files as well. For more information on the Link Checker, see Chapter 7.

To set up a local site root folder in Dreamweaver, follow these steps:

1. Select Site ➪ New Site from the main Dreamweaver menu.

   The Site window opens, followed shortly by the Site Definition dialog box, as shown in Figure 6-5.

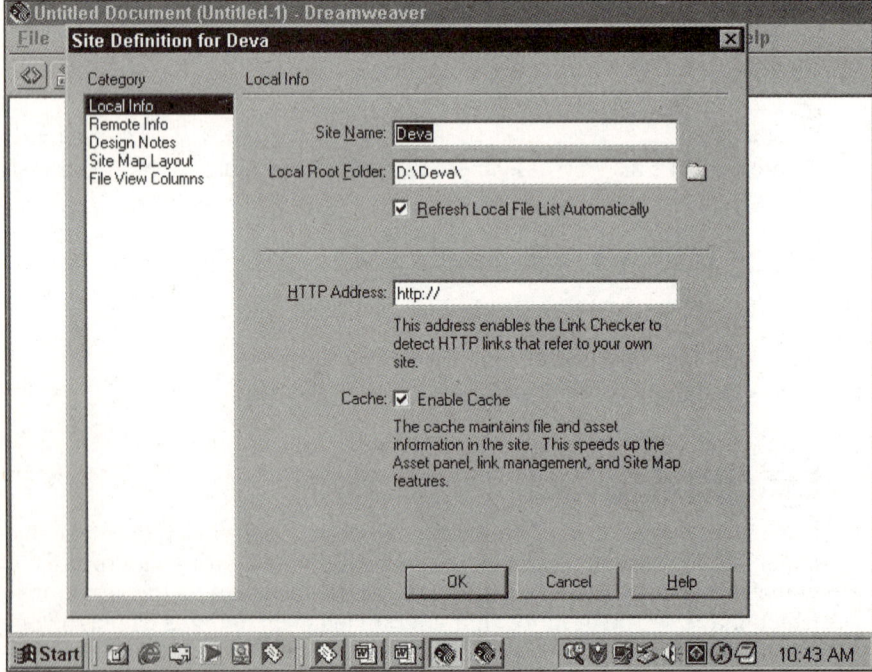

Figure 6-5: Set up your local site root through the Site Definition dialog box.

2. From the Local Info category, type a name for your site in the Site Name text box.

   This name appears in the user-defined site list displayed when you select File ⇨ Open Site.

3. Specify the folder to serve as the local site root, by either typing the path name directly into the Local Root Folder text box or clicking the folder button. The Browse button opens the Choose Local Directory dialog box. When you've made your choice there, click the Select button.

4. Leave the Refresh Local File List Automatically option selected. This option ensures that new files are automatically included in the list and relieves you from having to select the Refresh command.

5. Enter the full URL for your site in the HTTP Address text box.

   When checking links for your Web site, Dreamweaver uses the HTTP address to determine whether absolute links, such as `http://www.idest/ Dreamweaver/index.htm`, reference external files or files on your site.

6. For fastest performance, select the Cache option.

   Typically, the use of the cache speeds up link updates.

Specifying the remote site

In addition to defining the local site root, you also need to detail information pertaining to the remote site. The remote site may either be a folder accessed through the local network or via FTP (File Transfer Protocol). If your remote site is located on the local network — in this arrangement the remote site is often said to be on a *staging server* — all you need do is select or create the particular folder to house the remote site. At the appropriate time, the network administrator or other designated person from the Information Technology department, will migrate the files from the staging server to the Web or intranet server.

Note Many Dreamweaver developers have a Web server located on their development system making it possible to have both the local and remote site on the same machine.

If, on the other hand, you post your material to a remote site via FTP, you'll need various bits of information to complete the connection. In addition to the FTP host's name — used by Dreamweaver to find the server on the Internet — you'll also need, at a minimum, the user name and password to log into the server. The host's technical support staff will provide you with this and any other necessary info.

Caution Although it's entirely possible to develop your site locally without establishing a remote site root, it's not a recommended practice. Web sites require extensive testing in real-world settings — something that's just not possible with a local development setup. If you don't have the necessary information to establish a remote site root initially, you can still begin development locally; just be sure to transfer your files to your remote site and begin testing as soon as possible.

To enter the remote site information, follow these steps:

1. Continuing in the Site Definition dialog box, select the Remote Info category.

2. From the Remote Info category, as shown in Figure 6-6, choose the type of remote connection that applies to your site:

Figure 6-6: Choose whether your remote site is to be accessed via the local network or by FTP in the Web Server Info panel.

- **None:** Choose this option if your site is being developed locally and will not be uploaded to a Web server at this time.

  If you selected None for Server Access, proceed to entering the App Server Info as described in the next section.

- **Local/Network:** Select this option if you are running a local Web server and wish to store your remote site on your local drive or if your Web server is mounted as a network drive.

  If you selected Local/Network for Server Access, enter the name of the remote folder in the Remote Folder text box or click the Browse button to locate the folder. If you wish to automatically update the remote file list (recommended), leave the Refresh Remote File List Automatically option selected. Then proceed to entering the App Server Info as described in the following section.

- **FTP:** Select this option if you connect to your Web server via File Transfer Protocol (FTP).

- **SourceSafe Database:** Choose this option if your site is maintained within a SourceSafe database compatible with Microsoft Visual SourceSafe Client, version 6 on Windows or MetroWerks SourceSave version 1.10 on Macintosh.

- **WebDAV:** Select WebDAV (short for Web-based Distributed Authoring and Versioning) if your site is managed by a collaborative authoring system using WebDAV standards.

3. If FTP is selected, complete the following options:

- **FTP Host:** The host name of the FTP connection for your Web server, usually in the form `www.sitename.com`. Do not include the full URL, such as `ftp://www.sitename.com/index.html`.

- **Host Directory:** The directory in which publicly accessible documents are stored on the server. Typical Host Directory names are `www/public/docs/` and `public_html/htdoc/`. Your remote site root folder will be a subfolder of the Host Directory. If you are unsure of the exact name of the Host Directory, check with your Web server administrator for the proper directory path. Oftentimes the FTP Host connects to the correct directory automatically and this field is left blank.

- **Login:** The login name you have been assigned for access to the Web server.

- **Password:** The password necessary for you to gain access to the Web server. Many servers are case-sensitive when it comes to logins and passwords.

- **Save:** Dreamweaver automatically selects this option after you enter a password. Deselect this box only if you and others access the server from the current system.

- **Use Passive FTP:** Passive FTP establishes the FTP connection through the local software rather than the server. Certain firewall configurations use passive FTP; check with your network administrator to see if you need it.

- **Use Firewall:** This option will be selected for you if you've set the Preferences with the correct host and port information.

4. If SourceSafe Database is selected, choose Settings to display the Open SourceSafe Database dialog box. In the dialog box, complete the following:

- **Database Path:** Enter the path to the SourceSafe database; choose Browse to locate the database in a dialog box.

- **Project:** Enter the name of the project within the SourceSafe database; this will serve as the remote site's root directory.

- **Username:** Enter your login name.

- **Password:** Enter your password.

- **Save:** Keep the Save option enabled, unless you are sharing your system and want to log in into the database each time you access it.

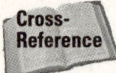

Cross-Reference For more information on team-building Web sites with SourceSafe and WebDAV, see Chapter 35.

5. If you're building your site with a team and using a WebDAV server, complete the following information:

- **URL:** Enter the absolute URL to the directory of your site on the WebDAV server.

- **Username:** Enter your login name.

- **Password:** Enter your password.

- **Email:** Enter your e-mail address. Unlike with Dreamweaver's own Check In/Check Out feature, an e-mail address is required with WebDAV.

- **Save:** Keep the Save option enabled, unless you are sharing your system and want to log in to the database each time you access it.

Note Dreamweaver doesn't save the Site Definition information until the program exits. If Dreamweaver should "unexpectedly quit"—the politically correct term for "crash"—any changes made to the Site Definition dialog box in the session will be lost.

Managing Site Info

You can change any of the information associated with your local site roots by selecting File ➪ Open Site ➪ Define Sites (Site ➪ Open Site ➪ Define Sites) from either the main Dreamweaver menu or from the Site Window menu. Choose the site you want to modify from the Site list box at the top of the Site Information dialog box; you'll see the corresponding information for you to edit.

After your participation in a project has ended, you can remove the site from your list. Select File ➪ Open Site ➪ Define Sites (Site ➪ Open Site ➪ Define Sites) to open the Site Information dialog box, choose the site you want to remove in the Site list box, and click the Delete Site button. Note that this action removes the site only from Dreamweaver's internal list; it does not delete any files or folders from your hard drive.

With the local site root folder established, Dreamweaver can properly manage links no matter which address format is used. The various address formats are explained in the following section.

Creating and Saving New Pages

You've considered message, audience, and budget issues. You've chosen a design. You've set up your site and its address. All the preliminary planning is completed, and now you're ready to really rev up Dreamweaver and begin creating pages. This section covers the basic mechanics of opening and saving Web pages in development.

Starting Dreamweaver

Start Dreamweaver as you would any other program. Double-click the Dreamweaver program icon, or single-click if you are using Internet Explorer's Desktop Integration feature in Windows.

Building Placeholder Pages

One technique that I've found helpful over the years—and especially so with the use of document relative addressing in Dreamweaver Web projects—is what I call *placeholder pages.* These placeholder pages can fill the need to include links as you create each Web page in as effortless a manner as possible.

Let's say, for example, you've just finished laying out most of the text and graphics for your home page and you want to put in some navigational buttons. You drop in your button images and align them just so. All that's missing is the link. If you're using document relative addressing, the best way to handle assigning the link would be to click the Browse for File button in the Property Inspector and select your file. But what do you do if you haven't created any other pages yet and there aren't any files to select? That's when you can put placeholder pages to work.

After you've designed the basics of your site and created your local site root, as described elsewhere in this chapter, start with a blank Dreamweaver page. Type a single identifying word on the page and save it in the local site root. Do this for all the Web pages in your plan. When it comes time to make your links, all you have to do is point and click to the appropriate placeholder page. This arrangement also gives you an immediate framework for link testing. When it comes time to work on the next page, just open up the correct placeholder page and start to work.

Another style of working involves using the Site window as your base of operations, rather than the Document window. It's very easy in Dreamweaver to choose File ⇨ New File from the Site Window menu several times and create the basic files of your site. You can even create a file and immediately link to it by choosing File ⇨ Link to New File; a dialog box opens, allowing you to specify the file name, title of the new document and text for the link. Moreover, any needed subfolders, such as ones for images or other media, can be created by selecting File ⇨ New Folder.

Opening Other Types of Files

Dreamweaver defaults to searching for HTML files with an extension of either .html or .htm. To look for other types of files, select the Files of Type arrow button. Dreamweaver allows several other file types, including server-side includes (.shtml, .shtm, or .stm), Active server pages (.asp), and Cold Fusion (.cfm or .cfml). If you need to load a valid HTML file with a different extension, select the All Files option.

If you are working consistently with a different file format, you can add your own extensions and file types to the Dreamweaver Open File dialog box. In the Configuration folder, there is an editable text file called Extensions.txt. Open this file in your favorite text editor to make any additions. If you use Dreamweaver, be sure to edit the file in the HTML Inspector to see the correct format.

The syntax must follow the format of the standard Extensions.txt file:

```
HTM,HTML,ASP,JSP,CFM,CFML,TXT,SHTM,SHTML,STM,LASSO,XML:
All Documents
HTM,HTML:HTML Documents
SHTM,SHTML,STM:Server-Side Includes
XML:XML Files
LBI:Library Files
DWT:Template Files
CSS:Style Sheets
ASP:Active Server Pages
CFM,CFML:Cold Fusion Templates
TXT:Text Files
PHP:PHP Files
LASSO:Lasso Files
JSP:Java Server Pages
```

After the splash screen, Dreamweaver opens with a new blank page. This page is created from the Default.html file found in the Dreamweaver/Configuration/Templates folder. Of course, it's possible that you'll want to replace the original Default.html file with one of your own—perhaps with your copyright information. All of your blank pages will then be created from a template that you've created.

 Tip   If you do decide to create your own Default template, it's probably a good idea to rename the Dreamweaver Default template—as Original-Default.html or something similar—prior to creating your new, personalized Default template.

Opening an existing file

If you're looking to work on a Web page in Dreamweaver that was created in another application, choose File ➪ Open, or the keyboard shortcut Ctrl+O (Command+O). From the standard Open File dialog box, you can browse to your file's location and select it.

If you have just started Dreamweaver or if your current document is blank, your selected file will load into the current window. If, however, you have another Web page open or have begun creating a new one, Dreamweaver opens your file in a new window.

When you first open an existing Web page, Dreamweaver checks the HTML syntax. If it finds any errors, Dreamweaver corrects them and then informs you of the corrections through the HTML Parser Results dialog box. As discussed in Chapter 4, you can turn off this HTML syntax-checking feature. Select Edit ⇨ Preferences and then, from the Code Rewriting category of the Preferences dialog box, deselect one or more of the checkbox options for HTML syntax-checking.

To add an entry, place your cursor at the end of the line above where you want your new file format to be placed, and press Enter (Return). Type in your file extension(s) in capital letters, followed by a colon and then the text description. Save the Extensions.txt file and restart Dreamweaver to see your modifications.

Opening a new window

You can work on as many Dreamweaver documents as your system memory can sustain. When you choose File ⇨ New or one of the keyboard shortcuts (Ctrl+N or Command+N), Dreamweaver opens a new blank page in a separate window. Once the window is open, you can switch among the various windows. To do this in Windows, you select the appropriate icon in the taskbar or use the Alt+Tab method. To switch between Dreamweaver windows on a Macintosh, click on the individual window or use the Window menu.

Opening a new page

After working for a while on a design, you sometimes need to start over or switch entirely to a new project. In either case, choose File ⇨ New or, in Windows, one of the keyboard shortcuts, Ctrl+Shift+N (Command+Shift+N). This closes the current document and opens a new blank page in the same window.

Tip   You can also drag and drop an HTML file onto the Dreamweaver Document window or — if you're just starting a session — onto the Dreamweaver icon on your desktop.

If you've made any modifications to your page, Dreamweaver asks if you would like to save the page. Click the Yes button to save the file or the No button to continue without saving it. To abort the new page opening, click Cancel.

Note   You can easily tell a page has been altered since the last save by looking at the title bar. Dreamweaver places an asterisk after the filename in the title bar for modified pages. Dreamweaver is even smart enough to properly remove the asterisk should you reverse your changes with the Undo command or the History palette.

Each time you open a new page, whether in the existing window or in a new window, Dreamweaver temporarily names the file "Untitled-n," where *n* is the next number in sequence. This prevents you from accidentally overwriting a new file opened in the same session.

Saving your page

Saving your work is very important in any computer-related task, and Dreamweaver is no exception. To initially save the current page, choose File ➪ Save or the keyboard shortcut Ctrl+S (Command+S). The Save dialog box opens; you can enter a filename and, if desired, a different path.

By default, all files are saved with a .htm filename extension for Windows and .html for Macintosh. To save your file with another extension, such as .shtml, change the Files of Type option to the specific file type and then enter your full filename, without the extension.

It seems kind of backward in this day and age of long filenames, but it's still a good idea to choose names for your files without spaces or punctuation other than an underscore or hyphen. Otherwise, not all servers will read the filename correctly and you'll have problems linking your pages.

Closing the page

When you're finished with a page you can close a file without quitting Dreamweaver. To close a page, select File ➪ Close or the keyboard shortcuts, Ctrl+W (Command+W). If you made any changes to the page since you saved it last, Dreamweaver prompts you to save it.

Windows users will note that if you only have one Dreamweaver window open and you close the current page, Dreamweaver asks you if you'd like to quit the program.

Quitting the program

Once you're done for the day — or, more often, the late, late night — you can close Dreamweaver by choosing File ➪ Exit (File ➪ Quit) or one of the standard keyboard shortcuts, Ctrl+Q (Command+Q).

In Windows systems, to make sure you're really ready to shut down the program, Dreamweaver asks you to confirm your desire to quit. If you're confident that you won't quit the program accidentally, select the Don't Warn Me Again option to stop this dialog box from reappearing.

You won't receive an opportunity to confirm your choice if you quit from the Site window in Windows or in Macintosh systems. That's because, on Windows, Dreamweaver's Site window and Document window are really separate applications.

Previewing Your Web Pages

When using Dreamweaver or any other Web authoring tool, it's important to constantly check your progress in one or more browsers. Dreamweaver's Document window offers a near-browser view of your Web page, but because of the variations among the different browsers, it's imperative that you preview your page early and often. Dreamweaver offers you easy access to a maximum of 20 browsers — and they're just a function key away.

Note Don't confuse Dreamweaver's Design view with the Preview in Browser feature. In Design view, Dreamweaver can only show you an approximation of how your page will look on the Web but not all aspects — such as links and rollovers — are active. You need to preview and test your page in a variety of browsers to truly see how your page looks and behaves on the Web.

You add a browser to your preview list by selecting File ⇨ Preview in Browser ⇨ Edit Browser List or by choosing the Preview in Browser category from the Preferences dialog box. Both actions open the Preview in Browser Preferences panel. The steps for editing your browser list are described in detail in Chapter 4. Here's a brief recap:

1. Select File ⇨ Preview in Browser ⇨ Edit Browser List.

2. To add a browser (up to 20), click the Add button and fill out the following fields:

   • **Name:** How you want the browser listed.

   • **Application:** Type in the path to the browser program or click the Browse button to locate the browser executable (.EXE) file.

   • **Primary Browser/Secondary Browser:** If desired, select one of these checkboxes to designate the current browser as such.

3. After you've added a browser to your list, you can easily edit or delete it. Choose File ⇨ Preview in Browser ⇨ Edit Browser List as before, and highlight the browser you want to modify or delete.

4. To alter your selection, click the Edit button. To delete your selection, click the Remove button.

5. After you've completed your modifications, click OK to close the dialog box.

Once you've added one or more browsers to your list, you can preview the current page in these browsers. Select File ⇨ Preview in Browser ⇨ BrowserName, where BrowserName indicates the particular program. Dreamweaver saves the page to a temporary file, starts the browser, and loads the page.

Note that in order to view any changes you've made to your Web page under construction, you must select the Preview in Browser menu option again (or press one of the function keys for primary/secondary browser previewing, described in the following paragraph). Clicking the Refresh/Reload button in your browser will not load in any modifications. The temporary preview files are deleted when you quit Dreamweaver.

Tip   Dreamweaver saves preview files with a file namelike this: TMP5c34jymi4q.htm; a unique name is generated with each preview to ensure that the browser does not load the page from the cache. If Dreamweaver unexpectedly quits, these TMP files are not deleted. Feel free to delete any TMP files you find in your site.

You can also use keyboard shortcuts to preview two different browsers, by pressing a function key: Press F12 to preview the current Dreamweaver page in your primary browser, and Ctrl+F12 (Command+F12) to preview the same page in your secondary browser. These are the Primary and Secondary Browser settings you establish in the Preferences/Preview in Browser dialog box, explained in Chapter 4.

In fact, with Dreamweaver's Preview in Browser Preferences you can so easily switch the designations of Primary and Secondary browser that you can use that setup for "debugging" a Web page in any browser, simply by changing the preferences. Go to the Preview in Browser Preferences pane, select the browser you want to use for debugging, and check the appropriate checkbox to designate the browser as Primary or Secondary. In the list of browsers in this Preferences pane, you'll see the indicator of F12 or Ctrl+F12 (Command+F12) appear next to the browser's name.

Tip   In addition to checking your Web page output on a variety of browsers on your system, it's also a good idea to preview the page on other platforms. If you're designing on a Macintosh, try to view your pages on a Windows system, and vice versa. Watch out for some not-so-subtle differences between the two environments, in terms of color rendering (colors in Macs tend to be brighter than in PCs) and screen resolution.

Putting Your Pages Online

The final phase of setting up your Dreamweaver site is publishing your pages to the Web. When you begin this publishing process is up to you. Some Web designers wait until everything is absolutely perfect on the local development site and then upload everything at once. Others like to establish an early connection to the remote site and extend the transfer of files over a longer period of time.

I fall into the latter camp. When I start transferring files at the beginning of the process, I find that I catch my mistakes earlier and avoid having to effect massive changes to the site after everything is up. For example, in developing one large site, I started out using filenames with mixed case, as in ELFhome.html. After publishing some early drafts of a few Web pages, however, I discovered that the host had switched servers; on the new server, filenames had to be all lowercase. Had I waited until the last moment to upload everything, I would have been faced with an unexpected and gigantic search-and-replace job.

Once you've established your local site root — and you've included your remote site's FTP information in the setup — the actual publishing of your files to the Web is a very straightforward process. To transfer your local Web pages to an online site, follow these steps:

1. Choose File ➪ Open Site ➪ Site Name (Site ➪ Open Site ➪ Site Name), where Site Name is the current site.

   The Site window opens, displaying the current site.

2. From the Site window, click the Connect button. (You may need to complete your connection to the Internet prior to choosing the Connect button.)

   Dreamweaver displays a message box showing the progress of the connection.

3. If you didn't enter a password in the Site Information dialog box, or if you entered a password but didn't opt to save it, Dreamweaver asks you to type in your password.

   Once the connection is complete, the directory listing of the remote site appears in the Remote (left-hand by default) pane of the Site window.

4. In the Local (right-hand by default) pane, highlight the HTML files you would like to transfer.

5. Click the Put button at the top of the Site window.

6. Dreamweaver asks if you would like to move the dependent files as well. Select Yes to transfer all embedded graphics and other objects, or No if you'd prefer to move these yourself. You can also select the Don't Ask Me Again box to make transfers of dependent files automatic in the future.

   Dreamweaver displays the progress of the file transfer in the Site window's status bar.

7. When each file transfer is finished, Dreamweaver places a green checkmark next to each file (if File Check In/Out has been enabled in the Site FTP Preferences pane).

8. When you've finished transferring your files, click the Disconnect button.

 Cross-Reference Some files, especially CGI programs, require that you set the file permissions before they can be used. For information about setting file permissions from within Dreamweaver, see Chapter 17.

Remember, the only files you have to highlight for transfer to the remote site are the HTML files. As noted previously, Dreamweaver automatically transfers any dependent files (if you allow it), which means that you'll never forget to move a GIF again! (Nor will you ever move an unnecessary file, such as an earlier version of an image, by mistake.) Moreover, Dreamweaver automatically creates any subfolders necessary to maintain the site's integrity. These two features combined will save you substantial time and worry.

So now your site has been prepped from the planning stages, through the local site root, and onto the Web. Congratulations — all that's left is to fill those pages with insightful content, amazing graphics, and wondrous code. Let's get to it!

Summary

In this chapter, you studied some options for planning your Web site and what you need to do in Dreamweaver to initialize the site. This planning and initialization process is not a detailed one, but there are particular steps to take that can greatly smooth your development path down the road.

✦ Put as much time into planning your site as possible. The more clearly conceived the site, the cleaner the execution.

✦ Set up your local site root in Dreamweaver right away. The local site root is essential for Dreamweaver to properly publish your files to the remote site later.

✦ Preview early, often, and with various browsers. Dreamweaver gives you quick function-key access to a primary and secondary browser. Check your pages frequently in these browsers, and then spend some time checking your pages against other available browsers and browser versions.

✦ Establish an early connection to the Web and use it frequently. You can begin publishing your local site through Dreamweaver's Site window almost immediately.

In the next chapter, you'll learn how to publish your site to the Internet in Dreamweaver.

✦   ✦   ✦

Publishing with the Site Window

Site management is an essential part of a Webmaster's job description. Far from static designs, the Web site is not like a magazine advertisement that you're finished with as soon as you send the file to the printer. Publishing your Web site pages on the Internet is really just the first step in an ongoing — often day-to-day — management task.

Dreamweaver includes an integrated but separate window known as the Site window to handle all your Web management needs. With the Site window, you can do the following:

✦ Transfer files to your remote site from your local development site and back again

✦ Issue system commands to enable CGI programs on the server

✦ Monitor your Web site for broken links and orphaned files

✦ Check a file in or out during team Web development

This chapter covers these site management functions and more. However, before you begin exploring the Site window features, it's helpful to know a little more about site management in Dreamweaver.

Site Management with Dreamweaver

At the simplest level, *site management* means transferring your files from the local drive to a publishing server. This is standard File Transfer Protocol (FTP), and many designers are accustomed to working with tools such as WS_FTP and Fetch. These utilities, however, only help you to move files back and forth. In a medium-to-large Web site, other issues must be addressed. For instance, consider the following:

✦ What happens when a large group is working on a single Web site? What prevents the graphics designer from altering the same file the JavaScript programmer is modifying?

✦ How can you tell which version of your logo is the final one among the 15 working versions in your local site root folder?

✦ Do you have to update all your files every time some change is made to a few? Or can you only update those that have changed? How can you tell which ones have changed?

To help the Dreamweaver developer cope with these issues and avoid the type of frustration they can produce, a useful site management tool is included within Dreamweaver: the Site window. Its key features include the following:

✦ A quick, visual view of the elements of your site on your local and remote directories

✦ Fast drag-and-drop functionality for transferring files with dependent file support

✦ Site management check-in and check-out tools for groups working on files within the same Web site

✦ A Link Checker that helps you identify broken or unused objects being posted to your site

✦ A Site Map that enables you to both visualize your Web site structure and alter it

On Windows systems, the Site window runs as a connected but independent process, so that you can close your document window when you're finished designing and then publish your files to the Web through the Site window.

Note   The Dreamweaver commands related to the Site window features are in different places on the Windows and Macintosh systems. In Windows, the Site window has its own menu bar; all the Windows-oriented references in this chapter refer to this menu. In addition, Dreamweaver includes a Site menu in the Document window that repeats many commands for easy access. Because Macintosh systems don't have a separate menu for a program's individual windows, Dreamweaver organizes the Site functions in a Site category of the main menu bar.

Setting Up a New Site

The first step in developing an effective site — one that links to other Web pages, uses images and library files, and offers other site root–relative links — is, of course, to establish a site. Dreamweaver has made this very easy to do.

Cross-Reference   For complete, detailed information on establishing your initial site, see Chapter 6.

You need to create a folder on your development system that contains the entire HTML, as well as graphics, media, and other files, needed by the site. To create a new site, choose Site ▷ New Site. The Site Definition dialog box opens with the Local Info category selected, as shown in Figure 7-1. Here you find the information and settings for the current site you are developing. Once you've entered this information, you seldom need to modify it.

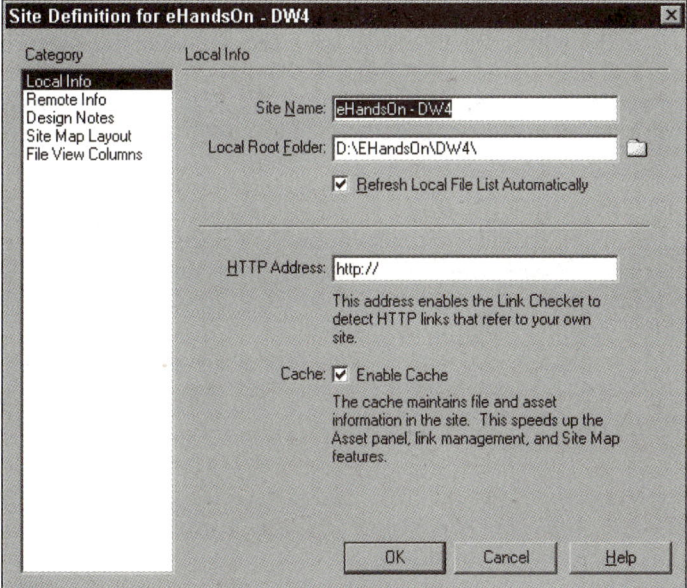

Figure 7-1: The Site Definition dialog box contains settings for the current site you are developing.

The data in the Site Definition dialog box is divided into five categories: Local Info, Remote Info, Design Notes, Site Map Layout, and File View Columns.

Local directory information

The local directory is in a folder on your development system, either on your own hard drive or on a network server.

Site Name

The site name is the name that appears in the Site ➪ Open Site list. The site name is a reference only you need to know, and it can be as fancy as you want. No hard-and-fast rules exist for creating a site name, except you should keep the name simple so you can easily reference it later. In a large Web design firm, you may need to develop more structured methods for naming various clients' Web sites.

Local Root Folder

The Local Root Folder is the location on your hard drive, or in a network folder, where you place your HTML pages, images, plug-in files, and Library items. Remember, the root folder is essential to an effective Dreamweaver site. As you add links to other Web pages and images, Dreamweaver needs to maintain the relative links between files. The benefit of this becomes apparent when you upload your files to a Web server. By maintaining a root-relative relationship, you ensure that all of the files and associated images can transfer seamlessly together onto any Web site. You won't have to go back and replace the code for any broken images.

Refresh Local File List Automatically

When the Refresh Local File List Automatically option is selected, Dreamweaver updates the list every time Dreamweaver or any other program adds a new file. Although it takes a bit more processing power to constantly watch and update the folder, it's a helpful option and I recommend always selecting it. Without the option checked, you need to choose View ➪ Refresh Local (Site ➪ Site Map View ➪ Refresh Local) or use the keyboard shortcut, Shift+F5, to see the latest files.

HTTP Address

The information entered in the HTTP Address field is used when you access the Link Checker. In this field, you enter the remote URL that corresponds to the local root folder, as if it were a regular Web address.

For example, say you are developing a Web site for My Frozen Custard, Inc. In the HTTP Address field, you would enter the URL for the Web site, as follows:

```
http://www.myfrozencustard.com/
```

With this information, the Link Checker can compare absolute addresses embedded in your Web page to see whether those addresses refer to internal or external files.

Cache

Put a checkmark in the Cache checkbox to speed up Dreamweaver's links and site management tasks.

Remote Info

The Remote Info category contains all of the information required for you to post your files to a remote server. The setup allows for any type of host directory. Typically, though, you upload your files to either a Unix or an NT Web server.

From the Remote Info category (see Figure 7-2), choose Local/Network from the Access drop-down menu to enter or select a folder on your hard drive or on the network from which your files will be served. If you're working on a big site in development with a team of Web-builders, you'll find Dreamweaver 4's new connectivity to SourceSafe databases and WebDAV servers extremely helpful. Should you choose either of these options for remote site access, you'll need to select the Settings button that appears and fill out the required information in the displayed dialog box.

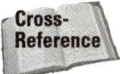

For greater detail on using Dreamweaver with SourceSafe databases or WebDAV servers, see Chapter 35.

Select FTP from the Access drop-down menu to be presented with a dialog box requesting information needed to access your remote site.

If you don't know the name of your FTP host server or any of the other required host site information (directory, login, password, and firewall preferences), contact your ISP or system administrator. If a hosting server is not yet established, keep Server Access set to None.

Figure 7-2: Information entered in the Remote Info category is essential for Dreamweaver to connect with your remote site.

FTP Host

The FTP Host is the name of the server on which you will be placing your files. The names for the host will be something like the following:

```
www.yourdomain.com
ftp.yourdomain.com
```

Do not include the protocol information, such as `http://` or `ftp://`, in the FTP host name.

Host Directory

The host directory is the one in which publicly accessible documents are stored on the server. Your remote site root folder will be a subfolder of the host directory. Here's an example of the host directory information:

```
/usr/www/htdocs/jlowery
```

If you don't know the proper directory path, check with your Web server administrator or ISP.

Login and Password

A login and password are required to transfer your files from your local root folder to the host. Your login is a unique name that tells the host who you are. Only you and the host should know your password. Every time you upload or download a file from the host server, you are asked for your password. If you don't want to have to retype your password each time you log on, just select the Save checkbox next to your password, and Dreamweaver remembers it.

Caution   For security reasons, it is highly recommended that you do not allow anyone to know your password.

Use Passive FTP

During a normal FTP process, one computer (the client) establishes a connection with another (the server) and then requests data to be sent. Firewall-protected servers do not allow the initial connection to be made, so no data can be transferred. Passive FTP establishes the FTP connection through the local software rather than the server. The majority of firewall configurations use passive FTP; check with your network administrator to see if you need it.

Use Firewall

Firewalls are security features used by many companies to prevent unwanted access to internal documents. Many different types of firewalls exist, and all have a multitude of security settings. For instance, some firewalls enable people within a company to move documents back and forth through the firewall without any problems. Other companies will not allow Java or ActiveX controls to be moved through the firewall.

If you have a firewall that requires additional security to upload and download files, you should enable the Use Firewall checkbox in the Site Definition window. Selecting this checkbox requires that you go to Dreamweaver Preferences and fill out additional information on proxy servers. A proxy server enables you to navigate files through a firewall.

To make the appropriate proxy server changes, go to Edit ➪ Preferences and choose the Site category from the Preferences dialog box. This category of settings contains selections for firewall information. Enter the firewall host name and port number, which can be provided to you by your ISP or system administrator. By default, most firewalls use port 21.

Check In/Out

You can enable or disable Dreamweaver's file management features by choosing the Check In/Out option. When you select Enable File Check In and Check Out, additional fields become available. You then can select the Check Out Files While Opening option, which automates the check-out process to some degree.

The name you enter in the Check Out Name field is used to inform others in your group when you have downloaded a file from the host server. Because the Check Out Name is one of several columns of information in the Local and Remote panes of the Site window, it's a good idea to keep the name relatively short. (Your initials are an ideal choice for Check Out Name, if that is appropriate.)

 If you enter your e-mail address in the aptly named field, Dreamweaver presents the check out name as a clickable link that invokes your system's e-mail editor to send a message. The E-mail Address feature enables team members to communicate directly with other team members who may have checked out a particular file.

Integrating Design Notes

Web sites can be complex creations, particularly when worked on by a team of designers, coders, and content providers. Dreamweaver offers a feature aimed at enhancing the communication between various team members: Design Notes. A Design Note can be attached to any Dreamweaver-created page, or any media inserted into a Dreamweaver page, and easily read from within Dreamweaver. Design Notes are also used extensively to facilitate the integration of Flash and Fireworks with Dreamweaver.

To be truly useful, the entire team needs to gain access to the Design Notes. Dreamweaver enables you to maintain the Design Notes on the remote server, as if another dependent file. The preferences in the Define Sites dialog box, shown in Figure 7-3, set up this option, and also give you a simple way to remove all unused Design Notes.

Figure 7-3: Use Design Notes to store information about HTML pages, graphics, or any other Web elements.

Options

Design Notes have only two options. The first option, Maintain Design Notes, enables Design Notes functionality for the site. It must be enabled to add or modify a Design Note for any page within the site. When a file is moved, this option also causes a Design Note to follow its associated file. The second option, Upload Design Notes for Sharing, "gets" or "puts" the Design Note when its associated file is transferred.

Tip   Design note files have an extension of .mno and are stored in a _notes folder. While they physically take up little room, typically under 1K, they greatly enhance your workflow, especially if you're using Fireworks and Flash. I strongly recommend that you keep Maintain Design Notes enabled.

Clean Up

If the Maintain Design Notes option is enabled and a Dreamweaver file is deleted from within Dreamweaver, the associated Design Note is removed also. However, if you delete, move, or rename your HTML files in any other way—with a file manager or other program—the Design Note remains. Select the Clean Up button to remove any Design Notes that no longer have associated HTML files.

Modifying the Site Map

You can control the way that Dreamweaver displays a Site Map in the Site Map Layout category (see Figure 7-4). In the Site Definition dialog box, select Site Map Layout from the Category list to access the Site Map options.

Figure 7-4: You can control what the Site Map shows as well as its overall appearance through the Site Map Layout category.

Home Page

By default, Dreamweaver looks for a file called index.html, index.htm, or default.htm (in that order) in your Local root folder from which to begin creating a Site Map. You can choose another page to appear at the top level of your Site Map by selecting a different file to serve as your home page.

Tip   It's best to include a home page if you plan on using the Site Map feature at all when defining the site. If one is not available, you can just enter the name for the file, like index.htm, in the Home Page field and press Tab; Dreamweaver will create the file for you.

Number of Columns/Column Width

These options (Number of Columns/Column Width) control the way your Site Map is displayed on your screen. You can modify these values in order to make the Site Map fit more easily onto a single page for printing.

Tip By default, the Site Map displays horizontally. You can switch the layout to vertical by changing the Number of Columns field to 1.

Icon Labels

The Icon Labels option enables you to select whether the icons in your Site Map should be displayed using their filenames or their page titles. Page titles are derived from the `<title>` tag in the `<head>` section of an HTML document. While this method can be more descriptive, you have to remember to insert the title, either through the Page Properties dialog box — by revealing the Head Content, selecting the Title icon, and entering the desired text in the Title Property Inspector — or entering it into the Title field of the Document window's toolbar. If you don't assign each page a title, Dreamweaver uses "Untitled Document" as the title.

Options

Checking Display Files Marked as Hidden includes hidden HTML files in your Site Map Layout; checking Display Dependent Files includes non-HTML files, such as graphics image files or external JavaScript files, in your Site Map Layout.

File View Columns

Building a major Web site can be an organizational nightmare. Different teams — consisting of graphic artists, coders, and layout designers — are often working on different sections of the site at the same time. While certain pages are finished, others are in process, or have yet to be drafted. Even relatively small Web-design shops need to track the progress of their various clients' sites in order to be productive.

New Feature   For Web developers, a major organizational advantage, now available in Dreamweaver 4, is the ability to create custom informational columns in the Site window's file view. The File View Columns feature works by storing information in an HTML or other file's Design Note; in essence, with a custom file view column, you can see what's in the Design Note at a glance. File view columns may also be re-ordered to put your project's most important details up front and less necessary built-in columns may be hidden.

Why are custom file view columns important? Let's say your team is working on a large site with a tight deadline. You need to keep track of which pages are completed and which need work. Create a custom file view column called Status, and then list for each file the percentage of completed work, such as 0%, 50%, or 100%. With one click of the Status column header, you can sort all the files, grouping them by the completed percentages, and instantly identifying which files need immediate attention. Add another custom column to include the name of the team member assigned to each page and you've got an instant contact list.

To add a new column in the file view, follow these steps:

1. Choose View ⇨ File View Columns from the Site window on a Windows system or Site ⇨ Site Files View ⇨ File View Columns on a Mac.

   The File View Columns category of the Site Definition dialog box appears.

2. Select the Add button.

   A new entry, initially called untitled, is added to the bottom of the column list.

3. In the Column Name field, enter a unique name to identify your column.

   There are no real restrictions for a column name, but it's best from a practical standpoint to keep them short.

4. In the Associate with Design Note field, enter a custom design note field or choose one of the existing fields from the drop-down list.

5. From the Align option, choose how the information is to be aligned in the column: Left, Center, or Right.

6. Make sure the Show option is selected.

7. To change the order in which your column is displayed on the screen — initially it's the final column, all the way on the right — use the Up and Down buttons to reposition the new column in the list.

   All of the built-in columns, except for Name, can also be moved to a new position. You can also hide a column by selecting it and deselecting the Show option.

8. Click OK when you're done.

With the custom column showing in the file view, enter information for that column in one of the following two ways:

✦ Right-click (control-click) on the filename and choose Design Notes. Then select the All Info tab of the Design Notes dialog box and enter the data in the Value field.

✦ In the file view pane of the Site window, click twice on the custom column for the file in question. The current information in the custom column, if any, will highlight and can be modified directly. Press Enter (Return) when you're done.

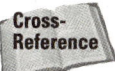
Cross-Reference   To see how else you can use the File View Column feature, turn to Chapter 35.

Using the Site Window

In Dreamweaver, some site commands, such as Put (which transfers a file from your local to remote site), can be called without using the Site window, but the Site window is "home base" for almost all of Dreamweaver's sitewide functions. You can open the Site window by any of the following methods:

✦ Choose Site ⇨ Open Site ⇨ Your Site.

✦ Select the Site button from the Launcher or Show Site from the Mini Launcher.

✦ Choose Window ⇨ Site Files.

✦ Press the keyboard shortcut F8.

The Site window is your vehicle for moving files back and forth between your local and remote folders. Figure 7-5 illustrates the various parts of the Site window.

Figure 7-5: The Site window is used for transferring files to and from your remote Web server.

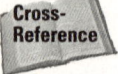

Cross-Reference   For detailed information on the Site Window preferences, see Chapter 4.

Remote Site and Local Root windows

The Site window is arranged in two main windows: By default, the remote site is on the left and the local root directory is on the right. These two windows enable you to view all the files contained within the two directories.

Another helpful view enables you to see which files have been most recently added or modified since the last FTP transfer. Choose either Select Newer Local or Select Newer Remote in the Edit menu (or on a Macintosh, Site ⇨ Site Files View ⇨ Select Newer Local or Site Files View ⇨ Select Newer Remote). Dreamweaver compares the files within the two folders to see which ones have been saved since the last FTP session. The newer files are highlighted and can be easily transferred by selecting the Get or Put button (described in a later section).

In large sites, the Select Newer Remote operation can take a fairly long time to complete. If possible, selecting individual folders to be checked, while leaving the others unscanned, can speed up the process.

Connect/Disconnect button

The Connect/Disconnect button to the right of the Site drop-down list enables you to begin or end a live session with a remote host server. By clicking the Connect button, you start a new FTP session. You must have a way to connect to the Internet, and you must have a Remote server defined, when you select Connect. You won't see any information in the Remote Site pane until you connect to it.

After Dreamweaver has made the connection to your remote site—as identified in the Site Information dialog box—the Connect button becomes the Disconnect button. To end your FTP session with the host server, click the Disconnect button.

You can monitor all of your site management transactions by looking at the FTP Log. Select Window ⇨ Site FTP Log (Windows) or Site ⇨ FTP Log (Macintosh) from within the Site window. A new window pops up and shows you all your transactions as you perform them.

Get and Put buttons

Two of the most useful controls on the Site window are the Get and Put buttons. The Get button retrieves selected files and folders from the host server. The Put button transfers selected files from your local root directory to the host server. Dreamweaver offers several ways to transfer files in the Site window during an active FTP session.

To transfer one or more files from the local directory to the host server, use one of the following methods:

✦ Select the files from the Local Folder pane and drag them over to the Remote Folder pane.

✦ Use the keyboard shortcut — select the files and press Ctrl+Shift+U (Command+Shift+U).

✦ Highlight the files and choose Site ➪ Put.

✦ Select the files in the Local Folder pane and click the Put button.

If the file you are transferring has any dependent files, such as inserted images or Java applets, the Dependent Files dialog box (see Figure 7-6) asks if you want to include dependent files. If you select Yes, all such files are transferred. Select No to move only the file you selected.

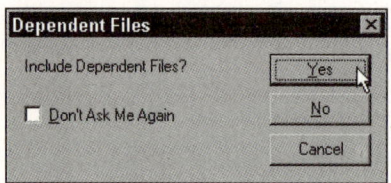

Figure 7-6: After selecting the HTML files, say Yes to the Dependent Files dialog box to transfer all the needed files.

Tip   The Dependent Files dialog box includes a checkbox that asks if you want to be reminded of this feature again. If you choose this option, but later want the reminder to reappear, you can select either of the Dependent Files options from the Site category of Preferences. To bring up the Dependent Files dialog box on a case-by-case basis, press Alt (Option) when selecting the Get, Put, Check In, or Check Out buttons.

To transfer one or more files from the host server to the local folder, use one of these techniques:

✦ Select the files you want from the Remote Site pane and drag them over to the Local Folder pane.

✦ Use the keyboard shortcut — select the files and press Ctrl+Shift+D (Command+Shift+D).

✦ Highlight the files and select Site ➪ Get.

✦ Select the files in the remote directory and click the Get button.

Caution   If you select either Site ➪ Get or the Get button without having selected any files in the Remote Site pane, all the files from your host server are moved. Dreamweaver does warn you, however.

Refresh button

As the name implies, the Refresh button re-reads the currently selected directory, whether locally or remotely. This can be useful when other people are working on the same site at the same time — refreshing your screen enables you to see if any additional files have been added or removed during your FTP session. You also need to refresh the Site window if you have modified a file during the FTP session. If you have enabled the Refresh Local Files Automatically option in the Define Site preferences, you only have to use this button to refresh the remote files. The Refresh button is found to the right of the Connect button.

The View (Windows) or Site ➪ Site Files View (Macintosh) menu options also enable you to refresh the two windows. You can choose from two refresh commands: Refresh Local and Refresh Remote.

Stop Current Task button

Use the Stop Current Task button to halt the current transfer of files in an active FTP session. The Stop Current Task button is the octagonal red X button located in the lower-right corner of the Site window; it appears only while you are actually moving files.

Check Out/Check In buttons

The Check In/Check Out buttons, which are visible to the right of the Get and Put buttons only if you've selected the Check In/Out category in the Site Definition window (as previously shown in Figure 7-2), enable a user to officially check out an item from either the local or host server. The Check Out button provides a visual cue to everyone with access to the server that a file is currently in use. Details on how to use this feature are covered in the next section.

Checking a File In and Out

Your control over the files used for your Web site is very important if you are developing a site with a team. On larger sites, the various Webmaster chores — design, programming, and management — are distributed among several people. Without proper check-in and check-out procedures, it's easy for the same HTML page to get updated by more than one person, and you can wind up with incompatible versions.

Dreamweaver's Check In/Check Out facility solves this file-control problem by permitting only one person at a time to modify a Web page or graphic. Once a file has been checked out — accessed by someone — the file must be checked in again before another person using the Site window can download it and work on it.

Dreamweaver handles the functionality of Check In/Check Out very efficiently. Whenever you establish an active FTP session between your local root folder and the remote server, any files you get or put are displayed with a green checkmark. If other people in your group are also moving files back and forth, their transferred files are marked with a red checkmark. This method provides a quickly recognized, visual representation of the status of files you and your teammates are handling. Files that do not have either a red or green checkmark are not currently checked out by anyone and are available to work on.

If you want to see who is working on what, you can view user names in the Remote Site window. (You may have to scroll the window horizontally to see the column.) The name shown is the Check Out name that they use for logging on to the remote server. The Check Out name is entered through the Site Information dialog box.

Knowing who is working on what, and when, is a good control mechanism, but to really prevent duplication, site file control has to go one step further. Under Dreamweaver's Check In/Check Out system, when you transfer a file from your local root folder to the host server, the file on your local folder becomes read-only. Making the file read-only enables others to see the Web page but prevents anyone else from overwriting the file. The file must be checked in again before others can modify it.

Dreamweaver accomplishes Check In/Check Out by using a set of special files. When a file is checked out, a text file of the same filename but with the extension .lck is placed on the server. The .lck file contains the name of the user who checked out the file, as well as the date and the time that the file was checked out. The .lck files cannot be viewed in the Site window display but can be seen when a third-party FTP program is used.

 Caution   Unfortunately, Dreamweaver is not able to make checked-out files in the host server read-only. This means someone in your group using an FTP program other than the Site window could easily overwrite the checked-out file on the server.

To check out one or more files, use any of the following methods:

✦ Select the files you want to transfer and then click the Check Out button at the top of the Site window. All the files are downloaded into your local folder and checked out in your name (denoted by a green checkmark).

✦ Select the files and choose Site ➪ Check Out.

✦ Select the files and use the keyboard shortcut Ctrl+Alt+Shift+D (Command+Option+Shift+D).

To check one or more files back in, do either of the following:

✦ Select the files you want to transfer and then click the Check In button at the top of the Site window. All of the selected files will be uploaded from your local folder to the remote site, and the green checkmark will be removed from their names.

✦ Select the checked-out files and choose Site ⇨ Check In.

✦ Select the files and use the keyboard shortcut Ctrl+Alt+Shift+U (Command+Option+Shift+U).

To change the checked-out status of a file, use one of these methods:

✦ Select the file that's checked out and then click the Check In button at the top of the Site window.

✦ Select the file and choose Site ⇨ Undo Check Out.

Synchronizing Local and Remote Sites

The necessity of having sets of files stored both locally and remotely often leads to confusion over which file is the most current. The problem is far more likely to occur if you're working in a team situation where numerous people are maintaining the same site.

Dreamweaver includes a one-step command to solve this local-remote dilemma: Synchronize. Found under the Site menu in Windows and on the menu bar in Macintosh systems, the Synchronize command ensures that the most current version of the same files is on both systems. Synchronize can also delete files on one site that do not appear on another. You can apply the Synchronize command sitewide or to selected files or folders.

To synchronize your files, follow these steps:

1. If you want to synchronize only selected files or folders, select those in the local pane of the Site window.

2. Choose Site ⇨ Synchronize.

The Synchronize Files dialog box opens, as shown in Figure 7-7.

Figure 7-7: The Synchronize command makes sure that both the local and remote sites contain the same files.

3. To synchronize the full site, select Entire *Site Name* Site from the Synchronize list, where *Site Name* is the current site. Otherwise, choose Selected Local Files Only.

4. Set the direction of the synchronization:

   • **Put Newer Files to Remote:** Examines local files and transfers those with more recent modification dates to the remote server.

   • **Get Newer Files from Remote:** Examines remote files and transfers those with more recent modification dates to the local server.

   • **Get and Put Newer Files:** Transfers the most current versions of all files to and from both sites.

5. By selecting the Delete Remote Files Not on Local Drive option, you can remove any local files without a corresponding file on the server side when using the Get Newer Files from Remote direction. If the Put Newer Files to Remote direction is chosen with the Delete option, files on the remote site without a local equivalent are removed.

Caution   As with all file deletions, these operations cannot be undone. Use this feature with extreme care.

6. When you're ready, click Preview to begin the process.

   Dreamweaver compares the local and remote sites and begins displaying files in a new Site dialog box for confirmation, as shown in Figure 7-8. If no files are mismatched, Dreamweaver tells you that no synchronization is necessary.

Figure 7-8: Confirm files to get, put, or to be deleted during the Synchronization process in the Site dialog box.

7. Deselect any file for action by removing its checkmark from the Action column.

8. Click OK when you're ready.

Dreamweaver displays the process of the synchronization in the dialog box and the status bar of the Site window.

9. When the synchronization is complete, you can keep a record of the changes by selecting the Save Log button; if you do, Dreamweaver asks for a file location. When you're done, select the Close button.

Caution On Windows, if you have Dreamweaver windows open other than just the Site window, the Site dialog box may not appear on top of the Site window. Select the other Dreamweaver windows to find the Site dialog box.

Synchronization is a powerful tool in Dreamweaver's site management arsenal. However, care needs to be taken when first using the feature to make sure that team members' system clocks are in sync.

Checking Links

During a Web site's development, hundreds of different files and links are often referenced from within the HTML code. Unfortunately, it's not uncommon for a user to enthusiastically follow a link only to encounter the dreaded Web server error 404: File Not Found. Broken links are one of a Webmaster's most persistent headaches, because a Web page may have not only internal links pointing to other pages on the Web site, but external links as well — over which the Webmaster has no control.

Orphaned files constitute a parallel nightmare for the working Web developer. An orphaned file is one that is included in the local or remote site but is no longer actively referenced by any Web page. Orphaned files take up valuable disk space and can erroneously be transferred from an old site to a new one.

Dreamweaver includes, for the Web designer, a useful feature to ease the labor in solving both of these problems: the Link Checker. The Link Checker command can be used to check a single page, selected pages, a subfolder, or an entire site. Once the Link Checker has completed its survey, you can view broken links, external files (links outside the site, such as absolute references and mailto: links), and orphaned files. You can also repair broken links immediately or save the Link Checker results in a file for later viewing.

To check for links, follow these steps:

1. Make sure that the most current versions of the files have been saved.

2. To check a single document from within Dreamweaver, open the file and then choose File ➪ Check Links, or use the keyboard shortcut Shift+F8.

3. To check for links on an entire site from within Dreamweaver, choose Site ➪ Check Links Sitewide or use the keyboard shortcut Ctrl+F8 (Command+F8).

After Dreamweaver checks all the links on your page or site, it opens the Link Checker dialog box. The Link Checker dialog box, shown in Figure 7-9, provides a summary report of the broken links, external links, and when an entire site is reviewed, orphaned files. You can also use the Save button to store for future reference, in a tab-delimited text file, a report of the problems that the Link Checker has found.

Figure 7-9: The Link Checker dialog box helps you determine which files have broken links and then fix the links directly.

When you list broken links, you can observe any file that is included as a link, inserted as an image, or embedded in the page, but which cannot be located. If you want to fix the broken link, you can do so by double-clicking the highlighted broken-link file. This brings up the file in Dreamweaver, where you can fix any problems using the Property Inspector. You can use the Property Inspector to locate the Src attribute. To open the page from the Link Checker, double-click the Dreamweaver icon next to the broken link.

You can also fix the link directly in the Link Checker window by following these steps:

1. Run the Link Checker command, either for the entire site or a single Web page.

2. In the Link Checker window, select the path and filename of the broken link you want to repair.

3. Enter the correct path for the missing file.

You can also access the Link Checker for both your local and remote folders. After you've selected your files or folders, choose File ➪ Check Links, from the main Dreamweaver menu, to check either the selected files or the entire Web site. Or, you can right-click (Control+click) any of the selected files to display the shortcut menu and choose the Check Link options from there.

Launching External Editors

As Web pages grow in complexity, many different types of media are involved in the creation of a page. Graphic editors, audio editors, word processors, spreadsheet programs, and database systems are all used in the creation and modification of files that can be included on a Web page — and the list grows daily. With Dreamweaver 4's capability to invoke editors for any file type, the workflow has been greatly simplified.

In Dreamweaver, you can assign an editor to any file type — actually you can assign multiple editors to the same file type for maximum flexibility. Because the editors are assigned according to file extension rather than kind of file, you can associate different editors for every different graphic format, if you so choose.

To launch a file's primary editor from the Site window, just double-click the filename. If you have multiple editors assigned to a file type, you can open the file with an alternative editor by right-clicking (Control+clicking) the filename and choosing the editor from the Open With menu option. There's even a Browse option under the Open With menu to enable you to select an unassigned editor.

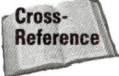

To learn how to set up editors for any media type, see the "External Editor Preferences" section in Chapter 4.

You may note that certain editors are preassigned on Windows systems. For example, on my system, if I double-click any .zip file, WinZip loads the archive. Dreamweaver recognizes file extension associations registered on your system. If a file extension has a particular association, it's listed under the Type category in the Site window. My file chap07.zip, for instance, is shown to be a WinZip file.

Macintosh users should check to see if the desired editor opens when the file is double-clicked before assigning new editors in Dreamweaver. On Macintosh, Dreamweaver uses system assignments through creator codes, if available.

Working with the Site Map

A Web site consists primarily of pages linked to other pages, which in turn can be linked to more pages. The more complex the site, the more difficult it becomes to comprehend — or remember — the entire structure when looking at just a directory listing.

With Dreamweaver, you can easily view your entire Web site and its links as a hierarchical tree using the Site Map feature. Not only do problems such as broken links jump out at you — after all, they're depicted in red — but also the Site Map can give you a much needed overview of the entire site. Poor site design can lead to visitors getting "lost" or frustrated with the number of links it takes to get to an important page. Dreamweaver's Site Map gives you a visual reference and enables you to create the structure for entire sites in a point-and-click environment.

The Site Map is a graphical representation of your site, with all its Web pages symbolized by icons, as shown in Figure 7-10. The Site Map resembles both an organizational chart and a flow chart. The Web site's home page is shown at the top of the chart. A link from one page to another is represented by a connecting line with an arrowhead. Any document, other than the home page, that is linked to additional pages indicates these pages with a plus or minus symbol in Windows systems and a right or down arrow in Macintosh systems. By default, Dreamweaver displays your Site Map only two levels deep. Selecting the plus/minus (arrow) symbols shows and hides the view of the linked pages on deeper levels.

Figure 7-10: Clicking the Site Map icon in the Site window brings up a graphical representation of your site.

To open the Site Map from the Document window, choose Window ⇨ Site Map or use the keyboard shortcut Alt+F8 (Option+F8). If the Site window is open, you can select the Site Map button to bring up the Site Map. The Site Map button has two settings, which you can activate by clicking and holding down the corresponding button. The Map Only setting displays just the Site Map. The Map and Files setting shows the Site Map in one pane of the Site window and the Local Files pane in the other.

The Site Map represents internal HTML pages with Dreamweaver page icons. If the link is good, the name is in blue type; if the link is broken, it's red. External files — files on another site — and special links, such as a `mailto:` or `javascript:` link, are indicated with globes. Initially, the Site Map displays only the HTML files, and not any hidden or dependent files, in a site. (Hidden and dependent files are covered later in this section.)

If your site has enabled Dreamweaver's Check In/Check Out features, you see additional symbols on the Site Map. A file checked out by you is indicated by a green checkmark. If someone else has checked out the file, the checkmark is red. It's not uncommon for teams to prevent an important Web page from being altered by making it read-only (Windows) or locking it (Macintosh). Such files are noted with a lock symbol.

To view a Site Map of your site, it must be in a local folder. To view a Site Map of a remote site, you must first download it to a local folder.

Storyboarding with the Site Map

Increasingly, Web designers lay out the structure of their sites in a process called storyboarding before filling in the details with text, image, and media content. This approach is all but essential on larger sites where development is divided among many people. In many ways, laying out the site's structure ahead of the content makes the content phase go much faster. You can, for example, pick an existing page (even if it is empty of content) from the Select File dialog box when building your links, rather than entering a nonexistent page's filename in the Link text box — and then trying to remember to create it later.

All you need to begin building your site with the Site Map is a single file, typically the site's home page. This home page is then defined as such in the Site Map Layout category of the Site Definition dialog box.

To create a Web site structure from the Site Map, follow these steps:

1. Open the Site Map by choosing Window ➪ Site Map or one of the other methods previously described.

2. Select the icon of the site's home page.

3. Choose Site ➪ Link to a New File (Site ➪ Site Map View ➪ Link to a New File). You can also right-click (Ctrl+click) the page's icon and choose Link to New File from the shortcut menu. Or use the key shortcut: Ctrl+Shift+N (Command+Shift+N).

   The Link to New File dialog box appears, as shown in Figure 7-11.

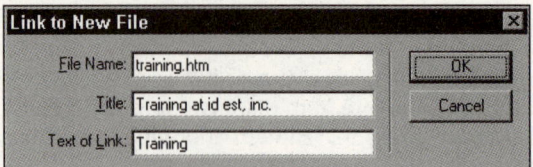

Figure 7-11: Use the Site Map to build the Web site's structure by creating new linked pages in one operation.

4. In the Link to New File dialog box, enter the correct filename, with an extension such as .htm or .html, in the File Name text box. Press Tab to move to the next text box.

5. Enter a title for the new page in the Title text box. Press Tab.

6. Enter the descriptive word or phrase to appear as a link on the original page in the Text of Link text box. Select OK or press Enter (Return) when you're done.

   The HTML page is created, and an icon for the new page appears, with a line connecting it to the original page.

7. To add another link to the home page, select the home page icon again and repeat Steps 3 through 6.

8. To add a new link to the newly created page, select its icon and repeat Steps 3 through 6.

When text links are added to a page, they are placed at the bottom of an existing page, one after another in the same line, like a text-only navigation bar. If the page is new, the text links are naturally the only items on the page.

Connecting to existing pages

Adding existing files to the Site Map is even easier than adding a new file, especially if the file to which you're linking is already in the same site. Part of building a Web-like structure is connecting from one page to another. With the Site Map, this is literally a drag-and-drop affair.

When an HTML icon is selected in the Site Map, a Point to File icon appears. The Point to File feature on the Site Map is basically used the same way it is on the Property Inspectors — just click the symbol and drag your pointer to another file. You can point and link to files in the current site whether or not they're already in the Site Map.

To link to a file that's in the current site but not on the Site Map (in other words, a file that's not linked to the home page or any connected pages), it's best to have both the Site Map and the Local Files panes displayed. To show both panes, select and hold down the Site Map button and then choose Map and Files from the drop-down list. Next, in the Site Map pane, select the file you want to link from—and a Point to File icon appears. Click and drag the Point to File icon from the Site Map to the Local Files pane to select the linking page. A line is drawn from the Point to File icon to the selected file, as shown in Figure 7-12. When your pointer is over the desired file, release the mouse button. The link is added, with a new icon appearing on the Site Map, and a text link is added to the originating page.

Figure 7-12: Quickly link to an existing file with Dreamweaver's Point to File feature.

If you're linking from one Site Map page to another, the Point to File icon is handy. Just select the originating page's icon and drag its Point to File symbol to the page you want to link to. Rather than draw another line across the screen—which would quickly render the Site Map screen indecipherable with crisscrossing lines—links to existing Site Map files are shown in italics.

Several other methods exist for linking to an existing file. First, you can open a Select File dialog box by selecting the originating file and then choosing Site ➪ Link to Existing File (Site ➪ Site Map View ➪ Link to an Existing File). The keyboard short-cut for this command is Ctrl+Shift+K (Command+Shift+K). You can also invoke the command by choosing Link to an Existing File from the shortcut menu, brought up by right-clicking (Control+clicking) the originating file's Site Map icon. Any of these techniques opens the Select File dialog box to enable you to browse for your file, which is useful for selecting files not in the current site.

If you want to drag and drop external files to create a link, you can use the Site Map in combination with the Windows Explorer or Finder, depending on your operating system. Instead of pointing from the originating file to the linked file, you drag the name or icon representing the external file from Windows Explorer (Finder) and drop it on the Site Map icon of the originating page. To accomplish this, it's best to either have the Site Map and Windows Explorer (Finder) windows side by side or, if they are overlapping, have the Windows Explorer (Finder) window in front.

Modifying links

If you have spent any time in Web site design and management, you know nothing is written in stone. Luckily, Dreamweaver 4 makes changing a link from one page to another a breeze and handles the tedious task of updating changes in all linked pages. Moreover, if you have multiple pages linking to a single page, you can make all the pages in the Web site link to a different page.

To change a link from one page to another, follow these steps:

1. Select the icon of the linked page you want to alter in the Site Map.

2. Choose Site ➪ Change Link (Site ➪ Site Map View ➪ Change Link) or use the keyboard shortcut Ctrl+L (Command+L).

   The Select File dialog box opens.

3. Enter the path and filename in the File Name text box or select the Browse (Choose) button to locate the file. Click OK when you've selected your file.

   Dreamweaver displays the Update Files dialog box with all the connecting pages, as shown in Figure 7-13.

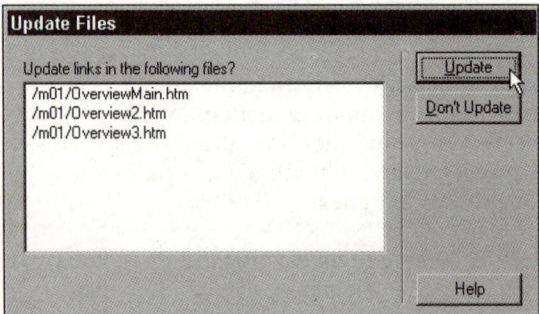

Figure 7-13: Changing a link in the Site Map brings up the Update Files dialog box.

4. To change the link in all the files, choose the Update button.

5. To change the link in some of the files, select the files first, using either the Shift+click or Ctrl+click (Command+click) method, and then choose the Update button.

6. To cancel the link change, choose the Don't Update button.

If you have multiple pages linking to a single page that you want to alter, you can change a link sitewide. Simply select the icon for the linked page you want to modify and choose Site ➪ Change Link Sitewide. As with the Change Link command, the Update Files dialog box opens; the balance of the procedure remains the same.

Tip

I recommend that you enable the Refresh Local File List Automatically option found in the Define Sites dialog box. Dreamweaver picks up changes made inside of its own program and outside of it — even the Site Map view is updated when a change is made on a page.

Deleting links

You can delete a link from one page in several ways. First, select the icon and then do any of the following:

✦ Press the Delete key (Windows only).

✦ Choose Site ➪ Remove Link (Site ➪ Site Map View ➪ Remove Link).

✦ Press Ctrl+Shift+L (Command+Shift+L).

✦ Right-click (Control+click) the icon and, from the shortcut menu, choose Remove Link.

In all cases, the link is deleted without confirmation, and the deletion cannot be undone.

Note

Deleting a link does not delete the file itself, just the link. For the text link, the href attribute is eliminated, but the actual text remains.

Changing titles

Dreamweaver 4 gives you an easy way to change a Web page's title right in the Site Map. Before you can use this feature, however, you must be sure the titles are used to identify the icons, rather than the filenames. Choose View ➪ Show Page Titles (Site ➪ Site Map View ➪ Show Page Titles) or use the keyboard shortcut, Ctrl+Shift+T (Command+Shift+T), to switch to a title view.

To retitle a Web page, click the title twice, slowly — make sure you don't double-click the title, which will open the file. Alternatively, you can select the icon and then click the title. You can also select the icon and then choose File ➪ Rename (Site ➪ Rename) from the menu. In Windows, F2 is the key shortcut. All of these methods make the title an editable field that you can then modify.

Modifying pages through the Site Map

Once you've created and refined your site structure, you're ready to begin adding the content. The Site Map enables you to open a single page or a collection of pages. You can even quickly locate the text or graphic that serves as the source for the link in the connecting page.

Open a page in Dreamweaver's Document window for editing by double-clicking the page's icon in the Site Map. To open more than one page, you must first select all icons. Multiple files can be selected by selecting one file and then Shift+clicking the additional files. Another method of multiple selection is to click into an empty area in the Site Map and then drag a rectangle around the desired files. After all the needed files are selected, choose File ➪ Open Selection (Site ➪ Open), and the key shortcut is Ctrl+Alt+Shift+O (Command+Option+Shift+O). Every file opens in a separate Dreamweaver Document window.

Occasionally, you need to go right to the source of a link. Dreamweaver 4 enables you to open the connecting page and instantly select the actual link used to make the connection. To view the actual text or graphic used to make a link, first select the file's icon in the Site Map. Then, choose Site ➪ Open Source of Link (Site ➪ Site Map View ➪ Open Source of Link). Dreamweaver loads the page containing the link, opens the Property Inspector, and selects the link.

Altering the home page

As noted earlier, the Site Map assigns a home page to use as the base for its organization. As with most items in Dreamweaver, this assignation can be changed. But why would you want to change a Web site's home page? One of the primary purposes for the Site Map is to provide a visual representation of a site's structure — one that can easily be presented to a client for discussion. You can set up multiple views of a site, each with its own structure, by just switching the home page.

You can replace the home page with an existing page or a new one. To create a new page and make it the home page, select Site ➪ New Home Page (Site ➪ Site Map View ➪ New Home Page). The New Home Page dialog box opens with two fields to fill out: File Name and Title. After you enter the needed information, the file is created, and the icon appears by itself in the Site Map. Now you can use the Link to Existing File and Link to New features to build your new site organization.

To change the home page to an existing file, choose Site ➪ Set as Home Page (Site ➪ Site Map View ➪ Set as Home Page). The Select File dialog box opens and enables you to choose a new file. Once you've selected a file, the Site Map is recreated using the new file as a base and displaying any existing links.

Viewing the Site Map

The more complex the site, the more important it is to be able to view the Site Map in different ways. To cut down on the number of pages showing, Dreamweaver 4 enables you to hide any pages you choose. For maximum detail, you can also display all the dependent files (such as a page's graphics) in the Site Map. You even have the option of temporarily limiting the view to a particular "branch" of the Site Map. Dreamweaver also enables you to zoom out to get the big picture of a particularly large site or save the Site Map as a graphic.

Tip   If the Site Map columns are too narrow to see the full title or filename, use the ToolTips feature. Enabling View ➪ Tool Tips (Site ➪ Tool Tips) causes Dreamweaver to display the full text of the title or filename in a ToolTip box when your pointer passes over the name.

Working with hidden and dependent files

Web sites are capable of containing several hundred, if not several thousand, pages. In these situations, the Site Map can become overcrowded. Dreamweaver can mark any file (and its associated linked files) as hidden with a single command, View ➪ Show/Hide Link (Site ➪ Site Map View ➪ Show/Hide Link). The key shortcut is Ctrl+Shift+Y (Command+Shift+Y). The Show/Hide Link command is a toggle — applying it a second time to a file removes the "hidden" designation.

To see previously hidden files, choose View ➪ Show Files Marked as Hidden (Site ➪ Site Map View ➪ Show Files Marked as Hidden). Hidden files made visible are displayed in italics.

Dependent files include any image, external style sheet, or media file (such as a Flash movie). By default, dependent files are not displayed in the Site Map; however, you can opt to view them by choosing View ➪ Show Dependent Files (Site ➪ Site Map View ➪ Show Dependent Files). Once visible on the Site Map, you can send any image to its designated image editor by double-clicking its icon. You can also open the Styles panel by double-clicking any external CSS file.

Focusing on part of a Site Map

Most of the time, the overall view, centered on the Web site's home page, is most useful. Sometimes, though, you want to examine a section of the site in greater detail. Dreamweaver enables you to set any page to be treated like a temporary home page or root, ignoring all linking pages above it.

To view just a portion of your Web site, first select the page you wish to choose as the new root. Next, choose View ➪ View As Root (Site ➪ Site Map View ➪ View As Root) or use the keyboard shortcut Ctrl+Shift+R (Command+Shift+R). The Site Map now depicts your selected file as if it were the home page. Notice also that the Site Navigation bar has changed, as shown in Figure 7-14. The Site Navigation bar shows the actual home page and any pages that have been chosen as roots, separated by right-pointing arrows. You can switch from one root to another, or to the actual home page, by clicking its icon in the Site Navigation bar.

Site Navigation bar

Figure 7-14: To view a section of your Site Map in detail, use the View As Root command.

Zooming out of your Site Map

What do you do when your site is so big that you can't see it all in one screen? Dreamweaver provides a Zoom feature that enables you to pull back for a more encompassing view. The Site Map Zoom button is located on the far left of the Site Window's status bar. Selecting the Zoom button reveals the magnification options to choose from: 100%, 75%, 50%, 25%, and 12%.

Tip   If you find that Dreamweaver is displaying page icons only, with no filenames or titles, you can expand the column width in the layout. Choose View ➪ Layout (Site ➪ Site Map View ➪ Layout) and change the value in the Column Width text box to a higher number. The default column width is 125 pixels.

Converting the Site Map into a graphic

Web designers like to believe that the whole world is wired and on the Web, but in truth, we're not there yet. Sometimes it's necessary to present a client or other interested party with a printout of a site design. Dreamweaver makes it possible to take a snapshot of the current Site Map and save it as a graphic file that can then be inserted into another program for printing—or attached to an e-mail for easy transmission.

To convert the Site Map into a graphic in Windows, choose File ➪ Save Site Map and then choose either BMP or PNG from the drop-down box in the Save box. On the Macintosh, choose Site ➪ Site Map View ➪ Save Site Map, and then the menu flies out to give you two file type options: Save Site Map as PICT or Save Site Map as JPEG.

When you save a Site Map as a graphic, the image is saved at the size necessary to contain all the displayed icons. Figure 7-15 shows a 352@ts1,118 pixel-sized graphic, saved from a Site Map, in Fireworks.

Figure 7-15: This Site Map image, ready for editing in Fireworks, was created in Dreamweaver.

Summary

With the Site window and Dreamweaver's site management tools, a group or an individual Web designer can manage even large and diverse sites.

✦ Setting up a new site is an essential element in managing a Dreamweaver Web site. Without the root directory for the local files, Dreamweaver cannot properly manage the Web pages and associated links.

✦ The Site window enables you to drag and drop files from the host server to the local root folder.

✦ All file check-in and check-out functions for teams can be handled through the Site window.

✦ Broken links can be quickly found and fixed with the Link Checker. You can also find orphaned files and identify external links.

✦ With Dreamweaver 's Synchronize command, keeping your local and remote sites in sync is easier than ever.

✦ Dreamweaver's Site Map enables you to quickly visualize your overall site structure.

✦ The Site Map is also useful for creating new pages and their associated links. You can storyboard the entire site structure — links and all — before adding any content.

In the next chapter, you'll see how to use Dreamweaver to begin coding your Web pages.

✦   ✦   ✦

Using Basic HTML in Dreamweaver

Understanding How HTML Works

In a perfect world, you could lay out the most complex Web site with a visual authoring tool and never have to see the HTML, much less code in it. Dreamweaver takes you a long way toward this goal—in fact, you can create many types of Web pages using only Dreamweaver's Document window. As your pages become more complex, however, you will probably need to tweak your HTML just a tad.

This chapter gives you a basic understanding of how HTML works and gives you the specific building blocks you need to begin creating Web pages. Also in this chapter, you get your first look at a Dreamweaver 4 innovation: the new Code view for altering the code, side-by-side with the visual environment. The other Dreamweaver-specific material in this chapter—which primarily describes how Dreamweaver sets and modifies a page's properties—is suitable for even the most accomplished Web designers. Armed with these fundamentals, you are ready to begin your exploration of Web page creation.

The Structure of an HTML Page

The simplest explanation of how HTML works derives from the full expansion of its acronym: HyperText Markup Language. *HyperText* refers to one of the World Wide Web's main properties—the capability to jump from one page to another, no matter where the pages are located on the Web. *Markup Language* means that a Web page is really just a heavily annotated text file. The basic building blocks of HTML, such as `<strong>` and `<p>`, are known as markup elements, or tags. The terms *element* and *tag* are used interchangeably.

An HTML page, then, is a set of instructions (the tags) suggesting to your browser how to display the enclosed text and images. The browser knows what kind of page it is handling based on the tag that opens the page, <html>, and the tag that closes the page, </html>. The great majority of HTML tags come in such pairs, in which the closing tag always has a forward slash before the keyword. Two examples of tag pairs are: <p>...</p> and <title>...</title>. A few important tags are represented by a single element: the image tag <img>, for example.

The HTML page is divided into two primary sections: the <head> and the <body>. Information relating to the entire document goes in the <head> section: the title, description, keywords, and any language subroutines that may be called from within the <body>. The content of the Web page is found in the <body> section. All the text, graphics, embedded animations, Java applets, and other elements of the page are found between the opening <body> and the closing </body> tags.

When you start a new document in Dreamweaver, the basic format is already laid out for you. Listing 8-1 shows the code from a Dreamweaver blank Web page.

Listing 8-1: **The HTML for a New Dreamweaver Page**

```
<html>
<head>
<title>Untitled Document</title>
<meta http-equiv="Content-Type" content="text/html; charset=iso-8859-1">
</head>

<body bgcolor="#FFFFFF" text="#000000">

</body>
</html>
```

Notice how the <head>...</head> pair is separate from the <body>...</body> pair, and that both are contained within the <html>...</html> tags.

Also notice that the <body> tag has two additional elements:

```
bgcolor="#FFFFFF"
```

and

```
text="#000000"
```

These types of elements are known as *attributes*. Attributes modify the basic tag and either can be equal to a value or can stand alone; in this example, the first attribute, bgcolor, is set to a hexadecimal number that represents the color white and the second, `text`, is set to the hexadecimal value for black. Thus, this attribute sets the background color of the body — the page — to white and the default text color to black. Not every tag has attributes, but when they do, the attributes are specific.

One last note about an HTML page: You are free to use carriage returns, spaces, and tabs as needed to make your code more readable. The interpreting browser ignores all but the included tags and text to create your page. Some minor, browser-specific differences in interpretation of these elements are pointed out throughout the book, but by and large, you can indent or space your code as you desire.

Defining <head> Elements

Information pertaining to the Web page overall is contained in the `<head>` section of an HTML page. Browsers read the `<head>` to find out how to render the page — for example, is the page to be displayed using the Western, the Chinese, or some other character set? Search engine spiders also read this section to quickly glean a summary of the page.

When you begin inserting JavaScript (or code from another scripting language such as VBScript) into your Web page, all the subroutines and document-wide declarations go into the `<head>` area. Dreamweaver uses this format by default when you insert a JavaScript behavior.

Dreamweaver enables you to insert, view, and modify `<head>` content without opening an HTML editor. Dreamweaver's View Head Content capability enables you to work with `<meta>` tags and other `<head>` HTML code as you do with the regular content in the visual editor.

Establishing page properties

When you first start Dreamweaver, your default Web page is untitled, with no background image but a plain white background. You can change all these properties and more through Dreamweaver's Page Properties dialog box.

New Feature
You can also change the document title in the Toolbar in Dreamweaver 4. Just enter the information in the Title field and press Enter (Return) to confirm the modification. You'll see the new title appear in the program's title bar and whenever you preview the page in a browser.

As usual, Dreamweaver gives you more than one method for accessing the Page Properties dialog box. You can select Modify ➪ Page Properties, or you can use the keyboard shortcut Ctrl+J (Command+J).

Tip
Here's the other way to open the Page Properties dialog box. Right-click (Control+click) any open area in the Document window — that is, any part of the screen not occupied by an image, table, or other object (text outside of tables is okay to click, however). From the bottom of the Shortcut menu, select Page Properties.

The Page Properties dialog box, shown in Figure 8-1, gives you easy control of your HTML page's overall look and feel.

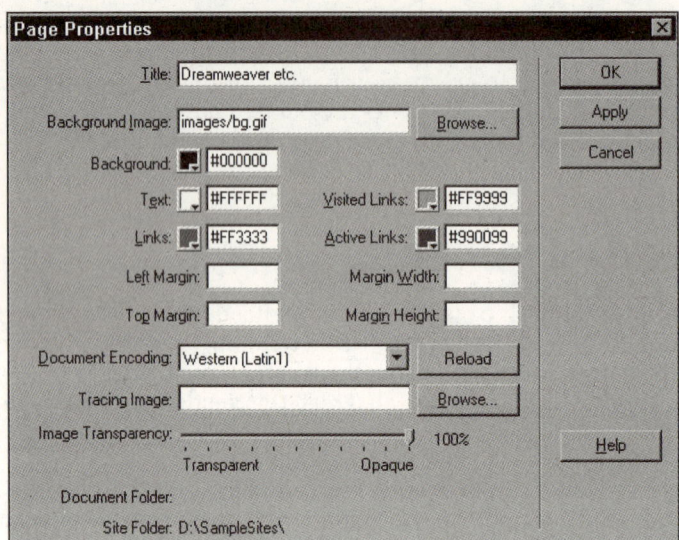

Figure 8-1: Change your Web page's overall appearance through the Page Properties dialog box.

Note   Technically, some of the values you assign through the Page Properties dialog box are applied to the `<body>` tag; because they affect the overall appearance of a page, however, they are covered in this `<head>` section.

The key areas of the Page Properties dialog box are as follows:

Page Property	Description
Title	The title of your Web page. The name you enter here appears in the browser's title bar when your page is viewed. Search engine spiders also read the title as one of the important indexing clues.
Background Image	The file name of the graphic you want in the page background. Either type in the path directly or pick a file by clicking the Browse (Choose) button. You can embed the graphic of your choice in the background of your page; if the image is smaller than your content requires, the browser tiles the image to fill out the page. Specifying a background image overrides any selection in the Background color field.

Page Property	Description
Background	Click this color swatch to change the background color of the Web page. Select one of the browser-safe colors from the pop-up menu, or enter its name or hexadecimal representation (for example, "#FFFFFF") directly into the text box.
Text	Click this color swatch to control the color of default text.
Links	Click this color swatch to modify the color of any text designated as a link, or the border around an image link.
Visited Links	Click this color swatch to select the color that linked text changes to after a visitor to your Web page has selected that link and then returned to your page.
Active Links	Click this color swatch to choose the color to which linked text changes briefly when a user selects the link.
Left Margin, Top Margin, Margin Width, Margin Height	Enter values here to change the default margin settings used by browsers. The Left and Top Margin settings are used by Microsoft, whereas Margin Width and Margin Height are used by Netscape.
Document Encoding	The character set in which you want your Web page to be displayed. Choose one from the drop-down list. The default is Western (Latin 1).
Tracing Image	Selects an image to use as a layout guide.
Image Transparency	Sets the degree of transparency for the tracing image.

The Page Properties dialog box also displays the document folder if the page has been saved, and the current site root folder if one has been selected.

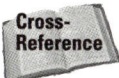

Cross-Reference
The Tracing Image option is a powerful feature for quickly building a Web page based on design comps. For details about this feature and how to use it, see the section "Tracing Your Design with Layers" in Chapter 28.

Choosing a Page palette

Getting the right text and link colors to match your background color has been largely a trial-and-error process. Generally, you'd set the background color, add a contrasting text color, and then add some variations of different colors for the three different link colors — all the while clicking the Apply button and checking your results until you found a satisfactory combination. This is a time-intensive chore, to say the least.

Choosing Colors from an Onscreen Image

One of the features found throughout Dreamweaver, the Eyedropper tool, is especially useful in the Page Properties options. The Eyedropper tool appears whenever you open any of Dreamweaver's color swatches, such as those attached to the Background, Text, and Links colors. You can not only pick a color from the Web-safe palette that appears, but also use the Eyedropper to select any color on any page — including system colors such as those found in dialog boxes and menu strips.

To use the Eyedropper tool to choose a color for the background (or any of the other options) from an onscreen image, follow these steps:

1. Insert your image on the page and, using the vertical scroll bar, position the Document window so that the image and the Page Properties dialog box can be viewed simultaneously.

   If your image is too big to fit both it and the Page Properties dialog box on the same screen, temporarily resize your image by dragging its sizing handles. You can restore the original image size when you're done by selecting the Refresh button on the Image Property Inspector.

2. Open the Page Properties dialog box by choosing Modify ⇨ Page Properties or using the keyboard shortcut Ctrl+J (Command+J).

3. Drag the Page Properties dialog box to a place where the image can be seen.

4. Select the Background color swatch (or whichever one you wish to change).

   The Dreamweaver color picker opens and the pointer becomes an eyedropper.

5. Move the Eyedropper tool over the image until you find the correct color. (On Windows, you must hold the mouse button down as you drag the Eyedropper off the Dreamweaver dialog box to the image.) As you move the Eyedropper over an image, its colors are reflected in the color well and its hex value is shown on the color picker. Click once when you've found the appropriate color.

   The color picker closes.

6. Repeat Steps 4 and 5 to grab other colors from the screen for other color swatches. Click OK when you've finished modifying the page properties.

You don't have to keep the image on your page to get its color. Just insert it temporarily and then delete it after you've used the Eyedropper to grab the shade you want.

However, Dreamweaver ships with a command that enables you to quickly pick an entire palette for your page in one fell swoop. The Set Color Scheme command, shown in Figure 8-2, features palette combinations from noted Web designers Lynda Weinman and Bruce Heavin. The colors available in the command are all Web safe — which means that they will appear the same in the major browsers on all Macintosh and Windows systems without dithering.

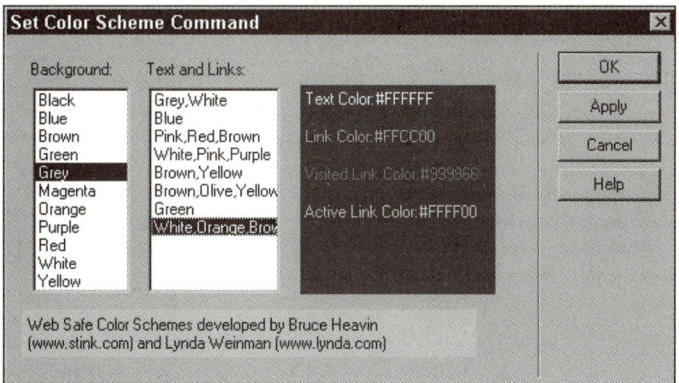

Figure 8-2: Get a Web-safe page palette with one click by using the Set Color Scheme command.

To use the Set Color Scheme command, follow these steps:

1. Choose Commands ➪ Set Color Scheme.

   The Set Color Scheme dialog box opens.

2. Select the background color from the Background column on the left.

   The Text and Links column is updated to show available combinations for the selected background color.

3. Select a color set from the Text and Links column to see various combinations in the Preview pane.

   The color names — such as White, Pink, Brown — refer to the Text, Link, and Visited Link colors, generally. If only one color name is offered, the entire color scheme uses shades of that color. Note that the background color changes slightly for various color combinations to work better with the foreground color choices.

4. Click Apply to see the effect on your current page. Click OK when you finish.

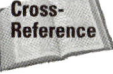

Cross-Reference

To learn more about commands in general — including how to build your own — check out Chapter 21.

Understanding <meta> and other <head> tags

Summary information about the content of a page — and a lot more — is conveyed through <meta> tags used within the <head> section. The <meta> tag can be read by the server to create a header file, which makes it easier for indexing software used by search engines to catalog sites. Numerous different types of <meta> tags exist, and you can insert them in your document just like other objects.

One `<meta>` tag is included by default in every Dreamweaver page. The Document Encoding option of the Page Properties dialog box determines the character set used by the current Web page and is displayed in the `<head>` section as follows:

```
<meta http-equiv="Content-Type" content="text/html; charset=iso-8859-1">
```

The preceding `<meta>` tag tells the browser that this page is, in fact, an HTML page and that the page should be rendered using the specified character set (the `charset` attribute). The key attribute here is `http-equiv`, which is responsible for generating a server response header.

Tip

Once you've determined your `<meta>` tags for a Web site, the same basic `<meta>` information can go on every Web page. Dreamweaver gives you a way to avoid having to insert the same lines again and again: templates. Once you've set up the `<head>` elements the way you'd like them, choose File ⇨ Save As Template. If you want to add `<meta>` or any other `<head>` tags to an existing template, you can edit the template and then update the affected pages. For more on templates, turn to Chapter 32.

In Dreamweaver, you can insert a `<meta>` tag or any other tag using the `<head>` tag objects, which you access via the Head category in the Objects panel or the Insert ⇨ Head Tags menu option. The `<head>` tag objects are described in Table 8-1 and subsequent subsections.

Table 8-1
Head Tag Objects

Head Tag Object	Description
Meta	Inserts information that describes or affects the entire document.
Keywords	Includes a series of words used by the search engine to index the current Web page and/or site.
Description	Includes a text description of the current Web page and/or site.
Refresh	Reloads the current document or loads a new URL within a specified number of seconds.
Base	Establishes a reference for all other URLs in the current Web page.
Link	Inserts a link to an external document, such as a style sheet.

Inserting tags with the Meta object

The Meta object is used to insert tags that provide information for the Web server, through the HTTP-equiv attribute, and other overall data that you want to include in your Web page but not make visible to the casual browser. Some Web pages, for example, have built-in expiration dates after which the content is to be considered outmoded. In Dreamweaver, you can use the Meta object to insert a wide range of descriptive data.

You can access the Meta object in the Head category of the Objects panel or via the Insert menu by choosing Insert ➪ Head Tags ➪ Meta. Like all the Head objects, you don't have to have the Head Content visible to insert the Meta object; although you do have to choose View ➪ Head Content if you wish to edit the object. To insert a Meta object, follow these steps:

1. Select Insert ➪ Head Tags ➪ Meta or select the Meta object from the Head category of the Objects panel. Your current cursor position is irrelevant.

   The Insert Meta dialog box opens, as shown in Figure 8-3.

Figure 8-3: The Meta object enables you to enter a full range of `<meta>` tags in the `<head>` section of your Web page.

2. Choose the desired attribute: Name or an HTTP-equivalent from the Attribute list box. Press Tab.

3. Enter the value for the selected attribute in the Value text box. Press Tab.

4. Enter the value for the content attribute in the Content text box.

5. Click OK when you're done.

Built-in Meta Commands

Although Dreamweaver presents six different Head objects, `<meta>` tags form the basis of four of them: Meta, Keywords, Description, and Refresh. By specifying different `name` attributes, the purpose of the `<meta>` tags changes. For example, a Keywords object uses this format:

```
<meta name="keywords" content="dreamweaver, web, authoring, ¬
HTML, DHTML, CSS, Macromedia">
```

whereas a Description object inserts this type of code:

```
<meta name="description" content="This site is devoted to ¬
extensions made possible by Macromedia's Dreamweaver, the ¬
premier Web authoring tool.">
```

It is possible to create all your `<meta>` tags with the Meta object by specifying the name attribute and giving it the pertinent value, but it's easier to just use the standard Dreamweaver Head objects.

You can add as many Meta objects as you need to by repeating Steps 1 through 4. To edit an existing Meta object, you must first choose View ⇨ Head Content to reveal the `<head>` code, indicated by the various icons. Select the Meta tag icon and make your changes in the Property Inspector.

Aiding search engines with the Keywords and Description objects

Let's take a closer look at the tags that convey indexing and descriptive information to search engine spiders. These chores are handled by the Keywords and Description objects. As noted in the sidebar, "Built-in Meta Commands," the Keywords and Description objects output specialized `<meta>` tags.

Both objects are straightforward to use. Choose Insert ⇨ Head Tags ⇨ Keywords or Insert ⇨ Head Tags ⇨ Description. You can also choose the corresponding objects from the Head category of the Objects panel. Once selected, these objects open similar dialog boxes with a single entry area, a large text box, as shown in Figure 8-4. Enter the values — whether keywords or a description — in the text box and click OK when you're done. You can edit the Keywords and Description objects, like the Meta object, by selecting their icons in the Head area of the Document window, revealed by choosing View ⇨ Head Contents.

Caution Although you can enter paragraph returns in your Keywords and Description objects, there's no reason to. Browsers ignore all such formatting when processing your code.

Figure 8-4: Entering information through the Keywords object helps search engines correctly index your Web page.

What you place in the Keywords and Description objects can have a big impact on your Web page's accessibility. If, for example, you want to categorize your Web page as an homage to the music of the early seventies, you could enter the following in the Content area of the Keywords object:

```
music, 70s, 70's, eagles, ronstadt, bee gees, pop, rock
```

In the preceding case, the content list is composed of words or phrases, separated by commas. Use sentences in the Description object, like this:

```
The definitive look back to the power pop rock stylings of early 1970s music, ¬
with special sections devoted to the Eagles, Linda Ronstadt, and the Bee Gees.
```

Keep in mind that the content in the Description should complement and extend both the Keywords and the Web page title. You have more room in both the Description and Keywords objects — really, an unlimited amount — than in the page title, which should be on the short side in order to fit into the browser's title bar.

Caution

When using `<meta>` tags with the Keywords or Description objects, don't stuff the `<meta>` tags with the same word repeated over and over again. The search engines are engineered to reject multiple words, and your description will not get the attention it deserves.

Refreshing the page and redirecting users

The Refresh object forces a browser to reload the current page or to load a new page after a user-set interval. The Web page visitor usually controls refreshing a page; if, for some reason, the display has become garbled, the user can choose Reload from the menu to redraw the screen. Impatient Web surfer that I am, I often stop a page from loading to see what text links are available and then — if I don't see what I need — hit Reload to bring in the full page. The code inserted by the Refresh object tells the server, not the browser, to reload the page. This can be a powerful tool but leads to trouble if used improperly.

To insert a Refresh object, follow these steps:

1. Choose Insert ➪ Head Tags ➪ Refresh or select the Insert Refresh object from the Head category of the Objects panel.

   The Insert Refresh dialog box, shown in Figure 8-5, opens.

Figure 8-5: Use the Refresh object to redirect visitors from an outdated page.

2. Enter the number of seconds you want to wait before the Refresh command takes effect in the Delay text box.

   The Delay value is calculated from the time the page finishes loading.

3. Select the desired Action:

- Go to URL

- Refresh This Document

4. If you selected Go to URL, enter a path to another page in the text box or select the Browse button to select a file.

5. Click OK when you're done.

The Refresh object is most often used to redirect a visitor to another Web page. The Web is a fluid place, and sites often move from one address to another. Typically, a page at the old address contains the Refresh code that automatically takes the user to the new address. It's good practice to include a link to your new URL on the "change-of-address" page because not all browsers support the Refresh option. One other tip: Keep the number of seconds to a minimum — there's no point in waiting for something to happen automatically when you could click a link.

Caution

If you elect to choose the Refresh This Document option, use extreme caution for several reasons. First, you can easily set up an endless loop for your visitors in which the same page is constantly being refreshed. If you are working with a page that updates often, enter a longer Refresh value, such as 300 or 500. You should be sure to include a link to another page to enable users to exit from the continually refreshed page. You should also be aware that many search engines will not index pages using the meta refresh tag because of wide-spread abuse by certain industries on the Web.

Changing bases

Through the Base object, the `<head>` section enables you to exert fundamental control over the basic HTML element: the link. The code inserted by this object specifies the base URL for the current page. If you use relative addressing (covered in Chapter 6), you can switch all your links to another directory — even another Web site — with one command. The Base object takes two attributes: `Href`, which redirects all the other relative links on your page; and `target`, which specifies where the links will be rendered.

To insert a Base object in your page, follow these steps:

1. Choose Insert ➪ Head Tags ➪ Refresh or select the Insert Base object from the Head category of the Objects panel.

The Insert Base dialog box opens.

2. Input the path that you want all other relative links to be based on in the Href text box or choose the Browse button to pick the path.

3. If desired, enter a default target for all links without a specific target to be rendered in the Target text box.

4. Click OK when you're done.

How does a <base> tag affect your page? Let's say you define one link as follows:

```
images/backgnd.gif
```

Normally, the browser looks in the same folder as the current page for a subfolder named images. A different sequence occurs, however, if you set the <base> tag to another URL in the following way:

```
<base href="http://www.testsite.com/client-demo01/">
```

With this <base> tag, when the same images/backgnd.gif link is activated, the browser looks for its file in the following location:

```
http://www.testsite.com/client-demo01/images/backgnd.gif
```

 Caution Because of the all-or-nothing capability of <base> tags, many Webmasters use them cautiously, if at all.

Linking to other files

The Link object is used to indicate a relationship between the current page and another page or file. Although many other intended uses exist, the <link> tag is most commonly used to apply an external Cascading Style Sheet (CSS) to the current page. This code is entered automatically in Dreamweaver when you create a new linked style sheet (as described in Chapter 27), but to apply an existing style sheet, you need to use the Link object. The Link tag is also used to include TrueDoc dynamic fonts.

To insert a Link object, first choose Insert ➪ Head Tags ➪ Link or select the Insert Link object from the Head category of the Objects panel. This opens the Insert Link dialog box, shown in Figure 8-6.

Insert Link		✕
Href: sheets/dba0ct.css	Browse...	OK
		Cancel
ID:	Title:	Help
Rel: stylesheet	Rev:	

Figure 8-6: The Link object is primarily used to include external style sheets.

Next, enter the necessary attributes:

Attribute	Description
Href	The path to the file being linked. Use the Browse button to open the Select File dialog box.
ID	The ID attribute can be used by scripts to identify this particular object and affect it if need be.
Title	The Title attribute is displayed as a ToolTip by Internet Explorer browsers.
Rel	A keyword that describes the relationship of the linked document to the current page. For example, an external style sheet uses the keyword `stylesheet`.
Rev	Rev, like Rel, also describes a relationship but in the reverse. For example, if home.html contained a link tag with a Rel attribute set to intro.html, intro.html could contain a link tag with a Rev attribute set to home.html.

Note   Aside from the style sheet use, there's little browser support for the other link functions. However, the World Wide Web Consortium (W3C) supports an initiative to use the `<link>` tag to address other media, such as speech synthesis and Braille devices, and it's entirely possible that the Link object will be used for this purpose in the future.

Adding to the \<body\>

The content of a Web page — the text, images, links, and plug-ins — is all contained in the `<body>` section of an HTML document. The great majority of `<body>` tags can be inserted through Dreamweaver's visual layout interface.

To use the `<body>` tags efficiently, you need to understand the distinction between logical styles and physical styles used in HTML. An underlying philosophy of HTML is to keep the Web as universally accessible as possible. Web content is intended to be platform- and resolution-independent, but the content itself can be styled by its intent as well. This philosophy is supported by the existence of logical `<body>` tags (such as `<code>` and `<cite>`), with which a block of text can be rendered according to its meaning, and physical style tags for directly italicizing or underlining text. HTML enables you to choose between logical styles, which are relative to the text, or physical styles, which can be regarded as absolute.

Logical styles

Logical styles are contextual rather than explicit. Choose a logical style when you want to ensure that the meaning, rather than a specific look, is conveyed. Table 8-2 shows a listing of logical style tags and their most common usage. Tags not supported through Dreamweaver's visual interface are noted.

Table 8-2
HTML Logical Style Tags

Tag	Usage
`<big>`	Increases the size of the selected text relative to the surrounding text. Not currently supported by Dreamweaver.
`<cite>`	Citations, titles, and references; usually shown in italic.
`<code>`	Code; for showing programming code, usually displayed in a monospaced font.
`<dfn>`	Defining instance; used to mark the introduction of a new term.
`<em>`	Emphasis; usually depicted as underlined or italicized text.
`<kbd>`	Keyboard; used to render text to be entered exactly.
`<s>`	Strikethrough text; used for showing text that has been deleted.
`<samp>`	Sample; a sequence of literal characters.
`<small>`	Decreases the size of the selected text relative to the surrounding text. Not currently supported by Dreamweaver.
`<strong>`	Strong emphasis; usually rendered as bold text.
`<sub>`	Subscript; the text is shown slightly lowered below the baseline. Not currently supported by Dreamweaver.
`<sup>`	Superscript; the text is shown slightly raised above the baseline. Not currently supported by Dreamweaver.
`<tt>`	Teletype; displayed with a monospaced font such as Courier.
`<var>`	Variable; used to distinguish variables from other programming code.

Logical styles are becoming increasingly important now that more browsers accept Cascading Style Sheets. Style sheets make it possible to combine the best elements of both logical and physical styles. With CSS, you can easily make the text within your `<code>` tags blue, and the variables, denoted with the `<var>` tag, green.

Caution

If a tag is not currently supported by Dreamweaver, you must enter the tag by hand — either through the Code Inspector, the Quick Tag Editor, or another text editor — and preview the result in a browser. For example, you can use the `<sub>` tag to create a formula for water (H20), but you don't see the subscripted 2 in the formula until you view the page through a browser.

Physical styles

HTML picked up the use of physical styles from modern typography and word processing programs. Use a physical style when you want something to be absolutely bold, italic, or underlined (or, as we say in HTML, `<b>`, `<i>`, and `<u>`, respectively).

You can apply the bold and the italic tags to selected text through the Property Inspector or by selecting Text ⇨ Style; the underline style is available only through the Text menu.

With HTML version 3.2, a fourth physical style tag was added: <font>. Most browsers recognize the size attribute, which enables you to make the selected text larger or smaller, relatively or directly. To change a font size absolutely, select your text and then select Text ⇨ Size; Dreamweaver inserts the following tag, where *n* is a number from 1 to 7:

```
<font size=n>
```

To make text larger than the default text, select Text ⇨ Size Increase and then choose the value you want. Dreamweaver inserts the following tag:

```
<font size=+n>
```

The plus sign (+) indicates the relative nature of the font. Make text smaller than the default text by selecting Text ⇨ Size Decrease; Dreamweaver inserts this tag:

```
<font size=-n>
```

You can also expressly change the type of font used and its color through the face and color attributes. Because you can't be sure what fonts will be on a user's system, common practice and good form dictate that you should list alternatives for a selected font. For instance, rather than just specifying Palatino — a sans serif font common on PCs but relatively unknown on the Mac — you could insert a tag such as the following:

```
<font face=" Palatino, Times New Roman, Times, sans-serif">
```

Caution   In the preceding case, if the browser doesn't find the first font, it looks for the second one (and so forth, as specified). Dreamweaver handles the font face attribute through its Font List dialog box, which is explained fully in Chapter 9.

Working with the Code View and Code Inspector

Although Dreamweaver offers many options for using the visual interface of the Document window, sometimes you just have to tweak the code by hand. Dreamweaver's acceptance by professional coders is due in large part to the easy access of the underlying code. Dreamweaver includes several methods for directly viewing, inputting, and modifying code for your Web page. For large-scale additions and changes, you might consider using an external HTML editor such as BBEdit or Homesite, but for many situations, the built-in Code view and Code Inspector are perfectly suited and much faster to work with.

New Feature   The Code view is the latest addition to Dreamweaver's code-savvy toolbox. With the addition of the Code view, you can either view your code full-screen in the Document Window, split-screen with the Design view, or in a separate panel, the Code Inspector. The underlying engine for all code views is the same — and, for Dreamweaver 4, the code editor has been rewritten from the ground up with significant enhancements to the feature set and performance.

To display the full-screen Code view:

✦ Select View ➪ Code.

✦ Choose the Show Code View button from the Toolbar.

The split-screen Code and Design view is revealed by:

✦ Choose View ➪ Code and Design.

✦ Select the Show Code and Design Views button on the Toolbar.

✦ Press Ctrl+Tab (Option+Tab) when in Design view and the Code Inspector is closed.

To change the relative size of the Code and Design views, drag the splitter bar up or down. In the split-screen Code and Design view, the Code view is shown on top of the Design view. You can reverse that order by choosing View ➪ Design View on Top or selecting Design View on Top from the View Options button on the Toolbar.

You have several ways to open the Code Inspector:

✦ Choose Window ➪ Code Inspector.

✦ Select the Show Code Inspector button in either Launcher.

✦ Use the keyboard shortcut F10.

Tip   To move between Design view and a code view, press Ctrl+Tab (Option+Tab). By default, this shortcut switches to Code view from Design view. However, if you are in the split-screen Code and Design view, this keyboard combination alternates focus between the two windows. If the Code Inspector is open, pressing Ctrl+Tab (Option+Tab) toggles the focus between Design view and the Code Inspector.

Once opened, the Code Inspector (Figure 8-7) behaves like any other floating panel in Dreamweaver: the window can be resized, moved, or hidden, and the inspector can be grouped with any other panel or dragged out onto its own. When the Code Inspector is opened initially, it is automatically selected. If you click in the Document window with the Code Inspector open, the inspector dims but still reflects changes made in the document.

Figure 8-7: To update the Design view while still working in Code view select the handy Refresh button on the Toolbar or choose F5.

In all code views, Dreamweaver does not update the Design view of the document immediately — whereas changes in the Design view are instantly reflected in any open code view. This delay is enforced to enable the code to be completed before being applied. To apply modifications made in the code, switch to the Design view; if the Design view is open, click anywhere in it to give it focus. Should Dreamweaver detect any invalid HTML, such as an improperly closed tag, the offending code is flagged with a yellow highlight in both Design and Code views. Select the marked tag to see an explanation and suggestions for correcting the problem in the Property Inspector.

You can also apply code changes to the Design view by saving the document or by choosing the Refresh button on the Toolbar. The Refresh button becomes active only when modifications are made in any code view. You also have a keyboard and menu alternative: pressing F5 has the same effect as choosing View ⇨ Refresh Design View.

By and large, the Code View and Code Inspector acts like a regular text editor. Simply click anywhere in the inspector to add or modify code. Double-click a word to select it. Select an entire line by moving your pointer to the left edge of the code — where the pointer becomes a right-pointing arrow — and clicking once.

Multiple lines can be selected in this same fashion by dragging the right-pointing arrow. Once a section of code is selected, you can drag and drop it into a new location; pressing the Ctrl (Option) key while dragging makes a copy of the selection. Moving from word to word is accomplished by pressing Ctrl (Command) in combination with any of the arrow keys.

There are, however, some special features in Dreamweaver's code editor to simplify the task of writing HTML and other types of code. When in Code or Code and Design view, some of these features can be toggled on and off by choosing the command from the View ⇨ Code View Options list or under the View Options button on the Toolbar:

✦ **Word Wrap** — Wraps lines within the boundaries of the Code View window or Code Inspector to eliminate the need for horizontal scrolling.

✦ **Line Numbers** — Displays a number for every line in the code; this feature is extremely helpful when used in combination with the JavaScript Debugger, which reports the line number of an error in the code.

✦ **Highlight Invalid HTML** — Toggles the highlighting of invalid tags in the Code view when the Design view is refreshed. Invalid tags are always highlighted in the Design view.

✦ **Syntax Coloring** — Syntax coloring makes code easier to read. Basic tags and keywords are shown in one color while text in another. Three different types of code are given different colors: Reserved Keywords, Other Keywords, and Strings. These colors are set in the Code Color category of Preferences. You can also set a color for an individual tag to further distinguish it if you like.

Caution   Disabling coloring in the code has a rather unexpected repercussion. With Syntax Coloring disabled, the Reference panel is no longer context-sensitive. In other words, you cannot select a tag, attribute, or CSS style rule in the Code view and then select the Reference button to find that particular entry in the Reference panel.

✦ **Auto Indent** — Auto Indent is another feature intended to improve code readability. With Auto Indent enabled, pressing Enter (Return) at the end of a line causes the new line to start at the same indentation as the preceding line. Press Backspace (Delete) to move the indented line closer to left margin. The number of characters for each indentation is set in the Code Format category of Preferences.

You can also change the indentation — in or out — for selected blocks of code with one command. To further indent a block of code, select it and then choose Edit ⇨ Indent Code or use the keyboard shortcut Ctrl+] (Command+]). To decrease the level of indentation for a selected code block, choose Edit ⇨ Outdent Code or the keyboard shortcut Ctrl+[(Command+[).

New Feature

As a further aid to help you find your way through a maze of code, Dreamweaver 4 includes the Balance Braces command. JavaScript is notorious for using parentheses, brackets, and curly braces to structure its code — and it's easy to lose sight of where one enclosing brace begins and it's closing mate ends. Dreamweaver highlights the content found within the closest pair of braces to the cursor when you select Edit ➪ Balance Braces or use the keyboard shortcut Ctrl-' (Command-'). If you select the command again, the selection expands to the set of surrounding braces. When the selection is not enclosed by parentheses, brackets, or curly braces, Dreamweaver sounds an alert.

Although most Web designers prone to using the code editor in Dreamweaver prefer to handwrite their code, the power of the Objects panel is still at your disposal for rapid code development. Any element available from the Objects panel can be inserted directly into the Code view or inspector. To use the Objects panel, you must first position your cursor where you would like the code for the object to appear and then select the element. You cannot, however, drag-and-drop an element from the Objects panel to the Code view or inspector.

Cross-Reference

Keep in mind that the Dreamweaver's code editor is highly customizable. You can change the way the lines wrap, by using indents for certain tag pairs; you can even control the amount of indentation. All the options are outlined for you in Chapter 4.

Rapid Tag Modification with the Quick Tag Editor

I tend to build Web pages in two phases: First, I generally lay out my text and images to create the overall design, and then I go back, adding details and alterations to get the page just right. The second phase of Web page design often requires that I make a small adjustment to the HTML code, typically through the Property Inspector, but occasionally I need to go right to the source — code, that is.

Dreamweaver offers a feature for making minor but essential alterations to the code: the Quick Tag Editor. The Quick Tag Editor is a small pop-up window that appears in the Document window and enables you to edit an existing tag, add a new tag, or wrap the current selection in a tag. One other feature makes the Quick Tag Editor even quicker to use: A handy list of tags or attributes appears to cut down on your typing.

To call up the Quick Tag Editor, use any of the following methods:

✦ Choose Modify ➪ Quick Tag Editor.

✦ Press the keyboard shortcut Ctrl+T (Command+T).

✦ Select the Quick Tag Editor icon on the Property Inspector.

The Quick Tag Editor has three modes: Insert HTML, Wrap Tag, and Edit HTML. Although you can get to all three modes from any situation, which mode appears initially depends on the current selection. The Quick Tag Editor's window (Figure 8-8) appears above the current selection when you use either the menu or keyboard method of opening it, or next to the Property Inspector when you select the icon. In either case, you can move the Quick Tag Editor window to a new location onscreen by dragging its Title bar.

Tip   Regardless of which mode the Quick Tag Editor opens in, you can toggle to the other modes by pressing the keyboard shortcut Ctrl+T (Command+T).

Title bar   Hint list

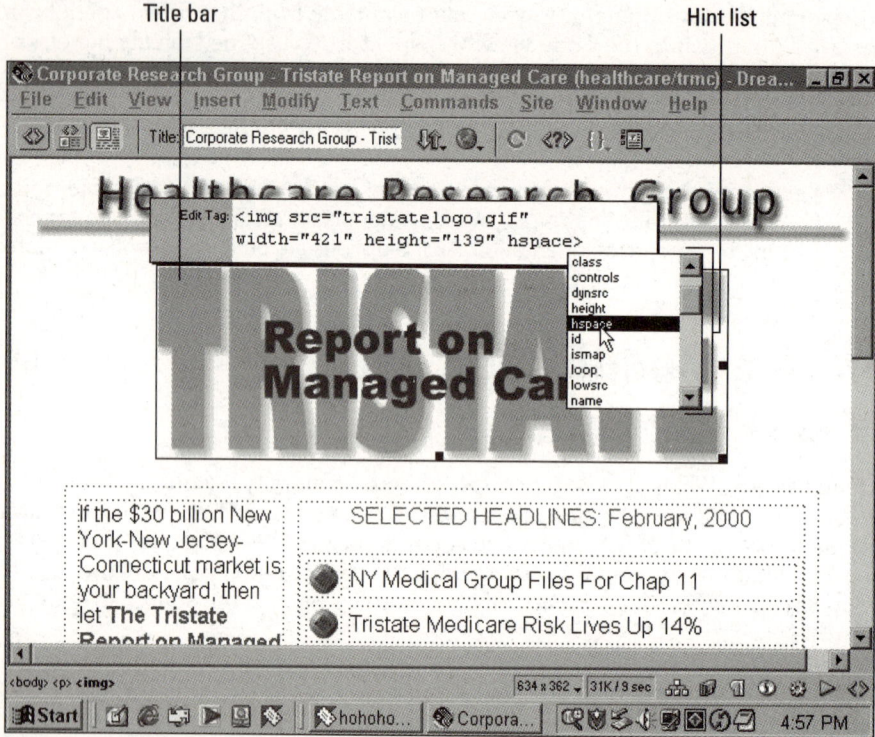

Figure 8-8: The Quick Tag Editor is great for quickly tweaking your code.

See the "Working with the Hint List" sidebar later in this chapter for details about this feature.

Insert HTML mode

The Insert HTML mode of the Quick Tag Editor is used for adding new tags and code at the current cursor position; it is the initial mode when nothing is selected. The Insert HTML mode starts with a pair of angle brackets enclosing a blinking cursor.

You can enter any desired tag—whether standard HTML or custom XML—and any attribute or content within the new tag. When you're done, just press Enter (Return) to confirm your addition.

To add new tags to your page using the Quick Tag Editor Insert HTML mode, follow these steps:

1. Position your cursor where you would like the new code to be inserted.

2. Choose Modify ⇨ Quick Tag Editor or use the keyboard shortcut, Ctrl+T (Command+T), to open the Quick Tag Editor.

    The Quick Tag Editor opens in Insert HTML mode, as shown in Figure 8-9.

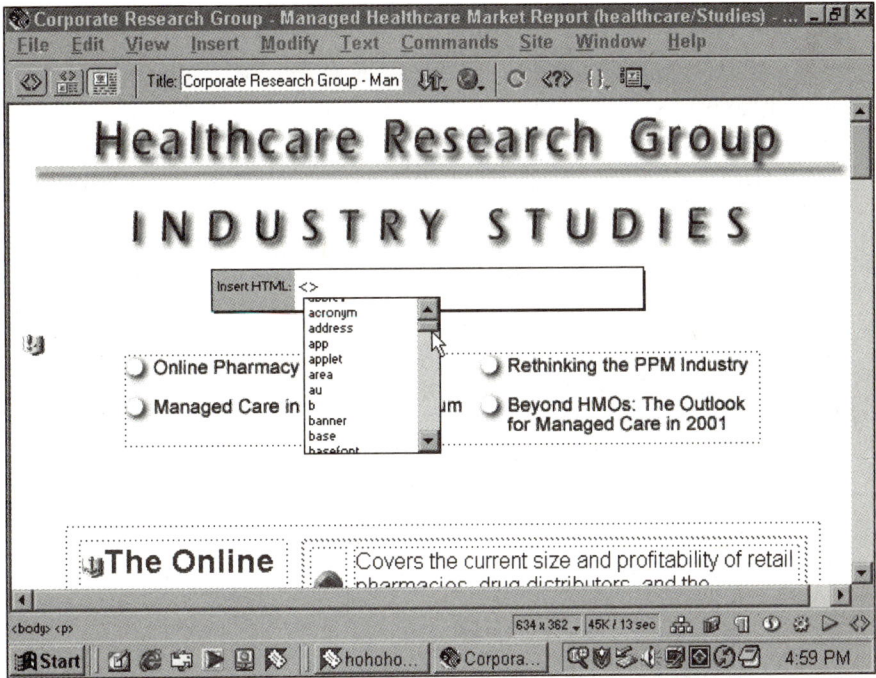

Figure 8-9: Use the Quick Tag Editor's Insert HTML mode to add tags not available through Dreamweaver's visual interface.

3. Enter your HTML or XML code.

Tip   Use the right-arrow key to move quickly past the closing angle bracket and add text after your tag.

4. If you pause while typing, the hint list appears, selecting the first tag that matches what you've typed so far. Use the arrow keys to select another tag in the list and press Enter (Return) to select a tag.

Working with the Hint List

The Quick Tag Editor has a rather nifty feature referred to as the *hint list*. To make it even quicker to use the Quick Tag Editor, a list of tags pops up when you pause in your typing. When you're entering attributes within a tag, a list of appropriate parameters pops up instead of tags. These lists are tied to what, if anything, you've already typed. Say, for instance, you've begun to enter **blockquote** and have only gotten as far typing **b** and **l**. When the hint list appears, it scrolls to "blink"—the first tag in the list starting with those two letters. If you continue typing "o," "blockquote" is selected. All you have to do to insert it into your code is to press Enter (Return).

Here's a few other hint list hints:

✦ Scroll to a tag by using the up- or down-arrow keys.

✦ Double-clicking the selected hint list item also inserts it into the code.

✦ Once the hint list is open, press Esc if you decide not to enter the selected tag or attribute.

✦ If an attribute has a set series of values that can be applied (for example, the <div> tag align attribute can only be set to left, right, or center), those values are accessible via the hint list.

✦ Control how quickly the hint list appears—or even if it appears at all—by altering the Quick Tag Editor preferences.

The tags and attributes that appear in the hint list are contained in the TagAttributeList.text file found in the Dreamweaver Configuration folder. The list is in a format known as Data Type Declaration (DTD), where each tag is listed as a separate element and any corresponding attributes are displayed under each of those elements. Here, for example, is the DTD listing for the background sound tag, <bgsound>:

```
<!ELEMENT BGSOUND Name="Background sound" >
<!ATTLIST BGSOUND
     Balance
     Loop
     Src
     Volume
>
```

As with almost all other Dreamweaver aspects, the TagAttribute.txt list can be modified to include any special tags and their attributes you might need to include on a regular basis. Just relaunch Dreamweaver after making your changes in a standard text editor and your modifications are included the next time you use the Quick Tag Editor.

   5. Press Enter (Return) when you're done.

   The Quick Tag Editor is fairly intelligent and tries to help you write valid HTML. If, for example, you leave off a closing tag, such as </b>, the Quick Tag Editor automatically adds it for you.

Wrap Tag mode

Part of the power and flexibility of HTML is the capability to wrap one tag around one or more other tags and content. To make a phrase appear bold and italic, the code is written this way:

```
<b><i>On Sale Now!</i></b>
```

Note how the inner `<i>...</i>` tag pair is enclosed by the `<b>...</b>` pair. The Wrap Tag mode of the Quick Tag Editor surrounds any selection with your entered tag in one easy operation.

The Wrap Tag mode appears initially when you have selected just text (with no surrounding tags) or an incomplete tag (the opening tag and contents but no closing tag). The Wrap Tag mode is visually similar to the Insert HTML mode, as can be seen in Figure 8-10. However, rather than just include exactly what you've entered into the Quick Tag Editor, Wrap Tag mode also inserts a closing tag that corresponds to your entry. For example, let's say I want to apply a tag not available in Dreamweaver's Document window, the subscript or `<sub>` tag. After highlighting the text I want to mark up as subscript (a "2" in the formula, H_2O, for example), I open the Quick Tag Editor and enter **sub**. The resulting code looks like this:

```
H<sub>2</sub>O
```

Caution
You can only enter one tag in Wrap Tag mode; if more than one tag is entered, Dreamweaver displays an alert informing you that the tag you've entered appears to be invalid HTML. The Quick Tag Editor is then closed, and the selection is cleared.

To wrap a tag with the Quick Tag Editor, follow these steps:

1. Select the text or tags you want to enclose in another tag.

2. Choose Modify ➪ Quick Tag Editor or use the keyboard shortcut, Ctrl+T (Command+T), to open the Quick Tag Editor.

   The Quick Tag Editor opens in Wrap Tag mode.

3. If you select a complete tag, the Quick Tag Editor opens in Edit HTML mode; press the keyboard shortcut, Ctrl+T (Command+T), to toggle to Wrap Tag mode.

4. Enter the desired tag.

5. If you pause while typing, the hint list appears, selecting the first tag that matches what you've typed so far. Use the arrow keys to select another tag in the list and press Enter (Return) to select a tag from the hint list.

6. Press Enter (Return) to confirm your tag.

   The Quick Tag Editor closes and Dreamweaver adds your tag before your selection and a corresponding closing tag after it.

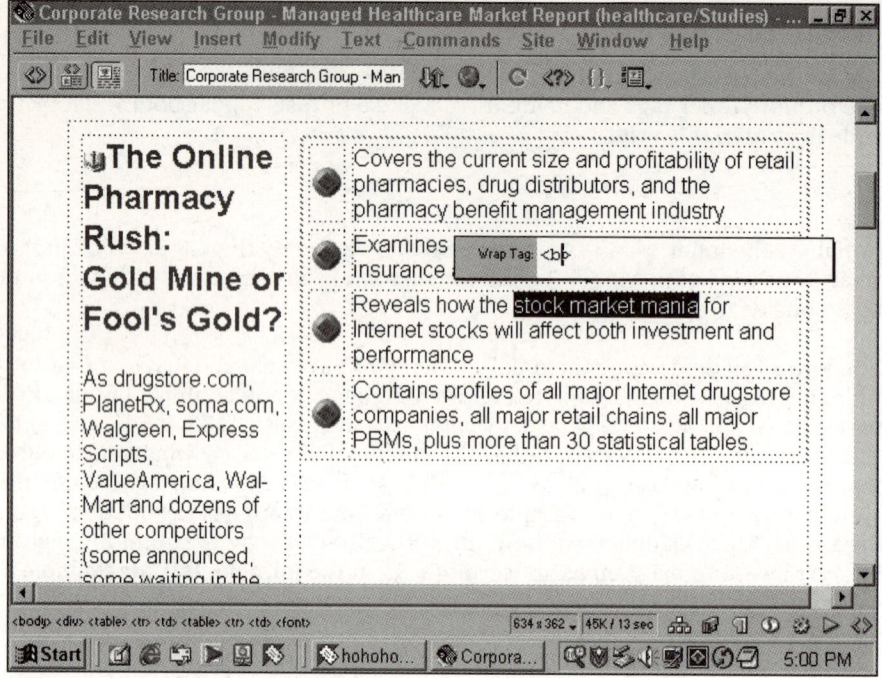

Figure 8-10: Enclose any selection with a tag by using the Quick Tag Editor's Wrap Tag mode.

Edit HTML mode

If a complete tag—either a single tag, such as `<img>`, or a tag pair, such as `<h1>...</h1>`—is selected, the Quick Tag Editor opens in Edit HTML mode. Unlike the other two modes where you are presented with just open and closing angle brackets and a flashing cursor, the Edit HTML mode displays the entire selected tag with all the attributes, if any. The Edit HTML mode is always invoked when you start the Quick Tag Editor by clicking its icon in the Property Inspector.

The Edit HTML mode has many uses. I've found it to be terrific for adding a parameter not found on Dreamweaver's Property Inspector. For example, when building a form that returns the information formatted, you need to declare the enctype attribute to be equal to "text/plain." However, the enctype attribute cannot be assigned from the Property Inspector for the `<form>` tag. So, I just select the tag from the Tag Selector and then click the Quick Tag Editor icon to open the Quick Tag Editor. The `<form>` tag appears with my current parameters, as shown in Figure 8-11.

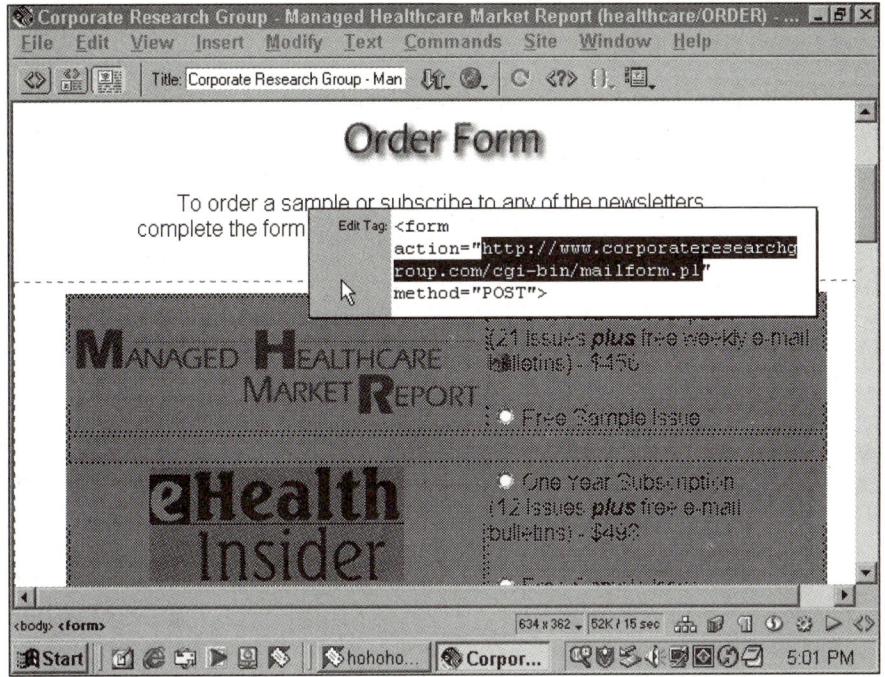

Figure 8-11: In Edit HTML mode, the Quick Tag Editor shows the entire tag with attributes and their values.

To use the Quick Tag Editor in Insert HTML mode, follow these steps:

1. Select an entire tag by clicking its name in the Tag Selector.

2. Choose Modify ➪ Quick Tag Editor.

3. To change an existing attribute, tab to the current value and enter a new one.

4. To add a new attribute, tab and/or use the arrow keys to position the cursor after an existing attribute or after the tag and enter the new parameter and value.

Tip If you don't close the quotation marks for a parameter's value, Dreamweaver does it for you.

5. If you pause briefly while entering a new attribute, the hint list appears with attributes appropriate for the current tag. If you select an attribute from the hint list, press Enter (Return) to accept the parameter.

6. When you're done editing the tag, press Enter (Return).

In addition to this capability to edit complete tags, Dreamweaver has a couple of navigational commands to help select just the right tag. The Select Parent Tag command — keyboard shortcut Ctrl+Shift+< (Command+Shift+<) — highlights the tag immediately surrounding the present tag. Going the other direction, Select Child Tag — keyboard shortcut Ctrl+Shift+> (Command+Shift+>) — chooses the next tag, if any, contained within the current tag. Both commands are available under the Edit menu. Exercising these commands is equivalent to selecting the next tag in the Tag Selector to the left (parent) or right (child).

Inserting Symbols and Special Characters

When working with Dreamweaver, you're usually entering text directly from your keyboard, one keystroke at a time, with each keystroke representing a letter, number, or other keyboard character. Some situations, however, require special letters that have diacritics or common symbols, such as the copyright mark, which are outside of the regular, standard character set represented on your keyboard. HTML enables you to insert a full range of such character entities through two systems. The more familiar special characters have been assigned a mnemonic code name to make them easy to remember; these are called *named characters*. Less typical characters must be inserted by entering a numeric code; these are known as *decimal characters*. For the sake of completeness, named characters also have a corresponding decimal character code.

Both named and decimal character codes begin with an ampersand (&) symbol and end with a semicolon (;). For example, the HTML code for an ampersand symbol follows:

&

Its decimal character equivalent follows:

&

Caution   If, during the browser-testing phase of creating your Web page, you suddenly see an HTML code onscreen rather than a symbol, double-check your HTML. The code could be just a typo; you may have left off the closing semicolon, for instance. If the code is correct and you're using a named character, however, switch to its decimal equivalent. Some of the earlier browser versions are not perfect in rendering named characters.

Named characters

HTML coding conventions require that certain characters, including the angle brackets that surround tags, be entered as character entities. Table 8-3 lists the most common named characters.

Table 8-3
Common Named Characters

Named Entity	Symbol	Description
&lt;	<	A left angle bracket or the less-than symbol
&gt;	>	A right angle bracket or the greater-than symbol
&amp;	&	An ampersand
&quot;	"	A double quotation mark
	°	A nonbreaking space
&copy;	(c)	A copyright symbol
&reg;	(r)	A registered mark
&trade;	(tm)	A trademark symbol, which cannot be previewed in Dreamweaver but is supported in Internet Explorer

Tip   Those characters that you can type directly into Dreamweaver's Document window, including the brackets and the ampersand, are automatically translated into the correct named characters in HTML. Try this with the Code Inspector open. Also, you can enter a nonbreaking space in Dreamweaver by typing Ctrl+Shift+spacebar (Command+Shift+spacebar) or by choosing the Non-breaking Space object.

Decimal characters

To enter almost any character that has a diacritic — such as á, ñ, or â — in Dreamweaver, you must explicitly enter the corresponding decimal character into your HTML page. As mentioned in the preceding section, decimal characters take the form of &#number;, where the number can range from 00 to 255. Not all numbers have matching symbols; the sequence from 14 through 31 is currently unused and the upper range (127 through 159) is only partially supported by Internet Explorer and Netscape Navigator. Also, not all fonts have characters for every entity.

Using the Character objects

Not only is it difficult to remember the various name or number codes for the specific character entity you need, it's also a bit of a process to enter the code by hand. The Dreamweaver engineers recognized this need and created a series of Character objects on their own category of the Objects panel.

Ease-of-use is the guiding principal for the new Character objects. Nine of the most commonly used symbols, such as © and ™ are instantly available as separate objects. And a single object exists offering access to 99 different character entities. Inserting the single Character objects is a straightforward point-and-click affair. Either drag the desired symbol to a place in the Document window or position your cursor and select the object.

The nine individual Character objects are detailed in Table 8-4.

	Table 8-4 Character Objects	
Icon	**Name**	**HTML Code Inserted**
©	Insert Copyright	`&copy;`
®	Insert Registered Trademark	`&reg;`
™	Insert Trademark	`&#153;`
£	Insert Pound	`&pound;`
¥	Insert Yen	`&yen;`
€	Insert Euro	`&euro;`
—	Insert Em-Dash	`&#151;`
"	Insert Left Quote	`&#147;`
"	Insert Right Quote	`&#148;`

Note   You may notice that the Character objects insert a mix of named and number character entities. Not all browsers recognize the easier-to-identify named entities, so for the widest compatibility, Dreamweaver uses the number codes for a few objects.

The final object on the Characters category is used for inserting these or any other character entity. The Other Characters object displays a large table with symbols for 99 different characters, as shown in Figure 8-12. Simply select the desired symbol and Dreamweaver inserts the appropriate HTML code into the current cursor position. By the way, the very first character — which appears to be blank — actually inserts the code for a nonbreaking space, also accessible via a keyboard shortcut, Ctrl+Shift+spacebar (Command+Shift+spacebar). The nonbreaking space is also available on the Characters category of the Objects panel.

Note   Keep in mind that the user's browser must support the character entity for it to be visible to the user. In the case of the Euro symbol, that support is still very haphazard.

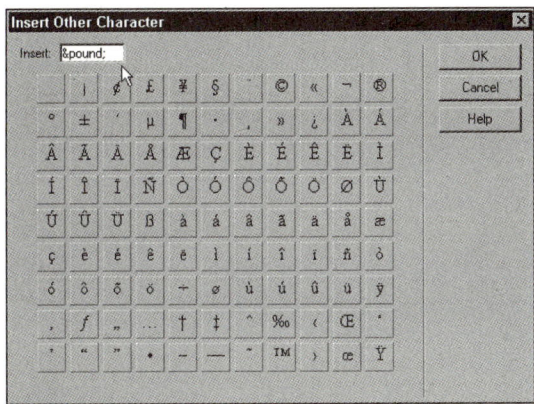

Figure 8-12: Use the Other Character objects to insert the character entity code for any of 99 different symbols.

Summary

Creating Web pages with Dreamweaver is a special blend of using visual layout tools and HTML coding. Regardless, you need to understand the basics of HTML so that you have the knowledge and the tools to modify your code when necessary. This chapter covered these key areas:

✦ An HTML page is divided into two main sections: the `<head>` and the `<body>`. Information pertaining to the entire page is kept in the `<head>` section; all the actual content of the Web page goes in the `<body>` section.

✦ You can change the color and background of your entire page, as well as set its title, through the Page Properties dialog box.

✦ Use `<meta>` tags to summarize your Web page so that search engines can properly catalog it. In Dreamweaver, you can use the View Head Contents feature to easily alter these and other `<head>` tags.

✦ When possible, use logical style tags, such as `<strong>` and `<cite>`, rather than hard-coding your page with physical style tags. Style sheets bring a great deal of control and flexibility to logical style tags.

✦ Special extended characters such as symbols and accented letters require the use of HTML character entities, which can either be named (as in ") or in decimal format (as in ").

In the next chapter, you learn how to insert and format text in Dreamweaver.

✦   ✦   ✦

Adding Text to Your Web Page

If content is king on the Web, then certainly style is queen — together they rule hand in hand. Entering, editing, and formatting text on a Web page is a major part of a Webmaster's job. Dreamweaver gives you the tools to make the task as clear-cut as possible. From headlines to comments, this chapter covers the essentials of working with basic text.

At first, Web designers didn't have many options for manipulating text. However, now the majority of browsers understand a number of text-related commands, and the designer can specify the font as well as its color and size. Dreamweaver includes a range of text manipulation tools. These topics are covered in this chapter, along with an important discussion of manipulating whitespace on the Web page.

Starting with Headings

Text in Hypertext Markup Language (HTML) is primarily composed of headings and paragraphs. Headings separate and introduce major sections of the document, just as a newspaper uses headlines to announce a story and subheads to provide essential details. HTML has six levels of headings; the syntax for the heading tags is ⟨h*n*⟩, where *n* is a number from 1 to 6. The largest heading is ⟨h1⟩ and the smallest is ⟨h6⟩.

Remember that HTML headings are not linked to any specific point size, unlike type produced in a page layout or word processing program. Headings in an HTML document are sized relative to one another, and their final, exact size depends on the browser used. The sample headlines in Figure 9-1 depict the basic headings as rendered through Dreamweaver and as compared to the default paragraph font size. As you can see, some headings are rendered in type smaller than that used for the default paragraph. Headings are usually displayed with a boldface attribute.

Figure 9-1: Standard HTML enables you to use up to six different size headings.

Two methods set text as a particular heading size in Dreamweaver. In both cases, you first need to select the text you want to affect. If you are styling a single line or paragraph as a heading, just position the cursor anywhere in the paragraph to select it. If you want to convert more than one paragraph, click and drag out your selection.

Tip   You can't mix heading levels in a single paragraph. That is, you can't have in the same line a word with an ⟨h1⟩ heading next to a word styled with an ⟨h4⟩ heading. Furthermore, headings belong to a group of HTML text tags called *block elements*. All block elements are rendered with a paragraph return both above and below, which isolates ("blocks") the text. To work around both of these restrictions, you can use ⟨font size=n⟩ tags to achieve the effect of varying sizes for words within the same line or for lines of different sizes close to one another. The ⟨font size=n⟩ tag is covered later in this chapter, in the section "Styling Your Text."

Once the text for the heading is selected, you can choose your heading level by selecting Text ⇨ Paragraph Format and then one of the Headings 1 through 6 from the submenu. Alternatively, you can make your selection from the Text Property Inspector. (If it's not already open, display the Property Inspector by selecting Window ⇨ Properties.) In the Text Property Inspector, open the Format drop-down list (see Figure 9-2) and choose one of the six headings.

Figure 9-2: You can convert any paragraph or line into a heading by using the Format options in the Text Property Inspector.

Headings are often used in a hierarchical fashion, largest to smallest — but you don't have to do it that way. You can have an `<h3>` line followed by an `<h1>` paragraph, if that's what your design needs. Be careful using the smallest headings, `<h4>`–`<h6>`; they are likely to be difficult to read on any resolution higher than 800×600.

Working with Paragraphs

Usually the bulk of text on any Web page is composed of paragraphs. Paragraphs in HTML are denoted by the `<p>` and `</p>` pair of tags. When your Web page is processed, the browser formats everything between those two tags as one paragraph and renders it to fit the user's screen, word wrapping as needed at the margins. Any additional line breaks and unnecessary whitespace (beyond one space between words and between sentences) in the HTML code are ignored.

Tip   In the early version of HTML, paragraphs used just the opening `<p>` tag, and browsers rendered everything between `<p>` tags as one paragraph; the closing tag was optional. As of HTML 3.2, however, an optional closing `</p>` tag was added. Because so many Web pages have been created with just the opening paragraph tag, most browsers still recognize the single-tag format. To be on the safe side in terms of future compatibility, enclose your paragraphs within both opening and closing tags when you do any hand-coding.

Dreamweaver starts a new paragraph every time you press Enter (Return) when composing text in the Document window. If you have the Code view or the Code Inspector open when you work, you can see that Dreamweaver inserts the following code with each new paragraph:

```
<p> </p>
```

The code between the tags creates a nonbreaking space that enables the new line to be visible. You won't see the new line if you have just the paragraph tags with nothing (neither a character nor a character entity, such as ` `) in between:

```
<p></p>
```

When you continue typing, Dreamweaver replaces the nonbreaking space with your input, unless you press Enter (Return) again. Figure 9-3 illustrates two paragraphs with text and a third paragraph with the nonbreaking space still in place.

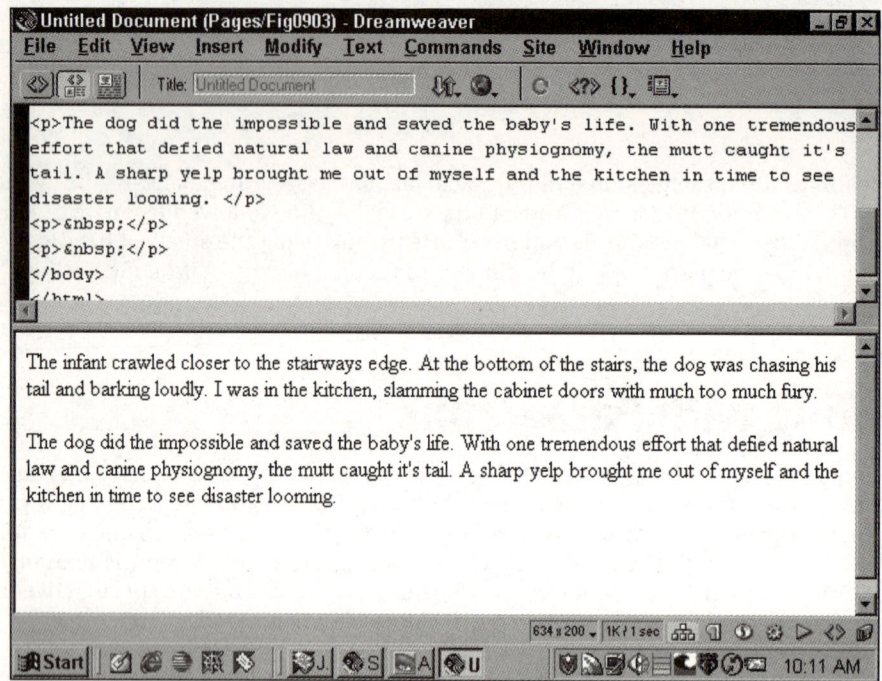

Figure 9-3: Dreamweaver automatically wraps any text inserted into the Document window. If you press Enter (Return) without entering text, Dreamweaver enters paragraph tags surrounding a nonbreaking space.

You can easily change text from most other formats, such as a heading, to paragraph format. First, select the text you want to alter. Then, in the Property Inspector, open the Format options drop-down list and choose Paragraph. You can also choose Text ⇨ Paragraph Format ⇨ Paragraph from the menu or use the keyboard shortcut Ctrl+Shift+P (Command+Shift+P).

All paragraphs are initially rendered on the page in the default font at the default size. The user can designate these defaults through the browser preferences, although most people don't bother to alter them. If you want to change the font name or the font size for selected paragraphs explicitly, use the techniques described in the upcoming section, "Styling Your Text."

Tip Remember, you can always use the Tag Selector on the status bar to select and highlight any tag surrounding your current cursor position. This method makes it easy to see exactly what a particular tag is affecting.

Editing paragraphs

By and large, the editing features of Dreamweaver are similar to other modern word processing programs — with one or two Web-oriented twists. Dreamweaver has Cut, Copy, and Paste options, as well as Undo and Redo commands. You can search for and replace any text on your Web page under construction and even check its spelling.

The "twists" come from the relationship between the Design and Code views of the Document window, which give Dreamweaver special functionality for copying and pasting text and code. Let's see how that works.

Inserting text

You've already seen how you can position the cursor on the page and directly enter text. In this sense, Dreamweaver acts like a word processing program, rather than a page layout program. On a blank page, the cursor starts at the top-left corner of the page. Words automatically wrap to the next line when the text exceeds the right margin. Press Enter (Return) to end the current paragraph and start the next one.

Indenting text

In Dreamweaver, you cannot indent text as you can with a word processor. Tabs normally have no effect in HTML. To indent a paragraph's first line, one method uses nonbreaking spaces, which can be inserted with the keyboard shortcut Ctrl+Shift+spacebar (Command+Shift+spacebar). Nonbreaking spaces are an essential part of any Web designer's palette because they provide single-character spacing — often necessary to nudge an image or other object into alignment. You've already seen the code for a nonbreaking space —   — that Dreamweaver inserts between the <p>...</p> tag pair to make the line visible.

Aside from the keyboard shortcut, two other methods involve inserting a nonbreaking space. You can enter its character code —   — directly into the HTML code. You can also style your text as *preformatted*; this technique is discussed later in this chapter.

Tip Another method exists for indenting the first line of a paragraph: Cascading Style Sheets. You can set an existing HTML tag, such as <p>, to any indent amount using the Text Indent option found on the Block panel of the Style Sheet dialog box. Be aware, however, that the various browsers support style sheets differently and to a different extent. A full discussion of text indent and other style sheet controls is in Chapter 27.

Inserting Text from Other Applications

The Paste command can also insert text from another program into Dreamweaver. If you cut or copy text from a file in any other program — whether it is a word processor, spreadsheet, or database program — Dreamweaver inserts it at the cursor position. The results of this Paste operation vary, however.

Dreamweaver can paste only plain, unformatted text — any bold, italic, or other styling in the original document are not retained in Dreamweaver. Paragraph breaks, however, are retained and reproduced in two different ways. A single paragraph return becomes a line break (a <br> tag) in Dreamweaver, whereas text separated by two returns is formatted into two HTML paragraphs, using the <p>... </p> tag pair.

If you need to import a great deal of text and want to retain as much formatting as possible, you can use another application, such as Microsoft Word, to save your text as an HTML file. Then open that file in Dreamweaver with the Import Word HTML command.

Cutting, copying, and pasting

Text can be moved from one place to another — or from one Web document to another — using the standard cut-and-paste techniques. No surprises here: Before you can cut or copy anything, you must select it. Select by clicking the mouse at the beginning of the text you want to cut or copy, drag the highlight to the end of your selection, and then release the mouse button.

Here are some other selection methods:

✦ Double-click a word to select it.

✦ Move the pointer to the left margin of the text until the pointer changes to a right-facing arrow. Click once to highlight a single line. Click and drag down the margin to select a group of lines.

✦ Position the cursor at the beginning of your selection. Hold down the Shift key and then click once at the end of the selection.

✦ You can select everything in the body of your document by using Edit ➪ Select All or the keyboard shortcut Ctrl+A (Command+A).

✦ Use the Tag Selector to select text or other objects contained within specific tags.

✦ You can also select text by holding down Shift and using the right- or left-arrow key to select one character at a time. If you hold down Ctrl+Shift (Command+Shift), you can press the right- or left-arrow key to select a word at a time.

When you want to move a block of text, first select it and then use Edit ➪ Cut or the keyboard shortcut Ctrl+X (Command+X). This sequence removes the text from the document and places it on your system's clipboard. To paste the text, move the pointer to the new location and click once to place the cursor. Then select Edit ➪ Paste or the keyboard shortcut Ctrl+V (Command+V). The text is copied from the clipboard to its new location. You can continue pasting this same text from the clipboard until another block of text is copied or cut.

To copy text, the procedure is much the same. Select the text using one of the preceding methods and then use Edit ➪ Copy or Ctrl+C (Command+C). The selected text is copied to the clipboard, and the original text is left in place. Then position the cursor in a new location and select Edit ➪ Paste (or use the keyboard shortcut).

Using drag-and-drop

The other, quicker method for moving or copying text is the drag-and-drop technique. Once you've selected your text, release the mouse button and move the cursor over the highlighted area. The cursor changes from an I-beam to an arrow. To move the text, click the selected area with the arrow cursor and drag your mouse to a new location. The arrow cursor now has a box attached to it, indicating that it is carrying something. As you move your cursor, a bar (the insertion point) moves with you, indicating where the text will be positioned. Release the mouse button to drop the text. You can copy text in the same manner by holding down the Ctrl (Option) key as you drag and drop your selected text. When copying this way, the box attached to the cursor is marked with a plus sign (on Macintosh computers the box is the same size as the text selection and no plus sign appears).

To remove text completely, select it and then choose Edit ➪ Clear or press Delete. The only way to recover deleted text is to use the Undo feature described in the following section.

Copying and Pasting Code

The "Editing paragraphs," section earlier in this chapter mentioned that Dreamweaver includes a couple of "twists" to the standard Cut, Copy, and Paste options. The combination of Dreamweaver's Design and Code views enables you to copy and paste both text and code. Previous versions of Dreamweaver used a couple of additional commands — Copy Text Only and Paste As Text — to accomplish what Dreamweaver 4 now does with the dual page views.

Put simply, to copy just text from Dreamweaver to another application, use the Design view; to copy both text and code, use the Code view. To understand how two views interact, let's examine how they are used. Table 9-1 explains the variations.

Table 9-1
Results of Copy/Paste from Design and Code views

Selected Text	Copy From	Paste To	Result
Example Text	Design view	Other program	Example Text
Example Text	Design view	Design view	**Example Text**
\<b\>Example Text\</b\>	Code view or other program	Code view	**Example Text** (Design view) \<b\>Example Text\</b\> (Code view)
\<b\>Example Text\</b\>	Code view or other program	Design view	\<b\>Example Text\</b\> (Design view) <b>Example Text</b> (Code view)

Notice that in the final row of Table 9-1, if you copy formatted text such as the bold-face "Example Text" sample and insert it in the Design view, you get the following:

```
&lt;b&gt;Example Text&lt;/b&gt;
```

If you remember the section on named character entities in Chapter 8, you may recognize < as the code for the less-than symbol (<) and > as the code for the greater-than symbol (>). These symbols are used to represent tags such as \<b\> and \</b\> to prevent a browser from interpreting them as tag delimiters.

So what possible real-life uses could there be for Dreamweaver's implementation of the regular Copy and Paste commands in the different views? First, these options are a major benefit for programmers, teachers, and writers who constantly have to communicate in both HTML code and regular text. If an instructor is attempting to demonstrate a coding technique on a Web page, for example, she can just copy the code in the Code view and Paste it into the Design view — instantly transforming the code into something readable online.

Undo, Redo, and the History panel

The Undo command has to be one of the greatest inventions of the twentieth century. Make a mistake? Undo! Want to experiment with two different options? Undo! Change your mind again? Redo! The Undo command reverses your last action, whether you changed a link, added a graphic, or deleted the entire page. The Redo command enables you to reverse your Undo actions.

Dreamweaver displays all of your previous actions on the History panel, so you can easily see what steps you took. To use the Undo command, you can either choose Edit ➪ Undo or press the keyboard shortcut Ctrl+Z (Command+Z); either command undoes a single action at a time. To undo multiple actions, drag the slider in the History panel to the last action you want to keep or just click the slider track at that action.

The complement to Undo is the Redo command. To reverse an Undo command, choose Edit ➪ Redo or Ctrl+Y (Command+Y). To reverse several Undo commands, drag the slider in the History panel back over the grayed-out steps; alternately, you can click the slider track once at the step up to which you'd like to redo.

Tip

The best use I've found for the Redo command is in concert with Undo. When I'm trying to decide between two alternatives, such as two different images, I'll replace one choice with another and then use the Undo/Redo combination to go back and forth between them. Because Dreamweaver replaces any selected object with the current object from the clipboard — even if one is a block of text and the other is a layer — you can easily view two separate options with this trick. The History panel enables you to apply this procedure over any number of steps.

Dreamweaver's implementation of the Undo command enables you to back up as many steps as set in the Maximum Number of History Steps found in Preferences. The History steps can even undo actions that had taken place before a document was saved. Note that the History panel has additional features besides multiple undos.

On the
CD-ROM

Although the History panel lets you replay any series of selected steps at the press of a button, you have to press that button every time you want to replay the steps. I developed a custom extension called Repeat History with which you can repeat any selected steps any number of times. You'll find Repeat History in the Additional Extensions folder on the CD-ROM.

Checking your spelling

A typo can make a significant impression. Not many things are more embarrassing than showing a new Web site to a client and having that client point out a spelling error. Dreamweaver includes an easy-to-use Spell Checker to help you avoid such awkward moments. I make it a practice to spell-check every Web page before it's posted online.

You start the process by choosing Text ➪ Check Spelling or you can press the keyboard shortcut Shift+F7. This sequence opens the Check Spelling dialog box, as seen in Figure 9-4.

Spell-Checking in Non-English Languages

Macromedia has made additional language dictionaries available. As of this writing, dictionaries in these other languages are also available: German, Spanish, French, Italian, Brazilian-Portuguese, Catalan, and Swedish. You can download these dictionaries from Macromedia's Dreamweaver Object Exchange at `www.macromedia.com/support/dreamweaver/dictionary.html`.

To use the dictionaries, download the compressed file to your system. After uncompressing them, store the file with the .dat extension in the Configuration\Dictionaries folder and restart Dreamweaver. Finally, open Preferences (Edit ➪ Preferences) and, from the General panel, select the Dictionary option button. Choose the new language from the drop-down list, and you're ready to spell correctly in another tongue.

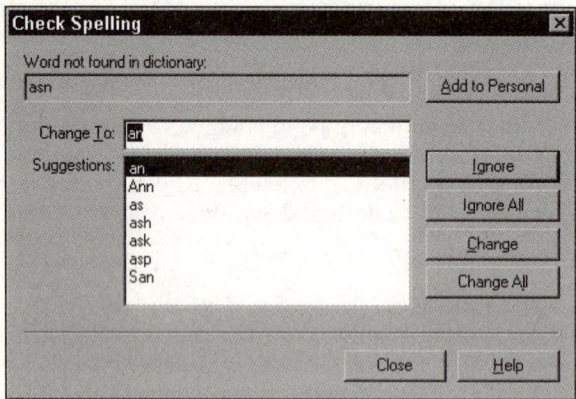

Figure 9-4: Dreamweaver's Spell Checker double-checks your spelling and can find the typos on any Web page.

Once you've opened the Check Spelling dialog box, Dreamweaver begins searching your text for errors. Unless you have selected a portion of your document, Dreamweaver checks the full document regardless of where your cursor is placed. When text is selected, Dreamweaver checks the selection first and then asks if you'd like to do the entire document.

Dreamweaver checks your Web page text against two dictionaries: a standard English (or your chosen language) dictionary and a personal dictionary, to which you can add words. If the Spell Checker finds any text not in either of the program's dictionaries, the text is highlighted in the Document window and appears in the Word not found in dictionary field of the dialog box. A list of suggested corrections appears in the Suggestions list box, with the topmost one highlighted and also displayed in the Change To box. If Dreamweaver cannot find any suggestions, the Change To box is left blank. At this point, you have the following options:

✦ **Add to Personal:** Select this button to include the highlighted word in your personal dictionary and prevent Dreamweaver from tagging it as an error in the future.

✦ **Ignore:** Select this button when you want Dreamweaver to leave the currently highlighted word alone and continue searching the text.

✦ **Ignore All:** Select this button when you want Dreamweaver to disregard all occurrences of this word in the current document.

✦ **Change:** If you see the correct replacement among the list of suggestions, highlight it and select the Change button. If no suggestion is appropriate, you can type the correct word into the Change To text box and then select this button.

✦ **Change All:** Choosing this button causes all instances of the current word to be replaced with the word in the Change To text box.

Have you ever accidentally added a misspelled word to your personal dictionary and then been stuck with the error for all eternity? Dreamweaver enables you to recover from your mistake by giving you access to the dictionary itself. The personal dictionary, stored in the Dreamweaver\Configuration\Dictionaries\ personal.dat file, can be opened and modified in any text editor.

Using Find and Replace

Dreamweaver's Find and Replace features are both timesaving and lifesaving (well, almost). You can use Find and Replace to cut your input time substantially by searching for abbreviations and expanding them to their full state. You can also find a client's incorrectly spelled name and replace it with the correctly spelled version—that's a lifesaver! However, that's just the tip of the iceberg when it comes to what Find and Replace can really do. The Find and Replace engine should be considered a key power tool for any Web developer. You can not only search multiple files but also easily check the code separately from the content.

Here's a short list of what the Find and Replace feature makes possible:

✦ Search the Document window to find any type of text.

✦ Search the underlying HTML to find tags, attributes, or text within tags.

✦ Look for text within specific tags with specific attributes — or look for text that's outside of a specific tag with specific attributes.

✦ Find and replace patterns of text, using wildcard characters called *regular expressions*.

✦ Apply any of the preceding Find and Replace operations to the current document, the current site, any folder, or any group of selected files.

The basic command, Find and Replace is found, with it's companion, Find Next (Find Again, on the Macintosh), under the Edit menu. You can use both commands in either Dreamweaver's Design or Code view, and — in Windows systems — the Site window. Although invoked by a single command, you can use the Find feature independently or in conjunction with Replace.

Find and Replace operations can be applied to one or a series of documents. In addition to searching the current document, you can also apply Find and Replace to all of the files in a folder or a site. Furthermore, individual files selected in the Site window are also searchable.

Finding and replacing text on the visual page

The most basic method of using Find and Replace takes place in the Document window. Whenever you need to search for any text that can be seen by the public on your Web page — whether it's to correct a spelling or change a name — Dreamweaver makes it fast and simple.

Tip The Find and Replace dialog box, unlike most of Dreamweaver's dialog boxes, is actually a *nonmodal window*. This technical term just means that you can easily move back and forth between your Document window and the Find and Replace dialog box without having to close the dialog box first, as you do with the other Dreamweaver windows.

To find some text on your Web page, follow these steps:

1. From the Document window, choose Edit ➪ Find and Replace or use the keyboard shortcut Ctrl+F (Command+F).

2. In the Find and Replace dialog box, shown in Figure 9-5, make sure that Text is the selected Search For option.

3. In the text box next to the Search For option, type the word or phrase you're looking for.

Tip If you select your text *before* launching the Find dialog box, it automatically appears in the Search For text box.

4. Select the appropriate search options, if any:

   • If you want to find an exact replica of the word as you entered it, select the Match Case checkbox; otherwise, Dreamweaver searches for all variations of your text, regardless of case.

   • To force Dreamweaver to disregard any whitespace variations, such as additional spaces, hard spaces or tabs, select the Ignore Whitespace Differences option. For most situations, it's a good idea to leave this default option enabled.

   • Selecting Use Regular Expressions enables you to work with Dreamweaver's wildcard characters (discussed later in this section). Use Regular Expressions and Ignore Whitespace Differences are mutually exclusive options.

Search For Options list   Search For Text box

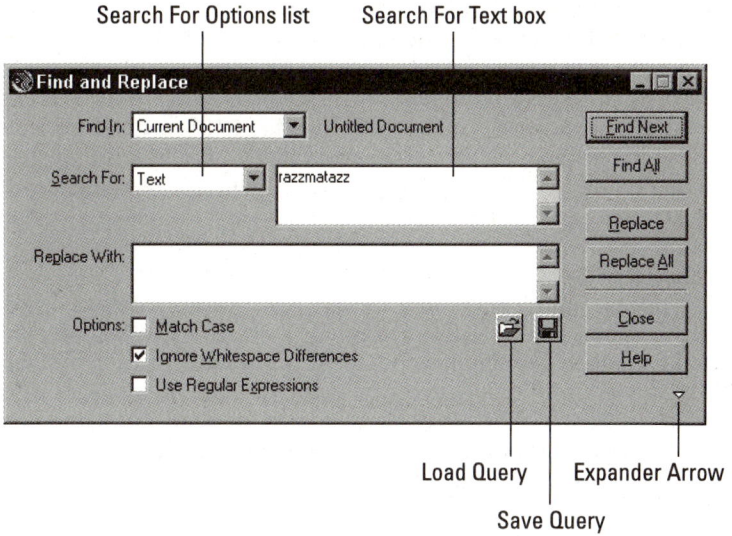

Load Query   Expander Arrow

Save Query

Figure 9-5: The Find and Replace dialog box.

5. Select the Find Next button to begin the search from the cursor's current position.

   • If Dreamweaver finds the desired text, it highlights the text in the Document window.

   • If Dreamweaver doesn't find the text in the remaining portion of the document, it asks if you want to continue searching from the beginning. Select Yes to continue or No to exit.

6. If you want to look for the next occurrence of your selected text, click the Find Next button again.

7. To look for all occurrences of your text, choose Find All.

   The Find dialog box expands to display the List window. Dreamweaver lists each found occurrence on a separate line in the List window.

 Tip

You can quickly move from one found selection to another by double-clicking the line in the List window. Dreamweaver highlights the selection, scrolling the Document window, if necessary.

After searching the page, Dreamweaver tells you how many occurrences of your selection, if any, were found.

8. You can enter other text to search or exit the Find dialog box by clicking the Close button.

The text you enter in the Find dialog box is kept in memory until it's replaced by your next use of the Find feature. After you have executed the Find command once, you can continue to search for your text without redisplaying the Find dialog box, by selecting Edit ⇨ Find Next (Find Again) or the keyboard shortcut F3 (Command+G). If Dreamweaver finds your text, it is highlighted — in fact, Dreamweaver acts exactly the same as when the Find dialog box is open. The Find Next (Find Again) command gives you a quick way to search through a long document — especially when you put the F3 (Command+G) key to work.

When you add the Replace command to a Find operation, you can search your text for a word or phrase and, if it's found, replace it with another word or phrase of your choice. As mentioned earlier, the Replace feature is a handy way to correct mistakes and expand abbreviations. Figure 9-6 shows an example of the latter operation. This example intentionally uses the abbreviation DW throughout the input text of a Web page article. Then the example uses the Replace All function to expand all the DWs to Dreamweaver — in one fell swoop. This technique is much faster than typing "Dreamweaver" nine times.

Figure 9-6: Use the Edit ⇨ Replace command to correct your text one item at a time or all at once.

When you replace text in the Document window, it is replaced regardless of its formatting. For example, suppose you had the following paragraph:

Mary's accusation reminded Jon of studying synchrones in high school. *Synchrones*, he recalled, were graphs in which the lines constantly approached zero, but never made it. "Yeah," he thought, "That's me, all right. I'm one big **synchrone**."

Upon discovering that "synchrone" should actually be "asymptote," you could use the Find and Replace feature to replace all the plain, italic, and bold versions of the "synchrone" text simultaneously.

Tip   It's possible to alter formatting as well — to change all the formatting to just under-lining for example — but for that, you need to perform your Find and Replace oper-ations in the Code Inspector, as discussed in the following section.

Follow these steps to use Dreamweaver's Replace feature in the Document window:

1. Choose Edit ➪ Find and Replace, or the keyboard shortcut Ctrl+F (Command+F).

2. In the Find and Replace dialog box, make sure that Text is the selected Search For option and then, in the text box next to the Search For option, type the word or phrase you're looking for.

3. In the Replace With text box, type the substitute word.

4. Click the Find Next button. Dreamweaver begins searching from the current cursor position. If Dreamweaver finds the text, it is highlighted.

   If the text is not found, Dreamweaver asks if you want to continue searching from the top of the document. Select Yes to continue or No to exit.

5. To replace the highlighted occurrence of your text, select the Replace button. Dreamweaver replaces the found text with the substitute text and then auto-matically searches for the next occurrence.

6. If you want to replace all instances of the Find text, select the Replace All button.

   When Dreamweaver has found all the occurrences of your Find text, it dis-plays the number of replacement operations and a line for each in the List window.

   Double-clicking a line in the List window highlights the changed text in the Document window.

7. When you've finished using the Replace dialog box, click the Close button to exit.

Tip   You can also rerun Find and Replace operations by highlighting the appropriate step in the History panel and choosing the Replay button.

Searching the code

The power curve ramps up significantly when you start to explore Dreamweaver's HTML Find and Replace capabilities. Should your client decide that he wants the company's name to appear in blue, bold, 18-point type throughout the 300-page site, you can accommodate him with a few keystrokes — instead of hours of mind-numbing grunt work.

Storing and Retrieving Queries

Dreamweaver enables you to develop extremely complex queries. Rather than forcing you to reenter queries over and over again, Dreamweaver enables you to save and load them when needed. You can store and retrieve Find and Replace queries; Dreamweaver saves them with .dwr file extensions, respectively.

To save a query, select the diskette icon on the Find and Replace dialog box. The standard Save Query (Save Query to file) dialog box appears for you to enter a file name; the appropriate file extension is appended automatically. To load a previously saved query, select the folder icon on the Find and Replace dialog box to open the Load Query dialog box. Although only queries with a .dwr extension are being saved in the current version, you can still load both .dwq and .dwr files saved from previous Dreamweaver versions.

Although saving and opening queries is an obvious advantage when working with complex wildcard operations, you can also make it work for you in an every day situation. If, for example, you have a set series of acronyms or abbreviations that you must convert repeatedly, you can save your simple text queries and use them as needed without having to remember all the details.

You can perform three different types of searches that use the HTML in your Web page:

✦ You can search for text anywhere in the HTML code. With this capability, you can look for text within Alt or any other attribute—and change it.

✦ You can search for text relative to specific tags. Sometimes you need to change just the text contained within the <b> tag and leave all other matching text alone.

✦ You can search for specific HTML tags and/or their attributes. Dreamweaver's Find and Replace feature gives you the capability to insert, delete, or modify tags and attributes.

Looking for text in the Code

Text that appears onscreen is often replicated in various sections of your off-screen HTML code. It's not uncommon, for example, to use the Alt attribute in an <img> tag that repeats the caption under the picture. What do you think would happen under those circumstances if you replaced the wording with the standard Find and Replace features in the Design view of the Document window? You're still left with the task of tracking down the Alt attribute and making that change as well. Dreamweaver enables you to act on both content and programming text in one operation—a major savings in time and effort, not to mention aggravation.

To find and replace text in both the content and the code, follow these steps:

1. Choose Edit ⇨ Find and Replace to open the dialog box.

2. Select the parameters of your search from the Find In option: Current Document, Current Site, or Folder.

   Remember, you can also search specific files if you launch the Find and Replace dialog box from the Site window.

3. Choose the Search For option button and select the Source Code option from the drop-down list.

4. Enter the text you're searching for in the text box next to the Search For option.

5. If you are replacing, enter the new text in the Replace With text box.

6. Select any options desired: Match Case, Ignore Whitespace Differences, or Use Regular Expressions.

7. Choose your Find/Replace option: Find Next, Find All, Replace, or Replace All

8. Select Close when finished.

Caution

As with all Find and Replace operations—especially those in which you decide to Replace All—you need to exercise extreme caution when replacing text throughout your code. If you're unsure about what's going to be affected, choose Find All first and, with your Code view or Inspector open, step through all the selections to be positive no unwanted surprises exist. Should you replace some code in error, you can always undo the operation — but only if the document is open. Replacing text or code in a closed file, as is done when the operation is performed on a folder, the current site, or selected files in the Site window, is not undoable.

Using advanced text options in Find and Replace

In Find and Replace operations, the global Replace All isn't appropriate for every situation; sometimes you need a more precise approach. Dreamweaver enables you to fine-tune your searches to pinpoint accuracy. You can look for text within particular tags—and even within particular tags with specific attributes. Moreover, you can find (and replace) text that is outside of particular tags with specific attributes.

Dreamweaver assists you by providing a drop-down list of every standard HTML tag, as well as numerous special function tags such as those used for Cold Fusion applications. You can also search for your own custom tags. You don't have to try to remember which attributes go with which tag either. Dreamweaver also supplies you with a context-sensitive list of attributes that changes according to the tag selected.

In addition to using the tag's attributes as a search filter, Dreamweaver can also search within the tag for text or another tag. Most HTML tags are so-called container tags that consist of an opening tag and a closing tag, such as <b> and </b>. You can set up a filter to look for text within a specific tag — or text outside of a specific tag. For example, if you were searching for the word *big*:

```
The big, red boat was a <b>big</b> waste of money.
```

you could build a Find and Replace operation that changed one instance of the one word (big, red) but not the other (big)—or vice versa.

To look for text in or out of specific tags and attributes, follow these steps:

1. Choose Edit ➪ Find and Replace to open the Find and Replace dialog box.

2. Select the parameters of your search from the Find In option: Current Document, Current Site, or Folder.

3. Choose the Search For option button and select the Text (Advanced) option from the drop-down list.

   The Add and Remove (+ and –) tag options are made available, as shown in Figure 9-7.

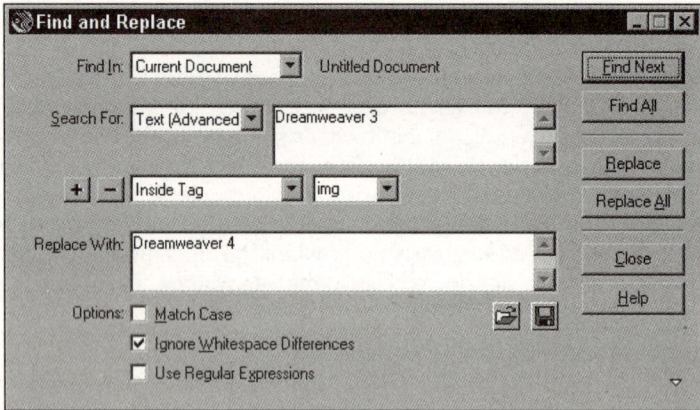

Figure 9-7: The advanced text features of Find and Replace enable you to manipulate text and code simultaneously.

4. Enter the text you're searching for in the text box next to the Search For option.

5. Select either Inside Tag or Not Inside Tag from the option list.

6. Select the tag to include or exclude from the adjacent option list.

7. To add a further restriction on the search, click the Add button (the plus sign).

   Another line of search options is added to the dialog box.

8. Select the additional search filter. The available options include the following:

Filter	Description
With Attribute	Enables you to select any attribute from the adjacent option list. You can set this attribute to be equal to, less than, greater than, or not equal to any given value by choosing from the available drop-down lists.
Without Attribute	Finds text within a particular tag that does not include a specific attribute. Choose the attribute to be equal to, less than, greater than, or not equal to any given value by choosing from the available drop-down lists.
Containing	Searches the tag for either specified text or another user-selectable tag found within the initial tag pair.
Not Containing	Searches the tag for either text or a tag not found within the initial tag pair.
Inside Tag	Enables you to look for text that is within two (or more) sets of specific tags.
Not Inside Tag	Enables you to look for text that is in one tag, but not in another tag, or vice versa.

 9. To continue adding filter conditions, select the Add button (the plus sign) and repeat Steps 7 and 8.

10. To remove a filter condition, select the Remove button (the minus sign).

11. If you are replacing, enter the new text in the Replace With text box.

12. Select any options desired: Match Case, Ignore Whitespace Differences, or Use Regular Expressions.

13. Choose your Find/Replace option: Find Next, Find All, Replace, or Replace All.

14. Select Close when finished.

Tip

You can continue to add conditions by clicking the Add (+) button. In fact, I was able to add so many conditions, the Find/Replace dialog box began to disappear off the screen! To erase all conditions, change the Search For option to Text or Source Code and then change it back to Text (Advanced).

Replacing HTML tags and attributes

Let's say a new edict has come down from the HTML gurus of your company: No longer is the `<strong>` tag to be used to indicate emphasis; from now on; use only the `<b>` tag. Oh, and by the way, change all the existing pages — all 3,000+ Web and intranet pages — so that they're compliant. Dreamweaver makes short work out of nightmare situations such as these by giving you the power to search and replace HTML tags and their attributes.

But Dreamweaver doesn't stop there. Not only can you replace one tag with another, you can also perform the following:

✦ Change or delete the tag (with or without its contents)

✦ Set an attribute in the tag to another value

✦ Remove any or all attributes

✦ Add text and/or code before or after the starting or the ending tag

To alter your code using Dreamweaver's Find and Replace feature, follow these steps:

1. As with other Find and Replace operations, choose Edit ➪ Find and Replace to open the dialog box.

2. Select the parameters of your search from the Find In option: Current Page, Current Site, or Folder.

3. Choose the Search For option button and select the tag option from the drop-down list.

   The dialog box changes to include the tag functions.

4. Select the desired tag from the option list next to the Search For option.

Tip   You can either scroll down the list box to find the tag or you can type the first letter of the tag in the box. Dreamweaver scrolls to the group of tags that begin with that letter when the list is visible (Windows only).

5. If desired, you can limit the search by specifying an attribute and value, or with other conditions, as discussed in detail in the previous section.

Note   If you want to search for just a tag, select the Remove button (the minus key) to eliminate the additional condition.

6. Make a selection from the Action list, shown in Figure 9-8. The options are as follows:

Action	Description
Replace Tag & Contents	Substitutes the selected tag and all included content with a text string. The text string can include HTML code.
Replace Contents Only	Changes the content between the specified tag to a given text string, which can also include HTML code.
Remove Tag & Contents	Deletes the tag and all contents.
Strip Tag	Removes the tag but leaves the previously enclosed content.

Action	Description
Change Tag	Substitutes one tag for another.
Set Attribute	Sets an existing attribute to a new value or inserts a new attribute set to a specific value.
Remove Attribute	Deletes a specified attribute.
Add Before Start Tag	Inserts a text string (with or without HTML) before the opening tag.
Add After End Tag	Inserts a text string (with or without HTML) after the end tag.
Add After Start Tag	Inserts a text string (with or without HTML) after the opening tag.
Add Before End Tag	Inserts a text string (with or without HTML) before the end tag.

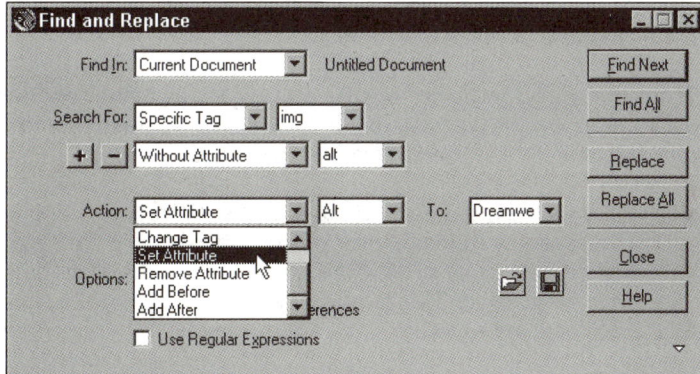

Figure 9-8: The Action list enables you to replace tags or modify them by setting the existing attributes or adding new ones.

Note

Not all the options listed in the preceding table are available for all tags. Some so-called empty tags, such as `<img>`, consist of a single tag and not tag pairs. Empty tags have only Add Before and Add After options instead of Add Before Start Tag, Add After Start Tag, Add Before End Tag, and Add After End Tag.

7. Select any options desired: Match Case, Ignore Whitespace Differences, or Use Regular Expressions.

8. Choose your Find/Replace option: Find Next, Find All, Replace, or Replace All.

9. Select Close when finished.

Tip You don't have to apply a single action to all the instances Dreamweaver locates if you choose Find All. In the list of found expressions, select a single item and then choose Replace. Dreamweaver makes the revision and places a green dot next to the item so you can tell it has been altered. If you want, you can then select another item from the list, choose a different action, and then select Replace.

Concentrating your search with regular expressions

As powerful as all the other Find and Replace features are, they are boosted to a higher level of flexibility with the addition of regular expressions. I've referred to regular expressions as being similar to wildcards in other programs, but their capabilities are really far more extensive.

Regular expressions are best described as a *text pattern matching system*. If you can identify any pattern in your text, you can manipulate it with regular expressions. What kind of pattern? Let's say you have a spreadsheet-like table with lots of numbers, showing both dollars and cents, mixed with explanatory text. With regular expressions, you can match the pattern formed by the dollar sign and the decimal point and reformat the entire table, turning all the figures deep blue with a new font — all in one Find and Replace operation.

Note   If you're into Unix, you recognize regular expressions as being very close to the grep utility — *grep*, by the way, stands for Get Regular Expressions and Print. The Find and Replace feature in BBEdit also features a grep-like syntax.

You can apply regular expressions to any of the types of Find and Replace operations previously discussed, with just a click of the Use Regular Expressions checkbox. Note that when you select Use Regular Expressions, the Ignore Unnecessary Whitespace option is deselected. This is because the two options are mutually exclusive and cannot be used together.

The most basic regular expression is the text itself. If you enable the feature and then enter **th** in the Search For text box, Dreamweaver locates every example of "th" in the text and/or source. Although this capability by itself has little use beyond what you can also achieve with standard Find and Replace operations, it's important to remember this functionality as you begin to build your patterns.

Using wildcard characters

Initially, it's helpful to be able to use what traditionally are know as *wildcards* — characters that match different types of characters. The wildcards in regular expressions represent single characters and are described in Table 9-2. In other words, no single regular expression represents all the characters, as the asterisk does when used in PC file searches (such as *.*). However, such a condition can be represented with a slightly more complex regular expression (described later in the "Matching character positions and repeating characters" section).

Table 9-2
Regular Expression Wildcard Characters

Character	Matches	Example
.	Any single character	**w.d** matches **wid**e but not world.
\w	Any alphanumeric character, including the underscore	**w\wd** matches **wid**e and **world**.
\W	Any nonalphanumeric character	**jboy\Widest.com** matches **jboy@idest.com**.
\d	Any numeric character 0–9	**y\dk** matches **Y2K**.
\D	Any nonnumeric character	**\D2\D** matches **Y2K** and **H20**.
\s	Any whitespace character, including space, tab, form feed, or line feed	**\smedia** matches **media** but not Macromedia.
\S	Any nonwhitespace character	**\Smedia** matches Macro**media** but not media.
\t	A tab	Matches any single tab character in the HTML source.
\f	Form feed	Matches any single form-feed character in the HTML source.
\n	Line feed	Matches any single line-feed character in the HTML source.
\r	Carriage return	Matches any single carriage-return character in the HTML source.

Tip
The backslash character (\) is used to escape special characters so that they can be included in a search. For example, if you want to look for an asterisk, you need to specify it in this way: *. Likewise, when trying to find the backslash character, precede it with another backslash character, as follows: \\.

Matching character positions and repeating characters

With regular expressions, not only can you match the type of character, but you can also match its position in the text. This feature enables you to perform operations on characters at the beginning, end, or middle of the word or line. Regular expressions also enable you to find instances in which a character is repeated an unspecified number of times or a specific number of times. Combined, these features broaden the scope of the patterns that can be found.

Table 9-3 details the options available for matching by text placement and character repetition.

<table>
<tr><td colspan="3">**Table 9-3**
Regular Expression Character Positions and
Repeating Characters</td></tr>
<tr><td>*Character*</td><td>*Matches*</td><td>*Example*</td></tr>
<tr><td>^</td><td>Beginning of a line</td><td>**^c** matches the first c in "**C**all me Ishmael."</td></tr>
<tr><td>$</td><td>End of a line</td><td>**d$** matches the final "d" in "Be afraid. Be very afrai**d**."</td></tr>
<tr><td>\b</td><td>A word boundary, such as a space or carriage return</td><td>**\btext** matches **text**book but not SimpleText.</td></tr>
<tr><td>\B</td><td>A nonword boundary inside a word</td><td>**\Btext** matches Simple**Text** but not textbook.</td></tr>
<tr><td>*</td><td>The preceding character zero or more times</td><td>**b*c** matches **BBC** and **c**old.</td></tr>
<tr><td>+</td><td>The preceding character one or more times</td><td>**b+c** matches **BBC** but not cold.</td></tr>
<tr><td>?</td><td>The preceding character zero or one time</td><td>**st?un** matches **stun** and **sun** but not strung.</td></tr>
<tr><td>{n}</td><td>Exactly *n* instances of the preceding character</td><td>**e{2}** matches reed and each pair of two e's in "Ai**ee**e**ee**ee!" but nothing in Dreamweaver.</td></tr>
<tr><td>{n,m}</td><td>At least *n* and *m* instances of the preceding character</td><td>**C{2,4}** matches #**CC**00FF and #**CCCC**00 but not the full string #CCCCCC.</td></tr>
</table>

Matching character ranges

Beyond single characters, or repetitions of single characters, regular expressions incorporate the capability of finding or excluding ranges of characters. This feature is particularly useful when you're working with groups of names or titles. Ranges are specified in set brackets. A match is made when any one of the characters, not necessarily all of the characters, within the set brackets is found.

Descriptions of how to match character ranges with regular expressions can be found in Table 9-4.

Table 9-4
Regular Expression Character Ranges

Character	Matches	Example
[abc]	Any one of the characters a, b, or c	**[lmrt]** matches the l and m's in **lemm**ings and the r and t in **r**oad**t**rip.
[^abc]	Any character except a, b, or c	**[^etc]** matches **GIFs** but not etc in the phrase "GIFs etc."
[a-z]	Any character in the range from a to z	**[l-p]** matches l and o in **lo**wery and m, n, o an p in **p**oint**m**an.
x|y	Either x or y	**boy|girl** matches both **boy** and **girl**.

Grouping with regular expressions

Grouping is perhaps the single most powerful concept in regular expressions. With it, any matched text pattern is easily manipulated — for example, the following list of names:

✦ John Jacob Jingleheimer Schmidt

✦ James T. Kirk

✦ Cara Fishman

could be rearranged so that the last name is first, separated by a comma, like this:

✦ Schmidt, John Jacob Jingleheimer

✦ Kirk, James T.

✦ Fishman, Cara

Grouping is handled primarily with parentheses. To indicate a group, enclose it in parentheses in the Find text field. Regular expressions can manage up to nine grouped patterns. Each grouped patterned is designated by a dollar sign ($) in front of a number (1–9), in the Replace text field, like this: **$3**.

Caution

Remember that the dollar sign is also used after a character or pattern to indicate the last character in a line.

Table 9-5 shows how regular expressions use grouping.

Table 9-5
Regular Expressions Grouping

Character	Matches	Example
(p)	Any pattern p	**(\b\w*)\.(\w*\b)** matches two patterns, the first before a period and the second, after — such as in a file name with an extension. The backslash before the period escapes it so that it is not interpreted as a regular expression.
$1, $2 . . . $9	The *n*th pattern noted with parentheses	The replacement pattern **$1's extension is ".$2"** would manipulate the pattern **(\b\w*)\.(\w*\b)** so that Chapter09.txt and Image12.gif would become **Chapter09's extension is ".txt"** and **Image12's extension is ".gif."**

The <br> tag

As with headings, the paragraph tag falls among the class of HTML objects called *block elements*. As such, any text marked with the <p>...</p> tag pair is always rendered with an extra line above and below the text, often called whitespace. To have a series of blank lines appear one after the other, use the break tag <br>. Multiple break tags may also be used to provide whitespace between elements.

Break tags are used within block elements, such as headings and paragraphs, to provide a line break where the <br> is inserted. Dreamweaver provides two ways to insert a <br> tag: You can choose the Enter Line Break button from the Characters panel of the Objects panel or you can use the keyboard shortcut Shift+Enter (Shift+Return).

Figure 9-9 demonstrates the effect of the <br> tag. The menu items in Column A on the left are the result of using the <br> tag within a paragraph. In Column B on the right, paragraph tags alone are used. The <h1> heading is also split at the top (modified through style sheet selections) with a break tag to avoid the insertion of an unwanted line.

By default, Dreamweaver marks <br> tags with a symbol: A gold shield with the letters BR and the standard Enter/Return symbol. You can turn off this display feature by choosing Preferences ➪ Invisible Elements and deselecting the Line Breaks checkbox.

Figure 9-9: Use break tags to wrap your lines without the additional line spacing brought about by <p> tags.

Other whitespace tags

If you can't get the alignment effect you want through the regular text options available in Dreamweaver, two other HTML tags can affect whitespace: <nobr> and <wbr>. Although a tad on the obscure side, these tags can be just the ticket in certain circumstances. Let's see how they work.

The <nobr> tag

Most of the time, you want the user's browser to handle word-wrapping chores automatically. Occasionally, however, you may need to make sure that a particular string of text is rendered in one piece. For these situations, you can use the no break tag <nobr>. Any text that comes in between the opening and closing tag pair — <nobr>...</nobr> — is displayed in one continuous line. If the line of text is wider than the current browser window, a horizontal scroll bar automatically appears along the bottom of the browser.

The <nobr> tag is supported only through the Netscape and Microsoft browsers and must be entered by hand into your HTML code. Use the <nobr> tag under very special circumstances.

Overcoming Line-Spacing Difficulties

Line spacing is a major issue and a common problem for Web designers. A design often calls for lines to be tightly spaced, and also of various sizes. If you use the break tag to separate your lines, you get the tight spacing required, but you won't be able to make each line a different heading size. As far as HTML and your browser are concerned, the text is still one block element, no matter how many line breaks are inserted. If, on the other hand, you make each line a separate paragraph or heading, the line spacing will be unattractively "open."

You can use one of several workarounds for this problem. First, if you're using line breaks, you can alter the size of each line by selecting it and choosing a different font size, either from the Property Inspector or the Text ⇨ Size menu.

A second option renders all the text as a graphics object and inserts it as an image. This gives you total control over the font's appearance and line spacing, at the cost of added download time.

For a third possible solution, take a look at the section on preformatted text later in this chapter. Because you can apply styles to a preformatted text block (which can include line breaks and extra whitespace), you can alter the size, color, and font of each line, if necessary.

Ultimately the best solution is to use Cascading Style Sheets (CSS). The majority of browsers now in use support line spacing through CSS; however, if 3.0 browser compatability is a site requirement, you'll have to use one of the other methods outlined here.

The <wbr> tag

The companion to the `<nobr>` tag is the word break tag `<wbr>`. Similar to a soft hyphen in a word processing program, the `<wbr>` tag tells the browser where to break a word, if necessary. When used within `<nobr>` tags, `<wbr>` is the equivalent of telling a browser, "Keep all this text in one line, but if you have to break it, break it here."

As with the `<nobr>` tag, `<wbr>` is supported only by Netscape and Microsoft browsers and must be entered by hand via the Quick Tag Editor, Code view, Code Inspector, or your external editor.

Importing Word HTML

Microsoft Word has offered an option to save its documents as HTML since the release of Word 97. Unfortunately, Microsoft's version of HTML output is, at best, highly idiosyncratic. Although you could always open a Word HTML file in

Dreamweaver, if you ever had to modify the page — which you almost always do — it took so long to find your way through the convoluted code that you were almost better off building the page from scratch. Fortunately, that's no longer the case with Dreamweaver.

The capability to Import Word HTML is a key workflow enhancement for Dreamweaver. Dreamweaver can successfully import and automatically clean up files from Microsoft Word 97, Word 98, or Word 2000. The cleanup takes place automatically upon import, but you can also finely tune the modifications that Dreamweaver makes to the file. Moreover, you can even apply the current Source Format profile so that the HTML is styled to look like native Dreamweaver code.

Naturally, before you can import a Word HTML file, you have to have created one. To export a document in HTML format in Word 97/98, choose File ➪ Save as HTML; in Word 2000, the command has changed to File ➪ Save as Web Page. Although the wording change may seem to be a move toward less jargon, what Word actually exports is significant. With Word 2000 (and all the Office 2000 products), Microsoft heartily embraced the XML standard and uses a combination of standard HTML and custom XML code throughout their exported Web pages. For example, here's the opening tag from a Word 2000 document, saved as a Web page:

```
<html xmlns:o="urn:schemas-microsoft-com:office:office"
xmlns:w="urn:schemas-microsoft-com:office:word"
xmlns:dt="uuid:C2F41010-65B3-11d1-A29F-00AA00C14882"
xmlns="http://www.w3.org/TR/REC-html40">
```

which Dreamweaver alters to:

```
<html>
```

If you accept the defaults, importing a Word HTML file is a two-step affair:

1. Choose File ➪ Import ➪ Import Word HTML.

   The Import Word HTML dialog box opens and Dreamweaver detects whether the HTML file was exported from Word 97/98 or 2000. The interface options change accordingly.

Caution If Dreamweaver can't determine what version of Word generated the file, an alert appears. Although Dreamweaver will still try to clean up the code, it may not function correctly. The same alert appears if you inadvertently select a standard nonHTML Word document.

2. Click OK to confirm the import operation.

   Dreamweaver creates a new HTML document, imports the file, and cleans up the code. If the Show Log on Completion option is selected, Dreamweaver informs you of the modifications made.

For most purposes, accepting the defaults is the best way to quickly bring in your Word HTML files. However, because Web designers have a wide range of code requirements, Dreamweaver provides a full set of options so you can tailor the Word-to-Dreamweaver transformation to your liking. Two different sets of options exist — one for documents saved from Word 97/98 and one for those saved from Word 2000. The different sets of options can be seen on the Detailed tab of the Import Word HTML dialog box; the Basic tab is the same for both file types. Table 9-6 details the Basic tab options, the Word 97/98 options, and the Word 2000 options.

Table 9-6
Import Word HTML Options

Option	Description
Basic	
Remove all Word-specific markup	Deletes all Word-specific tags, including Word XML, conditional tags, empty paragraphs, and margins in `<style>` tags.
Clean up CSS	Deletes all Word-specific CSS code, including inline CSS styles where styles are nested, "mso" designated styles, non-CSS style declarations, CSS style attributes from tables and orphaned (unused) style definitions.
Clean up `<font>` tags	Deletes `<font>` tags that set the default body text to an absolute font size 2.
Fix invalidly nested tags	Deletes tags surrounding paragraph and block-level tags.
Set background color	Adds a background color to the page. Word does not supply one. The default added color is white (#ffffff). Colors can be entered as hexadecimal triplets with a leading hash mark or as a valid color name — that is, red.
Apply source formatting	Formats the imported code according to the guidelines of the current Source Format profile used by Dreamweaver.
Show log on completion	Displays a dialog box that lists all alterations when the process is complete.
Detailed Options for Word 97/98	
Remove Word specific markup	Enables the general clean up of Word-inserted tags.
Word meta and link tags from `<head>`	Specifically enables Dreamweaver to remove Word-specific `<meta>` and `<link>` tags from the `<head>` section of a document.
Clean up `<font>` tags	Enables the general clean up of `<font>` tags.

Option	Description
Convert size [7-1] to	Specifies which tag, if any, is substituted for a `<font size=`*n*`>` tag. Options are:
	* `<h1>` through `<h6>`
	* `<font size=1>` through `<font size=7>`
	* Default size
	* Don't change

Detailed Options for Word 2000

Option	Description
Remove Word specific markup	Enables the general clean up of Word-inserted tags.
XML from `<html>` tag	Deletes the Word-generated XML from the `<html>` tag.
Word meta and link tags from `<head>`	Specifically enables Dreamweaver to remove Word-specific `<meta>` and `<link>` tags from the `<head>` section of a document.
Word XML markup	Enables the general clean up of Word-inserted XML tags.
`<![if...]>` `<![endif]>` conditional tags and their contents	Removes all conditional statements.
Remove empty paragraphs and margins from styles	Deletes `<p>` tags without a closing `</p>` and styles tags including margin attributes — for example, `style='margin-top:0in'`.
Clean up CSS	Enables the general clean up of Word inserted CSS tags.
Remove inline CSS styles when possible	Deletes redundant information in nested styles.
Remove any style attribute that starts with "mso"	Eliminates all Microsoft Office (mso) specific attributes.
Remove any non-CSS style declaration	Deletes nonstandard style declarations.
Remove all CSS styles from table rows and cells	Eliminates style information from `<table>`, `<tr>`, and `<td>` tags.
Remove all unused style definitions	Deletes any declared styles that are not referenced in the page.

You don't have to remember to run the Import Word HTML command to take advantage of Dreamweaver's cleanup features. If you've already opened a document saved as Word HTML, you can choose Commands ⇨ Clean Up Word HTML and gain access to the exact same dialog box for the existing page.

Styling Your Text

When the Internet was founded, its intended focus was to make scientific data widely accessible. Soon it became apparent that even raw data could benefit from being styled contextually, without detracting from the Internet's openness and universality. Over the short history of HTML, text styles have become increasingly important, and the World Wide Web Consortium (W3C) has sought to keep a balance between substance and style.

Dreamweaver enables the Web designer to apply the most popular HTML styles directly through the program's menus and Property Inspector. Less prevalent styles can be inserted through the integrated text editors or by hand.

Working with preformatted text

Browsers ignore formatting niceties considered irrelevant to page content: tabs, extra line feeds, indents, and added whitespace. However, you can force browsers to read all the text, including whitespace, exactly as you have entered it. By applying the preformatted tag, `<pre>`, you tell the browser that it should keep any additional whitespace encountered within the text. By default, the `<pre>` tag also renders its content with a monospace font such as Courier. For these reasons, the `<pre>` tag was used to lay out text in columns in the early days of HTML, before tables were widely available.

You can apply the preformatted tag either through the Property Inspector or the menus. Before you use either technique, however, be sure to select the text or position the cursor where you want the preformatted text to begin. To use the Property Inspector, open the Format list box and choose Preformatted. To use the menus, choose Text ⇨ Paragraph Format ⇨ Preformatted.

The `<pre>` tag is a block element format, like the paragraph or the headings tags, rather than a style. This designation as a block element format has two important implications. First, you can't apply the `<pre>` tag to part of a line; when you use this tag, the entire paragraph is altered. Second, you can apply styles to preformatted text — this enables you to increase the size or alter the font, but at the same time maintain the whitespace feature made possible with the `<pre>` tag. All text in Figure 9-10 uses the `<pre>` tag; the column on the left is the standard output with monospaced font; the column on the right uses a different font in a larger size.

Figure 9-10: Preformatted text gives you full control over the line breaks, tabs, and other whitespace in your Web page.

Depicting various styles

As explained in Chapter 8, HTML's logical styles are used to mark text relatively or within a particular context, rather than with a specific look. The eventual displayed appearance of logical styles is completely up to the viewer's browser. This is useful when you are working with documents from different sources — reports from different research laboratories around the country, for instance — and you want certain conformity of style. Logical styles are utilitarian; physical styles such as boldface and italic are decorative. Both types of styles have their uses in material published on today's Web.

All of Dreamweaver's styles are accessed by choosing Text ➪ Style and selecting from the 13 available style name options. A checkmark appears next to the selected tags. Style tags can be nested (put inside one another), and you can mix logical and physical tags within a word, line, or document. You can have a bold, strikethrough, variable style; or you can have an underlined, cited style. (Both variable and cite are particular logical styles covered later in this section.) If, however, you are trying to achieve a particular look using logical styles, you should probably use the Cascading Style Sheets feature.

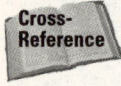

Cross-Reference   The styles that can be applied through regular HTML are just the tip of the iceberg compared to the possibilities with Cascading Style Sheets. For details on using this feature, see Chapter 27.

Take a look at Figure 9-11 for a comparison of how the styles are rendered in Dreamweaver, Internet Explorer 5.0, and Netscape Communicator 4.7. While the various renderings are mostly the same, notice the browser differences in the Definition styles and the difference in how the Keyboard style is rendered in Dreamweaver and either browser.

Figure 9-11: In this comparison chart, the various renderings of Dreamweaver style tags are from Dreamweaver, Netscape Communicator 4.7, and Internet Explorer 5.0 (from left to right).

Two of the three physical style tags — bold and italic — are both available from the Text Property Inspector and through keyboard shortcuts (Ctrl+B or Command+B, and Ctrl+I or Command+I, respectively). The Underline tag, <u>, is available only through the Text ⇨ Style menu. Underlining text on a Web page is generally discouraged in order to avoid confusion with links, which are typically displayed underlined.

Both physical and logical style tags are described, with examples, in Table 9-7.

Table 9-7
Dreamweaver Style Tags

Style	Tag	Description
Bold	`<b>`	Text is rendered with a bold style.
Italic	`<i>`	Text is rendered with an italic style.
Underline	`<u>`	Text is rendered underlined.
Strikethrough	`<s>`	Used primarily in edited documents to depict edited text. Usually rendered with a line through the text.
Teletype	`<tt>`	Used to represent an old-style typewriter. Rendered in a monospace font such as Courier.
Emphasis	`<em>`	Used to accentuate certain words relative to the surrounding text. Most often rendered in italic.
Strong Emphasis	`<strong>`	Used to strongly accentuate certain words relative to the surrounding text. Most often rendered in boldface.
Code	`<code>`	Used to depict programming code, usually in a monospaced font.
Sample	`<samp>`	Used to display characters in a literal sequence, usually in a monospaced font.
Variables	`<var>`	Used to mark variables in programming code. Most often displayed in italics.
Keyboard	`<kbd>`	Used to indicate what should be user input. Often shown in a monospaced font, sometimes in boldface.
Citation	`<cite>`	Used to mark citations, references, and titles. Most often displayed in italic.
Definition	`<dfn>`	Used to denote the first, defining instance of a term. Usually displayed in italic.

Using the <address> tag

Currently, Dreamweaver does not support one useful style tag: the `<address>` tag. Rendered as italic text by browsers, the `<address>`...`</address>` tag pair often marks the signature and e-mail address of a Web page's creator. The `<address>` tags should go around a paragraph tag pair; otherwise, Dreamweaver flags the closing `</p>` as invalid.

The easiest way to do this in Dreamweaver is to use the Quick Tag Editor. Select your text and press Ctrl+T (Command T) to automatically enter Wrap Tag mode. If Tag Hints is enabled, all you'll have to type is **ad** and press Enter (Return) twice to accept the hint and confirm the tag.

If you're applying the ⟨address⟩ tag to multiple lines, use ⟨br⟩ tags to form line breaks. The following example shows the proper use of the ⟨address⟩ tags:

```
<address><p>The President<br>
1600 Pennsylvania Avenue<br>
Washington, DC 20001</p></address>
```

This preceding code is shown on a Web browser as follows:

> *The President*
> *1600 Pennsylvania Avenue*
> *Washington, DC 20001*

Tip   To remove a standard style, highlight the styled text, choose Text ⇨ Style, and select the name of the style you want to remove. The checkmark disappears from the style name. To remove a nonstandard tag such as ⟨address⟩, choose the tag in the Tag Selector and right-click (Control+click) to open the shortcut menu and select Remove Tag.

Using HTML Styles

In the world of Web design, consistency is a good thing. A site where headings, subheads, and body text are consistent from page to page is far easier for the visitor to quickly grasp than one where each page has its own style. Although the best approach for a consistently designed site may be the use of Cascading Style Sheets, that approach requires 4.0 and later browsers, and many clients are not willing to write off those potential Web visitors using older software.

To bridge the gap between old and new — and to make it easier to apply the same set of tags over and over again — Dreamweaver includes HTML Styles. HTML Styles are similar to CSS in that you define a custom style for text and give it any attributes you want: font name, size, color, format, and so on. Then you apply that style to either a selection or an entire block of text. The primary difference is that, with HTML Styles, Dreamweaver adds the necessary standard HTML tags, instead of CSS style declarations, to recreate your style. In other words, if you always set your legal disclaimers in Verdana at a –1 size in a deep red color, you can define your "legal" style once and apply it over and over again with one step, anywhere on the site.

HTML Styles, however, are not a replacement for CSS styles, and you should keep in mind some important differences:

✦ Modifying a HTML Style definition affects only subsequent applications of the style. When a CSS style is altered, the change is immediately seen wherever the style has been applied on the current page as well as in all future applications.

✦ HTML Styles use standard text tags and cannot, therefore, create some of the special effects possible in CSS. For example, you could not create a HTML Style that eliminates the underline from a link or changes the leading of a paragraph.

✦ Although defined HTML Styles are accessible from anywhere within a site, they are applied on a document-to-document basis, whereas with CSS, an external style sheet could be defined and linked to pages anywhere on your site.

Even with these differences, however, HTML Styles are an enhancement to a designer's workflow and extremely easy to use.

Note   In the remainder of this section, when I refer to a style or styles, I'm referring to HTML Styles. CSS Style references are designated as such.

Applying HTML Styles

The HTML Styles panel, shown in Figure 9-12, displays all currently available styles as well as options for removing style formatting, editing existing styles, adding new styles, or removing styles from the panel.

Available styles

Figure 9-12: Manage your standard formatting through the HTML Styles panel.

HTML Styles are divided into two distinct types: paragraph and selection styles. A paragraph style affects an entire block element, whether it is a single heading, a paragraph, or another block element such as a block quote. Paragraph styles are designated with a ¶ symbol in the HTML Styles panel. A paragraph style is applied to the entire current block element, whether the cursor has selected the text or is just within the block. A selection style, on the other hand, applies formatting only to selected text. Selection styles are marked in the HTML Styles panel with an underlined lowercased *a*, like this (a̲).

It's possible for both paragraph and selection styles to either clear the existing style before adding the new formatting or add the new formatting to the existing style. The default behavior is for existing formatting to be removed; if the style is to be added, a small plus sign (+) is shown in front of the style name.

To apply an HTML Style, follow these steps:

1. Open the HTML Styles panel in one of the following ways:

    • Select Window ➪ HTML Styles.

    • Choose the HTML Styles button from either Launcher.

    • Press the keyboard shortcut, Ctrl+F11 (Command+F11).

2. To apply a style to the currently selected text, choose any designated (a̲) HTML Style.

Tip   It's easiest to always have the Auto Apply option selected, so that your choices immediately are applied; if this option is not selected, click the Apply button.

3. To apply a style to the current block element, choose any so-designated (¶) HTML Style.

Removing HTML Styles

As useful as applying new HTML Styles is, I find that the capability to remove all such formatting even more beneficial. It's not unusual for me to style a paragraph and then want to try a completely different approach — with the HTML Styles panel, I can wipe out all the formatting in one click and start fresh.

As with applying styles, you can remove either a paragraph or a selection style. Both are available as the first items in the HTML Styles panel. Clear Selection Style removes all <font> and other text formatting tags surrounding the current selection. Clear Paragraph Style eliminates all such tags from the current block element.

Caution   Removing a paragraph style removes all styles to the paragraph, not just ones you may have added via the HTML Styles panel. For example, if a line is styled in this way:

```
<h1><font color="#FFFF00">Welcome</font></h2>
```

Moving HTML Styles from Site to Site

Custom HTML styles are available from any page in your site. But what happens if you start a new site? Do you have to recreate your custom styles again? Every new site starts with the same set of default styles standard in Dreamweaver. (The next section describes how to alter even those defaults.) But you can easily transfer styles you've created for one site to another, just by copying the right file.

The information describing the custom HTML styles is stored in each site's Library folder in a file named styles.xml. To transfer the HTML styles, just copy the styles.xml file from one site's Library folder to the Library folder for another site. Library folders are created within a site when they are first needed, so if you've just defined your site, the Library folder may not exist yet. You can, however, safely create it within the local site root and move your styles.xml file into the folder.

Selecting Clear Paragraph Style converts the line to this:

```
<p>Welcome</p>
```

The Clear Selection Style command does not require that the formatting tags be adjacent to the selection. If you select some text in the middle of a paragraph styled in a particular color and font, choosing Clear Selection Style inserts appropriate tags before and after the selection so that the selection has no style whatsoever, but the surrounding text remains styled. A before and after view of the process is shown in Figure 9-13.

If you no longer wish to have a defined style displayed in the HTML Styles panel, select that style and choose the Delete Style button. Alternatively, you could select the style and choose Delete Style from the context-sensitive menu on the panel.

Defining HTML Styles

Naturally, the standard list of styles is just a jumping-off place for the HTML Styles panel. To get the most out the feature, you should design your own custom styles. Dreamweaver gives you a number of methods to define a style:

✦ **Style by Example** — Create a new style from formatted text onscreen.

✦ **Modify an Existing Style** — Edit a standard or custom style to your liking. You can even duplicate the style first, so both old and new versions are available.

✦ **Build a New Style** — Select all the desired attributes for your selection or paragraph style and try it out right away on selected text.

Clear Paragraph style   Clear Selection style

Figure 9-13: You can remove all styling from a bit of text and keep the surrounding styling with the Clear Selection Style command.

All style definitions are managed in the Define HTML Style dialog box, shown in Figure 9-14. How the dialog box is opened depends on which method you're using to create or modify your style.

✦ To create a style from example, select tags you want to include in the style from the Document window or the Tag Selector and then choose the New Style button from the HTML Styles panel.

✦ To modify an existing style, double-click its name in the HTML Styles panel list.

✦ To create a new style built on an existing one, select the style and then, from the context-sensitive menu of the HTML Styles panel, select Duplicate.

✦ To create a style from the ground up, choose the New Style button on the HTML Styles panel.

To define an HTML Style, follow these steps:

1. Open the Define HTML Style dialog box using one of the previously described methods.

2. Enter a unique name for your style, if creating a new one.

3. Choose whether your style is to apply to a selection or a paragraph.

4. Select whether your style will add to the existing style or clear existing style.

5. Choose the desired font attributes:

- Font

- Size

- Color

- Style: Bold, Italic, or Bold-Italic

- Other . . . (Additional Optional Styles): Underline, Strikethrough, Teletype, Emphasis, Strong, Code, Variable, Sample, Keyboard, Citation, Definition

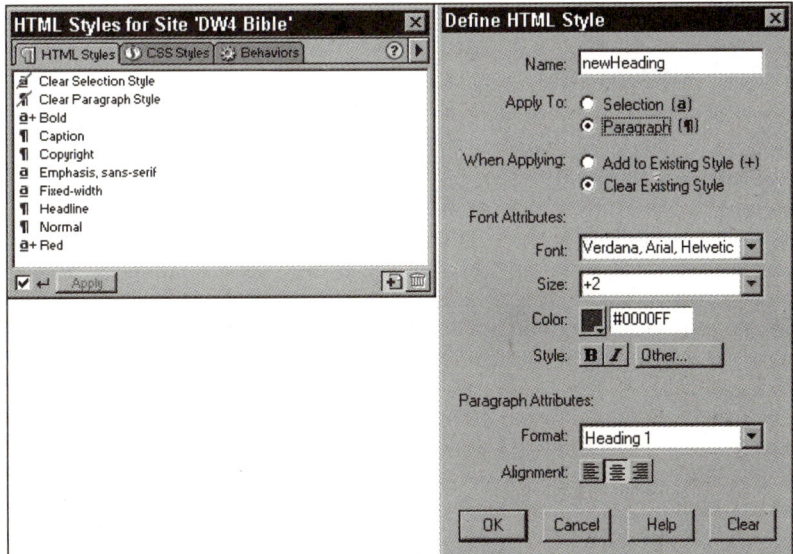

Figure 9-14: Build or modify styles in the Define HTML Style dialog box.

6. If defining a paragraph style, select from the following attribute options:

- Format: None, Heading 1 through Heading 6, or Preformatted

- Alignment: Right, Center, Left.

7. Click OK when you're done.

Tip

To start over at any time, select the Clear button.

Modifying Text Format

As a Web designer, you easily spend at least as much time adjusting your text as you do getting it into your Web pages. Luckily, Dreamweaver puts most of the tools you need for this task right at your fingertips. All the text-formatting options are available through the Text Property Inspector. Instead of hand-coding `<font>`, `<blockquote>`, and alignment tags, just select your text and click a button.

 Note   In HTML text formatting today, programmers are moving toward using Cascading Style Sheets and away from hard-coding text with `<font>` and other tags. Both 4.0+ versions of the major Web browsers support Cascading Style Sheets to some extent, and Internet Explorer has had some support since the 3.0 version. The current realities of browser competition, however, dictate that to take advantage of the widest support range, Web designers must continue to use the character-specific tags. Even after Cascading Style Sheets gain widespread acceptance, you'll probably still need to apply tags on the local level occasionally.

Adjusting font size

The six HTML heading types (H1 to H6) enable you to assign relative sizes to a line or to an entire paragraph. In addition, HTML gives you a finer degree of control through the size attribute of the font tag. In contrast to publishing environments, both traditional and desktop, font size is not specified in HTML with points. Rather, the `<font>` tag enables you to choose one of seven different explicit sizes that the browser can render (absolute sizing), or you can select one relative to the page's basic font. Figure 9-15 shows the default absolute and relative sizes, compared to a more page designer–friendly point chart (accomplished with Dreamweaver's Cascading Style Sheets features).

Which way should you go — absolute or relative? Some designers think that relative sizing gives them more options. As you can see by the chart in Figure 9-15, browsers are limited to displaying seven different sizes no matter what — unless you're using Cascading Style Sheets. Relative sizing does give you additional flexibility, though, because you can resize all the fonts in an entire Web page with one command. Absolute sizes, however, are more straightforward to use and can be coded in Dreamweaver without any additional HTML programming. Once again, it's the designer's choice.

Absolute size

You can assign an absolute font size through either the Property Inspector or the menus. In both cases, you choose a value, 1 (smallest) through 7 (largest), to which you want to resize your text; you might note that this order is the reverse of the heading sizes, which range from H1 to H6, largest to smallest.

Point Sizes	Absolute Sizes	Relative Sizes Base Font (Default = 3)	
8 pt.	Size 1	Size +1	Size -1
10 pt.	Size 2	Size +2	Size -2
12 pt.	Size 3	Size +3	Size -3
14 pt.	Size 4	Size +4	Size -4
18 pt.	Size 5	Size +5	Size -5
24 pt.	Size 6	Size +6	Size -6
36 pt.	Size 7	Size +7	Size -7

Figure 9-15: In this chart, you can see the relationships between the various font sizes in an HTML browser and as compared to "real-world" point sizes.

To use the Property Inspector to pick an absolute font size, follow these steps:

1. Select your text.

2. In the Property Inspector, open the Font Size drop-down list of options.

3. Choose a value from 1 to 7.

To pick an absolute font size from the menu, follow these steps:

1. Select your text.

2. Choose Text ➪ Size and pick a value from 1 to 7, or Default (which is 3).

Tip   You can also use the keyboard shortcuts for changing absolute font sizes. Headings 1 through 6 correspond to Ctrl+1 through Ctrl+6 (Command+1 through Command+6). The Paragraph option is rendered with a Ctrl+Shift+P (Command+Shift+P); you can remove all formatting with Ctrl+0 (Command+0).

Relative size

To what exactly are relative font sizes relative? The default font size, of course. The advantage of relative font sizes is that you can alter a Web page's default font size with one command, the `<basefont>` tag. The tag takes the following form:

```
<basefont size=value>
```

where value is a number from 1 to 7. The `<basefont>` tag is usually placed immediately following the opening `<body>` tag. Dreamweaver does not support previewing the results of altering the `<basefont>` tag and the tag has to be entered by hand or through the external editor.

You can distinguish a relative font size from an absolute font size by the plus or minus sign that precedes the value. The relative sizes are plus or minus the current `<basefont>` size. Thus, a `<font size=+1>` is normally rendered with a size 4 font because the default `<basefont>` is 3. If you include the following line in your Web page:

```
<basefont size=5>
```

text marked with a `<font size=+1>` is displayed with a size 6 font. Because browsers display only seven different size fonts with a `<basefont size=5>` setting—unless you're using Cascading Style Sheets—any relative size over `<font size=+2>` won't display differently when previewed in a browser.

Relative font sizes can also be selected from either the Property Inspector or the menus. To use the Property Inspector to pick a relative font size, follow these steps:

1. Select your text or position the cursor where you want the new text size to begin.

2. In the Property Inspector, open the Font Size drop-down list of options.

3. To increase the size of your text, choose a value from +1 through +7.

   To decrease the size of your text, choose a value from –1 to –7.

To pick a relative font size from the menus, follow these steps:

1. Select your text or position the cursor where you want the new text size to begin.

2. To increase the size of your text, choose Text ⇨ Size Increase and pick a value from +1 to +7.

   To reduce the size of your text, choose Text ⇨ Size Decrease and pick a value from –1 to –7.

Dreamweaver's Color Pickers

Dreamweaver includes a color picker for selecting colors for all manner of HTML elements: text, table cells, and page background. Dreamweaver's color picker—in keeping with the Macromedia common user interface—offers a number of palettes from the context menu to choose your colors: Color Cubes, Continuous Tone, Windows OS, Mac OS, and Grayscale. The most common choices for Web designers are Color Cubes and Continuous Tone, both of which display the 216 Web safe colors common to the Macintosh and Windows palettes. By default, the Snap to Web Safe option, also found in the context menu, is chosen.

Once you've opened the text color picker by selecting the color swatch on the Property Inspector, the cursor changes shape into an eye-dropper. This eye-dropper can sample colors from any of the displayed swatches or from any color on-screen. Simply click the color swatch and drag the eye-dropper over any graphic to choose a color.

If you choose a color outside of the "safe" range, you have no assurances of how the color is rendered on a viewer's browser. Some systems select the closest color in RGB values; some use dithering (positioning two or more colors next to each other to simulate another color) to try to overcome the limitations of the current screen color depth. So be forewarned: If at all possible, stick with the browser-safe colors, especially when coloring text.

Mac Users: The system color picker—brought up when the Palette icon on the color picker menu is selected—for Macintosh is far more elaborate than the one available for Windows. The Mac version has several color schemes to use: CMYK (for print-related colors), RGB (for screen-based colors), HTML (for Web-based colors), and Crayon (for kid-like colors). The CMYK, HTML, and RGB systems offer you color swatches and three or four sliders with text entry boxes, and accept percentage values for RGB and CMYK, and hex values for HTML. Both RGB and HTML also have a snap-to-Web color option for matching your chosen color to the closest browser-safe color. The Hue, Saturation, and Value (or Lightness) sliders also have color wheels.

Adding font color

Unless you assign a color to text on your Web page, the browser uses its own default, typically black. As noted in "Establishing Page Properties" in Chapter 8, you can change the font color for the entire page by choosing Modify ➪ Page Properties and selecting a new color from the Text Color swatch. You can also color any specific headings, words, or paragraphs that you have selected in Dreamweaver.

Tip

When adding a new font color, size, or name to text that already has one `<font>` tag applied to it, it's best to use the Tag Selector to highlight the text by selecting that `<font>` tag. If you select your text by clicking and dragging, you're likely to not select the entire contents of the tag, which results in multiple `<font>` tags being applied.

The `<font>` tag goes to work again when you add color to selected elements of the page — this time, with the color attribute set to a particular value. HTML color is expressed in either a hexadecimal color number or a color name. The hexadecimal color number is based on the color's red-green-blue value and is written as follows:

```
#FFFFFF
```

The preceding represents the color white. You can also use standard color names instead of the hexadecimal color numbers. A sample color code line follows:

```
I'm <font color="green">GREEN</font> with envy.
```

Dreamweaver understands both color names and hexadecimal color numbers, but its HTML code output is in hexadecimal color numbers only.

Again, you have two ways to add color to your text in Dreamweaver. The Property Inspector displays a drop-down list of the browser-safe colors and also gives you an option to choose from a full-spectrum Color dialog box. If you approach your coloring task via the menus, the Text ➪ Color command takes you immediately to the Color dialog box.

To use the Property Inspector to color a range of text in Dreamweaver, follow these steps:

1. Select the text you want to color or position the cursor where you want the new text color to begin.

2. From the Property Inspector, you can

   • Type a hexadecimal color number directly into the Font Color text box.

   • Type a color name directly into the Font Color text box.

   • Select the Font Color swatch to open the browser-safe color picker.

3. If you chose to type a color name or number directly into the Font Color text box, press Tab or click the Document window to see the color applied.

4. If you clicked the Font Color swatch, select your color from the browser-safe colors available. As you move your pointer over the color swatches, Dreamweaver displays the color in the corner and the color's hexadecimal number below.

5. For a wider color selection from the Color dialog box, select the Palette icon in the lower-right corner of the color swatch.

To access the full-spectrum color picker in Windows, follow these steps:

1. Select your text or position your cursor where you want the new text color to begin.

2. Choose Text ➪ Color to open the Color dialog box, as shown in Figure 9-16.

Figure 9-16: Use the Color dialog box in Windows to choose a color for your font outside of the browser-safe palette.

3. Select one of the 48 preset standard colors from the color swatches on the left of the Color dialog box, or use either of the following methods:

   • Select a color by moving the Hue/Saturation pointer and the Luminance pointer.

   • Enter decimal values directly into either the Red, Green, and Blue boxes or the Hue, Saturation, and Luminance boxes.

4. If you create a custom color, you can add it to your palette by selecting Add to Custom Colors. You can add up to 16 custom colors.

5. Click OK when you are finished.

Caution   When you add a custom color to your palette in Windows, the new color swatch goes into the currently selected swatch or, if no swatch is selected, the next available swatch. Make sure you have selected an empty or replaceable swatch before selecting the Add to Custom Color button. To clear the custom colors, first set the palette to white by bringing the Luminance slider all the way to the top. Then, select the Add to Custom Color button until all the color swatch text boxes are empty.

To access the full-spectrum color picker in Macintosh systems, follow these steps:

1. Select the text or position your cursor where you want the new text color to begin.

2. Choose Text ⇨ Color to open the Color dialog box.

3. From the Color dialog box, select the Color Palette icon.

   The Macintosh color picker opens.

4. In the Macintosh color picker, the list of available pickers is displayed in the left pane, and each particular interface is shown in the right. Choose the specific color picker icon from the left pane and create the color desired in the right.

The number and type of color pickers vary from system to system, depending on the version of the operating system and whether you've added any third-party color pickers.

5. When you've found the desired color, click OK.

Assigning a specific font

Along with size and color, you can also specify the typeface in which you want particular text to be rendered. Dreamweaver uses a special method for choosing font names for a range of selected text, due to HTML's unique way of handling fonts. Before you learn how to change a typeface in Dreamweaver, let's further examine how fonts in HTML work.

About HTML fonts

Page layout designers can incorporate as many different fonts as available to their own systems. Web layout designers, on the other hand, can use only those fonts on their viewers' systems. If you designate a paragraph to be in Bodoni Bold Condensed, for instance, and put it on the Web, the paragraph is displayed with that font only if that exact font name is on the user's system. Otherwise, the browser uses the default system font, which is often Times or Times New Roman.

Fonts are specified with the `<font>` tag, aided by the `name` attribute. Because a designer can never be certain of which fonts are on visitors' computers, HTML enables you to offer a number of options to the browser, as follows:

```
<font name="Arial, Helvetica, sans-serif">Swiss Maid Foundry</font>
```

The browser encountering the preceding tag first looks for the Arial font to render the enclosed text. If Arial isn't there, the browser looks for the next font in the list, which in this case is Helvetica. Failing to find any of the specified fonts listed, the browser uses whichever font has been assigned to the category for the font — sans-serif in this case.

The W3C and some Web browsers recognize five main categories of fonts: serif, sans-serif, monospace, cursive, and fantasy. Internet Explorer has a higher compliance rating on this issue than Netscape Communicator.

Selecting a font

The process for assigning a font name to a range of text is similar to that of assigning a font size or color. Instead of selecting one font name, however, you're usually selecting one font series. That series could contain three or more fonts, as previously explained. Font series are chosen from the Property Inspector or through a menu item. Dreamweaver enables you to assign any font on your system — or even any font you can name — to a font series, as covered in the section "Editing the Font List," later in this chapter.

To assign a specific font series to your text, follow these steps:

1. Select the text or position your cursor where you want the new text font to begin.

2. From the Property Inspector, open the drop-down list of font names. You can also choose Text ⇨ Font from the menu bar. Your font list is displayed.

3. Select a font from the Font List. To return to the system font, choose Default Font from the list.

It's also possible to enter the font name or font series directly in the Property Inspector's Font drop-down list.

Tip   Font peculiarities are one of the key reasons to always test your Web pages on several platforms. Macintosh and Windows have different names for the same basic fonts (Arial in Windows is almost identical to Helvetica in Macintosh, for instance), and even the standard font sizes vary between the platforms. On the plus side, standard Microsoft fonts (Arial, Verdana for example) are more common on the Macintosh since Mac OS 8.1, but differences still exist. Overall, PC fonts are larger than fonts on a Macintosh. Be sure to check out your page on as many systems as possible before finalizing your design.

Editing the Font List

With the Edit Font List dialog box, Dreamweaver gives you a point-and-click interface for building your font lists. Once the Edit Font List dialog box is open, you can delete an existing font series, add a new one, or change the order of the list so your favorite ones are on top. Take a look at Figure 9-17 to see the sections of the Edit Font List dialog box: the current Font List, the Available Fonts on your system, and the Chosen Fonts. The Chosen Fonts are the individual fonts that you've selected to be incorporated into a font series.

Let's step through the process of constructing a new font series and adding it to the Font List:

1. To open the Edit Font List dialog box, either choose Edit Font List through the Font Name option arrow in the Property Inspector, or select Text ⇨ Font ⇨ Edit Font List.

2. If the Chosen Fonts box is not empty, clear the Chosen Fonts box by selecting the plus (+) button at the top of the dialog box. You can also scroll down to the bottom of the current Font List and select "(Add fonts in list below)."

3. Select a font from the Available Fonts list.

4. Click the << button to transfer the selected font to the Chosen Fonts list.

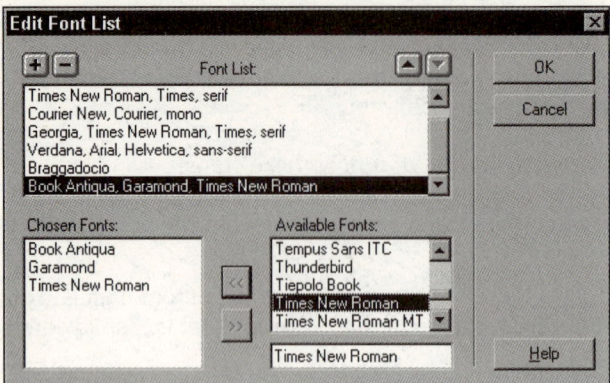

Figure 9-17: Dreamweaver's Edit Font List dialog box gives you considerable control over the fonts that you can add to your Web page.

5. To remove a font you no longer want or have chosen in error, highlight it in the Chosen Fonts list and select the >> button.

6. Repeat Steps 3 through 5 until the Chosen Fonts list contains the alternative fonts desired.

7. If you want to add another, separate font series, repeat Steps 2 through 5.

8. Click OK when you are finished adding fonts.

To change the order in which font series are listed in the Font List, follow these steps:

1. In the Font List dialog box, select the font series that you want to move.

2. If you want to move the series higher up the list, select the up-arrow button at the top-right of the Font List. If you want to move the series lower down the list, select the down-arrow button.

To remove a font series from the current Font List, highlight it and select the minus (–) button at the top-left of the list.

Remember, you need to have the fonts on your system to make them a part of your Font List. To add a font that's unavailable on your computer, type the name of the font into the text box below the Available Fonts list and press Enter (Return).

Aligning text

You can easily align text in Dreamweaver, just like in a traditional word processing program. HTML supports the alignment of text to the left or right margin, or in the center of the browser window. Like a word processing program, Dreamweaver aligns text one paragraph at a time. You can't left-align one word, center the next, and then right-align the third word in the same paragraph.

To align text, you can use one of three methods: a menu command, the Property Inspector, or a keyboard shortcut. To use the menus, choose Text ➪ Alignment and then pick the alignment you prefer (Left, Right, or Center). Table 9-8 explains the Text Property Inspector's Alignment buttons and the associated keyboard shortcuts.

<table>
<tr><td colspan="3" align="center">Table 9-8
Text Alignment Options in the Property Inspector</td></tr>
<tr><td>*Button*</td><td>*Alignment*</td><td>*Keyboard Shortcut*</td></tr>
<tr><td></td><td>Left</td><td>Ctrl+Alt+L (Command+Option+L)</td></tr>
<tr><td></td><td>Center</td><td>Ctrl+Alt+C (Command+Option+C)</td></tr>
<tr><td></td><td>Right</td><td>Ctrl+Alt+R (Command+Option+R)</td></tr>
</table>

Note   A fourth way to align text is through the Cascading Style Sheets. Any style can be set to align your text. Moreover, not only are Left, Right, and Center supported — so is Justify, which causes text to be flush against both left and right margins, creating a block-like appearance. The Justify value is supported in browsers 4.0 and later.

Cross-Reference   Traditional HTML alignment options are limited. For a finer degree of control, be sure to investigate precise positioning with layers in Chapter 28.

Indenting entire paragraphs

HTML offers a tag that enables you to indent whole paragraphs, such as inset quotations or name-and-address blocks. Not too surprisingly, the tag used is called the <blockquote> tag. Dreamweaver gives you instant access to the <blockquote> tag through the Indent and Outdent buttons located on the Text Property Inspector, as shown in Figure 9-18.

Outdent─   └─Indent

Figure 9-18: Indent paragraphs and blocks of text with the Indent and the Outdent buttons.

To indent one or more paragraphs, select them and click the Indent button in the Property Inspector. Paragraphs can be indented multiple times; each time you click the Indent button, another `<blockquote>...</blockquote>` tag pair is added.

Note   You can't control how much space a single `<blockquote>` indents a paragraph — that characteristic is determined by the browser.

If you find that you have over-indented, you can use the Outdent button, which is also located on the Property Inspector. The Outdent button has no effect if your text is already at the left edge.

You also have the option of indenting your paragraphs through the menus; choose Text ⇨ Indent or Text ⇨ Outdent.

Tip   You can tell how many `<blockquote>` tags are being used to create a particular look by placing your cursor in the text and looking at the Tag Selector.

Incorporating Dates

With the Web constantly changing, keeping track of when information is updated is important. Dreamweaver includes a new command that enables you to insert today's date in your page, in almost any format imaginable. Moreover, you can set the inserted date to be automatically updated every time the page is saved. This means every time you make a modification to a page and save it, the current date is added.

The Insert Date command uses your system clock to get the current date. In addition, you can elect to add a day name (for example, Thursday) and time to the basic date information. Once the date text is inserted, it can be formatted in the same way as any other text — adding color or a specific font type or changing the date's size.

To insert the current date, follow these steps:

1. Choose Insert ⇨ Date or select the Insert Date object from the Common panel of the Objects panel.

   The Insert Date dialog box, shown in Figure 9-19, is displayed.

2. If desired, select a Day Format to include in the date from the drop-down list. The options are:

[No Day]	Thu
Thursday,	thu,
Thursday	thu
Thu,	

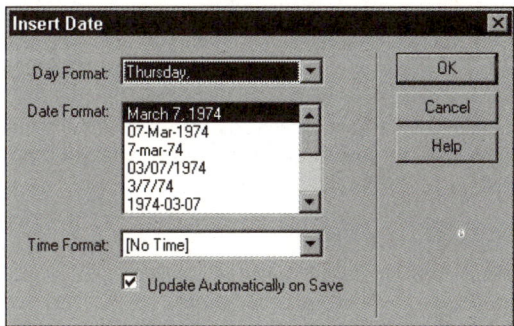

Figure 9-19: Keep track of when a file is updated by using the Insert Date command.

3. Select the desired date format from the drop-down list. The example formats are:

March 7, 1974	7./03/7.4
07.-Mar-1974	07.03.1974
7.-mar-7.4	07.03.74
03./07/1994	7.-03-197.4
3./7/747.	March, 197.4
1974.-03-07	74.-03-07
7./3/7.4	

Tip

If you are creating Web pages for the global market, consider using the format designated by the 1974-03-07 example. This year-month-day format is an ISO (International Organization for Standardization) standard and is computer sortable.

4. Select the desired time format, if any, from the drop-down list. The two example time formats are:

[No Time]

10.:18 PM

22.:18

5. If you want the date modified to include the current date every time the file is saved, select the Update Automatically on Save option.

6. Click OK when you're done.

Tip   It's no problem at all to format an inserted date when the Update Automatically on Save option is *not* selected—then it's just plain text and the formatting can be added easily through the Text Property Inspector. However, if the date is to be automatically updated, it's inserted as a special Macromedia datatype with its own Property Inspector. You can style it, however, by selecting options from the Text menu or applying an HTML or CSS style.

If your date object includes the Automatic Update option, you can modify the format. Select the date and, in the Property Inspector, choose the Edit Date Format button. The Edit Date Format dialog box opens and is identical to the Insert Date dialog box, except the Update Automatically on Save option is not available.

Commenting Your Code

When will you know to start inserting comments into your HTML code? The first time you go back to an earlier Web page, look at the code and say, "What on earth was I thinking?" You should plan ahead and develop the habit of commenting your code now.

Browsers run fine without your comments, but for any continued development—of the Web page or of yourself as a Webmaster—commenting your code is extremely beneficial. Sometimes, as in a corporate setting, Web pages are codeveloped by teams of designers and programmers. In this situation, commenting your code may not just be a good idea; it may be required.

An HTML comment looks like the following:

```
<!-- Created by Hummer Associates, Inc. -->
```

You're not restricted to any particular line length or number of lines for comments. The text included between the opening of the comment, <!--, and the closing, -->, can span regular paragraphs or HTML code. In fact, one of the most common uses for comments during the testing and debugging phase of page design is to "comment out" sections of code as a means of tracking down an elusive bug.

To insert a comment in Dreamweaver, first place your cursor in Code View, Design View, or in the Code Inspector where you want the comment to appear. Then select the Insert Comment button from the Invisibles panel of the Objects panel. This sequence opens the Insert Comment dialog box, where you can insert the desired text; click OK when you've finished. Figure 9-20 shows the Insert Comment dialog box, with the corresponding completed comment in the split Design/Code View.

Figure 9-20: Comments are extremely useful for inserting into the code information not visible on the rendered Web page.

By default, Dreamweaver inserts a Comment symbol in the Document window. As with the other Invisibles, you can hide the Comment symbol by choosing Edit ➪ Preferences and then deselecting the Comments checkbox in the Invisible Elements panel. You can also hide any displayed Invisibles by selecting View ➪ Invisible Elements or using the keyboard shortcut, Ctrl+Shift+I (Command+Shift+I).

When you need to edit a comment, double-click the Comment symbol to display the current comment in an editable window. After you've finished making your changes to the comment, select the Close button of the Comment window. A comment can be moved or duplicated by selecting its symbol and using the Cut, Copy, and Paste commands under the Edit menu. You can also right-click (Command+click) the Comment symbol to bring up the shortcut menu. Finally, you can click and drag Comment symbols to move the corresponding comment to a new location.

Summary

Learning to manipulate text is an essential design skill for creating Web pages. Dreamweaver gives you all the tools you need to insert and modify the full range of HTML text quickly and easily. This chapter covered the following topics related to adding text to your Web page:

✦ HTML headings are available in six different sizes: `<h1>` through `<h6>`. Headings are used primarily as headlines and subheads to separate divisions of the Web page.

✦ Blocks of text are formatted with the paragraph tag `<p>`. Each paragraph is separated from the other paragraphs by a line of whitespace above and below. Use the line break tag, `<br>`, to make lines appear directly above or below one another.

✦ Dreamweaver offers a full complement of text-editing tools — everything from Cut and Paste to Find and Replace. Two commands, Copy Text Only and Paste As Text, are unique to Dreamweaver and make short work of switching between text and code.

✦ Dreamweaver's Find and Replace feature goes a long way toward automating your work on the current page as well as throughout the Web site. Both content and code can be searched in a basic or very advanced fashion.

✦ Where possible, text in HTML is formatted according to its meaning. Dreamweaver applies the styles selected through the Text ➪ Style menu. For most styles, the browser determines what the user views.

✦ You can format Web page text much as you can text in a word processing program. Within certain limitations, you can select a font's size and color, as well as the font itself.

✦ Dreamweaver's HTML Styles feature enables you to consistently and quickly format your text.

✦ HTML comments are a useful (and often requisite) vehicle for embedding information into a Web page that remains unseen by the casual viewer. Comments can annotate program code or insert copyright information.

In the next chapter, you learn how to insert and work with graphics.

✦   ✦   ✦

Inserting Images

The Internet started as a text-based medium primarily used for sharing data among research scientists and among U.S. military commanders. Today, the Web is as visually appealing as any mass medium. Dreamweaver's power becomes even more apparent as you use its visual layout tools to incorporate background and foreground images into your Web page designs.

Completely baffled by all the various image formats out there? This chapter opens with an overview of the key Web-oriented graphics formats, including PNG. Also, this chapter covers techniques for incorporating both background and foreground images — and modifying them using new methods available in Dreamweaver 4. Animation graphics and how you can use them in your Web pages are also covered here, as are techniques for creating rollover buttons. Finally, this chapter introduces integration with Fireworks, Macromedia's award-winning Web graphics tool; Dreamweaver and Fireworks make a potent team for creating and publishing Web graphics.

Web Graphic Formats

If you've worked in the computer graphics field, you know that virtually every platform — as well as every paint and graphics program — has its own proprietary file format for images. One of the critical factors in the Web's rapid, expansive growth is the use of cross-platform graphics. Regardless of the system you use to create your images, these versatile files ensure that the graphics can be viewed by all platforms.

The trade-off for universal acceptance of image files is a restricted field: just two file formats, with a possible third just coming into view. Currently, only GIF and JPEG formats are fully supported by browsers. A third alternative, the PNG graphics format, is experiencing a limited but growing acceptance.

You need to understand the uses and limitations of each of the formats so you can apply them successfully in Dreamweaver. Let's look at the fundamentals.

GIF

GIF, the Graphics Interchange Format, was developed by CompuServe in the late 1980s to address the problem of cross-platform compatibility. With GIF viewers available for every system from PC and Macintosh to Amiga and NeXT, the format became a natural choice for an inline (adjacent to text) image graphic. GIFs are bitmapped images, which means that each pixel is given or mapped to a specific color. You can have up to 256 colors for a GIF graphic. These images are generally used for illustrations, logos, or cartoons—anything that doesn't require thousands of colors for a smooth color blend, such as a photograph. With a proper graphics tool, you can reduce the number of colors in a GIF image to a minimum, thereby compressing the file and reducing download time.

The GIF87a and GIF89a varieties

The GIF format has two varieties: "regular" (technically, GIF87a) and an enhanced version known as GIF89a. This improved GIF file brings three important attributes to the format. First, GIF89a supports transparency, in which one or more of the colors can become invisible. This property is necessary for creating nonrectangular-appearing images. Whenever you see a round or irregularly shaped logo or illustration on the Web, a rectangular frame is displayed as the image is loading— this is the actual size and shape of the graphic. The colors surrounding the irregularly shaped central image are set to transparent in a graphics-editing program (such as Fireworks or Adobe Photoshop) before the image is saved in GIF89a format.

 Note   Most of the latest versions of the popular graphic tools default to using GIF89a, so unless you're working with older, legacy images, you're not too likely to encounter the less flexible GIF87a format.

Although the outer area of a graphic seems to disappear with GIF89a, you won't be able to overlap your Web images using this format without using layers. Figure 10-1 demonstrates this situation. In this figure, the same image is presented twice—one lacks transparency, and one has transparency applied. The image on the left is saved as a standard GIF without transparency, and you can plainly see the shape of the full image. The image on the right was saved with the white background color made transparent, so the central figure seems to float on the background.

Interlacing capabilities of GIF89a

The second valuable attribute contributed by GIF89a format is *interlacing*. One of the most common complaints about graphics on the Web is lengthy download times. Interlacing won't speed up your GIF downloads, but it gives your Web page visitors something to view other than a blank screen. A graphic saved with the interlace feature turned on gives the appearance of "developing," like an instant picture, as the file is downloading. Use of this design option is up to you and your clients. Some folks swear by it; others can't abide it.

Figure 10-1: The same image, saved without GIF transparency (left) and with GIF transparency (right)

Animation capabilities of GIF89a

Animation is the final advantage offered by the GIF89a format. Certain software programs enable you to group your GIF files together into one large page-flipping file. With this capability, you can bring simple animation to your page without additional plug-ins or helper applications. Unfortunately, the trade-off is that the files get very big, very fast. For more on animated GIFs in Dreamweaver, see the section "Applying Simple Web Animation" later in this chapter.

JPEG

The JPEG format was developed by the Joint Photographic Experts Group specifically to handle photographic images. JPEGs offer millions of colors at 24 bits of color information available per pixel, as opposed to the GIF format's 8-bit and 256 colors. To make JPEGs usable, the large amount of color information must be compressed, which is accomplished by removing what the algorithm considers redundant information. This is often referred to as *lossy* compression—in which pixels are lost—as opposed to *lossless* compression, a characteristic of GIF images.

The more compressed your JPEG file, the more degraded the image. When you first save a JPEG image, your graphics program asks you for the desired level of compression. As an example, take a look at the three pictures in Figure 10-2. Here you can compare the effects of JPEG compression ratios and resulting file sizes to the original image itself. As you can probably tell, JPEG does an excellent job of compression, with even the highest degree of compression having only a little visible impact. Keep in mind that each picture has its own reaction to compression.

| 100% JPEG - 48K | 50% JPEG - 7K | 10% JPEG - 2K |

Figure 10-2: JPEG compression can save your Web visitors substantial download time, with little loss of image quality.

Tip   With the JPEG image-compression algorithm, the initial elements of an image "compressed away" are least noticeable. Subtle variations in brightness and hue are the first to disappear. When possible, preview your image in your graphics program while adjusting the compression level to observe the changes. With additional compression, the image grows darker and less varied in its color range.

With JPEGs, what is compressed for storage must be uncompressed for viewing. When a JPEG picture on your Web page is accessed by a visitor's browser, the image must first be downloaded to the browser and then uncompressed before it can be viewed. This dual process adds additional time to the Web-browsing process, but it is time well spent for photographic images.

JPEGs, unlike GIFs, have neither transparency nor animation features. A newer strand of JPEG called Progressive JPEG gives you the interlace option of the GIF format, however. Although not all browsers support the interlace feature of Progressive JPEG, they render the image regardless.

PNG

The latest entry into the Web graphics arena is the Portable Network Graphics format, or PNG. Combining the best of both worlds, PNG has lossless compression, like GIF, and is capable of millions of colors, like JPEG. Moreover, PNG offers an interlace scheme that appears much more quickly than either GIF or JPEG, as well as transparency support that is far superior to both the other formats.

One valuable aspect of the PNG format enables the display of PNG pictures to appear more uniform across various computer platforms. Generally, graphics made on a PC look brighter on a Macintosh, and Mac-made images seem darker on a PC. PNG includes gamma correction capabilities that alter the image depending on the computer used by the viewer.

Before the 4.0 versions, the various browsers supported PNG only through plug-ins. After PNG was endorsed as a new Web graphic format by the W3C, both 4.0 versions of Netscape and Microsoft browsers added native, inline support of the new format. Perhaps most important, however, Dreamweaver was among the first Web authoring tools to offer native PNG support. Inserted PNG images preview in the Document window just like GIFs and JPEGs. Browser support is currently not widespread enough to warrant a total switch to the PNG format (it's still lacking in Internet Explorer for Macintosh, for example), but its growing acceptance certainly bears watching.

Tip　If you're really excited about the potential of PNG, check out Macromedia's Fireworks, the first Web graphics tool to use PNG as its native format. Fireworks takes full advantage of PNG's alpha transparency features and enhanced palette.

Two excellent resources for more on the PNG format is the PNG home page at `www.freesoftware.com/pub/png/` and the W3C's PNG page at `www.w3.org/Graphics/PNG`.

Using Inline Images

An *inline image* can appear directly next to text — literally in the same line. The capability to render inline images is one of the major innovations of the World Wide Web's transition from the Internet. This section covers all the basics of inserting inline images into Dreamweaver and modifying their attributes.

Inserting inline images

Dreamweaver can open and preview any graphic in a GIF, JPEG, or PNG format. With Dreamweaver, you have six methods for placing a graphic on your Web page:

✦ From the Objects panel, select the Insert Image button.

✦ From the menu bar, choose Insert ⇨ Image.

✦ From the keyboard, press Ctrl+Alt+I (Command+Option+I).

✦ Point to an image file in the Site window using Dreamweaver's Point to File feature.

✦ Drag either the Insert Image button or an icon from your file manager (Explorer or Finder) to your page.

✦ Drag a *thumbnail* (a small version of an image) or filename from the Images category of the Assets panel onto your page. This capability is new in Dreamweaver 4 and is covered in detail in a following section.

The first four methods require that you first position the cursor at the point where you want the image to appear on the page; the drag-and-drop method enables you to place the image inline with any existing element.

For all but the method using the Assets panel, Dreamweaver opens the Select Image Source dialog box (shown in Figure 10-3) and asks you for the path or address to your image file. Remember that in HTML, all graphics are stored in separate files linked from your Web page. The image's address can be just a filename, a directory path and filename on your system, a directory path and filename on your remote system, or a full URL to a graphic on a completely separate Web server. You don't have to have the file immediately available to insert the code into your HTML.

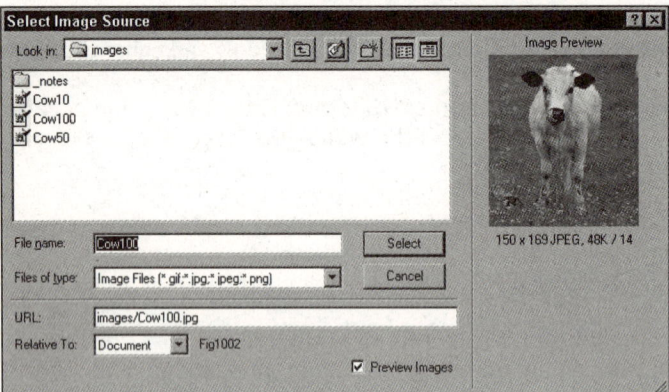

Figure 10-3: In this Select Image Source dialog box, you can keep track of your image's location relative to your current Web page.

From the Select Image Source dialog box, you can browse to your image folder, and preview images before you load them. To enable this feature, make sure the Preview Images option is selected. Dreamweaver can preview GIF, JPEG, or PNG files.

In the lower portion of the dialog box, the URL text box displays the format of the address Dreamweaver inserts into your code. Below the URL text box is the Relative To list box. Here you can choose to declare an image to be relative to the document you're working on (the default) or relative to the site root. (After you've saved your document, you see its name displayed beside the Relative To box.)

To take full advantage of Dreamweaver's site management features, you must open a site, establish a local site root, and save the current Web page before beginning to insert images. For more on how to begin a Dreamweaver project, and about document-relative and site root–relative addressing, see Chapter 6.

Relative to Document

Once you've saved your Web page and chosen Relative to Document, Dreamweaver displays the address in the URL text box. If the image is located in a folder on the same level as, or within, your current site root folder, the address is formatted with just a path and filename. For instance, if you're inserting a graphic from the sub-folder named images, Dreamweaver inserts an address like the following:

```
images/men10.jpg
```

If you try to insert an image currently stored outside of the local site root folder, Dreamweaver temporarily appends a prefix that tells the browser to look on your local system for the file. For instance, the file listing would look like the following in Windows:

```
file:///C|/Dreamweaver/Figs/men10.jpg
```

while on the Macintosh, the same file is listed as follows:

```
file:///Macintosh HD/Dreamweaver/Figs/men10.jpg
```

Dreamweaver also appends the `file:///C|` prefix (or just `file:///Macintosh HD` in Macintosh) if you haven't yet saved your document. It is strongly recommended that you save your file before you begin developing the Web page. You can easily upload Web pages with this `file:///C|` (`file:///Macintosh HD`) prefix in place—and miss the error completely. Because your local browser can find the referenced image on your system, even when you are browsing the remote site, the Web page appears perfect. However, anyone else browsing your Web site only sees placeholders for broken links. Saving your page before you begin enables Dreamweaver to help you avoid these errors. To this end, do not check the Don't show me this message again checkbox that appears when you're reminded to save your file the first time. This message can save you an enormous amount of grief!

After you select your image file, you see the prompt window shown in Figure 10-4. Dreamweaver asks if you want to copy this image to your local site root folder. Whenever possible, keep all of your images within the local site root folder so that Dreamweaver can handle site management efficiently. Click Yes, and you next see the Save Copy As dialog box, which points to the local site root folder. If you select No, the file is inserted with the `src` attribute pointing to the path of the file.

Figure 10-4: Dreamweaver reminds you to keep all your graphics in the local site root folder for easy site management.

Relative to Site Root

Should you select Site Root in the Relative To field of the Select Image Source dialog box, and you are within your site root folder, Dreamweaver appends a leading forward slash to the directory in the path so the browser can correctly read the address. Thus, the same men10.jpg file appears in both the URL box and the HTML code as follows:

```
/images/men10.jpg
```

When you use site root–relative addressing and you select a file outside of the site root, you get the same reminder from Dreamweaver about copying the file into your local site root folder — just as with document-relative addressing.

Dragging images from the Assets panel

Quite often, a Web designer works from a collection of images, much like a painter uses a palette of colors. Reusing images builds consistency in the site look and feel and makes it easier for a visitor to navigate through the site. However, trying to remember the differences between two versions of a logo — one named logo03.gif and another named logo03b.gif — often required inserting them both to find the correct image. Dreamweaver 4 eliminates the visual guesswork and simplifies the reuse of graphics with the new Assets panel.

New Feature

The Images category is key to the Assets panel. Not only does the Assets panel list all the GIF, JPEG, and PNG files found in your site — whether or not they are embedded in a Web page — selecting any graphic from the list instantly displays a thumbnail. Previewing the images makes it easy to select the proper one. Moreover, once you've found the correct image, all you need do it drag it from the Assets panel to the page.

Before you can use graphics from the Assets panel, you must catalog the site by choosing the Refresh Site List button, as shown in Figure 10-5. When you click the Refresh button (or choose Refresh Site List from the context menu on the Assets panel), Dreamweaver examines the current site and creates a list of the graphics, their sizes, file types, and full paths. To see an image, just click its name and a thumbnail appears in the preview area of the panel.

Thumbnail

Refresh

Refresh Site List button   Graphics list

Figure 10-5: Reuse any graphic in your site or from your Favorites collection by dragging it out from the Assets panel.

Tip

To increase the size of the thumbnail, make the preview area larger by dragging open the border between the preview and list areas. You can also expand the size of the entire panel by dragging its corner. Dreamweaver increases the size of the thumbnail while maintaining the width:height ratio so if you just move the border or resize the panel a little bit you may not see a significant change. Thumbnails are never displayed larger than their actual size.

You can insert an image from the Assets panel onto your Web page in two ways:

✦ Drag the image or the file listing onto the page.

✦ Place your cursor where you'd like the image to appear, and — once the listing of the desired image is highlighted in the Assets panel — select the Insert button.

The image you desire does not have to be in the current site, if you've added it to the Favorites collection. To retrieve an image from Favorites, first select the Favorites option at the top of the Assets panel. To switch back to the current site, choose the Site option.

Tip   In sites with many images, it's often difficult to scroll through all the names looking for a particular image. To aid your search, Dreamweaver enables you to sort the Images category by any of the columns displayed in the Assets panel: Name, Size, Type, or Full Path. Clicking once on the column heading sorts the assets in an ascending order by that criteria; click the column again to sort by that same criteria, but in a descending order.

If one or more objects are selected on the page, the inserted image is placed after the selection; Dreamweaver does not permit you to replace a selected image with another from the Assets panel. To change one image into another, double-click the graphic on the page to display the Select Image Source dialog box.

Caution   Do not double-click the image or listing in the Assets panel to insert it onto the page. Double-clicking invokes the designated graphics editor, whether it be Fireworks, Photoshop, or another program, and opens that graphic for editing.

One final note on adding images from the Assets panel: If you bring in a graphic from a location outside of the site, Dreamweaver asks that you copy the file to the current site. You must select the Refresh button to display this new image in the Assets panel.

Tip   When you select the Refresh button, Dreamweaver adds new images (and other assets) to the cache of current assets. If you add assets from outside of Dreamweaver, using, for example, a file manager, you might need to completely re-create the Assets panel by Ctrl-clicking (Command-clicking) the Refresh button.

Modifying images

When you insert an image in Dreamweaver, the image tag, `<img>`, is inserted into your HTML code. The `<img>` tag takes several attributes, all of which can be entered through the Property Inspector. Code for a basic image looks like the following:

```
<img src="images/Collection01.gif" width="172" height="180">
```

Dreamweaver centralizes all of its image functions in the Property Inspector. The Image Property Inspector, shown in Figure 10-6, displays a small thumbnail of the image as well as its file size. Dreamweaver automatically inserts the image filename in the Src text box (as the `src` attribute). To replace a currently selected image with another, click the folder icon next to the Src text box, or double-click the image itself. This sequence opens the Select Image Source dialog box. When you've selected the desired file, Dreamweaver automatically refreshes the page and corrects the code.

Size

Thumbnail   Image file name   Folder icon

Figure 10-6: The Image Property Inspector gives you total control over the HTML code for every image.

With the Property Inspector open when you insert your image, you can begin to modify it immediately.

Editing the image

Dreamweaver is a terrific Web authoring tool, but it's not a graphics editor. Quite often, after you've inserted an image into your Web page, you find that the picture needs to be altered in some way. Perhaps you need to crop part of the image or make the background transparent. Dreamweaver enables you to specify your primary graphics editor for each type of graphic in the File Types/Editors category of the Preferences.

Once you've picked an image editor, clicking the Edit button in the Property Inspector opens the application with the current image. After you've made the modifications, just save the file in your image editor and switch back to Dreamweaver. The new, modified graphic has already been included in the Web page.

Note   Dreamweaver seamlessly refreshed the images being edited in all the image editors I tested. However, there have been reports of images not reappearing in their modified form. If this happens, click the Refresh button in the Property Inspector after you select your image.

Adjusting height and width

The `width` and `height` attributes are important: Browsers build Web pages faster when they know the size and shape of the included images. Dreamweaver reads these attributes when the image is first loaded. The width and height values are initially expressed in pixels and are automatically inserted as attributes in the HTML code.

Browsers can dynamically resize an image if its height and width on the page are different from the original image's dimensions. For example, you can load your primary logo on the home page and then use a smaller version of it on subsequent pages by inserting the same image with reduced height and width values. Because you're only loading the image once and the browser is resizing it, download time for your Web page can be significantly reduced.

Note   Resizing an image just means you're changing its appearance onscreen; the file size stays exactly the same. To reduce a file size for an image, you need to scale it down in a graphics program such as Fireworks.

You don't have to use pixels to enter your resizing measurements into Dreamweaver's Property Inspector. You can also use inches (in), picas (pc), points (pt), millimeters (mm), or centimeters (cm). The values must be entered without spaces between the number and the measurement abbreviation, as follows:

```
72pt
```

You can also combine measurement systems. Suppose, for example, you want to resize a picture's height to 2 inches and 5 centimeters. In the Property Inspector, you enter the following value in the H text box:

```
2in+5cm
```

Dreamweaver translates both inches and centimeters to their equivalent in pixels and then adds them together. The measurements are system-dependent; on the Macintosh, an inch equals 72 pixels and on Windows, an inch is 96 pixels.

When you use values with a combined measurement system, you can only add values — you can't subtract them. When you press the Tab key or click outside of the height and width boxes, Dreamweaver converts your value to pixels.

Tip

With Dreamweaver, you can visually resize your graphics by using the click-and-drag method. A selected image has three sizing handles located on the right, bottom, and lower-right corners of its bounding box. Click any of these handles and drag it out to a new location — when you release the mouse, Dreamweaver resizes the image. Hold down the Shift key after dragging the corner sizing handle, and Dreamweaver maintains the current height/width aspect ratio.

If you alter either the height or the width of an image in the Property Inspector, Dreamweaver displays the values in bold in their respective fields. You can restore an image's default measurements by selecting the H or the W independently — or you can choose the Refresh button to restore both values.

Caution

If you elect to enable your viewer's browser to resize your image on the fly using the height/width values you specify, keep in mind that the browser is not a graphics-editing program and that its resizing algorithms are not sophisticated. View your resized images through several browsers to make sure that the results are acceptable.

Using margins

You can offset images with surrounding whitespace by using the margin attributes. The amount of whitespace around your image can be designated both vertically and horizontally through the vspace and hspace attributes, respectively. These margin values are entered, in pixels, into the V Space and H Space text boxes in the Image Property Inspector.

The V Space value adds the same amount of whitespace along the top and bottom of your image; the H Space value increases the whitespace along the left and right sides of the image. These values must be positive; HTML doesn't allow images to overlap text or other images (outside of layers). Unlike in page layout, "negative whitespace" does not exist.

Titling your image

When you first insert a graphic into the page, the Image Property Inspector displays a blank text box next to the thumbnail and file size. Fill in this box with a unique name for the image, to be used in JavaScript and other applications.

As a page is loading over the Web, the image is first displayed as an empty rectangle if the `<img>` tag contains the width and height information. Sometimes these rectangles include a brief title to describe the coming image. You can enter this alternative text in the Alt text box of the Image Property Inspector.

Tip

Good coding practice associates an Alt title with all of your graphics. Aside from giving the user some clue as to what's coming, these mini-titles are also used to display the screen tips that pop up in some browsers when the user's pointer passes over the graphic. The real benefit of mini-titles, however, is providing input for browsers not displaying graphics. Text-only browsers are still in use, and some users, interested only in content, turn off the graphics to speed up the text display. Moreover, the W3C is working toward standards for browsers for the visually impaired, and the Alt text can be used to describe the page.

Bordering a graphic

When you're working with thumbnails (a series of small versions of images) on your Web page, you may need a quick way to distinguish one from another. (Refer to Figure 10-5 for an example of a thumbnail.) The border attribute enables you to place a one-color rectangular border around any graphic. The width of the border is measured in pixels, and the color is the same as the default for the page's text color as specified in the Page Properties dialog box. To turn on the border, enter a value in the Border text box located on the lower half of the Image Property Inspector. Entering a value of zero explicitly turns off the border.

One of the most frequent cries for help among beginning Web designers (using Dreamweaver or another program) results from the sudden appearance of a bright blue border around their image. Whenever you assign a link to an image, HTML automatically places a border around that image; the color is determined by the Page Properties' Link color, where the default is bright blue. Dreamweaver intelligently assigns a zero to the border attribute whenever you enter a URL in the Link text box. If you've already declared a border value and enter a link, Dreamweaver won't zero-out the border. You can, of course, override the no-border option by entering a value in the Border text box.

Specifying a lowsrc

Another option for loading Web page images, the lowsrc attribute, displays a smaller version of a large graphic file while the larger file is loading. The lowsrc file can be a grayscale version of the original, or a version that is physically smaller or reduced in color or resolution. This option is designed to reduce the file size significantly for quick loading.

Select your `lowsrc` file by choosing the File icon next to the Low text box in the Image Property Inspector. The same criteria that applies to inserting your original image also applies to the `lowsrc` picture.

Tip

One handy `lowsrc` technique first proportionately scales down a large file in a graphics-processing program. This file becomes your `lowsrc` file. Because browsers use the final image's height and width information for both the `lowsrc` and the final image, your visitors immediately see a "blocky" version of your graphic, which is replaced by the final version when the picture is fully loaded.

Working with alignment options

Just like text, images can be aligned to the left, right, or center. In fact, images have much more flexibility than text in terms of alignment. In addition to the same horizontal alignment options, you can align your images vertically in nine different ways. You can even turn a picture into a floating image type, enabling text to wrap around it.

Horizontal alignment

When you change the horizontal alignment of a line — from left to center or from center to right — the entire paragraph moves. Any inline images that are part of that paragraph also move. Likewise, selecting one of a series of inline images in a row and realigning it horizontally causes all the images in the row to shift.

In Dreamweaver, the horizontal alignment of an inline image is changed in exactly the same way you realign text, with alignment buttons found on the Property Inspector. As with text, buttons exist for Left, Center, and Right. Although these are very conveniently placed on the lower portion of the Graphics Property Inspector, the alignment attribute is actually written to the `<p>` or other block element enclosing the image.

Vertical alignment

Because you can place text next to an image — and images vary so greatly in size — HTML includes a variety of options for specifying just how image and text line up. As you can see from the chart in Figure 10-7, a wide range of possibilities is available.

To change the vertical alignment of any graphic in Dreamweaver, open the Align drop-down list in the Image Property Inspector and choose one of the options. Dreamweaver writes your choice into the `align` attribute of the `<img>` tag.

The various vertical alignment options are listed in the following table, and you can see examples of each type of alignment in Figure 10-7.

Figure 10-7: You can align text and images in one of nine different ways using the Align option box on the Image Property Inspector.

Vertical Alignment Option	Result
Browser Default	No alignment attribute is included in the `<img>` tag. Most browsers use the baseline as the alignment default.
Baseline	The bottom of the image is aligned with the baseline of the surrounding text.
Top	The top of the image is aligned with the top of the tallest object in the current line.
Middle	The middle of the image is aligned with the baseline of the current line.
Bottom	The bottom of the image is aligned with the baseline of the surrounding text.
Text Top	The top of the image is aligned with the tallest letter in the current line.
Absolute Middle	The middle of the image is aligned with the middle of the text or object in the current line.

Vertical Alignment Option	Result
Absolute Bottom	The bottom of the image is aligned with the descenders (as in y, g, p, and so forth) that fall below the current line.
Left	The image is aligned to the left edge of the browser or table cell, and all text in the current line flows around the right side of the image.
Right	The image is aligned to the right edge of the browser or table cell, and all text in the current line flows around the left side of the image.

The final two alignment options, Left and Right, are special cases; details about how to use their features are covered in the following section.

Wrapping text

Long a popular design option in conventional publishing, wrapping text around an image on a Web page is also supported by most, but not all, browsers. As noted in the preceding section, the Left and Right alignment options turn a picture into a floating image type, so called because the image can move depending on the amount of text and the size of the browser window.

Tip   Using both floating image types (Left and Right) in combination, you can actually position images flush-left and flush-right, with text in the middle. Insert both images side by side and then set the leftmost image to align left and the rightmost one to align right. Insert your text immediately following the second image. Unless you place a <p> or <br> at the top, this arrangement does not render correctly in Dreamweaver (the first line overlaps the left image), but it does display as expected in most browsers.

Your text wraps around the image depending on where the floating image is placed (or anchored). If you have the feature enabled in the Invisibles pane of Preferences, Dreamweaver inserts a Floating Image Anchor symbol to mark the floating image's place. Figure 10-8 shows two examples of text wrapping. In the top case, the Floating Image Anchor symbol is placed in the midst of the first paragraph, which causes the three paragraphs to flow around the right-aligned image. In the bottom case, the image is left-aligned.

The Floating Image Anchor is not just a static symbol. You can click and drag the anchor to a new location and cause the paragraph to wrap in a different fashion. Be careful though — if you delete the anchor, you also delete the image it represents.

You can also wrap a portion of the text around your left- or right-aligned picture and then force the remaining text to appear below the floating image. However, the HTML necessary to do this task cannot currently be inserted by Dreamweaver and must be coded by hand. You have to force an opening to appear by inserting a break tag, with a special clear attribute, where you want the text to break. This special <br> tag has three forms:

Floating image anchor

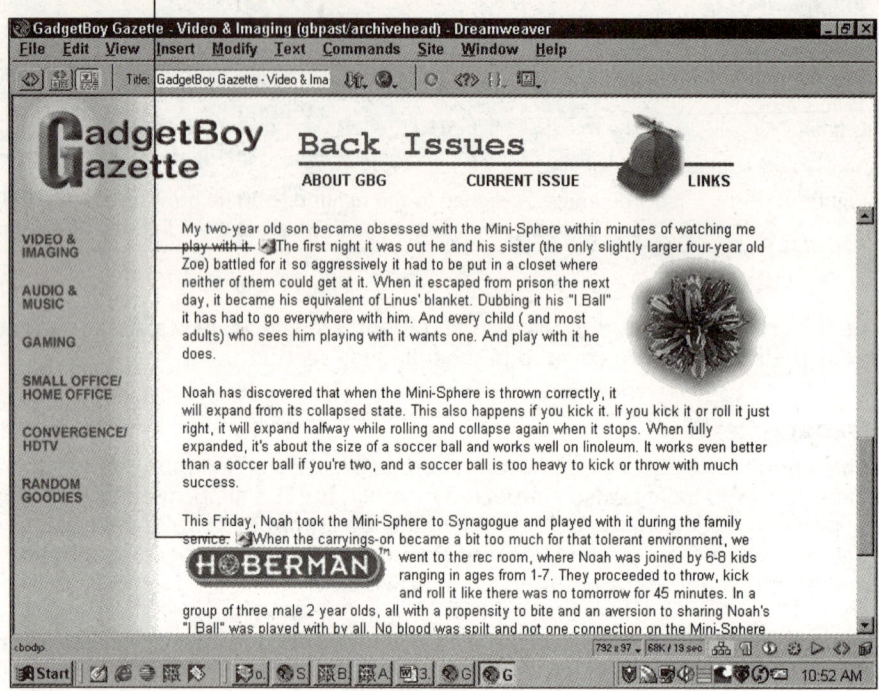

Figure 10-8: Aligning an image left or right enables text to wrap around your images.

`<br clear=left>`	Causes the line to break, and the following text moves down vertically until no floating images are on the left.
`<br clear=right>`	Causes the line to break, and the following text moves down vertically until no floating images are on the right.
`<br clear=all>`	Moves the text following the image down until no floating images are on either the left or the right.

On the CD-ROM

One of the Dreamweaver objects included on CD-ROM that accompanies this book is an enhanced break tag that enables you to include any version of the `clear` attribute. To access these objects, copy the new_break.htm and new_break.gif files from the Dreamweaver\Configuration\Objects\Invisibles folder into the same folder on your system, and then restart Dreamweaver.

Putting Pictures in the Background

In this chapter, you've learned about working with the surface graphics on a Web page. As seen in Chapter 8, you can also have an image in the background of an HTML page. This section covers some of the basic techniques for incorporating a background image in your Dreamweaver page.

Note
Remember, you add an image to your background in Dreamweaver by modifying the Page Properties. Either choose Modify ➪ Page Properties or select Page Properties from the contextual menu that pops up when you right-click (Command+click) any open area on the Web page. In the Page Properties dialog box, select a graphic by choosing the Browse (Choose) button next to the Background Image text box. You can use any file format supported by Dreamweaver — GIF, JPEG, or PNG.

Two key differences exist between background images and the foreground inline images discussed in the preceding sections of this chapter. First and most obvious, all other text and graphics on the Web page are superimposed over your chosen background image. This capability can bring extra depth and texture to your work; unfortunately, you have to make sure the foreground text and images work well with the background.

Cross-Reference
You can quickly try out a number of professionally designed background and foreground color combinations with the Set Color Scheme command. For more information on how to use this Dreamweaver command, see Chapter 8.

Basically, you want to ascertain that enough contrast exists between foreground and background. You can set the default text and the various link colors through the Page Properties dialog box. When trying out a new background pattern, you should set up some dummy text and links. Then use the Apply button on the Page Properties dialog box to test different color combinations. See Figure 10-9 for an example of this test at work.

The second distinguishing feature of background images is that the viewing browser completely fills either the browser window or the area behind the content of your Web page, whichever is larger. So, if you've created a splash page with only a 200×200 foreground logo, and you've incorporated an amazing 1,024×768 background that took you weeks to compose, no one can see the fruits of your labor in the background — unless they resize their browser window to 1,024×768. On the other hand, if your background image is smaller than either the browser window or what the Web page content needs to display, the browser and Dreamweaver repeat (or tile) your image to make up the difference.

Figure 10-9: If you're using a background image, be sure to check the default colors for text and links to make sure enough contrast exists between background and foreground.

Dividing the Web Page with Horizontal Rules

HTML includes a standard horizontal line that can divide your Web page into specific sections. The horizontal rule tag, `<hr>`, is a good tool for adding a little diversion to your page without adding download time. You can control the width (either absolutely or relative to the browser window), the height, the alignment, and the shading property of the rule. These horizontal rules appear on a line by themselves; you cannot place text or images on the same line as a horizontal rule.

To insert a horizontal rule in your Web page in Dreamweaver, follow these steps:

1. Place your cursor where you want the horizontal rule to appear.

2. From the Common pane of the Objects panel, select the Insert Horizontal Rule button or choose the Insert ➪ Horizontal Rule command.

   Dreamweaver inserts the horizontal rule and opens the Horizontal Rule Property Inspector, as shown in Figure 10-10.

3. To change the width of the line, enter a value in the width (W) text box. You can insert either an absolute width in pixels or a relative value as a percentage of the screen.

   • To set a horizontal rule to an exact width, enter the measurement in pixels in the width (W) text box and press the Tab key. Then select pixels in the drop-down list.

Tiling Images

Web designers use the tiling property of background images to create a variety of effects with very low file-size overhead. The columns typically found on one side of Web pages are a good example of tiling. Columns are popular because they enable the designer to place navigational buttons in a visual context. An easy way to create a column that runs the full length of your Web page uses a long, narrow background image.

Take a look at the following figure:

The background image is 45 pixels high, 800 pixels wide, and only 6K in size. When the browser window is set at 640×480 or 800×600, the image is tiled down the page to create the vertical column effect. You could just as easily create an image 1,000 pixels high by 40 pixels wide to create a horizontal column.

- To set a horizontal rule to a width relative to the browser window, enter the percentage amount in the width (W) text box and press Tab. Then select the percent sign (%) in the drop-down list.

Figure 10-10: The Horizontal Rule Property Inspector controls the width, height, and alignment for these HTML lines.

4. To change the height of the horizontal rule, type a pixel measurement in the height (H) text box.

For both the width and height values, you can also enter a value in inches (in), picas (pc), points (pt), millimeters (mm), or centimeters (cm), just as with images. When you press Tab to leave the text box, Dreamweaver converts your entry to pixels.

5. To change the alignment from the default (centered), open the Align drop-down list and choose another alignment.

6. To disable the default "embossed" look for the rule, deselect the Shading checkbox.

7. If you intend to address (call) your horizontal rule in JavaScript or another application, you can give it a unique name. Type it into the unlabeled name text box located directly to the left of the H text box.

To modify any inserted horizontal rule, simply click it. (If the Property Inspector is not already open, you have to double-click the rule.) As a general practice, size your horizontal rules using the percentage option if you are using them to separate items on a full screen. If the horizontal rules are being used to divide items in a specifically sized table column or cell, use the pixel method.

Tip

To use the Shading property of the horizontal rule properly, your background should be a shade of gray. The default shading is black along the top and left, and white along the bottom and right. The center line is generally transparent (although Internet Explorer enables you to assign a color attribute). If you use a different background color or image, be sure to check the appearance of your horizontal rules in that context.

Many designers prefer to create more elaborate horizontal rules; in fact, these rules are an active area of clip art design. These types of horizontal rules are regular graphics and are inserted and modified as such.

Applying Simple Web Animation

Why include a section on animation in a chapter on inline images? On the Web, animations are, for the most part, inline images that move. Outside of the possibilities offered by Dynamic HTML (covered in Part VI), Web animations typically either are animated GIF files or are created with a program such as Flash that requires a plug-in. This section takes a brief look at the capabilities and uses of GIF animations.

A GIF *animation* is a series of still GIF images flipped rapidly to create the illusion of motion. Because animation-creation programs compress all the frames of your animation into one file, a GIF animation is placed on a Web page in the same manner as a still graphic.

In Dreamweaver, click the Insert Image button in the Objects panel or choose Insert ⇨ Image and then select the file. Dreamweaver shows the first frame of your animation in the Document window. To play the animation, preview your Web page in any graphics-capable browser.

As you can imagine, GIF animations can quickly grow to be very large. The key to controlling file size is to think small: Keep your images as small as possible with a low bit-depth (number of colors) and use as few frames as possible.

To create your animation, use any graphics program to produce the separate frames. One excellent technique uses an image-processing program such as Adobe Photoshop and progressively applies a filter to the same image over a series of frames. Figure 10-11 shows the individual frames created with Photoshop's Lighting Effects filter. When animated, a spotlight appears to move across the word.

You need an animation program to compress the separate frames and build your animated GIF file. Many commercial programs, including Macromedia's Fireworks, can handle GIF animation. QuickTime Pro can turn individual files or any other kind of movie into an animated GIF, too. Most animation programs enable you to control the number of times an animation loops, the delay between frames, and how transparency is handled within each frame.

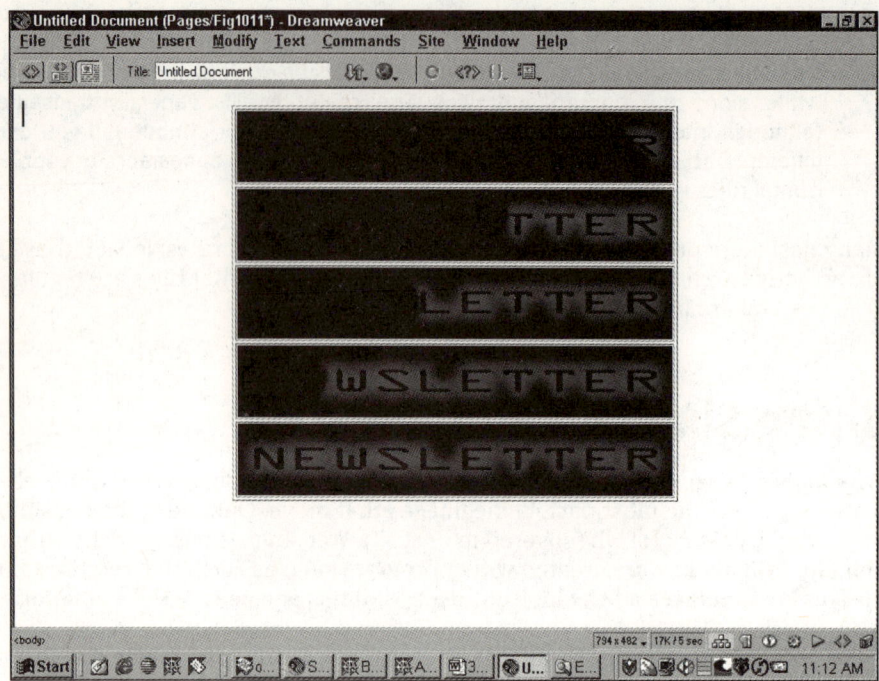

Figure 10-11: Five of twelve frames are compressed into one animated file.

Tip   If you want to use an advanced animation tool but still have full backward compatibility, check out Flash, from Macromedia. Flash is best known for outputting small vector-based animations that require a plug-in to view, but it can also save animations as GIFs or AVIs. The program is discussed in Chapter 25.

Dreamweaver Technique: Including Banner Ads

Banner ads have become an essential aspect of the World Wide Web; for the Web to remain, for the most part, freely accessible, advertising is needed to support the costs. Banner ads have evolved into the de facto standard. Although numerous variations exist, a banner ad is typically an animated GIF of a particular width and height and under a specified file size.

Two organizations, the Standards and Practices Committee of the Internet Advertising Bureau (IAB) and the Coalition for Advertising Supported Information and Entertainment (CASIE), established a series of standard sizes for banner ads. Although no law dictates that their guidelines have to be followed, the vast majority of commercial sites adhere to the suggested dimensions. The most common banner sizes (in pixels) and their official names are listed in Table 10-1.

Table 10-1 IAB/CASIE Advertising Banner Sizes	
Dimensions	**Name**
468×60	Full Banner
392×72	Full Banner with Vertical Navigation Bar
234×60	Half Banner
125×125	Square Button
88×31	Micro Button
120×90	Button 1
120×60	Button 2
120×240	Vertical Banner

File size for a banner ad is not as clearly determined, but it's just as important. The last thing a hosting site wants is for a large, too heavy banner to slow down the loading of its page. Usually a commercial site has an established maximum file size for a particular banner ad size. Generally banner ads are around 10K and no more than 12K. The lighter your banner ad, the faster it loads and — as a direct result — the more likely Web page visitors stick around to see it.

Inserting a banner ad on a Web page is very straightforward. As with any other GIF file, animated or not, all you have to do is insert the image and assign the link. As any advertiser can tell you, the link is as important as the image itself, and you should take special care to ensure that it is correct when inserted. Advertising links are often quite complex as they not only link to a specific page, but may also carry information about the referring site. Several companies monitor how many times an ad is selected — the *clickthru rate* — and often a CGI program is used to communicate with these companies and handle the link. Here's a sample URL from CNet's News.com site:

```
http://home.cnet.com/cgi-acc/clickthru.acc?¬
clickid=00001e145ea7d80f00000000&adt=003:10:100&edt=cnet&cat=1:1002:&site=CN
```

Obviously, copying and pasting such URLs is highly preferable to entering them by hand.

It's not unusual for an advertisement to come from an outside source, so a Web page designer often has to allow space for the ad without incorporating the actual ad. Some Web designers use special placeholder images. In Dreamweaver, placeholder ads can easily be maintained as a Library item and placed as needed from the Assets panel, as shown in Figure 10-12. If you'd prefer not to use placeholder graphics such as these, you could also just insert a plain `<img>` tag — with no `src` parameter — using the Quick Tag Editor. When an `<img>` tag without a `src` is in the code, Dreamweaver displays a broken image icon that could then be resized to the proper banner ad dimensions in the Property Inspector.

Figure 10-12: Use the Library to store standard banner ad images for use as placeholders.

Inserting Rollover Images

Rollovers are among the most popular of all Web page effects. A *rollover* (also known as a *mouseover*) occurs when the user's pointer passes over an image and the image changes in some way. It may appear to glow or change color and/or shape; when the pointer moves away from the graphic, the image returns to its original form. The rollover indicates interactivity and attempts to engage the user with a little bit of flare.

Rollovers are usually accomplished with a combination of HTML and JavaScript. Dreamweaver was among the first Web authoring tools to automate the production of rollovers through its Swap Image and Swap Image Restore behaviors. Later versions of Dreamweaver make rollovers even easier with the Rollover Image object. With the Rollover Image object, if you can pick two images, you can make a rollover.

Technically speaking, a rollover is accomplished by manipulating an <img> tag's src attribute. You'll recall that the src attribute is responsible for providing the actual file name of the graphic to be displayed; it is, quite literally, the source of the image. A rollover changes the value of src from one image file to another. Swapping the src value is analogous to having a picture within a frame and changing the picture while keeping the frame.

Caution The picture frame analogy is appropriate on one other level: It serves as a reminder of the size barrier inherent in rollovers. A rollover changes only one property of an <img> tag, the source — it cannot change any other property such as the height or width. For this reason, both your original image and the image that is displayed during the rollover should be the same size. If they are not, the alternate image is resized to match the dimensions of the original image.

Dreamweaver's Rollover Image object automatically changes the image back to its original source when the user moves the pointer off the image. Optionally, you can elect to preload the images with the selection of a checkbox. Preloading is a Web page technique that reads the intended file or files into the browser's memory before they are displayed. With preloading, the images appear on demand, without any download delay.

Rollovers are typically used for buttons that, when clicked, open another Web page. In fact, JavaScript requires that an image include a link before it can detect when a user's pointer moves over it. Dreamweaver automatically includes the minimum link necessary: the #target link. Although JavaScript recognizes this symbol as indicating a link, no action is taken if the image is clicked by the user; the #, by itself, is an empty link. You can, naturally, supply whatever link you want in the Rollover Image object.

To include a Rollover Image object in your Web page, follow these steps:

1. Place your cursor where you want the rollover image to appear and choose Insert ⇨ Rollover Image or select Insert Rollover Image from the Common panel of the Objects panel. You can also drag the Insert Rollover Image button to any existing location on the Web page.

   Dreamweaver opens the Insert Rollover Image dialog box shown in Figure 10-13.

2. If desired, you can enter a unique name for the image in the Image Name text box, or you can leave the name automatically generated by Dreamweaver.

3. In the Original Image text box, enter the path and name of the graphic you want displayed when the user's mouse is not over the graphic. You can also choose the Browse (Choose) button to select the file. Press Tab when you're done.

4. In the Rollover Image text box, enter the path and name of the graphic you want displayed when the user's pointer is over the graphic. You can also choose the Browse (Choose) button to select the file.

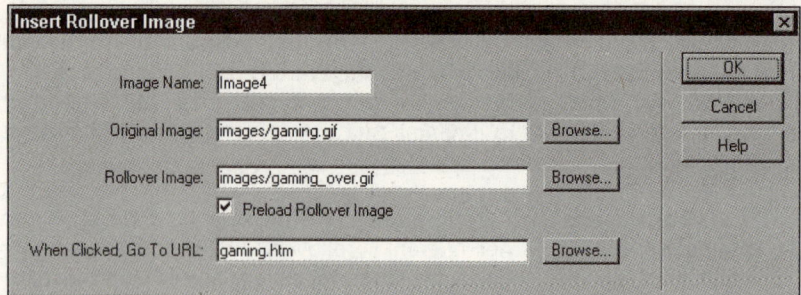

Figure 10-13: The Rollover Image object makes rollover graphics quick and easy.

5. If desired, specify a link for the image by entering it in the When Clicked, Go To URL text box. If you are entering a path and file by hand, be sure to delete the initial target link, #. If you use the Browse (Choose) button to select your file, the target link is deleted for you.

6. To enable images to load only when they are required, deselect the Preload Images option. Generally, it is best to leave this option selected (the default) so that no delay occurs in the rollover appearing.

7. Click OK when you're finished.

Tip

Keep in mind that the Rollover Image object inserts both the original image and its alternate, whereas the Swap Image technique is applied to an existing image in the Web page. If you prefer to use the Rollover Image object rather than the Swap Image behavior, nothing prevents you from deleting an existing image from the Web page and inserting it again through the Rollover Image object. Just make sure that you note the path and name of the image before you delete it so you can find it again.

Adding a Navigation Bar

Rollovers are nice effects, but a single button does not make a navigation system for a Web site. Typically, several buttons with a similar look and feel are placed next to each other to form a *navigation bar*. To make touring a site as intuitive as possible, the same navigation bar is usually repeated on each page or used once, as a frame element. Consistency of design and repetitive use of the navigation bar simplifies getting around a site — even for a first-time user.

Some designers build their navigation bars in a separate graphics program and then import them into Dreamweaver. Fireworks, with its capability to export both images and code, makes this a strong option. Other Web designers, however, prefer to build separate rollover images in a graphics program and then assemble all the pieces at the HTML layout stage. Dreamweaver now automates such a process with its Navigation Bar object.

The Navigation Bar object incorporates rollovers — and more. A Navigation Bar element can use up to four different images, each reflecting a different user action:

✦ Up — The user's pointer is away from the image.

✦ Over — The pointer is over the image.

✦ Down — The user has clicked the image.

✦ Over While Down — The user's pointer is over the image after it has been clicked.

You don't have to use all four states — it's up to you whether you use just the first two, like a standard rollover, or add the third and possibly the fourth. You can even skip the Over state and just use Up and Down. While it's possible to display an Over While Down state without a Down state, it doesn't make much sense to do so.

One key difference separates a fully functioning navigation bar from a group of unrelated rollovers. When the Down state is available, if the user clicks one of the buttons, any other Down button is changed to the Up state. The effect is like a series of mutually exclusive radio buttons: You can show only one selected in a group. The Down state is often used to indicate the current selection.

Tip　While you can use the Navigation Bar object on any type of Web design, it works best in a frameset situation with a frame for navigation and one for content. If you insert a navigation bar with Up, Over, Down, and Over While Down states for each button in the navigation frame, you can target the content frame and gain the full effect of the mutually exclusive Down states.

Before you can use Dreamweaver's Navigation Bar object, you have to create a series of images for each button — one for each state you plan to use. It's completely up to the designer how the buttons appear, but it's important that a consistent look and feel be applied for all the buttons. For example, if rolling over Button A reveals a green glow, rolling over Buttons B, C, and D should also cause the same green glow, as demonstrated in Figure 10-14.

To insert a navigation bar, follow these steps:

1. From the Objects panel, select the Insert Navigation Bar object.

   The Insert Navigation Bar dialog box appears, as shown in Figure 10-15.

2. Enter a unique name for the first button in the Element Name field and press Tab.

Caution　Be sure to use Tab rather than Enter (Return) when moving from field to field. When Enter (Return) is pressed, Dreamweaver attempts to build the navigation bar. If you have not completed the initial two steps (providing an Element Name and a source for the Up Image), an alert is displayed; otherwise, the navigation bar is built.

Figure 10-14: Before you invoke the Navigation Bar object, create a series of buttons with a separate image for each state to be used.

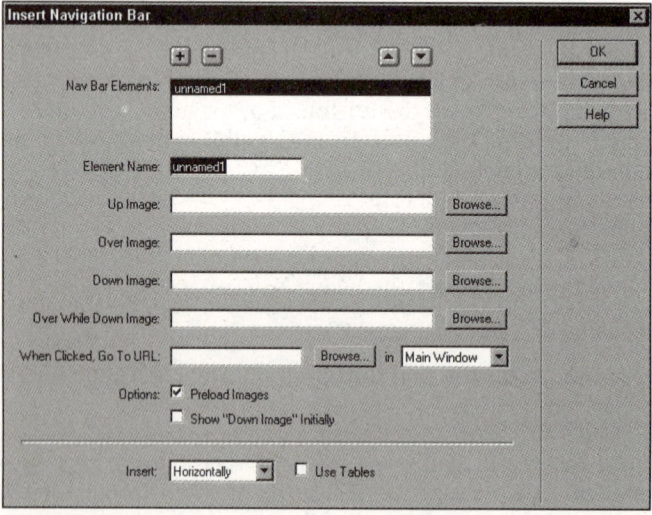

Figure 10-15: Add elements one at a time in the Insert Navigation Bar dialog box.

3. In the Up Image field, enter a path and filename or browse to a graphic file to use.

4. Select files for each of the remaining states you wish to use: Over, Down, and Over While Down.

5. Enter a URL or browse to a file in the When Clicked, Go To URL field.

6. If you're using a frameset, select a target for the URL from the drop-down list.

7. Enable or disable the Preload Images option as desired.

   For a multistate button to be effective, the reaction has to be immediate, and the images must be preloaded. It is highly recommended that the Preload Images option be enabled.

8. If you want the current button to display the Down state first, select the Show "Down Image" Initially option.

   When this option is chosen, an asterisk appears next to the current button in the Nav Bar Element list. Generally, you don't want more than one Down state showing at a time.

9. To set the orientation of the navigation bar, select either Horizontally or Vertically from the Insert drop-down list.

10. If you want to contain your images in a table, keep the Use Table option selected.

    If you decide not to use tables in a horizontal configuration, images are presented side by side; when a vertical navigation bar is built without tables, Dreamweaver inserts a line break (`<br>` tag) between each element.

11. Select the add (plus) button and repeat Steps 2 through 8 to add the next element.

12. To reorder the elements in the navigation bar, select an element in the Nav Bar Elements list and use the up and down buttons to reposition it in the Element list.

13. To remove an element, select it and click the delete (minus) button.

Each page can have only one Dreamweaver-built navigation bar. If you try to insert a second, Dreamweaver asks if you'd like to modify the existing series. Clicking OK opens the Modify Navigation Bar dialog box, shown in Figure 10-16, which is identical to the Insert Navigation Bar dialog box, except you can no longer change the orientation or table settings. You can also alter the inserted navigation bar by choosing Modify ➪ Navigation Bar.

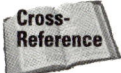

If you're looking for even more control over your navigation bar, Dreamweaver also includes the Set Navigation Bar behavior, which is fully covered in Chapter 19.

Figure 10-16: Once you've inserted your navigation bar, you can adjust it through the Modify Navigation Bar dialog box.

Summary

In this chapter, you learned how to include both foreground and background images in Dreamweaver. Understanding how images are handled in HTML is an absolute necessity for the Web designer. Some of the key points follow:

✦ Web pages are restricted to using specific graphic formats. Virtually all browsers support GIF and JPEG files. PNG is also gaining acceptance. Dreamweaver can preview all three image types.

✦ Images are inserted in the foreground in Dreamweaver through the Insert Image command of the Objects panel or from the Assets panel. Once the graphic is inserted, almost all modifications can be handled through the Property Inspector.

✦ You can use HTML's background image function to lay a full-frame image or a tiled series of the same image underneath your text and graphics. Tiled images can be employed to create columns and other designs with small files.

✦ The simplest HTML graphic is the built-in horizontal rule. Useful for dividing your Web page into separate sections, the horizontal rule can be sized either absolutely or relatively.

✦ With the Rollover Image object, you can easily insert simple rollovers that use two different images. To build a rollover that uses more than two images, you have to use the Swap Image behavior.

✦ Animated images can be inserted alongside, and in the same manner as, still graphics. The individual frames of a GIF animation must be created in a graphics program and then combined in an animation program.

✦ When used in conjunction with Fireworks, images can now be optimized from within Dreamweaver. Moreover, it's easier to integrate code generated from Fireworks — and you can even specify Dreamweaver-style HTML.

✦ You can add a series of interrelated buttons — complete with four-state rollovers — by using the Navigation Bar object.

In the next chapter, you learn how to use hyperlinks in Dreamweaver.

✦   ✦   ✦

Establishing Web Links

To me, links are the Web. Everything else about the medium can be replicated in another form, but without links, there would be no World Wide Web. As your Web design work becomes more sophisticated, you'll find more enhanced uses for links: sending mail, connecting to an FTP site — even downloading software. In this chapter, you learn how Dreamweaver helps you manage the various types of links, set anchors within documents to get smooth and accurate navigation, and establish targets for your URLs. But first, let's begin with an overview on Internet addresses to give you the full picture of the possibilities.

Understanding URLs

URL stands for Uniform Resource Locator. An awkward phrase, it nonetheless describes itself well — the URL's function is to provide a standard method for finding anything on the Internet. From Web pages to newsgroups to the smallest graphic on the most esoteric of pages, everything can be referenced through the URL system.

The URL can use up to six different parts, although all parts are not necessary for the URL to be read. Each part is separated by some combination of a slash, colon, and hash mark delimiter. When entered as an attribute's value, the entire URL is generally enclosed within quotes to ensure that the address is read as one unit. A generic URL using all the parts looks like the following:

```
method://server:port/path/file#anchor
```

Here's a real-world example that also uses every section:

```
http://www.idest.com:80/dreamweaver/index.htm#
bible
```

In order of appearance in the body of an Internet address, left to right, the parts denote the following:

✦ **The method used to access the resource.** The method to address Web servers is the HyperText Transport Protocol (HTTP). Other methods are discussed later in this section.

✦ **The name of the server providing the resource.** The server can either be a domain name (with or without the "www" prefix) or an Internet Protocol (IP) address, such as 199.227.52.143.

✦ **The port number to be used on the server.** Most URLs do not include a port number, which is analogous to a telephone extension number on the server, because most servers use the defaults.

✦ **The directory path to the resource.** Depending on where the resource (for example, the Web page) is located on the server, the following paths can be specified: no path (indicating that the resource is in the public root of the server), a single folder name, or a number of folders and subfolders.

✦ **The filename of the resource.** If the filename is omitted, the Web browser looks for a default page, often named index.html or index.htm. The browser reacts differently depending on the type of file. For example, GIFs and JPEGs are displayed by themselves; executable files and archives (Zip, StuffIt, and so on) are downloaded.

✦ **The named anchor in the HTML document.** This part is another optional section. The named anchor enables the Web designer to send the viewer to a particular section of an HTML page.

Because it is used to communicate with servers, the HTTP access method is far and away the most prevalent method on today's World Wide Web. In addition to the HTTP access method, other methods connect with other types of servers. Table 11-1 discusses some of these options.

Table 11-1
Various Internet Access Methods and Protocols

Name	Syntax	Usage
File Transfer Protocol	ftp://	Links to an FTP server that is generally used for uploading and downloading files. The server can be accessed anonymously, or it may require a user name and password.
Gopher	gopher://as	Connects to a directory tree structure primarily used for disseminating all-text documents.
HyperText Transfer Protocol	http://	Used for connecting to a document available on a World Wide Web server.

Name	Syntax	Usage
JavaScript	javascript://	Executes a JavaScript function.
Mailto	mailto:	Opens an e-mail form with the recipient's address already filled in. These links are useful when embedded in your Web pages to provide visitors with an easy feedback method.
News	news://	Connects to the specified Usenet newsgroup. Newsgroups are public, theme-oriented message boards where anyone can post or reply to a message.
Telnet	telnet://	Enables users to log directly onto remote host computers and interact directly with the operating system software.

Part of the richness of today's Web browsers stems from their capability to connect with all the preceding (and additional) services.

Tip

The mailto: access method enables you not only to open up a preaddressed e-mail form but also to specify the topic, with a little extra work. For example, if Joe Lowery wants to include a link to his e-mail address with the subject heading "Dreamweaver Bible," he can insert a link such as the following:

```
mailto:jlowery@idest.com?subject=Dreamweaver Bible
```

The question mark acts as a delimiter that enables a variable and a value to be passed to the browser. When you're trying to encourage feedback from your Web page visitors, every little bit helps. A note of caution: This method is not standardized HTML, and while it works with most browsers and mail programs, you could get unexpected results with some systems.

Surfing the Web with Hypertext

Most often, you assign a link to a word or phrase on your page, an image such as a navigational button, or a section of graphic for an image map (a large graphic in which various parts are links). Once you have created the link, you have to preview it in a browser; links are not active in Dreamweaver's Document window.

Designate links in HTML through the anchor tag pair: <a> and </a>. The anchor tag generally takes one main attribute—the hypertext reference, which is written as follows:

```
href="link name"
```

When you create a link in Dreamweaver, the anchor pair surrounds the text or object that is being linked. For example, if you link the phrase "Back to Home Page," it may look like the following:

```
<a href="index.html">Back to Home Page</a>
```

When you attach a link to an image, logo.gif, your code looks as follows:

```
<a href="home.html"><img src="images/logo.gif"></a>
```

Creating a basic link in Dreamweaver is easy. Simply follow these steps:

1. Select the text, image, or object you want to establish as a link.

2. In the Property Inspector, enter the URL in the Link text box as shown in Figure 11-1. You can use one of the following methods to do so:

   • Type the URL directly into the Link text box.

   • Select the folder icon to the right of the Link text box to open the Select File dialog box, where you can browse for the file.

   • Select the Point to File icon and drag your mouse to an existing page or link. This feature is explained later in this section.

   • Drag a link from the Assets panel onto a text or image selection.

Link text box┘   Point to File icon┘ └Folder icon

Figure 11-1: You can enter your link directly into the Link text box, point to it directly with the Point to File icon, or select the folder icon to browse for a file.

Only a few restrictions exist for specifying linked URLs. Dreamweaver does not support any letters from the extended character set (also known as High ASCII), such as ¡, à, or ñ. Complete URLs must have fewer than a total of 255 characters. You should be cautious about using spaces in path names and, thus, URLs. Although most browsers can interpret the address, spaces are changed to a %20 symbol for proper Unix usage, which can make your URLs difficult to read.

 Note   Whitespace in your HTML usually doesn't have an adverse effect. However, Netscape browsers are sensitive to whitespace when assigning a link to an image. If you isolate your image tag from the anchor tags as in the following example:

Links Without Underscores

To remove the underlined aspect of a link, you can use one of two methods. The classic method—which works for all graphics-capable browsers—uses an image rather than text as the link. You must make sure the `border` attribute of your image is set to 0 because a linked image usually displays a blue border if a `border` attribute exists. Dreamweaver adds border="0" to all image links now, as a default.

The second, newer method uses Cascading Style Sheets. While this is an excellent one-stop solution for 4.0 and later browsers, the links will still be seen with underlines on the earlier browser versions. Refer to the Dreamweaver Technique for eliminating the underlines in links in Chapter 27.

```
<a href="index.htm">
<img src="images/Austria.gif" width="34" height="24">
</a>
```

Netscape browsers attach a small blue underscore—a tail, really—to your image. Because Dreamweaver codes the anchor tag properly, without any additional whitespace, this odd case applies only to hand-coded or previously coded HTML.

Text links are most often rendered with a blue color and underlined. You can specify the document link color by choosing Modify ⇨ Page Properties and selecting the Link Color swatch. In Page Properties, you can also alter the color to which the links change after being selected (the Visited Link Color) and the color flashed when the link is clicked (the Active Link Color).

Tip

Want to add a little variety to your text links? You can actually change the color of the link on an individual basis. To do this, you have to enter the link in the Property Inspector before you apply the color. Be sure to exercise a little discretion though—you don't want to use so many different colors that your Web page visitors can't figure out the navigation.

Inserting URLs from the Assets panel

Internet addresses get more complicated every day. Trying to remember them all correctly and avoid typos makes the Web designer's job unnecessarily difficult. At least, it's unnecessary if you make use of the URLs category of Dreamweaver 4's new Assets panel. With the Assets panel, you can drag-and-drop the trickiest URLs with a flick of the mouse tail.

New Feature

As with other Assets panel categories, you'll need to select the Refresh Site List button to make available all the possible URLs in a site. Alternatively, you could choose Refresh Site List from the context menu on the panel. Either action causes

Dreamweaver to scan all the Web pages within the site and extract all the complete Internet addresses found. Only full Internet addresses—whether to files (such as `www.idest.com/dreamweaver`) or to e-mail addresses (for example, mailto:jlowery@idest.com)—are visible in the Assets panel. Document or site relative links are not listed as an Asset. To assign a link to a document or site relative page, use one of the other methods, such as pointing to a file, discussed in this chapter.

To assign a URL from the Assets panel, follow these steps:

1. If it's not already visible, select Window ➪ Assets or click the Assets icon on the Launcher to display the Assets panel. Alternatively, you show the Assets panel by pressing the keyboard shortcut, F11.

2. Select the URLs icon on the side of the Assets panel to show that category, as seen in Figure 11-2.

URLs icon

Figure 11-2: Banish typos from your absolute URLs by dragging a link from the Assets panel to any selected text or graphic.

3. If necessary, select the Refresh button on the Assets panel to list the most current links found in the site.

4. In the Document window, select the text or image you want the link assigned to.

5. Drag the desired link from the Assets panel onto the selected text or image; alternatively, highlight the link in the panel and then choose the Apply button.

You'll notice that the Edit button on the Assets panel is unavailable for the URLs category. Links cannot be edited; they can only be applied as shown in the preview area.

Pointing to a file

Dreamweaver has an alternative method of identifying a link — pointing to it. By using the Point to File icon on the Property Inspector, you can quickly fill in the Link text box by dragging your mouse to any existing named anchor or file visible in the Dreamweaver environment. The Point to File feature saves you from having to browse through folder after folder as you search for a file you can clearly see onscreen.

You can point to a file in another open Dreamweaver window or one in another frame in the same window. If your desired link is a named anchor located further down the page, Dreamweaver automatically scrolls to find it. You can even point to a named anchor in another page, and Dreamweaver enters the full syntax correctly. Named anchors are covered in detail later in this chapter.

Perhaps one of the slickest applications of the Point to File icon is when it is used in tandem with the Site window. The Site window lists all the existing files in any given Web site, and when both it and the Document window are onscreen, you can quickly point to any file.

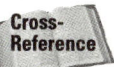 **Cross-Reference** For more details about using the Site window in this fashion, see Chapter 7.

Pointing to a file uses what could be called a "drag-and-release" mouse technique, as opposed to the more ordinary point-and-click or drag-and-drop method. To select a new link using the Point to File icon, follow these steps:

1. Select the text or the graphic that you'd want to make into a link.

2. In the Property Inspector, click and hold the Point to File icon located to the right of the Link text box.

3. Holding down the mouse button, drag the mouse until it is over an existing link or named anchor in the Document window or a file in the Site window.

   As you drag the mouse, a line extends from the Point to File icon, and the reminder "Point to a file to make a link" appears in the Link text box.

4. When you locate the file you want to link to, release the mouse button. The filename with the accompanying path information is written into the Link text box as shown in Figure 11-3.

Link   Point to File icon

Figure 11-3: The Point to File capability enables you to quickly insert a link to any onscreen page.

Addressing types

As you learned in Chapter 6, three types of URLs are used as links: absolute addresses, document-relative addresses, and site root–relative addresses. Let's briefly recap these address types.

✦ **Absolute addresses** require the full URL, as follows:

`http://www.macromedia.com/software/dreamweaver/`

This type is most often used for referencing links on another Web server.

✦ **Document-relative addresses** know the method, server, and path aspects of the URL. You need to include only additional path information if the link is outside of the current Web page's folder. Links in the current document's folder can be addressed with their filename only. To reference an item in a subfolder, just name the folder, enter a forward slash, and then enter the item's filename, as follows:

`images/background.gif`

✦ **Site root–relative addresses** are indicated with a leading forward slash. For example:

`/navigation/upndown.html`

The preceding address links to a file named upndown.html stored in the navigation directory at the current site root. Dreamweaver translates site-relative to document-relative links when the Preview in Browser feature is used.

A Webmaster often must perform the tedious but necessary task of verifying the links on all the Web pages in a site. Because of the Web's fluid nature, links can work one day and then be broken the next. Dreamweaver has enhanced its powerful link-checking capabilities with link-updating features.

To find out how to keep your site up to date with a minimum of effort, see Chapter 7.

Adding an E-Mail Link

E-mail links are very common on the Web. Rather than opening a new Web page like a regular link, when an e-mail link is clicked, a window for sending a new e-mail message is displayed. The message window is already preaddressed to the recipient, making it convenient to use. All the user has to do is add a subject, enter a message, and select Send.

E-mail links no longer need be added by hand. Dreamweaver includes an object that streamlines the process. Just enter the text of the line, and the e-mail address and the link is ready. E-mail links, like other links, do not work in Dreamweaver when clicked and must be previewed in the browser.

To enter an e-mail link with the new object, follow these steps:

1. Position your cursor where you want the e-mail link to appear.

2. From the Common category of the Objects panel, select the Insert E-Mail Link button.

   The Insert E-Mail Link dialog box, shown in Figure 11-4, appears.

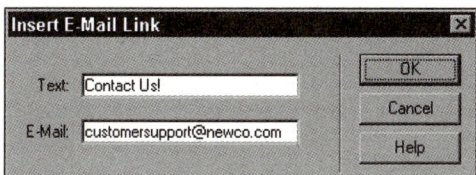

Figure 11-4: The Insert E-Mail Link object creates links that make it simple for your Web page visitors to send an e-mail.

3. In the Insert E-Mail Link dialog box, enter the visible text for the link in the Text field.

4. Enter the e-mail address in the E-Mail field.

 The e-mail address must be in the format name@company.com. Dreamweaver does not check to make sure you've entered the proper format.

5. Click OK when you're done.

Note If you already have the text for the e-mail link in the document, you can also use the Property Inspector to insert an e-mail link. Just highlight the text and in the Link field of the Property Inspector, enter the URL in this format:

```
mailto:name@company.com
```

Make sure that the URL is a valid e-mail address with the @ sign properly placed.

Here's a bit of the frustration that Web designers sometimes face: On some browsers, notably Internet Explorer, the user may see a dialog box when the e-mail link is first selected. The dialog box informs them that they are about to send an e-mail over the Internet. The user has an option to not see these warnings, but there's no way for the Web designer to prevent them from appearing.

Navigating with Anchors

Whenever you normally link to an HTML page, through absolute or relative address-ing, the browser displays the page from the top. Your Web visitors must scroll to any information rendered below the current screen. One HTML technique, however, links to a specific point anywhere on your page regardless of the display window's contents. This technique uses *named anchors*.

Using named anchors is a two-step process. First you place a named anchor some-where on your Web page. This placement is coded in HTML as an anchor tag using the name attribute, with nothing in between the opening and closing tags. In HTML, named anchors look like the following:

```
<a name="bible"></a>
```

The second step includes a link to that named anchor from somewhere else on your Web page. If used, a named anchor is referenced in the final possible portion of an Internet address, designated by the hash mark (#), as follows:

```
<a href="http://www.idest.com/dreamweaver/index.htm#bible>
```

You can include any number of named anchors on the current page or another page. Named anchors are commonly used with a table of contents or index.

To insert a named anchor in Dreamweaver, follow these steps:

1. Place the cursor where you want the named anchor to appear.

2. Choose Insert ➪ Named Anchor. You can also select the Insert Named Anchor button from the Invisibles category of the Objects panel. Or use the key short-cut Ctrl+Alt+A (Command+Option+A).

3. The Named Anchor dialog box opens. Type the anchor name into the text box.

Caution   Named anchors are case-sensitive and must be unique within the page.

When you press Enter (Return), Dreamweaver places a named anchor symbol in the current cursor location and opens the Named Anchor Property Inspector (shown in Figure 11-5).

Named Anchor symbol   Insert Named Anchor button

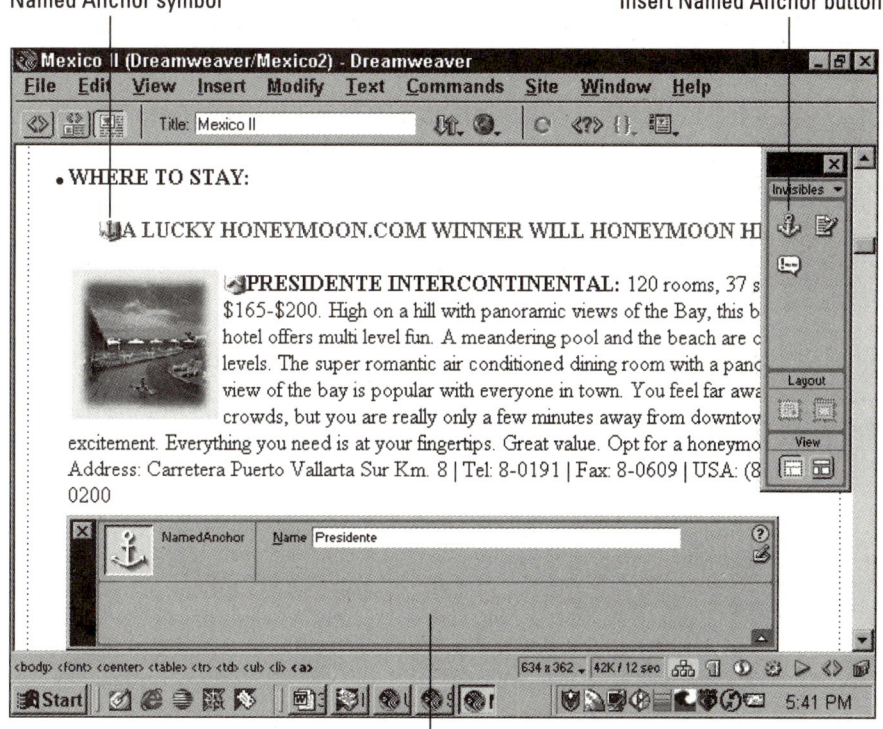

Named Anchor Property Inspector

Figure 11-5: The Named Anchor tag enables you to link to specific areas of a Web page.

4. To change an anchor's name, click the named anchor symbol within the page and alter the text in the Property Inspector.

As with other invisible symbols, the named anchor symbol can be cut and pasted or moved using the drag-and-drop method.

Moving within the same document

One of the major advantages of using named anchors is the almost instantaneous response the viewer receives when they click them. The browser only needs to scroll to the particular place in the document because the entire page is loaded. For long text documents, this capability is an invaluable time-saver.

Once you have placed a named anchor — or all of them at once — in your document, you can link to these anchors. Follow these steps to create a link to a named anchor in the same document:

1. Select the text or image that you want to designate as a link.

2. In the Link text box of the Property Inspector, type a hash mark, #, followed by the exact anchor name. For example:

   #top

   Remember, anchor names are case-sensitive and must be unique in each document.

Tip   You should place the named anchor one line above the heading or image to which you want to link the viewer. Browsers tend to be quite literal. If you place the named anchor on the same line, the browser renders it up against the top of the window. Placing your named anchor up one line gives your topic a bit of breathing room in the display.

In Dreamweaver, you can also use the Point to File icon to choose a named anchor link. If your named anchor is in the same document, just drag the Point to File icon to the named anchor symbol. When you release the mouse, the proper named anchor is inserted into the Link text box. If the named anchor is on the same page but offscreen, Dreamweaver automatically scrolls the Document window as you approach the edge. In Windows, the closer you move to the edge, the faster Dreamweaver scrolls. Dreamweaver even returns the screen to your original location, with the new link at the top of the screen, after you release the mouse button.

In long documents with a table of contents or index linking to a number of named anchors, it's common practice — and a good idea — to place a link back to the top of the page after every screen or every topic. This technique enables your users to return to the menu quickly and pick another topic without having to manually scroll all the way back.

Using named anchors in a different page

If your table of contents is on a separate page from the topics of your site, you can use named anchors to send the viewer anywhere on a new page. The technique is exactly the same as already explained for placing named anchors, but one minor difference exists when it comes to linking. Instead of placing a hash mark and name to denote the named anchor, you must first include the URL of the linked page.

Let's say you want to call the disclaimer section of a legal page from your table of contents. You could insert something like the following in the Link text box of the Property Inspector:

```
legal.htm#disclaimer
```

This link, when activated, first loads the referenced Web page (legal.htm) and then goes directly to the named anchor place (#disclaimer). Figure 11-6 shows how you would enter this in the Property Inspector. Keep in mind, you can use any form of addressing prior to the hash mark and named anchor.

Figure 11-6: You can also link to any part of a separate Web page using named anchors.

Tip One of the more obscure uses for named anchors comes into play when you are trying to use Dreamweaver's JavaScript Behavior feature. Because JavaScript needs to work with a particular type of tag to perform `onMouseOver` and other events, one trick marks some text or image with a link to #nowhere. You can use any name for the nonexistent named anchor. In fact, you don't even have to use a name—you can just use a hash mark by itself (#). One problem area: Netscape browsers have a tendency to send the page to the top if a link of this type is used. Many programmers have begun to substitute a JavaScript function instead, such as `javascript:;`. Dreamweaver itself now uses `javascript:;` instead of # when a new behavior is attached to an image.

Targeting Your Links

Thus far, all of this chapter's links have had a similar effect: They open another Web page or section in your browser's window. What if you want to force the browser to open another window and load that new URL in the new window? HTML enables you to specify the target for your links.

Targets are most often used in conjunction with frames — that is, you can make a link in one frame open a file in another. (Chapter 16 covers the subject of frames in depth.) Here, though, let's take a look at one of the HTML predefined targets useful in a situation where you want to load another URL into a new window.

To specify a new browser window as the target for a link in Dreamweaver, follow these steps:

1. Select the text or image you want to designate as your new link.

2. In the Property Inspector, enter the URL into the Link text box.

   After you've entered a link, the target option becomes active.

3. Choose the option button next to the Target list box and select _blank from the drop-down list. You can also type it in the list box.

   Dreamweaver inserts a _blank option in the Target list box, as shown in Figure 11-7. Now, when your link is activated, the browser spawns a new window and loads the referenced link into it. The user has both windows available.

Figure 11-7: You can force a user's browser to open a separate window to display a specific link with the Target command.

The _blank target is most often used when the originating Web page is acting as a jump station and has numerous links available. By keeping the original Web page open, the user can check out one site without losing the origin point.

Note   Three other system-wide targets exist: _top, _parent, and _self. Both _top and _parent are primarily used with framesets: _top target replaces the outermost frameset and _parent replaces the frameset containing the current page. These two have the same effect, except in the case of nested framesets. The _self target is the default behavior and only the current page is replaced.

You can even use the _blank target technique on named anchors in the same document, thereby emulating frames to some degree.

Caution   Some key online services, such as America Online and WebTV, don't enable their built-in browsers to open new windows. Every link that is accessed is displayed in the same browser window.

Summary

Whether they are links for Web site navigation or jumps to other related sites, hypertext links are an essential part of any Web page. Dreamweaver gives you full control over your inserted anchors.

✦ Through a unique URL, you can access virtually any Web page, graphic, or other item available on the Internet.

✦ The HyperText Transfer Protocol (HTTP) is the most common method of Web connection, but Web pages can link to other formats, including FTP, e-mail, and newsgroups.

✦ Any of the three basic address formats—absolute, document relative, or site root relative—can be inserted in the Link text box of Dreamweaver's Property Inspector to create a link.

✦ Dreamweaver has a quick linking capability through its Point to File feature.

✦ The Assets panel tracks all of your absolute and mailto: URLs and makes it easy to apply any of them to your pages. Document or site relative URLs are not displayed in the Assets panel, however.

✦ Named anchors give you the power to jump to specific parts of any Web page, whether the page is the current one or located on another server.

✦ With the _blank target attribute, you can force a link to open in a new browser window, leaving your original window available to the user.

In the next chapter, you learn how to use various types of lists in Dreamweaver.

✦   ✦   ✦

Creating Lists

Lists serve several different functions in all publications, including Web pages. A list can itemize a topic's points or catalog the properties of an object. A numbered list is helpful for giving step-by-step instructions. From a page designer's point of view, a list can break up the page and simultaneously draw the viewer's eye to key details.

Lists are an important alternative to the basic textual tools of paragraphs and headings. In this chapter, you study Dreamweaver's tools for designing and working with each of the three basic types of lists available under HTML:

✦ Unordered lists

✦ Ordered lists

✦ Definition lists

The various list types can also be combined to create outlines. Dreamweaver supplies a straightforward method for building these nested lists.

Creating Bulleted (Unordered) Lists

What word processing programs and layout artists refer to as *bulleted lists* are known in HTML as *unordered lists*. An unordered list is used when the sequence of the listed items is unimportant, as in a recipe's list of ingredients. Each unordered list item is set off by a leading character and the remainder of the line is indented. By default, the leading character is the bullet; in HTML, you also can specify two other symbols by conventional means and a custom bullet through Cascading Style Sheets (CSS).

You can either create the unordered list from scratch or convert existing text into the bulleted format. To begin an unordered list from scratch, position the cursor where you want to start the list. Next, click the Unordered List button supplied conveniently on the Text Property Inspector (see Figure 12-1) or use the Text ⇨ List ⇨ Unordered List command.

Unordered list button

Figure 12-1: An itemized list that doesn't need to be in any specific order is perfect for formatting as an unordered list.

If you are changing existing text into a list, select the paragraphs first and then execute the Unordered List button or menu command.

Dreamweaver creates one list item for every paragraph. As you can see from Figure 12-1, list items are generally rendered closer together than regular paragraphs. Unlike block elements such as paragraphs or headings, HTML doesn't insert additional lines above and space below each line of a list.

Caution

In terms of lists in Dreamweaver, the word *paragraph* is used literally to mean any text designated with a paragraph tag. Certainly you can apply a heading format to an HTML list, but you probably won't like the results: The heading format reinserts those additional lines below and above each list item—the ones generally not used by the list format. If you want your list items to appear larger in size, you should change the font size through the Property Inspector or with Text ⇨ Size Increase.

Editing unordered lists

Once a series of paragraphs is formatted as an unordered list, you can easily add additional bulleted items. The basic editing techniques are the same for all types of lists:

✦ To continue adding items at the end of a list, simply press Enter (Return) to create each new paragraph. Another bullet is inserted.

✦ To insert an item within an unordered list, place your cursor at the end of the item above the desired position for the added item and press Enter (Return).

✦ List items can be copied or cut and pasted in a different place on the list. Place your cursor in front of the list item below where you want the repositioned item to appear and choose Edit ⇨ Paste.

✦ To end a bulleted list, you can press Enter (Return) twice or deselect the Unordered List button on the Text Property Inspector.

List tags

You may occasionally need to tweak your list code by hand. Two HTML tags are used in creating an unordered list. The first is the outer tag, which defines the type of list; the second is the item delimiter. Unordered lists are designated with the `<ul>...</ul>` tag pair, and the delimiter is the `<li>...</li>` pair. The unordered list code in the HTML Inspector looks like the following:

```
<ul>
    <li>Cascading Style Sheet Support</li>
    <li>Roundtrip HTML</li>
    <li>JavaScript Behaviors</li>
    <li>Repeatable Library Elements</li>
</ul>
```

If a list item is too long to fit in a single line, the browser indents the line when it wraps. By inserting a line break code, you can emulate this behavior even when you're working with lines that aren't long enough to need wrapping. To insert a line break, choose the Insert Line Break button from the Invisibles panel of the Objects palette, or select Insert ⇨ Line Break. You can also use the key combination Shift+Enter (Shift+Return) or just type `<br>` in your code. Figure 12-2 shows examples of both approaches: the long paragraph that wraps naturally and the inserted line breaks to force the wrapping.

Using other bullet symbols

Although HTML doesn't include a wide range of different symbols to use in an unordered list, you have a few options. Most browsers recognize three different bullet styles: bullet (the default), circle, and square. You can apply the style to the entire unordered list or to one list item at a time.

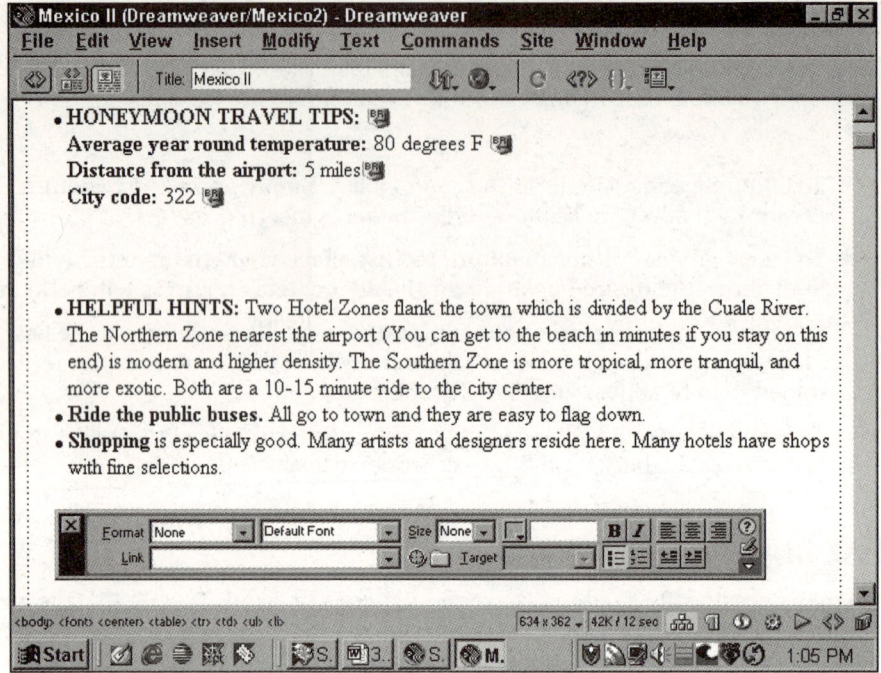

Figure 12-2: A list is indented if the text wraps around the screen or if you insert a line break.

Changing the overall style

To change the bullet style of the overall unordered list, follow these steps:

1. Position your cursor anywhere in an existing list.

2. If necessary, click the expander arrow on the Text Property Inspector to display the additional options. Click the List Item button.

3. In the List Properties dialog box that appears (see Figure 12-3), open the Style options list.

4. Select one of the four options:

   • **[Default]:** No style is listed, and the browser applies its default, usually rendered as a bullet.

   • **Bullet:** A solid circle.

   • **Circle:** An open circle.

   • **Square:** A solid square.

5. Click OK.

Figure 12-3: You can change the style of the entire list or just one list item through the List Properties dialog box.

Caution   If you find the List Item button inactive in your Text Property Inspector, make sure that you have — at most — one list item selected. Selecting more than one list item deactivates the List Item button.

When you try to change the style of just one list item, Dreamweaver alters all the successive list items as well. By default, list items don't specify a bullet style. Therefore, when a new style is inserted, all the following items adopt that style.

Changing the style for one item

When you need to change the bullet style of just one item in a list, follow these steps:

1. Select the list item you wish to change.

2. Make sure the Text Property Inspector is expanded and select the List Item button.

3. From the List Properties dialog box, in the List Item section, open the New Style drop-down list.

4. Select one of the four bullet options (described in the preceding steps).

You can alter the type of bullet used in two other ways. The time-tested solution substitutes a graphic for the bullet. Just as with graphical horizontal rules, the Web offers a substantial clip art collection of bullets. You have to insert a graphic for each bullet, however. The quickest method is the drag-and-drop copy technique: Hold down the Ctrl (Command) key and then click and drag the bullet graphic — this sequence places a copy of the bullet wherever you release the mouse.

Changing bullet styles with style sheets

The newer technique for installing bullet styles uses style sheets. Style sheets can switch a list or list item's bullet style the same as the List Properties dialog box can, but with a style sheet you can perform one additional task. You can assign the bullet style type to a specific file — in other words, you can customize your bullet image. The drawback to using this technique is that the list aspect of style sheets is currently supported only by Internet Explorer versions 4.0 and higher and Netscape 6. Netscape 4.*x* browsers display the regular bullet symbol.

Cascading Style Sheets are covered in depth in Chapter 27. Here is a brief version of the steps for using a style sheet to assign a new bullet symbol:

1. Select the CSS Styles panel button from the Launcher or choose Window ➪ CSS Styles.

2. In the CSS Styles panel, select the New Style button.

3. In the New Style dialog box, choose the li tag from the option list.

4. Choose the Redefine HTML Tag radio button from the Type section.

5. In the Define In section, choose the This Document Only radio button and click OK.

6. In the Style Definition dialog box that appears (see Figure 12-4), choose List in the Category list.

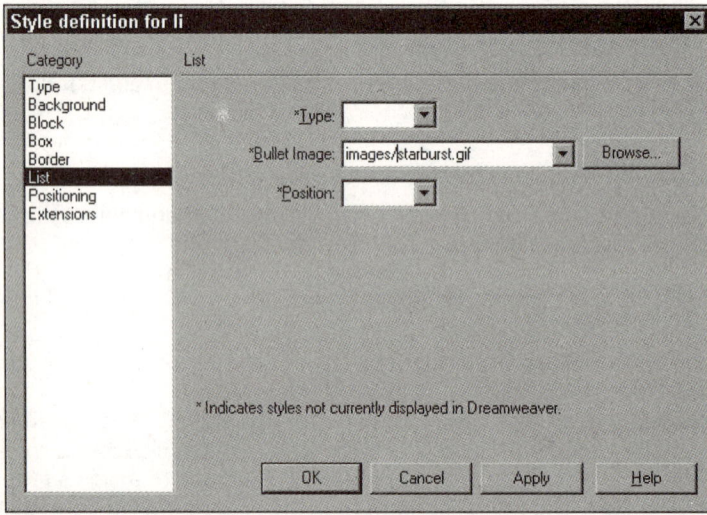

Figure 12-4: You can use Cascading Style Sheets to specify a bullet image for your Web page.

7. Find your graphics file by clicking the Browse (Choose) button next to the Button Image text box. Click OK when you're done.

Note   Your newly defined bullet image doesn't preview in Dreamweaver, but you can view it in Internet Explorer 4.0 or later.

Mastering Numbered (Ordered) Lists

Unlike a bulleted list, in which sequence is not vital, order is important in the numbered list. This relationship translates in HTML as: "The opposite of an unordered list is an ordered list." The major advantage of an ordered list is the automatic generation of list item numbers and automatic renumbering when you're editing. If you've ever had to renumber a legal document because paragraph 14.b became paragraph 2a, then you recognize the timesaving benefits of this feature.

Ordered lists offer a slightly wider variety of built-in styles than unordered lists, but you cannot customize the leading character further. For instance, you cannot surround a character with parentheses or offset it with a dash. Once again, the browser is the final arbiter of how your list is viewed.

Many of the same techniques used with unordered lists work with ordered lists. To start a new numbered list in Dreamweaver, place your cursor where you want the new list to begin. Then, in the Text Property Inspector, select the Ordered List button or choose Text ⇨ List ⇨ Ordered List.

As with unordered lists, you can also convert existing paragraphs into a numbered list. First select your text and then select either the Ordered List button or the Text ⇨ List ⇨ Ordered List command.

As shown in Figure 12-5, the default numbering system is Arabic numerals: 1, 2, 3, and so forth. In the following section, you learn how to alter this default.

Editing ordered lists

The HTML code for an ordered list is `<ol>`. Both `<ol>` and `<ul>` use the list item tag, `<li>`, to mark individual entries, and Dreamweaver handles the formatting identically:

```
<ol>
  <li>Stir in two sets of venetian blinds.</li>
  <li>Add one slowly rotating ceiling fan.</li>
  <li>Combine one flashing neon sign with one dangling light bulb.</li>
  <li>Toss in 150 cubic yards of fog.</li>
  <li></li>
</ol>
```

The empty list item pair, `<li>...</li>`, is displayed on the page as the next number in sequence.

Figure 12-5: Ordered lists are used on this page to create a numbered sequence.

Modifications to an ordered list are handled in the same manner as for an unordered list. The results are far more dramatic, however.

✦ To continue adding to the sequence of numbers, position your cursor at the end of the last item and press Enter (Return). The next number in sequence is generated, and any styles in use (such as font size or name) are carried over.

✦ To insert a new item in the list, put your cursor at the end of the item above where the new item will be positioned and press Enter (Return). Dreamweaver inserts a new number in sequence and automatically renumbers the following numbers.

✦ To rearrange a numbered list, highlight the entire list item you want to move. Using the drag-and-drop method, release the mouse when your cursor is at the front of the item below the new location for the moved item.

✦ To end an item in a numbered list, press Enter (Return) twice or press Enter (Return) and deselect the Ordered List button.

Using other numbering styles

In all, you can apply five different numbering styles to your numbered lists:

✦ **Arabic numerals:** 1, 2, 3, and so forth (this is the default style)

✦ **Roman Small:** i, ii, iii, and so forth

✦ **Roman Large:** I, II, III, and so forth

✦ **Alphabet Small:** a, b, c, and so forth

✦ **Alphabet Large:** A, B, C, and so forth

Changing single list items

You can restyle your entire list all at once, or you can just change a single list item. To change the style of the entire ordered list, follow these steps:

1. Position your cursor anywhere in an existing list.

2. If necessary, click the expander arrow on the Text Property Inspector to display the additional options. Select the List Item button.

   The List Properties dialog box opens, with Numbered List showing as the List Type.

3. Open the drop-down list of Style options and choose any of the five preceding numbering types.

4. Click OK.

Altering single and subsequent items

As with unordered lists, when you modify the style of one ordered list item, all the subsequent items adopt that style. To alter the style of a single and all subsequent items, follow these steps:

1. Select the item you wish to change.

2. In the expanded portion of the Text Property Inspector, select the List Item button.

3. In the List Properties dialog box from the List Item section, open the New Style list of options.

4. Select one of the five numbering options.

Although you can't automatically generate an outline with a different numbering system for each level, you can simulate this kind of outline with nested lists. See "Using Nested Lists" later in this chapter.

Making Definition Lists

A definition list is another list in HTML that doesn't use leading characters, such as bullets or numbers, in the list items. Definition lists are commonly used in glossaries or other types of documents in which you have a list of terms followed by their description or explanation.

Browsers generally render a definition list with the definition term flush left and the definition data indented, as shown in Figure 12-6. As you can see, no additional styling is added. You can, however, format either the item or the definition with the Text ⇨ Style options.

Definition term

Definition data

Figure 12-6: Definition lists are ideal for glossaries or other situations in which you have a list of terms followed by their definition.

To begin your definition list in Dreamweaver, follow these steps:

1. Choose Text ⇨ List ⇨ Definition List.

2. Type in the definition term and press Enter (Return) when you are finished. Dreamweaver indents the line.

3. Type in the definition data and press Enter (Return) when you are finished.

4. Repeat Steps 2 and 3 until you have finished your definition list.

5. Press Enter (Return) twice to stop entering definition list items.

Tip   If you have an extended definition, you may want to format it in more than one paragraph. Because definition lists are formatted with the terms and their definition data in alternating sequence, you have to use the line break tag, `<br>`, to create blank space under the definition if you want to separate it into paragraphs. Select the Insert Line Break button from the Objects palette to enter one or two `<br>` tags to separate paragraphs with one or two additional lines.

When you insert a definition list, Dreamweaver denotes it in code using the `<dl>`...`</dl>` tag pair. Definition terms are marked with a `<dt>` tag, and definition data uses the `<dd>` tag. A complete definition list looks like the following in HTML:

```
<dl>
  <dt>Capital</dt>
  <dd>Sum owed by a business to its owners. See Owner's Equity.</dd>
  <dt>Cash</dt>
  <dd>Total of currency, coins, money orders, checks, bank drafts, and letters
    of credit the firm has on hand or in bank accounts from which money can be
    drawn immediately.</dd>
  <dt>Cash Payments Journal</dt>
  <dd>Journal for recording payments made in cash.</dd>
</dl>
```

When originally proposed by the World Wide Web Consortium, the `<dt>` column was intended to take up only one-third of the browser window, but the latest, most common browsers don't follow this design specification.

Tip   You can vary the structure of a definition list from the standard definition term followed by the definition data format, but you have to code this variation by hand. For instance, if you want a series of consecutive terms with no definition in between, you need to insert the `<dt>`...`</dt>` pairs directly in the HTML Inspector.

Using Nested Lists

You can combine, or *nest,* lists in almost any fashion. For instance, you can mix an ordered and unordered list to create a numbered list with bulleted points. You can have one numbered list inside of another numbered list. You can also start with one numbering style such as Roman Large, switch to another style such as Alphabet Small, and then return to Roman Large to continue the sequence (as with an outline).

Dreamweaver offers an easy route for making nested lists. The Indent button in the Text Property Inspector — when used within a list — automatically creates a nested list. As an example, the ordered list in Figure 12-7 has a couple of bulleted points (or unordered list items) inserted within it. Notice how the new items are indented one level.

Figure 12-7: Dreamweaver automatically generates the code necessary to build nested lists when you use the Indent button on the Property Inspector.

Follow these steps to create a nested list in Dreamweaver:

1. Select the text in an existing list that you want to reformat with a different style.

2. In the Text Property Inspector, choose the Indent button. You can also select the Text ➪ Indent command. Dreamweaver indents the selected text and creates a separate list in the HTML code with the original list's properties.

3. Go to the List Properties dialog box and select another list type or style, as described in preceding sections.

Caution You can unnest your list and reverse the effects of the Indent button by selecting the Outdent button in the Text Property Inspector or choosing Text ⇨ Outdent. Be careful, however, when selecting your text for this operation. When you use the mouse to perform a click-and-drag selection, Dreamweaver tends to grab the closing list item tag above your intended selection. A better way to highlight the text in this case uses the Tag Selector on the status bar. Place the cursor in the indented list you want to outdent and choose the innermost ⟨ol⟩ or ⟨ul⟩ tag from the Tag Selector.

To examine the origins of the term *nested list*, take a look at the code created for this list type by Dreamweaver:

```
<ol>
   <li>Stir in two sets of venetian blinds.</li>
   <li>Add one slowly rotating ceiling fan.</li>
   <li>Combine one flashing neon sign with one dangling light bulb.</li>
     <ul>
       <li>Use a bare bulb, preferably swinging.</li>
       <li>The neon sign should throw contrasting shadows.</li>
     </ul>
   <li>Toss in 150 cubic yards of fog.</li>
</ol>
```

Notice how the unordered tag pair, ⟨ul⟩...⟨/ul⟩, is completely contained between the ordered list items.

Caution If you don't indent your list items before you change the list format, Dreamweaver breaks the current list into three separate lists: one for the original list above the selected text, another for the selected text itself, and a third list for the items following the selected text. If you don't want this arrangement, choose the Indent button in the Text Property Inspector, and Dreamweaver nests the list as described previously.

Accessing Special List Types

Dreamweaver gives you access to a couple of special-use list types: menu lists and directory lists. When the tags for these lists — ⟨menu⟩ and ⟨dir⟩, respectively — were included in the HTML 2.0 specification, they were intended to offer several ways to present lists of short items. Unfortunately, browsers tend to render both tags in the same manner: as an unordered list. You can use Cascading Style Sheets to restyle these built-in tags for use in 4.0 and later browsers.

Menu lists

A menu list generally comprises single items, with each item on its own individual line.

Tip   Because menu lists are rendered as unordered lists with leading bullets, you probably want to display the menu list in a more compact manner. Add the attribute compact as follows:

```
<menu compact>
```

To apply a menu list style, follow these steps:

1. In an existing list, select one item that you want to convert to a menu list.

2. In the expanded Text Property Inspector, select the List Item button.

3. In the List Properties dialog box, open the List Type drop-down list and choose Menu List, as shown in Figure 12-8.

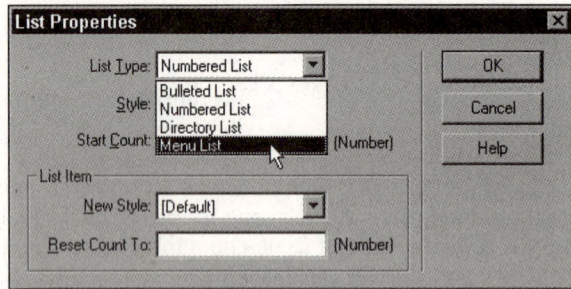

Figure 12-8: Making a menu list

4. Click OK.

Tip   To apply CSS techniques to either the `<menu>` or the `<dir>` tags in Dreamweaver, you must either hand-code all of the entry or use a little trick. Here's the trick: Because Dreamweaver doesn't list the menu or directory list tags in its list of HTML tags to redefine in the New Style dialog box, type **menu** or **dir** in the list box, instead of picking it from a list. But be certain you're entering the missing tag names in the text box when Redefine HTML Tag is selected; otherwise, Dreamweaver puts a period in front of your tag name, and it won't be recognized.

Directory lists

The directory list was originally intended to provide Web designers with an easy way to create multiple-column lists of short items. Unfortunately, the most current browsers present the directory list's items in one long list, rather than in columns.

The directory list format is applied in the same way as the menu list, and here as well, most browsers render the format as an unordered list with bullets.

To apply a directory list style, follow these steps:

1. In the current list, select one item you want to convert to a directory list.

2. In the expanded Text Property Inspector, select the List Item button.

3. In the List Properties dialog box, open the List Type list (previously shown in Figure 12-8) and choose Directory List.

4. Click OK.

Tip

Nested directory lists exhibit a cool feature in most browsers — they automatically change the list style for each level. In many browsers, the outermost level is displayed with a bullet, the second level with a circle, and the third level with a square. Automatic outlining from an unexpected source! One drawback to note: Dreamweaver doesn't preview the changing styles — it only shows the bullets.

Dreamweaver Technique: Building Graphical Bullets

HTML unordered lists are functional and often useful, but they're not particularly decorative. A Web designer might very well want to spice up a bulleted list of items with graphics. Although CSS offers the possibility of selecting an image to use as the bullet, this solution is not available to Netscape browsers or 3.0 versions of Internet Explorer. Moreover, you don't have much control over the vertical placement of the bullet, so the image often appears higher than desired.

On the
CD-ROM

The following technique is intended for designers working just with Dreamweaver and any graphics editor. However, if you have Fireworks 3 or later, you can automate the process of replacing an unordered list with graphical bullets. The Convert Bullets to Images command (originally developed by the author as BulletBuilder) converts list items to paragraph lines and places a custom bullet — available in ten different shapes and any Fireworks style — before the line. You'll find this extension on the CD-ROM that accompanies this book.

Substituting a graphical bullet for the HTML versions is practical and often desirable. Because a small, single image is used repeatedly, the impact on a Web page's size is negligible, and the image downloads quickly. You can include graphical bullets in two basic ways: inline and tables. Inline graphical bullets put the bullet image right next to the text, whereas the table technique keeps all the bullets in one column and the bullet items in another. Which technique you use depends on the length of the bulleted item. If your bulleted items are short enough so that they won't wrap, use the inline technique; on the other hand, if the text is likely or definitely wrapping from one line to the next, use the table technique.

To use graphic images as bullets in an inline technique, follow these steps:

1. Create your image in a graphics editor such as Fireworks and save the file so that it is accessible to your local site.

2. If necessary, convert your unordered list to standard paragraph format by selecting the entire list and deselecting the Bullet button on the Property Inspector.

3. Choose Insert Image from the Objects palette and place the graphic button before the first line item.

4. Select the correct vertical alignment for the image from the Align list on the image Property Inspector.

   Although your alignment choice may vary according to the height of your text and your image, Absolute Middle works in many situations.

5. If necessary, add a nonbreaking space or two between the image and the list item by pressing Ctrl+Shift+spacebar (Control+Shift+spacebar).

6. Select the image and any added nonbreaking spaces.

7. Ctrl+drag (Control+drag) the selection to copy it to the beginning of the next line item, as shown on Figure 12-9.

Figure 12-9: Copying your graphic bullets after you've set the alignment saves you many steps later.

8. Repeat Step 7 for each line item.

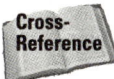

Cross-Reference

The following technique requires a basic understanding of tables in HTML in general and Dreamweaver in particular. If you're not familiar with inserting and formatting tables, you may want to look at Chapter 13 before proceeding.

If your text lines are too long, they wrap at the browser window and—here's the unsightly part—under the graphical bullet. To avoid this wrapping problem, use the table technique, detailed in the following steps:

1. Create your bullet in your favorite graphics program.

2. If necessary, convert your unordered list to standard paragraph format by selecting the entire list and deselecting the Bullet button on the Property Inspector.

3. Position your cursor above the first line item and choose the Insert Table object from the Objects palette.

4. In the Insert Table dialog box, set the Columns value to 2 and the Rows to the number of line items you have. If desired, turn off the borders by setting Border value to 0. Click OK when you're done.

The table is inserted in the Document window.

5. Select the first column of the table by dragging down its length.

6. In the Property Inspector, set the Horiz (horizontal alignment) value to Right and the Vert (vertical alignment) to Top.

7. Select the second column by dragging down its length.

8. In the Property Inspector, set the Horiz (horizontal alignment) value to Left and the Vert (vertical alignment) to Top.

9. Select the Insert Image object and place your bullet image in the first column, first row.

10. Select the first line item and drag it into the second column, first row.

11. Copy the bullet image from the first cell and paste it into the first column for every remaining row.

12. Repeat Step 10 for each of the remaining line items, putting each on its own row.

When you're done, the bullet images line up evenly as do the line items, as shown in Figure 12-10. You may find it necessary to adjust the vertical alignment on either the bullet or line item column to get the look you want.

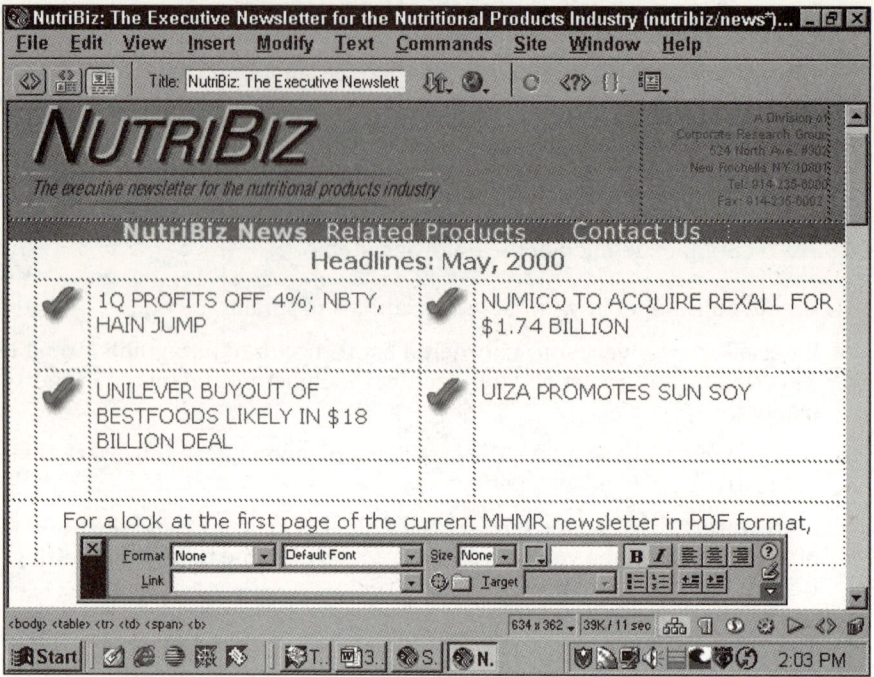

Figure 12-10: Placing bullet items in a table enables you to keep an equal spacing with longer, wrapping lines.

Summary

Lists are extremely useful to the Web site designer from the perspectives of both content and layout. Dreamweaver offers point-and-click control over the full range of list capabilities.

✦ The three primary list types in HTML are unordered, ordered, and definition lists.

✦ Use unordered lists when you want to itemize your text in no particular order. Dreamweaver can apply any of the three built-in styles to unordered lists, or you can customize your own list style through style sheets.

✦ An ordered list is a numbered list. Items are automatically numbered when added and the entire list is renumbered when items are rearranged or deleted. Dreamweaver gives you access to five different styles of numbering — everything from regular Arabic to Roman numerals.

✦ Definition lists are designed to display glossaries and other documents in which terms are followed by definitions. A definition list is generally rendered without leading characters such as bullets or numbers; instead, the list terms are displayed flush left, and the definitions are indented.

✦ Dreamweaver gives you the power to nest your lists at the touch of a button — the Indent button on the Text Property Inspector. Nested lists enable you to show different outline levels and to mix ordered and unordered lists.

✦ Menu and directory lists are also supported by Dreamweaver. Both of these special lists render in a similar fashion, but they can be adapted through style sheets for extensive use.

✦ It's easy to substitute graphic images for standard bullets in Dreamweaver. Two different techniques are used — inline and table — depending on the length of the line item.

In the next chapter, you learn how to create and use tables in Dreamweaver.

✦   ✦   ✦

Incorporating Advanced HTML

Setting Up Tables

Tables bring structure to a Web page. Whether used to align numbers in a spreadsheet or to arrange columns of text on a page, an HTML table brings a bit of order to otherwise free-flowing content. Initially, tables were implemented to present raw data in a more readable format. But it didn't take long for Web designers to take up tables as the most capable tool to control page layout.

Dreamweaver's implementation of tables reflects this current trend in Web page design. Drag-and-drop table sizing, easy organization of rows and columns, and instant table reformatting all help get the job done in the shortest time possible. Table editing features enable you to select and modify anything in a table from a single cell to multiple columns. Moreover, using Dreamweaver commands, you can sort your table in a variety of ways or completely reformat it.

Dreamweaver 4 introduces a new feature that takes table layout to the next level of ease-of-use and power. With the Layout view, designers are able to draw individual cells with a stroke of the mouse and Dreamweaver automatically creates a borderless, content-ready table. You can even add nested tables to maintain design integrity. While you still need to know the basics of table functionality to make the most out of this new tool, Layout view offers a fully backward-compatible technique for visually structuring your Web page.

Although the absolute positioning capabilities offered by Dynamic HTML give Web designers another route to precise layout control, many Web designers use a combination of tools to get desired effects and maintain wide browser compatibility. In other words, HTML tables are going to be around for a long time.

HTML Table Fundamentals

A table is basically a grid that expands as you add text or images. Tables consist of three main components: rows, columns, and cells. *Rows* go across a table from left to right, and *columns* go up and down. A *cell* is the intersection of a row and a column; it's where you enter your information. Cells expand to fit whatever they hold. If you have enabled the table border, your browser shows the outline of the table and all its cells.

In HTML, all the structure and all the data of a table are contained between the table tag pair, `<table>` and `</table>`. The `<table>` tag can take numerous attributes, determining a table's width and height (which can be given in absolute measurement or as a percentage of the screen) as well as the border, alignment on the page, and background color. You can also control the size of the spacing between cells and the amount of padding within cells.

HTML uses a strict hierarchy when describing a table. You can see this clearly in Listing 13-1, which shows the HTML generated from a default table in Dreamweaver.

Listing 13-1: Code for an HTML Table

```
<table border="1" width="75%">
  <tr>
    <td> </td>
    <td> </td>
    <td> </td>
  </tr>
  <tr>
    <td> </td>
    <td> </td>
    <td> </td>
  </tr>
  <tr>
    <td> </td>
    <td> </td>
    <td> </td>
  </tr>
</table>
```

Note   The ` ` seen in the table code is HTML for a nonbreaking space. Dreamweaver inserts the code in each empty table cell because some browsers collapse the cell without it. Enter any text or image in the cell, and Dreamweaver automatically removes the ` ` code.

Rows

After the opening `<table>` tag comes the first row tag `<tr>`. Within the current row, you can specify attributes for horizontal alignment or vertical alignment. In addition, browsers recognize row color as an added option.

Cells

Cells are marked in HTML with the `<td>...</td>` tag pair. No specific code exists for a column; rather, columns are seen as the number of cells within a row. For example, in Listing 1-1, notice the three sets of `<td>` tags between each `<tr>` pair. This means the table has three columns. A cell can span more than one row or column — in these cases, you see a `rowspan=value` or `colspan=value` attribute in the `<td>` tag.

Cells can also be given horizontal or vertical alignment attributes; these attributes override any similar attributes specified by the table row. When you give a cell a particular width, all the cells in that column are affected. Width can be specified in either an absolute pixel measurement or as a percentage of the overall table.

Tip   After the initial `<table>` tag, you can place an optional caption for the table. In Dreamweaver, you have to enter the `<caption>` tag by hand in the Code view or inspector. Here's an example to show how the tag works:

```
<caption align="center" valign="bottom">Table of
Periodic Elements</caption>
```

Column/row headings

A special type of cell called a *table header* is used for column and row headings. Information in these cells is marked with a `<th>` tag and is generally rendered in boldface, centered within the cell.

Inserting Tables in Dreamweaver

You can control almost all of a table's HTML features through Dreamweaver's point-and-click interface. To insert a Dreamweaver table in the current cursor position, use one of the following three methods:

✦ Select the Insert Table button on the Objects panel.

✦ Choose Insert ⇨ Table from the menus.

✦ Use the keyboard shortcut: Ctrl+Alt+T (Command+Option+T).

The Insert Table dialog box, shown in Figure 13-1, contains the following default values when it is first displayed:

Attribute	Default	Description
Rows	3	The number of horizontal rows.
Columns	3	The number of vertical columns.
Width	75%	Sets the preset width of the table. Available in a percentage of the containing element (screen, layer, or another table) or an absolute pixel size.
Border	1 pixel	The width of the border around each cell and the entire table.
Cell Padding	(Empty)	The space between a cell's border and its contents. Although not shown, Dreamweaver displays 1 pixel of cell padding unless a different value is entered.
Cell Spacing	(Empty)	The number of pixels between each cell. Although not shown, Dreamweaver displays 2 pixels of cell spacing unless a different value is entered.

Figure 13-1: The Insert Table dialog box starts out with a default of three columns and three rows; you can adjust as needed.

If you aren't sure of the number of rows and/or columns you need, put in your best guess — you can add or delete rows or columns as necessary.

The default table is sized to take up 75 percent of the browser window. You can alter this percentage by changing the value in the Width text box. The table maintains this proportion as you add text or images, except in two situations:

✦ When an image is larger than the specified percentage

✦ When the nowrap attribute is used for the cell or table row and there is too much text to fit

In either case, the percentage set for the table is ignored, and the cell and table expand to accommodate the text or image. (For further information on the nowrap attribute, see the section "Cell wrap," later in this chapter.)

Note The Insert Table dialog box uses what are called *sticky* settings and displays your previously used settings the next time you open the dialog box. This handy feature enables you to set the border width to zero and forget about resetting it each time.

If you prefer to enter the table width as an absolute pixel value, as opposed to the relative percentage, type the number of pixels in the Width text box and select pixels in the drop-down list of width options.

Figure 13-2 shows three tables: At the top is the default table with the width set to 75 percent. The middle table, set to 100 percent, will take up the full width of the browser window. The third table is fixed at 300 pixels — approximately half of a 640×480 window.

Tip You don't have to declare a width for your table at all. If you delete the value in the Width text box of the Insert Table dialog box, your table starts out as small as possible and only expands to accommodate inserted text or images. However, this can make it difficult to position your cursor inside a cell to enter content. You can always delete any set size — pixel or percentage — later.

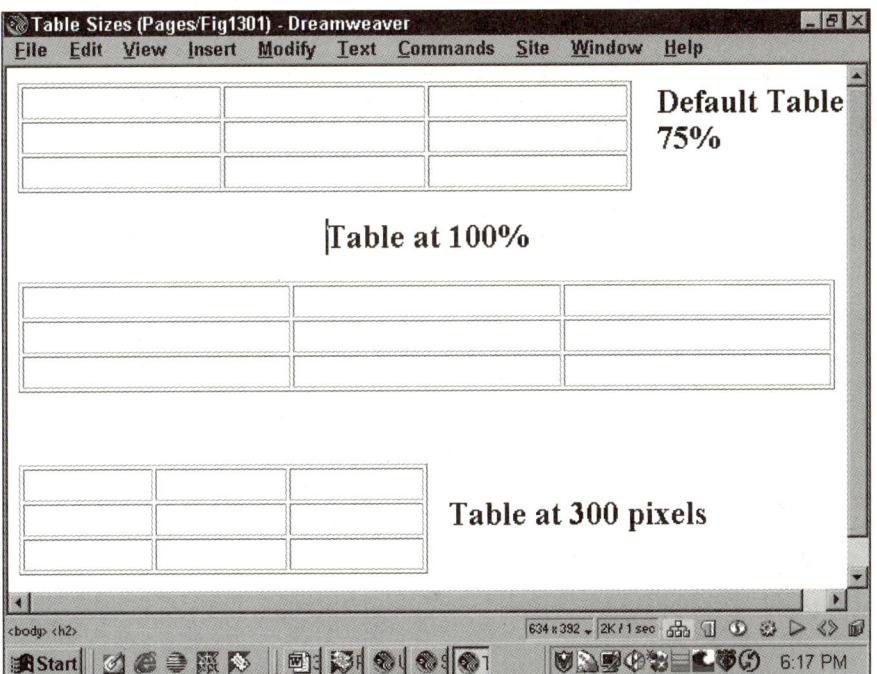

Figure 13-2: The width of a table can be relative to the browser window or set to an absolute width in pixels.

Setting Table Preferences

Two preferences directly affect tables. Both can be set by choosing Edit ⇨ Preferences and looking in the General category.

The first pertinent option is the Show Dialog when Inserting Objects checkbox. If this option is turned off, Dreamweaver always inserts a default table (3 rows by 3 columns at 75 percent width of the screen with a 1-pixel border), without displaying a dialog box and asking for your input. Should you wish to change these values, you can adjust them from the Table Property Inspector once the table has been inserted.

The second notable preference is labeled Faster Table Editing (Deferred Update). Because tables expand and contract dynamically depending on their contents, Dreamweaver gives you the option of turning off the continual updating. (Depending on the speed of your system, the updating can slow down your table input.) If the Faster Table Editing option is enabled, the table is updated whenever you click outside of it or when you press the keyboard shortcut, Ctrl+Space (Command+Spacebar).

 Note   If you have enabled Faster Table Editing and begin typing in one cell of your table, notice that the text wraps within the cell, and the table expands vertically. However, when you click outside of the table or press Ctrl+Space (Command+Spacebar), the table cells adjust horizontally as well, completing the redrawing of the table.

You should decide whether to leave the Faster Table Editing option on or turn it off, depending on your system and the complexity of your tables. Nested tables tend to update more slowly, and you may need to take advantage of the Faster Table Editing option if tables aren't getting redrawn quickly enough. I recommend turning off Faster Table Editing until it seems that you need it.

Modifying Tables

Most modifications to tables start in the Property Inspector. Dreamweaver helps you manage the basic table parameters — width, border, and alignment — and provides attributes for the other useful but more arcane features of a table, such as converting table width from pixels to percentage of the screen, and vice versa.

Selecting table elements

As with text or images, the first step in altering a table (or any of its elements) is selection. Dreamweaver simplifies the selection process, making it easy to change both the properties and the contents of entire tables, selected rows or columns, and even nonadjacent cells. You can change the font size and color of a row with a click or two of the mouse — instead of highlighting and modifying each individual cell.

Note   All of the following discussions about table selections pertain only to the Standard view and are not applicable in Layout view.

In Dreamweaver, you can select the following elements of a table:

✦ The entire table

✦ A single row

✦ Multiple rows, either adjacent or separate

✦ A single column

✦ Multiple columns, either adjacent or separate

✦ A single cell

✦ Multiple cells, either adjacent or separate

Once a table element is selected, you can modify its contents.

Selecting an entire table

Several methods are available for selecting the entire table, whether you're a menu- or mouse-oriented designer. To select the table via a menu, do one of the following:

✦ Choose Modify ➪ Table ➪ Select Table.

✦ With the cursor positioned in the table, choose Edit ➪ Select All or use the keyboard shortcut, Ctrl+A (Command+A).

✦ Right-click (Control+click) inside a table to display the shortcut menu and choose Table ➪ Select Table.

To select an entire table with the mouse, use one of these techniques:

✦ Click the bottom or right border of the table. You can also click anywhere along the table border when the pointer becomes a four-sided arrow.

✦ Select the <table> tag in the Tag Selector.

✦ Click immediately to one side of the table and drag the mouse over the table.

However you select the table, the selected table is surrounded by a black border with sizing handles on the right, bottom, and bottom-right corner (as shown in Figure 13-3), just as a selected graphic.

Selecting a row or column

Altering rows or columns of table text without Dreamweaver is a major time-consuming chore. Each cell has to be individually selected, and the changes applied. Dreamweaver has an intuitive method for selecting single or multiple columns and rows, comparable — and in some ways, superior — to major word processing programs.

Figure 13-3: A selected table can be identified by the black border outlining the table and the three sizing handles.

As with entire tables, you have several methods for selecting columns or rows. None of the techniques, however, use the menus; row and column selection is handled primarily with the mouse. In fact, you can select an entire row or column with one click.

The one-click method for selecting a single column or row requires that you position your pointer directly over the column or to the left of the row you want to choose. Move the pointer slowly toward the table — when the pointer becomes a single arrow, with the arrowhead pointing down for columns and to the right for rows, click the mouse. All the cells in the selected column or row are bounded with a black border. Any changes now made in the Property Inspector, such as a change in font size or color, affect the selected column or row.

You can select multiple, contiguous columns or rows by dragging the single arrow pointer across several columns or rows. To select a number of columns or rows that are not next to one another, use the Ctrl (Command) key. Press the Ctrl (Command) key while selecting each individual column, using the one-click method. (Not even Word 2000 can handle this degree of complex table selection.)

Tip If you have trouble positioning the mouse so that the single arrow pointer appears, you can use two other methods for selecting columns or rows. With the first method, you can click and drag across all the cells in a column or row. The second method uses another keyboard modifier, the Shift key. With this technique, click once in the first cell of the column or row. Then, hold down the Shift key while you click in the final cell of the column or row. You can also use this technique to select multiple adjacent columns or rows; just click in another column's or row's last cell.

Selecting cells

Sometimes you need to change the background color of just a few cells in a table, but not the entire row — or you might need to merge several cells to form one wide column span. In these situations, and many others, you can use Dreamweaver's cell selection capabilities. As with columns and rows, you can select multiple cells, whether they are adjacent to one another or separate.

Individual cells are generally selected by dragging the mouse across one or more cell boundaries. To select a single cell, click anywhere in the cell and drag the mouse into another cell. As you pass the border between the two cells, the initial cell is highlighted. If you continue dragging the mouse across another cell boundary, the second cell is selected, and so on. Note that you have to drag the mouse into another cell and not cross the table border onto the page; for example, to highlight the lower-right cell of a table, you need to drag the mouse up or to the left.

Tip You can also select a single cell by pressing the Ctrl (Command) key and clicking once in the cell, or you can select the rightmost <td> tag in the Tag Selector.

Extended cell selection in Dreamweaver is handled identically to extended text selection in most word processing programs. To select adjacent cells, click in the first desired cell, press and hold the Shift key, and click in the final desired cell. Dreamweaver selects all in a rectangular area, using the first cell as the upper-left corner of the rectangle and the last cell as the lower-right corner. You could, for instance, select an entire table by clicking in the upper-left cell and then Shift+clicking the lower-right cell.

Just as the Shift key is used to make adjacent cell selections, the Ctrl (Command) key is used for all nonadjacent cell selections. You can highlight any number of individual cells — whether or not they are next to one another — by pressing the Ctrl (Command) key while you click in the cell.

Tip If you Ctrl+click (Command+click) a cell that is already selected, that cell is deselected — regardless of the method you used to select the cell initially.

Editing a table's contents

Before you learn how to change a table's attributes, let's look at basic editing techniques. Editing text in Dreamweaver tables is slightly different from editing text outside of tables. When you begin to enter text into a table cell, the table borders expand to accommodate your new data, assuming no width has been set. The other cells appear to shrink, but they, too, expand once you start typing in text or inserting an image. Unless a cell's width is specified, the cell currently being edited expands or contracts, and the other cells are forced to adjust their width. Figure 13-4 shows the same table (with one row and three columns) in three different states. In the top table, only the first cell contains text; notice how the other cells have contracted. In the middle table, text has been entered into the second cell as well, and you can see how the first cell is now smaller. Finally, in the bottom table, all three cells contain text, and the other two cells have adjusted their width to compensate for the expanding third cell.

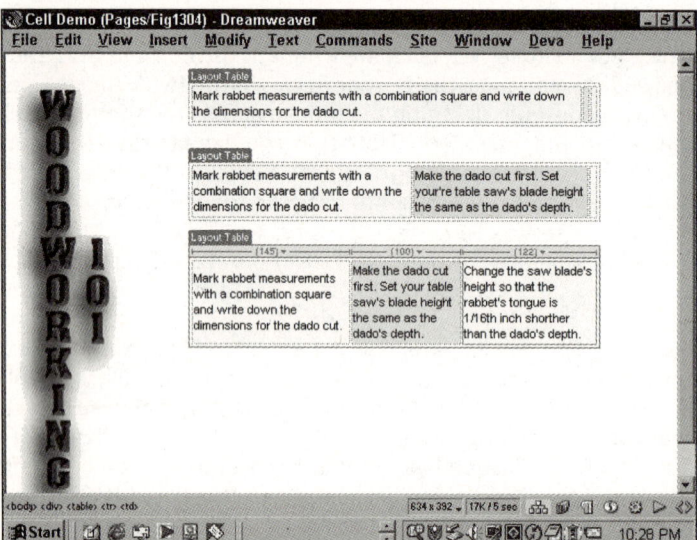

Figure 13-4: As text is entered into a cell, the cell expands; other cells contract, even if they already contain text.

If you look closely at the bottom table in Figure 13-4, you can also see that the text doesn't line up vertically. That's because the default vertical alignment in Dreamweaver, as in most browsers, provides for entries to be positioned in the middle of the cell. (Later in this section, you learn how to adjust the vertical alignment.)

Moving through a table

When you've finished entering your text in the first cell, you can move to the next cell in the row by pressing the Tab key. When you reach the end of a row, pressing Tab takes your cursor to the first cell of the next row. To go backward, cell to cell, press Shift+Tab.

Tip Pressing Tab has a special function when you're in the last cell of a row — it adds a new row, with the same column configuration as the current one.

The Home and End keys take you to the beginning and end, respectively, of the cursor's current line. If a cell's contents are large enough for the text to wrap in the cell, move to the top of the current cell by pressing Ctrl+Home (Command+up arrow or Command+Home). To get the bottom of the current cell in such a circumstance, press Ctrl+End (Command+down arrow).

When you're at the beginning or end of the contents in a cell, the arrow keys can also be used to navigate from cell to cell. Use the left and right arrows to move from cell to cell in a row, and the up and down arrows to move down a column. When you come to the end of a row or column, the arrow keys move to the first cell in the next row or column. If you're moving left to right horizontally, the cursor goes from the end of one row to the beginning of the next row — and vice-versa, if you move from right to left. When moving from top to bottom vertically, the cursor goes from the end of one column to the start of the next, and vice-versa when moving bottom to top.

Cutting, copying, and pasting in tables

In the early days of Web design (about four years ago), woe if you should accidentally leave out a cell of information. It was often almost faster to redo the entire table than to make room by meticulously cutting and pasting everything, one cell at a time. Dreamweaver ends that painstaking work forever with its advanced cutting and pasting features. You can copy a range of cells from one table to another and maintain all the attributes, such as color and alignment as well as the content — text or images — or you can copy just the contents and ignore the attributes.

Dreamweaver has one basic restriction to table cut-and-paste operations: Your selected cells must form a rectangle. In other words, although you can select non-adjacent cells, columns, or rows and modify their properties, you can't cut or copy them. Should you try, you get a message from Dreamweaver such as the one shown in Figure 13-5; the table above the notification in the figure illustrates an incorrect cell selection.

Copying attributes and contents

When you copy or cut a cell using the regular commands, Dreamweaver automatically copies everything — content, formatting, and cell format — in the selected cell. Then, pasting the cell reproduces it all — however, you can get different results depending on where the cell (or column or row) is pasted.

Figure 13-5: Dreamweaver enables you to cut or copy selected cells only when they form a rectangle, unlike the cells in the table depicted here.

To cut or copy both the contents and the attributes of any cell, row, or column, follow these steps:

1. Select the cells you wish to cut or copy.

   Remember that to cut or copy a range of cells in Dreamweaver, they must form a solid rectangular region.

2. To copy cells, choose Edit ➪ Copy or use the keyboard shortcut, Ctrl+C (Command+C).

3. To cut cells, choose Edit ➪ Cut or use the keyboard shortcut, Ctrl+X (Command+X).

   If you cut an individual cell, the contents are removed, but the cell remains. If, however, you cut an entire row or column, the cells are removed.

4. Position your cursor to paste the cells in the desired location:

   • To replace a cell with a cell on the clipboard, click anywhere in the cell to be replaced. If you cut or copied multiple cells that do not make up a full column or row, click in the upper-left corner of the cells you wish to replace. For example, a range of six cells in a 2×3 configuration replaces the same configuration when pasted.

Dreamweaver alerts you to the differences if you try to paste one configuration of cells into a different cell configuration.

- To insert a new row with the row on the clipboard, click anywhere in the row below where you'd like the new row to appear.

- To insert a new column with the column on the clipboard, click anywhere in the column to the right of where you'd like the new column to appear.

- To replace an existing row or column in a table, select the row or column. If you've cut or copied multiple rows or columns, you must select an equivalent size and shape of cells to replace.

- To insert a new table based on the copied or cut cells, click anywhere outside of the table.

5. Paste the copied or cut cells by choosing Edit ➪ Paste or pressing Ctrl+V (Command+V).

Tip

To move a row or column that you've cut from the interior of a table to the exterior (the right or bottom), you have to first expand the number of cells in the table. To do this, first select the table by choosing Modify ➪ Table ➪ Select Table or using one of the other techniques previously described. Next, in the Table Property Inspector, increase the number of rows or columns by altering the values in the Rows or Cols text boxes. Finally, select the newly added rows or columns and choose Edit ➪ Paste.

Copying contents only

It's not uncommon to need to move data from one cell to another, while keeping the destination cell's attributes, such as its background color or border, intact. For this, you need to use Dreamweaver's facility for copying just the contents of a cell.

To copy only the contents, select a cell as previously described and then choose Edit ➪ Copy or use the keyboard shortcut, Ctrl+C (Command+C). Then put your cursor in the destination cell and, instead of choosing Edit ➪ Paste, choose Edit ➪ Paste HTML, or use the keyboard shortcut, Ctrl+Shift+V (Command+Shift+V). Instead of selecting the entire cell to copy, you can also just select the text, or a portion of the text, and use the standard Edit ➪ Copy and Edit ➪ Paste commands to avoid pasting in the format of the copied text.

Unlike the copying of both contents and attributes described in the previous section, content-only copying has a couple of limitations:

- ✦ First, you can copy only the contents of one cell at a time. You can't copy contents only across multiple cells.

- ✦ Second, you can't replace the entire contents of one cell with another and maintain all the text attributes (font, color, and size) of the destination cell. If you select all the text to be replaced, Dreamweaver also selects the `<font>` tag that holds the attributes and replaces those as well. The workaround is to select all but one letter or word, paste the contents, and then delete the unwanted text.

Working with table properties

The <table> tag has a large number of attributes, and most of them can be modified through Dreamweaver's Property Inspector. As with all objects, the table must be selected before it can be altered. Choose Modify ⇨ Table ⇨ Select Table or use one of the other selection techniques previously described.

Once you've selected the table, if the Property Inspector is open, it presents the table properties as shown in Figure 13-6. Otherwise, you can open the Table Property Inspector by choosing Window ⇨ Properties Inspector.

Figure 13-6: The expanded Table Property Inspector gives you control over all the tablewide attributes.

Setting alignment

Aligning a table in Dreamweaver goes beyond the expected left, right, and center options — you can also make a table into a free-floating object around which text can wrap to the left or right.

With HTML, you can align a table using two different methods, and each gives you a different effect. Using the text alignment method (Text ⇨ Align) results in the conventional positioning (left, right, and center), and using the Table Property Inspector method enables you to wrap text around your realigned table. Figure 13-7 compares some of the different results you get from aligning your table with the two methods.

To align your table without text wrapping, follow these steps:

1. Select your table using one of the methods described earlier.

2. In the Property Inspector, make sure the Align option is set to Default.

3. Select the Text ⇨ Align command and then choose one of the three options: Left, Center, or Right.

   Dreamweaver surrounds your table code with a division tag pair, <div>...</div>, with an align attribute set to your chosen value.

To align your table with text wrapping, making your table into a floating object, follow these steps:

1. Select the table.

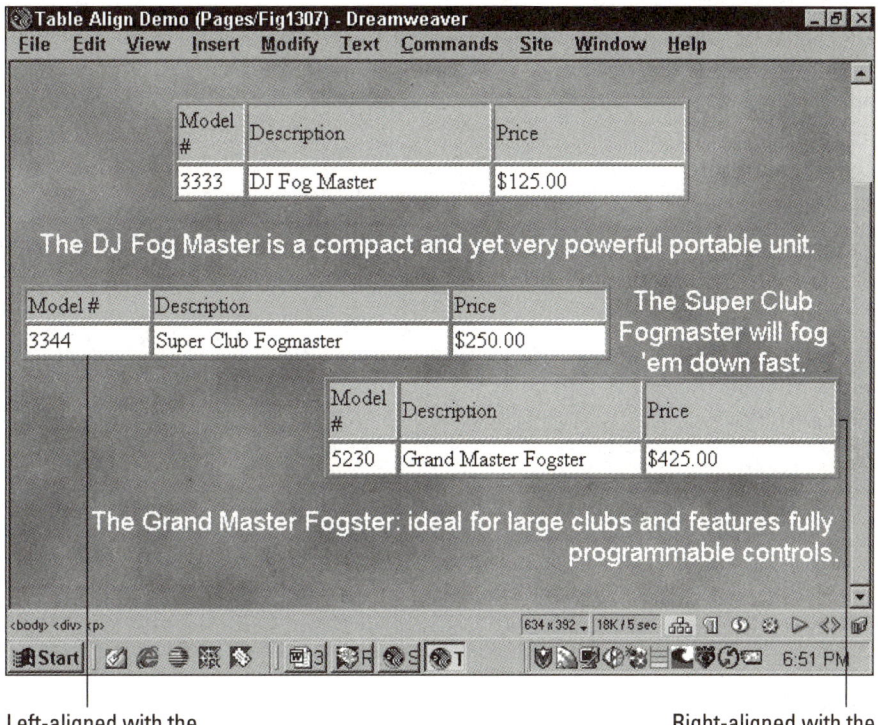

Left-aligned with the
Table Property Inspector

Right-aligned with the
Text Alignment command

Figure 13-7: Tables can be centered, as well as aligned left or right — with or without text wrapping.

2. In the Table Property Inspector, open the Align drop-down list and choose one of the four options:

Alignment Option	Result
Default	No alignment is written. Table aligns to the browser's default, usually left, with no text wrapping.
Left	Aligns the table to the left side of the browser window and wraps text around the right side.
Right	Aligns the table to the right side of the browser window and wraps text around the left side.
Center	The table aligns to the center of the browser window. Text does not wrap around either side. Note: This alignment option works only with 4.0 and above browsers.

Dreamweaver codes these alignment attributes in the `<table>` tag. As with floating images, Dreamweaver places an anchor point for floating elements on the Web page. However, you cannot drag-and-drop or cut-and-paste the anchor point, unlike most other Invisible symbols, for a floating table.

Resizing a table

The primary sizing control on the Table Property Inspector is the Width text box. You can enter a new width value for the entire table in either a screen percentage or pixels. Just enter your value in the Width text box and then select % or pixels in the drop-down list of options.

Dreamweaver also provides a quick and intuitive way to resize the overall table width, column widths, or row height. Pass your pointer over any of the table's borders, and the pointer becomes a two-headed arrow; this is the resizing pointer. When you see the resizing pointer, you can click and drag any border to new dimensions.

As noted earlier, tables are initially sized according to their contents. Once you move a table border in Dreamweaver, however, the new sizes are written directly into the HTML code, and the column width or row height is fixed — unless the contents cannot fit. If, for example, an inserted image is 115 pixels wide and the cell has a width of only 90 pixels, the cell expands to fit the image. The same is true if you try to fit an extremely long, unbroken text string, such as a complex URL, in a cell that's too narrow to hold it.

Dreamweaver enables you to set the height of a table using the Height text box in much the same way as the Width box. However, the height of a table — whether in pixels or a percentage — is maintained only as long as the contents do not require a larger size. A table's width, though, takes precedence over its height, and a table expands vertically before it expands horizontally.

Changes to a cell or column's width are shown in the `<td>` tags, as are changes to a row's height and width, using the `width` and `height` attribute, respectively. You can see these changes by selecting the table, cell, column, or row affected and looking at the W (Width) and H (Height) text box values.

For an overall view of what happens when you resize a cell, row, or column, it's best to look at the HTML. Here's the HTML for an empty table, resized:

```
<table border="1" width="70%">
  <tr>
    <td width="21%"> </td>
    <td width="34%"> </td>
    <td width="45%"> </td>
  </tr>
  <tr>
    <td width="21%" height="42"> </td>
```

```
      <td width="34%" height="42"> </td>
      <td width="45%" height="42"> </td>
   </tr>
   <tr>
      <td width="21%" height="42"> </td>
      <td width="34%" height="42"> </td>
      <td width="45%" height="42"> </td>
   </tr>
</table>
```

Notice how the width for each cell and the entire table is expressed as percentages. If the table width were initially set at a pixel value, the cell widths would have been, too. The row height values, on the other hand, are shown as an absolute measurement in pixels.

You can switch from percentages to pixels in all the table measurements, and even clear all the values at once — with the click of the right button. Four measurement controls appear in the lower-left portion of the expanded Table Property Inspector, as shown in Figure 13-8.

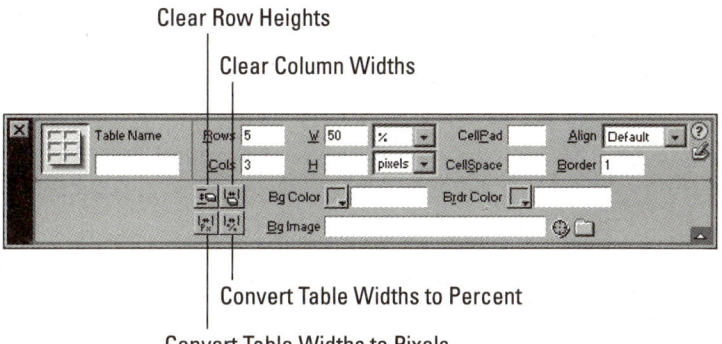

Figure 13-8: You can make tablewide changes with the four control buttons in the Table Property Inspector.

From left to right, the measurement controls are as follows:

Measurement Control Button	Description
Clear Row Heights	Erases all the `height` attributes in the current table
Clear Column Widths	Deletes all the `width` attributes found in the `<td>` tags
Convert Table Widths to Pixels	Translates the current widths of all cells and for the entire table from percentages to pixels
Convert Table Widths to Percent	Translates the current widths of all cells and for the entire table from pixels to percentages

Note Selecting Clear Row Heights doesn't affect the table height value.

If you clear both row heights and column widths, the table goes back to its "grow as needed" format and, if empty, shrinks to its smallest possible size.

Caution When converting width percentages to pixels, and vice versa, keep in mind that the percentages are relative to the size of the browser window — and in the development phase that browser window is Dreamweaver. Use the Window Size option on the status bar to expand Dreamweaver's Document window to the same sizes as what you expect to be seen in various browser settings.

Inserting rows and columns

The default Dreamweaver table configuration of three columns and three rows can be changed at any time. You can add rows or columns almost anywhere in a table, using various methods.

You have three methods for adding a single row:

✦ Position the cursor in the last cell of the last row and press Tab to add a new row below the present one.

✦ Choose Modify ➪ Table ➪ Insert Row to insert a new row above the current row.

✦ Right-click (Control+click) to open the shortcut menu and select Table ➪ Insert Row. Rows added in this way are inserted above the current row.

You have two ways to add a new column to your table:

✦ Choose Modify ➪ Table ➪ Insert Column to insert a new column to the left of the current column.

✦ Right-click (Control+click) to open the shortcut menu and select Table ➪ Insert Column from the shortcut menu. The column is inserted to the left of the current column.

You can add multiple rows and columns in one of two different ways:

✦ Increase the number of rows indicated in the Rows text box of the Table Property Inspector. All new rows added in this manner appear below the last table row. Similarly, you can increase the number of columns indicated in the Cols text box of the Table Property Inspector. Columns added in this way appear to the right of the last column.

✦ Use the Insert Rows or Columns dialog box.

The Insert Rows or Columns feature enables you to include any number of rows or columns anywhere relative to your current cursor position.

To add multiple columns using the Insert Rows or Columns dialog box, follow these steps:

1. Open the Insert Rows or Columns dialog box (shown in Figure 13-9) by selecting Modify ➪ Table ➪ Insert Rows or Columns or by choosing Table ➪ Insert Rows or Columns from the shortcut menu.

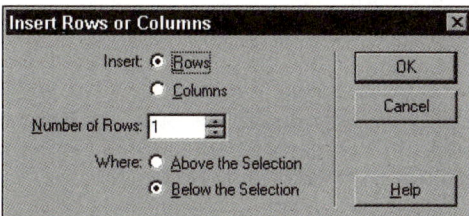

Figure 13-9: Use the Insert Rows or Columns feature to add several columns or rows simultaneously.

2. Select either Rows or Columns.

3. Enter the number of rows or columns you wish to insert — you can either type in a value or use the arrows to increase or decrease the number.

4. Select where you want the rows or columns to be inserted.

   • If you have selected the Rows option, you can insert the rows either Above or Below the Selection (the current row).

   • If you have selected the Columns options, you can insert the columns either Before or After the Current Column.

5. Click OK when you're finished.

Deleting rows and columns

When you want to delete a column or row, you can use either the shortcut menu or the Table Property Inspector. On the shortcut menu, you can remove the current column or row by choosing Delete Column or Delete Row, respectively. Using the Table Property Inspector, you can delete multiple columns and rows by reducing the numbers in the Cols or Rows text boxes. Columns are deleted from the right side of the table, and rows are removed from the bottom.

Caution Watch out — exercise extreme caution when deleting columns or rows. Dreamweaver does not ask for confirmation and removes these columns and/or rows whether or not data exists in them. You can, of course, undo the operation, if necessary.

Setting table borders and backgrounds

Borders are the solid outlines of the table itself. A border's width is measured in pixels; the default width is one pixel. This width can be altered in the Border field of the Table Property Inspector.

You can make the border invisible by specifying a border of 0 width. You can still resize your table by clicking and dragging the borders, even when the border is set to 0. When the View ⇨ Table Borders option is selected, Dreamweaver displays a thin dashed line to represent the border.

When the border is visible, you can also see each cell outlined. The width of the outline around the cells stays constant, regardless of the width of the border. However, you can control the amount of space between each cell with the CellSpace value in the Table Property Inspector, covered later in this chapter.

To change the width of a border in Dreamweaver, select your table and enter a new value in the Border text box. With a wider border, you can see the default shading: The top and left side are a lighter shade, and the bottom and right sides are darker. This gives the table border a pseudo-3D appearance. Figure 13-10 shows single-cell tables with borders of various widths.

Figure 13-10: Changing the width of the border can give your table a 3D look.

In Dreamweaver, you can directly assign colors to the border. To choose a color for the border, select the Border color swatch or enter a color name in the adjacent text box.

In addition to colored borders, a table can also have a colored background. (By default, the table is initially transparent.) Choose the background color in the Table Property Inspector by selecting a color in the Bg Color swatch or entering a color name in the adjacent text box. As you see later in the chapter, you can also assign background colors to rows, columns, and individual cells — if used, these specific colors all override the background color of the overall entire table.

Working with cell spacing and cell padding

HTML gives you two methods to add white space in tables. *Cell spacing* controls the width between each cell, and *cell padding* controls the margins within each cell. These values can be set independently through the Table Property Inspector.

Tip　　Although not indicated in the Table Property Inspector, the default value is 2 pixels for cell spacing and 1 pixel for cell padding. Some Web page designs call for a close arrangement of cells and are better served by changing either (or both) the CellSpace or CellPad values to 1 or 0.

To change the amount of white space between each cell in a table, enter a new value in the CellSpace text box of the Table Property Inspector. If you want to adjust the amount of white space between the borders of the cell and the actual cell data, alter the value in the CellPad text box of the Table Property Inspector. Figure 13-11 shows an example of a table with wide (10 pixels) cell spacing and cell padding values.

Merging and splitting cells

You have seen how cells in HTML tables can extend across (span) multiple columns or rows. By default, a cell spans one column or one row. Increasing a cell's span enables you to group any number of topics under one heading. You are effectively merging one cell with another to create a larger cell. Likewise, a cell can be split into multiple rows or columns.

Dreamweaver enables you to combine and divide cells in two different ways. If you're more comfortable with the concept of merging and splitting cells, you can use two handy buttons on the Property Inspector. If, on the other hand, you prefer the older method of increasing and decreasing row or column span, you can still access these commands through the main and shortcut menus.

To combine two or more cells, first select the cells you want to merge. Then, from the Property Inspector, select the Merge Cells button or press the keyboard shortcut Ctrl+Alt+M (Command+Option+M); Windows users also have the option of just pressing M. If the Merge button is not available, multiple cells have not been selected.

Cell padding   Cell spacing

Figure 13-11: You can add additional white space between each cell (cell spacing) or within each cell (cell padding).

To divide a cell, follow these steps:

1. Position your cursor in the cell to split.

2. From the Property Inspector, select the Split Cell button or press the keyboard shortcut, Ctrl+Alt+S (Command+Option+S).

   The Split Cell dialog box (shown in Figure 13-12) appears.

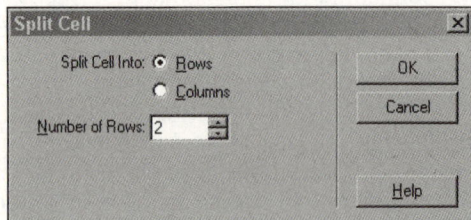

Figure 13-12: Use the Split Cell dialog box to divide cells horizontally or vertically.

3. Select either the Rows or Columns option to decide whether the cell will be split horizontally or vertically.

4. Enter the Number of Rows or Columns in the text box or use the arrows to change the value.

5. Select OK when you're done.

The same effect can be achieved by using the menus. To do so, first position the cursor in the cell to be affected and then choose one of the following commands from the Modify ⇨ Table menu:

Command	Description
Increase Row Span	Joins the current cell with the cell below it
Decrease Row Span	Separates two or more previously spanned cells from the bottom cell
Increase Column Span	Joins the current cell with the cell immediately to its right
Decrease Column Span	Separates two or more previously spanned cells from the right edge

Existing text or images are put in the same cell if the cells containing them are joined to span rows or columns. Figure 13-13 shows a table containing both row and column spanning.

Tip   When you need to build a complex table such as this one, it's best to map out your table before you begin constructing it, and complete it prior to entering your data.

Setting cell, column, and row properties

In addition to the overall table controls, Dreamweaver helps you set numerous properties for individual cells one at a time, by the column or by the row. When attributes overlap or conflict, such as different background colors for a cell in the same row and column, the more specific target wins out. The hierarchy, from most general to most specific, is as follows: tables, rows, columns, and cells.

You can call up the specific Property Inspector by selecting the cell, row, or column you want to modify. The Cell, Row, and Column Property Inspectors each affect similar attributes. The following sections explain how the attributes work in general and — if any differences exist — specifically in regard to the cell, column, or row.

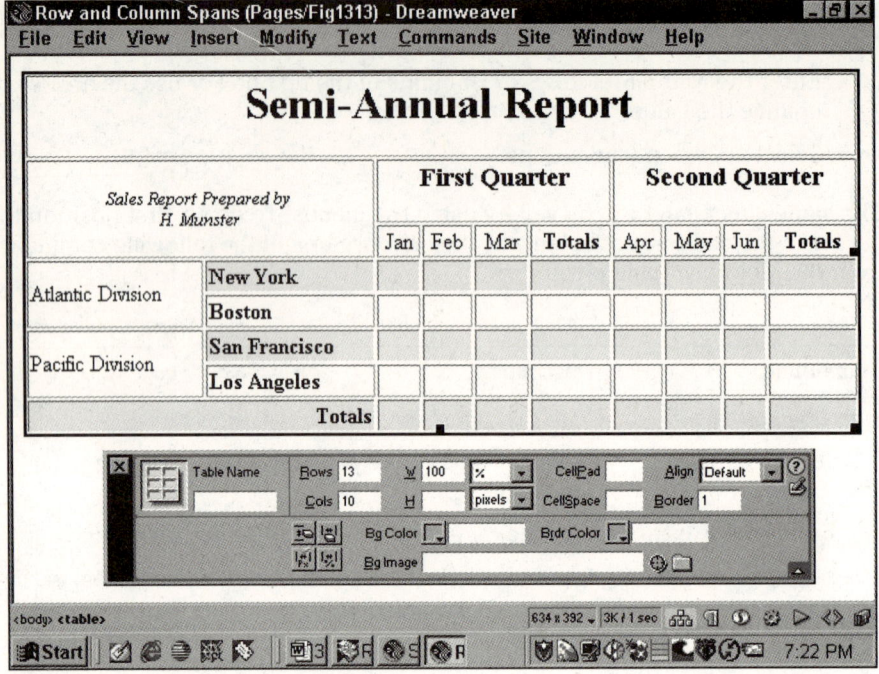

Figure 13-13: This spreadsheet-like report was built using Dreamweaver's row- and column-spanning features.

Horizontal alignment

You can set the Horizontal Alignment attribute, `align`, to specify the default alignment, or Left, Right, or Center alignment, for the element in the cell, column, or row. This attribute can be overridden by setting the alignment for the individual line or image. Generally, Left is the default horizontal alignment for cells.

Vertical alignment

The HTML `valign` attribute determines whether the cell's contents are vertically aligned to the cell's top, middle, bottom, or along the baseline. Typically, browsers align cells vertically in the middle by default. Select the Vertical Alignment option arrow in the Cell, Column, or Row Properties dialog box to specify a different alignment.

Top, Middle, and Bottom vertical alignments work pretty much as you would expect. A Baseline vertical alignment displays text near the top of the cell and positions the text—regardless of font size—so that the baselines of all the text in the affected row, column, or cell are the same. You can see how images and text of various sizes are displayed under the various vertical alignment options in Figure 13-14.

Figure 13-14: You can vertically align text and images in several arrangements in a table cell, row, or column.

Cell wrap

Normal behavior for any cell is to automatically wrap text or a series of images within the cell's borders. You can turn off this automatic feature by selecting the No Wrap option in the Property Inspector for cell, column, or row.

Note   I've had occasion to use this option when I absolutely needed three images to appear side by side in one cell. In analyzing the results, I found that on some lower-resolution browsers, the last image wrapped to the next line.

Table header cells

Quite often in tables, a column or a row functions as the heading for that section of the table, labeling all the information in that particular section. Dreamweaver has an option for designating these cells: the Header option. Table header cells are usually rendered in boldface and centered in each cell. Figure 13-15 shows an example of a table in which both the first row and first column are marked as table header cells.

Figure 13-15: Table header cells are a good way to note a category's label — either for a row or a column, or both.

Width and height

The gridlike structure of a table makes it impossible to resize only one cell in a multicolumn table. Therefore, the only way you can enter exact values for a cell's width is through the Width section available only in the Column Properties dialog box. In this section of the dialog box, you can enter values in pixels or as a percentage of the table. The default enables cells to automatically resize with no restrictions outside of the overall dimensions of the table.

Similarly, whenever you change a cell's height, the entire row is altered. If you drag the row to a new height, the value is written into the H (Height) text box for all cells in the row. On the other hand, if you specify a single cell's height, the row resizes, but you can see the value only in the cell you've changed.

Color elements

Just as you can specify color backgrounds and borders for the overall table, you can do the same for columns, rows, or individual cells. Corresponding color swatches and text boxes are available in all dialog boxes for the following categories:

✦ **Background Color:** Specifies the color for the selected cell, row, or column. Selecting the color swatch opens the standard color picker.

✦ **Border Color:** Controls the color of the single-pixel border surrounding each cell.

As with all Dreamweaver color pickers, you can use the Eyedropper tool to select a color from the Web-safe palette or from any item on a page. You can also select the Eraser tool to delete any previously selected color. Finally, choose the Palette tool to open the Color dialog box and select any available color.

Working with Table Formats

Tables keep data organized and generally make it easier to find information quickly. Large tables with many rows, however, tend to become difficult to read unless they are formatted with alternating rows of color or some other device. Formatting a large table is often an afterthought as well as a time-consuming affair. Unless, of course, you're using Dreamweaver's Format Table command.

The Format Table command enables you to choose from 17 preset formats or customize your own. This versatile command can style the top row, alternating rows in the body of the table, the left column, and the border. It's best to completely build the structure of your table—although you don't have to fill it with data—before formatting it; otherwise, you might have to reformat it when new rows or columns are added.

To apply one of the preset table formats, follow these steps:

1. Select your table by choosing Modify ⇨ Table ⇨ Select Table or by using one of the other techniques.

2. Choose Commands ⇨ Format Table.

   The Format Table dialog box (shown in Figure 13-16) opens.

3. Select any of the options from the scrolling list box on the left side of the Format Table dialog box.

   As you select an option, a representation of the table appears to the right, and the attribute values used are displayed below.

4. When you've found a table format that's appropriate, select OK to close the dialog box, and the format is applied.

The preset formats are divided into three groups: Simple, AltRows, and DblRows. The Simple formats maintain the same background color for all rows in the body of the table but change the top row and the left column. The AltRows formats alternate the background color of each row in the body of the table; you have eight different color combinations from which to choose. The final category, DblRows, alternates the background color of every two rows in the body of the table.

Figure 13-16: Select any one of 17 different preset formats from the Format Table dialog box or customize your own.

Although 17 different formats may seem as if there are plenty of choices, it's really just the jumping-off place for what's possible with the Format Table command. Each variable applied to create the preset formats can be customized. Moreover, you don't have to apply the changes to your selected table to see the effect — you can preview the results directly in the Table Format dialog box. Following are the variable attributes in the Table Format dialog box:

Attribute	Description
Row Colors: First	Enter a color (in color name or hexadecimal format) for the background colors of the first row in the body of a table. The Row Colors do not affect the top row of a table.
Row Colors: Second	Enter a color (in color name or hexadecimal format) for the background colors of the second row in the body of a table. The Row Colors do not affect the top row of a table.
Row Colors: Alternate	Establishes the pattern for using the specified Row Colors. Options are <do not alternate>, Every Other Row, Every Two Rows, Every Three Rows, and Every Four Rows.
Top Row: Align	Sets the alignment of the text in the top row of the table to left, right, or center.

Attribute	Description
Top Row: Text Style	Sets the style of the text in the top row of the table to Regular, Bold, Italic, or Bold Italic.
Top Row: Bg Color	Sets the background color of the top row of the selected table. Use either color names or hexadecimal values.
Top Row: Text Color	Sets the color of the text in the top row of the selected table. Use either color names or hexadecimal values.
Left Col: Align	Sets the alignment of the text in the left column of the table to Left, Right, or Center.
Left Col: Text Style	Sets the style of the text in the left column of the table to Regular, Bold, Italic, or Bold Italic.
Border	Determines the width of the table's border in pixels.
Options: Apply All Attributes to TD Tags Instead of TR Tags	Writes attribute changes at the cell level, `<td>`, rather than the default, the row level, `<tr>`.

The final option in the Format Table dialog box, Apply All Attributes to TD Tags Instead of TR Tags, should be used in only one of two situations: One, the selected table is nested inside another table and you want to override the outer table's `<tr>` format; or two, you anticipate moving cells from one table to another and want to maintain the formatting. Generally, the code produced by selecting this option is bulkier and could impact a page's overall download size, if the table is sufficiently large.

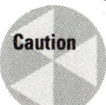

Caution Currently, there's no way to save your custom format without editing the tableFormats.js JavaScript file in the Commands folder. Otherwise, you need to reenter the selections each time you apply them.

Sorting Tables

Have you ever painstakingly built a table, alphabetizing every last entry by last name and first name, only to have the client call up with a list of 13 additional names that just have to go in? "Oh, and could you sort them by zip code instead of last name?" Dreamweaver contains a Table Sort command designed to make short work of such requests. All you need to do is select your table, and you're ready to do a two-level-deep sort, either alphabetically or numerically.

The Table Sort command can rearrange any size table; more important, it's HTML savvy and gives you the option of keeping the formatting of your table rows. This capability enables you to maintain a table with alternating row colors and still sort the data—something not even the most powerful word processors can handle. The Table Sort command is useful for generating different views of the same data, without having to use a database.

The Table Sort command is straightforward to use; just follow these steps:

1. Select your table by choosing Modify ⇨ Table ⇨ Select Table or by using one of the other techniques.

2. Choose Commands ⇨ Sort Table.

   The Sort Table dialog box (shown in Figure 13-17) opens.

Figure 13-17: Sort your tables numerically or alphabetically with the Sort Table command.

3. Choose the primary sort column from the Sort By option list.

   Dreamweaver automatically lists the number of columns in the selected table in the option list.

4. Set the type of the primary sort by choosing either Alphabetically or Numerically from the first Order option list.

5. Choose the direction of the sort by selecting either Ascending or Descending from the second Order option list.

6. If you wish to add a second level of sorting, repeat Steps 3 through 5 in the Then By section.

7. If your selected table does not include a header row, select the Sort Includes First Row option.

8. If you have formatted your table with alternating row colors, choose the Keep TR Attributes with Sorted Row option.

9. Click OK when you're finished.

Tip As with any sorting program, if you leave blank cells in the column you're basing the sort on, those rows appear as a group on top of the table for an ascending sort and at the end for a descending sort. Be sure that all the cells in your sort criteria column are filled correctly.

Importing Tabular Data

In the computer age, there's nothing much more frustrating than having information in a digital format and still having to enter it manually — either typing it in or cutting and pasting — to get on the Web. This frustration is multiplied when it comes to table data, whether created in a spreadsheet or database program. You have to transfer lots of small pieces of data, and it all has to be properly related and positioned.

Dreamweaver's Import Tabular Data goes a long way toward alleviating the tedium — not to mention the frustration — of dealing with tabular information. The Import Tabular Data command reads any delimited text file and inserts the information in a series of rows and columns. You can even set most characteristics for the table to be created, including the width, cell padding, cell spacing, and border.

Quite often, the first step in the process of importing table data into Dreamweaver is to export it from your other program. Most spreadsheet and database programs have some capability of outputting information in a text file; each bit of data (whether it's from a cell of a spreadsheet or field of a database) is separated — or *delimited* — from every other data by a special character, typically a tab or comma. In Dreamweaver, you can choose which delimiter is used in the Import Tabular Data dialog box to ensure a clean transfer with no loss of data.

Tip Although you have many types of delimiters to choose from, I generally default to exporting tab-delimited files. With a tab-delimited file, you usually don't have to worry if any of your data contains the delimiter — which would throw off the import. However, testing shows that Dreamweaver correctly handles comma-delimited files with and without quotes, so you could also use that format safely.

To import a tabular data file, follow these steps:

1. Be sure the data you wish to import has been saved or exported in the proper format: a delimited text file.

2. Choose File ➪ Import ➪ Import Tabular Data.

   The Import Table Data dialog box, shown in Figure 13-18, is displayed.

Figure 13-18: Any external data, saved in a delimited text file, can be brought into Dreamweaver through the Import Tabular Data command.

3. Select the Data File Browse button to find the desired file.

4. Choose the delimiter used to separate the fields or cells of data from the Delimiter option list. The choices are Tab, Comma, Semicolon, Colon, and Other.

Tip   If you select a file with a .csv extension, the Comma delimiter is automatically chosen. CSV is short for Comma Separated Values.

5. If you choose Other from the Delimiter list, a blank field appears to the right of the list. Enter the special character, such as a pipe (|), used as the delimiter in the exported file.

   Now that the imported file characteristics are set, you can predefine the table the information will be imported into, if desired.

6. If you want to set a particular table width, enter a value in the Set field and choose either Pixels or % from the option list. If you want the imported file to determine the size of the table, keep the Fit to Data option selected.

7. Enter any Cell Padding or Cell Spacing values desired, in their respective fields.

   As with standard tables, by default Cell Padding is set to 2 pixels and Cell Spacing to 1 if no specific values are entered.

8. If you'd like to style the first row, choose Bold, Italic, or Bold Italic from the Format Top Row option list.

   This option is typically used when the imported file contains a header row.

9. Set the Border field to the desired width, if any. If you don't want a border displayed at all, set the Border field to 0.

10. Click OK when you're done.

Even though the Import Tabular Data option is under the File menu, it doesn't open a new file — the new table is created at the current cursor position.

Caution If your data comes in wrong, double-check the delimiter used by opening the file in a text editor. If Dreamweaver is expecting a comma delimiter and your file uses tabs, data is not separated properly.

Designing with Layout Mode

As discussed earlier in this chapter, experienced Web designers regard tables as one of their primary layout tools because, outside of Dynamic HTML's layers, tables are the only way for you to get close to positioning your page elements the way you want them to appear. It's a lot of work to do this with raw tables, but designers are a persistent group — and for good reason: Persistence has a big payoff.

New Feature Thanks to the introduction of the Layout view in Dreamweaver 4, structuring your page with tables just got a whole lot easier. When you're in Layout view, you simply draw out separate areas to hold your content and Dreamweaver automatically converts these areas to cells and tables. The layout cells are very pliable and can be moved easily about the page, resized, and reshaped. Moreover, Layout view gives you professional design power with options such as tables that stretch to fit the browser window and transparent spacer images that maintain the structural integrity of tables across all browsers.

Although they share the same underlying HTML structure, tables and cells created in Layout view differ from those created in Standard view in the following ways:

✦ Borders are set to zero and, thus, turned off.

✦ Cell padding and cell spacing are also set to zero to enable content to appear directly next to each other.

✦ Layout tables optionally include a row for each column that holds a one pixel high transparent GIF image called a spacer.

✦ Columns in a layout table are set to either a fixed pixel width or designed to automatically stretch to the full width of the page.

In addition to these physical differences, Layout view has a different appearance. Each layout table is marked with a tab and the column width is identified at the top of each column as shown in Figure 13-19.

Dreamweaver puts the entrance to Layout view right up front on the Objects panel. At the bottom of the panel, two new areas have been added for Dreamweaver 4. To switch modes, click the Layout View button; to return to the traditional mode, select the Standard View button. If the Objects panel is not open, use the menu by choosing View ➪ Table View ➪ Layout View or the keyboard shortcut Ctrl+F6 (Command+F6). Once Layout view has been enabled, two buttons above the view modes become active: Draw Cell and Draw Table.

Layout Table tabs   Column widths

Draw Layout Cell button   Layout View button

Draw Layout Table button

Figure 13-19: In Layout view, tables and columns are immediately identifiable and extremely flexible.

Note By the way, don't fret about your existing pages: they'll show up just fine in Layout view. In fact, looking at a well-designed legacy page in Layout view is very helpful to understanding how the pages of a professional Web designer are built.

Drawing cells and tables

Although you can use the Layout view to modify the structure of existing pages, this mode is best when designing Web pages from the ground-up. The Draw Cell and Draw Table commands enable you to quickly layout the basic structure of your page by defining the key document areas. For example, with just four mouse moves in Layout view, I could design a page with sections for a logo, a navigation bar, a copyright notice, and a primary content area. Now I'm ready to fill out the design with graphics, text, and other assets.

Here's how it works:

1. On a blank page, choose the Layout View button from the bottom of the Objects panel.

   When you first enter Layout view, Dreamweaver displays a help screen to explain how the new feature works. After you get the hang of working in Layout view, feel free to select the Don't Show Me This Message Again option to prevent further appearances of the dialog box.

2. Select the Draw Cell button, directly above the View modes. The cursor changes to a plus (+) sign.

   Although it may seem backwards, it's best to initially use the Draw Cells rather than Draw Table. Dreamweaver automatically creates the HTML table necessary to hold any cells you draw, resulting in less tables and tighter code. The Draw Table command is best used to make a nested table.

3. Move your cursor anywhere on the page and drag out a layout cell, as shown in Figure 13-20.

Figure 13-20: Use the Draw Cell command to define the basic page structure in Layout view.

Dreamweaver creates a table around the cell; the cell is drawn in the current background color with the surrounding table shown in white. When the mouse moves over it, the outline of a layout cell highlights in red, and turns blue when selected; likewise a Layout table's outline is green. These colors can be user-defined in Preferences.

Tip   If you're within eight pixels of the edge of the Document window or another layout cell, the border of the new layout cell snaps to that edge. Press the Alt (Option) key when drawing a layout cell to temporarily disable snapping.

4. Repeat Step 3 until your layout is complete.

   Dreamweaver drops out of Draw Cell mode after your first cell is created to prevent unintentional cells. To create several layout cells in a row, hold down Ctrl (Command) while dragging.

As indicated earlier, the Draw Table command is best suited for creating nested tables. A table is said to be nested when it is placed within an existing table. Nested tables are useful when a design requires that a number of elements, for example, a picture and a related caption, remain stationary in relation to one another while text on the page flows according to the size of the browser window.

Tip   While the tabs designating a layout table are very handy, you may want to turn them off at a certain stage of your design. To hide them, choose View ⇨ Table View ⇨ Show Layout Table Tabs to disable the option. Select the command again to bring them back into view.

To create a nested table in Layout view, follow these steps:

1. Choose the Layout View button on the Objects panel.

2. Select the Draw Layout Table button, also from the Objects panel.

3. When the cursor is over an area of the table unoccupied by a layout cell, the cursor changes to a plus (+) sign and a layout table can be dragged out. When not over a valid area, the cursor is shown as a slashed circle—the universal sign for "not allowed."

   The new layout table is inserted as shown in Figure 13-21.

4. To divide the nested layout table into multiple areas, choose the Draw Cell button to drag out new cells.

5. As with the Draw Cell command, the Draw Table command defaults to dragging one table at a time. To draw several tables in a row, select Ctrl (Command) while dragging out a layout table.

Figure 13-21: Nested tables are easily added with the Draw Layout Table command.

While the Layout view is an excellent method for quickly structuring a page, there are some limitations you should be aware of:

✦ Layout tables and cells can only be drawn in the area of the Document window that does not have any code associated with it. In other words, you need to draw cells and tables below the apparent end of the document. The result is that the new table code is placed right before the closing body tag.

✦ Two objects are disabled in Layout view: the Standard Table and the Layer objects. To add either of these objects to the page, you need to return to Standard view.

✦ Layout cells and tables cannot be copied, cut, or pasted. These operations are available from the Standard view, however.

It's worthwhile to note that the Layout view works exceedingly well with Dreamweaver's Grid feature. With the Grid showing (View ⇨ Grid ⇨ Show Grid) and Snap to Grid enabled (View ⇨ Grid ⇨ Snap to Grid), precisely laying out cells and tables is quite literally a snap. With Dreamweaver's Layout view, complex but useful designs, such as the one shown in Figure 13-22, are within reach.

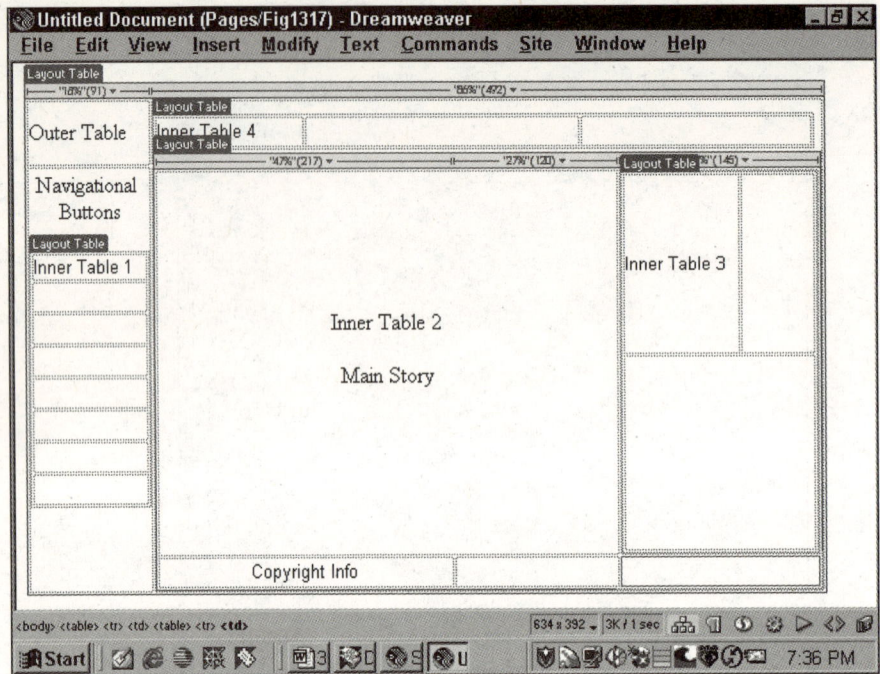

Figure 13-22: Nested tables — created in Dreamweaver's Layout view — offer the Web designer tighter command of Web page elements.

Modifying layouts

Layout view is not only a boon for creating the initial page design, but it also makes the inevitable modifications more straightforward. Cells are positionable within a layout table much the same as layers on a page. However, one difference exists; cells, unlike layers, cannot overlap. Resizing layout cells and tables is also easier. Unlike in Standard view where any table or cell border is draggable, in Layout view cells and tables have sizing handles — much the same as a selected image.

To easily manipulate layout and cells, they have to be easily selectable. Dreamweaver handles that chore with colorful flair. Pass your cursor over any layout cell, when you pass the border of a cell it changes from blue to red. Click once on the red highlight and the cell is selected. A selected cell is notable by the eight sizing handles placed on its perimeter. Once a cell is selected, the Property Inspector displays the available attributes.

Tip   To select a cell without moving the cursor over the border, Ctrl+click (Command+click) anywhere in the cell.

The Layout Cell Property Inspector (see Figure 13-23) offers six key attributes:

✦ **Width:** Enter a pixel value for a Fixed cell width or select the Autostretch option to enable the cell to grow as needed. (Autostretch is covered in the next section.) The width of each cell is shown on top of each column in Layout view. The column width property is an important one and is explained in greater detail later in this section.

✦ **Height:** Enter a pixel value for cell height. Percentages cannot be entered in Layout view.

✦ **Horz:** Select a horizontal alignment for the cell's content; the options are Default, Left, Center, and Right.

✦ **No Wrap:** When enabled, this option keeps content — text and images — from wrapping to the next line, which, if the column is in Autostretch mode, may alter the width of the cell.

✦ **Bg:** Choose a background color for the cell.

✦ **Vert:** Choose a vertical alignment for the cell's content; the options are Default, Top, Middle, Bottom, and Baseline.

Figure 13-23: Although similar to the standard Cell Property Inspector, the Layout Cell Property Inspector offers a different set of options.

Note   Not all the attributes of a table cell are available through the Layout cell Property Inspector. To add a background image, specify a border color, designate it as a header cell or split the cell, you need to switch to Standard view.

To reshape or resize a layout cell, drag any one of the sizing handles on the cell's border into the unused area of a table. Likewise, you can drag a cell into any open table area, for example, any area of the table unoccupied by another cell.

Tip   To maintain the width-height ratio of a cell, press Shift when resizing.

Tables may be similarly selected and resized. Layout tables are selected by clicking the title bar marking the table, or by clicking inside an open, gray-colored area within the table or on the table border. If the layout table is nested within another table, it can be dragged to a new location within the outer table. Non-nested tables cannot be dragged to a new location on the page, however.

Once a layout table is selected, the attributes in the Property Inspector become available as shown in Figure 13-24. These attributes include:

✦ **Width:** Enter a pixel value for a Fixed table width or select the Autostretch option to enable the table to grow as needed. (Autostretch is discussed in the next section.)

✦ **Height:** Enter a pixel value for table height. Percentages cannot be entered in Layout view.

✦ **CellPad:** Controls the amount of space between the content and the cell border throughout the table. The default value is zero.

✦ **CellSpace:** Controls the amount of space between cells throughout the table. The default value is zero.

✦ **Clear Row Heights:** Removes any set height values for all rows and reduces the table to existing content.

Caution   When the Clear Row Heights option is used with nested tables, Dreamweaver doesn't redraw the cell border to match the table border — in other words, the cell height is not cleared. To correct, drag the bottom cell border to match that of the table.

✦ **Make Cell Widths Consistent:** Reduces the width of all cells to the size of their respective content. If a cell is stretched beyond its original fixed size by an image or some text, the column header of the layout cell shows the fixed size next to the actual size in parenthesis. Choosing Make Cell Widths Consistent adjusts the fixed size to match the actual size.

✦ **Remove All Spacers:** Choosing this option deletes all single pixel images used to ensure browser compatibility for layout tables and their corresponding rows. Spacers are discussed in detail in a later section.

✦ **Remove Nesting:** Converts a nested table to rows and cells of the outer table.

Figure 13-24: The Layout Table Property Inspector includes important options for converting nested tables and sizing cells to fit existing content.

Altering column widths

The table elements in Layout view borrow a couple of pages from the professional Web designer's playbook. First, any column can easily be converted from a fixed width to a flexible width — in Dreamweaver this is known as *autostretch*. Second, when the autostretch option is chosen for a layout table, Dreamweaver inserts a spacer (a single-pixel high transparent GIF) in a new row along the bottom of the table. The spacer is sized to match the fixed width of each of the columns except for one — which is designated as an autostretch column. For a table to use the Autostretch option, one column must be flexible.

You can alter the width of a column in a number of ways:

✦ Visually, select the cell and then drag a sizing handle to a new position.

✦ For pixel precise width, use the Layout Cell Property Inspector and enter the desired size in the Width field. If the cell is currently in Autostretch mode, select the Fixed Width option to enable the value field.

✦ To convert an Autostretch column to its current on-screen pixel width, choose Make Column Fixed Width from the column header menu as shown in Figure 13-25.

✦ To make a fixed width column automatically stretch, choose Make Column
   Autostretch from the column header menu.

✦ Insert content wider than the set width and then choose Make Column Width
   Consistent from the Layout Table Property Inspector.

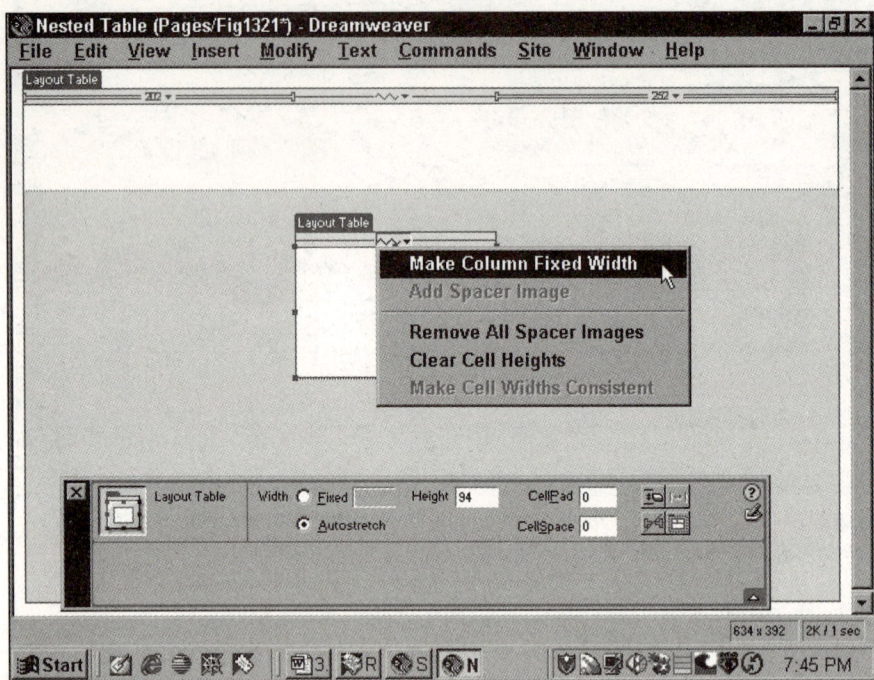

Figure 13-25: The switch between fixed width and autostretch through the column
header menu.

Working with the spacer image

If you've ever painstakingly created a complex table only to find that it looks great
in one browser but collapses into an unidentifiable mess in another, you're going to
love spacer images. Long used by Web site designers as a method of ensuring a
table's stability, a spacer image is simply an image — usually a single-pixel transparent GIF — that is resized to match the width of a column. Because no browser collapses a column smaller than the size of the largest image it contains, spacer
images retain a table's design under any circumstance.

Dreamweaver gives you several options when working with spacer images:

✦ You can have Dreamweaver create a spacer image for you.

✦ You can use an existing image as a spacer image.

✦ You can opt to never include spacer images.

The first time Autostretch is applied as an option in a table, Dreamweaver displays a dialog box (see Figure 13-26) that enables you to create or locate a spacer image. If you choose to create a new spacer image, you are then asked to select a location in the current site to store it. Generally you would save such a file in an images, assets, or media folder.

Figure 13-26: Spacer images essentially make layout tables browser-proof and Dreamweaver can either create one for you or enable you to use an existing image.

This image is then automatically inserted whenever an autostretch table or cell is created. One reason to use an existing image rather than a new one is if you work with sliced tables from Fireworks. Fireworks creates a single-pixel GIF image titled spacer.gif. The choice of a spacer image is a sitewide preference that can be viewed or changed by selecting the Layout View category of Preferences. Although it's not a commonly recommended practice, the Layout View category is also where you can disable spacer images.

Summary

Tables are an extremely powerful Web page design tool. Dreamweaver enables you to modify both the appearance and the structure of your HTML tables through a combination of Property Inspectors, dialog boxes, and click-and-drag mouse movements. Mastering tables is an essential task for any modern Web designer and worth the somewhat challenging learning curve. The key elements to keep in mind are as follows:

✦ An HTML table consists of a series of rows and columns presented in a grid-like arrangement. Tables can be sized absolutely, in pixels, or relative to the width of the browser's window, in a percentage.

✦ Dreamweaver inserts a table whose dimensions can be altered through the Objects panel or the Insert ⇨ Table menu. Once in the page, the table needs to be selected before any of its properties can be modified through the Table Property Inspector.

✦ Table editing is greatly simplified in Dreamweaver. You can select multiple cells, columns, or rows — and modify all their contents in one fell swoop.

✦ You can assign certain properties — such as background color, border color, and alignment — for a table's columns, rows, or cells through their respective dialog boxes. A cell's properties override those set for its column or row.

✦ Dreamweaver brings power to table building with the Format Table and Sort Table commands as well as a connection to the outside world with its Import Tabular Data option.

✦ Dreamweaver 4's new Layout view enables you to quickly prepare the basic structure of a page by drawing out layout cells and tables.

✦ Putting a table within another table — also known as *nesting tables* — is a powerful (and legal) design option in HTML. Nested tables are easily accomplished in Dreamweaver's Layout view by inserting a layout table.

In the next chapter, you learn how to create and use client-side image maps.

✦   ✦   ✦

Making Client-Side Image Maps

By their very nature, HTML images are rectangular. Although you can make portions of a rectangular graphic transparent, giving the impression of an irregularly shaped picture, the image itself — and thus its clickable region — is still a rectangle. For more complex images, in which shapes overlap and you want several separate areas of a picture to be hyperlinked, not just the overall graphic, you need an image map.

Dreamweaver puts its image map tools front and center so you can draw and manage your hotspots right on your graphics in the Document window. The onscreen image map tools make it much easier to manipulate your hotspots, but there's another major advantage: behaviors can easily be attached to hotspots.

This chapter introduces you to Dreamweaver's hotspot tools and also covers more advanced techniques for creating server-side and rollover image maps.

Client-Side Image Maps

As an almost literal example of an image map, imagine a map of the United States being used on a Web page. Suppose you want to be able to click each state and link to a different page in your site. How would you proceed? With the exception of Colorado and Wyoming, all the states have highly irregular shapes, so you can't use the typical side-by-side arrangement of rectangular images. You need to be able to specify a region on the graphic, to which you could then assign a link. This is exactly what an image map represents.

Two different kinds of image maps exist: client-side and server-side. With a server-side image map, all the map data is kept in a file on the server. When the user clicks a particular spot on the image, often referred to as a *hotspot*, the server compares the coordinates of the clicked spot with its image map data. If the coordinates match, the server loads the corresponding link. The key advantage to a server-side image map is that it works with any image-capable browser. The disadvantages are that it consumes more of the server's processing resources and tends to be slower than the client-side version.

With client-side image maps, on the other hand, all the data that is downloaded to the browser is kept in the Web page. The comparison process is the same, but it requires a browser that is image map savvy. Originally, only server-side image maps were possible. It wasn't until Netscape Navigator 2.0 was released that the client-side version was even an option. Microsoft began supporting client-side image maps in Internet Explorer 3.0. The vast majority of image maps used on the Web today are client-side, and server-side image maps should only be considered for special purposes.

In HTML, a client-side image map has two parts. In the `<img>` tag, Dreamweaver includes a `usemap=mapname` attribute. The mapname value refers to the second part of the image map's HTML, the `<map>` tag. One of the first steps in creating an image map is to give it a unique name. Dreamweaver stores all your mapping data under this map name. Here's an example of the code for an image map with three hotspots:

```
<img src="images/imagemap.jpg" width="640" height="480" ¬
usemap="#navbar"></p>
<map name="navbar">
  <area shape="poly"
coords="166,131,165,131,160,143,164,179,127,180,143,200,156,203,118,229,119,¬
236,158,229,177,217,199,238,212,247,220,242,196,203,232,190,241,189,241,182,¬
223,177,185,182,175,134,166,132" href="/starpro.html" alt="High Risk Funds">
  <area shape="circle" coords="312,202,56" href="/nestegg.html" ¬
alt="Mutual Funds">
  <area shape="rect" coords="389,138,497,244" href="/prodfunds.html" ¬
alt="Money Markets">
</map>
```

Dreamweaver directly supports client-side image maps. Once you've inserted an image into your Web page, it can be an image map. Select any image and open the expanded version of the Property Inspector. The image map tools are in the lower-left corner, as shown in Figure 14-1.

Map drawing tools — Map name field

Figure 14-1: From the Image Property Inspector, select the image map tools to draw hotspots directly on graphics within Dreamweaver.

Creating Image Hotspots

Image maps are created with tools similar to those you find in any drawing program. (They're described in detail in the section "Using the drawing tools," later in this chapter.) After you've selected your graphic, you can click a tool to describe a rectangle, oval, or polygon shape.

You can make an image map from any graphic format supported by Dreamweaver: GIF, JPEG, or PNG.

Follow these steps to create hotspots on an image in Dreamweaver:

1. Select your image and, if necessary, open the Image Property Inspector to full height by clicking the expander arrow.

2. Enter a unique name for your image map in the Map Name text box.

   Dreamweaver initially displays a placeholder name, Map, which you can use or replace. It's generally a good practice to use a name that is more meaningful, such as navMap.

3. Choose the appropriate drawing tool to outline your hotspot: Rectangle, Circle, or Polygon. Outline one hotspot.

   When you complete the hotspot, Dreamweaver displays the Hotspot Property Inspector, shown in Figure 14-2.

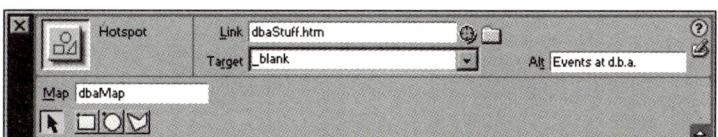

Figure 14-2: Enter image map attributes through the Hotspot Property Inspector.

4. Enter the URL for this image map in the Link text box or click the folder icon and browse for the file.

5. If desired, enter a frame name or other target in the Target text box.

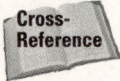

Cross-Reference

A target can refer to a specific section of a frameset or to a new browser window. For more information on using targets in frames, see Chapter 16. To learn more about targeting a new browser window, see the section "Targeting Your Links" in Chapter 11.

6. In the Alt text box, you can enter text you want to appear as a ToolTip that appears when the user's mouse moves over the area.

In Windows, the information taken from the Alt text box appears as a ToolTip only in Netscape browsers. Another attribute, `title`, is used in Microsoft browsers. Dreamweaver automatically adds both the `alt` and the `title` attributes for cross-browser compatibility.

7. Repeat Steps 3 through 6 to add additional hotspots to the graphic.

8. Click OK when you're finished.

Using the drawing tools

You'll find the hotspot drawing tools to be straightforward and easy to use. Each one produces a series of coordinates that are incorporated into the HTML code.

Outlining a hotspot

In the following steps, you use the hotspot drawing tools to outline a hotspot:

1. Select the Rectangle tool from the toolbar.

2. Click one corner of the area you want to map and drag toward the opposite corner to draw a rectangle.

3. Release the mouse button. Dreamweaver inverts the defined area.

4. Fill in the Link, Target, and Alt text boxes.

The Circle drawing tool

Follow these steps to use the Circle drawing tool in the Image Map Editor:

1. Select the Circle tool from the toolbar.

2. Click at one corner of the perimeter of the area you want to define and drag out the circle until it reaches the correct size.

3. Release the mouse button. Dreamweaver inverts the defined area.

4. As before, complete the Link, Target, and Alt text boxes.

The Polygon drawing tool

To define an irregularly shaped hotspot, use the Polygon drawing tool. Follow these steps:

1. Select the Polygon tool from the toolbar.

2. Click the first point for your hotspot object.

3. Release the mouse button and move the mouse to the next point.

4. Continue outlining the object by clicking and moving the mouse.

5. When the hotspot is completely outlined, double-click the mouse to close the area.

6. Fill in the Link, Target, and Alt text boxes.

Combining tools

You can use the drawing tools in any combination. In Figure 14-3, all three drawing tools have been used to create three different hotspots. The star-shaped image is currently selected, as indicated by the control points visible on that hotspot. The other two defined areas (the circular and rectangular objects) are shown with light blue overlays around them.

Figure 14-3: The image map drawing tools enable you to define both regular and irregularly shaped areas.

Setting the Default URL

What happens when Web site visitors pass their pointers over parts of your image that are not the primary hotspots? Prior to the fourth generation of browsers, a default URL property was supported to handle this issue. Now, however, the necessary code, `<area shape="default" href="url">`, is ignored by Internet Explorer 4 and above, although it remains supported by Netscape.

One workaround to this drawback is to completely cover the graphic with an area, using the Rectangle drawing tool, and then assign the desired default URL. If you add the overall rectangle hotspot after other hotspots have been created, be sure to send the full-graphic rectangle behind the other hotspots using the Modify ⇨ Arrange ⇨ Send to Back command. Where hotspots overlap, browsers detect only the uppermost hotspot.

Alternatively, open the Code view and locate the `<map>` tag. Next, place the code `<area shape="default" href="url">` —where *url* is replaced by a relative or absolute Web address— above the closing `</map>` tag. However, remember that this solution only works in Netscape browsers.

Tip

After you've created your hotspots, you may want to view your page without the highlighted areas. To turn off the overlays, choose View ⇨ Visual Aids ⇨ Image Maps; if the toolbar is visible, you can also choose the Options Menu button and then select Visual Aids ⇨ Image Maps.

Modifying an image map

Dreamweaver gives you several options for modifying the image maps you create. First, you can move any previously defined area by selecting it and then clicking and dragging to a new location. For precise pixel-by-pixel movement, select the area and use your keyboard arrow keys to move it in any direction.

Each of the hotspots has a number of control points that can be used to resize or reshape it. To move any of the control points, first select the hotspot Pointer tool.

✦ The rectangle has four control points, one at each corner. Drag any corner to resize or reshape the rectangle. Press Shift while dragging to constrain the rectangle's width-to-height ratio.

✦ Circle hotspots also have four control points. Dragging any of these points increases or decreases the diameter of the circle, leaving the opposing side stationary. For example, if you drag the top control point of a hotspot circle up, the hotspot expands from the bottom.

✦ Each point in a polygon hotspot is a control point that can be dragged into a new position to reshape the hotspot.

Hotspots can also be aligned with other hotspots or resized to match. The alignment commands are found under the Modify ⇨ Align menu and include the following:

Align Left	Aligns selected hotspots to the leftmost edge of the selection.
Align Right	Aligns selected hotspots to the rightmost edge of the selection.
Align Top	Aligns selected hotspots to the topmost edge of the selection.
Align Bottom	Aligns selected hotspots to the bottommost edge of the selection.
Make Same Width	Converts all selected hotspots to the width of the last selected hotspot.
Make Same Height	Converts all selected hotspots to the height of the last selected hotspot.

Caution

Although Dreamweaver lists keyboard shortcuts for all the alignment options under Modify ⇨ Align, these apply only to layers. You must use the menus (either the main or shortcut) to align hotspots.

Should your hotspots overlap, you can change the depth of any hotspot so that the desired hotspot is on top and has the focus in a particular area. These commands are found under the Modify ⇨ Arrange menu:

Bring to Front	Brings the selected hotspot in front of all other overlapping hotspots.
Send to Back	Sends the selected hotspot behind all other overlapping hotspots.

Of course, Dreamweaver also enables you to delete any existing area. Simply select the area and press the Delete or Backspace key.

Converting Client-Side Maps to Server-Side Maps

Although most Web browsers support client-side image maps, some sites still rely on server-side image maps. You can take a client-side image map generated by Dreamweaver and convert it to a server-side image map — you can even include pointers for both maps in the same Web page to accommodate older browsers as well as the newer ones. Such a conversion does require, however, that you use a text editor to modify and save the file. You also need to add one more attribute, ismap, to the <img> tag; this attribute tells the server that the image referenced in the src attribute is a map.

Adapting the server script

First, let's examine the differences between a client-side image map and a server-side image map from the same graphic. The HTML for a client-side image map looks like this:

```
<map name="navbar">
  <area shape="rect" coords="1,1,30,33" href="home.html" alt="Home Page">
  <area shape="circle" coords="65,64,62" href="contacts.html" ¬
alt="Information">
  <area shape="default" href="index.html">
</map>
```

The same definitions for a server-side image map are laid out like this:

```
rect home.html 1,1 30,33
circle contacts.html 65,64 62
default index.html
```

As you can see, the server-side image map file is much more compact. Notice first that all of the `alt="string"` code is thrown out because ToolTips can be shown only through client-side image maps.

A server expects the information in this form:

```
shape URL coordinates
```

So, you need to remove the `<area>` tag and its delimiters, as well as the phrases `shape=`, `coords=`, and `href=`. Then you reverse the order of the URL and the coordinates.

The last step in this phase of adapting the server-side script is to format the coordinates correctly. The format depends on the shape being defined:

✦ For rectangles, group the x, y points into comma-separated pairs with a single space in between each pair.

✦ For circles, separate the center point coordinates from the diameter with a space.

✦ For polygons, group the x, y points into comma-separated pairs with a single space in between each pair — just like rectangles.

Your new map file should be stored on your server, probably in a subfolder of the cgi-bin directory.

Caution   Not all servers expect server-side image maps in the same format. The format offered here conforms to the NCSA HPPD standard. If you're unsure of the required format, or of where to put your maps on your server, check with your server administrator before creating a server-side image map.

Attaching Behaviors to Image Maps

A hotspot is basically an interactive trigger. Although hotspots are used most frequently to open new Web pages, they can also be used to trigger other events. In Dreamweaver, behaviors assigned to linked text or images can perform a range of actions: swap an image on the page, show or hide a layer, or even open another smaller browser window. Dreamweaver 4, with its upfront image maps, makes it straightforward to assign behaviors to hotspots as well.

To attach a behavior to a hotspot, first select the hotspot and then choose the Add Action button from the Behaviors panel. Select your behavior from the list and enter its parameters. After you've confirmed your options, you may find it necessary to change the event from its default, which is often `onMouseDown` or `onMouseOver`. To do so, select the down triangle in-between the event and the action in the Behaviors panel and choose a new event from the list.

Here's a cool and useful feature: If you copy an image with defined hotspots and behaviors, all the associated behaviors are copied as well as the image map.

Including the map link

The second phase of converting a client-side map to a server-side one involves making the connection between the Web page and the map file. A client-side image map link directly calls the URL associated with it. In contrast, all references from a server-side link call the map file — which in turn calls the specified URL.

The connection to a server-side map is handled in the normal manner of adding a link to a graphic. You can, of course, do this directly in Dreamweaver. Simply select your graphic and, in the Image Property Inspector, insert the map file URL in the Link text box. Be sure the image's Border property is set to zero to avoid the link outline.

The final addition to your script is the `ismap` attribute. Place the `ismap` attribute in the `<img>` tag of the graphic being used for the image map, like this:

```
<img href="images/biglogo.gif" width="200" height="350" ismap>
```

Recall that it is entirely possible to use client-side and server-side image maps together. The easiest way to do it is to keep the image map data as written by Dreamweaver and add the `ismap` attribute. The HTML example in the previous section, "Client-Side Image Maps," would then read as follows:

```
<a href="http://www.idest.com/cgi-bin/maps/imap.txt">
<img src="images/imagemap.jpg" width="640" height="480" usemap="#navbar" ¬
ismap></a/>
```

Dreamweaver Technique: Building an Image Map Rollover

One of the most popular Web page techniques today is known as a *rollover*. A rollover occurs when a user's mouse moves over a button or graphic in the page, and the button or graphic changes in some way. You saw how to create these graphic rollovers in Chapter 10. In this section, let's try out one method for applying the same technique to an image map.

Note   The following method uses advanced techniques involving JavaScript behaviors and layers. If you're unfamiliar with these concepts, you might want to examine Chapters 19 and 28 before proceeding.

Before we get underway, keep in mind that this technique — because it uses layers — works only with 4.0 browsers and above.

Step 1: Create two images

As with behavior-based button rollovers, you use two images to represent the "off" and "over" states of the graphic. However, because we are using image maps here, rather than separate graphics, you only need a total of two images (versus two for every button). In our example, three buttons are "carved" from one graphic; but there could very easily have been eight or a dozen separate buttons, which would have required 16 or 24 separate images. All we need is our two image maps.

After building your first image, bring it into your favorite image processing program, such as Fireworks, and make the alterations necessary to create the second image. Figure 14-4 shows examples of the two images you need (above and below) inserted into Dreamweaver. As you can see, all that was necessary to make the "over" image was to add a glow effect to each of the three hotspots.

Tip   One of the methods used in this technique involves clipping a region of an image. Presently, layers support only rectangular clipping. Keep this in mind as you build your primary image and avoid placing hotspots too close together.

Step 2: Set up the layers

This technique takes advantage of three different layer properties: absolute positioning, visibility, and clipping. The idea is to display just a portion of a hidden layer during an `onMouseOver` event. To perform this function without rewriting the code, a layer for each of the hotspots is necessary. Each layer will later be clipped to show just that hotspot. The beauty of this technique is that while it uses multiple layers, only two images are required, as the single "over" image is used for each rollover.

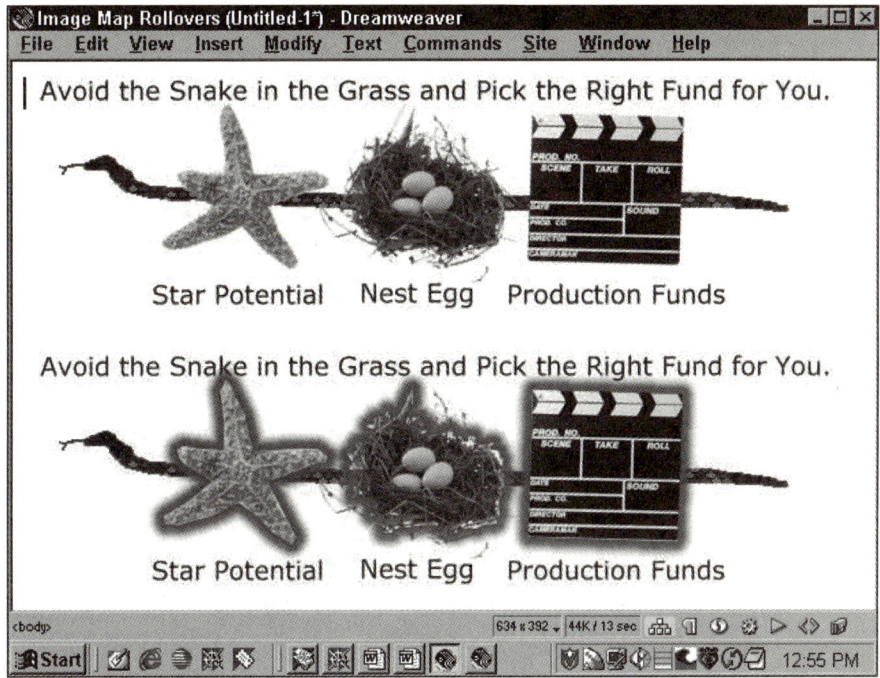

Figure 14-4: You need two separate images, representing "over" and "off," for a rollover image map.

To get started, you just need two layers — one for each of your images.

Follow these steps to establish the initial layers:

1. Choose Insert ⇨ Layer or select the Draw Layer button on the Objects panel to create the layer that will hold the image displayed when the mouse is over the graphic. I gave my layer the name overLayer.

   If you use the menu option instead of drawing out the layer, it is created at a standard size, and you won't have to spend as much time adjusting the layer sizes later.

2. Making sure the cursor is in the layer, choose Insert ⇨ Image or select the Insert Image button on the Objects panel. Load your "over" graphic. If the layer is smaller than the image, the layer automatically expands.

3. Repeat Step 1 to create the second layer that will hold the image displayed when the mouse is off the image; I named my example offLayer.

4. Repeat Step 2 and insert the "off" graphic.

5. If necessary, open the Layers panel by choosing Window ⇨ Layers or pressing F2, and make sure of the following:

- Both layers must have unique names. In this example, I use `offLayer` and `overLayer`.

- The `offLayer` must be visible.

- The `overLayer` must be hidden.

- The `overLayer` must be exactly on top of the `offLayer`, so that when you make a portion of the `overLayer` visible, it obscures the `offLayer`.

Figure 14-5 shows how the screen looks with both layers in place and the visibility properties set correctly.

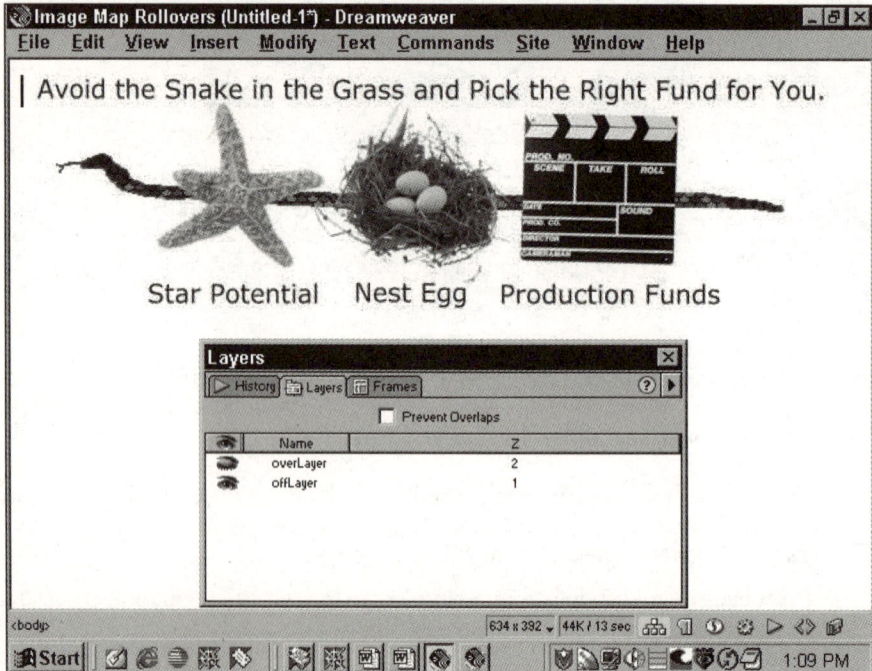

Figure 14-5: Two image maps are placed on top of each other in layers, and the top layer is hidden.

After you've created your initial layers, you need to create a layer for each remaining hotspot. I name these layers sequentially, such as overLayer02 and overLayer03. Then insert the "over" graphic in each of these layers. Finally, all the overLayers should be in the same position as, and on top of, the offLayer and hidden. Basically you have a stack of identical overLayers on top of the offLayer.

Aligning Layers

In Dreamweaver, you can use the layer alignment commands to easily line up the two layers. The commands are covered in detail in Chapter 25, but here are the steps briefly. Group the two windows by selecting both layers in the Layers panel while pressing the Shift key. Choose two of the Modify ➪ Align options — Align Left and Align Top, for example — so that they are in the same position. The layer alignment commands all work the same; all layers are aligned to the edge of the last layer selected. If the layers are different shapes, you can make them the same size by choosing Modify ➪ Align ➪ Make Same Width and/or Modify ➪ Align ➪ Make Same Height.

Tip

If you have many hotspots, you may want to name the overLayers something more recognizable. For example, with my three shapes, I could name the layers overLayerStar, overLayerNest, and overLayerClapboard. You need to be able to match the layers to the hotspot as part of the technique. And a proper naming scheme can smooth your workflow.

Step 3: Make the image map

The first part of this step is to make the actual image map that will eventually be used to activate the `onMouseOver` and `onMouseOut` events. Follow these steps to complete this task:

1. Select the image in one of the layers. You can use either image (the "over" or the "off") to draw the image map. I preferred the overLayer, with the slightly fuzzier edges.

2. In the Map Name field of the Property Inspector, give your map a unique name.

3. Draw out the image maps using the drawing tools.

4. In the Hotspot Property Inspector, give each area a URL in the Link box.

5. Complete the Target and Alt text boxes, if desired.

   Generally, when building an image map, this is where you would stop. However, because we're using multiple layers, we need to apply the same image map to each of the remaining layers in our technique.

6. Using the Layers panel, select the next layer and then choose the image.

7. In the Map Name field, enter the same name as previously assigned.

   This ensures that all the layers use the same image map; if you do not perform this step, the off and over images will appear to flicker.

8. Repeat Steps 6 and 7 for each of the remaining layers.

Step 4: Attach the behaviors

Dreamweaver includes a JavaScript behavior called Show/Hide Layers that does exactly what you need for this technique.

Follow these steps to assign the Show/Hide Layers behavior to the layers:

1. Be sure the offLayer (the layer holding the basic, unchanged image) is visible and all the overLayers are hidden. You can select the visibility options in the Layers panel to open and close the "eyes" of the respective layers.

2. Select the first hotspot of the image in the offLayer.

3. Open the Behaviors panel by clicking the Behavior button in the Launcher or selecting Window ➪ Behaviors.

4. Choose 4.0 and Later Browsers from the Show Events For submenu at the end of the Add Behavior list, if it's not already selected.

5. Still in the Behaviors panel, select the + (Add Behavior) button and choose Show-Hide Layers from the pop-up list.

6. When the Show-Hide Layers dialog box opens, Dreamweaver searches for all the layers in your document. After they are displayed, select overLayer and click the Show button (see Figure 14-6). Click OK when you've finished.

7. Now you need to change the event that triggers the behavior from onMouseDown to onMouseOver. To do this, click the Add Event button in the Behaviors panel. The Add Event button is the down arrow between the Event and Action lists. Choose onMouseOver from the Add Event drop-down list.

8. So far, you've assigned one behavior to make overLayer visible when the pointer is over the image. Now you have to assign another behavior to hide overLayer when the pointer moves away from the image.

9. Click the Add Behavior button and again select Show-Hide Layers from the option list.

10. Now select overLayer again and click the Hide button. Click OK when you're finished.

11. Finally, change the event to onMouseOut for this new behavior, following the same procedure as in Step 7.

So what you now have is two behaviors assigned to one image. Now, you need to repeat the attachment of the behaviors to each of the additional hotspots in your graphic. However, instead of showing and hiding overLayer, each hotspot has its own overLayer to show and hide. For example, after I've selected my second hotspot, I show and hide overLayer02, and so on.

Figure 14-6: Highlight overLayer and then choose the Show option to ensure that the Show-Hide Layer action makes the appropriate layer visible.

Step 5: Add the clipping

Let's review what you have done so far:

✦ Before you began working in Dreamweaver, you built two different images — one to depict the regular ("off") state, and another for the "over" state.

✦ You used Dreamweaver to create a series of identically sized and positioned layers. You then inserted your two images into the hidden layers, with the "over" graphic placed on top layers.

✦ Next, you created hotspots on your graphics and assigned the same image map name to each of the graphics in all the layers.

✦ Then, you used Dreamweaver to assign JavaScript behaviors that reveal the hidden layer when the user's pointer passes over the hotspot and hide it again when the pointer moves away from the hotspot.

If you test the image map rollover at this stage, you'll see the entire "over" graphic for every hotspot. To achieve the rollover effect, each of the overLayers must be clipped. All that is left to do now is assign the clipping values.

The clipping property of a layer essentially crops the visible portion of that layer. Four values are used to define the clipped section: Left, Top, Right, and Bottom. These values are pixel measurements relative to the upper-left corner of the layer. Although you could bring your image into an image editor to find the measurements, you can, with a slight bit of trickiness, also get the measurements right from Dreamweaver.

To get the relative pixel values within a layer, I use another temporary layer drawn over my clipped area. I can shape this temporary layer to the exact size of the clip and then note the layer's coordinates and dimensions. Because one layer can nest inside another, you can find the relative positioning—the Left and Top values—very easily. Finding the Right and Bottom values then requires only a minor calculation.

To add the clipping values to your overLayers, follow these steps:

1. From the Layers panel, select the first of the overLayers.

   Although it's not necessary, it's a good idea to select the Prevent Overlaps option from the Layers panel to stop your clipped sections from overlapping.

2. Click the graphic in the overLayer.

3. Press the left-arrow key once to move your cursor in front of the image but within the layer.

4. Choose Insert ⇨ Layer.

   This new layer is a temporary one that will be used for measurement purposes only and then deleted.

5. Drag the temporary layer into position for the first area to be clipped.

6. Use the resizing handles to reshape the temporary layer until it frames the area you want to clip, as shown in Figure 14-7.

7. In the Property Inspector, note the values for Left, Top, Width, and Height (L, T, W, and H, respectively) of the temporary layer.

8. From the Layers panel, select the overLayer.

9. In the Clip section of the Property Inspector, enter the Left and Top values as noted from the temporary layers.

10. For the Clip Right (R) value, enter the sum of the temporary layer's Left and Width values.

11. For the Clip Bottom (B) value, enter the sum of the temporary layer's Top plus its Height values.

    For example, the example temporary layer's initial values were: Left, 95; Top, 30; Width, 125; and Height, 125. This translates into the following clip values: Left, 95; Top, 30; Right, 220 (Left + Width); and Bottom, 155 (Top + Height).

    After you've entered the last clipping value (and pressed Tab or Enter/Return to confirm), Dreamweaver displays just the clipped area.

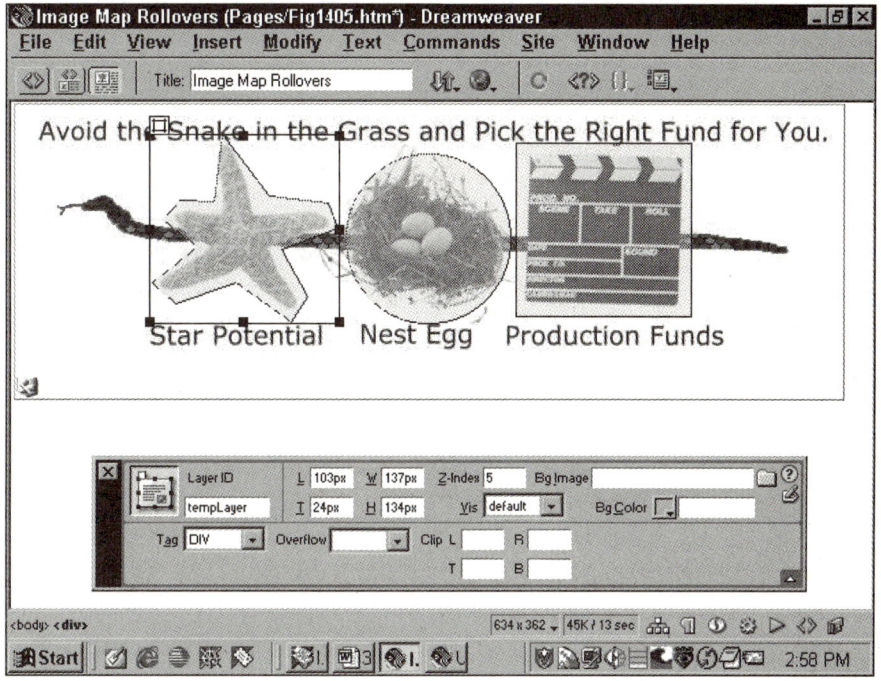

Figure 14-7: You can use a temporary layer to get the exact clipping measurements.

12. Repeat this procedure (Steps 1 through 11) for each of the remaining overLayers, until all have clip values.

Once you've implemented these changes, test your object. You should see the type of reaction demonstrated in Figure 14-8.

Note When you preview your work in a browser, make sure that visibility is set correctly for each layer.

Summary

Image maps provide a necessary capability in Web page design. Without them, you wouldn't be able to link irregularly shaped graphics or to group links all in one image. Dreamweaver's built-in Image Map Editor gives you all the tools you need to create simple, effective client-side image maps.

✦ Image maps enable you to define separate areas of one graphic and link them to different URLs. Image maps come in two varieties: client-side and server-side. Dreamweaver creates client-side image maps through its Image Map Editor.

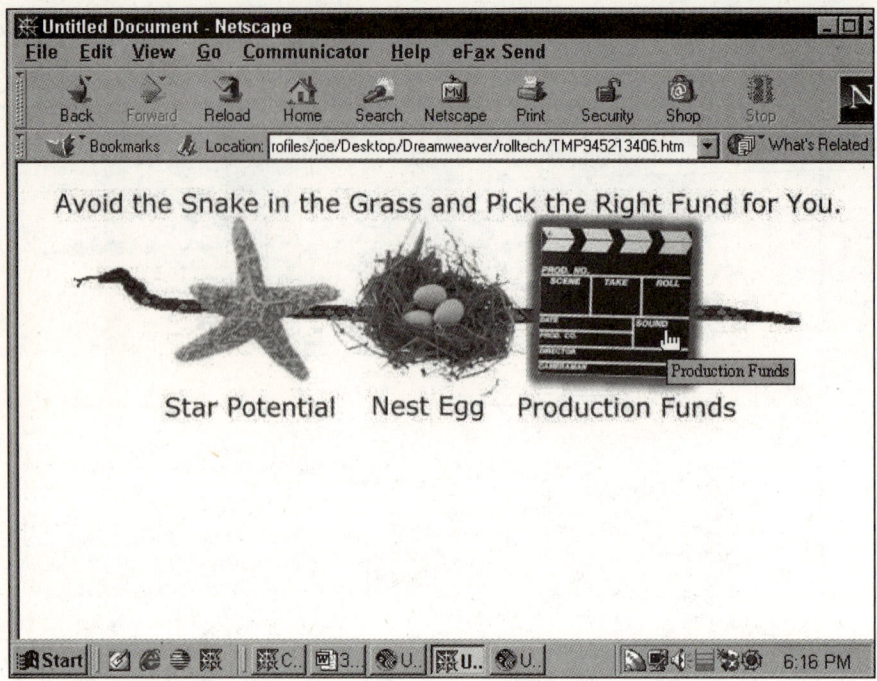

Figure 14-8: The completed image map rollover technique in action

✦ Dreamweaver offers three basic drawing tools for creating rectangular, circular, and irregularly shaped image maps, selectable from the Image Property Inspector.

✦ If your Web site uses server-side image maps, you can make them by modifying and converting Dreamweaver-generated client-side image maps.

✦ It's possible to create the effect of a graphic rollover, common on Web pages, using client-side image maps. This chapter's Dreamweaver Technique shows you how.

In the next chapter, you learn about forms in Dreamweaver.

✦   ✦   ✦

Interactive Forms

A form, in the everyday world as well as on the Web, is a type of structured communication. When you apply for a driver's license, you're not told to just write down all your personal information, you're asked to fill out a form that asks for specific parts of that information, one at a time, in a specific manner. Web-based forms are just as precise, if not more so.

Dreamweaver has a robust and superior implementation of HTML forms — from the dedicated Forms category in the Objects panel to various form-specific Property Inspectors. In addition to their importance as a tool for communication between the browsing public and Web site administrators, forms are integral to building some of Dreamweaver's own objects.

In this chapter, you learn how forms are structured and then created within Dreamweaver. Each form object is explored in detail — text fields, radio buttons, checkboxes, menus, list boxes, command buttons, hidden fields, and password fields.

How HTML Forms Work

Forms have a special function in HTML: They support interaction. Virtually all HTML elements apart from forms are concerned with design and presentation — delivering the content to the user, if you will. Forms, on the other hand, give the user the ability to pass information back to Web site creators and administrators. Without forms, the Web would be a one-way street.

Forms have many, many uses on the Web, such as for surveys, electronic commerce, guest books, polls, and even real-time custom graphics creation. For such feedback to be possible, forms require an additional component to what's seen onscreen so that each form can complete its function. Every form needs some type of connection to a Web server, and usually this connection uses a *common gateway interface (CGI)* script, although JavaScript and Java can also be used. This means that, in addition to designing your forms onscreen, you or someone who works with you must implement a program that collects and manages the information from the form.

Forms, like HTML tables, can be thought of as self-contained units within a Web page. All the elements of a form are contained within the form tag pair `<form>` and `</form>`. Unlike tables, you cannot nest forms, although there's nothing to stop you from having multiple forms on a page.

The `<form>` tag has three attributes, only two of which (method and action) are commonly used:

✦ The `method` attribute tells the server how the contents of the form should be presented to the CGI program. The two possible `method` values are `get` and `post`. `Get` passes the attached information to a URL; it is rarely used these days because it places limitations on the amount of data that can be passed to the gateway program. `Post` causes the server to present the information as standard input and imposes no limits on the amount of passed data.

✦ The second `<form>` attribute is `action`. The `action` attribute determines what should be done with the form content. Most commonly, `action` is set to a URL for running a specific CGI program or for sending e-mail.

✦ The third attribute for `<form>` is `enctype`, which specifies the MIME media type. It is used infrequently.

Typical HTML for a `<form>` tag looks something like this:

```
<form method="post" action="http://www.idest.com/_cgi-bin/mailcall.pl">
```

Tip   The .pl extension in the preceding example form tag stands for *Perl* — a scripting language often used to create CGI programs. Perl can be edited in any regular text editor.

Within each form is a series of input devices — text boxes, radio buttons, checkboxes, and so on. Each type handles a particular sort of input; in fact, the main tag for these elements is the `<input>` tag. With one exception, the `<textarea>` tag, all form input types are called by specifying the `type` attribute. The text box tag, for example, is written as follows:

```
<input type=text value="lastname">
```

All form input tags have `value` attributes. Information input by the user is assigned to the given value. Thus, if I were to fill out a form with a text box asking for my last name, such as the one produced by the foregoing tag, part of the message sent would include the following string:

```
lastname=Lowery
```

Web servers send all the information from a form in one long text string to whatever program or address is specified in the action attribute. It's up to the program or the recipient of the form message to parse the string. For instance, if I were to fill out a small form with my name, e-mail address, and a quick comment such as "Good work!" the server would send a text string similar to the following:

name=Joseph+Lowery&address=jlowery@idest.com&comment=Good+work%21

As you can see, the various fields are separated by ampersands, and the individual words within the responses are separated by plus signs. Characters outside of the lower end of the ASCII set — like the exclamation mark in the example — are represented by their hexadecimal values. Decoding this text string is called *parsing the response*.

Tip   If you're not using the mailto method for getting your Web feedback, don't despair. Most CGI programs parse the text string as part of their basic functionality before sending it on its way.

Inserting a Form in Dreamweaver

A form is inserted just like any other object in Dreamweaver. Place the cursor where you want your form to start and then either select the Insert Form button from the Forms category of the Objects panel or choose Insert ➪ Form from the menus. Dreamweaver inserts a red dashed outline stretching across the Document window to indicate the form.

If you have the Property Inspector open, the Form Property Inspector appears when you insert a form. As you can see from Figure 15-1, you can specify only three values regarding forms: the Form Name, the Action, and the Method.

Specifying a form name enables the form to be directly referenced by JavaScript or other languages. Because of the interactive nature of forms, Web programmers often use this feature to gather information from the user.

In the Action text box, you can directly enter a URL or mailto address, or you can select the folder icon and browse for a file.

Note   Sending your form data via a mailto address is not without its problems. Some browsers, most notably Internet Explorer, are set to warn the user whenever a form button using mailto is selected. While many users let the mail go through, they do have the option to stop it from being sent.

The Method defaults to POST, the most commonly used option. You can also choose GET or DEFAULT, which leaves the method up to the browser. In most cases, you should leave the method set to POST.

Form outline   Insert Form button

Figure 15-1: Inserting a form creates a dashed red outline of the form and displays the Form Property Inspector, if available.

 Note   Forms cannot be placed inline with any other element such as text or graphics.

Keep in mind a few considerations when it comes to mixing forms and other Web page elements:

✦ Forms expand as objects are inserted into them; you can't resize a form by dragging its boundaries.

✦ The outline of a form is invisible; there is no border to turn on or off.

✦ Forms and tables can be used together only if the form either completely encloses or is completely enclosed inside the table. In other words, you can't have a form spanning part of a table.

✦ Forms can be inserted within layers, and multiple forms can be in multiple layers. However, the layer must completely enclose the form. As with forms spanning tables, you can't have a form spanning two or more layers. (A workaround for this limitation is discussed in Chapter 28.)

Declaring the Enctype

The `<form>` attribute `enctype` is helpful in formatting material returned via a form. Enctype can have three possible values. By default `enctype` is set to `application/x-www-form-urlencoded`, which is responsible for encoding the form response with ampersands between entries, equal signs linking form element names to their values, spaces as plus signs, and all nonalphanumeric characters in hexadecimal, such as `%3F` (a question mark).

The second `enctype` value, `text/plain`, is useful for e-mail replies. Instead of one long string, your form data is transmitted in a more readable format with each form element and its value on a separate line as in this example:

```
fname=Joseph
lname=Lowery
email=jlowery@idest.com
comment=Please send me the information on your new products!
```

The final `enctype` value, `multipart/form-data`, is used only when a file is being uploaded as part of the form. There's a further restriction: The Method should be set to POST, instead of GET.

Dreamweaver doesn't include a space on the Form Property Inspector for the `enctype` attribute, so you have to add it manually either through the HTML Source Inspector or the Quick Tag Editor. To use the Quick Tag Editor, select the `<form>` tag in the Tag Selector and press Ctrl+T (Command+T). Tab to the end of the tag and enter `enctype="value"`, substituting one of the three possible values.

Tip You can turn off the red dashed form outline in Dreamweaver's preview, if you like. Choose Edit ⇨ Preferences and, in the Invisible Elements category, deselect the Form Delimiter option.

Using Text Boxes

Anytime you use a form to gather text information typed in by a user, you use a form object called a *text field*. Text fields can hold any number of alphanumeric characters. The Web designer can decide whether the text field is displayed in one line or several. When the HTML is written, a multiple-line text field uses a `<textarea>` tag, and a single-line text field is coded with `<input type=text>`.

Text fields

To insert a single-line text field in Dreamweaver, you can use any of the following methods:

✦ From the Forms category of the Objects panel, select the Insert Text Field button to place a text field at your current cursor position.

✦ Choose Insert ⇨ Form Objects ⇨ Text Field from the menu, which inserts a text field at the current cursor position.

✦ Drag the Insert Text Field button from the Objects panel to any existing location in the Document window and release the mouse button to position the text field.

When you insert a text field, the Property Inspector, when displayed, shows you the attributes that can be changed (see Figure 15-2). The size of a text field is measured by the number of characters it can display at one time. You can change the length of a text field by inserting a value in the Char Width text box. By default, Dreamweaver inserts a text field approximately 20 characters wide. The *approximately* is important here because the *final* size of the text field is ultimately controlled by the browser used to view the page. Unless you limit the number of possible characters by entering a value in the Max Chars text box, the user can enter as many characters as desired, and the text box scrolls to display them.

Note that the value in Char Width determines the visible width of the field, whereas the value in Max Chars actually determines the number of characters that can be entered.

Figure 15-2: The text field of a form is used to enable the user to type in any required information.

Neat Forms

Text field width is measured in a monospaced character width. Because regular fonts are not monospaced, however, lining up text fields and other form objects can be problematic at best. The two general workarounds are preformatted text and tables.

Switching the labels on the form to preformatted text enables you to insert any amount of white space to properly space (or *kern*) your text and other input fields. Previously, Web designers were stuck with the default preformatted text format — the rather plain-looking Courier monospaced font. Now, however, newer browsers (3.0 and later) can read the `face=fontname` attribute. So you can combine a regular font with the preformatted text option and get the best of both worlds.

Going the preformatted text route requires you to insert a lot of spaces. So when you are working on a larger, complex form, using tables is probably a better way to go. Besides the speed of layout, the other advantage that tables offer is the capability to right-align text labels next to your text fields. The top form in the following figure gives an example of using preformatted text to get different-sized form fields to line up properly, while the bottom form in the figure uses a table.

Combining differently sized text fields on a single row — for example, when you're asking for a city, state, and zip code combination — can make the task of lining up your form even more difficult. Most often, you'll spend a fair amount of time in a trial-and-error effort to make the text fields match. Be sure to check your results in the various browsers as you build your form.

The Init Value text box on the Text Field Property Inspector is used to insert a default text string. The user can overwrite this value, if desired.

Password fields

Generally, all text entered into text fields displays as you expect — programmers refer to this process as *echoing*. You can turn off the echoing by selecting the Password option in the Text Field Property Inspector. When a text field is designated as a password field, all text entered by the user shows up as asterisks in Windows systems or as dots on Macintoshes.

Use the password field when you want to protect the user's input from prying eyes (as your PIN number is hidden when you enter it at an ATM, for instance). The information entered in a password field is not encrypted or scrambled in any way, and when sent to the Web administrator, it displays as regular text.

Only single-line text fields can be set as password fields. You cannot make a multi-line `<textarea>` tag act as a password field without employing JavaScript or some other programming language.

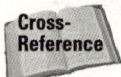

Cross-Reference Making sure that your user fills out the form properly is called validating the input. Dreamweaver includes a standard form validation behavior, covered in Chapter 19.

Multiline text areas

When you want to give your users a generous amount of room to write, set the text field to the Multiline option on the Text Field Property Inspector. This converts the default 20-character width for single-line text fields to a text area approximately 18 characters wide and 3 lines high, with a horizontal and vertical scroll bar. Figure 15-3 shows a typical multiline text field embedded in a form.

You control the width of a multiline text area by entering a value in the Char Width text box of the Text Field Property Inspector, just as you do for single-line text fields. The height of the text area is set equal to the value in the Num Lines text box. As with the default single-line text field, the user can enter any amount of text desired. Unlike the single-line text field, which can restrict the number of characters that can be input through the Max Chars text box, you cannot restrict the number of characters the user enters into a multiline text area.

By default, text entered into a multiline text field does not wrap when it reaches the right edge of the text area; rather, it keeps scrolling until the user presses Enter (Return). Dreamweaver 4 enables you to force the text to wrap by selecting Virtual or Physical from the Wrap drop-down list. The Virtual option wraps text on the screen but not when the response is submitted. To wrap text in both situations, use the Physical wrap option.

Multiline text box   Multiline option

Figure 15-3: The Multiline option of the Text Field Property Inspector opens up a text box for more user information.

One other option is to preload the text area with any default text you like. Enter this text in the Init Val text box of the Text Field Property Inspector. When Dreamweaver writes the HTML code, this text is not entered as a value, as for the single-line text field, but rather goes in between the `<textarea>...</textarea>` tag pair.

Providing Checkboxes and Radio Buttons

When you want your Web page reader to choose between a specific set of options in your form, you can use either checkboxes or radio buttons. Checkboxes enable you to offer a series of options from which the user can pick as many as desired. Radio buttons, on the other hand, enable your user to choose only one selection from a number of options.

Tip   You can achieve the same functionality as checkboxes and radio buttons with a different look by using the drop-down list and menu boxes. These options for presenting choices to the user are described shortly.

Checkboxes

Checkboxes are often used in a "Select All That Apply" type of section, when you want to enable the user to choose as many of the listed options as desired. You insert a checkbox in much the same way you do a text box: Select or drag the Insert Check Box object from the Objects panel or choose Insert ⇨ Form Objects ⇨ Check Box.

Like other form objects, checkboxes can be given a unique name in the text box provided in the Check Box Property Inspector (see Figure 15-4). If you don't provide one, Dreamweaver inserts a generic one, such as checkbox4.

Figure 15-4: Checkboxes are one way of offering the Web page visitor any number of options to choose.

In the Checked Value text box, fill in the information you want passed to a program when the user selects the checkbox. By default, a checkbox starts out unchecked, but you can change that by changing the Initial State option to Checked.

Radio buttons

Radio buttons on a form provide a set of options from which the user can choose only one. If users change their minds after choosing one radio button, selecting another one automatically deselects the first choice. You insert radio buttons in the same manner as checkboxes. Choose or drag Insert Radio Button from the Forms category of the Objects panel, or choose Insert ⇨ Form Objects ⇨ Radio Button.

Unlike checkboxes and text fields, each radio button in the set does not have a unique name — instead, each *group* of radio buttons does. Giving the entire set of radio buttons the same name enables browsers to assign one value to the radio button set. That value is determined by the contents of the Checked Value text box. Figure 15-5 shows two different sets of radio buttons. One is named computersRadio and the other, osRadio.

Figure 15-5: Radio buttons enable a user to make just one selection from a group of options.

To designate the default selection for each radio button group, you select the particular radio button and make the Initial State option Checked instead of Unchecked.

Because you must give radio buttons in the same set the same name, you can speed up your work a bit by creating one button, copying it, and then pasting the others. Don't forget to change the Checked Value for each button, though.

Creating Form Lists and Menus

Another way to offer your user options, in a more compact form than radio buttons and checkboxes, is with form lists and menus. Both objects can create single-line entries in your form that expand or scroll to reveal all the available options. You can also determine how deep you want the scrolling list to be; that is, how many options you want displayed at a time.

Drop-down menus

A drop-down menu should be familiar to everyday users of computers: The menu is initially displayed as a single-line text box with an option arrow button at the right end; when the button is clicked, the other options are revealed in a list or menu. (Whether the list "pops up" or "drops down" depends on its position in the browser window at the time it is selected. Generally, the list drops down, unless it is close to the bottom of the screen.) The user selects one of the listed options, and when the mouse is released, the list closes up and the selected value remains displayed in the text box.

Insert a drop-down menu in Dreamweaver as you would any other form object, with one of these actions:

✦ From the Forms category of the Objects panel, select the Insert List/Menu button to place a drop-down menu at the current cursor position.

✦ Choose Insert ➪ Form Objects ➪ List/Menu from the menu to insert a drop-down menu at the current cursor position.

✦ Drag the Insert List/Menu button from the Property Inspector to any location in the Document window and release the mouse button to position the drop-down menu.

With the List/Menu object inserted, make sure the Menu option (not the List option) is selected in the Property Inspector, as shown in Figure 15-6. You can also name the drop-down menu by typing a name in the Name text box; if you don't, Dreamweaver supplies a generic "select" name.

The HTML code for a drop-down menu uses the `<select>...</select>` tag pair surrounding a number of `<option>...</option>` tag pairs. Dreamweaver gives you a straightforward user interface for entering labels and values for the options on your menu. The menu item's *label* is what is displayed on the drop-down list; its *value* is what is sent to the server-side processor when this particular option is selected.

Menu option   Insert List / Menu button

Figure 15-6: Drop-down menus are created by inserting a List/Menu object and then selecting the Menu option in the List/Menu Property Inspector.

To enter the labels and values for a drop-down menu — or for a scrolling list — follow these steps:

1. Select the menu for which you want to enter values.

2. From the List/Menu Property Inspector, select the List Values button. The List Values dialog box appears (see Figure 15-7).

3. In the Item Label column, enter the label for the first item. Press the Tab key to move to the Value column.

4. Enter the value to be associated with this item. Press the Tab key.

5. Continue entering items and values by repeating Steps 3 and 4.

6. To delete an item's label *and* value in the List Values dialog box, highlight it and select the Remove button at the top of the list. To delete either the item's label or value, but not both, highlight either the label or the value and press the Delete or Backspace key.

7. To continue adding items, select the Add button or continue using the Tab key.

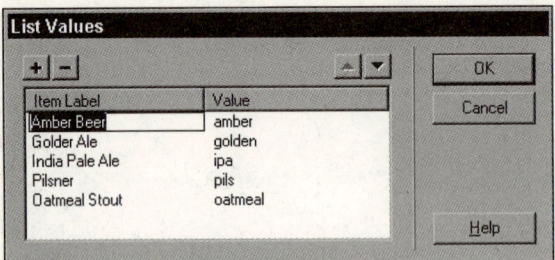

Figure 15-7: Use the List Values dialog box to enter and modify the items in a drop-down menu or scrolling list.

8. To rearrange the order of items in the list, select an item and then press the up- or down-arrow keys to reposition it.

9. Click OK when you've finished.

If you haven't entered a value for every item, the server-side application receives the label instead. Generally, however, it is a good idea to specify a value for all items.

You can preselect any item in a drop-down menu so that it appears in the list box initially and is highlighted when the full list is displayed. Dreamweaver enables you to pick your selection from the Initially Selected menu in the Property Inspector. The Initially Selected menu is empty until you enter items through the List Values dialog box. You can preselect only one item for a drop-down menu.

Scrolling lists

A scrolling list differs from a drop-down menu in three respects. First, and most obviously, the scrolling list field has up- and down-arrow buttons, rather than an option arrow button, and the user can scroll the list, showing as little as one item at a time, instead of the entire list. Second, you can control the height of the scrolling list, enabling it to display more than one item — or all available items — simultaneously. Third, you can enable the user to select more than one item at a time, as with checkboxes.

A scrolling list is inserted in the same manner as a drop-down menu — through the Objects panel or the Insert ⇨ Form Objects menu. Once the object is inserted, select the List option in the List/Menu Property Inspector.

You enter items for your scrolling list just as you do with a drop-down menu, by starting with the List Values button and filling in the List Values dialog box.

As it does for drop-down menus, Dreamweaver automatically shows the first list item in the scrolling list's single-line text box. However, all the list items are displayed in the Document window, as shown in Figure 15-8.

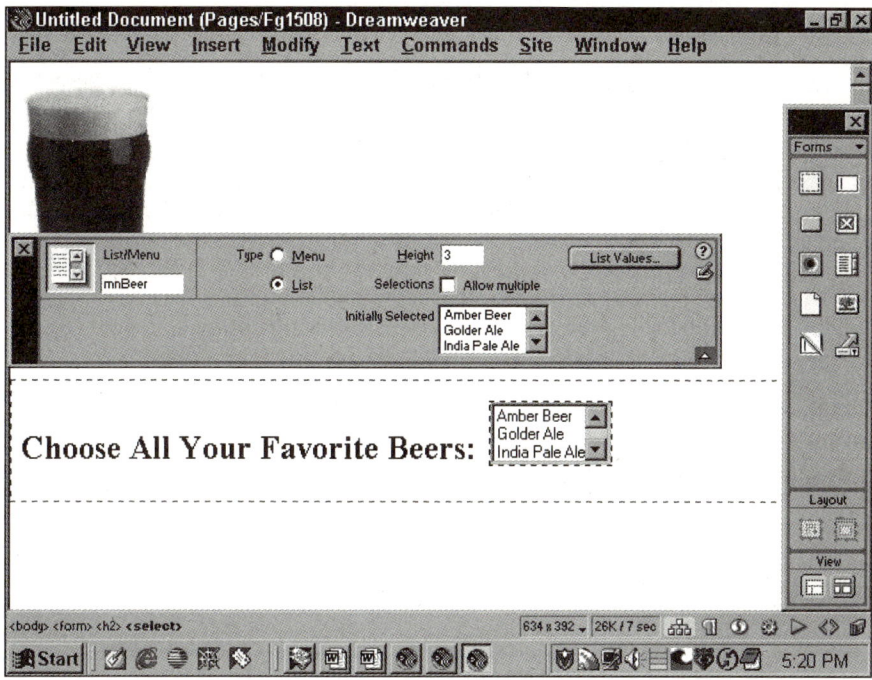

Figure 15-8: Scrolling lists enable multiple selections.

By default, the Selections checkbox for Allow multiple selections is enabled in the List/Menu Property Inspector, and the Height box (which controls the number of items visible at one time) is empty.

When multiple selections are enabled (by selecting the Allow multiple selections checkbox), the user can then make multiple selections by using two keyboard modifiers, the Shift and Control keys:

✦ To select several adjacent items in the list, the user must click the first item in the list, press the Shift key, and select the last item in the list.

✦ To select several nonadjacent items, the user must hold down the Control (Command) key while selecting the items.

Other than the highlighted text, no other acknowledgment (such as a checkmark) appears in the list. As with drop-down menus, the Web designer can preselect options by highlighting them in the Initially Selected menu. Use the same techniques with the Shift and Control (Command) keys as a user would.

Keep in mind several factors as you are working with scrolling lists:

✦ If you disable the Allow multiple selections box and do not set a Height value greater than 1, the list appears as a drop-down menu.

✦ If you do not set a Height value at all, the number of items that appear onscreen is left up to the browser. Internet Explorer, by default, shows four items at a time, and Navigator displays all the items in your list. To exercise control over your scrolling list, it is best to insert a Height value.

✦ The widths of both the scrolling list and the drop-down menu are determined by the number of characters in the longest label. To widen the List/Menu object, you must directly enter additional spaces ( ) in the HTML code; Dreamweaver does not recognize additional spaces entered through the List Values dialog box. For example, to expand the Favorite Beer List/Menu object in our example, you'd need to switch to Code view, or use the Code Inspector or an external text editor, to change the following code:

```
<option value="oatmeal">Oatmeal Stout</option>
```

to this:

```
<option value="oatmeal">Oatmeal Stout ¬
   </option>
```

Navigating with a Jump Menu

It's not always practical to use a series of buttons as the primary navigation tool on a Web site. For sites that want to offer access to a great number of pages, a *jump menu* can be a better way to go. A jump menu uses the menu form element to list the various options; when one of the options is chosen, the browser loads — or jumps to — a new page. In addition to providing a single mechanism for navigation, a jump menu is easy to update because it doesn't require relaying out the page. Because they are JavaScript-driven, jump menus can even be updated dynamically.

Dreamweaver includes a jump menu object that handles all the JavaScript coding for you — all you have to provide is a list of item names and associated URLs. Dreamweaver even drops in a Go button for you, if you choose. The Jump Menu object is easily used in a frame-based layout for targeting specific frames. Once inserted, the Jump Menu object is modified like any other list object, through the List/Menu Property Inspector.

To insert a jump menu, follow these steps:

1. Position your cursor in the current form, if one exists, where you'd like the jump menu to appear.

   If you haven't already inserted a form, don't worry. Dreamweaver automatically inserts one for you.

2. From the Forms category of the Objects panel, choose the Insert Jump Menu button.

   The Insert Jump Menu dialog box, shown in Figure 15-9, is displayed.

3. In the Insert Jump Menu dialog box, enter the label for the first item in the Text field.

When you confirm your entry by tabbing out of the field, Dreamweaver updates the Menu Items list.

4. Enter the path and filename of the page you want opened for the current item in the When Selected, Go To URL field; alternatively, you can select the Browse (Choose) button to select your file.

5. To add additional jump menu items, select the add (+) button and repeat Steps 3 and 4.

Figure 15-9: Consolidate your Web site navigation through a jump menu.

6. You can adjust the positioning of the items in the jump menu by selecting an item in the Menu List and using the up and down arrows to move it higher or lower.

7. Pick the destination target for the page from the Open URLs In list.

Unless you're working in a frameset, you have only one option — Main Window. When a Jump Menu object is added in a frameset, Dreamweaver displays all frame names as well as Main Window as options.

Tip

The Main Window option always replaces your current page with the new page. If you want to have your new page open in a separate window, and keep your current page active, you'll have to edit the HTML. Select the jump menu object on the page and open the Quick Tag Editor. In the code, locate the onChange event and change "parent" to "_blank." If you're working with a Go button, you need to follow the same procedure with the `onClick` event of the tag.

8. If desired, enter a unique name for the jump menu in the Menu Name field.

9. To add a button that activates the jump menu choice, select the Insert Go Button After Menu option.

10. To reset the menu selection to the top item after every jump, choose the Select First Item After URL Change.

11. Click OK when you're done.

Dreamweaver inserts the new jump menu with the appropriate linking code.

Modifying a jump menu

Once you've inserted your Jump Menu object, you can modify it in one of two ways: through the standard List/Menu Property Inspector or through the Jump Menu behavior. While the List Property Inspector uses a List Value dialog box, editing the Jump Menu behavior opens a dialog box similar to the one used to insert the jump menu object.

To alter the items in an existing jump menu via the List/Menu Property Inspector, select the jump menu and click the List Values button. In the List Values dialog box, you see the jump menu labels on the left and the URLs on the right. You can add, move, or delete items as you would with any other list.

Wrapping Graphics Around a Jump Menu

Jump menus are useful in many circumstances, but as a raw form element, they often stick out of a Web page design like a sore thumb. Some designers solve this dilemma by including their jump menu within a specially constructed graphic. The easiest way to create such a graphic is to use a program like Fireworks, which enables a single image to be sliced up into separate parts. The slices are then exported to an HTML file and reassembled in a table.

When you create your graphic, you need to leave room for the jump menu to be inserted in Dreamweaver. This usually entails designating one slice as a nongraphic or text-only slice in your graphics program. Fireworks uses a transparent GIF — called a *spacer image* — as a placeholder. Once you bring the HTML into Dreamweaver, delete the spacer image and insert the Jump Menu object in its place. The figure below shows a jump menu wrapped in a graphic.

Here are a few pointers for wrapping a graphic around a jump menu:

✦ Use a flat color — not a gradient — as the background for the menu.

✦ Select the background color of the graphic to be the background color of the cell of the table holding your jump menu.

✦ Make sure you leave enough height in your graphic to accommodate the jump menu in all browsers. Netscape displays a standard list/menu form element approximately 24 pixels high on a PC; I typically leave about 30 pixels in my graphic.

✦ Form elements are drawn by the user's operating system and are vastly different on each platform. Test your designs extensively.

✦ Integrate your Go button, if you're using one, right in the graphic. Be sure to set it as its own slice, so it comes in as a separate image and can be activated with a Jump Menu Go behavior.

Caution Note one caveat for adding new URLs to the jump menu through the Property Inspector: Any filenames with spaces or special characters should be URL-encoded. In other words, if one of your filenames is `about us.htm`, it should be entered using the hexadecimal equivalent for a space (%20): `about%20us.htm`.

If you'd prefer to work in the same environment as you did when creating the Jump Menu object, go the Behaviors panel route. Select the jump menu and from the Behaviors panel double-click the Jump Menu event. The Jump Menu dialog box opens — it is identical to the Insert Jump Menu dialog box except the Go button option is not available.

Activating Go buttons

The Dreamweaver jump menu is activated immediately whenever a user makes a choice from the list. So why would you want a Go button? The Go button, as implemented in Dreamweaver, is useful for selecting the first item in a jump menu list. To ensure that the Go button is the sole means for activating a jump selection, you need to remove an attached behavior. Select the jump menu item and then open the Behaviors panel. From the Behaviors panel, delete the Jump Menu event.

 Tip Some Web designers prefer to use a non-URL choice for the first item, such as "Please Select A Department." When entering such a non-URL option, set the Go to URL (or the Value in the List Value Properties) to #.

The generic Go button is a nice convenience, but it's a little, well, generic. To switch from a standard Go button to a graphical Go button of your choosing, follow these steps:

1. Insert the image that you want to use as your new Go button next to the jump menu.

2. With the new graphic selected, open the Behaviors panel.

3. Select Jump Menu Go from the Add Event drop-down list.

   Dreamweaver displays a dialog box showing all available jump menus.

4. Choose the name of the current jump menu from the Jump Menu Go dialog box list; click OK when you're done.

5. If necessary, delete the Dreamweaver-inserted Go button.

Activating Your Form with Buttons

Buttons are essential to HTML forms. You can place all the form objects you want on a page, but until your user presses that Submit button, there's no interaction between the client and the server. HTML provides three basic types of buttons: Submit, Reset, and Command buttons.

Submit, Reset, and Command buttons

A Submit button sends the form to the specified Action (generally the URL of a server-side program or a mailto address) using the noted Method (generally `post`). A Reset button clears all the fields in the form. Submit and Reset are both reserved HTML terms used to invoke specific actions.

A Command button permits the execution of functions defined by the Web designer, as programmed in JavaScript or other languages.

To insert a button in Dreamweaver, follow these steps:

1. Position the cursor where you want the button to appear. Then either select the Insert Button icon from the Form category of the Objects panel, or choose Insert ➪ Form Objects ➪ Button from the menu. Or you can simply drag the

Insert Button icon from the Objects panel and drop it into place on an existing form.

2. Choose the button Action type. As shown in Figure 15-10, the Button Property Inspector indicates that the Submit form button action is selected. (This is the default.) To make a Reset button, select the Reset form option. To make a Command button, select the None option.

3. To change the name of any button as you want it to appear on the Web page, enter the new name in the Label text box.

Tip

When working with Command buttons, it's not enough to just insert the button and give it a name. You have to link the button to a specific function. A common technique is to use JavaScript's `onClick` event to call a function detailed in the `<script>` section of the document:

```
<input type="BUTTON" name="submit2" value="yes" ¬
onClick="doFunction()">
```

Insert Button button

Figure 15-10: You can choose a function and a label for a button through the Button Property Inspector.

Graphical buttons

HTML doesn't limit you to the browser-style default buttons. You can also use an image as a Submit, Reset, or Command button. Dreamweaver has the capability to add an image field just like other form elements: Place the cursor in the desired position and choose Insert ➪ Form Objects ➪ Image Field, or select the Image Field icon from the Forms category of the Objects panel. You can use multiple image fields in a form to give the user a graphical choice, as shown in Figure 15-11.

When the user clicks the picture that you've designated as an image field for a Submit button, the form is submitted. Any other functionality, such as resetting the fields, must be coded in JavaScript or another language and triggered by attaching an onClick event to the button. This can be handled through the Dreamweaver behaviors, covered in Chapter 19 or by hand-coding the script and inserting the onClick code.

In fact, when the user clicks a graphical button, not only does it submit your form, but also it passes along the x, y coordinates of the image. The x coordinate is submitted using the name of the field and an .x attached; likewise, the y coordinate is submitted with the name of the field and a .y attached. Although this latter feature isn't often used, it's always good to know all the capabilities of your HTML tools.

Figure 15-11: Each flag in this page is not just an image; it's an image field that also acts as a Submit button.

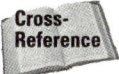 **Cross-Reference** For detailed information about how to use a graphic as a form button, see the section, "Posting Form Data with a Submit Button," in Chapter 17.

Using the Hidden Field and the File Field

You should also be aware of a couple of other special-purpose form fields. The *hidden field* and the *file field* are supported through all major browsers. The hidden field is extremely useful for passing variables to your gateway programs, and the file field enables the user to attach a file to the form being submitted.

The hidden input type

When passing information from a form to a CGI program, the programmer often needs to send data that should not be made visible to the user. The data could be a variable needed by the CGI program to set information on the recipient of the form, or it could be a URL to which the CGI program will redirect the user after the form is submitted. To send this sort of information unseen by the form user, you must use a hidden form object.

The hidden field is inserted in a form much like the other form elements. To insert a hidden field, place your cursor in the desired position and choose Insert ⇨ Form Objects ⇨ Hidden Field or choose the Insert Hidden Field icon from the Forms category of the Objects panel.

The hidden object is another input type, just like the text, radio button, and checkbox types. A hidden variable looks like this in HTML:

```
<input type="hidden" name="recipient" value="jlowery@idest.com">
```

As you would expect, this tag has no representation when it's viewed though a browser. However, Dreamweaver does display a Hidden Form Element Invisible symbol in the Document window. You can turn off the display of this symbol by deselecting the Hidden Form Element option from the Invisible Elements category of Preferences.

The file input type

Much more rarely used is the file input type, which enables any stored computer file to be attached to the form and sent with the other data. Used primarily to enable the easy sharing of data, the file input type has been largely supplanted by modern e-mail methods, which also enable files to be attached to messages.

The file field is inserted in a form much like the other form elements. To insert a file field, place your cursor in the desired position and choose Insert ⇨ Form Objects ⇨ File Field or choose the Insert File Field icon from the Forms category of the Objects panel. Dreamweaver automatically inserts a text box for the filename to be input, with a Browse (Choose) button on the right. In a browser, the user's selection of the Browse (Choose) button displays a standard Open File dialog box from which a file can be selected to go with the form.

Summary

HTML forms provide a basic line of communication from Web page visitor to Web page administrator. With Dreamweaver, you can enter and modify most varieties of form inputs, including text fields and checkboxes. This chapter covered the following important points:

✦ For the most part, a complete form requires two working parts: the form object inserted in your Web page and a CGI program stored on your Web server.

✦ To avoid using a server-side script, you can use a mailto address rather than a URL pointing to a program in a form's `action` attribute. However, you still have to parse the form reply to convert it to a usable format.

✦ The basic types of form input are text fields, text areas, radio buttons, checkboxes, drop-down menus, and scrolling lists.

✦ Dreamweaver includes a Jump Menu object, which uses a drop-down list as a navigational system.

✦ Once a form is completed, it must be sent to the server-side application. This is usually done through a Submit button on the form. Dreamweaver also supports Reset and user-definable Command buttons.

In the next chapter, you learn how to use Dreamweaver to develop frames and framesets.

✦   ✦   ✦

Using Frames and Framesets

Frames constitute one of the Webmaster's major design tools. A *frame* is a Web page that is subdivided into both static and changing HTML pages. Not too long ago, the evolution of frames was right where Dynamic HTML is today in terms of general acceptance. The use of frames and framesets has become even more widespread over the last year or so, and the technology is now supported through every major browser version. It's safe to say that every Web designer today needs a working knowledge of frames to stay competitive.

The first time I fully appreciated the power of frames, I was visiting a site that displayed examples of what the Webmaster considered "bad" Web pages. The site was essentially a jump-station with a series of links. The author used a frameset with three frames: one that ran all the way across the top of the page, displaying a logo and other basic information; one narrow panel on the left with a scrolling set of links to the sites themselves; and the main viewing area, which took up two-thirds of the center screen. Selecting any of the links caused the site to appear in the main viewing frame.

I was astounded when I finally realized that each frame was truly an independent Web page and that you didn't have to use only Web pages on your own site—you could link to any page on the Internet. That was when I also realized the amount of work involved in establishing a frame Web site: Every page displayed on that site used multiple HTML pages.

Dreamweaver takes the head-pounding complexity out of coding and managing frames with a point-and-click interface. You get easy access to the commands for modifying the properties of the overall frame structure as well as each individual frame. This chapter gives you an overview of frames, as well as all the specifics you need for inserting and modifying frames and framesets. Special attention is given to defining the unique look of frames through borders, scroll bars, and margins.

Frames and Framesets: The Basics

It's best to think of frames in two major parts: the frameset, and the frames themselves. The frameset is the HTML document that defines the framing structure — the number of individual frames that make up a page, their initial size, and the shared attributes among all the frames. A frameset by itself is never displayed. Frames, on the other hand, are complete HTML documents that can be viewed and edited separately or together in the organization described by the frameset.

A frameset takes the place of the `<body>` tags in an HTML document, where the content of a Web page is found. Here's what the HTML for a basic frameset looks like:

```
<frameset rows="50%,50%">
   <frame src="top.html">
   <frame src="bottom.html">
</frameset>
```

Notice that the content of a `<frameset>` tag consists entirely of `<frame>` tags, each one referring to a different Web page. The only other element that can be used inside of a `<frameset>` tag is another `<frameset>` tag.

Columns and rows

Framesets, much like tables, are made up of columns and rows. The columns and rows attributes (`cols` and `rows`) are lists of comma-separated values. The number of values indicates the number of either columns or rows, and the values themselves establish the size of the columns or rows. Thus, a `<frameset>` tag that looks like this:

```
<frameset cols="67,355,68">
```

denotes three columns of widths, 67, 355, and 68, respectively. And this frameset tag:

```
<frameset cols="270,232" rows="384,400">
```

declares that two columns exist with the specified widths (270 and 232) and two rows with the specified heights (384 and 400).

Sizing frames

Column widths and row heights can be set as absolute measurements in pixels, or expressed as a percentage of the entire screen. HTML frames also support an attribute that assigns the size relative to the other columns or rows. In other words, the relative attribute (designated with an asterisk) assigns the balance of the remaining available screen space to a column or row. For example, the following frameset:

```
<frameset cols="80,*">
```

sets up two frames, one 80 pixels wide and the other as large as the browser window allows. This ensures that the first column will always be a constant size — making it perfect for a set of navigational buttons — while the second is as wide as possible.

The relative attribute can also be used proportionally. When preceded by an integer, as in n*, this attribute specifies that the frame is allocated *n* times the space it would have received otherwise. So frameset code like this:

```
<frameset rows="4*,*">
```

ensures that one row is proportionately four times the size of the other.

Creating a Frameset and Frames

Dreamweaver offers several ways to divide your Web page into frames and make your frameset. The first method uses the menus. Choose Modify ⇨ Frameset and, from the submenu, select the direction in which you would like to split the frame: left, right, up, or down. Left or right splits the frame in half vertically; up or down splits it horizontally in half.

You can also create a frameset visually, using the mouse. To create frames with this method, follow these steps:

1. Turn on the frame borders in your Dreamweaver Document window by selecting View ⇨ Visual Aids ⇨ Frame Borders.

   A 3-pixel-wide inner border appears along the edges of your Document window.

2. Position the cursor over any of the frame borders.

3. Press Alt (Option).

   If your pointer is over a frame border, the pointer changes into a two-headed arrow when over an edge and a four-headed arrow (or a drag-hand on the Mac) when over a corner.

4. Drag the frame border into the Document window. Figure 16-1 shows a four-frame frameset being created.

Figure 16-1: After you've enabled the frame borders, you can drag out your frameset structure with the mouse.

Dreamweaver initially assigns a temporary filename and an absolute pixel value to your HTML frameset code. Both can be modified later, if you wish.

Tip   With the menu method of frameset creation, you can initially create only a two-way frame split. To further split the frame using the menu commands, you must first select each frame. However, by Alt+dragging (Option+dragging) the corner of the frame border, you can quickly create a four-frame frameset.

When the frameset is selected, Dreamweaver displays a black, dotted line along all the frame borders and within every frame. You can easily reposition any frameset border by clicking and dragging it. If you just want to move the border, make sure you don't press the Alt or Option key while dragging the border; this action creates additional frames.

Adding more frames

You're not at all limited to your initial frame choices. In addition to being able to move them visually, you can also set the size through the Frameset Property Inspector, as described in the next section. Furthermore, you can continue to split either the entire frame or each column or row as needed. When you divide a column or row into one or more frames, you are actually nesting one frameset inside another.

Tip Once you've created the basic frame structure, you can select View➪Frame Borders again (it's a toggle) to turn the borders off and create a more accurate preview of your page.

Using the menus

To split an existing frame using the menus, position the cursor in the frame you want to alter and choose Modify ➪ Frameset ➪ Split Frame Left, Right, Up, or Down. Figure 16-2 shows a two-row frameset in which the bottom row was split into two columns and then repositioned. The Frameset Property Inspector indicates that the inner frameset (2 columns, 1 row) is selected. The direction in the command (Left, Right, Up, and Down) indicates the frame the existing page will be placed in. For example, I selected Split Frame Right for Figure 16-2, and the current page is placed in the right frame.

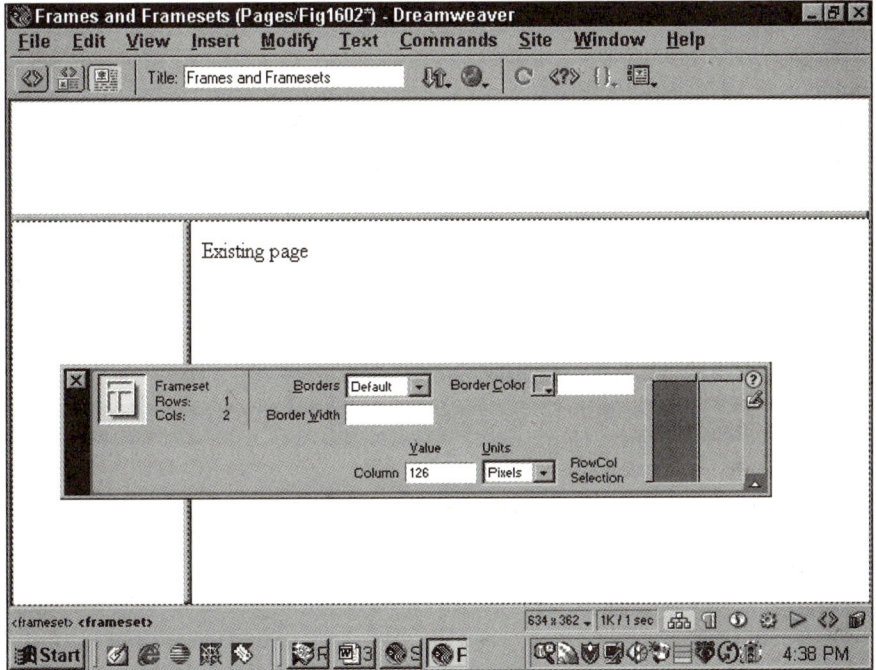

Figure 16-2: Use the Modify ➪ Frameset menu option to split an existing frame into additional columns or rows and create a nested frameset.

You can clearly see the "nested" nature of the code in this HTML fragment describing the frameset in Figure 16-2:

```
<frameset rows="163,333" cols="784">
  <frame src="file://Dev/UntitledFrame-34">
  <frameset cols="115,663" rows="*">
    <frame src="file://Dev/UntitledFrame-57">
    <frame src="file://Dev/UntitledFrame-35">
  </frameset>
</frameset>
```

 Tip   You can also split an existing frame by Alt+dragging (Option+dragging) the current frame's border, but you have to choose an inner border that does not extend across the page.

Using the mouse

When you need to create additional columns or rows that span the entire Web page, use the mouse method instead of the menus. Alt+drag (Option+drag) any of the current frame's borders that go across the entire page, such as one of the outer borders. Figure 16-3 shows a new row added along the bottom of our previous frame structure.

Figure 16-3: An additional frame row was added using the Alt+drag (Option+drag) method.

Tip   You can also split a smaller frame by first selecting it and then Alt+dragging or Option+dragging one of its borders. As you can see in this chapter, you select a frame by Alt+clicking (Windows) or Option+Shift+clicking (Macintosh) inside the frame.

Quick Framesets with the Frames Objects

Dragging out your frameset in Dreamweaver is a clear-cut method of setting up the various frames. However, now matter how easy it is, it can still be a bit of a chore to create even simple framesets by clicking and dragging. To hasten the development workflow, Dreamweaver uses Frame objects, which can build a frameset with a single click.

Although a frame-based Web design could potentially be quite complex with numerous nested framesets, most of the sites using frames follow a more simple, general pattern. Dreamweaver offers eight of the most common frameset configurations in the Frames category of the Objects panel, shown in Figure 16-4. Choose one of the basic designs, and you're ready to tweak the frame sizes and begin filling in the content. It's a great combination of ease-of-use mixed with design flexibility.

Figure 16-4: The Frames category of the Objects panel holds eight of the most commonly used frameset configurations.

The Frames category is roughly organized from simplest framesets to most complex. You might notice that each of the icons on the panel shows an example frameset with one blue section. The placement of the color is quite significant. The blue indicates in which frame the current page will appear when the frameset is constructed. For example, if I had begun to construct my main content page, and then decided to turn it into a frameset with a separate navigation strip frame beneath it, I would choose the Bottom Frames object. Figure 16-5 provides a before-and-after example with the preframe content on the left and the same content after a Bottom Frame object has been applied.

The eight different framesets available from the Frames category are:

✦ **Left:** Inserts a blank frame to the left of the current page.

✦ **Right:** Inserts a blank frame to the right of the current page.

✦ **Top:** Inserts a blank frame above the current page.

✦ **Bottom:** Inserts a blank frame below the current page.

✦ **Left and Top:** Makes a frameset with four frames where the current page is in the lower right.

✦ **Left Top:** Makes a frameset where the left spans the two rightmost frames; a nested frameset is used to create the right frames. The existing page is placed in the lower-right frame.

✦ **Top Left:** Makes a frameset where the top spans the lower two frames; the lower frames are created using a nested frameset. The existing page is placed in the lower-right frame.

✦ **Split:** Creates a frameset with four equal frames and moves the existing page to the lower right.

Using the Frames objects is quite literally a one-click operation. Just select the desired frameset, and Dreamweaver automatically turns on Frame Borders, if necessary, and creates and names the required frames. For all Frames objects, the existing page is moved to a frame where the scrolling option is set at Default, and the size is relative to the rest of the frameset. In other words, the existing page can be scrolled and expands to fill the content. For this reason, it's best to apply a Frames object to an existing page only if it is intended to be the primary content frame. Otherwise, it's better to select the Frames object while a blank page is open and then use the File ➪ Open in Frame command to load any existing pages into the individual frames.

Note

For almost all of the Frames objects, Dreamweaver creates one or more frames with a set size. Although by default, the set width or height is 80 pixels, you can easily resize the frame by dragging the frame border. The only frameset that does not have at least one set frame is the Split object where the four frames are divided equally. Dreamweaver also sets the Scroll option to No for frames with absolute sizes.

Before Bottom Frame object has been applied.

After Bottom Frame Object has been applied.

Figure 16-5: Existing content is incorporated in a new frameset when a Frames object is chosen.

Working with the Frameset Property Inspector

The Frameset Property Inspector manages those elements, such as the borders, that are common to all the frames within a frameset; it also offers more precise sizing control over individual rows and columns than you can do visually. To access the Frameset Property Inspector, choose Window ⇨ Properties, if the Property Inspector is not already open, and then select any of the frame borders.

Tip   When a browser visits a Web page that uses frames, it displays the title found in the frameset HTML document for the entire frame. The easiest method to set that title is to select the frameset and then enter the name directly in the Title field of the toolbar, if visible. You can also set the title by selecting the frameset and then choosing Modify ⇨ Page Properties. In the Page Properties dialog box, enter your choice of title in the Title text box, as you would for any other Web page. All the other options in the Page Properties dialog box — including background color and text color — apply to the <noframes> content, covered in the section "Handling Frameless Browsers," later in this chapter.

Resizing frames in a frameset

With HTML, when you want to specify the size of a frame, you work with the row or column in which the frame resides. Dreamweaver gives you two ways to alter a frame's size: by dragging the border or, to be more precise, by specifying a value in the Frameset Property Inspector.

As shown in Figure 16-6, Dreamweaver's Frameset Property Inspector contains a Row/Column selector to display the structure of the selected frameset. For each frameset, you select the tab along the top or left side of the Row/Column selector to choose the column or row you want to modify.

Row/Column selector tabs

Figure 16-6: In the Frameset Property Inspector, you use the Row/Column Selector tabs to choose which frame you are going to resize.

Tip   The Row/Column Selector shows only one frameset at a time. So if your design uses nested framesets, you won't see an exact duplicate of your entire Web page in the Row/Column Selector.

Whether you need to modify just a row, a column, or both a row and a column depends on the location of the frame.

✦ If your frame spans the width of an entire page, like the top or bottom row in Figure 16-3, select the corresponding tab on the left side of the Row/Column Selector.

✦ If your frame spans the height of an entire page, select the equivalent tab along the top of the Row/Column Selector.

✦ If your frame does not span either height or width, like the middle row in Figure 16-3, you need to select both its column and its row and modify the size of each in turn.

Once you have selected the row or column, follow these steps to specify its size:

1. To specify the size in pixels, enter a number in the Frameset Property Inspector's Value text box and select Pixels as the Units option.

2. To specify the size as a percentage of the screen, enter a number from 1 to 100 in the Value text box and select Percent as the Units option.

3. To specify a size relative to the other columns or rows, first select Relative as the Units option. Now you have two options:

   • To set the size to occupy the remainder of the screen, delete any number that may be entered in the Value text box; optionally, you can enter 1.

   • To scale the frame relative to the other rows or columns, type the scale factor in the Value text box. For example, if you want the frame to be twice the size of another relative frame, put a 2 in the Value text box.

Tip   The Relative size operator is generally used to indicate that you want the current frame to take up the balance of the frameset column or row. This makes it easy to specify a size without having to calculate pixel widths and ensures that the frame has the largest possible size.

Manipulating frameset borders

By default, Dreamweaver sets up your framesets so all the frames have gray borders that are 6 pixels wide. You can alter the border color, change the width, or eliminate the borders altogether. All of the border controls are handled through the Frameset Property Inspector.

Tip   Border controls for individual frames also exist. Just as table cell settings can override options set for the entire table, the individual frame options override those determined for the entire frameset, as described in the section "Working with the Frame Property Inspector," later in this chapter. Use the frameset border controls when you want to make a global change to the borders, such as turning them all off.

If you are working with nested framesets, it's important that you select the outer-most frameset before you begin making any modifications to the borders. You can tell that you've selected the outermost frameset by looking at the Dreamweaver Tag Selector; it shows only one <frameset> in bold. If you select an inner nested frame-set, you see more than one <frameset> in the Tag Selector.

Eliminating borders

When a frameset is first created, Dreamweaver leaves the borders display up to the browser's discretion. You can expressly turn the frameset borders on or off through the Frameset Property Inspector.

To eliminate borders completely, enter a zero in the Border Width text box. Even if no width value is displayed, the default is a border 6 pixels wide. If you turn off the borders for your frameset, you can still work in Dreamweaver with View ➪ Visual Aids ➪ Frame Borders enabled, which gives you quick access to modifying the frameset. The borders are not displayed, however, when your Web page is pre-viewed in a browser.

Border appearance options

You can control the appearance of your borders to a limited degree. In the Borders drop-down list of options, choosing Yes causes browsers to draw the borders with a 3D appearance. Select No, and the frameset borders are drawn as a single color. Browsers generally interpret the three-dimensional look as the default option.

Border color options

To change the frameset border color, select the Border Color text box and then enter either a color name or a hexadecimal color value. You can also select the color swatch and choose a new border color from the browser-safe color picker. Clicking the Palette icon on the color picker opens the extended color selector, just as for other color swatches in Dreamweaver.

Caution   If you have nested framesets on your Web page, make sure you've selected the correct frameset before you make any modifications through the Frameset Property Inspector. You can move from a nested frameset to its "parent" by using the keyboard shortcut Alt+up arrow (Command+up arrow). Likewise, you can move from a parent frameset to its "child" by pressing Alt+down arrow (Command+down arrow).

Saving a frameset and frames

As mentioned earlier, when you're working with frames, you're working with multi-ple HTML files. You must be careful to save not only all the individual frames that make up your Web page but also the frameset itself.

Dreamweaver makes it easy to save framesets and included frames by providing several special commands. To save a frameset, choose File ⇨ Save Frameset to open the standard Save File dialog box. You can also save a copy of the current frameset by choosing File ⇨ Save Frameset As. You don't have to select the frameset border or position your cursor in any special place to activate these functions.

Saving each frame in the frameset can be a chore unless you choose File ⇨ Save All Frames. The first time this command is invoked, Dreamweaver cycles through each of the open frames and displays the Save File dialog box. Each subsequent time you choose File ⇨ Save All Frames, Dreamweaver automatically saves every updated file in the frameset.

To copy an individual frame, you must use the regular File ⇨ Save As command.

Closing a frameset

There's no real trick to closing a Dreamweaver frameset: just choose File ⇨ Close. If the frameset is your last open file, Dreamweaver asks if you'd like to quit the program (unless you've previously selected the Don't Ask Me Again option).

Modifying a Frame

What makes the whole concept of a Web page frameset work so well is the flexibility of each frame.

✦ You can design your page so that some frames are fixed in size while others are expandable.

✦ You can attach scroll bars to some frames and not others.

✦ Any frame can have its own background image, and yet all frames can appear as one seamless picture.

✦ Borders can be enabled — and colored — for one set of frames but left off for another set.

Dreamweaver uses a Frame Property Inspector to specify most of a frame's attributes. Others are handled through devices already familiar to you, such as the Page Properties dialog box.

Page properties

Each frame is its own HTML document, and as such, each frame can have independent page properties. To alter the page properties of a frame, position the cursor in the frame and then choose Modify ⇨ Page Properties. You can also use the keyboard shortcuts, Ctrl+J or Command+J. Or you can select Page Properties from the shortcut menu by right-clicking (Control+clicking) any open space on the frame's page.

Joining Background Images in Frames

One popular technique is to insert background images into separate frames so they blend into a seamless single image. This takes careful planning and coordination between the author of the graphic and the designer of the Web page.

To accomplish this image consolidation operation, you must first "slice" the image in an image-processing program, such as Fireworks or Adobe Photoshop. Then save each part as a separate graphic, making sure that no border is around these image sections — each cut-up piece becomes the background image for a particular frame. Next, set the background image of each frame to the matching graphic. Be sure to turn off the borders for the frameset and set the Border Width to zero.

You can find a command on the CD-ROM that accompanies this book to help you eliminate your borders. Look for the Zero Page Borders Command in Andrew Wooldridge's folder.

Correct sizing of each piece is important to ensure that no gaps appear in your joined background. A good technique is to use absolute pixel measurements for images that fill the frame and, where the background images tile, set the frame to Relative spacing. In the following figure, the corner frame has the same measurement as the background image (107×126 pixels), and all the other frames are set to Relative.

From the Page Properties dialog box, you can assign a title, although it is not visible to the user unless the frame is viewed as a separate page. If you plan on using the individual frames as separate pages in your `<noframes>` content (see "Handling Frameless Browsers" at the end of this chapter), it's good practice to title every page. You can also assign a background and the various link colors by selecting the appropriate color swatch or entering a color name into the correct text box.

Working with the Frame Property Inspector

To access the Frame Property Inspector, you must first select a frame. Selecting a frame is different from just positioning the cursor in the frame. You have two ways to properly select a frame: using the Frames panel or using the mouse in the Document window.

The Frames panel shows an accurate representation of all the frames in your Web page. Open the Frames panel by choosing Window ➪ Frames. As you can see in Figure 16-7, the Frames panel displays names, if assigned, in the individual frames, and (no name) if not. Nested framesets are shown with a heavier border.

Figure 16-7: Use the Frames panel to visually select a frame to modify.

To select a frame, click directly on its represented image in the Frames panel. If the Frame Property Inspector is open, it reflects the selected frame's options. For more complex Web pages, you can resize the Frames panel to get a better sense of the page layout. To close the Frames panel, select the Close button or choose Window ➪ Frames again.

Tip

When you are working with multiple framesets, use the Tag Selector together with the Frames panel to identify the correct nested frameset. Selecting a frameset in the Tag Selector causes it to be identified in the Frames panel with a heavy black border.

To select a frame with the mouse, press Alt (Option+Shift) and click in the desired frame. Once the frame is selected, you can move from one frame to another by pressing Alt (Command) and then using the arrow keys.

Naming your frames

Naming each frame is essential to getting the most power from a frame-structured Web page. The frame's name is used to make the content inserted from a hyperlink appear in that particular frame. For more information about targeting a link, see the section "Targeting Frame Content," later in this chapter.

Frame names must follow specific guidelines, as explained in the following steps:

1. Select the frame you want to name. You can either use the Frames panel or Alt+click (Option+Shift+click) inside the frame.

2. If necessary, open the Property Inspector by choosing Window ➪ Properties.

3. In the Frame Property Inspector, shown in Figure 16-8, add the frame's name in the text box next to the frame logo. Frame names have the following restrictions:

   • You must use one word, with no spaces.

   • You may not use special characters such as quotation marks, question marks, and hyphens.

   • You may use the underscore character.

   • You may not use certain frame names: `_blank`, `_parent`, `_self`, and `_top`.

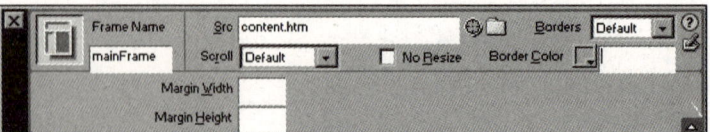

Figure 16-8: The Frame Property Inspector enables you to name your frame and control all of a frame's attributes.

Opening a Web page into a frame

You don't have to build all Web pages in frames from scratch. You can load an existing Web page into any frame. If you've selected a frame and the Frame Property Inspector is open, just type the link directly into the Src text box or choose the folder icon to browse for your file. Or you can position your cursor in a frame (without selecting the frame) and choose File ➪ Open in Frame.

Setting borders

You can generally set most border options adequately in the Frameset Property Inspector; you can also override some of those options, such as color, for each frame. These possibilities have practical limitations, however.

To set borders from the Frame Property Inspector for a selected frame, you can make the borders three-dimensional by choosing Yes in the Borders drop-down option list, or use the monochrome setting by choosing No. Leaving the Borders option at Default gives control to the frameset settings. You can also change a frame's border color by choosing the Border Color swatch in a selected frame's Property Inspector.

Now, about those limitations: They come into play when you try to implement one of your border modifications. Because frames share common borders, it is difficult to isolate an individual frame and have the change affect just the selected frame. As an example, Figure 16-9 shows a frameset in which the borders are set to No for all frames except the one on the lower right. Notice how the left border of the lower-right frame extends to the top, all the way over the upper frame. You have two possible workarounds for this problem. First, you can design your frames so that their borders do not touch, as in a multi-row frameset. Second, you can create a background image for a frame that includes a border design.

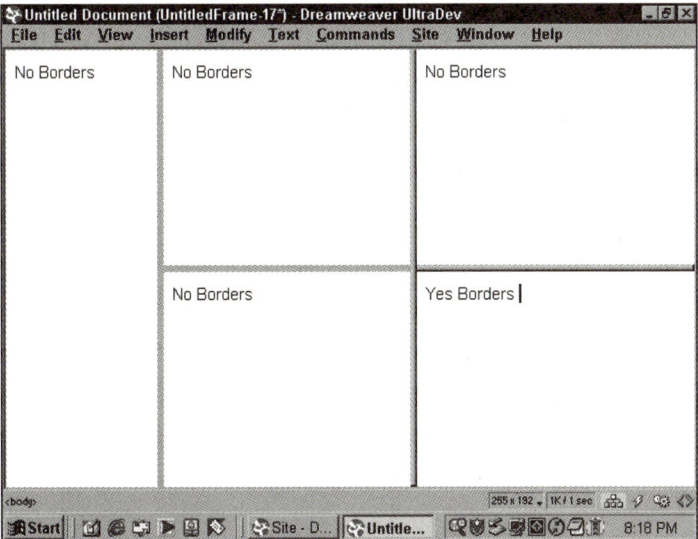

Figure 16-9: If you want to use isolated frame borders, you have to carefully plan your Web page frameset to avoid overlapping borders.

Adding scroll bars

One of the features that has given frames the wide use they enjoy is the capability to enable or disable scroll bars for each frame. Scroll bars are used when the browser window is too small to display all the information in the Web page frame. The browser window size is completely user controlled, so the Web designer must apply the various scroll bar options on a frame-by-frame basis, depending on the look desired and the frame's content.

Four options are selectable from the Scroll drop-down list on the Frame Property Inspector:

✦ **Default:** Leaves the use of scroll bars up to the browser.

✦ **Yes:** Forces scroll bars to appear regardless of the amount of content.

✦ **No:** Disables scroll bars.

✦ **Auto:** Turns scroll bars on if the content of the frame extends horizontally or vertically beyond what the browser window can display.

Figure 16-10 uses an automatic vertical scroll bar in the lower frame; you can see it on the far right.

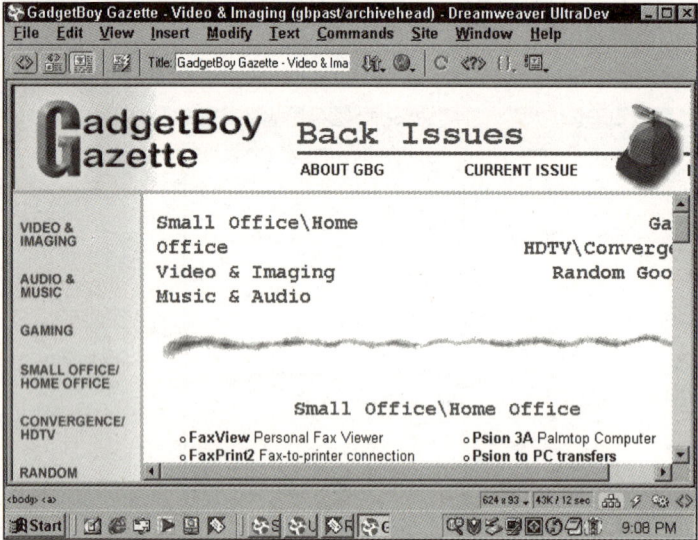

Figure 16-10: The top frame of the Web page has the scroll bars turned off, and the bottom-right frame has scroll bars enabled.

Resizing

By default, all frames are resizable by the user; that is, a visitor to your Web site can widen, narrow, lengthen, or shorten a frame by dragging the border to a new position. You can disable this resizing capability, however, on a frame-by-frame basis. In the Frame Property Inspector, select the No Resize option to turn off the resizing feature.

Tip

Although it might be tempting to select No Resize for every frame, it's best to enable resizing, except in frames that require a set size to maintain their functionality (for instance, a frame containing navigational controls).

Setting margins

Just as you can pad table cells with additional space to separate text and graphics, you can offset content in frames. Dreamweaver enables you to control the left/right margins and the top/bottom margins independently. By default, about 6 pixels of space are between the content and the left or right frame borders, and about 15 pixels of space are between the content and the top or bottom frame borders. You can increase or decrease these margins, but even if you set the values to zero, some room still exists between the borders and the content.

To alter the left and right margins, change the value in the Frame Property Inspector's Margin Width text box; to change the top and bottom margins, enter a new value in the Margin Height text box. If you don't see the Margin Width and Height text boxes, select the Property Inspector expander arrow.

Modifying content

You can update a frame's content in any way you see fit. Sometimes, it's necessary to keep an eye on how altering a single frame's content affects the entire frameset. Other times, it is easier — and faster — to work on each frame individually and later load them into the frameset to see the final result.

With Dreamweaver's multiwindow structure, you can have it both ways. Work on the individual frames in one or more windows and the frameset in yet another.

Although switching back to the frameset window won't automatically update it to show your changed frames, you can use one shortcut. After saving changes in the full frame windows, go to the frameset window. In any window you've altered elsewhere, make another small change, such as inserting a space. Then, choose File ➪ Revert. This command is normally used to revert to the previously saved version, but in this case, you're using it to update your frames.

Caution   To preview changes made to a Web page using frames, you must first save the changed files. Currently, Dreamweaver creates a temporary file of the frameset, but not any of the included frames.

Deleting frames

As you're building your Web page frameset, you inevitably try a frame design that does not work. How do you delete a frame once you've created it? Click the frame border and drag it into the border of the enclosing, or parent, frame. When no parent frame is present, drag the frame border to the edge of the page. If the frame being deleted contains any unsaved content, Dreamweaver asks if you'd like to save the file before closing it.

Tip Because the enclosing frameset and each individual frame are all discrete HTML pages, each keeps track of its own edits and other changes — and therefore each has its own Undo memory. If you are in a particular frame and try to undo a frameset alteration, such as adding a new frame to the set, it won't work. To reverse an edit to the frameset, you have to select the frameset and then choose File ⇨ Undo, or use one of the keyboard shortcuts (Ctrl+Z or Command+Z). To reverse the creation of a frameset, you must select Undo twice.

Targeting Frame Content

One of the major uses of frames is for navigational control. One frame acts as the navigation center, offering links to various Web pages in a site. When the user selects one of the links, the Web page appears in another frame on the page; and that frame, if necessary, can scroll independently of the navigation frame. This technique keeps the navigation links always visible and accessible.

When you assign a link to appear in a particular frame of your Web page, you are said to be assigning a target for the link. You can target specific frames in your Web page, and you can target structural parts of a frameset. In Dreamweaver, targets are assigned through the Text and Image Property Inspectors.

Targeting sections of your frameset

In the earlier section on naming frames, you learned that certain names are reserved. These are the four special names HTML reserves for the parts of a frameset that are used in targeting: _blank, _parent, _self, and _top. With them, you can cause content from a link to overwrite the current frame or to appear in an entirely new browser window.

To target a link to a section of your frameset, follow these steps:

1. Select the text or image you want to use as your link.

2. In the Text (or Image) Property Inspector, enter the URL and/or named anchor in the Link text box. Alternatively, you can select the folder icon to browse for the file.

3. Select the Target text box. You may need to expand the Image Property Inspector to see the Target text box.

4. Select one of the following reserved target names from the drop-down list of Target options (see Figure 16-11) or type an entry into the text box:

   • **_blank:** Opens the link into a new browser window and keeps the current window available.

   • **_parent:** Opens the link into the parent frameset of the current frame, if any.

- **_self:** Opens the link into the current frame, replacing its contents (the default).

- **_top:** Opens the link into the outermost frameset of the current Web page, replacing all frames.

Figure 16-11: Choose your frame target from the Property Inspector's Target drop-down list.

The generic nature of these reserved target names enables them to be used repeatedly on different Web pages, without your having to code a particular reference each time.

For an example of structural targeting, look at the code for the Dreamweaver Help system. The Index frame, for example, uses the implied _self target whenever a major Help topic is selected to open an HTML document that shows all the subtopics.

Caution A phenomenon known as *recursive frames* can be dangerous to your site setup. Let's say you have a frameset named index_frame.html. If you include in any frame on your current page a link to index_frame.html and set the target as _self, when the user selects that link, the entire frameset loads into the current frame — including another link to index_frame.html. Browsers can handle about three or four iterations of this recursion before they crash. To avoid the problem, set your frameset target to _top.

Targeting specific frames in your frameset

Earlier I stressed the importance of naming each frame in your frameset. Once you have entered a name in the Name text box of the Frame Property Inspector, Dreamweaver dynamically updates the Target list to include that name. This feature enables you to target specific frames in your frameset in the same manner that you target the reserved names noted previously.

Although you can always type the frame name directly in the Name text box, the drop-down option list comes in handy for this task. You avoid not only having to keep track of the various frame names in your Web page, but you avoid typing errors as well. Targets are case-sensitive, and names must match exactly or the browser won't be able to find the target.

Updating two frames or more at once

Sooner or later, most Web designers using frames have the need to update more than one frame with a single click. The problem is, you can't group two or more URLs together in an anchor tag. Here is an easy-to-implement solution, thanks to Dreamweaver's behaviors.

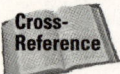 If you're not familiar with Dreamweaver's JavaScript behaviors, you might want to look over Chapter 19 before continuing.

To update more than one frame target from a single link, follow these steps:

1. Select your link in the frame.

2. Open the Behaviors panel from the Launcher or by choosing Window ⇨ Behaviors.

3. Make sure that 4.0 Browsers is selected in the Show Events For category of the add behavior button on the Behaviors panel.

4. Select the + (add behavior) button to display the list of available behaviors.

5. Choose Go To URL from the drop-down option list.

6. Dreamweaver displays the Go To URL dialog box (Figure 16-12) and scans your document for all named frames. Select a target frame from the list of windows or frames.

Figure 16-12: You can cause two or more frames to update from a single link by using Dreamweaver's Go To URL behavior.

 You won't be able to use this behavior until you name your frames as detailed in the section "Naming your frames" earlier in this chapter.

7. Enter a URL or choose the Browse (Choose) button to select one.

Dreamweaver places an asterisk after the targeted frame to indicate that a URL has been selected for it. You can see this in Figure 16-12.

8. Repeat Steps 6 and 7 for any additional frames you want to target.

9. Click OK when you're finished.

   Dreamweaver automatically selects the `onClick` event for the Go To URL behavior.

Now, whenever you click your one link, the browser opens the URLs in the targeted frames in the order specified.

Handling Frameless Browsers

Not all of today's browsers support frames. Netscape began supporting frames in Navigator version 2.0; Microsoft didn't start until IE version 3.0—and a few of the earlier versions for both browsers are still in use, particularly among AOL users. Some less prevalent browsers also don't support frames. HTML has a built-in mechanism for working with browsers that are not frame-enabled: the `<noframes>...</noframes>` tag pair.

When you begin to construct any frameset, Dreamweaver automatically inserts a `<noframes>` area just below the closing `</frameset>` tag. If a browser is not frames-capable, it ignores the frameset and frame information and renders what is found in the `<noframes>` section.

What should you put into the `<noframes>` section? To ensure the widest possible audience, Webmasters typically insert links to a nonframe version of the site. The links can be as obvious or as discreet as you care to make them. Perhaps a more vital reason is that most of the search engine indexing systems (called *spiders*) don't work with frames. If your frameset is index.html and you want the spider to find the rest of your site, you need to have a descriptive text from your home page as well as a link to each page in the noframes content. Many Webmasters also include links to current versions of Netscape or Internet Explorer, to encourage their nonframe-capable visitors to upgrade.

Dreamweaver includes a facility for easily adding and modifying the `<noframes>` content. Choose Modify ➪ Frameset ➪ Edit NoFrames Content to open the NoFrames Content window. As you can see in Figure 16-13, this window is identical to the regular Dreamweaver Document window, with the exception of the "NoFrames Content" in the title bar. In this window, you have access to all the same objects and panels that you normally do. When you have finished editing your `<noframe>` content, choose Modify ➪ Frameset ➪ Edit NoFrames Content again to deselect the option and return to the frameset.

Figure 16-13: Through the Edit NoFrames Content command, Dreamweaver enables you to specify what's seen by visitors whose browsers are not frame-capable.

Here are some pointers to keep in mind when working in the NoFrames Content window:

✦ The page properties of the `<noframes>` content are the same as the page properties of the frameset. You can select the frameset and then choose Modify ➪ Page Properties to open the Page Properties dialog box. While in the NoFrames Content window, you can also right-click (Control+click) in any open space to access the Page Properties command.

✦ Dreamweaver disables the File ➪ Open commands when the NoFrames Content window is onscreen. To move existing content into the `<noframes>` section, use Dreamweaver's Copy and Paste features.

✦ The `<noframes>` section is located in the frameset page, which is the primary page examined by search engine spiders. It's a good idea to enter `<meta>` tag information detailing the site, as described in Chapter 8, in the frameset page. While you're in the NoFrames Content window, you can switch to Code view, or open the Code Inspector, and add the `<meta>` tags.

Investigating Iframes

Iframes (short for inline frames) are an HTML 4.0 specification worth noting. An iframe is used to include one HTML document inside another — without building a frameset. What makes iframes visually arresting and extremely useful is their ability to display scroll bars automatically, as shown in Figure 16-14. While iframes are supported by Internet Explorer 4 and above and Netscape 6, you'll have to hand-code or use an extension to insert the tags into Dreamweaver; currently, no menu or object option exists within the standard configuration of Dreamweaver.

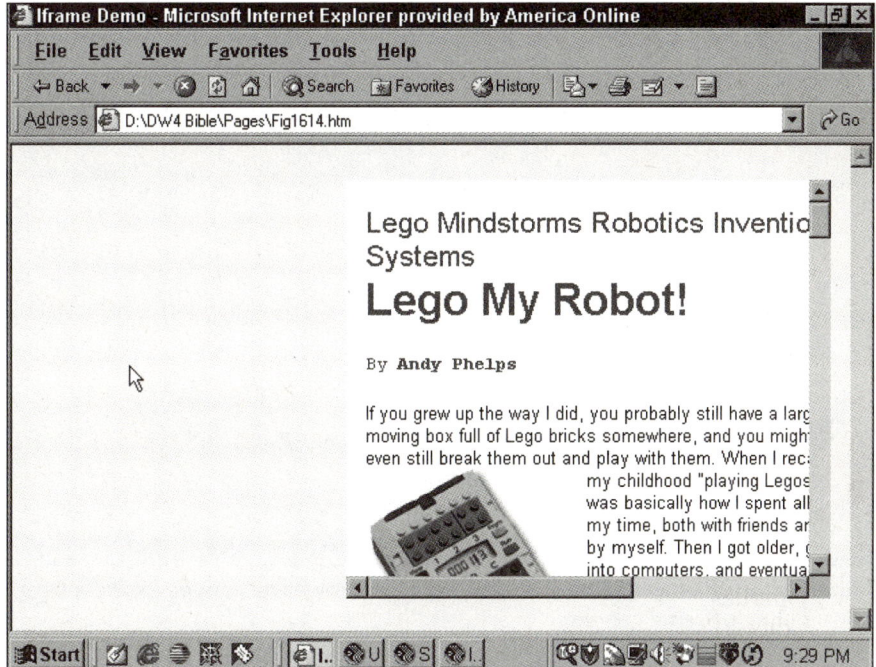

Figure 16-14: The iframe — also known as an inline frame — is a cutting-edge technique for including one HTML page within another.

The `iframe` tag uses the `src` attribute to specify which HTML file is to be included. Any content — whether text, images or whatever — found between the opening and closing `iframe` tags is displayed only if the browser does *not* support iframes. In other words, it's the no-iframe content. Here's an iframe code example:

```
<iframe src="/includes/salespromo.htm" name="promoFrame"
style="position:absolute; width:200px; height:300px; top:139px;
left:530px">Iframes are not supported by this browser.</iframe>
```

If you're familiar with Cascading Style Sheet layers, you'll notice that the style attribute is identical in iframes. This has an interesting effect in Dreamweaver: iframe code is displayed like a layer with the "no-iframe content" visible as shown in Figure 16-15. This makes positioning and resizing the iframe very straightforward. To see the actual iframe content, you'll need to preview the page in a compatible browser.

Figure 16-15: When you view an iframe tag in Dreamweaver, it appears like a layer showing the no-iframe content.

Can't wait to start using iframes but don't want to hand-code? Be sure to check out Massimo Foti's Iframe object, which takes advantage of Dreamweaver's interpretation of iframes as a layer. You'll find it under his name on the CD-ROM under Additional Extensions.

Summary

Frames are a significant Webmaster design tool. With frames and framesets, you can divide a single Web page into multiple, independent areas. Dreamweaver gives Web designers quick and easy access to frame design through the program's drag-and-drop interface.

✦ A framed Web page consists of a separate HTML document for each frame and one additional file that describes the frame structure, called the *frameset*.

✦ A frameset comprises columns and rows, which can be sized absolutely in pixels, as a percentage of the browser window, or relative to the other columns or rows.

✦ Dreamweaver enables you to reposition the frame borders by dragging them to a new location. You can also add new frames by Alt+dragging (Option+dragging) any existing frame border.

✦ Framesets can be nested to create more complex column and row arrangements. Selecting the frame border displays the Frameset Property Inspector.

✦ Select any individual frame through the Frames panel or by Alt+clicking (Option+Shift+clicking) within any frame. Once the frame is selected, the Frame Property Inspector can be displayed.

✦ You make your links appear in a specific frame by assigning targets to the links. Dreamweaver supports both structured and named targets. You can update two or more frames with one link by using a Dreamweaver JavaScript behavior.

✦ You should include information and/or links for browsers that are not frame-capable, through Dreamweaver's Edit NoFrames Content feature.

In the next chapter, you learn how to access external programs through your Web pages in Dreamweaver.

✦   ✦   ✦

Extending HTML Through Dreamweaver

♦ ♦ ♦ ♦

Accessing External Programs

Until recently, you could create relatively static Web pages made of text and images with "basic" HTML, but you needed additional code for more action. Without using some of the advanced capabilities of Dynamic HTML — viewable only with a fourth-generation browser — animated GIFs have been your sole option for any sort of motion on a self-contained Web page. HTML need not stand alone, however; the capabilities of the language can be extended using several methods.

You can do all of the following using external programs with HTML:

✦ Collect data from the user

✦ Add multimedia elements such as audio, video, animation, and virtual reality

✦ Enable a Web browser to present almost any kind of information in its native format

✦ Dynamically create Web pages based on a user's request

Dreamweaver gives you various methods — some specific to the file type and others more generic — for accessing a full range of external programs invaluable to the Web author. In this chapter, you learn how to send information to and from the server through CGI programs, install feature-extending Plugins and ActiveX controls, incorporate custom-built Java applets, and work with scripting languages such as JavaScript and VBScript.

Generally, the techniques for melding any of the external capabilities with your Web page are quite straightforward. Often, however, learning to use the outside program takes a fair amount of time — whether that program is writing your CGI script or encoding your digital video. You may want to approach each specific technique on a project-by-project basis, rather than try to master all the disciplines at once. No matter how you choose to work, you can always count on Dreamweaver's own extensibility to incorporate every new technology.

Using CGI Programs

When someone clicks a link to a Web page, a message is sent to a particular Web server, which then sends the components of that Web page — the HTML file and any associated graphic files — back to the user. Most information is usually sent over the Web from the server to the client. But how do you send information in the opposite direction, from the client to the server?

The standard method is to use a Common Gateway Interface (CGI) program. CGI programs, or scripts (the terms are used interchangeably), perform many different kinds of Internet functions, but they all entail collecting data from the user and passing it to the server. Whether the server stores the information in a database, manipulates it and passes it on to another system, or generates a new Web page to be sent to the user depends on the design of the CGI program.

Creating and calling scripts

CGI programs can be written in any number of computer languages, including C/C++, Fortran, Perl, TCL, Unix shell, Visual Basic, and AppleScript. The only requirement is that the program must be executable by the type of server processing the information. Perl (Program Extraction and Report Language) is one of the most popular languages used to write CGI programs. Perl is an interpreted language — that is, the source code is an ordinary text file compiled at runtime, unlike Java or C++ code, which are previously compiled. Because it is text-based, Perl is easy to modify and particularly strong in parsing and manipulating text — an important capability for interpreting data from forms and other Web-based tasks.

Perl, however, is difficult to debug — you don't get much in the way of error reporting from the Perl interpreter.

Note   Keep in mind that with CGI programs, you're essentially running a program on a different, remote computer and what's true for your computer setup may not be true for the server. Your best ally is the system administrator of your Web server. Chances are good that questions about running CGI programs have been asked many times before, and an FAQ or equivalent file is probably available.

Every CGI script must be customized to some extent in order to communicate with a particular server. You can develop your custom CGI program in two ways: build it from scratch yourself, or modify an existing script. Modifying an existing script is much easier and a customary practice on the Web. Someone else has probably already developed a CGI script for your situation, and it is probably available for download on the Internet.

Tip Three great sources for CGI scripts are Matt's Script Archives (`www.worldwidemart.com/scripts`); Extropia, formerly Selena Sol's Public Domain Archives (`www.extropia.com`); and—for all your scripting needs—The CGI-Resource Index (`www.cgi-resources.com`).

Once your CGI program is completed, three steps remain before it can be used:

✦ The CGI script must be uploaded to your Web server and stored in a special directory—often named cgi-bin.

✦ The file permissions need to be set depending on the program's function. File permissions determine whether a file can be read, written to, and/or executed and by whom. File permissions are explained in the following section.

✦ The CGI program must be referenced or called from the Web page.

Web designers most often use the HTML `<form>` structure to call a CGI script and simultaneously pass the data from the user to the server. Dreamweaver enables you to specify the necessary information through various form objects.

Setting file permissions in Dreamweaver

An important aspect of installing CGI programs is properly setting the file permissions for the CGI file. Because of security concerns, most Web servers restrict access on certain files to particular users. A file can be read, overwritten, or executed. With Unix servers, you can set these three operations for each of three different groups of people: the creator or owner of the file, the group administering the Web server, and outside visitors. These settings are called *file permissions*.

Typically, a CGI file is set to the following parameters:

✦ It can be read, overwritten, or executed by its owner.

✦ It can be read and executed by the administrative group but not overwritten.

✦ It can be read and executed by outside visitors but not overwritten.

File permissions are set on a Unix machine through the `site chmod` command issued directly to the server. The permissions previously listed are accomplished when the `site chmod` command is set to 755 and the filename is referenced, as follows:

```
site chmod 755 mailer.pl
```

To set the file permissions in Dreamweaver, follow these steps:

1. Open the Site window. Choose File ⇨ Open Site (Site ⇨ Open Site) and then select the site you want to work with from the submenu.

2. Go online and select the Connect button from the Site window.

3. From the Site window menus, choose Window ⇨ Site FTP Log (Site ⇨ FTP Log).

4. In the Site Log window's FTP command line, use the `site chmod` command with the appropriate code number and filename reference (see the example in Figure 17-1) and press Enter (Return).

The file permissions command

Figure 17-1: Before a CGI program can be used, the file permissions must be set through Dreamweaver's Site Log window.

On the CD-ROM   Jay London, a top Macromedia engineer, has created an extension that automates the procedure of setting permissions. After installing Set Permissions, right-click (Control-click) on any file on the remote site. From the context menu, choose Set Permissions and you'll be able to alter the file permissions through a graphical user interface. One caveat: The Set Permissions extension does not work with all servers.

Sending data to CGI programs

Two primary methods send data to the Web server for processing by a CGI script. The first technique attaches the information directly to a selected URL; another method uses a form to post the data when the user selects the Submit button.

The URL method is useful when you need to send known data. The form method is useful for sending variable or user-supplied information. Both techniques can be used within the Dreamweaver interface.

Passing data through a URL

Although the URL route is not as commonly employed as the forms method, certain information lends itself well to being passed to the server directly through a URL. Anytime you need to send a specific value to your CGI program, you can use the URL method.

Following is the general syntax of the statement that sends data to the URL. You use a question mark to separate the CGI program address from the data itself. The data takes the following form:

```
1st_field=value+2nd_field=value
```

In practice, information passed to a program via a link looks like the following:

```
<a href= "http://www.testcenter.com/cgi-bin/¬
response.pl?choice=left+entry=nada_ad">
```

In Dreamweaver, enter the data as part of the Link information, as shown in Figure 17-2. Most often, you should enter the URL to a CGI program as an absolute address, with the full "http://domain/path" attached, to properly reference the cgi-bin directory.

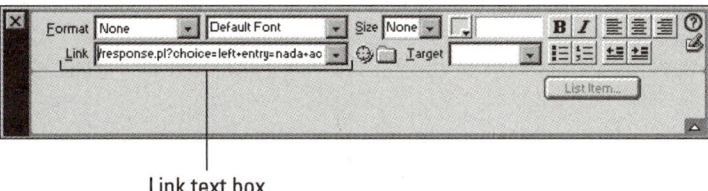

Link text box

Figure 17-2: In the Link text box, enter the specific information to be passed directly to a CGI program.

Using forms to send information

Forms are the most common method to transmit data from the user to a CGI program on a server. With the push of a single Submit button, all of the information the user has filled in or selected on the form — text, menu options, radio button options, and so forth — is sent. The data arrives in the program's standard input. The CGI script manipulates the data before sending it on to a database or in an e-mail message.

Cross-Reference　To find out more about building forms in Dreamweaver and the various form fields, see Chapter 15.

Most CGI scripts require that the form use the `post` method (as opposed to `get`) to send data to the server. When you first insert a form in Dreamweaver, you notice that the default method listed in the form's Property Inspector is POST, as shown in Figure 17-3.

Method option

Figure 17-3: Use the POST method to send information via a form to most CGI programs.

Aside from choosing a method, the only other task to ready a form for submission is to assign an action—which, oddly enough, is really the URL of the CGI program (see the Action box in Figure 17-3).

Again, this URL is most often supplied in absolute address form, like the following:

```
http://www.idest.com/cgi-bin/mailer.pl
```

Posting form data with a Submit button

Once you have set up the form properly and installed the Web page and corresponding CGI program, data is sent to the server when the user selects the Submit button. You don't need to assign an `onClick` or other event to the button.

As noted in Chapter 15, "Submit" and "Reset" are the default labels for these two buttons. You can easily modify the label of a button by entering new text in the Label text box, as shown in Figure 17-4.

With Dreamweaver, you can also use an image to create a graphical button for handling the submitting chores. However, it's necessary to use a little JavaScript—very little—to accomplish the task. Moreover, you currently have to hand-code the addition. Basically, you have to add a link tag (`<a>...</a>`) around the Image Field button that calls the JavaScript equivalent to Submit or Reset. The code refers to the form in which the button is located (here, "theForm") and uses the following format:

```
<a href="javascript:document.theForm.submit()"><img src=mySubmit></a>
```

I've bolded the additional code to make it easy to see. To make a Reset button, just substitute `reset()` for `submit()` in the preceding code.

Note   I've found it best to always be sure my form is named—doing so makes coding much simpler. Dreamweaver automatically names forms sequentially when they are inserted. The first form on a page, for example, is given the name `form1`. You can keep these names or give the forms your own names.

Label field

Figure 17-4: Change the text of the Submit and Reset buttons by entering a name in the Label field of the Property Inspector.

To use an image for a Submit button, follow these steps:

1. Choose Insert ➪ Image or select the Insert Image button from the Common category of the Objects panel.

2. In the Insert Image dialog box, enter the path to your image or select the folder icon to locate the file. The image can be in GIF, JPEG, or PNG format.

3. Give the image a name and, if desired, alternative text using the appropriate text boxes in the Property Inspector (see Figure 17-5).

4. In the Link field of the Property Inspector, enter the following code for a graphical Submit button:

```
javascript:document.form1.submit()
```

or this code for a Reset button:

```
javascript:document.form1.reset()
```

Note

Be sure to change the code to reflect your specifics: the name of your form as well as the name of your images.

Figure 17-5: You can substitute any valid graphic for the Submit button by using an image and JavaScript.

Using the Hidden Field

Many CGI scripts require that certain information not input by the user be submitted in order to process the form properly. A good example is a text string that tells the CGI program which fields of the form are required. This type of data is hidden from the user and passed to the program through the unseen form object, the appropriately named *Hidden Field*.

Although generally placed at the top of the form, Hidden Fields can be included anywhere between the <form> tag pair. You can include a Hidden Field by choosing the Insert Hidden Field button in the Forms category of the Objects panel or by selecting Insert ➪ Form Objects ➪ Hidden Field. Enter the information you want to pass to the CGI program in the Value text box of the Property Inspector, as shown in Figure 17-6.

When a Hidden Field is included in your form, Dreamweaver designates it with a Hidden Field icon. Like all invisible elements, the Hidden Field icon can be hidden by deselecting its option in the Invisible Elements category of Preferences.

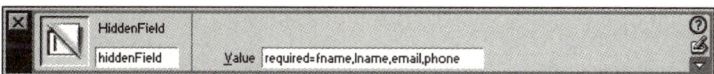

Figure 17-6: Pass variables that you want to remain unseen by your Web page visitor by using the Hidden Field in your form.

Incorporating Plugins

Plugins are small software programs introduced by Netscape to enable its browser to display many types of files, not only HTML. Although some of the most well-known Plugins are employed in the multimedia world — Macromedia's Shockwave, for example — hundreds of different kinds of Plugins are available for all kinds of files. Plugins are generally designed so that the document blends seamlessly with the other portions of the HTML page.

Note Keep in mind that you're not really inserting a Plugin; you're inserting a file that requires a Plugin. Although the Dreamweaver menus and dialog boxes refer to "inserting a Plugin," a reference to a specific file is actually inserted. That file is of a particular MIME (Multipurpose Internet Mail Extension), which tells the browser what kind of file is being called. Once the browser knows the file's MIME type, it can invoke the correct Plugin.

Just like Plugins, the code used to insert the Plugin was also originally developed by Netscape. Plugins are incorporated into HTML through the `<embed>` tag. Although Plugin features and their associated attributes vary widely, the minimum requirements for a Plugin are the source file and the dimensions (height and width) of the object. Typical HTML for a Plugin looks like the following:

```
<embed src="movies/oscars.avi" height="200" width="300">
```

Note Although Netscape developed the Plugin concept, Microsoft has embraced it to some degree. Internet Explorer recognizes the `<embed>` tag and works with some Plugins — even if an equivalent ActiveX control is unavailable.

Beyond the excitement and novelty that Plugins can add to your page, one inescapable fact remains: If a user doesn't have the Plugin installed, the Plugin file can't be experienced. Users generally have to download and install the Plugin — and then restart their browsers — before they can perceive any new material. Although this sequence is not a particularly difficult task, it nevertheless stops many people from viewing your creation in its entirety.

Tip Plugin Plaza (`http://browserwatch.internet.com/plug-in.html`) is an excellent resource for links to the entire spectrum of Plugins. You can access Plugins by category or by searching the entire list.

Dreamweaver has an open-ended approach to Plugins. After you've inserted the Plugin object, Dreamweaver displays a placeholder for it and enables you to enter the basic attributes through the Property Inspector (see Figure 17-7). Custom attributes are inserted through the Parameters dialog box. You can enter as many attributes as necessary.

Plugin Property Inspector   Plugin placeholder   Insert Plugin

Figure 17-7: Use the Plugin object from the Special category of the Objects panel to begin the process of embedding your Plugin.

Embedding a plugin and setting parameters

Dreamweaver provides a generic Plugin object available through the menus or through the Special category of the Objects panel. Like any other HTML object, a Plugin can be aligned with text or an image, or even included in a table. Some Plugins work automatically with no user interaction; others come with their own control panel.

To embed a Plugin into your Web page, follow these steps:

1. Insert the Plugin object by choosing Insert ➪ Media ➪ Plugin or by selecting the Plugin object from the Special category of the Objects panel. You can also drag the Insert Plugin object from the Objects panel to any place in the Document window with any existing text or object.

2. In the Select File dialog box, enter the path and filename for your Plugin file in the File Name text box, or select the Browse (Choose) button to locate your file.

   A placeholder icon for the Plugin appears in the Document window.

3. Size the Plugin placeholder with either of these methods:

   a. Enter the appropriate values in the W (Width) and the H (Height) text boxes of the Property Inspector.

   b. Click the resizing handles on the Plugin placeholder and drag out the placeholder to a new size.

4. In the Plg URL text box, enter the Internet address that visitors to your Web page can visit if they do not have the necessary Plugin installed. For example, in the case of QuickTime movies, you would use `http://quicktime.apple.com`.

5. To name the Plugin, enter a unique name in the unlabeled text box on the left side of the Property Inspector. Such names are useful when the Plugin is addressed from a JavaScript function.

6. To change the alignment relative to other inline objects, click the Align arrow button and choose one of the options in the drop-down list.

7. To add additional whitespace around the Plugin, enter pixel values in the V Space text box for the top and bottom of the object, and in the H Space text box for the left and right sides.

8. To surround the Plugin with a border, enter a pixel value in the Border text box.

9. To add additional attributes, select the Parameters button. These options are discussed in the following section.

Once you've entered the basic values for your Plugin, Dreamweaver enables you to preview it right in the Document window as well as through an appropriate browser. See the section "Playing Plugins," later in this chapter, for more details.

Because individual attributes for Plugins can take any form, Dreamweaver offers a completely generic method of entering parameters and associated values. Parameters generally fall into one of two categories: those that take a value and those that stand alone. You can enter both types through the Parameters dialog box.

To set additional parameters to a Plugin, follow these steps:

1. From the extended Property Inspector, select the Parameters button.

   The Parameters dialog box is displayed with its two columns: Parameters and Values.

2. Click the + (add) button and enter the first attribute in the Parameter column. Press Tab to move to the Value column and enter the desired value. If the attribute is a standalone and doesn't take a value, simply press Tab again to return to the Parameter column.

3. Repeat Step 2 until all parameters are entered. Press Shift+Tab to move backwards through the list.

4. To delete a parameter, highlight it and select the – (delete) button.

5. To move a parameter from one position in the list to another, highlight it and select the up- or down-arrow buttons in the Parameters dialog box, as shown in Figure 17-8.

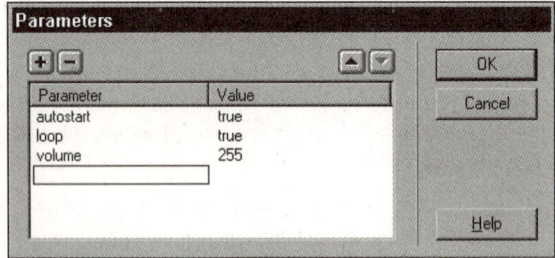

Figure 17-8: Enter specific attributes for each Plugin through the Parameters dialog box.

6. When you are finished inserting your parameters, click OK.

Caution Many Plugins require that the Web server recognize the affiliated MIME types. MIME types are a standard method of specifying various file formats. If your Plugin works locally but not remotely, the server probably needs to be configured for the particular MIME type. Contact your server administrator for further details.

Playing Plugins

Plugins were invented for browsers, by browsers. But you can play any file for which you have a Plugin right in Dreamweaver's Document window — and you can keep right on designing. Of course, you could use this capability to play an MP3 music file in the background as you work, but it really has far more practical uses.

One use for the Dreamweaver play Plugin feature is to align Web page elements with portions of your digitized video or Flash movie. Previously, this process involved flipping back and forth between the Dreamweaver Document window and the browser preview as you moved elements ever so slightly. Now, Dreamweaver's playback capabilities enable you to line up your static elements with the dynamic ones.

Dreamweaver can play any file that uses Plugins with the `<embed>` tag. Naturally, you have to have the Plugin installed on your local system. You can play any one selected Plugin file or all the Plugins on the page.

Tip   Dreamweaver looks in its own Configuration\Plugins folder as well as the Plugins folder of the installed Netscape browser to determine which Plugins are available. If you have it installed for Netscape, you don't have to reinstall it for Dreamweaver.

To play a selected Plugin, simply click the Play button (the green triangle) in the expanded Property Inspector. You can also choose View ➪ Plugins ➪ Play or use the keyboard shortcut Ctrl+Alt+P (Command+Option+P). To stop the Plugin from playing, click the red Stop button in the Property Inspector (Figure 17-9) or choose View ➪ Plugins ➪ Stop. The keyboard shortcut for stopping a Plugin from playing is Ctrl+Alt+X (Command+Option+X).

Figure 17-9: Files embedded in your Web page, such as this QuickTime movie, can be played back in the Document window as you design.

For the full effect on a media-rich page, play all the embedded Plugins at once. To do this, choose View ⇨ Plugins ⇨ Play All or use the keyboard shortcut Ctrl+Alt+Shift+P (Command+Option+Shift+P). You can stop any or all Plugins from playing by choosing View ⇨ Plugins ⇨ Stop All or by using the keyboard shortcut Ctrl+Alt+Shift+X (Command+Option+Shift+X).

Caution

Unfortunately, not all Plugins are created equal, and Dreamweaver can't play every one available. Dreamweaver maintains a list of those it can't play in the file UnsupportedPlugins.txt found in the Configuration/Plug-ins folder. As of this writing, no Plugins are noted as being "bad." Should you encounter any other Plugin that Dreamweaver cannot play, you can add its name to the UnsupportedPlugins.txt file, and Dreamweaver alerts you whenever you try to embed a file of this type.

Detecting particular Plugins

When a user visits your Web site via Netscape Navigator 3.0 or later, you can find out what Plugins are installed and act accordingly. You may, for example, want to redirect a user who can't accommodate Shockwave files to a separate, less media-intensive page. You can achieve this redirection by creating a mechanism within your page to recognize the Shockwave Plugin.

To detect the presence of a specific Plugin, you need to use a little JavaScript in the <head> section of your document. You also need to know either the official name of the Plugin or its MIME type. As an example, the following code checks for a Shockwave Plugin by name; if that name isn't found, the user is redirected to another page:

```
<script language="javascript">
if (!navigator.plugins['Shockwave for Director']){
location="http://www.nadaville.com/simple.html"
}
</script>
```

You can also have your document discover whether a particular MIME type is supported, regardless of which Plugin is used. This next example checks for anything that can play a .wav audio file and, if the means is found, plays some background music:

```
<script language="javascript">
if (navigator.mimetypes['audio/wav']){
document.write('<embed name="audioBG" src="moody.wav" loop=true
autostart=true hidden=true volume=100 height=2 width=2>');
}
</script>
```

Both of these if statements can be used to detect any Plugin and MIME type by simply substituting the appropriate Plugin name and the MIME type you are attempting to detect.

Tip   To see which Plugins are installed in your own system — and their proper names and MIME types — choose Help➪About Plug-ins from within Navigator or Communicator 4.*x*. In Netscape 6, type `about:plugins` in the Location bar and press Enter (Return).

Working with ActiveX Components

Microsoft developed ActiveX components largely in response to Netscape's Plugins, and although the two technologies are similar, some significant differences exist. Standing on the shoulders of Microsoft's Object Linking and Embedding (OLE) technology, ActiveX controls work only with Internet Explorer 3 and later. A Plugin that enables Navigator to run ActiveX components is available but not widely used. ActiveX technology is only available on the Windows platform.

ActiveX controls, although difficult to develop, are fairly easy to implement in any Web page. Aside from the usual attributes such as a source file and the object dimensions, ActiveX uses two special parameters: a Class ID and the `codebase` property.

The Class ID is a unique code used to identify the specific ActiveX control. Every ActiveX control has a Class ID that must be used when calling the control. The Class ID is a lengthy combination of numbers and letters; here's the RealPlayer ActiveX Class ID code:

```
CLSID:CFCDAA03-8BE4-11CF-B84B-0020AFBBCCFA
```

To escape the considerable risk of typing errors when entering a Class ID code, you should cut and paste the code.

The `codebase` property is an Internet location where the ActiveX control can be automatically downloaded and installed if the browser does not find the control on the user's system. The primary difference between ActiveX's `codebase` parameter and a Plugin's `pluginspage` attribute is that the ActiveX control can be transferred and installed without requiring the browser to close and restart. A typical `codebase` value follows — the Director 7 ActiveX control value:

```
http://download.macromedia.com/pub/shockwave/cabs/director/
sw.cab#version=7,0,2,0
```

Microsoft uses the `<object>...</object>` tag pair to include ActiveX controls in the HTML code. Unlike Netscape's `<embed>` tag, the `<object>` tag is recognized by the W3C as a valid specification for HTML 3.2 and later.

Note   Optimally, everyone would adhere to the same standard; however, because neither browser recognizes the other's tag 100 percent of the time, you can actually combine an `<object>` and an `<embed>` tag to cover both browsers. This procedure is explained in the following section.

Dreamweaver provides a separate object for adding ActiveX controls to your Web pages. In addition, Dreamweaver makes it easy to add those complex Class ID codes by maintaining a user-definable list — accessible right from the ActiveX Property Inspector.

Incorporating an ActiveX control

As with Plugins, Dreamweaver includes an ActiveX object to simplify inserting ActiveX controls. The primary difference between an ActiveX object and a Plugin object — aside from the two special ActiveX parameters previously noted — is the location for the ActiveX source file. For example, if you want to embed an ActiveX control to show a digital video in AVI format, you first insert the control object by selecting the Insert ActiveX button from the Special category of the Objects panel. Then you see the ActiveX Property Inspector (rather than an Insert ActiveX file dialog box). The source file is actually one of the parameters of the `<object>` tag, `FileName`, and must be entered through the Parameters dialog box (Embed Src text box).

Note   Although you see a Play button on the ActiveX Property Inspector, like the one on the Plugin Property Inspector, you can't actually play ActiveX files in the Document window. If you have checked the Embed option, the Play button uses the comparable Plugin to play the file if it's installed on your system.

Follow these steps to insert an ActiveX control into your Web page:

1. Position the cursor where you want the ActiveX file to appear. Choose Insert ⇨ Media ⇨ ActiveX or select the Insert ActiveX button from the Special category of the Objects panel.

   An ActiveX placeholder appears in the Document window, and the ActiveX Property Inspector displays (see Figure 17-10).

2. In the ClassID text box, enter the Microsoft ID for the ActiveX control.

Tip   If you've previously entered this particular Class ID, select the arrow button and choose the ID from the drop-down list, as shown in Figure 17-10.

3. Change the Width and Height values in the W and H text boxes to match the desired control display.

4. If you know the `codebase` URL, enter it in the Base text box.

5. Enter other relative parameters for the object as needed (see Table 17-1).

6. Click the Parameters button to display the Parameters dialog box.

7. Click the + (add) button and enter the first parameter: `FileName`. Press Tab to move to the Value column and enter the path and filename for your file.

8. Press Tab and continue entering the desired parameters in the left column, with their values in the right column. Click OK when you're finished.

9. Preview your ActiveX control in action through Internet Explorer 3 or 4.

Insert ActiveX   ActiveX Property Inspector   ActiveX placeholder

Figure 17-10: ActiveX controls are inserted with the help of Dreamweaver's ActiveX object and its Property Inspector.

Table 17-1 **ActiveX Object Properties**	
ActiveX Object Property	**Description**
Align	To alter the alignment of the ActiveX control, choose an option from the Align drop-down list. In addition to the Browser Default, your options include Baseline, Top, Middle, Bottom, Texttop, Absolute Middle, Absolute Bottom, Left, and Right.
Alt Image	Enter a path to an alternative image for display to browsers, such as Netscape, that don't understand the <object> tag. The Alt Image is available only if you are not using the Embed option. This image does not display in Dreamweaver.

Continued

	Table 17-1 *(continued)*
ActiveX Object Property	**Description**
Border	To place a border around your control, enter a number in the Border text box. The number determines the width of the border in pixels. The default is zero or no border.
Data	Specify a data file for the ActiveX control in this text box. Not all ActiveX controls use this attribute.
Embed	This property designates whether the matching code for the Plugin is to be included (see the following section "Combining ActiveX controls and Plugin objects," in this chapter).
H Space	You can increase the space to the left and right of the object by entering a value in the H (Horizontal) Space text box. The default is zero.
ID	The ID field is used to define the optional ActiveX ID parameter, most often used to pass data between ActiveX controls.
Name	If desired, you can enter a unique name in the unlabeled field at the left of the Property Inspector. JavaScript and VBScript use this name to identify the ActiveX control.
Src	This sets the source for the Plugin if the Embed checkbox is selected (as described in the following section).
V Space	To increase the amount of space between the top and bottom of the ActiveX object and the other elements on the page, enter a pixel value in the V (Vertical) Space text box. The default is zero.

Combining ActiveX controls and Plugin objects

Dreamweaver takes advantage of the fact that Netscape browsers do not recognize the <object> tag, and that Microsoft browsers ignore the <embed> tag placed inside the <object> tag. How could this be an advantage, you ask? Because of their mutual exclusivity, you can include both types of tags in the same Web page and still avoid conflicts.

The following example code shows you how the approach works in HTML. The <embed> section is bold to show how one tag fits within another.

```
<object width="137" height="136" classid="clsid:CFCDAA03-8BE4-11cf¬
-B84B-0020AFBBCCFA">
    <param name="FileName" value="images/braz.wav">
    <embed width="137" height="136" filename="images/braz.wav"
    src="images/braz.wav"></embed>
</object>
```

Notice the values common to both tags, including the dimensions and the source file. (The source file is the `src` attribute in `<embed>` and the `FileName` parameter in the `<object>` tag.) Dreamweaver automatically inserts these values when you enable the Embed option on the ActiveX Property Inspector.

Tip

If you're going to use the Embed option with your ActiveX object, you should wait until you've entered the necessary `FileName` parameter (through the Edit Parameters button) before you select the Embed checkbox. When the `FileName` parameter is already specified, Dreamweaver automatically writes the same value in the Embed Scr text box. If you forget and turn on the Embed option before entering the `FileName` parameter, just turn off Embed, reselect it, and the proper value appears as the Embed source file.

Adding Java Applets

Java is a platform-independent programming language developed by Sun Microsystems. Although Java can also be used to write entire applications, its most frequent role is on the Web in the form of an applet. An *applet* is a self-contained program that can be run within a Web page.

Java is a compiled programming language similar to C++. Once a Java applet is compiled, it is saved as a class file. Web browsers call Java applets through, aptly enough, the `<applet>` tag. When you insert an applet, you refer to the primary class file much as you call a graphic file for an image tag.

Each Java applet has its own unique set of parameters — and Dreamweaver enables you to enter as many as necessary in the same manner as Plugins and ActiveX controls. In fact, the Applet object works almost identically to the Plugin and ActiveX objects.

Caution

Keep two caveats in mind if you're planning to include Java applets in your Web site. First, most (but not all) browsers support some version of Java — the newest release has the most features but the least support. Second, all the browsers that support Java enable the user to disable it because of security issues. Make sure to use the Alt property to designate an alternative image or some text for display by browsers that do not support Java.

A Java applet can be inserted in a Web page with a bare minimum of parameters: the code source and the dimensions of the object. Java applets derive much of their power from their configurability, and most of these little programs have numerous custom parameters. As with Plugins and ActiveX controls, Dreamweaver enables you to specify the basic attributes through the Property Inspector, and the custom ones via the Parameters dialog box.

To include a Java applet in your Web page, follow these steps:

1. Position the cursor where you want the applet to originate and choose Insert ⇨ Media ⇨ Applet. You can also select the Insert Applet button from the Special category of the Objects panel.

   The Insert Applet dialog box opens.

2. From the Select File dialog box, enter the path to your class file in the File Name text box or select the Browse (Choose) button to locate the file.

   An Applet object placeholder appears in the Document window. In the Applet Property Inspector (Figure 17-11), the selected source file appears in the Code text box, and the folder appears in the Base text box.

Figure 17-11: Use the Insert Applet button to insert a Java Applet object and display the Applet Property Inspector.

 Note   The path to your Java class files cannot be expressed absolutely; it must be given as an address relative to the Web page that is calling it.

3. Enter the height and width of the Applet object in the H and W text boxes, respectively. You can also resize the Applet object by clicking and dragging any of its three sizing handles.

4. You can enter any of the usual basic attributes, such as a name for the object, as well as values for Align, V and/or H Space, and Alt in the appropriate text boxes in the Property Inspector.

5. If desired, enter the online directory where the applet code can be found in the Base text box. If none is specified, the document's URL is assumed to be this attribute, known as the *codebase*.

6. To enter any custom attributes, select the Parameters button to open the Parameters dialog box.

7. Select the + (add) button and enter the first parameter. Press Tab to move to the Value column.

8. Enter the value for the parameter, if any. Press Tab.

9. Continue entering desired parameters in the left column, with their values in the right. Click OK when you're finished.

Tip

Because of the importance of displaying alternative content for users not running Java, Dreamweaver provides a method for displaying something for everyone. To display an image, enter the URL to a graphics file in the Alt text box. To display text as well as an image, you have to do a little hand-coding. First, select a graphics file to insert in the Alt text box and then open the Code view. In the <img> tag found between the <applet> tags, add an alt="your_message" attribute by hand (where the text you want to display is the value for the alt attribute). Now your Java applet displays an image for browsers that are graphics-enabled but not Java-enabled, and text for text-only browsers such as Lynx.

Some Java class files have additional graphics files. In most cases, you need to store both the class files and the graphics files in the same folder.

Adding JavaScript and VBScript

When initially developed by Netscape, JavaScript was called LiveScript. This browser-oriented language did not gain importance until Sun Microsystems joined the development team and the product was renamed JavaScript. Although the rechristening was a stroke of marketing genius, it has caused endless confusion among beginning programmers — JavaScript and Java have almost nothing in common outside of their capability to be incorporated in a Web page. JavaScript is used primarily to add functionality on the client side of the browser (for tasks such as verifying form data and adding interactivity to interface elements) or to script Netscape's servers on the server side. Java, on the other hand, is an application development language that can be used for a wide variety of tasks.

Conversely, VBScript is a full-featured Microsoft product. Both VBScript and JavaScript are scripting languages — which means you can write the code in any text editor and compile it at runtime. JavaScript enjoys more support than VBScript — JavaScript can be rendered by both Netscape and Microsoft browsers (as well as other browsers such as WebTV, Opera, and Sun's HotJava), whereas VBScript is read only by Internet Explorer on Windows systems — but both languages have their fans. In Dreamweaver, both types of code are inserted in the Web page in the same manner.

Inserting JavaScript or VBScript

If only mastering JavaScript or VBScript itself were as easy as inserting the code in Dreamweaver! Simply go to the Objects panel's Invisibles pane and select the Insert Script button, or choose Insert ⇨ Invisible Tags ⇨ Script from the menus and enter your code in the small Insert Script window. After you click OK, a Script icon appears in place of your script.

Of course, JavaScript or VBScript instruction is beyond the scope of this book, but every working Web designer must have an understanding of what these languages can do. Both languages refer to and, to varying degrees, manipulate the information on a Web page. Over time, you can expect significant growth in the capabilities of the JavaScript and VBScript disciplines.

Cross-Reference   Dreamweaver, through the application of its behaviors, goes a long way toward making JavaScript useful for nonprogrammers. To learn more about behaviors, see Chapter 19.

Use the Script Property Inspector (Figure 17-12) to select an external file for your JavaScript or VBScript code. You can also set the language type by opening the Language drop-down list and choosing either JavaScript or VBScript. Because different features are available in the various releases of JavaScript, you can also specify JavaScript 1.1 or JavaScript 1.2. If you need to choose a specific version of JavaScript, you must do it when you initially insert the script — you cannot change the setting from the Script Property Inspector. Naturally, you could also make the adjustment in the Code view.

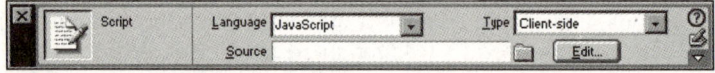

Figure 17-12: Insert either JavaScript or VBScript through the Objects panel's Script object available in the Invisibles category.

When you choose JavaScript or VBScript as your Language type, Dreamweaver writes the code accordingly. Both languages use the `<script>` tag pair, and each is specified in the `language` attribute, as follows:

```
<script language="JavaScript">alert("Look Out!")</script>
```

With Dreamweaver, you are not restricted to inserting code in just the `<body>` section of your Web page. Many JavaScript and VBScript functions must be located in the `<head>` section. To insert this type of script, first select View ⇨ Head Content or, from the Options menu of the toolbar, choose Head Content. Next, select the now-visible `<head>` window and choose Insert ⇨ Invisible Tags ⇨ Script, or click the Insert Script object. Enter your script as described earlier in this section and then select the main Document window, or choose View ⇨ Head Content again to deselect it.

You can also indicate whether your script is based on the client-side or server-side by choosing the Type option from the Property Inspector. If you choose server-side, your script is enclosed in `<server>`...`</server>` tags and is interpreted by the Web server hosting the page.

Editing JavaScript or VBScript

Dreamweaver provides a large editing window for modifying your script code. To open this Script Properties window, select the placeholder icon for the script you want to modify and then choose the Edit button on the Script Property Inspector. You have the same functionality in the Script Properties window as in the Script Property Inspector; namely, you can choose your language or link to an external script file (see Figure 17-13).

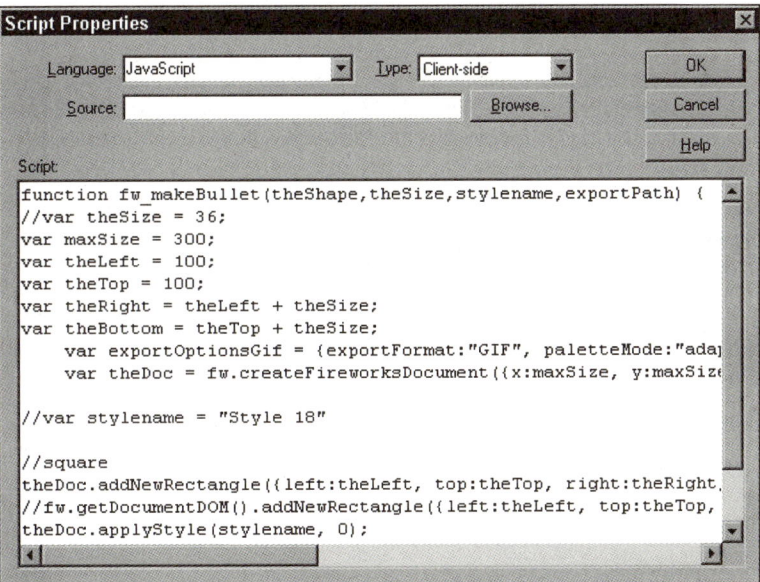

Figure 17-13: The generous Script Properties window provides plenty of room for modifying your JavaScript or VBScript.

Tip

Some older browsers "break" when loading a JavaScript Web page and display the code written between the `<script>...</script>` tag pair. Although Dreamweaver doesn't do it by default, you can use a trick to prevent this anomaly. In the Code view or inspector, insert the opening comment tag (`<--`) right after the opening `<script>` tag. Then insert the closing comment tag (`-->`), preceded by two forward slashes, right before the closing `</script>`. An example follows:

```
<script language="Javascript">
<!--
[JavaScript code goes here]
//-->
</script>
```

The comment tags effectively tell the older browser to ignore the enclosed content. The two forward slashes in front of the closing comment tag are JavaScript's comment indicator, which tells it to ignore the rest of the line.

Summary

To paraphrase a popular commercial, "Web pages aren't just for HTML anymore." The possibilities expand tremendously when you start to explore any of the technologies discussed in this chapter: CGI, Plugins, ActiveX, Java, and JavaScript or VBScript. Dreamweaver maintains an open-ended design for external programs.

✦ CGI scripts are primarily used to send information back and forth between the user and the Web server. The Web server can then, under the direction of the CGI program, store the information in a database or forward it to another URL or e-mail address.

✦ Plugins enable browsers to display formats other than HTML. A Plugin can display multimedia content inline with other HTML objects such as images and tables. Dreamweaver supports a Plugin object that enables the `<embed>` code to be customized through the Parameters dialog box.

✦ Dreamweaver enables you to play any or all of the Plugins — right in the Document window as you're creating your Web page.

✦ Microsoft browsers employ ActiveX controls in a manner similar to Netscape's Plugins. Each ActiveX control has its own unique Class ID, as well as a codebase attribute that enables users to get the control without interrupting their workflow. The Dreamweaver ActiveX object enables you to easily combine both ActiveX controls and their corresponding Plugin with the Embed option.

✦ Java applets can be inserted as Applet objects in a Dreamweaver Web page. Java source files, called *classes*, can be linked to the Applet object through the Property Inspector.

✦ Dreamweaver offers a simple method for including both JavaScript and VBScript code in the `<body>` section of your HTML page. Script functions that need to be inserted in the `<head>` section can now be added by selecting View ➪ Head Content.

In the next chapter, you learn how you can use and create your own Dreamweaver objects.

✦   ✦   ✦

Creating and Using Objects

Sometimes the simplest ideas are the most powerful. The Dreamweaver development team had a simple idea: Why not code the insertable objects in HTML? After all, when you choose to insert anything into a Web page — from a horizontal rule to a Shockwave movie — you are just putting HTML in the page. If the objects are just HTML files, what are the possible benefits? For one, the objects can be easily modified. Also, HTML requires no special program to code, and coding the language itself is not extraordinarily difficult. In addition, the core users of Dreamweaver are experts in HTML. Now, a simple idea is turned into a powerful tool.

All the objects included with Dreamweaver can be modified and customized to fit any Web designer's working preferences. Furthermore, custom objects can easily be created. This capability not only enables you to include regular HTML tags that repeatedly occur in your designs, but also opens the door to an impressive new level of expandability. Dreamweaver's capability to accommodate any number of custom objects means you can take advantage of new technologies immediately.

Building a site that needs the latest tags just released by the W3C? Go right ahead — make an object that inserts any or all of the tags. You may not be able to see the result in Dreamweaver, but if your browser can handle the tags, you can preview them there.

Find yourself including the same ActiveX control over and over again, with only one change in the parameters? Create a custom object that inserts that control, with all the constant attributes — and add a parameter form to enter the variable attributes.

This chapter shows you the tremendous potential of Dreamweaver objects. After studying the use of the standard objects, you learn how you can customize your object working environment. Then, you find out how to create your own objects and take advantage of the extensibility features in Dreamweaver.

Inserting Dreamweaver Objects

If you've been using Dreamweaver, you've been using objects. Even if your first exposure to Dreamweaver has been working through the first half of this book, you've already used several types of objects. Aside from text, everything inserted in a Web page can be considered an object: images, comments, plug-ins, named anchors—they're all objects, and are all extremely easy to use.

Dreamweaver offers several ways to include any object. For a few objects, you even have as many as four different techniques from which to choose:

✦ From the menu, choose Insert and then any of the listed objects.

✦ From the Objects panel (see Figure 18-1), click any button on the seven standard categories—Characters, Common, Forms, Frames, Head, Invisibles, and Special—to insert an object at the current cursor position.

✦ Drag any button off the Objects panel and drop it next to any existing content on your Web page.

Figure 18-1: You'll find yourself returning to the Objects panel as an easy way to include HTML elements.

✦ Many objects have a keyboard shortcut, such as Ctrl+Alt+I (Command+Option+I) for Image or Ctrl+Alt+F (Command+Option+F) for a Flash movie. Keyboard shortcuts insert the chosen object at the current cursor location.

Tip

When you insert one of the objects from the Invisibles category—such as a Comment or Named Anchor—Dreamweaver by default inserts an icon to show the object's placement. If you find these icons distracting, you can turn them all off by choosing the toggle command, View ⇨ Visual Aids ⇨ Invisible Elements. Alternatively, you can choose Visual Aids ⇨ Invisible Elements from the View Options button on the toolbar. If you have an invisible element "turned off" in Preferences, you never see the icon, regardless of the status of the View menu command.

Modifying the Objects Panel

The Objects panel is one of the most customizable of all of Dreamweaver's features. In addition to the flexibility of having it "float" anywhere on the screen, you can also resize and reshape the panel to your liking—you can even dock it with other floating panels. Most important, you can rearrange its contents, add new categories, and, as noted earlier, include custom objects.

Moving and reshaping the Objects panel

If you work with your Document window fully expanded, you often find yourself repositioning the Objects panel. Just click and drag the title bar on top of the panel to quickly move it out of the way. You can also press F4 to send the Objects panel (and any other open panels or inspectors) behind the Document window or Site window. Pressing F4 again brings them back to the front.

If you don't like the long, vertical shape that Dreamweaver uses by default for the Objects panel, you can change its appearance. Place your pointer over any border of the panel until the usual pointing arrow changes into a two-headed arrow—now you can click and drag the Objects panel into a new shape. You can drag any corner to form a rectangular shape in Windows, as shown in Figure 18-2 (with Macintosh, use the lower-right corner), or you can extend the panel horizontally instead of vertically.

When screen real estate is at a premium, you can reduce the overall size of the Objects panel—even down to just a two column by one button row size. If you shrink it down small enough so that all the buttons don't show at once, one or two scroll arrows appear. Click an arrow to see the next button in the panel.

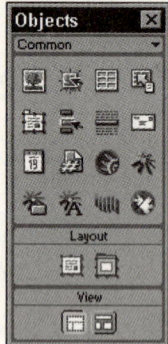

Figure 18-2: Reshape the Objects panel to your liking.

The Objects panel is the only one of the "big three" floating windows — Objects panel, Property Inspector, and Launcher — that can be included in Dreamweaver's docking system, but it's a one-way connection. You can dock any of the other panels to the Objects panel, but you can't dock the solo Objects panel to any of the others. If you're working with a variety of Dreamweaver's other features, such as layers, templates, behaviors, and so on, you might want to group the Objects panel with these other panels to reduce your workspace clutter.

Reorganizing the objects and adding categories

The seven categories of the Objects panel — Characters, Common, Forms, Frames, Head, Invisibles, and Special — correspond to the seven folders found in the Dreamweaver Configuration\Objects directory. Each folder has a minimum of two items for each object: an HTML file and a GIF file. The HTML file is the source code for the object, and the GIF file is the button image. Some of the objects also have a JavaScript file, with a .js extension associated with it. If you want to move an item from one Objects panel to another, just transfer the files related to that object from one folder to the other.

Note   Actually, there are eight folders in the Objects directory; the eighth one, Tools, holds the scripts and icons for the new Layout section of the Objects panel. Although it's possible to add objects to this folder and have the objects become available whenever you enter Layout mode, it's not the intended use and there's no guarantee that that particular folder will have that behavior.

For example, let's say you're doing a lot of JavaScript work and you want to move the Insert Script object from the Invisibles category to the Common category. To accomplish this task, you need to move script.htm, script.js, and script.gif from the Invisibles folder to the Common folder. You can click and drag the files or cut and paste them (Windows only). You must restart Dreamweaver to see the changes.

You're not limited to the seven categories on the Objects panel. As noted earlier, the standard categories correspond to identically named subfolders in the Objects directory. If you want to add another category, simply add a new subfolder. For example, I've developed a number of custom objects for inserting sound and digital video files, which I wanted to group on a new category of the Objects panel. In my file management program, I created a folder called Media within the Dreamweaver\Configuration\Objects folder and moved all my special object files into the new folder. After restarting Dreamweaver, Media appears as my eighth category in the Objects panel.

Caution Dreamweaver recognizes only one level of subfolders within the Objects folder as new Objects panel categories. You cannot, for instance, create a subfolder called Videos within the Media subfolder that will be recognized by Dreamweaver as a submenu.

Dreamweaver alphabetizes the Object categories by folder name. If you want your new custom category to appear first on the Objects panel, you must name its folder so that it appears further up alphabetically (that is, closer to A) than the Common folder. Use one of two tricks: You can start the custom folder name with a space or a tilde (~), such as ~Media, for instance; or you can rename the Common folder so that its name appears later in the alphabet.

Cross-Reference You can customize not only the Objects panel but also the menus. All menus are controlled via the menus.xml file found in the Configuration\Menus folder. For an in-depth look at how you can change your Insert — or any other — menu, as well as keyboard shortcuts, see Chapter 21.

Adding Other Objects

Before you begin building your own custom objects, you may want to look around and see if someone else has already created something similar. In addition to having the standard objects that ship with Dreamweaver, numerous Web sites have objects (and behaviors) that are available for download. Macromedia sponsors one of the largest collections at the Macromedia Exchange. You can also search another database of Dreamweaver objects (as well as behaviors, commands, and so on) at the Dreamweaver Extension Database, located on my site, Dreamweaver etc. (www.idest.com/dreamweaver). Of course, a variety of objects are available on the CD-ROM accompanying this book.

To facilitate the process of adding new objects and other extensions, Macromedia developed the aptly named Extension Manager. The Extension Manager is a cross-product utility that works with Dreamweaver, Dreamweaver UltraDev, and Flash. The Extension Manager works with extensions created in a special format, Macromedia Exchange Package or MXP. MXP files contain the necessary files for the extension, all the required information on where the files should be installed, how to access the extension, who the author is, and more, as shown in Figure 18-3. With a properly formatted MXP file, the Extension Manager can even adjust your menu and keyboard shortcut settings.

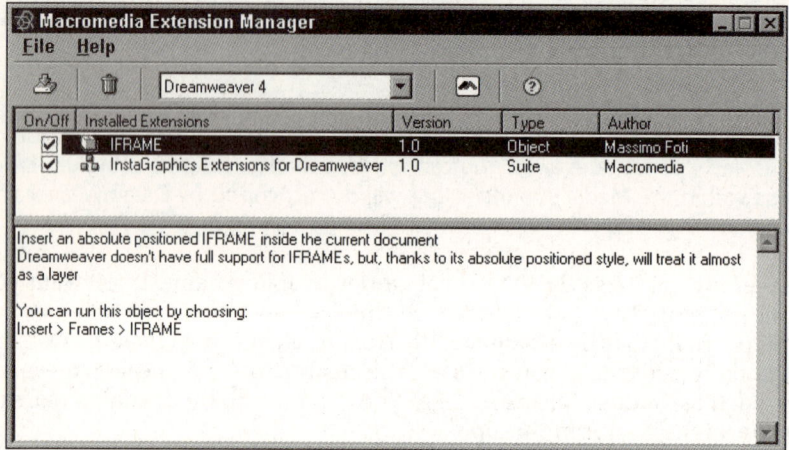

Figure 18-3: Use the Extension Manager to add additional objects without copying files.

The primary source for Macromedia Extension Package files is the Macromedia Exchange (`http://exchange.macromedia.com`), but you can also retrieve these files from other sources such as developers' sites or this book's CD-ROM. If you've located the MXP file from the Internet, your browser may offer you alternative methods to start the installation:

✦ Download the file to your system and complete the installation once that process is complete.

✦ Install the file directly from the Internet.

Tip   It's a matter of personal preference, but I prefer to store all the extensions locally. The vast majority of them tend to be fairly small and if I need to install them again or on a different machine, I don't have to go through the download process again. Macromedia recommends that you maintain your extensions in the Configuration\Downloaded Extensions folder, but there's no real benefit to doing so if you'd prefer to store them elsewhere.

To complete the installation, follow these steps:

1. If you chose to open the extension from the Internet, the Extension Manager is automatically launched. If you downloaded the extension, double-click the .mxp file to launch the Extension Manager. In either case, the Macromedia Exchange legal disclaimer is presented.

2. Select the Accept button to continue with the installation or Decline to cancel it.

After you accept the disclaimer, the Extension Manager informs you whether the installation is successful or alerts you to any errors it encounters, such as existing files with the same name.

If the installation succeeds, the extension is added to your list. The list displays the name of the installed extensions, their version number, the type, and the author.

Tip If you have a great number of extensions, you can sort the list in the Extension Manager by selecting the column heading. To change the display order from ascending to descending (to show, for example, the highest version numbers first) click the heading again under Windows; on Macintosh systems, select the sort-order button on top of the scroll bar.

You can also install an extension from within Dreamweaver by following these steps:

1. Choose Commands ➪ Manage Extensions to open the Extension Manager.

2. Select File ➪ Install Extension or use the keyboard shortcut, Ctrl+I (Command+O). Alternatively, Windows users can also select the Install New Extensionbutton.

The Select Extension to Install dialog box opens.

3. In the Select Extension dialog box, locate the desired .mxp file on your system and choose Install.

The legal disclaimer is presented.

4. Select the Accept button to continue with the installation or Decline to cancel it.

5. Once the installation is complete, choose File ➪ Exit (File ➪ Quit) to close the Extension Manager or click the Close button.

Caution Some extensions require Dreamweaver to be relaunched in order to take effect.

The Extension Manager is a relatively new addition to the Dreamweaver toolbox and many older extensions, while perfectly usable, have not been converted to the MXP format. To incorporate objects not in the Extension Manager format into your Dreamweaver system, follow these steps:

1. Uncompress the files if necessary. Object files come with an HTML file and a GIF file, and the two files are usually compressed for easy download or transfer.

Online Sources for Dreamweaver Extensions

You can find new objects and behaviors at numerous online sources aside from the Macromedia Exchange. However, like traditional Web development, creating Dreamweaver extensions is an ever-growing affair—if you can't find what you're looking for at any one site, visit the Dreamweaver Extension Database hosted by Dreamweaver etc.

Dreamweaver Depot

`http://weblogs.userland.com/dreamweaver`

Run by Andrew Wooldridge, the Dreamweaver Depot initially specialized in Netscape-only objects and behaviors, but the site now offers cross-browser and Internet Explorer-specific extensions as well. The Depot also has a forum and a chat room for Dreamweaver aficionados.

Massimo's Corner of the Web

`www.massimocorner.com`

Massimo Foti produces high-quality extensions that fulfill many specific functions faced by a Web developer. For example, his site features extensions devoted to redirecting browsers as well as controlling remote windows and scrolling layers.

Webmonkey Editor Extensions Collection

`www.hotwired.com/webmonkey/javascript/code_library/ed_ext`

Although this area on the Hot Wired site could potentially hold other Web authoring tools' extensions, Dreamweaver is currently the only one on the market with the capability. You can find several professional-quality objects and behaviors, both cross-browser and browser-specific ones.

Yaromat

`www.yaromat.com`

Featuring objects, commands, and behaviors by Jaro von Flocken, Yaromat houses some of the most creative Dreamweaver extensions on the Web. His Layer f(x) behavior brings mathematical precision to layer movements, and his other creations are equally dramatic.

Dreamweaver etc.

`www.idest.com/dreamweaver`

Maintained by Joseph Lowery, author of this book, the Dreamweaver etc. site includes all the objects found on this book's CD-ROM, plus new ones posted after this book's publication.

2. If necessary, make a new folder for your objects. All objects must be stored in a subfolder of the Dreamweaver\Configuration\Objects folder. You can either store the object files in a standard subfolder (Characters, Common, Forms, Frames, Head, Invisibles, or Special, for instance) or in a new folder that you create.

3. Transfer the object files to the desired folder. Be careful: Make sure you transfer both the HTML and the GIF file together.

Note The new object is automatically added as the last item on the Insert menu. If you want to customize the Insert menu to list the new object in a different location, you need to change the menus.xml file, found in the Configuration\Menus folder.

4. Restart Dreamweaver.

Creating Custom Objects

Each custom object, like standard objects, is made from at least two files: an HTML file describing the object, and a GIF file depicting the button. The complexity of the HTML depends on the complexity of the object. You can build just about anything—from a simple object that replicates a repeatedly used item, to a high-end object that uses advanced JavaScript techniques for creating special function layers and windows. You can even make objects that create other objects.

To support the "higher end" of the custom object scale, Dreamweaver includes proprietary extensions to JavaScript and a Document Object Model (DOM), which combines a subset of Netscape Navigator 4.0's DOM, a subset of the DOM Level 1 established by the W3C, and a host of custom Dreamweaver extensions. You study these techniques further into the chapter. As the following section shows, however, many objects don't require any JavaScript and are easy to construct.

Note While it's possible to split off the bulk of the JavaScript functionality into an included .js file as Macromedia does for many objects, it's not absolutely necessary. This separation of the user interface (the HTML file) and the underlying code (the JavaScript file) is usually undertaken for localization purposes and to allow one developer to work on the interface while another works on the code.

Making simple objects

To make a simple object that inserts any HTML-created item, put only the code necessary to create the object into a file and then save the file in one of the object folders. The key phrase in the preceding sentence is *only the code necessary*. Unlike a regular Web page, you don't have to include the framing <html>...<body>... </body>...</html> sections for a simple custom object—all you need is the essential code necessary to make the object.

For example, let's say you are asked to enhance 100 Web pages and make each page capable of showing a different QuickTime movie. Each of the .mov files is different, so you can't use Dreamweaver's Library feature. The easiest way to handle this situation is to create a dummy version of what you need and then turn that dummy into an object.

The whole process involves these four steps:

✦ Creating the item

✦ Creating the object

✦ Saving the object

✦ Creating a button for the object

Step 1: Creating the item

First, create your item as you normally would in Dreamweaver. For this example, let's insert a plug-in and add all the standard attributes: name, height and width, pluginspage, border, v space, and h space — and even a few special parameters such as autostart and stretch. The only attribute that the example omits is the attribute that changes: the file source. You also want the movie to be centered, wherever it's located, and you center the plug-in. When finished, the complete code for the page and plug-in, as generated by Dreamweaver, looks like the following:

```
<html>
<head>
<title>Untitled Document</title>
<meta http-equiv="Content-Type" content="text/html; charset=iso-8859-1">
</head>
<body bgcolor="#FFFFFF">
<div align="center">
  <embed src="" width="135" height="135" name="qtMovie" ¬
pluginspage="http://www.apple.com/quicktime/" vspace="5" hspace="5" ¬
border="5" stretch="true" autostart="false"></embed>
</div>
</body>
</html>
```

Step 2: Creating the object

The absolute simplest method available is to skip this step entirely and proceed to saving the HTML in an Objects subfolder as described in Step 3. Dreamweaver ignores the outer code and just inserts whatever is in the <body> tag. However, this technique might be confusing for future development of your object and I recommend, if you have the time, to complete this step and remove the unnecessary code.

To create a simple object from the preceding, just cut everything in the code but the item (or items) you want repeated. In Code view, or using the Code Inspector, select all the code from the opening <html> tag up to and including the <body> tag and then delete. Then delete the closing tags, </body> and </html>. The only remaining code is the following:

```
<div align="center">
  <embed src="" width="135" height="135" name="qtMovie" ¬
pluginspage="http://www.apple.com/quicktime/" vspace="5" hspace="5" ¬
border="5" stretch="true" autostart="false"></embed>
</div>
```

After you eliminate all the code except for your object's code and return to Design view, the Document window changes from a white background to a dark-gray background. This change occurs because Dreamweaver makes the `bgcolor` attribute of the `<body>` tag white by default — to create a simple object, you need to delete the entire `<body>` tag, including the color information.

Step 3: Saving the object

Now your object is ready to be saved. For Dreamweaver to recognize this or any other snippet of code as an object, the file must be saved in the Configuration\ Objects folder. You can choose to save your object in any of the existing subfolders or you can create a new subfolder within the Objects folder. For this example, create a new folder called Media for this and other similar objects.

Caution   You must save your new object in a subfolder within the Objects folder. Dreamweaver doesn't recognize objects saved individually in the Objects folder.

After the file is saved, you can restart Dreamweaver to test your object — or you can use the Reload Extensions feature.

To force Dreamweaver to reload objects, behaviors, inspectors, and commands, click the expander arrow on the Objects panel while holding down the Ctrl (Option) key. In addition to the different Objects panel categories, Dreamweaver displays the Reload Extensions menu item, as shown in Figure 18-4. Select this option, and soon your new objects will be available — although there's one final step to consider.

Step 4: Creating a button for the object

As shown in Figure 18-5, Dreamweaver displays an "unknown object" placeholder in the Objects panel because you haven't yet made a button image for the qtMovie object. In addition, unless you specifically include the new object in the menu configuration file, menus.xml, the object is listed in the bottom portion of the Insert menu. This arrangement is fine for debugging, but if you want to continue using your object, it's more efficient to create a button image for it and revise the menus.xml file to include it. The following section shows you how to complete this task.

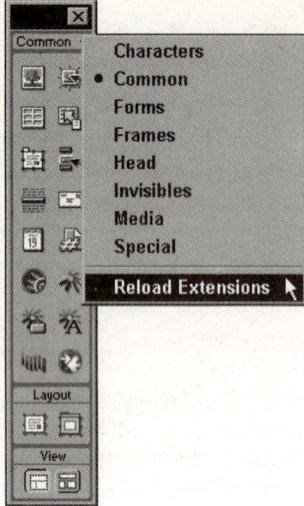

Figure 18-4: Press the Ctrl (Option) key and click the Objects panel expander arrow to access the Reload Extensions command.

The "unknown object" placeholder

Figure 18-5: You can create custom objects such as the qtMovie object shown here.

Building an object button

Object buttons are GIF files, ideally sized at 18 pixels square. To make the object button, you can use any graphics-creation program that can save GIF files. If your button image file is not 18 pixels by 18 pixels, Dreamweaver resizes it to those dimensions. Your button can be as colorful as you want — as long as it can still fit in an 18-pixel square.

Tip   To create an object button, you can open and modify any of the existing GIF files for the standard buttons. Just be sure to use the Save As command of your paint program — and not the Save command — to save your modified version.

After you've created your button image, save the GIF file in the same folder as the HTML file for the new object.

Cross-Reference   At this time, you may also want to modify the menus.xml file as described in Chapter 21.

Putting JavaScript to Work in Custom Objects

The remaining sections of this chapter deal with using JavaScript to create more complex objects.

Tip   If you're totally unfamiliar with JavaScript, you might want to review this section with a good supporting resource at hand. An excellent choice is Danny Goodman's *JavaScript Bible,* published by Hungry Minds, Inc. (formerly known as IDG Books Worldwide, Inc.).

Using the objectTag() function

When Macromedia built a JavaScript interpreter into Dreamweaver, a number of extensions were included to facilitate object and behavior creation. One of these functions, `objectTag()`, is the key to building advanced objects. All of the standard Dreamweaver-built objects use the `objectTag()` function. This function has a single purpose: It writes any specified value into the HTML document.

The `objectTag()` is multifunctional; it can insert code in the `<head>` as well as the `<body>`. Moreover, the function handles the placement intelligently; `objectTag()` knows which tags should be placed where. Consequently, you don't have to make any special declarations to place code in the `<head>` section.

You can see a simple use of the `objectTag()` function by looking at the source code for Dreamweaver's Insert Line-Break object. In the Objects\Common folder, open line_break.htm and look at the code for this object in the HTML Inspector.

Just like most JavaScript functions that can affect any portion of the page, the `objectTag()` function is written in the `<head>` section. Here's the function in its entirety:

```
function objectTag() {
  // Return the html tag that should be inserted
  return "<BR>";
}
```

Tip   You can designate a ToolTip to appear when your mouse passes over your new object's button. Enter the desired name in the `<title>` section of the HTML object file. The designated `<title>` also appears on any dialog boxes used by the object.

Aside from the comment line, `objectTag()` returns only one value. In the preceding example, the value happens to be "`<BR>`". You can insert any HTML code as the return value. However, because JavaScript formats any value as a string, you need to apply JavaScript string-formatting syntax, as follows:

✦ To use the `objectTag()` function to return an HTML tag and a variable, use quotes around each string literal, but not around the variable, and join the two with a plus sign. For example, the following `objectTag()` function code inserts `<img src=images/whatzit.gif>` in the current cursor position:

```
nada = "images/whatzit.gif"
return "<img src=" + nada + ">";
```

✦ To make an object that returns separate lines of code, put each tag on its own line, with the symbol for a newline, \n, at the end of the string, surrounded by quotes; then add a plus sign at the end of the line. For example, the following `objectTag()` function inserts a Flash movie of a particular size and shape:

```
function objectTag() {
  // Return the html tag that should be inserted
  return '\n' +
'<object classid="clsid:D27CDB6E-AE6D-11cf-96B8-444553540000"
\n' +
'codebase="http://active.macromedia.com/flash2/cabs/swflash.¬
cab#version=4,0,0,0". "width="145" height="135"> \n' +
' <param name="movie" value="newMovie.swf"> \n' +
' <param name="PLAY" value="false"> \n' +
' <embed src="newMovie.swf" \n' +
'pluginspage="http://www.macromedia.com/shockwave/download/¬
index.cgi?P1_Prod_Version=ShockwaveFlash" width="145"
height="135" play="false"></embed> \n' +
'</object>'
}
```

Some developers prefer to set the entire collection of strings to a variable and return that variable. In this case, you'd be better served by using JavaScript's add-by-value operator (+=), as in this example:

```
var retval = ''
retval += '<table width="' + newWidth + '" height="' +
newHeight + '" border="0" cellspacing="0" cellpadding="0">\n'
retval += '  <tr>\n'
retval += '    <td>' + newCode + '</td>\n'
retval += '  </tr>\n'
retval += '</table>\n'
return retval
```

✦ Use single quotes to surround the return values that include double quotes. For every opening quote of one kind, make sure a matching closing quote exists of the same kind. For example:

```
return '<img src="images/eiffel.jpg">'
```

✦ Use the backslash character, \, to display special inline characters such as double and single quotes or newline.

```
return "<strong>You\'re Right!</strong>"
```

Tip Unless you're mixing variables with the HTML you're using for your object, you should use the "object-only" method described in the earlier section, "Making simple objects." Reserve the `objectTag()` function for your intermediate-to-advanced object-creation projects.

Offering help

As objects grow in their features, they often grow in their complexity. An object with multiple parameters — especially if it is intended for public release — could potentially benefit from a Help button. Dreamweaver offers just such a button to aid custom object builders and their users.

Including the `displayHelp()` function causes Dreamweaver to display a Help button, directly beneath the OK and Cancel buttons found to the right of a user-created parameter form. When selected, this button calls whatever is defined in the function.

For example, if you wanted to define a Help button that would put up an informative message within Dreamweaver, you might code the `displayHelp()` function this way:

```
displayHelp() {
  alert("Be sure to name all your layers first")
}
```

You're not restricted to in-program alerts. If you have a much larger help file, you can display it in your primary browser by using Dreamweaver's built-in `browseDocument()` function. With the following definition, when the Help button is selected, Dreamweaver first opens the primary browser (if it's not already running) and shows the object-specific help file:

```
displayHelp() { dreamweaver.browseDocument¬
("http://www.idest.com/dreamweaver/help/entitiesHelp.htm")
}
```

Note that the preceding code includes an absolute URL that pulls a page off the Web. You can also reference a file locally. The best way to do this is to use another Dreamweaver JavaScript function, getConfigurationPath(). Just as it sounds, this function returns the current path to the Configuration folder. Using this as a base, you can reference other files installed on the system. In this example, the help file is stored in a folder called HelpDocs, which in turn is stored within the Configuration folder:

```
function displayHelp() {
  var helpPath = dreamweaver.getConfigurationPath() + ¬
"/HelpDocs/replicatorHelp.htm"
  dreamweaver.browseDocument(helpPath)
}
```

Attaching a parameter form

To be truly useful, many objects require additional attributes. Several of the standard objects in Dreamweaver use parameter forms to simplify entry of these attributes. A *parameter form* is the portion of the object code that creates a dialog box. Dreamweaver uses the HTML form commands for handling the parameter form duties.

To see how a parameter form is structured, look at the parameter forms used in the standard objects. Select the Insert Script button in the Invisibles category of the Objects panel. The Insert Script dialog box that appears on the screen is a basic parameter form.

Next, open the Script object source file (Objects\Invisibles\script.htm) in Dreamweaver to see how the parameter form is built. As shown in Figure 18-6, the <body> of the file consists of a single <form> element with two items inside, a text field and a menu list.

The <body> section of the HTML source code for the Script object contains only the <form> with two fields: a <select> field (the menu list used to select the language) and a <textarea> field for the actual script:

```
<FORM NAME="theform">
  <table>
    <tr>
      <td align="right" nowrap>Language:</td>
      <td>
        <select name="Language">
          <option value="JS" selected>JavaScript</option>
          <option value="JS11">JavaScript 1.1</option>
          <option value="JS12">JavaScript 1.2</option>
          <option value="VB">VBScript</option>
```

Parameter form

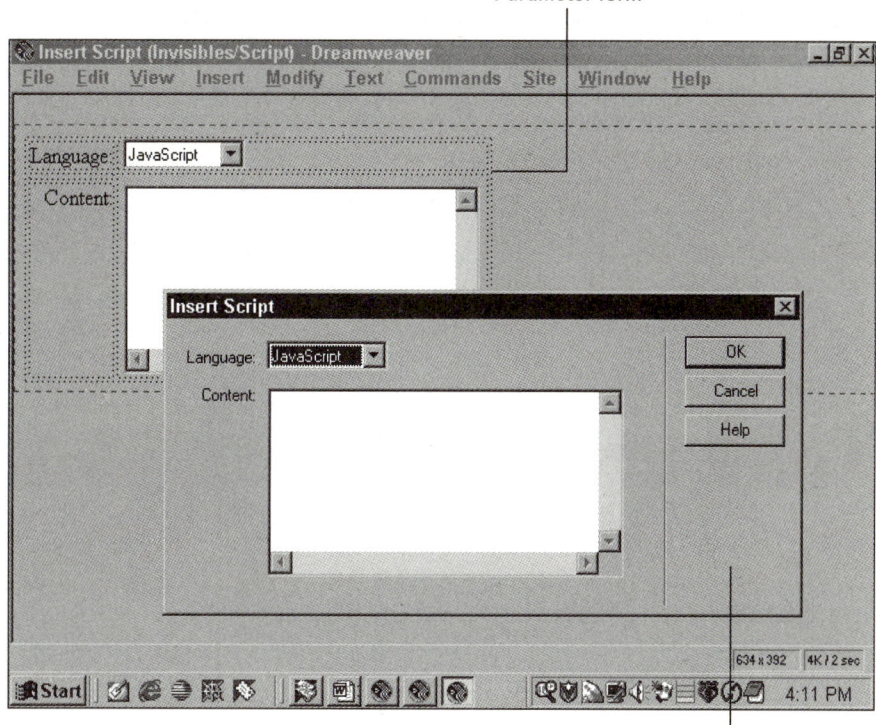

Insert Script dialog box

Figure 18-6: To see how the parameter form is used, compare the Script source file to its completed object.

```
      </select>
    </td>
  </tr>
  <tr>
    <td align="right" height="5"></td>
    <td rowspan="2">
      <textarea name="script" cols="50" rows="8"></textarea>
    </td>
  </tr>
  <tr>
    <td align="right" valign="top" nowrap>Content:</td>
  </tr>
  </table>
</FORM>
```

Sizing the Parameter Form Dialog Box

Although you cannot control all aspects of your parameter form—Dreamweaver automatically inserts the OK and Cancel buttons on the upper right—you can designate the dimensions of the parameter's dialog box. Generally, Dreamweaver sizes the dialog box automatically, but for a complex object, you can speed up the display by using the `windowDimensions()` function. Moreover, if your object is intended for general distribution, you can set different window dimensions for the Macintosh and Windows platforms.

The `windowDimensions()` function takes one argument, `platform`, and returns a string in the following form:

```
"width_in_Pixels,height_in_Pixels"
```

The size specified should not include the area for the OK and Cancel buttons. If the dimensions offered are too small to display all the options in the parameter form, scroll bars automatically appear.

The following example of the `windowDimensions()` function creates a parameter form dialog box 650 pixels by 530 pixels if viewed on a Macintosh, and 670 pixels by 550 pixels if viewed on a Windows system:

```
function windowDimensions(platform){
    if (platform.charAt(0) == 'm'){ // Macintosh
      return "650,530";
    }
    else { // Windows
      return "670,550";
    }
}
```

Macromedia recommends that you not use the `windowDimensions()` function unless you want your dialog box to be larger than 640 x 480 pixels. Like all Dreamweaver extensions to the Application Programming Interface (API), the `windowDimensions()` function can be used to build both objects and actions.

When the parameter form is displayed as an object, Dreamweaver automatically adds the OK and Cancel buttons; a Help button is added if the `displayHelp()` function is defined. When you select the OK button, the `objectTag()` function combines the values in the `<select>` and `<textarea>` tags with the necessary HTML tags to write the `<script>` code.

Using the form controls

Dreamweaver uses the HTML `<form>` tag and all of its various input types to gather attribute information for objects. To use the form elements in a parameter form, their input data must be passed to the JavaScript functions. Because Dreamweaver uses a subset of the Navigator 4.0 Document Object Model (DOM), as shown in Table 18-1, you are restricted to using specific methods for the various input types to gather this information. Properties marked with an asterisk are read-only.

Table 18-1
Form Elements in the Dreamweaver Document Object Model

Object	Properties	Methods	Events
form	elements* (an array of button, checkbox, password, radio, reset, select, submit, text, and text area objects); child objects by name	None	None
button	form*	blur()	OnClick
reset		focus()	
submit			
checkbox	checked	blur()	OnClick
radio	form*	focus()	
password	value	blur()	OnBlur
text	form*	focus()	OnFocus
textarea		select()	
select	form*	blur() (Windows only)	onBlur (Windows only)
	options[n].defaultSelected*	focus() (Windows only)	OnChange
	options[n].index*		onFocus() (Windows only)
	options[n].selected*		
	options[n].text*		
	options[n].value*		
	selectedIndex		

Note   JavaScript uses a hierarchical method of addressing the various elements on any given Web page. Moving from most general to most specific, each element is separated by a period. For example, the background color property of a page would be document.bgColor. The status of a checkbox named "sendPromo" on a form called "orderForm" would be document.orderForm.sendPromo.checked. The more complex your objects, the more important it is for you to master this syntax.

Input fields: Text, textarea, password, file, image, and hidden

When information is entered in one of the input type fields, the data is stored in the value property of the specific object. For example, look again at the code for the Plug-in object and notice the text field where the selected file's name is displayed:

```
<INPUT TYPE="text" name="pluginfilename" size="30">
```

When the `objectTag()` function is run, the contents of that text box are assigned to a variable, and that variable is included in the output written to the Web page:

```
function objectTag() {
  // Return the html tag that should be inserted
  var retval = '<EMBED SRC="' +
escape(document.forms[0].pluginfilename.value) + '"></EMBED>';

  // clear the field for next insertion
  clearForm();
  return retval;
}
```

In the preceding case, the input filename is located in:

```
document.forms[0].pluginfilename.value
```

Because the form was also named ("theForm"), this same value could also be written as follows:

```
document.theForm.pluginfilename.value
```

Note The "escape" function is an internal JavaScript function that converts a text string so that it can be read by a Web server. Any special characters are encoded into their hexadecimal ASCII equivalents. A single space between words, for instance, is converted to %20.

The text input types recognize two events in the Dreamweaver DOM: `onBlur` and `onFocus`. When a user selects a text field, either by tabbing to or clicking it, that text field is said to have focus — and the `onFocus` event is fired. When the user leaves that field, the field loses focus or blurs — and the `onBlur` event is triggered. Because the DOM does not recognize the `onChange` event handler with text fields, you can use a combination of `onFocus` and `onBlur` to check for changes and act accordingly.

Submit, Reset, and Command buttons

The button input types are used in parameter forms to trigger custom JavaScript functions. Instead of sending data to an external server, the data is sent to a specified internal function. The buttons respond only to `onClick` events and cannot pass any particular properties of their own, such as value or name.

Command buttons are used extensively in the Character Entities object shown in Figure 18-7. (The object is available on this book's CD-ROM and was developed before Dreamweaver's Other Characters object was created.) Each character entity is a separate Command button, written in the following form:

```
<input type="BUTTON" value="&#161;"
onClick="getChar('&amp;#161;','&#161;')">
```

Figure 18-7: This custom Character Entities object uses 97 separate Command buttons.

Each character entity symbol in each line has a specific purpose. The value is the character displayed on the button; the first argument in the getChar() function is written to a hidden field and eventually sent to the Web page; and the second argument is used to display the selected character in a text box.

```
function getChar(val,val2) {
  document.theForm.charValue.value=val
  document.theForm.txChar.value=val2
}
```

When this object is at work, the user makes a selection and clicks OK, and the objectTag() function reads the value from the hidden field and writes it into the Web page:

```
function objectTag() {
  return document.theForm.charValue.value;
}
```

Command buttons can be used to fire any custom JavaScripts and pass any necessary information to be eventually processed by the objectTag() function.

Checkboxes

Checkboxes enable an option to be selected or deselected, so the only information that a function needs from a checkbox is whether it has been selected. Dreamweaver's DOM enables you to read the checked property of the Checkbox object and act accordingly. The Character Entities object discussed in the preceding section, for instance, uses a checkbox to turn on and off the Multiple Characters option. If the checkbox (named cbMultiple) is selected, then `document.theForm.cbMultiple.checked` is true, and one set of statements is executed; otherwise, the second set of statements is run. The code for checkboxes follows:

```
function getChar(val,val2) {
if(document.theForm.cbMultiple.checked) {
  document.theForm.charValue.value=
  document.theForm.charValue.value+val
  document.theForm.txChar.value=
  document.theForm.txChar.value+val2
  } else {
  document.theForm.charValue.value=val
  document.theForm.txChar.value=val2
  }
}
```

Checkboxes are excellent for setting up either/or situations. You can also use checkboxes to set (turn on) particular attributes. You may, for instance, use a checkbox to make it possible for the user to enable an automatic startup for a QuickTime movie, or to turn the control panel on or off.

Radio buttons

Radio buttons offer a group of options, from which the user can only select one. The group is composed of `<input type=radio>` tags with the same name attribute; there can be as few as two in the group or as many as necessary.

The input type `radio`, like `checkbox`, makes use of the checked property to see which option was selected. The method used to figure out which of the radio buttons was chosen depends on the number of buttons used on the form:

✦ With just two or three buttons, you may want to use a simple if-else construct to determine which radio button was selected.

✦ If you are offering many options, you can use a loop structure to look at the `checked` property of each radio button.

With only a couple of radio buttons in a group, you can examine the one radio-type item in the array (starting with 0) and see if it was checked. In the following code, if one radio button is selected, the variable (`theChoice`) is set to one value — otherwise, it is set to the other value:

```
if (document.forms[0].comm[0].checked == "1")
```

```
        theChoice = "left";
    else
        theChoice = "right";
```

When you have many radio buttons, or you don't know how many radio buttons you will have, use a counter loop such as this next example from the Enhanced LineBreak object (available on the CD-ROM that accompanies this book):

```
for (var i = 0; i < document.theForm.lbreak.length; i++) {
    if (document.theForm.lbreak[i].checked) {
        break
    }
}
```

In this example, lbreak is the name of the group of radio buttons on the parameter form, and the length property tells you how many radio buttons are in the group. When the loop finds the selected radio button in the array, the loop is broken, and the program proceeds to the next group of statements.

Unfortunately, once you know which radio button is checked, there's no easy way to get its value. The Dreamweaver DOM doesn't support the value property for the radio input type. As a result, you have to assign the value to a variable based on which radio button was selected. You can complete this task in a simple series of if-else statements:

```
if (i == 0){
val = ""
    } else {
    if (i == 1) {
    val = "left"
        } else {
        if (i == 2) {
        val = "right"
            } else {
            val = "all"
            }
        }
    }
```

Alternatively, you can put all the values in an array and assign them in a statement like the following:

```
return "<br clear=" + newValue[i].name + ">"
```

List boxes and drop-down menus

List boxes and drop-down menus are perfect for offering a variety of options in a compact format. Drop-down menus enable the user to choose an option from a scrolling list; list boxes offer multiple choices from a similar list. Both use the `<select>` tag to set up their available options. When you include a list box or drop-down menu from Dreamweaver, you enter the options by selecting the List Value button and entering the item labels and their associated values in the dialog box. The code for the Direction list box—taken from Matthew David's Marquee object, which is shown in Figure 18-8 and is available on the CD-ROM that accompanies this book—is written as follows:

```
<select name="direction">
     <option value="LEFT" selected>LEFT</option>
     <option value="RIGHT">RIGHT</option>
     <option value="UP">UP</option>
     <option value="DOWN">DOWN</option>
</select>
```

Figure 18-8: The Marquee custom object is designed to take advantage of an Internet Explorer special function: the capability to make a scrolling text display.

Each list box or drop-down menu must have a unique name—in the preceding code, that name is "direction," given in the `<select>` tag. To discover which option the user selected when working with a drop-down menu, you need to examine the selectedIndex property of the named `<select>` object. Each `<option>` in a `<select>` tag is placed in an array in the order listed in the displayed menu. Remember, arrays always start with a 0 in JavaScript.

The following code looks at each member of the array; if that option is the one in which the `selectedIndex` property is `true`, then the proper value is assigned to a variable:

```
if(document.forms[0].direction.selectedIndex == 0) {
  direct_choice = 'LEFT'
    } else {
    if(document.forms[0].direction.selectedIndex == 1) {
    direct_choice = 'RIGHT'
    } else {
        if(document.forms[0].direction.selectedIndex == 2) {
        direct_choice = 'UP'
    } else {
        if(document.forms[0].direction.selectedIndex == 3) {
        direct_choice = 'DOWN'
    }
  }
 }
}
```

The process is slightly different when you have multiple options in a list box. In this situation, you should set up a loop to examine the `options[n].selected` property. All the options in a `<select>` tag set have additional properties that can be read by Dreamweaver's DOM, as follows:

Select Option	Description
`options[n].defaultSelected`	Returns `true` for the option (or options, when multiple selections are enabled) for every `<option>` tag with a selected attribute.
`options[n].index`	Returns the option's position in the array.
`options[n].selected`	Returns `true` if the option is chosen by the user.
`options[n].text`	Returns the text of the item as it appears in the list.
`options[n].value`	Returns the value of the item assigned in the `<option>` statement.

The following method cycles through all of the `<options>` to find which one(s) were selected:

```
for (var i = 0; i < document.theForm.optList.length; i++) {
  if (document.theForm.optList.options[i].selected) {
      result += "n\ " + document.theForm.optList.options[i].
      value
      }
  }
return result
}
```

Adding images to your objects

Custom objects don't have to be just text, of course. You can include images in your object, just as you would in a regular Web page — with one catch: Dreamweaver has to be able to find your image files. If you are not distributing your custom object, you can use images from any folder on your system. On the other hand, if your objects are going out to other users, you have to either include the image files with the object or use existing graphics stored in known locations.

What existing graphics are on every Dreamweaver system in specific locations? The GIF files for each object, of course. The button for the custom Character Entities object (previously shown in Figure 18-7) is used in the dialog box for the object itself. Because the two files always have to be in the same folder, you can include the image file on the same level. The size of the GIF files is fairly small (18 pixels by 18 pixels), so you can simply double the size of the image and have Dreamweaver rescale it.

Tip   The opposite approach for using one image for both the Objects panel and your dialog box is to make a larger image, say 32×32. Often this results in a better looking graphic in both places.

Of course, you can create your own custom graphics for your objects and include those files with the associated HTML and GIF button files. You can even spice up your Dreamweaver standard objects, as shown in Figure 18-9.

Figure 18-9: You can include graphics in custom objects; in this Insert Table dialog box, the standard Dreamweaver object is altered to add a brick background.

Tip   You can count on several other useful graphical objects, all found in the Configuration\Shared\MM\Images folder. In addition to the plus and minus buttons used in the Dreamweaver dialog boxes for behaviors and parameters, there are GIF files for standard up and down arrows, a transparent 1-pixel image to use for spacing, and more.

Using layers and Flash movies in objects

Standard HTML layout options are fairly limiting. You can, however, use layers in your custom Object dialog boxes. With the expansive possibilities of layers, you can build a Wizard-type object that leads users through a series of complex steps, with instructions on every screen. You can also use layers to describe the effect of the user's choices.

For an excellent example of the use of layers to create a Dreamweaver extension, take a look at the Drag Layer behavior, discussed in Chapter 19. This behavior uses five different layers to reveal new options as the user makes certain choices; there's even an error layer to inform the user of a precondition to using the object.

Note

Layers enable you to pack in a lot of information—and amass a great deal of input—in a single parameter form. One of the best examples of a multilayered object is Dreamweaver CourseBuilder Knowledge Object. CourseBuilder is a version of the program customized for Web learning, and the Knowledge object is the primary interface. Amazingly enough, all the key functionality of the program is contained in the one object.

Another available option in Dreamweaver objects is the capability to use Flash movies—or any plug-in on the system—within the parameter form. All that's required is that the user have the same plug-in available on their system.

With Flash's scalable vector graphics, animation capabilities, and interactivity, user interfaces have the potential to take a tremendous leap forward. Instead of a Help message, you could build in a training video that demonstrates particularly difficult concepts.

Incorporating a Flash file in your object's parameter form is no different from using it in your Web page. Just choose Insert ⇨ Flash or select the Insert Flash button from the Objects panel. Dreamweaver automatically reads the correct size from the Flash file. Make sure any other parameters you desire are set, and you've just created an advanced user interface! To get an idea of what's possible, take a look at Figure 18-10, which shows an Insert Flash 3 object that uses Flash as the interface, playing in Dreamweaver.

Figure 18-10: Spice up your object's user interface like this Insert Flash 3 object from the Web designer team of Spooky and the Bandit at www.spookyandthebandit.com.

Summary

In one sense, objects are analogous to the macros in a word processing program that enable repetitive work to be greatly simplified. Objects can be so much more than just duplication tools, however — they can extend the reach of Dreamweaver's power and instantly incorporate new standards and technology. The standard Dreamweaver objects can be used effortlessly. Just like all objects, they are simply HTML files, and thus provide excellent examples for creating custom objects.

✦ Objects can be inserted from either the Objects panel or the Insert menu.

✦ Both the Objects panel and the Insert menu can be easily modified by adjusting the menus.xml file.

✦ Simple objects can be created by inserting the HTML code necessary to make the object into a file and then saving the file in one of the object's subfolders.

✦ More complex objects can take advantage of Dreamweaver's built-in JavaScript interpreter, its Document Object Model (DOM), special JavaScript functions, and enhanced Application Programming Interface (API). In Dreamweaver, you can even use layers to construct custom objects.

In the next chapter, you learn how to use Dreamweaver behaviors.

✦   ✦   ✦

Using Behaviors

Behaviors are truly the power tools of Dreamweaver. With Dreamweaver behaviors, any Web designer can make layers appear and disappear, execute any number of rollovers, or control a Shockwave movie — all without knowing even a snippet of JavaScript. In the hands of an accomplished JavaScript programmer, Dreamweaver behaviors can be customized or created from scratch to automate the most difficult Web effect.

Creating behaviors is one of the more challenging Dreamweaver features to master. Implementing these gems, however, is a piece of cake. This chapter examines the concepts behind and the reality of using behaviors — detailing the use of all the behaviors included with Dreamweaver and some from other notable third-party sources. This chapter also contains tips on managing your ever-increasing library of behaviors.

Here's a guarantee for you: Once you get the hang of using Dreamweaver behaviors, your Web pages will never be the same.

Understanding Behaviors, Events, and Actions

A *behavior*, in Macromedia parlance, is the combination of an event and an action. In the electronic age, one pushes a button (the event), and something (the action) occurs — such as changing the channel on the TV. In Dreamweaver, events can be anything as interactive as a user's click of a link or something as automatic as the loading of a Web page. Behaviors are said to be *attached* to a specific element on your page, whether it's a text link, an image, or even the <body> tag.

Dreamweaver has simplified the process of working with behaviors by including default events in every possible object on the Web page. Instead of having to think about both *how* you want to do something and *what* you want to do, you only have to focus on the *what* — the action.

◆   ◆   ◆   ◆

In This Chapter

Behavior basics

Adding a behavior's event and action

Looking at the standard behaviors

Managing behaviors

◆   ◆   ◆   ◆

To help you understand conceptually how behaviors are structured, let's examine the four essential steps for adding a behavior to your Web page:

✦ **Step 1: Pick a tag.** All behaviors are connected to a specific HTML element. You can attach a behavior to everything from the `<body>` to the `<textarea>` of a form. If a certain behavior is unavailable, it's because the necessary element isn't present on the page.

✦ **Step 2: Choose your target browser.** Different browsers — and the various browser versions — support different events. Dreamweaver enables you to choose either a specific browser, such as Internet Explorer 4, or a browser range, such as version 3 and 4 browsers.

✦ **Step 3: Select an action.** Dreamweaver makes active only those actions available to your specific page. You can't, for instance, choose the Show-Hide Layer action until you insert one or more layers. Behaviors guide you to the workable options.

✦ **Step 4: Enter the parameters.** Behaviors get their power from their flexibility. Each action comes with a specific parameter form (which represents the dialog box that the user sees) designed to customize the JavaScript code output. Depending on the action, you can choose source files, set attributes, and enable features. The parameter form can even dynamically update to reflect your current Web page.

Dreamweaver 4 comes with 25 cross browser–compatible actions, and both Macromedia and third-party developers have made many additional actions available, with even more in the works. Behaviors greatly extend the range of possibilities for the modern Web designer — without learning to program JavaScript. All you need to know about attaching behaviors is presented in the following section.

Attaching a Behavior

When you see the code generated by Dreamweaver, you understand why setting up a behavior is also referred to as *attaching* a behavior. As previously noted, Dreamweaver needs a specific HTML tag in order to assign the behavior (Step 1). The link tag `<a>` is often used because, in JavaScript, links can respond to several different events, including `onClick`. Here's an example:

```
<a href="#" onClick="MM_popupMsg('Thanks for coming!')">Exit Here</a>
```

You're not restricted to one event per tag or even one action per event. Multiple events can be attached to a tag to handle various user actions. For example, you may have an image that does all of the following things:

✦ Highlights when the user's pointer moves over the image

✦ Reveals a hidden layer in another area of the page when the user clicks the mouse button on the image

✦ Makes a sound when the user releases the mouse button over the image

✦ Starts a Flash movie when the user's pointer moves away from the image

Likewise, a single event can trigger several actions. Updating multiple frames through a single link used to be difficult — but no more. Dreamweaver makes it easy by enabling you to attach several Go to URL actions to the same event, onMouseClick. In addition, you are not restricted to attaching multiple instances of the same action to a single event. For example, in a site that uses a lot of multimedia, you could tie all of the following actions to a single onClick event:

✦ Begin playing an audio file (with the Play Sound action).

✦ Move a layer across the screen (with the Play Timeline action).

✦ Display a second graphic in place of the first (with the Swap Image action).

✦ Show the copyright information for the audio piece in the status bar (with the Set Text of Status Bar action).

You can even determine the order in which the actions connected to a single event are executed.

With Dreamweaver behaviors, hours of complex JavaScript coding is reduced to a handful of mouse clicks and a minimum of data entry. All behavior assigning and modification is handled through the Behaviors panel.

Using the Behaviors panel

The Behaviors panel is a two-columned window (see Figure 19-1) that neatly sums up the behaviors concept in general. After attaching a behavior, the triggering event (onClick, onMouseOver, and so on) is shown on the left and its associated action — what exactly is triggered — is on the right. A down arrow between the event and action, when clicked, displays other available events for the current browser model. Double-click the action to open the associated parameter window, where you can modify the action's attributes.

As typical in Dreamweaver, you have your choice of methods for opening the Behaviors panel:

✦ Choose Window ➪ Behaviors.

✦ Select the Show Behaviors button from either Launcher.

✦ Use the keyboard shortcut Shift+F3 (an on/off toggle).

Expert Tip   The Behaviors panel can be closed by toggling it off with Shift+F3 or hidden with the other floating panels by pressing F4.

Selected tag

Events   Actions

Down arrow to display options

Figure 19-1: You can handle everything about a behavior through the Behaviors panel.

After you have attached a behavior to a tag and closed the associated action's parameter form, Dreamweaver writes the necessary HTML and JavaScript code into your document. Because it involves functions that can be called from anywhere in the document, the JavaScript code is placed in the <head> section of the page, and the code that links the selected tag to the functions is written in the <body> section. A few actions, including Play Sound, place additional HTML code at the bottom of the <body>, but most of the code — there can be a lot of code to handle all the cross-browser contingencies — is placed in the <head> HTML section.

Adding a behavior

Now let's look more closely at the procedure for adding (or attaching) a behavior. As noted earlier, you can assign only certain events to particular tags, and those options are further defined by the type of selected browser.

Note Even in the latest browsers, key events such as onMouseDown, onMouseOver, and onMouseOut work only with anchor tags. To circumvent this limitation, Dreamweaver can enclose an element, such as <img>, with an anchor tag that links to nowhere — src="javascript:;". Events that use the anchor tag in this fashion are seen in parentheses in the pop-up menu of events.

To add a behavior to your Web page, follow these steps:

1. Select an object in the Document window.

Expert Tip If you want to assign a behavior to the entire page, select the <body> tag from the Tag Selector.

2. Open the Behaviors panel by choosing Window ➪ Behaviors or selecting the Show Behaviors button from either Launcher. You can see the selected tag at the top of the Behaviors panel.

3. Select the + (add action) button to reveal the available options, as shown in Figure 19-2. Choose one from the pop-up menu.

Figure 19-2: The Add Action pop-up menu dynamically changes according to what's on the current page and which tag is selected.

4. Enter the necessary parameters in the Action's dialog box.

5. Click OK when you're finished to close the dialog box.

Dreamweaver adds a line to the Behaviors panel displaying the added action and its default action.

A trigger — whether it's an image or a text link — may have multiple behaviors attached to it. One graphical navigation element could, for instance, perform a Swap Image when the user's mouse moves over it, a Swap Image Restore when the mouse moves away and, when clicked, show another Web page in an additional smaller window with the Open Browser Window behavior.

Dreamweaver includes a menu item at the bottom of the Add Action list: Get More Behaviors. To use this feature, go online and then choose the option. You will be connected with the Dreamweaver Exchange, a service from Macromedia with a huge selection of extensions of all flavors, including behaviors.

Managing events

Every time Dreamweaver attaches a behavior to a tag, it also inserts an event for you. The default event that is chosen is based on two selections: the browser type and the tag selected. The different browsers in use have widely different capabilities, notably when it comes to understanding the various event handlers and associated tags.

For every browser and browser combination shown in the Browser drop-down list, Dreamweaver has a corresponding file in the Configuration\Behaviors\Events folder. Each of the tags listed in each file, such as I.E. 4.0.htm, has at least one event associated with it. The entries look like this:

```
<INPUT TYPE="Text" onBlur="*" onChange="" onFocus="" onSelect="">
```

The default event for each tag is marked with an asterisk; in the example, onBlur is the default event. After you've selected an action and completed the dialog box, the default event appears in the Events column alongside the action in the Actions column.

If you find yourself changing a particular default event over and over again to some other event, you might want to modify the Event file to pick your alternative as the default. To do this, open the relevant browser file found in the Configuration\Behaviors\Events folder in a regular text editor (not Dreamweaver) and move the asterisk to a different event for that particular tag. Resave the file and restart Dreamweaver to try out your new default behavior.

Should the default event not be the one you prefer to use, you can easily choose
another. Choose a different event by selecting the down arrow next to the displayed
default event in the Behaviors panel and select any event in the drop-down list (see
Figure 19-3).

Figure 19-3: You can change the event
by selecting the Events arrow button.

Which events are available depends on the browser model selected. By default, 3.0
and Later Browsers is chosen. To change browser models, choose Show Events For
from the Events list and select one of the following:

✦ 3.0 and Later Browsers

✦ 4.0 and Later Browsers

✦ IE 3.0

✦ IE 4.0

✦ IE 5.0

✦ Netscape 3.0

✦ Netscape 4.0

The Dreamweaver\Configuration\Behaviors\Events folder contains HTML files
corresponding to the six browsers offered in the Show Events For submenu. You
can open these files in Dreamweaver, but Macromedia asks that you not edit
them — with one exception. Each file contains the list of tags that have supported
event handlers (the JavaScript term for events) in that browser.

The older the browser, the fewer event handlers are included—unfortunately, this also means that if you want to reach the broadest Internet audience, your event options are limited. In the broadest category, 3.0 and Later Browsers, only 13 different tags can receive any sort of event handler. This is one of the reasons why, for example, Internet Explorer 3 can't handle rollovers: the browser doesn't understand what an onMouseOut event is, and so the image can't revert to its original state.

If you do open and examine an event file in Dreamweaver, notice a group of yellow tags and a few form objects (see Figure 19-4). The yellow tags identify what Dreamweaver sees as invalid HTML. Those form objects—the buttons, checkbox, radio button, and text—render normally but aren't active.

Caution   It's far better to use a standard text editor such as HomeSite or BBEdit to open and modify an event file than to use Dreamweaver. By default, Dreamweaver attempts to correct the invalid HTML it finds in the file, and if you save the file with these unwanted corrections in place, your file will be corrupted, and you'll lose access to certain events.

In this case, viewing the HTML is far more instructive than the Document window, as you can see by looking at Listing 19-1. This example gives the event handler definitions for the 3.0 and Later Browsers category.

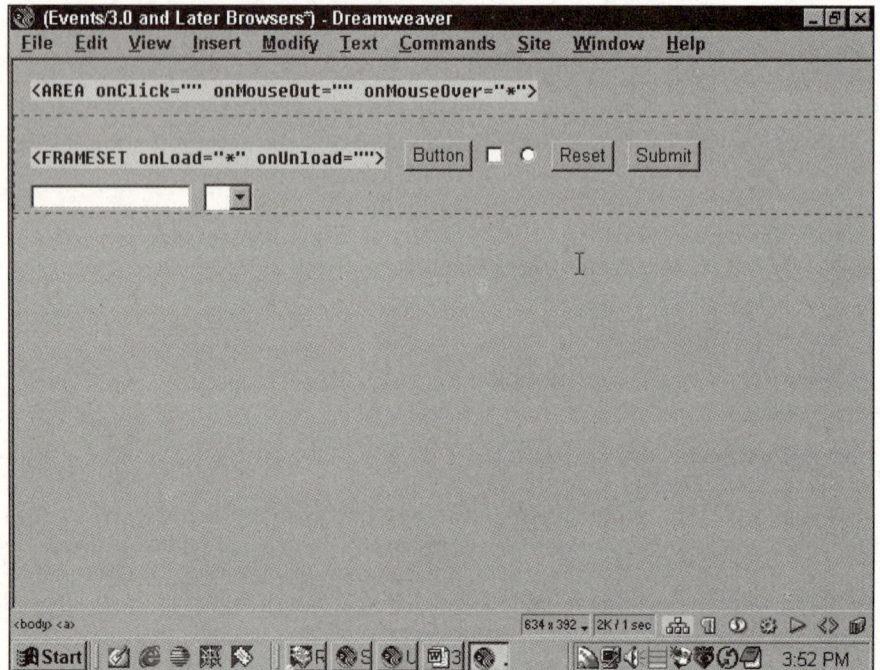

Figure 19-4: The event files define the tags that support particular event handlers in a selected browser.

Listing 19-1: The Events File for 3.0 and Later Browsers

```
<A onMouseOver="*">
<AREA onClick="" onMouseOut="" onMouseOver="*">
<BODY onLoad="*" onUnload="">
<FORM onReset="" onSubmit="*">
<FRAMESET onLoad="*" onUnload="">
<INPUT TYPE="Button" onClick="*">
<INPUT TYPE="Checkbox" onClick="*">
<INPUT TYPE="Radio" onClick="*">
<INPUT TYPE="Reset" onClick="*">
<INPUT TYPE="Submit" onClick="*">
<INPUT TYPE="Text" onBlur="*" onChange="" onFocus=""
onSelect="">
<SELECT onBlur="" onChange="*" onFocus="">
<TEXTAREA onBlur="" onChange="*" onFocus="" onSelect="">
```

By contrast, the events file for Internet Explorer 5.0 shows support for every tag under the HTML sun — 92 in all — with almost every tag able to handle any type of event.

Expert Tip   Although any HTML tag could potentially be used to attach a behavior, the most commonly used by far are the `<body>` tag (for entire-page events such as `onLoad`), the `<img>` tag when used as a button, and the link tag, `<a>`.

To locate the default events for any tag as used by a particular browser, consult Table 19-1. The table also shows, at a glance, which browsers support which tags to receive events.

Standard actions

The following 25 standard actions ship with Dreamweaver 4:

Call JavaScript	Open Browser Window	Show-Hide Layers
Change Property	Play Sound	Swap Image
Check Browser	Popup Message	Swap Image Restore
Check Plugin	Preload Images	Play Timeline
Control Shockwave or Flash	Set Nav Bar Image	Stop Timeline
Drag Layer	Set Text of Frame	Go to Timeline Frame
Go to URL	Set Text of Layer	Validate Form
Jump Menu	Set Text of Status Bar	
Jump Menu Go	Set Text of Text Field	

Table 19-1
Default Events by Browser

Tag	3.0 and Later Browsers	4.0 and Later Browsers	IE 3.0	IE 4.0	IE 5.0	Netscape 3.0	Netscape 4.0
<a>	onMouseOver	onClick	OnMouseOver	onClick	onClick	onClick	onClick
<acronym>					onClick		
<address>					onClick		
<applet>				onLoad	onLoad		
<area>	onMouseOver	onMouseOver		onMouseOver	onMouseOver	onMouseOver	onMouseOver
<b>				onClick	onClick		
<bdo>				onMouseOver	onMouseOver		
<big>				onMouseOver	onMouseOver		
<blink>							
<body>	onLoad	onLoad	OnLoad	onLoad	onLoad	onLoad	onLoad
<button>				onClick	onClick		
<caption>				onMouseOver	onMouseOver		
<center>				onMouseOver	onMouseOver		
<cite>				onMouseOver	onMouseOver		
<code>				onMouseOver	onMouseOver		
<col>				onMouseOver	onLoseCapture		
<colgroup>				onMouseOver	onLoseCapture		
<dd>				onMouseOver	onMouseOver		
<del>				onMouseOver	onMouseOver		
<dfn>				onMouseOver	onMouseOver		
<dir>				onMouseOver	onMouseOver		
<div>				onClick	onClick		
<dl>				onMouseOver	onMouseOver		
<dt>				onMouseOver	onMouseOver		
<em>				onMouseOver	onMouseOver		
<embed>				onLoad	onLoad		
<fieldset>				onClick	onClick		
<font>				onMouseOver	onMouseOver		
<form>	onSubmit	onSubmit	OnSubmit	onSubmit	onSubmit	onSubmit	onSubmit
<frame>	onLoad	onLoad	OnLoad	onLoad	onLoad	onLoad	onLoad
<frameset>				onLoad	onLoad		
<h1>...<h6>				onMouseOver	onMouseOver		
<hr>				onMouseOver	onMouseOver		
<i>				onMouseOver	onMouseOver		
<iframe>				onFocus	onFocus		
<ilayer>							
<img>	onClick	onMouseDown	OnClick	onClick	onClick	(None selected)	onLoad onMouseDown
<input type=button | checkbox | image | radio | reset | submit>	onClick	onClick	OnClick	onClick	onClick	onClick	onClick

Tag	3.0 and Later Browsers	4.0 and Later Browsers	IE 3.0	IE 4.0	IE 5.0	Netscape 3.0	Netscape 4.0
`<input type=file | password>`		onChange		onChange	onChange	onChange	onChange
`<input type=text>`	onBlur	onBlur	OnBlur	onBlur	onBlur	onBlur	onBlur
`<ins>`				onMouseOver	onMouseOver		
`<kbd>`				onClick	onClick		
`<label>`				onClick	onClick		
`<layer>`							onMouseOver
`<legend>`					onClick		
`<li>`				onMouseOver	onMouseOver		
`<listing>`				onMouseOver	onMouseOver		
`<map>`				onClick	onClick		
`<marquee>`				onMouseOver	onMouseOver		
`<menu>`				onMouseOver	onMouseOver		
`<nobr>`				onMouseOver	onMouseOver		
`<object>`				onLoad	onLoad		
`<ol>`				onMouseOver	onMouseOver		
`<p>`				onMouseOver	onMouseOver		
`<plaintext>`				onMouseOver	onMouseOver		
`<pre>`				onMouseOver	onMouseOver		
`<q>`				onMouseOver	onMouseOver		
`<rt>`					onClick		
`<s>`				onMouseOver	onMouseOver		
`<samp>`				onMouseOver	onMouseOver		
`<select>`	onChange	onChange	OnChange	onChange	onChange	onChange	onChange
`<small>`				onMouseOver	onMouseOver		
`<span>`				onMouseOver	onMouseOver		
`<strike>`				onMouseOver	onMouseOver		
`<strong>`				onMouseOver	onMouseOver		
`<sub>`				onMouseOver	onMouseOver		
`<sup>`				onMouseOver	onMouseOver		
`<table>`				onMouseOver	onMouseOver		
`<tbody>`				onMouseOver	onMouseOver		
`<td>`				onMouseOver	onMouseOver		
`<textarea>`	onChange	onChange	onChange	onChange	onChange	onChange	onChange
`<tfoot>`				onMouseOver	onMouseOver		
`<th>`				onMouseOver	onMouseOver		
`<thead>`				onMouseOver	onMouseOver		
`<tr>`				onMouseOver	onMouseOver		
`<tt>`				onMouseOver	onMouseOver		
`<u>`				onMouseOver	onMouseOver		
`<ul>`				onMouseOver	onMouseOver		
`<var>`				onMouseOver	onMouseOver		
`<xmp>`				onMouseOver	onMouseOver		

Each action operates independently and differently from the others, although many share common functions. Each action is associated with a different dialog box or parameter form to enable easy attribute entry.

The following sections describe each of the standard actions: what the action does, what requirements must be met for it to be activated, what options are available, and most important of all, how to use it. Each action is written to work with all browser versions 4 and above; however, some actions do not work as designed in the older browsers. The charts included with every action show the action's compatibility with older browsers. (The information in these charts was adapted from the Dreamweaver Help pages and is used with permission.)

Note The following descriptions assume that you understand the basics of assigning behaviors and that you know how to open the Behaviors panel.

Call JavaScript

With Call JavaScript, you can execute any JavaScript function — standard or custom — with a single mouse click or other event. As your JavaScript savvy grows, you'll find yourself using this behavior again and again.

Call JavaScript is straightforward to use; simply type in the JavaScript code or the name of the function you want to trigger into the dialog box. If, for example, you wanted to get some input from a visitor, you could use JavaScript's built-in `prompt()` method, like this:

```
result=prompt("Whom shall I say is calling?","")
```

When this code is triggered, a small dialog box appears with your query (here, "Whom shall I say is calling?") and a space for an input string. The second argument in the `prompt()` method enables you to include a default answer — to leave it blank, just use two quotes.

Note You can use either single or double quotes in your Call JavaScript behavior; Dreamweaver automatically adjusts for whichever you choose. However, I find it easier to use single quotes because Dreamweaver translates double quotes into character entities; that is, " becomes `&quot;`.

Naturally, you could use Call JavaScript to handle much more complex chores as well. To call a specific custom function that is already in the `<head>` section of your page, just enter its name — along with any necessary arguments — in the Call JavaScript dialog box, shown in Figure 19-5.

Figure 19-5: Trigger any JavaScript function by attaching a Call JavaScript behavior to an image or text.

To use the Call JavaScript behavior, follow these steps:

1. Select the object to trigger the action.

2. From the Behaviors panel, select the add action button and choose Call JavaScript.

3. In the Call JavaScript dialog box, enter your code in the text box.

4. Click OK when you're done.

Note   In the following charts that detail action behaviors for both newer and older browsers, the phrase "Fails without error" means that the action won't work in the older browser, but that it doesn't generate an error message for the user to see. Where the table indicates "error," it means the user receives a JavaScript alert message.

Here's the browser compatibility chart for the Call JavaScript behavior:

Call JavaScript	Netscape 3.x	Internet Explorer 3.0	Internet Explorer 3.01
Macintosh	Okay	Fails without error	
Windows	Okay		Okay

Change Property

The Change Property action enables you to dynamically alter a property of one of the following tags:

```
<layer>        <div>        <form>        <textarea>
<span>         <img>        <select>
```

You can also alter the following `<input>` types:

```
radio          checkbox         text          password
```

Exactly which properties can be altered depends on the tag as well as on the browser being targeted. For example, the `<div>` tag and Internet Explorer 4.0 combination enables you to change virtually every style sheet option on the fly. The Change Property dialog box (see Figure 19-6) offers a list of the selected tags in the current page.

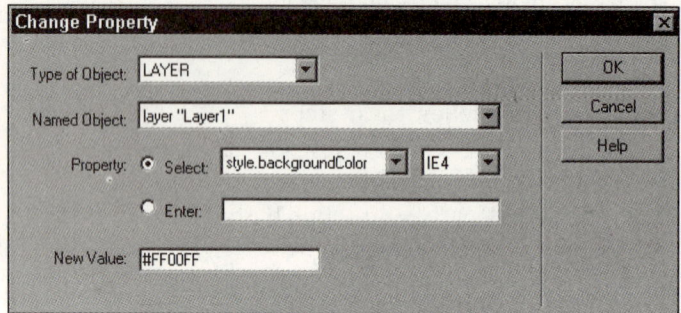

Figure 19-6: The Change Property action enables you to alter attributes of certain tags dynamically.

It's important that you name the objects you want to alter so that Dreamweaver can properly identify them. Remember to use unique names that begin with a letter and contain no spaces or special characters.

This behavior is especially useful for changing the properties of forms and form elements. Be sure to name the form if you wish to use Change Property in this manner.

To use the Change Property action, follow these steps:

1. Select the object to trigger the action.

2. From the Behaviors panel, select the add action button and choose Change Property.

3. In the Change Property dialog box, choose an object type, such as FORM or SELECT, from the Type of Object drop-down list.

4. In the dynamic Named Object drop-down list, choose the object on your page you wish to affect.

5. Click the Select radio button. Select the target browser in the small list box on the far right and then choose the property to change. If you don't find the property in the drop-down list box, you can type it yourself into the Enter text box.

Many properties in the various browsers are read-only and cannot be dynamically altered. Those properties listed in the option list are always dynamic.

6. In the New Value text box, type the property's new value to be inserted when the event is fired.

7. Click OK when you're done.

Here's the browser compatibility chart for the Change Property behavior:

Change Property	Netscape 3.x	Internet Explorer 3.0	Internet Explorer 3.01
Macintosh	Okay	Fails without error	
Windows	Okay		Okay

Check Browser

Some Web sites are increasingly split into multilevel versions of themselves to gracefully handle the variety of browsers in operation. The Check Browser action acts as a type of browser "router" capable of sending browsers to appropriate URLs, or just letting them stay on the current page. The Check Browser action is generally assigned to the `<body>` tag and uses the `onLoad` event. If used in this fashion, it's a good idea to keep the basic page accessible to all browsers, even those with JavaScript disabled.

The Check Browser parameter form (see Figure 19-7) is quite flexible and enables you to specify decimal version numbers for the two main browsers. For instance, you may want to let all users of Navigator 4.04 or later stay on the current page and send everyone else to an alternative URL. The URLs can be either relative, such as `alt/index.html`, or absolute, such as `www.idest.com/alt/index.html`.

Figure 19-7: The Check Browser action is a great tool for segregating old and new browsers.

To use the Check Browser action, follow these steps:

1. Select the object to trigger the action.

2. From the Behaviors panel, select the add action button and choose Check Browser.

3. Specify the Netscape Navigator and Internet Explorer versions and whether you want the browser to stay on the current page, go to another URL, or proceed to a third alternative URL.

Note   With both major browsers, you can specify the URL that the lower version numbers should visit.

4. Set the same options for all other browsers, such as Opera or OMNIWeb.

5. Enter the URL and alternative URL options in their respective text boxes or select the Browse (Choose) button to locate the files.

Cross-Reference   The Check Browser action works well with another Dreamweaver feature: Convert to 3.0 Compatible. Learn all about this capability in Chapter 34.

Here's the browser compatibility chart for the Check Browser behavior:

Check Browser	*Netscape 3.x*	*Internet Explorer 3.0*	*Internet Explorer 3.01*
Macintosh	Okay	Fails without error	
Windows	Okay		Okay

Check Plugin

If certain pages on your Web site require the use of one or more plug-ins, you can use the Check Plugin action to see if a visitor has the necessary plug-in installed. Once this has been examined, Check Plugin can route users with the appropriate plug-in to one URL, and users without it to another URL. You can look for only one plug-in at a time, but you can use multiple instances of the Check Plugin action, if needed.

By default, the parameter form for Check Plugin (see Figure 19-8) offers five plug-ins: Flash, Shockwave, LiveAudio, Netscape Media Player, and QuickTime Plug-in. You can check for any other plug-in by entering its name in the Enter text box; use the name that appears when choosing Help ⇨ About Plugins in the Navigator menus.

Figure 19-8: Running a media-intensive site? Use the Check Plugin action to divert visitors without plug-ins to alternate pages.

Expert Tip If you use a particular plug-in regularly, you may want to also modify the Check Plugin.js file found in your Actions folder. Add your new plug-in name to the PLUGIN_NAMES array and the corresponding PLUGIN_VALUES array in the initGlobal function.

Although Check Plugin cannot check for specific ActiveX controls, this action can route the Internet Explorer user to the same page as users who have plug-ins. The best way to handle both browsers is to use both ActiveX controls and plug-ins, through the `<object>` and `<embed>` methods explained in Chapter 17.

On the CD-ROM Another method for determining whether a plug-in or other player is available is to use the Check MIME action included on the CD-ROM that accompanies this book. This action works in the same way as the Check Plugin action, except you enter the MIME type.

To use the Check Plugin action, follow these steps:

1. Select the object to trigger the action.

2. From the Behaviors panel, select the add action button and choose Check Browser.

3. Select a plug-in from the drop-down list. You can also type another plug-in name in the Enter text box.

Note The names presented in the drop-down list are abbreviated, more recognizable names, and not the formal names inserted into the code. For example, when the option Shockwave is selected, the phrase Shockwave for Director is actually input into the code. On the other hand, any plug-in name you enter manually into the Enter field is inserted verbatim.

4. If you want to send users who are confirmed to have the plug-in to a different page, enter that URL (absolute or relative) in the If Found, Go To URL text box or use the Browse (Choose) button to locate the file. If you want them to stay on the current page, leave the text box empty.

5. In the Otherwise, Go To URL text box, enter the URL for users who do not have the required plug-in.

6. Should the browser detection method fail — as with certain browsers, such as some versions of Internet Explorer on the Macintosh — you can keep the user on the initial page by enabling the "Always go to first URL if detection is not possible" option. Otherwise, if the detection fails, for any reason, the users are sent to the URL listed in the Otherwise field.

Here's the browser compatibility chart for the Check Plugin behavior:

Check Browser	Netscape 3.x	Internet Explorer 3.0	Internet Explorer 3.01
Macintosh	Okay	Fails without error	
Windows	Okay		Okay

Control Shockwave or Flash

The Control Shockwave or Flash action enables you to command your Shockwave and Flash movies through external controls. With Control Shockwave or Flash, you can build your own interface for your Shockwave or Flash material. This action can be used in conjunction with the autostart=true attribute (entered through the Property Inspector's Parameter dialog box for the Shockwave or Flash file) to enable a replaying of the movie.

You must have a Shockwave or Flash movie inserted in your Web page in order for the Control Shockwave or Flash action to be available. The parameter form for this action (see Figure 19-9) lists all the Shockwave or Flash movies by name that are found in either an <embed> or <object> tag. You can set the action to control the movie in one of four ways: Play, Stop, Rewind, or Go to Frame. You can choose only one option each time you attach an action to an event. If you choose the last option, you need to specify the frame number in the text box. Note that specifying a Go to Frame number does not start the movie there; you need to attach a second Control Shockwave or Flash action to the same event to play the file.

Figure 19-9: Build your own interface and then control a Shockwave and Flash movie externally with the Control Shockwave or Flash action.

Expert Tip

Be sure to name your Shockwave or Flash movie. Otherwise, the Control Shockwave or Flash action lists both `unnamed <embed>` and `unnamed <object>` for each file, and you cannot write to both tags as you can with a named movie.

To use the Control Shockwave or Flash action, follow these steps:

1. Select the object to trigger the action.

2. From the Behaviors panel, select the add action button and choose Control Shockwave or Flash.

3. In the Control Shockwave or Flash dialog box, select a movie from the Named Shockwave Object drop-down list.

4. Select a control by choosing its radio button:

   • **Play:** Begins playing the movie at the current frame location.

   • **Stop:** Stops playing the movie.

   • **Rewind:** Returns the movie to its first frame.

   • **Go to Frame:** Displays a specific frame in the movie. Note: For this option, you must enter a frame number in the text box.

5. Click OK when you're done.

Here's the browser compatibility chart for the Control Shockwave or Flash behavior:

Control Shockwave or Flash	Netscape 3.x	Internet Explorer 3.0	Internet Explorer 3.01
Macintosh	Okay	Fails without error	
Windows	Okay		Fails without error

Drag Layer

The Drag Layer action provides some spectacular — and interactive — effects with little effort on the part of the designer. Drag Layer enables your Web page visitors to move layers — and all that they contain — around the screen with the drag-and-drop technique. With the Drag Layer action, you can easily set up the following capabilities for the user:

✦ Enable layers to be dragged anywhere on the screen.

✦ Restrict the dragging to a particular direction or combination of directions — a horizontal sliding layer can be restricted to left and right movement, for instance.

✦ Limit the drag handle to a portion of the layer such as the upper bar or enable the whole layer to be used.

✦ Provide an alternative clipping method by enabling only a portion of the layer to be dragged.

✦ Enable changing of the layers' stacking order while dragging or on mouse release.

✦ Set a snap-to target area on your Web page for layers that the user releases within a defined radius.

✦ Program a JavaScript command to be executed when the snap-to target is hit or every time the layer is released.

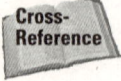

Cross-Reference   Layers are one of the more powerful features of Dreamweaver. To get the most out of the layer-oriented behaviors, familiarize yourself with layers by examining Chapter 28.

Layers must be inserted in your Web page before the Drag Layer action becomes available for selection from the Add Action pop-up menu. You must attach the action to the <body> — you can, however, attach separate versions of Drag Layer to different layers for different effects.

Drag Layer's parameter form (see Figure 19-10) includes a Get Current Position button that puts the left and top coordinates of a selected layer into the appropriate boxes for the Drop Target parameters. If you plan on using targeting, place your layer at the target location before attaching the behavior.

Figure 19-10: With the Drag Layer action, you can set up your layers to be repositioned by the user.

To use the Drag Layer action, follow these steps:

1. Select the <body> tag.

2. From the Behaviors panel, select the add action button and choose Drag Layer.

3. In the Layer drop-down list of the parameter form in the Basic tabbed panel, select the layer you want to make draggable.

4. To limit the movement of the layer, change the Movement option from Unconstrained to Constrained. Text boxes for Up, Down, Left, and Right appear. Enter pixel values in the text boxes to control the range of motion:

   • To constrain movement vertically, enter positive numbers in the Up and Down text boxes and zeros in the Left and Right text boxes.

   • To constrain movement horizontally, enter positive numbers in the Left and Right text boxes and zeros in the Up and Down text boxes.

   • To enable movement in a rectangular region, enter positive values in all four text boxes.

5. To establish a location for a target for the dragged layer, enter coordinates in the Drop Target: Left and Top text boxes. Select the Get Current Position button to fill these text boxes with the layer's present location.

6. To set a snap-to area around the target coordinates where the layer falls, if released in the target location, enter a pixel value in the Snap if Within text box.

7. For additional options, select the Advanced tab.

8. If you want to limit the area to be used as a drag handle, select the radio button for Drag Handle: Area Within Layer. Left, Top, Width, and Height text boxes appear. In the appropriate text boxes, enter the Left and Top coordinates of the drag handle in pixels, as well as the Width and Height dimensions.

Note If you want to enable the whole layer to act as a drag handle, make sure the Drag Handle: Entire Layer radio button is selected.

9. To control the positioning of the dragged layer, set the following While Dragging options:

   • To keep the layer in its current depth and not bring it to the front when it is dragged, deselect the checkbox for While Dragging: Bring Layer to the Front.

   • To change the stacking order of the layer when it is released, select either Leave on Top or Restore z-order from the drop-down list.

10. To execute a JavaScript command while the layer is being dragged, enter the command or function in the Call JavaScript text box.

11. To execute a JavaScript command when the layer is dropped on the target, enter the code in the When Dropped: Call JavaScript text box. If you want the JavaScript to execute only when the layer is snapped to its target, select the Only if snapped option — this option requires that a value be entered in the Snap if Within text box.

12. Click OK when you're done.

Note   If you—or someone on your team—has the JavaScript programming skills, you can gather information output from the Drag Layer behavior to enhance your pages. Dreamweaver declares three variables for each draggable layer: MM_UPDOWN (the y coordinate), MM_LEFTRIGHT (the x coordinate), and MM_SNAPPED (true, if the layer has reached the specified target). Before you can get any of these properties, you must get an object reference for the proper layer. Another function, MM_findObj (layername), handles this chore.

Here's the browser compatibility chart for the Drag Layer behavior:

Drag Layer	*Netscape 3.x*	*Internet Explorer 3.0*	*Internet Explorer 3.01*
Macintosh	Fails without error	Fails without error	
Windows	Fails without error		Fails without error

Go to URL

Dreamweaver brings the same power of links — with a lot more flexibility — to any event with the Go to URL action. One of the trickier tasks in using frames on a Web page is updating two or more frames simultaneously with a single button click. The Go to URL action handily streamlines this process for the Web designer. Go to URL can also be used as a preload router that sends the user to another Web page once the onLoad event has finished.

The dialog box for Go to URL (see Figure 19-11) displays any existing anchors or frames in the current page or frameset. To load multiple URLs at the same time, open the drop-down list and select the first frame that you want to alter; then enter the desired page or location in the URL text box. Select the second frame from the list and enter the next URL (or Browse/Choose to find it). If you select a frame to which you have previously assigned a URL, that address appears in the URL text box.

Figure 19-11: Update two or more frames at the same time with the Go to URL action.

To use the Go to URL action, follow these steps:

1. Select the object to trigger the action.

2. From the Behaviors panel, select the add action button and choose Go to URL.

3. From the Go to URL dialog box, select the target for your link from the list in the Open In window.

4. Enter the path of the file to open in the URL text box or click the Browse (Choose) button to locate a file.

   An asterisk appears next to the frame name to indicate that a URL has been chosen.

5. To select another target to load a different URL, repeat Steps 3 and 4.

6. Click OK when you're done.

Here's the browser compatibility chart for the Go to URL behavior:

Go to URL	Netscape 3.x	Internet Explorer 3.0	Internet Explorer 3.01
Macintosh	Okay	Fails without error	
Windows	Okay		Okay

Jump Menu and Jump Menu Go

Although most behaviors insert original code to activate an element of the Web page, several behaviors are included to edit code inserted by a Dreamweaver object. The Jump Menu and Jump Menu Go behaviors both require a previously inserted Jump Menu object before they become active. The Jump Menu behavior is used to edit an existing Jump Menu object, while the Jump Menu Go behavior adds a graphic image as a "Go" button.

To use the Jump Menu behavior to edit an existing Jump Menu object, follow these steps:

1. Select the Jump Menu object previously inserted into the page.

2. In the Behaviors panel, double-click the listed Jump Menu behavior.

3. Make your modifications in the Jump Menu dialog box, as shown in Figure 19-12.

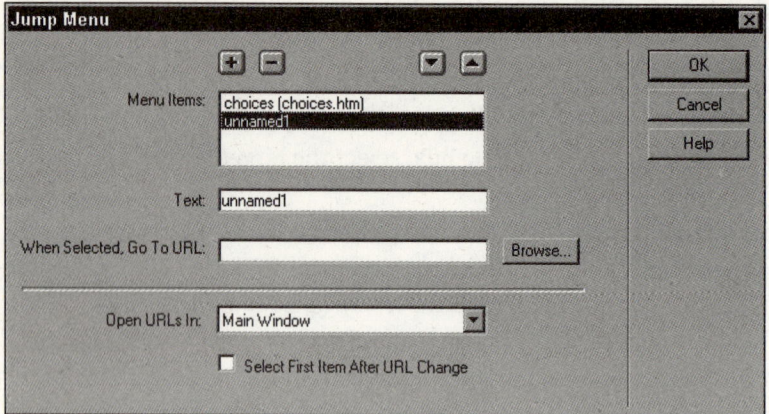

Figure 19-12: The Jump Menu behavior is used to modify a previously inserted Jump Menu object.

You can alter the existing menu item names or their associated URLs, add new menu items, or reorder the list through the Jump Menu dialog box.

4. Click OK when you're done.

To add a button to activate the Jump Menu object, follow these steps:

1. Select the image or form button you'd like to make into a Go button.

A Jump Menu object must be on the current page for the Jump Menu Go behavior to be available.

2. From the Behaviors panel, select Jump Menu Go from the Add behavior list.

The Jump Menu Go dialog box, shown in Figure 19-13, is displayed.

Figure 19-13: Add a graphic or standard button as a Go button with the Jump Menu Go behavior.

3. Select the name of the Jump Menu object you want to activate from the option list.

4. Click OK when you're done.

Here's the browser compatibility chart for both Jump Menu behavior:

Jump Menu	Netscape 3.x	Internet Explorer 3.0	Internet Explorer 3.01
Macintosh	Okay	Fails without error	
Windows	Okay		Fails without error

Open Browser Window

Want to display your latest design in a borderless, nonresizable browser window that's exactly the size of your image? With the Open Browser Window action, you can open a new browser window and specify its exact size and attributes. You can even set it up to receive JavaScript events.

You can also open a new browser window with a regular link by specifying target="_blank", but you can't control any of the window's attributes with that method. You do get this control with the parameter form of the Open Browser Window action (see Figure 19-14); here you can set the window width and height, and whether or not to display the Navigation Toolbar, Location Toolbar, Status Bar, Menu Bar, Scrollbars, and Resize Handles. You can also name your new window, a necessary step for advanced JavaScript control.

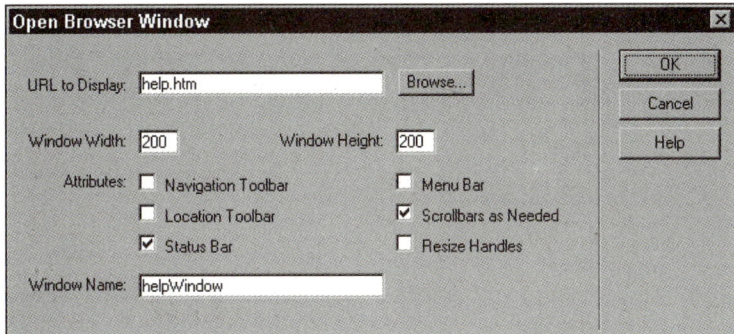

Figure 19-14: Use the Open Browser Window action to program in a pop-up advertisement or remote control.

You have to explicitly select any of the attributes you want to appear in your new window. Your new browser window contains only the attributes you've checked, plus basic window elements such as a title bar and a Close button.

To use the Open Browser Window action, follow these steps:

1. Select the object to trigger the action.

2. From the Behaviors panel, select the add action button and choose Open Browser Window.

3. In the URL to Display text box, enter the address of the Web page you want to display in the new window. You can also select the Browse (Choose) button to locate the file.

4. To specify the window's size and shape, enter the width and height values in the appropriate text boxes.

   You must enter both a width and height measurement, or the new browser window opens to its default size.

5. Check the appropriate Attributes checkboxes to enable the parameters you want.

6. If you plan on using JavaScript to address or control the window, type a unique name in the Window Name text box. This name cannot contain spaces or special characters. Dreamweaver alerts you if the name you've entered is unacceptable.

7. Click OK when you're done.

Here's the browser compatibility chart for the Open Browser Window behavior:

Open Browser Window	*Netscape 3.x*	*Internet Explorer 3.0*	*Internet Explorer 3.01*
Macintosh	Okay	Fails without error	
Windows	Okay		Okay

Play Sound

The Play Sound action is used to add external controls to an audio file that nor-mally uses the Netscape LiveAudio plug-in or the Windows Media Player. Supported audio file types include .wav, .mid, .au, and .aiff files — generally to add background music with a hidden sound file. The Play Sound action inserts an `<embed>` tag with the following attributes set:

✦ loop=false

✦ autostart=false

✦ mastersound

✦ hidden=true

✦ width=0

✦ height=0

Instead of automatically detecting which sound files have been inserted in the current Web page, Play Sound looks for the sound file to be inserted though the action's dialog box (see Figure 19-15).

Figure 19-15: Give your Web page background music and control it with the Play Sound action.

Note   Dreamweaver can detect if a visitor's browser has the Windows Media Player installed and, if so, issue the appropriate commands.

To use the Play Sound action, follow these steps:

1. Select the object to trigger the action.
2. From the Behaviors panel, select the add action button and choose Play Sound.
3. To play a sound, enter the path to the audio file in the Play Sound text box or select the Browse (Choose) button to locate the file.
4. Click OK when you're done.

Here's the browser compatibility chart for the Play Sound behavior:

Play Sound	Netscape 3.x	Internet Explorer 3.0	Internet Explorer 3.01
Macintosh	Okay	Fails without error	
Windows	Okay		Fails without error

Popup Message

You can send a quick message to your users with the Popup Message action. When triggered, this action opens a JavaScript Application Alert with your message. You enter your message in the Message text box on the action's parameter form (see Figure 19-16).

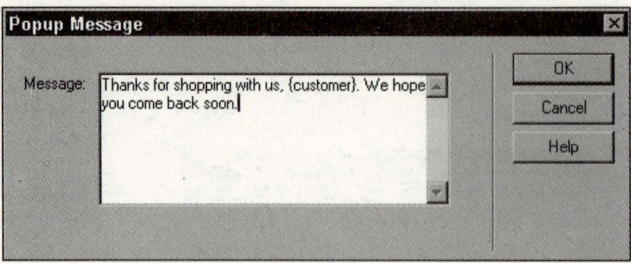

Figure 19-16: Send a message to your users with the Popup Message action.

To use the Popup Message action, follow these steps:

1. Select the object to trigger the action.

2. From the Behaviors panel, select the add action button and choose Popup Message.

3. Enter your text in the Message text box.

4. Click OK when you're done.

Expert Tip

You can include JavaScript functions or references in your text messages by surrounding the JavaScript with curly braces. For example, today's date could be incorporated in a message like this:

```
Welcome to our site on {new Date()}!
```

You could also pull data entered into a form to incorporate into a message, as in this example:

```
Thanks for filling out our form, ¬
{document.theForm.firstname.value}.
```

If you need to display a curly brace in a message, you must precede it with a back-slash character, \.

Here's the browser compatibility chart for the Popup Message behavior:

Popup Message	Netscape 3.x	Internet Explorer 3.0	Internet Explorer 3.01
Macintosh	Okay	Fails without error	
Windows	Okay		Okay

Preload Images

Designs commonly require a particular image or images to be displayed immediately when called by an action or a timeline. Because of the nature of HTML, all graphics are separate files that normally are downloaded when needed. To get the snappy response required for certain designs, graphics need to be preloaded or cached so that they will be available. The Preload Images action performs this important service. You designate the images you want to cache for later use through the Preload Images parameter form (see Figure 19-17).

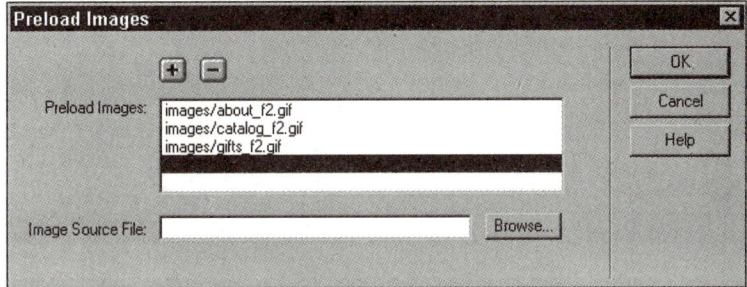

Figure 19-17: Media-rich Web sites respond much faster when images have been cached with the Preload Images action.

 Note You don't need to use the Preload Images action if you're creating rollovers. Both the Rollover object and the Swap Image action enable you to preload images from their dialog boxes.

To use the Preload Images action, follow these steps:

1. Select the object to trigger the action.

2. From the Behaviors panel, select the add action button and Preload Images.

3. In the action's parameter form, enter the path to the image file in the Image Source File text box or select the Browse (Choose) button to locate the file.

4. To add another file, click the + (add) button and repeat Step 2.

 Caution After you've specified your first file to be preloaded, be sure to press the + (add) button for each successive file you want to add to the list. Otherwise, the highlighted file is replaced by the next entry.

5. To remove a file from the Preload Images list, select it and click the – (delete) button.

6. Click OK when you're done.

Here's the browser compatibility chart for the Preload Images behavior:

Preload Image	Netscape 3.x	Internet Explorer 3.0	Internet Explorer 3.01
Macintosh	Okay	Fails without error	
Windows	Okay		Fails without error

Set Nav Bar Image

The Set Nav Bar Image action, like the Jump Menu actions, enables you to edit an existing Dreamweaver object. The Nav Bar object, inserted from the Common category of the Objects panel, consists of a series of user-specified images acting as a group of navigational buttons. The Set Nav Bar Image action enables you to modify the current Nav Bar object, adding, reordering, or deleting images as buttons as well as setting up advanced rollover techniques. In fact, the Set Nav Bar Image action could be thought of as a superduper Swap Image behavior.

Cross-Reference   To refresh your memory about the capabilities of the Nav Bar Image, see Chapter 10.

The main aspect that sets a nav bar apart from any other similar series of rollover images is that the nav bar elements relate to one another. When you select one element of a nav bar, by default, all the other elements are swapped to their up state. The Set Nav Bar Image action enables you to modify that default behavior to a rollover in another area or any other image swap desired. You can also use the Set Nav Bar Image to include another image button in the nav bar.

To modify an existing Nav Bar object, follow these steps:

1. Choose any image in a Nav Bar object.

2. From the Behaviors panel, double-click any of the Set Nav Bar Image actions displayed for the image.

    The same Set Nav Bar Image dialog box (see Figure 19-18) opens regardless of whether you select an action associated with the onClick, onMouseOver, or onMouseOut event.

3. Make any desired edits — changing the Up, Over, Down, or Over While Down state images or their respective URLs or targets — from the Basic tab of the dialog box.

4. To change any other images when the current image is interacted with, select the Advanced tab.

5. On the Advanced tab of the dialog box, choose which state you want to trigger any changes from the drop-down list:

    • Over Image or Over While Down

    • Down State

Figure 19-18: Modify an existing Nav Bar element through the Set Nav Bar Image action.

6. Select the image you wish to change from the Also Set Image list.

   Dreamweaver lists all the named images on the current page, not just those in the nav bar.

7. Select the path of the new image to be displayed in the To Image Field text field.

   An asterisk appears after the current image in the list box, signifying that a swap image has been chosen.

8. If you chose Over Image or Over While Down as the triggering event, an optional field, If Down, enables you to specify another graphic to swap the image of the down state image as well.

9. To alter other images with the same triggering event, repeat Steps 6 through 8.

Here's the browser compatibility chart for the Set Nav Bar Image behavior:

Set Nav Bar Image	*Netscape 3.x*	*Internet Explorer 3.0*	*Internet Explorer 3.01*
Macintosh	Okay	Fails without error	
Windows	Okay		Fails without error

Set Text of Frame

Dreamweaver has grouped together four similar behaviors under the Set Text heading:

- ✦ Set Text of Frame
- ✦ Set Text of Layer
- ✦ Set Text of Status Bar
- ✦ Set Text of Text Field

Set Text of Frame enables you to do much more than change a word or two — you can dynamically rewrite the entire code for any frame. You can even incorporate JavaScript functions or interactive information into the new frame content.

The Set Text of Frame action replaces all the contents of the `<body>` tag of a frame. Dreamweaver supplies a handy "Get Current HTML" button that enables you to easily keep everything you want to retain and change only a heading or other element. Naturally, you must be within a frameset to use this behavior, and the frames must be named correctly — that is, uniquely without special characters or spaces.

To change the content of a frame dynamically, follow these steps:

1. Select the triggering object.

2. In the Behaviors panel, choose Set Text ➪ Set Text of Frame from the Add Behavior list.

   The Set Text of Frame dialog box opens as shown in Figure 19-19.

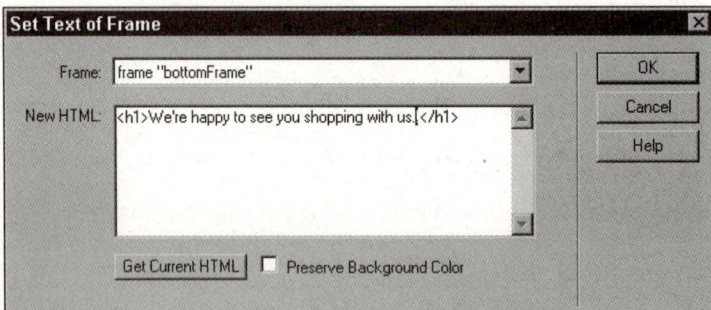

Figure 19-19: The Set Text of Frame behavior enables you to interactively update the contents of any frame in the current frameset.

3. Choose the frame you wish to alter from the Frame option list.

4. Enter the code for the changing frame in the New HTML text area.

   Keep in mind that you're changing not just a word or phrase, but all the HTML contained in the `<body>` section of the frame.

5. If you want to keep the majority of the code, select the Get Current HTML button and change only those portions necessary.

Expert Tip

The same JavaScript capabilities outlined in the Popup Message section are available in the Set Text of Frame behavior.

6. To maintain the frames <body> attributes, such as the background and text colors, select the Preserve Background Color option.

If this option is not selected, the frames background and text colors are replaced by the default values (a white background and black text).

7. Click OK when you're done.

Here's the browser compatibility chart for the Set Text of Frame behavior:

Set Text of Frame	Netscape 3.x	Internet Explorer 3.0	Internet Explorer 3.01
Macintosh	Okay	Fails without error	
Windows	Okay		Okay

Set Text of Layer

The Set Text of Layer behavior is similar to the previously described Set Text of Frame behavior in that it replaces the entire HTML contents of the target. The major difference, of course, is that with one you're replacing the code of a layer and with the other, the <body> tag of a frame. You're also able to include any valid JavaScript functions within a pair of curly braces, { }, in the HTML code as with other Set Text behaviors. You should also note that, unlike Set Text of Frame, no button exists for getting the current HTML in Set Text of Layer.

To set the text of a layer dynamically, follow these steps:

1. Make sure that the layer you want to change has been created and named properly.

2. Select the tag, link, or image you want to trigger the behavior.

3. From the Behaviors panel, select the add action button and choose Set Text ⇨ Set Text of Layer from the option list.

The Set Text of Layer dialog box opens, as shown in Figure 19-20.

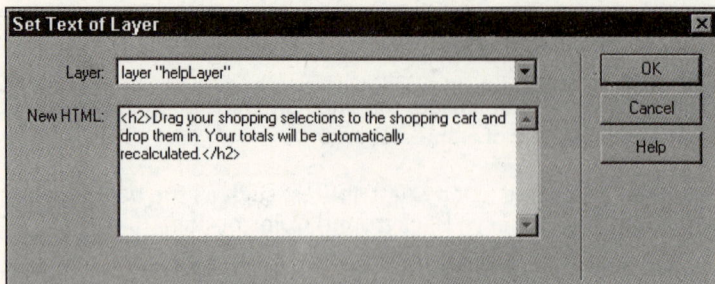

Figure 19-20: Replace all the HTML in a layer with the Set Text of Layer behavior.

4. Select the layer to modify from the Layer option list.

5. Enter the replacement code in the New HTML text area.

 Expert Tip Although no "Get Current HTML" button exists here as with the Set Text of Frame behavior, a workaround does exist. Before invoking the behavior, select and copy all the elements inside the layer. Because Dreamweaver copies tags as well as text in the Document window, you can then just paste the clipboard into the New HTML text area. Be careful not to select the layer tag, <div>, or the layer's contents — if you do, you are pasting a layer in a layer.

6. Click OK when you're done.

Here's the browser compatibility chart for the Set Text of Layer behavior:

Set Text of Layer	Netscape 3.x	Internet Explorer 3.0	Internet Explorer 3.01
Macintosh	Fails without error	Fails without error	
Windows	Fails without error		Fails without error

Set Text of Status Bar

Use the Set Text of Status Bar action to show your choice of text in a browser's status bar, based on a user's action such as moving the pointer over an image. The message stays displayed in the status bar until another message replaces it. System messages, such as URLs, tend to be temporary and visible only when the user's mouse is over a link.

The only limit to the length of the message is the size of the browser's status bar; you should test your message in various browsers to make sure that it is completely visible.

Expert Tip To display a message only when a user's pointer is over an image, use one Set Text of Status Bar action, attached to an `onMouseOver` event, with your associated text. Use another Set Text of Status Bar action, attached to an `onMouseOut` event, that has a null string (a couple of spaces) as the text.

All text is entered in the Set Text of Status Bar parameter form (see Figure 19-21) in the Message text box.

Figure 19-21: Use the Set Text of Status Bar action to guide your users with instructions in the browser window's status bar.

To use the Set Text of Status Bar action, follow these steps:

1. Select the object to trigger the action.

2. From the Behaviors panel, select the add action button and choose Set Text of Status Bar.

 Expert Tip As with the other Set Text behaviors, you can include valid JavaScript functions and variables in the Set Text of Status Bar behavior by offsetting them with curly braces.

3. Enter your text in the Message text box.

4. Click OK when you're done.

Here's the browser compatibility chart for the Set Text of Status Bar behavior:

Set Text of Status Bar	Netscape 3.x	Internet Explorer 3.0	Internet Explorer 3.01
Macintosh	Okay	Fails without error	
Windows	Okay		Okay

Set Text of Text Field

The final Set Text behavior enables you to update any text or textarea field, dynamically. The Set Text of Text Field behavior accepts any text or JavaScript input. (JavaScript functions and variables must be enclosed in a set of curly braces.) A text field must be present on the page for the behavior to be available.

To change the displayed text of a text field, follow these steps:

1. From the Behaviors panel, choose Set Text ⇨ Set Text of Text Field from the Add Action list.

   The Set Text of Text Field dialog box is displayed, as shown in Figure 19-22.

Figure 19-22: Dynamically update text form elements with the Set Text of Text Field behavior.

2. Choose the desired text field from the drop-down list.

3. Enter the new text and/or JavaScript in the New Text area.

4. Click OK when you're done.

Here's the browser compatibility chart for the Set Text of Text Field behavior:

Set Text of Text Field	*Netscape 3.x*	*Internet Explorer 3.0*	*Internet Explorer 3.01*
Macintosh	Okay	Fails without error	
Windows	Okay		Okay

Show-Hide Layers

One of the key features of Dynamic HTML layers is their capability to appear and disappear on command. The Show-Hide Layer action gives you easy control over the visibility attribute for all layers in the current Web page. In addition to explicitly showing or hiding layers, this action can also restore layers to the default visibility setting.

The Show-Hide Layers action typically reveals one layer while concealing another; however, you are not restricted to hiding or showing just one layer at a time. The action's parameter form (see Figure 19-23) shows you a list of all the layers in the current Web page, from which you can choose as many as you want to show or hide.

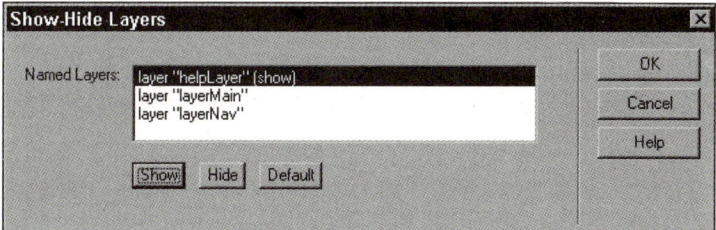

Figure 19-23: The Show-Hide Layers action can make any number of hidden layers visible, hide any number of visible layers, or both.

To use the Show-Hide Layers action, follow these steps:

1. Select the object to trigger the action.

2. From the Behaviors panel, select the add action button and choose Show-Hide Layer.

   When the dialog box opens, the parameter form shows a list of the available layers in the open Web page.

3. To reveal a hidden layer, from the Show-Hide Layer dialog box, select the layer from the Named Layers list and click the Show button.

4. To hide a visible layer, select its name from the list and click the Hide button.

5. To restore a layer's default visibility value, select the layer in the list and click the Default button.

Here's the browser compatibility chart for the Show-Hide Layers behavior:

Show-Hide Layer	Netscape 3.x	Internet Explorer 3.0	Internet Explorer 3.01
Macintosh	Fails without error	Fails without error	
Windows	Fails without error		Fails without error

Swap Image and Swap Image Restore

Button rollovers are one of the most commonly used techniques in Web design today. In a typical button rollover, a user's pointer moves over one image, and the graphic appears to change in some way, seeming to glow or change color. Actually, the onMouseOver event triggers the almost instantaneous swapping of one image for another. Dreamweaver automates this difficult coding task with the Swap Image action and its companion, the Swap Image Restore action.

In recognition of how rollovers most commonly work in the real world, Dreamweaver makes it possible to combine Swap Image and Swap Image Restore in one easy operation—as well as to preload all the images. Moreover, you can use a link in one frame to trigger a rollover in another frame without having to tweak the code as you did in early versions.

When the parameters form for the Swap Image action opens, it automatically loads all the images it finds in the current Web page (see Figure 19-24). You select the image you want to change—which could be the same image to which you are attaching the behavior—and enter the address for the file you want to replace the rolled-over image. You can swap more than one image with each Swap Image action. For example, if you want an entire submenu to change when a user rolls over a particular option, you can use a single Swap Image action to switch all of the sub-menu button images.

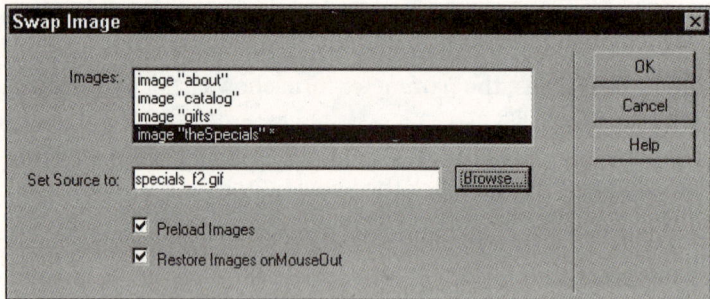

Figure 19-24: The Swap Image action is used primarily for handling button rollovers.

If you choose not to enable the Restore Images `onMouseOut` option, which changes the image back to the original, you need to attach the Swap Image Restore action to another event. The Swap Image Restore action can be used only after a Swap Image action. No parameter form exists for the Swap Image Restore action—just a dialog box confirming your selection.

Note   If the swapped-in image has different dimensions than the image it replaces, the swapped-in image is resized to the height and width of the first image.

To use the Swap Image action, follow these steps:

1. Select the object to trigger the action.

2. From the Behaviors panel, select the add action button and choose Swap Image.

3. In the parameter form, choose an available image from the Named Images list of graphics on the current page.

4. In the Set Source To text box, enter the path to the image that you want to swap in. You can also select the Browse (Choose) button to locate the file.

   An asterisk appears at the end of the selected image name to indicate an alternate image has been selected.

5. To swap additional images using the same event, repeat Steps 3 and 4.

6. To preload all images involved in the Swap Image action when the page loads, make sure the Preload Images option is checked.

7. To cause the selected images to revert to their original source, make sure that the Restore Images onMouseOut option is selected.

8. Click OK when you're done.

Here's the browser compatibility chart for the Swap Image and Swap Image Restore behaviors:

Swap Image and Swap Image Restore	Netscape 3.x	Internet Explorer 3.0	Internet Explorer 3.01
Macintosh	Okay	Fails without error	
Windows	Okay		Fails without error

Timelines: Play Timeline, Stop Timeline, and Go to Timeline Frame

Any Dynamic HTML animation in Dreamweaver happens with timelines, but a timeline can't do anything without the actions written to control it. The three actions in the timeline set — Play Timeline, Stop Timeline, and Go to Timeline Frame — are all you need to set your Web page in motion.

Before the Timeline actions become available, at least one timeline must be on the current page. All three of these related actions are located in the Timeline pop-up menu. Generally, when you are establishing controls for playing a timeline, you first attach the Go to Timeline Frame action to an event and then attach the Play Timeline action to the same event. By setting a specific frame before you enable the timeline to start, you ensure that the timeline always begins at the same point.

Cross-Reference

For more detailed information on using timelines, see Chapter 29.

The Play Timeline and Stop Timeline actions have only one element on their parameter form: a drop-down list box offering all timelines in the current page.

The Go to Timeline Frame action's parameter form (see Figure 19-25), aside from enabling you to pick a timeline and enter a specific go-to frame, also gives you the option to loop the timeline a set number of times.

Figure 19-25: Control your timelines through the three Timeline actions. The Go to Timeline Frame parameter form enables you to choose a go-to frame and designate the number of loops for the timeline.

Expert Tip   If you want the timeline to loop an infinite number of times, leave the Loop text box empty and turn on the Loop option in the Timelines panel.

To use the Go to Timeline Frame action, follow these steps:

1. Select the object to trigger the action.

2. From the Behaviors panel, select the add action button and choose Go to Frame.

3. In the dialog box Timeline list, choose the timeline for which you want to set the start frame.

4. Enter the frame number in the Go to Frame text box.

5. If you want the timeline to loop a set number of times, enter a value in the Loop text box.

6. Click OK when you're done.

To use the Play Timeline action, follow these steps:

1. Select an object to trigger the action and then choose Timeline ⇨ Play Timeline from the Add Action pop-up menu in the Behaviors panel.

2. In the parameter form's Timeline list, choose the timeline that you want to play.

To use the Stop Timeline action, follow these steps:

1. Select an object to trigger the action and then choose Timeline ⇨ Stop Timeline from the Add Action pop-up menu in the Behaviors panel.

2. In the parameter form's Timeline list, choose the timeline that you want to stop.

Note   You can also choose All Timelines to stop every timeline on the current Web page from playing.

Here's the browser compatibility chart for the Timeline behaviors:

Timelines: Play Timeline, Stop Timeline, and Go to Timeline Frame	Netscape 3.x	Internet Explorer 3.0	Internet Explorer 3.01
Macintosh	Image source animation and invoking behaviors work, but layer animation fails without error.	Fails without error	
Windows	Image source animation and invoking behaviors work, but layer animation fails without error.		Fails without error

Validate Form

When you set up a form for user input, each field is established with a purpose. The name field, the e-mail address field, the zip code field — each has its own requirements for input. Unless the CGI program is specifically written to check the user's input, forms usually take input of any type. Even if the CGI program can handle it, this server-side method ties up server time and is relatively slow. The Validate Form action checks any text field's input and returns the form to the user if any of the entries are unacceptable. You can also use this action to designate any text field as a required field.

The Validate Form action can be used to check either individual fields or multiple fields for the entire form. Attaching a Validate Form action to an individual text box alerts the user to any errors as the form is being filled out. To check the entire form, the Validate Form action must be linked to the form's Submit button.

The Validate Form dialog box (see Figure 19-26) enables you to designate any text field as required, and you can evaluate its contents. You can require the input of a text field to be a number, an e-mail address (for instance, jdoe@anywhere.com), or a number within a range. The number range you specify can include positive whole numbers, negative numbers, or decimals.

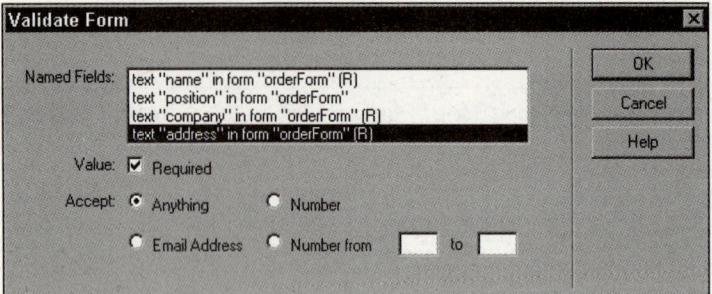

Figure 19-26: The Validate Form action can check your form's entries without CGI programming.

To use the Validate Form action, follow these steps:

1. Select the form object, such as a Submit button or text field, to trigger the action.

Expert Tip

You can also attach the Validate Form to a checkbox or radio button, but it's really useful only if you want to require the field.

2. From the Behaviors panel, select the add action button and choose Validate Form.

3. If validating an entire form, select a text field from the Named Fields list.

   If you are validating a single field, the selected form object is chosen for you and appears in the Named Fields list.

4. To make the field required, select the Value: Required checkbox.

5. To set the kind of input expected, choose from one of the following Accept options:

   • **Anything:** Accepts any input.

   • **Number:** Enables any sort of numeric input. You cannot mix text and numbers, however, as in a telephone number such as (212) 555-1212.

   • **Email Address:** Looks for an e-mail address with the @ sign.

   • **Number from:** Enables you to enter two numbers, one in each text box, to define the number range.

6. Click OK when you're done.

On the CD-ROM

Date validation is currently problematic when attempted with Dreamweaver's Validate Form action — you can't enter a date such as "011200" and have it recognize the entry as a number because of the leading zero. For easy date validation, use the Validate Form Plus action included on this book's CD-ROM. If you need more detailed validation, check out the JavaScript Integration Kit for Flash 5, also on the CD-ROM. One of the key components of this extension is a set of 17 validation behaviors that can be used to check form entries in Flash or in a regular HTML page.

Here's the browser compatibility chart for the Validate Form behavior:

Validate Form	Netscape 3.x	Internet Explorer 3.0	Internet Explorer 3.01
Macintosh	Okay	Fails without error	
Windows	Okay		Okay

Managing and Modifying Your Behaviors

The standard behaviors that come with Dreamweaver are indeed impressive, but they're really just the beginning. Because existing behaviors can be modified and new ones created from scratch, you can continue to add behaviors as you need them.

The process of adding a behavior is simplicity itself. Just copy the HTML file to the Configuration\Behaviors\Actions folder and restart Dreamweaver.

If you find that your Add Action pop-up list is starting to get a little unwieldy, you can create subfolders to organize the actions better. When you create a folder within the Actions folder, that subfolder appears on the Add Action pop-up menu as a submenu, as you saw when you worked with the Timelines actions in the preceding section. Figure 19-27 shows a sample arrangement. This example has a subfolder called Beatnik - Advanced and another called Tracks to organize these diverse behaviors from Beatnik. You can even create sub-subfolders to maintain several levels of nested menus.

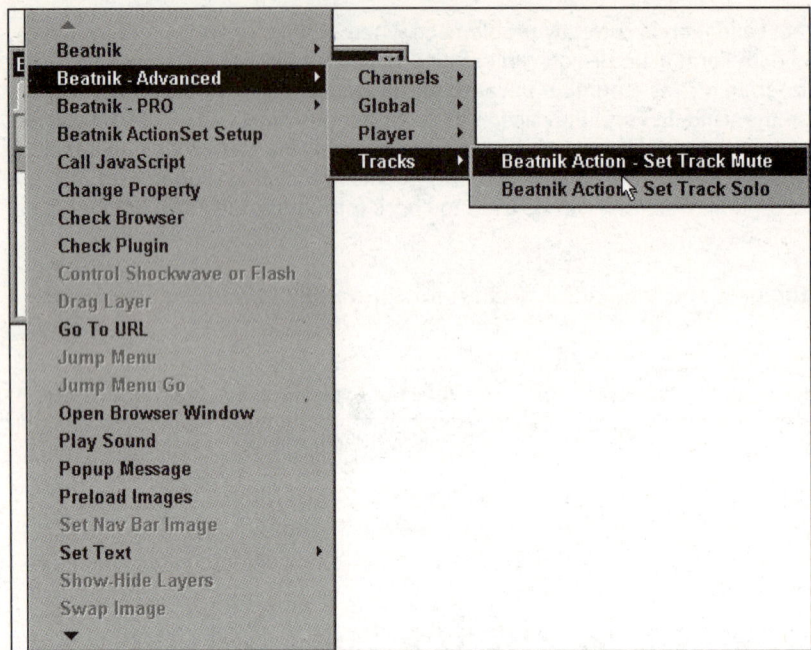

Figure 19-27: To create a new submenu in the Actions pop-up menu, just create a folder in the Actions directory.

Altering the parameters of a behavior

You can alter any of the attributes for your inserted behaviors at any time. To modify a behavior you have already attached, follow these steps:

1. Open the Behaviors panel (go to Window ⇨ Behaviors or click the Show Behaviors button in either Launcher, or press Shift+F3).

2. Select the object in the Document window or the tag in the Tag Selector to which your behavior is attached.

3. Double-click the action that you want to alter. The appropriate dialog box opens, with the previously selected parameters.

4. Make any modifications to the existing settings for the action.

5. Click OK when you are finished.

Sequencing your behaviors

When you have more than one action attached to a particular event, the order of the actions is often important. For example, you should generally implement the Go to Timeline Frame action ahead of the Play Timeline action. To specify the sequence in which Dreamweaver triggers the actions, reposition as necessary in the Actions page by highlighting one and using the up and down arrow buttons to reposition it in the list.

Deleting behaviors

To remove a behavior from your list of actions attached to a particular event, simply highlight the behavior and select the – (delete) button. If the removed behavior is the last action added, the event is also removed from the list; this process occurs after you select any other tag or click anywhere in the Document window.

Summary

Dreamweaver behaviors can greatly extend the Web designer's palette of possibilities — even a Web designer who is an accomplished JavaScript programmer. Behaviors simplify and automate the process of incorporating common, and not so common, JavaScript functions. The versatility of the behavior format enables anyone proficient in JavaScript to create custom actions that can be attached to any event. When considering behaviors, keep the following points in mind:

✦ Behaviors are a combination of events and actions.

✦ Behaviors are written in HTML and are completely customizable from within Dreamweaver.

✦ Different browsers support different events. Dreamweaver enables you to select a specific browser or a browser range, such as all 4.0 browsers, on which to base your event choice.

✦ Dreamweaver includes 25 standard actions. Some actions are not available unless a particular object is included on the current page.

In the next chapter, you learn how to create your own behaviors using Dreamweaver's custom JavaScript extensions.

✦   ✦   ✦

Creating a Behavior

The technology of a Dreamweaver behavior is open, and anybody with the requisite JavaScript and HTML skills can write one. To talk about "writing" a behavior, though, is a bit of a misnomer. You never actually touch the event portion of the behavior — you work only on the action file. To help the creation process, Macromedia has a complete Extending Dreamweaver document covering all the custom functions, JavaScript extensions, and the Document Object Model (DOM) that Dreamweaver recognizes.

Behaviors in Dreamweaver have been greatly expanded in their functionality and implementation over the original release. By incorporating a much broader DOM, Dreamweaver can now read and affect virtually any element on the current HTML page. You can even use behaviors to open other existing documents or create new Web pages from scratch. Perhaps more importantly, the JavaScript API (built-in JavaScript extensions) has, in the words of Dreamweaver engineers, "exploded" to over 400 functions affecting every area of extensibility. Although this chapter covers the primary features pertaining directly to behaviors, the majority of the JavaScript API is beyond the scope of this book. But before we delve into the nuts-and-bolts of behavior building, let's first get an overview of the process of creating a behavior.

Creating a Behavior from Scratch

Writing a behavior is not so complex when you take it one step at a time. In all, you need to follow just six basic steps to create a behavior from scratch:

◆ **Step 1: Define your behavior.** A behavior is an automatic method of incorporating a particular JavaScript function. The best way to begin building your behavior is to write that function. The function that you write is actually incorporated into the Dreamweaver action.

✦ **Step 2: Create the action file.** One of the key functions in Dreamweaver behaviors is, aptly enough, behaviorFunction(), which inserts your function into the <head> section of the Web page. Dreamweaver enables you to include multiple functions as well as single ones.

✦ **Step 3: Build the user interface.** As you look through the standard Dreamweaver behaviors, you see a dialog box that acts as the user interface in all but a few instances. The user interface that you create is based on HTML forms and is alternately referred to as a *parameter form* and seen by the user as a dialog box.

✦ **Step 4: Apply the behavior.** Both an event and an action are required to make up a behavior. The applyBehavior() function ties your new function to a specific tag and event. The applyBehavior() function also passes the necessary arguments to the function in the <head> section.

✦ **Step 5: Inspect the behavior.** From a user's point of view, building a Web page is often a trial-and-error process. You try one setting and if it doesn't work, you try another. To modify settings for a particular behavior, the user double-clicks the behavior name to reopen the dialog box and change the settings. The inspectBehavior() function handles the restoration of the previous values to the parameters form for easy editing.

✦ **Step 6: Test your behavior.** The final step, as in any software development, is testing. You need to try out your new behavior in a variety of Web browsers and debug it, if necessary (and it's always necessary).

To demonstrate the process of creating a behavior, the next few sections take you through a real-world example: the construction of a Set Layer Z Index action by Massimo Foti. Although it's easy to change the depth of a layer — its Z index — in the design phase, having a layer pop to the front is also a desirable dynamic effect. Massimo has designed a cross-browser behavior that enables Web designers to control layer depth interactively. Set Layer Z Index is a relatively simple, but elegant behavior and as such, perfect for understanding how behaviors in general are constructed.

 Note   Dreamweaver includes a standard behavior — Change Property — that can also change the Z index of a layer, but it isn't cross-browser. To get the same effectiveness as Massimo's behavior, you'd have to apply Change Property twice: once for Netscape browsers and again for Internet Explorer.

Step 1: Define your behavior

Behaviors are born of need, desire, or a combination of both. After repeating a single operation a thousand times, you probably find yourself thinking, "there's got to be a better way." The better way usually automates the process in any possible manner. In the case of inserting JavaScript functions into Web pages, the better way is to create a behavior.

Starting from this vantage point already accomplishes the first phase of behavior creation: defining the behavior. If one were to add the necessary code to a single page to change the Z index of a layer dynamically, it would look like this:

```
<html>
<head>
<title>Untitled Document</title>
<meta http-equiv="Content-Type" content="text/html; charset=iso-8859-1">
<script language="JavaScript">
<!--
function tmt_LayerIndex(theTarget, theValue) {
    if (document.layers) {
        target = eval(theTarget);
        target.zIndex = theValue;
    }
    if (document.all) {
        eval("theTarget=theTarget.replace(/.layers/gi, '.all')");
        eval(theTarget + ".style.zIndex = theValue");
    }
}
//-->
</script>
</head>
<body bgcolor="#FFFFFF">
<a href="#" onClick="tmt_LayerIndex('document.layers[\'backLayer\']','4')" ¬
>Click to Bring Layer to Front</a>
<div id="backLayer" style="position:absolute; left:125px; top:95px; ¬
width:327px; height:142px; z-index:1; background-color: #CCCCFF; ¬
layer-background-color: #CCCCFF; border: 1px none #000000">
  <p>Back layer</p>
</div>
<div id="frontLayer" style="position:absolute; left:238px; top:45px; ¬
width:162px; height:258px; z-index:2; background-color: #FFCCCC; ¬
layer-background-color: #FFCCCC; border: 1px none #000000">
  <p>Front Layer</p>
</div>
</body>
</html>
```

Notice the lines in boldface. These are the key parts in the file: the function in the `<script>` section (the action) and the runtime function call attached to the text (the event). After being tested in several browsers, the function is judged to be sound and can be made into a behavior.

When you define your behavior in this manner, it tells you the arguments you need to generalize. In this example, two exist: `theTarget` and `theValue`. Ideally, your action should be flexible enough to enable any argument to be user defined. Here there are at most two attributes to take in through my parameter form and pass to my function.

Once you've created and tested your function in Dreamweaver, save it. I've found it helpful to go back to the original file as I build my action and verify that I have everything in working order.

Step 2: Create the action file

In the next phase of behavior creation, you build the skeleton of the action file and begin filling in the necessary JavaScript functions. Each action file must have, at a minimum, the following four functions:

✦ `canAcceptBehavior()`: Determines if the behavior should be available. If it is not to be available, the entry in the Add Action pop-up menu is not selectable.

✦ `behaviorFunction()`: Inserts the general function in the `<head>` section of the Web page.

✦ `applyBehavior()`: Attaches the runtime function to the selected tag and inserts the chosen event.

✦ `inspectBehavior()`: Enables the user to reopen the parameter form and make modifications to the original settings.

Note   One of the easiest ways to start an action file is to adapt one that is already built. You can open and modify any of the existing Dreamweaver standard actions, as long as you remember to use the File ⇨ Save As feature command and give your file a new name.

Behaviors and other extensions can include external JavaScript files through the `<script language="javascript" src="script.js"></script>` construct. All of the Dreamweaver behaviors take advantage of this facility. The key benefit of this approach is to enable easy sharing of JavaScript code between functions. Although you can still combine the user interface and JavaScript aspects of a behavior in one file, the standard practice is to store your parameter form instructions in the HTML file, such as Control Sound.htm, and the JavaScript in a .js file with an identical name, such as Control Sound.js.

Note   The current example is fairly straightforward and does not incorporate the external JavaScript file technique.

Here are the steps to follow in the initial behavior creation phase:

1. Choose File ⇨ New to open a new file.

2. Select Modify ⇨ Page Properties to change the title of your behavior.

3. Choose File ⇨ Save to save the HTML file under a new name in the Configuration\Behaviors\Action folder.

4. Switch to Code view, open the Code Inspector, or use your favorite text editor to work on the code for your new action.

Tip   It's best to work on the parameter form — the user interface — in Dreamweaver's Design view and work on your JavaScript file in Code view.

5. Enter a new `<script language='javascript'>...</script>` tag pair in the `<head>` section of the document.

6. Open your original function test file.

7. Copy the function from the original file to the new behavior file.

   In our example, the function `tmt_LayerIndex()` is copied.

Caution   Make sure your behavior name is unique. Whenever you first open the Behaviors panel, Dreamweaver checks to see if multiple function names exist. In the case of repetitive function names, Dreamweaver recognizes the earlier file but not the later one.

8. Add the following functions to the `<script>` tag:

```
function canAcceptBehavior(){
    return true;
}

function behaviorFunction(){
    return tmt_LayerIndex;
}

function applyBehavior(){
    return "";
}

function inspectBehavior(msgStr){
}
```

   Only one function, `behaviorFunction()`, is completed at this time; the rest are placeholders for necessary functions.

Tip   The `behaviorFunction()` is not limited to returning just one function; it can also return multiple functions. For more on this capability, see the section "Dreamweaver Behavior Techniques," later in this chapter.

After you've laid out the basic behavior structure, the next step is to define when the behavior can be used. This is handled by the `canAcceptBehavior()` function. If the behavior has no special requirements — such as needed images on the page — you can leave the function as is. Our example behavior uses layers so the behavior should be available only if layers exist on the current page. To check for layers, use this code:

```
function canAcceptBehavior(){
  var nameArray = getObjectRefs("NS 4.0","document","LAYER");
  return (nameArray.length > 0);
}
```

Here, if the Dreamweaver function `getObjectRefs()` finds any layer objects, the `nameArray` length is greater than zero, and the `canAcceptBehavior` function returns true; otherwise, false is returned, and the behavior name in the Add Action list of the Behaviors panel is dimmed and inactive.

Step 3: Build the user interface

The user interface of a behavior is a parameter form, constructed with HTML form elements. The key indicator of what you need to include in your action's parameter form is the number and type of arguments required by your completed function.

In the Set Layer Z Index example, the function requires two primary arguments: `theTarget` and `theValue`. The interface needs to enable the user to choose the target parameter — the layer being affected — and the value of the Z index. To be useful, the action should list all available layers by name.

All user interface constructions are contained in the `<body>` section of your HTML action file. You can use Dreamweaver's visual editor to create and modify your form quickly. Many Web designers use tables to line up the various form elements; if you use this approach, be sure to place the table inside the form and not the other way around. Although you could insert a form in the cell of a table, you are limited to just entering form elements in that cell — and you return to no structure at all.

Follow these steps to create your user interface:

1. Open your HTML action file in Dreamweaver.

2. In the Document window, choose Insert ⇨ Form or select the Insert Form button from the Forms category of the Objects panel. Name the form in the Property Inspector for easy JavaScript identification.

3. For better alignment, place a table in your form by choosing Insert ⇨ Table or by selecting the Insert Table button from the Common category of the Objects panel.

4. Enter your form elements as needed. Be sure to name each one individually (with the exception of a radio button grouping) for JavaScript purposes.

Note   As with Dreamweaver objects, you don't see the OK, Cancel, and Help buttons that appear when the parameter form is actually used. Dreamweaver automatically applies these buttons to the upper-right part of your interface.

The interface for the Set Layer Z Index action, as shown in Figure 20-1, uses a drop-down menu form element to list all available layers and a text box to get the desired Z index from the user.

Figure 20-1: The basic part of this parameter form uses text boxes to gather the user input and transmit it to the proper functions. This behavior also uses layers to create a tabbed interface.

The last part of setting up the user interface writes a function that initializes the interface and sets the cursor in the right field, or whatever is applicable. To complete this task, use the `initializeUI()` function, generally located in the Local Functions section of the JavaScript code. For the Set Layer Z Index action, all the layers in the current page must be displayed in the drop-down list. To do this, the `initializeUI()` function a number of specialized functions:

```
function initializeUI() {
  var niceNamesArray;
  //Get all the layers available including parent frames
  //Then turn those objects references into nice names
  niceNamesArray = niceNames(getAllObjectRefs("NS
4.0","LAYER"),TYPE_Layer);
  //Populate the select element
  populateSelect("LAYER_LIST",niceNamesArray);
  //Set focus on textbox
  findObject("Z-INDEX").focus();
  //Set insertion point into textbox
  findObject("Z-INDEX").select();
}
```

Massimo uses a combination of Macromedia functions and his own to initialize the dialog box. The Macromedia-designed niceNames( ) function changes JavaScript object references such as `document.layers['onLayer'].document.theForm` to a more readable format such as `form "theForm" in layer "onLayer"`. The results of the niceNames( ) function then is used to fill a drop-down list via Massimo's own populateSelect( ) function. The remaining two lines that start with the findObject( ) function are used to place the user's cursor in the text field when the dialog box opens — it's a nice touch that demonstrates Massimo's absolute professionalism.

Finally, you need to attach the `initializeUI( )` to `<body>` with an `onLoad` event in the HTML file. Again, you can proceed in one of two ways. First, you can locate the `<body>` tag and amend it so that it reads as follows:

```
<body onLoad="initializeUI()">
```

The second method uses the Call JavaScript behavior (as detailed in Chapter 19). In this case, enter only the code `intializeUI( )` in the Call JavaScript dialog box.

Step 4: Apply the behavior

Now you can write the code that links your function to a specific tag and event. You can think of this as a three step process:

1. Make sure that the user entered information in the right places.

2. Put the user's input on the parameter form into a more usable format.

3. Return the runtime function call.

All of these steps are contained in the `applyBehavior( )` function maintained in the JavaScript file.

You gather information from an action's parameter form in the same way that you gather data from a custom object. Using the same techniques discussed in Chapter 18, you receive the input information and usually convert it to local variables that are easier to handle. The number of variables is equal to the number of arguments expected.

Tip If any of the input from the parameter form may be sent out to a Web server — say, a URL or a file — you need to encode the text string so that it can be read by Unix servers. Use the built-in JavaScript function `escape` to convert space and special characters in the URL to Unix-friendly strings. The companion function, `unescape( )`, reverses the process and is used in the `inspectBehavior( )` function.

Follow these steps to build your `applyBehavior( )` function:

1. Make the necessary variables:

```
var theTarget
var theValue
```

2. Get the information from the form. This process depends on the type of input field used. For the drop-down list, you need to find the value from an array of all layers, such as this:

```
divArray = getObjectRefs("NS 4.0", "document", "LAYER");
theTarget="'" + escQ(divArray[theForm.le.selectedIndex]) +
"'";
```

The escQ() is another custom function for putting the layer name in the proper format.

3. Return the function runtime call, incorporating the variables. The applyBehavior() function must return a complete string. Enclose the argument variables with single quotes. If you use any internal quotes, they should be preceded by or escaped with a backslash.

4. Run an error check to see if values are entered where necessary; if not, inform the user.

```
myErr = (myErr=="")? "":"The following fields must be ¬
filled: "+myErr;
if (!myErr)
return "tmt_LayerIndex("+ theTarget+ ", " + theValue ¬
+ ")";
else return myErr;
```

Only one more step remains before you're ready to begin testing your action.

Step 5: Inspect the behavior

Now it's time to add the inspectBehavior() function to the JavaScript file. Basically, this function is called when the user double-clicks the action in the Behaviors panel. It restores the information already entered through the parameter form and enables the user to change the parameters. In many ways, inspectBehavior() can be considered the reverse of the applyBehavior() function: rather than reading the form and writing the information to the Web page, inspectBehavior() reads the information and writes it back to the form.

Interpreting the string of information from a form is referred to as *parsing the string*. The Set Layer Z Index action passes a message string similar to the following:

```
onClick="tmt_LayerIndex('document.layers[\'backLayer\']','4')"
```

Dreamweaver uses several built-in functions to aid the parsing process, but the key function is getTokens(). The getTokens() function accepts a string to parse and the separators for which to look. It returns an array of strings. You can call getTokens(), passing the function call string as the first argument. The second argument should contain parentheses, a quote, and a comma as separators, as follows:

```
var argArray = getTokens(msgStr,"()',",");
```

Once the string arguments are in an array, they can be extracted and placed back in the parameter form. Follow these steps to write the inspectBehavior() function:

1. Declare a variable and set it equal to the getTokens() function.

2. Assign the array elements to the same variables you used in the applyBehavior() function:

```
var theValue=unescQ(argArray[1]);
```

3. Now put the variables back in the form:

```
theForm.le.selectedIndex=j;
theForm.theZvalue.value=argArray[2]
```

4. The complete inspectBehavior() function looks like the following:

```
function inspectBehavior(msgStr){
    aargArray = extractArgs(msgStr);
    var argArray = getTokens(msgStr,"()',",");
    var ii=0; var j=0;
    divArray = getObjectRefs("NS 4.0", "document", "LAYER");
    for (j=0;j<divArray.length;j++){
        myImg=unescQ(argArray[1]);
        if (myImg==divArray[j]){
            theForm.le.selectedIndex=j;
        }
    }
    theForm.theZvalue.value=argArray[2]
}
```

Tip   This example is a fairly simple inspectBehavior() function. Keep in mind that the more input you allow from your user, the more complicated it is to restore the information through this function. As with many aspects of building behaviors, one of the best ways to construct your inspectBehavior() function is by examining the code of working examples provided in the Macromedia-built behaviors, as well as examples contributed by other developers.

Step 6: Test your behavior

Testing and debugging is the final, necessary phase of building an action. To test your behavior, follow these steps:

1. Restart Dreamweaver.

2. Insert an image or a link in a blank Web page.

3. Select the element to use as your trigger.

4. Open the Behaviors panel.

5. Select the + (add action) button and choose your behavior.

6. Fill out the parameters form as required.

Your action's name appears in the Actions column, as shown with the Set Layer Z Index example in Figure 20-2.

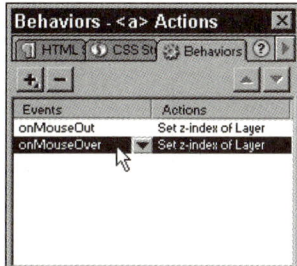

Figure 20-2: Even custom behaviors appear in the Behaviors panel when created properly.

7. Select onClick from the Add Event pop-up menu.

8. Double-click the action to verify that your prior choices have been restored.

9. Test the behavior in various Web browsers.

Caution

When you first select an event to add, Dreamweaver examines all of the actions in the Actions folder. If a problem is found, such as two files having the same function name, you are alerted to the conflict, and the list displays only the older file. You have to correct the problem with the other action and restart Dreamweaver before the file appears in the list again.

If your action is intended for distribution and not your own personal use, you should expand your testing considerably, especially on the user-interface side. As the action programmer, you know what values are expected and know — often subconsciously — how to avoid the pitfalls into which a new user may easily stumble. Be especially mindful of accepting input through a text box. Unless you're just passing a message to be displayed onscreen or in the browser status bar, you often have to validate the incoming text string. Telling the user to enter a number in a particular range doesn't guarantee correct results.

Debugging the behavior

Finding a bug is every programmer's least favorite moment — but getting rid of that bug can be the best. Basic JavaScript debugging techniques, including using the `alert()` function to keep track of variables, are without a doubt your first course of action. With its built-in JavaScript interpreter, Dreamweaver can give you error messages in the same manner as a browser. Dreamweaver's error handling is very good, with many error messages pointing directly to the problem code.

If the errors are severe enough to stop Dreamweaver from recognizing your action file as such, the file is not listed in the Action pop-up menu until the problem is resolved. Generally, this situation means that you must restart Dreamweaver after each modification until the problem is resolved. Once you are debugging and modifying the minor errors, the following technique enables you to make changes without restarting Dreamweaver:

1. First, open your Action file and make the necessary changes. Save the file.

2. Assign your action to a tag and open the behavior's dialog box. Without entering any parameters, click Cancel to close the parameter form.

3. Remove the action from the Actions column by selecting the Delete button.

4. Reassign your action, and Dreamweaver loads the new version.

Tip   Remember that JavaScript is case sensitive. If you get a message that a function cannot be found, make sure the names match exactly.

Extending Dreamweaver Documentation

To help developers create behaviors, Macromedia has released the Extending Dreamweaver documentation. Extending Dreamweaver is the background documentation of the various functions available for building behaviors. As such, it provides a useful framework for discussing the underpinnings of Dreamweaver behaviors and how you can use the extensions and built-in functions. The Extending Dreamweaver documentation can be found by choosing Help ⇨ Extending Dreamweaver from the menus.

Although Extending Dreamweaver covers all types of Dreamweaver extensions, behavior developers are interested in three main sections: the Document Object Model and JavaScript, the Dreamweaver JavaScript API, and the behaviors sections. If your behavior is intended to interact with Fireworks then you may want to become familiar with the Fireworks Integration API section. The more you understand about each of the various components and their included functions, the more flexibility you have in building your behaviors.

Caution The material in this section is intended for programmers familiar with JavaScript and, as such, is fairly advanced.

Document Object Model

JavaScript is an interpreted programming language that addresses elements in the browser and on the Web page in a hierarchical fashion. To access the properties of any object on the page, JavaScript employs a Document Object Model (DOM). The DOM breaks down the page into successively smaller parts, until each element and its specific properties are identified.

As noted in the introduction, Dreamweaver 4 integrates a subset of the Netscape 3 DOM from the earlier version of Dreamweaver with a subset of the W3C's implementation of the DOM. They've also tossed in a couple of features not implemented in either specification, but incredibly useful nonetheless. The largest area of the DOM comes from the integration of the History panel. In order to make any user action repeatable, every user action needed a JavaScript equivalent.

Understanding nodes

Dreamweaver's DOM makes available, or *exposes*, virtually every element on a Web page. The DOM is often described using a tree metaphor, with the HTML document as the trunk. Instead of regarding the <head> and the <body> as the major branches, however, Dreamweaver's DOM, along with the W3C DOM, uses four separate branches, or *nodes*, to divide the document:

✦ **DOCUMENT_NODE:** Enables access to objects directly relating to the overall document.

✦ **ELEMENT_NODE:** Contains references to all tags in the HTML document.

✦ **TEXT_NODE:** Describes the contiguous block of text within tags.

✦ **COMMENT_NODE:** Represents the comments within an HTML document and the text strings they contain.

Just as one tree branch can lead to another, nodes can contain other nodes. For example, a layer can contain a table that holds table rows that, in turn, hold table data. One node containing another is said to be in a *parent-child* relationship, and a node that cannot contain any other node is referred to as a *leaf node*, as it is incapable of supporting any more "branches." Figure 20-3 illustrates the node concept.

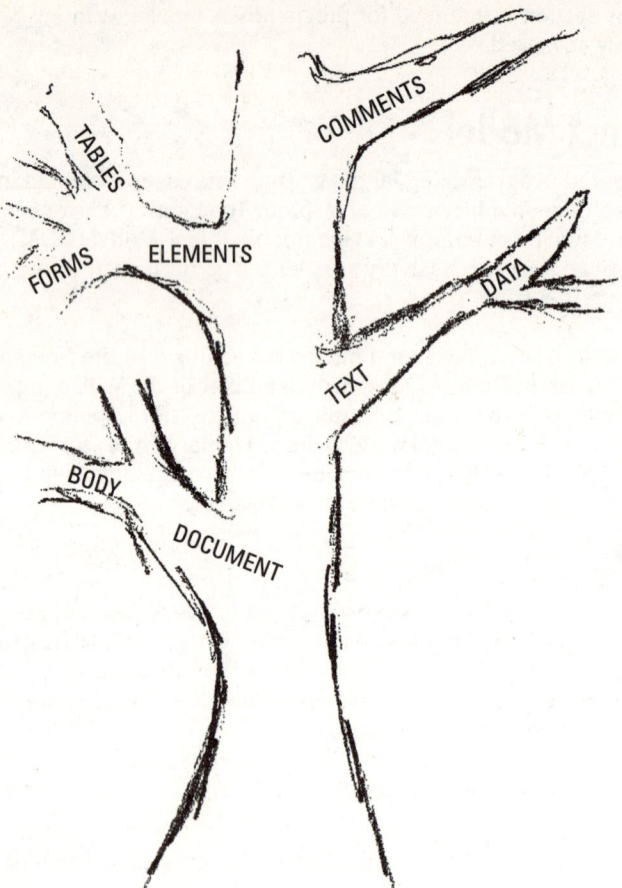

Figure 20-3: Nodes are used to express the structure of the
HTML document and its relationship to the browser.

DOM properties

When referencing a specific tag, the DOM syntax goes from the most general to the
most specific. For example, let's say you want to find out what a user entered into a
specific text box, a property called *value*. You need to start from the document
itself and work your way down, as follows:

```
var theText = document.theForm.textboxName.value
```

The DOM dictates what properties are accessible and in what form. Not all properties and methods are supported. You can't, for instance, directly reference the value
of a button on a form. Instead, you have to assign that value to a hidden or other
text field and access that value.

The portion of the DOM relating directly to forms and form elements is discussed in Chapter 18. The same rules of use and the same restrictions for implementing forms in objects apply likewise to implementing forms in behaviors. Additionally, the Dreamweaver DOM addresses other major objects as outlined in Table 20-1. Read-only properties are marked with an asterisk; otherwise, properties can be both read and set.

Table 20-1
Dreamweaver Document Object Model Properties

Property	Nodes	Description	Return Values
nodeType*	All	Returns the node of the current selection	DOCUMENT_NODE
			ELEMENT_NODE
			TEXT_NODE
			COMMENT_NODE
parentNode*	All	Returns the parent tag or, if the HTML tag is selected, the document object	Any node
parentWindow*	DOCUMENT_NODE	Returns the JavaScript object of the document's parent window	A string
childNodes*	All	Returns the nodelist of immediate children to the current selection	An array
documentElement*	DOCUMENT_NODE	Corresponds to the `<html>` tag of the current document	"`<html>`
			`<head>`... `</body>`
			`</html>`" (when used with outerHTML)
body*	DOCUMENT_NODE	Corresponds to `<body>` tag of the current document	"`<body>`... `</body>`" (when used with outerHTML)
URL*	DOCUMENT_NODE	Returns the current document's path	"FILE://C|/ DOCS/NEW.HTML" for example

Continued

Table 20-1 *(continued)*

Property	Nodes	Description	Return Values
tagName*	ELEMENT_NODE	Returns the HTML name for a tag	"IMG" or "TABLE", for example
attrName	ELEMENT_NODE	Returns the value of the named attribute	"grey" or "#33CC66", for example
innerHTML	ELEMENT_NODE	Returns the HTML source within the specified tag	"<b>First Name</b>"
outerHTML	ELEMENT_NODE	Returns the HTML source, including the specified tag	"<p><b>First Name</b></p>"
data	TEXT_NODE	Returns the text string contained within a specified tag or comment	"J. Lowery" where the tag reads <p>J. Lowery</p>
	COMMENT_NODE		

* Read-only.

DOM methods

Methods, in programming, are functions attached to a particular object, such as the document object. Dreamweaver includes several methods in the DOM to help manipulate the HTML page. With the node structure, you can apply these methods to the current document, frameset, frame, or a selected object.

Using these methods, your behaviors can inspect the current page and, if desired, change or even delete any attributes found. Table 20-2 outlines the methods contained in the Dreamweaver DOM.

Table 20-2
Dreamweaver DOM Methods

Method	Returns	Description
getElementsByTagName(tagName)	A nodelist	Builds an array of the specified tag on the current page
getTranslatedAttribute(attrName)	The value	Gets the translated value of the named attribute; used in conjunction with Dreamweaver translators

Method	Returns	Description
`hasChildNodes()*`	Boolean value	Determines if current selection has children
`hasTranslatedAttributes()`	Boolean value	Determines if the tag has translated attributes; used in conjunction with Dreamweaver translators
`getAttribute(attrName)`	The value	Gets the value of a named attribute
`setAttribute(attrName,attrValue)`	Nothing	Sets a particular attribute to the specified value
`removeAttribute(attrName)`	Nothing	Deletes the specified iattribute

Dreamweaver JavaScript API extensions

With the release of Dreamweaver 3, the JavaScript API was expanded tremendously with functions for virtually everything Dreamweaver does. Because of this, more than 400 custom Dreamweaver functions now exist, many of which were created to facilitate the History panel. Although in-depth discussion of the full API is beyond the scope of this book, behavior programmers should be familiar with what is available in the API. The JavaScript API section of Extending Dreamweaver is categorized within the following areas:

Behaviors	General Editing	Quick Tag Editor
Clipboard	Global Applications	Selection
Command	Global Document	Site
Conversion Manipulation	History	String
CSS Style	HTML Style	Table Editing
External Application	Keyboard	Toggle
File Manipulation	Layer and Image Map	Translation
Find/Replace	Menu	Visual Layout
Frame and Frameset	Path	Window

Behavior writers will find the API functions under Behaviors, File Manipulation, Global Document, Path, Selection, and String Manipulation to be of particular interest.

The Macromedia engineers didn't stop with just Dreamweaver document APIs; there are also specific APIs for file I/O, Source Control integration, JavaBean management, Design Notes, Fireworks integration, Flash objects, and more. Extending Dreamweaver has basic documentation about them all.

To make the behavior programmer's life a little easier, I've included coverage of some of the most often used API extensions. Although the following sections are in no way exhaustive, they do give a good example of how API functions work in Dreamweaver in general and behaviors in particular.

Note   Notice that the API extensions have "dreamweaver." or "dom" as a prefix. The dreamweaver prefix can also be abbreviated as "dw" as in "dw.getDocumentDOM()." The "dom" functions refer to the DOM of a document returned by the `getDocumentDOM()` function as explained in the following section.

The dreamweaver.getDocumentDOM() function

The `getDocumentDOM()` function is the starting point for many Dreamweaver JavaScript manipulations. Setting this function equal to a variable returns the entire Document Object Model of the specified document, enabling the DOM (and thus the document) to be read and edited. Generally, `getDocumentDOM()` is used in this fashion:

```
var theDom = dreamweaver.getDocumentDOM("document")
```

Here, `theDom` now represents the root of the current document and everything connected to it. Once you have accessed the DOM in this manner, you need to request more specific information. If, for example, you wanted to examine the `<body>` of the current document, you could code it this way:

```
var theDom = dreamweaver.getDocumentDOM("document")
var theBody = theDom.body
```

You could also use JavaScript dot notation to shorten the code:

```
var theBody = dreamweaver.getDocumentDOM("document").body
```

Tip   Many behaviors require repeated access to the DOM; it's good practice to set it to one variable early on in your script.

The `getDocumentDOM()` function requires one argument, *sourceDoc*, which, as expected, refers to the source document. The argument must be one of the following:

✦ **"document"**: Sets the reference to the current document. Although the `"document"` argument can be used from anywhere to read the DOM, any edits applied using it must be ultimately called from within the `applyBehavior()`, `deleteBehavior()`, or `objectTag()` functions — or any function in a Command or Property Inspector file.

✦ **"parent":** Sets the source document to the parent of the current document. This argument is generally used to determine if a document is within a frameset, such as this:

```
var frameset = dreamweaver.getDocumentDOM("parent");
if (frameset) { ... do code ... }
```

✦ **"parent.frames[number]" or "parent.frames['framename']":** To access another document in the frameset of which the current document is a member, use one of these two argument forms. The first, "parent.frames[number]", is usually used when the names of the current frames are unknown or to cycle through any number of frames. The second, "parent.frames['framename']", is applied in specific cases where the names of the other frames are known and modifications need to be made only to them.

✦ **A URL:** Occasionally, the behavior builder needs to reference existing documents, either locally or on the Web. Using a URL — either absolute or relative — as an argument enables you to retrieve information on almost any document you can specify. When using a relative URL, such as this one from Dreamweaver's displayHelp.js file,

```
var idRoot = dreamweaver.getDocumentDOM¬
('../../../Help/contextID.html')
```

the URL is relative to the location of the behavior or other extensibility file.

Note   Where API functions require the DOM object, such as the `dom.getSelection()` function and others that are discussed in the following sections, you must first get the DOM of the applicable document. In all examples that follow, the variable the DOM is understood to have been established, such as this:

```
var theDOM = dreamweaver.getDocumentDOM("document")
var theSel = theDOM.getSelection()
```

The dom.getSelection() function

How a behavior performs is quite often dictated by what tag the user selects prior to attaching the behavior. The `getSelection()` function is the *first step* toward getting all the information necessary to control your behavior based on a user selection. I emphasize "first step" because this function returns the selection in the form of *byte offsets in memory*. A *byte offset* is a number that points to a memory address. In the case of the `getSelection()` function, the two byte offsets that are returned mark the beginning and end of the selection in memory. For example, say you open a new page in Dreamweaver, type in a phrase such as "The Key Points," and then select the first word. If you used the `getSelection` function like this:

```
var selArray = theDOM.getSelection()
alert(selArray)
```

the message box would return

```
161,164
```

which denotes the beginning byte (161) and the ending byte (164) offset of the selected word, "The." If your beginning and ending byte offsets are the same (as in "164,164"), then nothing is selected. This fact comes in handy when you want to make sure that the user has selected something before proceeding.

To examine what is contained within the byte offsets returned by the getSelection() function, you have to use the offsetsToNode() function, explained later in this section.

The dom.setSelection() function

Just as getSelection() retrieves the memory offsets of the current selection, the setSelection() function sets a new pair of memory offsets and thus a new selection. The setSelection() function takes two arguments: *offsetBegin* and *offsetEnd*.

setSelection() is most often used to restore a user's selection after various document manipulations have taken place. In this example, the selection is first stored in a variable via getSelection() and then, after much document modification, restored by setSelection:

```
var currSelection = theDOM.getSelection()
// document altering code goes here
theDom.setSelection(currSelection[0],currSelection[1])
```

Note   Should the new setting not conform to a valid HTML selection, such as the attributes within a tag, the selection expands to include the entire tag.

You can also use setSelection to deselect anything on the page after completing a behavior. All that's required is that the two arguments be equal. Using the preceding example, the following code:

```
theDOM.setSelection(currSelection[1],currSelection[1])
```

would place the cursor after the previous selection, while

```
theDOM.setSelection(currSelection[0],currSelection[0])
```

would place it before.

The dom.offsetsToNode() function

The offsetsToNode() function serves as a translator, converting the byte memory offsets retrieved by getSelection() into readable data. For this reason, you often see the following code combination:

```
selArr = theDOM.getSelection();
selObj = theDOM.offsetsToNode(selArr[0],selArr[1]);
```

where `getSelection()` returns the array of the selection and the object referenced by that array. As indicated, `offsetsToNode()` takes two arguments: *offsetBegin* and *offsetEnd*, usually expressed as the initial (0) and next (1) array elements.

Once you've used `offsetsToNode` to get the selected object, you can examine or manipulate it. For example, in the custom Replicator command (included on the CD-ROM that accompanies this book), I used `offsetsToNode` to see if the selection made was appropriate (text only) and, if not, call a help function:

```
var offsets = theDOM.getSelection()
var selObj = theDOM.offsetsToNode(offsets[0],offsets[1])
if (selObj.nodeType == Node.TEXT_NODE) {
  helpMe2()
}
```

The dom.nodeToOffsets() function

As the name indicates, `nodeToOffsets()` is the inverse of `offsetsToNode()`. Instead of converting memory offsets to an object, `nodeToOffsets` takes an object reference and returns its memory offsets. This is useful when you need to manipulate a substring of the selection, usually text.

For example, in the custom command Change Case (included on the CD-ROM that accompanies this book), after the selected object is retrieved via `getSelection` and `offsetsToNode`, `nodeToOffsets` expresses it in an array that can be upper-cased or lowercased at the click of a button. Here's a fragment of the code from the custom `upperCase()` function:

```
var theDom = dreamweaver.getDocumentDOM("document");
var offsets = theDom.getSelection()
var theNode = theDom.offsetsToNode(offsets[0],offsets[1])
if (theNode.nodeType == Node.TEXT_NODE) {var nodeOffsets = ¬
theDom.nodeToOffsets(theNode)
offsets[0] = offsets[0]-nodeOffsets[0]
offsets[1] = offsets[1]-nodeOffsets[0]
var nodeText = theNode.data
theNode.data = nodeText.substring(0,offsets[0]) +
  nodeText.substring(offsets[0], offsets[1]).toUpperCase() +
  nodeText.substring(offsets[1], nodeText.length);
```

Because `nodeToOffsets` returns two memory offsets, you can use these as the arguments in `setSelection` to choose an object on the page. If, for instance, you wanted to select the first link on the page, you could use the code as follows:

```
var theDom = dreamweaver.getDocumentDOM("document")
var theLink = theDom.links[0]
var offsets = theDom.nodeToOffsets(theLink)
theDom.setSelection(offsets[0],offsets[1])
```

The dreamweaver.getTokens() function

The `getTokens()` function is often used in the `inspectBehavior()` function because it does such a good job of parsing a string. A *token* is a group of text characters that do not contain any of the specified separators. Generally, the *separators* in a function are the parentheses that surround the arguments and the commas that separate them.

The `getTokens()` function takes two arguments — the string to be parsed and the separators — and puts the results in an array. For example, note the following string:

```
doGroovoid('false','Fanfare-Arrival')
```

To extract the two arguments from this statement, use the `getTokens()` function as follows:

```
getTokens("doGroovoid('false','Fanfare-Arrival')","'(),")
```

If you set this function equal to an array called `argArray`, you get the following results:

```
argArray[0] = 'doGroovoid'
argArray[1] = 'false'
argArray[2] = 'Fanfare-Arrival'
```

Usually the first element of the array, the function name, is ignored.

The dreamweaver.getElementRef() function

The `getElementRef()` function is used to gather browser-specific references to a particular object and placing them into an array.

The `getElementRef()` function takes two arguments: the first argument is either *NS 4.0* or *IE 4.0,* which reference the Netscape and Internet Explorer formats, respectively, and the second argument is the tag being examined. The string returned puts the specified tag in the format of the named browser. If, for example, `getElementRef()` is used to get the object reference to a specific layer in Netscape terms, such as:

```
var theObjNS = dreamweaver.getElementRef("NS 4.0", tagArr[i])
```

the variable, `theObjNS`, would be set to something such as:

```
document.layers['newLayer']
```

On the other hand, the same layer, in Internet Explorer terms, such as this:

```
var theObjNS = dreamweaver.getElementRef("IE 4.0", tagArr[i])
```

would return a string such as `document.all.newLayer1`.

Both getElementRef() and getObjectRefs() return browser-correct references for both browsers for the following tags: <a>, <area>, <applet>, <embed>, <select>, <option>, <textarea>, <object>, and <img>. Additionally, references for the tags <div>, <span>, and <input> are returned correctly for Internet Explorer, as <layer> and <ilayer> are for Netscape. Absolutely positioned <div> and <span> tags are also returned correctly for Netscape, but others return the message "cannot reference <tag>".

Caution   Naming objects and layers is often critical in JavaScript, as it certainly is with getElementRef() and getObjectRef(). Dreamweaver can't return references for unnamed objects; you get back an "unnamed <tag>" message for those. Furthermore, Dreamweaver can't handle references to a named object if it is in an unnamed layer or form. Although Dreamweaver automatically names layers as they are created, forms require that names be entered by the designer, in the Property Inspector.

The dreamweaver.getBehaviorTag() function

The getBehaviorTag() function returns the tag selected to implement the current behavior. The getBehaviorTag() function can also be incorporated into the behavior setup code to steer the user in the appropriate direction.

The getBehaviorTag() function returns the entire tag—attributes, values, and any text selected. For this reason, you need to seek out only the relevant portion of tag. One technique for doing this is to use JavaScript's indexOf property to determine if the tag is within the returned string. To make this even easier, it's best to uppercase or lowercase the tag. For example, the following code looks to see if the tag selected for the behavior is an <img> tag and, if it's not, alerts the users to what's required:

```
function initializeUI(){
var theTag = dreamweaver.getBehaviorTag().toUpperCase();
if (theTag.indexOf('IMG') != -1)){
// Behavior UI initilaization goes here
} else{
alert("This behavior requires you select an IMAGE to proceed.")
}
}
```

Note   This is different from using the canAcceptBehavior function to block access to a behavior. With the getBehaviorTag() technique, the user is informed of what the problem is, rather than simply being denied access.

The dreamweaver.getBehaviorElement() function

Another method to discover which tag was selected for the invoked behavior is the getBehaviorElement() function. The major difference between this function and the getBehaviorTag() function is that the former returns the DOM reference to the tag, whereas the latter returns the tag itself. Once you have the DOM reference of the behavior tag, you can uncover a terrific amount of information about the tag and its attributes.

As with getBehaviorTag(), getBehaviorElement() is most often used to determine if the user has selected an appropriate tag for the chosen behavior. If the tag is inappropriate, a helpful message can be displayed to guide the user to a better option. The getBehaviorElement() function returns either a DOM reference or null. Circumstances under which null is returned by getBehaviorElement() are as follows:

✦ The function was not invoked from a script called by the Behaviors panel.

✦ The behavior called is part of a timeline.

✦ The function was invoked from a script called by dreamweaver.popupAction().

✦ The function was invoked as part of a Behaviors panel that is attaching an event to a link wrapper (<a href="#">...</a>), and the link wrapper has not yet been created.

✦ The function is called outside of a behavior.

The following example assumes that the required tag must be an embedded plug-in that is visible on the page:

```
function initializeUI(){
var theTag = dreamweaver.getBehaviorElement();
var tagGood = (theTag.tagName == "EMBED" && theTag.getAttribute("HIDDEN") ¬
== null);
if (tagGood) {
// Behavior User Interface code goes here
} else{
alert("This behavior can not be applied to hidden plug-ins")
}
}
```

The dreamweaver.browseForFileURL() function

The browseForFileURL() function enables the user to locate a file via a dialog box, rather than enter the entire path by hand. You can specify whether you want an Open, Save, or Select style dialog box, as well as the label in the title bar. You can even enable the Preview panel for images. No matter which options you choose, the browseForFileURL() function returns the path and filename in the form of a relative URL.

The browseForFileURL() function follows this syntax:

```
browseForFileURL('Open'|'Save'|'Select', 'Title Bar Label', true|false)
```

The first argument, either Open, Save, or Select, specifies the type of dialog box. The Select File dialog box displays additional local root information in its lower portion. The second argument is displayed in the title bar of the dialog box; if you don't want to insert your own title, you must use two quotes, as in this example:

```
browseForFileURL('open','',false)
```

The final argument is a Boolean and indicates whether or not the Preview dialog box for selecting images is to be displayed. If no title bar label is given and the Preview dialog box argument is true, the title displayed is "Select Image Source."

The `browseForFileURL()` function is generally contained within another function that is called by an `onClick` event attached to a Browse (Choose) button, which in turn is next to a text field that enables the user to enter the path by hand. Standard in the _common.js file, is the `browseFile()` function, which takes one argument, `fieldToStoreURL`. For instance, the code for a Browse (Choose) button may read as follows:

```
<input type="text" name="textFile">
<input value="Browse..." type="button" ¬
onClick="browseFile(document.theForm.textFile.value)" name="button">
```

The `browseFile()` function then calls the built-in `browseForFileURL()` function, which opens the Select File dialog box and, if the dialog box is returned with a filename, assigns that filename to a variable. In the standard `browseFile()` function, shown here, the returned filename is then assigned to a text box value for the given field, which makes the name appear in the text box:

```
function browseFile(fieldToStoreURL){
  var fileName = "";
  fileName = browseForFileURL();  //returns a local filename
  if (fileName) fieldToStoreURL.value = fileName;
}
```

The `browseForFileURL()` function does not return absolute URLs.

The dreamweaver.getDocumentPath() function

Dreamweaver includes several local document functions that aid in the reading, editing, and storing of current and external documents. The `getDocumentPath()` function is one of these; as the name states, this function returns the path of the specified document. The path returned is in the file://URL format, so that a file located at c:\sites\index.html would return file://c|/sites/ as its path.

The `getDocumentPath()` function takes one argument: the source document. This argument can be `"document"`, `"parent"`, `"parent.frames[number]"`, or `"parent. frames[framename]"` as described earlier in the `getDocumentDOM()` function. If the document specified has not been saved, `getDocumentPath()` returns an empty string.

The dreamweaver.getConfigurationPath() function

The Configuration folder can be considered the hub of Dreamweaver extensibility. It contains not only all the standard HTML files, such as the behaviors and objects, that are read into the system when Dreamweaver starts, but also various other files that control the look and feel of the menus in other areas. As such, it's often useful to be able to find the path to the Configuration folder so that other files can be created, read, edited, and stored. And that's exactly what `getConfigurationPath()` does.

One sample use of this function included with Dreamweaver is part of the secret behind the Rollover object. To a trained eye, the Rollover object is unlike any other — in fact, it's not really an object at all; it's a command masquerading as an object. The `getConfigurationPath()` function plays a key role in the JavaScript file, rollover.js, with this code:

```
var rolloverCmdURL = dreamweaver.getConfigurationPath() + ¬
"/Commands/Rollover.htm";
    var rolloverDoc   = dreamweaver.getDocumentDOM( rolloverCmdURL );
```

In the first line, `getConfigurationPath`, is used to locate the Rollover.htm file in the Command subfolder and assign it to a variable. This then enables the object to retrieve the DOM for manipulation with the `getDocumentDOM()` function.

Note   As with `getDocumentPath()`, `getConfigurationPath()` **formats the path as a file://URL.**

The dreamweaver.getSiteRoot() function

Dreamweaver depends on the establishment of a local site root for much of its Web site management facility: all site root-relative links and references are based upon the location of the site root folder. The capability to uncover its file location is important for any behaviors or other extensibility files that work on the site root level. Dreamweaver supplies such a capability with the `getSiteRoot()` function.

Very straightforward to use, `getSiteRoot()` does not take an argument and returns a file://URL format reference to the local site root of the currently selected document. If an empty string is returned, it means that the file has not been saved.

The dreamweaver.releaseDocument() function

If you're working with a complex document with a lot of images, layers, tables, and text, you're going to have a lot of HTML to deal with. Accessing the DOM for that page can take up a significant chunk of your memory. If you're working with multiple pages, you could begin to run low on memory before the behavior closes and the memory is automatically freed. With the `releaseDocument()` function, you can get back the memory as soon as possible, whenever you request it.

The `releaseDocument` function's one argument is the DOM of the document in question. This is acquired by using the `getDocumentDOM()` function. You can see this function demonstrated in Dreamweaver's displayHelp.js file, which is used to direct all the help requested, contextually.

The dreamweaver.browseDocument() function

Should a help file get too big for an alert dialog box, you might need to provide access to a larger file. Dreamweaver enables you to open any specified file —

including an expanded help file—within the primary browser. The browseDocument() function takes one argument, the path to the required file:

```
dreamweaver.browseDocument("http://www.idest.com/help/etable.htm")
```

As noted in Chapter 18, you can use browseDocument to access an absolute URL from the Web or a file from a local drive. To display a local file, you need to combine browseDocument with another function such as getConfigurationPath(). The example offered here shows how to use the two functions together to programmatically display Dreamweaver's InsertMenu.htm file:

```
function displayMenu() {
   var menuPath = dreamweaver.getConfigurationPath() + ¬
"/Objects/InsertMenu.htm"
   dreamweaver.browseDocument(menuPath)
}
```

The dreamweaver.openDocument() and dreamweaver.createDocument() functions

The openDocument() and createDocument() functions provide similar capabilities while possessing similar restrictions. The openDocument() function is equivalent to selecting File ⇨ Open and selecting a file from the dialog box. The createDocument() function, as the name implies, creates a new, blank document, based on the standard Default.htm file. In either case, the document loads into a Dreamweaver window and is brought forward.

The createDocument() function does not need an argument to work and automatically returns the DOM of the new document. For example, the following code:

```
var theNewDoc = dreamweaver.createDocument()
```

is the same as using getDocumentDOM() for a new page.

The openDocument() function requires an argument in the form of a file://URL. If the URL is given in relative terms, the file is relative to the extensibility file calling the function. For instance, to open a file located one directory up from the Commands folder, you need to refer to it as follows in a custom command:

```
dreamweaver.openDocument("../Extensions.txt")
```

You can also use the same technique referred to earlier in the browseDocument() function to access files with the Configuration folder as a base.

Note Although this function and its companion, createDocument(), cannot be used within a behavior, they can be called from a custom command or Property Inspector. Therefore, it's possible to use the popupCommand() function to access a command that employs openDocument() or createDocument().

The dreamweaver.saveDocument() function

Once all your edits and modifications have been finished, you need a way to store that file. The aptly named `saveDocument()` function performs just that chore for you. This function takes two arguments, *documentObject* and *fileURL*; the first corresponds to the DOM of the file desired to be saved, and the second is the address for it to be saved to. Again *fileURL* is relative to the extensibility file.

The `saveDocument` function returns true if successful and false if the file-storing attempt fails. If the file specified is noted as read-only, Dreamweaver attempts to check it out; if it is unsuccessful, an error message appears.

The dreamweaver.editLockedRegions() function

Dreamweaver templates are based on a combination of locked and editable regions. Normally, these regions are designated in the Document window, but you can use the `editLockedRegions()` function to lock and unlock a template's regions programatically. The `editLockedRegions()` function works by entering true as the function's argument if you want to unlock all of the current document's locked regions, and false to lock them again. After the routine calling `editLockedRegions()` ends, all regions revert to their default status.

Caution   Due to the potentially undesirable results using this function, Macromedia recommends that only custom data translators use the `editLockedRegions()` function.

The dreamweaver.popupAction() and dreamweaver.runCommand() functions

Although the `popupAction()` and `popup.Command()` functions are not directly useful to behavior creators because they cannot be called from within a behavior, they do enable considerable cross-pollination of Dreamweaver extensible objects. Invoking these functions calls an existing behavior or command and presents its dialog box to the user — except you use these functions to call the behaviors or commands from within a custom object, command, or Property Inspector.

The `popupAction()` function takes two arguments: the name of the action file and the general function call of the action. The action chosen must be in the Action subfolder. For example, code to call the Control Sound behavior could appear as the following:

```
var goCS = dreamweaver.popupAction("Control Sound.htm","MM_controlSound(,,)")
```

Tip   To call an action in a subfolder of the Action subfolder, you need to specify the path. For example, if you want to call one of the standard Timeline actions, it's necessary to state the action name as "Timeline/Go to Frame.htm."

The general function call can be found near the end of the `applyBehavior()` function, where the return value is specified, or as the `behaviorFunction()` return value. The `popupAction()` function returns the completed function call, including whatever parameters are selected by the user. In the previous example, if the user had chosen "Play" and selected "brazil.mid" as the file, the result (goCS) would be similar to the following:

```
"MM_controlSound('play',document.CS911946210190.'brazil.mid')"
```

Note The second argument is a unique name generated by Dreamweaver as part of the function.

Everything is written into the user's page, except the event handler and its corresponding function call. This is left to the calling object, command, or Property Inspector to handle.

The `runCommand()` function is a bit simpler; this function requires only one argument: the name of the command file. Any file named must be located in the Commands folder. The `runCommand()` function does not return a value but simply executes the specified command.

The dreamweaver.latin1ToNative() and dreamweaver.nativeToLatin1() functions

Dreamweaver provides two functions to help with the localization of your behaviors around the globe. Many countries use font encodings other than Latin 1, which is standard in the United States and several Western European countries. To convert a string of text for a user interface from Latin 1 encoding to that of the user's machine, use the `latin1ToNative()` function. The argument, a text string, should be already translated into the other language. To convert a text string from the user's encoding system to Latin 1, use the inverse function, `nativeToLatin1()`.

Note Neither of these functions has an effect in Windows systems, which are already based on Latin 1.

The dreamweaver.relativeToAbsoluteURL() function

As more programs such as Fireworks and Director are capable of outputting HTML, behaviors and other extensions are being employed to access their documents. It's often necessary to find the absolute URL of a selected file in order to get the document's DOM or open it. The `relativeToAbsoluteURL()` function returns this needed information, given three arguments:

✦ **docBaseURL:** The portion of the current document's relative path name excluding the filename. For example, if the file in question were to be found at images\austria.gif, the docBaseURL would be images/.

✦ **siteRootURL:** The file URL of the current site root, as returned from the `getSiteRoot()` function.

✦ **relativeURL:** The full relative path name of the selected file (for example, images/austria.gif).

The syntax for the function is as follows:

```
var absoluteURL = dreamweaver.relativeToAbsoluteURL( docBaseURL, ¬
siteRootURL, relativeURL )
```

Of the three arguments, only *docBaseURL* is a little tricky to get. Once you have the *relativeURL*, which can be returned from the browseForFileURL() function, you need to examine the path name and extract the first part of the path leading up to the actual filename. To do so, use the JavaScript function lastIndexOf to find the final "/" character and extract the previous substring. For example:

```
function docBase() {
var docURL = dreamweaver.getDocumentPath("document");
var index = docURL.lastIndexOf('/');
if ( -1 == index ){ // If there is no additional path
  return "";       // return nothing.
  }
  else {
  return docURL.substring(0, index);
  }
}
```

Behavior API

You've seen most of the behavior API functions applied in a previous section, "Step 2: Create the action file." The API is used to create a behavior. The primary functions are as follows:

Function	Role
canAcceptBehavior()	Determines whether an action is available
windowDimensions()	Sets the width and height of the parameter form
applyBehavior()	Attaches the behavior function to the selected tag
inspectBehavior()	Restores user-selected values to the parameter form for reediting
behaviorFunction()	Writes a function into the <head> of the HTML file
deleteBehavior()	Removes a behavior from the HTML file
identifyBehaviorArguments()	Notes the behavior arguments that need to be altered if the file is moved
displayHelp()	Attaches a Help button to the behavior's dialog box

For discussions of the uses of the canAcceptBehavior(), applyBehavior(), inspectBehavior(), and behaviorFunction() functions, see the preceding sections. Following are discussions of the other behavior API functions.

The windowDimensions() function

To speed display, the `windowDimensions()` function sets specific dimensions for the parameters form that the user sees as the dialog box. If this function is not defined, the window dimensions are computed automatically. This function takes one argument, *platform*, which is used to specify whether the user's system is Macintosh or Windows. The function returns a string with the width and height in pixels. For example:

```
function windowDimensions(platform){
if (platform.charAt(0) == 'm'){ // Macintosh
     return "650,500";
     }
     else { // Windows 95 or NT
     return "675,525";
}
}
```

You can see this function in some of the standard behaviors. However, Macromedia recommends that it be used only when you need the behavior's dialog box to be larger than 640×480.

The deleteBehavior() function

Normally, Dreamweaver automatically handles removal of a behavior's event handler and associated JavaScript when the user chooses the Remove Behavior button in the Behaviors panel. However, as behaviors grow in complexity and become capable of adding additional support code to the HTML document, it becomes necessary to use the `deleteBehavior()` function on a case-by-case basis. To better understand how `deleteBehavior()` is used, it's best to look at a couple of examples.

Two standard behaviors, Control Sound and Swap Image, use the `deleteBehavior()` function. Control Sound inserts an `<embed>` tag that contains a unique ID. To remove the code, `deleteBehavior()` first reads a function call string, just as the one returned by `applyBehavior()`. If the function finds an `<embed>` tag with the matching ID that is not referenced elsewhere on the page, the code is deleted. Here's the implementation of `deleteBehavior()` for Control Sound:

```
function deleteBehavior(fnCallStr) {
  var argArray,sndName,doc,tagArray,i,embedName;

  argArray = extractArgs(fnCallStr);
  if (argArray.length > 2) {
    sndName = dreamweaver.getTokens(argArray[2],".")[1]; //remove ¬
"document.", use unique name
    //Find all EMBED calls that we created (name starts with "CS"), add ¬
to menu
    doc = dreamweaver.getDocumentDOM("document"); //get all
    tagArray = doc.getElementsByTagName("EMBED");
    for (i=0; i<tagArray.length; i++) {  //with each EMBED tag
      embedName = tagArray[i].name;
```

```
          if (embedName == sndName) { //if same embed
            if ( -1 == doc.body.outerHTML.indexOf( argArray[2] ) ) // and embed ¬
ref'd no where else
                tagArray[i].outerHTML = "";
            break;
    } } }
}
```

Swap Image doesn't insert additional `<embed>` or other tags; it inserts additional event handlers to make implementing rollovers a one-step process. When a Swap Image behavior is deleted from the page, all the additional event handlers must be stripped out as well. To do so, the `deleteBehavior()` function first reads in the behavior function call string and then searches for the *Preload ID*. This is a unique name inserted by Dreamweaver if the user checked the Preload option when running the behavior. If the preload ID is found, the preload handler, such as `onLoad = MM_preloadImages()`, is removed. Next, the Swap Image `deleteBehavior()` searches to see if the Swap Image Restore code was added — and if so, deletes that event handler as well.

The identifyBehaviorArguments() function

If you've ever had to relocate a Web site from one directory to another, you know the laborious job of making sure all your references are intact. Dreamweaver takes some of the tedium out of this chore. When you use Save As from Dreamweaver, all of the file paths within HTML attributes, such as the image source files and links, are automatically updated. Dreamweaver extends the same functionality to URLs contained within behaviors.

For example, suppose you have constructed a Web page that uses the Check Browser action to route users to various URLs, depending on the browser they are using. Should you elect to save your Web page in a different folder, for whatever reason, Dreamweaver automatically updates the referenced URLs.

For this property to work correctly, a new function must be included in the behavior. The function, `identifyBehaviorArguments()`, passes the argument structure to Dreamweaver so it can update the URLs, if necessary. The function also identifies the layer objects in the behavior that Dreamweaver must correct if the Convert Layers to Tables command is used.

The `identifyBehaviorArguments()` function accepts a string that contains the behavior function call, with arguments. The function then extracts the arguments into an array and identifies which arguments in the array are URLs, which ones are layer objects, and which ones are neither. Four identifying values are returned:

✦ **URL:** When the argument is a file or file path

✦ **NS4.0ref:** When the argument identifies a layer in Netscape syntax, such as `document.layers[\'Layer1\']`

✦ **IE4.0ref:** When the argument identifies a layer in Internet Explorer syntax, such as `document.all[\'Layer1\']`

✦ **Other:** When the argument is none of the preceding

You can see an example of the `identifyBehaviorArguments()` function in the Check Plugin action:

```
function identifyBehaviorArguments(fnCallStr) {
  var argArray;

  argArray = extractArgs(fnCallStr);
  if (argArray.length == 5) {
    return "other,URL,URL,other";
  }
}
```

As with the `inspectBehavior()` function, the array for the function call string is one element longer than the number of arguments — the initial array element is the function name itself.

The displayHelp() function

The `displayHelp()` function inserts a Help button on your custom behavior dialog boxes, below the standard OK and Cancel buttons. This function takes no arguments and is usually defined to display a help message or file. The two typical techniques are to use either the `alert()` method or the Dreamweaver JavaScript extension, `browseDocument()`.

To display a brief message, use the `alert()` method, as in the following code:

```
function displayHelp() {
  alert("This behavior works only with .rmf files.")
}
```

When you need to bring up a much longer file, use the `browseDocument()` function:

```
function displayHelp() {
  dreamweaver.browseDocument("http://www.idest.com/help/rep.htm")
}
```

You can also reference local files using `browseDocument()`. See the `browseDocument()` description in the section "Dreamweaver JavaScript API Extensions," earlier in this chapter.

 Caution   Do not include the JavaScript file displayHelp.js in your behaviors. This is the Dreamweaver file used for calling its own Help pages.

Useful Common Functions

As with most other object-oriented programming languages, it's good programming practice to build a function once and recall it when needed. Dreamweaver includes a large library of such useful functions, which are maintained in the Shared\ Macromedia\Scripts\CMN folder. The functions are grouped by category into JavaScript files; currently 13 such files exist, including docInfo.js, DOM,js, file.js, and string.js. Although they are used extensively throughout the standard behaviors, nothing prevents you from using them in your own routines. To access them, you need to insert only a line in your behavior JavaScript file such as this:

```
<SCRIPT SRC="../../Shared/MM/Scripts/CMN/string.js"></SCRIPT>
```

Table 20-3 shows a breakdown of some of the most commonly used functions available in the Shared folder and the file in which they can be found.

<table>
<tr><td colspan="3" align="center">Table 20-3
Useful Common Functions</td></tr>
<tr><td>**Function**</td><td>**File**</td><td>**Description**</td></tr>
<tr><td>extractArgs()</td><td>string.js</td><td>Takes a function call and extracts the arguments into an array without quotes.</td></tr>
<tr><td>escQuotes()</td><td>string.js</td><td>Reviews a string and adds the escape character, /, in front of any single quote, double quote, or backslash found.</td></tr>
<tr><td>unescQuotes()</td><td>string.js</td><td>Removes any escape characters found in a string.</td></tr>
<tr><td>browseFile()</td><td>file.js</td><td>Opens the Select File dialog box and inserts the results into a specified text box.</td></tr>
<tr><td>stripStar()</td><td>menuItem.js</td><td>Removes asterisks from the end of a string.</td></tr>
<tr><td>stripValue()</td><td>menuItem.js</td><td>Removes any specified value from the end of a string.</td></tr>
<tr><td>addStarToMenuItem()</td><td>menuItem.js</td><td>Adds an asterisk to a selected menu item on the end, as in Swap Image.</td></tr>
<tr><td>addValueToMenuItem()</td><td>menuItem.js</td><td>Adds any specified value to a selected menu item, as (show), (hide), and (default) are added in Show/Hide Layers.</td></tr>
<tr><td>niceNames()</td><td>niceName.js</td><td>Changes JavaScript object references such as document.layers['onLayer']. document.theForm to a more readable format such as form "theForm" in layer "onLayer".</td></tr>
</table>

Function	File	Description
`nameReduce()`	niceName.js	Extracts object names and array numbers and quotes them, if necessary.
`errMsg()`	errmsg.js	Concatenates strings given in an argument. For example, `errMsg("Now is the %s for %s to fight", var1, var2)` returns `"Now is the time for all men to fight"` if var1 is set to `"time"` and var2 is set to `"all men"`. However, if var1 is set to `"not the time"` and var2 is set to `"anyone"`, then `errMsg` returns `"Now is not the time for anyone to fight."`
`findObject()`	UI.js	Returns the JavaScript object reference for any named object. For example, if you have an image named `imgOne` in a form in a layer, `onLayer`, `findObject("imgOne")` returns `document.layers['onLayer'].imgOne`.
`getParam()`	string.js	Returns an array of named objects within a given tag found on the current page.
`badChars()`	string.js	Removes inappropriate characters such as `~!@#$%^&*()_+|`-=\\{}[]:\";'<>,./` and space.
`getAllObjectRefs()`	docInfo.js	Returns an array of object references for any specified tag in the current document or, if the document is in a frameset, in all frames.
`getAllObjectTags()`	docInfo.js	Returns an array of tags for any specified tag in the current document or, if the document is in a frameset, in all frames.

Dreamweaver Behavior Techniques

Creating a behavior is often far more than just stringing together a number of pre-defined functions. Specific techniques exist for many special needs, and if you don't know them, you can spend many hours redeveloping the wheel. In this section, you learn several methods that can help you streamline your work.

Specifying an event

In Dreamweaver, every tag capable of being used to launch a behavior has a default event. Although you can alter the default events for various tags by editing the HTML files in the Events folder, as described in Chapter 19, these changes affect only your own system, not those of other users. You can, however, specify the desired event on a behavior-by-behavior basis — in fact, you can specify a series of desired events.

The event specification takes place in the `canApplyBehavior()` function. Usually, this function returns either true or false, depending on whether the proper conditions for implementing the behavior have been met. If, however, the conditions have been met *and* you want to specify an event to use, `canApplyBehavior()` can be set to return a string of acceptable events.

In the following example, the page is inspected, and if a layer is found, the default event is overridden in favor of `onKeyDown`:

```
function canAcceptBehavior(){
  var nameArray = dreamweaver.getObjectRefs("NS 4.0","document","LAYER");
  if (nameArray.length > 0){
    return "onKeyDown";
  }else{
  return FALSE;

  }
```

It's also possible to specify a series of preferred events, in reverse order of preference, such as this:

```
    return "onKeyDown, onKeyPress, onKeyUp"
```

If one event handler is not available — perhaps because the user specified an older browser — the next is selected.

Returning a value

Most event handlers don't require a return value to be implemented, but some, such as `onMouseOver` and `onMouseOut`, do. Generally, Dreamweaver behaviors don't take this into account, but you can by declaring a special variable, `document.MM_returnValue`. You can see the return value variable in operation in the standard Display Status Message behavior.

The `document.MM_returnValue` variable is declared as the last line in the function definition. Thus, Display Status Message reads as follows:

```
    function MM_displayStatusMsg(msgStr) { //v2.0
      status=msgStr;
      document.MM_returnValue = true;
    }
```

Naturally, the return value can also be `false`.

Including multiple functions

Although little known, the capability to return multiple functions began in Dreamweaver 1.2. Previously, all behavior functions had to be self-contained, and one could not call on any helper functions. Now, however, multiple functions can easily be defined and returned via `behaviorFunction()`. Once written into the user's page, all the returned functions are stored in a single `<script>...</script>` tag pair.

The technique for inserting multiple functions is fairly straightforward. First, list your defined functions in a comma-delimited string in `behaviorFunction()`. The one trick is to make sure that your primary function — the one called by the event handler — is listed last. This technique is illustrated in the following code for my custom Resize Layer Patch behavior:

```
function behaviorFunction(){
   return 'reDo,resizePatch';
}
```

Here, my primary function is `resizePatch()` and is used as such in `applyBehavior()`:

```
function applyBehavior() {
   return 'resizePatch()';   //return fn call with args
}
```

Summary

Although creating a custom behavior is not a simple task, it is a vastly rewarding one — both from the programmer's and the user's perspective. Dreamweaver gives you tremendous power to automate advanced Web page techniques with access to the Document Object Model. As you ponder building your own behaviors, remember the following:

✦ If you can achieve a result in JavaScript, chances are good you can make a behavior to automate that task.

✦ Dreamweaver includes an expanded Document Object Model (DOM) that enables the programmer to examine and modify virtually every aspect of an HTML page.

✦ You can use Dreamweaver's built-in JavaScript extensions and API functions to build your own actions.

✦ Dreamweaver's JavaScript extensions enable you to open existing documents, as well as create and save new ones.

✦ Many useful functions can be found in the Configuration\Shared\CMN folder.

In the next chapter, you learn how to customize Dreamweaver further through commands, Property Inspectors, and more.

✦   ✦   ✦

Customizing Dreamweaver

The Web is a dynamic environment, with new technologies continually emerging. Until recently, HTML standards were changing every year or so, and even now, products are routinely introduced that use the Web as a jumping-off place for new methods and tools. Keeping pace with the constantly shifting work environment of the Web was beyond the capabilities of any suite of Web authoring tools, much less a single one — until Dreamweaver debuted, of course.

The initial version of Dreamweaver had a high degree of extensibility built right in, with its customizable HTML objects and JavaScript behaviors. Macromedia continues to take this core of flexibility to new heights with each release. With the implementation of the W3C Document Object Model and a tremendous number of API functions, objects and behaviors have been beefed up so that they are much more powerful than ever. In addition, Dreamweaver presents a host of ways to extend its power:

✦ **Menus:** The entire menu system is completely customizable. You can add context menu items, rearrange the main menu, and even add completely new menus, all by modifying a single XML file.

✦ **Keyboard Shortcuts:** Macromedia makes it easy to use the same keyboard shortcuts across their product line — even extending that ease to other products — with the Keyboard Shortcut editor. In addition to adopting the most comfortable set of key combinations, shortcuts for individual commands can be personalized.

✦ **Commands:** Commands are JavaScript and HTML code that manipulate the Web page during the design phase, much as behaviors are triggered at runtime.

✦ **Custom tags:** With the rapid rise of XML, custom tag support becomes essential in a professional Web authoring tool. Dreamweaver gives you the power to create any custom tag and control how it displays in the Document window.

✦ **Property Inspectors:** Custom Property Inspectors go hand-in-hand with custom tags, enabling the straightforward entry of attributes and values in a manner consistent with the Dreamweaver user interface.

✦ **Floating panels:** Property Inspectors are limited to a specific size and shape, but custom floating panels are not. Floating panels also have the advantage of being onscreen with other elements, unlike Command dialog boxes.

✦ **Translators:** Translators enable server-side content to be viewed in the Document window at design time, as well as in the browser at runtime.

✦ **C-level extensions:** Some special uses require a root-level addition to Dreamweaver's capabilities. Macromedia's engineers have "popped the hood" on Dreamweaver and made it possible for a C or C++ language library to interface with it through C-level extensions.

While a few of these extension features require programming skills outside of those common to the typical Web designer, most are well within the reach of an HTML — and JavaScript-savvy coder — and the keyboard shortcut editor employs a graphical user interface making it accessible to all. As with behaviors and objects, the source code for all but the C-level extensions is readily available and serves as an excellent training ground. This chapter, combined with these standard scripts, provides all the tools you need to begin carving out your own personalized version of Dreamweaver.

Adding New Commands

By their very nature, objects and behaviors are single-purpose engines. A custom object inserts a single block of HTML into the `<body>` of a Web page, while custom behaviors add JavaScript functions to the `<head>` and attributes of one tag. Commands, on the other hand, are multifaceted, multipurpose, go-anywhere and do-anything mechanisms. Commands can do everything objects and behaviors can do, combined — and more. In fact, commands can even masquerade as objects.

For all their power, however, commands are one of the most accessible of the Dreamweaver extensions. This section describes the basic structure of commands as well as the use of the standard commands that ship with Dreamweaver. You can also find information about how to create your own commands and control their integration into Dreamweaver.

Understanding Dreamweaver commands

When I first encountered commands, I thought, "Great! Dreamweaver now has a macro language," and I envisioned instantly automating simple Web design tasks. Before long, I realized that commands were even more powerful — and a bit trickier than a macro recorder. Dreamweaver's adoption of the W3C Document Object Model (DOM) is one of the factors that makes commands feasible. The DOM in Dreamweaver makes available, or *exposes*, every part of the HTML page — every tag, every attribute, every bit of content — which can then be read, modified, deleted, or added to. Moreover, Dreamweaver commands can open, read, and modify other files on local systems.

The command can have a parameter form or not, depending on how the command was written. Generally, commands are listed in the Commands menu, but by altering the menus.xml file (as described later in the chapter), you can cause your command to appear as part of any other menu — or to not appear at all. Because one command can call another, such hidden commands are more easily modified.

My vision of a macro recorder came true with the Start Recording and Play Recording commands. Now, any onscreen action can be instantly logged and replayed — and through the History panel, even converted into a permanent, repeatable command.

But how specifically are commands being used? Here's a short list of the commands that have been built by Web designers outside of Macromedia:

✦ **Tag Killer:** Removes all instances of any tag from a Web page. By Massimo Foti.

✦ **Scratch Pad:** Keeps snippets of code available for easy cutting and pasting on a single page or across Web sites. By Andrew Wooldridge.

✦ **Borderless Frames:** Sets all frames in a frameset to no borders. By Massimo Foti.

✦ **Quick Site:** Prototypes a simple Web site by creating files and generating a navigation bar to all pages. By Andrew Wooldridge.

✦ **Replicator:** Duplicates any selected element any number of times. By this book's author, Joseph Lowery.

As should be obvious from this list, commands come close to being limited only by the author's imagination. The next section takes a brief look at the commands that ship with Dreamweaver 4 and their uses.

Dreamweaver 4 comes with nine standard commands that, in addition to adding some extra functionality, give you a taste of just how powerful commands can be:

✦ **Apply Source Formatting:** Styles HTML in Web pages created outside of Dreamweaver to resemble Dreamweaver-created code.

✦ **Clean Up HTML:** Removes unnecessary or redundant HTML for a smaller file size and more readable code.

✦ **Clean Up Word HTML:** Deletes unnecessary XML or redundant HTML from a Microsoft Word file saved as a Web page.

✦ **Add/Remove Netscape Resize Fix:** Initially inserts code necessary to work around a problem with layers in Netscape browsers. When a Netscape 4.*x* browser is resized, all layers created with ⟨div⟩ tags lose their precise positioning; the inserted code causes browsers to reload whenever necessary. Reapplying the command deletes the code.

✦ **Optimize Image in Fireworks:** Opens the Fireworks Export Preview dialog box, which enables images to be rescaled, cropped, color-corrected, or exported in a different format. Requires Fireworks 3.

✦ **Create Web Photo Album:** Turns a folder of images into a Web page of thumbnail images, each linked to the original image. Requires Fireworks 3.

✦ **Set Color Scheme:** Selects the colors for the current page's background, text, and link states.

✦ **Format Table:** Applies one of 17 different predesigned formats or any designated custom format to the selected table.

✦ **Sort Table:** Performs a one- or two-level sort on any table, using any column in an ascending or descending manner.

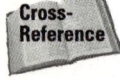

All but the first two of the standard commands are described in detail elsewhere in the book. You can find a description of Set Color Scheme in Chapter 8, and Chapter 13 covers the two Table commands. Chapter 4 explains the use of the Netscape Layer Fix, and you can find information on the two Fireworks commands in Chapter 22.

The Apply Source Formatting command

All the code created by Dreamweaver is structured according to a document called the "Source Format Profile." The Source Format Profile controls which codes are indented and which are on their own line, as well as numerous other specifications of HTML writing. Occasionally, a Web designer must work with Web pages created earlier or by other designers using other programs, or even by hand. The Apply Source Formatting command can rewrite the original code so that it is structured according to the current Source Format Profile. The more accustomed your eye is to following Dreamweaver-style HTML, the more you value this command.

To learn more about the Source Format Profile, see Chapter 4.

The Apply Source Formatting command is an example of a Dreamweaver command that doesn't display a dialog box to gather the user's selected parameters — because you have no parameters to set. To invoke the command, choose Commands ⇨ Apply Source Formatting. The command is applied immediately, with no confirmation or feedback offered, indicating that it is complete.

The Clean Up HTML command

Even if you never switch to Code view, open the Code Inspector, or touch the code in an external editor, your HTML can still become unwieldy. One of the most common problems is redundant `<font>` tags that result from doing something such as selecting some text and then first changing the font itself, and next the font size, and finally the font color. This is likely to give you code that resembles the following:

```
<font face="Arial"><font size="4">¬
<font color="green">Bonanza!</font></font></font>
```

The Clean Up HTML command is, quite literally, custom made to consolidate code such as this and remove some of the code clutter that can accumulate during a page's design. In all, you have six different cleansing operations from which to choose. The Clean Up HTML command is applicable only to the current page and cannot be applied sitewide.

To use the Clean Up HTML command, follow these steps:

1. Choose Commands ➪ Clean Up HTML.

   The Clean Up HTML dialog box appears, as shown in Figure 21-1.

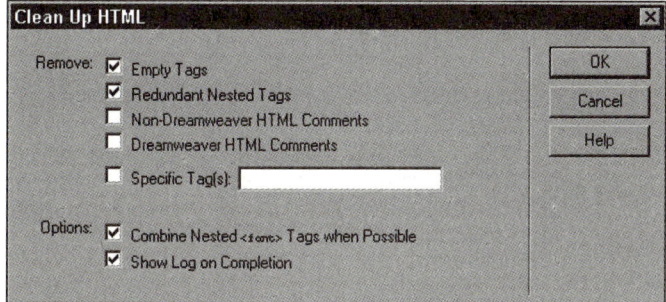

Figure 21-1: Reduce your page's file size and make your HTML more readable with the Clean Up HTML command.

2. To delete tag pairs with no code between them (such as `<i></i>`), make sure the Remove: Empty Tags option is selected.

3. To eliminate superfluous tags that repeat the same code as the tags surrounding them, as in this example:

   ```
   <font color="white">And the <font color="white">¬
   truth</font> is plain to see.</font>
   ```

   choose the Remove: Redundant Tags option.

4. To delete any HTML comments not created by Dreamweaver to mark a Library or Template item, choose Remove: Non-Dreamweaver HTML Comments.

5. To clear all Dreamweaver-specific comments, such as:

```
<! #BeginEditable "openingPara" -->
```

select the Remove: Dreamweaver HTML Comments option.

6. To erase any specific tag and its attributes, select the Remove: Specific Tag(s) option and enter the tag name(s) in the text box.

Note　　Tag names are entered without angle brackets; separate multiple tags with a comma.

7. To consolidate `<font>` tags, select the Combine Nested `<font>` Tags When Possible option.

8. To view a report of the changes applied to your document, select the Show Log on Completion option.

9. Click OK when you're done.

Dreamweaver performs the actions requested on the current document. If the Show Log option has been selected, an alert displays the changes made, if any.

Recording and replaying commands

I'm a big fan of any kind of work-related automation and consider myself a power user of word processing macros, so you can imagine my delight when a similar capability was added to Dreamweaver. The capability to record your onscreen actions and then replay them instantly — with the option of saving them as a command or simply pasting them into another document — is a tremendous work-saver. Most every onscreen action can be replicated.

How could you use such a macro-like capability in Dreamweaver? Let's say you have a series of ten images on a page, and you want to surround each of them with a 2-pixel border and center them on the page. Now, you could do this one at a time entering in the same border value and selecting the center alignment button, but it would get pretty tedious after the third or fourth image. With Dreamweaver, here's the basic automation procedure:

1. Select the first image.

2. Choose Commands ⇨ Start Recording or use the keyboard shortcut, Ctrl+Shift+X (Command+Shift+X).

The cursor changes to a recording tape symbol, indicating you're in recording mode.

3. Enter the new values in the Property Inspector.

4. Choose Commands ⇨ Stop or the same keyboard command again: Ctrl+Shift+X (Command+Shift+X).

5. Select another image.

6. Choose Commands ⇨ Play Recorded Command or use the keyboard shortcut Ctrl+P (Command+P).

7. Repeat Steps 5 and 6 for every image you want to affect as shown in Figure 21-2.

Figure 21-2: After the steps for formatting the first image were recorded, formatting the other images is a one-step process with Dreamweaver's command recorder.

Most of the commands and onscreen moves can be replicated in this manner, but not always. The major exception is the use of the mouse. Dreamweaver cannot repeat mouse moves and selections. You could not, for example, begin to create a drop-cap by recording the drag selection of the first letter in each paragraph. You can, however, use the arrow keys and any keyboard-related combination.

For example, let's say you had a standard list of names in your document, such as the following:

```
Joseph Lowery
Andrew Wooldridge
Al Sparber
Simon White
Derren Whiteman
```

that you wanted to change to *Lastname, Firstname* format. To do this with command recording, you'd follow this procedure.

1. Position your cursor at the beginning of the first name.

2. Choose Commands ➪ Start Recording.

3. Press Shift+right arrow to select the first word.

   Dreamweaver highlights the first word and the following space.

4. Press Ctrl+X (Command X) to cut the selected word.

5. Press End to move to the end of the line.

6. Type a comma and a space.

7. Press Ctrl+V (Command+V) to paste the previously cut word.

8. Press Backspace to remove the trailing space.

   Now that the first line is complete, it's important to position the cursor to perform the recorded command again.

9. Press right arrow to move to the start of the next line.

   Because the cursor was left at the end of the last line, the right-arrow key moves it to the front of the following line.

10. Choose Commands ➪ Stop Recording.

11. Choose Commands ➪ Play Recorded Command for each name in the list.

If you try to include a mouse move or selection when recording a command or playing back a recorded command, Dreamweaver issues a warning and asks if you'd like to stop recording. If you choose to continue, Dreamweaver ignores the attempted mouse move and resets the pointer in its previous position.

Tip   If you try to record your navigations around a table, Dreamweaver does not record the Tab or Shift+Tab keys. However, you can still record your table moves by using Home and End in combination with the arrow keys. To move from cell to cell, from left to right, press End and then right arrow. To move right to left, press Home and then left arrow. You can also move up and down columns by pressing Home or End and then either up or down arrow.

Recorded actions are maintained in memory and when you issue the Start Recording command again, the previously recorded steps are replaced. You can, however, convert recorded steps to a command to use over and over in any document or site you'd like by using the History panel.

1. Record a series of actions as described previously.

2. Play the recorded actions at least once by choosing Commands ⇨ Play Recorded Command.

   On the History panel, the collective recorded actions are displayed as a single step, Run Command.

3. In the History panel, select Run Command.

4. Select the Save As Command button from the bottom of the History panel.

New commands saved in this manner are dynamically added to the Commands menu.

Scripting commands

Commands, as with most behaviors, are a combination of JavaScript functions and HTML forms; the HTML provides the user interface for any parameters that need to be set, and JavaScript carries out the particular command. Although you can combine both languages in a single HTML file, many programmers, including those from Macromedia, keep the JavaScript in a separate .js file that is incorporated in the HTML file with a `<script>` tag, such as this one:

```
<SCRIPT LANGUAGE="javascript" SRC="Clean Up HTML.js">
```

This separation enables easy modification of the user interface and the underlying code, and the sharing of the JavaScript functions.

Commands are very open-ended. In fact, only two Dreamweaver functions are specific to commands — `canAcceptCommand()` and `commandButtons()` — and neither function is required. Two other command-oriented functions, `receiveArguments()` and `windowDimensions()`, are also used elsewhere, but again, neither is required.

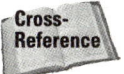 **Cross-Reference** The DOM in Dreamweaver is covered in great detail in Chapter 20.

The `canAcceptCommand()` function controls when the command is active in the menus and when it is ghosted. If `canAcceptCommand()` is not defined, the command is always available. This function returns true or false; if false is returned, the command is ghosted in the menus.

You can see `canAcceptCommand()` in action in both the Sort Table and Format Table commands. For either of these commands to be effective, a table must be indicated. Rather than require that a table be selected, the `canAcceptCommand()` function calls a subroutine, `findTable()`, which returns true if the user's cursor is positioned inside a table:

```
function canAcceptCommand(){
  if (findTable())
    return true;
  else
    return false;
}

function findTable(){
  var tableObj="";
  var selArr = dreamweaver.getSelection();
  var selObj = dreamweaver.offsetsToNode(selArr[0],selArr[1]);

  while (tableObj=="" && selObj.parentNode){
    if (selObj.nodeType == Node.ELEMENT_NODE && selObj.tagName=="TABLE")
    tableObj=selObj;
    else
      selObj = selObj.parentNode;
    }
  return tableObj;
}
```

Macromedia recommends that the `canAcceptCommand()` function not be defined unless at least one case exists in which the command should not be available. Otherwise, the function is asked to run for no purpose, which degrades performance.

The `commandButtons()` function defines the buttons that appear on the parameter form to the right. This expanded functionality is extremely useful when developing commands. Some commands require that an operation be enabled to run repeatedly and not just the one time an OK button is selected. As noted earlier, you don't have to declare the function at all, in which case the form expands to fill the dialog box entirely.

Each button that is declared has a function associated with it, which is executed when the user selects that particular button. All the buttons for a command are listed in an array, returned by `commandButtons()`. The following example declares three buttons: OK, Cancel, and Help:

```
function commandButtons() {
    return new Array("OK","goCommand()","Cancel","window.close()","Help",¬
"displayHelp()")
}
```

Notice that two of the buttons, OK and Help, call custom functions, but the Cancel button simply calls a built-in JavaScript function to close the window. No real limitations exist to the number of buttons a command can hold other than user interface design sense.

The `receiveArguments()` function is used in conjunction with `runCommand()`. Whenever `runCommand()` calls a specific command — from a behavior, object, or other command — it can pass arguments. If `receiveArguments()` is set up, that function is executed, and the arguments read into `receiveArguments()`. This function enables the same command to be called from different sources and have different effects, depending on the arguments passed. The `receiveArguments()` function is used extensively in menu commands and is explained more fully in that section later in this chapter.

As with behaviors and objects, the `windowDimensions()` function can be used with commands to set a specific size for the associated dialog box. If windowDimensions is not defined, the dialog box's size is set automatically. Macromedia recommends that `windowDimensions()` not be used unless your parameter form exceeds 650×480.

The remainder of the user interface for a command — the parameter form — is constructed in the same manner, using the same tools as objects and behaviors. A command parameter form or dialog box uses an HTML `<form>` in the `<body>` of the file. If no `<form>` is declared, the command executes without displaying a dialog box. All of the form elements used in objects — text boxes, radio buttons, checkboxes, and lists — are available in commands.

Cross-Reference For detailed information about how to retrieve information in a parameter form, see Chapter 18.

Dreamweaver techniques: Useful command routines

When programming a command, I often get stuck on one small point. "If only I knew how to _____, I'd be home free," is my usual refrain. The following routines and explanations are presented in the interest of helping you "fill in the blank" as you begin to construct your own custom commands.

Getting a user's selection

Although many commands work with the entire HTML document, some require just a portion of text or an object that has been selected by the user. While it seems a simple task, some quirks in the API make getting a selection a little tricky.

Selecting text

The usual method for finding out — and acting on — what the user has selected requires the `getSelection()` function. As discussed in Chapter 20, `getSelection()` returns two-byte offsets that mark the beginning and end of the user's selection. The difficulty appears when you try to extract the character data that corresponds to those byte offsets. The `offsetsToNode()` function, which is used to make this translation, expands the offsets to the nearest tag—the `innerHTML`, in other words. For example, the following function attempts to get the user's selection and report it in an alert:

```
function testCase() {
  var theDom = dreamweaver.getDocumentDOM("document");
  var offsets = dreamweaver.getSelection()
  var theNode = dreamweaver.offsetsToNode(offsets[0],offsets[1])
  var nodeText = theNode.data
  alert(nodeText)
}
```

If a user selects the word "gray" in the paragraph "The old gray mare just ain't what she used to be," the function returns the entire line. To get just what is selected, you need to use the `nodeToOffsets()` function in combination with `offsetsToNode()` and the JavaScript `substring()` function.

The example code in Listing 21-1 demonstrates the proper substring technique; it is taken from the Change Case command, included on the CD-ROM that accompanies this book:

Listing 21-1: **Getting Selected Text**

```
function lowerCase(){
  var theDom=dreamweaver.getDocumentDOM("document");
  var offsets = dreamweaver.getSelection()
  var theNode = dreamweaver.offsetsToNode(offsets[0],offsets[1])
  if (theNode.nodeType == Node.TEXT_NODE) {
  var nodeOffsets = dreamweaver.nodeToOffsets(theNode)
  offsets[0] = offsets[0]-nodeOffsets[0]
  offsets[1] = offsets[1]-nodeOffsets[0]
  var nodeText = theNode.data
  theNode.data = nodeText.substring(0,offsets[0]) +
   nodeText.substring(offsets[0], offsets[1]).toLowerCase() +
   nodeText.substring(offsets[1], nodeText.length);
  window.close()
  } else { //it's not a TEXT_NODE
  var nodeOffsets = dreamweaver.nodeToOffsets(theNode)
  offsets[0] = offsets[0]-nodeOffsets[0]
  offsets[1] = offsets[1]-nodeOffsets[0]
  var nodeText = theNode.innerHTML
  theNode.innerHTML = nodeText.toLowerCase()
  window.close()
  }
}
```

Notice two conditions in the example function—either the selected string is text (a TEXT_NODE), or it's not. If the node is something other than a TEXT_NODE, the data property is not available, and innerHTML must be used instead. This situation occurs when a user selects an entire paragraph. In fact, all the user has to select is the last character before the closing tag—such as a period at the end of a paragraph—and the node type switches to ELEMENT_NODE.

Selecting objects

By comparison, you have far fewer hoops to jump through to reference a selected object. To find a selected object, you need to get only its outerHTML property, as shown in Listing 21-2.

Listing 21-2: **Getting a Selected Object**

```
function replicate(){
  var theDom = dreamweaver.getDocumentDOM("document");
  var offsets = dreamweaver.getSelection()
  var selObj = dreamweaver.offsetsToNode(offsets[0],offsets[1])
  if (selObj.nodeType == Node.TEXT_NODE) {
    helpMe2()
    window.close()
    return;
  }
  var theCode = selObj.outerHTML
```

Listing 21-2 also includes a small error routine that looks to see if the user's selection is text (selObj.nodeType == Node.TEXT_NODE) and, if so, puts up an advisory and then closes the window to enable the user to reselect.

Using a command as an object

Commands offer a tremendous range of power and can perform actions not available to behaviors or objects. To take advantage of this power with a point-and-click interface, it's best to "disguise" your command as an object. As an object, your command appears in both the Objects panel and the Insert menu.

A Dreamweaver object usually consists of two files: an HTML file for the code and a GIF image for the button, all in the Object folder. When using a command as an object, however, you can have as many as five files split between the Object and Command folders. The standard Rollover object is a good example: three associated Rollover files are in the Object folder and two in the Command folder. Here is how they are used:

✦ **Object/Rollover.gif:** The image for the Rollover button that appears in the Objects panel

✦ **Object/Rollover.htm:** A shell file (called by the Rollover button) that reads Object/Rollover.js

✦ **Object/Rollover.js:** Contains the `objectTag()` function, which references the Command/Rollover.htm file

✦ **Command/Rollover.htm:** Builds the user interface for the "object" and reads all external JavaScript files, including Command/Rollover.js

✦ **Command/Rollover.js:** Contains the actual code for the function that performs the required operations, which returns its value to the Object/Rollover.htm file by way of the Object/Rollover.js file

The key to understanding how to use a command as an object is the code linking the two. In the Object/Rollover.js file is the `objectTag()`, which is used to write an object into an existing Web page with its return value. In this case, the function first gets the Document Object Model of the relevant Command file (Command/Rollover.htm); this procedure enables the current function to reference any variable set in the other file. Then the `popupCommand` is executed, which runs Command/Rollover.htm — which, in turn, launches the dialog box and gets the user parameters. Finally, a result from that command is set to the return value of `objectTag()` and written into the HTML page. Here's the `objectTag()` function in its entirety from Object/Rollover.js:

```
function objectTag() {
   var rolloverCmdURL = dreamweaver.getConfigurationPath() + ¬
"/Commands/Rollover.htm";
   var rolloverDoc    = dreamweaver.getDocumentDOM( rolloverCmdURL );
   dreamweaver.popupCommand( "Rollover.htm" );
   return( rolloverDoc.parentWindow.getRolloverTag() );
}
```

Some custom commands disguised as objects make the DOM connection in the command file, rather than the object file. The iCat objects, for example, all establish the link in the primary functions of their command JavaScript files, in this manner:

```
   var dom = dreamweaver.getDocumentDOM("../Objects/iCat/Add To Cart.htm");
   dom.parentWindow.icatTagStr = icatTagStr;
```

Then, the corresponding `objectTag()` function simply returns the `icatTagStr` variable.

Placing code in the <head> section

It's fairly straightforward to insert text wherever the cursor has been set in the document — you just set a text string equal to the [`innerHTML | data`] property of the DOM at that point. But how do you insert code in the <head> section of a Web page where the cursor is generally not found? Certain code, such as `<script>` tags that hold extensive JavaScript functions, must be inserted in the `<head>`. By design, behaviors return code specifically intended for the `<script>` tag—except you can't easily use a behavior to include a line such as

```
<script language="Javascript" src="extend.js"></script>
```

You can insert such a line with commands, however, and this technique, developed by Dreamweaver extensions author Massimo Foti, shows the way.

Unfortunately, no equivalent to the .body property exists in the Dreamweaver DOM for the `<head>` section. The way around this minor limitation is to first locate the sole `<head>` tag in a document. This task can be accomplished in two lines of JavaScript code:

```
theDom = dreamweaver.getDocumentDOM("document")
theHeadNode = theDom.getElementsByTagName("HEAD")
```

Now the script variable needs to be set. Whenever Dreamweaver encounters a closing `<script>` tag (such as `</script>`) in a JavaScript function, the tag is flagged because it seems to be missing a mate. To avoid this problem, split the tag up into two concatenated strings, such as this:

```
theScript = '<script language="Javascript" src="extend.js"><' + '/script>'
```

Finally, find the first item in the `<head>` section and append the script to its `innerHTML` property:

```
theHeadNode.item(0).innerHTML = theHeadNode.item(0).innerHTML + theScript
```

The full function looks like this:

```
function insertScript() {
  var theDom, theHeadNode, theScript
  theDom = dreamweaver.getDocumentDOM("document")
  theHeadNode = theDom.getElementsByTagName("HEAD")
  theScript = '<script language="Javascript" src="extend.js"><' + 'script>'
}
```

On the CD-ROM You can find numerous examples of Massimo Foti's commands and other extensions on the CD-ROM that accompanies this book. Just look in the Additional Extensions folder under his name.

Using commands to call other commands

In the earlier section "Using a Command as an Object," the `runCommand()` function plays a key role. It's worth emphasizing that this same function is used when you want one command to invoke another command. The proper syntax is

```
var doNew = dw.runCommand("commandFileName")
```

where *commandFileName* is the name of an HTML file in the Command folder. No value is returned with `runCommand()`; the function executes whatever command is called, passing any optional arguments. The function takes the format

```
dreamweaver.runCommand("myCommand.htm","argument01", "argument02")
```

The called command's dialog box is presented and must be completed or canceled before the originating command is able to continue.

Tip　Many commands—especially those disguised as objects—are not intended to be directly accessed by the user. However, Dreamweaver lists any valid command found in the Command folder on the menu—unless you add a comment as the first line of your HTML file in this format:

```
<!-- MENU-LOCATION=NONE -->
```

This code line inhibits the command name from being automatically displayed in the Commands menu list.

Creating a blank document

Commands aren't limited to working on the current document—you can use a command to read, modify, and even create new files. Any new file created using the `createDocument()` function is an HTML page based on the Default.htm file found in the Configuration\Templates folder—this is the same file used as the base for any files created when File ⇨ New is chosen.

Occasionally, however, a command needs to make a new non-HTML document, such as an XML or SMIL file or other file type that doesn't use the `<html>...</html>` structure. To accomplish this task, you first create an HTML file and then replace its entire contents with your own data—or nothing at all. The following custom function, developed by Andrew Wooldridge, makes and saves a new, blank text file:

```
function doNew() {
var newDOM = dreamweaver.createDocument();
var theDoc = newDOM.documentElement;
theDoc.outerHTML = ".";
theDoc.innerHTML = " ";
dreamweaver.saveDocument(newDOM, '../../empty.txt');
}
```

Remember, all the Dreamweaver document functions—such as `saveDocument()`—use addresses relative to the file calling them. For example, if the `doNew()` function just described is included in a command, and therefore stored in the Commands folder, the empty.txt document is saved two folders above the Commands folder or in the Dreamweaver root directory, as the full path to the Commands folder is Dreamweaver\Configuration\Commands.

Note　You'll find all of Hava's commands to be heavily commented and very worthwhile for programmers of any level.

Commands from a Developer's Developer

Hava Edelstein, a JavaScript engineer with Macromedia, has contributed five commands especially valuable for developers. You can find them on the Dreamweaver Exchange as well as on the CD-ROM accompanying this book. Here is an overview of these very useful commands:

✦ **Eval:** This command enables you to quickly spot-check JavaScript statements and perform one-time alterations to your document. A must-have for the serious command developer.

✦ **Show Browser References:** Navigator and Internet Explorer handle objects' references — especially those objects in layers — quite differently. This command enables you to select any object on the page and then find its proper JavaScript reference, which can be easily cut and pasted into your code.

✦ **Show Document Tree:** Want to see how the current document is structured from a DOM point of view? Run this command to create a new document with all the details, most notably the Node_Type of each node. Included in this command is a useful subroutine, `traverseNodes()`, which travels recursively through a document's nodes.

✦ **Set All Checkboxes:** If you've ever had to work with a large form with many checkboxes, you can appreciate this command. Each checkbox on the page is presented and can be set as checked or unchecked. Of special note to programmers is the included function, `setSingleWordAttribute()`, which enables an attribute such as hidden or checked to be set; this functionality is not present in the standard Dreamweaver function `setAttribute()`.

✦ **Show Table Properties:** While the capability to display the properties of a selected table may not seem all that compelling, it's what's under the hood here that counts. This command encompasses three useful utility functions: `getTagAttributes()`, `stripQuotesIfTheyExist()`, and `deleteExtraWhiteSpace()`.

 You can find a command incorporating this technique on the CD-ROM that accompanies this book along with many other commands by Andrew Wooldridge. Andrew has a deep understanding of commands and continually stretches the boundaries of what they can accomplish.

Managing Menus and Keyboard Shortcuts

Dreamweaver offers numerous ways to perform most every task: through the Property Inspector, pop-up context menus, keyboard shortcuts, and even entering code directly. However, in the search for ever-faster, more efficient ways of working, it's often desirable to take control of the menus and other command methods and make them work the way you or your team prefer to work. If, for example, you insert a great number of layers and always define your links via the Property Inspector, you'd probably be better off redefining Ctrl+L (Command+L) to Insert Layer rather than its default, Insert Link.

Dreamweaver completely places all menus and keyboard shortcuts under your control. Not only can you add new items but you can also rename menu items, change their keyboard shortcuts, determine when a menu item is active or dimmed — and even add entirely new menu strips. Moreover, all of this functionality is available with the context pop-up menus as well.

One file — menus.xml, found in the Configuration/Menus folder — is responsible for menu and keyboard shortcut set-up. While you have to edit the XML file by hand to reconfigure the menus, Dreamweaver includes a Keyboard Shortcut editor for modifying the keystroke commands. Details on using the Keyboard Shortcut editor are found later in this section.

This menu customization brings a whole new level of functionality to Dreamweaver. It's entirely possible for a company to create custom subsets of the program for certain departments. For example, let's assume each of several departments in a large firm is responsible for its own section of the Web site. A customized version of Dreamweaver could include a predefined site and disable the Define Site commands in the Site menu, as well as offer a specialized menu for calling up help screens, tied to the standard F1 keyboard shortcut for Help.

In addition to the fully open architecture of the menus.xml file, command menu items, created by the History panel, can be managed right in the Document window. Before we delve into the relatively more complex menus.xml structure, let's take a look at the Edit Command List function.

Handling History panel commands

Whenever you save a series of History panel steps as a command, it is instantly added to the bottom of the Commands menu list. Dreamweaver enables you to manage these custom added items — renaming them or deleting them — through the Edit Command List feature.

To manage History panel recorded commands, follow these steps:

1. Choose Commands ⇨ Edit Command List.

   The Edit Command List dialog box appears as shown in Figure 21-3.

2. To remove a command, select it and choose Delete.

3. To rename a command, select it and enter the new name or alter the existing one.

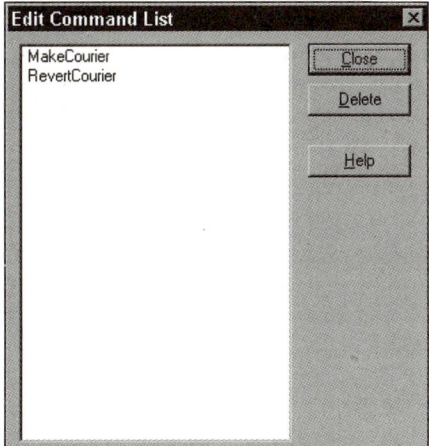

Figure 21-3: Manage your recorded commands through the Edit Command List dialog box.

Note The Edit Command List affects only those commands saved from the History panel. To manage other commands — whether included in Dreamweaver or added later — you have to alter the menus.xml file, as discussed later in this chapter. This procedure is also required to reorder the Commands menu list.

Using the Keyboard Shortcut editor

When I'm learning a new program, one of the tasks I set for myself is to memorize the half-dozen or so essential keyboard shortcuts of the software. Keyboard shortcuts are terrific for boosting productivity — so terrific, in fact, that almost every program uses them. While this is a good thing from a single-program user's perspective, in reality no Web designer uses just one program and having to remember the keyboard shortcuts for every needed program can be an absolute nightmare.

New Feature To put the brakes on keyboard shortcut overload, Macromedia has implemented a standard keyboard shortcut editor for their key Web products — Flash, Fireworks, and Dreamweaver. Where possible, common features share the same shortcut across the product line. For example, opening the Behaviors panel is now accomplished with the same keyboard shortcut in Dreamweaver and Fireworks, Shift+F3. Dreamweaver also includes a set of shortcuts matching those from HomeSite and BBEdit to smooth your transition from those text-based editors. Best of all, you can personalize any existing set of shortcuts to truly work with the way you work best.

To access the Keyboard Shortcuts editor, shown in Figure 21-4, choose Edit ⇨ Keyboard Shortcuts. The Keyboard Shortcuts editor comes standard with four different sets of shortcuts:

✦ **BBEdit:** Keyboard shortcut set matching those found in BBEdit 6.0.

✦ **Dreamweaver 3:** This set uses the standard shortcuts found in Dreamweaver 3, supplemented with additional shortcuts for Dreamweaver 4 features, such as the Assets panel. These additional shortcuts will not necessarily be the same as those in the Macromedia Standard set.

✦ **HomeSite:** Keyboard shortcut set matching those found in HomeSite 4.5.

✦ **Macromedia Standard:** The default set of shortcuts incorporating common keyboard combinations in Dreamweaver 4, Fireworks 4 and Flash 5.

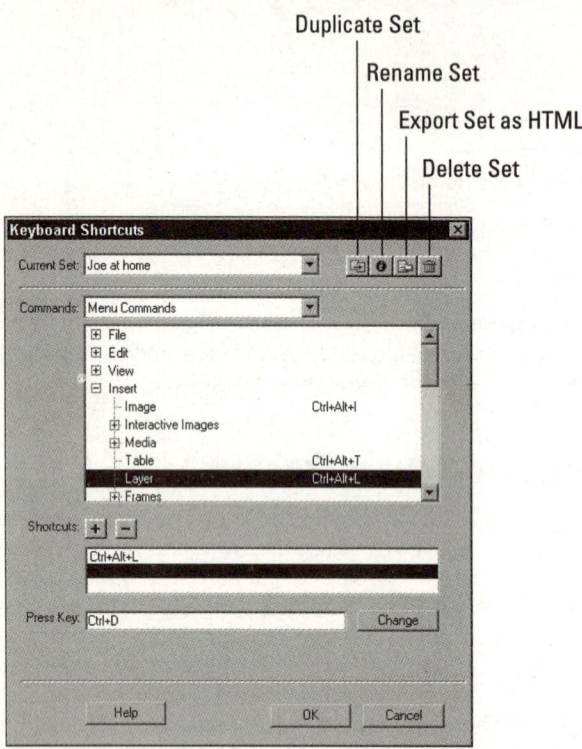

Figure 21-4: Use the Keyboard Shortcuts editor to establish the easiest-to-remember mnemonics.

To change from one set to another, open the Keyboard Shortcuts editor and choose the desired set from the Current Set drop-down list. The changes take effect immediately upon closing the dialog box; there's no need to relaunch Dreamweaver.

The standard sets are locked and cannot be altered — you can only customize a copy of one of the standard sets. Dreamweaver provides all the controls you need to accomplish this on top of the Keyboard Shortcuts editor. The four buttons are:

✦ **Duplicate Set:** Copies the current set (standard or custom) and appends the word "copy." The duplicate set can be fully customized.

✦ **Rename Set:** Renames the current shortcut set.

✦ **Export Set as HTML:** Saves out a listing of the keyboard shortcuts of the current set in an HTML format that can be viewed or printed in a browser.

✦ **Delete Set:** Removes a keyboard shortcut set. When Delete Set is chosen, a listing of all custom sets is displayed and any set except the active one may be removed. To remove a sole custom set, select any of the standard shortcut sets prior to choosing Delete Set.

Each command has up to two shortcuts assigned to it. This facility makes it possible to retain the originally assigned keyboard shortcut and to add a more personal one. Use the following steps to create a custom keyboard shortcut set:

1. Choose Edit ⇨ Keyboard Shortcuts to open the editor.

> **Note**
>
> A brief note from the Department of Pointless Nonsense, Irony Division: the Keyboard Shortcuts feature is one of the few commands without a keyboard shortcut.

2. Select a standard keyboard shortcut set upon which to base your custom set from the Current Set drop-down list.

3. Click the Duplicate Set button and type in an appropriate name for your custom shortcut set and click OK. The Current Set drop-down list changes to the new name and you are ready to edit.

4. Choose the type of commands you wish to modify from the Commands drop-down list.

   Dreamweaver has five different command types in Windows — Menu Commands, Site Menu Commands, Code Editing, Document Editing, and Site Window — and three under the Macintosh system (Menu Commands, Code Editing, and Document Editing).

5. Select the command to modify from the listings. If you're altering a Menu or Site Menu Command (Windows only), select the plus (+) sign next to the menu heading containing the command.

   The listing expands to show the first level of menu items. If the command you want to alter is contained within a submenu, click the plus (+) sign next to the submenu. Select the minus (-) sign to collapse an expanded listing.

6. With the desired command selected, click the Add (+) button in the Shortcuts section.

   The cursor moves into the Press Key field.

7. Press the keyboard combination you want to assign to the command.

If Dreamweaver detects a conflict with an existing keyboard shortcut, an alert is displayed beneath the Press Key field telling you which command that shortcut is currently assigned to.

8. Select Change to confirm your choice.

If the shortcut you selected is already in use, Dreamweaver brings up an alert dialog box warning you that the shortcut is in use, telling you which command is using it, and asking if you want to reassign it to the command you are editing. To reassign the keystroke, click OK. To choose a new keyboard shortcut, click Cancel.

9. Click OK when you're done to save your keyboard shortcut set.

If a command already has two shortcuts assigned to it, you need to select the one you want to change.

Tip　The personalized keyboard shortcut files are stored in the Configuration/ Menus/Custom Sets folder as XML files. To make a keyboard shortcut set available on another system, copy the appropriate XML file to the corresponding folder.

Adjusting the Menu XML file

When Dreamweaver is launched, the menus.xml file is read by the program and the menu system is built. You can even customize menus.xml and then reload the file from within Dreamweaver — and instantly update your menu and shortcuts. The key, of course, is in editing the XML file.

Caution　Before you begin editing the menus.xml file, it's important that you create a backup of the file. The syntax for menus.xml is fairly sophisticated, and Dreamweaver ignores any incorrect entries, which could result in numerous menu items being made inoperative. Also, it's best to use a robust text editor, rather than Dreamweaver itself, to make changes to the menus.xml file.

The typical procedure for changing an existing menu item or shortcut is to open the file in a text editor (after making a backup of the original) and make the necessary changes. When adding menus or menu items, you need to follow the file's syntax, as described in the following sections.

Generic shortcuts

Although Dreamweaver now provides a user interface for editing the keyboard shortcuts, sometimes power-users need to go to the source for major modifications — and the source for shortcuts is menus.xml. The menus.xml file is divided into two main sections: `<shortcutlist>` and `<menubar>`. The `<shortcutlist>` divisions are, as you might suspect, a list of keyboard shortcuts, while the

`<menubar>` areas are concerned with the various menu bars, in the main Document window, in the Site window (Windows only), and the numerous context menus. `<shortcutlist>` and `<menubar>` share several characteristics. They both follow the same basic structure:

```
<shortcutlist id=shortcutListID>
    <shortcut attributeName = value/>
    <shortcut attributeName = value/>
    <shortcut attributeName = value/>
</shortcutlist>

<menubar name=name id=menubarID platform=win|mac>
    <menu attributeName = value>
        <menuitem attributeName = value/>
        <menuitem attributeName = value/>
        <menuitem attributeName = value/>
    </menu>
</menubar>
```

Shortcuts for menu items are primarily defined within the `<menubar>` code; the `<shortcutlist>` is primarily concerned with those shortcuts that do not have a menu item associated with them, such as moving from one word to another. By default, Dreamweaver defines four `<shortcutlist>` sections: one for the Document window, the Site window (Windows only), the Code Inspector, and the Timelines panel.

Note   The key difference between the `<shortcutlist>` and the `<menubar>` sections is that while you can define new menu items or change existing ones in the `<menubar>` portion of the code, you can only alter existing shortcuts—you cannot add new shortcuts.

Each `<shortcutlist>` tag has one required attribute, the ID. The ID refers to a specific window or floating panel and must be unique within the `<shortcutlist>` section. The same ID is repeated in the `<menubar>` section to refer to the same window or panel. For example, the Document window ID is DWMainWindow, while the one for the context menu of the Timelines panel is DWTimelineContext. The `<shortcutlist>` tag can also have another attribute, platform, which must be set to either win or mac, for Windows and Macintosh systems, respectively. If no platform attribute is listed, the `<shortcutlist>` described applies to both platforms. Here, for example, is the beginning of the shortcutlist definition for the Site window, which only appears in the Windows version of the software:

```
<shortcutlist id="DWMainSite" platform="win">
```

A separate `<shortcut>` tag exists for every keystroke defined in the `<shortcutlist>`. The `<shortcut>` tag defines the key used, the tag's ID, the command or file to be executed when the keyboard shortcut is pressed, and the applicable platform, if any. Shortcuts can be defined for single special keys or key combinations using modifiers. The special keys are:

✦ F1 through F12

✦ PgDn, PgUp, Home, End

✦ Ins, Del, BkSp, Space

✦ Esc and Tab

Modifiers can be used in combination with standard keys, special keys, or themselves. A combination keyboard shortcut is indicated with a plus sign between keys. Available modifiers include those described in Table 21-1.

Table 21-1
Dreamweaver Shortcut Modifier Keys

Key	Example	Use
Cmd	Command+S	Indicates the Ctrl (Windows) and the Command (Macintosh) key modifier
Alt or Opt	Alt+V; Option+V	Indicates the Alt (Windows) or Option (Macintosh) key modifier
Shift	Shift+F1	Indicates the Shift key on both platforms
Ctrl	Ctrl+U	Indicates the Ctrl (Windows) or Control (Macintosh)

You can also combine multiple modifiers, as in this example:

Cmd+Shift+Z

The balance of the `<shortcut>` tag is identical in format to that used in the `<menuitem>` tag and is described in the section that follows.

Menubar definitions

Each `<menubar>` section of the menus.xml file describes a different menu strip, either on a window or the context menu associated with a floating panel. Nested within the `<menubar>` tag are a series of `<menu>` tags, each detailing a drop-down menu. The individual menu items are defined in the `<menuitem>` tags contained within each `<menu>` tags. Here, for example, is the context menu for the HTML Styles panel (I've abbreviated the complete `<menuitem>` tag for clarity):

```
<menubar name="" id="DWHtmlStyleContext">
    <menu name="HTML Style Popup" id="DWContext_HTMLStyle">
        <menuitem name="Edit..." />
        <menuitem name="Duplicate..." />
        <menuitem name="Delete" />
        <menuitem name="Apply" />
        <separator />
```

```
            <menuitem name="New..." />
        </menu>
    </menubar>
```

`<menubar>` and `<menu>` tags are alike in that they both require a name — which is what appears in the menu system — and an ID. The ID must be unique within the `<menubar>` structure to avoid conflicts. If a conflict is found (that is, if one item has the same ID as another), the first item in the XML file is recognized, and the second item is ignored.

Note You can put a dividing line between your menu items by including a `<separator/>` tag between any two `<menuitem>` tags.

Numerous other attributes exist for the `<menuitem>` tag. The required attributes are name, ID, and either file or command as marked with an asterisk in Table 21-2.

Table 21-2
Menuitem Tag Attributes

Attribute	Possible Value	Description
name*	Any menu name	The name of the menu item as it appears on the menu. An underscore character causes the following letter to be underlined for Windows' shortcuts — for example, "_Frames" becomes "Frames."
id*	Any unique name	The identifying term for the menu item.
key	Any special key or keyboard key plus modifier(s)	The keyboard shortcut used to execute the command.
platform	win or mac	The operating system valid for the current menu item. If the platform parameter is omitted, the menu item is applicable for both systems.
enabled	JavaScript function	If present, governs whether a menu item is active (the function returns true) or dimmed (the function returns false). Including enabled=true assures that the function is always available.
command* (required if file is not used)	JavaScript function	Executed when the menu item is selected. This inline JavaScript function capability is used for simple functions.
file* (required if command is not used)	Path to a JavaScript file	The JavaScript file is executed when the menu item is selected; the path is relative to the Configuration folder.

Continued

	Table 21-2 (continued)	
Attribute	**Possible Value**	**Description**
`checked`	JavaScript function	Displays a checkmark next to the menu item if the function returns true.
`dynamic`	N/A	Specifies that the menu item is set dynamically by the function(s) found in the `file`.

Tip   The menus.xml file is quite extensive. The main menu for Dreamweaver — the one you most likely want to modify — can be found by searching for the second instance of its ID, `DWMainWindow`. The first instance is used by the corresponding `<shortcutlist>` **tag.**

You can create submenus by nesting one set of `<menu>` tags within another. For example, here's a simplified look at the File ➪ Import commands, as structured in menus.xml:

```
<menu name="_File" id="DWMenu_File">
[other menu items...]
    <menu name="_Import" id="DWMenu_File_Import">
        <menuitem name="Import _XML into Template..."/>
        <menuitem name="Import _Word HTML..."/>
        <menuitem name="Import _Table Data..."    />
    </menu>
[other menu items...]
</menu>
```

Note how within the `<menu>` tag that defines the File menu, another `<menu>` tag defining the Import submenu is nested.

Building menu commands

When examining the menu.xml file, notice that many of the menu items have JavaScript functions written right into the `<menuitem>` tag, such as this one for File ➪ Open:

```
<menuitem name="_New" key="Cmd+N" enabled="true" command="dw.createDocument()" ¬
id="DWMenu_File_New" />
```

Here, when the user selects File ➪ New, Dreamweaver executes the API function, `dw.createDocument()` in what is referred to as a *menu command*. Menu commands are used to specify the action of every menu item; what makes them unique is that they can be used to create and activate dynamic menus. Dynamic menus update according to user selections; the Preview in Browser list and HTML Styles menu items are both dynamic menus.

A menu command, as with most of the other Dreamweaver extensions, is a combination of HTML and JavaScript. If the menu command is extensive and cannot be referenced as one or two functions directly in the menus.xml file, it is contained in an HTML file, stored in the Configuration\Menus folder. Menu commands can even use a dialog box such as standard commands for accepting user input.

Tip Many examples of menu commands, written by the Dreamweaver engineers, are to be found in the MM subfolder of the Menus folder.

Menu commands have access to all of the Dreamweaver API functions and a few of their own. None of the seven menu command API functions, listed in Table 21-3, are required, and three are automatically called when the menu command is executed.

Table 21-3
Command Menu API Functions

Function	Returns	Description
canAcceptCommand()	Boolean	Determines whether the menu item is active or dimmed.
commandButtons()	An array of labels and functions, separated by commas	Sets the name and effect of buttons on the dialog box.
getDynamicContent()	An array of menu item names and unique IDs, separated by a semicolon	Sets the current listing for a menu.
isCommandChecked()	Boolean	Adds a checkmark next to item if true is returned.
receiveArguments()	N/A	Handles any arguments passed by <menuitem> tag.
setMenuText()	A text string	Sets the name of the menu item according to the given function. Not to be used in conjunction with getDynamicContent().
windowDimensions()	"Width,Height" (in pixels)	Determines the dimensions of the dialog box.

Working with Custom Tags

With the advent of XML—in which no standard tags exist—the capability to handle custom tags is essential in a Web authoring tool. Dreamweaver incorporates this capability through its third-party tag feature. After you've defined a third-party tag, Dreamweaver displays it in the Document window by highlighting its content, inserting a user-defined icon, or neither. Third-party tags are easily selected through the Tag Selector on the status bar and, thus, easy to cut, copy, and paste or otherwise manipulate. Perhaps most important, once a third-party tag is defined, you can apply a custom Property Inspector that enables tag attributes to be entered in a standardized user interface.

Third-party tags can be defined directly within Dreamweaver. Just as Object files use HTML to structure HTML code for easy insertion, Dreamweaver uses XML to make an XML definition for the custom tag. A custom tag declaration consists solely of one tag, `<tagspec>`, with up to seven attributes. The attributes for `<tagspec>` are as follows:

✦ **tag_name:** Defines the name of the tag as used in the markup. Any valid name — no spaces or special characters allowed — is possible. A tag with the attribute `tag_name="invoice"` is entered in the document as `<invoice>`.

✦ **tag_type:** Determines whether the tag has a closing tag (`nonempty`) and is thus capable of enclosing content or if the tag describes the content itself (`empty`). For example, the `<invoice>` tag could have a `tag_type="nonempty"` because all the content is between `<invoice>` and `</invoice>`.

✦ **render_contents:** Sets whether the contents of a nonempty type tag are displayed or not. The `render_contents` attribute value is either true or false; if false, the tag's icon is displayed instead of the contents.

✦ **content_model:** Establishes valid placement and content for the tag in the document. The possible options are as follows:

- **block_model:** Tags defined with `content_model="block_model"` only appear in the `<body>` section of a document and contain block-level HTML tags, such as `<p>`, `<div>`, `<blockquote>`, and `<pre>`.

- **head_model:** To define a tag that appears in the `<head>` section and can contain text, set `content_model="head_model"`.

- **marker_model:** Tags with the attribute `content_model=marker_model` are capable of being placed anywhere in the document with no restrictions on content. The `marker_model` value is most often used for inline tags that are placed within a paragraph or division.

- **script_model:** Like the `marker_model`, `script_model` tags can be placed in either the `<head>` or `<body>` section. All content within a `script_model` tag is ignored by Dreamweaver, which enables server-specific scripts to be included without alteration.

✦ **start_string:** The initial delimiter for a custom string-delimited tag; `start_string` and `end_string` must both be defined if one is declared. Lasso tags, for example, use a `start_string` of a left bracket, [.

✦ **end_string:** The closing delimiter for a custom string-delimited tag. The `end_string` for a Lasso tag is the right bracket,].

✦ **detect_in_attribute:** A Boolean value that sets whether or not Dreamweaver should ignore string-delimited tags used as attributes in other tags. While the default is `false`, for most string-delimited functions, the `detect_in_attribute` value should be set to `true`.

✦ **parse_attribute:** A Boolean value that determines if Dreamweaver should inspect and parse the attributes within string-delimited tags. By default, Dreamweaver parses all attributes; set `parse_attribute` to `false` to force Dreamweaver to ignore the attributes.

✦ **icon:** Empty tags or nonempty custom tags with `render_content` disabled require a GIF file to act as an icon in the Document window. The icon attribute should be set to any valid URL, relative or absolute (as in `icon="images/invoice.gif"`).

✦ **icon_width:** Sets the width in pixels of the icon used to represent the tag. The value can be any positive integer.

✦ **icon_height:** Sets the height in pixels of the icon used to represent the tag. The value can be any positive integer.

Tip The icons used by Dreamweaver to represent the Invisible Elements such as the `<br>` tag are 16 pixels wide by 14 pixels high.

Here's the complete code for a sample custom tag, the ColdFusion Directory tag:

```
<tagspec tag_name="CFDIRECTORY" tag_type="empty" render_contents="false" ü
content_model="marker_model" icon="ColdFusion.gif" icon_width="16" ü
icon_height="16"></tagspec>
```

You can see an example of the ColdFusion custom tags in Figure 21-5.

Tip If the content is to be rendered for a custom tag, you can easily view it in the Document window by enabling the Third-Party Tags Highlighting option in Preferences. Make sure that View ⇨ Invisible Elements is enabled.

Once a custom tag is defined, the definition is saved in an XML file in the ThirdPartyTags folder, in Dreamweaver's Configuration folder. If you are establishing a number of custom tags, you can place all the definitions in the same file. Macromedia refers to this as the Tag DB or Database.

On the CD-ROM Andrew Wooldridge has created an extremely useful command called `Build_Custom_Tag` for defining XML third-party tags. You can find it on the CD-ROM that accompanies this book.

Custom icon   Highlighted content for third-party tags

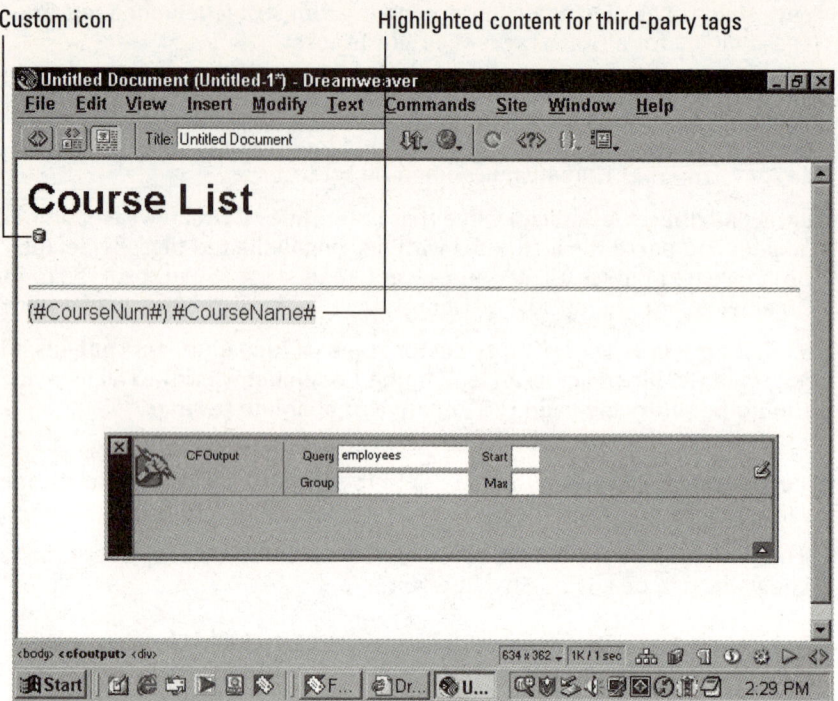

Figure 21-5: Third-party tags such as these from ColdFusion can be displayed—and manipulated—in the Document window.

Customizing Property Inspectors

The Property Inspector is used throughout Dreamweaver to display the current attributes of many different types of tags: text, images, layers, plug-ins, and so on. Not only do Property Inspectors make it easy to see the particulars for an object, they make it a snap to modify the same parameters. With the inclusion of custom tags in Dreamweaver, the capability to add custom Property Inspectors is a natural parallel. Moreover, you can create custom Property Inspectors for existing tags, which display in place of the built-in Property Inspectors.

As with objects, commands, and behaviors, custom Property Inspectors are composed of HTML and JavaScript; the Property Inspector HTML file itself is stored in the Configuration\Inspectors folder. However, the layout of the Property Inspector is far more restrictive than it is with the other Dreamweaver extensions. The dialog box for an object, command, or behavior can be any size or shape desired—any custom Property Inspector must fit the standard Property Inspector dimensions and design. Because of the precise positioning necessary to insert parameter form items such as text boxes and drop-down menu lists, layers are used extensively to create the layout.

Quite elaborate Property Inspectors are possible. The XSSI IF Property Inspector built by Webmonkey, shown in Figure 21-6, has three separate tabs (Browser, Basic, and Advanced) based on layers for accessing different possible parameters of the object. Property Inspectors, as other extension types, can also incorporate CSS styles, Flash movies, and Shockwave files.

Figure 21-6: Some custom Property Inspectors, such as this one from Webmonkey, take advantage of Dreamweaver's layer and CSS styles support.

Coding a Property Inspector

As with many of the other standard extension files, most of the Property Inspector files that ship with Dreamweaver are composed of an HTML file that calls a separate JavaScript file. It is entirely possible, however, to combine HTML and JavaScript into a single file. No matter how it's structured, a custom Property Inspector HTML file needs the following three key elements to be properly defined:

✦ An initial HTML comment line that identifies which tag the Property Inspector is for.

✦ The function `canInspectSelection()`, which determines if the Property Inspector should be displayed according to the current selection.

✦ A second function, inspectSelection(), that updates the tag's HTML when new values are entered in the Property Inspector.

If any of these elements are missing or incorrectly declared, Dreamweaver ignores the file and does not display the Property Inspector.

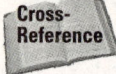

Cross-Reference

In addition to the mandatory functions and definition, custom Property Inspectors are capable of using any of the other Dreamweaver JavaScript functions described in Chapter 20, with the exception of the getBehaviorTag() and getBehaviorElement functions. If you include the displayHelp() function, a small question mark in a circle appears in the upper-right corner of your custom Property Inspector, which, when selected by the user, executes whatever routines your Help function has declared.

The Property Inspector definition

The initial HTML comment — placed above the <html> tag — defines the Property Inspector. More than one Property Inspector can be defined for a particular tag, making it possible for separate Inspectors to be used if different attributes are specified. Therefore, each Property Inspector is assigned a priority that determines the one to be displayed. Property Inspectors are further defined by whether the current selection is within the tag indicated or contains the entire tag; this feature enables two different Property Inspectors to be defined, as with the <table> tag. Finally, optional graphic elements are definable: a horizontal line to delineate the upper and lower portions of a Property Inspector, and a vertical line to separate the object's name from the other parts of the Property Inspector.

The Property Inspector definition follows this syntax:

```
<!-- tag:ID,priority:Number,selection:Type,hline,vline -->
```

For example, the Property Inspector for the <link> tag (a <head> element) is defined as follows:

```
<!-- tag:LINK,priority:5,selection:within,vline,hline -->
```

The individual sections of the definition are as follows:

✦ **tag:** The name of the tag for which the Property Inspector is intended. Although it's not mandatory, the tag name is customarily uppercased. The tag ID can also be one of three keywords: *COMMENT*, when a comment class tag is indicated; *LOCKED*, when a locked region is to be inspected; or *ASP*, for all ASP elements.

Note

The asterisks on either side of the tag keywords are mandatory.

✦ **priority:** The priority of a Property Inspector is given as a number from 1 to 10. The highest priority, 10, means that this Property Inspector takes precedence over any other possible Property Inspectors. The lowest priority, 1, marks the Property Inspector as the one to use when no other Property Inspector is available.

Note

An example of how `priority` is used can be found in the `<meta>` tag and the Description and Keyword objects. The Property Inspectors for Description and Keyword have a higher priority than the one for the basic `<meta>` tag, which enables those Inspectors to be shown initially if the proper criteria is met; if the criteria is *not* met, the Property Inspector for the `<meta>` tag is displayed.

✦ **selection:** Depending on the current selection, the cursor is either within a particular tag or exactly enclosing it. The selection attribute is set to within or exact, according to the condition under which the Property Inspector should be displayed.

✦ **hline:** Inserts a one-pixel horizontal gray line (see Figure 21-7) dividing the upper and lower halves of the expanded Property Inspector.

✦ **vline:** Places a one-pixel vertical gray line (see Figure 21-7) between the tag's name field and the other properties on the upper half of the Property Inspector.

h line   v line

Figure 21-7: The Property Inspector for the `<img>` tag uses both the `hline` and `vline` attributes.

The canInspectSelection() function

To control the circumstances under which your custom Property Inspector is displayed, use the `canInspectSelection()` function. Like `canAcceptBehavior()` and `canAcceptCommand()` for behaviors and commands, respectively, if `canInspectSelection()` returns true, the Property Inspector is shown; if it returns false, the custom Property Inspector is not shown.

As noted earlier, the `canInspectSelection()` function is mandatory. If no conditions exist under which the Property Inspector should not be displayed, use the following code:

```
function canInspectSelection(){
    return true;
}
```

Several of the standard Dreamweaver <head> elements have Property Inspector files that use the `canInspectSelection()` function to limit access to specific tags. In this example, drawn from the <meta> Description object, the current selection is examined to see if a <meta> tag is selected, and the `name` attribute is set to description:

```
function canInspectSelection(){
  var selArr=dreamweaver.getSelection();
  var metaObj = dreamweaver.offsetsToNode(selArr[0],selArr[1]);
  return (metaObj.tagName && metaObj.tagName == "META" &&
      metaObj.getAttribute("name") &&
    metaObj.getAttribute("name").toLowerCase()=="description");
}
```

The inspectSelection( ) function

The `inspectSelection()` function is the workhorse of the custom Property Inspector code and is responsible for pulling the information from the selected tag for display in the various Property Inspector fields. Depending on the code design, the `inspectSelection()` function can also be used to update the HTML code when the attribute values are modified in the Property Inspector.

Here's a simple example of how the `inspectSelection()` function is used, drawn from the Link Property Inspector file:

```
function inspectSelection(){
  var Href = findObject("Href");

  if (linkObj.getAttribute("href"))
    Href.value=linkObj.getAttribute("href");
  else
    Href.value = "";
}
```

In this example, if an attribute (`href`) exists, its value is assigned to the Property Inspector's appropriate text box value (`Href.value`). The remainder of the `inspectSelection()` function for the <link> tag consists of a series of statements such as those in the example code.

Tip

You can design a Property Inspector that displays a different interface depending on whether or not it is expanded, as the Keywords Property Inspector does. If an inspector is not expanded, the `argument(0)` property is set to the value `min`; when it is expanded, `argument(0)` is equal to the value `max`.

Many Property Inspectors update their HTML tags when a change occurs in one of the input boxes. No real standard method exists to accomplish this, due to the many possible variations with Property Inspectors. However, one of the most commonly used events is `onBlur()`, as in this example, again taken from the Link Property Inspector file:

```
<input type="text" name="Rel" onBlur="setLinkTag()" style="width:120">
```

The `setLinkTag()` function that is called is a local one that reads the new value in the current text box and sets it equal to the corresponding attribute.

Designing a Property Inspector

All the attributes for a Property Inspector must fit into a tightly designed space. While it's helpful to look at examples found in the Inspectors folder, many of the standard Property Inspectors are built-in to the core functionality of the program and are not immediately accessible on the design level. The following specifications and tips are offered to make it easier to design your own custom Property Inspectors:

✦ The full dimensions of available layout space in a Property Inspector are 482 pixels wide by 87 pixels high.

✦ The top (unexpanded) portion of the Property Inspector is 42 pixels high, while the bottom portion is 44 pixels high.

✦ If the `hline` attribute is specified in the Property Inspector definition, a single-pixel line is drawn the entire width of the Inspector, 43 pixels from the top.

✦ If the `vline` attribute is specified, a single-pixel line is drawn across the top half of the Property Inspector, 118 pixels from the left.

✦ The background color for the Property Inspector is a light gray, which translates into #D0D0D0FF in hexadecimal, or an RGB value of 208, 208, 208.

✦ The default text displayed within a Property Inspector is from the Arial, Helvetica, sans-serif font families, sized at 8 points. If you enter text with the standard default text selected, it is rendered in this style. For this reason, I often temporarily change my Proportional Font settings (found in the Fonts/Encoding category of Preferences) to match those of the Property Inspector when building extensions.

✦ The image placed on the upper left of the Property Inspector is generally sized at 36 pixels square and placed 3 pixels from the top and 2 pixels from the left. Although you are under no requirement to keep this size image — or its placement — following these guidelines helps make your custom Property Inspectors resemble the standard Dreamweaver ones.

✦ It's a good idea to lay out your Property Inspector with the View ➪ Invisible Elements command disabled. The small icons that indicate layers can alter the perceived spacing.

✦ Keep the Layers panel visible. Many custom Property Inspectors use multiple layers to position the elements exactly — several of the Webmonkey-designed XSSI Property Inspectors employ upwards of 20 layers, as shown in Figure 21-8 — and the Layers panel makes selecting individual layers for adjustment a snap.

✦ Use nested layers to position and group associated items in the Property Inspector. Almost all form objects used in Property Inspectors for user input, such as text boxes and drop-down lists, are identified by labels. Placing both label and text boxes in their own layers, while grouping them under one parent layer, provides maximum flexibility and ease of placement.

✦ Apply CSS styles within the Property Inspector to easily manage font sizes and design your Property Inspector in a WYSIWYG environment.

Figure 21-8: Property Inspectors, such as Webmonkey's custom XSSI IF Inspector, use parent and child layers to position layout components and toggle different options.

Making Custom Floating panels

Property Inspectors are an excellent way to manage the attributes of most elements in a single consistent user interface. The Property Inspector user interface, however, is not the best solution for all situations. Recognizing this, the Macromedia engineers have added another extension type for Dreamweaver: floating panels.

A *floating panel* is a cross between a Property Inspector and a command. As with Property Inspectors, floating panels can stay on the screen while you work on the Web page; as with commands, floating panels are not restricted to a set size and shape. Custom floating panels have the same basic interface as standard Dreamweaver panels. Any floating panel can be resized or grouped with other floating panels, standard or custom. Once grouped, a custom floating panel also has a tab which, when selected, brings the floating panel interface to the front. The only minor difference between a built-in and a custom floating panel is that only the standard floating panels can have icons in the tabs; custom floating panels display only their names.

Floating panels, as with most other extensions, are a combination of HTML and JavaScript: HTML is the main file that is called and provides the user interface via an HTML form, while JavaScript provides the functionality from the `<head>` of the HTML page. Floating panels are stored in the Configuration\Floaters folder. However, unlike commands or objects, it's not enough just to save your custom floating panel in a particular folder to make it accessible. A function that displays the floating panel, either `dw.setFloaterVisibility(floaterName,true)` or `dw.toggleFloater(floaterName)` must be called. Most often these functions are called from a `<menuitem>` tag in the menus.xml file, as with this custom floating panel:

```
<menuitem name="HelpBuilder" enabled="true" ü
command="dw.toggleFloater('helpBuilder')" ü
checked="dw.getFloaterVisibility('helpBuilder')" />
```

The checked attribute assures that a checkmark is displayed next to the menu item if the floating panel is visible.

Caution When naming your custom floating panel, be sure to avoid names reserved for Dreamweaver's built-in elements: objects, properties, launcher, site files, site map, assets, library, CSS styles, html styles, behaviors, timelines, html, layers, frames, templates, timelines, reference, or history.

As indicated in the preceding paragraphs, floating panels have their own API functions, and several methods of the Dreamweaver object are applicable. The API functions, none of which are required, are listed in Table 21-4.

Table 21-4
Floating panel API Functions

Function	Returns	Use
documentEdited()	N/A	Executes after the current document has been edited.
selectionChanged()	N/A	Executes after the current selection has been altered.
initialPosition(platform)	A string in the format "left,top"	Sets the position of the floating panel onscreen when it is first called. If left onscreen when Dreamweaver quits, it reopens in the last location.

Continued

Table 21-4 *(continued)*		
Function	**Returns**	**Use**
`initialTabs()`	A string in the format "floating panel1, floating panel2"	Indicates what other floating panels are grouped with the current floating panel when it first appears.
`IsAvailableInCodeView()`	Boolean	Determines if the floating panel is enabled when Code view is active.

Caution Macromedia strongly cautions programmers from using `documentEdited()` and `selectionChanged()` unless absolutely needed. Both functions — because they constantly watch the document — can have an adverse affect on performance if implemented. Macromedia suggests programmers incorporate the `setTimeout()` method to temporarily pause these functions so that the user can continue to interact with the program.

Within the Dreamweaver API are two pairs of methods and a single function, which relate to floating panels as follows:

✦ `getHideAllFloaters()`: Reads the Show/Hide Floating panel menu option state to determine if all floating panels should be hidden (true) or shown (false).

✦ `setHideAllFloaters()`: Sets the Show/Hide Floating panel to a particular state to Hide (true) or Show (false).

✦ `getFloaterVisibility(floaterName)`: Reads whether the given floating panel is currently displayed and frontmost (true) or hidden (false).

✦ `setFloaterVisibility(floaterName,isVisible)`: Brings the named floating panel forward if the `isVisible` argument is true.

✦ `toggleFloater(floaterName)`: Toggles the visibility state of the given floating panel between hiding and bringing to the front.

Floating panels have a great deal of potential with their flexible interface and constant onscreen presence. The example shown in Figure 21-9, built by the author, scans an entire Web site, looking for items marked with a custom table of contents tag and then lists the object, with its corresponding link.

Developing Translators

In order for any markup tag to be depicted in the Document window — whether it's `<b>` for bold or a custom third-party tag such as Tango's `<@cols>` — it must be translated. Dreamweaver's built-in rendering system translates all the standard

HTML code, along with a few special custom tags such as those for ASP and ColdFusion. However, in order to display any other custom tags, or those that perform special functions such as server-side includes, a special translator must be built.

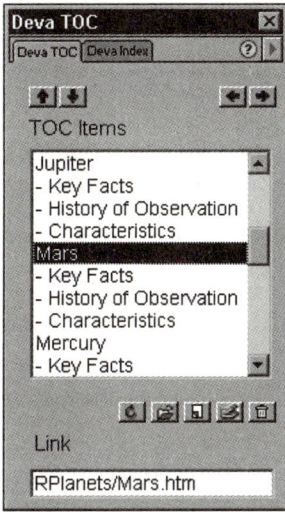

Figure 21-9: The custom floater, built for the Deva help authoring extension, lists phrases marked with a `<toc>` tag.

As part of its expansion efforts, Dreamweaver enables the inclusion of custom *translators*. This enhancement enables programs that output nonstandard HTML to be displayed onscreen integrated with the regular code. One of Dreamweaver's main claims to fame is its capability to accept code without rewriting it. With Dreamweaver translators, custom code can not only be inserted but also shown — and edited — visually.

Here's a brief overview of how translators work:

1. When Dreamweaver starts, all the properly coded translators in the Configuration\Translators folder are initialized.

2. If a document is loaded with nonstandard HTML, the code is checked against the installed translators.

3. The translators are enabled.

Note   Starting in Dreamweaver 4, all translators are automatically active all the time — there is no Preference setting that determines their availability.

4. The code is processed with the translator and temporarily converted to a format acceptable to Dreamweaver.

5. Dreamweaver renders the code onscreen.

6. If a change is made to the page, Dreamweaver retranslates the document and refreshes the screen.

7. When the page is saved, the temporary translation is discarded, and the original code, with any modifications, is stored.

Developers continue to break new ground with the use of translators. Some of the translators that have been developed so far include those for the following:

✦ **Server-Side Includes:** Standard with Dreamweaver, the SSI translator effortlessly inserts, at design time, files that you normally don't see until delivered by the Web server. (To learn more about SSI, see Chapter 33.)

✦ **XSSI:** The Extended Server-Side Include (XSSI) extension, developed by Webmonkey authors Alx, Nadav, and Taylor for Macromedia, includes a translator that brings the Apache-served code right in the Document window. (See the XSSI sidebar in Chapter 33.)

✦ **Tango:** Developed by Pervasive Software, the Tango translator compensates for differences between their database-oriented code and standard HTML. Additionally, Tango includes a manually controlled Sample Data translator that enables the Web designer to view the page complete with example database.

Translator functions

As with other Dreamweaver extensions such as behaviors and commands, translators are HTML files with JavaScript. Translators have no user interface. Other than deciding when to invoke it, you have no parameters to set or options to choose from; all the pertinent code is in the `<head>` section of a translator. In the translator's `<head>`, along with any necessary support routines, you can find two essential JavaScript functions: `getTranslatorInfo()` and `translateMarkup()`. Any other Dreamweaver JavaScript API functions not specific to behaviors can be used in a translator as well.

Note   Due to the limitations of JavaScript, much of the heart of custom translation is handled by specially written C-level extensions. These compiled code libraries enhance Dreamweaver's capabilities so that new data types can be integrated. C-level extensions are covered later in this chapter.

The getTranslatorInfo( ) function

The settings that appear for each selected translator in the Translation category of Preferences are determined by the `getTranslatorInfo()` function. The function itself simply sets up and returns an array of text strings that are read by Dreamweaver during initialization.

The structure of the array is fairly rigid. The number of array elements is specified when the `Array` variable is declared, and a particular text string must correspond to the proper array element. The array order is as follows:

✦ **translatorClass:** The translator's unique name used in JavaScript functions. The name has to begin with a letter and can contain alphanumeric characters as well as hyphens or underscores.

✦ **title:** The title listed in the menu and the Translation category. This text string can be no longer than 40 characters.

✦ **nExtensions:** The number of file extensions, such as .cfml, to follow. This declaration tells Dreamweaver how to read the next portion of the array. If this value is set to zero, then all files are acceptable.

✦ **extension:** The actual file extension without the leading period.

✦ **nRegularExpressions:** The number of regular expressions to be declared. Should this value be equal to zero, the array is closed.

✦ **RegularExpression:** The regular expression to be searched for by Dreamweaver.

The number of array elements — and thus, the detail of the function — depends entirely on the translator. Here, for example, is the code for `getTranslatorInfo()` from Live Picture's translator, where a file must have a particular `<meta>` tag to be translated:

```
function getTranslatorInfo(){
  returnArray = new Array( 5 )
  returnArray[0] = "FPX";          // translatorClass
  returnArray[1] = "Flashpix Image Translator";     // title
  returnArray[2] = "0"          // number of extensions
  returnArray[3] = "1";         // number of expressions
  returnArray[4] = "<meta http-equiv=\"refresh\" content=\"0;url=http://";
  return returnArray
}
```

By comparison, the standard SSI translator's `getTranslatorInfo()` function has 10 array elements, and Webmonkey's XSSI has 17.

The translateMarkup() function

While the `getTranslatorInfo()` function initializes the translator, the `translateMarkup()` function actually does the work. As noted earlier, most of the translators rely on a custom C-level extension to handle the inner workings of the function, but `translateMarkup()` provides the JavaScript shell.

The `translateMarkup()` function takes three arguments, which must be declared but whose actual values are provided by Dreamweaver:

✦ **docName:** The file URL for the file to be translated.

✦ **siteRoot:** The site root of the file to be translated. Should the file be outside the current site, the value would be empty.

✦ **docContent:** A text string with the code for the page to be translated.

Typically, the *docContent* text string is parsed using either JavaScript or a C-level extension within the `translateMarkup()` function that returns the translated document. This translated document is then displayed by Dreamweaver.

Here's the `translateMarkup()` function from the standard SSI translator:

```
function translateMarkup( docNameStr, siteRootStr, inStr ) {
  var outStr = ""
  if ( inStr.length > 0 )
  {
  outStr = SSITranslator.translateMarkup( docNameStr, siteRootStr, inStr )
  }
  return outStr
}
```

In this example, notice that the translated document in the form of `outStr` is created by the custom function `SSITranslator.translateMarkup()`. The `SSITranslator` portion of this function calls the C-level extension, built by Macromedia for this purpose.

Locking code

Translations are generally intended for onscreen presentation only. Although there's no rule saying that translated content can't be written out to disk, most applications need the original content to run. To protect the original content, Dreamweaver includes a special locking tag. This XML tag pair, `<MM:BeginLock>...<MM:EndLock>`, stops the enclosed content (the translation) from being edited, while simultaneously storing a copy of the original content in a special format.

The `<MM:BeginLock>` tag has several attributes:

✦ **translatorClass:** The identifying name of the translator as specified in `getTranslatorInfo()`. Required.

✦ **type:** The type or tag name for the markup to be translated.

✦ **depFiles:** A comma-separated list of any files on which the locked content depends. If any of the listed dependent files are altered, the page is retranslated.

✦ **orig:** A text string with the original markup before translation. The text string is encoded to include three standard HTML characters. The < becomes %3C;, the > becomes %3E;, and the quote character is converted to %22;.

To see how the special locking tag works, look at an example taken from the Tango Sample Data translator. Tango uses what are called "meta tags" that begin with an @ sign, such as the <@TOTALROWS> tag. The Tango Sample Data translator replaces what will be a result drawn from a database with a specified sample value. The original code is

```
<@TOTALROWS samptotalrows=23>
```

Once the code is translated, Dreamweaver refreshes the screen with this code:

```
<MM:BeginLock translatorClass="TANGO_SAMPLEDATA"  type ="@TOTALROWS ü
orig="%3C@TOTALROWS samptotalrows=23%3E">23<MM:EndLock>
```

The "23" in bold is the actual translated content that appears in Dreamweaver's Document window.

Note   You don't actually see the locking code — even if you open the Code Inspector when a page is translated. To view the code, select the translated item, copy it, and then paste it in another text application, or use the Paste As HTML feature to see the results in Dreamweaver.

Extending C-Level Libraries

All programs have their limits. Most limitations are intentional and serve to focus the tool for a particular use. Some limitations are accepted because of programming budgets — for both money and time — with the hope that the boundaries can be exceeded in the next version. With Dreamweaver, one small section of those high, sharply defined walls has been replaced with a doorway: C-level extensions. With the proper programming acumen, you can customize Dreamweaver to add the capabilities you need.

As with most modern computer programs, the core of Dreamweaver is developed using C and C++, both low-level languages that execute much faster than any non-compiled language, such as JavaScript. Because C is a compiled language, you can't just drop in a function with a few lines of code and expect it to work — it has to be integrated into the program. The only possible way to add significant functionality is through another compiled component called a *library*. With the C-level extensions capability, Dreamweaver enables the incorporation of these libraries, known as DLLs (Dynamic Link Libraries) on Windows systems and CFMs (Code Fragment Managers) on Macintosh systems.

One excellent example of the extended library is DWfile. This C-level extension is used by several Dreamweaver partners, including RealNetworks and iCat, to perform tasks outside the capabilities of JavaScript; namely, reading and writing external text files. By adding this one library, Dreamweaver can now work with the support files necessary to power a wide range of associated programs. DWfile is described in detail later in this section.

C-level extensions are also used in combination with Dreamweaver's translator feature. As discussed earlier in this chapter, translators handle the chore of temporarily converting nonstandard code to HTML that Dreamweaver can present onscreen — while maintaining the original code in the file. Although much of this functionality isn't impossible for JavaScript, the conversion would be too slow to be effective. C-level extensions are definitely the way to go when looking for a powerful solution.

Note　Programming in C or C++, as required by C-level extensions, is beyond the scope of this book. Developers are encouraged to examine Macromedia's Extending Dreamweaver PDF file found on the Dreamweaver Web site.

Calling a C-level extension

C-level extensions, properly stored in the Configuration\JSExtensions folder, are read into Dreamweaver during initialization when the program first starts. The routines contained within the custom libraries are accessed through JavaScript functions in commands, behaviors, objects, translators, and other Dreamweaver extensions.

Let's take a look at how Macromedia's C-level extensions DWfile is used. DWfile has ten main functions:

✦ exists(): Checks to see if a specified filename exists. This function takes one argument, the filename.

✦ read(): Reads a text file into a string for examination. This function also takes one argument, the filename.

✦ write(): Outputs a string to a text file. This function has three arguments; the first two — the name of the file to be created and the string to be written — are required. The third, the mode, must be the word "append." This argument, if used, causes the string to be added to the end of the existing text file; otherwise, the file is overwritten.

✦ getAttributes(): Returns the attributes of a specified file or folder. Possible attributes are R (read-only), D (directory), H (hidden), and S (system file or folder).

✦ getModificationDate(): Returns the date a specified file or folder was last modified.

✦ createFolder(): Creates a folder, given a file URL.

✦ listFolder(): Lists the contents of a specified folder in an array. This function takes two arguments: the file URL of the desired folder (required) and a Keyword, either "files" (which returns just filenames) or "directories" (which returns just directory names). If the Keyword argument is not used, you get both files and directories.

✦ copy(): Copies a file from one file URL (the first argument) to another (the second argument). DWfile.copy() may be used to copy any type of file, not just text files.

✦ remove(): Places the referenced file in the Recycling Bin (Windows) or Trash (Macintosh) without requesting confirmation.

✦ getCreationDate(): Returns the date when the file was initially created.

The following JavaScript function, which could be included in any Dreamweaver extension, uses DWfile to see if a file, named in a passed argument, exists. If it does, the contents are read and presented in an alert; if the file doesn't exist, the function creates it and writes out a brief message.

```
function fileWork(theFile) {
   var isFile = DWfile.exists(theFile)
   if (isFile) {
        alert(DWfile.read(theFile))
   } else {
     DWfile.write(theFile,"File Created by DWfile")
   }
}
```

Note how the C-level extension name, DWfile, is used to call the library and its internal functions. Once the library has been initialized, it can be addressed as any other internal function, and its routines are simply called as methods of the function using JavaScript dot notation, such as DWfile.exists(theFile).

Building C-level extensions

A C-level extension must follow strict guidelines in order to be properly recognized by Dreamweaver. Specifically, two files must be included in the library when created in C, and each function must be declared for correct interpretation by Dreamweaver's JavaScript interpreter.

Macromedia engineers have developed a C-Level Extension API in the form of a C header, mm_jsapi.h. This header contains definitions for over 20 data types and functions. To insert mm_jsapi.h in your custom library, add the following statement:

```
#include "mm_jsapi.h"
```

You can find the latest version of mm_jsapi.h in the Dreamweaver 4\Help\Extending\c_files folder.

After you've included the JavaScript API header, you need to declare a specific macro, MM_STATE. This macro, contained within the mm_jsapi.h header, holds definitions necessary for the integration of the C-level extension into Dreamweaver's JavaScript API. The MM_STATE must be defined only once.

Each library can be composed of numerous functions available to be called from within Dreamweaver. For Dreamweaver's JavaScript interpreter to recognize the functions, each one must be declared in a special function, JS_DefineFunction(), defined in the library. All of the JS_DefineFunction() functions are contained in the MM_Init() function. The syntax for JS_DefineFunction() is as follows:

```
JS_DefineFunction(jsName, call, nArgs)
```

where *jsName* is the JavaScript name for the function, *call* is a pointer to a C-level function, and *nArgs* is the number of arguments that the function can expect. For example, the MM_Init() function for DWfile might appear as this:

```
void
MM_Init()
{
   JS_DefineFunction("exist", exist, 1);
   JS_DefineFunction("read", exist, 1);
   JS_DefineFunction("write", exist, 2);
}
```

Because MM_Init() depends on definitions included in the C header, mm_jsapi.h, it must be called after the header is included.

Tip If you're building cross-platform C-level extensions, consider using Metrowerks CodeWarrior integrated development environment. CodeWarrior can edit, compile, and debug C, C++, and even Java or Pascal for both Windows and Macintosh operating systems. Perhaps, most important, Macromedia engineers used CodeWarrior to test C-level extensions.

Summary

Dreamweaver's commitment to professional Web site authoring is at its most profound when examining the program's customization capabilities. Virtually every Web site production house can benefit from some degree of personalization — and some clients absolutely require it. As you consider making your productive life easier by extending Dreamweaver, keep the following points in mind:

✦ Dreamweaver includes a full range of customizable features: objects, behaviors, commands, third-party tags, Property Inspectors, and translators. You can even extend the program's core feature set with the C-Level Extensibility option.

✦ You can use commands to affect any part of your HTML page and automate repetitive tasks.

✦ In addition to accessing custom commands through the Command menu, you can configure them as objects for inclusion in the Objects panel. You can also make a command appear in any other standard Dreamweaver menu by altering the menus.xml file.

✦ To make it easy to work with XML and other non-HTML tags, Dreamweaver enables you to create custom tags complete with individual icons or highlighted content.

✦ Attributes for third-party tags are viewable — and modifiable — by creating a custom Property Inspector.

✦ Dreamweaver's C-Level Extensibility feature enables C and C++ programmers to add new core functionality to a program.

✦ Tags from server-side applications can be viewed in the Document window, just as they would be when browsed online, when a custom translator is used. A custom translator often requires a C-level extension.

In the next chapter, you see how Dreamweaver and Fireworks work closely together to smooth your workflow.

✦   ✦   ✦

Adding Multimedia Elements

Fireworks Integration

Imagine demonstrating a newly completed Web site to a client who *didn't* ask for an image to be a little bigger, or the text on a button to be reworded, or the colors for the background to be revised. In the real world, Web sites — particularly the images — are constantly being tweaked and modified. This fact of Web life explains why Fireworks, Macromedia's premier Web graphics tool, is so popular. One of Fireworks' main claims to fame is that everything is editable all the time. If that were all that Fireworks did, the program would have already earned a place on every Web designer's shelf just for its sheer expediency. But Fireworks is far more capable a tool — and now, that power can be tapped directly in Dreamweaver.

With the release of Dreamweaver 4 and Fireworks 4, an even greater level of integration between the two Macromedia products has been achieved. You can optimize your images — reduce the file size, crop the graphic, and make colors transparent — within Dreamweaver using the Fireworks interface. Moreover, you can edit your image in any fashion in Fireworks and, with one click of the Update command, automatically export the graphic with its original export settings. Perhaps most importantly, now Dreamweaver can control Fireworks — creating graphics on the fly — and then insert the results in Dreamweaver.

A key Fireworks feature is its capability to output HTML and JavaScript for easy creation of rollovers, sliced images, and image maps with behaviors. With Fireworks, you can specify Dreamweaver-style code, so that all your Web pages are consistent. Once HTML is generated within Fireworks, Dreamweaver's Insert Fireworks HTML object makes code insertion effortless. Dreamweaver now recognizes images — whether whole or sliced — as coming from Fireworks and displays a special Property Inspector.

Web pages and Web graphics are closely tied to one another. With the tight integration between Dreamweaver and Fireworks, the Web designer's world is moving toward a single design environment.

Easy Graphics Modification

It's not uncommon for graphics to need some alteration before they fully integrate into a Web design. In fact, I'd say it's far more the rule than the exception. The traditional workflow generally goes like this:

1. Create the image in one or more graphics-editing programs.

2. Place the new graphic on a Web page via your Web authoring tool.

3. Note where the problems lie — perhaps the image is too big or too small, maybe the drop shadow doesn't blend into the background properly, or maybe the whole image needs to be flipped.

4. Reopen the graphics program, make the modifications, and save the file again.

5. Return to the Web page layout to view the results.

6. Repeat Steps 3 through 5 ad infinitum until you get it right.

Although you're still using two different programs even with Dreamweaver and Fireworks integration, there is a feature that enables you to open a Fireworks window on the Dreamweaver screen: Optimize Image in Fireworks. Now you can make your alterations with the Web page noticeable in the background. I've found that this small advantage cuts my trial-and-error to a bare minimum and streamlines my workflow.

If you're not familiar with Fireworks, you're missing an extremely powerful graphics program made for the Web. Fireworks combines the best of both vector and bitmap technologies and was one of the first graphics programs to use PNG as its native format. Exceptional export capabilities are available in Fireworks with which images can be optimized for file size, color, and scale. Moreover, Fireworks is terrific at generating GIF animations, rollovers, image maps, and sliced images.

With the latest versions of Dreamweaver and Fireworks, you have two ways to alter your inserted graphics: the Optimize Image in Fireworks command and the Edit button in the Image Property Inspector.

Note   The full integration described in this chapter requires that Fireworks 4 be installed after Dreamweaver 4. Certain features, such as the Optimize Image in Fireworks command, work with Dreamweaver 4 and Fireworks 2 and above, but any others requiring direct communication between the two programs work only with Fireworks 4.

Optimizing an image in Fireworks

Although you can design the most beautiful, compelling image possible in your graphics program, if it's intended for the Internet, you need to view it in a Web page. Not only must the graphic work in the context of the entire page, but the file size of the Web graphic must also be taken into account. All these factors mean that most, if not all, images need to undergo some degree of modification once they're included in a Web page. Fireworks makes these alterations as straightforward as possible by including a command for Dreamweaver during its installation.

The Optimize Image in Fireworks command opens the Export module of Fireworks, as shown in Figure 22-1, right in Dreamweaver's Document window.

Figure 22-1: With Fireworks 4 installed, you can optimize your images from within Dreamweaver.

The Export module consists of three tabbed panels: Options, File, and Animation. Although a complete description of all of its features is beyond the scope of this book, here's a breakdown of the major uses of each area:

✦ **Options:** The Options panel is primarily used to try different export options and preview them. You can switch file formats from GIF to JPEG (or Animated GIF or PNG) as well as alter the palette, color depth, and dithering. Transparency for GIF and PNG images is set in the Options panel. Fireworks also has an Export to Size wizard that enables you to target a particular file size for your graphic.

✦ **File:** An image's dimensions are defined in the File panel. Images can be rescaled by a selected percentage or pixel size. Moreover, you can crop your image either numerically—by defining the export area—or visually with the Cropping tool.

✦ **Animation:** Frame-by-frame control for animated GIFs is available on the Animation panel. Each frame's *delay* (how long it is onscreen) is capable of being defined independently, and the entire animation can be set to either play once or loop a user-determined number of times.

If you crop or rescale an inserted image in Fireworks, you need to update the height and width in Dreamweaver. The easiest way to accomplish this is to select the Refresh button in the image's Property Inspector.

Fireworks saves its source files in an expanded PNG format to maintain full editability of the images. Graphics for the Web must be exported from Fireworks in GIF, JPEG, or standard PNG format. Dreamweaver's Optimize Image in Fireworks command can modify either the source or exported file. In most situations, better results are achieved from using the source file, especially when optimizing includes rescaling or resampling. However, some situations require that you leave the source file as is and modify only the exported files. Let's say, for example, that one source file is used to generate several different export files, each with different backgrounds (or *canvases*, as they are called in Fireworks). In that case, you'd be better off modifying the specific exported file rather than the general source image.

Dreamweaver enables you to choose which type of image you'd like to modify. When you first execute the Optimize Image in Fireworks or the Edit Image command, a Find Source dialog box (Figure 22-2) appears. If you want to locate and use the source file, choose Yes; to use the exported image that is inserted in Dreamweaver, select No. If you opt for the source file — and the image was created in Fireworks — Dreamweaver reads the Design Note associated with the image to find the location of the source file and open it. If the image was created with an earlier version of Fireworks or the image has been moved, Dreamweaver asks you to locate the file with a standard Open File dialog box. By setting the Fireworks Source Files option, you can always open the same type of file: source or exported. Should you change your mind about how you'd like to work, open Fireworks and select Edit ➪ Preferences, and then choose the desired option from the Launch and Edit category.

There's one exception to Fireworks always following your Launch and Edit preferences. If the image chosen is a sliced image, Fireworks always optimizes the exported file rather than the source, regardless of your settings.

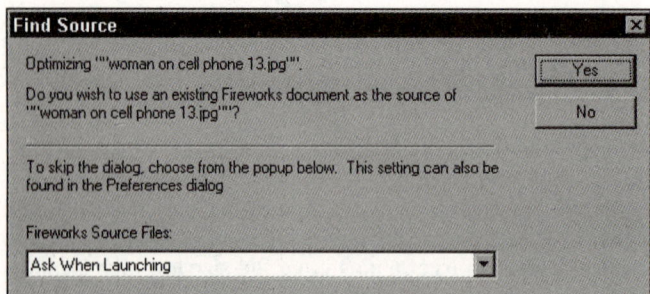

Figure 22-2: Set the Find Source dialog box to always use the source graphics image or the exported image, or to choose from a popup menu for each optimization.

Exploring Fireworks Source and Export Files

The separate source file is an important concept in Fireworks, and its use is strongly advised. Generally, when working in Fireworks, there is a minimum of two files for every image output to the Web: your source file and your exported Web image. Whenever major alterations are made, it's best to make them to the source file and then update the export files. Not only is this an easier method of working, but also you get a better image this way.

Source files are always Fireworks-style PNG files. Fireworks-style PNG files differ slightly from regular PNG format because they include additional information, such as paths and effects used that can be read only by Fireworks. The exported file is usually in GIF or JPEG format, although it could be in standard PNG format. Many Web designers keep their source files in a separate folder from their exported Web images so the two don't get confused. This source-and-export file combination also prevents you from inadvertently re-editing a lossy compressed file such as a JPEG image and reapplying the compression.

To use the Optimize Image in Fireworks command, follow these steps:

1. In Dreamweaver, select the image that you'd like to modify.

You must save the current page at least once before running the Optimize Image in Fireworks command. The current state of the page doesn't have to have been saved, but a valid file must exist for the command to work properly. If you haven't saved the file, Dreamweaver alerts you to this fact when you call the command.

2. Choose Commands ➪ Optimize Image in Fireworks.

You can also invoke the Optimize Image in Fireworks command from the context menu — just right-click (Control+click) on the image.

3. If your Fireworks Preferences are set to ask whether a source file should be used in editing, the Find Source dialog box opens. Choose Yes to use the PNG format source file and No to work with the exported file.

The Optimize Images dialog box appears.

4. Make whatever modifications are desired from the Options, File, or Animation tabs of the Optimize Images dialog box.

5. When you're finished, select the Update button.

If you're working with a Fireworks source file, the changes are saved to both your source file and exported file; otherwise, only the exported file is altered.

Editing an image in Fireworks

Optimizing an image is great when all you need to do is tweak the file size or to rescale the image. Other images require more detailed modification — as when a client requests that the wording or order of a series of navigational buttons be changed. Dreamweaver enables you to specify Fireworks as your graphics editor; and if you've done so, you can take advantage of Fireworks' capability to keep every element of your graphic always editable. And believe me, this is a major advantage.

In Dreamweaver, external editors can be set for any file format; you can even assign more than one editor to a file type. When installing the Dreamweaver/Fireworks Studio, Fireworks is preset as the primary external editor for GIF, JPEG, and PNG files. If Fireworks is installed outside of the Studio setup, the external editor assignment is handled through Dreamweaver Preferences.

To assign Fireworks to an existing file type, follow these steps:

1. Choose Edit ⇨ Preferences.

2. Select the External Editors category.

3. Select the file type (GIF, JPEG, or PNG) from the Extensions list as shown in Figure 22-3.

Figure 22-3: Define Fireworks as your External Editor for GIF, JPEG, and PNG files to enable the back-and-forth interaction between Dreamweaver and Fireworks.

4. Click the Add (+) button above the Editors list. The Add External Editor dialog box opens.

5. Locate the editor application and click Open when you're ready.

Note The default location in Windows systems is in C:\Program Files\Macromedia\ Fireworks 4\Fireworks 4.exe; on the Macintosh it's Macintosh HD:Applications: Fireworks 4:Fireworks 4. (The .exe extension may or may not be visible in your Windows system.)

6. Click Make Primary while the editor is highlighted.

Now, whenever you want to edit a graphic, select the image and click the Edit button in the Property Inspector. You can also right-click (Control+click) the image and select Edit Image to start editing it. Fireworks starts up, if it's not already open. As with the Optimize Image in Fireworks command, if the inserted image is a GIF or a JPEG and not a PNG format, Fireworks asks if you'd like to work with a separate source file, if that option in Fireworks Preferences is set. If so, Fireworks automatically loads the source file.

When the image opens in Fireworks, the graphic's window indicates that this particular graphic is being edited from Dreamweaver in Fireworks as shown in Figure 22-4. In the same title bar, a Done button is available for completing the operation after you've made your alterations to your file in Fireworks. Alternatively, you can choose File ➪ Update or use the keyboard shortcut Ctrl+S (Command+S). If you're working with a Fireworks source file, both the source file and the exported file are updated and saved.

Figure 22-4: Fireworks now graphically depicts where the current image being edited is from.

Inserting Rollovers

The rollover is a fairly common, but effective, Web technique that you can use to indicate interactivity. Named after the user action of "rolling the mouse pointer over" the graphic, this technique uses from two to four different images per button. With Fireworks, you can both create the graphics and output the necessary HTML and JavaScript code from the same program. Moreover, Fireworks has some sophisticated twists to the standard "on/off" rollovers to further easily enhance your Web page.

Rollovers created in Fireworks can be inserted into Dreamweaver through several methods. First, you can use Fireworks to just build the images and then export them and attach the behaviors in Dreamweaver. This technique works well for graphics going into layers or images with other attached behaviors. The second method of integrating Fireworks-created rollovers involves transferring the actual code generated by Fireworks into Dreamweaver — a procedure that can be handled with one command: Insert Fireworks HTML.

Using Dreamweaver's behaviors

With its full-spectrum editability, Fireworks excels at building consistent rollover graphics simply. The different possible states of an image in a rollover — Up, Over, Down, and Over While Down — are handled in Fireworks as separate frames. As with an animated GIF, each frame has the same dimensions as the document, but the content is slightly altered to indicate the separate user actions. For example, Figure 22-5 shows the different frame states of a rollover button, side by side.

Many Web designers use just the initial two states — Up and Over — in their rollover buttons. The third state, Down, takes place when the user clicks the button, and it is useful if you want to indicate that moment to the user. The Down state also indicates which button has been selected (which is "down") when a new page appears, but the same navigation bar is used, notably with frames. The fourth state, Over While Down, is called when the previously selected button is rolled over by the user's pointer.

Figure 22-5: A Fireworks-created rollover can be made of four separate frames.

To insert Fireworks-created graphics using Dreamweaver behaviors, follow these steps:

1. Create your graphics in Fireworks, using a different frame for each rollover state.

Caution You cannot use Fireworks's Insert ➪ New Button command to build your button for this technique because the separate states are now stored as frames.

2. In Fireworks, choose File ➪ Export. The Export dialog box opens (see Figure 22-6).

3. Enter a new filename in the Base Name text box, if desired.

   In this operation, Fireworks uses the filename as a base name to identify multiple images exported from a single file. When exporting frames, the default settings append "_fn", where n is the number of the frame. Frame numbers 1 to 9 are listed with a leading zero (for example, MainButton_f01).

Figure 22-6: From Fireworks, you can export each frame as a separate file to be used in Dreamweaver rollovers.

4. In the Save As Type list box, select Frames to Files.

5. If desired, select the Trim Images option. I recommend that the default practice be to trim your images when exporting frames as files. This option results in smaller, more flexible files.

6. Select the Save button to store your frames as separate files.

Note   You can attach the rollover behaviors to your images in several ways in Dreamweaver. The following technique uses Dreamweaver's Rollover object.

7. From the Common panel of the Objects palette, choose the Insert Rollover Image object.

8. In the Insert Rollover Image dialog box, choose the Original Image Browse (Choose) button to locate the image stored with the first frame designation, _f01.

9. If desired, give your image a different unique name than the one automatically assigned in the Image Name text box.

10. Choose the Rollover Image Browse button to locate the image stored with the second frame designation, _f02.

11. Click OK when you're done.

12. If you'd like to use the Down (_F03) and Over While Down (_F04) images, attach additional swap image behaviors by opening the Swap Image behavior and following the steps outlined in Chapter 19.

Note

Many Web designers build their entire navigation bar — complete with rollovers — in Fireworks. Rather than create and export one button at a time, all the navigation buttons are created as one graphic, and slices or hotspots are used to make the different objects or areas interact differently. You learn more about slices and hotspots later in this chapter under "Using Fireworks' Code."

Using Fireworks' code

In some ways, Fireworks is a hybrid program, capable of simultaneously outputting terrific graphics and sophisticated code. You can even select the type of code you want generated in Fireworks 4: Dreamweaver; Dreamweaver Library compatible; or code compatible with other programs such as GoLive and FrontPage. You'll also find a Generic code option. You can choose these options during the Export procedure.

For rollovers, Fireworks generally outputs to two different sections of the HTML document, the `<head>` and the `<body>`; only the FrontPage style keeps all the code together. The `<head>` section contains the JavaScript code for activating the rollovers and preloading the images; `<body>` contains the HTML references to the images themselves, their links, and the event triggers (`onClick` or `onMouseOver`) used.

The general procedure is to first create your graphics in Fireworks and then export them, simultaneously generating a page of code. Now, the just-generated Fireworks HTML page can be incorporated in Dreamweaver. Dreamweaver includes two slick methods for including your Fireworks-output code and images. The Insert Fireworks HTML object places the code — and the linked images — right at your current cursor position. You also have the option of exporting your Fireworks HTML directly to the clipboard and pasting it, verbatim, into Dreamweaver.Just as an image requires a link to create a rollover in Dreamweaver, Fireworks images need to be designated as either a *slice* or a *hotspot*. Slices are rectangular areas that permit different areas of the same graphic to be saved as separate formats — the entire graphic is formatted as an HTML table. Each slice can also be given its own URL; Fireworks requires either slices or hotspots to attach behaviors.

A Fireworks *hotspot* is a region defined for an image map. Hotspots can be rectangular, elliptical, or polygonal — just like those created by Dreamweaver by using the Image Map tools. Because Fireworks is an object-oriented graphics program, any selected image (or part of an image) can be automatically converted to a hotspot. Like slices, hotspots can have both URLs and behaviors assigned to them.

The Fireworks program describes slices and hotspots as being part of the graphic's Web layer. The Web layer can be hidden or locked, but not deleted. Figure 22-7 shows the same button with both a slice and a hotspot attached.

Figure 22-7: The Fireworks image on the left uses a slice object, whereas the image on the right uses a polygon hotspot.

Note

In addition to the technique outlined in the text that follows, you could also use Fireworks's Button Editor (available by choosing Insert ➪ New Button) to create your rollover images and behaviors.

To include Fireworks-generated code in your Dreamweaver document, first follow these steps in Fireworks:

1. Create your graphics in Fireworks, placing the image for each interactive state on its own frame.

2. When the object is selected, choose Insert ➪ Hotspot or Insert ➪ Slice to add the item to your Web layer for attaching behaviors. Alternatively, you can use any of the Hotspot or Slice tools found in the Fireworks toolbox.

3. Select the hotspot or slice and use Fireworks' Object Inspector to assign an Internet address to the selected graphic.

4. Click the target symbol displayed in the center of the hotspot or hotspot to display a menu of available behaviors. Alternatively, you could open Fireworks' Behavior Inspector and choose the Add Behavior button (the + sign).

5. Select Simple Rollover.

Tip The Simple Rollover behavior is used to create single-button or multiple-button rollovers in which one image is replaced by another image in the same location; only two frames are used for a Simple Rollover. Use Swap Image to create more complex rollovers such as those in which the rollover triggers an image change in another location. A third alternative, Nav Bar, should be used in situations where the navigation system is to be placed in a frameset; Nav Bar can hold all four states (Up, Over, Down, and Over While Down).

6. Export the object by choosing File ➪ Export.

7. From the Export dialog box, enter a name in the filename text box and make sure HTML and Images is displayed in the Save as Type drop-down list.

   If you intend to use the graphics in several places on your site, choose Dreamweaver Library (*.lbi) from the Save as Type list.

8. To change the type of HTML code generated, choose the Options button and make a choice from the Style drop-down list.

   Dreamweaver code is the default Style; other options include GoLive, FrontPage, and Generic.

9. Choose the location to store your HTML code by navigating to the desired folder. Note that Dreamweaver 4 Library code must be saved in a site's Library folder.

   If you'd prefer to not save your HTML, choose Copy to Clipboard from the HTML drop-down list.

10. To save your graphics in a separate folder, select the Put Images in Subfolder option.

Caution Fireworks defaults to placing the graphics in the images subfolder, even if one does not exist. Select a folder by choosing Browse.

11. Click Export when you're done.

When Fireworks completes the exporting, you have one HTML file (unless you've chosen the Copy to Clipboard option) and one object file for each slice and frame. Now you're ready to integrate these images and the code into your Dreamweaver page. Which method you use depends on the HTML style selected when the graphics were exported from Fireworks:

✦ If you chose Dreamweaver, use the Insert Fireworks HTML object.

✦ If you chose Dreamweaver Library, open the Library palette in Dreamweaver and insert the corresponding Library item.

✦ If you chose Copy to Clipboard, position your cursor where you'd like the graphics to appear and select Edit ➪ Paste or press Ctrl+V (Command+V).

Both the Library and Clipboard methods are one-step, self-explanatory techniques — and the Insert Fireworks HTML is hardly more complex. To insert the

Fireworks code and images into your Dreamweaver page using the Insert Fireworks HTML object, follow these steps:

1. Make sure that you've exported your graphics and HTML from Fireworks with Dreamweaver HTML Style selected.

2. Select the Insert Fireworks HTML object from the Common panel of the Objects palette or choose Insert ➪ Interactive Media ➪ Fireworks HTML.

   The Insert Fireworks HTML dialog box, shown in Figure 22-8, appears.

Figure 22-8: Import Fireworks code directly into Dreamweaver with the Insert Fireworks HTML object.

3. If you want to remove the Fireworks-generated HTML file after the code is inserted, select the Delete file after insertion option.

4. Enter the path to the Fireworks HTML file or select the Browse button to locate the file.

5. Click OK when you're done. Dreamweaver inserts the Fireworks HTML and graphics at the current cursor location.

Note If you're a hands-on kind of Web designer, you can also use the HTML Inspector to copy and paste the JavaScript and HTML code. If you do, you can find helpful comments in the Fireworks file such as "Begin copying here" and "Stop copying here."

All the methods for inserting Fireworks HTML work with images with either hotspots or sliced objects (or both), with or without behaviors attached.

Modifying sliced images

Placing sliced images on your Web page couldn't be simpler, thanks to the Insert Fireworks HTML command. But, like standard nonsliced graphics, sliced images often need to be modified. One technique that many designers use is to create a framing graphic that encompasses HTML text; in Fireworks, a sliced area designated as a text slice can hold any HTML content. Text is often modified, and if it's in a framing graphic, that could mean that the images need to be changed or the table will separate making the separate slices apparent.

New Feature   In Dreamweaver 4, sliced images from Fireworks are recognized as a Fireworks Table and may be modified through a dedicated Property Inspector.

The Fireworks Table Property Inspector shown in Figure 22-9 displays the PNG source file and an Edit button for sending the entire table back to Fireworks for alterations. As with nonsliced graphics, select Done from the document title bar in Fireworks when your modifications are complete to update the source and exported files. The newly exported images are then reloaded into Dreamweaver.

 Caution   While Fireworks attempts to honor any changes that you make to the HTML table, certain alterations may result in Fireworks overwriting your table. If, for example, you add or remove one or more cells from the table in Dreamweaver, Fireworks recognizes that the tables no longer match. An alert is displayed indicating that Fireworks will replace the table in Dreamweaver. To keep your table the same in Dreamweaver, make no changes in Fireworks and select Done.

Figure 22-9: Modify sliced graphics by first selecting the surrounding table and then choosing Edit from the Fireworks Table Property Inspector.

Controlling Fireworks with Dreamweaver

Dreamweaver and Fireworks integration extends deeper than just the simplified insertion of code and graphics. Dreamweaver can communicate directly with Fireworks, driving it to execute commands and return custom-generated graphics. This facility enables Web designers to build their Web page images based on the existing content. This interprogram communication promises to streamline the work of the Webmaster — and that promise is already beginning to come through with existing Dreamweaver commands.

Web photo album

Online catalogs and other sites often depend on imagery to sell their products. Full-scale product shots can be large and time-consuming to download, so it's not uncommon for Web designers to display a thumbnail of the images instead. If the viewer wants to see more detail, clicking the thumbnail loads the full-size image. Although it's not difficult to save a scaled-down version of an image in a graphics program and link the two in a Web layout program, creating page after page of such images is an overwhelming chore. The Dreamweaver/Fireworks interoperability offers a way to automate this tedious task.

A new Dreamweaver command, Create Web Photo Album, examines any user-specified folder of images and then uses Fireworks to scale the graphics to a set size. When the scaling is completed, the thumbnail graphics are brought into a Dreamweaver table, complete with links to a series of pages with the full-size image. Create Web Photo Album is an excellent example of the potential that Dreamweaver and Fireworks intercommunication offers.

The Create Web Photo Album command works with a folder of images in any format that Fireworks reads: GIF, JPEG, TIFF, Photoshop, PICT, BMP, and more. The images can be scaled to fit in a range of sizes, from 36×36 to 200×200. These thumbnails are exported in one of four formats:

- ✦ **GIF WebSnap 128:** Uses the WebSnap Adaptive palette, which is limited to 128 colors or fewer
- ✦ **GIF WebSnap 256:** Same as preceding format but with as many as 256 colors available
- ✦ **JPEG Better Quality:** Sets the JPEG quality setting at 80 percent with no smoothing
- ✦ **JPEG Smaller File:** Sets the JPEG quality setting at 60 percent with a smoothing value of 2

The images are also exported in one of the same four settings, at a user-selected scale; the default scale is 100 percent.

To create a thumbnail gallery using Create Web Photo Album, follow these steps:

1. Choose Commands ➪ Create Web Photo Album.

   The Create Web Photo Album dialog box appears, as shown in Figure 22-10.

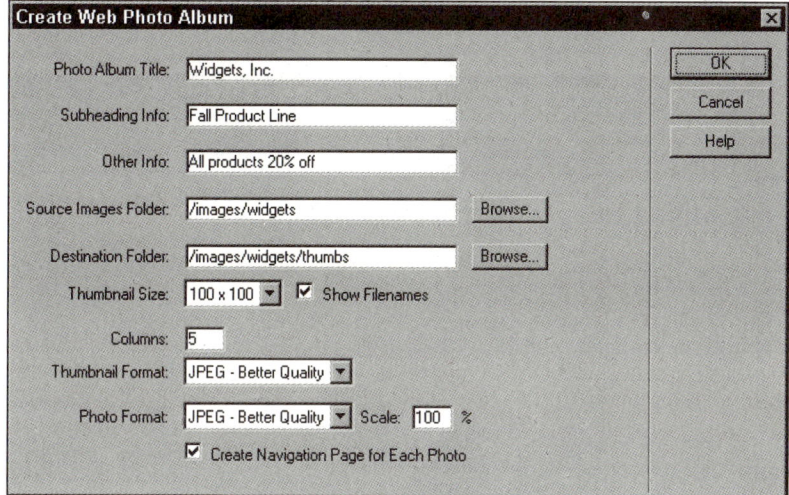

Figure 22-10: Use the Creat Web Photo Album dialog box to build a thumbnail gallery page, linked to full-size orignals.

2. Enter the Photo Album Title, Subheading Info, and Other Info into their respective text fields, if desired.

3. Enter the path to the folder of source images or select the Browse (Choose) button to locate the folder in the Source Images Folder field.

4. Enter the path to the Destination Folder or select the Browse (Choose) button to locate the folder in its field.

   Dreamweaver creates up to three subfolders in the Destination Folder: one for the original, rescaled images, another for the thumbnail images, and a third for the HTML pages created.

5. Select the desired thumbnail size from the drop-down list with the following options: 36×36, 72×72, 100×100, 144×144, and 200×200.

6. Select the Show Filenames option if you want the file name to appear below the image.

7. Choose the number of Columns for the table.

8. Select the export settings for the thumbnail images from the Thumbnail Format option list.

9. Select the export settings for the linked large-sized images from the Photo Format option list.

10. Choose the size of the linked large-sized images in the Scale field.

11. Select the Create Navigation Page for Each Photo option, if desired. Each photo's navigation page includes links to the Next and Previous images as well as the Home (main thumbnail) page, as shown in Figure 22-11.

Figure 22-11: You can add simple, clear navigation options to your Web Photo Album.

12. Click OK when you're done.

If Fireworks is not open, the program launches and begins processing the images. When all the images are created and exported, Fireworks returns control to Dreamweaver. Dreamweaver then creates a single HTML page with the title, sub-heading, and other information at the top, followed by a borderless table. As shown in Figure 22-12, each image is rescaled proportionately to fit within the limits set in the dialog box.

Custom Graphic Makers: Convert Text to Graphics and Convert Bullets to Graphics

Excited by the potential of Dreamweaver and Fireworks communication, I built two custom extensions that I originally called StyleBuilder and BulletBuilder. Macromedia took these extensions, enhanced them, and then released them as two-thirds of the InstaGraphics Extensions. StyleBuilder — now called Convert Text to Graphics — enables you to convert any standard text in your Dreamweaver Web page to a graphic. The command converts all text in a standard HTML tag, such as <h1> or <b>, any custom XML tag, or any selection. The graphics are based on Fireworks styles, displayed in a small swatch in the dialog box; you can specify a font on your system as well as a text size to be used. Fireworks styles can be updated at any time, and the swatch set recreated on the fly in Fireworks.

Convert Bullets to Graphics (nee BulletBuilder) is similar to Convert Text to Graphics, but instead of changing text to graphics, this command converts the bullets of an unordered list to different graphic shapes. Choose from 10 different shapes, including diamonds, stars, starbursts, and 4 different triangles. The chosen shape is rendered in any available Fireworks style at a user-selected size. You have the option to convert the current bullet list or all such lists on the page.

You can find both commands in the Additional Extensions folder on the CD-ROM that accompanies this book or online at the Dreamweaver Exchange.

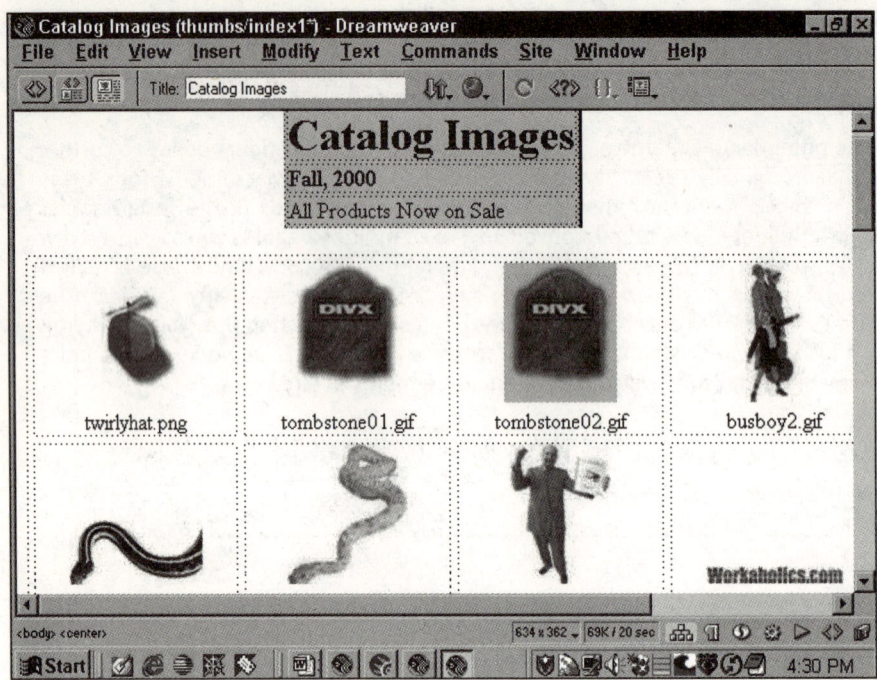

Figure 22-12: Build a thumbnail gallery with Fireworks right from Dreamweaver with the Create Web Photo Album command.

Building Dreamweaver/Fireworks extensions

To make communication between Dreamweaver and Fireworks viable, two conditions had to be met. First, Fireworks had to be scriptable. Second, a link between the two programs needed to be forged. The Dreamweaver 4/Fireworks 4 combination meets both criteria—and then some.

As with Dreamweaver 4, almost every operation is under command control in Fireworks 4. This is most apparent when using either program's History palette. If your action appears as a repeatable item in the History palette, a corresponding JavaScript function controls it. Fireworks' wealth of JavaScript functions also serves to expose its control to Dreamweaver—and the first condition for interoperability is handled. To create a strong link between programs, Dreamweaver engineers expanded on the Fireworks API used in the Optimize Image in Fireworks command, where Dreamweaver actually launches a streamlined version of Fireworks. This operation is controlled by a C-level extension called FWLaunch.

Here's a step-by-step description of how Dreamweaver is typically used to communicate with Fireworks:

1. The user selects a command in Dreamweaver.

2. Dreamweaver opens a dialog box, as with other extensions.

3. After the user has filled in the dialog box and clicked OK, the command begins to execute.

4. All user-supplied parameters are read and used to create a JavaScript scriptlet or function, which serve as instructions for Fireworks.

5. If used, the scriptlet is stored on the disk.

6. Fireworks is launched with a command to run the Dreamweaver-created scriptlet or function.

7. Fireworks processes the scriptlet or function, while Dreamweaver tracks its progress via a cookie on the user's machine.

8. Once Fireworks is finished, a positive result is returned. The Fireworks API includes several error codes if problems such as a full disk are encountered.

9. While tracking the Fireworks progress, Dreamweaver sees the positive result and integrates the graphics by rewriting the DOM of the current page.

10. The dialog box is closed, and the current page is refreshed to correctly present the finished product.

To successfully control Fireworks, you need a complete understanding of the Fireworks DOM and its extension capabilities. Macromedia provides documentation for extending Fireworks at its support site: www.macromedia.com/support/fireworks.

 Tip   I've also found the History palette in Fireworks to be useful — especially the Copy Command to Clipboard function. To see the underlying JavaScript used to create an object in Fireworks, first make the object. Then highlight the History palette steps and select the Copy to Clipboard button. Paste the clipboard contents in a text editor to see the exact steps Fireworks used; you can then begin to generalize the statements with variables and other functions.

On the Dreamweaver side, six useful methods are in the FWLaunch C Library. Table 22-1 details the methods.

Table 22-1
FWLaunch Methods

Method	Returns	Use
bringDWToFront()	N/A	Brings the Dreamweaver window in front of any other application running.
bringFWToFront()	N/A	Brings the Fireworks window in front of any other application running.
execJsInFireworks (javascriptOrFileURL)	Result from running the scriptlet in Fireworks. If the operation fails, returns an error code: 1: The argument proves invalid 2: File I/O error 3: Improper version of Dreamweaver 4: Improper version of Fireworks 5: User canceled operation	Executes the supplied JavaScript function or scriptlet.
mayLaunchFireworks()	Boolean	Determines whether Fireworks may be launched.
optimizeInFireworks (fileURL, docURL, {targetWidth}, {targetHeight})	Result from running the scriptlet in Fireworks. If the operation fails, returns an error code: 1: The argument proves invalid 2: File I/O error 3: Improper version of Dreamweaver 4: Improper version of Fireworks 5: User canceled operation	Performs an Optimize in Fireworks operation, opening the Fireworks Export Preview dialog box.
validateFireworks (versionNumber)	Boolean	Determines if the user has a specific version of Fireworks.

Summary

Creating Web pages is almost never done with a single application: In addition to a Web layout program, you need a program capable of outputting Web graphics — and Fireworks is a world-class Web graphics generator and optimizer. Macromedia has integrated several functions with Dreamweaver and Fireworks to streamline production and ease modification. Here are some of the key features of the integration:

✦ You can update images placed in Dreamweaver with Fireworks in two ways: Optimize or Edit. With the Optimize Image in Fireworks command, just the Export Preview portion of Fireworks opens; with the Edit Image command, the full version of Fireworks is run.

✦ Graphics and HTML exported from Fireworks can be incorporated into a Dreamweaver page in numerous ways: as a Library item, an HTML file (complete with behavior code), or just pasted from the clipboard.

✦ New interapplication communication between Dreamweaver and Fireworks makes commands such as Create Web Photo Album possible.

✦ Dreamweaver includes a special C-level extension called FWLaunch, which provides the primary link to Fireworks.

In the next chapter, you see how you can add downloaded or streaming video to your Dreamweaver-created Web pages.

✦   ✦   ✦

Inserting Flash and Shockwave Elements

Animated splash screens, sound-enabled banners, button bars with special fonts, and other exciting Web elements are often built with Macromedia's Flash. Flash combines vector graphics and streaming audio into great-looking, super–low bandwidth files that can be viewed in a browser using the Flash player plug-in. Flash's vector graphics have also turned out to be just the thing for Web-based cartoons. Beginning with version 4, Flash gained its own scripting language, ActionScript, and added MP3 compression to its streaming audio. With a huge base of installed players — as of this writing, well over 90 percent of browsers can view basic Flash content — Flash is an excellent way to liven up a Web page.

But Flash is not Macromedia's only solution for building interactive presentations for the Web. To many Web designers, Shockwave has represented the state of the art in Web interactivity since Macromedia first created the format in 1995. With Shockwave, multimedia files created in Macromedia's flagship authoring package, Director, can be compiled to run in a browser window. This gives Web designers the capability to build just about anything — from interactive Web interfaces with buttons that look indented when pushed, to arcade-style games, multimedia Web front-ends, and complete Web sites built entirely in Director — bringing a CD-ROM "look and feel" to the Web. Today, Shockwave continues to be an important force on the Web, as the enormous success of Macromedia's Shockwave.com amply demonstrates.

The final component in Macromedia's vector-graphic tool chest is a server-side technology called Generator. Generator works with templates built in Flash to display customized graphics, built on-demand. In its initial release, Generator was available only to designers working on big-budget, high-end sites and did not gain a sizeable foothold in the market.

However, Macromedia has recently changed its pricing policy on Generator and made the technology much more accessible to developers.

As you might expect, Macromedia makes it easy to incorporate Shockwave, Flash and Generator files into your Dreamweaver projects. All of these formats have special objects that provide control over virtually all of their parameters through the Property Inspector — and each format is cross-browser compatible by default. In Dreamweaver 4, Macromedia has moved to capitalize on the popularity of Flash and the flexibility of Generator with the introduction of two new tools: Flash Buttons and Flash Text. Now, it's easier than ever to incorporate customized, well-crafted Flash elements in your Web page without knowing a bit of Flash.

To take full advantage of the enhanced graphics potential of Flash and Shockwave's multimedia capabilities, you need to understand the differences between Director and Flash, as well as the various parameters available to each format. In addition to covering this material, this chapter also shows you how to use independent controls — both inline and with frames — for your Shockwave and Flash movies.

Shockwave and Flash: What's the Difference?

Director and Flash share many features: interactivity, streaming audio, support for both bitmaps and vector graphics, and "shocked fonts." Both can save their movies in formats suitable for viewing on the Web. So how do you choose which program to use? Each has its own special functions, and each excels at producing particular types of effects. Director is more full featured, with a complete programming language called Lingo that enables incredible interactivity. And Director movies can include Flash animations. Director also has a much steeper learning curve than does Flash. Flash is terrific for short, low-bandwidth animations with or without a synchronized audio track; however, the interactive capabilities in Flash are limited compared to Director.

Director is really a multimedia production program used for combining various elements: backgrounds, foreground elements called *sprites*, and various media such as digital audio and video (see Figure 23-1). With Director's Lingo programming language, you can build extraordinarily elaborate demos and games, with Internet-specific commands. When you need to include a high degree of interactivity, build your movie with Shockwave.

One of the primary differences between Director and Flash is the supported graphic formats. Director is generally better for bitmap graphics, in which each pixel is mapped to a specific color; both GIF and JPEG formats use bitmap graphics. Flash, on the other hand, uses primarily vector graphics, which are drawing elements described mathematically. Because vector graphics use a description of a drawing — a blue circle with a radius of 2.5 centimeters, for instance — rather than a bitmap, the resulting files are much smaller. A fairly complex animation produced with Flash might be only 10K or 20K, whereas a comparable digital video clip could easily be 10 times that size.

Figure 23-1: Director works mainly with bitmaps and video, and enables "multimedia programming" using Lingo.

Aside from file size, the other feature that distinguishes vector graphics from bitmap graphics is the smoothness of the line. When viewed with sufficient magnification, bitmap graphics always display telltale "stair-steps" or "jaggies," especially around curves. Vector graphics, on the other hand, are almost smooth. In fact, Flash takes special advantage of this characteristic and enables users to zoom into any movie — an important effect that saves a lot of bandwidth when used correctly.

However, these differences were significantly blurred with the release of Director 7, which incorporates its own native vector graphics and introduces the capability to include Flash movies within Director movies. Flash 4 blurred the line the other way by incorporating streaming MP3-encoded audio and QuickTime integration, both things that were traditionally the province of Director. In Flash 5, Flash's scripting capabilities have been significantly beefed up with the expansion of ActionScript into a JavaScript-based programming language.

Flash animations can be used as special effects, cartoons, and navigation bars within (or without) frames (see Figure 23-2). Although Flash isn't the best choice for games and other complex interactive elements, you can use Flash to animate your navigation system — complete with sound effects for button-pushing feedback.

Figure 23-2: Flash movies tend to look more cartoon-like, thanks to Flash's lightweight vector graphics.

If Flash is a power tool, Director is a bulldozer. Director has been significantly expanded to handle a wide variety of file types, such as QuickTime and MP3, with advanced streaming capabilities. Supporting multimedia interactivity is Director's own programming language, Lingo, which has also been enhanced. Furthermore, Director now includes multiplayer support for network game play and chat rooms, XML parsing, embedded compressed fonts, up to 1,000 sprite channels, and a potential frame rate of 999 frames per second. Luckily, Dreamweaver enables you to pack all that power into a Web page with its Shockwave object.

Including Flash and Shockwave Movies in Dreamweaver Projects

Dreamweaver makes it easy to bring Shockwave and Flash files into your Web pages. The Objects panel provides an object for each type of movie, both located in the Common category.

Because Shockwave and Flash objects insert both an ActiveX control and a plug-in, Dreamweaver enables you to play the movie in the Document window. First it displays a plug-in placeholder icon (see Figure 23-3).

Flash placeholder　　　　　　　　　Insert Flash object

Insert Shockwave object

Flash property inspector

Figure 23-3: Dreamweaver includes many interface elements for working with Shockwave and Flash.

Before you can successfully include a Shockwave file, you need to know one small bit of information — the dimensions of your movie. Dreamweaver automatically reads the dimensions of your Flash file when you use the Insert Flash Movie object. Unfortunately, if you're incorporating a Shockwave movie, you still need to enter the dimensions by hand in the Shockwave Property Inspector.

To check the width and height of your movie in Director, load your file and then choose Modify ➪ Movie ➪ Properties to open the Movie Properties dialog box.

Note　It is essential to know the movie's height and width before you can include it successfully in Dreamweaver-built Web pages. During the development phase of a Dreamweaver project, I often include the movie dimensions in a file name, as an instant reminder to take care of this detail. For example, if I'm working with two different Shockwave movies, I can give them names such as navbar125x241.dcr and navbar400x50.dcr. (The .dcr extension is automatically appended by Director when you save a movie as a Shockwave file.) Because I consistently put width before height in the filename, this trick saves me the time it would take to reopen Director, load the movie, and choose Modify ⇨ Movie to check the measurements in the Movie Properties dialog box. The alternative to keeping track of the Director movie's dimensions is to choose File ⇨ Save as Shockwave Movie in Director; this creates an HTML file with all the necessary parameters—including width and height—that can be inserted into Dreamweaver. You'll find a detailed description of this process later in this chapter.

To include either a Shockwave or Flash file in your Web page, follow these steps:

1. Position the cursor in the Document window at the point where you'd like the movie to appear.

2. Insert the movie using any of these methods:

   • Choose Insert ⇨ Media ⇨ Shockwave or Insert ⇨ Media ⇨ Flash from the menus.

   • In the Common category of the Objects panel, select either the Insert Shockwave or Insert Flash button.

   • Drag the movie object from the Objects panel to any location in the Document window.

3. In the Select File dialog box, enter the path and the filename in the File Name text box or select the Browse (Choose) button to locate the file. Click OK.

   Dreamweaver inserts a small plug-in placeholder in the current cursor position, and the Property Inspector displays the appropriate information for Shockwave or Flash.

4. Preview the Flash or Shockwave movie in the Document window by selecting the Play button found in the Property Inspector. You can also choose View ⇨ Plugins ⇨ Play.

5. End the preview of your file by selecting the Stop button in the Property Inspector or selecting View ⇨ Plugins ⇨ Stop.

Tip   If you have more than one Flash or Shockwave movie on your page, you can control them all by choosing View ⇨ Plugins ⇨ Play All and View ⇨ Plugins ⇨ Stop All. If your files appear in different pages in a frameset, you have to repeat the Play All command for each page.

As noted earlier, you must specify the dimensions of your file in the Property Inspector before you can preview the movie in a browser; again, Dreamweaver supplies this information automatically for Flash files, but you have to enter it yourself for Shockwave movies. Shockwave and Flash have some different features in the Dreamweaver Property Inspector. These differences are covered separately in the following sections.

Specifying Shockwave Properties

Once you've inserted your Shockwave file, you're ready to begin entering the specific parameters in the Property Inspector. The Property Inspector takes care of all but one Shockwave attribute, the palette parameter. Some of the information, including the ActiveX Class ID, is automatically set in the Property Inspector when you insert the movie.

 You can find a custom command called Insert Shockwave HTML that automates the process of inserting a Shockwave movie and its Director-generated HTML. Look in the Configuration\Commands folder on the CD-ROM that accompanies this book. If you'd prefer a version developed by Macromedia that does the same job, visit the Dreamweaver Exchange to download the Insert Shockwave extension.

To set or modify the parameters for a Shockwave file, follow these steps:

1. Select the Shockwave placeholder icon.

2. In the Shockwave Property Inspector, enter the width and the height values in the W and H text boxes, respectively, as shown in Figure 23-4. Alternatively, you can click and drag any of the three resizing handles on the placeholder icon.

Generating HTML Within Director

In Director, you can generate a file with all the appropriate HTML code at the same time that you save your Shockwave movie, with just the selection of a checkbox. When you choose File ⇨ Save as Shockwave Movie in Director, the dialog box contains a Generate HTML option. Selecting this option causes Director to save an HTML file with the same name as your Shockwave movie but with an appropriate file extension (.html for Macintosh and .htm for Windows). You can easily copy and paste this HTML code directly into Dreamweaver.

When you open the Director-generated HTML file, you see the name of your file and the Shockwave placeholder, correctly sized and ready to preview. To move this object into another Web page in progress, just select the Shockwave object and choose Edit ⇨ Copy. Then switch to your other page and choose Edit ⇨ Paste. Naturally, you can also use the keyboard shortcuts or, if both pages are accessible, just drag and drop the object from one page to another.

Figure 23-4: Modify parameters for a Shockwave property through the Shockwave Property Inspector.

 Tip   Pressing the Shift key while dragging the corner resizing handle maintains the current aspect ratio.

3. To designate how the Shockwave HTML code is written, select one of these three options from the Tag drop-down list:

   • **Object and Embed:** This is the default option and ensures that code is written for both Internet Explorer and Netscape. Use this option unless your page is on an intranet where only one browser is used.

   • **Object only:** Select this option to enable your movie to be viewed by Internet Explorer–compatible browsers.

   • **Embed only:** Select this option to enable your movie to be viewed by Netscape-compatible browsers.

4. Set and modify other object attributes as needed; see Table 23-1 for a list.

Table 23-1
Property Inspector Options for Shockwave Objects

Shockwave Property	Description
Align	Choose an option to alter the alignment of the movie. In addition to the browser default, your options include Baseline, Top, Middle, Bottom, Texttop, Absolute Middle, Absolute Bottom, Left, and Right.
Alt Image	The Alt Image file is displayed in browsers that do not support the `<embed>` tag and is available if you select Embed Only. This image does not display in Dreamweaver. Enter the path to the alternative image, or select the Folder icon to open a Select Image Source dialog box.
BgColor	The background color is visible only if the width and height of the plug-in are larger than the movie. To alter the background color of your plug-in, choose the color swatch and select a new color from the pop-up menu; or enter a valid color name in the BgColor text box.
Border	To place a border around your movie, enter a number in the Border text box. The number determines the width of the border in pixels. The default is zero or no border.
H Space	You can increase the space to the left and right of the movie by entering a value in the H (Horizontal) Space text box. The default is zero.
ID	The ID field is used to define the optional ActiveX ID parameter, most often used to pass data between ActiveX controls.
(Name)	If desired, you can enter a unique name in this unlabeled field on the far left of the Property Inspector. The name is used by JavaScript and other languages to identify the movie.
V Space	To increase the amount of space between other elements on the page and the top and bottom of the movie plug-in, enter a pixel value in the V (Vertical) Space text box. Again, the default is zero.

Additional parameters for Shockwave

As you can with other plug-ins, you can pass other attributes to the Shockwave movie via the Parameters dialog box — available by clicking the Parameters button on the Property Inspector. Press the add (+) button to begin inserting additional parameters. Enter the attributes in the left column and their respective values in the right. To remove an attribute, highlight it and select the delete (–) button.

Automatic settings for Shockwave files

When you insert a Shockwave or Flash file, Dreamweaver writes a number of parameters that are constant and necessary. In the `<object>` portion of the code, Dreamweaver includes the ActiveX Class ID number as well as the `codebase` number; the former calls the specific ActiveX control, and the latter enables users who don't have the control installed to receive it automatically. Likewise, in the `<embed>` section, Dreamweaver fills in the `pluginspage` attribute, designating the location where Navigator users can find the necessary plug-in. Be sure you don't accidentally remove any of this information — however, if you should, all you have to do is delete and reinsert the object.

Only one other general attribute is usually assigned to a Shockwave file, the `palette` parameter. This parameter takes a value of either foreground or background.

✦ If `palette` is set to background, the movie's color scheme does not override that of the system; this is the default.

✦ When `palette` is set to foreground, the colors of the selected movie are applied to the user's system, which includes the desktop and scroll bars.

Note that `palette` is not supported by Internet Explorer.

Caution   Web designers should take care when specifying the `palette=foreground` parameter. This effect is likely to prove startling to the user; moreover, if your color scheme is sufficiently different, the change may render the user's system unusable. If you do use the `palette` parameter, be sure to include a Director command to restore the original system color scheme in the final frame of the movie.

Designating Flash Attributes

Flash movies require the same basic parameters as their Shockwave counterparts — and Flash movies have a few additional optional ones as well. As it does for Shockwave files, Dreamweaver sets almost all the attributes for Flash movies through the Property Inspector. The major difference is that several more parameters are available.

To set or modify the attributes for a Flash file, follow these steps:

1. After your Flash movie has been inserted in the Document window, make sure it's selected. Dreamweaver automatically inserts the correct dimensions for your Flash movie.

2. Set any attributes in the Property Inspector as needed for your Flash movie. (Refer to the previous descriptions of these attributes in the section "Specifying Shockwave Properties.") In addition, you can also set the parameters described in Table 23-2.

Table 23-2
Property Inspector Options for Flash Objects

Flash Parameter	Possible Values	Description
Autoplay	Checked (default)	Enables the Flash movie to begin playing as soon as possible.
Loop	Checked (default)	If Loop is checked, the movie plays continuously; otherwise, it plays once.
Quality		Controls antialiasing during playback.
	High	Antialiasing is turned on. This can slow the playback frame rate considerably on slower computers.
	Low	No antialiasing is used; this setting is best for animations that must be played quickly.
	AutoHigh (default)	The animation begins in High (with antialiasing) and switches to Low if the host computer is too slow.
	AutoLow	Starts the animation in Low (no antialiasing) and then switches to High if the host machine is fast enough.
Scale		Scale determines how the movie fits into the dimensions as specified in the width and height text boxes
	ShowAll (default)	Displays the entire movie in the given dimensions while maintaining the file's original aspect ratio. Some of the background may be visible with this setting.
	ExactFit	Scales the movie precisely into the dimensions without regard for the aspect ratio. It is possible that the image could be distorted with this setting.
	NoBorder	Fits the movie into the given dimensions so that no borders are showing and maintains the original aspect ratio. Some of the movie may be cut off with this setting.

Setting the scale in Flash movies

Be careful with your setting for the Scale parameter, in order to avoid unexpected results. If you have to size a Flash movie out of its aspect ratio, the Flash player needs to know what to do with any extra room it has to fill. Figure 23-5 demonstrates the different results that the Scale attribute can provide. Only the figure in the lower right is at its proper dimensions. The gray box is the actual size of the authoring canvas.

Show All   No Border (note cut off figure)

Exact fit   Show All (not scaled)

Figure 23-5: Your setting for the Scale attribute determines how your movie is resized within the plug-in width and height measurements.

Tip   Dreamweaver makes it easy to rescale a Flash movie. First, from the Property Inspector, enter the precise width and height of your file in the W and H text boxes. Then, while holding down the Shift key, click and drag the corner resizing handle of the Flash placeholder icon to the new size for the movie. By Shift+dragging, you retain the aspect ratio set in the Property Inspector. This enables you to quickly enlarge or reduce your movie without distortion.

Additional parameters for Flash

Flash has two additional attributes that can be entered through the Parameters dialog box (click the Parameters button on the Property Inspector): salign and swliveconnect. The salign attribute determines how the movie aligns itself to the surrounding frame when the Scale attribute is set to ShowAll. In addition, salign determines which portion of the image gets cut off when the Scale attribute is set to NoBorder. The alignment can be set to L (left), R (right), T (top), or B (bottom). You can also use these values in combination. For example, if you set salign=RB, the movie aligns with the right-bottom edge or the lower-right corner of the frame.

The swliveconnect attribute comes into play when you're using FSCommands or JavaScripting in your Flash movies. FSCommands are interactive commands, such as Go to URL, issued from inside the Flash movie. The latest versions of the Netscape browser initialize Java when first called — and if your Flash movie uses FSCommands or JavaScript, it uses Java to communicate with the Netscape plug-in interface, LiveConnect. Because not all Flash movies need the LiveConnect connection, you can prevent Java from being initialized by entering the swliveconnect attribute in the Parameters dialog box and setting its value to false. When the swliveconnect=false parameter is found by the browser, the Java is not initialized as part of the loading process — and your movie loads more quickly.

Creating Flash Buttons and Crafting Templates

The primary argument against using Flash has always been, "Not everyone has the Flash plug-in, so not everyone can see Flash movies." When Macromedia began promoting the 96.4 percent and above market penetration of the Flash Player, that argument started to fade. True, this almost universally installed base applies to the Flash 2 player — as of this writing, over 88 percent of browsers have Flash 4 players and almost 40 percent, Flash 5 — but the basic ability to play back .swf files is all that's necessary to display simple animations and enable sounds.

While Flash is often used to create standalone movies, cartoons, and interactive games, it is also capable of making excellent navigation aids. One feature of traditional user interfaces — audio feedback, the "click" that one hears when a button has been chosen onscreen — has been long missing on the Web because of the lack of a universally available sound engine. With navigation buttons created in Flash, sound is very easy to incorporate, as are animation effects and smooth blends. Best of all, these effects are extremely low bandwidth and often weigh less on a page than a comparable animated GIF file, even without the sound.

New Feature Dreamweaver designers may now add the power and beauty of Flash objects to their Web page design palette. Both animated Flash Buttons and static Flash Text (covered later in this chapter) may now be created directly within Dreamweaver. Flash Buttons are based on template designs created in Flash and customized in Dreamweaver. This separation of design and implementation allows Flash graphic designers to create the overall look for a navigational button or button series and

Dreamweaver layout artists to incorporate them into the proper page design, adding the appropriate button text, links, and background color where needed. Flash Buttons, like any Flash movie, may be previewed in Dreamweaver and resized as needed.

Dreamweaver comes with 44 different Flash Button templates with additional styles available at the Macromedia Exchange. The buttons are primarily intended to be used as links to other Web pages although some are designed as VCR-like player controls. To insert a Flash Button, follow these steps:

1. Make sure that the current document has been previously saved.

   If you're working on a new document, Dreamweaver requires that you save it before adding a Flash Button.

2. Choose Insert Flash Button from the Common category of the Objects panel or select Insert ⇨ Interactive Images ⇨ Flash Button.

   The Insert Flash Button dialog box, shown in Figure 23-6, is displayed.

Figure 23-6: Choose Apply to test typeface and text size variations when creating your Flash Button.

3. Select a button type from the Style list.

   The previews shown in the Sample area are live demonstrations and will play as designed when moused-over and/or clicked. There is, however, one exception: no sound is heard in preview; you'll have to preview the Flash Button in the browser to get the full effect.

4. If it's a navigation button, enter the custom text desired in the Button Text field.

   The Button Text field is physically limited to 50 characters, although for most practical purposes, your text will be shorter. Certain symbols, such as those in the Control group, ignore the text and font settings.

5. Select a typeface from the Font drop-down list.

   The fonts listed are TrueType fonts found on your system. Most of the button templates have a preselected font and text size. If the preselected font is not found on your system, a small alert appears at the bottom of the dialog box.

6. Enter the desired font size, in points, in the Size field.

7. If the button is to link to another page, enter the absolute or document relative URL in the Link field. Alternatively, you can choose the Browse button to locate the file.

   Flash movies don't handle site root–relative links correctly, so your link needs to either be absolute, such as `www.idest.com/contact.htm`, or document relative. Use document relative links only if the Flash Button is to be stored in the same folder as the page referenced.

8. If working in a frame-based site or you want the link to open in another page, select an option from the Target drop-down list.

   The standard system targets — _blank, _self, _parent, and _top — are always available. Additional frame names appear if the Flash Button is inserted in an existing frameset.

9. If the Flash Button is to be placed on a page or in a table with a background color other than white, select the Bg Color swatch to choose an appropriate background. Alternatively, the hexadecimal color number or standard color name may be entered directly into the Bg Color text field.

10. Enter a path and filename for the Flash Button file. If you like, you can use the suggested default name in the site root or select the Browse button to choose a different location.

11. Choose Apply to insert the button in the cursor location on the page.

12. Click OK when you're done.

Tip

If you'd like to see what other styles are available, open the Insert Flash Button dialog box and choose Get More Styles. Your primary browser will launch and go to the Dreamweaver Exchange where you can search for new styles. Once you've installed the additional extensions using the Extension Manager, you'll need to relaunch Dreamweaver to see the new styles. One word of caution: selecting Get More Styles immediately closes the dialog box without creating a button.

Once your Flash Button is inserted, it can be modified on the page. Choose the Flash Button to activate the specific Property Inspector that, along with standard Flash object parameters, offers a couple of new controls: Edit and Reset Size. Selecting Edit reopens the Insert Flash Button dialog box and allows you to modify any of the settings. Use Reset Size if you have altered the dimensions of the Flash Button — by dragging one of the sizing handles or entering new values in the Width and/or Height fields — and want to return to the preset size.

Tip   If you've moved an existing Flash Button to a frame-based design, select the button and choose Edit from the Property Inspector. Under Target, you'll find names for all the frames in your new frameset to make it easy to position your content.

The Flash Button samples that ship with Dreamweaver are nice, but to be truly useful, you — or someone on your team — must be able to create your own templates that fit the design of your site. The Flash Button templates you see previewed in Dreamweaver are actually Generator templates, created in Flash.

To create the Generator templates, you'll need Flash, of course, and the free Generator authoring extensions from Macromedia. The authoring extensions are included in Flash 5 or can be downloaded from the Macromedia site at `www.macromedia.com/software/generator/trial`. Additionally, you'll need to copy two Generator object files from the Dreamweaver CD-ROM to their proper place in the Flash and Generator installations. From the Dreamweaver 4/More Extensions/Flash Objects/Generator Text Object folder, copy these files:

✦ InsertText.def to Flash 5/generator/template folder

✦ InsertText.class to Generator 2/extras

If you don't have the Dreamweaver CD-ROM, you can download these files from the same Macromedia site listed previously.

Once you have the Generator Text object files in place, the next step is to create your button in Flash. As with other Flash Buttons, your graphic should be converted to a button-type symbol and it may use all four keyframes: Up, Over, Down, and Hit. Once you've built the button, follow these steps to add the Generator functionality:

1. In Flash, choose Window ➪ Generator Objects.

2. From the Generator Objects panel, drag the Insert Text object over the previously built button.

   Position the Insert Text object so that its center is over where you'd like your button text to appear.

3. When the Insert Text object is in place and selected, the Generator Insert Text panel displaying the appropriate properties appears. Double-click the Insert Text object to bring the panel to the front if necessary.

   Within the panel, you'll need to set several parameters to placeholder values so that the Insert Flash Button dialog box in Dreamweaver can function properly. In each case, enter the value in the right column.

4. Enter the following values in the Generator Insert Text panel:

- **Text:** Enter {Button Text}
- **Font:** Enter {Button Font}
- **Font Size:** Enter {Button Size}
- **Alignment:** Enter either left, right, center or justified.
- **Vertical Alignment:** Enter either top, center or bottom.
- **URL:** Enter {Button URL}
- **Window:** Enter {Button Target}

5. Shrink the movie to the size of your button by dragging the button to the upper-left corner of the stage and choosing Modify ⇨ Movie. In the Movie Properties dialog box, select the Match Contents option.

6. Save the movie as a .fla file so that you may adjust it later.

7. Choose File ⇨ Export Movie and select Generator Template as the file type. Save the template in the Dreamweaver/Configuration/Flash Objects/Flash Buttons folder.

Now your Flash Button is almost ready to use. If you like, you can choose the Insert Flash Button object in Dreamweaver and see your button; however, no sample text will be displayed. There's one last procedure that's required if you want to preview your Flash Button with example text. Interestingly enough, you use the Insert Flash Button object to create the preview:

1. Open Dreamweaver and save a blank page.

2. Choose the Insert Flash Button object.

3. Select your newly inserted button from the Style list.

New buttons are found at the end of the list.

4. Enter desired default values in the Text, Font, and Size fields.

These values will be preset whenever this particular Flash Button is chosen.

5. In the Save As field, store the file under the same name as your style in the Dreamweaver/Configuration/Flash Objects/Flash Buttons Preview folder.

6. Click OK when you're done.

The next time you access the Flash Button object, your custom template will display a full preview, with text.

Working with Flash Text

The addition of Flash Text to Dreamweaver goes a long way toward solving one of the Web designer's most perplexing problems: how to achieve good-looking text that uses non-standard fonts. While standard HTML text allows font families — a series of fonts offered in hopes that one of them is installed on the user's system — few designers stray outside of tried and true options such as Arial, Helvetica, and Times New Roman for the majority of their content. This is especially grating to print designers coming to the Web who rely on typography as a primary design tool. The advent of Dynamic HTML promised to bring a wider selection of typefaces with so-called dynamic font technology, but lack of built-in cross-browser support for any one system dashed those hopes.

New Feature   The new Flash Text feature allows the designer to use any TrueType font to create low-weight, jaggie-free headings, right from within Dreamweaver itself. The ubiquitous nature of the Flash Player ensures cross-browser support without resorting to GIF images, which are often not as crisp as required. Moreover, with Flash Text, you can easily declare a second color for automatically enabled rollovers — you don't even have to attach a Dreamweaver behavior.

The Flash Text feature is especially useful for creating headings in a corporate-approved typeface. Because it doesn't involve downloading a font resource as dynamic font technologies do, there is no concern about the misuse of copyrighted fonts. The only downside to Flash Text over a dynamic font technology is that unlike dynamically created fonts, Flash Text cannot be searched on a page. To overcome this limitation, Web designers can include key phrases in `<meta>` tags.

To use the Flash Text object, follow these steps:

1. Make sure your page has been saved before proceeding.

2. Choose Insert Flash Text from the Common category of the Objects panel or select Insert ⇨ Interactive Images ⇨ Flash Text.

   The Insert Flash Text dialog box appears, as shown in Figure 23-7.

3. Select the desired typeface from the Font drop-down list.

4. Enter the font size desired in the Size field.

5. Choose Bold and/or Italic styles for your text.

6. Select the alignment on the page: left, center, or right.

7. Select a basic color from the color swatch or enter a hexadecimal value or valid color name in the Color field.

8. If desired, choose a secondary color for the text to change to when the user moves his or her mouse over the Flash Text from the Rollover Color swatch.

Figure 23-7: Use the Insert Flash Text object to create headlines with a non-standard or custom font.

9. Enter the desired text in the Text field.

   There's no real limit to the amount of text that can be entered other than practical considerations, and line returns are acceptable.

10. If you want to see the text in the default font in the Text field, disable the Show Font option.

11. If desired, enter an absolute or document relative URL in the Link field.

   As with Flash Buttons, site relative links are not available in Flash Text objects.

12. If you're working in a frame-based site or want the link to open in a new browser window, choose the appropriate Target from the drop-down list.

13. Optionally, choose a background color from the Bg Color swatch.

14. Enter a filename and path to store the object in the Save As field. Alternatively, select the Browse button to locate a folder.

   If you're using document relative links in the Flash Text object, be sure to store the object in the same folder as the current document.

15. Click Apply to preview what your button will look like in your document and then click OK when you're done.

As with Flash Buttons, you can resize a Flash Text object by dragging the resizing handles; press the Shift key while dragging to constrain the dimensions to their initial width and height ratio. Click Reset Size on the Property Inspector to restore the original dimensions. To edit a Flash Text object, choose Edit from the Property Inspector; alternatively, you can double-click the object to open the Insert Flash Text dialog box again.

When you create a Flash Text object, Dreamweaver makes a GIF representation for display during layout — you may notice some roughness in the lines, especially if you resize the object. You can, at any time, select Play from the Flash Text Property Inspector (or choose Preview in Browser) to see the true Flash object with its smooth vector shape.

Configuring MIME Types

As with any plug-in, your Web server has to have the correct MIME types set before Shockwave files can be properly served to your users. If your Web page plays Shockwave and Flash movies locally, but not remotely, chances are good the correct MIME types need to be added. The system administrator generally handles configuring MIME types.

The system administrator needs to know the following information in order to correctly configure the MIME types:

✦ **Shockwave:** application/x-director (.dcr, .dir, .dxr)

✦ **Flash:** application/x-shockwave-flash (.swf)

Both Shockwave and Flash are popular plug-ins, and it's likely that the Web server is already configured to recognize the appropriate file types.

Tip   Movies made by an earlier version of Flash, called FutureSplash, can also be played by the Flash plug-in — but only if the correct MIME type is added: `application/futuresplash` with the file extension .spl.

Adding Generator Objects

Generator is Macromedia's tool for personalizing and delivering Flash content. While developers create Flash movies on their own systems, Generator graphics are built on-demand, by the server. Generator works with a series of variables in each template, which is filled in when the page containing the Generator object is requested by the browser. Think of Generator as a graphic mail-merge system in which the basic letter is the animation and the form fields can be anything from a user's name to data returned from a database. Although Generator is largely used to customize Flash content on the fly, it can also output other formats including GIF, JPEG, PNG, and QuickTime.

Inserting a Generator template into a Web page is very straightforward in Dreamweaver. Most of the work comes from providing values for the variables through a name/value pair interface. To add a Generator template, follow these steps:

1. Position your cursor where you'd like the Generator object to appear and choose Insert Generator from the Common category of the Objects panel or select Insert ⇨ Media ⇨ Generator.

   The Insert Generator dialog box, shown in Figure 23-8, appears.

Figure 23-8: Generator templates allow Flash movies and other graphics to be personalized by the server.

2. Enter the path to the Generator template file or choose the Browse button to locate the file.

   Generator templates have a .swt file extension.

3. Choose the kind of media to be created by Generator from the Type drop-down list: SWF (Flash), GIF, JPEG, MOV (QuickTime), or PNG.

4. To enter parameters for the object, first select the Add button.

   In the Parameters list, the temporary name=value listing appears.

5. Enter the name for your parameter in the Name field.

6. Enter the value of your parameter in the Value field.

7. Repeat Steps 4 through 6 for each parameter.

8. To remove a parameter, highlight it in the Parameters list and choose the Remove button.

9. Click OK when you're done.

Managing Links in Flash Movies with Dreamweaver

Many Web sites rely heavily on Flash movies, substituting movies for entire pages that would otherwise be created with HTML. Others take advantage of Flash's interactivity in their main navigation buttons. Adding links to buttons in Flash is easy, but embedding multiple URLs into multiple SWF files can make modifying a site's structure a nightmare, forcing you to re-create every SWF file in your site. Luckily, Dreamweaver comes to the rescue, with link management features that are SWF-savvy.

Dreamweaver extends its link management to include the links contained in Flash SWF movies. Edit links within a SWF file manually in the Site Map, or move SWF files in the Site Files view and let Dreamweaver clean up behind you.

Within the Site window, you can drag SWF files to new folders just as you would an HTML file. Unless your Update Links preference is set to Never, Dreamweaver will either modify the links in the SWF file accordingly or prompt you for permission to do so.

Be careful with the type of links you use — Flash (or, more accurately, browser playback of Flash) can't handle them all. Absolute URLs are very common in Flash movies because they can be used in every situation. Document relative links may be used successfully in all cases if the Web page and the Flash file are stored in the same folder. Site root relative links, such as /products/widgets.htm, should not be used in Flash movies.

To modify the links in a SWF file manually, follow these steps:

1. Choose Window ⇨ Site Map to view the Site Map.

2. Choose View ⇨ Show Dependent Files (Site ⇨ Site Map View ⇨ Show Dependent Files) to include dependent files such as Flash movies in the Site Map.

3. Locate the SWF file that you want to modify. If it contains any links, a plus sign is shown next to its icon. Click the plus sign to expand a branch of links from the SWF file, as shown in Figure 23-9.

4. To change a link, select it and choose Site ⇨ Change Link (Site ⇨ Site Map View ⇨ Change Link) or use the key shortcut Ctrl+L (Command+L). Alternatively, you can right-click (Control+click) the link and choose Change Link from the contextual menu. Dreamweaver displays a Select HTML File dialog box.

5. Select a new file by navigating to an HTML file or entering an URL. Click OK when you're done.

Figure 23-9: Dreamweaver's Site Map displays links contained in Flash SWF movies.

 Note If your preferences call for Dreamweaver to prompt you before updating links, Dreamweaver will ask you to confirm that you want this link changed.

The link in your SWF file is changed.

Just as with HTML files, you can also remove links from a SWF file by selecting the link and choosing Site ➪ Remove Link (Site ➪ Site Map View ➪ Remove Link) or use the keyboard shortcut Ctrl+Shift+L (Command+Shift+L).

 Caution Dreamweaver changes links within SWF files, but the links in the original Flash document that you edit in Flash itself will remain unchanged. Make sure to update your Flash document before exporting a revised SWF file.

Providing User Interaction with Shockwave Movies

What happens once you've installed your Director or Flash Shockwave files? Many movies are set to play automatically or upon some action from the user, such as a mouse click of a particular hotspot within the page. The Show Me movies used in

Dreamweaver are good examples of the kind of interactivity you can program within a Director Shockwave movie. But what if you want the user to be able to start or stop a movie in one part of the page, using controls in another part? How can controls in one frame affect a movie in a different frame?

Dreamweaver includes a Control Shockwave or Flash behavior that makes inline controls — controls on the same Web page as the movie — very easy to set up. However, establishing frame-to-frame control is slightly more complex in Dreamweaver and requires a minor modification to the program-generated code.

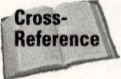 **Cross-Reference** Both of the following step-by-step techniques rely on Dreamweaver behaviors. If you're unfamiliar with using behaviors, you should review Chapter 19 before proceeding.

Dreamweaver technique: Creating inline Shockwave controls

Certainly it's perfectly acceptable to make your Director or Flash movies with built-in controls for interactivity, but sometimes you want to separate the controls from the movie. Dreamweaver includes a JavaScript behavior called Control Shockwave or Flash. With this behavior, you can set up external controls to start, stop, and rewind Shockwave and Flash movies.

To create inline Shockwave or Flash controls:

1. Insert your Shockwave or Flash file by choosing either the Insert Shockwave or Insert Flash button from the Objects panel.

2. From the Select File dialog box, enter the path to your file in the File Name text box or select the Browse (Choose) button to locate your file.

3. For Shockwave, enter the width and height of your movie in the W and H text boxes, respectively, in the Property Inspector. The dimensions for Flash movies are entered automatically.

4. Enter a unique name for your movie in the text box provided.

5. If you are inserting a Flash movie, deselect the Autoplay and Loop options.

6. To insert the first control, position the cursor where you'd like the control to appear on the page.

7. Select Insert Image from the Objects panel or select some text.

8. In the Link box of the Property Inspector, enter a dummy link or just a hash symbol, #, to create an empty target.

9. Open the Behaviors panel by selecting the Show Behaviors button from the Launcher or by pressing Shift+F3.

10. If necessary, change the selected browser to 4.0 Browsers; you can do this by selecting an option from the Show Events For submenu of the Add Behavior menu.

11. Select the + (Add Action) button and choose Control Shockwave or Flash from the drop-down list.

12. In the Control Shockwave or Flash dialog box (see Figure 23-10), select the movie you want to affect from the Movie drop-down list.

Figure 23-10: In the Control Shockwave or Flash dialog box, you assign a control action to an image button or link.

13. Now select the desired action for your control. Choose from the four options: Play, Stop, Rewind, and Go to Frame. If you choose the Go to Frame option, enter a frame number in the text box.

14. Click OK to close the Control Shockwave or Flash dialog box.

15. Repeat Steps 6 through 14 for each movie control you'd like to add. Figure 23-11 shows a sample Web page with Play and Stop controls.

Dreamweaver technique: Playing Shockwave movies in frames

Framesets and frames are great for Web sites in which you want your navigation and other controls kept in one frame and the freedom to vary the content in another frame. It's entirely possible to set up your movie's playback buttons in one frame and the Shockwave movie in another. The method and the tools used are similar to those used in the preceding technique for adding same-page controls to a Shockwave movie. For this technique using frames, some HTML hand-coding is necessary, but it is relatively minor — only one additional line per control!

As you saw in the previous section, Dreamweaver's Control Shockwave or Flash behavior lists all the Shockwave and Flash movies in the page and enables you to choose the one you want to affect (as previously shown in Figure 23-11). Unfortunately, the behavior looks on only one page and not through an entire frameset. However, with a little sleight-of-hand and a bit of JavaScript, you can get the effect you want.

Figure 23-11: This Web page contains Play and Stop controls using the Control Shockwave or Flash behavior.

 Note   Before you begin applying this technique, you should construct (and save) your frameset and individual frames. Be sure to name each frame uniquely, because you have to provide the names in order to address the correct frames.

To place Shockwave controls in frames:

1. In one frame, insert the images or links that are going to act as the Shockwave controls. (For this demonstration, the control frame is named `frControl`.)

2. In another frame, insert the Shockwave file (either Shockwave or Flash) by choosing the appropriate object from the Objects panel. (For this demonstration, the movie frame is named `frMovie`.)

3. Be sure to modify the Shockwave Property Inspector with the necessary parameters: name, width, height, and source; and, if you're inserting a Flash file, deselect the Autoplay and Loop checkboxes.

4. Copy the Shockwave placeholder by selecting it and choosing Edit ⇨ Copy.

5. Position the cursor in the `frControl` frame and paste the placeholder in a temporary position by choosing Edit ⇨ Paste. At this point, the placement for the placeholder is not critical, as long as it is in the same frame as the images or links you are going to use as controls. The placeholder will be deleted shortly.

Instead of using the Copy and Paste commands, you can hold down Ctrl (Command) and click and drag the placeholder to its new temporary position.

6. Now select the first image or link you want to use as a control. As described in the preceding technique, attach the Control Shockwave or Flash behavior to the selected object. As you learned in the preceding exercise, this entails the following actions:

- With the image or link selected, open the Behaviors panel.

- Add the Control Shockwave or Flash action.

- In the Control Shockwave or Flash dialog box, specify the movie and select the required action (Play, Rewind, Stop, or Go to Frame).

7. The major work is finished now. All you still need to do is add a little HTML. Switch to Code view, open the Code Inspector, or use your favorite external editor to edit the file.

8. Locate the image or link controls in the code. Each JavaScript routine is called from within an `<a>` tag and reads something like the following, where `fMovie` is the name of the Flash movie:

```
<a href="#" onClick="MM_controlShockwave ¬
('document.fMovie', 'document.fMovie','Play')">
```

9. Wherever you see the JavaScript reference to document, change it to

```
parent.frameName.document
```

where `frameName` is the unique name you gave to the frame in which your movie appears. In our example, `frameName` is `frMovie`, so after the replacement is made, the tag reads as follows:

```
<a href="#" onClick="MM_controlShockwave('parent.ù
frMovie.document.fMovie','document.fMovie','Play')">
```

By making this substitution, you've pointed the JavaScript function first to the "parent" of the current document — and the parent of a frame is the entire frameset. Now that we're looking at the entire frameset, the next word (which is the unique frame name) points the JavaScript function directly to the desired frame within the frameset.

Tip   If you have a number of controls, you might want to use Dreamweaver's Find and Replace features to ensure that you've updated all the code.

10. Finally, delete the temporary Shockwave movie that was inserted into the frame containing the controls.

Test the frameset by pressing F12 (primary browser) or Shift+F12 (secondary browser). If you haven't changed the Property Inspector's default Tag attribute (the default is Object and Embed), the Shockwave movie should work in both Netscape and Internet Explorer.

Dreamweaver technique: Triggering behaviors from Flash movies

Flash includes a number of its own behaviors for creating interactivity, but Flash behaviors don't do JavaScript as Dreamweaver behaviors do. A Flash-heavy project might benefit from Dreamweaver's Open Browser Window or Pop-up Message behaviors as much as the next site. The technique in this section shows you how to trigger Dreamweaver behaviors from buttons in a Flash movie.

What Flash buttons do is specified in the Flash authoring environment, not in Dreamweaver. Dreamweaver can attach behaviors to HTML elements such as anchor tags and body tags but not to plug-ins. The solution lies in creating dummy "buttons" in Dreamweaver and copying the JavaScript code from those links into the actions attached to Flash buttons, within Flash itself.

Note The following technique can be used for any Dreamweaver behavior. The JavaScript Integration Kit for Flash 5 (JIK) extension, covered later in this chapter, has several built-in functions including Open Browser Window and Swap Image. Use the following procedure if you don't want to use the JIK extension or need to incorporate a behavior not included in that extension.

To trigger Dreamweaver behaviors from Flash buttons, follow these steps:

1. Create a new Dreamweaver document or open an existing one.

2. Create a dummy link that represents a button in your Flash movie. If you want a Flash button to open a new browser window, attach the Open Browser Window behavior to your dummy link, as in Figure 23-12.

3. Place your cursor within the dummy link and choose the ⟨a⟩ tag from the Tag Chooser in Dreamweaver's status bar to completely select the link.

4. Click the Show Code and Design views button on the toolbar or choose View ⇨ Code and Design from the menus. Note that the dummy link is selected in both the Code and Design portions of the document window and looks something like this:

```
<a href="#"
onClick="MM_openBrWindow('myBuddy.htm','','scrollbars=yes','w
idth=250,height=200')">popup copywrite message</a>
```

5. Select everything between the quotes in the onClick attribute—including the parentheses—as shown in Figure 23-13, and copy it to the clipboard. This is the actual JavaScript that we want the Flash button to execute.

6. In Flash, double-click the button you want to add the Dreamweaver behavior to. The Instance Properties dialog box opens. Select the Object Actions tab, as shown in Figure 23-14.

Figure 23-12: Attach a behavior you want to trigger from Flash to a dummy link in Dreamweaver.

7. Click the + (add) button and choose Get URL from the Basic Actions category to add a Flash Get URL behavior to your Flash button. In the URL box, type:

```
javascript:
```

and then paste the contents of the clipboard—your JavaScript code—so that you have something like this (refer back to Figure 23-14):

```
javascript:MM_openBrWindow('myBuddy.htm','','scrollbars=yes',
'width=250,height=200')
```

Click OK when you're done.

8. Repeat Steps 2 through 7 for each additional button or behavior you'd like to use.

9. Export your Flash movie as a SWF file and place it into the same page in Dreamweaver where you built your dummy links. Note that the `<head>` tag of this page contains JavaScript functions that match your dummy links and the JavaScript inside your Flash movie, as shown in Figure 23-15.

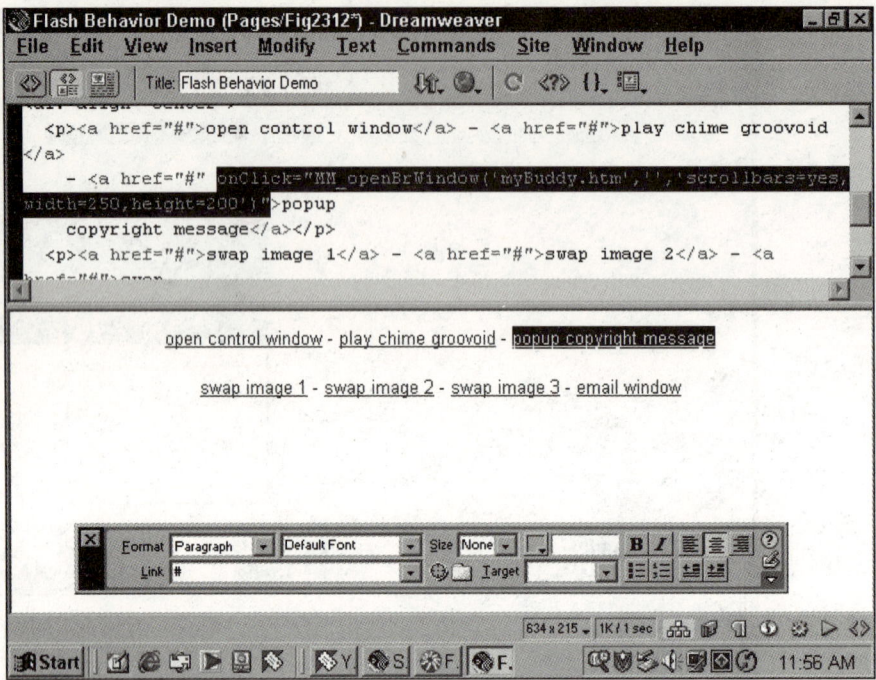

Figure 23-13: Select the JavaScript that the Flash button should execute from within the `onClick` attribute of your anchor tag.

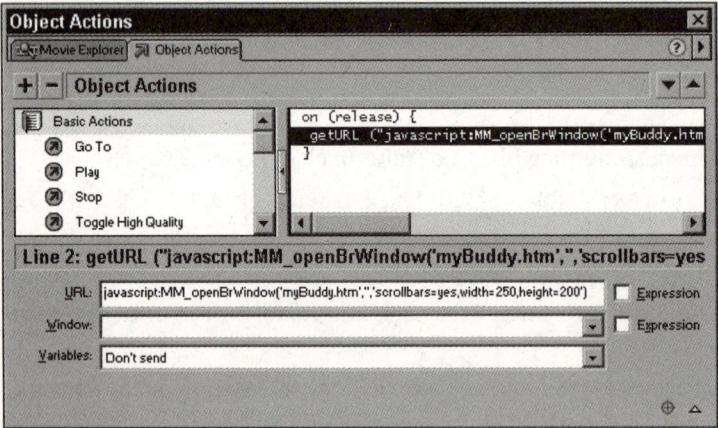

Figure 23-14: Add your JavaScript code to a Flash button Get URL behavior in the Instance Properties dialog box in Flash.

Figure 23-15: The JavaScript in your Flash movie relies on the same JavaScript functions that Dreamweaver inserted in the `<head>` tag as you built your dummy links.

10. Delete your dummy links — but not the JavaScript functions in the `<head>` tag — and publish your page.

When users click the buttons in your Flash movie, `javascript: URL` sends the commands to the browser, executing the JavaScript functions in your Web page. Flash buttons open new browser windows, pop-up messages, and so on. This works in Netscape and in Internet Explorer.

 Tip   Shockwave authors can also use JavaScript URLs from Lingo to trigger Dreamweaver behaviors in a manner similar to the preceding. The JavaScript-savvy can also reference their own JavaScript functions using this method.

Dreamweaver Technique: Using the JavaScript Integration Kit for Flash 5

With an eye toward smoothing the integration between Flash and Dreamweaver, Macromedia released the JavaScript Integration Kit for Flash 5 (JIK). The JIK is a suite of commands and behaviors installable in Dreamweaver — versions 3 and above — via the Extension Manager. You can download the current version from the Macromedia Exchange; choose Commands ⇨ Get More Commands to go directly online.

The JavaScript Integration Kit for Flash 5 consists of four main components:

✦ **Macromedia Flash Player Controls:** Allows the designer to include interactive control over Flash movies in a Web page. New Dreamweaver behaviors assign play, stop, rewind, fast-forward, pan, and zoom actions to any graphic element. In addition, an HTML drop-down menu can be turned into a Flash movie selector.

✦ **Advanced Form Validations:** Ensures that your visitors are entering the proper type of information in your Flash form. You can apply any of 18 client-side form validations — everything from a required, non-blank to an International Phone Validation.

✦ **Browser Scripts for Flash:** Embeds up to 10 different JavaScript functions in the Dreamweaver page, callable from any Flash 5 movie. With these functions, your Flash movie can control form elements such as text fields and select lists, open remote browser windows, set cookies, and swap images on the Web page.

✦ **Flash Dispatcher Behavior:** Detects the visitor's Flash Player version and redirects to a suitable Web page.

The beauty of the JIK is that its various components can be mixed and matched to achieve a wide range of effects and control. The resulting Web page offers a greater degree of interactivity for the visitor as well as for the Flash designer.

Macromedia Flash Player Controls

One method of engaging your Web page visitors is to give them more control over their viewing experience. Rather than just displaying a movie from beginning to end, allow the viewer to pause, rewind, and play the animation at will. Flash's vector-based nature even allows you to zoom in and out, without loss of image clarity. While all of this functionality is available through Flash ActionScripting, not all designs require the controls to be maintained within a Flash movie. The Flash Player Controls allow all of the common VCR-like functionality — and then some — to be assigned to HTML elements such as images or hotspots.

When the JavaScript Integration Kit is installed, 10 different behaviors are grouped under the MM Flash Player Controls:

✦ Fast Forward Flash

✦ Go To Flash Frame

✦ Go To Flash Frame Based on Cookie

> ✦ Load Flash Movie
>
> ✦ Pan Flash
>
> ✦ Play Flash
>
> ✦ Rewind Flash
>
> ✦ Set Flash by List
>
> ✦ Stop Flash
>
> ✦ Zoom Flash

As with any other Dreamweaver behavior, the player controls must be assigned to a target: a text link, an image map hotspot, or a graphic with a link attached. Typically, such a graphic button would use a false link, such as # or javascript:; so that it may act as a trigger but not actually open a URL.

You must have at least one Flash movie in the page before the Flash Player Controls become available, as shown in Figure 23-16. Once activated, the user interfaces for the Flash Player Controls vary according to their function as detailed below. With the Play, Stop, Rewind Flash behaviors, you just pick the Flash movie you want to control from the drop-down list. All the other behaviors include this option as well so you can affect any movie on the page.

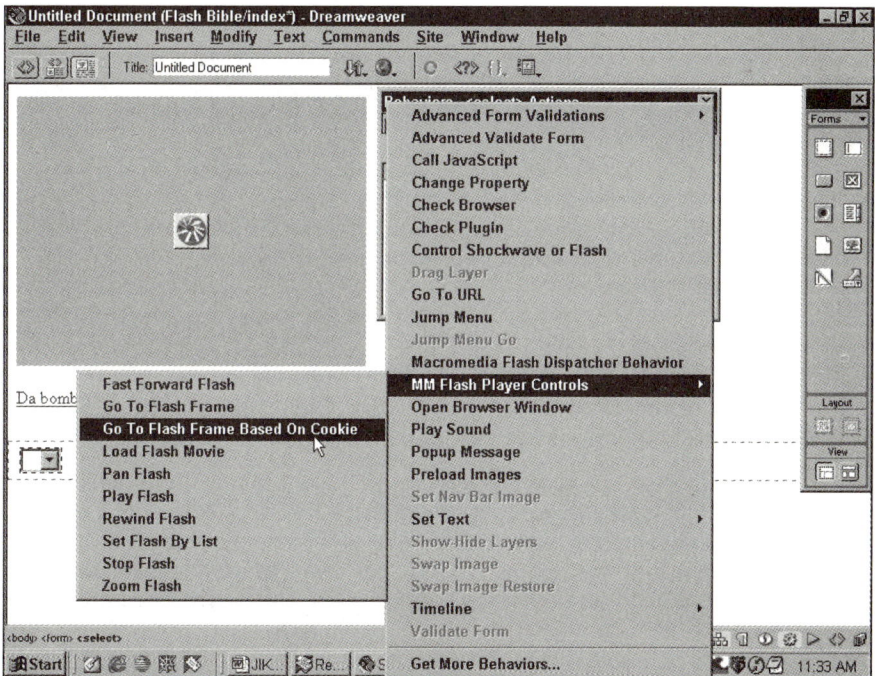

Figure 23-16: The Flash Player Controls become active once a Flash movie is present in the current Dreamweaver document.

To use the Flash Player Controls, follow these steps:

1. Insert at least one Flash movie by choosing an animation from the Assets panel or applying the Insert Flash object.

2. Enter a unique name in the ID field of the Flash Property Inspector for each movie. A distinct ID avoids browser compatibility problems; if one is not initially supplied, Dreamweaver offers to make one for you when any of the behaviors are applied.

3. Select the text link, hotspot, or image to trigger the behavior.

   If you'd like to apply the Set Flash by List behavior, select a form list object.

4. Choose Window ⇨ Behaviors to open the Behaviors panel, if necessary. Alternatively, you can select the Show Behavior icon from the Launcher or use the keyboard shortcut, Shift+F3.

5. Choose the Add button from the Behaviors panel and select the desired behavior under the MM Flash Player Controls heading.

   The chosen behavior's dialog box appears, similar to the one shown in Figure 23-17.

Figure 23-17: With the Pan Flash behavior, your viewer can move around a Flash movie in any direction. As shown, this behavior pans in a diagonal direction, down and to the right, every time it is triggered.

6. Select the parameters for your behavior.

   • For the Play Flash, Rewind Flash, and Stop Flash behaviors, select the desired animation to affect from the Movie drop-down list.

   • For the Fast Forward Flash behavior, select the desired animation to affect from the Movie drop-down list. In the first blank field, enter the desired value you want the movie to advance by. Select either Frames or Percent from the drop-down list. For example, to advance the movie by 5 percent each time the behavior is called, enter 5 in the first field and choose Percent from the list.

   • For the Go To Flash Frame behavior, select the desired animation to affect from the Movie drop-down list and then enter the frame number to move to in the Go To Frame field.

- For the Go To Flash Frame Based on Cookie behavior, select the desired animation to affect from the Movie drop-down list, enter the name of the cookie to read in the Cookie Name field, enter the value to look for in the Cookie Value field, and then enter the frame number to advance to when the cookie name and value are read in the Go To Frame field.

- For the Load Flash Movie behavior, select the desired animation to you want to replace from the Replace Movie drop-down list. Enter the file-name for the movie to load in the With Movie field or locate the movie by selecting the Browse button. Input the level to load the movie into in the Level field.

To replace an existing movie with the loaded movie, enter a level number that is currently occupied by another movie. To replace the original movie and unload every level, choose 0 for the Level. To begin playing the movie immediately, set the Play option to Yes; otherwise, set Play to No.

 As Dreamweaver warns you, the Load Flash Movie behavior is not supported for Netscape browsers.

- For the Pan Flash behavior, select the desired animation to affect from the Movie drop-down list, choose the Horizontal and/or Vertical direction — up, down, right, or left — to pan to from the drop-down lists, and then select the degree of the pan by entering a value in the fields below each direction. You can pan diagonally by entering non-zero values for both the Horizontal and Vertical direction. Choose whether you'd like the pan values to operate in either Pixel or Percent mode.

- For the Set Flash by List behavior, select the desired animation to affect from the Movie drop-down list, choose the list object from the Select Box drop-down list, and input the level to load the movie into in the Level field. To replace an existing movie with the loaded movie, enter a level number that is currently occupied by another movie. To replace the original movie and unload every level, choose 0 for the Level.

To begin playing the movie immediately, set the Play option to Yes; otherwise, set Play to No. For the Set Flash by List behavior to work properly, you'll also need to set the values of each of the list items to a relative or absolute file URL pointing to a .swf file. Click the Parameters button on the List/Menu Property Inspector to enter new labels and their corresponding values.

 As Dreamweaver warns you, the Set Flash by List behavior is not supported for Netscape browsers.

- For the Zoom Flash behavior, select the desired animation to affect from the Movie drop-down list. Enter the value desired in the Zoom field. To zoom in, enter a number greater than 100; to zoom out, enter a number below 100. To reset the movie to the original zoom level, enter 0.

7. After you've chosen all the desired parameters from the dialog box, select OK to close it.

   The Behaviors panel displays the event and action for the behavior just applied.

8. By default, onClick is the selected event. To change the triggering event to onMouseOver or onMouseOut, select the down arrow between the event and the action and choose the desired event from the list.

Advanced Form Validations

HTML forms can be tricky: The more you use forms to gather information from your visitors, the greater the possibility for user error. In a sense, forms are a classic double-edged sword and a few people taking advantage of Flash's increased interactivity are getting nicked by them. If, for example, your online form includes two fields for a telephone number, one for the U.S. and one for international visitors, you'll want to be sure that the proper data is entered in the correct field. To ensure that a user enters the type of information you're expecting in your Flash form, that information needs to be validated. The JavaScript Integration Kit includes methods for validating 18 different types of data.

For the Advanced Form Validations to work, you'll need to work both with your Flash movie and with the Dreamweaver page the movie is embedded in. Here's an overview of the process:

On the Dreamweaver side:

1. Create a form with hidden fields — one for each of the Flash fields you want to validate.

2. Attach the Advanced Validate Form behavior to the form itself.

3. Add one of the Browser Scripts for Flash functions, FDK_setFormText, to the page.

4. Attach the desired validation behavior to the <body> tag of the current document.

On the Flash side:

1. Make sure every form field has a unique variable name assigned to it.

2. Add a getURL action to the on (press) event of the submit button, calling the FDK_setFormText function inserted into the Dreamweaver page.

3. Add another getURL action to the on (release) event of the submit button, which invokes the FDK_Validate function — which was put on the Dreamweaver document by the Advanced Validate Form behavior.

You'll need to keep track of the names of the Hidden field inputs inserted in Dreamweaver, as well as the name of the form itself; they both are referenced when the functions are added in Flash.

Now that you have an overview, let's go through the process with a little more detail. Again, we'll start with the Dreamweaver page:

1. Choose Insert ➪ Form to add a form to your document.

   In Dreamweaver, the form is automatically named.

2. Within the form, add a Hidden form field for every Flash field you'd like to validate. Give each Hidden field a unique name and leave the Value blank.

3. Select the ⟨form⟩ tag in the Tag Selector and, from the Behaviors panel, choose the Advanced Validate Form behavior.

   The Advanced Validate Form dialog box appears, as shown in Figure 23-18.

Figure 23-18: The Advanced Validate Form behavior controls how validations overall are applied.

4. In the Advanced Validate Form dialog box:

   • Select the form containing the Hidden elements you want to use from the Validate drop-down list.

   • To stop validating when an incorrect entry is encountered, check the Stop on First Error option.

   • Enter any desired message in the Error Header text area. The Error Header is displayed in addition to any validation-specific error messages.

   • If your behavior is assigned to an onSubmit event (the default) choose the Stop Submission If Errors Occur option; otherwise, select the Automatically Submit If No Errors Occur option.

   • Select OK to close the dialog box when you're done.

5. Choose Commands ➪ Browser Scripts for Flash.

The Browser Scripts for Flash command, discussed in more detail later in this section, embeds functions in the Dreamweaver page for communicating with Flash.

6. When the Browser Scripts for Flash dialog box opens, select the `FDK_setFormText` option; close the dialog box when you're done.

Our final preparation in Dreamweaver is to add the individual validation behaviors required.

7. Select the `<body>` tag from the Tag Selector and choose the Add (+) button in the Behaviors panel. From the drop-down list, select a validation behavior from the Advanced Form Validations category.

Most of the Advanced Form Validation behaviors have similar dialog boxes in which you can choose the particular form element (the Hidden field relating to the Flash form field) affected, make the field required, and set the error message. The differences between the various behaviors are detailed in Table 23-3.

8. Repeat Step 7 for every validation you'd like to apply in the form.

Table 23-3
Advanced Form Validation Behaviors

Behavior	Description
Alphanumeric Validation	Displays an error if non-alphanumeric characters are entered.
Credit Card Validation	Removes any spaces or hyphens and then displays an error message if the card number is not valid. This behavior does not authorize credit card purchases.
Date Validation	Optionally allows dates in the future, past, or in a particular range and specific format.
E-mail Validation	Makes sure that the entry contains an @ and a period.
Entry Length Validation	Accepts a defined number range of characters — for example, from 5 to 10.
Floating Point Validation	Displays an error if a non-number is entered; floating point numbers can contain decimals.
Integer Validation	Displays the message if a non-number or a number with decimals is entered. You can also set an acceptable number range.
International Phone Validation	Removes parentheses, spaces, and hyphens and then makes sure at least six digits are entered.
Like Entry Validation	Checks one form field entry against another; typically used for password verification.

Behavior	Description
Mask Validation	Allows the designer to require a specific pattern of text, and numbers to be entered. Use A to indicate a letter, # for numbers and ? if the entry could be either a letter or a number. For example, the mask A###?? would require a letter followed by three numbers, followed by two other alphanumeric characters.
Nonblank Validation	Displays a message if the field is left empty.
Radio Button Validation	Ensures that at least one option in a specified radio button group is selected. Note: This behavior is only used with HTML form elements.
Selection Made in List Validation	Displays an error if the user does not make a selection from a specific drop-down list. Note: This behavior is only used with HTML form elements.
Social Security Validation	Removes any hyphens, checks for a proper length and then reformats the number into a 3-2-4 configuration, as in 123-45-6789.
Time Validation	Displays an error if a valid time with minutes within a certain range is not entered. Military time and most variations of a.m. and p.m. are accepted.
URL Validation	Looks for valid URL protocols and displays an error message if one is not found at the start of the entry. Accepted URLs include: `ftp://`, `http://`, `javascript:`, `file://`, `gopher://`, `https://`, `mailto:`, `rlogin://`, `shttp://`, `snews://`, `telnet://`, `tn3270://`, `swais://`
US Phone Validation	Verifies that the entered information is either 7 or 10 digits after removing any parentheses and hyphens.
Zip Code Validation	Requires the entry to be either 5 or 9 digits.

Now that the Dreamweaver page is prepped, you're ready to prepare the Flash movie:

1. In Flash, add the required form fields as text input fields

2. In the Text Options panel, enter a unique name in the Variable field.

3. Make sure your form has a graphic that acts as a submit button.

4. Select the submit button graphic and open the Object Actions panel.

5. Add an `on (press)` event and attach a `getURL` function to the event.

6. In the `getURL` function, call the `FDK_setFormText` function that was embedded into the Dreamweaver page. The `FDK_setForm Text` function takes three arguments: the name of the form, the name of the field to be validated, and the variable name assigned to the corresponding field in Flash.

   For example, let's say the form is named `theForm` and you've created a field for gathering an e-mail address and given it a name in Dreamweaver such as `emailHidden`. In Flash, the variable assigned to the corresponding text field might be called `emailField`. In this case, the `getURL` function would read:

```
getURL("javascript:FDK_setFormText('theForm','emailHidden','"
add emailField add "')";)
```

Note the addition of the word `add` on either side of the variable name, as shown in the code and Figure 23-19. This syntax is required for the parameters to be passed correctly.

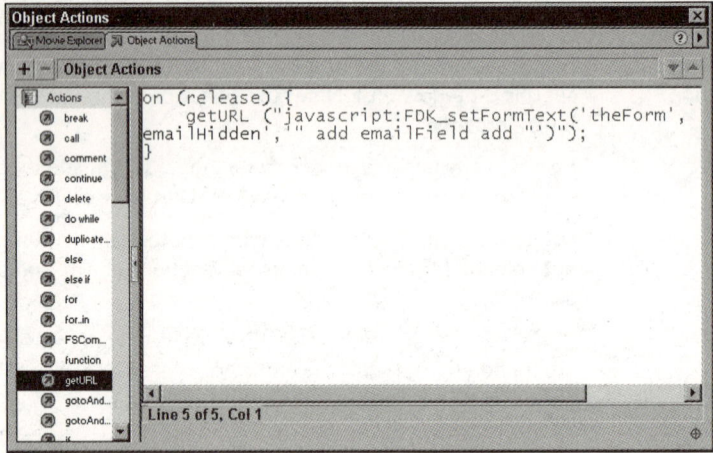

Figure 23-19: Enter a `FDK_setFormText` function for every Flash field you need to qualify.

7. Continue adding as many `FDK_setFormText` functions as you have fields to validate to the same `getURL` action. Separate each function with a semicolon.

   After you've entered all the required `FDK_setFormText` functions, you'll need to add one last event and function.

8. In the Object Actions panel for the submit button graphic, add an `on (release)` event and attach a `getURL` action to it.

9. In the `getURL` action, insert the `FDK_Validate` function. This function takes four arguments, which correspond to the options available in Dreamweaver's Advanced Validate Form dialog box: FormName, stopOnFailure, AutoSubmit, and ErrorHeader. Both stopOnFailure and AutoSubmit are Booleans and accept either true or false.

   As an example, suppose the form is again called `theForm`, that you'd like the form to stop processing when an error is encountered as well as automatically be submitted, and that your general error message reads, "Attention!! I found an error on the form!" Here, the `getURL` function would look like this:

```
getURL("javascript:FDK_Validate('theForm',true,true,'Attentio
n!! I found an error on the form!\\n\\n');");
```

The \n\n after the function call acts as a hard return in the alert box to separate the generic message header and the specific validation error.

The final step is to cross the bridge again from Flash to Dreamweaver, bringing your exported Flash movie into the Dreamweaver page. Be sure to give it both a name and ID (both of which can be the same) in the Property Inspector.

Browser Scripts for Flash

With the JavaScript Integration Kit, integration is a two-way street: not only is it easier to control Flash movies, the Flash movies can also affect the HTML page. The JIK includes one overall command called Browser Scripts for Flash, which offers over 5 different types of control:

- ✦ Setting a form element's value
- ✦ Setting a cookie
- ✦ Opening a remote browser window
- ✦ Swapping images for rollovers
- ✦ Setting list menu items

Implementing these functions in Dreamweaver is simplicity itself: Just choose Commands ➪ Browser Scripts for Flash and check off the desired options you see in Figure 23-20. The various functions are grouped into five different categories. If you open a page with these functions already in place, you'll find the option already selected; deselecting the checkbox removes the function from the page when the dialog box is closed.

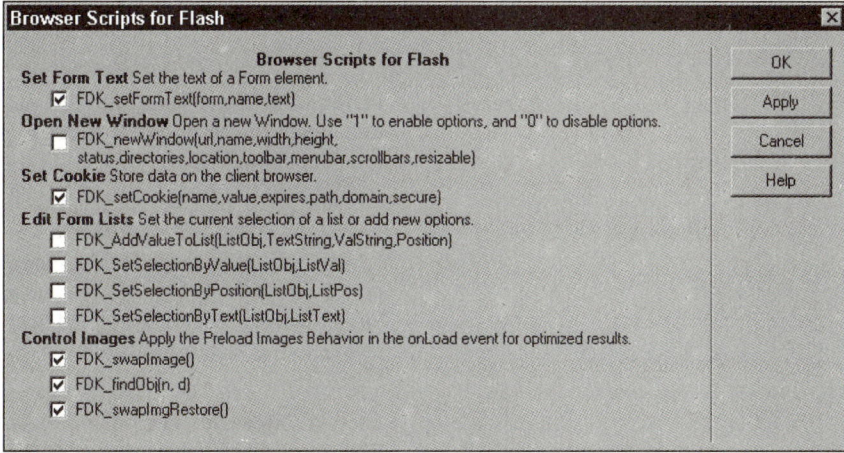

Figure 23-20: The Browser Scripts for Flash dialog box enables you to easily insert or remove functions that you can call from Flash.

Like the form validations, using the Browser Scripts is a two-program process. Once you've installed them in Dreamweaver you need call the function in a Flash action. Each of the functions takes its own series of parameters and typically, each one is invoked using an action such as getURL. The functions and their arguments are explained in Table 23-4.

Table 23-4
Browser Scripts for Flash Functions

Function	Arguments	Description
FDK_setFormText elementName variableName	FormName	Sets the value of a form element.
FDK_newWindow windowName width height status directories location toolbar menubar scrollbars resizable	URL	Opens a remote browser window. The width and height values are entered in pixels; for all other parameters (except URL and windowName) enter a 0 to disallow the element and a 1 to include it.
FDK_setCookie cookieValue expiresWhen path domain secureBoolean	CookieName	Sets a cookie from within a Flash movie and can be used in conjunction with the Go To Flash Frame Based on Cookie behavior.
FDK_swapImage [blank] replacementPath 1	ImageName	Performs an image swap in the HTML document. The second parameter is intentionally left blank.
FDK_swapImgRestore	n/a	Restores a previously executed image swap. For complex pages using multiple image swaps, it's best to explicitly swap the image from its replacement to its original source rather than use the FDK_SwapImgRestore behavior.
FDK_findObj	n/a	Used in conjunction with the FDK_SwapImage behavior.

Function	Arguments	Description

`FDK_AddValueToList`
`TextString`
`ValString`
`Position`
	`ListObj`	Inserts a new value into a form list element.

`FDK_SetSelectionByValue` `ListValue`	`ListObj`	Determines the selection of a list item with a given value.
`FDK_SetSelectionByPosition` `ListPos`	`ListObj`	Determines the selection of a list item in a particular list position.
`FDK_SetSelectionByText` `ListText`	`ListObj`	Determines the selection of a list item with a given label.

Flash Dispatcher Behavior

The final component of the JavaScript Integration Kit, the Flash Dispatcher Behavior, is designed to smooth visitor access to your Web-based Flash content. The Flash Dispatcher checks to see if the visitor to your site already has the Flash player and, if so, what version. If the proper version — or no player at all — is found, this behavior gives you several options. The visitor's browser can be redirected to a Flash-less page or to a site for downloading an appropriate version, if an automatically downloaded version is not possible.

To apply this behavior, select the <body> tag from the Tag Selector and, from the Behaviors panel, choose Macromedia Flash Dispatcher Behavior. In the dialog box (see Figure 23-21), you have the following options:

- ✦ **Macromedia Flash Content URL:** Enter or locate the path to the page containing the Flash movie.

- ✦ **Alternate URL:** Enter or locate the path to a Web page the visitor should go to if the proper Flash player is not found.

- ✦ **Macromedia Flash Version:** Choose the lowest permissible version from 2.0, 3.0, 4.0, or 5.0

- ✦ **Require Latest Plugin:** Select this option to require the latest version of the Flash Player.

- ✦ **No Player Options:** Any visitors who do not have the Flash Player installed are sent to a selectable download page or are directed to use the Alternate URL.

- ✦ **Improper Version Options:** Any visitors who do not have the required version of the Flash Player installed will be sent to a selectable upgrade page or are directed to use the Alternate URL.

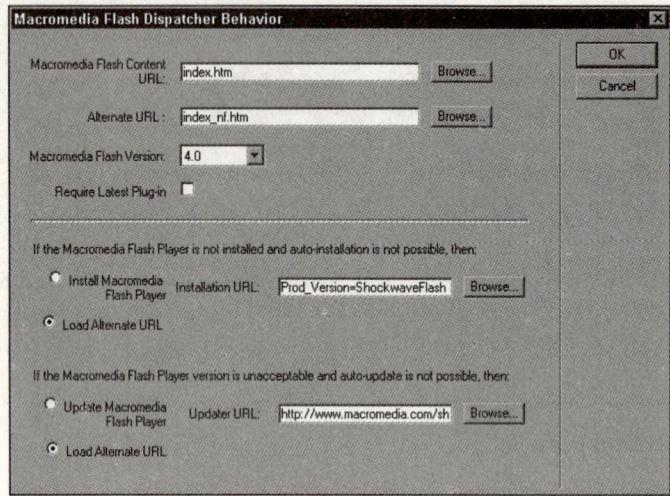

Figure 23-21: Make sure that only visitors with the proper Flash player can see your movies with the Flash Dispatcher Behavior.

The Flash Content URL can be the same page that the behavior is applied to or, in the case of what is referred to as a gateway script, another page.

Summary

Together, the interactive power of Shockwave and the speedy glitz of Flash can enliven Web content like nothing else. Dreamweaver is extremely well-suited for integrating and displaying Shockwave and Flash movies. Here are some key pointers to keep in mind:

✦ Saving your Director movies as Shockwave enables them to be played on the Web with the help of a plug-in or ActiveX control.

✦ Flash movies are a way to enhance your Web pages with vector animations, interactivity, and streaming audio. Flash movies require the Flash player plug-in or ActiveX Control.

✦ Dreamweaver has built-in objects for both Director and Flash movies. All the important parameters are accessible directly through the Property Inspector.

✦ You need only three parameters to incorporate a Shockwave movie: the file's location, height, and width. Dreamweaver automatically imports a Flash movie's dimensions. You can get the exact measurements of a Shockwave movie from within Director.

✦ Dreamweaver comes with a JavaScript behavior for controlling Shockwave and Flash movies. This Control Shockwave or Flash behavior can be used as-is for adding external controls to the same Web page or — with a minor modification — for adding the controls to another frame in the same frameset.

✦ Dreamweaver behaviors can be triggered from a Shockwave or Flash movie.

✦ The JavaScript Integration Kit for Flash 5 is a powerful set of extensions that enable Flash movies to control Dreamweaver behaviors and for HTML elements to activate Flash movies.

In the next chapter, you begin to learn how to add video to your Web pages.

✦   ✦   ✦

Adding Video to Your Web Page

In a world accustomed to being entertained by moving images 50 feet high, it's hard to understand why people are thrilled to see a grainy, jerky, quarter-screen sized video on a Web page. And in truth, it's the promise of video on the Web, not the current state of it, that has folks excited. Many of the industry's major players, including Microsoft and Apple, are spending big bucks to bring that promise a little closer to reality.

QuickTime and RealVideo are the most popular formats on the Web, and both are cross-platform. Video can be downloaded to the user and then automatically played with a helper application, or it can be streamed to the user so that it plays while it's downloading.

This chapter looks at the many different methods for incorporating video — whether you're downloading an MPEG file or streaming a RealVideo movie — into your Web pages through Dreamweaver.

Video on the Web

It may be hard for folks not involved in the technology of computers and the Internet to understand why the high-tech Web doesn't always include something as "low-tech" as video. After all, television has been around forever, right? The difficulties arise from the fundamental difference between the two media: television and radio signals are analog, and computers are pure digital. Sure, you can convert an analog signal to a digital one — but that's just the beginning of the solution.

The amount of information stored on a regular (analog) VHS cassette is truly remarkable. Moving that amount of information about in the ones and zeros of the digital world is a formidable task. For example, storing the digital video stream from any digital video camcorder uses up storage space at the rate of about 1 gigabyte every five minutes, and that video is already compressed. Large file sizes also translate into enormous bandwidth problems when you are transmitting video over the Web.

To resolve this issue of megasized files, industry professionals and manufacturers have developed various strategies, or *architectures*, for the creation, storage, and playback of digital media. Each architecture has a different file format, and thus each requires the user to have a playback system — whether a plugin, ActiveX control, or Java applet — capable of handling that particular format.

In an effort to keep file sizes as small as possible, Web videos are often presented in very small dimensions. It's not uncommon to display a video at a puny 180 by 120 pixels. Furthermore, you'll notice a major difference between conventional and Web-based video in terms of quality. Television video displays at roughly 30 frames per second, film at 24 frames per second; but the best Web video rarely gets above 15 frames per second — virtually guaranteeing choppy motion in scenes with any action in them. Lossy compression also leads to *artifacting* — visible flaws introduced by the compression itself.

Given all the restrictions that video suffers on the Web, why use it at all? Simply because nothing else like it exists, and when you need video, you have to use video. Take heart, though. Advances are occurring at a rapid rate, both in the development of new video architectures and codecs and in new, higher-speed Internet delivery systems, such as cable modems and DSL phone lines. What you learn in this chapter enables you to include video in your Dreamweaver-built Web pages today and gives you a good foundation for accommodating future enhancements.

The Streaming Media Big Three

Technologies — and the companies that create them — come and go on the Internet. Over the past few years, quite a few different streaming media solutions have presented themselves and then faded away, leaving us with the current "Big Three": RealMedia, QuickTime, and Windows Media. These three technologies together represent almost the entire streaming media market, and the vast majority of Internet users have at least one of the corresponding players; many have two or even all three.

RealMedia

RealNetworks released the first streaming media system — RealAudio — in 1995. Over the years, RealAudio has evolved into RealMedia and now supports video, images, text, Flash movies, and standard audio types such as AIFF and MP3. All of these media types can be combined into a single presentation using SMIL (Synchronized Multimedia Integration Language).

The three primary software components of RealMedia are as follows:

✦ **RealPlayer:** The client software for viewing RealMedia. RealPlayer Basic is free, and RealPlayer Pro offers the user more features for $30. Either one can view all RealMedia content. A user who enjoys streaming media could quite easily browse the Web with RealPlayer 8 (see Figure 24-1) because its many Web links and ads, as well as the Flash navigation elements that often sur-round presentations, offer the user a lot of choices. RealPlayer 8 is available at `www.real.com/player`.

Figure 24-1: RealPlayer 8's busy interface enables the user to forego a Web browser completely when browsing for streaming media.

✦ **RealProducer:** Encoding software that turns standard MPEG and QuickTime Video into RealMedia files, which have the filename extension .rm. Again, you can pay for a free RealProducer Basic and an enhanced Pro version, available at `www.realnetworks.com/products/producer`.

✦ **RealServer:** Server software for serving RealMedia over RTSP (Real-Time Streaming Protocol). You can still offer RealMedia to your users over the Web's regular HTTP without any special server software. RealServer Basic is limited to 10 users; to upgrade from that, you pay by the number of users. It's available at `www.realnetworks.com/products/basicserverplus`.

RealNetworks has led the way in cross-platform authoring and playback. Versions of RealPlayer are available for Windows, Macintosh, Unix, Linux, and OS/2, and versions of RealProducer for almost as many platforms. WebTV even plays RealAudio 3.0. By contrast, QuickTime is limited to Windows and Macintosh, and Microsoft's streaming video solution is basically Windows-only.

RealNetworks has also led the way in sheer numbers of eyeballs; for years they were the only option for large-scale streaming media sites. Even now, when they face the stiffest competition they've ever had, their market share is still about 55 percent. RealPlayer is included with major browsers, as well as with Windows, Mac OS and Red Hat Linux.

Tip   See `www.real.com` for examples of RealMedia content.

QuickTime

What "QuickTime" refers to is widely misunderstood. Some people confuse the video format QuickTime Video with QuickTime itself, but QuickTime Video is just one of the things a QuickTime movie might contain. Sometimes the high-profile QuickTime Player 4 is confused with QuickTime, but it is just one dependent application.

The best way to explain QuickTime is to say that it's a multimedia operating system, enabling applications such as CD-ROM titles to run on top of it and use the features it provides. These features include support for audio, video, images, 3D objects, MIDI music (including a software wavetable synthesizer) and — with QuickTime 4 — streaming video, Flash movies, and MP3 audio. Once you have QuickTime 4 installed on your computer, suddenly Director can access digital video. Flash 4 can export complete QuickTime presentations, and otherwise pedestrian applications can suddenly play synthesized music.

With the inclusion of streaming video in QuickTime, Apple dressed up QuickTime 3's MoviePlayer with an eye-catching brushed aluminum look and changed its name to QuickTime Player 4. Apple positioned itself as a competitor to RealNetworks in the Web broadcasting field and now has almost 35 percent of the streaming market. QuickTime movies have a .mov filename extension.

Like RealMedia, QuickTime streaming has three main software components:

✦ **QuickTime and QuickTime Player:** All the viewing goodness of QuickTime and QuickTime Player (see Figure 24-2) is free and is available for Macintosh and Windows at `www.apple.com/quicktime`. QuickTime is also included with all Macintosh computers and installed on Windows by CD-ROM titles. Just as they can with RealPlayer, users can spend more time in QuickTime Player and less in a browser because of the favorites storage and Flash navigation elements in many streaming presentations.

Figure 24-2: QuickTime Player has an uncluttered appearance that focuses the eye on the content.

✦ **QuickTime Pro and QuickTime Player Pro:** For about $30, Apple sells you a key code that unlocks the content creation features of QuickTime and turns it into QuickTime Pro, enabling QuickTime-dependent applications to create a vast range of QuickTime content. QuickTime Player becomes QuickTime Player Pro: a great piece of software that provides easy content conversion and cut-and-paste video compositing, although the interface is spartan and sometimes hides functionality.

✦ **QuickTime Streaming Server:** QuickTime Streaming Server delivers video over the Web using the standard RTSP, just like RealPlayer. Apple released QuickTime Streaming Server as open source software, and it is available completely free — no per stream charge, either — for Mac OS X, Darwin, and Linux. See www.apple.com/quicktime/products/qtss.

Tip

Examples of QuickTime streaming content can be found on the QuickTime home page at www.apple.com/quicktime.

Windows Media

Microsoft has released a succession of media technologies over the years in an effort to gain some sort of foothold in content creation and delivery. The history of Microsoft multimedia is an incredible story of acquisitions, rebranding, orphaned technologies, and outright copying everybody else.

With Windows Media, however, Microsoft has gone all out, providing a solid — if unexciting — solution with lots of partners. Still, Windows Media's greatest asset is its automatic inclusion with every Windows PC, virtually guaranteeing it a huge installed base as time goes on. Windows Media files have filename extensions of .asf or .asx.

The software involved in Windows Media includes:

✦ **Windows Media Player:** The supercharged Windows Media Player (see Figure 24-3) received a complete face-lift for version 7 — and with the new change-able skins feature, it's quite the literal face-lift. In addition to Web streaming, the Windows Media Player accesses many other media types including audio CDs, Internet radio, and portable devices. Currently only an earlier version, 6.3, is supported on the Macintosh. The Windows Media Player home page is at `www.microsoft.com/windows/mediaplayer`.

Figure 24-3: The Windows Media Player offers instant access to many media types as well as switchable skins.

✦ **Content creation and server software:** A directory of tools for working with Windows Media can be found at `www.microsoft.com/windows/ windowsmedia`. Most are from Microsoft themselves, and all are Windows-only.

Tip The Windows Media home page is located at `www.windowsmedia.com` and includes example content.

Working with Video Clips

If you have short video clips you'd like to put on the Web, you may not need the industrial strength — or the hassle and expense — of a streaming media solution. Short video clips can be included in a Web page just by linking to them or embedding them.

Depending on the viewer's software setup, video clips either download completely and then start playing, start playing right away and stutter as they wait for data, or start playing as soon as enough of the video has arrived that uninterrupted playback is possible, as shown in Figure 24-4.

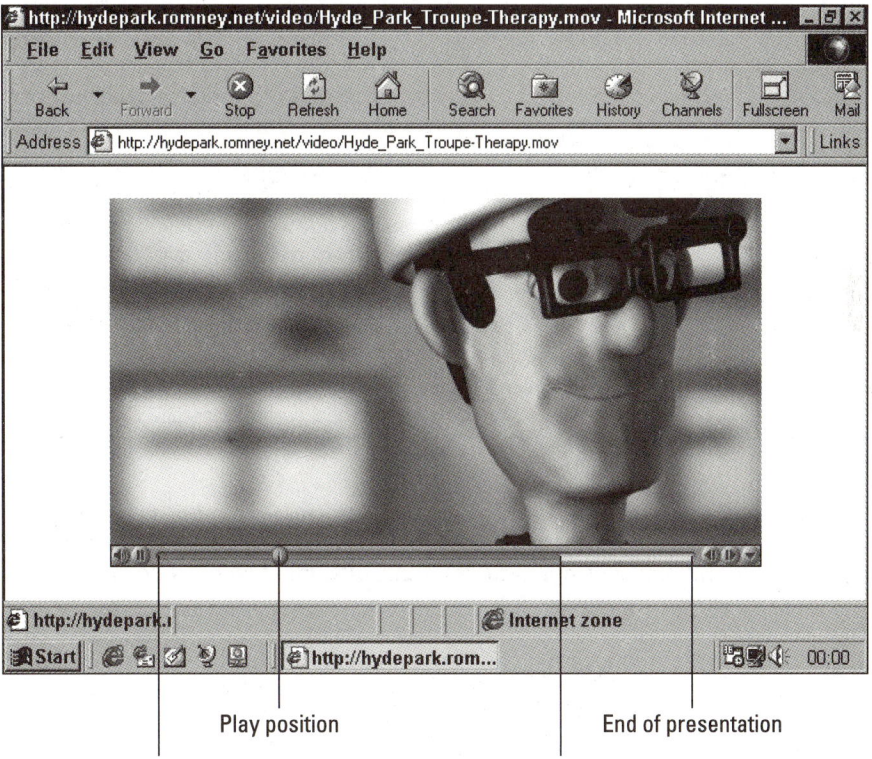

Figure 24-4: QuickTime Player starts playing video clips when it has downloaded enough that playback will be uninterrupted.

Video clips come in a few common formats, detailed in Table 24-1. In addition to the video format itself, what *codec* (en**co**der/**dec**oder) a particular video clip uses is also important. A codec provides video compression and is required for the decompression at playback time. Many codecs are included with Windows and with QuickTime, so codecs are not usually a problem, unless you're authoring for platforms other than Windows and Macintosh.

Table 24-1
Video Clip File Formats

Video Format	Typical Filename Extension	Description
MPEG	.mpg, .mpeg .mpe	The MPEG video format is the work of the Motion Picture Experts Group. Windows computers play MPEG video clips with Windows Media Player or another, older Microsoft player. Macintosh systems play MPEG clips with QuickTime.
QuickTime	.mov	QuickTime movies can contain a multitude of media types and usually require QuickTime for playback.
QuickTime Video	.mov	A QuickTime movie that contains plain video only, and can be played by almost any video player on a machine that doesn't have QuickTime installed, as long as the right codec is available.
Video for Windows (AVI)	.avi	The popular but now officially unsupported format used by Microsoft's Video for Windows (aka ActiveMovie, aka NetShow). As with QuickTime Video, clips can be played in almost any player, as long as the right codec is installed.

Caution   One codec to watch out for if you're making cross-platform movies is the Intel Indeo Video codec, sometimes used for Video for Windows (AVI) files. The Indeo codec for Macintosh is not included with QuickTime and must be installed manually by Macintosh users.

MPEG, QuickTime Video, or AVI clips are good candidates for linking or embedding due to the wide variety of players on multiple platforms that can play them. QuickTime movies are best aimed squarely at the QuickTime Player because of the multiple media types that they contain.

Linking to video

To include a video clip in your Dreamweaver Web page, follow these steps:

1. Select the text or image that you want to serve as the link to the video file.

Tip   If you use an image as a link, you might want to use a frame from the video clip in order to provide a preview.

2. In the Property Inspector, enter the name of the video file in the Link text box or select the folder icon to browse for the file.

3. Because video files can be quite large, it's also good practice to note the file size next to the link name or enter it in the Alt text box, as shown in Figure 24-5.

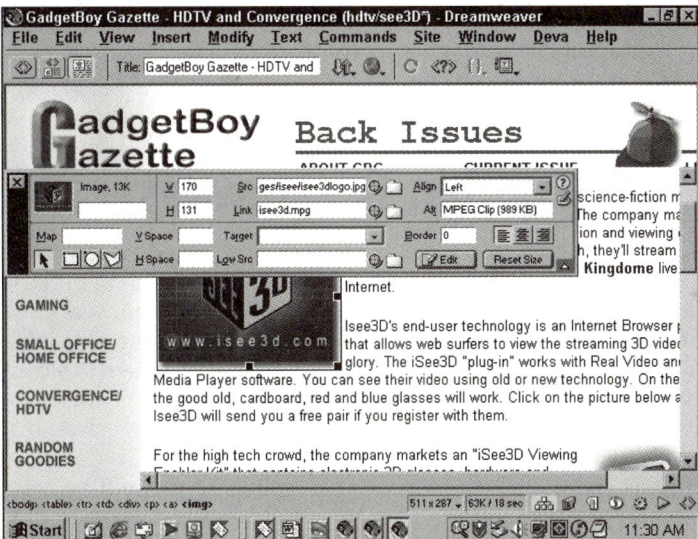

Figure 24-5: You can insert any video file for user download by creating a link to it, as if it were a simple Web page.

Embedding video

You can gain more control over the way your video clip plays by embedding it in the Web page with the `<embed>` tag. Modifying the attributes of the `<embed>` tag enables you to modify how the video is presented. Video clips inserted this way play back in whatever players are available, just as linked video clips do.

New Feature The new Assets panel includes a Movies category, which holds QuickTime movies, MPEG videos and Windows Media file types. As with all the other Assets panel categories, you must select the Refresh Site List button to initially populate the panel with all the movies in the current site. The preview pane includes a play button for reviewing the movies before they are inserted in the page.

To embed a simple video clip in a Web page, follow these steps:

1. Choose Insert ➪ Plugin or select the Plugin object from the Common pane of the Objects palette, or drag the file from the Movies category of the Assets panel to a location on your Web page.

2. If you inserted a Plugin object, enter the path to the video clip in the Plugin Src text box of the dialog box, or select the folder icon to browse for the file.

   Movies dragged onto the page from the Asset panel already include the source path. The plugin placeholder is displayed as a 32×32 icon.

3. In the Plugin Property Inspector, enter the dimensions of your video clip in the width and height boxes, marked W and H, respectively.

Playing Videos Within Dreamweaver

Dreamweaver can access and use Netscape plugins to display video right in the Document window at design-time. These plugins can be installed in Netscape's Plugins folder, in Internet Explorer's Plugins folder, or in Dreamweaver's own Plugins folder. Dreamweaver checks all three every time it starts up. Installing the correct plugins into Netscape and enabling Dreamweaver to use them from there can make maintaining your plugins easier because many come with browser-specific installation programs that are hard to adapt to Dreamweaver.

Whenever a file is embedded for playback via a plugin, a green Play button appears in the Property Inspector. To play a particular video in Dreamweaver's Document window, all you have to do is select the plugin placeholder and click the Play button. The video begins playing, and the green Play button, shown in Figure 24-6, becomes a red Stop button. To stop playback—surprise—just click the Stop button.

Tip How can playing a video during the design phase be useful? I've used this capability to sample the background color of the page from the background of a video's title or ending frame so that the video clip fits seamlessly into the page.

You can also use the menus and the corresponding keyboard shortcuts to control the digital video in the Document window: View ➪ Plugins ➪ Play or Ctrl+Alt+P (Command+Option+P), and View ➪ Plugins ➪ Stop or Ctrl+Alt+X (Command+Option+X). If you have multiple videos inserted on the page, you can play them all by choosing View ➪ Plugins ➪ Play All or by using the keyboard shortcut Ctrl+Alt+Shift+P (Command+Option+Shift+P), and stop them with View ➪ Plugins ➪ Stop All or Ctrl+Alt+Shift+X (Command+Option+Shift+X).

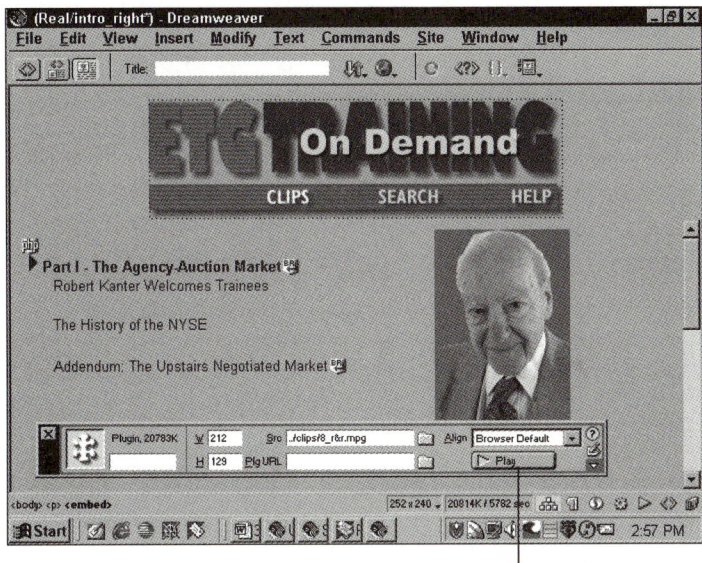

Play/Stop button

Figure 24-6: Playing video within Dreamweaver is as simple as having the right plugin installed and clicking Play.

Caution

Unsupported plugins are listed in the UnsupportedPlugins.txt file in Dreamweaver's Configuration folder. The one plugin identified by Macromedia as not working with Dreamweaver is the Video for Windows plugin on Windows. If you're relying on this plugin for video playback, you still have to preview your video files through a browser.

Inserting QuickTime Movies

The HTML command for incorporating a QuickTime movie (or any other media that requires a plugin) is the <embed> tag. Because so many different types of plugins exist, Dreamweaver uses a generic Plugin Inspector that enables an unlimited number of parameters to be specified. If you regularly work with QuickTime movies, a custom QuickTime Dreamweaver object such as the one from Brendan Dawes (available on the CD-ROM that comes with this book) in Figure 24-7 can streamline the process. Although you still need to add some parameters by hand, having easy access to the most common ones can be a real time-saver.

On the CD-ROM

You can find Brendan Dawes' QuickTime 4 object in a folder on the CD-ROM that accompanies this book. Copy the folder to your own Objects folder and restart Dreamweaver.

Figure 24-7: Add a third-party QuickTime object to Dreamweaver to simplify embedding QuickTime movies.

Only three <embed> tag parameters are absolutely required for a QuickTime movie: the source of the file, the movie's width, and the movie's height, but the QuickTime plugin also offers an amazing array of additional <embed> tag attributes to enable you to fine-tune the way content is presented.

Note   The QuickTime Plugin is used by both Netscape and Internet Explorer on both Windows and Macintosh to enable the browser to interface with QuickTime.

To insert a QuickTime movie in your Web page, follow these steps:

1. First, insert the Plugin object. Choose Insert ⇨ Plugin or select the Plugin object from the Common pane of the Objects palette, or drag the Plugin object to a location on your Web page.

2. In the Insert Plugin dialog box, enter the QuickTime movie's path and filename in the Plugin Source text box, or select the folder to browse for the file.

Tip   If you're working on a Macintosh and your QuickTime movie doesn't have a file-name extension, add **.mov** to the end of its name before embedding it or placing it on the Web.

3. In the Plugin Property Inspector (see Figure 24-8), enter the width and height values in the W and H text boxes, respectively. Alternatively, you can drag any of the sizing handles on the Plugin placeholder in the Document window to a new size.

Width box

Height box   Plug-in Source text box

Figure 24-8: When inserting a QuickTime movie, specify the properties and values in the Plugin Property Inspector.

Tip

If you don't know the dimensions of your QuickTime movie, open it in the QuickTime Player and choose Movie ⇨ Get Info and select Size from the options list on the right of the dialog box that appears.

4. In the Plg URL text box, enter `www.apple.com/quicktime`. This is the Web address that users who don't have QuickTime are directed to by their browser.

5. Select the Parameters button to open the Parameters dialog box, where you can enter additional `<embed>` tag attributes. Enter the attribute name in the left column and the value in the right column. Press Tab to move from one column to another. Table 24-2 describes the available parameters for a QuickTime movie. Add any additional parameters that you may require and click OK when you're done.

Table 24-2
QuickTime 4 Plugin Parameters

QuickTime Plugin Parameter	Possible Values	Description
autoplay	true (the default) or false	When set to false, a movie won't play until the user presses play in the controller. Otherwise, it starts playing as soon as enough data is downloaded to ensure uninterrupted playback.
bgcolor	RGB colors in hexadecimal such as "#FFFFFF", or valid HTML color names, such as "red"	Sets the color of the space set aside by the width and height attributes but not taken up by the QuickTime movie. Add a border to a QuickTime movie by setting the appropriate bgcolor and increasing the width and height attributes by a few pixels.
cache	true (the default) or false	Specifies whether the browser should store the movie in its cache for later retrieval. Doesn't work in IE.
controller	true (default for most movies) or false (the default for Flash only or QuickTime VR movies)	Displays the controller panel attached to the bottom of the movie.
dontflatten whensaving	Does not take a value. Include the parameter only.	When included, saving the movie using the Save As QuickTime option on the QuickTime Plugin's controller menu saves the movie without resolving references (not self-contained).
endtime	30 frame SMPTE timecode (hours:minutes :seconds:thirtieths of a second)	Indicates the point in the movie at which playback should stop.
height	A value in pixels; usually the height of the movie	Reserves a space in the page for the QuickTime movie.
hidden	Does not take a value; include the parameter only	Tells the QuickTime Plugin not to show the movie. Audio is played, though.

QuickTime Plugin Parameter	Possible Values	Description
`href`	A URL	A link to go to when the movie is clicked. You can supply either an absolute or a relative URL. QuickTime movies replace the current movie in-place; Web pages open in the browser.
`kioskmode`	true and false (the default)	Eliminates the QuickTime Plugin's controller menu when set to true.
`loop`	true, false (the default), or palindrome	Causes the movie to loop continuously when set to true. The palindrome value causes the QuickTime Player to play alternately forward and backward.
`movieid`	A number	A number identifying the movie so another wired sprite movie can control it.
`moviename`	A number	A name identifying the movie so another wired sprite movie can control it.
`playeveryframe`	true and false (the default)	When set to true, forces the movie to play every frame, even if it must do so at a slower rate than real time. Disables audio and QuickTime Music tracks.
`pluginspage`	`www.apple.com/ quicktime`	Where users who don't have QuickTime should be sent to get it.
`qtnext{n}`	A URL	Specifies a movie as being {n} in a sequence of movies. The movie specified in the `src` attribute is movie zero.
`qtnext`	goto{n}	Tells the QuickTime Plugin to open movie {n} in an already specified sequence of movies.
`qtsrc`	A URL	Tells the QuickTime Plugin to open this URL instead of the one specified by the `src` attribute. A way to open files that don't have a .mov filename extension — such as MP3 files — with the QuickTime Plugin, regardless of how the user's system is set up. Use a dummy movie in the `src` attribute.
`qtsrcchokespeed`	movierate, or a number in bytes per second	Downloads the movie specified in the `qtsrc` attribute in chunks; movierate indicates to use the movie's data rate.

Continued

Table 24-2 *(continued)*		
QuickTime Plugin Parameter	**Possible Values**	**Description**
scale	tofit, aspect, or a number (default is 1)	Resizes the QuickTime Player movie. By setting scale as tofit, you can scale the movie to the dimensions of the embedded box as specified by the height and width values. Setting scale to aspect resizes the movie to either the height or the width while maintaining the proper aspect ratio of the movie. Set to a number, the size of the movie is multiplied by that number.
starttime	30 frame SMPTE timecode (hours:minutes:seconds: thirtieths of a second)	Indicates the point in the movie at which playback should start.
target	_self, _parent, _top, _blank, a frame or window name or QuickTimePlayer	Enables the link specified in the href attribute to be targeted to a specific frame or window. The value QuickTimePlayer causes the movie specified in the href attribute to be opened in the QuickTime Player.
targetcache	true (the default) or false	Same as the cache attribute but for the movie called by a poster movie using the href attribute.
volume	0 to 256 (the default)	Controls the volume of the audio track(s). Zero is softest; 256 is loudest.
width	A value in pixels; usually the width of the movie	Reserves a space in the page for the QuickTime movie.

Tip   Dreamweaver's Plugin Property Inspector also enables you to enter several other attributes generally used with other objects, such as images. These include Align (alignment), V Space (vertical space), H Space (horizontal space), and Border (border). You can also enter a name in the Plugin text box if you plan on referring to your QuickTime movie in a JavaScript or other program.

QuickTime versions

Before inserting a QuickTime movie into a Web page, it's helpful to know what version of QuickTime your movie requires. Because QuickTime movies can contain a variety of track types, each containing a different type of media, some movies may play back with QuickTime 3, while others require QuickTime 4.

You can identify the different tracks in a QuickTime movie by opening it in QuickTime Player and choosing Movie ⇨ Get Info. In the dialog box that appears, the options list on the left details the various tracks, as shown in Figure 24-9. If your movie has Flash or MP3 audio tracks, it requires QuickTime 4 for playback. It's a good idea to note this somewhere in your Web page and offer users a link to www.apple.com/quicktime so that they can upgrade if necessary.

Figure 24-9: In addition to the Video track, this QuickTime movie also has a (MIDI) Music track, a Flash track that provides the opening titles and closing credits, and an MP3 audio Sound track.

Playing QuickTime VR

QuickTime VR (QTVR) enables the user to "look around" in a virtual space created from a panoramic image or to rotate an object around its center point in three dimensions ("object movies"). The QuickTime VR author can also designate certain areas in the movie as hotspots that, when selected by the user, activate a link to another page or another movie. Although purists argue that QTVR is not really virtual reality, the technology is a low-bandwidth quick-and-dirty virtual reality that makes sense on today's Web. QTVR is commonly used to show homes, cars, and other products to potential buyers.

QuickTime VR movies open in their own special QuickTime Player window, shown in Figure 24-10. Instead of the more familiar brushed aluminum and round buttons, the QTVR controller has zoom and pan buttons.

Figure 24-10: QuickTime VR's panoramic views enable the user to look around in a panoramic picture by moving the cursor right, left, up, and down.

QuickTime VR <embed> tag attributes are entered in the same manner as other QuickTime Plugin attributes: Click the Parameters button in the Plugin Property Inspector to open the Parameters dialog box (see Figure 24-11) and enter attributes and values. As with a regular QuickTime Player movie, the only required parameters for a QTVR movie are the source file, movie width, and movie height.

Figure 24-11: Use the Plugin Parameters dialog box to enter attributes for any plugin. This example is for a QuickTime VR movie.

Using a Poster Movie

One of the nicest features of the QuickTime Plugin is the capability to have one movie replace itself with another. This enables you to place very lightweight (low file size), single-image "poster movies" into your Web pages instead of the full clips, so that the rest of the elements in your page load quickly. When the user clicks a poster movie, it replaces itself with your full movie, which begins downloading or streaming immediately. A poster movie can be a preview of the full movie that replaces it or a generic QuickTime image. It's possible to use poster movies to place a number of movies in a single page, enabling the user to pick and choose which ones to view without downloading the rest, as in the following figure.

Creating a poster movie requires QuickTime Pro. Simply open your movie in QuickTime Player Pro, move to the frame you'd like to use as a preview and choose File ⇨ Export and select Movie to Picture from the Export options list and Photo-JPEG from the Use options list. This exports the current frame as a QuickTime Image using JPEG compression. Choose File ⇨ New Player to create a new untitled movie and then File ⇨ Import to import your picture into this new movie. Save your work as a self-contained movie. A good idea for a filename might be the name of your full movie with "poster" prefixed.

Embed your poster movie in your Web page as discussed previously in this chapter and use the Plugin Property Inspector's Parameters button to add the href attribute with the value set to the URL of your full movie, so that the <embed> tag looks like this:

```
<embed src="my_poster_movie.mov" width="360" height="180" ¬
href="my_full_movie.mov"></embed>
```

You can also make multiple frame poster movies if you like. As long as you keep the file size low, your pages will seem to load more quickly, and you'll provide your users more control over the way they experience them.

Table 24-3 details QuickTime Plugin <embed> tag attributes that work with QuickTime VR only.

Table 24-3 Additional Parameters for QuickTime VR Movies		
QuickTime VR Parameter	**Possible Values**	**Description**
correction	none, partial, or full (the default)	Applies the correction filter.
fov	0 (the default) to 360	Specifies the initial field-of-view angle, in degrees.
hotspot(n)	A URL	Defines the URL for any designated hotspot. Replace *n* with the identification number given to the hotspot during QTVR authoring.
node	A number less than or equal to the number of nodes in the movie	Specifies which node of a multinode movie is opened first.
pan	0 (the default) to 360	Sets the initial pan angle, in degrees.
target(n)	_self, _parent, _top, _blank, a frame, or window name	Targets the URL of the similarly numbered hotspot at a specific frame or window.
tilt	−42.5 to 42.5 (0 is the default)	Sets the initial tilt angle, in degrees.

Caution Some parameters meaningful to regular QuickTime Player movies are not appropriate for QuickTime VR movies. These include autoplay, controller, hidden, href, loop, playeveryframe, target, and volume.

Streaming with RealMedia

If you've ever downloaded a few minutes of digital video over a slow modem connection, you know the reason why streaming video was invented. In an age when immediacy rules, waiting until the complete video file is transferred and then loaded into the video player can seem to last an eternity. *Streaming*, on the other hand, enables the multimedia content to begin playing as soon as the first complete packet of information is received, and then to continue playing as more digital information arrives. Video is just one form of media to get the streaming treatment: You can also stream audio, animation, text, and other formats.

Regardless of which streaming video protocol you use, the procedure for incorporating the file on your Web page is basically the same, although the details (such as filename extensions) differ. In order to demonstrate the general technique and still offer some specific information you can use, the next section details how to include streaming RealMedia clips with Dreamweaver. Check with the developer of the streaming video format you plan to use to get the precise installation details. Typically, lots of information is available for free on the developers' Web sites.

A RealMedia example

When incorporating RealMedia into your Web pages, you have a variety of playback options. You can set the video so that a free-floating RealPlayer is invoked, or you can specify that the video appears inline on your Web page. You can also customize the controls that appear on your Web page so that only the ones you want — at the size you want — are included.

Tip   Dreamweaver includes a full set of Real media objects — collectively called *RealSystem G2 objects* — that were developed in partnership with RealNetworks. You can find instructions for using these Dreamweaver extensions later in this chapter.

Creating RealMedia metafiles

RealMedia uses its own specialized server software called RealServer to transmit encoded video files. Rather than call this server and the digital video file directly, RealMedia uses a system of *metafiles* to link to the RealMedia server and file. A metafile is an ordinary text file containing the appropriate URL pointing to the RealServer and video file.

The metafiles are distinguished from the media files by their filename extensions:

✦ RealMedia files: .rm, .ra, .rp, .rt, .swf

✦ Metafile that launches the independent RealPlayer: .ram

✦ Metafile that launches the RealPlayer plugin: .rpm

To create the metafile, open your favorite text editor and insert one or more lines pointing to your server and the video files. Instead of using the `http://` locator seen with most URLs, RealMedia files address the RealServer with an `rtsp://` (Real-Time Streaming Protocol) indicator. The contents of the file should take the following form:

```
rtsp://hostname/path/file
```

where *hostname* is the domain name of the server where the RealMedia files are stored, *path* is the path to the file, and *file* is the name of the RealMedia file. For example, to display a training video, the metafile contents might look like the following:

```
rtsp://www.trainers.com/videos/training01.rm
```

You can include multiple video clips by putting each one on its own line, separated by a single return. RealMedia plays each clip in succession, and the user can skip from one clip to another.

Inserting RealMedia in your Web page

Once you've created both the encoded RealMedia file and the metafiles, you're ready to insert them into your Web page. You have two basic techniques for including RealMedia: as a link and using the `<embed>` tag.

Using a link

Generally, if you want to invoke the free-floating RealPlayer, you use a link; the `href` attribute is set to an address for a metafile, like this:

```
<a href="videos/howto01.ram">Demonstration</a>
```

When the link is selected, it calls the metafile that, in turn, calls the video file on the RealServer. As the file begins to download to the user's system, the RealPlayer program is invoked and starts to display the video as soon as possible through the independent video window, as shown in Figure 24-12. The link can be inserted in Dreamweaver through either the Text or Image Property Inspector.

Figure 24-12: You can set up your RealMedia clip so that it plays in its own RealPlayer window. This is RealPlayer's "Compact" view (compare to Figure 24-1).

Using <embed>

If, on the other hand, you'd like to make the video appear inline with the Web page's text or graphics, you use Dreamweaver's Plugin object to insert an `<embed>` tag. Position the pointer where you want the RealMedia to be displayed, and either choose Insert ⇨ Plugin or select Insert Plugin from the Objects palette. After the

Insert Plugin dialog box appears, enter the path and filename for the video's metafile in the Plugin Source text box.

When the Plugin object representing the RealMedia clip is selected, you can enter values for the <embed> tag in the Property Inspector. The only attributes required for a RealMedia clip, as with the QuickTime Player object, are the file source and the width and height of the movie. And, as you can with QuickTime Player, you can choose from a healthy number of attributes to control your RealMedia movie. Enter attributes by selecting the Parameters button on the Plugin Inspector and entering attributes and their values in the Parameters dialog box (shown earlier in Figure 24-11).

RealMedia attributes are listed in Table 24-4.

Table 24-4 **Parameters for RealMedia Movies**		
RealMedia G2 Parameter	**_Possible Values_**	**_Description_**
Autostart	true (the default) or false	Tells RealPlayer to start playing as soon as content is available.
Console	{name}, _master, _unique	Determines the console name for each control in a Web page that has multiple controls. Force controls on a page to refer to the same file by giving them all the same name. A value of _master links to all controls on a page, whereas _unique connects to no other instances.
Controls	all, controlpanel, imagewindow, infovolumepanel, infopanel, playbutton, positionslider, positionfield, statuspanel, statusbar, stopbutton, statusfield, volumeslider	Enables the placement of individual control panel elements in the Web page. You can use multiple controls in one attribute or multiple <embed> tags to build a custom RealMedia interface.
nolabels	true or false (the default)	Suppresses the Title, Author, and Copyright labels in the Status panel. If you set nolabels to true, the actual data is still visible.

Using the RealSystem G2 Objects for Dreamweaver

Macromedia has partnered with RealNetworks to provide a full set of objects to ease the implementation of RealMedia in Dreamweaver. The RealSystem G2 Objects for Dreamweaver include drop-in objects for RealAudio, RealVideo, RealPix,

RealText, RealFlash, and SMIL presentations. You can also find an array of control panel options for building your own interfaces.

Note   Find the RealSystem G2 Objects for Dreamweaver at www.macromedia.com/software/dreamweaver/download/extensions/obj_05.html.

Installing RealSystem G2 objects

The RealSystem G2 objects need to be installed before they can be used. Naturally, you need the RealPlayer G2 version 6 or above on your system as well. To install the objects, follow these steps:

Tip   Making a backup copy of your Dreamweaver 4/Configuration folder before using an installer to add extensions helps to guard against accidentally losing custom menu settings or other unforeseen problems.

1. Decompress your RealSystem G2 objects installer (if it isn't already) using one of the following methods:

   • On Windows, open the g2_obj.zip file using WinZip or a similar unzipping utility.

   • On Macintosh systems, use Stuffit Expander or a similar program to open the realg2.sit.hqx file.

HTTP Streaming

To gain the maximum throughput of your RealVideo files, it's best to use the RealServer software. However, you occasionally encounter Web site clients who must economize and can't afford the specialized server. Not widely known is the fact that you can use a regular World Wide Web server to stream RealVideo and other RealMedia files over HTTP.

Two prerequisites exist for HTTP streaming: Your system administrator must first correctly configure the MIME types, and you must provide multiple files to match the right user-selectable modem speeds. The proper MIME types are as follows:

✦ audio/x-pn-RealAudio (for .ra, .rm, or .ram files)

✦ audio/x-pn-RealAudio-plugin (for .rpm files)

✦ video/x-pn-RealVideo (for .ra, .rm, or .ram files)

✦ video/x-pn-RealVideo-plugin (for .rpm files)

RealServer automatically selects the right file for the user's modem connection. If you are using HTTP streaming capabilities, you should offer multiple files to accommodate the various modem connection rates, such as 28.8K and 56K.

Other than a reduction in download speed, the other disadvantage to using HTTP streaming over RealServer streaming is the reduced number of simultaneous users who can be served. RealServer can handle hundreds of connections at the same time; HTTP streaming is far more limited.

2. Run the setup program (setup.exe for Windows and RealSystem G2 Objects Installer for Macintosh) and follow the onscreen instructions.

Caution

The RealSystem G2 objects were originally developed for Dreamweaver 2. The Windows Installer complains that it can't find Dreamweaver and offers you a path of C:\Program Files\Dreamweaver 2. Use the Browse button to choose your Dreamweaver 4 folder. The Macintosh Installer says it will install into your Dreamweaver 2 folder but will find Dreamweaver wherever it is. If you have multiple copies and/or versions of Dreamweaver, the installer asks you to pick one.

3. Restart Dreamweaver.

A RealSystem G2 pane has been added to the Objects palette. Objects exist for six media types, including RealVideo, and seven control panel options. You may need to expand or scroll the Objects palette to see buttons for all the objects.

You can also use the RealSystem G2 objects to build your own interface that incorporates parts of the standard control panel. A separate control panel element works with any file or other element with the same console name. For example, if you have two RealVideo files on your Web page, you could have separate Play buttons (each pointing to a different console value, say video1 and video2), while having one volume slider controlling all sound with the console name _master. Table 24-5 displays the various control options available to all RealSystem G2 objects.

	Table 24-5	
	RealSystem G2 Control Options	
Icon	**G2 Object**	**Description**
	Insert Full Controls	Shows the Control panel, Information and Volume panel, and the status bar.
	Insert Control Panel	Shows the Play/Pause button, the Stop button, Fast Forward and Rewind controls, and the position slider.
	Insert Play Button	Shows the Play and Pause buttons.
	Insert Stop Button	Shows only the Stop button.
	Insert Volume Slider	Shows the vertical volume control slider.
	Insert Status Panel	Shows the Status panel, which displays messages, current place in the presentation timeline, and total clip length.
	Insert InfoVolumePanel Control	Shows the title, author, and copyright information panel, as well as the volume slider.

Inserting a RealVideo object

With the RealVideo object, all you need to know is the name of your source file and its dimensions — all the other factors are handled for you. The RealVideo object inserts a combination of tags to call both an ActiveX control and a plugin so that the file can be played with both Internet Explorer and Netscape Navigator. You can also add new parameters after the object has been inserted through the Property Inspector's Parameters button.

To insert a RealVideo object, follow these steps:

1. Choose Insert ➪ RealSystem G2 Object ➪ RealVideo or select the Insert RealVideo button from the RealSystem G2 panel of the Objects palette.

    The Insert RealVideo dialog box (shown in Figure 24-13) opens.

Figure 24-13: The RealVideo object makes inserting streaming video a simple process.

2. Enter the source file by choosing one of the following radio buttons:

    • **Local File:** Enter the path name of a file found on the local system in the Local File text box or choose the Browse (Choose) button to locate the file.

    • **URL:** Enter the absolute address of a file located on the Internet in the URL text box. The example address, `rtsp://g2home.real.com/install/welcome.rm`, is displayed beneath the URL text box.

3. Enter the dimensions of the RealVideo movie in the Width and Height text boxes.

   The default measurements of 192 pixels wide by 112 pixels high are suggestions only and do not necessarily reflect the accurate size of your file.

4. If you don't want your file to begin playing automatically, deselect the Autostart option.

5. The remaining text boxes, Region name, Metafile, and SMIL file, are automatically filled out. Alter any name by entering the modification in the text box.

6. Click OK when you're done.

Note   The RealVideo object creates both a metafile and a SMIL presentation file. When selected by the user to play (or when playing automatically), the original file first calls the metafile, which in turn calls the SMIL file. For this reason, if you ever need to change the source of the original file, you have to open and edit the referenced SMIL file—or delete the RealVideo object and reinsert it with the new filename.

By default, the RealVideo object is inserted with the controls set to the ImageWindow option, which shows only the RealVideo movie with no control panel. To incorporate a control panel into the video file, you need to first choose the Edit Parameters button from the Property Inspector. Next, change the controls attribute from imagewindow to one of the other options, such as All, ControlPanel, or PlayButton.

Cross-Reference   The RealAudio object is covered in Chapter 25.

Summary

Digital video on the Web is in its infancy. Bandwidth is still too tight to enable full-screen, full-motion movies, no matter what the format. However, you can include downloadable as well as streaming video content through Dreamweaver's Plugin object and Plugin Inspector. In this chapter, you learned:

✦ Even with compression, digital video has steep storage and download requirements.

✦ You can include a digital video movie to be downloaded in your Web page by linking to it as if it were a Web page.

✦ Use Dreamweaver's Plugin object when you want your video to be presented inline on your Web page. The Plugin Property Inspector then enables you to alter the video's parameters for any video architecture.

✦ QuickTime is a cross-platform multimedia architecture that offers much more than just video. QuickTime movies can include QuickTime VR, MIDI music, 3D objects, Flash movies, and more.

✦ To enable your visitors to view your digital video clips as soon as possible, use a streaming video technology such as RealMedia, QuickTime, or Windows Media. Streaming video files can be displayed in a separate player or embedded in the Web page.

In the next chapter, you learn how Dreamweaver helps you incorporate sound and music into your Web pages.

✦   ✦   ✦

Using Audio on Your Web Page

Web sites tend to be divided into two categories: those totally without sound, and those that use a lot of it — there's not much middle ground. Many music and entertainment sites rely heavily on both streaming audio and downloadable audio files such as MP3.

In this chapter, you learn how to use audio in the Web pages you design with Dreamweaver. We look at traditional digital audio formats such as AIFF and WAV, and how you can turn these into files suitable for publishing on the Web, in formats such as MP3 and RealAudio. We also look at music formats such as Standard MIDI files and QuickTime Music.

Lest we forget that we're Dreamweaving here, we look at some Dreamweaver extensions you can use to get audio-enabled sites up and running in no time. But before we leap into those deep waters, let's get an overview of digital audio and its place on the Web.

Cross-Reference Because the primary technologies for distributing streaming audio are also the primary technologies for streaming video, you may find it helpful to familiarize yourself with the Big Three streaming media technologies — RealMedia, QuickTime, and Windows Media — introduced in Chapter 24.

Digital Audio Fundamentals

Digital audio files are digitized representations of sound waves. While not as heavy as digital video, digital audio files — even those that have been compressed — are still a strain for today's Web. As usual, minimizing file sizes wherever possible makes for a better experience for users of your Web site.

File formats

Many different formats for digital audio files are in use today across the various computer platforms. The most common formats are described in Table 25-1 and can be identified by their unique filename extensions and/or by their icons on Macintosh systems.

	Table 25-1	
	Web Digital Audio File Formats	
Audio Format	**Typical File Name Extension**	**Description**
AU	.au, .snd	Very common on the early Unix-dominated Web. Uncompressed and no longer suitable for Web use.
AIFF	.aif, .aiff	Apple developed the Audio Interchange File Format. Uncompressed versions can be played in most browsers, but using AIFF on the Web should be avoided when possible.
Flash	.swf	Not just an animation format, Flash streams PCM- or MP3-compressed audio at various bit rates.
MP3	.mp3, .mp2	The MPEG Audio Layer 3 format features high-quality digital audio files with excellent compression. MP3 has become the standard for downloadable music. It plays in QuickTime Player 4+, RealPlayer G2 6+, Windows Media Player 5.2+, and a whole range of standalone players that work as browser helper apps.
QuickTime	.mov	A QuickTime movie with a soundtrack only.
RealAudio	.ra or .ram	The audio component of RealNetworks' RealMedia. Lots of players. Good quality at low bit rates, but not as good as MP3.
Rich Music Format	.rmf	Beatnik's hybrid audio/music format. Samples are either PCM or MP3 compressed.
Shockwave Audio	.swa	The audio component of Shockwave, they're low bit rate MP3 files with a different file header. They stream over HTTP, and any MP3 player can play them locally.
WAV	.wav	Codeveloped by Microsoft and IBM, the default audio format for Windows. Uncompressed versions play in browsers, but their use on the Web should be avoided whenever possible.
Windows Media	.asf, asx, .wma, .wmv	Microsoft's streaming media solution.

Which audio format should you choose? That depends on a combination of factors, including your target audience, available bandwidth, and the purpose of the audio's content.

Although most browsers can play standard digital audio files such as AIFF and WAV, the sheer uncompressed bulk of these files makes them unsuitable for the Internet, now that so many highly compressed formats exist. In the early days of the Web, with slower computers and less advanced compression technologies, these uncompressed audio files were the only game in town. But today, fast computers are capable of easily decoding MP3 and RealAudio, and free players for those formats are common.

A live Internet broadcast dictates a streaming solution such as RealAudio, QuickTime, or Windows Media. If you're offering complete songs for download, you may not have to look any further than MP3. It's not uncommon to offer a sound file in multiple formats. Although many users have more than one player, offering your audio in a few formats gives you a better chance of reaching everybody.

Converting one audio file format to another typically involves opening the source file in an audio editor that can read the format and exporting it in another format. If you lack a professional audio editor such as SoundForge or Peak, a simple alternative is to use QuickTime Pro; it reads and writes a lot of formats. You can also easily cut and paste sections of files, to remove or add a few seconds of silence, for example.

Making audio files lighter

As well as categorizing by file format, we can also think of audio on the Web as being in one of two categories: uncompressed and compressed.

Uncompressed files

AIFF and WAV audio files come in compressed and uncompressed formats, but only the uncompressed versions play in Web browsers. If you can't compress an audio file in some way, the only way to lower its file size is to lower its quality in one of three ways:

✦ **Convert a stereo file into a mono file:** A stereo file has two audio channels, while a mono file has only one. Converting a stereo file to mono halves its file size.

✦ **Lower the bit depth:** A lower bit depth — for example, from 16-bit to 8-bit — reduces the accuracy of the stored audio waveforms.

✦ **Lower the sample rate:** From 44 kHz to 22 kHz, for example. This lowers the range of audio frequencies in the recording, chopping off the "high end" or treble frequencies.

You can make the preceding conversions by opening the audio file in an application such as QuickTime Player Pro and exporting the file with new properties, as shown in Figure 25-1.

Figure 25-1: Exporting an AIFF as a WAV in QuickTime Player Pro. Converting stereo to mono, 16-bit to 8-bit, and lowering the sample rate from 44.1 kHz to 8 kHz lowers the file size but drastically lowers the quality.

Compressed files

Network-ready audio file types that were specifically created for the Internet, such as MP3 and RealAudio, are compressed through encoding. Rather than arbitrarily lowering the quality of the file to make it lighter, you pick a target bit rate, as in Figure 25-2, and the encoding software produces the best quality file it can at that bit rate. If you've ever exported a JPEG graphic from an image editor and specified a target file size, the principle is the same.

When working with a compressed audio format, you ideally start with the best "master copy" that you have in an uncompressed format, such as AIFF, and then encode that audio file as MP3 or RealAudio. If you want your audio to move quickly, even over dial-up connections, choose a low bit rate such as 24 Kbps.

Caution Always keep a master copy of your audio file when you're encoding. Encoding a file is often a "lossy" compression; in other words, information is thrown away in order to create smaller files. Although you can convert an MP3 to an AIFF, it will not be the same quality as the original AIFF that the MP3 was made from. The process is similar to converting a TIFF to a JPEG, rather than zipping and unzipping files.

Figure 25-2: Choosing a 32-Kbps bit rate when exporting an AIFF as an MP3 from QuickTime Player Pro with the Terran Interactive MP3 Plugin

Music Files

In the 19th century, before the technology to electronically record audio existed, a musical performance could be "recorded" by making a series of stipples on a cylinder. The performance could then be played "live" for the listener through a music box. Later, player pianos used rolls of paper with appropriate holes punched in them to cause the piano keys to mimic the performances of far away or long dead musicians. In the early 1980s, electronic musical instrument manufacturers created MIDI (Musical Instrument Digital Interface) to enable the keys of one electronic keyboard to trigger the sounds in another. It wasn't long before somebody realized that the MIDI information that all electronic keyboards were putting out could be recorded and could thus turn any electronic instrument into a modern-day music box or player piano.

The key to using music files on the Web is their very small file size. A music file is the ultimate in compressed sound: the musical instruments aren't even included! For example, a three-minute, full-fidelity, 128 bps stereo MP3 file would weigh in at just under 3MB. A QuickTime movie that only contains a music track could give you ten minutes of music for 60K and have similar fidelity, although you're limited to the sounds contained in the QuickTime synthesizer, of course.

Today, music files appear on the Web in one of three ways:

✦ **QuickTime Music:** MIDI information is stored as a music track within a QuickTime movie, and it is played back through the QuickTime software synthesizer (or through a hardware synthesizer such as a sound card if the user has configured QuickTime to use one). The QuickTime synthesizer sounds have often been criticized for being a little bland. Music tracks can coexist with all other kinds of QuickTime media in one movie, so they make excellent soundtracks for digital video tracks. QuickTime movies have a filename extension of .mov.

✦ **Rich Music Format:** Beatnik's hybrid audio/music format. MIDI information is played through the Beatnik player's software synthesizer, which contains generally excellent and often original sounds. Additionally, further instrument sounds can be included in an RMF by adding digital audio samples with the Beatnik Editor for Macintosh. RMF files are unique among music file formats in that the user cannot get the raw MIDI data out of them. Some content authors see this is as an advantage. RMF files have an .rmf file name extension.

✦ **Standard MIDI files:** This is the "raw data" of MIDI music files. The biggest downside is that the Web author has absolutely no idea what kind of synthesizer the user will use to play back a MIDI file. On older Windows machines, this synthesizer may not even include actual instrument sounds, but instead use FM synthesis to come up with very poor approximations. Standard MIDI files have a filename extension of .mid, .midi, or .smf.

Occasionally, you may want to render a music file as a digital audio file, in order to play it in a situation where a synthesizer is unavailable. Doing this the hard way involves playing the file through a synthesizer and recording the output to a digital audio file. You have an easier way, however, if you have QuickTime Player Pro. Open your QuickTime Music or import your Standard MIDI file into QuickTime Player Pro and then choose File ⇨ Export and specify Music to AIFF. QuickTime Player Pro creates a digital audio file of its "performance" of the music using the QuickTime software synthesizer. You can also convert a QuickTime Music track back into a Standard MIDI file. Choose Music to Standard MIDI when you export.

Caution   RMF files are designed to disallow this conversion. Always keep the original Standard MIDI file when you create an RMF.

MP3 Mini-Primer

The MP3 audio format has quite simply taken the Web — and the world — by storm. While other downloadable music formats come with caveats such as ownership by one company or built-in limitations on how users can use the files they purchase, MP3 just did the work and got the job done. MP3 software players are common. A range of manufacturers offers MP3 hardware, such as home, car, and personal stereos.

Tip
MP3.com remains the one-stop place for information about MP3. Visit `www.mp3.com`.

Generally, the MP3 "scene" has shown interest in new and/or unusual artists, offered a selection of dynamic, full-featured players (see Figure 25-3), and maintained an attitude of music appreciation. Conversely, non-MP3 downloadable music has generally featured bland players, corporate music, proprietary technologies, and an unhealthy fascination with watermarking and controlling content. It's not hard to see why the market chose MP3.

Winamp (Windows)   Audion (Macintosh)

Figure 25-3: Many standalone MP3 players feature dynamic looks that can even be changed by applying a new "skin."

Player support

Table 25-2 lists common MP3 player software — including old friends like RealPlayer that now handle MP3 — and the URLs where they can be found. Many of these applications offer to set themselves up as browser helper applications. You might feature some of these links at the bottom of pages with MP3 content, so users who are new to MP3 can get a leg up.

Table 25-2 Common MP3 Players	
Player Software	**URL**
Audion (Mac only)	`www.panic.com/ppack/audion`
QuickTime Player 4+	`www.apple.com/quicktime`

Continued

Table 25-2 *(continued)*	
Player Software	**URL**
RealJukebox	`www.real.com/jukeboxplus`
RealPlayer G2 6.0+	`www.real.com/player`
SoundJam MP (Mac only)	`www.soundjam.com`
Winamp (Windows only)	`www.winamp.com`
Windows Media Player 5.2+	`www.microsoft.com/windows/` `windowsmedia/en/download`

Note   Providing users with a link to MP3.com is another way to offer them a great selection of players.

Encoding MP3

The most common MP3 files are downloadable music files. These files aim for "CD quality" and so are recorded with a bit rate of 128 Kbps. This works out to a little less than one megabyte per minute for a stereo, 44.1 kHz file, which is too heavy to move quickly for non-broadband users on today's Web. You can encode an MP3 using a variety of bit rates, though. Lower bit rates mean lower quality, but even at 16 Kbps, speech sounds pretty good, and the 60K per minute bulk of a mono file will be music to your ears.

Caution   Beware of MP3 encoders that sacrifice quality for speed. Many encoders simply throw out the upper audio frequency range so that they can encode the rest in record time. While this might be fine if you're encoding your CD collection into a massive jukebox on your computer, it is less than ideal for content creators who want the best quality encoded files.

Linking to Audio Files

The simplest way to add sound to a Web page is to create a link to an audio file. You enter the path to your audio file in the Link text box in the Text or Image Property Inspector, or select the folder icon to browse for the file. When the user clicks that link, the sound file downloads, and whatever program has been designated to handle that type of file opens in a separate window. The exception to this is the QuickTime Plugin. Instead of opening linked audio files in the QuickTime Player, it opens them within the browser window, as if they were a new Web page. To get back to your Web page, the user clicks the browser's Back button.

Netscape Navigator 4.*x*'s LiveAudio player is the only major audio player that does not yet support MP3, but Netscape has also shipped with RealPlayer G2 for quite some time now, which does play MP3, as shown in Figure 25-4.

Figure 25-4: A link to an MP3 file in this Web page downloaded and then opened the file in RealPlayer, which was specified as a helper application for MP3 files.

To create a link to an audio file in Dreamweaver, follow these steps:

1. Select the text or image that you want to serve as the link to the audio file.

2. In the Property Inspector, enter the name of the audio file in the Link text box, or select the folder icon to browse for the file.

3. Because audio files can be large, it's good practice to note the file size next to the link name or enter it in the Alt text box for your image.

When you use the link technique for incorporating sound, you have no control over the position or appearance of the player. However, you can control these factors and more by embedding your audio.

Embedding Sounds and Music

Embedding a sound file truly integrates the audio into your Web page. Embedding the sound files also gives you a much higher degree of control over the presentation of the audio player itself, including the following:

✦ The clip's play volume

✦ Which part, if any, of the player's controls is visible

✦ The starting and ending points of the music clip

As with any other embedded object, you can present the visual display inline with other text elements — aligned to the top, middle, or bottom of the text, or blocked left or right to enable text to flow around it. Dreamweaver controls all of these parameters through two different objects: the Plugin object and the ActiveX object. Each type of object calls a specific type of player. For example, the default Plugin object calls the LiveAudio Plugin in a Netscape browser and the Windows Media Player control in Internet Explorer. Calling the Windows Media Player as an ActiveX object explicitly enables you to modify a great number of parameters for Internet Explorer — which are completely ignored by Navigator. You learn all of your embedding options, including techniques for cross-browser audio, in the next few sections.

Note Unfortunately, the Assets panel does not include a Sound or Audio category. You'll have to continue inserting audio elements via the Insert Plugin object.

As with the basic video file, Dreamweaver uses the generic Plugin object to embed audio in your Web page. The object requires only three parameters: the source of the audio file, the width and the height of the object. To embed an audio file in your Web page, follow these steps in Dreamweaver:

1. Position the cursor where you want the control panel for the audio file to appear.

2. Insert the Plugin object by choosing Insert ⇨ Media ⇨ Plugin or by selecting the Plugin object from the Special category of the Objects panel.

3. In the Select File dialog box that appears, choose the audio file.

4. Use either of the following techniques to size the Plugin placeholder:

   • Enter the appropriate values in the W (Width) and the H (Height) text boxes of the Property Inspector.

   • Or click the resizing handles on the Plugin placeholder and drag it out to a new size.

For a default audio Plugin, use a width of 144 pixels and a height of 60 pixels. These dimensions are slightly larger than necessary for Internet Explorer's audio controls, as shown in Figure 25-5, but they fit Navigator's controls perfectly, and the control panel does not appear to be "clipped" when viewed through any browser.

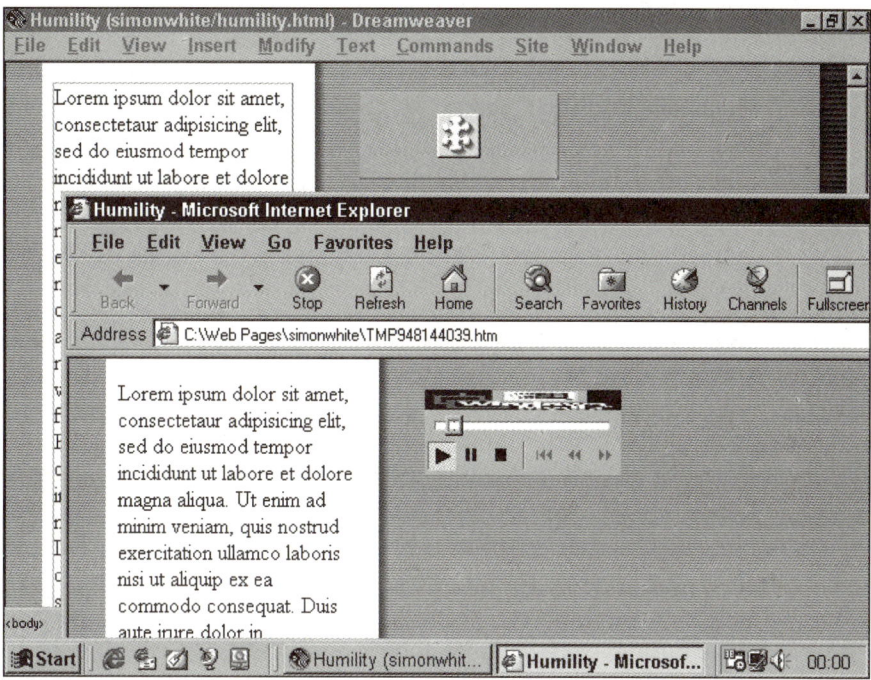

Figure 25-5: Windows Media Player needs less space than Netscape's LiveAudio for its controls, so it fills the rest with a crushed version of its logo.

When the Plugin object is inserted, Dreamweaver displays the generic Plugin placeholder.

Playing Background Music

Background music, played while the user is viewing online material, is one of the Web's hidden treasures. When used tastefully, background music can enhance the overall impact of the page.

Making a regular embedded sound into a background sound is as simple as adding a few parameters to the embed tag: hidden tells the browser not to display any controls, autostart tells it to start playback automatically, and loop tells it to play the audio continuously. Although you can add these attributes to the embed tag manually in Code View, or in the Code Inspector, it's easier to add them using the Parameters button of the embed tag Property Inspector.

Follow these steps to embed background music in a Web page:

1. Position the cursor near the top of your Web page. Choose Insert ⇨ Media ⇨ Plugin or select the Plugin object from the Special category of the Objects panel.

2. Enter the path to your audio file in the Plugin Source text box or select Browse to locate the file.

3. In the Property Inspector, enter **2** in both the H (Height) and W (Width) text boxes.

Note

Entering a width and height attribute is necessary for compatibility with older browsers.

4. Click Parameters.

5. In the Parameters dialog box, select the add (+) button and enter **hidden** in the Parameter column. Press Tab and enter **true** in the Value column.

6. Enter autostart as the next parameter and give it the value **true**.

7. To make the audio clip repeat, enter **loop** as the next parameter, and in the Value column, enter the number of times you want the sound to repeat. To make the audio repeat indefinitely, enter **true** as the value.

8. Click OK to finish.

Targeting Specific Plugins

You can exercise a much finer degree of control of the audio in your pages by calling specific Plugins. The trade-off, unfortunately, is that by designating a Plugin, you reduce the size of your potential audience. Some Plugins are specific to a browser or browser version. Moreover, Plugins that aren't distributed with the major browsers face an uphill battle in terms of market penetration. If you use a Plugin, you can always expect some folks to be resistant to downloading the necessary software. Before you incorporate any Plugin, you must weigh these issues against your overall design plan.

Tip

A great number of audio Plugins are available and offer a broad variety of functionality and features. A good place to see a list of those available is the Plugin Plaza (`browserwatch.internet.com/plugin.html`). In addition to offering complete descriptions, this site also has links directly to the download areas.

Windows Media Player audio

The Windows Media Player is Internet Explorer's multimedia player. As such, you can use it to play the standard audio formats, including MP3, WAV, AIFF, AU, or MIDI files. In fact, when you add an audio file as a link, or embed it without any other specifications, Internet Explorer automatically calls Windows Media Player to play the file. Calling Windows Media Player directly as an ActiveX control, however, gives you far more flexibility over the player's appearance and functionality.

 If you're unfamiliar with ActiveX Controls, you might want to look over the section "Incorporating an ActiveX Control" in Chapter 17 before proceeding.

Calling the Windows Media Player ActiveX control

To incorporate the Windows Media Player ActiveX control, follow these steps:

1. Position the cursor where you would like the Windows Media Player control panel to appear. Choose Insert ⇨ Media ⇨ ActiveX or select Insert ActiveX from the Special category of the Objects panel.

   The Property Inspector displays the ActiveX options.

2. In the ClassID text box, enter the ID for the Windows Media Player control: **CLSID:22d6f312-b0f6-11d0-94ab-0080c74c7e95**.

 If you've entered this long Windows Media Player class ID previously, you can click the arrow button and choose the ID from the drop-down list.

3. Change the width and height values in the W and H text boxes to match the desired control display.

   The Windows Media Player display resizes to match your dimensions as closely as possible.

4. Click Parameters in the Property Inspector.

5. Select the add (+) button and enter the first parameter: `FileName`. Press Tab to move to the Value column.

6. Enter the path and filename for your audio file. Press Tab.

7. Continue entering the desired parameters and values for your audio file.

8. Click OK when you're finished.

The Windows Media Player ActiveX Control has many parameters to choose from — 34, to be exact. Explaining all of these parameters is beyond the scope of this book, but Table 25-3 lists the key parameters that parallel the LiveAudio attributes.

	Table 25-3	
	Windows Media Player Parameters	
WMP Parameter	**Possible Values**	**Description**
AutoStart	true (default) or false	Determines if the sound begins playing when the download is complete.
FileName	Any valid URL	Specifies the sound file to be played.
PlayCount	Any integer	Sets the number of times the file should repeat. If the value is 0, the sound loops continuously. The default is 1.
SelectionStart	Number of seconds	Determines the beginning point for the audio clip, relative to the start of the file.
SelectionEnd	Number of seconds	Determines the ending point for the audio clip, relative to the start of the file.
ShowControls	true or false (default)	Hides the control panel if set to true.
ShowDisplay	true or false (default)	Hides the display panel if set to true.
Volume	Any integer, from 10,000 to 0 (the default).	Sets the loudness of the audio.

Caution   Windows Media Player's default volume setting is 0, but this is the highest setting, not the lowest setting. Specifying a higher number for the volume parameter lowers the volume of the sound.

Using Embed with ActiveX

All ActiveX controls are included in HTML's <object>...</object> tag pair. Dreamweaver codes this for you when you insert any ActiveX control. Netscape doesn't recognize the <object> tag, and Internet Explorer doesn't recognize the <embed> tag when it's within an <object> tag, so it's possible to target both browsers with one <object> and <embed> pair.

After you've entered the FileName parameter and value for the Windows Media Player ActiveX Control, select the Embed checkbox in the Property Inspector. The same name that you specified as the FileName now appears in the Embed text box. Dreamweaver takes advantage of the fact that Netscape doesn't recognize the <object> tag by inserting the <embed> tag inside the <object>...</object> tag pair. The resulting HTML looks like the following:

```
<object width="200" height="18" classid="CLSID:05589FA1-C356-11CE-BF01-¬
00AA0055595A" border="2">
 <param name="FileName" value="images/BrazMIDI file">
 <param name="ShowDisplay" value="False">
```

```
<embed width="200" height="18" border="2" filename="images/BrazMIDI¬
file" showdisplay="False" src="images/BrazMIDI file"></embed>
</object>
```

Note that Dreamweaver picks up the attributes and parameters from the ActiveX control to use in the `<embed>` tag. You often have to adjust these, especially when specifying a narrow ActiveX control and a taller Netscape object.

Using Netscape's LiveAudio Plugin

LiveAudio is Netscape's default audio player and is used when you do basic embedding of an audio file, as well as when you attach a sound file to a URL. Both of these methods of incorporating audio, however, barely scratch the surface of what LiveAudio is capable of doing. LiveAudio uses up to 13 different parameters to shape its appearance and functionality in the Web page, and also accepts a full range of JavaScript commands.

To take advantage of LiveAudio's full capabilities, you must enter the audio file's parameters and values through Dreamweaver's Property Inspector. Follow these steps to specify the parameters for your Plugin object:

1. Insert the Plugin object — either by choosing Insert ⇨ Media ⇨ Plugin or by dragging the Plugin object from the Special Category of the Objects panel to a place on your Web page.

2. From the extended Property Inspector, select Parameters.

   The Parameter dialog box is displayed with its two columns: Parameter and Value.

3. Click in the Parameter column and type in the first parameter. Press Tab to move to the Value column and enter the desired value. Press Tab again to move to the next parameter.

   • Press Shift+Tab if you need to move backwards through the list.

   • To delete a parameter, highlight it and select the minus (–) button at the top of the parameters list.

   • To add a new parameter, select the plus (+) button to move to the first blank line and press Tab to move to the next parameter.

   • To move a parameter from one position in the list to another, highlight it and select the up or down arrow buttons at the top of the parameters list.

   For most Plugins, including LiveAudio, the order of the parameters is irrelevant.

4. Repeat Step 3 until all parameters are entered.

5. Click OK when you're done.

The parameters for LiveAudio affect either the look of the player or the qualities of the sound. The main parameter for altering the player's appearance is `controls`. Depending on the value used, you can display the default control panel, a smaller version, or individual controls.

You can embed individual controls anywhere on your Web page. To link the various controls, you use the `mastersound` keyword in each `<embed>` statement and set the name parameter to one unique value for all files. Finally, set the source in one `<embed>` tag to the actual sound file, and the other sources in the other files to a dummy file called a *stub* file.

Table 25-4 contains all the parameters available for LiveAudio, except those set by Dreamweaver's Property Inspector (source, height, width, and alignment).

Table 25-4
LiveAudio Parameters

Parameter	Acceptable Values	Description
autostart	true or false (default)	If autostart is set to true, the audio file begins playing as soon as the download is completed.
controls	console (default), smallconsole, playbutton, pausebutton, stopbutton, or volumelever	Sets the sound control to appear.
endtime	minutes:seconds; for example, 00:00	Determines the point in the sound clip at which the audio stops playing.
hidden	true	Expressly hides all the audio controls; sound plays in the background.
loop	true, false, or an integer	Setting loop to true forces the sound file to repeat continuously until the Stop button is selected or the user goes to another page. To set the number of times the sound repeats, set loop equal to an integer. The default is false.
mastersound	None	Enables several `<embed>` tags to be grouped and controlled as one. Used in conjunction with the name attribute.
name	A unique name	Links various `<embed>` tags in a file to control them as one. Used in conjunction with the `<mastersound>` attribute.

Parameter	Acceptable Values	Description
`starttime`	minutes:seconds; for example, 00:00	Determines the point in the sound clip at which the audio begins playing.
`volume`	1 to 100	Sets the loudness of the audio clip on a scale from 1 to 100 percent.

Installing Streaming Audio

Although audio files are not as time consuming as video, downloading them can take a long time. Audio-on-demand — or *streaming audio* — is an alternative to such lengthy downloads.

Streaming audio files have a lot in common with streaming video files, as covered in Chapter 24.

For streaming audio, you have the same Big Three choices as with streaming video — RealMedia, QuickTime, and Windows Media — plus Shockwave streaming audio and Flash movies.

Shockwave and Flash are covered in Chapter 23.

Using the RealAudio object

Embedding a streaming audio file has been greatly simplified with the introduction of the RealAudio object. As with RealVideo, you can have the RealAudio player appear either free-floating or embedded in the Web page. Embedding a RealAudio file is explained in the next section. To insert a RealAudio streaming audio file with a free-floating player, follow these steps:

1. Select the link or image that you want to use to begin the RealAudio file.

2. In the Property Inspector, enter the path to the RealAudio metafile in the Link text box or select Browse to locate the file.

Make sure that the metafile has the .ram extension.

To learn how to install the RealSystem G2 objects (and attach individual controls), see Chapter 24.

After you've installed the RealSystem G2 objects, you can insert the RealAudio object in one of two ways. You can choose Insert ⇨ RealAudio, or you can select the Insert RealAudio object from the RealSystem G2 category of the Objects panel. Once you've inserted the object, the Insert RealAudio dialog box appears, as shown in Figure 25-6. All you need to do is to enter the path to the streaming audio file either in the Local File text box or in the URL text box; be sure to select the appropriate radio buttons for your choice. After you click OK, the object verifies the creation of two additional support files, the metafile and the SMIL file, and your file is ready to stream.

Figure 25-6: The Insert RealAudio object, part of the RealSystem G2 object set, makes embedding a streaming file into your Web page a snap.

Accessing RealAudio parameters

Only the source of the player and the dimensions are required, but it probably comes as no surprise to you that a great number of attributes are available for a RealAudio file. You can add any of the attributes found in Table 25-5 through the Parameters button of the selected RealAudio file's Property Inspector.

<table>
<tr><td colspan="3" align="center">Table 25-5
RealAudio Parameters</td></tr>
<tr><td>***RealPlayer Attribute***</td><td>***Possible Values***</td><td>***Description***</td></tr>
<tr><td>autostart</td><td>true (the default) or false</td><td>Enables the RealAudio clip to start playing as soon as content is available.</td></tr>
<tr><td>console</td><td>_master or _unique</td><td>Determines the console name for each control in a Web page that uses multiple controls. To force controls on a page to refer to the same file, use the same console=name attribute. The console name _master links to all controls on a page; _unique connects to no other instances.</td></tr>
</table>

RealPlayer Attribute	Possible Values	Description
controls	all, controlpanel, infovolumepanel,	infopanel, statuspanel, statusbar, playbutton, stopbutton, volumeslider, positionslider, positionfield, or statusfield Enables the placement of individual control panel elements in the Web page. You can use multiple controls in one attribute, or multiple <embed> tags to build a custom RealAudio interface.
nolabels	true or false (the default)	Suppresses the Title, Author, and Copyright labels in the Status panel. If you set nolabels to true, the actual data is still visible.

Sonifying with the Beatnik ActionSet Pro

While other technologies enable you to use the Web to download or listen to audio, Beatnik is focused solely on making interactive audio part of the Web itself. The Beatnik player links directly with JavaScript to enable a Web author to "sonify" almost any element within a Web page. Add sounds to rollover buttons, form elements, or add tasteful background music to heighten the immersive experience. Because the Beatnik player contains many built-in sounds — called "Groovoids" — the user doesn't need to download anything to hear audio immediately.

The best part of Beatnik for a Dreamweaver user is the free Beatnik ActionSet Pro, a comprehensive collection of Dreamweaver behaviors — 48 in all — that makes sonifying a Web site a point-and-click affair.

 Note Beatnik now offers the Beatnik ActionSet Pro 1.2 for free at www.beatnik.com.

The only downside to Beatnik is that it is subject to the problems inherent in using browser Plugins. Your audience has to have the Beatnik Plugin (or ActiveX Control) installed before it can experience the RMF and Groovoid sounds. The Beatnik player is included with all Intel Pentium III machines, though, and installs automatically on Internet Explorer 4 or above for Windows and on Netscape Navigator 4 or above.

 Tip Beatnik is nothing if not well documented. Comprehensive help files, instructional examples, and user forums are available on the Beatnik Web site. If you want to go further with Beatnik than this chapter takes you, check out www.beatnik.com.

Making RMFs

Beatnik's proprietary audio format is Rich Music Format (RMF) files. RMF files can contain digital audio or MIDI data, or a mixture of the two. MIDI data is played back through the Beatnik player's built-in synthesizer, providing consistent fidelity for every user. Digital audio can be MP3 encoded to minimize file size.

You don't have to make your own RMF files to sonify a page — the Beatnik player's built-in sounds are excellent in their own right — but if you want to, Beatnik offers the free Beatnik Converter for Windows and Beatnik Editor for Macintosh. Either one can turn any standard audio format or MIDI file into an RMF. The Macintosh version can also integrate with other music and audio software through Open Music System (OMS), the standard MIDI communication system on the Macintosh. Both tools also come in reasonably priced Pro versions that add MP3 compression features.

Installing the Beatnik ActionSet Pro

Before you can use the Beatnik ActionSet Pro in Dreamweaver, you have to install it. Follow these steps:

1. Close Dreamweaver if it is running.

2. Double-click the installer file to begin the installation process.

> **Note** The Beatnik ActionSet Pro installers contain a license that says "Beatnik ActionSet Lite" instead of "Beatnik ActionSet Pro," which seems to be a simple mistake and should not affect the installation.

3. Follow the onscreen instructions. On Windows, you are prompted to browse to and select your Dreamweaver installation folder. On Macintosh, the installer finds Dreamweaver for you but asks you to confirm which copy of Dreamweaver you want the installer to target if you have multiple copies or versions.

   When the installation is complete, the documentation for the Beatnik ActionSet Pro automatically opens in your system browser. On Windows, an entry is added to the Add/Remove Programs panel to make uninstallation easier. On Macintosh, the Beatnik Installer leaves a standard installer log called "Beatnik ActionSet Installer Log" in the root folder of your startup drive. It details the names and locations of the files it has installed.

4. When you're ready to begin investigating the Beatnik ActionSet Pro, start Dreamweaver.

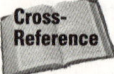

> **Cross-Reference** If you've never worked with behaviors before, you might want to review Chapter 19 before proceeding.

Using the Beatnik ActionSet Pro

As befits a revolutionary technology, the Beatnik ActionSet Pro must be used with special care. While it's still possible to use the <embed> tag to insert Beatnik RMF files as detailed later in this chapter, the Beatnik ActionSet Pro works in a significantly different fashion. Following are the key points:

✦ **Players:** Beatnik, unlike many other Web audio technologies, is capable of playing eight different audio files simultaneously, which is what has enabled it to become so popular for remixing songs in a Web page. When the Beatnik ActionSet is initialized, the eight different voices are established, although one is reserved to play musical notes. Many of the Beatnik behaviors enable you to assign a specific player or use the next available player. Unless you wish to exercise ongoing control over a specific voice, it's generally best to choose the available player option.

✦ **Interface:** Under the new Beatnik ActionSet philosophy, you won't find a series of control panels from which to choose — in fact, you won't find one. Rather than hard-code a VCR-like panel into the system, all Beatnik audio events occur via user interaction, using either a custom interface or no interface whatsoever. While this may seem daunting at first, it actually gives the Web designer tremendous freedom and works effectively to better integrate the sound design into the page.

✦ **Settings:** Adding music to the Web page often requires much fine-tuning and trial-and-error. The Beatnik ActionSet includes a series of settings that recognize this real-world requirement. At the least, you'll find Default Settings for using preset configurations, Previously Used Settings from your last configuration, and New Settings, which reflect the latest modifications. You can switch back and forth between these settings to find exactly the right sound.

Initializing a page

Each of the behaviors in the Beatnik ActionSet Pro uses a JavaScript library found in the file beatnik-actionset.js as well as a dummy music file stub.rmf. In order to use any of the behaviors, a page must first be initialized and these files located. To simplify this task, Beatnik includes a special behavior, the Beatnik ActionSet Setup.

To initialize a page for Beatnik behaviors, follow these steps:

1. Select the <body> tag from the Tag Selector in the status bar.

2. Open the Behaviors panel by choosing Window ➪ Behaviors or selecting the Show Behaviors button from either Launcher.

3. Click the add behavior button (the + sign) and choose Beatnik ActionSet Setup from the drop-down list.

The Beatnik ActionSet Setup dialog box opens, as shown in Figure 25-7.

Figure 25-7: You must initialize your Web page with the Beatnik ActionSet Setup before you can use any of the Beatnik behaviors.

4. Enter the path to the beatnik-actionset.js file in the appropriate text box or select the Locate button to browse for the file.

   Initially, the beatnik-actionset.js file is located in the Configuration\ Behaviors\Help\Beatnik-ActionSet\javascript folder. It's good practice to copy the file to the local root folder of your working site and assign that file in the Setup behavior. Keeping it in the local root folder makes it easier to upload when publishing the page.

5. Next, enter the path to the stub.rmf file in the text box or select the Locate button to browse for the file.

   You'll find a copy of the stub.rmf file in the Configuration\Behaviors\Help\ BeatnikActionSet\music folder. Again, it's a good idea to copy this file to your working site directory and choose that file in the Beatnik Setup.

6. Click OK when you're done.

Caution   Should you ever relocate a page that has been Beatnik-initialized, Beatnik (the company) recommends that you use Dreamweaver's advanced Find and Replace features to update the pages with the new location for these two files. Currently, it's not possible to delete and reapply the Setup behavior.

Adding Groovoids

As mentioned earlier, Groovoids are short musical riffs and sound effects intended to add an interactive sound dimension to your Web page. The Beatnik player includes 72 such samples in five categories: User Interface, Hits, Fanfare, Background, and Miscellaneous. Groovoids are used in two different ways:

✦ As a repeating background theme, generally begun when the page is loading

✦ As an interactive audio cue based on a user's actions and attached to a specific button or link

The Beatnik ActionSet has a section devoted to Groovoids with three behaviors:

✦ **Play Groovoid:** Starts a specified Groovoid when triggered.

✦ **Pause Groovoid:** Pauses or restarts a Groovoid. The pause can incorporate a fade of user-definable length.

✦ **Stop Groovoid:** Stops the specified Groovoid from playing; the Stop action can also fade out.

To insert a Play Groovoid behavior, follow these steps:

1. Set up the Web page as outlined in the section "Initializing a Page," earlier in this chapter, if you've not done so already.

2. Select the tag you'd like to attach the Play Groovoid behavior to.

3. From the Behaviors panel, choose Beatnik ➪ Groovoid ➪ Play Groovoid.

   The Play Groovoid dialog box opens, as shown in Figure 25-8.

Figure 25-8: Use the Play Groovoid behavior to insert ongoing background music or short user-interface sounds.

4. If desired, enter a unique player name in the Target Player text box. Generally, Groovoids use the [available player] setting.

5. Select the looping option. Choose Yes to cause the Groovoid to repeat, No for it to play once, and Auto for automatic looping. Under the Auto setting, background music loops, and user interface selections do not.

6. Choose the Groovoid Name from the drop-down list. The Groovoids are grouped by category.

7. Select the Volume from the drop-down list, where 100 is the loudest and 0 is mute.

8. To return to the original settings, choose Default Settings from the Presets option box. If you are editing a behavior, you can choose Previous Settings to return to your prior options or New Settings to display the latest changes.

9. Click OK when you're done.

Because of the ongoing nature of the Groovoid background music, it is sometimes helpful to pause the audio. The Pause Groovoid behavior enables you to stop and restart the music from where it stopped. Applying a second Pause Groovoid behavior causes the music to restart, as can triggering the behavior again. Moreover, you can fade the music out and back in again. Naturally, a Groovoid must be playing before it can be paused.

To insert a Pause Groovoid behavior, follow these steps:

1. Select the tag to which you'd like to attach the Pause Groovoid behavior.

2. From the Behaviors panel, choose Beatnik ➪ Groovoid ➪ Pause Groovoid.

   The Pause Groovoid dialog box opens.

3. Enter the Target Player in the text box, if specified earlier. Otherwise, leave Target Player with its default setting [matching Groovoid].

4. Select the name of the Groovoid you wish to pause.

5. If desired, enter the fade out/fade in time in the Fade Time text box, in milliseconds.

   You can use the VCR-like controls to choose a Fade Time. The Go To Beginning, Fast Reverse, and Reverse buttons decrement your value (0, –1,000, and –100, respectively), while the Play button increases it 100 milliseconds; the Fast Forward button, 1,000 milliseconds; and the Go to End button, 100,000 milliseconds (100 seconds or 1.6 minutes).

6. Click OK when you're done.

The Stop Groovoid behavior is structured exactly like Pause Groovoid and is implemented in the same fashion.

Playing Beatnik music

While Groovoids are great for providing aural feedback or "canned" background music, you can't use them to play user-designated music files. Beatnik supports Rich Music Format (.rmf) and MIDI files (.mid, .midi, and .smf). Unlike Groovoids, these file types have to be completely downloaded before they can begin playing on the user's system. To prevent unwanted delays in playback, Beatnik includes a Preload behavior.

In all, the Beatnik ActionSet provides four commands for working with music files:

✦ **Play Music File:** Starts the selected file to play. The file can also be designated as looping or nonlooping.

✦ **Pause Music File:** Pauses and restarts the selected file with or without fades.

✦ **Stop Music File:** Stops the music from playing with or without a fade.

✦ **Preload Music File:** Loads the selected file into memory before it begins to play.

All of the behaviors function in a similar fashion. Like the Groovoids, a Target Player is chosen initially; however, in the case of music files, it is often better to designate a Target Player, rather than leave the default selection of [available player]. By designating a Target Player, you reserve one of the eight voices for the particular file and are assured of uninterrupted play. You can also adjust the parameters of the music file while it is playing by referring to the Target Player in another behavior.

To use the Play Music File behavior, follow these steps:

1. Set up the Web page as outlined in the section "Initializing a Page," earlier in this chapter, if you've not done so already.

2. Select the tag to which you'd like to attach the Play Music File behavior.

3. From the Behaviors panel, choose Beatnik ➪ Music File ➪ Play Music File.

   The Play Music File dialog box opens, as shown in Figure 25-9.

4. If desired, enter a unique player name in the Target Player text box. Otherwise, leave the default [available player] setting.

5. To cause a file to play repeatedly, change the Looping option to Yes.

6. Enter the path to the music file in the File URL text box or use the Browse (Choose) button to the right of the text box to locate the file.

7. Select the loudness setting for the file from the Volume option box, where 100 is the loudest and 0 is mute.

Tip   The mute or zero setting should be chosen only if you intend to fade up the music at a later time.

Figure 25-9: Start any RMF or MIDI file through the Play Music File behavior.

8. You can inspect previous configurations by choosing one of the Preset options: Default Settings, Previous Settings, or New Settings.

9. Click OK when you're finished.

The Pause Music File and Stop Music File are used in exactly the same manner as Pause Groovoid and Stop Groovoid. If you've given the music file a unique Target Player name, use that in the Pause and Stop Music File behaviors. If, on the other hand, you left the Target Player at the [available player] setting, choose [matching file] for Target Player and enter the file's path in the File URL text box.

Hitting all the notes

If you're a musician first and a Web designer second, you'll appreciate the total control Beatnik gives you over music. Beatnik has a fully functional built-in software synthesizer that is capable of playing notes over the 16 MIDI channels using any one of over 500 instruments. Moreover, you can alter the velocity, duration or sustain, volume, and pan settings of any note.

Tip   You can easily play chords by assigning multiple Play Musical Note behaviors to a single tag and event. Just change the note settings while maintaining the same instrument in all behaviors. Of course, you could also have multiple instruments playing the same note as well.

Only two behaviors are in this category: Play Musical Note and Stop Musical Note. All settings are established in the Play Musical Note dialog box, shown in Figure 25-10. Generally, it's best to leave the Target Player setting at its default [reserved player] setting, although you can also specify a player already declared for a Groovoid or music file. You cannot enter a new, previously unused value. Likewise, leaving the Channel Number parameter set to [auto] enables the Beatnik Music Management System to handle note assignment. Change this setting to a specific MIDI channel only if you want to halt its playing with the Stop Musical Note behavior at some point.

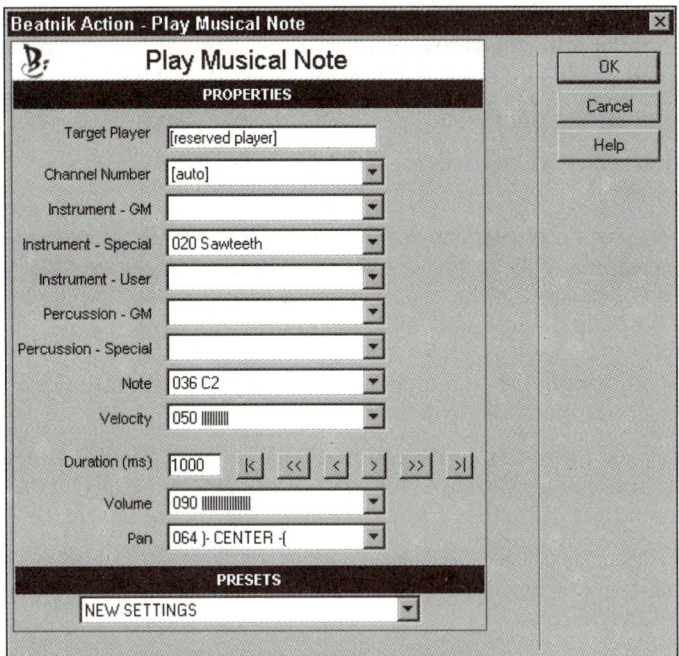

Figure 25-10: Choose from more than 500 musical MIDI instruments to play any of 128 notes over a ten-octave range with the Play Musical Note behavior.

To assign a Play Musical Note behavior, follow these steps:

1. Set up the Web page as outlined in the section "Initializing a Page," earlier in this chapter, if you've not done so already.

2. Select the tag to which you'd like to attach the Play Musical Note behavior.

3. From the Behaviors panel, choose Beatnik ⇨ Musical Note ⇨ Play Musical Note.

   The Play Musical Note dialog box opens.

4. Enter a unique name in Target Player text box, if desired. Otherwise, leave the default [reserved player] setting.

5. If a specific MIDI channel is desired, choose a new number from the Channel Number drop-down list. Otherwise, leave the default [auto] setting.

6. Choose a musical instrument from one of the following five categories:

   • **Instrument - GM:** The general MIDI soundbank, modeled after industry-standard instruments.

   • **Instrument - Special:** Variations on the general MIDI soundbank.

- **Instrument - User:** User-defined instrumentation for RMF music files, set up by Beatnik authoring software. (These files are dependent on the selected music file and not present when the stub.rmf file is used.)

- **Percussion - GM:** General MIDI percussive instruments.

- **Percussion - Special:** Variations on the general MIDI percussive instruments.

Caution

Although the behavior's user interface enables you to choose multiple instruments from different categories, only the first one is valid. Therefore, make sure that only the final choice is displayed in the chosen category list box; all other list boxes should display the blank value, found at the top of the list options.

7. Choose a note pitch from C-1 (C in octave –1) to G9 (G in the ninth octave) by selecting an option from the Note drop-down list.

   The notes are shown with the corresponding MIDI number (0–127), followed by the musical note name. Middle C, for example, is displayed as 060 C4 — which represents the C note in the fourth octave. Sharps are designated with a hash mark (#).

8. Select the velocity (how hard the note is struck) of the musical note from the Velocity drop-down list.

   The Beatnik velocity scale goes from the hardest note struck (100) to the softest (0) and corresponds to the MIDI rates of 127–0. The default is 100.

9. Select the duration for the musical note from the Duration (ms) VCR-style controls.

   The duration is given in milliseconds. The default is 1,000 or 1 second.

10. Choose the loudness setting for the musical note from the Volume option box.

11. Choose the pan setting from the Pan option box.

    The default pan setting is the audio center, between the left and right speakers. Beatnik enables you to choose from 21 pan positions in all, from all the way to the left to all the way to the right.

12. You can inspect previous configurations by choosing one of the Preset options: Default Settings, Previous Settings, or New Settings.

13. Click OK when you're finished.

Incorporating advanced Beatnik features

Beatnik really gets its power from making your Web page audio interactive — and much of that interactivity comes from using the behaviors found under the Beatnik Advanced category. In all, 22 different behaviors are divided into the four main advanced sections: Channels, Global, Player, and Tracks. Virtually any of the attributes previously explored in the music file or musical note behaviors can be modified on the fly with the advanced behaviors, including the volume, pan setting, and instrument. Moreover, you can adjust the tempo, transpose the music, and instantly mute all but one of the instruments for a solo.

All the behaviors function in a similar fashion to those already described. Rather than detailing the use of each of the 22 behaviors, the remainder of this section describes their effects. The advanced Beatnik behaviors are categorized according to what they control:

✦ **Channel behaviors:** Control individual MIDI channels.

✦ **Global behaviors:** Affect all Beatnik sounds.

✦ **Player behaviors:** Pinpoint specific, named voices or players.

✦ **Track behaviors:** Target any one of the possible 64 tracks in a Beatnik MIDI or RMF composition.

Tip   Any behavior that starts with the word *Adjust*, such as Adjust Channel Pan, is used relatively, while any one that starts with *Set*, such as Set Channel Pan, is used absolutely.

Table 25-6 describes the Beatnik Channel behaviors. These behaviors are applied by selecting a tag and, from the Behaviors panel, choosing Beatnik Advanced ⇨ Channels and then the desired behavior. In all cases, choose either the matching Target Player or the number of the MIDI channel already playing that you wish to alter.

Table 25-6
Beatnik Advanced Channel Behaviors

Behavior	*Description*
Adjust Channel Pan	Moves the left-to-right speaker pan relative to the current setting.
Adjust Channel Volume	Changes the loudness of the selected player or channel relative to the current setting.
Set Channel Instrument	Selects a different instrument for the selected player or channel.
Set Channel Monophonic	Changes the MIDI setting from polyphonic (multivoiced) to monophonic (single-voiced) or vice versa. A Toggle option enables the setting to alternate each time it is selected.
Set Channel Mute	Turns the mute setting on or off for the selected channel or player. A Toggle option enables the setting to alternate each time it is selected.
Set Channel Pan	Selects a new left-to-right speaker pan setting for the selected player or channel.
Set Channel Solo	Changes the solo status from the unsolo setting to solo or vice versa. A Toggle option enables the setting to alternate each time it is selected.
Set Channel Volume	Selects a new loudness setting for the specified channel or player.

The Global Beatnik behaviors apply to all eight-player voices, affecting every sound emanating from the Beatnik sound engine. Only two behaviors are in this category:

✦ **Set Global Mute:** This behavior effectively mutes or unmutes all Beatnik sound. The behavior can be set to one option or the other, or used as a toggle to alternate between the two states.

✦ **Set Reverb Type:** Reverb can be thought of as the amount of echo in a sound. Beatnik has one reverb setting for all of its sounds, which can be altered globally through this behavior. The six different reverb options are each expressed as the size of a room, ranging from zero to the most reverb:

- No Reverb (Default)
- Closet
- Garage
- Acoustic Lab
- Cavern
- Dungeon

Caution

The Global Reverb setting should be judiciously applied. If an instrument relies heavily on reverb for its effect, changing the Global setting significantly alters what is heard.

When you want to alter one of Beatnik's eight players on a page, use one of Beatnik's Advanced Player behaviors. These behaviors can be used in concert with the Channel behaviors to affect the sound experience. Before any of the Player behaviors can be used, a Groovoid, music file, or musical note must be inserted with a named player. Table 25-7 describes the Advanced Player behaviors.

Table 25-7 Beatnik Advanced Player Behaviors	
Behavior	**Description**
Adjust Position	Resets the playback position relative to its current position. This behavior can be used to build a VCR-like control with fast-forward and reverse features. A positive value (measured in milliseconds) moves the position forward, and a negative value moves it backward.
Adjust Tempo	Alters the playback speed of a selected player relative to the current speed. Values are measured in beats per minute; a positive number speeds up the music, while a negative number slows it down.

Behavior	Description
Adjust Transposition	Alters the pitch of a selected player relative to the current setting. Possible values range from up three octaves to down three octaves.
Adjust Volume	Modifies the current loudness setting relative to the current setting for a selected player.
Release Player	Frees one of the eight Beatnik player slots previously reserved.
Set Position	Resets the playback position to an absolute position. This behavior can be used to build a VCR-like control with a Rewind feature. A positive value (measured in milliseconds) moves the position forward, and a negative value moves it backward.
Set Tempo	Resets the playback speed of a selected player to a new speed. Values are measured in beats per minute; a positive number speeds up the music, while a negative number slows it down.
Set Transposition	Resets the pitch of a selected player to a new setting. Possible values range from up three octaves to down three octaves.
Set Volume	Resets the current loudness setting relative to a new setting for a selected player.
Show Copyright Info	Displays the detailed copyright information available in every RMF file in a separate system window.

The final advanced Beatnik category affects music tracks. Both RMF and Beatnik MIDI files enable composers to create their music with up to 64 different tracks. The tracks are identified by their number, 1 to 64. The two Track behaviors are as follows:

✦ **Set Track Mute:** Mutes or unmutes the sound on a specified track. The behavior can be set to one option or the other, or used as a toggle to alternate between the two states.

✦ **Set Track Solo:** Sets a specified track to solo or unsolo status. A toggle option enables the choice to alternate.

Exploring the Pro behaviors

Four more categories of behaviors are included in the Beatnik ActionSet Pro, found under the PRO menu of the behaviors menu:

✦ **Compatibility:** This enables the Web page designer to specify a specific minimum version requirement for the Beatnik player. Without this behavior, any system with the Beatnik player installed — regardless of version — attempts to run the page.

✦ **Dynamic:** Often the difference between a great sound effect and an annoying one is the number of times the same sound is heard. The Dynamic category enables Groovoids, music files, and musical notes to be chosen for a specified group and played randomly, thus varying the musical experience of a Web page.

✦ **Sonification Wizards:** The form is perhaps the most interactive of all Web page elements. Rather than undergo the tedious procedure of adding feedback sounds to each and every form checkbox, radio button, or text box, Beatnik provides a Sonify Forms With Groovoids Wizard (shown in Figure 25-11) for an all-in-one solution. Additionally, form elements can be used to trigger any JavaScript function by using Beatnik's Sonify Forms with Handlers. This behavior extends beyond an audio capability and enables, for example, a layer to be made visible when a text box receives focus, and disappear when it loses focus.

✦ **Synchronization:** With the Synchronization category of behaviors, Beatnik can use events in the music — such as a chorus change or the beginning of lyrics — to trigger specific JavaScript functions. These music events are incorporated into the RMF file by the composer and can be referenced generically (such as all the choruses in a song) or specifically (such as one particular lyric).

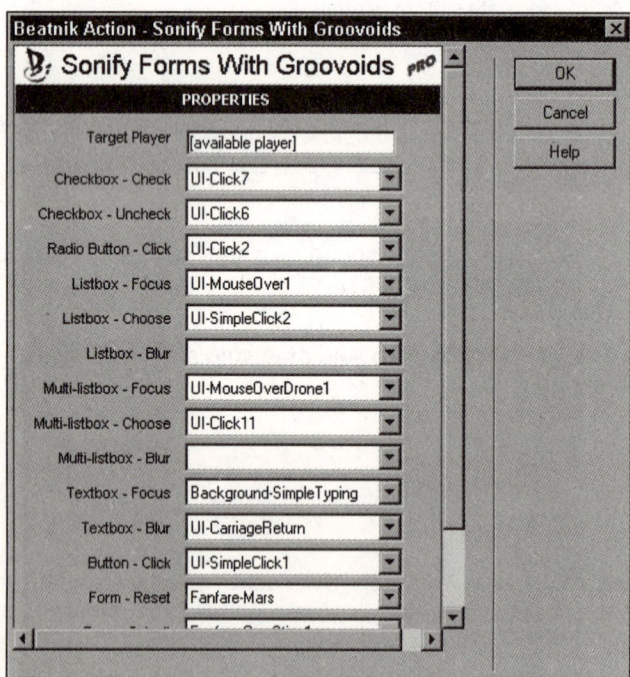

Figure 25-11: The Sonify Forms with Groovoids behavior enables you to attach aural feedback cues to any or all form elements in a page.

The Pro Beatnik behaviors are extremely powerful and enable an integration of music and visuals limited only by the imagination — and, because they're Dreamweaver behaviors, you can do it all without coding the JavaScript.

Embedding a Beatnik object in your page

If you're working with Beatnik, be sure to install the Beatnik object from Brendan Dawes. You'll find the object available on the Macromedia Exchange as well on the CD that accompanies this book. Once the Beatnik object is installed in Dreamweaver, incorporating RMF and other files to use the Plugin is a very straightforward process. As with other Plugins, simply position the cursor where you want the Beatnik object to appear and select it from the Beatnik category of the Objects panel. (You can also choose Insert ➪ Beatnik from the menus.) When the Insert Beatnik dialog box opens, enter a file source in the RMF File Source text box. This can be the name of any RMF file or other audio format file. As usual, you can also select Browse to choose your file from a Select File dialog box. Click OK when you're finished.

After you've picked your file, the Property Inspector displays your file name in the src text box, along with other information about the Beatnik object, including the following attributes:

✦ **Width and Height:** The preset dimensions conform to the size of the default Beatnik controls. As you can with LiveAudio objects, you can vary the size and number of Beatnik controls through the parameters.

✦ **Plg URL:** When a user doesn't have the appropriate Plugin, this attribute provides a link to get one. The Beatnik Plugin URL address is www.beatnik. com/to/?player.

Caution   At a minimum, always keep the width and height attributes set to a value of at least 2, even when using the hidden parameter. Enter the width and height pixel sizes in the W and H text boxes, respectively, on the Property Inspector. Otherwise, your Plugins are not backwardly compatible with earlier versions of Netscape Navigator.

When you click Parameters in the Beatnik object's Property Inspector, you get access to the parameters described in Table 25-8.

<table>
<tr><td colspan="2" align="center">Table 25-8
Beatnik Object Parameters</td></tr>
<tr><td>**Beatnik Parameter**</td><td>**Description**</td></tr>
<tr><td>autostart</td><td>This attribute is set to true, which enables the audio to begin playing as soon as the file has completely downloaded. Use false if you want to control the playing of the audio independently.</td></tr>
</table>

Continued

Table 25-8 *(continued)*	
Beatnik Parameter	**Description**
`Display`	Determines which graphic is used to represent the Beatnik object. Options are song, which shows copyright information, or system (the default), which enables the user to toggle between the song information, output meters, or oscilloscope.
`Hidden`	Hides the controls; no value is specified.
`Type`	Sets the MIME type. If the audio file is in RMF format, this attribute is set to audio/rmf.
`mode`	Sets which of three graphics is to be displayed initially as the Beatnik Plugin—scope, meters, or copyright. When `display=song`, only the copyright value is available.
`loop`	If set to true, this attribute causes the file to repeat continuously. If set to false (the default), the file plays once only. The value for loop can also be an integer to determine the number of times the file repeats.
`volume`	Preset to the loudest value (100); this attribute can be any number from 1 to 100.

Summary

Adding sound to a Web page brings it into the realm of multimedia. Dreamweaver gives you numerous methods to handle the various different audio formats, both static and streaming. With custom Dreamweaver objects and actions, enhancing your Web site with audio is a snap.

✦ The common downloadable audio file formats are MP3, AIFF, WAV, AU, and RMF.

✦ The common downloadable music file formats are MIDI, QuickTime Music, and RMF.

✦ You can either link to a sound or embed it in your Web page. With standard audio, the linking technique calls an independent, free-floating player; the embedding technique incorporates the player into the design of the page. Hiding the player creates background music or sound.

✦ Third-party Plugins offer far greater control over the appearance and functionality of the sound than relying on a browser's default Plugin; to use a third-party Plugin, however, your user must download it.

✦ The Beatnik Plugin provides incredible JavaScript interaction, excellent fidelity, and low file sizes.

✦ Streaming audio gives almost instant access to large audio files; RealAudio is the leader in player deployment, and the inclusion of the RealSystem G2 objects simplifies embedding streaming players.

In the next chapter you're given an overview of Dynamic HTML.

Working with Dynamic HTML and Dreamweaver

Defining Dynamic HTML

Dynamic HTML sounds like an ad slogan for the latest technology, doesn't it? In this case, the word *dynamic* refers to the capability to change, evolve, grow, shift, and otherwise metamorphose into a different state. With Dynamic HTML (or DHTML), almost everything on the heretofore static Web page can change. Moreover, these dynamic transitions are not generated from the server side of the Internet; they are inherent in the programming language itself.

Depending on the implementation, Dynamic HTML enables an amazing range of effects:

+ Objects fly in from all corners of the screen and assemble into a coherent, integrated portion of the page.

+ Text and logos suddenly materialize and instantly disappear from the screen.

+ Web pages aren't two-dimensional — now objects can be in front of or behind other objects.

+ Outlines expand to reveal details and collapse to provide an overview; content changes with the interactive click of a button.

+ The design on the Web appears as it was designed off the Web; designers can make their Web layouts appear just the way they want, without complicated tables or single-pixel spacers.

+ Tables are automatically generated according to the data returned from a query and then updated globally with input from the user.

These capabilities barely scratch the surface of Dynamic HTML possibilities. With Dreamweaver's advanced interface, challenging and code-intensive projects become intuitively achievable. Dreamweaver was among the first Web authoring tools to take full advantage of Dynamic HTML capabilities.

With its history of open standards and competing commercial visions, however, the Web doesn't yet have a smooth road with Dynamic HTML. In theory, both Netscape and Microsoft have fully embraced DHTML, but the reality is that both companies have adopted divergent models of the standard. Dreamweaver rises above the fray and makes cross-browser Dynamic HTML really work—with little or no assistance from the Web designer.

This chapter has a dual purpose. First and foremost, it introduces you to the concepts behind DHTML and provides an overview of the current state of implementation in the two primary browsers. Second, it examines the browser-specific Dynamic HTML features and shows you how to employ them in Dreamweaver.

Tip   For a taste of the possibilities with Dynamic HTML, visit Macromedia's Dynamic HTML Zone at www.dhtmlzone.com and select the Tutorials option. Once you're in the tutorial screen, click the Launch Superfly button. This demo not only shows the excitement Dynamic HTML can generate, but also acts as an excellent tutorial. (While you're in the Dynamic HTML Zone, be sure to also check out the Spotlight sites for further demonstrations.)

Fundamentals of Dynamic HTML

What makes Dynamic HTML so, well . . . dynamic? No single factor can take all the credit. Rather, DHTML is really a combination of technologies that are coming to be regarded as the next generation of Web development. In this section, you examine the roles of the components that make up DHTML:

- ✦ **Cascading Style Sheets:** These give the Web designer control over the many characteristics of the Web page, whether designated by a standard or custom HTML tag.

- ✦ **Absolute positioning:** This feature enables pixel-precise placement of any Web object.

- ✦ **Dynamic content:** The Web page can have content added or deleted on the fly.

- ✦ **Downloadable fonts:** Web designers can embed specific fonts to control a Web page's typography.

- ✦ **Data binding:** Server-side data is linked to a table or form on a Web page, which can dynamically update without redrawing the entire page.

Not all of this functionality is cross-browser, but all these features are possible in one configuration or another. As a whole, Dynamic HTML brings a more responsive, media-rich Web environment to the Web designer's palette—one that more closely resembles multimedia CD-ROM productions, while still maintaining the unique hyperconnectivity of the Internet. Best of all, Dynamic HTML is far more internalized than earlier HTML implementations, relying less on Helper applications and plug-ins to achieve its state-of-the-art effects.

Cascading Style Sheets

As sanctioned by the HTML governing body, the World Wide Web Consortium (W3C), the Cascading Style Sheet (CSS) specification is at the core of DHTML. CSS was the first step toward making traditional HTML more flexible and malleable. In a nutshell, CSS enables a Web designer to specify the attributes of an HTML tag — whether in a single page or through an entire site — with one command.

Take the <h1> tag, for instance. Does management want all headlines across the company's Web site during July to be 24-point Helvetica and blue-green? CSS can handle this request in one line:

```
h1 {  font: 24pt Helvetica; color: green}
```

If you're a print-oriented layout artist who has been trying to adjust to HTML, you'll appreciate not only the flexibility and control of Cascading Style Sheets, but also their implementation. CSS uses the well-established language of print designers. Fonts, for example, can be sized in points or picas, instead of with relative sizes 1–6.

The Cascading Style Sheet technology not only affects the standard attributes of HTML tags, but also extends the number and variety of properties that can be modified. For instance, CSS now enables Web designers to specify the line height of any given tag, to make a paragraph of text double-spaced, or to tighten the leading (line-spacing) for subheads. CSS offers entire categories of new elements, such as boxes, that can be added to the designer's palette and the Web page. Moreover, CSS power is not limited to existing standard tags — you can create custom styles and assign them special characteristics. For instance, a large organization may define a "legal" style to be used in disclaimers and other fine print.

The important aspect of CSS from the standpoint of DHTML is that CSS begins to control the elements on the page in a systematic fashion. In the fullest implementation of CSS, scripting languages such as JavaScript can address any declared style and modify its properties interactively.

Cross-Reference Dreamweaver uses an intuitive interface for working with CSS. To learn more about this topic, see Chapter 27.

Absolute positioning

From a print designer's viewpoint, perhaps the single most aggravating aspect of working on the Web has been the inability to easily place type or graphics anywhere on the page. Designers have had to go to elaborate lengths, using complex nested tables and one-pixel images as spacers, in attempts to achieve a faithful online representation of their designs.

An extension of Cascading Style Sheets now provides a more elegant solution: absolute positioning. Initially known as CSS-P, the standard for positioning has been adopted fully by Microsoft and by Netscape, starting in version 6. CSS-P formed the basis for layers.

Layers are invisible containers that can hold any type and amount of Web elements — and most important, they can be positioned anywhere on a Web page to exact pixel coordinates.

The power of layers goes farther than absolute positioning, however. Layers and their contents can be made invisible or visible with a change of one property. Because CSS employs a concept known as *inheritance*, in which related styles take on the characteristics of the parent style, many layers can be manipulated at once. As the term implies, layers bring an illusion of depth to the Web page. By design, each layer exists in its own three-dimensional plane. You can stack one layer on top of another, or you can change their stacking order interactively.

Just as regular CSS elements can be updated dynamically, the position of layers can, too — which makes the look of animation possible. Just as one second in a movie is actually 24 static images shown rapidly, layers can be quickly repositioned, appearing to move from point A to point B. This animation quality is one of the most striking features of Dynamic HTML. For the first time, movement on the Web is not generated from a source external to the Web page itself, whether it is server-push, an animated GIF, or a plug-in. This capability accelerates the display of pages online and enables Web pages to be viewed offline in a more easy and complete manner.

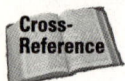 To learn more about absolute positioning and layers, refer to Chapter 28.

Dynamic content

So far, Dynamic HTML can change the look of a Web page's elements with CSS and control the placement of a Web page's objects with layers — but what about the content? Only Microsoft has currently taken the challenge of creating dynamic content. Because Internet Explorer has complete control over the Document Object Model (DOM), any element or tag can be updated on the fly. This capability includes the content or value of tags.

Dynamic content is extremely useful when working with outline-based documents. With dynamic content links, you can show only the heading of a document, which when selected by the user, expands to present the substance — no matter how many paragraphs exist. Select the same heading again, and the expanded outline collapses. Expanding and collapsing outlines can be implemented in all primary DHTML-capable browsers. Microsoft and Netscape 6 both use true dynamic content; Netscape's 4.*x* browsers use a technique involving layers.

When you build an expanding outline in a Web page, you initially include all the content. Then, you designate the heading and the content and apply the appropriate styles, as illustrated in Figure 26-1.

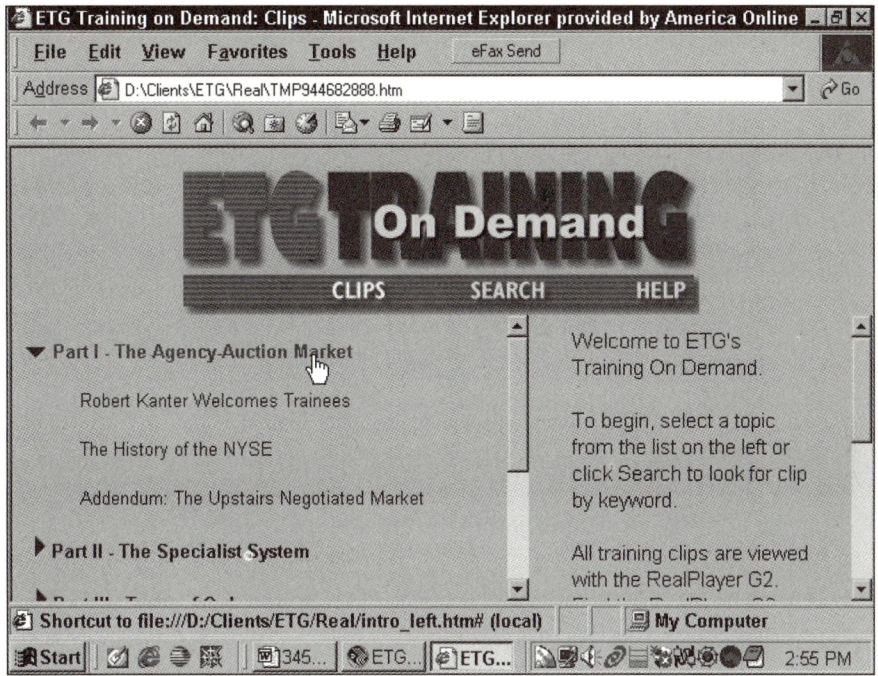

Figure 26-1: Dynamic content enables you to create expanding and collapsing outlines.

Downloadable fonts

Increased font control tops the wish list for most Web designers — and this capability does not mean font size or color. For too long, Web pages have been limited to the most generic of typefaces (primarily Arial, Times, and Helvetica) because HTML could access only the fonts on the user's system. Dynamic HTML promises to change this deficiency with downloadable fonts. As the term implies, downloadable fonts enable the Web designer to embed a specific font within a DHTML page, and the font is temporarily transferred to the Web site visitor's system.

Unfortunately, at the present time, the key word in the preceding paragraph is *promises*. Both Microsoft and Netscape have implemented their own mutually incompatible versions of downloadable fonts. The demand for this capability is so strong, however, that it is only a matter of time before downloadable fonts become a cross-browser reality and a working standard. In the meantime, you can apply Open Font in Internet Explorer and Dynamic Font technology in Communicator simultaneously.

Tip

You can embed fonts capable of being read by both browsers on the PC with the help of Bitstream's TrueDoc technology; unfortunately, it does not work on Macintosh systems. Although it's native to Communicator, Internet Explorer users need only an ActiveX control, which can be automatically downloaded. See Bitstream's Web site at www.truedoc.com for more details.

Data binding

Tying an online database to a Web page has never been a trivial matter. Any Web page had to be generated on the server side in order to post the most current information — until the emergence of Dynamic HTML's data binding feature. With data binding, the tables, forms, and other elements of the page that present the information can also receive information and can be dynamically restructured. Once data has been received on the client side, data binding enables the information to be filtered, sorted, and represented — only the elements affected need be redrawn, rather than the entire page.

Presently, only Internet Explorer 4.0 and later support data binding. Microsoft's support is extensive, however; key innovations include the following:

✦ **Full object model access to data binding attributes:** Enables Web designers to use JavaScript to add, delete, and modify bindings at runtime.

✦ **Table paging:** Provides the capability to limit the number of records displayed in a repeated table and move the starting record forward and backward in the data set.

✦ **Table and form generation:** Offers automatic building of table rows from data records and data-bound form fields.

For more on data binding, see the section "Delivering Data Binding" later in this chapter.

Accessing DHTML in Netscape Communicator

The Navigator component of Communicator contains three features that comprise Netscape's Dynamic HTML effort: style sheets, positionable content, and downloadable fonts. The Netscape version of DHTML only partially conforms to the standard outlined by the W3C. For instance, Netscape supports two different types of style sheets: the W3C-standard Cascading Style Sheets, and the company's own JavaScript Style Sheets (JSS).

The following sections discuss Netscape's methods of implementing Dynamic HTML and show you how to implement those methods in Dreamweaver.

Creating style sheets

Let's take a closer look at Netscape's support of the standard Cascading Style Sheet as well as its own proprietary JSS method (used in Netscape 4.*x* but not in Netscape 6). In brief, CSS uses the `<style>` tag to apply new attributes to an existing HTML tag or a custom tag known as a *class*. The CSS style tag format looks like the following:

```
<STYLE TYPE="text/css">
<!--
P {font-size:18pt; margin-left:20pt;}
H1 {color:blue;}
-->
</STYLE>
```

For me, the big news in Netscape 6 is the breadth of Cascading Style Sheet support. The CSS support in Netscape 6 matches the W3C CSS1 standards. This means that designers can begin to use CSS capabilities to their fullest extent rather than working with a narrow subset of functionality previously supported by both major browsers. Although it will be some time before Netscape 6 is prevalent enough to safely code for, designers can look forward to an easier and more productive future.

JavaScript Style Sheets also use the `<style>` tag but take advantage of the DOM to format the JSS specifications. The DOM is a hierarchical system that identifies each page element by its type of object (or by its assigned name). Once you have properly identified an element, you can then change its properties. The preceding CSS style sheet example looks like the following in JSS:

```
<STYLE TYPE = "text/javascript">
tags.P.fontSize = "18pt";
tags.P.marginLeft = "20pt";
tags.H1.color = "blue";
</STYLE>
```

Caution   You cannot use the HTML comment tags with JavaScript Style Sheets.

Dreamweaver outputs CSS-formatted code and previews the changes as well. Although you cannot preview JSS-formatted code within Dreamweaver, JSS renders properly when previewed in a compatible browser.

To be frank, JSS has not received serious support in the Web developer community, and because the standard CSS format works in both browsers, JSS has little chance of becoming popular, a fact recognized by Netscape's dropping support of it for version 6. If, however, you develop pages that use JSS, you can continue to code them in Dreamweaver — just not as conveniently.

Making positionable content

With positionable content, Netscape again supports two possibilities. Although Navigator 4.0 essentially supports the CSS-P style layers created using the `<div>` and `<span>` tags with the style attributes, it also puts forth its own proprietary `<layer>` and `<ilayer>` tags. Aside from these syntax differences, some differences also exist between what Navigator 4.0 supports in the properties for CSS-P style positioning and the proprietary `<layer>` tags. That said, all of the tags form the basis for layers, which can be placed anywhere on the page.

Caution   Netscape has given up on the `<layer>` and `<ilayer>` tag; neither are supported in Navigator 6. Unless you are building a Netscape 4.x intranet site, it is highly recommended that you avoid both of these tags.

Relative positioning represents perhaps the biggest difference between the two implementations. Usually when you place a layer in your Web page, the left and top attributes define the layer's absolute position on the screen. When the position attribute is set to relative, however, the left and top values relate to whatever contains the layer, whether it is a table or another layer. In Navigator 4.x, the `<layer>` tag is used for absolute positioning, and `<ilayer>` is used for relative positioning — or what Netscape calls *inflow-positioning*. Dreamweaver supports these as well as the CSS standard `<div>` and `<span>` layer tag variations.

Although Netscape 6 handles CSS in a standard fashion, several properties for positionable content are supported differently in Netscape 4.x. In most cases, when Netscape 4.x doesn't support the CSS standard, it offers its own variation for the `<layer>` and `<ilayer>` tags and for the CSS style use. Table 26-1 describes these equivalents.

Table 26-1
Differences Between CSS and Netscape 4.x Layer Properties

CSS Term	Layer Property	Netscape 4.x Equivalent
`include-source:` `url("filename.htm")`	`SRC="filename.htm"`	`source-include:` `url("filename.htm")`
`background-color:` `colorname`	`BGCOLOR="colorname"`	`layer-background-color:` `colorname`
`background-image:` `url("filename")`	`BACKGROUND="filename"`	`layer-background-image:` `filename`

Tip   You can include both the CSS standard and the Netscape 4.x variation of an attribute in a `<style>` tag for cross-browser compatibility without dire consequences. For the `background color` and `background image` attributes applied to a layer, Dreamweaver automatically includes both the standard and Netscape 4.x specific; the `include source` attribute would have to be added by hand.

Using downloadable fonts

Fonts in HTML have only recently started to get a little respect. A `<font>` tag wasn't supported until HTML 3.2 — and the support is still strictly limited. Attributes for the `<font>` tag enable you to specify a number of font face options from which the user's system can choose, such as the following:

```
<font face="Arial, Helvetica, sans-serif">
```

Until Dynamic HTML, however, a designer could not use a typeface that users did not have on their system and still expect to have the layout viewed correctly. Netscape's method for implementing downloadable fonts requires that the fonts be contained in a font definition file on the same Web server as the Web page. When the page is served to the user, the font definition file is downloaded with the HTML file in the same way as a GIF or JPEG file. The font definition file is loaded asynchronously so that the HTML page doesn't have to wait while the fonts are loading.

Note To protect the copyrights of font designers, the downloaded font remains on the user's system only while the page is in the browser's cache; the fonts cannot be copied for personal use.

Font definition files are generated with a special authoring tool, such as Bitstream's WebFont Maker (`www.truedoc.com`), or the Font Composer Plug-in for Communicator or CorelDraw 8 and later. The process involves opening your Web page in the authoring tool, selecting text, and applying the font to it. You then burn (process) the file, which saves the document, creates a font definition file containing the fonts used by the file, and also links the font definition file to the document. Font definition files can be used by only one domain at a time and the domain is specified at the time you burn the file.

Once the font definition file is created, you link the font through a style tag, such as the following:

```
<STYLE TYPE="text/css"><!--
@fontdef url(http://home.netscape.com/fonts/sample.pfr);
--></STYLE>
```

You can also use a `<link>` tag, as follows:

```
<LINK REL="fontdef" SRC="fontdef1.pfr">
```

The final step in getting the user's system to recognize Netscape downloadable fonts adds a new Multipurpose Internet Mail Extension (MIME) type to the Web server, `application/font-tdpfr`, with a file name extension of .pfr (Portable Font Resource).

Once you've linked the font to your page, you can include it in a font tag, as with a regular system font. For example, if you've included a font called "BurnOut," you could include a font family definition by choosing Text ➪ Font ➪ Edit Font List. Then, when applying the font to a particular bit of text, the HTML could read as follows:

```
"<font face="BurnOut, Arial, Helvetica, sans-serif">
```

To support the new capabilities of downloadable fonts, Netscape includes two new attributes: point-size and weight. The point-size attribute enables you to set exact sizes for your font (unlike the regular `size` attribute for the `<font>` tag, which works relatively). The weight attribute enables you to alter the boldness of the font. The weight value is from 100 to 900, inclusive (in steps of 100), where 100 indicates the least bold value and 900 indicates the boldest value. Specifying the `<b>` tag causes Netscape to render the boldest font possible.

The amount of work involved to achieve downloadable fonts is a factor in Web designers' reluctance to use the technique. As you can see in Figure 26-2, however, the results can be spectacular.

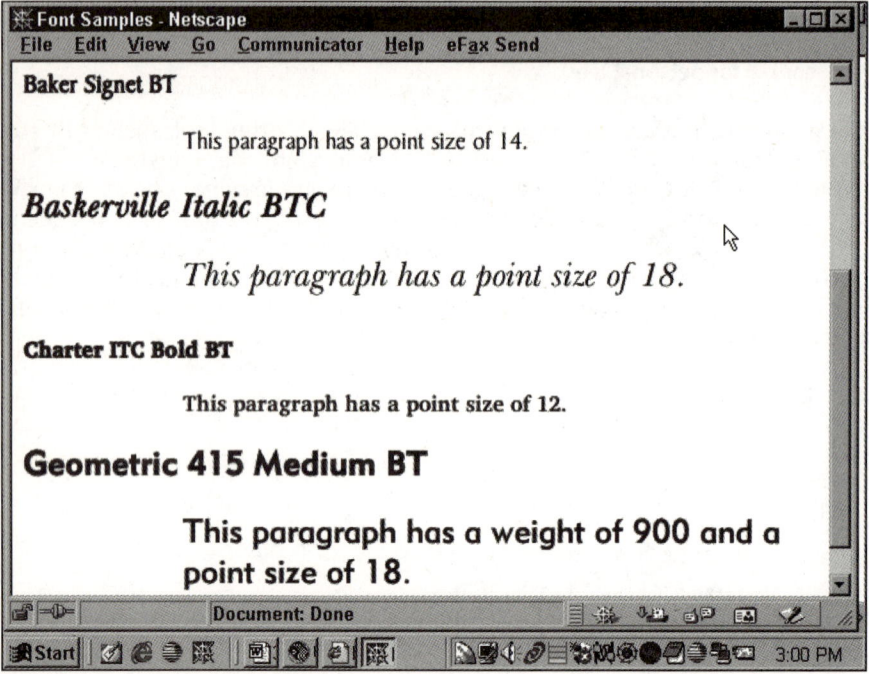

Figure 26-2: You can access a wide range of fonts and font sizes with Netscape's downloadable font technology.

You can certainly use Netscape's downloadable fonts in Dreamweaver, but Simon White has an extension that inserts the necessary code for you; you'll find it on the CD-ROM under his name in the Additional Extensions folder. Keep in mind that Dreamweaver does not preview the font changes.

Viewing Netscape Embedded Fonts in Internet Explorer

Recall that Internet Explorer browsers can use Netscape embedded fonts with the aid of a small ActiveX control. The ActiveX control is added by simply inserting the following lines after the `<link>` code:

```
<script language="JavaScript" ü
src="http://www.truedoc.com/activex/tdserver.js"></script>
```

When the Internet Explorer browser loads the page, the user's system is inspected to determine if the proper ActiveX control is already installed. If not, the user is asked if the ActiveX control should be downloaded.

Remember that the easiest way to include TrueDoc fonts in a page is to use Simon White's PFR (Portable Font Resource) command, included on this book's CD-ROM. The command searches for a PFR file and then inserts the necessary code for the link and the ActiveX control. Unfortunately the TrueDoc system is not compatible with Internet Explorer on the Macintosh.

Working with DHTML and Internet Explorer

Starting with Internet Explorer 4.0, Microsoft adopted Dynamic HTML with a vengeance. At least partially supporting all the W3C official recommendations as well as numerous proposals, Internet Explorer advances DHTML to the extreme. Included in Microsoft's rendition are the following features:

✦ **Dynamic Styles:** Includes a robust implementation of the CSS Level 1 specification for controlling style sheets.

✦ **Dynamic Content:** Enables the Web page to be redrawn after it has been downloaded.

✦ **Positioning and animation:** Provide a full implementation of the CSS-P specification for layers and movement.

✦ **Filters and transitions:** Permit designers to use special effects applied to images, text, or entire Web pages.

✦ **Open fonts:** Enable the Web page to specify a font that is automatically downloaded, used for that page, and then discarded.

✦ **Data binding:** Links Web elements such as tables to an external source, either a server database or a comma-delimited file, for automatic updating.

✦ **Dynamic HTML Object Model:** Gives complete access to all of the page elements and their properties through an extensive list of events.

Dreamweaver directly supports all the Internet Explorer Dynamic HTML features that are cross-browser compatible, including style sheets, layers, and a large portion of the Object Model. Other elements, such as filters and transitions, can be applied through Dreamweaver's Style Sheet Inspector but cannot be previewed in the Document window.

This book does not cover all the details of Internet Explorer's DHTML implementation, but the remainder of this section covers those features not duplicated in any other browser.

Creating dynamic content

Dynamic content has been made possible by Internet Explorer's complete support of the Dynamic HTML Object Model, a superset of Netscape's own Document Object Model (DOM). Essentially, the DHTML Object Model gives you full access to all the elements in a document — and here's the innovation — even after the document has been downloaded to the user.

The most obvious use for dynamic content is with outline-oriented Web pages. Dynamic content enables outlines to expand and collapse at the click of a mouse. The key property to activate dynamic content is the `display` property, because you can name or identify any block of text or element and then alter its `display` property on the fly.

The following code hides the `<ul>` list elements until the user clicks the heading above them, and then hides the list again when the same heading is double-clicked:

```
<a href=# onClick="javascript:document.all.MyList.style.display = ''" ü
onDblClick="javascript:document.all.MyList.style.display='none'" border=0>
<h1>Notes on Installation</h1>
</a>
<ul ID=MyList STYLE="display:none" >
  <li>Item #1...</li>
  <li>Item #2...</li>
  <li>Item #3...</li>
</ul>
<p>More information to follow...</p>
```

You see all the elements when viewed in Dreamweaver's Document window, and you must preview it in Internet Explorer to see the dynamic content in action. Currently, you have to code this sort of structure in Dreamweaver by hand or through a custom object.

Using filters and transitions

Looking for a little sparkle in your Web page? Internet Explorer's filters and transitions are quite spectacular. A filter is a special effect, such as a drop shadow, that you can apply to an element (usually text or an image) through CSS. Transitions are used when one image is exchanged with another, or one Web page with another.

The number of available filters and the range of their parameters is mind boggling. The list in Table 26-2 gives an overview of the filters but doesn't hint at the amount of variety available from changing their attributes due to the length that such coverage would require.

	Table 26-2 CSS/Internet Explorer 4+ Filters	
Filter	*Description*
Alpha	Sets a uniform transparency level.
Blend	Sets a transition blending between two objects.
Blur	Creates the impression of moving at high speed.
Chroma	Makes a specific color transparent.
DropShadow	Creates a solid silhouette of the object.
FlipH	Creates a horizontal mirror image.
FlipV	Creates a vertical mirror image.
Glow	Adds radiance around the outside edges of the object.
Gray	Drops color information from the image.
Invert	Reverses the hue, saturation, and brightness values.
Light	Projects a light source onto an object.
Mask	Creates a transparent mask from an object.
Shadow	Creates an offset solid silhouette.
Reveal	Sets a transition's revealing of a hidden object.
Wave	Creates a sine wave distortion along the horizontal axis.
Xray	Shows just the edges of the object.

Filters can be coded in the `<style>` tag or as a `style` attribute and are generally applied to a class object. The syntax follows:

```
filter:filtername(parameter_1, parameter_2, ...)
```

As you can see from Figure 26-3, the effects are quite amazing — especially when you consider that they all can be performed interactively.

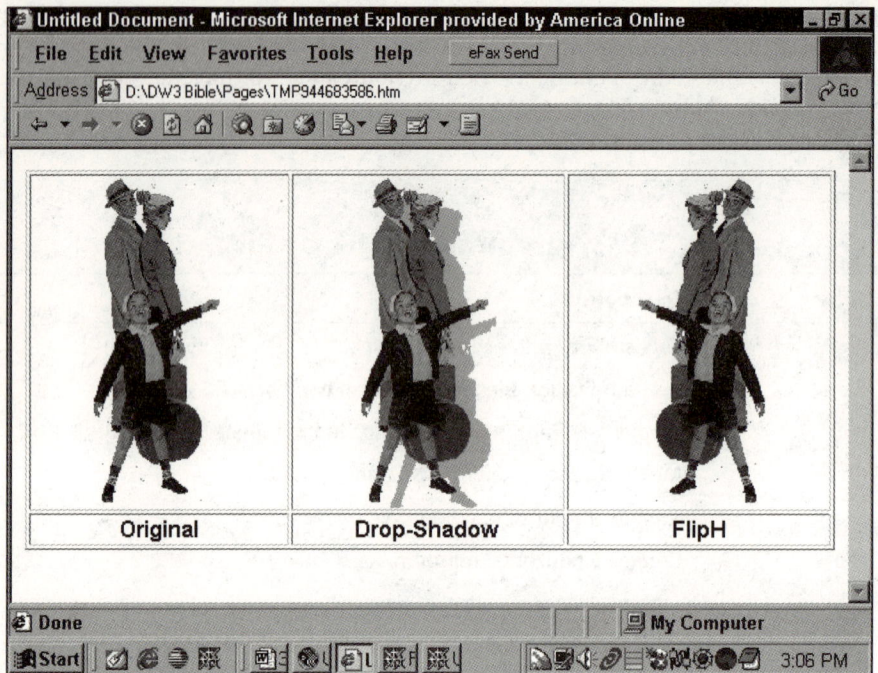

Figure 26-3: Internet Explorer's filters and transitions offer a full spectrum of graphic effects.

Delivering data binding

Much of the business of the Web depends on database-driven Web sites; virtual storefronts, online catalogs, and special information servers all require a strong connection between client-side requests and server-side answers. Microsoft's Dynamic HTML data binding links individual elements in your document, such as tables and forms, to data from another source, such as a database on a server or a comma-delimited text file. When the Web page with the data-bound tag is loaded, the data is automatically retrieved from the source, formatted, and displayed within the tag.

You can use Internet Explorer's data binding feature to generate tables in your Web page automatically and dynamically by binding a `<table>` tag to a data source. When the Web page is viewed, a new row is created in the table for each record retrieved from the source, and the cells of each row are filled with text and data from the fields of the record. Because this generation is dynamic, the user can view the document even while new rows in the table are being created. Moreover, once all the table data is present, you can sort or filter it without requiring the server to send additional data. The table is simply regenerated, using the previously retrieved data to fill the new rows and cells of the table.

You can also bind one or more tags in the Web page to specific fields of a record. When the page is browsed, the tags are filled with text and data from the fields in the current record. This technique can be used to generate form letters on the Web from a remote database. You can also bind the form tags to record fields, which gives the user the opportunity to view the information and, if necessary, change it. Then the record can be submitted to the server and reentered into the database.

Data binding requires that a data source object be included in the Web page. A *data source object* is an ActiveX control (or a Java applet) capable of communicating with the data source. Internet Explorer offers two data source objects: one for comma-delimited data in text files, and the other for structured query language (SQL) data in SQL servers and other open database connectivity (ODBC) sources.

Summary

Dynamic HTML is a quantum leap forward in Web development. Style sheets, layers, dynamic content, downloadable fonts, and other features make the latest generation of browsers faster, more client-side oriented, and more designer friendly. To sum up:

✦ Dynamic HTML features work only with Internet Explorer 4.0 and Navigator 4.0 browsers and later.

✦ Much of the DHTML feature set is based on the Cascading Style Sheet specification recommended by the World Wide Web Consortium.

✦ The Dynamic HTML components of Netscape Navigator 4.*x* are a blend of W3C standards and proprietary tags.

✦ Microsoft's Internet Explorer offers wide support of Dynamic HTML innovations through its Dynamic HTML Object Model, combined with comprehensive support of the CSS Level 1 standard.

✦ Netscape 6 has the greatest level of compliance to a number of W3C standards, including the Document Object Model and CSS Level 1.

In the next chapter, you study more specifics about how to use Cascading Style Sheets.

✦   ✦   ✦

Building Style Sheet Web Pages

All publications, whether on paper or the Web, need a balance of style and content to be effective. Style without content is all flash with no real information. Content with no style is flat and uninteresting, thus losing the substance. Traditionally, HTML has tied style to content wherever possible, preferring logical tags such as `<strong>` to indicate emphasis to physical tags such as `<b>` for bold. Although this emphasis on the logical worked for many single documents, its imprecision made it unrealistic, if not impossible, to achieve style consistency across a broad range of Web pages.

The Cascading Style Sheets specification has changed this situation—and much more. As support for Cascading Style Sheets (CSS) grows, more Web designers can alter font faces, type size and spacing, and many other page elements with a single command—and have the effect ripple not only throughout the page, but also throughout a Web site. Moreover, an enhancement of CSS called CSS-P (for positioning) is the foundation for what has become commonly known as *layers*.

Dreamweaver was one of the first Web authoring tools to make the application of Cascading Style Sheets user friendly. Through Dreamweaver's intuitive interface, the Web designer can access over 70 different CSS settings, affecting everything from type specs to multimedia-like transitions. Dreamweaver enables you to work the way you want: Create your style sheet all at once and then link it when you're ready, or make up your styles one-by-one as you build your Web page.

In this chapter, you find out how CSS works and why you need it. A Dreamweaver Technique for removing underlines from links walks you through a typical style sheet session. With that experience under your belt, you're ready for the sections with detailed information on the current CSS commands and how to apply them to your Web page and site. Also, the section on defining styles helps you understand what's what in the Style Definition dialog box. Finally, you learn how you can create external style sheets to create — and maintain — the look and feel of an entire Web site with a single document.

Understanding Cascading Style Sheets

The Cascading Style Sheets system significantly increases the design capabilities for a Web site. If you are a designer used to working with desktop publishing tools, you will recognize many familiar features in CSS, including the following:

✦ Commands for specifying and applying font characteristics

✦ Traditional layout measurement systems and terminology

✦ Pinpoint precision for page layout

Cascading Style Sheets are able to apply many features with a simple syntax that is easy to understand. If you're familiar with the concept of using styles in a word processing program, you'll have no trouble grasping style sheets.

Here's how the process works: CSS instructions are given in rules; a style sheet is a collection of these rules. A rule is a statement made up of an HTML or custom tag, called a *selector*, and its defined properties, referred to as a *declaration*. For example, a CSS rule that makes the contents of all <h1> tags (the selector) red in color (the declaration) looks like the following:

```
h1 {color:red}
```

In the following sections, you see the various characteristics of CSS — grouping, inheritance, and cascading — working together to give style sheets their flexibility and power.

Grouping properties

A Web designer often needs to change several style properties at once. CSS enables declarations to be grouped by separating them with semicolons. For example:

```
h1 {color:red; font-family:Arial,Helvetica,sans-serif; font-size:18pt}
```

The Dreamweaver interface provides a wide range of options for styles. Should you ever need to look at the code, you'll find that Dreamweaver groups your selections exactly as shown in the preceding example. Although Dreamweaver keeps each selector in its own rule, when you are hand-coding your style sheets, you can group selectors as well as declarations. Separate grouped selectors with commas, rather than semicolons. For example:

```
h1, h2, p, em {color:green; text-align:left}
```

Inheritance of properties

CSS rules can also be applied to more than one tag through inheritance: the ability of a parent or outer tag to pass on characteristics to the child or inner tags. Most, but not all, CSS declarations can be inherited by the HTML tags enclosed within the CSS selector. Suppose you set all <p> tags to the color red. Any tags included within a <p>...</p> tag pair then inherit that property and are also colored red.

Inheritance is also at work within HTML tags that involve a parent-child relationship, as with a list. Whether numbered (ordered, <ol>) or bulleted (unordered, <ul>), a list comprises any number of list items, designated by <li> tags. Each list item is considered a child of the parent tag, <ol> or <ul>. Take a look at the following example:

```
ol {color:red}
ul {color:blue}
```

With the preceding example, all ordered list items appear in red, whereas all unordered list items appear in blue. One major benefit to this parent-child relationship is that you can change the font for an entire page with one CSS rule. The following statement accomplishes this change:

```
body {font-family: Arial}
```

The change is possible in the previous example because the <body> tag is considered the parent of every HTML element on a page.

Tip

There's one exception to the preceding rule: tables. Netscape browsers (through version 4.75) treat tables differently than the rest of the HTML <body> when it comes to style sheets. To change the font of a table, you'd have to specify something such as the following:

```
td {font-family: Arial}
```

Because every cell in a table uses the <td> tag, this style sheet declaration affects the entire table. Dreamweaver is uneven in its application of this treatment. Setting the entire <body> to a particular font family is displayed correctly in the Document window, with even tables being affected. However, changing the color of a font in the <body> style sheet declaration does not alter the font color of text in a table in the Document window.

Cascading characteristics

The term *cascading* describes the capability of a local style to override a general style. Think of a stream flowing down a mountain; each ledge encountered by the stream has the potential to change its direction. The last ledge determines the final direction of the stream. In the same manner, one CSS rule applying generally to a block of text can be overridden by another rule applied to a more specific part of the same text.

For example, let's say you've defined, using style sheets, all normal paragraphs —
<p> tags — as a particular font in a standard color, but you mark one section of the
text using a little-used tag such as <samp>. If you make a CSS rule altering both the
font and color of the <samp> tag, the section takes on the characteristics of that
rule.

The cascading aspect of style sheets also works on a larger scale. One of the key
features of CSS is the capability to define external style sheets that can be linked to
individual Web pages, acting on their overall look and feel. Indeed, you can use the
cascading behavior to fine-tune the overall Web site style based on a particular
page or range of pages. Your company may, for instance, define an external style
sheet for the entire company intranet, and each division could then build upon that
overall model for its individual Web pages. For example, let's say that the company
style sheet dictates that all <h2> headings are in Arial and black. One department
could output their Web pages with <h2> tags in Arial, but colored red rather than
black, while another department could make them blue.

Defining new classes for extended design control

Redefining existing HTML tags is a step in the right direction toward consistent
design, but the real power of CSS comes into play when you define custom tags. In
CSS-speak, a custom tag is called a *class*, and the selector name always begins with
a period. Here's a simple example: To style all copyright notices at the bottom of all
pages of a Web site to display in 8-point Helvetica all caps, you could define a tag as
follows:

```
.cnote {font-family:Helvetica; font-size:8pt; font-transform:uppercase}
```

If you define this style in an external style sheet and apply it to all 999 pages of your
Web site, you have to alter only one line of code (instead of all 999 pages) when the
edict comes down from management to make all the copyright notices a touch
larger. Once a new class has been defined, you can apply it to any range of text,
from one word to an entire page.

How styles are applied

CSS applies style formatting to your page in one of three ways:

   ✦ Via an external, linked style sheet
   ✦ Via an internal style sheet
   ✦ Via embedded style rules

External style sheets

An *external* style sheet is a file containing the CSS rules; it links one or more Web
pages. One benefit of linking to an external style sheet is that you can customize
and change the appearance of a Web site quickly and easily from one file.

Two different methods exist for working with an external style sheet: the `link` method and the `import` method. Dreamweaver defaults to the link method, but you can also choose import if you prefer.

For the `link` method, a line of code is added outside of the `<style>` tags, as follows:

```
<link rel="stylesheet" href="mainstyle.css">
```

The `import` method writes code within the style tags, as follows:

```
<style type="text/css">
@import "newstyles.css";
</style>
```

Between the `link` and the `import` methods, the `link` method is better supported among browsers.

Internal style sheets

An *internal* style sheet is a list of all the CSS styles for a page.

Dreamweaver inserts all the style sheets at the top of a Web page within a `<style>...</style>` tag pair. Placing style sheets within the header tags has become a convention that many designers use, although you can also apply a style sheet anywhere on a page.

The `<style>` tag for a Cascading Style Sheet identifies the type attribute as `text/css`. The following is a sample internal style sheet:

```
<style type="text/css">
<!--
p {  font-family: "Arial, Helvetica, sans-serif"; color: #000000}
.cnote {  font: 8pt "Arial, Helvetica, sans-serif"; text-transform: uppercase}
h1 {  font: bold 18pt Arial, Helvetica, sans-serif; color: #FF0000}
-->
</style>
```

The HTML comment tags `<!--` and `-->` prevent older browsers that can't read style sheets from displaying the CSS rules.

Embedded style rules

The final method of applying a style inserts it within HTML tags using the `style` attribute. This method is the most "local" of all the techniques; that is, it is closest to the tag it is affecting and therefore has the ultimate control — because of the cascading nature of style sheets as previously discussed.

When you create a layer within Dreamweaver, you notice that the positioning attribute is a Cascading Style Sheet embedded within a `<div>` tag such as the following:

```
<div id="Layer1" style="position:absolute; visibility:inherit; left:314px; ¬
top:62px; width:194px; height:128px; z-index:1">
</div>
```

For all its apparent complexity, the Cascading Style Sheets system becomes straightforward in Dreamweaver. You often won't have to write a single line of code. But even if you don't have to write code, you should understand the CSS fundamentals of grouping, inheritance, and cascading.

Creating and Applying a Style Sheet in Dreamweaver

Dreamweaver uses three primary tools to implement Cascading Style Sheets: the CSS Styles panel, the Edit Style Sheet dialog box, and the Style Definition dialog box. Specifically, the CSS Styles panel is used to apply styles created in the Edit Style Sheet dialog box and specified with the Style Definition dialog box. With these three interfaces, you can accomplish the following:

✦ Link or import all your styles from an external style sheet

✦ View and edit most of the attributes included in the official release of CSS Level 1

✦ Modify any styles you have created

✦ Apply styles to selected text or to a particular tag surrounding that text

Caution

The fourth-generation browsers (and above) support many of the attributes from the first draft of the Cascading Style Sheets standard. Neither Netscape Navigator 4.0 nor Microsoft Internet Explorer 4.0 fully supports CSS Level 1, however. Of the earlier browsers, only Internet Explorer 3.0 supports a limited set of the CSS Level 1 features: font attributes, indents, and color. However, this support is rendered differently in Internet Explorer 3.0 and 4.0. Netscape Navigator 3.0 does not support any of the features of CSS Level 1. On the brighter side, Netscape Navigator 6.0 offers virtually complete compliance of CSS 1 and quite a lot of CSS 2. The current version of Internet Explorer for Windows (5.5 for Windows and 5.0 for Macintosh) is not as complete, but better than the 4.x versions.

Dreamweaver technique: Eliminating underlines from links

Because Dreamweaver's interface for CSS has so many controls, initially creating and applying a style can be a little confusing. Before delving into the details of the various panels, dialog boxes, and floating windows, let's quickly step through a typical style sheet session. Then, you can have an overall understanding of how all the pieces fit together.

 Note   Don't panic if you encounter unfamiliar elements of Dreamweaver's interface in this introductory technique. You see them at work again and again as you work through the chapter.

Disabling the underline for the anchor tag, <a>, which is normally associated with hyperlinked text, is one modification commonly included in style sheets. To accomplish this task, follow these steps:

1. Open the CSS Styles panel by choosing Windows ➪ CSS Styles or selecting the Show CSS Styles button from either Launcher.

2. In the CSS Styles panel, select the New Style button. This sequence opens the New Styles dialog box.

3. In the New Styles dialog box, select Redefine HTML Tag and choose the anchor tag, a, from the drop-down list. Finally select Define In This Document Only to create an internal CSS style sheet. Click OK, and the Style Definition window opens.

 Tip   You can also select the Use CSS Selector option and choose a:link from the drop-down list. You can even employ the a:hover style, which enables text to change color or style on rollover. You must, however, define the four CSS Selector styles in a particular order for them to work correctly. Start by defining the a:link class and then proceed to define a:active, a:visited, and a:hover, in that order. Note that these altered styles do not preview in Dreamweaver.

4. In the Style Definition window, select Type from the list of categories.

5. In the Decoration section of the Type category, select the option none. You can also make any other modifications to the anchor tag style, such as color or font size. Click OK when you're done.

 Tip   Many designers, myself included, like to make the link apparent by styling it bold and in a different color.

The Style Definition window closes, and any style changes instantly take effect on your page. If you have any previously defined links, the underline disappears from them.

Now, any links that you insert on your page still function as links — the user's pointer still changes into a pointing hand, and the links are active — but no underline appears.

Tip   This technique works for any text used as a link. To eliminate the border around an image designated as a link, the image's border must be set to zero in the Image Property Inspector. Dreamweaver handles this automatically when a graphic is made into a link.

Using the CSS Styles panel to apply styles

The CSS Styles panel, shown in Figure 27-1, is a flexible and easy-to-use interface with straightforward command buttons listing all available style items. As with all of Dreamweaver's primary panels, you can open the CSS Styles panel in several ways:

✦ Choose Windows ⇨ CSS Styles.

✦ Select the New Style button from either Launcher.

✦ Press Shift+F11.

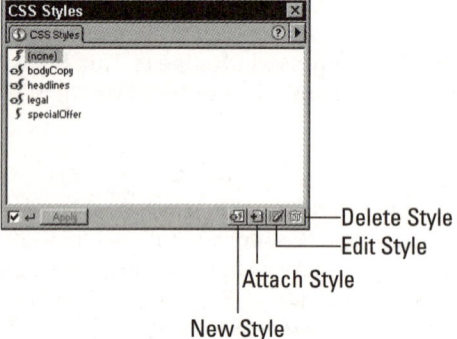

Figure 27-1: The Dreamweaver CSS Styles panel helps you apply consistent styles to a Web page.

The main part of the CSS Styles panel is the list of defined custom styles or classes. Every custom tag you create is listed alphabetically in this window. Once you've chosen the portion of your HTML document that you're stylizing, you can choose one of the custom styles listed here by simply selecting it, if the Apply option is selected. If the option is not checked, select the desired style and choose the Apply button.

At the bottom right-hand corner of the CSS Styles panel are four buttons. The first of these, Attach Style Sheet is a new addition in Dreamweaver 4 and is used for quickly linking the current Web page to an existing style sheet. Clicking the second—the New Style button—begins the process of defining a new CSS style, either in an external or internal style sheet. The third button, Edit Style Sheet, opens the multifaceted Edit Style Sheet dialog box, in which you can create a new style, link a style sheet, edit or remove an existing style, or duplicate a style that you can then alter. Before you can begin applying styles to a Web page or site, the styles must be defined, and using the Edit Style Sheet dialog box is the pain-free method of accomplishing this task. You can, of course, switch to Code view or open the Code Inspector and add the style by hand, but you can avoid this process with the Edit Style Sheet dialog box. You get a close look at this tool in the upcoming section "Editing and managing style sheets." The final button is for deleting styles once they are defined.

Attaching an external style sheet

As CSS-enabled browsers begin to become predominant, more Web designers are encountering clients with existing external style sheets. To apply the site's design specifications to a new page, all the designer need do is link the current page to the CSS document. Dreamweaver 4 provides a streamlined method for doing just that.

New Feature

The Attach Style Sheet button, found on the CSS Styles panel, is a one-step solution for linking external style sheets to the current document. When Attach Style Sheet is selected, a standard Select File dialog box appears with the *.css filter set. Simply locate the desired style sheet and select it: Dreamweaver inserts the necessary code into the <head> of your document. If any HTML tags—such as <p> or any of the heading tags—on your page are defined in the style sheet, you'll see an immediate change in your document.

When the Attach Style Sheet feature is applied, Dreamweaver uses the link attribute to connect style sheet to Web page. The link attribute is much more widely used by professional designers than the import attribute; however, if you'd prefer to use import instead, you can still attach a style sheet with this method as described in a section later in this chapter, "Importing an External Style Sheet."

Applying, changing, and removing a style

As noted above, any HTML tags redefined as CSS styles in an attached style sheet will automatically be applied to your document. However, any custom CSS styles must be applied on a case-by-case basis. Most Web designers use a combination of HTML and custom CSS styles. Only custom CSS styles appear in the CSS Styles panel.

New Feature

Dreamweaver 4 enables you to tell where a custom style is from—whether it's from a linked external style sheet or included in the current document—at a glance. The CSS Styles panel now displays a small chain-link symbol next to the listing if the style can be found on a separate style sheet. In larger sites, it's often important to differentiate between two similarly named custom styles.

To apply an existing custom style, follow these steps:

1. Choose Windows ⇨ CSS Styles or select the Show CSS Styles button from either Launcher to open the CSS Styles panel.

2. To apply the style to a section of the page enclosed by an HTML tag, select the tag from the Tag Selector.

   To apply the style to a section that is not enclosed by a single HTML tag, use your mouse to select that section in the Document window.

3. Select the desired custom style from the CSS Styles panel.

   Dreamweaver applies the custom style either by setting the `class` attribute of the selected tag to the custom style or — if just text is selected, not an enclosing tag — to a `<span>` tag which wraps around the text.

As you might expect, Dreamweaver offers a second way of applying a style to your pages. The following method, using the menus, does not employ the CSS Styles panel:

1. Highlight the text to which you're applying the style, either through the Tag Selector or by using the mouse.

2. Select Text ⇨ CSS Styles ⇨ Your Style.

   The same dynamic CSS Styles list is maintained in the context menu, accessible through a right-click (Ctrl+click) on the selected text.

Changing styles

In prior versions of Dreamweaver, multiple `<span>` tags were a common phenomenon as designers tried out different styles without properly selecting the `<span>` tag. It was not unusual to see this type of code:

```
<span class="head1"><span class="head2"><span
class="head3">News of the Moment</span></span></span>
```

In situations such as these, the CSS style in the span tag closest to the text, in this example head3, is rendered. The other span tags are just so much cluttered code. Dreamweaver 4 now strives to prevent nested `<span>` tags, automatically.

New Feature

Changing from applied custom style to another is extremely straightforward in Dreamweaver4. No longer do you have to be sure to select the enclosing tag — whether it's a `<span>` or other tag — to replace the style. In fact, you don't have to select anything: just place your cursor anywhere within the styled text and select a different custom style from the CSS Styles panel. Dreamweaver changes the old style to the new without adding additional `<span>` tags.

But what if you want to apply a new style to a text range within an existing `<span>` tag? Again, Dreamweaver's default is to avoid nested span tags. Here's how it works. Let's say you're working with the following code:

```
<span class="bodyCopy">Developing strategies to survive
requires industry insight and forward thinking in this
competitive marketplace.</span>
```

If you apply a custom style called hype to the phrases industry insight and forward thinking by first selecting those phrases and then choosing hype from the CSS Styles panel, the code looks like this:

```
<span class="bodyCopy">Developing strategies to survive
requires </span><span class="hype">industry insight</span> and
<span class="hype">forward thinking</span><span
class="bodyCopy"> in this competitive marketplace.</span>
```

Dreamweaver wraps each phrase in a distinct <span> tag so that nesting is entirely avoided. This behavior enables the style of each phrase to be altered more easily.

Tip   If you positively, absolutely would prefer to nest your <span> tags, you can do so by Shift+clicking on the desired style in the CSS Styles panel.

If your cursor is positioned within a tag without an existing style, you can still quickly apply the custom CSS style. Dreamweaver now automatically applies the chosen style to the following tags:

✦ <p>

✦ <h1>-<h6>

✦ <td>

✦ <th>

✦ <caption>

✦ <li>

✦ <ul>

✦ <ol>

✦ <pre>

✦ <blockquote> or <bq>

Caution   In most cases, this new functionality means that it's far easier to apply — and change — CSS styles than ever before. However, should your cursor be in a tag other than those listed above, such as an <address> tag, Dreamweaver wraps the text in a paragraph tag and assigns the style to the <p> tag. If your text is not within a span or one of the tags listed above, be sure to select the tag you want to apply the style to from the Tag Selector.

Removing applied styles

Getting rid of an applied style also gets a whole lot simpler in Dreamweaver 4. Now, just position your cursor anywhere in the stylized text and select (none) from the

CSS Styles panel. Dreamweaver removes the class attribute if the style was attached to a tag other than `<span>` while surrounding `<span>` tags are completely deleted. Naturally, if you choose the tag containing the style through the Tag Selector, selecting (none) also eliminates the style from the tag.

Note   Be sure your cursor is just positioned within styled text and not selecting any. Selecting (none) from the CSS Styles panel when text alone — no tags — is highlighted, has no effect.

Defining new styles

Selecting the New Style button in the CSS Styles panel brings up a new dialog box (see Figure 27-2) where you specify the type of style you're defining. You can opt to create the new styles in an external style sheet or in the current document. After you've chosen the type of style desired, select the Define In This Document Only option to create an internal style sheet. Any style sheets already linked to (or imported into) the current document appear in the drop-down list along with the New Style Sheet File option. If you choose Define In New Style Sheet File, a standard file dialog box opens for you to name and store your new .css file.

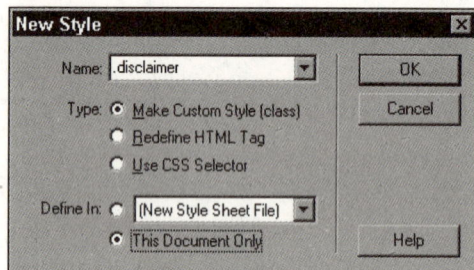

Figure 27-2: The first step in defining a new style is to select a style type and enter a name for the style, if it's a custom one.

The following sections explain the three style types in depth:

✦ Make Custom Style (class)

✦ Redefine HTML Tag

✦ Use CSS Selector

Make Custom Style (class)

Making a custom style is the most flexible way to define a style on a page. The first step in creating a custom style is to give it a name; this name is used in the `class` attribute. The name for your class must start with a period and must be alphanumeric without punctuation or special characters. If you do not begin the name of your custom style with a period, Dreamweaver inserts one for you.

Following are typical names you can use:

```
.master
.pagetitle
.bodytext
```

Caution Although you can use names such as body, title, or any other HTML tag, this approach is not a good idea. Dreamweaver warns you of the conflict if you try this method.

Redefine HTML Tags

The second radio button in the New Style dialog box is Redefine HTML Tag. This type of style is an excellent tool for making quick, global changes to existing Web pages. Essentially, the Redefine HTML Tag style enables you to modify the features of your existing HTML tags. When you select this option, the drop-down list displays over 40 HTML tags in alphabetical order. Select a tag from the drop-down list and click OK.

Use CSS Selector

When you use the third style type, Use CSS Selector, you define what are known as *pseudo-classes* and *pseudo-elements*. A pseudo-class represents dynamic states of a tag that may change under user action or over time. Several standard pseudo-classes associated with the <a> tag are used to style hypertext links.

When you choose Use CSS Selector, the drop-down list box contains four customization options, which can all be categorized as pseudo-classes:

✦ a:active customizes the style of a link when the user selects it.

✦ a:hover customizes the style of a link while the user's mouse is over it.

Note The a:hover pseudo-class is a CSS Level 2 specification and is currently supported only by Internet Explorer 4.0 and above as well as Netscape 6.

✦ a:link customizes the style of a link that has not been visited recently.

✦ a:visited customizes the style of a link to a page that has been recently visited.

Tip Dreamweaver does not preview pseudo-class styles, although they can be previewed through a supported browser.

A pseudo-element, on the other hand, enables control over contextually defined page elements: for example, pseudo-elements enable you to style paragraphs within a table differently than paragraphs outside of a table. Similarly, text that is nested within two blockquotes (giving the appearance of being indented two levels) can be given a different color, font, and so on than text in a single blockquote.

Because of their specific nature, Dreamweaver does not display any pseudo-elements in the Use CSS Selector list. You can, however, enter your own. For example, to style text within nested blockquotes, enter the following in the Use CSS Selector field of the New Style dialog box:

```
blockquote blockquote
```

Basically, you are creating a custom style for a set of HTML tags used in your document. This type of CSS selector acts like an HTML tag that has a CSS style applied to it; that is, all page elements fitting the criteria are automatically styled.

Editing and managing style sheets

The Edit Style Sheet dialog box, shown in Figure 27-3, displays all your current styles — including HTML tags and custom styles — and provides various controls to link a style sheet and edit, create, duplicate, or remove a style. To access the Edit Style Sheet dialog box, choose the Edit Style Sheet button on the CSS Styles panel.

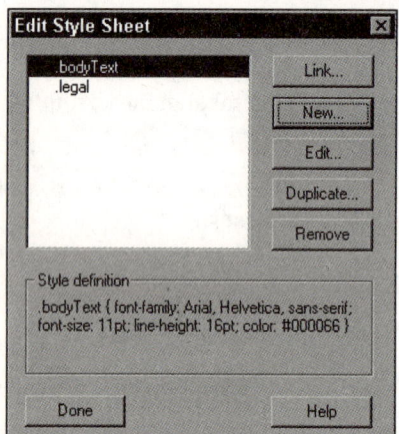

Figure 27-3: The Edit Style Sheet dialog box lists and defines any given style, in addition to presenting several command buttons for creating and managing styles.

 Tip   To start editing one of your styles immediately, double-click the style in the list window of the Edit Style Sheet dialog box. This sequence takes you to the Style Definition dialog box, in which you redefine your selected style.

Use the following five command buttons along the right side of the Edit Style Sheet dialog box to create new external sheets or manage your existing style sheets:

✦ **Link:** Enables you to create an external style sheet or link to (or import) an existing external style sheet.

✦ **New:** Begins the creation of a new style by first opening the New Style dialog box, described in the following section.

✦ **Edit:** Modifies any existing style.

✦ **Duplicate:** Makes a copy of the selected style as a basis for creating a new style.

✦ **Remove:** Deletes an existing style.

Importing an external style sheet

As noted earlier, most Web designers prefer the link method of including an external style sheet to the import method. However, Dreamweaver offers both options, albeit in a slightly more difficult to get to place.

To import a separate style sheet, follow these steps:

1. Open the CSS Styles panel by choosing Windows ➪ CSS Styles or selecting the Show CSS Styles button from either Launcher.

2. Select the Edit Style Sheet button.

3. In the Edit Style dialog box, select the Link command button.

   The Link External Style Sheet dialog box pops up, where you can access all your style sheets, by browsing and linking.

4. Either type in the File/URL path or select the Browse button to locate a style sheet; the Cascading Style Sheet file has the .css file name extension on your hard drive. If you have not already created a style sheet, you can do so by locating the place you want the style sheet and then creating a name for it. Useful names for style sheets can be master.css, contents.css, or body.css.

5. Choose the Import option.

   Naturally, you could also, at this point, choose the Link option

When you go back to the Edit Style Sheet dialog box, you see a link file referenced in the listing above all the styles, followed by (link) or (import). You can double-click the file listing to open a new Edit Style Sheet dialog box for your external style sheet file. The defined styles within the style sheet then appear in the CSS Styles panel.

Tip
Once you've defined your external style sheet, a couple of shortcuts exist for the Edit Style Sheet dialog box. First, you can press the Ctrl (Option) key and click the Edit Style Sheet button in the CSS Styles panel. Rather than displaying the Edit Style Sheet dialog box with a link to your external style sheet (which you'd have to double-click or highlight and select Edit to modify), you'll see the dialog box for the external style sheet immediately.

The second method is useful if you have the Site window open. Just double-click any .css file, and the Edit Style Sheet dialog box for that file opens instantly.

If you've already defined styles in the current document and you want to convert them to an external style sheet, Dreamweaver has you covered. Just choose File ⇨ Export ⇨ Export CSS Styles and enter a file name in the Export Styles as CSS File dialog box. Follow the directions in this section for linking this newly created file to your other Web pages as a style sheet.

Tip
You can also export internal styles to an external style sheet by pressing Ctrl (Option) while clicking the Done button in the Edit Style Sheet dialog box.

Styles and Their Attributes

After you've selected a type and name for a new style or chosen to edit an existing style, the Style Definition dialog box opens. A Category list from which you select a style category (just as you select a category in Dreamweaver's Preferences dialog box) is located on the left side of this dialog box.

Dreamweaver offers you eight categories of CSS Level 1 styles to help you define your style sheet:

- ✦ Type
- ✦ Background
- ✦ Block
- ✦ Box
- ✦ Border
- ✦ List
- ✦ Positioning
- ✦ Extensions

You can apply styles from one or all categories. The following sections describe each style category and its available settings.

Note Dreamweaver doesn't preview all the possible CSS attributes. Those attributes that can't be seen in the Document window are marked with an asterisk in the Style Definition dialog box.

Type options

The Type category (see Figure 27-4) specifies the appearance and layout of the typeface for the page in the browser window. The Type category is one of the most widely used and supported categories — it can be rendered in Internet Explorer 3.0 and above and Netscape Navigator 4.0 and above. Table 27-1 explains the settings available in this category.

<table>
<tr><td colspan="2" align="center">Table 27-1
CSS Type Attributes</td></tr>
<tr><td>*Type Setting*</td><td>*Description*</td></tr>
<tr><td>Font</td><td>Specifies the font or a collection of fonts, known as a *font family*. You can edit the font list by selecting Edit Font List from the drop-down list. (This sequence opens the Edit Font List dialog box, as described in Chapter 9.)</td></tr>
<tr><td>Size</td><td>Selects a size for the selected font. If you enter a value, you can then select the measurement system in the adjacent text box (the default is points). The relative sizes, such as small, medium, and large, are set relative to the parent element.</td></tr>
<tr><td>Style</td><td>Specifies a normal, oblique, or italic attribute for the font. An oblique font may have been generated in the browser by electronically slanting a normal font.</td></tr>
<tr><td>Line Height</td><td>Sets the line height of the line (known as *leading* in traditional layout). Typically, line height is a point or two more than the font size, although you can set the line height to be the same as or smaller than the font size, for an overlapping effect.</td></tr>
<tr><td>Decoration</td><td>Changes the decoration for text. Options include underline, overline, line-through, blink, and none. The blink decoration is displayed only in Netscape browsers.</td></tr>
<tr><td>Weight</td><td>Sets the boldness of the text. You can use the relative settings (light, bold, bolder, and boldest) or apply a numeric value. Normal is around 400; bold is 700.</td></tr>
<tr><td>Variant</td><td>Switches between normal and small caps. Small caps is a font style that displays text as uppercase, but the capital letters are a slightly larger size. The Variant option is not currently fully supported by either primary browser.</td></tr>
<tr><td>Case</td><td>Forces a browser to render the text as uppercase, lowercase, or capitalized.</td></tr>
<tr><td>Color</td><td>Sets a color for the selected font. Enter a color name or select the color swatch to choose a browser-safe color from the pop-up menu.</td></tr>
</table>

Figure 27-4: Type settings for your style

Figure 27-5: You can achieve a number of different tiling effects by using the Repeat attribute of the CSS Background category.

Background options

Since Netscape Navigator 2.0, Web designers have been able to use background images and color. Thanks to CSS Background attributes, designers can now use background images and color with increased control. Whereas traditional HTML background images are restricted to a single image for the entire browser window, CSS backgrounds can be specified for a single paragraph or any other CSS selector. (To set a background for the entire page, apply the style to the <body> tag.) Moreover, instead of an image automatically tiling to fill the browser window, CSS backgrounds can be made to tile horizontally, vertically, or not at all (see Figure 27-5). You can even position the image relative to the selected element.

Currently only Netscape 6 fully supports the CSS Background attributes shown in Figure 27-6 and listed in Table 27-2. The Repeat attribute enjoys full support across 4.*x* browsers and above, but Positioning and Attachment are rendered only in Internet Explorer 4.0 and above and Netscape 6.

Figure 27-6: The CSS Background options enable a much wider range of control over background images and color.

Table 27-2
CSS Background Attributes

Background Setting	Description
Background Color	Sets the background color for a particular style. Note that this setting enables you to set background colors for individual paragraphs or other elements.
Background Image	Specifies a background image.
Repeat	Determines the tiling options for a graphic:
	no repeat displays the image in the upper-left corner of the applied style
	repeat tiles the background image horizontally and vertically across the applied style
	repeat-x tiles the background image horizontally across the applied style
	repeat-y tiles the background image vertically down the applied style
Attachment	Determines whether the background image remains fixed in its original position or scrolls with the page. This setting is useful for positioned elements. If you use the overflow attribute, you often want the background image to scroll in order to maintain layout control.
Horizontal Position	Controls the positioning of the background image in relation to the style sheet elements (text or graphics) along the horizontal axis.
Vertical Position	Controls the positioning of the background image in relation to the style sheet elements (text or graphics) along the vertical axis.

Block options

One of the most common formatting effects in traditional publishing long absent from Web publishing is justified text — text that appears as a solid block. Justified text is possible with the Text Align attribute, one of the six options available in the CSS Block category, as shown in Figure 27-7. Indented paragraphs are also a possibility. Table 27-3 lists the CSS Block options.

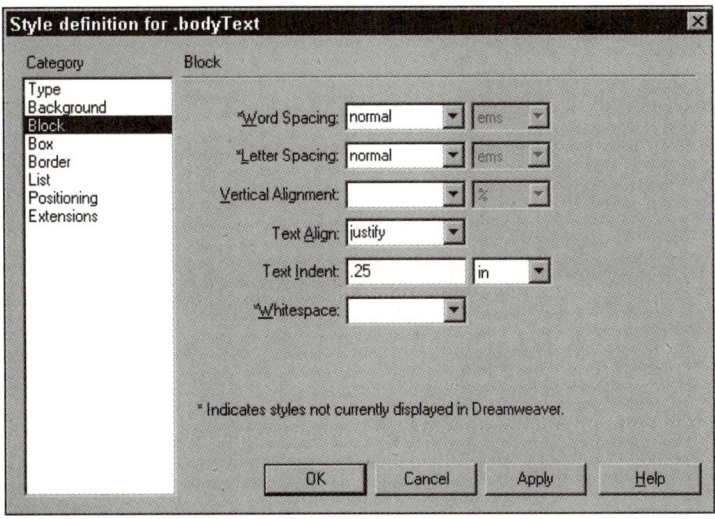

Figure 27-7: The Block options give the Web designer enhanced text control.

	Table 27-3
	CSS Block Attributes

Block Setting	Description
Word Spacing	Defines the spacing between words. You can increase or decrease the spacing with positive and negative values, set in ems.
Letter Spacing	Defines the spacing between the letters of a word. You can increase or decrease the spacing with positive and negative values, set in ems.
Vertical Alignment	Sets the vertical alignment of the style. Choose from baseline, sub, super, top, text-top, middle, bottom, or text-bottom, or add your own value.
Text Align	Sets text alignment (left, right, center, and justified).
Text Indent	Indents the first line of text on a style by the amount specified.
Whitespace	Controls display of spaces and tabs. The normal option causes all whitespace to collapse. The pre option behaves similarly to the `<pre>` tag; all white space is preserved. The nowrap option enables text to wrap if a ` ` tag is detected.

Box options

The Box attribute defines the placement and settings for elements (primarily images) on a page. Many of the controls (shown in Figure 27-8) emulate spacing behavior similar to that found in `<table>` attributes. If you are already comfortable using HTML tables with cell padding, border colors, and width/height controls, you can quickly learn how to use these Box features, which are described in Table 27-4.

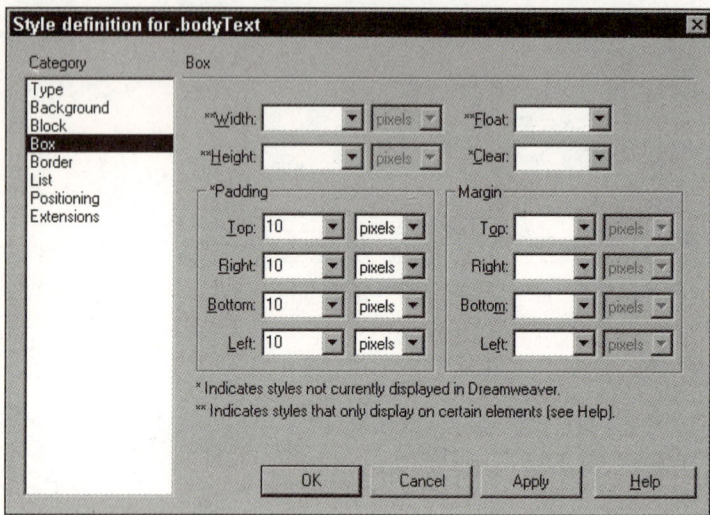

Figure 27-8: The CSS Box attributes define the placement of HTML elements on the Web page.

Table 27-4
CSS Box Attributes

Box Setting	Description
Width	Sets the width of the element.
Height	Defines the height of the element.
Float	Places the element at the left or right page margin. Any text that encounters the element wraps around it.
Clear	Sets the side on which layers cannot be displayed next to the element. If a layer is encountered, the element with the Clear attribute places itself beneath the layer.
Padding	Sets the amount of space between the element and the border or margin, if no border is specified. You can control the padding for the left, right, top, and bottom independently.
Margin	Defines the amount of space between the borders of the element and other elements in the page.

Dreamweaver imposes some specific restrictions on which Box attributes can and cannot be previewed in the Document window. For example, the Float and Clear attributes can be previewed only when applied to an image. The Margin attributes can be previewed when applied to block-level elements, such as any of the <h1> through <h6> tags or the <p> tag. Padding is not displayed within Dreamweaver.

Border options

With Cascading Style Sheets, you can specify many parameters for borders surrounding text, images, and other elements such as Java applets. In addition to specifying separate colors for any of the four box sides, you can also choose the width of each side's border, as shown in the CSS Border category (see Figure 27-9). You can use eight different types of border lines, including solid, dashed, inset, and ridge. Table 27-5 lists the Border options.

Figure 27-9: Borders are useful when you need to highlight a section of text or a graphic.

	Table 27-5
	CSS Border Attributes

Border Setting	Description
Top	Sets the color and settings for a border along the top of an element.
Right	Sets the color and settings for a border along the right side of an element.
Bottom	Sets the color and settings for a border along the bottom of an element.
Left	Sets the color and settings for a border along the left side of an element.
Style	Sets the style of the border. You can use any of the following as a border: Dotted, Dashed, Solid, Double, Groove, Ridge, Inset, and Outset.

Tip   CSS Border attributes are especially useful for highlighting paragraphs of text with a surrounding box. Use the Box category's Padding attributes to inset the text from the border.

List options

CSS gives you greater control over bulleted points. With Cascading Style Sheets, you can now display a specific bulleted point based on a graphic image, or you can choose from the standard built-in bullets, including disc, circle, and square. The List category also enables you to specify the type of ordered list, including decimal, Roman numerals, or A-B-C order.

Figure 27-10 shows, and Table 27-6 describes, the settings for lists.

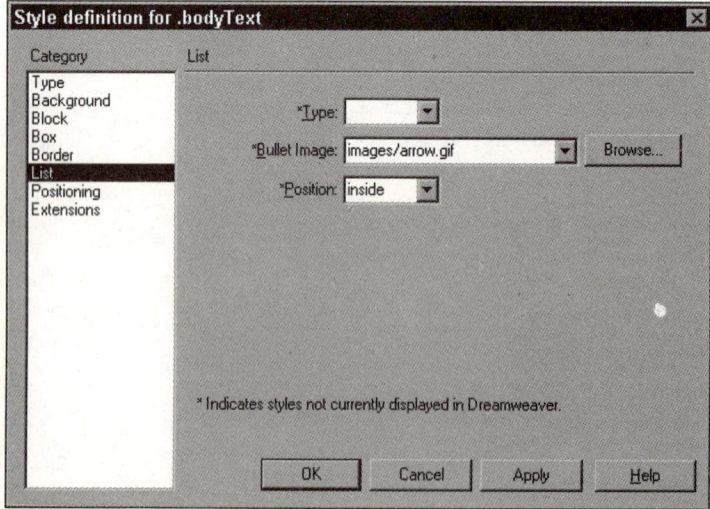

Figure 27-10: Specify a graphic to use as a bullet through the List category.

Table 27-6
List Category for Styles

List Setting	Description
Type	Selects a built-in bullet type. The options include disc, circle, square, decimal, lowercase roman, uppercase roman, lowercase alpha, and uppercase alpha.
Bullet Image	Sets an image to be used as a custom bullet. Enter the path to the image in the text box.
Position	Determines if the list item wraps to an indent (the default) or to the margin.

Positioning options

For many designers, positioning has increased creativity in page layout design. With positioning, you have exact control over where an element is placed on a page. Figure 27-11 shows the various attributes that provide this pinpoint control of your page elements. The options are described in Table 27-7.

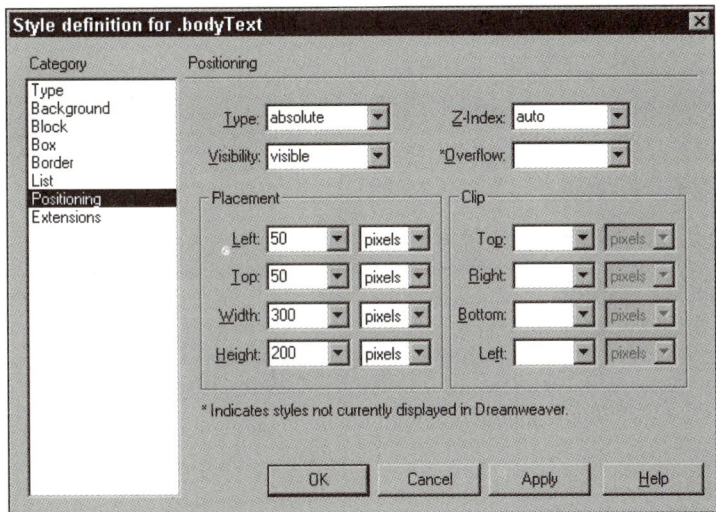

Figure 27-11: Control over the placement of elements on a page frees the Web designer from the restrictions imposed with HTML tables and other old-style formats.

Table 27-7
CSS Positioning Attributes

Positioning Setting	Description
Type	Determines whether an element can be positioned absolutely or relatively on a page. The third option, static, does not enable positioning.
Visibility	Determines whether the element is visible or hidden, or inherits the property from its parent.
Z-Index	Sets the apparent depth of a positioned element. Higher values are closer to the top.
Overflow	Specifies how the element is displayed when it's larger than the dimensions of the element. Options include the following: Clip, where the element is partially hidden; none, where the element is displayed and the dimensions are disregarded; and Scroll, which inserts scroll bars to display the overflowing portion of the element.
Placement	Sets the styled element's placement with the left and top attributes, and the dimensions with the width and height attributes.
Clip	Sets the visible portion of the element through the top, right, bottom, and left attributes.

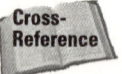

Cross-Reference   Dreamweaver layers are built upon the foundation of CSS positioning. For a complete explanation of layers and their attributes, see Chapter 28.

Extensions options

The specifications for Cascading Style Sheets are rapidly evolving, and Dreamweaver has grouped some cutting-edge features in the Extensions category. As of this writing, the majority of the Extensions attributes (see Table 27-8) are supported only by Internet Explorer 4.0 and above; Netscape 6 supports only the cursor property. The Extensions settings shown in Figure 27-12 affect three different areas: page breaks for printing, the user's cursor, and special effects called *filters*.

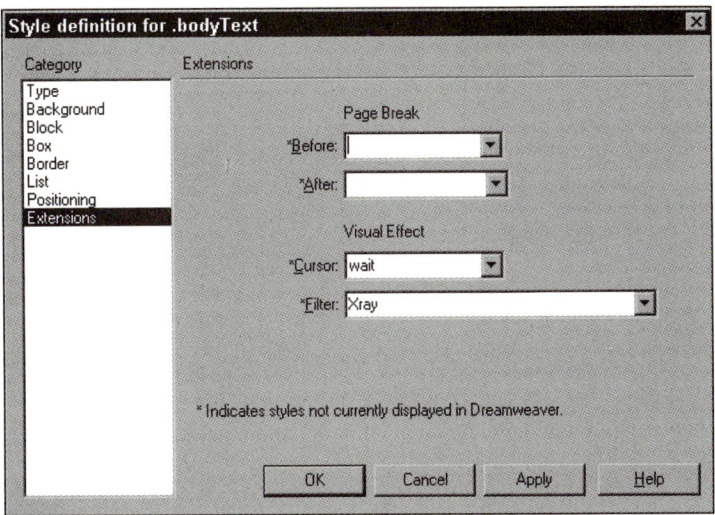

Figure 27-12: The Extensions category is currently supported only by Internet Explorer 4 and above, as well as Netscape 6.

Table 27-8
CSS Extensions Attributes

Extensions Setting	Description
Pagebreak	Inserts a point on a page where a printer sees a page break. Not supported by any current browser.
Cursor	Defines the type of cursor that appears when the user moves the cursor over an element. Currently supported only by Internet Explorer 4.0 and above, as well as Netscape 6.
Filter	Filters enable you to customize the look and transition of an element without having to use graphic or animation files. Currently supported only by Internet Explorer 4.0 and above.

Note   One of the problems with the Web's never-ending evolution of page design is evident when you begin to print the page. The Pagebreak attribute alleviates this problem by enabling the designer to designate a style that forces a page break when printing; the break can occur either before or after the element is attached to the style. Although no browser currently supports this feature, it's a good candidate for support by future browsers.

The Filter attribute offers 16 different special effects that can be applied to an element. Many of these effects, such as wave and xray, are quite stunning. Several effects involve transitions, as well. Table 27-9 details all these effects.

Table 27-9 CSS Filters		
Filter	**Syntax**	**Description**
Alpha	alpha(Opacity=*opacity*, FinishOpacity=*finishopacity*, Style=*style*, StartX=*startX*, StartY=*startY*, FinishX=*finishX*, FinishY=*finishY*)	Sets the opacity of a specified gradient region. This can have the effect of creating a burst of light in an image.
	Opacity is a value from 0 to 100, where 0 is transparent and 100 is fully opaque.	
	Style can be 0 (uniform), 1 (linear), 2 (radial), or 3 (rectangular).	
BlendTrans*	blendtrans(duration=*duration*)	Causes an image to fade in or out over a specified time.
	Duration is a time value for the length of the transition, in the format of *seconds.milliseconds*.	
Blur	blur(Add=*add*, Direction=*direction*, Strength=*strength*)	Emulates motion blur for images.
	Add is any integer other than 0.	
	Direction is any value from 0 to 315 in increments of 45.	
	Strength is any positive integer representing the number of pixels. affected.	
Chroma	chroma(Color= *color*)	Makes a specific color in an image transparent.
	Color must be given in hexadecimal form, for example, #rrggbb.	
DropShadow	dropshadow(Color=*color*, OffX=*offX*, OffY=*offY*, Positive=*positive*)	Creates a drop shadow of the applied element, either image or text, in the specified color.
	Color is a hexadecimal triplet.	

Filter	Syntax	Description
	OffX and *OffY* are pixel offsets for the shadow.	
	Positive is a Boolean switch; use 1 to create shadow for nontransparent pixels and 0 to create shadow for transparent pixels.	
FlipH	FlipH	Flips an image or text horizontally.
FlipV	FlipV	Flips an image or text vertically.
Glow	Glow(Color=*color*, Strength=*strength*)	Adds radiance to an image in the specified color.
	Color is a hexadecimal triplet.	
	Strength is a value from 0 to 100.	
Gray	Gray	Converts an image in grayscale.
Invert	Invert	Reverses the hue, saturation, and luminance of an image.
Light*	Light	Creates the illusion that an object is illuminated by one or more light sources.
Mask	Mask(Color=*color*)	Sets all the transparent pixels to the specified color and converts the nontransparent pixels to the background color.
	Color is a hexadecimal triplet.	
RevealTrans*	RevealTrans(duration=*duration*, transition=*style*)	Reveals an image using a specified type of transition over a set period of time.
	Duration is a time value that the transition takes, in the format of *seconds.milliseconds*.	
	Style is one of 23 different transitions.	
Shadow	Shadow(Color=*color*, Direction=*direction*)	Creates a gradient shadow in the specified color and direction for images or text.
	Color is a hexadecimal triplet.	

Continued

Table 27-9 *(continued)*

Filter	Syntax	Description
	Direction is any value from 0 to 315 in increments of 45.	
Wave	Wave(Add=*add*, Freq=*freq*, LightStrength=*lightstrength*, Phase=*phase*, Strength=*strength*)	Adds sine wave distortion to the selected image or text.
	Add is a Boolean value, where 1 adds the original object to the filtered object and 0 does not.	
	Freq is an integer specifying the number of waves.	
	LightStrength is a percentage value.	
	Phase specifies the angular offset of the wave, in percentage (for example, 0% or 100% = 360 degrees, 25% = 90 degrees).	
	Strength is an integer value specifying the intensity of the wave effect.	
Xray	Xray	Converts an image to inverse grayscale for an X-rayed appearance.

* These three filters require extensive documentation beyond the scope of this book.

Note   Although only Internet Explorer uses the filters described here, Netscape 6 does have the capability to control opacity. The MozOpacity property of the style command may be set programmatically to a percentage value as in this code:

```
document.myImage.style.MozOpacity = '50%';
```

You can also declare the MozOpacity property as part of a CSS style. The following code example shows a CSS style that changes the opacity to 77% to whatever it's applied for both Internet Explorer 4 (and above) and Netscape 6.

```
.myOpacity { filter: alpha(opacity=77); -moz-opacity:
77% }
```

Summary

In this chapter, you discovered how you can easily and effectively add and modify Cascading Style Sheets. You can now accomplish all of the following:

✦ Update and change styles easily with the CSS Styles panel.

✦ Easily apply generated styles to an element on a page.

✦ Apply a consistent look and feel with linked style sheets.

✦ Position fonts and elements, such as images, with pinpoint accuracy.

✦ Exercise control over the layout, size, and display of fonts on a page.

✦ Define external style sheets to control the look and feel of an entire site.

In the next chapter, you learn how to position elements on a page in Dreamweaver using layers.

✦　　✦　　✦

Working with Layers

For many years, page designers have taken for granted the capability to place text and graphics anywhere on a printed page—even enabling graphics, type, and other elements to "bleed" off a page. This flexibility in design has eluded Web designers until recently. Lack of absolute control over layout has been a high price to pay for the universality of HTML, which makes any Web page viewable by any system, regardless of the computer or the screen resolution.

Lately, however, the integration of positioned layers within the Cascading Style Sheets specification has brought true absolute positioning to the Web. Page designers with a yen for more control can move to the precision offered with Cascading Style Sheets-Positioning (CSS-P).

Dreamweaver's implementation of layers turns the promise of CSS-P into an intuitive, designer-friendly, layout-compatible reality. As the name implies, layers offer more than pixel-perfect positioning. You can stack one layer on another, hide some layers while showing others, move a layer across the screen—and even move several layers around the screen simultaneously. Layers add an entirely new dimension to the Web designer's palette. Dreamweaver enables you to create page layouts using layers and then convert those layers to tables that are viewable by earlier browsers.

This chapter explores every aspect of how layers work in HTML—except for animation with timelines, which is saved for Chapter 29. With the fundamentals under your belt, you learn how to create, modify, populate, and activate layers on your Web page.

Layers 101

When the World Wide Web first made its debut in 1989, few people were concerned about the aesthetic layout of a page. In fact, because the Web was a descendant of SGML — a multiplatform text document and information markup specification — layout was trivialized. Content and the capability to use hypertext to jump from one page to another were emphasized. After the first graphical Web browser software (Mosaic) was released, it quickly became clear that a page's graphics and layout could enhance a Web site's accessibility and marketability. Content was still king, but design was moving up quickly.

The first attempt at Web page layout was the server-side image map. This item was a typically large graphic (usually too hefty to be downloaded comfortably) with hotspots. Clicking a hotspot sent a message to the server, which returned a link to the browser. The download time for these files was horrendous, and the performance varied from acceptable to awful, based on the server's load.

The widespread adoption of tables, released with HTML 2.0 and enhanced for versions 3.2 and 4.0, radically changed layout control. Designers gained the capability to align objects and text — but a lot of graphical eye candy was still left to graphic files strategically located within the tables. The harder designers worked at precisely laying out their Web pages, the more they had to resort to workarounds such as nested tables and 1-pixel-wide GIFs used as spacers. To relieve the woes of Web designers everywhere, the W3C included a feature within the new Cascading Styles Sheet specifications that allows for absolute positioning of an element upon a page. Absolute positioning enables an element, such as an image or block of text, to be placed anywhere on the Web page. Both Microsoft Internet Explorer 4.0 (and above) and Netscape Navigator 4.0 (and above) support layers under the Cascading Style Sheets-Positioning specification.

The addition of the third dimension, depth, truly turned the positioning specs into layers. Now objects can be positioned side-by-side, and they have a *z-index* property as well. The z-index gets its name from the practice in geometry of describing three-dimensional space with x, y, and z coordinates; z-index is also called the *stacking order* because objects can be stacked upon one another.

A single layer in HTML looks like the following:

```
<div id="Layer1" style="position:absolute; visibility:inherit; width:200px; ¬
height:115px; z-index:1"></div>
```

Positioned layers are most commonly placed within the `<div>` tag. Another popular location is the `<span>` tag. These tags were chosen because they are seldom used in the HTML 3.2 specification (Dreamweaver supports both tags). Both Microsoft and Netscape encourage users to employ either of these tags, because the two primary browsers are designed to credit full CSS-P features to either the `<div>` or `<span>` tag. You should generally use these tags when anything but specific Navigator 4.*x* compatibility is desired.

Positioning Measurement

The positioning of layers is determined by aligning elements on an x-axis and a y-axis. In CSS, the x-axis (defined as "Left" in CSS syntax) begins at the left side of the page, and the y-axis (defined as "Top" in CSS syntax) is measured from the top of the page down. As with many of the other CSS features, you have your choice of measurement systems for Left and Top positioning. All measurements are given in Dreamweaver as a number followed by the abbreviation of the measurement system (without any intervening spaces). The measurement system options follow:

Unit	Abbreviation	Measurement
Pixels	px	Relative to the screen
Points	pt	1 pt = $1/72$ in
Inches	in	1 in = 2.54 cm
Centimeters	cm	1 cm = 0.3937 in
Millimeters	mm	1 mm = 0.03937 in
Picas	pc	1 pc = 12 pt
EMS	em	The height of the element's font
Percentage	%	Relative to the browser window

If you don't define a unit of measurement for layer positioning, Dreamweaver defaults to pixels. If you decide to edit out the unit of measurement, the Web browser defaults to pixels.

Note Netscape has developed two additional proprietary tags for using layers in its 4.x browser: `<layer>` and `<ilayer>`. The primary difference between the two tags has to do with positioning: the `<layer>` tag is used for absolute positioning, and the `<ilayer>` tag for relative positioning. Unfortunately, layers created by the `<div>` tag and the `<layer>` tag have different feature sets. These tags are no longer supported in Navigator 6.0; instead Netscape's latest browser fully supports the CSS standard tags, `<div>` and `<span>`.

Creating Layers with Dreamweaver

Dreamweaver enables you to create layers creatively and precisely. You can drag out a layer, placing and sizing it by eye, or choose to do it by the numbers — it's up to you. Moreover, you can combine the methods, quickly eyeballing and roughing out a layer layout and then aligning the edges precisely. For Web design that approaches conventional page layout, Dreamweaver even includes rulers and a grid to which you can snap your layers.

You can handle the creation of layers in Dreamweaver in one of three ways:

✦ You can drag out a layer, after selecting the Draw Layer button from the Objects panel.

✦ You can put a layer in a predetermined size by choosing Insert ➪ Layer.

✦ You can create a layer with mathematical precision through the CSS Styles panel.

The first two methods are quite intuitive and are explained in the following section. The CSS Styles panel method is examined later in this chapter in the section "Embedding a Layer with Style Sheets."

Inserting a layer object

When you want to draw out your layer quickly, use the object approach. If you come from a traditional page-designer background and are accustomed to using a program such as QuarkXPress or PageMaker, you're already familiar with drawing out frames or text boxes with the click-and-drag technique. Dreamweaver uses the same method for placing and sizing new layer objects.

To draw out a layer as an object, follow these steps:

1. From the Common category of the Objects panel, select the Draw Layer button. Your pointer becomes a crosshair cursor. (If you decide not to draw out a layer, you can press Shift+Esc at this point or just click once without dragging to abort the process.)

2. Click anywhere in your document to position the layer and drag out a rectangle. Release the mouse button when you have an approximate size and shape with which you're satisfied (see Figure 28-1).

After you've dragged out your layer, notice several changes to the screen. First, the layer now has a small box on the outside of the upper-left corner. This box, shown in Figure 28-2, is the selection handle, which you can use to move an existing layer around the Web page. When you click the selection handle, eight sizing handles appear around the perimeter of the layer.

Layer icon   Selected layer   Draw Layer button

Layer Property Inspector

Figure 28-1: After selecting the Drag Layer object in the Objects panel (Common), the pointer becomes crosshairs when you are working on the page. Click and drag to create the layer.

Selection handle

Sizing handles

Figure 28-2: Once a layer is created, you can move it by dragging the selection handle and size it with the sizing handles.

Another subtle but important addition to the screen is the Layer icon. Like the other Invisibles icons — so named because they represent the unseen code — the Layer icon can be cut, copied, pasted, and repositioned. When you move the Layer icon, however, its corresponding layer does not move — you are actually only moving the code for the layer to a different place in the HTML source. Generally, the layer code's position in the HTML is immaterial — however, you may want to locate your layer source in a specific area to be backwardly compatible with 3.0 browsers. Dragging and positioning Layer icons one after another is a quick way to achieve this task.

Using the Insert ⇨ Layer command

The second method to create a layer is through the menus. Instead of selecting an object from the Objects panel, choose Insert ⇨ Layer. Unlike the click-and-drag method, inserting a layer through the menu automatically creates a layer in the upper-left corner; the default size is 200 pixels wide and 115 pixels high.

Although the layer is by default positioned in the upper-left corner of the Document window, it does not have any coordinates listed in the Property Inspector. The position coordinates are added when you drag the layer into a new position. If you repeatedly add new layers through the menus without moving them to new positions, each layer stacks directly on top of one another, with no offset.

It's important for every layer to have a specific position (left and top) assigned to it. Otherwise, the browser displays all layers directly on top of one another. To give a layer measurements, after you've inserted it through the menu, be sure to drag the layer, even slightly.

Setting default characteristics of a layer

You can designate the default size — as well as other features — of the layer that is inserted with Insert ⇨ Layer. Choose Edit ⇨ Preferences or use the keyboard shortcut Ctrl+U (Command+U) to open the Preferences dialog box. Select the Layers category. The Layers Preferences category (see Figure 28-3) helps you to set the layer attributes listed in Table 28-1.

Table 28-1 Layer Preferences	
Layer Preference	*Description*
Tag	Sets the HTML code to use when creating layers. The options are `<div>` (the default), `<span>`, `<layer>`, and `<ilayer>`.
Visibility	Determines the initial state of visibility for a layer. The options are default, inherit, visible, and hidden.

Layer Preference	Description
Width	Sets the width of the layer in the measurement system of your choice. The default is 200 pixels.
Height	Sets the height of the layer in the measurement system of your choice. The default is 115 pixels.
Background Color	Sets a color for the layer background. Select the color from the pop-up menu of Web-safe colors.
Background Image	Sets an image for the layer background. In the text box, enter the path to the graphics file or click the Browse (Choose) button to locate the file.
Nesting Option	If you want to nest layers when one layer is placed in the other automatically, check the Nest when Created Within a Layer checkbox.
Netscape 4 Compatibility	To add code for a workaround to a known problem in Navigator 4.x browsers, which causes layers to lose their positioning coordinates when the user resizes the browser window, select this option.

Figure 28-3: If you're building layers to a certain specification, use the Layers Preferences category to designate your options.

Embedding a layer with style sheets

In addition to laying out your layer by eye, or inserting a default layer with Insert ⇨ Layer, you can also specify your layers precisely through style sheets. Although this method is not as intuitive as either of the preceding methods, creating layers through style sheets has notable advantages:

✦ You can enter precise dimensions and other positioning attributes.

✦ The placement and shape of a layer can be combined with other style factors such as font family, font size, color, and line spacing.

✦ Layer styles can be saved in an external style sheet, which enables similar elements on every Web page in a site to be controlled from one source.

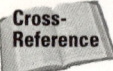

Cross-Reference If you haven't yet read Chapter 27, which discusses building style sheet Web pages, you may want to look it over before continuing here.

To create a layer with style sheets, follow these steps:

1. Choose Window ⇨ CSS Styles or select the Show CSS Styles button from the Launcher. This selection opens the CSS Styles panel.

2. From the CSS Styles panel, select the New Style button. This selection opens the New Style dialog box.

3. From the New Style dialog box, set the Type option set to Make Custom Style (class). Enter a name for your new style and then choose Define In This Document Only. Click OK.

4. This opens the Style Definition dialog box. Select the Positioning category.

5. From the Positioning category (see Figure 28-4), enter desired values for these attributes: Type, Visibility, Z-Index, Overflow, Placement (Left, Top, Width, and Height), and Clip settings (Top, Right, Bottom, Left). Overflow and Clip settings are optional.

   The Type attribute offers three options: Absolute, Relative, and Static. While you are familiar with the first two options, the third option, Static, is probably new to you. Use Static when you don't want to add content to a layer, but you still want to specify a rectangular block. Static <div> types ignore the Left and Top attributes. Dreamweaver does not display a static <div> type, so you'll have to preview your page in a browser to see the results.

6. If appropriate, select other categories and enter any additional style sheet attributes desired. Click OK when you're done.

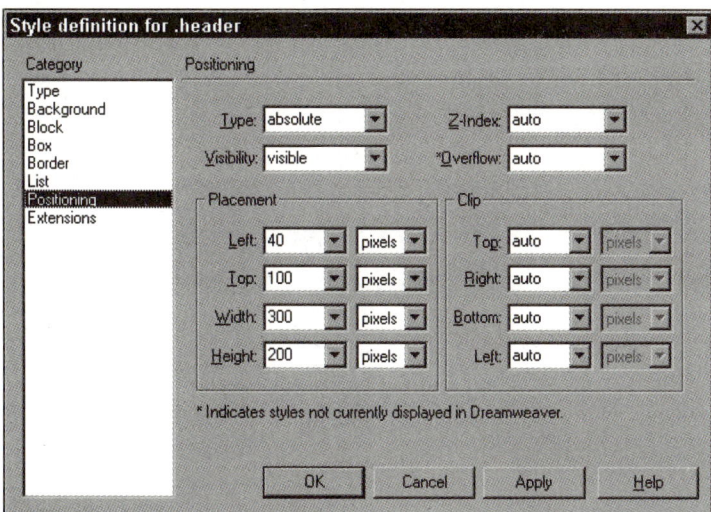

Figure 28-4: Use the Positioning category of the Style Definition dialog box to set layer attributes in an internal or external style sheet.

Keep in mind that layers are part of the overall Cascading Style Sheet specification and can benefit from all of the features of style sheets. You may decide that a specific area of text — a header, for instance — must always be rendered in a bold, red, 18-point Arial font with a green background, and that it should always be placed 35 pixels from the left margin and 25 pixels from the top of the page. You can place the style sheet within a .css file, link your Web pages to this file, and receive a result similar to what's shown (in black and white) in Figure 28-5. Within one component — the Cascading Style Sheet file — you can contain all of your positioning features for a page's headers, titles, and other text, graphics, or objects. This capability gives you the benefit of controlling the position and look of every title linked to one style sheet.

Choosing relative instead of absolute positioning

In most cases, absolute positioning uses the top-left corner of the Web page or the position where the `<body>` tag begins as the point of origin from which the Web browser determines the position of the text, image, or object. You can also specify measurements relative to objects. Dreamweaver offers two methods to accomplish relative positioning: the relative attribute and nested layers.

Using the relative attribute

In the first method, you select Relative as the Type attribute in the Style Sheet Positioning category. Relative positioning does not force a fixed position; instead, the HTML tags around it guide the positioning. For example, you may place a list of some items within a table and set the positioning relative to the table. You can see the effect of this sequence in Figure 28-6. In this illustration's Positioning category, the Type attribute is set to Relative and the Placement/Left value is set to 0.5 inch for a style applied to the listed items.

Figure 28-5: You can apply the layer style to any element on any Web page linked to the style sheet.

Note   Dreamweaver 4 doesn't preview relative positioning unless you're working with a nested layer, so you should check your placement by previewing the page in a browser, as shown in Figure 28-6.

Relative attributes can be useful, particularly if you want to place the positioned objects within free-flowing HTML. Free-flowing HTML repositions itself if the browser window is larger or smaller than the designer is aware. When you're using this technique, remember to place your relative layers within absolutely positioned layers. Otherwise, when the end user resizes the browser, the relative layers position themselves relative to the browser and not to the absolutely positioned layers. This situation can produce messy results — use relative positioning with caution when mixed with absolute layers.

Figure 28-6: Relative positioning through styles can give your document a clean look, although the effect is not previewed in Dreamweaver.

Using nested layers

The second technique for positioning layers relatively uses nested layers. Once you nest one layer inside another, the inner layer uses the upper-left corner of the outer layer as its orientation point. For more details about nesting layers, refer to the section "Nesting with the Layers panel," later in this chapter.

Modifying a Layer

Dreamweaver helps you deftly alter layers once you have created them. Because of the complexity of managing layers, Dreamweaver offers an additional tool to the usual Property Inspector: the Layers panel. This tool enables you to select any of the layers on the current page quickly, change layer relationships, modify their visibility, and adjust their stacking order. You can also alter the visibility and stacking order of a selected layer in the Property Inspector, along with many other attributes. Before any modifications can be accomplished, however, you have to select the layer.

Selecting a layer

You can choose from several methods to select a layer for alteration (see Figure 28-7).

Figure 28-7: You have four different methods for selecting a layer to modify.

Your method of choosing a layer most likely depends on the complexity of your page layout:

✦ When you have only a few layers that are not overlapping, just click the selection handle of the layer with which you want to work.

✦ When you have layers placed in specific places in the HTML code (for example, a layer embedded in a table using relative positioning), choose the Layer icon.

✦ When you have many overlapping layers that are being addressed by one or more JavaScript functions, use the Layers panel to choose the desired layer by name.

✦ When you're working with invisible layers, click the `<div>` (or `<span>`) tag in the Tag Selector to reveal the outline of the layer.

Resizing a layer

To resize a layer, position the pointer over one of the eight sizing handles surrounding the selected layer. When over the handles, the pointer changes shape to a two- or four-headed arrow. Now click and drag the layer to a new size and shape.

You can also use the arrow keys to resize your layer with more precision. The following keyboard shortcuts change the width and height dimensions while the layer remains anchored by the upper-left corner:

✦ When the layer is selected, press Ctrl+arrow (Command+arrow) to expand or contract the layer by one pixel.

✦ Press Shift+Ctrl+arrow (Shift+Command+arrow) to increase or decrease the selected layer by the current grid increment. The default grid increment is five pixels.

Tip   You can quickly preview the position of a layer on a Web page without leaving Dreamweaver. Deselecting the View ⇨ Visual Aids ⇨ Layer Borders option leaves the layer outline displayed only when the layer is selected, but otherwise it is not shown.

Moving a layer

The easiest way to reposition a layer is to drag the selection handle. If you don't see the handle on a layer, click anywhere in the layer. You can drag the layer anywhere on the screen — or off the bottom or right side of the screen. To move the layer off the left side or top of the screen, enter a negative value in the left and top (L and T) text boxes of the Layer Property Inspector.

Tip   To hide the layer completely, match the negative value with the width or height of the layer. For example, if your layer is 220 pixels wide and you want to position it offscreen to the left (so that the layer can slide on at the click of a mouse), set the Left position at –220 pixels.

As with resizing layers, you can also use the arrow keys to move the layer more precisely:

✦ Press any arrow key to move the selected layer one pixel in any direction.

✦ Use Shift+arrow to move the selected layer by the current grid increment.

Using the Layer Property Inspector

You can modify almost all the CSS-P attributes for your layer right from the Layer Property Inspector (see Figure 28-8). Certain attributes, such as width, height, and background image and color are self-explanatory or recognizable from other objects. Other layers-only attributes such as visibility and inheritance require further explanation. Table 28-2 describes all the Layer properties, and the following sections discuss the features unique to layers.

Figure 28-8: The Layer Property Inspector makes it easy to move, resize, hide, and manipulate all of the visual elements of a layer.

	Table 28-2	
	Layer Property Inspector Options	
Layer Attribute	**Possible Values**	**Description**
BgColor	Any hexadecimal or valid color name	Background color for the layer.
BgImage	Any valid graphic file	Background image for the layer.
Clip (Top, Bottom, Left, Right)	Any positive integer region of the layer. If the values are not specified, the entire layer is visible.	Measurements for the displayable
H (Height)	Any integer measurement in pixels, centimeters, millimeters, inches, points, percentage, ems, or picas	Vertical measurement of the layer.
L (Left)	Any integer measurement in pixels, centimeters, millimeters, inches, points, percentage, ems, or picas	Distance measured from the origin point on the left.
Name	Any unique name without spaces or special characters	Labels the layer so that it can be addressed by style sheets or JavaScript functions.
Overflow	visible, scroll, hidden, or auto	Determines how text or images larger than the layer should be handled.
T (Top)	Any integer measurement in pixels, centimeters, millimeters, inches, points, percentage, ems, or picas	The distance measured from the origin point on the top.

Layer Attribute	Possible Values	Description
Tag	span, div, layer, or ilayer	Type of HTML tag to use for the layer.
Vis (Visibility)	default, inherit, visible, or hidden	Determines whether a layer is displayed. If visibility is set to inherit, then the layer takes on the characteristic of the parent layer.
W (Width)	Any integer measurement in pixels, centimeters, millimeters, inches, points, percentage, ems, or picas	The horizontal measurement of the layer.
Z-Index	Any integer	Stacking order of the layer in relation to other layers on the Web page. Higher numbers are closer to the top.

Name

Names are important when working with layers. To refer to them properly for both CSS and JavaScript purposes, each layer must have a unique name: unique among the layers and unique among every other object on the Web page. Dreamweaver automatically names each layer as it is created in sequence: Layer1, Layer2, and so forth. You can enter a name that is easier for you to remember by replacing the provided name in the text box on the far left of the Property Inspector.

Caution

Netscape Note: Netscape Navigator 4.x is strict with its use of the ID attribute. You must ensure that you call the layer with an alphanumeric name that does not use spacing or special characters such as the underscore or percentage sign. Moreover, make sure your layer name begins with a letter and not a number—in other words, layer9 works but 9layer can cause problems.

Tag attribute

The Tag drop-down list contains the HTML tags that can be associated with the layer. By default, the positioned layer has <div> as the tag, but you can also choose <span>, <layer>, or <ilayer>. As previously noted, the <div> and <span> tags are endorsed by the World Wide Web Consortium group as part of their CSS standards. The <layer> and <ilayer> tags are Netscape Navigator 4.x proprietary tags, although Netscape also supports the CSS tags.

Indeed, if you are working on a Navigator 4.x-based intranet, you may want to change the default layer tag. Choose Edit ➪ Preferences and then, from the Layers category, select either <layer> or <ilayer> from the Tag drop-down list.

Visibility

Visibility (Vis in the Property Inspector) defines whether or not you can see a layer on a Web page. The following four values are available:

✦ **Default:** Enables the browser to set the visibility attribute. Most browsers use the inherit value as their default.

✦ **Inherit:** Sets the visibility to the same value as that of the parent layer, which enables a series of layers to be hidden or made visible by changing only one layer.

✦ **Visible:** Causes the layer and all of its contents to be displayed.

✦ **Hidden:** Makes the current layer and all of its contents invisible.

Remember the following when you're specifying visibility:

✦ Whether or not you can see a layer, you must remember that the layer still occupies space on the page and demands some of the page loading time. Hiding a layer does not affect the layout of the page, and invisible graphics take just as long to download as visible graphics.

✦ When you are defining the visibility of a positioned object or layer, you should not use default as the visibility value. A designer does not necessarily know whether the site's end user has set the default visibility to visible or hidden. Designing an effective Web page can be difficult without this knowledge. The common browser default is for visibility to be inherited, if not specifically shown or hidden.

Overflow

Normally, a layer expands to fit the text or graphics inserted into it. You can, however, restrict the size of a layer by changing the height and width values in the Property Inspector. What happens when you define a layer to be too small for an image, or when an amount of text depends on the setting of the layer's overflow attribute? CSS layers (the <div> and <span> tags) support four different overflow settings:

✦ **Visible (Default):** All of the overflowing text or image is displayed, and the height and width settings established for the layer are ignored.

✦ **Hidden:** The portion of the text or graphic that overflows the dimensions is not visible.

✦ **Scroll:** Horizontal and vertical scroll bars are added to the layer regardless of the content size or amount, and regardless of the layer measurements.

✦ **Auto:** When the content of the layer exceeds the width and/or height values, horizontal and vertical scroll bars appear.

Currently, support for the overflow attribute is spotty at best. Dreamweaver doesn't display the result in the Document window; it must be previewed in a browser to be seen. Navigator offers limited support: Only the attribute's hidden value works correctly and, even then, just for text. Only Internet Explorer 4.0 or above and Netscape 6 render the overflow attribute correctly, as shown in Figure 28-9.

Figure 28-9: When your contents are larger than the dimensions of your layer, you can regulate the results with the overflow attribute.

 Caution   Netscape Note: The Overflow property is not recognized by the Netscape Navigator 4.*x* proprietary layer tags, `<layer>` and `<ilayer>`.

Clipping

If you're familiar with the process of cropping an image, you'll quickly grasp the concept of clipping layers. Just as desktop publishing software hides but doesn't delete the portion of the picture outside of the crop marks, layers can mask the area outside the clipping region defined by the Left, Top, Right, and Bottom values in the Clip section of the Layer Property Inspector.

All clipping values are measured from the upper-left corner of the layer. You can use any CSS standard measurement system: pixels (the default), inches, centimeters, millimeters, ems, or picas.

The current implementation of CSS only supports rectangular clipping. When you look at the code for a clipped layer, you see the values you inserted in the Layer Property Inspector in parentheses following the clip attribute, with the `rect` (for rectangular) keyword, as follows:

```
<div id="Layer1" style="position:absolute; left:54px; top:24px; ¬
width:400px; height:115px; z-index:1; visibility:inherit; ¬
clip:rect(10 100 100 10)">
```

Generally, you specify values for all four criteria: Left, Top, Right, and Bottom. You can also leave the Left and Top values empty or use the keyword `auto`—which causes the Left and Top values to be set at the origin point: 0,0.

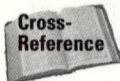

Cross-Reference   Clipping is a powerful function that can be employed in interesting ways. This property is the basis for the image map rollover technique discussed in Chapter 14.

Z-index

One of a layer's most powerful features is its capability to appear above or below other layers. You can change this order, known as the *z-index*, dynamically. Whenever a new layer is added, Dreamweaver automatically increments the z-index—layers with higher z-index values are positioned above layers with lower z-index values. The z-index can be adjusted manually in either the Layer Property Inspector or the Layers panel. The z-index must be an integer, either negative or positive.

A Visual Clipping Technique

In Dreamweaver, you cannot draw the clipping region visually—the values have to be explicitly input in the Clip section of the Layer Property Inspector. That said, a trick using a second temporary layer makes it easier to position your clipping. Follow these steps to get accurate clipping values:

1. Insert your original layer and image.

2. Nest a second, temporary layer inside the first, original layer (select the Draw Layer button in the Objects panel and draw out the second layer inside the first).

   If you have your Layer Preferences set so that a layer does not automatically nest when created inside another layer, press the Ctrl (Command) key while you draw your layer, to override the preference.

3. Position the second layer over the area you want to clip. Use the layer's sizing handles to alter the size and shape, if necessary.

4. Note the position and dimensions of the second layer (the Left, Top, Width, and Height values).

5. Delete the second layer.

6. In the Property Inspector for the original layer, enter the Clip values as follows:

- **L:** Enter the Left value for the second layer.

- **T:** Enter the Top value for the second layer.

- **R:** Add the second layer's Left value to its Width value.

- **B:** Add the second layer's Top value to its Height value.

Dreamweaver displays the clipped layer after you enter the final value. The following figure shows the original layer and the temporary layer on the left, and the final clipped version of the original layer on the right.

Tip

Although some Web designers use high values for the z-index, such as 3,000, the z-index is completely relative. The only reason to increase a z-index to an extremely high number is to ensure that that particular layer remains on top.

The z-index is valid for the CSS layer tags as well as the Netscape 4.*x* proprietary layer tags. Netscape 4.*x* also has two additional attributes that can affect the apparent depth of either the `<layer>`- or `<ilayer>`-based content: above and below. With above and below, you can specify which existing layer is to appear directly on top of or beneath the current layer. You can only set one of the depth attributes, the z-index, or above or below.

Caution   Certain types of objects—including Java applets, plug-ins, and ActiveX controls—ignore the z-index setting when included in a layer and appear as the uppermost layer. However, certain ActiveX Controls—most notably Flash—can be made to respect the z-index.

When you designate the layer's tag attribute to be either `<layer>` or `<ilayer>`, the Property Inspector displays an additional field: the A/B attribute for setting the above or below value, as shown in Figure 28-10. Choose either attribute from the A/B drop-down list and then select the layer from the adjacent list. The layer you choose must be set up in the code before the current layer. You can achieve this condition in the Document window by moving the icon for the current layer to a position after the other layers. Although you must use either `<layer>` or `<ilayer>` to specify the above or below attribute, the layer specified can be either a CSS or Netscape type.

Figure 28-10: Choosing the Netscape-specific tags LAYER or ILAYER from the Property Inspector causes several new options to appear, including the A/B switch for the above/below depth position.

Caution   Working with the above and below attributes can be confusing. Notice that they determine which layer is to appear on top of or underneath the current layer, and not which layer the present layer is above or below.

Background image or color

Inserting a background image or color with the Layer Property Inspector works in a similar manner to changing the background image or color for a table (as explained in Chapter 13). To insert an image, enter the path to the file in the Bg Image text box or select the Folder icon to locate the image file on your system or network. If the layer is larger than the image, the image is tiled, just as it would in the background of a Web page or table.

To give a layer a background color, enter the color name (either in its hexadecimal or nominal form) in the Bg Color text box. You can also select the color swatch to pick your color from the color picker.

Additional Netscape 4.x properties

In addition to the above and below values for the z-index attribute, two other Netscape 4.x variations must be noted for the sake of completeness — both of which appear as options in the Property Inspector when either $\langle$layer$\rangle$ or $\langle$ilayer$\rangle$ is selected as the layer tag.

When either $\langle$layer$\rangle$ or $\langle$ilayer$\rangle$ is selected, the Page X, Page Y option becomes available as a radio button in the Property Inspector in addition to Left, Top. With Netscape 4.x layers, Left, Top places the layer relative to the top-left corner of its parent (whether that's the page or another layer if the layer is nested). Page X, Page Y positions the layer based on the top-left corner of the page, regardless of whether the layer is nested.

The other additional Netscape 4.x layer attribute is the source property. You can specify another HTML document to appear within a $\langle$layer$\rangle$ or $\langle$ilayer$\rangle$ — much like placing other Web pages in frames. To specify a source for a Netscape 4.x layer, enter the path to the file in the Src text box or select the Folder icon to locate the file.

Caution   Although these properties are available in Dreamweaver, they should really only be used if your Web site is used as a Netscape 4.x intranet. Neither of these properties is supported by Internet Explorer or Netscape 6.

The Layers panel

Dreamweaver offers another tool to help manage the layers in your Web page: the Layers panel. Although this tool doesn't display as many properties about each element as the Property Inspector, the Layers panel gives you a good overview of all the layers on your page. It also provides a quick method of selecting a layer — even when it's offscreen — as well as enabling you to change the z-index and the nesting order.

The Layers panel, shown in Figure 28-11, can be opened either through the Window menu (Window ➪ Layers) or by pressing the keyboard shortcut F2.

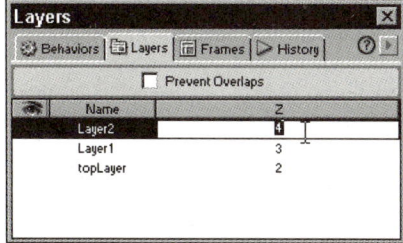

Figure 28-11: Use the Layers panel to select quickly or alter the visibility or relationships of all the layers on your page.

Modifying properties with the Layers panel

The Layers panel lists the visibility, name, and z-index settings for each layer. All of these properties can be modified directly through the Layers panel.

The visibility of a particular layer is noted by the eye symbol in column one of the Layers panel. Selecting the eye symbol cycles you through three different visibility states as follows:

✦ **Eye closed:** Indicates that the layer is hidden.

✦ **Eye open:** Indicates that the layer is visible.

✦ **No eye:** Indicates that the visibility attribute is set to the default (which, for both Navigator and Internet Explorer, means inherit).

Tip To change all of your layers to a single state simultaneously, select the eye symbol in the column header. Unlike the individual eyes in front of each layer name, the overall eye toggles between open and shut.

You can also change a layer's name (in the second column of the Layers panel). Just double-click the current layer name in the Layers Property Inspector; the name is highlighted. Type in the new name and press Enter (Return) to complete the change.

The z-index (stacking order) in the third column can be altered in the same manner. Double-click the z-index value; then type in the new value and press Enter (Return). You can enter any positive or negative integer. If you're working with the Netscape proprietary layer tags, you can also alter the above or below values previously set for the z-index through the Property Inspector. Use A for above and B for below.

Tip To change a layer's z-index interactively, you can drag one layer above or below another in the Layers panel.

Nesting with the Layers panel

Another task managed by the Layers panel is nesting or unnesting layers. This process is also referred to as *creating parent-child layers*. To nest one layer inside another through the Layers panel, follow these steps:

1. Choose Window ➪ Layers or press F2 to open the Layers panel.

2. Press the Ctrl (Command) key, then click the name of the layer to be nested (the child), and drag it on top of the other layer (the parent).

3. When you see a rectangle around the parent layer's name, release the mouse.

   The child layer is indented underneath the parent layer, and the parent layer has a minus sign (a down-pointing triangle on the Mac) attached to the front of its name.

4. To hide the child layer from view, select the minus sign (down-pointing triangle) in front of the parent layer's name. Once the child layer is hidden, the minus sign turns into a plus sign (a right-pointing triangle on the Mac).

5. To reveal the child layer, select the plus sign (right-pointing triangle on the Mac).

6. To undo a nested layer, select the child layer and drag it to a new position in the Layers panel.

When it comes to nested layers, Netscape 4.*x* does not "play well with others." In fact, the expected results are so rarely achieved that it's best to avoid nested layers in cross-browser sites for the time being.

You can use the nesting features of the Layers panel to hide many layers quickly. If the visibility of all child layers is set to default — with no eye displayed — then by hiding the parent layer, you cause all the child layers to inherit that visibility setting and also disappear from view.

You can also delete a layer from the Layers panel. Just highlight the layer to be removed and press Delete. Dreamweaver does not enable you to delete nested layers as a group, however — you have to remove each one individually.

Aligning layers with the ruler and grid

With the capability to position layers anywhere on a page comes additional responsibility and potential problems. In anything that involves animation, correct alignment of moving parts is crucial. As you begin to set up your layers, their exact placement and alignment becomes critical. Dreamweaver includes two tools to simplify layered Web page design: the ruler and the grid.

Rulers and grids are familiar concepts in traditional desktop publishing. Dreamweaver's ruler shows the x-axis and y-axis in pixels, inches, or centimeters along the outer edge of the Document window. The grid crisscrosses the page with lines to support a visual guideline when you're placing objects. You can even enable a snap-to-grid feature to ensure easy, absolute alignment.

Using the ruler

With traditional Web design, "eyeballing it" was the only option available for Web page layout. The absolute positioning capability of layers filled this deficiency. Now online designers have a more precise and familiar system of alignment: the ruler. Dreamweaver's ruler can be displayed in several different measurement units and with your choice of origin point.

To enable the ruler in Dreamweaver, choose View ➪ Rulers ➪ Show or use the keyboard shortcut Ctrl+Alt+R (Command+Option+R). Horizontal and vertical rulers appear along the top and the left sides of the Document window, as shown in Figure 28-12. As you move the pointer, a light-gray line indicates the position on both rulers.

Figure 28-12: Use the horizontal and vertical rulers to assist your layer placement and overall Web page layout.

By default, the ruler uses pixels as its measurement system. You can change the default by selecting View ➪ Rulers and choosing either inches or centimeters.

Dreamweaver also enables you to move the ruler origin to a new position. Normally, the upper-left corner of the page acts as the origin point for the ruler. On some occasions, it's helpful to start the measurement at a different location — at the bottom-right edge of an advertisement, for example. To move the origin point, select the intersection of the horizontal and the vertical rulers and drag the crosshairs to a new location. When you release the mouse button, both rulers are adjusted to show negative values above and to the right of the new origin point. To return the origin point to its default setting, choose View ➪ Rulers ➪ Reset Origin, or you can simply double-click the intersection of the rulers.

Tip   You can access a ruler shortcut menu by right-clicking (Command+clicking) the ruler itself. The shortcut menu enables you to change the system of measurement, reset the origin point, or hide the rulers.

Lining up with the grid

Rulers are generally good for positioning single objects, but a grid is extremely helpful when aligning one object to another. With Dreamweaver's grid facility, you can align elements visually or snap them to the grid. You can set many of the grid's other features, including grid spacing, color, and type.

To turn on the grid, choose View ➪ Grid ➪ Show Grid or press Ctrl+Alt+G (Command+Option+G). By default, the grid is displayed with mustard-yellow (#CCCC99) lines set at 50-pixel increments.

The snap-to-grid feature is enabled by choosing View ➪ Grid ➪ Snap To Grid or with the keyboard shortcut Ctrl+Alt+Shift+G (Command+Option+Shift+G). When activated, Snap to Grid causes the upper-left corner of a layer to be placed at the nearest grid intersection when the layer is moved.

Like most of Dreamweaver's tools, the grid can be customized. To alter the grid settings, choose View ➪ Grid ➪ Edit Grid. In the Grid Settings dialog box, shown in Figure 28-13, you can change any of the following settings (just click OK when you're done):

Grid Setting	Description
Color	Change the default color by selecting the color swatch to open the Dreamweaver color picker where you can click on a new swatch, or type a new value in the text box.
Show Grid	Show or hide the grid with this checkbox toggle.
Snap to Grid	Checkbox toggle to enable or disable the Snap to Grid feature.
Spacing	Adjust the distance between grid points by entering a numeric value in the text box.
Spacing Unit of Measure	Select Pixels, Inches, or Centimeters from the Spacing drop-down list.
Display	Choose either solid lines or dots for the gridlines.

Adding elements to a layer

Once you have created and initially positioned your layers, you can begin to fill them with content. Inserting objects in a layer is just like inserting objects in a Web page. The same insertion methods are available to you:

✦ Position the cursor inside a layer, choose Insert in the menu bar, and select an object to insert.

✦ With the cursor inside a layer, select any object from the Objects panel. Note: you cannot select the Draw Layer object.

✦ Drag an object from the Objects panel and drop it inside the layer.

A known problem exists with Netscape Navigator 4.*x* browsers and nested layers — and layers in general — using the `<div>` tag. Whenever the browser window is resized, the layers lose their left and top position and are displayed along the left edge of the browser window or parent layer. Dreamweaver includes the capability to insert code that serves as a workaround for this problem. With this code in place, if the browser is resized, the page reloads, repositioning the layers. If you want the code to be automatically inserted the first time you add a layer to your page, select the Add Resize Fix When Inserting Layers option found on the Layers category of Preferences. You can also insert it on a case-by-case basis by choosing Commands ➪ Add/Remove Netscape Resize Fix. As the name implies, this command also deletes the Netscape Resize Fix code.

Figure 28-13: Dreamweaver's grid feature is extremely handy for aligning a series of objects.

Forms and layers

When you're mixing forms and layers, follow only one rule: Always put the form completely inside the layer. If you place the layer within the form, all form elements after the layer tags are ignored. With the form completely enclosed in the layer, the form can safely be positioned anywhere on the page and all form elements still remain completely active.

Although this rule means you can't split one form onto separate layers, you can set up multiple forms on multiple layers — and still have them all communicate to one final CGI or other program. This technique uses JavaScript to send the user-input values in the separate forms to hidden fields in the form with the Submit button. Let's say, for example, that you have three separate forms gathering information in three separate layers on a Web page. Call them formA, formB, and formC on layer1, layer2, and layer3, respectively. When the Submit button in formC on layer3 is selected, a JavaScript function is first called by means of an onClick event in the button's <input> tag. The function, in part, looks like the following:

```
function gatherData() {
   document.formC.hidden1.value = document.formA.text1.value
   document.formC.hidden2.value = document.formB.text2.value
}
```

Notice how every value from the various forms gets sent to a hidden field in formC, the form with the Submit button. Now, when the form is submitted, all the hidden information gathered from the various forms is submitted along with formC's own information.

Note

Netscape Note: The code for this separate-forms approach, as written in the preceding listing, works in Internet Explorer. Netscape 4.x, however, uses a different syntax to address forms in layers. To work properly in Netscape 4.x, the code must look like the following:

```
document.layers["layer3"].document.formC.hidden1.value=¬
document.layers["layer1"].document.formA.text1.value
```

To make the code cross-browser compatible, you can use an initialization function that allows for the differences, or you can build it into the onClick function. (For more information on building cross-browser compatible code, see Chapter 34.)

Creating Your Page Design with Layers

While the advantage to designing with layers is the greater flexibility it affords, one of the greatest disadvantages of using layers is that they are viewable in only the most recent generation of browsers. Dreamweaver enables you to get the best of both worlds by making it possible for you to use layers to design complex page layouts, and then to transform those layers into tables that can be viewed in earlier browsers. Designing this way has some limitations — you can't, for example, actually layer items on top of each other. Nevertheless, Dreamweaver's capability to convert layers to tables (and tables to layers) enables you to create complex layouts with ease.

Using the Tracing Image

Page-layout artists are often confronted with Web-page designs that have been mocked up in a graphics program. Dreamweaver's Tracing Image function enables you to use such images to guide the precise placement of graphics, text, tables, and forms in your Web page, enabling you to match the original design as closely as possible.

In order to use a Tracing Image, the graphic must be saved in either JPG, GIF, or PNG format. Once the Tracing Image has been placed in your page, it is viewable only in Dreamweaver — it will never appear in a browser. A placed Tracing Image hides any background color or background graphic in your Web page. Preview your page in a browser, or hide the tracing layer, to view your page without the Tracing Image.

Adding the Tracing Image to your page

To add a Tracing Image to your Dreamweaver page, select View ⇨ Tracing Image ⇨ Load. This brings up a Select Image Source dialog box that enables you to select the graphic you would like to use as a Tracing Image. Clicking Select brings up the Page Properties dialog box, shown in Figure 28-14, where you may specify the opacity of the Tracing Image, from Transparent (0%) to Opaque (100%). You can change the Tracing Image or its transparency at any point by selecting Modify ⇨ Page Properties to bring up the Page Properties dialog box. You can toggle between hiding and showing the Tracing Image by selecting View ⇨ Tracing Image ⇨ Show. The Tracing Image can also be inserted directly in the Page Properties dialog box by entering its path in the Tracing Image text box or selecting the Browse button to locate the image.

Moving the Tracing Image

The Tracing Image cannot be selected and moved the same way as other objects on your page. Instead, you must move the Tracing Image using menu commands. You have several options for adjusting the Tracing Image's position to better fit your design. First, you can align the Tracing Image with any object on your page by first selecting the object and then choosing View ⇨ Tracing Image ⇨ Align with Selection. This lines up the upper-left corner of the Tracing Image with the upper-left corner of the bounding box of the object you've selected.

To precisely or visually move the Tracing Image to a specific location, select View ⇨ Tracing Image ⇨ Adjust Position. Then enter the x and y coordinates into the boxes in the Adjust Tracing Image Position dialog box, shown in Figure 28-15. For more hands-on positioning, use the arrow keys to nudge the tracing layer up, down, left, or right one pixel at a time. Holding down the Shift key while pressing the arrow keys moves the Tracing Image in five-pixel increments. Finally, you can return the Tracing Image to its default location of 9 pixels down from the top and 11 pixels in from the left by selecting View ⇨ Tracing Image ⇨ Reset Position.

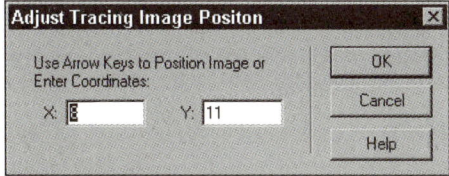

Figure 28-14: Setting the transparency of the Tracing Image to a setting such as 51 percent can help you differentiate between it and the content layers you are positioning.

Figure 28-15: Use the Adjust Tracing Image Position dialog box to precisely place your graphic template.

Preventing overlaps

In order to place layers on your page that can later be converted to a table, the layers must not overlap. Before you begin drawing out your layers, open the Layers panel — either by selecting Windows ⇨ Layers or pressing F2 — and put a checkmark in the Prevent Overlap box at the top of the Inspector window. You can also select Modify ⇨ Arrange ⇨ Prevent Layer Overlaps to toggle overlap protection on and off.

Designing precision layouts and converting content to layers

As noted earlier, layers brought pixel-perfect positioning to the Internet. Now, Web designers can enjoy some of the layout capabilities assumed by print designers. Unfortunately, you need a 4.0 browser or better to view any page created with layers, and a portion of the Web audience is still using 3.0 or older browsers. Dreamweaver includes layers-to-tables and back again as part of its round-trip repertoire.

Web designers can freely design their page and then lock it into position for posting. Moreover, if the design needs adjustment — and all designs need adjustment — the posted page can be temporarily converted back to layers for easy repositioning. The Convert Tables to Layers and Convert Layers to Table menu commands work together terrifically and greatly enhance the designer's workflow.

The two commands are described in detail in the following sections, but let's examine a typical Dreamweaver layout session to see how they function together:

1. The Web designer is handed a comp or layout design created by another member of the company or a third-party designer.

2. After creating the graphic and type elements, the Web designer is ready to compose the page in Dreamweaver.

3. Ideally, the comp is converted to an electronic graphic format and brought into Dreamweaver as a Tracing Image.

4. If at all possible, it's best for conversion purposes not to overlap any layers, so the Web designer enables the Prevent Overlap option.

5. Each element is placed in a separate layer and placed in position, following the Tracing Image, if any.

6. With one command (Convert Layers to Table), the layout is restructured from appearing in layers to being in tables for backward browser compatibility.

7. After the client has viewed the page — and made the inevitable changes — the page is converted from tables to layers. Again, in Dreamweaver, this process is triggered by one command (Convert Tables to Layers) and takes seconds to complete.

8. The trip from tables to layers and back again is made as many times as necessary to get the layout pixel-perfect.

Convert Tables to Layers and Convert Layers to Table is a one-two combination that cuts layout time tremendously and frees the designer to create visually instead of programmatically.

Dreamweaver enables you to take any page and enclose all the contents in layers for easy design layout with drag-and-drop ease. Convert Tables to Layers is very flexible and enables the designer to convert pages previously constructed either partially or totally with tables or ones that already have layers in place. You can even quickly convert an all-text page into a layer.

Tip   One valuable use for this command is to better prepare a page to use another Dreamweaver feature: Convert to 3.0 Browser Compatible. While you no longer have to have every page element in a layer to use this feature, if you use the Convert Tables to Layers command first, you get better results.

With the page open in Dreamweaver, select Modify ➪ Convert ➪ Tables to Layers to view the command's dialog box, shown in Figure 28-16.

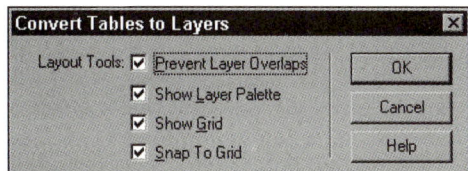

Figure 28-16: Choose the appropriate Layout Tools to help you reposition your content using layers.

By default, each of the following Layout Tools options are enabled:

✦ **Prevent Layer Overlaps:** You want this option turned on if you plan to convert the layers back to a table.

✦ **Show Layer Palette:** This automatically opens the Layers panel for you with each layer given a default name by Dreamweaver.

✦ **Show Grid:** This option reveals the grid overlay that can help with precision layout.

✦ **Snap to Grid:** With this turned on, layers snap to the nearest gridlines as they are moved onscreen.

You can uncheck any of these options before you convert the page.

Tip   Turn off Show Grid and Snap to Grid if you are laying out objects on top of a Tracing Image, as they may interfere with the absolute positions that you are trying to achieve.

Converting layers to tables

To convert a Web page that has been designed with layers into a table for viewing in older browsers, simply select Modify ⇨ Convert ⇨ Layers to Table. This opens the Convert Layers to Table dialog box, shown in Figure 28-17, with the following options:

✦ **Most Accurate:** This creates as complex a table as is necessary to guarantee that the elements on your Web page appear in the exact locations that you've specified. This is the default setting.

✦ **Smallest:** Collapse empty cells less than *n* pixels wide: Selecting this option simplifies your table layouts by joining cells that are less than the number of pixels wide that you specify. This may result in a table that takes less time to load; however, it also means that the elements on your page may not appear in the precise locations where you've placed them.

✦ **Use Transparent GIFs:** When you select this option, Dreamweaver fills all empty cells with a transparent spacer graphic to ensure that the table looks the same across a variety of browsers. When Dreamweaver creates the table layout, it places a file called transparent.gif in the same folder as your Web page. You must make sure to include this file when you upload your page to your server in order for it to display correctly.

✦ **Center on Page:** Selecting this option puts `<div align=center>` tags around your table so that it displays in the middle of a browser window. Deselecting this option leaves out those tags so that the table starts from its default position in the upper-left corner of a browser.

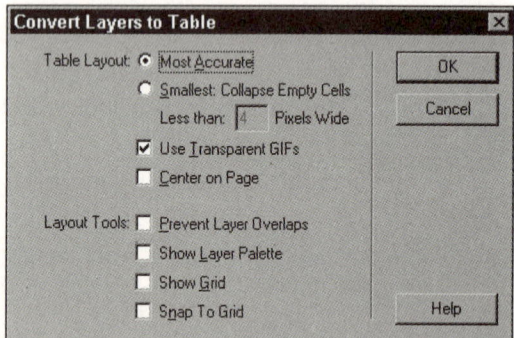

Figure 28-17: Check off the right Layout Tools options to help reposition your content as a table.

Once you have converted your layout into a table, as shown in Figure 28-18, you should preview it in your browser. If you aren't happy with the way your layout looks, or if you wish to do further modifications, you can convert the table back into layers by selecting Modify ⇨ Convert ⇨ Tables to Layers as described previously, selecting the layers to drag and drop the contents into new positions. Finally, transform your layout back into a table and preview it again.

Figure 28-18: The results of transforming layers into a table, using the default settings.

Tip

It's worth pointing out that the two Modify ➪ Convert commands can be easily reversed by choosing Edit ➪ Undo, whereas the effectively similar File ➪ Convert ➪ 3.0 Browser Compatible command cannot.

Activating Layers with Behaviors

While absolute positioning is a major reason to use layers, you may have other motives for using this capability. All the properties of a layer—the coordinates, size and shape, depth, visibility, and clipping—can be altered dynamically and interactively as well. Normally, dynamically resetting a layer's properties entails some fairly daunting JavaScript programming. Now, with one of Dreamweaver's hallmarks—those illustrious behaviors—activating layers is possible for nonprogrammers as well.

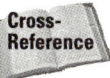

Cross-Reference

In case you missed it, Chapter 19 describes Dreamweaver's rich behaviors feature.

Behaviors consist of two parts, the event and the action. In Dreamweaver, three standard actions are designed specifically for working with layers:

✦ **Drag Layer:** Enables the user to move the layer and get a response to that movement.

✦ **Set Text of Layer:** Interactively alter the content of any layer to include any HTML, not just text.

✦ **Show-Hide Layers:** Controls the visibility of layers, either interactively or through some preprogrammed action on the page.

You can find detailed information about these actions in their respective sections in Chapter 19. The following sections outline how to use these behaviors to activate your layers.

Note   Netscape 6 was released just before Dreamweaver 4; consequently some of the layer-oriented behaviors do not work properly with that version of Netscape's browser. As of this writing, there are third-party replacements for the Drag Layer behavior, written by Jaro von Flocken; and the Set Text of Layer and Show-Hide Layers behavior, both contributed by Al Sparber. You can find these extensions on the CD-ROM that accompanies this book or on the Macromedia Exchange.

Drag Layer

For the Web designer, positioning a layer is easy: click the selection handle and drag the layer to a new location. For the readers of your pages, moving a layer is next to impossible — unless you incorporate the Drag Layer action into the page's design.

With the Drag Layer action, you can set up interactive pages in which the user can rearrange elements of the design to achieve an effect or make a selection. Drag Layer includes an option that enables you to execute a JavaScript command if the user drops the layer on a specific target. In the example shown in Figure 28-19, each pair of shoes is in its own layer. When the user drops a pair in the bag, a one-line JavaScript command opens the desired catalog page and order form.

After you've created all your layers, you're ready to attach the behavior. Because Drag Layer initializes the script to make the interaction possible, you should always associate this behavior with the <body> tag and the onLoad event.

Follow these steps to use the Drag Layer action, and to designate the settings for the drag operation:

1. Choose the <body> tag from the Tag Selector in the status bar.

2. Choose Window ➪ Behaviors or select the Show Behaviors button from either Launcher. The Behaviors panel opens.

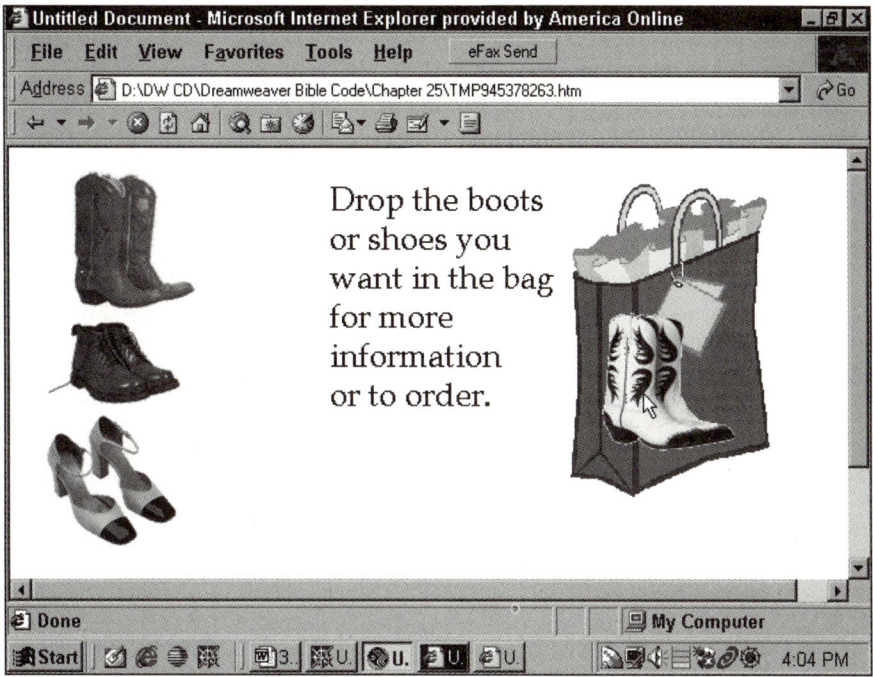

Figure 28-19: On this interactive page, visitors can drop merchandise into the shopping bag; this feature is made possible with the Drag Layer action.

3. In the Behaviors panel, make sure that 4.0 and Later Browsers is displayed in the Show Events For Submenu of the Add Behavior pop-up menu.

4. Click the + (add) action button and choose Drag Layer from the Add Behavior pop-up menu.

5. In the Drag Layer dialog box, select the layer you want to make available for dragging.

6. To limit the movement of the dragged layer, select Constrained from the Movement drop-down list. Then enter the coordinates to specify the direction to which you want to limit the movement in the Up, Down, Left, and/or Right text boxes.

7. To establish a location for a target, enter coordinates in the Drop Target: Left and Top text boxes. You can fill these text boxes with the selected layer's present location by clicking the Get Current Position button.

8. You can also set a snap-to area around the target's coordinates. When released in the target's location, the dragged layer snaps to this area. Enter a pixel value in the Snap if Within text box.

9. Click the Advanced tab.

10. Designate the drag handle:

   • To enable the whole layer to act as a drag handle, select Entire Layer from the drop-down menu.

   • If you want to limit the area to be used as a drag handle, select Area within Layer from the drop-down menu. Enter the Left and Top coordinates as well as the Width and Height dimensions in the appropriate text boxes.

11. If you want to keep the layer in its current depth and not bring it to the front, deselect the checkbox for While Dragging: Bring Layer to the Front. To change the stacking order of the layer when it is released after dragging, select either Leave on Top or Restore z-index from the drop-down list.

12. To execute a JavaScript command when the layer is dropped on the target, enter the code in the Call JavaScript text box. If you want the script to execute every time the layer is dropped, enter the code in the When Dropped: Call JavaScript text box. If the code should execute only when the layer is dropped on the target, make sure there's a check in the Only if Snapped checkbox.

13. Click OK.

14. To change the event that triggers the action (the default is onLoad), select an event from the drop-down menu in the Events column.

Set Text of Layer

We've seen how layers can dynamically move, change their visibility, and their depth — but did you know that you could also change a layer's *content* dynamically? With Dreamweaver, you can do it easily. A standard behavior, Set Text of Layer, enables you to swap the entire contents of one layer for whatever you'd like. You're not limited to exchanging just text either. Anything you can put into HTML, you can swap — which, is pretty much everything!

This behavior is extremely useful for putting up context-sensitive help and other information. Rather than construct a series of layers which you show and hide, a single layer is used, and just the contents change. To use Set Text of Layer, follow these steps:

1. Insert and name your layers as desired.

2. Select the graphic, button, or text link you'd like to act as the trigger for your changing the content of the layer.

3. Choose Window ⇨ Behaviors or select the Show Behaviors button from either Launcher to open the Behaviors panel.

4. Choose Set Text ⇨ Set Text of Layer from the + (add) action pop-up menu.

   The dialog box (see Figure 28-20) shows a list of the available layers in the current Web page as well as providing a space for the new content.

Targeted JavaScript Commands

The following simple yet useful JavaScript commands can be entered in the Snap JavaScript text box of the Drag Layer dialog box:

✦ To display a brief message to the user after the layer is dropped, use the `alert()` function:

```
alert("You hit the target")
```

✦ To send the user to another Web page when the layer is dropped in the right location, use the JavaScript location object:

```
location = "http://www.yourdomain.com/yourpage.html"
```

The location object can also be used with relative URLs.

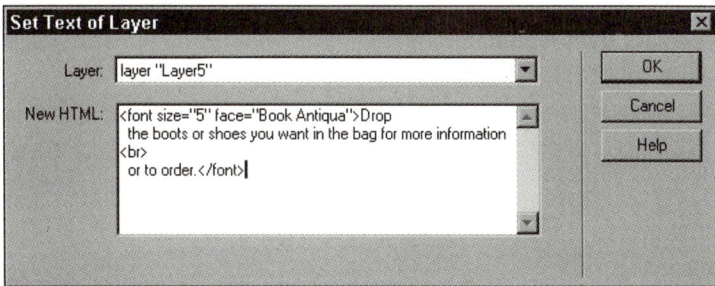

Figure 28-20: Swap out all the contents of a layer using the Set Text of Layer behavior.

5. Select the layer you want to alter from the Layer option list.

6. Enter the text or code in the New HTML text area.

   You can enter either plain text, which is rendered in the default paragraph style, or any amount of HTML code, including `<img>`, `<table>`, or other tags.

Tip   If you're entering a large amount of HTML, don't bother doing so by hand—Dreamweaver can do it for you. On a blank page, create your HTML content and then select and copy it. Then, in the Set Text of Layer dialog box, paste the code using Ctrl+V (Command+V).

7. Click OK when you're done.

If you want several layers to change when a single event is triggered, just add more Set Text of Layer behaviors to the same object.

Note   You may need to change the behavior event from its default; to do so select the down arrow in between the Event and Action columns on the Behaviors panel and choose a new event from the list.

Show-Hide Layers

The capability to implement interactive control of a layer's visibility offers tremendous potential to the Web designer. The Show-Hide Layers action makes this implementation straightforward and simple to set up. With the Show-Hide Layers action, you can simultaneously show one or more layers while hiding as many other layers as necessary. Create your layers and give them a unique name before invoking the Show-Hide Layers action.

To use Show-Hide Layers, follow these steps:

1. Select an image, link, or other HTML tag to which to attach the behavior.

2. Choose Window ➪ Behaviors or select the Show Behaviors button from either Launcher to open the Behaviors panel.

3. Choose Show-Hide Layers from the + (add) action pop-up menu. The parameters form (see Figure 28-21) shows a list of the available layers in the open Web page.

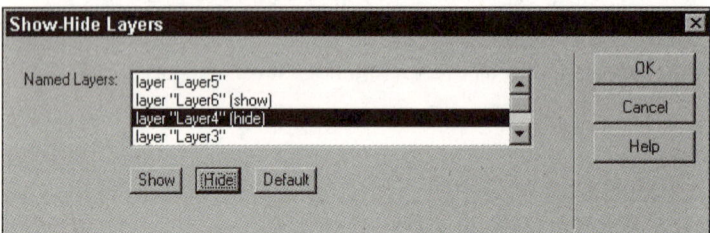

Figure 28-21: With the Show-Hide Layers behavior attached, you can easily program the visibility of all the layers in your Web page.

4. To cause a hidden layer to be revealed when this event is fired, select the layer from the list and click the Show button.

5. To hide a visible layer when this event is fired, select its name from the list and click the Hide button.

6. To restore a layer's default visibility value when this event is fired, select the layer and click the Default button.

7. Click OK when you are done.

8. If the default event is not suitable, use the drop-down menu in the Events column to select a different one.

Dreamweaver Technique: Creating a Loading Layer

As Web creations become more complex, most designers want their layers to zip on and off screen or appear and disappear as quickly as possible for the viewer of the page. A layer can act only when it has finished loading its content — the text and images. Rather than have the user see each layer loading in, some designers use a loading layer to mask the process until everything is downloaded and ready to go.

A loading layer is fairly easy to create. Dreamweaver supplies all the JavaScript necessary in one behavior, Show-Hide Layers. Keep in mind that because this technique uses layers, it's good only for 4.0 browsers and above. Use the following steps to create a loading layer:

1. Create all of your layers with the contents in place and the visibility property set as normal.

2. Create the loading layer. (Choose Insert ⇨ Layer or select the Draw Layer button from the Objects panel.)

3. Enter and position whatever contents you want displayed in the loading layer while all the other layers are loading.

4. Open the Layers panel (F2).

5. Turn off the visibility for all layers except the loading layer. In essence, you're hiding every other layer.

6. Select the <body> tag from the Tag Selector.

7. Choose Window ⇨ Behaviors or select Show Behaviors from either Launcher to open the Behaviors panel.

8. Select the + (add) action button and choose Show-Hide Layers from the pop-up menu.

9. In the Show-Hide Layers dialog box, select the loading layer and then click the Hide button.

10. Select all the other layers and set them to Show. Click OK when you are done.

11. Leave onLoad (the default) as the event to trigger this action.

Now, when you test your Web page, you should see only your loading layer until everything else is loaded, then the loading layer disappears, and all the other layers are made visible.

Note A loading layer may be the last bastion of the <blink> tag. Created by Netscape fairly early in the history of the Web, the <blink>...</blink> tag pair was grossly overused and is today generally shunned. However, if you apply it (by switching to Code view, using the Code Inspector or through the Quick Tag Editor) just to the ellipse following the term "Loading . . ." like this:

```
<h2>Loading<blink>...</blink></h2>
```

you get a small bit of movement on the page, similar to a blinking cursor. Only Netscape Navigator supports the `<blink>` tag. You could also use an animated GIF to create the pulsing image for a cross-browser effect.

Summary

Layers are effective placement tools for developing the layout of a page. Anyone used to designing with desktop publishing tools can quickly learn to work layers effectively. The following points will help guide your way:

✦ Layers are visible only on fourth-generation and above browsers.

✦ Layers can be used to place HTML content anywhere on a Web page.

✦ You can stack layers on top of one another. This depth control is referred to as the *stacking order* or the *z-index*.

✦ Dreamweaver can convert layers to tables for viewing in earlier browsers, and back again for straightforward repositioning.

✦ Layers can be constructed so that the end user can display or hide them interactively, or alter their position, size, and depth dynamically.

✦ Dreamweaver gives you rulers and grids to help with layer placement and alignment.

✦ Layers can easily be activated by using Dreamweaver's built-in JavaScript behaviors.

In the next chapter, you learn how to develop timelines, which enable layers and their contents to move around the Web page.

✦   ✦   ✦

Working with Timelines

Motion implies time. A static object, such as an ordinary HTML Web page, can exist either in a single moment or over a period of time. Conversely, moving objects (such as Dynamic HTML layers flying across the screen) need a few seconds to complete their path. All of Dreamweaver's Dynamic HTML animation effects use the Timeline feature to manage this conjunction of movement and time.

Timelines can do much more than move a layer across a Web page, however. A timeline can coordinate an entire presentation: starting the background music, scrolling the opening credits, and cueing the voice-over narration on top of a slideshow. These actions are all possible with Dreamweaver because, in addition to controlling a layer's position, timelines can also trigger any of Dreamweaver's JavaScript behaviors on a specific frame.

This chapter explores the full and varied world of timelines. After an introductory section brings you up to speed on the underlying concepts of timelines, you learn how to insert and modify timelines to achieve cutting-edge effects. A Dreamweaver Technique shows you, step by step, how to create a multiscreen slideshow complete with fly-in and fly-out graphics. From complex multilayer animations to slideshow presentations, you can do it all with Dreamweaver timelines.

Cross-Reference Because timelines are so intricately intertwined with behaviors and layers, you need to have a good grasp of these concepts. Before examining the topic of timelines, make sure to read Chapter 19 and Chapter 28.

Entering the Fourth Dimension with Timelines

Web designers in the early days had little control over the fourth dimension and their Web pages. Only animated GIFs, Java, or animation programs such as Macromedia's Flash could create the illusion of motion events. Unfortunately, all of these technologies have some limitations.

The general problem with animated GIF images is related to file size. An animated GIF starts out as an image for every frame. Therefore, if you incorporate a three-second, 15-frames-per-second animation, you are asking the user to download the compressed equivalent of 45 separate images. Even though an animated GIF is an index color file with a limited 256 colors and uses the format's built-in compression, the GIF file is still a relatively large graphic file. Moreover, for all their apparent animated qualities, GIFs enable no true interaction other than as a link to another URL. Animations created with Dynamic HTML and Dreamweaver's timelines, on the other hand, do not significantly increase the overall size of the Web page and are completely interactive. DHTML is not the only low-bandwidth approach to animations with interactive content for the Web. You can create animations, complete with user-driven interactions, with Java — as long as you're a Java programmer. Certainly Java development tools are making the language easier to use, but you still must deal with the rather long load time of any Java applet and the increasing variety of Java versions. As another option, Macromedia Director movies can be compressed or "shocked" to provide animation and interactivity in your pages. As with Java, the Director approach requires a bit of a learning curve. Shockwave movies can also have long load times and require the user to have a plug-in application.

While all of Part VI of this book discusses DHTML and Dreamweaver, see Chapter 26 for a discussion of DHTML, specifically.

Macromedia's Flash might be the best alternative to GIF images, even though Flash has its own set of caveats to keep in mind. On the plus side, Flash files are small and can be streamed through their own player. This arrangement is tempting, and if you just want animation on a page, Flash is probably a superior choice to any of the approaches previously described. On the minus side, Flash is limited to its own proprietary features and functions, and every user must have the Flash plug-in or ActiveX control installed — although Flash player is rapidly becoming ubiquitous, making this point moot. However, you cannot layer Flash animation on top of other layers on a page. Moreover, once you, or another designer, have created a Flash animation, the animation must be edited with the same animation package.

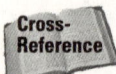

See Chapter 23 for a discussion of Flash.

Timeline capabilities

Dreamweaver timelines are part of the HTML code. For the movement of one layer straight across a Web page, Dreamweaver generates about 70 lines of code devoted to initializing and playing the timeline. But just what is a timeline? A timeline is composed of a series of frames. A frame is a snapshot of what the Web page, more specifically, the objects on the timeline, look like at a particular moment. You probably know that a movie is made up of a series of still pictures; when viewed quickly, the pictures create the illusion of movement. Each individual picture is a frame; movies show 24 frames per second, and video uses about 30 frames per second. Web animation, on the other hand, generally displays about 15 frames per second (fps). Not surprisingly, Dreamweaver's timeline is similar to the one used in Macromedia's timeline-based, multimedia authoring tool and animation package, Director.

If you have to draw each frame of a 30-second animation, even at 15 fps, you won't have time for other work. Dreamweaver uses the concept of *keyframes* to make a simple layer movement workable. Each keyframe contains a change in the timeline object's properties, such as position. For example, let's say you want your layer to start at the upper left (represented by the coordinates 0,0) and travel to the lower right (at 750,550). To accomplish this task, you need only specify the layer's position for the two keyframes — the start and the finish — and Dreamweaver generates all the frames in between.

Timelines have the following three primary roles:

✦ A timeline can alter a layer's position, dimensions, visibility, and depth.

✦ Timelines can change the source for any image on a Web page and cause another graphic of the same height and width to appear in the same location.

✦ Any of Dreamweaver's JavaScript behaviors can be triggered on any frame of a timeline.

A few ground rules

Keep the following basic guidelines in mind when you're using timelines in the Web pages you create with Dreamweaver:

✦ Timelines require a 4.0 or later browser.

✦ For a timeline to be able to animate an object, such as text, the object must be within a layer. If you try to create a timeline with an element that is not in a layer, Dreamweaver warns you and prevents you from adding the object to the timeline.

✦ Events don't have to start on the beginning of a timeline. If you want to have an action begin five seconds after a page has loaded, you can set the behavior on frame 60 of the timeline, with a frame rate of 15 frames per second.

✦ The selected frame rate is a "best-case scenario" because the actual frame rate depends on the user's system. A slower system or one that is simultaneously running numerous other programs can easily degrade the frame rate.

✦ You can include multiple animations on one timeline. The only restriction? You can't have two animations affecting the same layer at the same time. Dreamweaver prevents you from making this error.

✦ You can have multiple timelines that animate different layers simultaneously or the same layer at different times. Although you can set two or more timelines to animate the same layer at the same time, the results are difficult to predict and generally unintended.

Creating Animations with Timelines

Dreamweaver provides an excellent tool for managing timelines — the Timelines panel. Open this tool by choosing Window ➪ Timelines or using the keyboard shortcut Shift+F9.

The Timelines panel uses VCR-style controls combined with a playback head, which is a visual representation showing which frame is the current one. As shown in Figure 29-1, the Timelines panel gives you full control over any of the timeline functions.

Figure 29-1: Dreamweaver's Timelines panel enables you to quickly and easily master animation control.

The Timelines panel has four major areas:

✦ **Timeline Controls:** Includes the Timeline pop-up menu for selecting the current timeline; the Rewind, Back, and Play buttons; the Fps (frame rate) text box; and the Autoplay and Loop checkboxes.

- ✦ **Behavior Channel:** Shows the placement of any behaviors attached to specific frames of the timeline.

- ✦ **Frames:** Displays the frame numbers for all timelines and the playback head showing the current frame number.

- ✦ **Animation Channels:** Represents the animations for any included layers and images.

Adding Layers to the Timelines Panel

As with many of Dreamweaver's functions, you can add a layer or an image to the Timelines panel in more than one way. You can either insert a layer into a timeline through the menus (Modify ➪ Timeline ➪ Add Object to Timeline), or you can drag and drop an object into a timeline or use the keyboard shortcut, Ctrl+Alt+Shift+T (Command+Option+Shift+T). The default timeline is set at a frame rate of 15 fps. When you add an object to a timeline, Dreamweaver inserts an animation bar of 15 frames in length, labeled with the object's name. The animation bar shows the duration (the number of frames) for the timeline's effect on the object. An animation bar is initially created with two initial keyframes: the start and the end.

To add a layer or image to the Timelines panel through the menus, follow these steps:

1. Choose Window ➪ Timelines or use the keyboard shortcut, Shift+F9, to open the Timelines panel.

2. In the Document window, select the layer or image you want to add to the timeline.

3. Choose Modify ➪ Timeline ➪ Add Object to Timeline. An animation bar appears in the first frame of the timeline, as shown in Figure 29-2.

4. To add another object, repeat Steps 2 and 3. Each additional animation bar is inserted beneath the preceding bar.

Tip

The first time you add an image or layer to the Timelines panel, Dreamweaver displays an alert message that details the limitations of timelines. If you don't want to see this alert, turn it off by checking the Don't Show Me This Message Again checkbox.

As previously noted, you can add as many objects to a timeline as you desire. If necessary, increase the size of the Timelines panel by dragging any border of its window.

You have a little more flexibility when you add an object by dragging it into the timeline. Instead of the animation bar always beginning at frame one, you may drop the object in to begin on any frame. This approach is useful, especially if you are putting more than one object into the same animation channel.

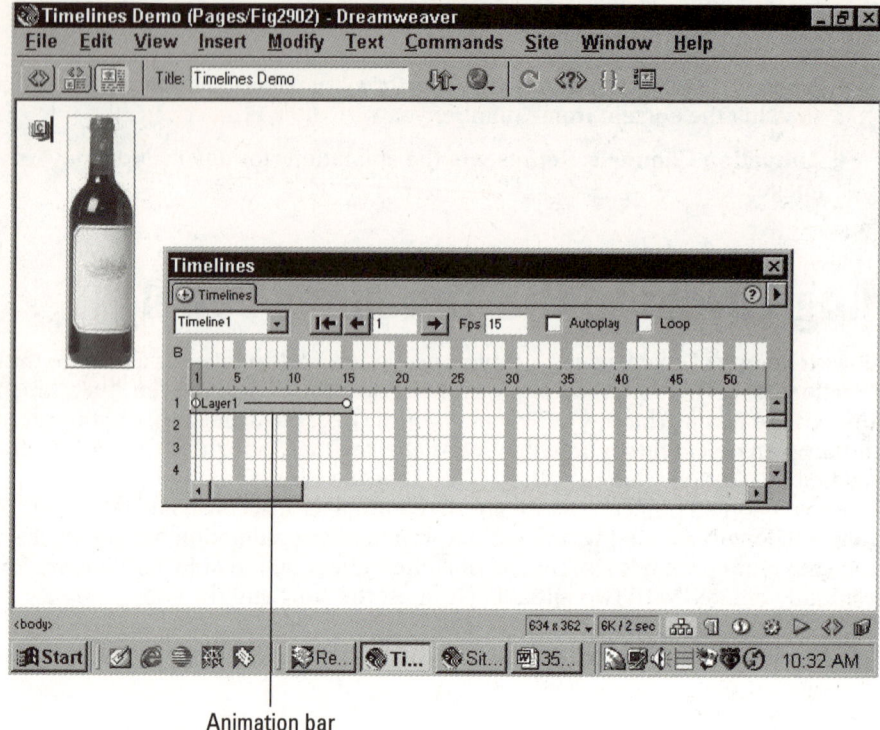

Animation bar

Figure 29-2: The default animation bar is set at 15 frames but can be easily modified.

To place an object in a timeline with the drag-and-drop method, follow these steps:

1. Open the Timelines panel by choosing Window ⇨ Timelines or using the keyboard shortcut, Shift+F9.

2. In the Document window, select the object — layer or image — you want to add to the timeline and drag it to the Timelines panel. As soon as the object is over the Timelines panel, a 15-frame animation bar appears.

3. Holding the mouse button down, position the animation bar so that the animation begins in the desired frame. Release the mouse button to drop the object into the timeline.

Note Your placement does not have to be exact; you can modify it later.

Placing a layer or image on a timeline is just the beginning. To begin using your timeline in depth, you have to make changes to the object for the keyframes and customize the timeline.

Modifying a Timeline

When you add an object—either an image or a layer—to a timeline, notice that the animation bar has an open circle at its beginning and end. An open circle marks a keyframe. As previously explained, the designer specifies a change in the state of the timeline object in a keyframe. For example, when you first insert a layer, the two generated keyframes have identical properties—the layer's position, size, visibility, and depth are unchanged. For any animation to occur, you have to change one of the layer's properties for one of the keyframes.

For example, let's move a layer quickly across the screen. Follow these steps:

1. Create a layer. If you like, add an image or a background color so that the layer is more noticeable.

2. Open the Timelines panel.

3. Drag the layer into the Timelines panel and release the mouse button.

4. Select the ending keyframe of the layer's animation bar.

   The playback head moves to the new frame.

5. In the Document window, grab the layer's selection handle and drag the layer to a new location. A thin line connects the starting position of the layer to the ending position, as shown in Figure 29-3. This line is the animation path.

6. To play your animation, first click the Rewind button in the Timelines panel and then click and hold down the Play button.

If you want to change the beginning position of your layer's movement, select the starting keyframe and then move the layer in the Document window. To alter the final position of your layer's movement, select the ending keyframe and then move the layer.

Tip   For more precise control of your layer's position in a timeline, select a keyframe and then, in the layer's Property Inspector, change the Left and/or Top values. You can also select the layer and use the arrow keys to move it.

Altering the animation bars

A Web designer can easily stretch or alter the range of frames occupied by a layer or image in an animation bar. You can make an animation longer or smoother, or have it start at an entirely different time. You can also move the layer to a different animation channel so it runs before or after another animation.

Use the mouse to drag an animation bar around the timeline. Click any part of the bar except on the keyframe indicators and move it as needed. To change the length of an animation, select the first or final keyframe and drag it forward or backward to a new frame.

Figure 29-3: When you move a layer on a timeline, Dreamweaver displays an animation path.

You can remove an animation bar in two ways: select it and press Delete, or choose Modify ➪ Timeline ➪ Remove Object.

Using the Timeline controls

As you probably noticed if you worked through the example in the preceding section, you don't have to use a browser to preview a timeline. The Timeline controls shown in Figure 29-4 enable you to fine-tune your animations before you view them through a browser.

At the top-left corner is the Timeline pop-up menu, which is used to indicate the current timeline. By default, every new timeline is given the name Timeline*n*, where *n* indicates how many timelines have been created. You can rename the timeline by selecting it and typing in the new name. As you accumulate and use more timelines, you should give them recognizable names.

Tip   If you change the timeline name, you must enter a one-word name using alphanumeric characters that always begin with a letter. Netscape Navigator 4.*x* cannot read spaces or special characters in JavaScript.

Figure 29-4: The Timeline controls enable you to move back and forth in your timeline, easily and precisely.

The next three buttons in the control bar enable you to move through the frames of a timeline. From left to right:

✦ **Rewind:** Moves the playback head to the first frame of the current timeline.

✦ **Back:** Moves the playback head to the previous frame. You can hold down the Back button to play the timeline in reverse.

✦ **Play:** Moves the timeline forward one frame at a time; hold down the Play button to play the timeline normally. When the last frame is reached, the playback head moves to the first frame of the current timeline and continues playing it.

The field between the Back and Play buttons is the frame indicator text box. To jump to any specific frame, enter the frame number in this box.

The next item in the control bar is the Fps (frames per second) text box. To change the frame rate, enter a new value in the Fps text box and press Tab or Enter (Return). The frame rate you set is an ideal number that a user's browser attempts to reach. The default rate of 15 frames per second is a good balance for both Macintosh and Windows systems.

Tip Because browsers play every frame regardless of the frame rate setting, increasing the frame rate does not necessarily make your animations smoother. A better method for creating smooth animations is to drag the end keyframe farther out and therefore increase the number of frames used by your animation.

The next two checkboxes, Autoplay and Loop, affect how the animation is played.

Autoplay

If you mark the Autoplay checkbox, the current timeline begins playing as soon as the Web page is fully downloaded. Dreamweaver alerts you to this arrangement by telling you that the Play Timeline action is attached to an onLoad event. Autoplay is achieved by inserting code into the <body> tag that looks similar to the following:

```
<body bgcolor="#FFFFFF" onload="MM_timelinePlay('timeline1')">
```

Caution   If you don't use the Autoplay feature, you must attach the Play Timeline action to another event and tag, such as an onMouseClick event and a button graphic. Otherwise, the timeline does not play.

Looping

Mark the Loop checkbox if you want an animation to repeat once it has reached the final frame. When Loop is enabled, the default setting causes the layer to replay itself an infinite numbers of times; however, you can change this setting.

When you first enable the Loop checkbox, Dreamweaver alerts you that it is placing a Go to Frame action after the last frame of your current timeline. To set the number of repetitions for a timeline, follow these steps:

1. In the Timelines panel, check the Loop checkbox.

2. Dreamweaver displays an alert informing you that the Go to Timeline Frame action is being added one frame past your current final frame. To disable these alerts, select the Don't Show Me This Message Again option.

3. In the Behavior channel (above the Frame numbers and playback head), double-click the behavior you just added.

Note   When you first add a behavior to a timeline, Dreamweaver presents a dialog box reminding you how to perform this action. Select the Don't Show Me This Message Again option when you've mastered the technique.

The Behaviors panel opens, with an onFrame event in the Events column and a Go To Timeline Frame action showing in the Actions column.

4. Double-click the onFrame event. The Go to Timeline Frame dialog box opens (see Figure 29-5).

5. Enter a positive number in the Loop text box to set the number of times you want your timeline to repeat. To keep the animation repeating continuously, leave the Loop text box blank.

6. Click OK when you are finished.

Tip   Your animations don't have to loop back to the beginning each time. By entering a different frame number in the Go to Frame text box of the Go to Timeline Frame dialog box, you can repeat just a segment of the animation.

Figure 29-5: Selecting the Loop option on the Timelines panel adds a Go to Timeline Frame action, which you can customize.

Adding keyframes

Animating a timeline can go far beyond moving your layer from point A to point B. Layers (and the content within them) can dip, swirl, zigzag, and generally move in any fashion—all made possible by keyframes in which you have entered some change for the object. Dreamweaver calculates the differences between each keyframe, whether the change is in a layer's position or size. Each timeline starts with two keyframes, the beginning and the end; you have to add other keyframes before you can insert the desired changes.

You can add a keyframe to your established timeline in a couple of different ways. The first method uses the Add Keyframe command, and the second method uses the mouse to click a keyframe into place.

Adding keyframes with the Add Keyframe command

To add a keyframe with the Add Keyframe command, follow these steps:

1. In the Timelines panel, select the animation bar for the object with which you are working.

2. Select the frame in which you want to add a keyframe.

3. Add your keyframe by either of the following methods:

 a. Choose Modify ⇨ Timeline ⇨ Add Keyframe.

 b. Right-click (Control+click) the frame in the animation bar and, from the shortcut menu, choose Add Keyframe.

A new keyframe is added on the selected frame, signified by the open circle in the animation bar.

While your new keyframe is selected, you can alter the layer's position, size, visibility, or depth. For example, if your animation involves moving a layer across the screen, you can drag the layer to a new position while the new keyframe is selected. The animation path is redrawn to incorporate this new position, as illustrated in Figure 29-6.

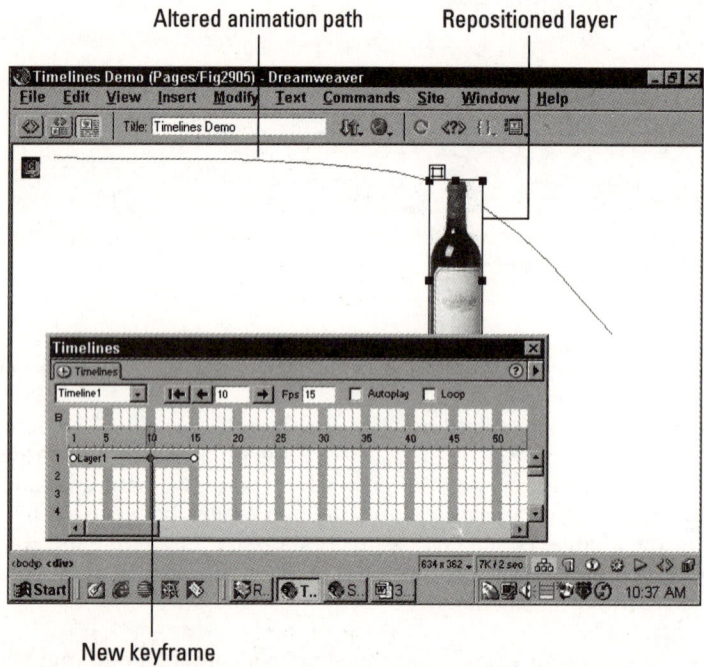

Figure 29-6: Repositioning a layer while a keyframe is selected can redirect your animation path.

Adding a keyframe with the mouse

The second method for adding a keyframe is quicker. To add a keyframe using the mouse, simply hold down the Ctrl (Command) key. Then click anywhere in the animation bar to add a keyframe. Your cursor turns into a small open circle when it is over the Timeline window to show that it is ready to add a new keyframe.

What if you want to move the keyframe? Simply click and drag the keyframe to a new frame, sliding it along the animation bar in the Timelines panel.

Tip   If, after plotting out an elaborate animation with a layer, you discover that you need to shift the entire animation — say, six pixels to the right — you don't have to redo all your work. Just select the animation bar in the Timelines panel and then, in the Document window, move the layer in question. Dreamweaver shifts the entire animation to your new location.

Removing timeline elements

The easiest way to remove an object, keyframe, or behavior from the Timelines panel is to select the element and press Delete. You cannot use this technique to delete individual frames or entire timelines, however. For these situations, you must use the menus as follows:

✦ To remove the whole timeline, choose Modify ➪ Timeline ➪ Remove Timeline.

✦ To remove an individual frame, choose Modify ➪ Timeline ➪ Remove Frame.

The Timelines panel's shortcut menu also contains all the removal commands. Right-click (Control+click) the Timelines panel anywhere below the control bar and, in the shortcut menu (see Figure 29-7), choose the removal command you need: Remove Keyframe, Remove Behavior, Remove Object, Remove Frame, or Remove Timeline.

Figure 29-7: The Timelines panel's shortcut menu is extremely handy for doing quick edits.

You can also Cut, Copy and Paste Timelines between documents. The Delete command in the shortcut menu is the same as Remove Timeline.

Changing animation speed

You can alter your Dynamic HTML animation speed with two different methods that can be used separately or together.

✦ Drag the final keyframe in the animation bar out to cover additional frames, or back to cover fewer frames. Any keyframes within the animation bar are kept proportional to their original settings. This method works well when altering the speed of an individual animation bar.

✦ Change the frames per second value in the Fps text box of the Timelines panel. Increasing the number of frames per second accelerates the animation, and vice versa. Adjusting the Fps value affects every layer contained within the timeline; you cannot use this method for individual layers.

Browsers play every frame of a Dynamic HTML animation, regardless of the system resources. Some systems, therefore, play the same animation faster or slower than others. Don't depend on every system to have the same timing.

Recording a layer's path

Plotting keyframes and repositioning your layers works well when you need to follow a pixel-precise path, but it can be extremely tedious when you're trying to move a layer more freely on the screen. Luckily, another, easier method exists for defining a movement path for a layer. In Dreamweaver, you can simply drag your layer around the screen to create a path and refine the path or its timing afterward.

The Record Path of Layer command automatically creates the necessary series of keyframes, calculated from your dragging of the layer. To fine-tune your work, you can select any keyframes and reposition the layer or even delete it entirely. This feature is a definite time-saver for quickly inserting your DHTML animation.

Keep in mind that a timeline represents not only positions but also positions over time, and thus, movement. The Record Path of Layer command is very smart when it comes to time; the slower you drag the layer, the more keyframes are plotted. You can vary the positioning of the keyframes by changing the tempo of your dragging. Moreover, the duration of the recorded timeline reflects the length of time spent dragging the layer.

To record a layer's path, do the following:

1. In the Document window, select the layer you are going to move.

Make sure that you've selected the layer itself and not its contents. If you've correctly selected the layer, it has eight selection boxes around it.

2. Drag the layer to the location in the document where you want it to be at the start of the movement.

3. From the menu bar, select Modify ⇨ Timeline ⇨ Record Path of Layer. You can also right-click (Control+click) the selected layer and choose Record Path from the shortcut menu.

   If it's not already open, the Timelines panel appears.

4. Click the layer and drag it around onscreen to define the movement. As you drag the layer, Dreamweaver draws a gray dotted line that shows you the path it is creating (see Figure 29-8).

Figure 29-8: To record a layer's path, Select Modify ⇨ Timeline ⇨ Record Path of Layer and then drag your layer in the Document window.

   Each dot represents a keyframe. The slower you draw, the closer the keyframes are placed; moving quickly across the Document window causes Dreamweaver to space out the keyframes.

5. Release the mouse. This ends the recording.

   Unless Dreamweaver is instructed not to, Dreamweaver displays an alert reminding you of the capabilities of the Timelines panel. If the alert dialog box does appear, you can select the Don't Show Me This Message Again option to prevent this dialog box from reappearing.

After you've finished recording a layer's movement, you see a new animation bar in the Timelines panel, representing the motion you just recorded. The duration of the new timeline matches the duration of your dragging of the layer. A number of keyframes that define your layer's movement already are inserted in this animation bar. You can use any of the procedures described earlier in this chapter to modify the timeline or its keyframes. If you select the same layer at the end of the generated timeline and perform the Record Path operation again, another animation bar is added at the end of the current timeline.

Caution   Any new paths recorded with the same layer are added after the last animation bar. You can't select a keyframe in the middle of a path and then record a path from that point; the starting keyframe of the newly recorded path corresponds to the position of the layer in the last keyframe.

Triggering Behaviors in Timelines

Adding a behavior to a timeline is similar to adding behaviors to any object on a Web page. Because timelines are written in JavaScript, they behave exactly the same as any object enhanced with JavaScript.

Use the Behavior channel section of the Timelines panel to work with behaviors in timelines.

You can attach a behavior to a timeline in four ways:

✦ Highlight the frame in which you wish to have the behavior and then right-click (Control+click). Select Add Behavior from the shortcut menu.

✦ Highlight the frame in which you want to activate the behavior and choose Modify ➪ Timeline ➪ Add Behavior to Timeline.

✦ Open the Behaviors panel and click the frame you wish to modify in the Behavior channel.

✦ Double-click the frame for which you want to add a behavior in the Behavior channel.

After a behavior is attached to a frame and you open the Behaviors panel, you see that the event inserted in the Events pane is related to a frame number — for example, onFrame20. Each frame can trigger multiple actions.

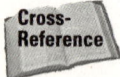

Cross-Reference   For more specifics about Dreamweaver behaviors, see Chapters 19 and 20.

Behaviors are essential to timelines. Without these elements, you cannot play or stop your timeline-based animations. Even when you select the Autoplay or Loop options in the Timelines panel, you are enabling a behavior. The three behaviors always deployed for timelines are Play Timeline, Stop Timeline, and Go to Timeline Frame.

If you are not using the Autoplay feature for your timeline, you must explicitly attach a Play Timeline behavior to an interactive or another event on your Web page. For example, a timeline is typically set to start playing once a specific picture has loaded, if the user enters a value in a form's text box or — more frequently — when the user selects a Play button. You could use the Stop Timeline behavior to pause an animation temporarily.

 Caution   If you find your Behaviors panel locked on the timeline and you're unable to attach a behavior to any other object, you've encountered a known Dreamweaver issue. Click on any other frame in your timeline — besides the one with the attached behavior — to free up the Behaviors panel.

To use the Play Timeline or Stop Timeline behavior, follow these steps:

1. In the Document window, select a tag, link, or image that you want to trigger the event.

2. Choose Window ⇨ Behaviors or select the Show Behavior button from the Launcher to open the Behaviors panel.

3. In the Behaviors panel, click the + (add) Action button, and from the pop-up menu choose either of the following methods:

    a. Timeline ⇨ Play Timeline to start a timeline.

    b. Timeline ⇨ Stop Timeline to end a timeline.

4. In the Play Timeline or Stop Timeline dialog box (see Figure 29-9), choose the timeline that you want to play (or stop) from the appropriate Timeline drop-down list.

Figure 29-9: You can use the Stop Timeline behavior to stop all timelines or a specific timeline.

5. Click OK when you are finished.

6. Select an event to trigger the behavior from the drop-down menu in the Events column.

When you select the option to loop your timeline, Dreamweaver automatically inserts a Go to Frame behavior—with the first frame set as the target. You can display any frame on your timeline by inserting the Go to Frame behavior manually. To use the Go to Frame behavior, follow these steps:

1. In the Document window, select a tag, link, or image that you want to have trigger the event.

2. Choose Window ➪ Behaviors or select the Show Behavior button from the Launcher to open the Behaviors panel.

3. In the Behaviors panel, select the + (add) Action button and choose Timeline ➪ Go to Timeline Frame from the drop-down list.

4. Choose the timeline you want to affect from the Timeline drop-down menu.

5. Enter the frame number in the Go to Frame text box.

6. If you'd like the timeline to loop a set number of times, enter a value in the Loop text box. Click OK when you are finished.

    Remember, if you don't enter a value, the timeline loops endlessly.

Tip   Depending on the type of effect desired, you may want to use two of the Timeline behaviors together. To ensure that your timeline always starts from the same point, first attach a Go to Timeline Frame behavior to the event and then attach the Play Timeline behavior to the same event.

Dreamweaver Technique: Creating a Multiscreen Slideshow

Moving layers around the screen is pretty cool, but you've probably already figured out that you can do a lot more with timelines. One of the possibilities is a graphics slideshow displaying a rotating series of pictures. To demonstrate the range of potential available to timelines, the following sample project shows you how to construct a slideshow with more than one screen, complete with moving layers and triggered behaviors.

This technique has four steps:

1. **Prepare the graphic elements.** The process is easier if you have most (if not all) of your images for the slideshow—as well as the control interface— ready to go.

2. **Create the slideshow timeline.** In this project, one timeline is devoted to rotating images on four different "screens."

3. **Create the moving layers timeline.** The slideshow begins and ends with a bit of flair, as the screens fly in and fly out.

4. **Add the behaviors.** The slideshow includes controls for playing, pausing, restarting, and ending the slideshow, which then takes the user to another Web page.

This technique is intended to act as a basis for your own creations, not as an end in itself. You can add many variations and refinements; for example, you can preload images, make rollover buttons, and add music to the background. Following is a fundamental structure focused on the use of timelines, which you can expand with additional objects as needed.

Note   The end result of this Dreamweaver Technique can be viewed only by 4.0 browsers or later.

Step 1: Preparing the graphic elements

Using a timeline for a slideshow presentation has only one restriction, but this qualification is significant — all the graphics in one "screen" must have the same dimensions. The timeline doesn't actually change the image tag; it only changes the file source for the tag. Thus, the height and width of the last image inserted overrides all the values for the foregoing graphics.

Luckily, all major image-processing software can resize and extend the canvas of a picture with little effort. When creating a slideshow, you may find it useful to do all of the resizing work at one time. Load in your images with the greatest width and height — they may or may not be the same picture — and use these measurements as your common denominators for all graphics.

Go ahead and create your interface buttons earlier rather than later. Experience shows that the more design elements you prepare ahead of time, the less adjusting you have to do later. Also, activating a timeline with a behavior is a straightforward process, and a finished interface enables you to incorporate the buttons quickly.

Finally, you should create and place the layers you want to use. The sample Web page in this technique is built of four screens, all of the same dimensions. The four different layers are uniquely named, but they all have the same size.

Tip   If you are making multiple versions of the same layer, consider changing the default layer size to fit your design. Choose Edit ⇨ Preferences and select the Layers category. Once you've customized the height and width values, all the layers incorporated in the Web page with the Insert ⇨ Layer command automatically size correctly. You only have to position those layers once they are created.

To recap, use the following steps to prepare your graphics:

1. Create all the images to be used as slides. All the slides must be the same height and width.

2. Prepare and place your interface buttons.

3. Create the number of layers that you need for the different screens in the slideshow.

4. Position your layers so that each can hold a different slide. The preceding example has four layers, centered on the screen in two rows.

5. Insert your opening slides into each of the layers.

 Note   Your opening slide doesn't have to be a graphic image. You could also use a solid-colored GIF or a slide with text.

Try to work backward from a final design whenever layer positioning is involved. At this stage, all of the elements are in their final placement, ready for the slideshow to begin (see Figure 29-10). Next, you can activate the slideshow.

Figure 29-10: Before activating any layers or setting up the slideshow, design the layout.

Step 2: Creating the slideshow timeline

For all the attention that timelines and layers receive, you may be surprised that one of the best features of Dreamweaver timelines has nothing to do with layers. You can use timelines to change images anywhere on your Web page — whether or not they are in layers. As explained in Step 1, the timeline doesn't actually replace one <img> tag with another, but rather alters an image by swapping the src attribute value. The src attribute changes just as changes in a layer's position, shape, or depth must happen at a keyframe.

In planning your slideshow, you need to decide how often a new slide appears, because you need to set keyframes at each of these points. If you are changing your slides every few seconds, you can change the frame rate to 1 fps. This setting helps you easily keep track of how many seconds occur between each slide change (and because no animation is involved with this timeline, a rapid frame rate is irrelevant). Note, however, that on the timeline described previously in this chapter that involved moving layers, the frame rate should be maintained at around 15 fps. Each timeline can have its own frame rate.

The only other choices involve the Autoplay and Loop options. As with frame rate, you can set each timeline to its own options without interfering with another timeline. This example has the slideshow loop but does not start automatically. Use the Play button to enable the user to start the show. But first, let's add the images to the slides.

To put images into a slideshow on a timeline, follow these steps:

1. Choose Window ⇨ Timelines to open the Timelines panel.

2. If desired, rename Timeline1 by selecting the name and typing your own unique name.

3. Select one image from those onscreen in the positioned layers and drag the graphic to the Timelines panel.

Caution　　　Be sure to grab the image, not the layer.

4. Release the animation bar at the beginning of the timeline.

5. Repeat Steps 3 and 4 for each image until all images are represented on the timeline.

6. Change the frame rate by entering a new value in the Fps text box. This example changes the frame rate to 1.

7. Select the Loop or Autoplay options, if desired.

8. On one of the animation bars representing images, select the frame for a keyframe.

9. Choose Modify ➪ Timeline ➪ Add Keyframe, or right-click (Control+click) the frame on the timeline and choose Add Keyframe from the shortcut menu.

10. In the Image Property Inspector, select the Src folder to locate the graphic file for the next slide image.

11. Repeat Steps 9 and 10 until every animation bar has keyframes for every slide change and each keyframe has a new or different image assigned.

This example changes slides every five seconds, as you can see in Figure 29-11 by looking at the keyframe placement. Although the slideshow has all four images changing simultaneously, you can also stagger the timing of the image changes. Simply drag one or more of the animation bars a few frames forward or backward after the keyframes have been set.

Figure 29-11: Each keyframe on each animation bar signals a change of the slide image.

Tip   To preview your slide changes, you don't have to go outside of Dreamweaver. Just click and hold down the Play button on the Timelines panel.

Step 3: Creating the moving layers timeline

At this stage, the slideshow is functional but a little dull. To add a bit of showmanship, you can "fly in" the layers from different areas of the Web page to their final destination. This task is easy—to complete the effect, the layers "fly out" when the user is ready to leave.

You can achieve these fly-in/fly-out effects in several ways. You can put the opening fly-in on one timeline and the ending fly-out on another. A more concise method combines the fly-in and fly-out for each layer on one timeline—separating them with a Stop Timeline behavior. After the fly-in portion happens when the page has loaded (because the example selects the Autoplay option for this timeline), the fly-out section does not begin to play until signaled to continue with the Play Timeline behavior.

To create the moving layers' opening and closing for the slideshow, follow these steps:

1. Choose Modify ⇨ Timeline ⇨ Add Timeline, or right-click (Ctrl+click) the Timelines panel and choose Add Timeline from the shortcut menu.

2. Rename your new timeline if desired.

3. Select the Autoplay checkbox so that this timeline begins playing automatically when the Web page is loaded.

4. Select any one of the layers surrounding your images and drag it onto the Timelines panel.

Caution   This time, make sure you move the layers—not the images.

5. To set the amount of time for the fly-in section to span, drag the final keyframe of the animation bar to a new frame. The example sets the end at 30 frames, which at 15 fps lasts two seconds.

6. From the Document window, select the same layer again and drag it to the Timelines panel. Place it directly after the first animation bar. This animation bar becomes the fly-out portion.

7. Drag the final keyframe to extend the time, if desired.

8. At this point, all four keyframes—two for each animation bar—have exactly the same information. Now change the positions for two keyframes to enable the layer to move. Select the first keyframe in the opening animation bar.

9. Reposition the layer so that it is offscreen. Although you can complete this task manually to the right or bottom of the screen by dragging the layer to a new location, you can also use the Layer Property Inspector to input new values directly for the Left and Top attributes.

Tip   Use negative numbers to move a layer offscreen to the left or top of the browser window.

10. From the Timelines panel, select the last keyframe of the closing animation bar.

11. Reposition the layer offscreen. If you want the layer to return in the same manner as it arrived, enter the same values for the Left and Top attributes as in the first keyframe of the opening animation bar.

12. Repeat Steps 4 through 11 for every layer.

Now, when you preview this timeline, the layers fly in and immediately fly out again. Figure 29-12 shows the layers in the example in mid-animation. In the final phase of the technique, you add behaviors to put the action under user control.

Figure 29-12: You can use two animation bars side by side to achieve a back-and-forth effect.

Step 4: Adding the behaviors

Although it may be fun to watch an unexpected effect take place, giving the user control over aspects of a presentation is much more involving — for the designer as well as the user. The example is ready to incorporate the user-interaction aspect by attaching Dreamweaver behaviors to the user interface and to the Behavior channel of the Timelines panel.

Two timeline behaviors have already been attached to the example. When the Loop option is selected in Step 2 for the slideshow timeline, Dreamweaver automatically includes a Go to Timeline Frame behavior after the final frame that sends the timeline back to the first frame. In the moving layers timeline, enabling the Autostart option causes Dreamweaver to attach a Play Timeline behavior to the onLoad event of the Web page's <body> tag. To complete the project, five behaviors need to be added.

First, you need a behavior to stop the moving layers from proceeding after the fly-in portion of the animation:

1. From the Timelines panel, double-click the final frame of the first animation bar in the Behavior channel.
2. In the Behaviors panel, select Timeline ⇨ Stop Timeline from the + (add) Actions pull-down menu.
3. From the Stop Timeline dialog box, select the timeline that contains the moving layers.
4. Click OK. An onFrame event is set for the Stop Timeline action by default.

Second, you need a behavior to enable the user to begin playing the slideshow:

1. In the Document window, select the Play button.
2. In the Behaviors panel, select the Timeline ⇨ Play Timeline action from the + (add) Action drop-down list.
3. In the Play Timeline dialog box, choose the timeline representing the slideshow.
4. Click OK. An onMouseDown event is set to trigger the action by default.

The next behavior enables the user to stop the slideshow temporarily:

1. In the Document window, select the Pause button.
2. In the Behaviors panel, select Timeline ⇨ Stop Timeline from the + (add) Actions drop-down list.
3. Choose the layer representing the slideshow in the Stop Timeline dialog box.
4. Click OK. An onMouseDown event is set to trigger the action by default.

To enable the user to begin the slideshow from the beginning, follow these steps:

1. In the Document window, select the Restart button.

2. In the Behaviors panel, add the Timeline ⇨ Go to Timeline Frame action.

3. In the Go to Timeline Frame dialog box, choose the layer representing the slideshow.

4. Enter a 1 in the Frame text box.

5. Click OK. An onMouseDown event is set to trigger the action by default.

6. Add the next action. In the Behaviors panel, select Timeline ⇨ Play Timeline from the + (add) Action drop-down list.

7. In the Play Timeline dialog box, choose the layer representing the slideshow.

8. Click OK. An onMouseDown event is attached to the action by default.

To end the presentation and move the user on to the next Web page, follow these steps:

1. In the Document window, select the End button.

2. In the Behaviors panel, select the Timeline ⇨ Play Timeline action from the + (add) Action drop-down list.

3. Choose the timeline representing the moving layers in the Play Timeline dialog box and click OK. The timeline begins playing where it last stopped — just before the layers are about to fly out. An onMouseDown event is set to trigger the action by default.

4. Add the next behavior. Select the Go to URL action from the + (add) drop-down list.

5. In the Go to URL dialog box, enter the path to the new page in the URL text box or select the Browse button to locate the file. Click OK when you are finished.

The project is complete and ready to test. Feel free to experiment, trying out different timings to achieve different effects.

You can test the final working version by using your browser to view the Multiscreen Slideshow Demo in the Code section of the CD-ROM that accompanies this book.

Summary

Timelines are effective tools for developing pages in which events need to be triggered at specific points in time.

✦ Timelines can affect particular attributes of layers and images, or they can start any Dreamweaver behavior.

✦ Use the Timelines panel to set an animation to play automatically, to have it loop indefinitely, and to change the frames-per-second display rate of the timeline.

✦ You must use one of the timeline behaviors to activate your timeline if you don't use the Autoplay feature.

In the next chapter, you learn how you can use Dreamweaver to explore the brave new world of XML, the Extensible Markup Language.

✦   ✦   ✦

Creating Next-Generation Code with Dreamweaver

Extending with XML

XML, short for Extensible Markup Language, is quickly becoming a powerful force on the Web and an important technology for Web designers to master. XML enables the parts of any document — from Web page to invoice — to be defined in terms of how those parts are used. When a document is defined by its structure rather than its appearance, as it is with HTML, the same document can be read by a wide variety of systems and put to use far more efficiently.

Dreamweaver adds *Roundtrip XML* as a complement to its Roundtrip HTML core philosophy. Roundtrip HTML ensures that the defined tags of HTML remain just as you've written them. With XML, no one defined set of tags exists — XML tags can be written for an industry, a company, or just a Web site. Roundtrip XML permits Web designers to export and import XML pages based on their own structure.

You can find XML all throughout Dreamweaver, just under the hood. The Design Notes feature is based on XML, as is the completely customizable menu system and even the HTML Styles feature. The Third-party Tags file is pure XML and can describe any kind of tag. In fact, XML can be used to describe most anything, even HTML. This chapter explores the basics of XML, as well as the implementation of Roundtrip XML in Dreamweaver.

Understanding XML

XML is to structure what Cascading Style Sheets (CSS) are to format. While Cascading Style Sheets control the look of a particular document on the Web, XML makes the document's intent paramount. Because there are almost as many ways to describe the parts of documents as there are types of documents, a set language, such as HTML, could never provide enough specification to be truly useful. This is why, with XML, you create your own custom tags to describe the page — XML is truly an extensible language.

XML became a W3C Recommendation in February 1998, after a relatively brief two-year study. The speed with which the recommendation was approved speaks to the need for the technology. XML has been described as a more accessible version of SGML (Standard Generalized Markup Language), the widely used text processing standard. In fact, the XML Working Group that drafted the W3C Recommendation started out as the SGML Working Group.

What can XML do that HTML can't? Let's say you have a shipping order that you want to distribute. With HTML, each of the parts of the document — such as the billing address, the shipping address, and the order details, to name a few — are enclosed in tags that describe their appearance, like this:

```
<h2 align="center"><bold>Invoice</bold></h2>
<p align="left">Ship to:</p>
<p>J. Lowery<br>
101 101st Avenue, Ste. 101<br>
New York, NY 10000</p>
```

With XML, each section of the page is given its own set of tags, according to its meaning, like this:

```
<documentType>Invoice</documentType>
<ship-toHeader>Ship to:</ship-toHeader>
<customer>J. Lowery<br></customer>
<ship-toAddress>101 101st Avenue, Ste. 101<br>
New York, NY 10000</ship-toAddress>
```

Like HTML, XML is a combination of content and markup tags. Markup tags can be in pairs, such as `<customer>...</customer>`, or they can be singular. A single tag is called an *empty tag* because no content is included. Single tags in XML must include an ending slash — as in `<noTax/>`, for example — and are used to mark where something occurs. Here, `<noTax/>` indicates that no sales tax is to be applied to this invoice.

XML tags, again like HTML, can also include attributes and values. As with HTML, XML attributes further describe the tag, much like an adjective describes a noun. For example, another way to write the `<ship-toHeader>` tag would be

```
<header type="Ship To">
```

With a more generalized tag such as this one, you could easily change values, as in `<header type="Bill To">`, rather than include another new tag.

In all, XML recognizes six kinds of markup:

✦ **Elements:** Elements are more commonly known as *tags* and, as in HTML, are delimited by a set of angle brackets `<>`. As noted previously, elements can also have attributes set to particular values.

Caution

While surrounding values with quotes—such as in `color="white"`—is optional in HTML, it's mandatory in XML.

✦ **Entity References:** Certain characters in XML, such as the delimiting angle brackets, are reserved in order to permit markup to be recognized. These characters are represented by entities in XML. As in HTML, character entities begin with an ampersand and end with a semicolon. For example `&lt;Content&gt;` is XML code to represent `<Content>`.

✦ **Comments:** XML comments are identical to HTML comments; they both begin with `<!--` and end with `-->`.

✦ **Processing instructions:** XML processing instructions are similar to server-side includes in that the XML processor (like the server) passes them on to the application (like the browser).

✦ **Marked sections:** XML can pass blocks of code or other data without parsing the markup and content. These blocks of character data are marked with `<![CDATA[` at the beginning and `]]>` at the end. For example:

```
<![CDATA[If age < 19 and age > 6, then the kids are in ¬
school]]>
```

Communication between XML and HTML is greatly eased because large blocks of data can be passed in this fashion.

✦ **Document type declarations:** Because every XML document is capable of containing its own set of custom tags, a method for defining these tags must exist. Although a discussion of the formats of such document-type declarations is beyond the scope of this book, it's helpful to know that such declarations can be made for elements, attributes, character entities, and notations. Notations refer to external binary data, such as GIFs, that are passed through the XML parser to the application.

XML documents may begin with an XML declaration that specifies the version of XML being used. The XML declaration for a document compliant with the 1.0 specification looks like the following:

```
<?xml version="1.0"?>
```

A much more detailed document type declaration (DTD), in which each tag and attribute is described in SGML, is also possible. XML documents including these types of DTDs are labeled *valid XML documents*. Other documents that respect the rules of XML regarding nesting of tags and other matters, but don't include DTDs for the elements, are known as *well-formed XML*. Dreamweaver exports well-formed XML documents but can import either well-formed or valid XML.

Exporting XML

How do you make an XML page? In Dreamweaver, you can convert an existing document into XML format with one command. Currently, Dreamweaver creates its XML pages based on a template's editable regions. With this approach, the true content of a page — what distinguishes it from all other pages of the same type — can be separated and applied independently of the original Web page. In other words, once the XML information is culled from a Web page, it can be imported into any other application to be displayed, read, spoken, translated, or acted upon.

Dreamweaver templates are composed of *locked* and *editable* regions; the locked regions are repeated for each page created from the template, while the content in the editable regions is added per page. The connection between XML and templates is similar to the relationship between a database form and its data. In a database, each field has a unique name, such as LastName, FirstName, and so on. When you create a database form to present the data, the placeholders for the data use the same field names. Then, when data from one record flows into the form, the information from the field goes into the areas with the corresponding field names. Likewise, each editable region has a unique name — in essence, a field name. The content within the editable region is the field's data. When exported as an XML file, the name of the editable region is converted to an XML tag that surrounds its data.

For example, Figure 30-1 shows a Dreamweaver template for a purchase order. On the left are the headings (To, Company, Address, and so on) for the information in a locked area, while the specific shipping data on the right resides in a series of editable regions, each with its own name.

When exported as XML by Dreamweaver, the resulting XML file looks like the following:

```
<?xml version="1.0"?>
<doctitle><![CDATA[<title>Purchase Order</title>]]></doctitle>
<Customer><![CDATA[Jose Bleau]]></Customer>
<Company><![CDATA[Kreamhorn, Inc. ]]></Company>
<Address><![CDATA[155 Somerton Ave.<br>
                  West Therea, TX]]></Address>
<PO_Date><![CDATA[January 2, 1999]]></PO_Date>
<Ship_Via><![CDATA[FedEx]]></Ship_Via>
```

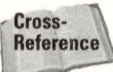

Cross-Reference To get a better idea of how to use XML, you need to understand Dreamweaver templates, which are discussed in Chapter 32.

Note several important items about the XML file. First, notice the use of self-evident labels for each of the tags, such as <Customer> and <Ship_Via>; such names make it easy to understand an XML file. Even the one tag not based on a user-defined name, <doctitle>, is straightforward. Second, all the data included in the XML tags is marked as a CDATA area; this ensures that the information is conveyed intact, just as it was entered. Finally, if you look at the `<Address>` tag data, you see that even HTML tags (here, a `<br>` tag) are included in the `CDATA` blocks. This practice enables basic formatting to be carried over from one page to the next. You can avoid this by selecting just the inner content — without any of the formatting tags — to be marked as an editable region.

Figure 30-1: Dreamweaver 4 creates XML pages based on templates and editable regions.

Dreamweaver can create one of two different types of XML tags during its export operation. The first is referred to as *Dreamweaver Standard XML* and uses an `<item>` tag with a name attribute set to the editable region's name. For example, if the editable region were named Ship_Via, the Dreamweaver Standard tag would be

```
<item name="Ship_Via">Content</item>
```

The Dreamweaver Standard XML file has one other distinguishing characteristic. The XML file is saved with a reference to the defining Dreamweaver template, like this:

```
<templateItems template="/Templates/PO.dwt">
```

When importing a Dreamweaver Standard XML file, if the specified template cannot be found, a dialog box appears asking that you select another template.

The other option is to use what Dreamweaver refers to as *Editable Region Name tags*. This method uses the editable region names themselves as tags. In the case of the editable region name Ship_Via, the tag pair under this method would be `<Ship_Via>...</Ship_Via>`.

To create an XML file from within Dreamweaver, follow these steps:

1. Open a Dreamweaver document based on a template that has at least one editable region.

2. Choose File ➪ Export ➪ Export Editable Regions As XML.

   The Export Editable Regions as XML dialog box opens, as shown in Figure 30-2.

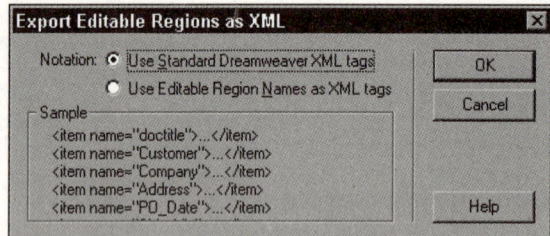

Figure 30-2: Convert any template-based page to an XML document with the Export Editable Regions as XML dialog box.

3. Choose the format for the XML tags by selecting one of the Notation options:

   • **Use Standard Dreamweaver XML tags:** Select this option to produce `<item>` tags with `name` attributes set to the names of the editable regions.

   • **Use Editable Region Names as XML tags:** Select this option to produce XML tags that use the editable region names directly.

   Selecting either option displays sample tags in the preview area of the dialog box.

4. Select OK when you're done.

   An Export Editable Regions as XML Save File dialog box appears.

5. Enter the path and name of the XML file you wish to save in the File Name text box or select the Browse (Choose) button to locate another folder. Click Save when you're done.

Importing XML

As part of Roundtrip XML, Dreamweaver 4 includes an Import XML command. Like the Export XML command, Import XML works with Dreamweaver templates. The content information in the XML document fills out the editable regions in the template, much as data fills out a form in a database.

With this import capability, content can be independently created and stored in an XML file and then, to publish the page to the Web, simply imported into the Dreamweaver template.

XML files to be imported must follow either one of the two structures used when exporting a template to XML: Standard Dreamweaver XML or Editable Region Names used as XML tags. Although it's a matter of personal preference, I find the Editable Region Names format to be easier to read and, in general, simpler to work with.

How does one create an XML file? Naturally, you could open a template for your XML document and fill in the data by hand — but that, in a sense, defeats the purpose of automating your workflow via XML. A more likely scenario is to use a database to accept and store content; the database entry form could easily be accessible over a network or over the Internet. A report, generated by the database application, blends the content data and the XML structure, resulting in an XML file to be imported into Dreamweaver.

To import an XML file into a Dreamweaver template, follow these steps:

1. If desired, open a file based on a Dreamweaver template.

You don't have to have a page created from a template open in order to access the XML information — Dreamweaver automatically opens one for you.

2. Choose File ➪ Import XML into Template.

The Import XML dialog box opens.

Any existing information in the Dreamweaver document in the editable regions is replaced by the information in the corresponding tags of the XML document.

3. Select an XML file from the Import XML dialog box.

4. Choose Open when you're done.

The XML file is imported into Dreamweaver, and the editable region placeholder names are replaced with the data in the XML document.

Summary

XML is a vital future technology that is knocking on the door of virtually every Web designer in business. As the development tools become more common, the Roundtrip XML capability within Dreamweaver makes interfacing with this new method of communication straightforward and effortless. Keep the following points in mind:

✦ XML (Extensible Markup Language) enables content to be separated from the style of a Web page, creating information that can be more easily used in various situations with different kinds of media.

✦ Tags in XML reflect the nature of the content, rather than its appearance.

✦ Dreamweaver includes a Roundtrip XML facility that makes it possible to export and import XML files through Dreamweaver templates.

In the next chapter, you learn how Dreamweaver can be used to build database-connected Web pages.

✦   ✦   ✦

Building Active Web Sites

C H A P T E R

31

The Internet was initially a vehicle for simple documents — basic communication, reports on laboratory findings, and scholarly papers — and the Web consisted of basically static pages, each one separate and independent. As the Web exploded and the need for more up-to-date information grew, the practice of building or continually modifying a Web page soon became impractical. Not only were special skills required, such as an understanding of HTML coding, but also data was often taken from an existing system and reentered onto a Web page, thus duplicating effort unnecessarily. A link between the Web and existing database structures was forged to create dynamic Web pages capable of displaying the most current content in a structured, easy-to-navigate format.

Database connectivity is a strong and growing aspect of the Web. Without a strong connection between the Web and databases, e-commerce could not thrive, news bureaus would be buried under a glut of information, and intranets would be continually out of date. Numerous companies are involved in the field: Microsoft pioneered Active Server Pages for their servers, while companies such as Allaire, Oracle, and Tango produce alternative technologies for others.

Until recently, Internet database connectivity was an art form practiced only by the most adept programmers. If you didn't understand the inner workings of ODBC, SQL, and other database acronyms, you could forget it. However, if you want to keep your client base happy and growing, that won't be an option for long — many businesses are demanding database connectivity for their Web sites. Now, with Dreamweaver, bringing a page to life through active database content is only a click or two away. Dreamweaver has partnered with several of the top companies to smooth this tortuous path. Although specific examinations of all the solutions possible is beyond the scope of this book, this chapter explains the ins and outs of database connectivity and e-commerce — even as more are on the way, thanks to Dreamweaver's inherent extensibility.

Note   Perhaps, Macromedia's Dreamweaver UltraDev is the ultimate solution for Dreamweaver users who desire to build active Web sites. UltraDev is a superset of Dreamweaver: The program retains all of Dreamweaver's features and user interface while adding numerous drag-and-drop Web application abilities. UltraDev outputs code for Active Server Pages, ColdFusion pages, and Java Server Pages. While UltraDev deserves a book of its own, the balance of this chapter is focussed on what you need to know if you use Dreamweaver UltraDev to build your active Web applications or if you just use Dreamweaver.

Understanding Active Content

For many Web designers, databases are a completely foreign territory — and how you build a bridge from a Web page to a database is a total mystery. Before you implement a database-oriented Web site, it's helpful to understand the fundamentals of databases and gain an overview of the connectivity processes involved. For some Web production companies, the designer is responsible for all aspects of site creation; here, a firm understanding of the new possibilities and technologies of an active content page is essential.

Database basics

Databases store information systematically. Here, the key word is *systematically*. Many other technologies, both low- and high-end, store information — a shelf of books, a shoebox full of receipts, even a collection of Web pages — but few store the information in such a way that retrieval is structured and uniform. Naturally, the precise nature of the structure varies from one type of database to another, but fundamentally, they are all the same.

A database is made up of a series of *records*. Each record can be thought of as a snapshot of a particular set of details. These details are known as *fields*, and each field contains the pertinent information or data. A single database record can be made up of any number of fields of varying types — some fields hold only numbers or only dates, whereas others are open-ended and can hold any type of information. A series of database records, all with the same fields, is commonly referred to as a *table* — a simple table is also known as a *flat-file database*. As with a word processing or an HTML table, a database table has rows and columns. Each column represents a field, while each row represents a record. For example, the following table that I call `BookTitles` describes a series of books:

Title	Author	Pages	Published
JavaScript Bible	Danny Goodman	1,015	1998
HTML Manual of Style	Larry Aronson and Joseph Lowery	385	1997
Netrepreneur	Joseph Lowery	424	1998

The first row in the table contains the field names: Title, Author, Pages, and Published. Each subsequent row contains a complete record. As presented here, this table is in no particular order; however, one of the reasons databases are so powerful is their sorting ability. If I were to sort the `BookTitles` table by page count, listing the books with the fewest pages first, it would look like this:

Title	Author	Pages	Published
HTML Manual of Style	Larry Aronson and Joseph Lowery	385	1997
Netrepreneur	Joseph Lowery	424	1998
JavaScript Bible	Danny Goodman	1,015	1998

Most modern databases can sort a table on any field, using any criteria. Many databases require that a table have an *index field* where each entry is unique, to simplify data manipulation. In the prior table example, the Title field could serve as an index because each title is unique; however, this is often not the case, and a separate field is created.

Index fields, also referred to as *key fields,* become an absolute necessity when two or more tables — or flat-file databases — are combined to create a *relational database*. As the name implies, a relational database presents information that is related. For example, let's say we created another table called `BookSales` to accompany our previous book database example, like this:

Region	Sales	Book
East	10,000	*JavaScript Bible*
South	20,500	*JavaScript Bible*
West	42,000	*JavaScript Bible*
North	25,000	*JavaScript Bible*
East	15,000	*Netrepreneur*
South	12,000	*Netrepreneur*

Continued

Region	Sales	Book
West	8,000	*Netrepreneur*
North	21,000	*Netrepreneur*
East	8,330	*HTML Manual of Style*
South	6,500	*HTML Manual of Style*
West	8,000	*HTML Manual of Style*
North	7,400	*HTML Manual of Style*

To get a list of authors, sorted according to sales figures, you have to combine or join the two databases. A field common to both tables is used to create the juncture, or *join* — here, the common field is the index field Title. While flat-file databases can be used in many situations, most industrial-strength applications use relational databases to access information.

In addition to changing the sort order of a table, database information can also be selectively retrieved by using a *filter*. A filter is often represented by a *where* statement, as in "Show me the books where regional sales were over 10,000 but under 20,000." Applying this filter to the BookSales table would result in the following table:

Region	Sales	Book
East	10,000	*JavaScript Bible*
East	15,000	*Netrepreneur*
South	12,000	*Netrepreneur*

The common language understood by many Web-available databases is SQL, which stands for *Structured Query Language*. A SQL statement tells the database precisely what information you're looking for and what form you want it in. Although SQL statements can become quite complex, a relatively simple SQL statement has just four parts, as follows:

✦ **Select:** Picks the fields to display.

✦ **From:** Chooses the databases from which to gather the information.

✦ **Where:** Describes the filter criteria and/or the joins.

✦ **Order:** Gives the sorting criteria.

A sample SQL statement translation of our "Show me the books where regional sales were over 10,000 but under 20,000" example would look like this:

```
SELECT Title
FROM BookSales
WHERE (Sales > 10000) & (Sales < 20000)
ORDER by Sales
```

Joins between two or more tables are depicted in SQL with an equal sign and are considered part of the filter in the WHERE statement. To show the sales by author's name, I'd have to revise my SQL statement to read as follows:

```
SELECT Title, Author
FROM BookTitles, BookSales
WHERE BookTitles = BookSales & ((Sales > 10000) & (Sales < 20000))
ORDER by Author
```

Tip　The quick way to display all the fields in a table is to use a SQL statement with a wildcard, like this:

```
SELECT * FROM Booktitles
```

The asterisk indicates that you want to choose every field.

How active content pages work

The journey for a static Web page from user to server is straightforward, even for the most complex, graphics- and JavaScript-laden page. The user clicks a link that sends a signal to the server to send that page. An active content page — with full database connectivity — travels a much different route, however.

An active content page is a blend of traditional HTML and a database server language, such as Active Server Pages (ASP) or Cold Fusion Markup Language (CFML). When a user accesses an active content page, the requested page is passed through the database server where the code is processed and a new HTML page is generated. This page is then returned to the regular Web server and sent on to the user. Figure 31-1 illustrates this process.

Active content servers can connect to more than databases, however. Other possibilities include the following:

✦ **Directory servers:** Directory servers control the permissions for large corporations and determine who is granted access to what group of files. With a directory server, two people — with different clearances — could see two different pages when clicking the same link.

✦ **Mail servers:** E-mail communication can be fully automated through a mail server: Responses to forms are categorized and forwarded to the proper parties, mass mailings can go out at the click of a button, and messages can be automatically incorporated into Web pages.

Dreamweaver Database Partners

Developing connectivity for a Web authoring tool requires a close alliance with the database company. Macromedia has established partnerships with several of the leaders in Internet database technology and has released a series of solutions with each of them. As of this writing, the partnership with Allaire has brought the Cold Fusion extensions to fruition — and the recent merger between Macromedia and Allaire promises many more cross-overs — as has a partnership with Pervasive and their Tango extensions. Blueworld built an entirely new product, Lasso Studio for Dreamweaver, around their set of extensions.

Macromedia has instituted similar arrangements with Oracle, Broadvision, and Apple. Oracle has many adherents, and their Web-oriented technology, Oracle8i, combined with Dreamweaver, is a possible winning combination. Broadvision is a developer of high-end database solutions used for tracking personal access on the Web; their primary Web development tool is Dreamweaver. Database integration for Broadvision means a much smoother workflow for complex Web sites.

Dreamweaver's extensibility makes it the ideal Web authoring tool for customization and use by the various connectivity solutions. Be sure to keep an eye on the official Dreamweaver Web site (www.dreamweaver.com) for further announcements and software releases.

Figure 31-1: An active content page is processed by a database server prior to being sent to the user.

✦ **File servers:** By and large, HTML by itself has no file manipulation capabilities. However, with a file server, files can be uploaded, copied, renamed, moved, deleted, and more.

The primary HTML vehicle for interfacing with a database server is the form.

Most Web databases are Open Database Connectivity (ODBC) compliant. ODBC is a standard that enables virtually any type of database to be accessed — if the database has an ODBC driver. Similar to printer drivers that enable your computer to communicate with a wide variety of printers, an ODBC driver translates data to and from the database program. When setting up your database on the Web server, you may need to declare the ODBC driver for the file, as well as establish the Data Source Name (DSN). The DSN is used to simplify query building by giving each database a unique name to be referenced. Most servers require that the ODBC driver and DSN name be handled by the system administrator, or someone with that level of access.

E-Commerce Solutions

Although the first age of the Internet was widely devoted to information — gathering, storing, archiving, and sharing it — the next era increasingly seems devoted to transactions and business. E-commerce is on the rise; online retail purchases are doubling and tripling each year as consumers feel more secure about shopping over the Web and business-to-business sales are skyrocketing. You'll find numerous explanations for this explosive growth, but the bottom line is this: Buying and selling online is here to stay.

More and more, Web designers are asked to build storefronts on the Web. Enabling a Web site for e-commerce is not a trivial task, as it requires a blend of Internet security, database connectivity, and marketing savvy. Macromedia has partnered with several leaders in electronic commerce, including iCat, NetStores, and Miva, to develop a series of commands and objects, available on the Dreamweaver Web site, that simplify creating and hosting an online store. Specific discussions of these integration capabilities are beyond the scope of this book; however, the balance of this chapter includes an overview of e-commerce from a Web designer's point of view. Also, along the way, you learn how Dreamweaver can help you with another e-commerce necessity: tracking customers with JavaScript cookies.

Understanding E-Commerce

Although there are almost as many variations to how shopping works as there are stores on the Web, many transactions take a similar path. Here's how a typical transaction makes its way around the Internet:

1. The user sees something desirable in the online store and clicks the "Buy" button to put the item in their shopping cart.

   The "Buy" triggers a cookie containing the item number and quantity to be written to the user's system.

2. After shopping for a bit more, the user decides to proceed to the checkout area of the site.

   The link on the Checkout Counter button is to a page on a secure server that employs Secure Sockets Layer (SSL) protocol. An icon on the user's browser — usually a locked padlock or a solid key — indicates the change. All communication between a user and secure server is coded or encrypted.

3. The user is given an opportunity to confirm the current contents of the shopping cart — and, if desired, change the quantity of any item.

   The cookie information (with the information about the selected products) that has been stored during the online shopping trip is read back into the browser. (See the sidebar, "Passing Cookies," later in this chapter for details.)

4. If the customer has shopped at the online store before, a user ID and password are all that are required to retrieve all the pertinent account information: billing and shipping address, credit card numbers, e-mail address, and so forth.

   If the buyer is a first-time customer, forms with the applicable information are filled out, and the data — along with a new user ID and password — is transferred to the store's system over the secure network.

5. The system at the online shop retrieves the order information and decodes it. The transactional information (credit card number, amount of purchase, and so on) is reencrypted and sent over secure phone lines to the credit card clearinghouse with an authentication certificate from the store.

   The order information is entered into the database. Some systems deduct the order from inventory at this point, whereas others wait for the transaction to be confirmed by the bank.

6. The credit card clearinghouse authenticates the merchant and forwards the transaction data to the bank.

7. The bank accepts or declines the charge and sends the result back to the clearinghouse, which then forwards it to the merchant.

8. The merchant sends two electronic confirmations to the customer: one to the browser as a thank-you and one via e-mail with full details of the order and shipping information. Any links from here, back to the main store, end the secure server connection.

As you can see, online selling requires a great deal of behind-the-scenes communication and coordination. However, it all boils down to two primary factors: security and connectivity.

Encryption

The facet of the Web that makes it so compelling — global access — is one of the factors that keeps consumers wary. The common fear is, "If anyone in the world can get online, can't they also get my credit card information?" Grabbing any data as it passes by on the Internet is certainly not a trivial task and is possible for only the most dedicated hackers. Even with the information in hand, however, cyberthieves still haven't made off with the loot — because whatever data they have is meaningless unless it is decoded.

Encryption is handled automatically, with all data passed through a *secure server*. A secure server is one that uses some form of coding, or *encryption*, technology. The most common form of Internet encryption comes from servers with a Secure Sockets Layer (SSL). To secure any information passed over the Web, the page with the form must access a secure server. Links for secure servers begin with `https://`, instead of the usual `http://` — the additional *s* stands, of course, for security.

> **Note** Depending on the user's browser settings, messages can appear when going from a secure server to a nonsecure server. As these alerts can be disconcerting to the novice user, it's a good idea to continue using the secure server for all Web pages accessed during the sales checkout procedure — even those pages that are purely informational and don't require the secure server to pass data.

Authentication

Encryption solves only half of the problem with online security — the other half requires *authentication*. It accomplishes nothing to receive an encrypted message from someone if you're not sure they are who they are supposed to be. Because online communication is largely anonymous — there's no visual or aural confirmation of identity — another method of identification is necessary.

The current basic method of authentication involves *digital certificates*. A digital certificate is a type of identity card for companies, Web sites, and online individuals. Digital certificates are issued by established certificate authorities, such as VeriSign (`www.verisign.com`), and are generally automatically transferred by browsers. Companies (or individuals) applying for a digital certificate must prove their identity. With companies, the process is similar to applying for a merchant bank account; you must supply the companies' articles of incorporation, tax ID number, and so forth. With individuals, you need enter only an e-mail address. Higher classes of digital certificates include insured protection, which requires a more rigorous identification procedure. Digital certificates are typically offered when a user enters a secure server.

Passing Cookies

As noted earlier, cookies are used to track user information — such as what's in a shopping cart — from one Web page. A *cookie* is a small piece of information that can be passed along with the HTTP header that accompanies every Web page: The Web page is displayed by the browser, and the cookie information is stored on the user's hard drive in a special file. Don't get the idea that cookies are just text files that can be used in any situation. Cookies have a very special format and definite limits.

Each domain is limited to 20 cookies, and a 4-megabyte or 300-total cookie limit imposed by the browser. A cookie generally conveys four pieces of information:

✦ **Domain of origin:** All cookies are domain specific (sent from one particular Internet domain). Only the domain sending the cookie can retrieve it.

✦ **Expiration date:** Many cookies are intended to be active for a single online session; when you leave the Web site, the cookie is no longer of any value. These cookies are maintained in memory only and never written to a file. Other cookies use specified expiration dates to keep the number of cookies down, so new ones can be added.

✦ **Path of URL:** You can specify where a cookie is active on your site. Generally, it's best to keep the cookies available in the current directory.

✦ **Name and value pairs:** The name and value pairs are the real content of a cookie. Each variable or name is set equal to a particular value, generally user supplied either directly through a text box or by an action, such as selecting an Add to Shopping Cart button. The name and value pairs are later retrieved by a JavaScript or CGI program when the cookie is read.

Although Dreamweaver 4 doesn't come with any standard cookie behaviors, third-party developers have created a number of them. Generally, cookie behaviors come in a set — one behavior to set the cookie, another to read it, and yet another to remove it entirely. Nadav Silvio of the Webmonkey Web site built one of the better cookie behavior sets. With the Webmonkey Set and Read Cookie behaviors, you can even choose a form field on the Web page, such as a text box, to get the cookie from or set it to.

One of the drawbacks to cookies is that they're not universally accepted. Because of the possible security risk involved with any outside system writing and reading information to a local hard drive, browsers enable the user to choose whether they will accept cookies or be warned every time one is passed to their system. Using another third-party extension, the Check Cookie behavior by Jaro von Flocken, you can redirect to another page visitors whose browsers do not have cookies enabled.

On the CD-ROM   You'll find all these cookie behaviors and more on the CD-ROM.

Working with shopping carts

Whenever a customer selects an item online with the intent to buy it, the item goes into an online *shopping cart*. Although commonly thought of as a single object, a shopping cart is composed of several key components of a program or programs. Basically, the shopping cart enables the potential customer to tag selected items for purchase and continue shopping. When the customer decides to finalize the purchase, the items are listed on the checkout screen, and a total cost is calculated.

Generally, shopping cart functionality includes the capability to include any number of items and modify the quantity of the items — including changing the number to zero, thus removing it from the shopping cart. Most stores are set up so that items can be added to the shopping cart at any time in one session and checkout is always available.

> **Note**
>
> As well as the numerous high-end e-commerce products from such companies as Open Market (www.openmarket.com), Netscape (www.netscape.com), and ICVerify (www.icverify.com), you can also find several full-featured CGI online shopping solutions from such resources as Extropia (www.extropia.com) and the CGI Resource Index (www.cgi-resources.com) for free or at relatively low cost.

Because of the complexity of handling complete online shopping transactions and store management — and the inherent expense — several e-commerce solutions have separated the shopping cart component from the all-in-one store solution. Under a shopping cart–only arrangement, your Web pages include Add to Shopping Cart and Proceed to Checkout links that access the e-commerce solution's secure server instead of your own. This is an excellent route for a small business that wants to sell online, but whose business volume doesn't rate an in-house server.

Ensuring Dreamweaver Compatibility

Since its first release, one of Dreamweaver's primary selling points has been its claim that it does not alter your code. Unfortunately for many Web designers working with middleware server-side systems that use custom tags for programming, Dreamweaver's claim only extended to HTML code — any other nonstandard tags were often marked as Invalid HTML or, worse, altered significantly.

Recognizing that Web pages aren't just for HTML anymore, Dreamweaver incorporates several new methods to ensure that server-side markup is as protected as HTML. By adjusting Preferences, Dreamweaver can be instructed to adopt a "hands-off" policy for any Web page with a particular file extension, such as .cfm or .asp. Moreover, you can turn off Dreamweaver's automatic encoding of URLs and/or attributes.

To understand the overall rewriting problem better, let's look at an example. One of the major benefits of active content pages is being able to use a variable as an image's source on catalog-like pages. To do so, you need something like this ASP code:

```
<img src="images/<% = Replace(varGrade," ","%20") %>.jpg">
```

If you tried to include ASP code such as this in Dreamweaver 2 or earlier, the crucial %20 value would be stripped out because Dreamweaver interprets %20 as hexadecimal for a space character. Although workarounds exist for situations such as this — you could always assign the offending character or its overall string to a variable and use that within the HTML tag — workarounds take time to implement. An overall solution is far better.

Dreamweaver solves this problem by enabling the user to specify file types that should remain unchanged such as HTML. By default, Dreamweaver includes the following file types as being protected when the Never Rewrite Code option is selected from the Code Rewriting category of Preferences:

File Type	Server-Side System
.asp	Active Server Pages
.cfm, .cfml	Cold Fusion Application Server
.ihtml	Inline HTML
.jsp	JavaServer Pages
.php	PHP: Hypertext Preprocessor

You can add as many file extensions as you'd like, although I recommend including only those file types you actually use.

Another potential problem with HTML rewriting stems from URL encoding. In order to ensure universal acceptance of URLs, regardless of the type of server, Dreamweaver automatically encodes nonstandard characters, such as spaces or tildes, entered through the Property Inspector in hexadecimal. Thus, a space is represented as %20 and a tilde as %7E. While this practice is good for standard Web servers, it can raise havoc with application servers. Dreamweaver also extends a similar type of encoding to attributes containing special characters such as angle brackets (< and >), ampersands, and quote marks. Both of these types of encoding can be disabled via an option in Dreamweaver preferences.

Caution It's best to disable the encoding options only if you encounter HTML rewriting issues involving URLs or attributes.

If you find that your active content page code is being rewritten when opened in Dreamweaver, follow these steps:

1. Choose Edit ➪ Preferences.

    The Preferences dialog box is displayed.

2. Select the Code Rewriting category, shown in Figure 31-2.

Figure 31-2: Lock out any file type from Code Rewriting through Dreamweaver Preferences.

3. Enable the Never Rewrite Code option.

4. Adjust the In Files with Extensions field to include your file type's extension.

    Add new file types separated by a space with a leading period, as in .lasso. Be sure to include all possible variations of the file types, such as .phtm and .phtml.

5. To prevent Dreamweaver from encoding special characters in URLs with hexadecimal values, disable the Encode Special Characters in URLs using % option.

6. To prevent Dreamweaver from encoding special characters in attributes with hexadecimal values, disable the Encode <, >, &, and " in Attribute Values Using & option.

All these Preference changes take place immediately; there's no need to relaunch Dreamweaver.

Summary

It's a pretty safe bet that active content is an issue in every Web designer's future. Not only can database-connected pages serve up simple data in an organized fashion, but images, links, streaming video, and other media are also targetable content. Dreamweaver's extensibility makes it the ideal choice for a Web designer who needs to connect to the ever-expanding world of databases. When you're considering building an active content page, keep the following in mind:

✦ A database is a structured file for maintaining data. Databases are made up of tables, fields, and records. A database that can use two or more tables together is called a *relational database*.

✦ Web pages that link standard HTML and elements drawn from a database are referred to as *active content pages*. With an active content page, you change the data, and the Web page is presented with the new information automatically.

✦ All specialized servers — whether for database-generated pages or e-commerce — use non-HTML code. Dreamweaver offers several Preference options for preserving both HTML and non-HTML code.

In the next chapter, you learn how to create reusable templates within Dreamweaver.

✦   ✦   ✦

Enhancing Web Site Management and Workflow in Dreamweaver

Using Dreamweaver Templates

Let's face it: Web design is a combination of glory and grunt work. Creating the initial design for a Web site can be fun and exciting, but when you have to implement your wonderful new design on 200 or more pages, the excitement fades as you try to figure out the quickest way to finish the work. Enter templates. Properly using templates can be a tremendous time-saver. Moreover, a template ensures that your Web site has a consistent look and feel, which, in turn, generally means that it's easier for users to navigate.

In Dreamweaver, new documents can be produced from a standard design saved as a template, as in a word processing program. Furthermore, you can alter a template and update all the files that were created from it earlier; this capability extends the power of the repeating element Libraries to overall page design. Templates also form the bridge to one of the hottest technologies shaping the Web—XML (Extensible Markup Language).

Dreamweaver makes it easy to access all kinds of templates—everything from your own creations to the default blank page. This chapter demonstrates the mechanism behind Dreamweaver templates and shows you strategies for getting the most out of them.

Understanding Templates

Templates exist in many forms. Furniture makers use master patterns as templates to create the same basic design repeatedly, using new wood stains or upholstery to differentiate the end results. A stencil, in which the inside of a letter, word, or design is cut out, is a type of template as well. With computers, templates form the basic document into which specific details are added to create new, distinct documents.

Dreamweaver templates, in terms of functionality, are a combination of traditional templates and updateable Library elements. Once a new page is created from a template, the new document remains attached to the original template unless specifically separated or detached. Because the new document maintains a connection to previous pages in a site, if the original template is altered, all the documents created from it can be automatically updated. This relationship is also true of Dreamweaver's repeating elements Libraries. In fact, templates can even include Library elements.

Cross-Reference Library items can work hand-in-hand with templates. See Chapter 33 for a detailed discussion of Library items.

Templates are composed of two types of regions: *locked* and *editable*. Every element on the Web page template falls into one category or the other. When a template is first created, all the areas are locked. Part of the process of defining a template is to designate and name the editable regions. Then, when a document is created from that template, the editable regions are the only ones that can be modified.

Naturally, templates can be altered to mark additional editable areas or to relock editable areas. Moreover, you can detach a document created from a template at any point and edit anything in the document — you cannot, however, reattach the document to the template without losing newly inserted content. On the other hand, a document based on one template can be changed to a completely different look but with the same content, if another template with identical editable regions is applied.

Dreamweaver ships with a tutorial that illustrates the power of templates. The tutorial, found in the Dreamweaver/Tutorial folder, is based on an example Web site for a travel company called Compass. Previewing the site in a browser shows that all the sample pages for the different trips in the Destinations section are basically the same — only the destination title, description, and Flash movie vary. The layout, background, and navigation controls are identical on every page. Each of these pages was created from the template page shown in Figure 32-1. Notice the highlighting surrounding certain areas; in a template, the editable regions are highlighted, and the locked areas are not. A tab further identifies each editable region to make it easier to add the right content in the right area.

Creating Your Own Templates

You can use any design that you like for your own template. Perhaps the best course to take is to finalize a single page that has all the elements that you want to include in your template. Then, convert that document to a template and proceed to mark all the changeable areas — whether text or image — as editable regions.

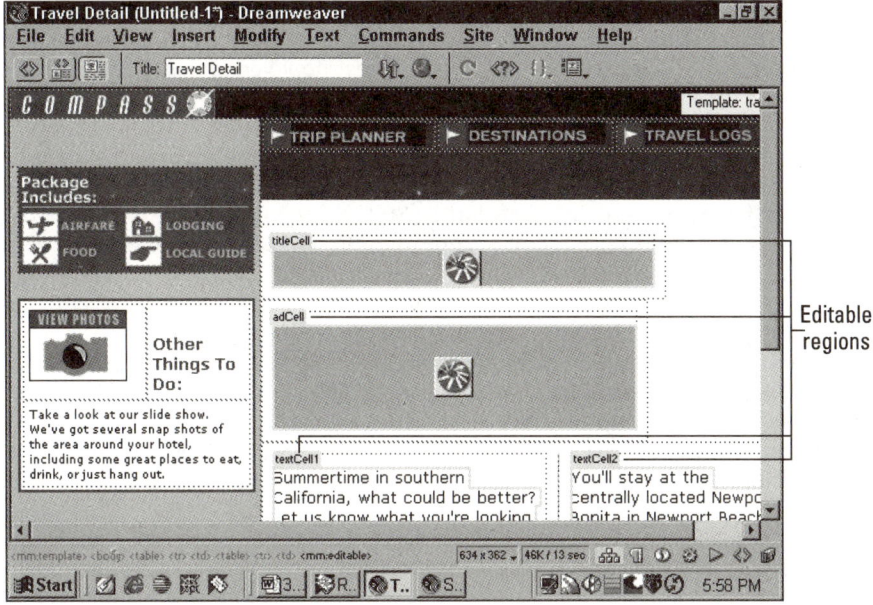

Figure 32-1: In this sample template from the Dreamweaver tutorial, editable regions are highlighted.

Before saving your file as a template, consider these points when designing your basic page:

✦ **Use placeholders where you can.** Whether it's dummy text or a temporary graphic, placeholders give shape to your page. They also make it easier to remember which elements to include. If you are using an image placeholder, set a temporary height and width through the Property Inspector or by dragging the image placeholder's sizing handles; of course, you can also just insert a sample graphic.

✦ **Finalize and incorporate as much content as possible in the template.** If you find yourself repeatedly adding the same information or objects to a page, add them to your template. The more structured elements you can include, the faster your pages can be produced.

✦ **Use sample objects on the template.** Often you have to enter the same basic object, such as a plug-in for a digital movie, on every page, with only the file-name changing. Enter your repeating object with all the preset parameters possible on your template page as an editable region, and you only have to select a new filename for each page.

✦ **Include your** `<meta>` **information.** Search engines rely on `<meta>` tags to get the overview of a page and then scan the balance of the page to get the details. You can enter a Keyword or Description object from the Head panel of the Objects palette so that all the Web pages in your site have the same basic information for cataloging.

Note   You cannot enter separate `<meta>` tag information into template-derived pages without inserting it directly into the code. Dreamweaver defines one editable area for the title—your hand-entered `<meta>` tags should go in this region. This procedure is described in detail later in this chapter.

✦ **Apply all needed behaviors and styles to the template.** When a document is saved as a template, all the code in the `<head>` section is locked. Because most behaviors and CSS (Cascading Style Sheet) styles insert code here, documents created from templates cannot easily apply new behaviors or create new styles.

You can create a template from a Web document with one command: File ⇨ Save As Template. Dreamweaver stores all templates in a Templates folder created for each defined site, with a special file extension, .dwt. After you've created your page and saved it as a template, notice that Dreamweaver inserts `<<Template>>` in the title bar to remind you of the page's status. Now you're ready to begin defining the template's editable regions.

Note   You can also create a template from an entirely blank page if you like. To do so, open the Assets panel and select the Templates category. From the Templates category, select the New Template button. You can find more information on how to use the Assets panel's Templates category later in this chapter.

Using Editable Regions

As noted earlier, when you convert an existing page into a template via the Save As Template command, the entire document is initially locked. If you attempt to create a document from a template at this stage, Dreamweaver alerts you that the template doesn't have any editable regions, and you cannot change anything on the page. Editable regions are essential to any template.

Marking existing content as editable

Two techniques exist for marking editable regions. First, you can designate any existing content as an editable region. Second, you can insert a new editable region anywhere you can place your cursor. In both cases, you must give the region a unique name. Dreamweaver uses the unique name to identify the editable region when entering new content, applying the template, and exporting or importing XML.

Note   As noted, each editable region must have a unique name, but the names need only be different from any other editable region on the same page. The name could be used for objects or JavaScript functions, or for editable regions on a different template.

To mark an existing area as an editable region, follow these steps:

1. Select the text or object that you wish to convert to an editable region.

Tip

The general rule of thumb with editable regions is that you need to select a complete tag pair, such as `<table>...</table>`. This has several implications. For instance, while you can mark an entire table or a single cell as editable, you can't select multiple cells, a row, or a column to be so marked. You have to select each cell individually (`<td>...</td>`). Also, you can select the content of a layer to be editable and keep the layer itself locked (so that its position and other properties cannot be altered), but if you select the layer to be editable, you can't lock the content.

2. Choose Modify ⇨ Templates ⇨ New Editable Region. You can also use the keyboard shortcut Ctrl+Alt+W (Command+Option+W), or right-click (Control+click) the selection and choose Editable Regions ⇨ New Editable Region from the shortcut menu. Dreamweaver displays the New Editable Region dialog box.

Tip

If you want the flexibility of adding returns to your editable region, make sure it includes at least one return. The easiest method is to select the <p> tag in the Tag Selector. If just text is selected, Dreamweaver does not allow any returns, although line breaks are accepted.

3. Enter a unique name for the selected area. Click OK when you're done or Cancel to abort the operation.

Caution

While you can use spaces in editable region names, some characters are not permitted. The illegal characters are the ampersand (&), double quote ("), single quote ('), and left and right angle brackets (< and >).

Dreamweaver outlines the selection with the color picked in Preferences on the Highlighting panel. The name for your newly designated region is displayed on a tab marking the area; the region is also listed in the Modify ⇨ Templates submenu. If still selected, the region name has a checkmark next to it in the Templates submenu. You can jump to any other editable region by selecting its name from this dynamic list.

Tip

Make sure you apply any formatting to your text — either by using HTML codes such as `<font>`, or by using CSS styles — before you select it to be an editable region. Generally, you want to keep the defined look of the content while altering just the text, so make just the text an editable region and exclude the formatting tags. It's helpful to have the HTML Inspector open for this detailed work.

Inserting a new editable region

Sometimes it's helpful to create a new editable region where no content currently exists. In these situations, the editable region name doubles as a label identifying the type of content expected, such as {CatalogPrice}. Dreamweaver always puts new region names in curly braces as just shown and highlights the entry in the template.

To insert a new editable region, follow these steps:

1. Place your cursor anywhere on the template page.

2. Choose Modify ➪ Templates ➪ New Editable Region. You can also use the keyboard shortcut Ctrl+Alt+V (Command+Option+V), or right-click (Control+click) the selection and choose New Editable Region from the shortcut menu.

   Dreamweaver displays the New Editable Region dialog box.

3. Enter a unique name for the new region. Click OK when you're done or Cancel to abort the operation.

Dreamweaver inserts the new region name in the document, surrounded by curly braces, marks it with a named tab and adds the name to the dynamic region list (which you can display by choosing Modify ➪ Templates).

Tip   One editable region, the Web page's title, is automatically created when you save a document as a template. The title is stored in a special editable region called doctitle. To change the title (which initially takes the same title as the template), enter the new text in the Title field of the Toolbar. You can also use the keyboard shortcut Ctrl+J (Command+J) to open the Page Properties dialog box. Finally, you can select View ➪ Head Elements and choose the Title icon to enter the new text in the Property Inspector.

Locking an editable region

Inevitably, you'll mark a region as editable that you'd prefer to keep locked, or you may discover that every page constructed to date has required inputting the same content, so it should be entered on the template and locked. In either event, converting an editable region to a locked one is a simple operation.

To lock an editable region, follow these steps:

1. Place your cursor in the editable region you want to lock.

2. Choose Modify ➪ Templates ➪ Remove Editable Region. The Unmark Editable Region dialog box, shown in Figure 32-2, appears with the selected region highlighted.

Note   You don't have to preselect the editable region to unmark it. If you don't, the Unmark Editable Region dialog box opens but doesn't highlight any selection; you have to choose it by name.

Creating Links in Templates

A common problem that designers encounter with Dreamweaver templates centers on links. People often add a link to their template and discover that it doesn't work when the new page is derived from the template. The main cause of this error stems from linking to a nonexistent page or element by hand—that is, typing in the link rather than using the Select File dialog box to choose it. Designers tend to set the link according to their final site structure without taking into account how templates are stored in Dreamweaver.

For example, when creating a template, let's say that you have links to three pages, products.htm, services.htm, and about.htm, all in the root of your site. Both products.htm and services.htm have been created, so you select the folder icon in the Property Inspector and select those files in turn. Dreamweaver inserts those links like this: `../products.htm` and `../services.htm`. The `../` indicates the directory above the current directory—which makes sense only when you remember that all templates are stored in a subfolder of the site root called Templates. These links are correctly resolved when a document is derived from this template to reflect the stored location of the new file.

Let's assume that the third file, about.htm, has not yet been created, and so that link is entered by hand. The common mistake is to enter it as it should be when it's used: about.htm. However, because the page is saved in the Template folder, Dreamweaver converts that link to /Templates/about.htm for any page derived from the template—and the link will fail. This type of error also applies to dependent files, such as graphics or other media.

The best solution is to always use the folder icon to link to an existing file when building your templates. If the file does not exist, and if you don't want to create a placeholder page for it, link to another existing file in the same folder and modify the link manually.

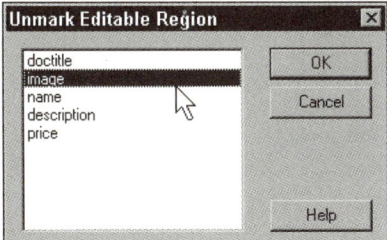

Figure 32-2: Convert an editable region to a locked one with the Unmark Editable Region command.

3. Click OK in the Unmark Editable Region dialog box to confirm your choice.

The editable region highlight is removed, and the area is now a locked region of the template.

Caution If you are removing a newly inserted editable region that is labeled with the region name in curly braces, then the label is not removed and must be deleted by hand on the template. Otherwise, it appears as part of the document created from a template and won't be accessible.

Adding Content to Template Documents

Constructing a template is only half the job — using it to create new pages is the other half. Because your basic layout is complete and you're only dropping in new images and entering new text, pages based on templates take a fraction of the time needed to create regular Web pages. Dreamweaver makes it easy to enter new content as well — you can even move from one editable region to the next, much like filling out a form (which, of course, is exactly what you're doing).

To create a new document based on a template, follow these steps:

1. In the Template category of the Assets panel, select the desired template and choose the New from Template from the panel's context menu. Alternatively, choose File ⇨ New from Template.

   If you chose the command from the File menu, the Select Template dialog box, shown in Figure 32-3, appears.

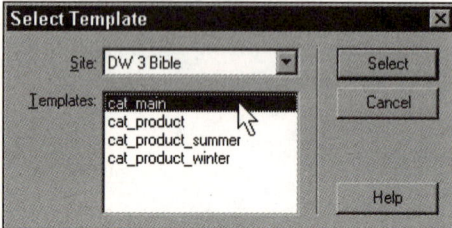

Figure 32-3: Create a new document based on any template listed in the Select Template dialog box.

2. If you wish to create a template from a local site other than the current one, select it from the Site drop-down list.

3. Select the desired template from those in the Templates list box.

4. Click OK when you're done.

When your new page opens, the editable regions are again highlighted; furthermore, the cursor is only active when it is over an unlocked region. If you have the Code view open, you also will see that the locked region is highlighted in a different color as shown in Figure 32-4. The highlighting makes it easy to differentiate the two types of regions.

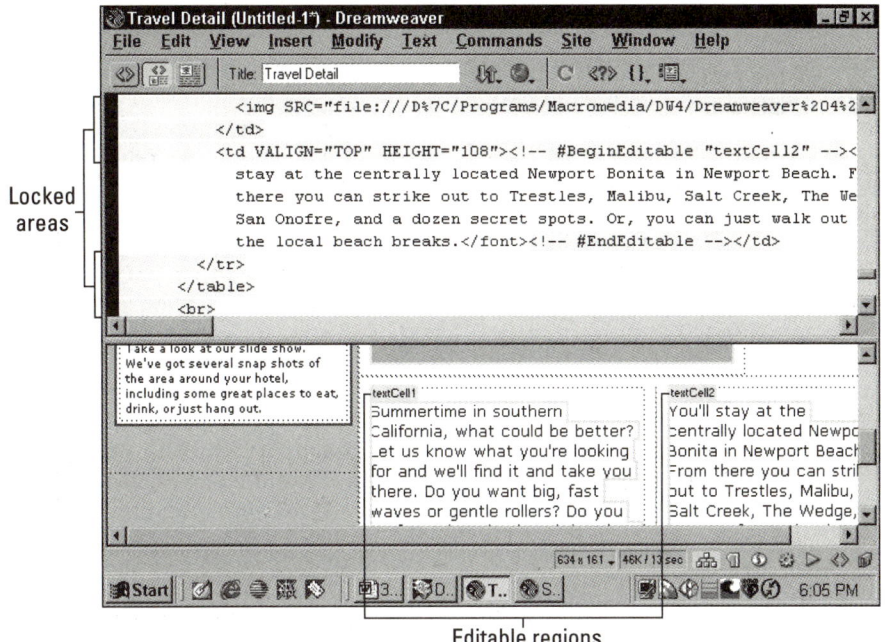

Figure 32-4: In a document based on a template, the editable regions are clearly marked, as are the locked portions in the Code view.

Generally, it is easiest to select the editable region name or placeholder first and then enter the new content. Selecting the editable regions can be handled in several ways:

✦ Highlight each editable region name or placeholder with the mouse.

✦ Position your cursor inside any editable region and then select the `<mm:editable>` tag in the Tag Selector.

✦ Choose Modify ➪ Templates and then select the name of your editable region from the dynamic list.

Note If all your editable regions are separate cells in a table, you can tab forward and Shift+Tab backward through the cells. With each press of the Tab key, all the content in the cell is selected, whether it is an editable region name or a placeholder.

Naturally, you should save your document to retain all the new content that's been added.

Adding behaviors to template-derived documents

The current implementation of Dreamweaver templates does not enable behaviors to be added to any document created from — and still linked to — a template. If you try, Dreamweaver plays a single note, as it does anytime that you try to select a locked region. With behaviors, the `<head>` section — where the code needs to go — is locked in a template.

You have three ways to handle the problem, however. First, if you're just using the template to get the basic layout of the page and don't need to maintain its link for updating, you can detach the Web page from the template by choosing Modify ⇨ Templates ⇨ Detach from Template. Second, if all your pages require the same behavior, as in a Navigation Bar, for example, you can simply add the behavior to the template itself.

The final method is the most involved, but also the most flexible. By adding some code to the original template, new behaviors can be attached, either to the template or to any template-based document. Here are the steps required for the modification:

1. Open the template for editing.

2. Display the HTML Inspector and scroll to the closing `</head>` tag.

   If you select the `<body>` tag from the Tag Selector, the closing `</head>` tag is just above the selected region.

3. Enter this code above the `</head>` tag:

   ```
   <mm:editable>
   <script>
   </script>
   </mm:editable>

   <mm:editable>
   <!-- Dummy comment, to be deleted by Dreamweaver -->
   </mm:editable>
   ```

4. Choose File ⇨ Save and update any documents linked to the template.

When a document is derived from this modified template, Dreamweaver removes the dummy comment but maintains the `<script>...</script>` pair, enabling behaviors to be added.

Inserting meta tags in documents based on templates

With the exception of the `<title>` tag, Dreamweaver locks the entire head section when a template is made. Therefore, a special procedure must be used to add page-specific `<meta>` tags to a document derived from a template. While it is considered a best practice to include as many `<meta>` tags as possible in the general template, often special keyword or description `<meta>` tags must be included on a page-by-page basis. If you try to add any item from the Head category of the Objects panel, Dreamweaver notifies you with a beep that the insertion is not allowed.

To work around the locked `<head>` region, the `<meta>` tag is added within the editable region surrounding the title. Here's the most direct method for accomplishing this task:

1. Choose Show Code and Design Views or Show Code View from the Toolbar.

   You also have the option of selecting the Code Inspector button from the Launcher or pressing the keyboard shortcut F10.

2. In the Code view, scroll up to the top of the document until the `<!-- #BeginEditable -->` ... `<!-- #EndEditable -->` tags surrounding the `<title>` tag are visible.

3. Place the cursor behind the closing `</title>` tag.

4. From the Head category of the Objects panel, choose the desired `<meta>` tag: Insert Meta, Insert Keywords, Insert Description, or Insert Refresh.

   The appropriate dialog box opens.

5. Enter the desired attributes for the `<meta>` tag in the dialog box and select OK when you're done.

   Dreamweaver inserts the completed `<meta>` tag behind the `<title>` tag, but within the editable region.

By using this technique, any updates to the general template will still be reflected in the derived document and you'll have the added advantage of unique `<meta>` tags where necessary.

Working with Templates in the Assets Panel

As a site grows, so does the number of templates it employs. Overall management of your templates is conducted through the Templates category of the Assets panel. You can open the Templates palette by choosing Windows ➪ Templates or by pressing the keyboard shortcut Ctrl+F11 (Command+F11). The Templates category, shown in Figure 32-5, displays a list of the current site's available templates in the lower pane and a preview of the selected template in the upper pane.

The Templates palette has five buttons along the bottom of its window:

✦ **Apply** — Creates a document derived from the currently selected template if the current document is blank, or, if the current document is based on a template, changes the locked regions of the document to match the selected template.

✦ **Refresh Site List** — Displays the list of all the templates currently in the site.

Figure 32-5: Use the Templates category of the Assets panel to preview, delete, open, create, or apply your current site's templates.

✦ **New Template** — Creates a new blank template.

✦ **Edit** — Loads the selected template for modification.

✦ **Delete** — Removes the selected template.

The Assets panel's context menu offers all of these options and more as explained in Table 32-1:

Table 32-1 Template Category Context Menu	
Command	**Description**
Refresh Site List	Displays the list of all the templates currently in the site.
New Template	Starts a new blank template.
New from Template	Creates a new document based on the currently selected template.
Edit	Opens the current template for modifying.
Apply	Creates a document derived from the currently selected template if the current document is blank or, if the current document is based on a template, changes the locked regions of the document to match the selected template. The same effects can also be achieved by dragging the template from the Assets panel to the current document.
Rename	Renames the selected template

Command	Description
Delete	Removes the selected template.
Update Current Page	Applies any changes made in the template to the current page, if the current page is derived from a template.
Update Site	Applies any changes made in any templates to all template-based documents in the site.
Copy to Site	Copies the highlighted template, but none of the dependent files, to the selected site.
Locate in Site	Opens the Site window and highlights the selected template.

Creating a blank template

Not all templates are created from existing documents. Some Web designers prefer to create their templates from scratch. To create a blank template, follow these steps:

1. Open the Templates category of the Assets panel by selecting its symbol or by choosing Window ⇨ Templates.

2. From the Templates category, select New Template. A new, untitled template is created.

3. Enter a title for your new template and press Enter (Return).

4. While the new template is selected, press the Edit button. The blank template opens in a new Dreamweaver window.

5. Insert your page elements.

6. Mark any elements or areas as editable regions using one of the methods previously described.

7. Save your template.

Deleting and opening templates

As with any set of files, there comes a time to clean house and remove files that are no longer in use. To remove a template, first open the Templates category of the Assets panel. Next, select the file you want to remove and choose the Delete button.

Caution Be forewarned: Dreamweaver does not alert you if files exist that were created from the template that you're about to delete. Deleting the template, in effect, "orphans" those documents, and they can no longer be updated via a template.

You can edit a template—to change the locked or editable regions—in several ways. To use the first method, choose File ⇨ Open and, in the Select File dialog box, change the Files of Type to Template Files (*.dwt) on Window systems and choose Template Files from the Show drop-down list on Macintosh systems. Then, locate the Templates folder in your defined site to select the template to open.

The second method of opening a template for modification uses the Templates category of the Assets panel. Select a template to modify and choose the Edit button. You can also double-click your template to open it for editing.

Finally, if you're working in the Site window, open a template by selecting the Templates folder for your site and open any of the files found there.

Tip

After you've made your modifications to the template, you don't have to use the Save As Template command to store the file—you can use the regular File ⇨ Save command or the keyboard shortcut Ctrl+S (Command+S). Likewise, if you want to save your template under another name, use the Save As command.

Applying templates

Dreamweaver makes it easy to try a variety of different looks for your document while maintaining the same content. Once you've created a document from a template, you can apply any other template to it. The only requirement is that the two templates have editable regions with the same names. When might this feature come in handy? In one scenario, you might develop a number of possible Web site designs for a client and create templates for each different approach, which are then applied to the identical content. Or, in an ongoing site, you could completely change the look of a catalog seasonally but retain all the content. Figure 32-6 shows two radically different schemes for a Web site with the same content.

To apply a template to a document, follow these steps:

1. Open the Templates category of the Assets panel.

2. Make sure the Web page you want to apply the style to is the active document.

3. From the Templates category, select the template you want to use and click the Apply button.

Tip

You can also drag onto the current page the template you'd like to apply or choose Modify ⇨ Templates ⇨ Apply Template to Page from the menus.

4. If content exists without a matching editable region, Dreamweaver displays the Choose Editable Region for Orphaned Content dialog box. To receive the content, select one of the listed editable regions from the template being applied and click OK.

The new template is applied to the document, and all the new locked areas replace all the old locked areas.

Figure 32-6: You can apply a template to a document created from another template to achieve different designs with identical content.

Updating Templates

Anytime you save a change to an existing template—whether or not any documents have been created from it—Dreamweaver asks if you'd like to update all the documents in the local site attached to the template. As with Library elements, you can also update the current page or the entire site at any time. Updating documents based on a template can save you an enormous amount of time—especially when numerous changes are involved.

To update a single page, open the page and choose Modify ⇨ Templates ⇨ Update Current Page or select the same command from the context menu of the Assets panel. Either way, the update is instantly applied.

To update a series of pages or an entire site, follow these steps:

1. Choose Modify ⇨ Templates ⇨ Update Pages.

   The Update Pages dialog box, shown in Figure 32-7, appears.

Figure 32-7: Any changes made to a template can be automatically applied to the template's associated files by using the Update Pages command.

2. To update all the documents using all the templates for an entire site, choose Entire Site from the Look In option and then select the name of the site from the accompanying drop-down list.

3. To update pages using a particular template, choose Pages Using from the Look In option and then select the name of the template.

4. To view a report of the progress of the update, make sure that the Show Log option is enabled.

5. Click Start to begin the update process.

The log window displays a list of the files examined and updated, the total number of files that could not be updated, and the elapsed time.

Changing the Default Document

Each time you open a new document in Dreamweaver—or even just start Dreamweaver—a blank page is created. This blank page is based on an HTML file called Default.html that is stored in the Configuration\Templates folder. The default page works in a similar fashion to the templates in that you can create new documents from it, but no editable or locked regions exist—everything in the page can always be altered.

The basic blank-page document is an HTML structure with only a few properties specified: a document type, character set, and white background for the body:

```
<html>
<head>
<title>Untitled Document</title>
<meta http-equiv="Content-Type" content="text/html; charset=iso-8859-1">
</head>

<body bgcolor="#FFFFFF">

</body>
</html>
```

Naturally, you can change any of these elements — and add many, many more — after you've opened a page. But what if you want to have a <meta> tag with creator information in every page that comes out of your Web design company? You can do it in Dreamweaver manually, but it's a bother, and chances are that you'll forget. Luckily, Dreamweaver provides a more efficient solution.

In keeping with its overall design philosophy of extensibility, Dreamweaver enables you to modify the Default.htm file as you would any other file. Just choose File ➪ Open and select the Configuration\Templates\Default.htm file. As you make your changes, save the file as you would normally. Now, to test your modifications, choose File ➪ New — your modifications should appear in your new document.

Summary

Much of a Web designer's responsibility is related to document production, and Dreamweaver offers a comprehensive template solution to reduce the workload. When planning your strategy for building an entire Web site, remember that templates provide these advantages:

✦ Templates can be created from any Web page.

✦ Dreamweaver templates combine locked and editable regions. Editable regions must be defined individually.

✦ After a template is declared, new documents can be created from it.

✦ If a template is altered, pages built from that template can be automatically updated.

✦ The default template that Dreamweaver uses can be modified so that every time you select File ➪ New, a new version of your customized template is created.

In the next chapter, you learn how to streamline production and site maintenance with repeating page elements from the Dreamweaver Library.

✦   ✦   ✦

Using the Repeating Elements Library

One of the challenges of designing a Web site is ensuring that buttons, copyright notices, and other cross-site features always remain consistent. Fortunately, Dreamweaver offers a useful feature called *Library items* that helps you insert repeating elements, such as a navigation bar or a company logo, into every Web page you create. With one command, you can update and maintain Library items efficiently and productively.

In this chapter, you examine the nature and the importance of repeating elements and learn how to effectively use the Dreamweaver Library feature for all your sites.

Dreamweaver Libraries

Library items within Dreamweaver are another means for you, as a designer, to maintain consistency throughout your site. Suppose you have a navigation bar on every page that contains links to all the other pages on your site. It's highly likely that you'll eventually (and probably more than once) need to make changes to the navigation bar. In a traditional Web development environment, you must modify every single page. This creates lots of opportunities for making mistakes, missing pages, and adding code to the wrong place. Moreover, the whole process is tedious — ask anyone who has had to modify the copyright notice at the bottom of every Web page for a site with over 200 pages.

One traditional method of updating repeating elements is to use *server-side includes*. A server-side include causes the server to place a component, such as a copyright notice, in a specified area of a Web page when it's sent to the user. This arrangement, however, increases the strain on your already overworked Web server and many hosting companies do not permit server-side includes for this reason. To add to the designer's frustrations, you can't lay out a Web page in a WYSIWYG format and simultaneously see the server-side scripts (unless you're using a Dreamweaver translator). So you either take the time to calculate that a server-side script will take up a specific space on the Web page, or you cross your fingers and guess.

A better way in Dreamweaver is to use an important innovation called the *Library*. The Library is designed to make repetitive updating quick, easy, and as error-free as possible. The Library's key features include the following:

✦ Any item—whether text or graphic—that goes into the body of your Web page can be designated as a Library item.

✦ Once created, Library items can be placed instantly in any Web page in your site, without your having to retype, reinsert, or reformat text and graphics.

✦ Library items can be altered at any time. After the editing is complete, Dreamweaver gives you the option to update the Web site immediately or postpone the update until later.

✦ If you are making a number of alterations to your Library items, you can wait until you're finished with all the updates and then make the changes across the board in one operation.

✦ You can update one page at a time, or you can update the entire site all at once.

✦ A Library item can be converted back to a regular non-Library element of a Web page at any time.

✦ Library items can be copied from one site to another.

✦ Library items can combine Dreamweaver behaviors—and their underlying JavaScript code—with onscreen elements, so you don't have to rebuild the same navigation bar every time, reapplying the behaviors over and over again.

Using the Library Assets Panel

Dreamweaver's Library control center is located on the Assets panel in the Library category. There you find the tools for creating, modifying, updating, and managing your Library items. Shown in Figure 33-1, the Library category is as flexible and easy to use as all of Dreamweaver's primary panels, with straightforward command buttons, a listing of all available Library items, and a handy Preview pane.

Insert Library item   Library item preview   New Library button

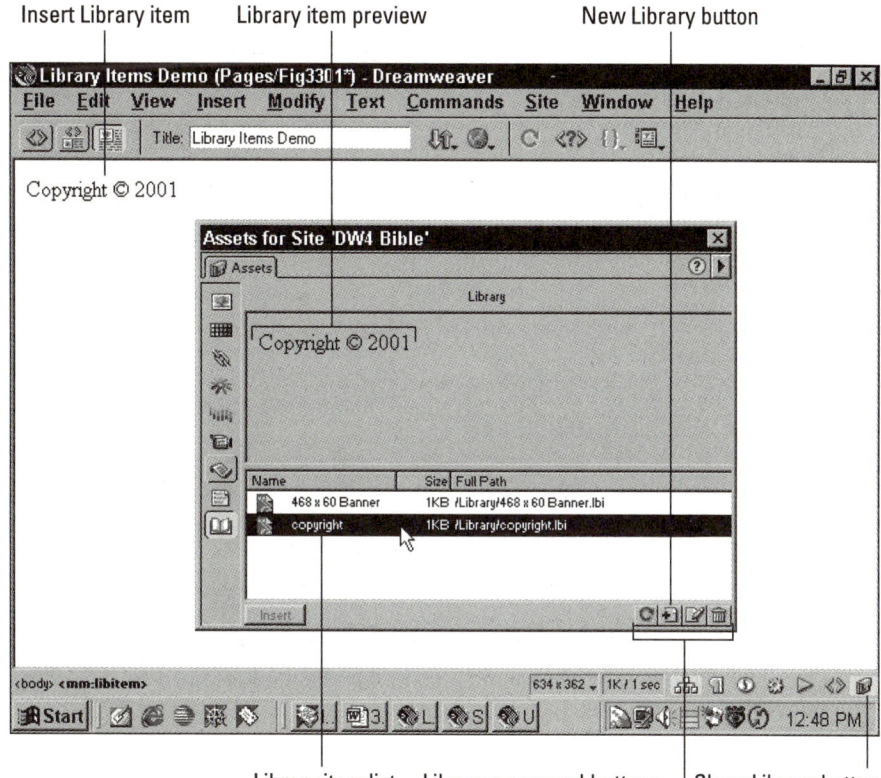

Library item list   Library command buttons ⌐ Show Library button

Figure 33-1: With the Dreamweaver Library feature, you can easily add and modify consistent objects on an entire Web site.

As usual, you can open the Library panel in several ways:

✦ Choose Window ⇨ Library.

✦ Select the Library symbol on the Assets panel.

✦ Select the Library button from the Launcher.

Cross-Reference

To use Library items, you must first create a site root folder for Dreamweaver, as explained in Chapter 6. A separate Library folder is automatically created to hold the individual Library items and is used by Dreamweaver during the updating process.

Ideally, you could save the most time by creating all your Library items before you begin constructing your Web pages, but most Web designers don't work that way. Feel free to include, modify, and update your Library items as much as you need to as your Web site evolves — that's part of the power and flexibility you gain through Dreamweaver's Library.

Adding a Library item

Before you can insert or update a Library item, that item must be designated as such within the Web page. To add an item to your site's Library, follow these steps:

1. Select any part of the Web page that you want to make into a Library item.

2. Open the Library category of the Assets panel with any of the available methods: the Window ⇨ Library command, the Library symbol in the Assets panel or the Library button in the Launcher.

3. From the Library category (see Figure 33-1), select the New Library Item button.

   The selected page element is displayed in the upper pane of the Library category. In the lower pane — the Library item list — a new entry is highlighted with the default name "Untitled."

Note   If the text you've selected has been styled by a CSS rule, Dreamweaver warns you that the appearance may be different because the style rule is not included in the Library item. To ensure that the appearance is the same, include the Library item only on those pages with the appropriate CSS styles.

4. Enter a unique name for your new Library item and press Enter (Return).

   The Library item list is resorted alphabetically, if necessary, and the new item is included.

When a portion of your Web page has been designated as a Library item, a yellow highlight is displayed over the entire item within the Document window. The highlight helps you to quickly recognize what is a Library item and what is not. If you find the yellow highlight distracting, you can disable it. Go to Edit ⇨ Preferences and, from the Highlighting category of the Preferences dialog box, deselect Show check box for Library Items. Alternatively, deselecting View ⇨ Visual Aids ⇨ Invisible Elements hides Library Item highlighting, along with any other invisible items on your page.

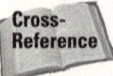

Cross-Reference   Dreamweaver can include Library items only in the <body> section of an HTML document. You cannot, for instance, create a series of <meta> tags for your pages that must go in the <head> section.

Moving Library items to a new site

Although Library items are specific to each site, they can be used in more than one site. When you make your first Library item, Dreamweaver creates a folder called Library in the local root folder for the current site. To use a particular Library item in another site, simply open the Library folder from your system's desktop and copy the item to the new site's Library folder.

Drag-and-Drop Creation of Library Items

A second option for creating Library items is the drag-and-drop method. Simply select an object or several objects on a page and drag them to the Library category (either the top or bottom pane); release the mouse button to drop them in.

You can drag any object into the Library category: text, tables, images, Java applets, plug-ins, and/or ActiveX controls. Essentially anything in the Document window that can be HTML code can be dragged to the Library. And, as you might suspect, the reverse is true: Library items can be placed in your Web page by dragging them from the Library category and dropping them anywhere in the Document window.

Cross-Reference Be sure to also move any dependent files or other assets such as images and media files associated with the Library items.

Inserting a Library item in your Web page

When you create a Web site, you always need to incorporate certain features, including a standard set of link buttons along the top, a consistent banner on various pages, and a copyright notice along the bottom. Adding these items to a page from the Library can be as easy as dragging and dropping them.

You must first create a Web site and then designate Library items (as explained in the preceding section). Once these items exist, you can add the items to any page created within your site.

To add Library items to a document, use the following steps:

1. Position the cursor where you want the Library item to appear.

2. From the Library category, select the item you wish to use.

3. Select the Insert button. The highlighted Library item appears on the Web page.

Tip As noted earlier, you can also use the drag-and-drop method to place Library items in the Document window.

When you add a Library item to a page, you notice a number of immediate changes. As mentioned, the added Library item is highlighted. If you click anywhere on the item, the entire Library item is selected.

It's important to understand that Dreamweaver treats the entire Library item entry as an external object being linked to the current page. You cannot modify Library items directly on a page. For information on editing Library entries, see the section "Editing a Library Item," later in this chapter.

While the Library item is highlighted, notice also that the Property Inspector changes. Instead of displaying the properties for the HTML object that is selected, the item is identified as a Library item, as shown in Figure 33-2.

Figure 33-2: The Library Item Property Inspector identifies the source file for any selected Library entry.

You can also see evidence of Library items in the HTML for the current page. Open the Code Inspector, and you see that several lines of code have been added. The following code example indicates one Library item:

```
<!-- #BeginLibraryItem "/Library/title.lbi" -->
<font color="#FF6633" face="Verdana, Arial, Helvetica, sans-serif" ¬
size="-4">
<b>Copyright &copy; 2000</b></font>
<!-- #EndLibraryItem -->
```

In this case, the Library item happens to be a phrase: "Copyright (c) 2000." (The character entity © is used to represent the c-in-a-circle copyright mark in HTML.) In addition to the code that specifies the font face, color, and size, notice the text before and after the HTML code. These are commands within the comments that tell Dreamweaver it is looking at a Library item. One line marks the beginning of the Library item:

```
<!-- #BeginLibraryItem "/Library/title.lbi" -->
```

and another marks the end:

```
<!-- #EndLibraryItem -->
```

Two items are of interest here. First, notice how the Library demarcation surrounds not just the text ("Copyright (c) 2000") but all of its formatting attributes. Library items can do far more than just cut and paste raw text. The second thing to note is that the Library markers are placed discreetly within HTML comments. Web browsers ignore the Library markers and render the code in between them.

The value in the opening Library code, "/Library/title.lbi", is the source file for the Library entry. This file is located in the Library folder, inside of the current site root folder. Library source (.lbi) files can be opened with a text editor or in Dreamweaver; they consist of plain HTML code without the <html> and <body> tags.

The .lbi file for our title example would contain the following:

```
<font color="#FF6633" face="Verdana, Arial, Helvetica, sans-serif" ¬
size="-4">
<b>Copyright &copy; 2000</b></font>
```

The power of repeating elements is that they are simply HTML. There is no need to learn proprietary languages to customize Library items. Anything, except for information found in the header of a Web page, can be included in a Library file.

The importance of the `<!-- #BeginLibraryItem>` and `<!-- #EndLibraryItem>` tags becomes evident when you start to update Library items for a site. You examine how Dreamweaver can be used to automatically update your entire Web site in the section "Updating Your Web Sites with Libraries," later in this chapter.

Deleting an item from the Library

Removing an entry from your site's Library is a two-step process. First, you must delete the item from the Library category. Then, if you want to keep the item on your page, you must make it editable again. Without completing the second step, Dreamweaver maintains the Library highlight and, more importantly, prevents you from modifying the element.

To delete an item from the Library, follow these steps:

1. Open the Web page containing the Library item you want to delete.

2. Open the Library category by choosing Window ⇨ Library or by selecting the Library button from the Launcher.

3. Select the Library item in the list and click the Delete button.

4. Dreamweaver asks if you are sure you want to delete the item. Select Yes, and the entry is removed from the Library item list. (Or select No to cancel.)

5. In the Document window, select the element you are removing from the Library.

6. In the Property Inspector, click Detach from Original.

7. As shown in Figure 33-3, Dreamweaver warns you that if you proceed, the item cannot be automatically updated (as a Library element). Select OK to proceed. The Library highlighting vanishes, and the element can now be modified individually.

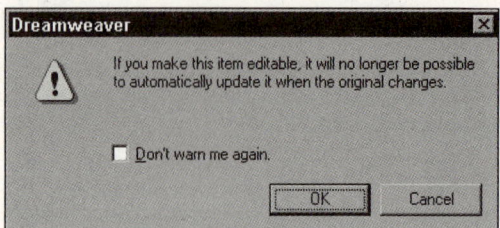

Figure 33-3: When making an item editable from the Library, Dreamweaver alerts you that, if you proceed, you won't be able to update the item automatically using the Library function.

Note   Should you unintentionally delete a Library item in the Library category, you can restore it if you still have the entry included in a Web page. Select the element within the page and, in the Property Inspector, choose the Recreate button. Dreamweaver restores the item to the Library item list, with the original Library name.

Renaming a Library item

It's easy to rename a Library item, both in the Assets panel and across your site. Dreamweaver automatically updates the name for any embedded Library item. To give an existing Library entry a new name, open the Library category and click the name of the item twice, slowly — do not double-click. Alternatively, you could choose Rename from the context menu of the Assets panel. The name is highlighted, and a small box appears around it. Enter the new name and press Enter (Return).

Dreamweaver then displays the Update Files dialog box with a list of files in which the renamed Library item is contained. Select Update to rename the Library item across the site. If you select Don't Update, the Library item will be renamed only in the Library category. Furthermore, your embedded Library items will be orphaned — that is, no master Library item will be associated with them and they will not be updateable.

Editing a Library Item

Rarely do you create a Library item that is perfect from the beginning and never needs to be changed. Whether it is due to site redesign or the addition of new sections to a site, you'll find yourself going back to Library items and modifying them, sometimes over and over again. You can use the full power of Dreamweaver's design capabilities to alter your Library items, within the restraints of Library items in general. In other words, you can modify an image, reformat a body of text, add new material to a boilerplate paragraph, and have the resulting changes reflected across your Web site. However, you cannot add anything to a Library item that is not contained in the HTML `<body>` tags.

To modify Library items, Dreamweaver uses a special editing window identifiable by the double angle brackets surrounding the phrase "Library Item" in the title bar. You access this editing window through the Library category or the Property Inspector. Follow these steps to modify an existing Library item:

1. In the Library category, select the item you wish to modify from the list of available entries.

2. Click the Open Library Item button. The Library editing window opens with the selected entry, as shown in Figure 33-4.

3. Make any necessary modifications to the Library entry.

4. When you are finished with your changes, choose File ⇨ Save or press Ctrl+S (Command+S).

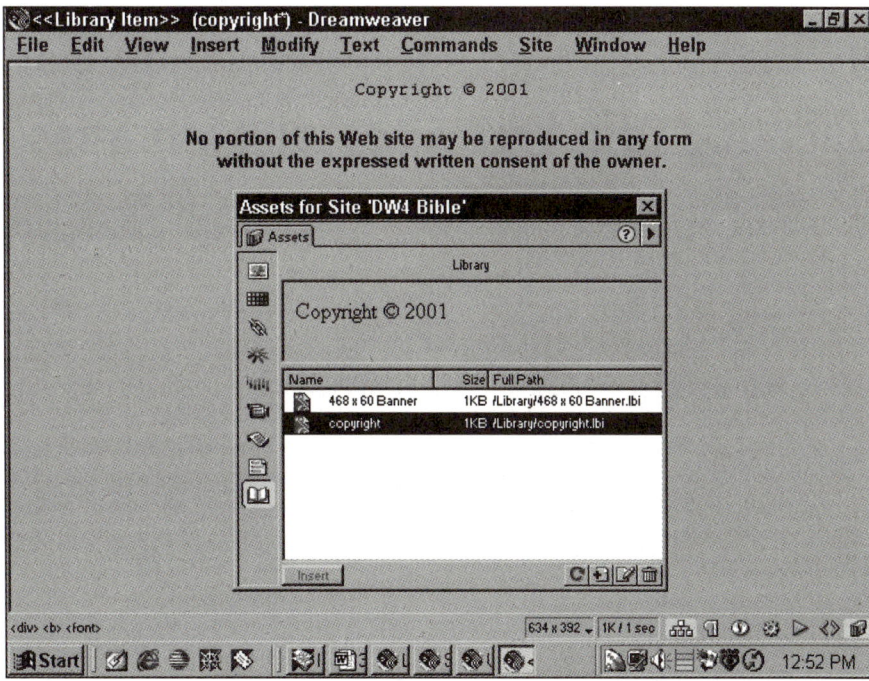

Figure 33-4: Use the Library editing window to modify existing Library items.

5. Dreamweaver notes that your Library item has been modified and asks if you would like to update all of the Web pages in your site that contain the item. Select Yes to update all of the Library items, including the one just modified, or select No to postpone the update. (See the next section, "Updating Your Web Sites with Libraries.")

6. Close the editing window by selecting the Close button or choosing File ➪ Close.

Once you've completed the editing operation and closed the editing window, you can open any Web page containing the modified Library item to view the changes.

Cross-Reference

You cannot use some features to their fullest when editing Library items. These include timelines, behaviors, and styles. Each of these modifications requires a JavaScript function to be placed in the `<head>` tags of a page — a task that the Dreamweaver Library function cannot handle. If you add a behavior to a Library item while editing it, the JavaScript function will be copied to your page next to the Library item itself. While this will work in some instances — a pop-up message for example — other behaviors will perform erratically. One workaround is to use a Dreamweaver template to add entire pages with JavaScript functions included, as described in Chapter 32. You could, of course, also add behaviors to a page element before converting it to a Library item.

Updating Your Web Sites with Libraries

The effectiveness of the Dreamweaver Library feature becomes more significant when it comes time to update an entire multipage site. Dreamweaver offers two opportunities for you to update your site:

✦ Immediately after modifying a Library item, as explained in the preceding steps for editing a Library item

✦ At a time of your choosing, through the Modify ➪ Library command

An immediate update to every page on your site can be accomplished when you edit a Library item. After you save the alterations, Dreamweaver asks if you'd like to apply the update to Web pages in your site. If you click Yes, Dreamweaver not only applies the current modification to all pages in the site, but it also applies any other alterations that you have made previously in this Library.

The second way to modify a Library item is by using the Modify ➪ Library command, and when you use this method, you can choose to update the current page or the entire site.

To update just the current page, choose Modify ➪ Library ➪ Update Current Page. Dreamweaver makes a quick check to see what Library items you are managing on the current page and then compares them to the site's Library items. If any differences exist, Dreamweaver modifies the page accordingly.

To update an entire Web site, follow these steps:

1. Choose Modify ➪ Library ➪ Update Pages. The Update Pages dialog box opens (see Figure 33-5).

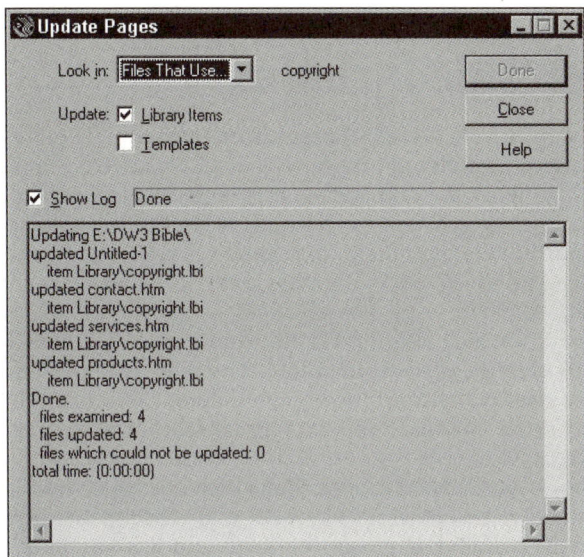

Figure 33-5: The Update Pages dialog box enables you to apply any changes to your Library items across an entire site and informs you of the progress.

2. If you want Dreamweaver to update all of the Library items in all of the Web pages in your site, select Entire Site from the Look In drop-down list and choose the name of your site in the drop-down list on the right. You can also have Dreamweaver update only the pages in your site that contain a specific Library item. Select the Files That Use option from the Look In drop-down list and then select the Library item that you would like to have updated across your site from the drop-down list on the right.

3. If you want to see the results from the update process, leave the Show Log checkbox selected. (Turning off the Log reduces the size of the Site Update dialog box.)

4. Choose the Start button. Dreamweaver processes the entire site for Library updates. Any Library items contained are modified to reflect the changes.

Note   Although Dreamweaver does modify Library items on currently open pages during an Update Site operation, you have to save the pages to accept the changes.

The Update Pages log displays any errors encountered in the update operation. A log containing the notation

```
item Library\Untitled2.lbi -- not updated, library item not found
```

indicates that one Web page contains a reference to a Library item that has been removed. Though this is not a critical error, you might want to use Dreamweaver's Find and Replace feature to search your Web site for the code and remove it.

Applying Server-Side Includes

In some ways, the server-side include (SSI) is the predecessor of the Dreamweaver Library item. The difference is that with Library items, Dreamweaver updates the Web pages at design time, whereas with server-side includes, the server handles the updating at runtime (when the files are actually served to the user). Server-side includes can also include server variables, such as the current date and time (both locally and Greenwich mean time) or the date the current file was last saved.

Because server-side includes are integrated in the standard HTML code, a special file extension is used to identify pages using them. Any page with server-side includes is most often saved with either the .shtml or .shtm extension. When a server encounters such a file, the file is read and processed by the server.

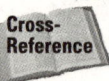

Not all servers support server-side includes. Some Web hosting companies disable the function because of potential security risks and performance issues. Each .shtml page requires additional processing time, and if a site uses many SSI pages, the server can slow down significantly. Be sure to check your Web host's policy before including SSIs in your Web pages.

Server-side includes are often used to insert header or footer items into the <body> of an HTML page. Typically, the server-side include itself is just a file with HTML. To insert a file, the SSI code looks like the following:

```
<!-- #include file="footer.html" -->
```

Note how the HTML comment structure is used to wrap around the SSI directive. This ensures that browsers ignore the code, but servers do not. The file attribute defines the path name of the file to be included, relative to the current page. To include a file relative to the current site root, use the virtual attribute, as follows:

```
<!-- #include virtual="/main/images/spaceman.jpg" -->
```

As evident in this example, you can use SSIs to include more than just HTML files — you can also include graphics.

With Dreamweaver's translator mechanism, server-side includes can be visible in the Document window during the design process. All you need to do is make sure that the Translation preferences are set correctly, as described in the section "Modifying Translators," later in this chapter.

One of the major benefits of SSIs is inserting information from the server itself, such as the current file size or time. One tag, `<!-- #echo -->`, is used to define a custom variable that is returned when the SSI is called, as well as numerous *environmental variables*. An environmental variable is information available to the server, such as the date a file was last modified or its URL.

Table 33-1 details the possible server tags and their attributes.

Table 33-1
Server-Side Include Variables

Tag	Attribute	Description
`<!-- #config -->`	`errmsg`, `sizefmt`, or `timefmt`	Used to customize error messages, file size, or time and date displays
`<!-- #echo -->`	`var` or environmental variables, such as `last_modified`, `document_name`, `document_url`, `date_local`, or `date_gmt`	Returns the specified variable
`<!-- #exec -->`	`cmd` or `cgi`	Executes a system command or CGI program
`<!-- #flastmod -->`	`file` or `virtual`	Displays the last modified date of a file other than the current one
`<!-- #fsize -->`	`file` or `virtual`	Displays the size of a file other than the current one
`<!-- #include -->`	`file` or `virtual`	Inserts the contents of the specified file to the current one

Adding server-side includes

Dreamweaver has made inserting a server-side include in your Web page very straightforward. You can use a Dreamweaver object to easily select and bring in the files to be included. Any other type of SSI, such as declaring a variable, must be entered in by hand, but you can use the Comment object to do so without switching to Code View, or opening the Code Inspector.

To use server-side includes to incorporate a file, follow these steps:

1. In the Document window, place your cursor in the location where you would like to add the server-side include.

2. Select Insert ⇨ Server-Side Include or choose Insert Server-Side Include from the Common category of the Objects panel.

   The standard Select File dialog box appears.

3. In the Select File dialog box, type in the URL of the HTML page you would like to include in the File Name text box or use the folder icon to locate the file. Click OK when you're done.

   Dreamweaver displays the contents of the HTML file at the desired location in your page. Should the Property Inspector be available, the SSI Property Inspector is displayed (see Figure 33-6).

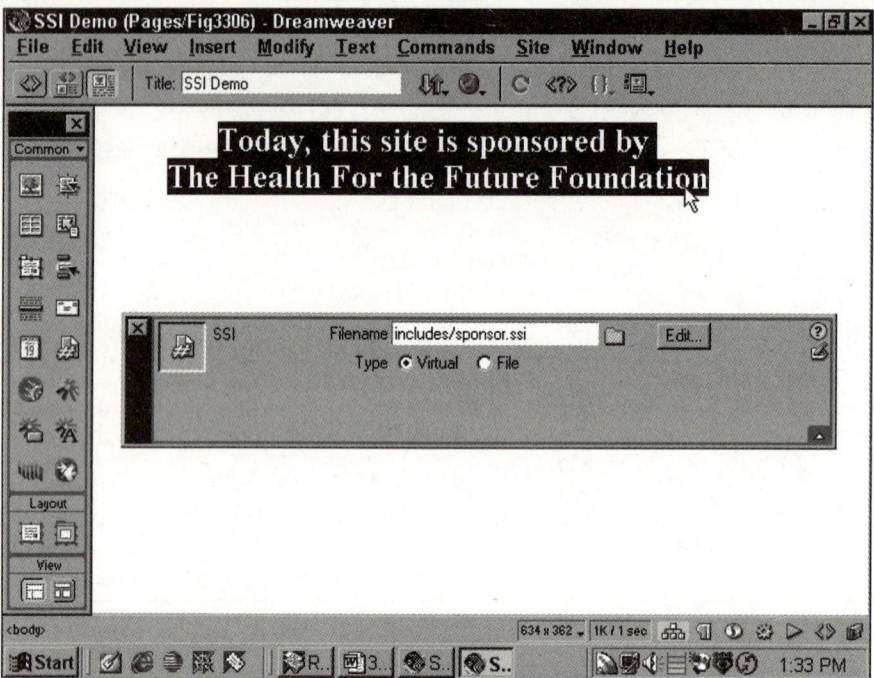

Figure 33-6: The selected text is actually a server-side include automatically translated by Dreamweaver, as is evident from the SSI Property Inspector.

4. In the Property Inspector, if the server-side include calls a file-relative document path, select the Type File option. Or, if the SSI calls a site root-relative file, choose the Type Virtual option.

Tip

Because server-side includes can be placed only within the body of a Dreamweaver file, the contents of the HTML page that you wish to include should not have any tags that are not readable within the body section of a document, such as <head>, <title>, or <meta>—or the <body> tag itself. You can, however, design your HTML page in Dreamweaver, and then use Code View, or the Code Inspector, to remove any such tags before inserting the page into your document with a server-side include.

Editing server-side includes

As is the case with Library items, it is not possible to directly edit files that have been inserted into a Web page using server-side includes. In fact, should you try, the entire text block highlights as one. The text for a server-side included file is not editable through Dreamweaver's Code View, or Code Inspector, although the SSI code is.

To edit the contents of the server-side included file, follow these steps:

1. Select the server-side include in the Document window.

2. Select the Edit button from the SSI Property Inspector.

   The file opens in a new Dreamweaver window for editing.

3. When you've finished altering the file, select File ➪ Save or use the keyboard shortcut Ctrl+S (Command+S).

4. Close the file editing window by choosing File ➪ Close.

Dreamweaver automatically reflects the changes in your currently open document.

Unlike when editing Library items, Dreamweaver does not ask if any other linked files should be updated because all blending of regular HTML and SSIs happens at runtime or when the file is open in Dreamweaver and the SSI translator is engaged.

Extending Dreamweaver with XSSI

Both Dreamweaver Library items and server-side includes are useful for easily updating a range of pages when changing one item. But what if you have to change that one item several times a day — or based on which domain the user is coming from? To handle these tasks automatically, a system must support some form of conditional tags, such as if-then statements. Such a system is now available through Apache servers and XSSI, extended server-side includes. Most importantly, a full set of XSSI objects, translators, and Property Inspectors for Dreamweaver have been built by the wonderful programmers at Webmonkey (www.webmonkey.com). You can find the XSSI extensions on the CD-ROM that comes with this book.

In addition to handling standard server-side includes, the XSSI extensions offer a series of conditional statements: if, elif (else-if), else, and endif. The beauty of the Webmonkey objects is that you can construct or edit these conditional statements through their graphical user interface. The basic syntax of the conditional statements is as follows:

Continued

Continued

```
<!--#if expr="text_expression" -->
If the above is true, perform this action
<!--#elif expr="text_expression" -->
Else if the above is true, do this
<!--#else -->
Otherwise, do this
<!--#endif -->
```

The XSSI extensions also have the capability of setting an environmental variable so that you can view your page under various conditions. For example, let's say you've written a script that includes a particular file that greets the visitor in a proper way, depending on which browser is being used. Your conditional script would look to the HTTP_USER_AGENT variable to see which message to serve. With the XSSI Set Env Variables command, you could test your script during the design phase without having to visit the server at different times of the day. The following figure displays the Set XSSI Environment Variables dialog box.

One note of caution: Due to a potential conflict between the two translators, installing the XSSI extensions disables the standard SSI translator. Make sure your system is XSSI compatible (it uses Apache server software) before incorporating the XSSI extensions.

Summary

In this chapter, you learned how you can easily and effectively create Library items that can be repeated throughout an entire site to help maintain consistency.

✦ Library items can consist of any text, object, or HTML code contained in the `<body>` of a Web page.

✦ The quickest method to create a Library item is to drag the code from the Dreamweaver Document window into the Library category's list area.

✦ Editing Library items is also easy: just click the Edit button in the Assets panel or choose Open from the Property Inspector, and you can swiftly make all of your changes in a separate Dreamweaver Library Item window.

✦ The Modify ⇨ Library ⇨ Update Pages command enables easy maintenance of your Web site.

✦ Server-side includes enable files to be inserted into the final HTML at runtime by the server. Dreamweaver's translation feature enables you to preview these effects.

In the next chapter, you learn how to ensure cross-browser compatibility with Dreamweaver.

✦　　✦　　✦

Maximizing Browser Targeting

♦ ♦ ♦ ♦

In This Chapter

Maintaining different versions of Web pages

Handling cross-browser compatibility

Planning for backward compatibility

Dreamweaver technique: Browser checking

Creating your own browser profile

♦ ♦ ♦ ♦

Each new release of a browser is a double-edged sword. On the one hand, an exciting new array of features is made possible. On the other, Web designers have to cope with yet another browser-compatibility issue. In today's market, you find all of the following in use:

♦ A rapidly increasing number of 5.0 — and above — browsers that, although fairly standards compliant, are still different from each other in implementation

♦ Browsers for different platforms which interpret code differently, even though the browsers are the same version number and from the same company

♦ A host of fourth-generation browsers, widely varying in their capabilities

♦ A decreasing number of 3.0 browsers, limited in some basic functionality

♦ A small group of 2.0 browsers in the machines of determined users who have never (and may never be) upgraded

♦ A diverse assortment of browsers outside the mainstream, including Opera, WebTV, OmniWeb for Mac OS X, and Navigator for Linux

♦ Various versions of America Online browsers, which range from being completely proprietary to being a blend of current and special technologies; as a specific example, AOL 4.0 is not the same as Internet Explorer 4.0, although it is based on it

Browser-compatibility is one of a Web designer's primary concerns (not to mention the source of major headaches); and many strategies are evolving to deal with this matter. Dreamweaver is in the forefront of cross-browser Web page design, both in terms of the type of code it routinely outputs and in its specialty functions. This chapter examines the browser-targeting techniques available in Dreamweaver. From multibrowser code to conversion innovations to browser validation capabilities, Dreamweaver helps you get your Web pages out to the widest audience, and with the most features.

Converting Pages in Dreamweaver

DHTML's gifts of layers and Cascading Style Sheets are extremely tempting to use because of their enhanced typographic control and absolute-positioning capabilities. Many Web designers, however, have resisted using these features because only fourth-generation browsers can view them. Though Dreamweaver can't change the capabilities of 3.0 browsers, it can make it easy for you to create alternative content for them.

Dreamweaver makes it possible to convert Web pages designed with layers and CSS into pages that can be rendered by 3.0 browsers. Moreover, if you're looking to upgrade your site from nested tables to layers, you don't have to do it by hand. Dreamweaver also includes a command to convert tables to layers, preserving their location but enabling greater design flexibility and dynamic control. A Webmaster's life just got a tad easier.

To see how to use Dreamweaver's Layers-to-Tables roundtrip features, see Chapter 28.

Making 3.0-compatible pages

It's a slight misstatement that Dreamweaver converts 4.0 feature-laden pages into pages that can be read by 3.0 browsers. Actually, Dreamweaver creates a new 3.0-compatible page based on the 4.0 page — and does it in almost no time at all. Once you've converted your page, you can use Dreamweaver's Check Browser behavior to route users to the appropriate pages, based on their browser version.

Preparing your page for conversion

When Dreamweaver makes a new 3.0-compatible page, layers are converted to nested tables, and Cascading Style Sheet references are converted to inline character styles. You have the option to convert either or both features. To accomplish this conversion of your 4.0 Web page, the document must meet the following conditions:

✦ **All content must be in layers:** Because Dreamweaver converts layers to tables, it must start with everything absolutely positioned.

✦ **Layers must not overlap:** During the conversion process, Dreamweaver warns you when it finds overlapping layers and even tells you which ones they are.

A feature in Dreamweaver prevents you from encountering the problem of overlapping layers in the design stage. Enable the option by choosing Modify ⇨ Arrange ⇨ Prevent Layer Overlaps or clicking the Prevent Overlaps checkbox on the Layers panel. While this can't separate layers that are currently overlapping — you have to do that by hand — it does stop you from accidentally laying one layer on top of another and makes 3.0 conversion a breeze.

✦ **Nesting layers are not allowed:** When one layer is inside another, the inner layer is placed relative to the outer layer. Dreamweaver cannot convert relatively positioned layers.

✦ **The** `<ilayer>` **tag cannot be used:** Because the `<ilayer>` tag is based on relative positioning, Dreamweaver cannot convert it. Use `<layer>`, `<div>`, or `<span>` instead.

Some Web pages you might like to convert — or devolve — from 4.0 to 3.0 applicability have content both in and out of layers. And, as noted, Dreamweaver needs to have all the Web page elements in a layer before proceeding with conversion. Previously, it was necessary to cut elements outside of a layer and paste them in to prepare the page for conversion. Dreamweaver does it for you — just choose Modify ⇨ Convert ⇨ Tables to Layers. In the dialog box that appears, be sure to choose the Select Layer Overlap option to avoid that problem. Click OK, and Dreamweaver places everything in a layer, automatically — without generating a new page. For more on using this capability, see Chapter 28.

Running the conversion

Once your page is prepped, generating a 3.0-compatible Web page from a 4.0+ version is straightforward. You have only a couple of options — whether to convert layers, CSS styles, or both — and once you make your choice and click OK, the rest of the process is almost instantaneous.

To create a 3.0-compatible version of a Web page with 4.0 or above features, follow these steps:

1. Choose File ⇨ Convert ⇨ 3.0 Browser.

   The Convert to 3.0 Browser Compatible dialog box opens, as shown in Figure 34-1.

Figure 34-1: Begin to build your cross browser–compatible site with Dreamweaver's Convert Layers to Table command.

2. From the Convert to 3.0 Browser Compatible dialog box, select your options:

   • If you are converting layers to tables only, choose the Layers to Table radio button.

   • If you are converting Cascading Style Sheet styles to HTML tags only, choose the CSS Styles to HTML Markup radio button.

   • If you are making all conversions, select the Both radio button.

3. Click OK, and Dreamweaver starts the conversion. A dialog box informs you if a problem is encountered, such as a nested layer or overlapping layers. If the Web page has overlapping layers, another dialog box (shown in Figure 34-2) tells you which layers are overlapping. Dreamweaver cannot proceed until all conflicts are resolved. If no problems occur, Dreamweaver creates the page in a new window.

Figure 34-2: On a page with multiple layers, Dreamweaver spots the "illegal" overlapping ones when you try to convert the page to tables.

Note   The CSS-to-HTML conversion disregards any CSS feature, such as line spacing, that is not implemented in regular HTML. In addition, the exact point size that can be specified in CSS is roughly translated to the relative size equivalents in HTML. Any font over 36 points is set to the largest HTML size, which is 7.

Making a Web Page Netscape 6 Compliant

Netscape 6's compliance with W3C standards offers many long-term advantages to Web developers, but in the short-term, it presents one more hurdle for today's designers. In addition to conforming their latest browser to industry standards, Netscape also decided to break with their own past and withdraw support for some of their own proprietary tags and syntax. Consequently, JavaScript behaviors that are set up to work with Netscape 4.x need to be modified to work properly with Netscape 6. Moreover, additional work is necessary to make the page viewable on all the major browser versions in use today: Internet Explorer 4, 5, 5.5, and Netscape versions 4.x and 6.

Netscape 6 does not support the <layer> and <ilayer> tags in Netscape 4.x. When a page contains at least one of these two tags, developers have two choices:

✦ Use a browser sniffer to detect which browser is being used to view the page and redirect the non-Netscape 4.x user to another page.

✦ Recode the existing page and change the <layer> and <ilayer> tags to <div> tags, which are supported to some degree by all 4.0 and above browsers.

A somewhat more involved solution is required for pages with Dynamic HTML effects, especially those involving layers and timelines. The Document Object Module for Netscape 4.x referred to objects inside of layers with this type of syntax:

```
document.layers.forms[0].firstNameText.value
```

There are a couple of ways this syntax could be rendered according to the W3C DOM. One version of this code reads:

```
document.getElementsByTagName("*").forms[0].firstNameText.value;
```

Another method looks at the id attribute of an element on the page. If, for example, the first name text field in the previous code had an id of firstNameText, the code could read like this:

```
document.getElementById('firstNameText').value
```

While some code may require handtooling, if you've used Dreamweaver behaviors, the easiest way to upgrade your pages is to delete the existing layer behaviors and replace them with Netscape 6 compatible behaviors. Although Dreamweaver 4 did not ship with all Netscape 6 behaviors, you can find viable replacements on the Dreamweaver Exchange.

Evolving 3.0 pages to 4.0 standards

Web sites are constantly upgraded and modified. You'll eventually need to enhance a more traditional site with new features, such as layers. Some of the older 3.0-oriented sites used elaborately nested tables on their pages to create a semblance of absolute positioning; normally, upgrading these Web pages takes hours and hours of tedious cutting and pasting. Dreamweaver can bring these older pages up to speed with the Convert Tables to Layers command, found under the Modify ➪ Convert submenu item.

The Convert Tables to Layers command can also be used to convert a page created by another Web authoring program (Net Objects Fusion, for example) that uses nested tables for positioning. Once tables have been transformed into layers, the layout of the entire page is much easier to modify. It's even possible to make the switch from 3.0 to 4.0 capabilities, modify your page, and then, with the Convert Layers to Tables command, re-create your 3.0-compliant page.

The name of the Convert Tables to Layers command is another one that's a little misleading. Once you issue this command, every HTML element in the new page — not just the tables — is placed in a layer. Moreover, every cell with content in every table is converted into its own layer. In other words, if you are working with a 3×3 table in which one cell is left empty, Dreamweaver creates eight different layers for just the table.

Note   If you want to convert a 3.0-compatible page to a page with layers, but the page has no tables, Dreamweaver places all the content in one layer, as if the `<body>` tag was one big single-cell table.

To convert a 3.0-browser-compatible Web page with tables to a 4.0-browser-compatible Web page with layers, choose Modify ⇨ Convert ⇨ Tables to Layers. If you need to return to a table-based layout, choose Modify ⇨ Convert ⇨ Layers to Table.

Ensuring Browser Compatibility

As more browsers and browser versions become available, a Web designer has two basic options to stay on the road to compatibility: *internal* and *external*.

✦ The **internal** method uses scripts on the same Web page; the scripts deliver the proper code depending on the browser detected. Many of Dreamweaver's own behavior functions manage the browser issue internally.

✦ The **external** approach examines each visitor's browser right off the bat and reroutes the user to the most appropriate Web page.

Both the internal and the external methods have their pluses and minuses, and both are better suited to particular situations. For example, it is impractical to use the external method of creating multiple versions of the same Web pages when you are working with a large site. Suddenly, you've gone from managing 300 pages of information to 900 or 1,200. Of course, you don't have to duplicate every page — but because of the open nature of the Web, where any page can be bookmarked and entered directly, you have to plan carefully and provide routing routines at the key locations. Conversely, sometimes you have no choice but to use multiple versions, especially if a page employs many browser-specific features.

Don't get the idea that the internal and external strategies are mutually exclusive. Several sites today are routing 3.0 browsers to one page and using internal coding methods to differentiate between the various 4.0 browser versions on another page. This section examines techniques for implementing browser-compatibility from both the internal and external perspective.

Internal coding for cross-browser compatibility

Imagine the shouts of joy when the Web development community learned that the 4.0 versions of Navigator and Internet Explorer both supported Cascading Style Sheet layers! Now imagine the grumbling when it became apparent that each browser uses a different JavaScript syntax for calling them. You get the picture: It all boils down to differences in each browser's Document Object Model.

Note — Navigator 6.0 incorporates the W3C standard for layers, which is also largely supported by Internet Explorer 4.0 and above. Although this will eventually simplify compatibility issues for Web designers, Navigator 4.x browsers will remain in use for some time and the code for handling layers in those browsers must be accounted for.

Calling layers

When referring to a layer, Navigator 4.x uses this syntax:

```
document.layers["layerName"]
```

whereas Internet Explorer uses this syntax:

```
document.all["layerName"]
```

The trick to internal code-switching is to assign the variations — the "layers" from Navigator and the "all" from Internet Explorer — to the same variable, depending on which browser is being used. Here's a sample function that does just that:

```
function init(){
if (navigator.appName == "Netscape") {
var layerRef="document.layers";
}else {
var layerRef="document.all";
}
}
```

In this function, if the visitor is using a Netscape 4.x browser, the variable `layerRef` is assigned the value `document.layers`; otherwise, `layerRef` is set to `document.all`.

Calling properties

If you're looking to assign or read a layer property, one variable is only half the battle. Another difference exists in the way properties are called. With Navigator, it's done like this:

```
document.layers["layerName"].top
```

and with Internet Explorer, it's as follows:

```
document.all["layerName"].style.top
```

Internet Explorer inserts another hierarchical division, called style, whereas Navigator doesn't use anything at all. The solution is another variable, styleRef, which for Internet Explorer is set like this:

```
var styleRef="style"
```

And the Navigator styleRef is actually set to a *null string*, or nothing. You can combine the two variables into one initialization function, which is best called from an onLoad event in the <body> tag:

```
function init(){
if (navigator.appName == "Netscape") {
var layerRef="document.layers";
var styleRef = "";
}else {
var layerRef="document.all";
var styleRef="style";
}
}
```

Once these differences are accommodated, the variables are ready to be used in a script. To do this, you can use JavaScript's built-in eval() function to combine the variables and the object references. Here's an example that sets a new variable, varLeft, to whatever is the left value of a particular layer:

```
varLeft = eval(layerRef + '["myLayer"]' + styleRef + '.left');
```

Luckily, the variations between the Navigator and Internet Explorer DOM are consistent enough that a JavaScript function can assign the proper values with a minimum of effort.

Calling objects within layers

There's one other area where the two DOMs diverge. When you are attempting to address almost any entity inside a layer, Navigator uses an additional hierarchical layer to reference the object. Thus, a named image in a named layer in Navigator is referenced like this:

```
document.layers["layerName"].document.imageName
```

whereas the same object in Internet Explorer is called like this:

```
document.imageName
```

This is why the Show-Hide Layers behavior passes two arguments with the affected layers' name: one in the Navigator format and the other in the Internet Explorer syntax.

Designing Web pages for backward compatibility

The previous section describes a technique for dealing with the differences between 4.0 and above browsers, but how do you handle the much larger gap between third- and fourth-generation browsers? When this gap becomes a canyon, with DHTML-intensive pages on one side and incompatible browsers on the other, the ultimate answer is to use redirection to send a particular browser to an appropriate page. However, browsers can coexist in plenty of cases — with a little planning and a little help from Dreamweaver.

When designing backwardly compatible Web pages, browsers generally offer one major advantage: ignorance. If a browser doesn't recognize a tag or attribute, it just ignores it and renders the rest of the page. Because many of the newer features are built on new tags, or on tags such as `<div>` that previously were little used, your Web pages can gracefully devolve from 4.0 to 3.0 behavior, without causing errors or grossly misrendering the page.

Take layers, for instance. One advantage offered by this DHTML feature is the capability to make something interactively appear and disappear. Although that's not possible in 3.0 browsers (without extensive image-swapping), it is possible to display the same material and even enable some degree of navigation. The key is proper placement of the layer code, and not the layer itself.

Browsers basically read and render the code for a Web page from top to bottom. You can, for example, make several layers appear one after another in a 3.0 browser, even if they appear to be stacked on top of one another in a 4.0 browser. All you have to do is make sure the code — not the position of the layers — appears in the document sequentially. You can see this effect in Figure 34-3, where all three layers have the same `left` coordinates. However, the layer symbols inserted by Dreamweaver to represent the actual code appear one after the other with a little whitespace in between. The navigational links in the upper left have two roles: They are linked to the named anchor next to the layer's code and, through the Behavior Inspector, are set to show and hide the appropriate layers when selected (using the `onClick` event).

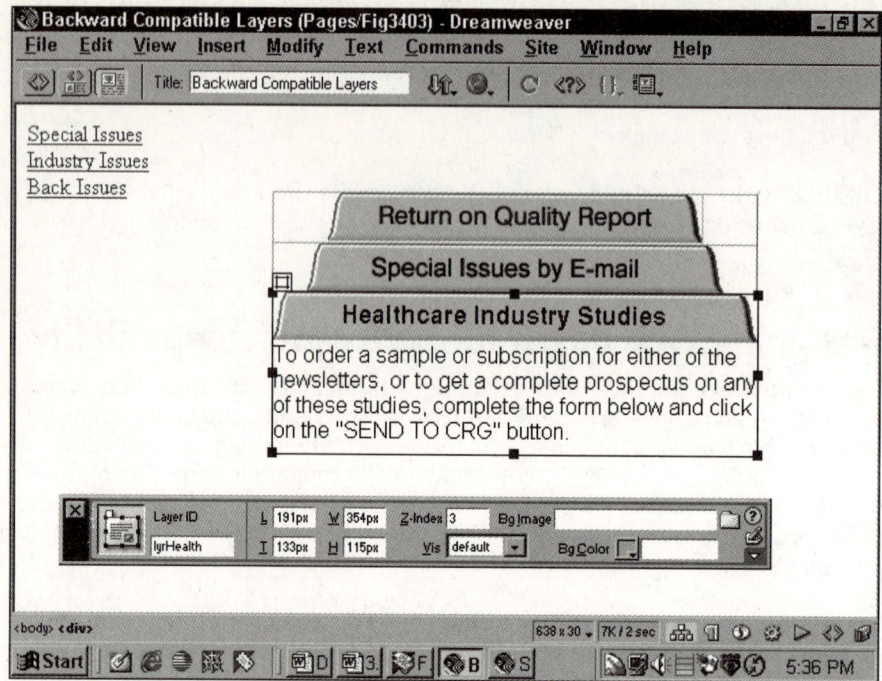

Figure 34-3: Careful placement of the code for layers can be an effective tool for backward compatibility.

Because the code for the three layers is spaced one after the other, browsers that do not understand the `style` attribute in the `<div>` tags — which create the layers — simply render the information contained within all three tags, one after another.

Note Although it may seem obvious, it bears mentioning that you must preview your pages in a 3.0 browser to see the results of these positioning techniques.

The Dreamweaver Technique in the upcoming section is based on methods used by George Olsen, Design Director of 2-Lane Media (`www.21m.com`), and on an article by Trevor Lohrbeer in the Dynamic HTML Zone (`www.dhtmlzone.com`).

Tip It's even possible to animate your layers for the benefit of Dynamic HTML-enabled browsers and, at the same time, enable 3.0 browsers to just show the static images. The key is to make sure that your animations begin and end in the same locations.

Dreamweaver technique: Browser checking

Because of the major differences between third- and fourth-generation and beyond browsers, it is an increasingly popular practice to create a Web page geared to each browser and then use a *gateway* script to direct users to the proper page. A gateway script uses JavaScript to determine a visitor's browser version and route the page accordingly. Dreamweaver includes the Check Browser behavior (see Chapter 19), which makes this process relatively effortless.

For maximum efficiency, the best strategy is to use three pages: one page for 4.0 and above browsers, one page for 3.0 browsers, and a blank page that serves as your home page. Then, the Check Browser action can be assigned to the onLoad event of the blank page and can execute immediately. The other alternative is to use only two pages, one for each browser, and then run the Check Browser routine after the page is loaded and send the users of one browser version off to the other page. The disadvantage to this approach is that many of your visitors have to sit through the loading process of one page, only to be whisked off to another to start again.

Other variations besides those encountered in different browser versions may cause you to redirect a visitor to a different Web page. Screen resolution, color depth, MIME types — each comes in myriad possibilities. Using different behaviors, you can detect the differences and direct your users accordingly. You can find a host of these redirection helpers on the Additional Extensions section of the CD-ROM that accompanies this book, in the various Behavior folders under each author's name.

The following technique takes you through the conversion of a layers-based page to a 3.0-compatible page, the creation of a new gateway page, and the incorporation of a Check Browser action that automatically directs users to a new page depending on their browser type:

1. In Dreamweaver, construct the fourth-generation browser version of your Web page — the one that uses layers and Cascading Style Sheets — first.

Be sure no layers overlap and that the Web page otherwise meets the criteria noted in the section "Preparing your page for conversion," earlier in this chapter.

2. Choose File ➪ Convert ➪ 3.0 Browser Compatible. Save the new version of the page, created by Dreamweaver, with a name similar to the original (4.0) page but with a different prefix or suffix. For example, you might call the page intended for 4.0 browsers index40.html and the 3.0 version index30.html.

3. Choose File ➪ New to create a new page. This page serves as the gateway for the other two pages.

4. By default, Dreamweaver makes new pages with a white background. To make the gateway page as unobtrusive as possible, it's best to use the same background color as your target pages. To do this, choose Modify ⇨ Page Properties. In the Page Properties dialog box, select the color value in the Background Color text box that corresponds to your other pages. You could even position the two pages side-by-side and sample the background color. Click OK to close the Page Properties dialog box.

5. In your blank gateway page, choose Window ⇨ Behaviors to open the Behavior Inspector.

6. From the Tag Selector in the status bar of the Document window, select the `<body>` tag.

7. In the Behavior Inspector, select the + (Add Behavior) button and choose the Check Browser action from the pop-up menu.

8. In the Check Browser parameter form:

   • Enter the URL for your 4.0 browser page in the URL text box or select the Browse (Choose) button to locate the file.

   • Enter the URL for your 3.0 browser page in the Alt URL text box or select the Browse (Choose) button to locate the file.

   Click OK when you are done. If you haven't changed any of the other Check Browser default settings, both 4.0 browsers go to the address in the URL text box, and all other browser versions are directed to the address in the Alt URL text box (see Figure 34-4).

9. Save your gateway page. If this page is to serve as the gateway for the home page(s) for your domain, save it as index.html or whatever name your server uses for default documents.

Figure 34-4: The Check Browser behavior can build a gateway script for you with no coding.

10. The gateway can now be preliminarily tested. However, because any Web page can be an entry point to a site, you also have to use the Check Browser action on each of the version-specific pages. Reopen the 4.0 browser page.

11. If necessary, open the Behavior Inspector by choosing Window ➪ Behaviors or selecting the Show Behaviors button from the Launcher.

12. Repeat Steps 6 and 7 to get to the Check Browser parameter form.

13. This time, enter the URL for your 3.0 browser page in the Alt URL text box or select the Browse (Choose) button to locate the file.

14. In the sections for both Netscape and Internet Explorer 4.0 (or above), choose the Stay on this Page option from the drop-down list.

15. Select OK when you are finished and save the file.

16. Open the 3.0 browser page. Repeat Steps 12 through 15, but when you get to the Check Browser parameter form, enter the URL for the 4.0 browser page in the Alt URL text box.

Now visitors can come in through the front door of your home page, or through any side door, and be served the correct page. Generally, not all the pages in your site will use the high-end features available to the 4.0 browsers, so you have to create gateways for only those pages that do. If you plan your site with this strategy in mind — and avoid putting a moving layer on every page as a logo, for instance — you can manage your site more effectively.

Testing Your Page with a Targeted Browser

Testing is an absolute must when building a Web site. It's critical that you view your pages on as many browsers and systems as possible. Variations in color, gamma, page offset, and capabilities must be observed before they can be adjusted.

A more basic, preliminary type of testing can also be done right from within Dreamweaver: code testing. Browsers usually ignore tags and attributes they do not understand. However, sometimes these tags can produce unexpected and undesirable results, such as exposing code to the viewer.

Dreamweaver's Browser Targeting feature, File ➪ Check Target Browsers, enables you to check a Web page — or an entire Web site — against any number of browser profiles. Currently, Dreamweaver comes with profiles for the following browsers:

✦ Internet Explorer 2.0

✦ Internet Explorer 3.0

✦ Internet Explorer 4.0

✦ Internet Explorer 5.0

✦ Navigator 2.0

✦ Navigator 3.0

✦ Navigator 4.0

You can choose to check your page or site against a single browser profile, all of them, or anything in-between. Though not a substitute for real-world testing, Browser Targeting gives you an overview of potential errors and problematic code to look out for.

Testing browser compatibility for a Web page

To check a single Web page against specific browser targets, follow these steps:

 With Browser Targeting, Dreamweaver checks the saved version of a Web page. So if you've made any modifications to your current page, save it *before* beginning the following process.

1. Choose File ⇨ Check Target Browsers.

   The Check Target Browsers dialog box opens as shown in Figure 34-5.

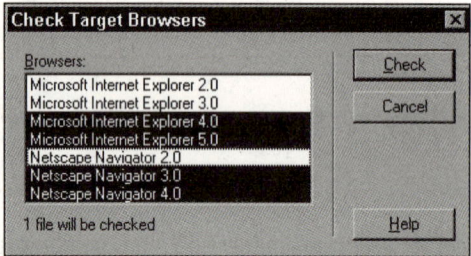

Figure 34-5: Select the browsers on which you'd like to check the code of your current page.

2. Select the browsers against which you want the current page to be checked. The usual selection techniques work in this list: To choose various browsers, press Ctrl (Command) while selecting. To specify a contiguous range of browsers, select the first one, press Shift, and then select the last one.

3. After you've chosen the target browsers, click the Check button. Dreamweaver opens your primary browser, if necessary, and outputs the report to the browser window (see Figure 34-6).

4. Dreamweaver stores the Target Browser Check report only temporarily and deletes the file after its use. To keep a record of the report, use your browser's File ⇨ Print or File ⇨ Save command.

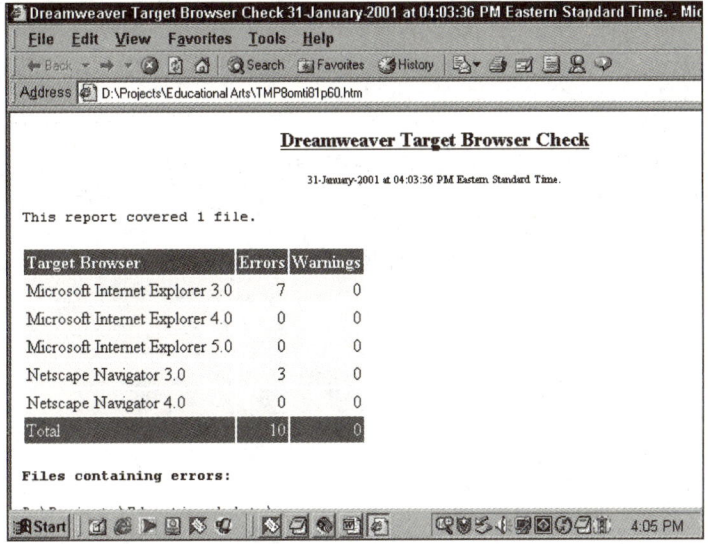

Figure 34-6: The Dreamweaver Target Browser Check report displays a summary of all the errors it finds in your selected page. It's a good idea to print the report or save it in a file.

The Dreamweaver Target Browser Check report offers both a summary and a detail section. The summary, previously shown in Figure 34-6, lists the browser being tested and any errors or warnings. Totals for each category are listed beneath the columns.

The detail section of the Target Browser Check report, shown in Figure 34-7, lists the following:

✦ Each offending tag or attribute

✦ The browsers that do not support the tag or attribute

✦ An example HTML line

✦ Additional line numbers where the error occurred

Testing browser compatibility for an entire site

With Dreamweaver, you can check browser compatibility for an entire Web site as easily as you can check a single page. Dreamweaver checks all the HTML files in a given folder, whether or not they are actually used in the site.

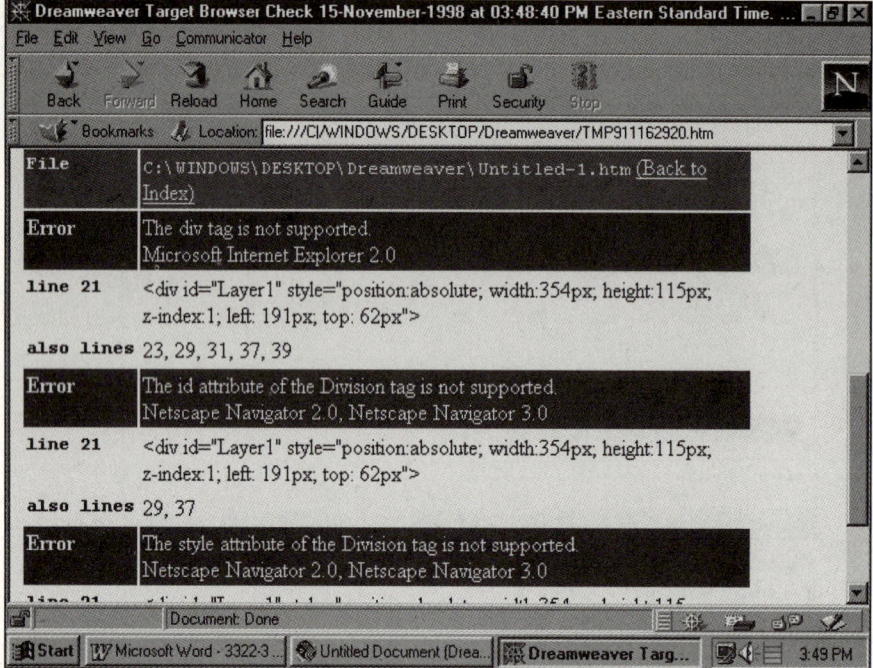

Figure 34-7: You can find detailed information on the lower half of the Dreamweaver Target Browser Check report.

To check an entire site against specific browser targets, follow these steps:

1. Choose Window ⇨ Site Files or select the Show Site FTP button from the Launcher. The Site window opens.

2. In the Site window, select a folder from the Local Folder pane, choose one of the listed sites from the Remote Site pane, or select any number of individual files.

3. Choose File ⇨ Check Target Browsers from the Site window menu (while the Site window has focus). The Check Target Browsers dialog box opens, shown earlier in Figure 34-5. Below the list of Browsers is a statement of how many pages are to be checked.

4. Select the browsers against which you want the current site checked.

5. When you're ready, select the Check button. Dreamweaver opens your primary browser, if necessary, and outputs the report to the browser window.

6. Dreamweaver stores the Target Browser Check file only temporarily and deletes the file after its use. To keep a record of the report, use your browser's File ⇨ Print or File ⇨ Save command.

When you're checking more than one page, the summary section of the Dreamweaver Target Browser Check gives you a list of the files containing errors as well as an error count. The summary section displays the errors for each file grouped together.

Using the results of the browser check

How you handle the flagged errors in Dreamweaver's Target Browser Check report is entirely dependent on the design goals you have established for your site. If your mission is to be totally accessible to every browser on the market, then you need to look at your page/site with the earliest browsers and pay special attention to those areas of possible trouble noted by the report. On the other hand, if your standards are a little more relaxed, then you can probably ignore the 2.0 browser warnings and concentrate on those appearing in the 3.0 and 4.0 categories.

 Note Many items flagged as errors aren't incorrect code — they're just not supported in the targeted browser. For example, checking a page with rollovers against an Internet Explorer 3 profile will always display an error stating "The onMouseOut attribute of the Hyperlink Anchor tag is not supported." Although this means that the rollover won't work in this browser, it also won't create an error message.

Customizing a Browser Profile

In order for Dreamweaver's Browser Targeting feature to be effective, you must have access to profiles for all the browsers you need to check. You can create custom browser profiles to cover any new browser versions or browsers as they become available. The browser profile file is a text file and can be created or altered in any text editor.

This section examines the required structure and format for a browser profile file and the steps for building one based on an existing file.

Understanding the browser profile structure

In order for Dreamweaver to properly process an HTML file using any browser profile, the profile must follow a precise format. Here's a sample taken from the Internet Explorer 3.0 browser profile:

```
<!ELEMENT H1 name="Heading 1" >
<!ATTLIST H1
        Align ( left | center | right )
        Class
        ID
        Style
>
```

As you can see, the HTML tag is listed in a very specific syntax. Here's how the syntax is formed:

```
<!ELEMENT htmlTag Name="tagName" >
<!ATTLIST htmlTag
unsupportedAttribute1 !Error !msg="The unsupportedAttribute1 of the htmlTag ¬
is not supported. Try using thisAttribute for a similar effect."
supportedAttribute1
supportedAttribute2 ( validValue1 | validValue2 | validValue3 )
unsupportedAttribute2 !Error !htmlmsg="<b>Don't ever use this ¬
unsupportedAttribute2 of the  htmlTag !!</b>"
>
```

The variables in the syntax are as follows:

✦ `htmlTag`: The tag as it appears in an HTML document.

✦ `tagName`: Optional; how the tag is known. For example, the `<applet>` tag is called the "Java Applet." If it's noted in the file, the `tagName` is used in the error message; otherwise, `htmlTag` is used.

✦ `unsupportedAttribute`: Indicates invalid attributes so that a custom error message can be offered. Otherwise, all attributes not specifically listed are assumed to be unsupported.

✦ `supportedAttribute`: A valid attribute; all valid attributes must be listed. Only attributes listed without an `!Error` designation are supported.

✦ `validValue`: A value supported by the attribute.

Several other, not-so-obvious rules must be followed for Dreamweaver to correctly read the profile:

✦ The name of the profile must appear in the first line of the file, followed by a single carriage return. This is the profile name that appears in the Check Target Browser(s) dialog box and in the report.

✦ The key phrase `PROFILE_TYPE=BROWSER_PROFILE` must appear in the second line.

✦ On the `!ELEMENT` line, a single space must be used before the closing angle (>) bracket, after the opening parentheses, before the closing parentheses, and before and after each pipe (|) character in the list of values.

✦ An exclamation point, without an intervening space, must be placed before the words `ELEMENT`, `ATTLIST`, `Error`, `msg`, and `htmlmsg`. For example:

`!ELEMENT, !ATTLIST, !Error, !msg, and !htmlmsg.`

✦ You can only use plain text in `!msg` messages, but an `!htmlmsg` message can use any valid HTML, including links.

✦ Don't use HTML comment tags, `<!-- -->`, because they interfere with the regular Dreamweaver processing of the file.

Creating a browser profile

As you can see, Dreamweaver browser profiles have a specific structure. Consequently, it's far easier to modify an existing profile than to write one from scratch. The basic procedure takes three steps:

1. Choose an existing profile for a browser similar to the one for which you are creating a new profile. Open the profile in a text editor.

Numerous custom browser profiles appear on this book's accompanying CD-ROM. You can copy them directly to your BrowserProfiles folder found in the Configuration folder or use them as models for modification.

2. Add any tags and attributes that are supported in the target browser but not in the existing profile.

3. Remove any tags or attributes not supported by your target browser. Or, you can add an !Error message after any attribute to flag it for Dreamweaver's Target Browser Check operation.

For example, take a look at the code fragment illustrated in Listing 34-1; it contains a portion of the browser profile I created for WebTV. Note the custom error messages after the <applet> tag and the rel attribute of the <a> tag.

When saving a new browser profile in Windows, there's a small trick to getting the version number to appear correctly at the end of the browser name, as in "Navigator 3.0." Choose File ⇨ Save As from your text editor. Then, in the Filename text box, enter your browser name with the filename extension (.txt), all enclosed in quotes. For example, to save the WebTV 1.0 file, I entered "WebTV_1.0.txt" in the Filename text box.

Listing 34-1: **Excerpt from Browser Profile File for WebTV**

```
WebTV 1.0
PROFILE_TYPE=BROWSER_PROFILE
-- Copyright 1997 Macromedia, Inc. All rights reserved.

<!ELEMENT A Name="Hyperlink Anchor" >
<!ATTLIST A
        Class              !Error
        HREF
        ID
        Name
        OnClick
        OnMouseOut
        OnMouseOver
        Rel                !Warning !msg "The rel attribute has been modified by ¬
WebTV."
```

Continued

Listing 34-1: *(continued)*

```
        Style           !Error
        Selected        !Error
        Target          !Error
>

<!ELEMENT Address >
<!ATTLIST Address
        Class           !Error
        ID              !Error
        Style           !Error
>

<!ELEMENT APPLET Name="Java Applet" > !Error !msg "WebTV does not support ¬
Java Applets."
<!ATTLIST APPLET
        Align ( top | middle | bottom | left | right | absmiddle | ¬
absbottom | baseline | texttop )
        Alt
        Archive         !Error
        Code
        Codebase
        Height
        HSpace
        Name
        VSpace
        Width
        Class
        ID
        Style
>

<!ELEMENT AREA Name="Client-side image map area" >
<!ATTLIST AREA
        Alt             !Error
        Class           !Error
        Coords
        HREF
        ID
        Name
        NoHREF
        NoTab
        OnMouseOut
        OnMouseOver
        Shape
        Style           !Error
        Target
>
```

```
<!ELEMENT AUDIOSCOPE Name="Audioscope" >
<!ATTLIST AUDIOSCOPE
        Align
        Border
        Gain
        Height
        LeftColor
        LeftOffset
        MaxLevel
        RightColor
        RightOffset
        Width
>

<!ELEMENT B Name="Bold" >
<!ATTLIST B
        Class           !Error
        ID              !Error
        Style           !Error
>

<!ELEMENT Base >
<!ATTLIST Base
        HREF
        Target
>

<!ELEMENT BaseFont >
<!ATTLIST BaseFont
        Size
>
<!ELEMENT BGSOUND Name="Background sound" >
<!ATTLIST BGSOUND
        Loop
        Src
>

<!ELEMENT Big >
<!ATTLIST Big
        Class
        ID
        Style
>

<!ELEMENT Blackface >

<!ELEMENT Blink !Error >

<!ELEMENT Blockquote >
```

Continued

Listing 34-1: *(continued)*

```
<!ELEMENT Body >
<!ATTLIST Body
        ALink                   !Error
        Background
        BGColor
        BGProperties
        Credits
        LeftMargin
        Link
        Logo
        OnBlur                  !Error
        OnFocus                 !Error
        OnLoad
        OnUnload
        Style                   !Error
        Text
        VLink
>

<!ELEMENT BQ Name="Block Quote" >

<!ELEMENT BR Name="Line break" >
<!ATTLIST BR
        Clear ( left | right | all )
>
```

Summary

Unless you're building a Web site for a strictly controlled intranet, in which case you know everyone is using the BrandX 4.03 browser, it's critical that you address the browser-compatibility issues that your Web site is certain to face. Whether it's cross-browser or backward compatibility you're trying to achieve, Dreamweaver has features and techniques in place to help you get your Web pages viewed by the maximum number of users. This chapter covered the following points, specifically:

✦ Dreamweaver takes a Web page built with 4.0 and above features, including layers and CSS, and creates another Web page that is 3.0-compatible.

✦ Dreamweaver can take a Web page created with layers and create another Web page that uses tables instead. Tools in Dreamweaver, such as Convert Layers to Tables, make it quick and straightforward.

✦ You can use JavaScript within a Web page to handle cross-browser compatibility problems with 4.0 and above browsers.

✦ Careful placement of your DHTML objects can help with backward compatibility.

✦ Dreamweaver enables you to check your Web page, selected pages, or an entire Web site against a browser profile to look for tags and attributes that will not work in a particular browser version.

✦ Browser profiles can be customized or copied and modified for a new browser or browser version.

In the next chapter, you'll learn how Dreamweaver may be used in a team environment to develop Web sites.

✦   ✦   ✦

Building Web Sites with a Team

Major Web sites designed, developed, and maintained by a single person are, increasingly, few and far between. Once a site has reached a certain complexity and size, it's far more timely and cost effective to divide responsibility for different areas among different people. For all of its positive aspects, team development has an equal number of shortcomings — as anyone who has had their work overwritten by another developer working on the same page will attest.

Dreamweaver includes a number of features to make it easy for teams to work together. Team-oriented features have increased significantly in Dreamweaver 4. In addition to the existing Check In/Check Out facility, version control and collaborative authoring have been enabled in Dreamweaver through the connectivity to Microsoft's Visual SourceSafe and the WebDAV (Web Distributed Authoring and Versioning) standard.

In addition to providing a link to industry standard protocol used in team development, Dreamweaver 4 also includes a more accessible Design Notes feature. When custom file columns are set up — which rely on Design Notes to store their information — a project's status is just a glance away. For more detailed feedback, Dreamweaver's Reports command provides an interactive method of uncovering problems and offering a direct link to fixing them. As with many Dreamweaver features, the Reports mechanism is extensible which means it's possible for JavaScript-savvy developers to create their own custom reports to further assist their teamwork. In this chapter we'll look at the various Dreamweaver tools — both old and new — for developing Web sites with a team. We begin with the essential team-based feature: Check In/Check Out.

Following Check In/Check Out Procedures

Site development can be broken up as many different ways as there are site development teams. In one group, all the graphics may be handled by one person or department while layout is handled by another and JavaScript coding by yet another. Or, one team may be given total responsibility over one section of a Web site — the products section, for example — as another team handles the services division. However the responsibilities are shared, there's always the danger of overlap: that two or more team members will unknowingly work on the same page, graphic, or other Web element — and that one person's work will replace the other's when transferred to the remote site. Suddenly, the oh-so-efficient division of labor becomes a logistical nightmare.

Dreamweaver's core protection for team Web site development is its Check In/Check Out system. When properly established and adhered to, the Check In/Check Out system not only stops files from improperly being overwritten, it also lets everyone on the team know who is working on what file and provides a direct method of contacting them, right from within Dreamweaver.

As with any team effort, to get the most out of the Check In/Check Out system everybody must follow the rules:

✦ **Rule Number 1:** All team members must have Check In/Check Out set up for their Dreamweaver-defined sites.

✦ **Rule Number 2:** All team members must have Design Notes enabled in their site definition.

And, arguably the most important rule:

✦ **Rule Number 3:** All team members must use Dreamweaver to transfer files to and from the remote server.

Should the Check In/Check Out system fail and a file be accidentally overwritten, it is invariably because Rule Number 3 was broken: someone got or put a file from the Web server using a tool other than Dreamweaver.

Check In/Check Out overview

Before discussing the Check In/Check Out setup procedure, let's take a look at how the process actually works with two fictional team members, Eric and Bella:

1. Eric gets an e-mail with a note to update the content on the About Our Company page with news of the merger that has just occurred.

2. Bella receives a similar note — except Bella is the graphic artist and needs to change the logo to reflect the new organization.

3. Eric connects to the remote site, selects the about.htm file, and chooses the Check Out button on Dreamweaver's Site window Toolbar.

   If Eric had chosen Get instead of Check Out, he would have received a read-only file on his system.

4. Dreamweaver asks if Eric would like to include dependent files in the transfer. As he doesn't know that Bella needs to work on the site also, he selects OK.

   The file on the remote system is downloaded to Eric's machine and a small green check mark appears next to the name of each file transferred in both the remote and local File views as shown in Figure 35-1.

Figure 35-1: For a checked out file, a check mark is placed next to the filename on both the local and remote sites. The check mark is green if you checked it out and red if someone else checked it out.

5. Bella connects to the remote site in Dreamweaver and sees a red check next to the file she needs to work on, about.htm. Next to the file is the name of the person who currently has the file, Eric, as well as his e-mail address.

6. Bella selects the link to Eric's e-mail address and drops him a note asking him to let her know when he's done.

7. Eric finishes adding the content to the page and chooses the Check In button to transfer the files back to the remote server.

The checkmarks are removed from the File views and the local version of about.htm is marked as read-only by Dreamweaver as indicated with a closed padlock symbol. This is to prevent Eric from working on the file without first checking it out.

8. Bella receives Eric's "I'm done!" e-mail and retrieves the file by selecting the Check Out button from the Site window.

Now on Bella's machine, the transferred files have a green check mark and her name while on Eric's screen the check marks are displayed in red.

9. After she's finished working on the graphics side of the page, ensuring that Eric's new content wraps properly around her new logo, she's selects the HTML file and then clicks Check In. By opting to transfer the dependent files as well, all of her new graphics are properly transferred. Again, the check marks are removed and the local files are set to read-only.

10. The work is completed without anyone stepping on anyone else's toes — or files.

 Caution   Dreamweaver places a small text file with a .lck (lock) extension on both the server and local site for each checked out document. The .lck file stores the Check Out name of the person transferring the files and, if available, their e-mail address. It's important that these files not be deleted from the server as their very existence signals to Dreamweaver that a file has been checked out.

Enabling Check In/Check Out

Dreamweaver's Check In/Check Out system is activated through the Site Definition dialog box. The Check In/Check Out settings must be input individually for each site; there's no global option for all sites. Although it's generally best to set it up when the site is initially defined, you can enable Check In/Check Out at any time.

To establish the Check In/Check Out feature, follow these steps:

1. Choose Site ➪ Define Sites or select Define Sites from the site drop-down list in the Site window.

2. From the Define Sites dialog box, select the desired site in the list and choose Edit or select the New button to define a new site.

3. Select the Remote Info category in the Site Definition dialog box.

4. From the Access list, choose either FTP or Local/Network.

5. Choose the Enable File Check In and Check Out option.

6. If you want to automatically check out a file when opening it from the Site window, select the Check Out Files when Opening option.

When the Check Out Files when Opening option is selected, double-clicking a file in the local site File view or selecting it and then choosing File ➪ Open Selection, transfers the corresponding remote file to the local system and notes the file as being checked out. Choosing File ➪ Open does not automatically check out a file whether this option is chosen or not.

7. Enter the name you displayed under the Checked Out By column in the Check Out Name field.

   It's a good idea to use the name that not only identifies yourself, but also identifies the system you're working on. Thus, `jlowery-laptop` or `jlowery-iMac` is a better choice than just `jlowery`.

8. To allow team members to send you a message from within Dreamweaver, enter your full e-mail address in the E-mail Address field.

   Entering an e-mail address converts the Checked Out By name to an active link. Selecting the link prompts the default e-mail program to display a new message form where the To field contains the supplied e-mail address and the Subject field contains the site name and filename as shown in Figure 35-2.

Figure 35-2: Dreamweaver lets you contact the team member working on a file with the e-mail address feature. The subject line is automatically added to reference a particular file and site.

9. Make sure that the other necessary information for establishing an FTP or network connection is entered. If so, select OK to close the Site Definition dialog box.

10. From the Define Sites dialog box, choose Done.

Note The preceding procedure works for both FTP and network connected remote sites. If you are working within a Visual SourceSafe or WebDAV environment, see their corresponding sections later in this chapter for enabling check in and check out protocols.

Checking Files In and Out

Once the Check In/Check Out feature is enabled, additional buttons and commands become available. The Site window Toolbar shows both a Check Out File(s) button and Check In one, as shown in Figure 35-3. The Site ⇨ Check Out and Site ⇨ Check In commands become active as do those options under the File Management button on the Toolbar. The redundancy of these commands makes it feasible to check files in and out from wherever you happen to be working in the Dreamweaver environment.

Figure 35-3: The Check In and Check Out buttons do not appear unless Enable Check In/Check Out has been selected in the Site Definition.

To check out a file or series of files from the Site window, follow these steps:

1. Choose Window ➪ Site Files or click the Show Site button from the Launcher to open the Site window. If you prefer to use keyboard shortcuts, press F8.

2. If necessary, select the desired site — where Check In/Check Out has been enabled — from the site drop-down list.

3. Click the Connect button in the Site window toolbar or choose Site ➪ Connect.

   If you've chosen Local/Network as your remote access method, you're connected automatically.

4. Choose the HTML or other Web documents you want to check out from the Remote file listing.

   It's not necessary to select the dependent files; Dreamweaver will transfer those for you automatically.

5. Choose Check Out File(s) from the Toolbar or select Site ➪ Check Out.

   If you Get the files instead of checking them out, either by choosing the Get button or dragging the files from the Remote to the Local file listing, the local file will become read-only, but the remote file will not be marked as checked out.

6. If the Prompt on Get/Check Out option is selected in Preferences, Dreamweaver asks if you'd like to transfer the dependent files. Choose Yes to do so or No to transfer only the selected files.

   When Dreamweaver has completed the transfer, green check marks appear next to each primary file (HTML, ASP, ColdFusion, and so on) in both the Remote and File views; dependent files are made read-only locally as designated by a padlock symbol.

I find that it's better to check out all the files I believe I'll need in a work session right at the start. While it's possible to check out an open document — by choosing Site ➪ Check Out or selecting Check Out from the File Management button on the Toolbar — Dreamweaver needs to transfer the remote file to your local system, possibly overwriting any changes you've made, because you are checking out a file from the remote server. Dreamweaver does ask you if you want to replace the local version with the remote file; to abort the procedure, choose No.

Tip   If you need to edit a graphic or other dependent file that has been locked as part of the check out process, you can unlock the file from the Site window. Right-click (Control+click) the file in the Site window and, from the context menu, choose Unlock. One related tip: to quickly select the file for an image, choose the image in the Assets panel and from the context menu choose Locate in Site.

Once you've completed your work on a particular file, you're ready to check it back in. To check in the current file, follow these steps:

1. Choose Site ➪ Check In or select Check In from the File Management button on the Toolbar.

2. If you haven't saved your file and if you've enabled the Save Files Before Putting option from the Site category in Preferences, your file will be automatically saved; otherwise, Dreamweaver asks if you want to store the file before transferring it.

3. If Prompt on Put/Check In is enabled, Dreamweaver will ask if you want to transfer the dependent files as well. If any changes have been made to the dependent files, select Yes.

Once the files are transferred, Dreamweaver removes the check marks from the files and makes the local files read-only.

Note Ever start working on a file only to realize you're working on the wrong one? If you make this or any other mistake that makes you wish you could go back to the original version when working with a checked out file, don't worry. Even if you've saved your changes locally, you can choose Site ➪ Undo Check Out (or select Undo Check Out from the File Management button on the Toolbar) to retransfer the posted file from the remote site. The local file will be made read-only and the file will no longer be checked out under your name.

Integrating Dreamweaver with Visual SourceSafe

Microsoft's Visual SourceSafe (VSS) is an industrial strength version control tool. With VSS, not only can team members check files in and out, as with Dreamweaver, but other valuable features are also available such as the ability to get a history of changes, compare two or more versions to one another to see the differences and the restoration of a previous version. Visual SourceSafe is generally used in larger corporations where many different departments are involved in a Web development project. VSS is bundled with the Enterprise edition of Visual InterDev as well as being sold separately.

New Feature Dreamweaver now integrates it's own Check In/Check Out system with that of Visual SourceSafe. When a Dreamweaver site is connected to a VSS database, checking out a file in Dreamweaver checks out a file from the VSS project. Likewise, when a file is checked back in Dreamweaver, it is noted as being checked in the VSS database. This integration allows Dreamweaver to be smoothly integrated into a large-scale Web development project where both Dreamweaver users and non-users may be working together, accessing the same files.

Visual SourceSafe is available on both the Macintosh and Windows platforms, and there are special requirements on each platform as follows:

✦ For Windows systems, the Visual SourceSafe version 6 client must be installed on the local machine.

✦ Macintosh users should have the MetroWerks SourceSafe version 1.1.0 client installed. In addition, you must have the ToolServer utility from the Macintosh Programmer's Workshop installed. ToolServer is found on the Dreamweaver 4 CD or it can be downloaded from Apple Developer's site at http://developer.apple.com/tools/mpw-tools/.

Caution There are several versions of ToolServer, and you must have the correct version for VSS integration to work properly. If you already have ToolServer on your Macintosh, make sure that the file mwcm tool is included in the ToolServer/Tools folder.

Once set up, the Dreamweaver/VSS integration is virtually seamless. Files are checked in and out, just as they would be if VSS were not involved. Dreamweaver performs what SourceSafe sees as an Exclusive file check out; to enable a Multiple Check Out — which allows several people to check out the same file — you must go through VSS. Other VSS administrative features, such as Show History and Differences, must be handled from within SourceSafe by a user with administrator privileges.

Note There are two Dreamweaver site commands that are not accessible with a SourceSafe connection: Synchronize and Select Newer. In order to use these commands, Dreamweaver must know how the local system and remote server relate time-wise — are they in the same time zone or is one behind the other? It's not feasible in the current implementation to get time stamp information from a VSS database and consequently the features that depend on this information are not available.

As noted earlier, the Visual SourceSafe connection is managed through the Site Definition dialog box. To set up VSS connectivity, follow these steps:

1. Choose Site ⇨ Define Sites.

2. From the Define Sites dialog box, choose the site to be connected to the VSS database from the list and select Edit.

3. Select the Remote Info category.

4. From the Access drop-down list, choose SourceSafe Database.

5. Select the Settings button.

   All of the connection information is entered through the displayed Open SourceSafe Database dialog box, shown in Figure 35-4.

Figure 35-4: Visual SourceSafe projects require a user name and password for access.

6. Enter the path and filename of the SourceSafe database in the Database Path field. Alternatively, select Browse to locate the file.

7. Enter the VSS project name in the Project field.

The name of all VSS projects begins with a $/ prefix — for example, $/bigco — and Dreamweaver supplies this prefix in the Project field.

8. Enter your VSS login name in the Username field.

9. Enter your VSS password in the Password field.

10. To circumvent automatic logon to the VSS database when connecting in Dreamweaver — and cause Dreamweaver to prompt you for a password every time — deselect the Save option.

11. Click OK when you're done to close the Open SourceSafe Database dialog box.

12. If you want to automatically check out a file when opening it from the Site window, select the Check Out Files when Opening option.

When this option is enabled, double-clicking a file in the local site File view or selecting it and then choose File ⇨ Open Selection, automatically performs the check out procedure.

13. Click OK to close the Site Definition dialog box.

14. Choose Done to close the Define Sites dialog box.

As mentioned earlier, the procedures for checking out and checking in files are almost identical to those described in the "Checking Files In and Out" section. Simply select the files desired in the Remote files area of the Site window and click the Check Out button or use the menu command, Site ⇨ Check Out.

Note   When Multiple Check Out is enabled, the file view column, Checked Out By, displays a list of names separated by commas.

Similarly, you can check a file back in by choosing the Check In button. There is one difference, however: Dreamweaver gives you an opportunity to attach a comment (which will be written into the VSS database) to a file when it is checked in. To view the comments in Visual SourceSafe, select the file and then choose the Show History button; in the History dialog box, choose Details and check the Comments field of the History Details dialog box.

Caution   There is a known problem with the initial version of Dreamweaver 4 that prevents the local file from being replaced when the Check Out feature is used under Visual SourceSafe integration. This means that, potentially, the file you're working on could be different from the one posted on the remote site. Macromedia plans to release an updater on their support site (www.macromedia.com/support/dreamweaver) to address this problem. Without the updater, Macromedia suggests that you first back up your local file and then delete it. Now, when the remote file is checked out, the posted version is ready to be edited locally.

Communicating with WebDAV

WebDAV — shorthand for Web-based Distributed Authoring and Versioning — is an Internet protocol that allows Web developers to collaborate over the Web itself. Just as Visual SourceSafe allows teams to work together over a network, WebDAV lets developers log in over the Web to work on a common set of files. Normally, the HTTP protocol, the basis for most Internet communication, only permits files to be read. With the WebDAV set of extensions installed, files may also be written to the server. More important, files may also be locked to prevent multiple, simultaneous edits; in other words, files may be checked out for modification and checked in when the update is complete.

New Feature   Dreamweaver 4 supports the WebDAV protocol enabling developers and designers around the world to work together on a single site. The WebDAV setup is, as with VSS, handled through the Remote Info category of the Site Definition dialog box. Once established, the Dreamweaver/WebDAV connection is transparent and the Check In/Check Out features work as they do on a standard FTP or network connection.

Dreamweaver's implementation of WebDAV connectivity is geared toward Microsoft IIS and Apache servers. Both have been fully tested and are supported. WebDAV implementations on other servers may interact erratically, or not at all, with Dreamweaver. For more in-depth information on WebDAV, including a list of publicly available servers, visit www.webdav.org.

To establish a WebDAV connection, follow these steps:

1. Choose Site ➪ Define Sites.

2. From the Define Sites dialog box, choose the site to be connected to the WebDAV server from the list and select Edit.

3. Select the Remote Info category.

4. From the Access drop-down list, choose WebDAV.

5. Select the Settings button.

   All of the connection information is entered through the displayed WebDAV Connection dialog box, shown in Figure 35-5.

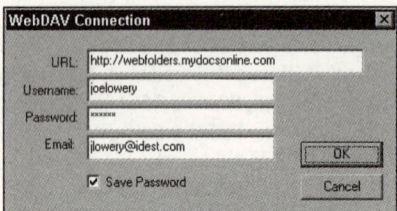

Figure 35-5: Once the WebDAV is enabled, team members can collaborate over the Web itself to develop Web sites.

6. Enter the absolute URL to the WebDAV server in the URL field.

7. Enter your WebDAV login name in the Username field.

8. Enter your WebDAV password in the Password field.

9. Enter your e-mail address in the E-mail field.

   The username and e-mail address will be displayed for checked out files.

10. To circumvent automatic logon to the VSS database when connecting in Dreamweaver — and cause Dreamweaver to prompt you for a password every time — deselect the Save option.

11. Click OK when you're done to close the WebDAV Connection dialog box.

12. If you want to automatically check out a file when opening it from the site window, select the Check Out Files when Opening option.

    When this option is enabled, double-clicking a file in the local site File view or selecting it and then choosing File ➪ Open Selection, automatically performs the check out procedure.

13. Click OK to close the Site Definition dialog box.

14. Choose Done to close the Define Sites dialog box.

To use the WebDAV server, select the Connect button on the Site window toolbar or choose Site ➪ Connect.

Note   WebDAV is a technology that should definitely remain on every Web developer's radar screen whether they are currently involved in a WebDAV project or not. WebDAV technology is the underpinnings for Microsoft's Web Folder feature found in Internet Explorer 5 and above and in Office 2000 products. Furthermore, Macromedia is said to be supporting the WebDAV through their upcoming content management system, code-named Whirlwind.

Keeping Track with Design Notes

When several people are working are on a site, they can't just rely on the Web pages to speak for themselves. In any team collaboration, there is much organizational information that needs to be communicated behind the scenes: Who's working on what areas, what's the status of any given file, when is the project due, what modifications are needed, and so on. Dreamweaver includes a feature called Design Notes that is designed to facilitate team communication in a very flexible manner.

Dreamweaver Design Notes are small files that, in a sense, attach themselves to the Web pages or objects they concern. A Design Note may be attached to any HTML page, graphic, or media file inserted into a page. Design Notes follow their corresponding file whenever that file is moved or renamed using the Dreamweaver Site window; moreover, a Design Note is deleted if the file it is related to is deleted. Design Notes have the same base name as the file to which they are attached — including that file's extension — but are designated with an .mno extension. For example, the Design Note for the file index.html would be called index.html.mno; Design Notes are stored in the _notes subfolder.

Design Notes may be entered and viewed through the Design Notes dialog box as shown in Figure 35-6. The dialog box may optionally be set to appear when a file is opened, thus passing instructions from one team member to another automatically. In addition to the Design Notes dialog box, you can configure File view columns to display Design Note information right in the Site window; the File view columns feature is covered later in this chapter.

Figure 35-6: You can configure a Design Note to pop up whenever a file is opened to alert a fellow team member of work to be done.

Setting up for Design Notes

Design Notes are enabled by default but can be turned off on a site-by-site basis. To disable Design Notes, follow these steps:

1. Choose Site ⇨ Define Sites or select Define Sites from the site listing.

2. In the Define Sites dialog box that opens, select the site you wish to alter and choose Edit.

3. In the Site Definition dialog box, select the Design Notes category (see Figure 35-7).

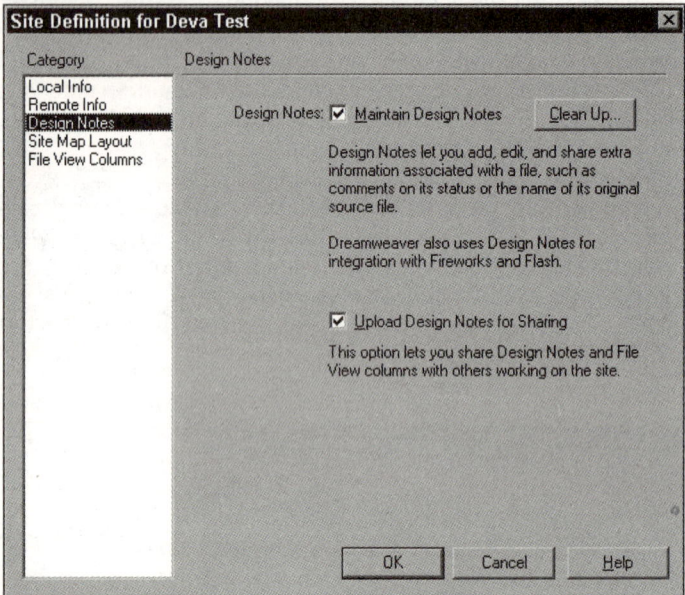

Figure 35-7: Although it's not recommended, it is possible to disable Design Notes through the Site Definition dialog box.

4. Deselect the Maintain Design Notes option to stop Dreamweaver from creating Design Notes completely.

   Dreamweaver alerts you to the consequences of disabling Design Notes. Click OK to continue.

5. If you want to work with Design Notes locally, but don't want to automatically transfer them to the remote site, leave Maintain Design Notes checked and uncheck Upload Design Notes for Sharing.

6. To remove Design Notes that no longer have an associated file —
which can happen if a file is deleted or renamed by a program other than
Dreamweaver — click the Clean Up button. Dreamweaver gives you an
opportunity to confirm the delete operation.

7. Click OK to close the Site Definition dialog box and Done to close the Define
Sites dialog box.

Design Notes really serve two different purposes. From a team perspective they're
invaluable for tracking a project's progress and passing information between team
members. However, Design Notes are also used by Dreamweaver and other Macromedia products, including Fireworks and UltraDev, to pass data between programs
and program commands. For example, Fireworks uses Design Notes to store the
location of a Fireworks source file that is displayed in the Image Property Inspector
when the exported graphic is selected in Dreamweaver.

It's important to realize the dual nature of Design Notes. I strongly recommend —
whether you work on a large team or if you're a "team of one" — that you keep
Design Notes enabled and fully functioning.

Setting the status with Design Notes

What is the one thing a Web site project manager always wants to know? The status
of every page under development: What's still in the planning stages, what has been
drafted, what's made it to beta, and what's ready to go live? An awareness of each
page's status allows the manager to prioritize appropriately and put additional
resources on the development of a page if necessary. It's also helpful for individual
team members working on a page to know how far along that page is.

Design Notes put the Status category front and center for all files. It's the one standard field that is always available and offers eight different values and one custom
value. Entries may be date stamped in the full note area to show a history of revisions, as shown in Figure 35-8. Optionally, you can elect to display the Design Note
the next time the file is opened by anyone.

To enter the status of a file, follow these steps:

1. Choose File ➪ Design Notes to open the Design Notes dialog box.

   To insert a Design Note for an object embedded on a Web page, such as a
   graphic, Flash movie, or other multimedia element, right-click (Control+click)
   the object and then, from the context menu, choose Design Notes.

2. On the Basic Info tab of the Design Notes dialog box, choose from one of
   these standard options from the Status drop-down list: `draft`, `revision1`,
   `revision2`, `revision3`, `alpha`, `beta`, `final`, or `needs attention`.

3. To add today's date (in m/d/yy format, such as 3/7/01) to the Notes field, click
   the Calendar icon.

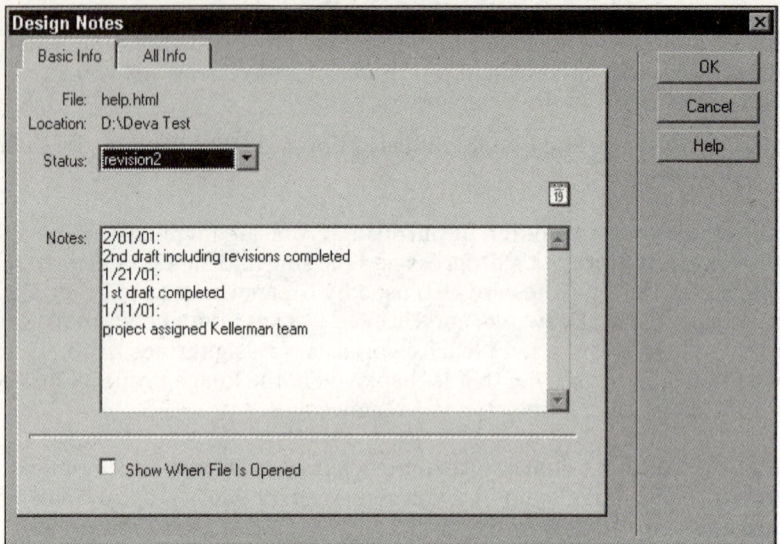

Figure 35-8: Design Notes can maintain a history of revisions for any Web page.

4. Enter any desired text into the Notes field.

   The same Notes text is displayed regardless of which Status option you choose.

5. If you'd like the Design Notes dialog box with the current information to appear the next time the page is loaded, choose the Show When File is Opened option.

   The Show When File is Opened option is only available for Design Notes attached to pages, not for Design Notes attached to page elements such as images.

6. Click OK when you're done.

Creating custom Design Notes

Aside from monitoring the status of a project, a Design Note may be used to describe any single item. The All Info tab of the Design Notes dialog box allows you to enter any number of name/value pairs, which can be viewed in the Design Note itself or — more effectively — in the File view columns. This mechanism might be used to show which graphic artist in your department has primary responsibility for the page or how many billable hours the page has accrued. You can also use the All Info tab to set a custom value for the Status list on the Basic Info tab.

To enter a new name/value pair, follow these steps:

1. Choose File ⇨ Design Notes to open the Design Notes dialog box.

2. Select the All Info tab.

   If a Status and/or Notes entry has been made on the Basic Info tab, you'll see their values listed in the Info area.

3. Choose the Add button (plus sign) to start a new name/value pair.

4. In the Name field, enter the term you wish to use.

5. In the Value field, enter the information you want associated with the current term.

6. To edit an entry, select it from the list in the Info area and alter either the Name or Value field.

7. To delete an entry, select it and press the Remove button (minus sign).

8. Click OK when you're done.

As noted earlier, you can create a custom Status list option in the All Info tab. To do so, just enter status in the Name field of a new name/value pair and enter the desired listing in the Value field. If you switch to the Basic Info tab, you'll find your new Status entry listed as the last item. You can only add one custom Status entry; if you add another it will replace the previous one.

Viewing Design Notes

To fully view a Design Note, you have several choices. You can choose File ⇨ Design Notes to open the dialog box; in Windows, this option is available from either the Document or the Site window. Another possibility is to right-click (Control+click) the file in the File or the Site Map view of the Site window and choose the Design Notes option from the context menu. Finally, if a Design Note is attached to a file, you'll see an icon in the Notes column of the File view as shown in Figure 35-9. Double-clicking the Notes icon will open the Design Note associated with that file.

Browsing File View Columns

While Design Notes can hold a lot of information about a Web page or element, the details are kept out of sight. With an eye toward heightening the visibility of Design Notes data—thus making it more useful—Dreamweaver has tied the columns of the Site window's file view directly to Design Notes. In the previous section, you saw how the Notes column indicated that a Design Note existed for a particular file and now you'll learn how to create custom file view columns to display any value stored in a Design Note.

Design Note icon

Figure 35-9: Get immediate access to previously created Design Notes by double-clicking the icon in the Notes column.

New Feature

With custom columns in the file view, a quick glance at the Site window can reveal which files are completed, which are in revision, and which need attention. Moreover, custom columns may be sorted, just as regular columns, so you could, for instance, easily group all the files with the same due date together or those coded by the same programmer. File view columns—even the built-in ones such as Type and Modified—may be re-aligned, re-ordered, or hidden. Only the Name column may not be altered or moved. With this level of customizability, virtually the entire file view could be reshaped as the one in Figure 35-10 has been.

The six standard columns—Name, Notes, Size, Type, Modified, and Checked Out By—may be supplemented by any number of custom columns. Modification of the column setup is handled in the File View Columns category of the Site Definition dialog box. File views are managed on a per-site basis; when defining the file views, you can determine if the views are to be seen by anyone accessing the development site. Likewise, any custom column may optionally be shared among team members.

Figure 35-10: File view columns can be substantially reorganized to reflect the concerns of your team on a project-by-project basis.

To create a custom file view, follow these steps:

1. Open the File View Columns category with one of these methods:

   • Choose Define Sites and open the Site Definition for the desired site. Then, select the File View Column option from the category list.

   • Select View ➪ File View Columns from the Site window on Windows systems or, on the Macintosh, choose Site ➪ Site Files View ➪ File View Columns.

2. If you'd like team members to see the custom columns you're developing, select Enable Column Sharing.

   You'll also need to choose the Share with All Users of this Site option for each custom column you want to share.

3. To add a custom column, click the Add button.

   A new entry at the end of the list is created.

4. Enter a unique name for the column in the Column Name field.

   If you enter an existing name, Dreamweaver warns you and requires a new name before proceeding.

5. Pick a Design Note field to link to the new column from the Associate with Design Note list.

   You can choose one of the suggested Design Note fields (assigned, due, priority, or status) or you can enter your own. Design Note fields may be upper-, lower-, or mixed-case; multiple words are also allowed.

6. Select an Alignment option from the list: Left, Center, or Right.

   Columns expecting numeric or date values should be aligned to the right.

7. Make sure the Show option is selected.

8. To share this column with fellow team members, choose the Share with All Users of this Site option.

   Selecting this option causes Dreamweaver to create a file called dwSiteColumnsAll.xml within the _notes folder on the Remote Site. When another member of your team connects to the site, Dreamweaver reads this file and incorporates it into that person's site definition. This allows any other user to see the same column set up on their system.

9. Use the Up and Down arrows to reposition the column.

10. To add additional columns, repeat Steps 3 through 9.

11. Click OK when you're done.

How might a team benefit from custom file view columns? Some of the possibilities for custom columns include:

✦ Project Manager   ✦ Date Created

✦ Lead Designer   ✦ Date Due

✦ Lead Programmer   ✦ Percentage Complete

✦ Template Used   ✦ Client Contact

Caution   File view columns are sorted alphabetically even if the values are numeric. For example, if you have three files with the numeric values 100%, 50%, and 10%, an ascending sort displays 10%, 100%, 50%. As a work-around, use decimal values (.10, .50, and 1.00) to represent percentages, and the files will sort correctly. If your columns require date values, use leading zeros in dates, such as 01/03, to ensure that the columns may be properly sorted.

While having the Design Notes information visible in file view columns is extremely helpful for maintaining an overview of a Web site, Dreamweaver takes the feature a step further. Once a custom file column is established, additions and modifications to the Design Note may be handled from the Site window. Click into the custom column of the file; the existing information, if any, is highlighted and can be altered. If there is no data in the column, the column becomes editable.

Note Although the Design Note is actually a separate file, you cannot change file view columns for a locked file. One solution is to turn off read-only temporarily by right-clicking (Control-clicking) the file and choosing Unlock, then add the file view info and relock if necessary.

Generating Reports

While custom file view columns can present a tremendous degree of detail, the data is only viewable from the Site window. Often managers and team members need to abstract certain bits of information about a site to know where they stand and fix problems in an organized, timely fashion. Some Webmasters use third-party utilities to comb their sites and generate lists of errors that can then be assigned to be resolved. Such utilities may also be used to establish workflow patterns as they gather information, such as which pages have yet to be completed or who is currently working on what site elements.

New Feature Dreamweaver Reports, introduced in version 4, give the Webmaster and team members a new tool for efficiently building Web sites. The information from a Dreamweaver Report may be instantly used — double-clicking on any report detail opens the referenced file — or stored as an XML file for later output. Dreamweaver 4 includes seven standard reports that may be generated individually or combined into one. As with many Dreamweaver features, the Reports command is extensible allowing custom reports to be built.

How do Dreamweaver Reports work? The user must first choose from a variety of scopes: the current document, selected files in the site, all the files in a particular folder, or the entire site. Once the scope has been selected, the report elements — what the report will actually cover — are selected. The report is then run and Dreamweaver outputs the results into a floating panel, as shown in Figure 35-11. Each entry in the Results panel is capable of opening the listed file; in the case of reports querying the underlying HTML, the entries lead directly to the referenced code.

Generated reports may also be saved for later use. The reports are saved in an XML file format that can be imported into a Web page, database, or spreadsheet program. Although this information could be extracted by hand, the structured format of the XML file makes it a perfect candidate for an automated process handled by an extension or other utility.

On the CD-ROM An extension, Import Report, by Dreamweaver engineer Tim Christensen that converts saved Dreamweaver Reports to a Web page is available on the CD-ROM in the Additional Extensions section.

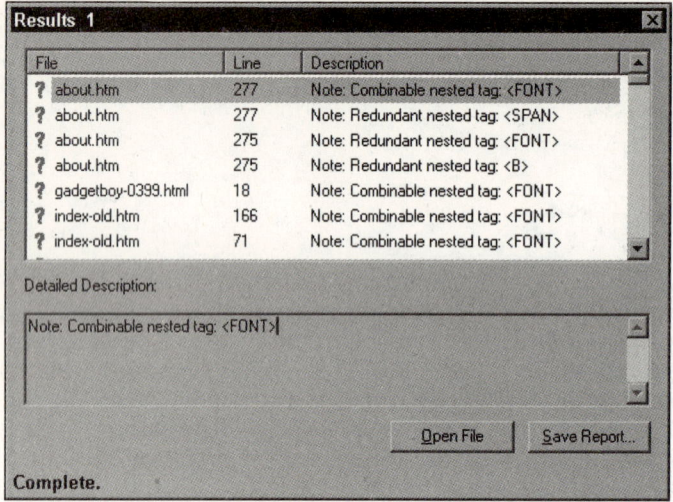

Figure 35-11: Dreamweaver Reports return interactive results — just double-click on any listed entry to open the related file.

There are two different types of Dreamweaver Reports: those concerned with the code in the pages themselves and those accessing workflow details. Choosing Site ⇨ Reports displays the available reports in both categories.

To access a Dreamweaver Report, follow these steps:

1. Choose Site ⇨ Reports. Windows users may choose the command from either the Document or the Site window menus.

Caution

If run from the Site window, the Results dialog box appears behind the Site window and is not immediately obvious; select the Document window to see the Results dialog box. If no Document window is open, you need to open a new or existing file to view the Results dialog box.

2. From the Reports dialog box (see Figure 35-12), choose the scope of the report from the Report On drop-down list.

   Dreamweaver remembers the Report On setting each time you run this command.

3. Select which reports you'd like to include from either the Workflow or the HTML Reports categories.

4. If you choose an option from the Workflow category, the Report Settings button activates. Select it to define the report search.

   The Report Settings options are covered in detail later in this section under "Workflow Reports."

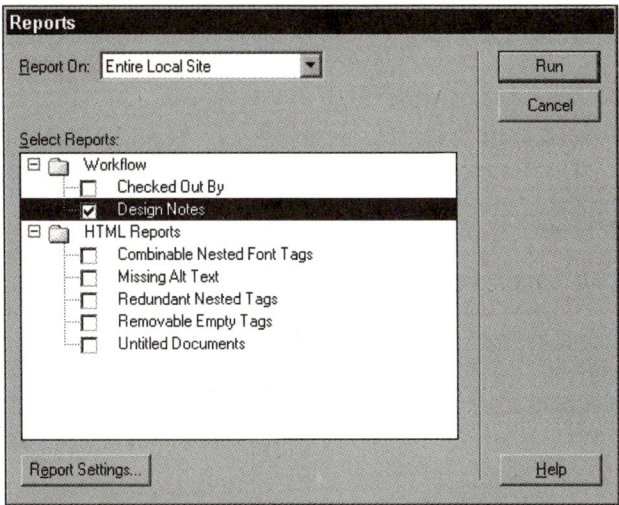

Figure 35-12: The Design Notes report uses the search criteria established in the Report Settings dialog box.

5. Click the Run button.

The Results dialog box appears. As the report is processed, results are listed in the upper window.

6. From the Results dialog box, you can choose the Stop icon to halt the report.

7. To open any referenced file, double-click the entry or select the entry and choose Open File.

8. To store the report as an XML file, choose Save Report and enter a file and path in the Save File dialog box.

9. To close the Results dialog box, click the Close icon in the top-right corner on Windows or the top left on the Mac.

The Results dialog box is a floating window that may remain open as you work.

Entries in the Results dialog box are initially sorted by filename in an ascending order; however, selecting any column heading (File, Line, or Description) re-sorts the list accordingly. If many result listings are returned, the Results dialog box may be resized to display more of them.

Outputting HTML reports

Dreamweaver includes five options under the HTML Reports category:

✦ **Combinable Nested Font Tags:** This query looks for code where the font tag has been applied to the same text at different times as in this example:

```
<font color="#000000"><font size=+1>Monday, December 15th
@7pm</font></font>
```

✦ **Missing Alt Text:** This report searches for `<img>` tags where the `alt` attribute is empty or missing entirely. To comply with accessibility guidelines established by the W3C, all images should have `alt` attributes that describe the graphic.

✦ **Redundant Nested Tags:** This report identifies tags nested within themselves. For example,

```
<b><b>On Sale!</b></b>
```

✦ **Removable Empty Tags:** This search finds nonempty tags (i.e., tags with both an opening and closing element) with no content as in this code:

```
<div align="center"> </div>
```

✦ **Untitled Documents:** This report looks for pages that have no title or use the default "Untitled Document" text.

You can run any or all of the HTML Reports at once — just select the desired one(s) from the Reports dialog box. The Results dialog box lists the name of the file, the line number where the search condition was found, and an error message for each entry; selecting a file displays the error message with additional detail, if available, in the Detailed Description area. Choosing Open File or double-clicking on an entry loads the file, if possible; if the file is currently locked, Dreamweaver asks if you'd like to view the read-only file or unlock it. All HTML Report files are displayed in the split-screen Code and Design View.

Using Workflow reports

Workflow Reports, unlike HTML Reports, don't examine the code of Web pages, they look at the meta-data — the information about the information — of a site. There are two standard reports available under the Workflow heading:

✦ **Checked Out By:** This report displays any file checked out by a particular person as designated in the Report Settings dialog box. If nothing is entered in the Settings dialog box, a list of all files in the selected scope that have been checked out by anyone is returned.

Caution   To run this report, you must be able to connect to your Remote site.

✦ **Design Notes:** This report examines the designated files according to search criteria set up in the Report Settings dialog box, shown in Figure 35-12. Searches may be conducted on up to three criteria. If no criterion is entered, a list of all files with Design Notes in the selected scope is returned.

The Report Settings dialog box for the Design Notes reports is fairly flexible as it enables "and" type searches. To use the Design Notes Report Settings dialog box, follow these steps:

1. In the Reports dialog box, select the Design Notes option under the Workflow category.

   The Report Settings button is made available.

2. Select Report Settings.

   The Report Settings dialog box opens; the previous Design Notes Settings are restored.

3. In the Report Settings dialog box, enter the name of the Design Notes field in the first column.

   The name of the Design Notes field is case-sensitive: In other words, entering `Status` in the Report Settings dialog box will not match `status` in the Design Note.

4. Choose a criteria type from the middle column drop-down list. The choices are: `contains`, `does not contain`, `is`, `is not`, and `matches regex`.

Cross-Reference

The final criteria type, `matches regex`, **enables regular expression pattern matching. For a full discussion of Regular Expressions in Dreamweaver, see Chapter 9.**

5. In the third column enter the value of the Design Notes field being sought.

   As with the Design Notes field, the value search is also case-sensitive.

6. To add a second or third condition to the query, repeat Steps 3 through 5 in the second and third line of the Report Settings dialog box.

   Additional conditionals are applied in an "and" type search. For example, settings where the first line reads:

   `status is revision3`

   and the second line reads

   `done is 1.00`

   will return all Design Notes where both conditions are true. Currently, there is no way to perform an "or" type search.

7. Click OK when you're done.

8. Choose Run to execute the search.

Of all the criteria options — is, is not, contains, and so on — available in the Report Settings dialog box for Design Notes, the most powerful is `matches regex`. **Regular Expressions are a pattern matching mechanism and, as such, are extremely flexible. The syntax, however, is quite unique and requires a bit of use before it becomes second nature. Here are some examples you might find useful:**

Regular Expression	Matches
`.*`	Any text
`[^.]`	An empty string
`\d`	Any single number
`[0-5]`	Any digit from 0 to 5
`graphics|code`	Either the word `graphics` **or the word** `code`

Summary

The expression "many hands make light work" certainly applies to Web site production and maintenance — but without some type of authoring management, the "many hands" may soon create a disaster. Dreamweaver offers both built-in and industry-standard authoring management solutions to aid in the development of Web sites. In addition to the precautions against overwriting files, Dreamweaver includes several other key features to help with team communication and to keep those many hands working together. To get the most out of Dreamweaver for your team, keep these thoughts in mind:

✦ For Dreamweaver's standard Check In/Check Out feature to be effective, everybody on the team must have the system engaged and in use for all file transfers.

✦ Dreamweaver can tie into existing development projects through the Visual SourceSafe integration or the WebDAV standard support.

✦ Meta-data — information about the information — about the project can be tied to any Web page or Web object through Dreamweaver's Design Notes feature. Again, to get the most out of this feature, it is key for all team members to use Dreamweaver's Site window to manage their files.

✦ Dreamweaver includes interactive Report capabilities that enable team members to quickly check the status of various HTML and workflow conditions, which can, if necessary, enable them to open the file directly for repair.

✦   ✦   ✦

What's on the CD-ROM?

The CD-ROM that accompanies *Dreamweaver 4 Bible* contains the following:

◆ Fully functioning trial versions of Dreamweaver 4, Fireworks 4, and Flash 5

◆ Code examples used in the book

Also included are hundreds of Dreamweaver extensions designed to make your work more productive, from the leaders in the Dreamweaver community:

◆ Behaviors

◆ Objects

◆ Commands

◆ Browser profiles

◆ Inspectors

◆ Floaters

Using the Accompanying CD-ROM

The CD-ROM is what is known as a *hybrid CD-ROM*, which means it contains files that run on more than one computer platform — in this case, both Windows and Macintosh computers.

Several files, primarily the Macromedia trial programs and the other external programs, are compressed. Double-click these files to begin the installation procedure. Most other files on the CD-ROM are uncompressed and you can simply copy them to your system by using your file manager. A few of the Dreamweaver extensions with files that must be placed in different folders are also compressed.

In the Configuration folder, the file structure replicates the structure that Dreamweaver sets up when it is installed. For example, objects found in the Dreamweaver\Configuration\Objects folder should be in that location for both the CD-ROM, and the installed program. One slight variation: In the Additional Extensions folder, you'll find the various behaviors, objects, and so on, filed under their author's name.

Files and Programs on the CD-ROM

The *Dreamweaver 4 Bible* contains a host of programs and auxiliary files to assist your exploration of Dreamweaver, as well as your Web page design work in general. The following is a description of the files and programs on the CD-ROM that comes with this book.

Macromedia demos

If you haven't had a chance to work with Dreamweaver (or Fireworks or Flash), the CD-ROM offers fully functioning trial versions of three key Macromedia programs for both Macintosh and Windows systems. Each of the demos will run for 30 days; they cannot be reinstalled in order to gain additional time. The three trial programs are:

✦ Dreamweaver 4

✦ Fireworks 4

✦ Flash 5

To install any of the programs, just double-click the program icon in the main folder of the CD-ROM where the program is located and follow the installation instructions on your screen.

Caution   The trial versions of Macromedia programs are very sensitive to system date changes. If you alter your computer's date, the programs will time-out and no longer function. It is a good idea to check your system's date and time before installing them. Moreover, if you've previously run the trial version of the same program from another source (such as downloading it from the Internet), you won't be able to run the trial version again.

Dreamweaver extensions

Dreamweaver is amazingly extendible, and the Dreamweaver community has built some amazing extensions. In the Additional Extensions folders of the CD-ROM, you'll find hundreds of behaviors, objects, commands, inspectors, and more. The extensions are grouped according to author, and within each author's folder they are organized by function. Almost all of these extensions were written prior to the availability of the Extension Manager and do not require that program for installation. Extensions that contain files that must be placed in different folders, such as the Commands and Inspectors directories, are compressed in a Zip format.

Note Within the Additional Extensions folder, all behaviors are stored in the Behaviors folder to make it easy to access them. When installing, make sure to put them in the Configuration\Behaviors\Action folder on your system and not just the Behaviors folder.

You'll find a ReadMe.htm file in each author's folder, with links to the author's Web site and more information about their creations.

Following is a partial list of extension authors featured on the CD-ROM (alphabetized by first word to match how you'll see them on the disc):

- ✦ Andrew Wooldridge
- ✦ Brendan Dawes
- ✦ Eddie Traversa
- ✦ Fantastic Corporation
- ✦ Jaro von Flocken
- ✦ Lucas Lopatin
- ✦ Machax FX
- ✦ Olle Karneman
- ✦ Project Seven Development
- ✦ Robert Sherman — SnR Graphics
- ✦ Simon White — Derren Whiteman
- ✦ Stefan vanAs
- ✦ Webmonkey

Dreamweaver Bible extensions

The majority of the following extensions were built specifically for this book. You can find these extensions in the Configuration folder on the CD-ROM.

Note   Where available, extensions are packaged in an .mxp file that can easily be installed using the Extension Manager. To run the Extension Manager from Dreamweaver, choose Commands ⇨ Manage Extensions. Then choose File ⇨ Install Extension, and browse to the location of the extension's .mxp file. Other extensions need to be installed by copying the required files to your Dreamweaver\Configuration folder as described below.

Behaviors

Dreamweaver behaviors automate many functions that previously required extensive JavaScript programming. The behaviors included on the CD-ROM are in addition to the standard set of behaviors included with Dreamweaver and discussed in Chapter 19. The behaviors on the CD-ROM are stored in the Configuration\Behaviors\Actions folder. Copy the behaviors to the similarly named folder in your system installation of Dreamweaver, and restart Dreamweaver to access the new behaviors.

Objects

Much of Dreamweaver's power is derived from its extensibility. Each of the standard Dreamweaver objects is based on an HTML file. The CD-ROM contains various Dreamweaver objects designed to help you create your Web pages faster and more efficiently.

Each Dreamweaver object consists of two files, an HTML file and a GIF file with the same name that is used to create the button on the Objects Palette. For example, the Character Entities object comprises the two files char_entities.htm and char_entities.gif.

To install the Dreamweaver objects, go to Dreamweaver\Configuration\Objects and copy any pair of files from the subfolders Common, Forms, Media, and New to similarly named folders in your system installation of Dreamweaver. (The Media and New folders are not included in the standard release of Dreamweaver and must be created on your system.) Restart Dreamweaver to access the new objects.

Commands

Commands are proving to be the real workhorses of Dreamweaver extensibility. Not only can they do pretty much everything that behaviors and objects do, but they also have their own capabilities as well. Command files come in many shapes and sizes—from a single file to five or more files split across multiple folders. The commands found in the Configuration\Commands folder on the CD-ROM go into the equivalent Dreamweaver folder on your system. The commands are as follows:

✦ **Repeat History:** Repeats any selected actions in the History palette any number of times. This command requires the Extension Manager to install.

✦ **Replicator:** Duplicates any selected object, any number of times. Be sure to copy both Replicator.htm and Replicator.js into the Commands folder.

✦ **Install Shockwave HTML:** Reads an HTML file generated by Director to insert a Shockwave object, complete with proper dimensions and other needed parameters.

✦ **Change Case:** Converts the case of the selected text to uppercase or lowercase.

Browser profiles

Dreamweaver recognizes the proliferation of browsers on the market today and makes it easy for you to check your Web page creations against specific browser types. The browser targeting capability is available through the use of browser profiles, covered in Chapter 34. In addition to the standard profiles that come with Dreamweaver, the CD-ROM contains several browser profiles for checking various implementations of HTML, including the following:

✦ HTML 2.0

✦ HTML 3.0

✦ HTML 4.0

✦ Opera 3.2

✦ Pocket Internet Explorer 1.0 (for Windows CE 1.0)

✦ Pocket Internet Explorer 1.1 (for Windows CE 1.0)

✦ Pocket Internet Explorer 2.0 (for Windows CE 2.0)

Each additional browser profile is contained in the Dreamweaver\Configuration\ BrowserProfiles folder of the CD-ROM. To install the browser profiles, the files must be copied to a similarly named folder in your system installation of Dreamweaver. Restart Dreamweaver to access the new browser profiles.

Dreamweaver 4 Bible code examples

You can find the example code listed by chapter number used in the *Dreamweaver 4 Bible* Code folder of the CD-ROM. Also included and of particular note are the Dreamweaver Techniques from various chapters throughout the book. Each technique contains all the requisite example HTML files and graphics files within its own folder. You can easily view the files through Dreamweaver or your browser without transferring the files to your system. If you do wish to transfer the files, copy the entire folder over to your system.

Dreamweaver style sheets

Dreamweaver makes using Cascading Style Sheets (CSS) a point-and-click operation. One of the great features of CSS is the capability to link your Web site to external style sheets. The CD-ROM contains several external style sheets that you can customize for your Web sites. Each external style sheet comes with an example HTML file that you can view in your browser.

To incorporate the external style sheets in your Web sites, copy files with .css extension into your local site's root folder. Then follow the instructions in the section "External Style Sheets" in Chapter 27.

Dreamweaver examples

One of the best ways to begin working in Web design is to customize another's designs. The CD-ROM includes several Web page examples aimed at giving you a running start in creating your own pages. Each example is found in its own sub-folder in the Dreamweaver Bible Code\Examples folder. You can use these examples from within Dreamweaver by opening them directly from the CD-ROM by using the File ➪ Open command, or by transferring the files to your system and opening them from there.

Online learning

What better place to learn an Internet technology than online? eHandsOn is an online learning company that brings students together with the Web's leading experts. It specializes in media-rich content delivered by industry experts. eHandsOn was founded by Lisa Lopuck, a professional Web graphics designer and instructor. On the CD, go to Software: eHandsOn: eHandsOn.html. When you scroll to the bottom, you'll see "visit ehandon.com to learn more about our expert courses and take your free trial. Begin learning today!" Click on the link and register for the free course.

Web resource directory

The World Wide Web is a vital resource for any Web designer, whether a seasoned professional or a beginner. The CD-ROM contains an HTML page with a series of links to resources on the Web; the series contains general as well as Dreamweaver-specific references.

Dreamweaver 4 Bible in PDF Format

Can't find the exact reference that you know you read earlier? Search for it in the *Dreamweaver 4 Bible* in PDF format located on the CD-ROM. You'll need Adobe

Acrobat Reader to view the PDF files; if you don't have it installed on your system, you'll find it on the CD-ROM also.

✦　　✦　　✦

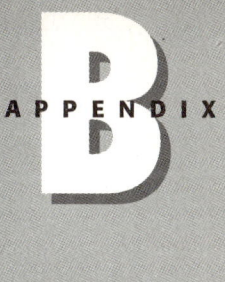

BBEdit 6.0.2 Primer (for Macintosh Users)

Creating great-looking Web sites is easy thanks to Dreamweaver's visual layout interface. Even so, sometimes it's helpful to switch from Dreamweaver's visual editing mode, called Design view, to edit the underlying HTML (Hypertext Markup Language) source code — particularly when you're troubleshooting HTML documents.

Dreamweaver's new Code view makes the task of getting under the hood, to the raw source of your page, much easier than simply using the Code Inspector. Even with this new, robust code editing mode available, there will always be those people who prefer a standalone, dedicated code editor. In these situations, Macintosh users can always rely on BBEdit from Bare Bones Software (www.barebones.com or www.bbedit.com). A trial version of this standalone editor is included on the CD-ROM that accompanies the full version of Dreamweaver.

BBEdit 6.0.2 is the most recent version of this popular Macintosh programmer's text editor. In recent years, the program has evolved into a feature-packed, text-based, pre-Web HTML editor that elegantly exploits the ease-of-use capabilities of the Mac OS. BBEdit is the choice of many Webprofessionals.

This appendix is written as a basic beginner's guide to BBEdit. The software has myriad features and capabilities; some of BBEdit's more advanced features are not covered here.

Note The trial version of BBEdit included on the CD-ROM is fully functional; however, you can launch it only 24 times. After that, you can either upgrade to the full version of BBEdit, by visiting its Web site, or you can use BBEdit Lite, also available there.

If you plan on using BBEdit with Dreamweaver, then you should be sure to install the BBEdit 6.0.2 update as there are known issues that it corrects. This patch can be downloaded from the BBEdit Web site and it is also included on the Dreamweaver 4 CD-ROM. You cannot apply the patch to the BBEdit 6.0 demo, only to the full version.

Getting Started

You can easily switch between Dreamweaver and BBEdit. A simple click of a button, or a quick keystroke, toggles you from one application to the other. Elements selected in one application are automatically highlighted in the other. This capability makes it easy to find your place in the code, and modifications can be made quickly.

Key features

BBEdit is wonderfully full-featured and adaptable to your style of working. Just a few of BBEdit's many advantages are

- ✦ HTML syntax checking
- ✦ Multiple layers of Undo and Redo
- ✦ Spell-checking
- ✦ Multiple-file Search and Replace
- ✦ Multiple clipboards for easier copying and pasting
- ✦ Support for files up to 2GB
- ✦ A file comparison feature for locating differences among files
- ✦ HTML syntax coloring
- ✦ "Open from" and "Save to" FTP servers from the File menu
- ✦ Table builder
- ✦ Web-safe color palette
- ✦ One-click preview in any browser
- ✦ Support for Unicode (UTF-8 and UTF-16) files
- ✦ Scriptable, recordable, and attachable OSA support

BBEdit installation

BBEdit 6.0.2, like Dreamweaver, runs on Power Macintoshes and compatible computers. Install BBEdit by launching the BBEdit Demo application on the CD-ROM supplied with the full version of Dreamweaver.

BBEdit creates several special folders during the installation process that provide additional functionality. These folders can be removed if you don't need their features. The folders listed in Table B-1 are created within a folder called BBEdit Support, located in the main BBEdit 6.0.2 folder.

Table B-1
Folders Within BBEdit Support

Folder	Contents
Dictionaries	Dictionaries used by BBEdit's Spell Checker. The User Dictionary stores words you add to this personal dictionary. See the section "Spell-checking," later in this appendix, for more information.
Glossary	Text files that can be inserted into an active editing window. Simply add text files to the folder and then use the Glossary command in the Windows menu to insert the contents of a text file.
Help	Contains all of the Apple Guide help files that are called from BBEdit's Help menu.
HTML Templates	Example templates and files to be used.
Language Modules	Contains plug-ins to tell BBEdit about programming, scripting, and markup languages. This allows for correct coloring and status bar pop-ups.
MacPerl Support	Support files for MacPerl, a CGI language.
Plug-Ins	Modules that offer additional BBEdit features written and contributed by BBEdit users.
Scripts	AppleScripts ready for execution through the Scripts menu, represented by a script icon, located just to the left of the Help menu.
Search Scripts	Contains compiled OSA scripts, which return a list of files. These are listed in the Find dialog box's pop-up.
Shutdown Items	Contains scripts that are run when you exit BBEdit.
Startup Items	On launch, BBEdit opens items in this folder, such as text files and scripts. Aliases to applications, such as Web browsers or WYSIWYG editors, may also be here and BBEdit will ask the Finder to launch them.
Stationary	Macintosh stationary files are stored here so that new documents can be opened based on any of these files.
ToolServer Tools	Support files for the ToolServer integration.

Working with Dreamweaver and BBEdit

Although Dreamweaver 4 enables you to assign any HTML editor as your external editor, Dreamweaver integrates optimally with BBEdit. Once you set up BBEdit as your default editor, switching between the two editors is just a button click or keyboard shortcut away.

Setting up BBEdit as your default editor

Before Dreamweaver can access BBEdit, you must make BBEdit your default HTML editor. You can make this assignment through the Dreamweaver Preferences by following these steps:

1. In Dreamweaver, choose Edit ⇨ Preferences, or use the keyboard shortcut Command+U, to open the Preferences dialog box.

2. From the Category list on the left, choose File Types / Editors to display that panel.

3. In the File Types / Editors panel, use the Browse (Choose) button next to the External Code Editor field to find BBEdit. Once you pick BBEdit, Dreamweaver offers to enable integration; click Yes and you will be returned to the Preferences dialog box. Notice that BBEdit is now listed as the External Code Editor and that there is a checkmark in the box that says Enable BBEdit Integration. Click OK to close the Preferences dialog box and return to Dreamweaver. The Edit menu option changes from Launch External Editor to Edit with BBEdit.

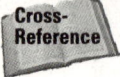

The External Code Editor options that control file synchronization between Dreamweaver and BBEdit are explained in Chapter 4.

Switching between Dreamweaver and BBEdit

You have several ways to switch to BBEdit while in Dreamweaver:

- ✦ Use the Finder.
- ✦ Choose Edit ⇨ Edit with BBEdit.
- ✦ Use the keyboard shortcut, Command+E.

Depending on the file reloading options chosen in the File Types / Editors preferences, Dreamweaver may ask if you want to save the file first before you switch to BBEdit. If you do not save your Dreamweaver file, your modifications do not appear in BBEdit, and vice versa. For this reason, you should set your Reload Modified File option to Always.

After you've made your code modifications in BBEdit and you're ready to return to Dreamweaver, just click the Dreamweaver button near the center of BBEdit's HTML Tools palette (see Figure B-1). The section "HTML Tools Palette," later in this appendix, provides more information about this window.

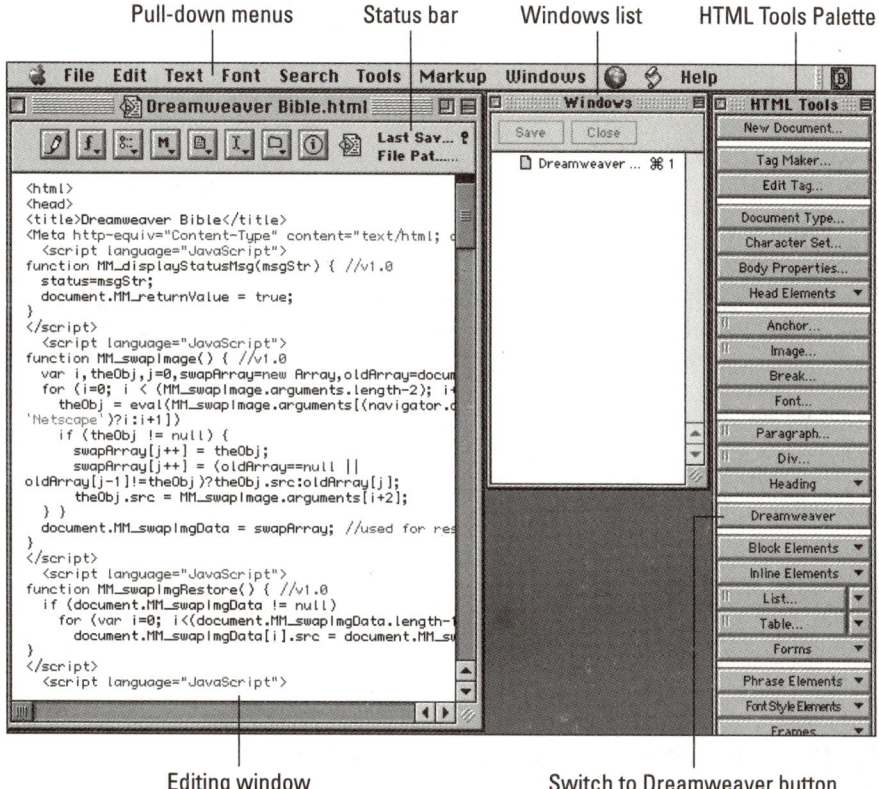

Figure B-1: BBEdit's interface puts everything you need right where you can easily get to it.

Disabling BBEdit integration

You may disable BBEdit integration if you prefer working with an older version of BBEdit or if you use a different HTML text editor. Follow these steps:

1. Choose Edit ➪ Preferences.

2. Select File Types / Editors from the category list on the left.

3. Deselect the Enable BBEdit Integration option and click OK.

4. If you like, you can now choose a different HTML editor.

Note Text selections are not tracked if integration is turned off.

BBEdit menus

BBEdit is chock-full of features and has the menus to prove it. Here's an overview of their structure:

Dynamic menus: BBEdit uses an advanced menu system called *dynamic menus*. This system uses the Shift or Option keys to alter menu options while a menu is open.

Keyboard shortcuts: Many of BBEdit's commands have keyboard equivalents. Pull-down menus show keyboard shortcuts. To see the keyboard equivalents for options in a dialog box, hold down the Command key. After a brief delay, the keyboard equivalents appear next to the buttons in the dialog box.

Set Menu Keys: For those menu items that don't have keyboard shortcuts, or if you are accustomed to using a different keystroke for the same function in another program, you have the Set Menu Keys option on the Edit menu. This allows you to change the existing keyboard shortcuts, or to add shortcuts to menu items that don't already have them.

BBEdit preferences

BBEdit offers a wealth of options for customizing the application to meet your needs. Use the Edit pull-down menu to select Preferences. A dialog box appears with several categories of options listed on the left side. When you select a category, a short description of the category is displayed at the top of the dialog box. Figure B-2 displays BBEdit's Editor Defaults in the Preferences.

Getting Help

BBEdit provides assistance with its functions with the Help pull-down menu. You can choose the BBEdit Guide to show a window that offers Help by topic, through an index, or via searching. This choice activates the Apple Guide-style interactive Help in BBEdit. Use the Show Balloons option to display the functions of many buttons and features as you move your mouse over various parts of BBEdit windows. To open the manuals in the BBEdit Documentation folder, the Adobe Acrobat Reader must be installed on your machine.

HTML Document Basics

Once the BBEdit software is installed, you're ready to author HTML documents destined to become great-looking Web pages. This section explains the basics of creating, saving, and opening BBEdit documents.

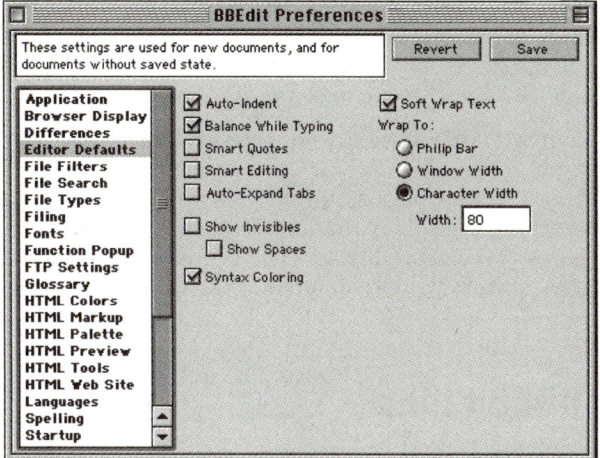

Figure B-2: BBEdit's Preferences dialog box showing the Editor Defaults category

Creating and saving new documents

Use the File menu to select New; then follow the pointer to the submenu. The most common options are Text Document and HTML Document.

Text Document

This command opens an empty text file with two suboptions:

✦ **With Selection:** Creates a new document containing text selected in another currently open BBEdit document. This is handy for quickly producing multiple pages that have common elements, such as a sitewide menu or background image.

✦ **With Clipboard:** Creates a new document containing text copied into the Mac OS clipboard. The text could originate from any application.

HTML Document

Choose HTML Document, and you get a dialog box with options for creating a new HTML-formatted document. This option automatically places the HTML tags you need to begin building a page. This is the best option if you're starting a document from scratch.

Saving your work

When you're ready to save your newly created document, choose File ➪ Save and BBEdit opens a standard Mac OS dialog box. Give the document a name and choose the location where you wish to save the document. At the bottom of this dialog box are two checkboxes offering you these choices:

+ **Save As Stationery:** Saves the document as a Mac OS stationery document. Later, when you open this document, BBEdit uses it as a template for a new untitled document. This option is useful for creating multiple Web pages with common elements, such as a sitewide menu or background image.

+ **Save Selection Only:** Instructs BBEdit to save only the selected text.

To the right of these checkboxes is the Options button. This button opens another dialog box that gives you control over the way that many of the file's attributes will be saved. Some of the attributes you can modify are the Macintosh creator code and whether the file will be saved with Macintosh, UNIX, DOS, or Unicode line breaks.

Opening existing BBEdit files

You have four ways to open existing BBEdit documents:

+ Drag a file's icon to the BBEdit application icon, or to an alias of the icon. You can place the alias on your desktop for easy access. This option takes advantage of the Mac OS drag-and-drop feature and works for any document with a file type of TEXT.

+ Simply double-click a BBEdit file. You can identify BBEdit documents by the associated BBEdit icon.

+ With BBEdit launched, use the Open or Open Recent commands from the File menu.

+ With BBEdit launched, and the Window List open, drag a file from the Finder and drop it on an empty portion of the Window List floater.

Let's take a look at these File ⇨ Open commands.

File ⇨ Open

When you select Open from the File pull-down menu, a dialog box gives you the following options:

+ **Open Read Only:** This command opens the file so it can be viewed but not edited. To make a file editable, simply click the pencil icon in the status bar located at the top of each BBEdit document. (For a description of the status bar, see the section "Editing Documents," later in this appendix.)

+ **LF Translation:** Translates DOS or UNIX line breaks when you open a file. If this option is not selected, BBEdit leaves the original line breaks untranslated. If your preferred line endings are set to UNIX, then the preceding option translates Mac endings to UNIX as well.

+ **File Types:** A pop-up menu enables you to select types of files to open. When the default file type All Available is chosen, BBEdit uses its built-in translation system to open any files it can translate.

If you want to open multiple files, you can do that right from the standard Open dialog box by holding down Shift while you select the documents to open. If you accidentally select a file, or change your mind after selecting it, simply click it again to deselect it.

File ➪ Open Recent

The Open Recent menu contains a list of files recently opened. To open one of these files, simply choose it from the submenu.

Using file groups

BBEdit enables you to group files in a way that makes managing your Web site easier. You may want to group all the files that make up your Web site or divide them into logical subsections that make sense to you.

A *file group* is a special BBEdit file that references other files in the file group. Any type of file can be included in a file group.

To start a file group, select File ➪ New ➪ File Group. BBEdit opens a new empty file group (see Figure B-3).

Figure B-3: An empty file group window

To add files to a file group, simply drag any file or folder from the Finder into the file group window (shown previously in Figure B-3). Alternatively you can click the Add Files or Add Folder button to open a dialog box (Figure B-4) that enables you to actually navigate through your hard drive to select files or folders.

Figure B-4: Clicking Add Folder opens the Add Folder to Group dialog box.

To open a file within a file group, double-click the file. Or you can select the file and click the Open button.

Note If the file is a BBEdit document, then BBEdit opens it. If the file is not a BBEdit document, then the application that created the file is launched.

Editing Documents

This section guides you through BBEdit's menus, windows, and functions.

Basic text manipulation

BBEdit handles text in a way similar to many Macintosh text editors and word processors. Characters typed in BBEdit appear at the blinking vertical insertion point. The insertion point is controlled by placing the mouse in the desired location and clicking.

Click and drag the mouse to select several characters or words. If you select some text and then type, the new entry replaces the selected text. Use the Delete key to remove selected text.

Moving text

To easily move text from one location to another, follow these steps:

1. With the mouse, select the text you want to move.

Tip If you wish to select all the text within a document choose Edit ⇨ Select All or press Command+A.

2. Choose Edit ⇨ Cut (Command+X) to remove the text from the window and store it in the Mac OS clipboard.

3. Find the place where you wish to move the text and click your mouse at the insertion point.

4. Choose Edit ⇨ Paste (Command+V) to place your text.

To copy text into the clipboard without deleting it from its original location, select Copy from the Edit pull-down menu (Command+C).

Dragging and dropping text

A fast and simple method to move text from one place to another takes advantage of the Mac OS drag-and-drop feature. Follow these steps:

1. Select the desired text.

2. Place the mouse pointer within the selected area.

3. Click and hold down the mouse button.

4. Drag the mouse pointer to the new position for the text.

5. Release the mouse button to drop in the text.

You can also use drag-and-drop to copy text to any other open BBEdit window.

Tip BBEdit enables you to drag and drop a text file from the Finder onto an editing window. Doing so inserts the file's contents where it's dropped.

Undo/Redo

The Edit ➪ Undo command (Command+Z) reverses changes — in chronological order — made to your file. The amount of available memory is the only limit to the number of edits that can be undone.

BBEdit also enables multiple redo's. Choose the Edit ➪ Redo command or use the keyboard shortcut Command+Shift+Z.

Text wrapping

BBEdit wraps text in two ways: *soft wrapping* and *hard wrapping*. You can choose the option that works best for you and have it take effect globally or for just one document.

✦ **Soft wrapping:** Soft wrapping handles text like most word processing software. As the insertion point reaches the limit of the right margin, it automatically moves to the next line. You never need to type a Return at the end of a line unless you are beginning a new paragraph.

✦ **Hard wrapping:** Hard wrapping enables you to type as far as you wish on a single line. You have to enter a Return to end each line in order to begin a new line of text.

To change the text-wrapping option in BBEdit, select Soft Wrap Text from the Window Options pop-up menu in the status bar (see the section "The status bar" coming up). Or you can choose Text Options via the Edit menu and select (or deselect) the Soft Wrap Text option from the dialog box.

What's in the BBEdit windows

Basic operation of BBEdit windows follows the standard Mac OS format. BBEdit offers two extra features: the status bar and the split bar.

The status bar

The status bar (see Figure B-5) resides at the top of each editing window. This bar contains buttons and pop-up menus that help you work with the text in the window. Using the status bar you can save your work, show line numbers, display document information, and more.

Figure B-5: BBEdit's status bar gives you quick access to advanced features and also provides lots of information about your document.

Like the asterisk, also referred to as the "dirty dot," that appears after the filename of an unsaved Dreamweaver document, BBEdit also gives a visual clue as to the saved state of its files. This visual clue comes in the form of a solid black diamond that appears on the left side of the status bar (see Figure B-6). This allows you to easily determine whether or not a document has been modified.

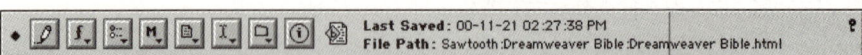

Figure B-6: BBEdit's status bar shows a solid diamond to indicate that the document has not been saved.

Tip   You can toggle the status bar on and off by clicking the Key icon on the right side of the status bar.

The split bar

Each editing window contains a split bar — it's a small black bar located just above the vertical scroll bar. The split bar divides the window into two panes, which is particularly helpful when you're editing a document in two places. Figure B-7 shows an editing window split into two panes.

To split the window, drag the split bar from the top of the vertical scroll bar into the main window area. You can scroll both windows independently. Return to a full window by dragging the split bar to its original location.

Tip   Double-clicking the split bar divides a window into two equal panes or removes the division from a split window.

Markup menu

The Markup pull-down menu and associated HTML Tools palette together offer powerful assistance in designing the layout of your Web pages. In most respects, the Markup menu and the HTML Tools palette function similarly. Following are descriptions of some of the basic Markup menu functions.

Tag Maker command

The Tag Maker command brings up a list of HTML tags or HTML tag attributes that are available for insertion in your file. The command is context-sensitive — that is, the list of tags displayed is specific to the location in your document where your cursor is positioned when you choose this command. Select the desired tag or tag attribute from the list and click Insert to add the tag to your file.

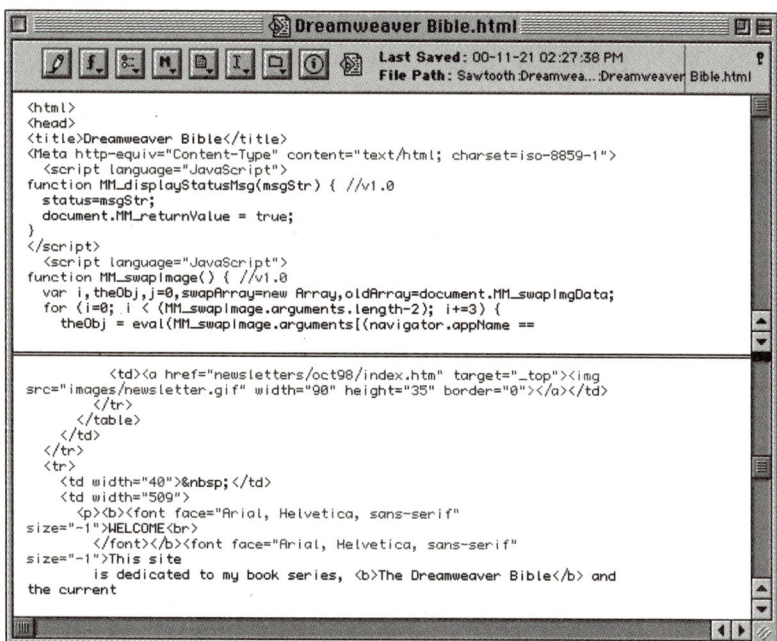

Figure B-7: Use the split bar to divide a window for editing a document in two places.

Edit Tag command

To use the Edit Tag command, your cursor must be located inside an HTML tag in your document. Selecting the Edit Tag command brings up a context-sensitive dialog box that enables you to edit the attributes of that specific tag.

Head Elements menu

The Head Elements menu contains a variety of commands that enable you to set the properties of an entire HTML page. Examples of head elements are `<meta>` and `<title>` tags.

Body Properties command

The Body Properties command enables you to specify a document's background image, background color, and default text and link colors as follows:

- ✦ Select a background graphic by typing the file's name into the Background field or by pressing the File button to bring up a standard Macintosh dialog box.

- ✦ Assign a color for the background, default text, and links by checking the box next to the desired attribute and then selecting a color from the pop-up window of 216 Web-safe colors. Hold down the Option key while clicking a color to access the Apple color picker.

Block Elements menu

Insert HTML block elements, such as `<blockquote>`, `<address>`, and `<pre>`, into your page by accessing this menu.

Heading menu

Use this menu to insert the HTML tags appropriate for heading levels 1 through 6, to distinguish the various titles and subheadings within a page.

Lists menu

This menu enables you to organize lists of textual items, with optional indentation and a choice of bullets. BBEdit supports five list types: Unordered, Ordered, Definition, Menu, and Directory.

Tables menu

Tables are a great way to organize your Web page layout. The Tables menu provides the following table-creation tools:

- ✦ **Table Builder:** Displays the Table Builder utility. If the cursor is currently positioned within a table, the table is first selected.

- ✦ **Table:** Opens a dialog box that enables a variety of table attributes to be specified, including Border, Width, Spacing, Padding, Frame, Rules, Align, Background color, the number of columns, and the number of rows. Inserts a `<table>...</table>` tag pair with the selected attributes, or encloses selected text with the same tag pair.

✦ **Row:** Opens a dialog box that enables a variety of row attributes to be speci-fied, including Align, Valign, and Background color. Inserts a `<tr>...</tr>` tag pair with the selected attributes, or encloses selected text with the same tag pair.

✦ **TD:** Opens a dialog box that enables a variety of table cell attributes to be specified, including Rowspan, Colspan, Width, Height, Align, Valign, and Background color; it also determines whether text wrapping is to be turned on or off. Inserts a `<td>...</td>` tag pair with the selected attributes, or encloses selected text with the same tag pair.

✦ **TH:** Opens a dialog box that enables a variety of table header cell attributes to be specified, including Rowspan, Colspan, Width, Height, Align, Valign, and Background color and determines whether text wrapping is to be turned on or off. Inserts a `<th>...</th>` tag pair with the selected attributes, or encloses selected text with the same tag pair.

✦ **Caption:** Inserts a `<caption>...</caption>` tag pair, or encloses selected text with the same tag pair.

✦ **Convert to Table:** Converts the currently selected text to a table format using the parameters set by the displayed dialog box.

Inline Elements menu

An inline element is one that can be inserted next to another element without requiring a paragraph break. Following are some of the most commonly used tags:

✦ **Anchor:** Inserts an anchor tag with the associated attributes for creating a link or a base anchor.

✦ **Image:** Places a graphic image at the current insertion point. Size attributes are handled automatically for GIF, JPEG, and PNG files.

✦ **Font:** Opens a dialog box that enables the specification of a font face, size, and color for the selected text. Click and hold the color chip to bring up a pull-down menu of Web-safe colors, or hold down the Option key while clicking the color to open the Apple color picker.

Font Style Elements menu

Set the size and style of your font through the Font Style Elements menu. You can also open a separate Font Style palette, which contains all of the Font Style Elements commands, by selecting Font Palette from the Font Style Elements drop-down menu on the HTML Tools palette.

The following font style options are available on this menu:

✦ **Big:** Sets the current text to use the `<big>...</big>` tag pair.

✦ **Small:** Sets the current text to use the `<small>...</small>` tag pair.

✦ **Bold:** Sets the current text to use the `<b>...</b>` tag pair.

✦ **Italic:** Sets the current text to use the `<i>...</i>` tag pair.

✦ **Strike-Through:** Sets the current text to use the `<strike>...</strike>` tag pair.

✦ **Teletype Text:** Sets the current text to use the `<tt>...</tt>` tag pair.

✦ **Underline:** Sets the current text to use the `<ul>...</ul>` tag pair.

Check menu

This set of commands helps you find problems such as bad links and HTML coding errors in your Web documents. Errors are shown in a new window, complete with the line number of the offending HTML code. The Check menu contains the following commands:

✦ **Document Syntax:** Checks the current document for HTML syntax errors. Faulty HTML may work fine when viewed in one browser but display incorrectly when viewed by another, and this command helps you avoid that problem.

Tip

One HTML error can result in the report of multiple subsequent errors. It's best to correct errors from the top of the document and then recheck the document after you correct each error.

✦ **Document Links:** Verifies that documents linked to a file actually exist, to help you identify bad links in your Web site. The command does not verify that these documents exist on your Web server, but rather that the documents exist in your site root folder (as defined in the HTML Preferences section of BBEdit's Preferences). See the section "Internet menu," later in this appendix, for information on checking external Web links.

✦ **Site Syntax:** Similar to the Document Syntax command but checks the syntax of every HTML file in the site root folder.

✦ **Site Links:** Operates like the Document Links command but checks the validity of link references in every HTML file in the site root folder. No attempt is made to validate external links (such as sites on a remote Web server). See the section "Internet menu," later in this appendix, for information on checking external Web links.

✦ **Balance Tags:** Selects the pair of container tags nearest the cursor, highlighting the tags and all the HTML text in between. If you select Balance Tags again, the next pair of tags is selected.

Update menu

This menu replaces all placeholders and includes in the current document (or the current site). See the BBEdit Help system for detailed information on using placeholders and includes.

Utilities menu

The Utilities menu offers a variety of page-oriented tools especially useful for preparing a regular text document for publication on the Web. You can open a separate palette that contains all of the Utilities commands by selecting Utilities Palette from the Utilities pull-down menu in the HTML Tools palette.

The Utilities commands are as follows:

✦ **Format:** Reformats the structure and display of the HTML text. Choose from the following:

- *Hierarchical* — Each set of tags is indented, and tag pairs appear on separate lines.

- *Gentle Hierarchical* — Similar to Hierarchical but anchors within other tags are not indented.

- *Document Skeleton* — Hierarchical style but with everything removed that is not a tag or tag specification (such as all the text). Use this format to create a template.

- *Plain* — Each tag appears on a separate line.

- *Compact* — Deletes any unnecessary whitespace, including tabs, spaces, and carriage returns.

✦ **Optimize:** The Optimize command is similar to the Compact option under the Format command in that it deletes any unnecessary whitespace, but it also removes empty `<font>...</font>` tags, naturalsizeflag attributes, as well as quotes from around tag attributes that don't need them.

✦ **Translate:** Enables a variety of translation options, including conversions between the ISO Latin-1 and Macintosh character set, conversion of 8-bit characters to ASCII equivalents, and conversion of HTML standard characters such as `<` and `>` to character entities (and back). Adds or deletes `<p>` tags to or from paragraphs.

✦ **Remove Comments:** Deletes all commented material from the current page.

✦ **Remove Markup:** Deletes all HTML code from the file, yielding a clean text file.

✦ **Comment:** Surrounds selected text with HTML comment tags.

✦ **Uncomment:** Deletes comment tags from selected text.

✦ **Make Tags Upper Case:** Uppercases all HTML tags. Attribute values, such as filenames and functions, remain the same case.

✦ **Make Tags Lower Case:** Lowercases all HTML tags. Attribute values, such as filenames and functions, remain the same case.

Misc menu

The Misc menu holds a hodgepodge of special-purpose tools, including the following:

+ **Dreamweaver:** Returns current document to Dreamweaver.

+ **Document Size:** Returns the size of the current document and estimated download times over a variety of modems.

+ **Index Document:** Creates an unordered list of all the links and images in every HTML page in the current page. The list appears at the current cursor position.

+ **Index Site:** Creates an unordered list of all the links and images in every HTML page in the current site. Aside from the unordered list, four other predefined index styles are available.

+ **CyberStudio Cleaner:** Fixes problems associated with Web pages created or edited in GoLive CyberStudio.

+ **PageMill Cleaner:** Fixes problems associated with Web pages created or edited in Adobe PageMill, including replacing multiple instances of the `<br>` tag with a single `<p>` tag. Removes the `naturalsize` attribute from image tags and removes empty anchor tags.

Preview menu

This menu loads the active document into the default Web browser defined in the Web Browser section of BBEdit's Preferences.

Preview With menu

This menu enables the selection, from a drop-down menu, of a browser in which to preview the active document. Available browsers can be specified in the Web Browser section of BBEdit's Preferences.

HTML Tools palette

The HTML Tools palette (see Figure B-8) gives you a quick path to the most frequently used functions of BBEdit. You can place this floating palette anywhere on your desktop for easy access.

Several buttons have submenus that appear when you click the button, presenting additional related options. A downward-pointing arrow on the right side of a button indicates a submenu. For example, the Heading button enables the user to select the desired heading level.

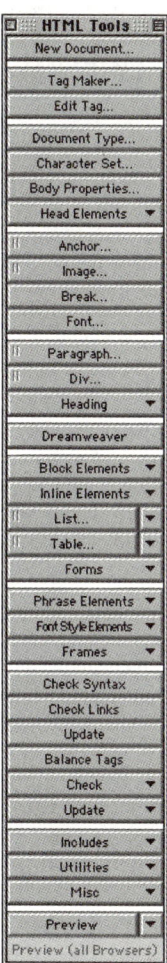

Figure B-8: The HTML Tools palette puts all of your key HTML features in one convenient place, always just a mouse-click away.

A double vertical bar on the left side of some buttons (the grip strip) indicates that the button supports drag-and-drop. For example, you can drag the Table button into a document window to place a table at the insertion point. This action brings up the Table dialog box.

Windows menu

It can get confusing when you have many BBEdit windows open simultaneously. The Windows menu helps you manage the clutter.

The Window List

BBEdit's Window List helps you gain quick access to the files that make up your Web site. A special floating window (see Figure B-9) lists the names of all the open files.

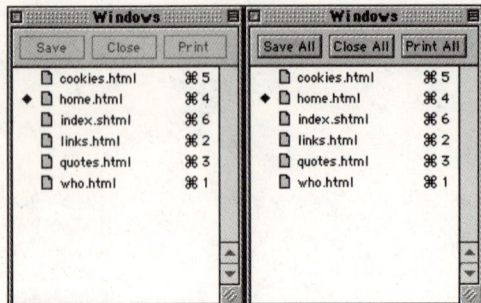

Figure B-9: On the left is BBEdit's standard Window List; on the right is the same Window List with the Option key held down.

To make a window active, simply double-click its name within the Window List or press Command and the number that's listed beside the document. You can open a file from the Finder by dragging it into the Window List. Buttons at the top of the window offer Save, Close, and Print options. The Window List displays the same diamond icon to indicate the modification state of the document (refer to Figure B-6). Here, the document home.html has not been saved.

Use your keyboard's Option key to make the action of any button at the top of the window apply to all the files in the Window List.

HTML Entities

This command displays the HTML Entities dialog box, which enables easy entry of HTML character entities.

Web-Safe Colors

This command displays a palette of 216 browser-safe colors. Drag any color swatch from the palette to the document to insert a color value.

Arrange

BBEdit's Arrange command is a tool for organizing multiple windows in the editor. This is particularly helpful if you're using a small monitor to create your Web pages. When you select Window ⇨ Arrange, you get a dialog box from which to choose an arrangement for the windows.

Get Info

This command displays a dialog box that lists the number of characters, words, lines, and pages in any selected text (as well as the document). This same information is available by clicking the Info button on the status bar.

Reveal in Finder

Reveal in Finder is a handy feature with which you can quickly find a particular file without leaving the BBEdit application. This command opens the Mac OS Finder window that contains the active file.

> **Tip**
>
> Select the text of a filename (for example, index.html) within a document and hold down the Option key while opening the File pull-down menu. Choose the Reveal Selection command to open the Finder folder that contains that file. You can also click once on the document's icon in the status bar for the same effect.

Send to Back

This command places the front window behind all other windows.

Exchange with Next

This command enables you to switch your screen between the front two windows.

Synchro Scrolling

Synchro Scrolling enables multiple files to scroll in unison — the files in all open windows scroll when you scroll just one. This feature is great for comparing two versions of the same file.

Window Names

All the open windows are listed at the bottom of the Windows pull-down menu. Simply select one to make it active.

Internet menu

If your computer is connected to the Internet — and it undoubtedly is — BBEdit offers additional valuable features. In order to use these features, you must you have the Mac OS Internet Control Panel installed in your System folder and configured for your Internet preferences.

The Internet menu is identified by a globe icon in the menu bar. An especially helpful feature of the Internet menu is Resolve URL.

Follow these steps to check the validity of a URL:

1. Make sure you have an active connection to the Internet.

2. Place the insertion point anywhere within the URL.

3. Open the Text menu and choose the Resolve URL command. BBEdit launches your default Web browser. (If the Web browser can't be found, an alert beep sounds.)

4. If the URL is valid, you can view the site in your browser. If it is invalid, your browser displays the standard dialog box indicating that the server could not be found.

Tip You can Command+click anywhere in a URL to resolve it, or you can Control+click to bring up the contextual menu and then choose Resolve URL.

Printing

To print a document, select the Print command from the File menu. A standard Mac OS Print dialog box appears, with a number of advanced BBEdit printing options. Each printer type presents its own dialog box, of course; Figure B-10 shows the printer dialog box for Adobe's Acrobat PDFWriter.

Figure B-10: Acrobat PDFWriter's Print dialog box showing BBEdit's various printing options

Some printer drivers offer you a drop-down list with other formatting and layout options. If your printer does, make any necessary changes there, select the BBEdit category from the drop-down list, and then click the Options button. The available options are outlined in the following table.

Print Option	Description
Print Backwards	With this option selected, BBEdit will print from the last page to the first page rather than from the first to the last.
Frame Printing Area	BBEdit prints a frame around the text on your page.
Print Page Headers	Prints the page number, filename, time, and date from the header of each page.
Print Line Numbers	Displays line numbers along the left margin of the document. This is useful when debugging a file because error reports point to actual line numbers within a file.
Print Two-Up	Use this option to save resources by printing two BBEdit pages on one sheet of paper.
1-Inch Gutter	Leaves a one-inch margin along the left side of the paper. Allows space for notes in the margin, for instance, or to accommodate placement in three-ring binders.
Print Full Pathname	Prints the full path name of the file, from the header.
Time Stamp:	This option enables you to decide whether the header date is the date the file was last modified or the date the file was printed.
Date Last Saved	
Date of Printing	
Print Rubber Stamp	You can specify a message to be printed diagonally across the page, in gray if your printer supports grayscale, otherwise in outline, like a watermark. This feature may not work on all printers. You can also select any font on your system for this Rubber Stamp to be printed in.

Other Useful BBEdit Features

This section takes a look at some selected BBEdit features that you may find useful.

Spell-checking

The Check Spelling command on the Text menu launches BBEdit's built-in spelling checker. The Spell Checker compares each word in the document with words in the Spell Checker's dictionaries. If a word can't be found in a dictionary, BBEdit attempts to offer a possible correction.

If the questioned word is actually spelled correctly, you can add the word to the User Dictionary or simply skip the word. BBEdit ignores HTML code and checks only the text that will actually appear in your Web page.

If you've used any spell-checkers at all, these steps are familiar:

1. Select Text ⇨ Check Spelling (Command+F12).

2. To limit spell-checking to only selected text, choose the Selection Only option.

3. Click Start to begin spell-checking.

4. If a Questioned Word is misspelled, choose the correct word from the Guesses list or type a replacement word in the Replace With box.

5. If a Questioned Word is not misspelled, choose the Skip command or use the Add command to enter the word into your personal User Dictionary.

Altering the User Dictionary

BBEdit's User Dictionary is a simple, editable text file that you can alter yourself. You can add and delete words quickly and easily.

Open the User Dictionary by double-clicking the file located inside the BBEdit Support/Dictionaries folder within the main BBEdit 6.0.2. folder. Each dictionary word must be entered on a separate line. Edit the file just as you would any other BBEdit text file.

Caution Do not alter the coded number that appears at the top of the file. This code enables BBEdit to recognize the file as the User Dictionary.

Comparing files

BBEdit's Search menu contains a Find Differences command for comparing two files. For example, you may want to compare a file you have been working on locally to a file you just retrieved from a server to find differences between the two. Figure B-11 demonstrates this feature at work.

Follow these steps to use the comparison features of the Find Differences command:

1. Choose Search ⇨ Find Differences. The Find Differences dialog box appears.

2. Use the New and Old pop-up menus to choose the files you wish to compare. You can also drag file icons from the Finder into the New and Old portions of the dialog box.

3. Select the appropriate options — Case Insensitive or Ignore Leading Space — for your situation.

4. Click Compare to start the file-comparison operation.

Figure B-11: Comparing differences in BBEdit files

If BBEdit finds differences, the two files appear side by side. In addition, a Differences pane detailing the found differences appears at the bottom of the screen (as previously shown in Figure B-11). You can copy a line from one file to another by selecting the line and choosing either Apply to Old or Apply to New. BBEdit italicizes the line in the Differences pane to indicate the change has been applied.

Search menu

BBEdit's Search and Search and Replace features work on a single file or multiple files. Follow these steps to search and/or replace text in the active window:

1. Select Search ⇨ Find. The Find and Replace dialog box will appear, as shown in Figure B-12.

2. Enter the text you wish to locate in the Search For box.

3. To enter a replacement string, do so in the Replace With box. Otherwise, leave this box empty.

4. Choose any options you wish to apply to the search, including the direction of the search (Start at Top, Wrap Around, or Backwards), the selection, and case sensitivity.

5. Click any of the buttons along the right side of the dialog box to begin the search operation: Find, Find All, Replace, Replace All, Don't Find, or Cancel. Don't Find saves the settings of your search without actually performing the search.

Figure B-12: BBEdit's formidable Find & Replace dialog box

One of the options in the Search command's dialog box enables you to search and/or replace text in multiple files. A handy use for this feature is updating each occurrence of a revised filename in several related HTML documents.

Follow these steps to perform multifile searches:

1. Select Search ⇨ Find.

2. Enter the text you wish to locate in the Search For box.

3. To enter a replacement string, do so in the Replace With box. Otherwise, leave this box empty.

4. Find the Multi-File Search option and click the triangle to reveal the Multi-File Search options. (This portion of the dialog box may already be visible.)

5. Choose the files you wish to search, using the buttons and pop-up menus in the bottom part of the dialog box.

6. Select any other options you wish to apply to the search, as you would in a single-file search.

7. Click the appropriate button along the right side of the dialog box to begin the operation.

Go To Line command

It's easy to move the insertion point instantly to a specific line in your document. Use the Go To Line command under the Search menu. Enter the line number in the dialog box and click Go To (see Figure B-13).

Figure B-13: The Go To Line dialog box

Markers icon

BBEdit's markers enable you to quickly and easily move to a particular section of your file. You can give the marker a unique name that makes sense to you and helps you find it later. This feature helps you stay on track in a large HTML file.

To set markers:

1. First select the section of your document you wish to mark.

2. Click the Markers icon in the status bar and select Set Marker from the pop-up menu.

3. In the Set Marker dialog box, enter a name for the marker and click the Set button.

   Once markers are established, the marker names appear at the bottom of the Mark pull-down menu. Simply select the marker name to take you to that location in your document.

4. When you want to clear markers you don't need anymore, click the Markers icon and select Clear Markers from the pop-up menu. In the Clear Markers dialog box, choose the marker you want to delete and click the Clear button.

Syntax coloring

To make editing easier, BBEdit displays HTML tags in colored text. Be sure to save your HTML documents with the .html or .htm extensions to enable this feature. If you want to change the colors BBEdit uses for syntax coloring, you can do so in the Text Colors portion of the Preferences dialog box.

Working with servers

You will be placing your completed Web files on a public server that enables people to view your masterpiece worldwide. The public server uses the File Transfer Protocol (FTP) to send and receive files. Dreamweaver has built-in FTP capabilities that enable you to connect to a remote server to save (upload) and open (download) files; see Chapter 7 for more information on FTP publishing. In addition, BBEdit offers the following FTP capabilities.

Saving files to a server (uploading)

Follow these steps to upload files to a server:

1. With a document open in BBEdit, select File ➪ Save to FTP Server (see Figure B-14).

2. To connect to a server, enter the name of the server. You can choose from previously used servers in the pop-up Server menu.

3. Enter your user name and password.

4. Click the Connect button to begin an FTP session.

5. Choose the destination directory on the server by using the standard Mac OS directory pop-up menu.

Tip

BBEdit remembers your password if you desire. Auto-Connect instructs BBEdit to automatically connect to a server using your saved password the next time you begin an FTP session.

Figure B-14: The Save to FTP Server dialog box

Opening files from a server (downloading)

If you wish to retrieve files from a server, use the File ⇨ Open From FTP Server command (see Figure B-15). The steps are similar to those for saving to an FTP server in the preceding section.

Once the connection is made, use a standard Mac OS directory pop-up menu to navigate through the folders — just as you would if the files were stored locally on your Mac. Once you have located the file you desire, choose Save to begin the downloading process. After the file is completely downloaded, BBEdit displays the file in a new text-editing window.

Figure B-15: The Open from FTP Server dialog box

Notice that the Open from FTP Server dialog box is very similar to its Save to FTP Server counterpart. It's this kind of ease-of-use, with only subtle changes in the user interface when they're required, that makes BBEdit such a powerful tool and keeps it a breeze to learn.

✦   ✦   ✦

HomeSite 4.5 Primer (for Windows Users)

Designing and creating Web sites is intuitive and easy with Dreamweaver's visual interface. Yet you may want to leave the visual editor at times and get your hands on the underlying HTML code. In some cases, Dreamweaver's built-in HTML editor is all you need. Whenever you need a more advanced HTML editor to add features or troubleshoot your page, the Windows version of Dreamweaver includes a complete registered version of HomeSite 4.5. This standalone HTML editor package for Windows works with Dreamweaver. HomeSite is one of the most popular HTML editors available today. It enables you to produce HTML files without actually memorizing HTML tag commands.

This appendix provides instructions about how to access HomeSite's basic features. You can also access an Online User Manual and other invaluable help resources by clicking the Help tab in the Resources area of the HomeSite screen. (Remember that you can resize this frame by clicking and dragging the borders to make reading the help resources easier.) Also, you can visit Allaire's HomeSite 4.5 Web site at www.allaire.com.

Note

Dreamweaver ships with HomeSite version 4.5.1. Users may upgrade to the just-released 4.5.2 for free. While there are numerous bug fixes and enhancements in 4.5.2, only one directly affects Dreamweaver users: If both UltraDev and Dreamweaver are installed on the same machine, UltraDev will open when you click the Macromedia icon on the Editor toolbar.

Getting Started

It's easy to switch between Dreamweaver and HomeSite. A simple click of an icon toggles you from one application to the other. Elements selected in one application are automatically highlighted in the other, making it easy to keep your project organized.

Key features

"Full-featured" just scratches the surface when it comes to describing HomeSite. Many of the tools are the perfect complement to Dreamweaver's visual editor; others serve to make straight coding as efficient as possible. Here are just a few of the HomeSite highlights:

✦ Multiple layers of Undo

✦ Spell-checker

✦ Site link validation

✦ Automatic color-coding of HTML, CFML, and other scripts

✦ Collapsible code

✦ Extended Find and Replace capabilities for making global edits

✦ Tag Insight, offering a list of attributes and attribute values as you enter tag code

✦ Customization of main and tag toolbars

✦ Wizards for complex tasks, including incorporating Dynamic HTML, RealAudio, and RealVideo

✦ Toggle capability between multiple documents

✦ Drag-and-drop from image libraries into the page

✦ Access to remote sites via built-in FTP

✦ Estimates of document sizes and download times

✦ Management for Cascading Style Sheets, CFML server-side tags, Netscape and Internet Explorer HTML extensions, embedded multimedia and plug-ins, and ActiveX and Java controls

✦ Web-safe color palette

✦ HTML syntax checking

✦ One-click preview in any browser

✦ Design View WYSIWYG Need Editing

✦ Style Editor for applying CSS styles

✦ SMIL support, with tags for multimedia applications

The HomeSite 4.5 interface

The HomeSite interface is simple and logical, making even the most demanding programming projects easier to accomplish. The workspace (see Figure C-1) has three primary areas: the Editor/Browser and Resource windows, and the command bars.

Figure C-1: The HomeSite 4.5 workspace

Editor/Browser window

Toggle between these two screens with F12. The Editor screen is where you enter HTML tags and place page content. The Browser screen is where you render the current document in the browser you choose.

Resource window

Click the tab buttons at the bottom of the Resource window to access areas where you manage files, custom tags, and online help areas. From left to right, the tabs represent the following groups of resources:

    ✦ **Local:** Use the Directory and File panes to access local and network drives.

    ✦ **Projects:** Create and manage HomeSite projects.

    ✦ **Site View:** Provides a graphic view of the links in a document.

◆ **Snippets:** Store code for later use; see the section "Inserting Tags in a Document," later in this appendix.

◆ **Help:** Access help files, including user manual, FAQ, HTML reference files, and more.

◆ **Tag Inspector:** Displays all the tags in your document in a hierarchical tree, along with a list of properties for editing them.

Command bars

A rich supply of menus and toolbars is available throughout the HomeSite workspace, which you read about as you work through this appendix.

Working with Dreamweaver and HomeSite

Although Dreamweaver enables you to assign any HTML editor as your external editor, it integrates best with HomeSite. Once you've set up HomeSite as your default editor, switching between Dreamweaver and HomeSite is just a button click or keyboard shortcut away.

Setting up HomeSite as your default editor

Before Dreamweaver can access HomeSite, you must make HomeSite your default HTML editor. You can make this assignment through the Dreamweaver Preferences by following these steps:

1. In Dreamweaver, choose Edit ⇨ Preferences to open the Preferences dialog box.

2. From the Category list on the left, choose File Types / Editors to display that category's information.

3. In the File Types / Editors category, enter the path to the HomeSite executable in the External Code Editor field. The easiest way to do this is to select the Browse button and locate the file. If you installed HomeSite according to the defaults, this path should read C:\Program Files\Allaire\HomeSite 4.5\homesite45.exe.

4. Click OK when you've finished.

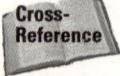
Cross-Reference
The External Editor options that control file synchronization between Dreamweaver and HomeSite are explained in detail in Chapter 4.

Switching between Dreamweaver and HomeSite

When you're in Dreamweaver, you have two ways to switch to HomeSite:

✦ Choose Edit ➪ Edit with Homesite.

✦ Use the keyboard shortcut, Ctrl+E.

You can also select the other program's button on the taskbar or use the Alt+Tab method to switch between applications, but the file integration does not work under these circumstances.

Caution Depending on the synchronization options chosen in the File Types / Editors category of the Preferences, Dreamweaver may ask if you want to save the files first before you switch to HomeSite. If you do not save your Dreamweaver file first, your modifications do not appear in HomeSite (and vice versa). For this reason, I recommend setting your synchronization options to Always.

After you've made your code modifications in HomeSite and you're ready to return to Dreamweaver, you have three methods for switching back:

✦ Select the Macromedia Dreamweaver button on HomeSite's Editor toolbar.

✦ Choose View ➪ Open in Macromedia Dreamweaver.

✦ Use the keyboard shortcut, Ctrl+D.

Caution If HomeSite doesn't switch to Dreamweaver using any of the methods just given, check your HomeSite settings. In HomeSite, choose Options ➪ Settings (or press F8) to open the HomeSite Settings dialog box and select the HomeSite reload options from the Dreamweaver and File Settings categories.

Disabling HomeSite integration

You can disable HomeSite integration if you prefer working with an older version of HomeSite or if you use a different HTML text editor. Here's how:

1. Choose Options ➪ Settings.

2. Select the Dreamweaver category.

3. Turn off Enable Dreamweaver Integration and click OK.

Creating Pages: Making HTML Files

You have a couple of ways to work with HTML files. You can either create a new file or open an existing one and edit it. This section shows you how to create, open, apply tags to, and save Web pages in HomeSite. Remember: Even if you create a Web page in another application, you can still edit the page with HomeSite.

If you're starting from scratch to create a new file, HomeSite offers the following ways to create a new document:

✦ Select File ➪ New to open the New HTML Document dialog box. Select a blank document, one of the templates, or use any HTML file as a template. Template files are stored separately from the source documents, so you can modify the template files without worrying about changing the originals.

✦ Click the New button on the main toolbar to open a new document based on your default template. Change the default template by choosing Options ➪ Settings (F8) and selecting the Locations category. Then enter the address of the file you would like to use as a template in the Default Template field.

✦ Use the Quick Start Wizard. Click the Quick Start button on the Common tab of the Tag Chooser (see Figure C-2) and follow the steps to design a new page or build your own template.

✦ Select File ➪ Convert Text File to convert an ASCII text file to an HTML file.

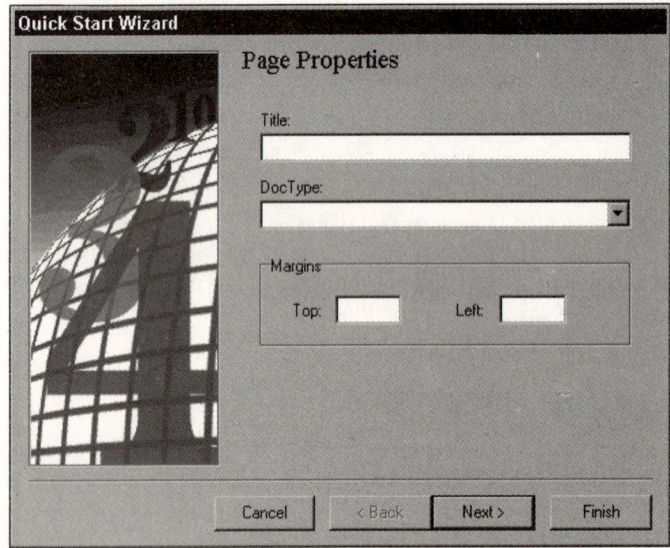

Figure C-2: Use the Quick Start Wizard to build a new page or template.

Opening an existing Web page

Another way to create a new HTML document is to start with an existing Web page. Use any of the following methods to open files:

✦ Select File ➪ Open (Ctrl+O).

✦ Click the Open button on the main toolbar.

✦ In the Open HTML Document dialog box, double-click a file listed in the Local Files view of the Resource tab.

✦ To open Web files directly, select File ➪ Open from the Web. Type in a URL or select a URL from your Favorites or Bookmarks list.

✦ Select File ➪ Recent Files to see a list of recently used files.

Note HomeSite treats read-only files differently from other files. These files are marked with a small red dot in the Resource window file list, and a warning message pops up if you try to open one. You cannot edit read-only files, but you can change the attribute on the file by right-clicking it, selecting Properties in the shortcut menu, and then deselecting the read-only attribute.

Inserting tags in a document

Of course, you can type codes directly into the document in the Edit screen, but the following methods are usually more efficient. To have HomeSite add tags for you, choose among these commands:

✦ Select Tools ➪ Tag Chooser (Ctrl+E). Select from the Chooser list (see Figure C-3), which contains the complete HTML tag set as well as CFML, JSP, WML, HDML, SMIL, VTML, and custom tag sets. Double-click a tag to insert or to display a dialog box in which you can add tag-specific attributes and then click OK to add the tag to your document.

✦ From the Tags menu, choose from a basic set of formatting tags.

✦ Select Options ➪ Settings (F8), click on the Editor category and ensure that Tag Insight and Tag Completion sections are both enabled. The following sections describe these three tools and their benefits.

✦ Select Options ➪ Settings (F8) and open the HTML tab to set alignment and centering tags and to toggle the case of inserted tags.

✦ To repeat the previous tag, select Edit ➪ Repeat Last Tag (Ctrl+Q).

Using Tag Insight

The Tag Insight tool is a valuable aid to all Web designers, even beginners. It's a quick way to develop a tag as you type it by displaying a drop-down list of attributes and values for each tag. Click the Tag Insight button on the Editor toolbar to enable this feature. Or you can turn off Tag Insight in the Editor category of the Settings dialog box (Options ➪ Settings, or F8). Finally, you can use it only when needed by pressing Shift+F2 when your cursor is in the first tag of a tag pair.

When Tag Insight is turned on, follow these steps to use this helpful feature:

1. Place the cursor in front of the start tag's end bracket (>). Press the spacebar to open the attribute list.

Figure C-3: Access any HTML tag — and many other varieties —
through the Tag Chooser.

2. To add an attribute to the tag, double-click the attribute in the list. The cursor then moves between the double quotes of the attribute's value.

3. A list of values appears if the attribute has a fixed set of allowed values. To select a value from the list, press the spacebar. Once the value is inserted, the cursor moves in front of the closing bracket.

   If no allowed values appear, the attribute accepts programmer-specified values.

4. Continue selecting attributes until the tag code is complete.

Using Tag Completion

The Tag Completion feature automatically inserts the end tag after you type the start tag. Here are the steps to use this feature:

1. To enable Tag Completion, choose Options ➪ Settings (F8), click the Editor category, and then check the Enable Tag Completion box in the Tag Completion section.

2. In the Tag Completion section of the Editor category, select Edit to change the syntax of a selected tag.

3. You can use the Add and Delete buttons in the Tag Completion section to manage the list.

Tag Snippets

You can save portions of HTML code for easy recall in other files, using the valuable Tag Snippets feature. It's a lot easier than copying and pasting blocks of code from various files.

To save HTML code as a Tag Snippet, follow these steps:

1. Click the Tag Snippets tab at the bottom of the Resources panel to open the Tag Snippets window.

2. Right-click in the empty pane and select Create Folder from the drop-down menu.

3. Name the folder from which you want to save code and press Enter.

4. From the Tag Snippets window, right-click the folder and select Add Snippet from the shortcut menu to open the Custom Tag dialog box.

5. Type the start and end tags or paste them from another file. Click OK to save the tag in the folder created in Step 2.

To add more snippets to a folder, right-click the snippet folder in the Tag Snippets window and select Add Snippet from the shortcut menu. You can delete or rename folders as well, from the right-click shortcut menu.

To insert a Tag Snippet you've saved, follow these steps:

1. In the Editing window, place the cursor where you want to insert the tag.

2. Open the Tag Snippet window using one of the methods described previously.

3. Double-click the folder that holds the snippet you'd like to enter.

4. Double-click the snippet you wish to insert into your document.

Entering text in a document

In HomeSite's Editor window, you can type in page content and tags directly or use the numerous shortcuts to speed up the process. To check your work, toggle to the Browse mode by pressing F12 or click the Browse tab button on the Editor toolbar. Here are some examples of entering text in a document:

✦ To change the defaults for paragraph tags and filename cases, access the HTML tab by selecting Options ➪ Settings (F8).

✦ To create a link, drag and drop a document file into the Editor window.

✦ To insert an image or other media file, drag and drop it into the Editor window to insert it.

✦ To insert an HTML, ASCII text, or Cascading Style Sheet file into a document, select File ➪ Insert File.

✦ To display a menu of special and extended characters, select View ➪ Extended and Special Characters (Ctrl+Shift+X). In the Special dialog box (see Figure C-4), click a character to insert it into your document.

✦ To insert text from any application into your document, use the standard Windows Copy, Cut, and Paste commands.

Figure C-4: Insert extended ASCII characters through the Extended and Special Characters dialog box.

Saving files

When you view an unsaved document in either the internal or external browser, HomeSite saves a temporary copy of the file in memory. Thus, you should always save documents with new links in them before viewing them in a browser, to ensure that the file paths are identified.

To set the default file format:

1. Select Options ➪ Settings and click the File Settings icon, shown in Figure C-5.

2. Check a format radio button among the Format When Saving options.

3. Now select one of the four Save commands from the File pull-down menu:

   • **Save (Ctrl+S):** Saves the current document.

   • **Save As (Ctrl+Shift+S):** Select a filename and click the Local tab to save the document locally, or click Remote to save the document to a server.

   • **Save All:** Saves all open documents.

   • **Save As Template:** Saves the HTML file as a template. Template files have the .hst extension and are stored separately. Later changes to the source document do not affect the corresponding template file in any way.

Browsing pages

It's imperative that you view your HTML pages in more than just one browser. HomeSite provides many browser options so you can test your pages against the array of available browsers.

Mapping Your Web Site

HomeSite's Default Mapping feature sends a document through the specified Web server. If you don't run your own Web server, leave the mapping settings blank. If you do run your own server, here's how to set a default mapping for your Web server:

1. Access the Browse category of the Settings by selecting Options ⇨ Settings.

2. Check the Use Microsoft Internet Explorer box.

3. Select the Enable Server Mappings option.

4. Select the Add button to open the Mapping dialog box.

5. In the Mapping dialog box, enter the path of the folder to be mapped in the Map From text box.

6. Enter the URL of the server in the Map To text box. Click OK when you're done.

7. To add additional mappings, select the Add button again and repeat Steps 5 and 6.

You also have the option to map any particular path to a file with a specific URL. This mapping capability enables you to use your remote server to preview server-side includes and other types of files. To define a separate mapping for a project:

1. In the Projects panel of the Resources window, right-click a project and select Properties.

2. In the Project Properties dialog box, access the Server Mapping tab. Enter the local path in the first text box and the URL you want to use for that project in the second text box. Click OK.

Now, if you open this file from the project tree, the project mapping overrides the default mapping.

Internal browser

If HomeSite 4.5 detects Microsoft Internet Explorer on your system during installation, you have the option of selecting it as the default HTML browser (see Figure C-6). Netscape Navigator cannot be used as the internal browser in HomeSite.

If you don't want to have to toggle between the Editor and Browser windows, you can view both at once by clicking the Show Browser Below Editor button in the Editing toolbar (the magnifying glass icon above the Dreamweaver button). You must be in the Editing pane for this button to be available. When you have HomeSite set up this way, you can see the changes you make to your code reflected in the Browser window instantly—without having to toggle the display. Remember that you can resize the Browser view by clicking and dragging the borders.

Figure C-5: HomeSite's Settings dialog box features many different options for customizing your work environment.

Figure C-6: Use HomeSite's internal browser to preview your Web pages.

External browser

HomeSite makes it easy to add browsers — and browser versions — to the External Browser list. To add, delete, or reconfigure an external browser, open the External Browsers dialog box by selecting Options ➪ Configure External Browsers. When you add a new browser to your list, you have the following options in the External Browsers dialog box (shown in Figure C-7), which affect your current document when you launch an external browser:

✦ Prompt to save changes to current document.

✦ Automatically save changes to the current document.

✦ Browse using a temporary copy (no need to save). This is the default setting; it enables you to view your current document without having to save the document itself. Thus, you can get a quick look at your current code without saving over the previous version of the file, in case you don't like what you see.

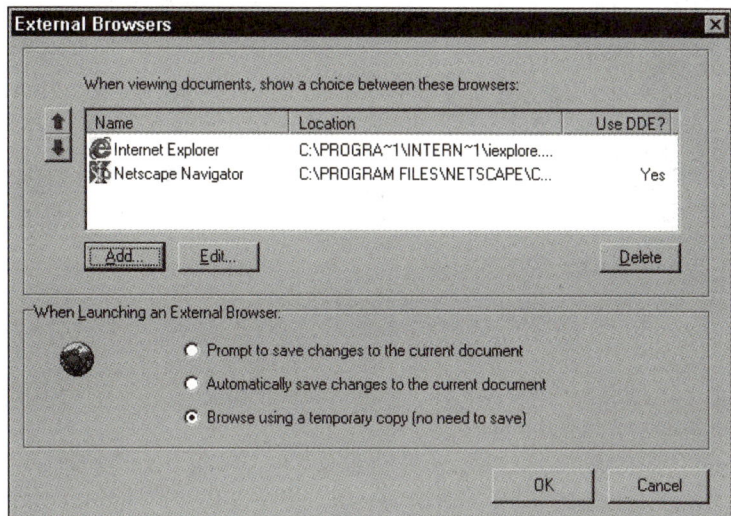

Figure C-7: Add more browsers for testing in the External Browsers dialog box.

Once you add at least one external browser to HomeSite, you can then choose a browser from the list when you click the Launch External Browser button on the main toolbar. Alternately, pressing F11 loads the current document in the first listed browser. To place your preferred browser at the top of the list, open the Configure External Browsers dialog box, click the browser, and click the blue arrow buttons to move it to the top. Then click OK to save the change.

Setting up an FTP server

To establish an FTP server, follow these steps:

1. Select the Files tab in the Resources section.

2. Select the Drives drop-down list, above the list of folders, and choose Allaire FTP & RDS.

3. Right-click on Allaire FTP & RDS in the folder list, and select Add FTP Server to open the Configure FTP Server dialog box (see Figure C-8).

Figure C-8: Set up your FTP server so you can publish directly to the Web from within HomeSite.

4. At a minimum, complete the following fields:

   • **Description:** The name of the server

   • **Host Name:** The FTP address

   • **Username:** Your login name

   • **Password:** Your password, if any

5. Change the default Remote Port entry as needed.

6. Click OK to close the dialog box and the server you configured will appear below Allaire FTP & RDS.

7. Once you've set up an FTP server, right-click the server name and then select Connect, if you're not already connected to the Internet via a DSL, cable modem, or network. You can double-click the server name to expand the directory tree if you've connected correctly to the server.

To open a file on a server, you access the remote server's files directly. (To change server settings, right-click a server name and then select Properties to open the Properties dialog box.) Here are the steps for opening a file:

1. Click the Files tab in the Resources section, navigate to the FTP & RDS entry, and double-click it to display the server's directory tree.

2. If you're not already connected to the Internet, double-click an FTP icon to open a connection to the server.

3. Double-click a file to open it in the Editor window.

Remote files have a small dot on their filename tab at the bottom of the Editor window. To save changes to a remote file, click the Save button on the main toolbar.

Editing and Enhancing Your Pages

HomeSite makes it easy to customize your working space, modify HTML code, and add bells and whistles to your pages.

Changing how the Editor window looks and works

You can customize the Editor window's appearance as well as its operation to your liking.

✦ To remove any of the three toolbars from the screen, toggle them off from the View menu.

✦ To switch between open documents, click the tabs at the bottom of the window. If you've made changes to a document since the last time it was saved, the filename is blue.

✦ To adjust the size of the text line in the Editor window, click the Toggle Word Wrap button on the Editor toolbar or select Options ➪ Word Wrap.

✦ To view your document with an internal browser, press F12 or click the Browser button on the Editor toolbar. To enable the internal browser to Microsoft Internet Explorer, select Options ➪ Settings and open the Browse tab.

✦ To view your document with an external browser, press F11 to open the current document in the first browser in your External Browser list. Or click View External Browser List on the main toolbar and select a browser from the list.

✦ To have HomeSite insert ending tags automatically after you type in a start tag, toggle the Tag Completion button on the Editor toolbar.

Tag attribute values

Many HTML tags have attribute values that may enable you to define the tag's appearance or its usefulness. You can set attribute values as you create a tag, or later after you've previewed the page in a browser and you need to adjust the display. You can edit a tag with the Tag Inspector using any of the following methods:

✦ Right-click any start tag and select Edit Tag.

✦ Place the cursor in a start tag and press F4.

✦ Select Tags ⇨ Inspect Current Tag.

To set or change attribute values with the Tag Editor, follow these steps:

1. Select a start tag, or place the cursor inside it and then right-click and select the Edit Tag option or choose Tags ⇨ Edit Current Tag.

2. Enter new values or edit the existing values in the Tag Editor panel; the options for `<body>` are shown in Figure C-9.

Figure C-9: The Tag Editor shows all of the options for any selected HTML tag.

3. Complex tags may have multiple tabs in the Tag Editor dialog box. Click the tab names at the top of the Tag Editor dialog box to access the other attributes.

4. Click the OK button to close the Tag Editor and have the attribute changes appear in the document.

Using bookmarks

You can set up to ten bookmarks in a document — very handy for finding a given spot in a large HTML file. To set and use bookmarks, follow these steps:

1. Select Edit ⇨ Toggle Bookmark (Ctrl+K) to add a bookmark.

2. To go to the next bookmark, select Edit ⇨ GoTo Next Bookmark (Ctrl+Shift+K).

Using search

HomeSite has two levels of search and replace. Basic searches scan only the currently open document. Extended searches scan more than just the open document. Thus, it's easy to make global changes.

Performing basic searches

To search for a string in the currently open document, select Search ⇨ Find (Ctrl+F). Then, if you want to replace a matching string in the currently open document, select Search ⇨ Replace (Ctrl+R).

If the search dialog box is closed and you want to resume the previous search, select Search ⇨ Find Next (F3).

Performing extended replaces

To search for and replace a string among all open documents (or all HTML files in a particular directory, folder, or project), follow these steps:

1. Select Search ⇨ Extended Replace (Ctrl+Shift+R).

2. Enter your selections in the Extended Replace dialog box, shown in Figure C-10.

3. Click the corresponding radio button to search all open documents or to specify a folder or project in which to search.

4. Select the Replace button.

5. You can see all of the matches in the Search Results tab. Double-click any match in the list to go directly to that file. Note that read-only files are not searched and that you are not prompted to confirm each replacement.

Extended Searches work in the same manner as Extended Replaces.

Figure C-10: HomeSite's Extended Find and Replace feature is extremely powerful and flexible.

Spell Check

HomeSite takes the normal spell-checking operation to the next level by providing a multilanguage Spell Check feature. When you install HomeSite, you can select additional language dictionaries to use. To run Spell Check, use any of the following methods:

✦ Select Tools ⇨ Spell Check (F7) to scan your current document for spelling errors.

✦ You can also have Spell Check go through all of your open documents and then present you with any mistakes all at once. To do this, select Tools ⇨ Spell Check All (Shift+F7).

✦ To configure the Spell Checker to skip all text within HTML tags, select Options ⇨ Settings and select the Spelling category. In this category, you can also select the dictionaries you want the Spell Checker to use.

Using color-coded tags

To facilitate the quick scanning of documents, HomeSite displays tags in distinct colors. This includes all HTML tags, quoted attributes, and script and object tags. You can change the default colors used and create custom colors as well.

Changing colors

To change color coding, select Options ⇨ Settings and then click on the Color Coding section of the Editor category (see Figure C-11). Click HTML in the scheme column and select Edit Scheme.

Figure C-11: Color-code your HTML to easily find specific or different kinds of tags.

You can assign a color from the Basic color palette to any tag. To change the tag's color, follow these steps:

1. Open the Color Coding section in the Settings dialog box as described previously. Select HTML from the Scheme column and click the Edit Scheme button.

2. Select the tag group to change from the Elements list.

3. Open the color palette by clicking the Foreground or Background button.

4. Pick a basic color and click OK.

Creating new colors

To create a custom color for a tag, follow these steps:

1. Open the Color Coding section in the Settings dialog box as described previously. Select HTML from the Scheme column and click the Edit Scheme button.

2. Select the tag group to change from the Elements list.

3. Open the color palette by clicking the Foreground or Background button.

4. Drag the arrow on the brightness scale to set a level.

5. Drag the color pointer to define a color. The color values display as you move the pointer, and the color displays in the Preview box.

6. Click Add to Custom Colors; then click OK to enter the color for the tag.

Adding colors

Wise use of color can make the difference between uninspired and exciting Web pages. HomeSite provides some easy ways to add and change colors in your pages. To insert a color value using Tag Insight:

1. Open Tag Insight by placing the cursor in front of the start tag's closing bracket and pressing the spacebar.

2. Double-click Color from the pop-up list.

3. Double-click a color from the drop-down menu.

HomeSite provides a list of colors to choose from, or you can select a specific color from a variety of color palettes. To insert a color from a palette:

1. To open a color palette, double-click the Custom button from the Colors drop-down list. This opens the Palette dialog box.

2. Position the cursor over any palette color to display its name or hexadecimal value.

3. Click a color to insert it into your document.

Working with palettes

To open a different palette from which to select colors, follow these steps:

1. Access the Palette drop-down menu, shown in Figure C-12, by clicking the Open Palette button on the left side of the Palette dialog box.

Figure C-12: Switch among any number of color sets through the Palette drop-down menu.

2. Click a palette to open it in the Palette dialog box.

You can edit and delete existing palettes from the Open Palette drop-down menu. You can create a new palette, too. Follow these steps:

1. From the Open Palette drop-down menu, select Edit Palette.

2. In the Palette dialog box, click the New Palette button.

3. Select RGB values, or click the Eyedropper button and drag the dropper over the color spectrum to create a color.

4. Once you create a color you want to add to your palette, click the Add button.

5. When you are done creating a new palette, click the Save button and enter a name for the palette. The new file is saved with a default .pal extension in the Palettes subdirectory.

Adding a palette from Paint Shop Pro

Paint Shop Pro is an excellent graphic editor that comes free with HomeSite and is available to Dreamweaver users who register HomeSite online. Follow these steps to bring a Paint Shop Pro palette into HomeSite:

1. In Paint Shop Pro, select Colors ⇨ Save Palette to open the Save Palette panel.

2. Enter a name for the palette.

3. Set the Save As type to PAL-JASC Palette.

4. Save the file in the HomeSite\Palettes directory.

Adding images

HomeSite supports the standard Web graphics formats: GIF, JPG, PNG graphics files, and BMP (Internet Explorer only). To see all of your image files, right-click in one of the file list resource tabs, select Filter, and then select Web Images to limit the file display to images only. If you want to view thumbnails of the image files, click the Thumbnail button in the Resources menu bar.

To add an image to the current document, follow these steps:

1. Select an image in the file list and drag it directly into your document. The default image width and height appear in the tag code.

2. Place the cursor anywhere in the image tag, right-click, and select Edit Tag.

3. Change the image settings in the editor as needed. You can click the Clear button to delete the current entries.

Testing Your Pages

Before you launch your Web site, you should test your code. HomeSite has several key features — HTML Validation, Link Checking, and Document Weighting — to put your Web page through its paces.

HTML validation

Before you FTP your files up to the remote server, it's a good idea to verify that your HTML code is sound. HomeSite includes a powerful tool for checking and reporting on HTML syntax errors. Although it won't automatically correct errors, it identifies them and gives you a list of errors and comments. Double-click an error message to highlight the offending code in your document.

To set the HTML Validator options:

1. Select Options ⇨ Settings and choose the Validation category. Click the Validator Settings button to open the dialog box shown in Figure C-13.

2. Complete the settings for Options and then do the same for the Tags, Versions, and Values tabs.

3. Click OK to save your changes.

Figure C-13: Set up the HTML Validator to your specific parameters with the Validator options.

When you have validation set up as desired, you're ready to use it to test code in your current document. Click the Validate Document button on the main toolbar or select Tools ➪ Validate Document. The results from the validation test appear in a new window below the current document. To find the code that corresponds to any error message, double-click it in the list.

Testing your links

Links change often, so it's important to do regular testing of your documents' links. HomeSite makes the task easier with its built-in Link Checker. Besides testing URLs, it also checks directory paths of images and other Web page elements specified in the current HTML document.

Note that the Link Checker can't verify links to secure pages, FTP links, and mailto: links. You need an active Internet connection to check remote URLs.

Follow these steps to use the Link Checker:

1. To start the Link Checker working on your current document, click the Verify Links button on the main toolbar or select Tools ➪ Verify Links. A list is generated with each link's URL or path.

2. If you need to change the URL or the local directory, do this by first selecting the Set Root URL button next to the list of links. Next enter the new root URL in the Set Root URL text box that is displayed, or select the folder icon to set the root directory and drive against which local links should be tested.

3. Click the Start Link Verification button, the right-pointing triangle found next to the list of links, to begin the verification. The status of each link is updated as it is processed.

4. A checkmark tells you that the link works. An X indicates that it's a failed link, which means that the document or file couldn't be located. Double-click an item in the Verifier List to find the code that corresponds to the failed link.

Document weight

This handy feature estimates the upload time of your current page. To find out how long it takes to upload a page, select Tools ➪ Document Weight. The Root URL setting in your FTP configuration is used to determine the relative path to files, and the results are displayed in the Document Weight dialog box (see Figure C-14).

Creating Projects

If your Web site contains multiple files, you can probably benefit by grouping the files as projects. HomeSite contains powerful project management features that help you organize your site or a collection of sites.

Figure C-14: It's a good idea to check on the probable download time for your Web page.

To create a new project, start by clicking the Projects tab at the bottom of the Resources window. From there, you have several alternatives. You can create a new project or import a project from an existing directory folder. To open the New Project dialog box shown in Figure C-15, click the New Project icon, right-click anywhere in the Project folder area or select Project ⇨ New Project.

The project workspace gives you easy and organized access to related documents and files. The files in the project folders are pointers to your HTML documents. The documents are not physically moved or modified in any way.

Projects toolbar

When the Projects tab is open in the Resources window, you have access to the following tools:

- ✦ **Open Project:** Opens up a project from a local or remote folder.
- ✦ **New Project:** Brings up the New Project dialog box.
- ✦ **Deployment Wizard:** Launches a wizard that aids you in the uploading of your site to a local or remote server.

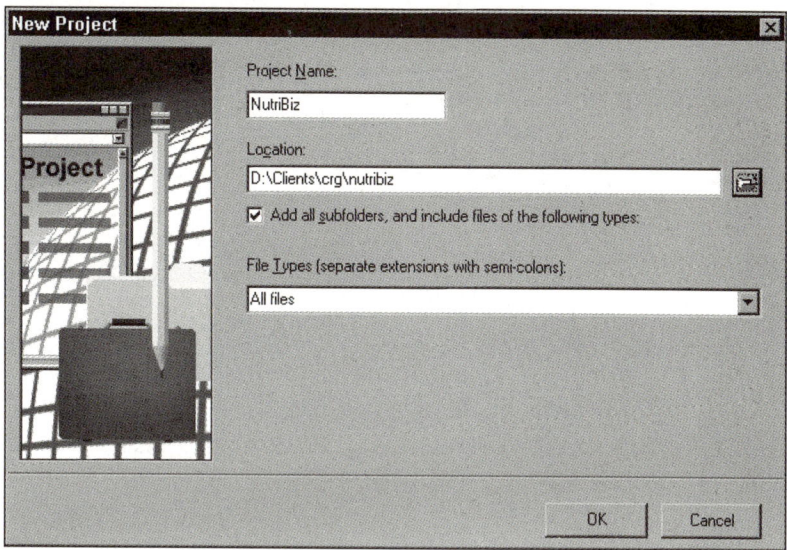

Figure C-15: Use the New Project dialog box to start your new Web site.

Uploading a project to a server

Use the Upload Project icon to select and upload project files to a server. You can select from the list of server connections you have established in the Remote tab.

To upload a project, follow these steps:

1. First, open the Upload Project dialog box by clicking the Upload Project button in the Project tab.

2. In the Upload Project dialog box, select whether you want to upload the entire site or upload only new or modified pages. Click Next.

3. Select the target server from the list in the Upload locations. (If the server you want is not on the list, close the dialog box and set up a protocol for an FTP connection as described earlier.)

4. Click OK to start the upload. The uploaded files are displayed in the file list.

Keyboard Shortcuts

As an alternative to using the pull-down menus, HomeSite 4.5 provides a full complement of keyboard commands, listed in Tables C-1 through C-4.

Table C-1
File Menu Keyboard Shortcuts

Command	Keyboard Shortcut
New document	Ctrl+N
Open an HTML document	Ctrl+O
Save current document	Ctrl+S
Save As	Ctrl+Shift+S
Close current document	Ctrl+W
Close All	Ctrl+Shift+W
Print current document	Ctrl+P

Table C-2
Tag Selector Keyboard Shortcuts

Action	Keyboard Shortcut
Open the Tag Chooser	Ctrl+E
Open the Editor for the selected tag	Ctrl+F4
Open the Quick Anchor dialog box	Ctrl+Shift+A
Open the Image dialog box	Ctrl+Shift+I
Insert a paragraph tag	Ctrl+Shift+P
Insert a break tag	Ctrl+Shift+B
Insert a nonbreaking space	Ctrl+Shift+spacebar
Insert a bold tag	Ctrl+B
Insert an italic tag	Ctrl+I
Insert a center tag (div align="center") by default	Ctrl+Shift+C
Insert a comment tag	Ctrl+Shift+M
Find matching tag	Ctrl+M
Repeat last tag	Ctrl+Q

Table C-3
Edit and Search Menu Keyboard Shortcuts

Command	Keyboard Shortcut
Select all text in the current document	Ctrl+A
Copy selected text to the clipboard	Ctrl+C
Cut the selection to the clipboard	Ctrl+X
Paste selection from the clipboard	Ctrl+V
Insert bookmark at the current line	Ctrl+K
Go to the next bookmark	Ctrl+Shift+K
Open the Find dialog box	Ctrl+F
Run the Find command again	F3
Open the Find dialog box	Ctrl+F
Open the Replace dialog box	Ctrl+R
Open the Extended Find dialog box	Ctrl+Shift+F
Open the Extended Replace dialog box	Ctrl+Shift+R
Open the Go To line number dialog box	Ctrl+G
Undo the previous edit	Ctrl+Z
Redo the previously undone edit	Ctrl+Shift+Z
Validate HTML in the current document	Shift+F6
Spell-check the current document	F7
Open the special/extended character list	Ctrl+Shift+X
Indent the selected text block	Ctrl+Shift+. (period)
Unindent the selected text block	Ctrl+Shift+, (comma)

Table C-4
General Workspace Keyboard Shortcuts

Command	*Keyboard Shortcut*
Toggle the Quick toolbar	Ctrl+H
Display Help for current tag	F1
Open the Options ⇨ Settings menu	F8
Toggle the Resources tab	F9
Toggle Full Screen view	Ctrl+F12
Toggle Editor/Browser views	F12

✦   ✦   ✦

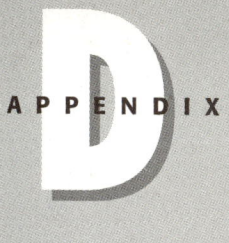
CourseBuilder for Dreamweaver

Web-based training is an explosive field. With the rise of the Internet, a potential learning delivery system is on every desktop: the browser. To meet the growing needs of corporate trainers, remote educators, and Internet instructors, Macromedia developed a special extension of Dreamweaver called CourseBuilder for Dreamweaver. CourseBuilder for Dreamweaver extends the standard HTML authoring interface with a CourseBuilder Interaction dialog box designed to simplify the task of creating and testing instructional Web pages. In its earlier versions, CourseBuilder was known both as Dreamweaver Attain and Attain Objects for Dreamweaver.

CourseBuilder for Dreamweaver enables the Web educator to take advantage of the enhancements in Dreamweaver and greatly eases the creation and editing chores. The program now employs Property Inspectors and special Interaction menu commands to facilitate the instructional design. Moreover, any modifications to Interaction parameters are reflected in real time in the Document window, which helps to cut development time significantly.

The intent of this appendix is twofold. First, I'd like to offer an overview of the product for the Web designer unfamiliar with the distance learning market; the need for designers with Web-training savvy is growing by leaps and bounds. Second, this appendix is intended to bridge the gap for educators beginning to explore the Internet as a delivery medium, who may be completely at home with the testing concepts but unfamiliar with Web design possibilities. This appendix is definitely not intended as a CourseBuilder for Dreamweaver instruction manual — a task beyond the scope of this book.

Understanding the CourseBuilder Interface

At the heart of CourseBuilder for Dreamweaver is the CourseBuilder Interaction dialog box. The CourseBuilder Interaction dialog box enables the Web designer to easily insert seven different types of testing objects, ranging from simple multiple-choice questions to complex drag-and-drop representations. The CourseBuilder Interaction dialog box also serves as the command center for interactions between testing conditions and makes it possible for the answer to one question to affect how another is posed. You can also enable tracking with a Computer Managed Instruction (CMI) system such as Macromedia's Pathware or another database setup. Most important, the CourseBuilder Interaction dialog box handles all this complex interactivity through its point-and-click interface without the need for hand-coding HTML or JavaScript.

On the CD-ROM
To install CourseBuilder, choose Commands ⇨ Manage Extensions to open the Extension Manager. In the Extension Manager, choose File ⇨ Install Extension and navigate to the CourseBuilder.mxp file on the CD-ROM. After the installation is complete, you'll need to relaunch Dreamweaver to use the extension—which, by the way, is not a trial version, but a fully functioning free copy of CourseBuilder.

Although the Insert CourseBuilder Interaction is seen as a single object on Dreamweaver's Objects panel, it acts as the gateway for inserting all the different types of Interactions, such as multiple-choice questions, timers, and text entry boxes. Most of the individual Interactions have a variety of options associated with them—and as you would expect given Dreamweaver's extensibility, new templates can be custom-built and called from within the overall CourseBuilder Interaction dialog box.

With CourseBuilder for Dreamweaver, the CourseBuilder Interaction dialog box and the test question structures it generates are far more integrated into Dreamweaver. Special menu options have been added that enable inserted questions to be moved or deleted—without losing the associated code. You can even move any Interaction into a layer to gain the benefits of absolute positions and visibility control.

Using the CourseBuilder Interaction dialog box: An overview

The CourseBuilder Interaction dialog box is a sophisticated tool that interactively assists your Web instructional design. To give you some measure of its complexity, the CourseBuilder Interaction dialog box consists of over 80 layers—most of which are populated at runtime—and uses more than 20 separate HTML and JavaScript scripts. However, for all its behind-the-scenes intricacy, using the CourseBuilder Interaction dialog box is straightforward.

After you've installed CourseBuilder for Dreamweaver, a new object, Insert CourseBuilder Interaction, is added to a newly created Learning category, which is accessed from Objects panel. Selecting this object opens the CourseBuilder Interaction dialog box, shown in Figure D-1. Alternatively, choose Insert ⇨ CourseBuilder Interaction. The actual interface of the CourseBuilder Interaction dialog box varies depending on which implementation of the eight different Interactions you choose to insert; however, you always make your selections from a series of tabbed panels.

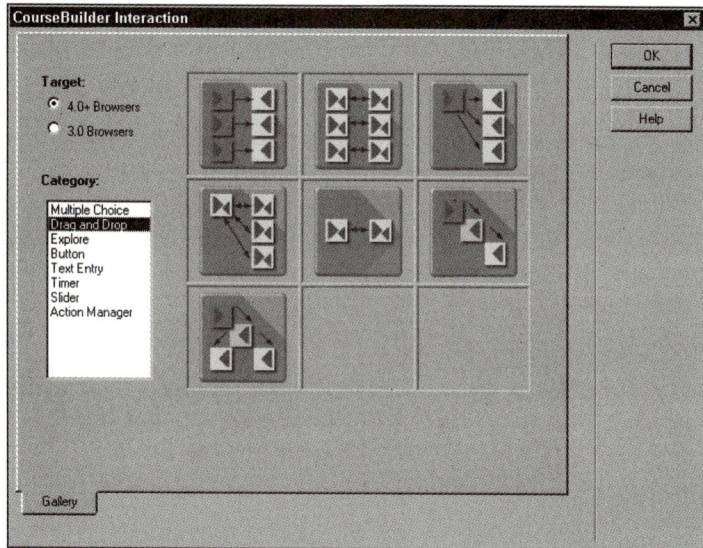

Figure D-1: The CourseBuilder Interaction dialog box is the control panel for almost all of CourseBuilder for Dreamweaver's power.

Caution Be sure to save your document before opening the CourseBuilder Interaction dialog box; if you start to insert the CourseBuilder Interaction without saving, Dreamweaver gives you the option to store your file.

To give you a better idea of how the CourseBuilder Interaction dialog box works, here are the steps for inserting a relatively simple multiple-choice question that offers visual cues:

1. Position your cursor wherever you'd like the multiple-choice question to appear.

   Make sure you've saved your page before continuing; if you haven't, CourseBuilder reminds you to do so.

2. From the Objects panel's Learning category, choose Insert CourseBuilder Interaction.

3. If this is the first time you used CourseBuilder, you are asked if you'd like to copy the support files to the suggested folders.

Note It's recommended that you copy the support files within your site. Dreamweaver uploads only those dependent files actually used.

After the support files are copied, the CourseBuilder Interaction dialog box opens, displaying the Gallery tab.

4. Select the version of browser your Web learning project is targeting by choosing either 4.0+ Browsers or 3.0 Browsers under the Target option.

Tip While choosing the 3.0 Browsers option offers the greatest compatibility, none of the 4.0 capabilities, such as layers or CSS, are available to your design.

5. Choose Multiple Choice from the list of Categories on the left.

The available templates appear in the grid on the right of the CourseBuilder Interaction dialog box.

6. Select the lower-left template with the three graphic symbols.

The other tabs of the CourseBuilder Interaction dialog box appear, created in response to your selection. Also, the initial design for the multiple-choice question is displayed in the Document window, as shown in Figure D-2.

7. Select the General tab.

8. Enter the particular options that identify this test item, including the following:

   • A unique name, used to identify this particular Interaction.

   • The actual multiple-choice question.

   • The circumstances that determine when the question is judged correct or incorrect. Questions can be judged each time a selection is made or after an entire page of questions is submitted.

   • Whether the results of the question are to be tracked by a test management program.

   • The number of attempts allowed for answering the question.

   • A time limit for answering the question.

   • Whether a Reset button is to be made available for this question.

   • Whether the question should be placed within a layer.

9. If you've opted to send the results of the test question to a management system, select the Tracking tab and enter the necessary identifiers, as well as the relative weight of the question.

Figure D-2: As you build your Interaction, the elements appear in the Document window.

10. Select the Choices tab.

11. For each of the placeholders in the Choices list, enter its name, any optional text, the path to the image you want used, and whether or not the choice is correct. If the choice is correct, you can also enter the number of points to add to the user's score.

    Additional choices can be added, or the number of preset choices reduced, by using the Add and Delete buttons at the top of the panel, respectively.

12. Select the Action Mgr (Manager) tab.

    The Action Manager tab lists what actions are taken when the user interacts with the question. Actions can generally be thought of as a series of *If . . . then* statements. *If* a certain condition is met, *then* a defined action is taken. Actions are separated into different *segments*, such as when a particular option is selected. Figure D-3 shows the Action Manager listing for a four-option multiple-choice question.

13. Segments can be added, deleted, renamed, or repositioned in the Action Manager panel. By accessing the drop-down list at the top of the panel, you can also insert special CourseBuilder behaviors, as well as any standard Dreamweaver behaviors.

14. Click OK when you're done.

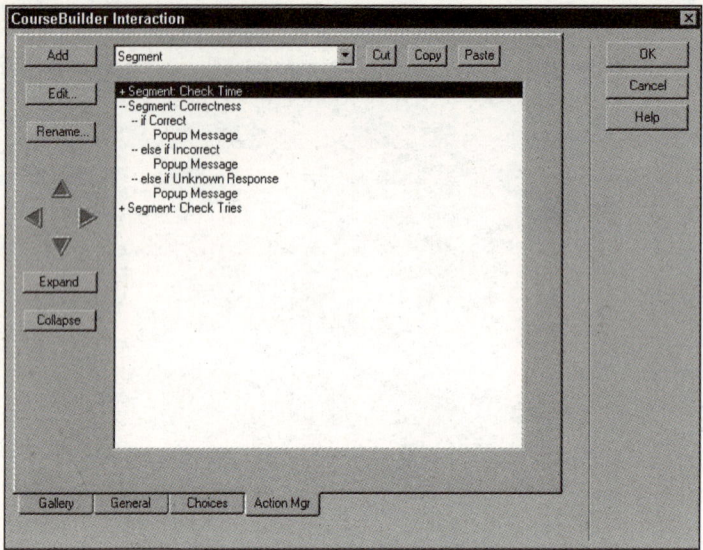

Figure D-3: The Action Manager tab provides an overview of how each question is evaluated at runtime.

Identifying tags and icons

Now that your multiple-choice question has been inserted into your Web page, you can modify its appearance using any of the standard Dreamweaver methods, such as selecting the text of the question and applying a new font face or size. You can also construct an entire page of questions and then use the Style Sheet Inspector to apply a uniform style. CourseBuilder for Dreamweaver makes it easy to identify and select individual Interactions through unique icons and a special tag.

Any inserted Interaction can be chosen by selecting the icon or the tag shown in Figure D-4. The Interaction icon is similar to a layer or form in that, when it is selected, all of the contents of the object — the text, images, form elements, and so on — are selected as well. This ensures that any editing includes the whole object. CourseBuilder for Dreamweaver also inserts a special tag, `<interaction>`, which can be chosen from the Tag Selector to achieve the same effect.

Working with the Interaction Property Inspectors

When an Interaction is selected, a special CourseBuilder Interaction Property Inspector is displayed. The Interaction Property Inspector, shown in Figure D-5, has three basic functions:

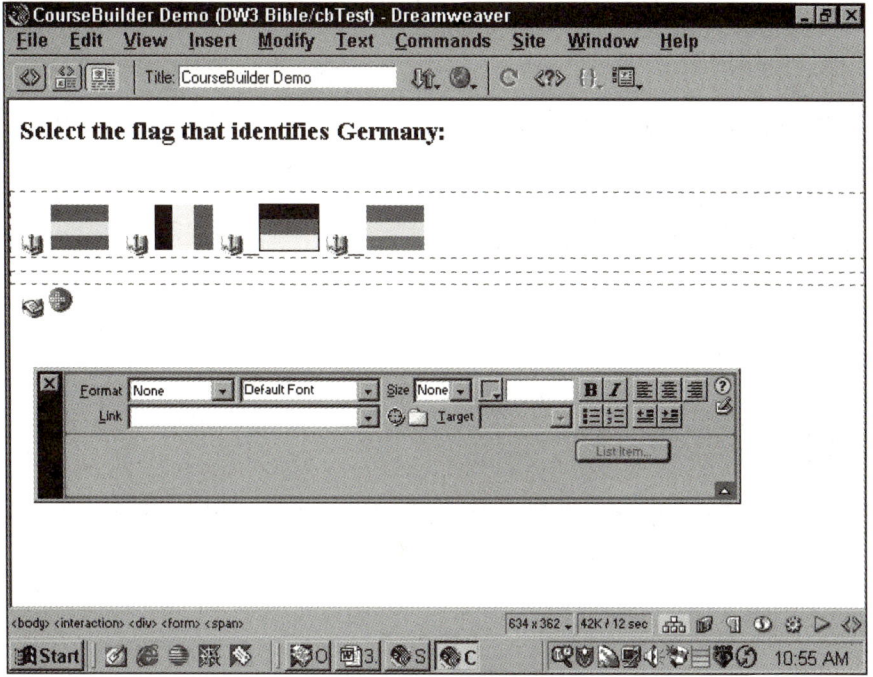

Figure D-4: Select the Interactions by choosing the icon in your Document window or the `<interaction>` tag in the Tag Selector on the status bar.

✦ Editing the current Interaction

✦ Selecting other Interactions in the page

✦ Moving the selected Interaction into or out of a positionable layer

To modify an inserted Interaction, select its icon or tag; then, from the Property Inspector, choose the Edit button. A dialog box similar to the CourseBuilder Interaction dialog box opens. The particular options displayed depend on the configuration of the Interaction, but they are generally a subset of the options offered when the object was constructed. The initial Interaction Gallery and its accompanying template variations are not available.

If you have a fair number of Interactions on the current page, you can use the Property Inspector as a navigator of sorts between them. Select the Interaction Property Inspector's drop-down list to reveal a dynamically generated list of the current Interactions. Select any one, and the Document window scrolls to its location, if necessary, and highlights the object.

Figure D-5: The Interaction Property Inspector enables you to quickly move from one Interaction to another or to edit the current selection.

Finally, the Interaction Property Inspector is useful for moving the individual Interactions into — or out of — layers. In CourseBuilder for Dreamweaver, all Interactions offer you the option of placing the object in a layer at design time. The Property Inspector enables you to change your mind if you so choose by selecting or deselecting the Layer option. Once in a layer, the Interaction can be positioned anywhere on the page, but, of course, layers can be used only in conjunction with 4.0 or later browsers.

Accessing the menus

CourseBuilder takes advantage of Dreamweaver's facility to insert menus wherever appropriate. After installing CourseBuilder, you can find new menu additions in the Modify menu.

Under the Modify menu, you'll find a new CourseBuilder menu option with seven submenu offerings:

✦ **Edit Interaction:** Opens the CourseBuilder Interaction dialog box with the settings for the currently selected Interaction.

✦ **Add Interaction to Gallery:** One of the easiest ways to add new options to the CourseBuilder Interaction dialog box is to customize an existing object and then use this command. Custom Interactions can be stored under an existing category (such as Multiple Choice) or under a new category. It's even possible to select and store an entire page as a Gallery item.

✦ **Copy Support Files:** If you're moving CourseBuilder for Dreamweaver files from one site to another, all you have to do is save the HTML page and then execute this command. All your dependent files, such as graphics and scripts, are copied to the current folder. This command is also used with the next command for updating previous versions of CourseBuilder for Dreamweaver files.

✦ **Add Template Fix:** Inserts code necessary for attaching Interactions to documents derived from templates.

✦ **Create Tracking Frameset:** Makes a two-frame frameset for tracking user results to be used by CMI programs other than Pathware.

✦ **Create Pathware Frameset:** Pathware is Lotus's Computer Managed Instruction program and can be used in conjunction with CourseBuilder for Dreamweaver to track user results. Pathware uses a two-frame frameset structure to display content in one frame and test results in another. The Create Pathware Frameset automatically builds this frameset and loads the current page in the content frame.

✦ **Convert from Previous Versions:** Files created in the earlier versions of CourseBuilder for Dreamweaver cannot be edited in the current version without conversion. After you've loaded the Web page with the Interactions to convert and invoke this command, Dreamweaver stores your old files with a .bak file extension and the converted file under the original name. According to Macromedia, it's best to copy old scripts to a new folder and delete the Scripts folder before beginning the conversion.

Surveying the Interactions

To better understand the capabilities of CourseBuilder for Dreamweaver, you need to know how the various Interactions are used. In all, eight different Interactions exist: Multiple Choice, Drag and Drop, Explore, Button, Text Entry, Timer, Slider, and Action Manager. All but the Action Manager insert an actual object or series of objects in your Web page — the Action Manager controls the interactions between Interactions on the same Web page.

Most of the Interactions have multiple templates to choose from, and all vary in terms of which parameters are available. Some of the objects, such as the Timer and the Slider, are far more useful when working in conjunction with another object. By combining a variety of Interactions, your Web training pages can encompass a wide variety of models and simulations.

Multiple Choice Interaction

The Multiple Choice Interaction encompasses all types of choice questions, not just the traditional pop-quiz type of text questions. This object has four templates:

✦ **Graphic:** Displays images for choices with an optional text line.

✦ **Radio buttons:** Enables one answer to be chosen from a group of possibilities.

✦ **True/False:** Permits an answer to be one of two possibilities.

✦ **Checkboxes:** Enables the user to select any number of answers from a group of possibilities.

All the options enable the designer to specify the text of the question during object setup. You can alter the font face, size, and color — or specify a style — from the Document window.

Drag and Drop Interaction

Computer-based training can be used to simulate the assembly of components or to demonstrate knowledge of the relationship of one object to another. The Drag and Drop Interaction (shown in Figure D-6) enables the user to move one onscreen item and drop it on another. The specified graphics can appear to fit together or lay on top of one another.

Figure D-6: The Drag and Drop Interaction uses draggable layers that can snap to their targets.

CourseBuilder for Dreamweaver ships with a variety of Drag and Drop Interaction templates:

✦ **One to one matching:** Establishes a series of objects on the left and targets on the right, which must be correctly paired.

✦ **One to one both ways:** Places objects in pairs and enables either object to be dropped on its pair.

✦ **One object to multiple targets:** Used to demonstrate that the object can be associated with any of the onscreen targets.

✦ **One object to many, many to one matching:** Uses four draggable items onscreen; the first object can be dropped on any of the other three items, each of which can in turn be dropped on the first object.

✦ **One object to one, two ways:** Provides two draggable objects, each of which can be a target for the other.

✦ **One object to two targets, in two steps:** Used to demonstrate two-phased operations.

✦ **One object to target, with two steps and one distracter:** Similar to the previously described template, except the second step has one correct and one incorrect target.

The Drag and Drop Interaction is accomplished using layers, and like Dreamweaver's standard Drag Layer behavior, the layer being dragged can be made to snap to specific coordinates when the correct target is approached. Moreover, if the wrong target is chosen, the dragged layer can snap back to its original position.

Explore Interaction

The Explore Interaction uses an image map and a series of hotspots to permit the user to "explore" the onscreen graphic. A click in a particular area — or on a certain part — generates a specific response, which could take the form of a pop-up message or a jump to another URL. Any of the available Dreamweaver behaviors can be attached to a defined hotspot by using the Action Manager tab of the Explore Interaction.

Three templates are available for the Explore Interaction:

✦ **Hotspots at various locations:** Five different hotspots are initially identified, although these can be customized to represent any graphic.

✦ **Transparent hotspots at various locations:** Same as preceding template but with five transparent areas instead of placeholders.

✦ **Hotspots in quadrants:** Use this template when you want to divide an image into four equal areas that cover the entire graphic.

Button Interaction

The Button Interaction is generally used in conjunction with other Interactions on the page to represent selections or choices. One button, when selected, could initiate a series of actions with another button; clicking a button, for example, could start or stop a timer. One bank of buttons could activate another bank of buttons as well.

Although only two templates exist for the Button Interaction — an on/off-type switch and a push button — CourseBuilder for Dreamweaver includes 11 different appearances from which to choose, as shown in Figure D-7. The buttons can be set to highlight like a rollover and/or be initially deactivated, if desired.

Figure D-7: Choose from any of the 11 different types of buttons included with the Button Interaction.

Text Entry Interaction

While multiple-choice and true/false questions are often used to handle text-based questions, sometimes you want to test a user's retention. The Text Entry Interaction enables you to request information to be keyed in by the user, which can then be judged correct by comparing the input to a specified list of possible answers. You can also use the Text Entry Interaction to request a user ID and password.

The two templates for the Text Entry Interaction are as follows:

✦ Single line of text

✦ Multiple lines of text

Timer Interaction

With the Timer Interaction, questions can be judged incorrect if the answer is not chosen within the time limit. An onscreen timer — such as an hourglass, a clapboard, or a set of rising bars — can visually mark off seconds or be used as a countdown. Specific triggers can be set at any point in the timeline to activate behaviors such as a pop-up message or a custom function. The two templates for the Timer Interaction enable you to easily choose a count up or count down scenario.

Slider Interaction

The Slider Interaction is similar to the Button Interaction in that it is generally used with other Interactions on the page. However, whereas a button is used to represent a binary set of values, a slider is used to show a linear range of values. CourseBuilder for Dreamweaver includes almost 20 different slider appearances from which to choose; generally, one type of slider is offered in both a horizontal and vertical format. Like the Timer, the Slider Interaction can trigger behaviors at specified points.

You have two Slider Interaction templates to choose from:

✦ **Range of values:** Actions are triggered when the slider is moved anywhere within a set range of values.

✦ **Specific values:** Actions are triggered when the slider is moved to specific values within a specified range.

Action Manager Interaction

The Action Manager Interaction is used to coordinate information from the various Interactions on a given page, whether it is to send all the answers to a database or to switch the Interactions from a tutorial to a test. Bear in mind that the Action Manager Interaction is different from the Action Manager panel found in the dialog box, which is used to control a single Interaction.

Generally, the Action Manager object is placed first on the HTML page so that it is set up to interact with all Interactions that follow. Because all customization occurs within the Action Manager object, it has only one template.

✦   ✦   ✦

Index

Continued

Continued

Continued

Continued

Continued

Continued

Q

Continued

Hungry Minds, Inc.
End-User License Agreement

READ THIS. You should carefully read these terms and conditions before opening the software packet(s) included with this book ("Book"). This is a license agreement ("Agreement") between you and Hungry Minds, Inc. ("HMI"). By opening the accompanying software packet(s), you acknowledge that you have read and accept the following terms and conditions. If you do not agree and do not want to be bound by such terms and conditions, promptly return the Book and the unopened software packet(s) to the place you obtained them for a full refund.

1. **License Grant.** HMI grants to you (either an individual or entity) a nonexclusive license to use one copy of the enclosed software program(s) (collectively, the "Software") solely for your own personal or business purposes on a single computer (whether a standard computer or a workstation component of a multi-user network). The Software is in use on a computer when it is loaded into temporary memory (RAM) or installed into permanent memory (hard disk, CD-ROM, or other storage device). HMI reserves all rights not expressly granted herein.

2. **Ownership.** HMI is the owner of all right, title, and interest, including copyright, in and to the compilation of the Software recorded on the disk(s) or CD-ROM ("Software Media"). Copyright to the individual programs recorded on the Software Media is owned by the author or other authorized copyright owner of each program. Ownership of the Software and all proprietary rights relating thereto remain with HMI and its licensers.

3. **Restrictions On Use and Transfer.**

   (a) You may only (i) make one copy of the Software for backup or archival purposes, or (ii) transfer the Software to a single hard disk, provided that you keep the original for backup or archival purposes. You may not (i) rent or lease the Software, (ii) copy or reproduce the Software through a LAN or other network system or through any computer subscriber system or bulletin-board system, or (iii) modify, adapt, or create derivative works based on the Software.

   (b) You may not reverse engineer, decompile, or disassemble the Software. You may transfer the Software and user documentation on a permanent basis, provided that the transferee agrees to accept the terms and conditions of this Agreement and you retain no copies. If the Software is an update or has been updated, any transfer must include the most recent update and all prior versions.

4. Restrictions on Use of Individual Programs. You must follow the individual requirements and restrictions detailed for each individual program in Appendix A of this Book. These limitations are also contained in the individual license agreements recorded on the Software Media. These limitations may include a requirement that after using the program for a specified period of time, the user must pay a registration fee or discontinue use. By opening the Software packet(s), you will be agreeing to abide by the licenses and restrictions for these individual programs that are detailed in Appendix A and on the Software Media. None of the material on this Software Media or listed in this Book may ever be redistributed, in original or modified form, for commercial purposes.

5. Limited Warranty.

(a) HMI warrants that the Software and Software Media are free from defects in materials and workmanship under normal use for a period of sixty (60) days from the date of purchase of this Book. If HMI receives notification within the warranty period of defects in materials or workmanship, HMI will replace the defective Software Media.

(b) HMI AND THE AUTHOR OF THE BOOK DISCLAIM ALL OTHER WARRANTIES, EXPRESS OR IMPLIED, INCLUDING WITHOUT LIMITATION IMPLIED WARRANTIES OF MERCHANTABILITY AND FITNESS FOR A PARTICULAR PURPOSE, WITH RESPECT TO THE SOFTWARE, THE PROGRAMS, THE SOURCE CODE CONTAINED THEREIN, AND/OR THE TECHNIQUES DESCRIBED IN THIS BOOK. HMI DOES NOT WARRANT THAT THE FUNCTIONS CONTAINED IN THE SOFTWARE WILL MEET YOUR REQUIREMENTS OR THAT THE OPERATION OF THE SOFTWARE WILL BE ERROR FREE.

(c) This limited warranty gives you specific legal rights, and you may have other rights that vary from jurisdiction to jurisdiction.

6. Remedies.

(a) HMI's entire liability and your exclusive remedy for defects in materials and workmanship shall be limited to replacement of the Software Media, which may be returned to HMI with a copy of your receipt at the following address: Software Media Fulfillment Department, Attn.: *Dreamweaver 4 Bible*, Hungry Minds, Inc., 10475 Crosspoint Blvd., Indianapolis, IN 46256, or call 1-800-762-2974. Please allow four to six weeks for delivery. This Limited Warranty is void if failure of the Software Media has resulted from accident, abuse, or misapplication. Any replacement Software Media will be warranted for the remainder of the original warranty period or thirty (30) days, whichever is longer.

(b) In no event shall HMI or the author be liable for any damages whatsoever (including without limitation damages for loss of business profits, business interruption, loss of business information, or any other pecuniary loss) arising from the use of or inability to use the Book or the Software, even if HMI has been advised of the possibility of such damages.

(c) Because some jurisdictions do not allow the exclusion or limitation of liability for consequential or incidental damages, the above limitation or exclusion may not apply to you.

7. **U.S. Government Restricted Rights.** Use, duplication, or disclosure of the Software for or on behalf of the United States of America, its agencies and/or instrumentalities (the "U.S. Government") is subject to restrictions as stated in paragraph (c)(1)(ii) of the Rights in Technical Data and Computer Software clause of DFARS 252.227-7013, or subparagraphs (c) (1) and (2) of the Commercial Computer Software - Restricted Rights clause at FAR 52.227-19, and in similar clauses in the NASA FAR supplement, as applicable.

8. **General.** This Agreement constitutes the entire understanding of the parties and revokes and supersedes all prior agreements, oral or written, between them and may not be modified or amended except in a writing signed by both parties hereto that specifically refers to this Agreement. This Agreement shall take precedence over any other documents that may be in conflict herewith. If any one or more provisions contained in this Agreement are held by any court or tribunal to be invalid, illegal, or otherwise unenforceable, each and every other provision shall remain in full force and effect.

CD-ROM Installation Instructions

Dreamweaver 4 Bible CD-ROM contain trial versions of Dreamweaver 4, Dreamweaver UltraDev 4, CourseBuilder for Dreamweaver 4, Fireworks 4, and Flash 5, in addition to a host of extensions, objects, and commands, and code from this book.

Accessing the Programs on the CD-ROM

The CD-ROM is what is known as a *hybrid CD-ROM*, which means it contains files that run on more than one computer platform—in this case, both Windows and Macintosh computers.

Several files, primarily the Macromedia trial programs and the other external programs, are compressed. Double-click these files to begin the installation procedure. Most other files on the CD-ROM are uncompressed and you can simply copy them to your system by using your file manager. A few of the Dreamweaver extensions with files that must be placed in different folders are also compressed.

In the Configuration folder, the file structure replicates the structure that Dreamweaver sets up when it is installed. For example, objects found in the Dreamweaver\Configuration\ Objects folder should be in that location for both the CD-ROM, and the installed program. One slight variation: In the Additional Extensions folder, you'll find the various behaviors, objects, and so on, filed under their author's name.

For a detailed synopsis of the contents of the CD-ROMs, see Appendix A, "What's on the CD-ROM?"

Installing Dreamweaver

To install Dreamweaver on your Windows system, follow these steps:

1. Insert the *Dreamweaver 4 Bible* CD-ROM into your CD-ROM drive.
2. Double-click the Dreamweaver.exe file to unpack it and begin the installation process.
3. Follow the onscreen instructions. Accept the default options for program location.

Changing the Windows read-only attribute

You may not be able to access files on the CD-ROMs after you copy the files to your computer. After you copy or move the entire contents of the CD-ROMs to your hard disk or another storage medium (such as a Zip disk), you may get the following error message when you attempt to open a file with its associated application:

```
[Application] is unable to open the [file]. Please make sure the
drive and file are writable.
```

Windows sees all files on a CD-ROM drive as read-only. This normally makes sense because a CD-ROM is a read-only medium—that is, you can't write data back to the CD-ROM. However, when you copy a file from a CD-ROM to your hard disk or to a Zip disk, Windows doesn't automatically change the file attribute from read-only to writable.

Installation software normally takes care of this chore for you, but in this case, because the files are intended to be manually copied to your disk, you have to change the file attribute yourself. Luckily, it's easy—just follow these steps:

1. Click the Start menu button.
2. Select Programs.
3. Choose Windows Explorer.
4. Highlight the file name(s) on the hard disk or Zip disk.
5. Right-click the highlighted file name(s) to display a pop-up menu.
6. Select Properties to display the Properties dialog box.
7. Click the Read-only option so that it is no longer checked.
8. Click the OK button.

You should now be able to use the file(s) with the specific application without getting the annoying error message.